Quantum Leap

Innovative Strategies for Trade Finance in the 21st Century and Beyond

Andrea Frosinini
Venu Borra

Quantum Leap: Innovative Strategies for Trade Finance in the 21st Century and Beyond

Andrea Frosinini
Florence, Italy

Venu Borra
Chennai, Tamil Nadu, India

ISBN-13 (pbk): 979-8-8688-1217-0　　　　ISBN-13 (electronic): 979-8-8688-1218-7
https://doi.org/10.1007/979-8-8688-1218-7

Copyright © 2025 by Andrea Frosinini, Venu Borra

This work is subject to copyright. All rights are reserved by the Publisher, whether the whole or part of the material is concerned, specifically the rights of translation, reprinting, reuse of illustrations, recitation, broadcasting, reproduction on microfilms or in any other physical way, and transmission or information storage and retrieval, electronic adaptation, computer software, or by similar or dissimilar methodology now known or hereafter developed.

Trademarked names, logos, and images may appear in this book. Rather than use a trademark symbol with every occurrence of a trademarked name, logo, or image we use the names, logos, and images only in an editorial fashion and to the benefit of the trademark owner, with no intention of infringement of the trademark.

The use in this publication of trade names, trademarks, service marks, and similar terms, even if they are not identified as such, is not to be taken as an expression of opinion as to whether or not they are subject to proprietary rights.

While the advice and information in this book are believed to be true and accurate at the date of publication, neither the authors nor the editors nor the publisher can accept any legal responsibility for any errors or omissions that may be made. The publisher makes no warranty, express or implied, with respect to the material contained herein.

　　Managing Director, Apress Media LLC: Welmoed Spahr
　　Acquisitions Editor: Shivangi Ramachandran
　　Development Editor: James Markham
　　Editorial Assistant: Gryffin Winkler

Cover designed by eStudioCalamar

Distributed to the book trade worldwide by Springer Science+Business Media New York, 1 New York Plaza, Suite 4600, New York, NY 10004-1562, USA. Phone 1-800-SPRINGER, fax (201) 348-4505, e-mail orders-ny@springer-sbm.com, or visit www.springeronline.com. Apress Media, LLC is a California LLC and the sole member (owner) is Springer Science + Business Media Finance Inc (SSBM Finance Inc). SSBM Finance Inc. is a **Delaware** corporation.

For information on translations, please e-mail booktranslations@springernature.com; for reprint, paperback, or audio rights, please e-mail bookpermissions@springernature.com.

Apress titles may be purchased in bulk for academic, corporate, or promotional use. eBook versions and licenses are also available for most titles. For more information, reference our Print and eBook Bulk Sales web page at http://www.apress.com/bulk-sales.

Any source code or other supplementary material referenced by the author in this book is available to readers on GitHub. For more detailed information, please visit https://www.apress.com/gp/services/source-code.

If disposing of this product, please recycle the paper

To Bo "Bosse" Ericsson, in loving memory

Table of Contents

About the Authors vii

Acknowledgments ix

Preface xi

Introduction xiii

Chapter 1: Gateway to Global Commerce: Unlocking the Secrets of Trade and Supply Chain Finance 1

Chapter 2: Letters of Credit: The Lifeline of Global Trade 19

Chapter 3: Cashing In on the Opportunity: The Dynamic World of Receivables Finance 77

Chapter 4: The Interplay Between Banks and Stakeholders in Trade Finance 169

Chapter 5: Empowering SMEs in Trade and Supply Chain Finance 181

Chapter 6: Unlocking Value: The Potential of Deep-Tier Supply Chain Finance (DTSCF) 209

Chapter 7: Merging the Seas: The Imperative of Digital Transformation and Legal and Regulatory Reform 293

Chapter 8: Bits, Bytes, and Legal Bites: Navigating the Digital Frontier of Trade Law and Practice 359

Chapter 9: Blockchain Breakthrough: Rewiring Trade Finance for the Digital Age 405

Chapter 10: Rising Titans, Falling Empires: The Epic Saga of Trade Finance Consortia in the Digital Age 437

Chapter 11: Shaping Tomorrow's Markets: The Future of Trade Finance Through Innovations 499

TABLE OF CONTENTS

Chapter 12: Achieving Financing Resilience and Influence on Trade Finance Through DORA 569

Chapter 13: Navigating the New Normal: Reinventing Trade Finance with Blockchain, AI, and IoT in a Zero-Trust Era 603

Chapter 14: Credit Revolution: The Tokenization Tidal Wave in Global Trade 667

Chapter 15: The Nexus of Trade, Environment, and Sustainable Development 695

Chapter 16: Pioneering Greener Trade: Practices and Innovations in Sustainable Finance 791

Chapter 17: Thriving Together: A Regenerative Power for Small and Mighty Businesses 837

Chapter 18: Data-Driven Dynamics: Linking Real-World Insights to Trade Finance 913

Chapter 19: Afterword: Digital Trade As an Evolved Digital Governance 987

Bibliography 997

Index 1007

About the Authors

Andrea Frosinini is a seasoned trade finance and business development professional, deeply rooted in the quest for innovation and progress within the industry. His career journey has been marked by a continuous pursuit of excellence and an eagerness to embrace and drive change. Recently, he took an exciting leap by joining the Hyperledger community. This strategic move aligns with his commitment to contribute to the modernization of the trade finance sector.

Andrea is particularly focused on harnessing the potential of blockchain technology. This passion lies in exploring and developing new products that leverage these cutting-edge technologies. He believes that blockchain and DLTs hold the key to unlocking unprecedented efficiency, transparency, and security in trade finance processes. As a professional, Andrea brings to the table a wealth of experience and a keen insight into the complexities of trade finance. He's driven by the challenge of integrating traditional financial systems with innovative digital solutions, aiming to revolutionize how trade finance operates.

Venu Borra is a passionate and skilled technical architect with expertise in analysis, architecture, and development of solutions using blockchain, distributed computing, artificial intelligence, smart contracts, digital assets, and IoT. He brings a wealth of insightful experience to the table, navigating the intricate landscapes of DLTs and blockchain technologies across diverse sectors, including Fintech, trade finance, supply chain, agri-tech, and healthcare. Fluent in an array of programming languages such as Solidity, Go-lang, Python, and more, Venu Borra possesses a versatile technical skill set encompassing AI, ML, IoT integration, and DLT.

ABOUT THE AUTHORS

With a career marked by proficiency in analysis, architecture, and solution development, he stands at the forefront of innovation, championing the principles of self-sovereign identity (SSI) and zero knowledge. Beyond technical prowess, Venu excels in bridging the gap between business requirements and technical solutions. With a keen focus on collaboration and innovation, Venu fosters a culture of excellence within teams, motivating individuals to surpass corporate objectives and achieve collective goals. Through strategic leadership and a commitment to excellence, he continues to shape the future of blockchain technology.

Acknowledgments

We would like to extend our heartfelt gratitude to all those who have supported us throughout the journey of writing our book.

First and foremost, we express our deep appreciation to each other for the unwavering collaboration, dedication, and shared vision that formed the foundation of this book. Writing this work together has been an inspiring and rewarding experience, and we could not have asked for a better partner in this endeavor.

We would also like to thank our families for their love and patience. To our parents for instilling in us a passion for learning and innovation, and to our partners for their constant support and encouragement, which allowed us to pursue this ambitious project.

Our heartfelt thanks go to the many experts and professionals of ICC UK, XDC Foundation, XDC Trade Network, and Circularity Finance who graciously shared their insights with us over the years, providing invaluable perspectives that have enriched the content of this book. Your knowledge has been instrumental in shaping our understanding of trade finance and its potential for creating global prosperity.

We are grateful to the editorial team, whose hard work and attention to detail helped refine and bring clarity to our ideas. Your professionalism and dedication have made this book what it is today.

Lastly, we extend our gratitude to the readers who have joined us on this journey through the evolving landscape of trade finance. We hope this book serves as a guide, inspiring new strategies and fostering a future where global prosperity is accessible to all.

Thank you all for your support.

Preface

The financial foundations that support trade and supply chain activities have, for the most part, remained steady and unaltered for decades in the ever-evolving environment of global trade. Traditional trade finance systems, which are based on layers of paper trails, manual checks, and laborious verifications, have provided the foundation of international trade, enabling the transportation of goods and services across borders. But as a new era approaches, digital technology—especially blockchain—has the potential to completely transform this field. The book *Quantum Leap: Innovative Strategies for Trade Finance in the 21st Century and Beyond* is an investigation that shows how these traditional methods will change over time to a future where cutting-edge technologies and the ideas of Regenerative Finance (ReFi) will make trade finance faster, safer, and more efficient overall. The idea behind this book is to guide the reader on an in-depth "journey" through the present transformations taking place in the trade and supply chain finance sectors. It starts with a thorough examination of the traditional trade finance techniques for setting the scene. These centuries-old mechanisms have facilitated large-scale international trade, but they are not without flaws. These include inefficiencies, fraud vulnerabilities, and a lack of transparency that can hinder trade, particularly for smaller players in developing economies. Trade finance is at a crucial stage in the digital age that is sweeping through several industries. With the potential to improve transparency and streamline procedures, digitalization has started to permeate this traditionally conservative area. The book explores the way technologies such as blockchain, artificial intelligence (AI), and the Internet of things (IoT) are mainly accountable for these advancements. Blockchain technology particularly provides an unprecedented level of security and transparency due to its immutable record, potentially eliminating many of the long-standing issues with trade finance. Following this point, the narrative switches to discuss the fascinating possibilities that exist at the intersection of trade finance and regenerative financing (ReFi). ReFi is a concept that extends outside financial services to tackle wider economic and social issues with potential environmental implications. This has a strong connection to the concepts of sustainability and ethical finance. In the second part, we'll look into how blockchain technology can help create more sustainable and equitable trade financing

PREFACE

procedures. It will eventually end up in a more renewable system that's beneficial to all parties involved. Through this book, we hope to give readers an in-depth review of trade finance's past, present, and future while serving as an inspiration for the coming generations of leaders, thinkers, and innovators. This book will indeed be of interest to anyone with an interest in trade and finance in the future, whether they are a student, a professional in the sector, a legislator, or a technological enthusiast.

Introduction

Global trade is a thread that has spun together the fabric of human civilization from the very beginning; it is not only the interchange of commodities and services. Early human tribes using primitive barter systems traded products including grain, cattle, and tools, therefore starting the path of commerce in ancient times. These simple exchanges were the initial steps toward creating sophisticated commercial networks; every level of progress marks a significant turning point in the evolution of mankind.

Trade practices changed with cultures to reflect their development. First in the form of precious metals and then paper money, the introduction of money enabled standardized trades, hence enabling bigger and more complex systems of commerce. Transforming events that changed the global economic scene were the Silk Road, the Age of Discovery, and the Industrial Revolution. Innovations in communication, transportation, and—above all—finance—the lifeblood of every modern economy—drove these benchmarks.

New ideas have led commerce to grow both geographically and conceptually in every age and have produced new financial instruments. Notwithstanding this rich legacy of change, trade finance—the foundation of the world economy—has persistently stayed bound to antiquated methods. Even with technology, paper-based procedures, bureaucratic red tape, and poor transaction speeds endure. The book will look at this contradiction as we head toward a day where such inefficiencies will be relics of the past. In a world where technology has transformed almost every facet of life—from smartphones to artificial intelligence—the continuation of paper-based trade finance is amazing. Letters of credit, trade invoices, and other instruments—among the tools supporting worldwide trade—still mostly rely on manual, paper-driven procedures. Not just sluggish but also prone to mistakes, fraud, and inefficiencies, these systems create slow transactions and stunt economic development.

The book explores why trade finance has been so firmly ingrained in the past. Is it the industry's level of complexity? The enormity of worldwide transactions? Maybe it's the regulatory obstacles causing a sluggish and tough transition. *Quantum Leap* investigates the shortcomings of the present system and flags up the areas of hindrance to world commerce and environmentally friendly development. It also looks at how

INTRODUCTION

these antiquated methods restrict tracking of the social and environmental effects of trade, something that will become even more crucial as we head toward a more cognizant, environmentally conscious global market.

Already, the emergence of digital technology is starting to bring about a change in corporate behavior. From artificial intelligence to blockchain, the instruments are now accessible to eradicate the inefficiencies long afflicting trade finance. *Quantum Leap* sees a period when trade finance will be completely digital, paperless, and linked in real-time with worldwide supply networks. We will examine closely the promise of blockchain technology—allowing transparent, safe, and speedy transactions—in particular. Digitalization is the way to release the actual potential of international trade in a world where demand for speed, accuracy, and security is at an all-time high.

The book does, however, also go one step further by including in the digital revolution the growing impact of environmental, social, and governmental (ESG) elements. The worldwide drive toward sustainability is about reevaluating how trade finance may match world environmental goals, not only about better energy or fewer carbon footprints. As we investigate how finance may help to bring about a sustainable future, green financing, sustainable trade practices, and carbon-neutral trade paths will be important to the story.

Readers will go chronologically through the development of trade finance as the chapters roll out. From its early, simple forms in the ancient world to the sophisticated, highly controlled buildings of today, we will investigate the historical events, people, and ideas that have formed the present terrain. We will also explore the developments in recent years—digital payments, supply chain financing, and AI-driven trade solutions—that are preparing the ground for the direction of trade going forward.

Crucially, every chapter will place the past against a future vision. We will take into account the technological, social, and environmental changes that must take place if we explore the prospects of a paperless, seamless ecosystem for trade finance to take hold. From the emergence of digital trade platforms and decentralized finance (DeFi) to the acceptance of blockchain for transparent and effective transactions, we will investigate how invention might break down the barriers that have long hampered world commerce. We will also examine the legislative frameworks and alliances required to sustain this new age of trade financing alongside these technical innovations.

INTRODUCTION

This book's goal is not only about technology; it's about building a linked society in which trade moves ethically, quickly, and effortlessly. In the future, we see all transactions—including those involving financial assets, products, or services—being carried out digitally, securely, and sustainably. Along with speedier, more transparent trade, this future world will be very vital for the larger goal of environmental stewardship.

Trade finance crosses with environmental objectives here. The book will look at how green finance methods, together with digital technology, will enable trade finance to become a major driver for sustainable world development. A key component of this trip will be the inclusion of environmental standards into trade agreements and financial instruments. *Quantum Leap* sees a day when trade finance will be a real partner in solving the global environmental challenge, guiding companies toward decisions that support not only economic development but also planetary health.

By the end of the book, readers will have not only acquired insight into the transforming possibilities that lay ahead but also a thorough awareness of the past and present of trade finance. *Quantum Leap* sees a future whereby finance itself becomes a vehicle for sustainability and global prosperity, not only one whereby trade finance is digital and paperless. The book contends that the world may enter a new age of commerce, one that is quicker, fairer, and more sustainable than ever before with the correct mix of technical innovation, imaginative financial methods, and a dedication to environmental stewardship.

The book's last message is unambiguous: trade finance as we know it is about to make a quantum future leap. And this jump is about a reinterpretation of what commerce may be in the 21st century, not only about the digital revolution. The future resides in a digital, green, interconnected ecosystem; there are almost endless options, and the moment of transformation is right here now.

This closer examination adds further layers of historical background, digital and ecological change, and a future trade finance perspective. Every part prepares the foundation for a thorough investigation of the developments and inventions transforming this industry.

We do hope you're going to enjoy the reading!

CHAPTER 1

Gateway to Global Commerce: Unlocking the Secrets of Trade and Supply Chain Finance

This chapter provides a thorough roadmap for the development, processes, and future direction of trade and supply chain finance as the portal to worldwide business by blending history, contemporary practices, and future prospects. It follows the evolution of trade finance from prehistoric societies to contemporary business, therefore highlighting the continuing relevance of trust and documentation in enabling world trade. The chapter ends with a forward-looking viewpoint stressing the transforming power of technology in linking conventional trade finance systems with creative digital ecosystems.

A Look Back into the History

From the Middle Ages to the present, the evolution of international trade finance presents an intriguing prism that allows us to examine broader transformations in global finance, governance, and economic interaction. In a world where economic powers are shifting and environments are becoming more interesting, the way that unique instruments made by local merchants got turned into the complicated, decentralized market systems we have now shows how centralization, standardization, and eventually globalization are becoming more powerful trends.

CHAPTER 1   GATEWAY TO GLOBAL COMMERCE: UNLOCKING THE SECRETS OF TRADE AND SUPPLY CHAIN FINANCE

Trade finance throughout the Middle Ages has been defined by the issue of unique assets by local bankers and merchants. Individual relationships served as the primary form of financing, supplemented by small-scale, locally applicable mechanisms like bills of exchange. The conventions of the specific trade regions largely governed the conditions and enforcement of those agreements. The need for a more consistent and reliable source of funding intensified as trade expanded.

As a consequence, major trading centers like Antwerp, Amsterdam, and ultimately London emerged in the 16th century. The concentration and standardization of credit tools brought about by each of these institutions strengthened the efficiency and dependability of trade finance. Particularly, Antwerp and Amsterdam played a significant role in the early development of the financial markets and banking systems that underpinned global trade.

London emerged as the world's financial center for worldwide trade by the 19th century, partly thanks to the pound bill of exchange's widespread adoption and Britain's dominance as a maritime nation.

This instrument, which provided a standardized, widely accepted method for payment and credit, turned into the cornerstone of international trade finance. The pound bill of exchange was simple to use anywhere because Britain had such a large colonial empire. The English legal system also provided a strong legal base, which gave merchants a high level of predictability and confidence. These were the primary factors that made the sterling bill of exchange superior.

An era of significant disruption in the financing of international trade started with the outbreak of World War I. The conflict fragmented the world's financial system and retreated from the globalization of the previous period, paving the way for the Great Depression and World War II. Trade finance decentralized throughout the interwar era as nations adopted stringent capital controls and turned toward autarky.

Despite its role in establishing a new international monetary order during World War II, the Bretton Woods system initially did not significantly influence the reunification of the world's trade and finance markets. Yet the ensuing collapse of Bretton Woods in the early 1970s, along with improvements in technology and the opening up of international financial markets, made it simpler to rebuild international trade finance.

Given the advent of a number of tools, players, and regulatory frameworks, an open market structure for trade financing emerged after 1970. Recent developments like distributed ledger technology and blockchain have further changed the game by making it possible to finance international commerce in a way that is more transparent, safe, and profitable.

Today, the broad category of goods and services that makes up international trade finance includes supply chain financing, trade credit insurance, conventional letters of credit, and bills of exchange. Since banks, financial institutions, and fintech startups operating globally provide international trade finance, the market is distinctive for its global reach.

The development of international trade finance from the Middle Ages to the decentralized market structure of today is indicative of larger trends in technical innovation, regulatory change, and economic globalization. The core function of trade finance in promoting international trade has not altered, despite changes to its tools and procedures. International trade finance will surely continue to adapt as the world economy changes, overcoming obstacles and grasping possibilities in the constantly shifting context of international commerce.

From Parchment to Power: A Paper-Based Instrument and Its Voyage Through History

The development of a variety of financial instruments and the evolution of centers of trade finance are hallmarks of this intriguing past, which encompasses many centuries. The bill of exchange is unique among these tools because it plays a crucial role in enabling business by providing channels for both credit and payment. Analyzing the rise of the bill of exchange from its medieval roots to its use in contemporary trade finance as well as the market's initial centralization and eventual decentralization is essential. In the Middle Ages, this instrument became a vital part of commercial financing.

Story of London as Trade Finance Hub and Changes Post-World Wars

These were formerly unique assets that regional bankers and merchants distributed to promote transactions across various areas. Over time, as global trade expanded, the need for standards became evident, leading to the gradual centralization of trade finance in major commercial cities such as Antwerp, Amsterdam, and ultimately London. The market for pounds bills of exchange was so liquid that by the 19th century, London had grown into the world's hub for global trade finance. Britain's extensive trade networks and the pound's status as an international reserve currency reinforced the city's supremacy. A number of investors, including banks, merchants, and private financiers, gathered in London's financial district to fund a sizable portion of international trade. During the interwar years, the global trade finance market's coherent structure began to fall apart. A period of declining global trade volumes, protectionist policies, and economic volatility damaged the centralized trade finance structure that had thrived in the 19th century.

The trade finance industry underwent reconstruction after World War II, culminating in the market structure that exists today. Local banks in the nations of exporters and importers typically provide trade finance instruments, as trade finance operations have shifted away from a single global center. During this period, the introduction and adoption of new finance mechanisms and processes, tailored to the evolving needs of global commerce, also occurred.

The present-day trade finance industry makes use of an extensive variety of resources and methods, including supply chain financing and digital platforms, as well as more conventional instruments like letters of credit. These developments are a reflection of both the complexity of the global economy and the progress made in technology since World War I.

This illustrates how financial practices have proven able to innovate and adapt to evolving trade patterns and economic conditions. Trade finance has grown from the medieval bill of exchange to the much more complex platforms of today, reflecting broader trends in globalization, technical advancement, and the changing nature of international trade. The architecture and tools of trade finance will evolve along with trade, highlighting the ongoing significance of financial innovation in promoting international trade and spearheading an internationally recognized system largely influenced by the evolving legal, social, and economic landscapes of Western Europe.

The history of trade finance that spans from the 12th to the 19th centuries is a compelling narrative of innovation, globalization, and the evolution of financial instruments that facilitated commerce across continents. This extended period saw the creation and improvement of the bill of exchange, a crucial tool in trade finance. At the same time, there were big changes in the locations and types of institutions that handled international trade finance.

The complex banking systems of the Greek Mediterranean and the ancient Middle Eastern civilizations are the sources of trade finance. The specific financing of trade arrangements employed throughout this era, however, still remains mostly unknown.

CHAPTER 1 GATEWAY TO GLOBAL COMMERCE: UNLOCKING THE SECRETS OF TRADE AND SUPPLY CHAIN FINANCE

Trade finance flourished again in Western Europe after the year 1000, among an interconnected network of conflicting legal frameworks bound together through the Canon Law and Roman legal legacy.

A collection of business precepts known as the "law merchant" (lex mercatoria) developed to direct commerce throughout Europe. The financing of commerce initially took on a more formal shape with the establishment of solid networks of correspondents, particularly by Italian companies. The transition from sedentary to local trading signified the emergence of contemporary trade finance frameworks. Within these networks, the bill of exchange developed into a private credit contract, changing from a simple certificate to an advanced, negotiable credit instrument. This change was essential for giving wider access to trade finance by removing the constraints of restricted company networks. Due in large part to economic events in the Flanders region, the bill of exchange underwent a transition in the early modern age with the realization of its negotiability.

With the adoption of negotiable bills of exchange in the 16th century, Antwerp in particular emerged as a key center that enabled the mobilization of capital for commerce across various locations. Bills' negotiability made it possible to break away from the medieval paradigm by allowing trading enterprises to lend directly to one another and lessening the need for bankers to act as intermediaries.

The commercial rules and practices of this city established a new global benchmark for trade financing, inspiring the adoption of ideas throughout Europe. As Antwerp declined, Amsterdam and then London emerged as the primary hubs for trade finance. Throughout Europe, the negotiable bill of exchange continued to be an essential instrument and gained universal support. Even after negotiable bills of exchange gained widespread acceptance and circulation to facilitate payments and credit within this network, trade finance remained somewhat fragmented, with merchants and companies specializing in foreign commerce providing the majority of the financing.

The bill of exchange was a key part of this global change because it became a negotiable instrument. This made it possible for trade to grow and for modern financial instruments and practices to emerge that support international trade today.

The evolution ran in parallel with another significant development, notably the centralization of the market around London and the standardization of credit instruments. As a result, London emerged as the actual global hub for international trade finance, transforming the sector from a specialized domain into a widely accessible market.

CHAPTER 1 GATEWAY TO GLOBAL COMMERCE: UNLOCKING THE SECRETS OF TRADE AND SUPPLY CHAIN FINANCE

A significant driver was the emergence of a sizable discount market in London in the second part of the 18th century for bills of exchange. This market, which initially focused on inland bills, a domestic credit instrument, helped mobilize local credits and established the framework for the financing of international trade. Bills of exchange drawn on London started to finance worldwide commercial transactions during the early 20th century. The inland bill vanished with the introduction of standardized, internationally traded pound bills of exchange as the market's focus switched from domestic to global. A set of governance guidelines and the rise of important companies, such as acceptance houses, which controlled market access, helped to facilitate this shift.

As intermediaries, acceptance houses played a crucial role in facilitating foreign clients' access to the London market by ensuring the accuracy of their bills. These organizations essentially controlled admission into the biggest trade financing market in the world by screening potential borrowers. The Bank of England's rediscount policy increased the market's liquidity and safety for sterling bills.

The Bank enhanced the credit and liquidity characteristics of pound bills by establishing qualifying criteria and closely monitoring market players, thereby reinforcing their status as global "safe assets." London dominated international trade financing from 1870 to 1914, and bills were the most popular short-term financial product globally as a result of the adoption of the international gold standard and the London market's stability. Through this market, a wide spectrum of investors, including foreign central and commercial banks, participated in funding international commerce. Despite appearing to be open, local gatekeepers regulated entry and took profits from the London market.

Acceptance houses in particular played a significant role in the regulation of international trade finance and made use of their position to extort fees for bill acceptance. A crucial piece of legislation, the Bills of Exchange Act of 1882, codified market behaviors without drastically altering the structure of the market. The only significant statutory innovation that lasted was the concept of negotiability, which originated in Antwerp in the 16th century. During this time, market forces and the roles of organizations such as the Bank of England and acceptance houses shaped the development of informal rules and market practices. These helped build the industry we know today and set up systems and structures of governance that would impact the sector for decades to come.

The period spanning between the two main war events of the 20th century, i.e., from 1914 to 1939, was characterized by significant upheavals in global trade finance, largely catalyzed by World War I, the subsequent economic revival of the 1920s, and finally, the

CHAPTER 1   GATEWAY TO GLOBAL COMMERCE: UNLOCKING THE SECRETS OF TRADE AND SUPPLY CHAIN FINANCE

debilitating effects of the Great Depression. This era marked the decline of London's preeminence in trade finance, the rise of New York as a competing financial center, and the eventual disintegration of the structured international trade finance system that had flourished in the 19th century.

The outbreak of World War I and the ensuing political unrest seriously impacted the London discount market, which was an essential part of world trade financing. The sterling bill, which was the most widely used trade finance instrument in worldwide circulation at the time, experienced challenges regarding its liquidity and effectiveness when capital controls and a halt on foreign exchange payments prevented international debtors from transferring money to London acceptors. Urgent actions were implemented to avert a financial disaster, enabling accepting houses to postpone bill payments and get direct government borrowing. Although these actions avoided a financial catastrophe, they raised doubts about the pound bill's dependability and, consequently, London's place in the world's trade finance system.

The financing of trade became more and more vital after World War I. On the other hand, the recovery also saw New York becoming a serious rival to London, creating a dual market framework. As the most powerful commercial force globally, the United States endeavored to emulate London's financial framework, most prominently by enacting the Federal Reserve Act of 1913, which sparked the growth of a dollar-denominated bankers' acceptances market in New York. London remained a major player in the international trade finance market despite competition because of its advantageous location, the knowledge of British acceptance houses, and the structural benefits of its money market. In the aftermath of the Great Depression, there was a significant drop in international trade, which in turn decreased demand for financing.

European liquidity issues, particularly for London's acceptance houses, put bills drawn on banks in London and New York at risk of non-payment. The emergence of bilateral clearing agreements, regional trading blocs, and stronger government oversight of global trade in the latter part of the 1930s drastically fragmented the world trade finance market. During the interwar period, Treasury bills, backed by government debt, gradually replaced bankers' acceptances as the primary money market instrument, signifying a shift from privately to publicly supported securities.

During that period, the League of Nations spearheaded efforts to codify the laws regulating international bills of exchange, which eventually led to the Geneva Convention. However, Anglo-Saxon nations refused to ratify the Convention, which was primarily based on Continental legal practices, underscoring the continued legal distinctions in the oversight of payment instruments.

CHAPTER 1 GATEWAY TO GLOBAL COMMERCE: UNLOCKING THE SECRETS OF TRADE AND SUPPLY CHAIN FINANCE

The post-World War II era brought about significant changes to the global trade finance scenario, including improvements to financial instruments and procedures, market evolution, and regulatory reforms. We can divide the era in question into three distinct phases: the period after the war, marked by governmental control over finance and trade; the post-Bretton Woods period, marked by market liberalization; and the current state of trade finance.

The Bretton Woods System

American and British banks revived old-fashioned techniques for funding foreign commerce, such as acceptances. However, the establishment of the new Bretton Woods system completely transformed the inner workings of trade finance by imposing stringent government regulations on capital flows and international payments. Financial institutions had to negotiate a complex web of regulations, which was particularly challenging in the years following World War II.

One of the most notable examples of the regulatory hurdles that financial institutions encountered was the UK's requirement for official approval before granting overseas loans. As the Bretton Woods system collapsed and capital restrictions lifted, trade between nations revived, leading to a soaring demand for trade finance. With its robust currency and lax banking laws, the United States became a major hub for trade funding and saw a spike in bankers' acceptances. Regulations governing US banks in the 1970s made accepting bills appealing because they qualified for discounts, the Federal Reserve could acquire them on the open market, and there were no reserve requirements.

Trade finance has transitioned from regulated marketplaces, like those in London before World War II, to a more decentralized model where regional financial institutions in the countries of importers and exporters primarily act as intermediaries. Direct loans, overdraft facilities, commercial paper markets, and specialized trade finance instruments like documentary collections and letters of credit are only a few of the methods by which trade funding is facilitated nowadays. The modern era's localized trade finance poses difficulties, especially for businesses operating in nations with weak banking infrastructure, creating a "trade finance gap." Furthermore, access to trade credit is more susceptible to domestic financial shocks due to dependence on local banks.

Unlike the pre-World War I era, where trade finance instruments circulated widely among a diverse range of investors, modern trade finance sees a narrower investor base, primarily consisting of local banks and, to some extent, branches of global banks.

CHAPTER 1   GATEWAY TO GLOBAL COMMERCE: UNLOCKING THE SECRETS OF TRADE AND SUPPLY CHAIN FINANCE

The global financial crisis of 2008 starkly highlighted the vulnerabilities of the current trade finance system, as the drying up of financing facilities contributed significantly to the collapse in global trade.

It is fair to argue that the bill of exchange, a key tool in trade finance history, displays a resilient nature, which reflects the enormous shifts in the global economy from antiquity to the modern digital era. Its roots are in the trading traditions of ancient civilizations, and it first appeared in the West around the 13th century. From humble beginnings as a simple financial instrument, it has grown to become a vital component of global trade.

A network of merchant bankers operating within the confines of localized trading hubs crafted this bespoke financial instrument in medieval Europe. These instruments were the lifeblood of bank-intermediated trade finance, facilitating transactions across the diverse mercantile cities of Europe. However, the geographical and relational proximity of the trading parties involved inherently limited their scope.

The Advent of the Negotiable Bill of Exchange

The introduction of the negotiable bill of exchange at the beginning of the modern era triggered a profound upheaval in the field of trade finance. With the help of this innovation, trade finance products may now circulate more widely among organizations engaged in global commerce, reaching beyond the boundaries of merchant networks. However, the distribution of these instruments remained largely restricted to those directly involved in international trade, despite this advancement. The bill of exchange entered a new phase with the advent of the 19th century.

The process of standardization somehow led to the disassociation of the location of a lender and the borrower, especially with the London acceptance market becoming a world's central money market, showing how crucial standardized invoices or acceptances are to enabling the mobility of credit across borders. These financial instruments, stripped of local idiosyncrasies and rendered uniform in form and enforcement, allowed banks and investors to assess and price risk independently of geographic proximity. As a result, trade financing evolved into a network of trust built on documentation, not on the familiarity or physical closeness of transacting parties. This shift laid the groundwork for the modern global financial architecture—where credibility, rather than location, governs access to liquidity. The global financial system broke down during the interwar and post-World War II eras, almost completely eliminating the acceptance market. During the economic boom of the 1980s, trade finance experienced a temporary upsurge, but ultimately, the London market's centralized approach gave way to a more diffused framework. Banks or their international branches offer a wide range of trade finance products locally in today's market. This bears resemblance to the nascent days of the bill of exchange, yet stands in stark contrast to the initial globalization period characterized by centrally regulated trade finance.

The evolution of the financial system architecture significantly influences the governance of international trade finance. Being the dominant political and economic force in the 19th century, the UK had an enormous amount of influence over the trade finance market, with the banking institutions in London defining the standards for obtaining trade financing facilities. Following World War I, the United States emerged as a rival hub for trade finance, posing a challenge to the centralized control that Britain's hegemony had enabled.

Today's environment makes worldwide oversight extremely challenging since local governments establish the standards for trade finance eligibility and regulate the organizations that provide these services. The British-regulated worldwide system of the 19th century contrasts sharply with the regionally customized goods of today's trade finance industry. This move toward a more dispersed governance framework casts doubt on the idea of a unified worldwide supervision framework and ushers in a new period of regulatory "anarchy" in the field of international trade finance.

Foundations of Prosperity and the Essentials of Tradition: The Pivotal Role of Financial Institutions in Banking on Trade

Far back in the history we've just narrated, a crude type of documentary credit was already facilitating trade along the historic Silk Road, long before the contemporary complexity of global banking. This earliest form of what we know today as a letter of credit dates back to the time of Babylonian dominance in Mesopotamia and supported trade between the vibrant markets of the Mediterranean and the remote regions of China. These antiquated trading tools demonstrate the inventiveness of early trade as well as the ongoing need for confidence in business dealings.

The development of documentary credits, which became essential to the period of exploration and empire and eventually resembled modern traveler's checks, is the most memorable aspect of the Age of Exploration and Expansion, spanning from the 17th through the 19th century. British banks essentially monopolized trade finance, capitalizing on the growing financial dominance of London and the widespread acceptance of the Pound Sterling. During this time, the ease of conducting business internationally underwent a substantial transformation, with documentary credits turning into a vital resource for dealers and merchants visiting far-off markets.

The start of World War I sparked change by upending long-standing economic networks and drawing attention to the weaknesses in global trade. The documentary credit went from being a convenience to being essential in this uncertain time. Exporters were more and more dependent on documentary credits to ensure payment for their goods as a result of unfamiliar, unproven trading networks and inaccurate counterparty information. This change emphasized the importance of the documentary credit as the foundation of safe international trade.

The Lifeblood of International Commerce

Documentary credits expanded so rapidly in the 20th century that Sir Michael Kerr called them "the lifeblood of international commerce." At this time, regulations and systematization ensured the vital role of documentary credit in promoting international trade. Modern terminology defines a documentary credit as an irreversible bank guarantee that, provided the seller provides the required documentation, the buyer will pay the seller.

This financial tool showcases the system's adaptability and durability by limiting transaction completion to specific requirements. "Uniform Customs and Practice for Documentary Credits, Revision 600" (UCP 600) regulates this. Despite these advancements, analyzing the paperwork associated with a credit remains exceedingly challenging, often slowed down by tedious, sluggish manual processes. The meticulous scrutiny required to ensure compliance with the "International Standard Banking Practice for the Examination of Documents under UCP 600" (ISBP 821) and UCP 600 both stress how complicated it is to finance international trade.

The persistence of human verification processes and paper-based documentation demonstrates the necessity for immediate digital transformation of documentary credits. Along with other digital advancements, blockchain technology promises to address these inefficiencies and create new avenues for global trade. By automating document analysis and compliance checks, digital solutions provide access to a more efficient, transparent, and secure trade finance environment.

Sticking to documentary credits, they have had a remarkable metamorphosis from the days of the Silk Road to the digital era, all driven by the fundamental requirement for security and confidence in international trade. With digital innovation defining our future, there is immense opportunity to further improve the integrity and efficiency of international trade. In addition to demonstrating the flexibility of trade financing arrangements, the shift from paper to pixels portends a revolutionary advance and a new era of cooperation and opportunity in the international economy

Defining Traditional Trade Finance

Traditional trade finance is an umbrella term for a number of different financial tools and solutions that make it easier to make cross-border trade deals happen while reducing the risks that come with them, such as changes in exchange rates, unstable governments, and not being able to trust your trading partner.

Trade credit insurance provides a layer of protection to protect exporters against the threat of nonpayment by overseas customers. This particular kind of coverage is crucial, particularly when doing business with new or dubious partners. When exporters cover a sizable amount of the receivable, they can boost their competitiveness in overseas markets by extending credit to purchasers with a higher level of trust.

The insurance typically covers commercial risks like the buyer's insolvency and political risks like war or the enactment of export restrictions. Premiums are calculated after taking account of an array of variables, which includes those related to his financial standing,

Bank guarantees provide an additional layer of protection to global trade transactions. These are enforceable promises from a bank to the exporter, provided on behalf of the importer, that the exporter will comply with payment or performance requirements. In the event that the importer infringes on the terms of the contract, the bank will reimburse the damage up to a predefined sum.

Thanks to its flexibility, this specific type of financial product can provide a range of guarantees, including payment, performance, and advance payment guarantees. It is particularly useful in situations where the seller requires evidence demonstrating the buyer's commitment to the terms of the contract and ability to pay.

Last but certainly not least, although still providing a certain level of protection in international commerce transactions, Documentary Collections offer a more straightforward, cheaper option to Letters of Credit. In this scenario, the exporter ships the products, entrusting their bank with the responsibility of collecting money and transferring the necessary paperwork, including invoices, bills of lading, and insurance documents, to the importer's bank, along with payment instructions.

CHAPTER 1   GATEWAY TO GLOBAL COMMERCE: UNLOCKING THE SECRETS OF TRADE AND SUPPLY CHAIN FINANCE

Securing Global Trade: The Role of Payment Terms and Financial Instruments in Mitigating Risk

Payment can be arranged against documents on sight, i.e., D/P—Documents against Payment, or after a certain period, i.e., D/A—Documents against Acceptance. It also reduces the risk for exporters by preventing the importer from acquiring ownership of the products until full payment or by agreeing to pay at a later date.

Combined, these resources provide a comprehensive framework that promotes the safety and efficiency of international transactions. Conventional trade finance is essential to the global economy because it helps businesses expand their markets and capture opportunities for expansion by lowering the potential dangers associated with cross-border transactions. The core of the trade finance ecosystem consists of financial institutions that facilitate trade, provide loans, and oversee risk.

The distribution of various financial instruments that encourage activities involving global trade is primarily reliant on banking institutions. Along with, but not limited to, bank guarantees and letters of credit, banks offer a range of additional tools to ease the trade lifecycle. For instance, standby letters of credit serve as a safety net for contractual payments and performance.

Mitigating Risk in Global Trade: Documentary Credits and Institutional Solutions

Documentary Credits offer a secure means for payment but require an amount of paperwork attesting that there was a delivery of the merchandise. In order to ensure the financial stability of the parties involved and the viability of the underpinning business relationships, the steps consist of a comprehensive assessment and underwriting. By minimizing payment risk, these instruments not only make trade simpler but also strengthen trade interactions between parties by providing a bank's guarantee.

Banking institutions provide a broad range of short-term financial solutions for filling the payment gaps that naturally occur between importers and exporters as a result of different trade cycles. Trade loans, for instance, enable importers who have to make payments to suppliers upfront or exporters who are waiting for payment to have instant liquidity. Factoring and invoice financing are additional popular methods that allow companies to borrow against the value of their accounts receivable, thereby strengthening liquidity and shortening operational cycles.

Solutions such as Import Letters of Credit Funding support importers in financing their purchases of goods while providing prompt payment to suppliers and allowing the importer to schedule payment outflows in line with their financial cycles. These financing options, tailored to meet the needs of the trade transaction, enable companies to operate effortlessly and efficiently.

Advanced risk management techniques are required for coping with all of the dangers linked to global trade, from credit and payment risks to political and country risks. In order to safeguard themselves from these dangers, financial institutions deploy a combination of internal evaluations, insurance policies, and derivatives. As an example, they might utilize credit futures to shift credit risk to a third party or provide currency hedging products to guard against fluctuations in foreign exchange.

Furthermore, banks use comprehensive industry and country evaluations to guide their borrowing choices, ensuring a deep comprehension of the outside variables that may impact the deal. Banking institutions play a vital role in stabilizing the trade finance landscape by implementing risk mitigation strategies that minimize potential losses for businesses engaging in foreign trade.

Mastering the Flow of Commerce from Concept to Execution

Traditional trade finance, which has its roots in centuries-old customs, is an extremely essential approach to funding international trade, with banks serving as critical intermediaries. The primary goal of this approach is documented trade, whereby banks oversee the exchange of cash against shipping documentation to facilitate operations. This transaction-based strategy places a strong emphasis on risk minimization and ensuring the timely payment of products sold internationally.

Trade finance is subject to a complex international system of regulation that includes international treaties, national laws, and standards developed by global financial institutions, which have a lot of legal responsibilities to follow, including know your customer (KYC) standards, sanctions legislation, and anti-money laundering (AML) regulations.

International Chambers of Commerce (ICC) and various other entities establish standards and guidelines, such as UCP 600 (Uniform Customs and Practice for Documentary Credits), that harmonize international banking procedures. Banks must keep up with these changing regulations so as to ensure compliance and to promote policies that foster the growth and sustainability of global trade. Financial institutions are vital elements that propel international trade; they are more than just middlemen in the trade finance ecosystem, since they facilitate cross-border business expansion, global economic growth, and development by managing a wide range of risks, offering vital financing solutions, issuing crucial financial instruments, and navigating the complex regulatory landscape.

Global rules and regulations that are very strict, like the Uniform Customs and Practice for Documentary Credits (UCP600), control the process and make sure it is done correctly and safely. Its complexity, higher transaction costs, and requirement for manual processing of physical documents, which may result in longer execution times, are among its key features.

The environment of global commerce is changing rapidly; projections point to a notable increase in trade flows and a growing trend toward open account operations. This change suggests that supply chain finance will become more important, maybe surpassing traditional trade finance techniques in terms of volume and effectiveness. However, because of their advantages in risk avoidance, conventional trade systems have briefly regained attention in light of the continuing COVID-19 epidemic.

For conventional trade finance, the digital revolution presents both a significant challenge and an opportunity. Integrating digital technologies could revitalize this outdated system, enhancing its ability to rival the efficiency and scalability of supply chain finance. The future of trade finance will ultimately depend on how eager the sector is to accept new technologies and adjust to shifting trade dynamics.

Future Unfolded: The Rise of Digital Ecosystems

Supply chain finance and trade finance are essential parts of the global trade ecosystem that support economic growth and ease commerce. As digital technology develops and becomes more effective, secure, and accessible, these financial disciplines stand to undergo further revolution. Leveraging these technologies to create a more robust, transparent, and interconnected global trading environment is key to the future of trade finance.

Trade finance is undergoing a digital revolution that is a significant step toward more efficient, open, and inclusive financial procedures. Emerging technologies like blockchain, AI, and ML, along with the creation of digital platforms and ecosystems, are driving this transition. These developments create new opportunities for growth and innovation, in addition to addressing long-standing inefficiencies.

CHAPTER 1   GATEWAY TO GLOBAL COMMERCE: UNLOCKING THE SECRETS OF TRADE AND
            SUPPLY CHAIN FINANCE

The Technology Streamline: Blockchain, AI, and IoT

By utilizing blockchain technology, a group of banks and shipping businesses were able to complete a cross-border trade transaction with outstanding success, cutting down on the amount of time needed for document processing and verification. This illustrated how blockchain technology may not only increase productivity but also security and transparency throughout the supply chain. By providing predictive insights, improving risk assessment, and automating repetitive processes, AI and ML are redefining trade finance's capabilities.

Artificial intelligence (AI) algorithms are capable of analyzing enormous volumes of data to forecast market trends, evaluate a party's creditworthiness, and spot possible fraud or compliance problems. This allows for better informed decision-making.

The Internet of things (IoT) can significantly enhance trade finance digitization by providing real-time visibility and transparency across the supply chain. IoT devices, such as sensors and GPS trackers, can monitor the condition and location of goods, ensuring compliance with contractual terms and improving risk management. Blockchain technology can integrate this data to create immutable records, enhancing trust among parties and reducing the need for manual documentation and verification.

Automated data collection and analysis streamline processes such as inventory management, shipment tracking, and quality control, leading to faster, more accurate trade finance operations. IoT-enabled systems can also find and report strange things, like changes in temperature or unauthorized access, so that steps can be taken to stop fraud and losses. Overall, IoT facilitates a more efficient, secure, and transparent trade finance ecosystem, promoting better decision-making and reducing operational costs.

Financial institutions are using AI to create more accurate and dynamic credit scoring models. These models provide a more comprehensive picture of a borrower's financial health and risk profile by accounting for non-traditional data sources, including social media activity and real-time supply chain information.

The capacity of blockchain technology to provide safe, open, and effective trade finance transactions sets it apart. Blockchain lowers costs and increases speed by reducing the need for middlemen and enabling decentralized transaction verification. By automating the execution of agreements when predetermined criteria are satisfied, smart contracts further streamline workflows and lower the likelihood of disputes.

The emergence of digital trade finance platforms has led to the creation of interconnected ecosystems that facilitate seamless connections between lenders, suppliers, and buyers. These platforms enhance efficiency and accessibility by offering a comprehensive range of financial services, including foreign payments and invoice finance. A leading international trade finance platform has changed the way that businesses interact with their financial supply chains. The platform provides SMEs with improved access to financing, improved visibility throughout the supply chain, and smoother transactions by providing a full suite of digital trade finance products.

Digitalization has revolutionary potential, but many obstacles stand in its way. There's a chance that the trade finance industry's digital revolution could exacerbate the divide between big, technologically sophisticated corporations and smaller, less capable enterprises. It will need focused efforts to increase digital literacy and technological access to close this gap. It continues to be difficult to negotiate the many and diverse regulatory environments across jurisdictions.

The broad acceptance of digital trade finance solutions depends on regulatory harmonization and the creation of digital-friendly legal frameworks. The danger of cyberattacks increases with the digitization of trade finance procedures. It is imperative to allocate resources toward strong cybersecurity protocols and cultivate a security-conscious mindset in order to safeguard confidential data and uphold confidence in digital channels. The strategic use of digital advances to overcome these obstacles and seize new opportunities will determine the direction of trade finance in the future.

Digital technologies promise to improve the efficiency and accessibility of trade finance by fostering a more integrated, transparent, and resilient global trading environment. This will drive economic growth and facilitate global commerce in the digital era. Before going deeper into the realm of digital trade, it may be worth setting the traditional scenario through the next chapter, where we'll dive into the world and trade finance and the strategies and instruments helping the stakeholders involved: the *Buyer/Importer, The Seller/Exporter, and The Enabler*.

Summary

This chapter reviewed trade and supply chain finance as the portal to worldwide business by blending history, contemporary practices, and future prospects. It followed the evolution of trade finance from prehistoric societies to contemporary business, therefore highlighting the continuing relevance of trust and documentation in enabling world trade. It then examines the historical relevance and the transforming effect of the World Wars on world trade patterns and financial leadership and the part financial institutions play in guaranteeing economic stability and thereby supporting trade financing. It also explores how the digital revolution is altering the trading environment.

CHAPTER 2

Letters of Credit: The Lifeline of Global Trade

The significance of traditional documented trade in the dynamic world of international trade, tools such as documentary credits, or letters of credit (LCs), is becoming increasingly important. LCs provide the sector security and confidence in cross-border transactions as we traverse challenging macroeconomic landscapes and unstable geopolitical environments. Examining its mechanics, advantages, and development as a reliable financial tool, this chapter explores the indispensible role LCs play in world commerce. It begins by asking, "How does a letter of credit work?" to clarify how the guarantee of payment helps buyers and sellers reduce risks.

How Does a Letter of Credit Work?

When a Buyer, referred to as the "Applicant," pays a Seller, referred to as the "Beneficiary," a certain amount at the time of purchase or at a later date, i.e., the "maturity date," the Issuer, usually referred to as the "issuing bank," irrevocably undertakes to pay the Seller, provided that the documents listed under the documentary credit are issued and submitted in compliance with the terms and conditions specified in the LC itself. The issuing bank may grant the documentary credit on its own account or on behalf of the Applicant. People commonly refer to these types of instruments as "documentary credits" because they necessitate the submission of specific documents to receive credit.

Given that they were formerly printed papers, irrevocability is the documentary credits' feature. The issuer irrevocably undertakes to settle for payment(s) with these documentary credits; once issued, the issuing bank cannot take them back or alter the credit. The Beneficiary, the issuing bank, and the confirming bank (if any) can only approve changes or cancellations to a credit. Their nature is quite peculiar since, as stated in the credit terms and conditions, documentary credits are "documentary in nature," and any payment promises they contain are contingent upon the receipt of supporting documentation.

Only when the beneficiaries acknowledge the documents they submitted in accordance with the documentary's terms and conditions are documentary credits paid out. As a result, the recipient must provide documentation that satisfies the terms and conditions of each credit in order to receive payment under a documentary credit. If any discrepancies arise, the issuing bank has the right to refuse to honor the request and pay only if the non-compliant documents are amended and made compliant before the credit expires, or if both the Applicant and the issuing bank agree to waive the discrepancy(ies). They are intended to speed up the settlement of an underlying trade transaction in which the Applicant receives payment via credit, which subsequently fulfills the Applicant's payment obligations against the underlying sales or other contract on which it may be based. (The buyer) receives the products or services.

Documentary credits can be defined as a payment mechanism whose purpose is to speed up the settlement of an underlying trade transaction. In such a scenario, the Beneficiary receives payment via credit, which then fulfills his payment obligations under any applicable contracts or sales agreements. On the other hand, the applicant, as the buyer, receives the goods or services. They exist independently of the sale or other contract they are based on. They are "independent commitments" made by the issuing bank and, if applicable, the confirming bank. Globally respected, the ICC Uniform Customs and Practice for Documentary Credits 2007 Revision (also known as "UCP 600") articulates the notion of autonomy in this regard.

An instrument or agreement, known as a documentary credit, facilitates the settlement of local or international commercial transactions through the use of bank undertakings. Banks involved in such transactions do not deal with products, services, or performances related to the documents; instead, they merely handle records. When a compliant presentation is generated, the Applicant is obligated to effect payment(s) to the issuing bank based on the terms and conditions of the documentary credit. Documentary credits guarantee payment to the recipient, provided they submit the necessary paperwork to the originating bank, the designated bank, or the confirming bank, as applicable.

The Power of Documentary Credits: Safeguarding Transactions and Reaping Benefits

The parties involved in international business transactions frequently originate from countries with numerous exchange control regulations, legal frameworks, market behaviors, currencies, and cultures. In addition to having to assume the risk of the Seller defaulting on the contract, Buyers may find it difficult to assess the reliability of overseas suppliers. Products that fail to meet the contract's quality standards, or those that arrive slowly or not at all, can fall under this category. Due to the challenge of solving these issues in a foreign legal system, purchasers would naturally want to commit to paying only once they are satisfied with the items. In a similar way, Sellers are exposed to the threat of nonpayment and would have to assume the responsibility for legal action in the buyer's nation against the buyer. This implies that vendors typically demand payment prior to shipment. The system becomes unbalanced as a result of this dynamic, where Purchasers only want to pay after delivery, while Sellers want payment prior to shipping. Documentary credits offer a way to talk about and work toward resolving these competing interests. UCP 600 and ISBP publication 821, which additionally provide guidelines and procedures for document verification, govern documentary credits. As a result of this, whenever traders follow these guidelines, there is less opportunity for miscommunication or misinterpretation, which reduces the likelihood of unforeseen conflicts. In order to take advantage of the benefits offered by such a method, the Beneficiary must explicitly specify the terms and conditions expressed therein, including what documents must be submitted and who should provide them. In a similar way, the Beneficiary needs to provide the documentation listed in the terms and conditions of the documentary credit. Depending on which side of the transaction a party is on, documentary credits have different benefits. The main advantages for the Buyer/Applicant in an overseas transaction are the guarantee that they will only have to pay after the shipping has been made.

The Beneficiary/Seller will provide the documentation that is required by the credit, which ought to satisfy the requirements for customs clearance. The issuing bank will review the submitted documents to ensure compliance with the credit's terms and conditions before processing payment. The primary advantage of a documentary credit for the Beneficiary/Seller in an overseas transaction is that it transfers the buyer's risk of payment under the sales contract to the issuing bank, which may have a credit rating higher than the Applicant's. The beneficiary's consent is required to withdraw or alter a documentary credit due to its irreversible nature. If the issuing, confirming, or designated bank receives compliant documentation and agrees to act upon its designation, it will issue payment. Further remedies may be available to a confirming bank. This is useful if the Beneficiary/Seller has concerns regarding the Applicant/Buyer's nation's political or legal climate or the issuing bank's credit standing.

The Key Players in Documentary Credit Transactions: Roles and Relationships

A documentary credit may include parties that are different from one another. While some parties are essential, others are discretionary, included solely to achieve specific goals or requirements for that specific contact. The potential parties in the documentary credits are as follows.

The Buyer of the products typically submits the application or request to the issuing bank to get a documentary credit issued on its behalf. Now referred to as the Applicant, he provides the applicable terms and conditions along with the necessary documents to establish the documentary credit. Since a credit is a bank undertaking, even when he initiates the request, he is not a party to the documentary credit.

In accordance with the Applicant's request, **the issuing bank** issues the documentary credit. In line with the terms and conditions of the documentary credit, this bank irrevocably agrees to pay the Beneficiary as soon as the required documentation is received.

The beneficiary is the person or entity that has received the documentary credit. In an international trade transaction, it is typically the Seller.

Along with adhering to the originating bank's irrevocable commitment, a **confirming bank** may also provide one to honor the documentary credit. In other words, it promises to pay right away, take on a deferred payment obligation, or accept a bill of exchange when it receives the documents that meet the terms and conditions of the credit. This depends on whether the credit is available.

Upon receiving the documentary credit from the issuing bank, an **advising bank** advises the recipient to take steps to verify its legitimacy. The advising bank makes sure the advice properly reflects the terms and conditions of the documentary credit as received and authenticates the documentary credit by offering guidance. The advising bank declines any further obligation or responsibility until it has verified the documented credit.

The issuing bank may authorize a different bank, known as **the nominated bank**, to pay a presenter at sight or undertake a deferred payment obligation with the agreement that the amount will be paid at maturity.

The nominated bank is only bound by the originating bank's nomination if it has verified the documentary credit or if it has explicitly informed the Beneficiary that it would be carrying out its nomination.

The other entity that provides the reimbursement is often the issuing bank's **correspondent bank**, with which it keeps an account in the document credit's currency.

As stated in the documentary credit, the nominee bank or the confirming bank (referred to as the "claiming bank") will be required to submit a reimbursement claim on behalf of the reimbursing bank. With approval from the originating bank, the reimbursement bank may honor a reimbursement claim from the claiming bank.

The ICC Uniform Rules for Bank-to-Bank Reimbursements under Documentary Credits (URR 725) are often applicable to the reimbursement authorization. Reimbursement is subject to UCP 600 article 13 (Bank-to-Bank Reimbursement Arrangements) unless otherwise stated in the credit.

Beneficiaries of documentary credits occasionally act as middlemen, acquiring items from other vendors and asking their buyers to set up a transferable documentary credit. The documentary credit would subsequently be transferred by the issuing bank, designating a **transferring bank**.

The first beneficiary, the Beneficiary, will ask the transferring bank to assign the documentary credit, in whole or in part, to the other beneficiary, the beneficiary's own supplier.

In such a case, the documentary credit must expressly indicate that it is transferable so that such a transfer can take place.

Orchestrating Trust: The Ensemble of Parties in a Letter of Credit

A number of parties conduct an LC, and each one of them has specific duties for making sure that the transaction goes successfully from start to finish.

The **Applicant** is typically the buyer in a trade transaction. Businesses request that the issuing bank start an LC on the beneficiary seller's behalf. He goes over the documentary credit's terms and conditions as well as the paperwork needed to finish the deal.

CHAPTER 2   LETTERS OF CREDIT: THE LIFELINE OF GLOBAL TRADE

The bank that approves the LC at the Applicant's request is known as the **Issuing Bank**; it assumes responsibility for paying the **Beneficiary** in line with the terms of the LC upon presentation of the necessary documentation. This latter party is typically the seller in the transaction, in whose favor the LC is issued; in order to be paid, he must provide the necessary documentation within the allotted period.

In addition to the issuing bank's assurance, the **Confirming Bank** adds its own one since it is essentially in charge of committing to reimburse the beneficiary upon the presentation of compliant documents, providing the recipient with an additional layer of security.

By definition, the **Advising Bank** advises the Beneficiary on the LC, guaranteeing its legitimacy. Unless it is also the confirming bank, it validates and forwards the LC to the recipient without taking on any payment obligations.

The **Nominated Bank** is the one authorized by the issuing bank to make payments or accept drafts under the documentary credit. If it has confirmed the LC or agreed to act upon its nomination, it must honor the payment.

Since the **Reimbursing Bank** has been given permission by the Issuing Bank to reimburse the Claiming Bank following presentation of compliance documentation, it manages the reimbursement claims from the nominated or confirming banks.

In transactions involving intermediary merchants, the **Transferring Bank** enables the transfer of an LC from the first beneficiary to one or more second beneficiaries. It transfers the LC as instructed by the first beneficiary.

Emphasizing the LC's independence from the underlying contract between the buyer and seller, despite the applicant initiating it, is crucial. The LC must clearly include specific provisions for certain elements like transferability and confirmation to be applicable.

When they apply, international rules such as the ICC Uniform Rules for Bank-to-Bank Reimbursements (URR 725) and the UCP 600 spell out how LCs work and what each party's role and responsibility is. By combining these different organizations into a safe and well-organized system for doing business across international borders, documentary credits do lower risk and make sure that everyone knows what their duties are.

Risk mitigation in international trade transactions with documentary credits addresses the inherent uncertainties and challenges arising from the financial, legal, and geographic separation between buyers and sellers. The goal is to keep disagreements and financial losses to a minimum while still making sure that both parties keep their end of the deal. Documentary credits are a safe way to achieve this balance.

In simple terms, they operate as a crucial instrument of finance in worldwide trade, bridging the trust gap between individuals living in different countries with disparate legal frameworks. Cultural norms and financial stability levels play a significant role. They instill confidence in both parties by effectively binding the buyer's bank to make payments to the seller under specified conditions.

The primary danger to the buyer is that it's possible that the seller fails to provide the items in a timely and high-quality manner as stipulated in the contract. By requiring the seller to provide evidence of shipping and manufacturing compliance prior to payment, documentary credits mitigate this risk. The process guarantees that clients only approve payment after verifying the dispatch of items in line with the contract's terms.

The primary risk for the seller is not receiving payment after shipping. Documentary credits guarantee payment to sellers, provided they provide the necessary documentation that meets the credit's requirements. Sellers benefit from increased financial security as a result of the buyer's bank taking on the payment risk instead of the buyer.

Ensuring Clarity and Compliance: The Role of ISBP and UCP 600

The two main frameworks that control documentary credits are the International Standard Banking Practice (ISBP) publication 821 and the Uniform Customs and Practice for Documentary Credits (UCP 600). By standardizing document examination procedures and guaranteeing precise documentary credit conditions, these standards lessen the possibility of misunderstandings and conflicts. All parties will be fully aware of their responsibilities and the terms under which money will be issued if these criteria are followed.

The beneficiary must carefully define the credit terms, including the necessary papers and their issuers, in order to leverage documentary credits. By making sure that everyone understands their duties and responsibilities, this clarity reduces the possibility of noncompliance and disagreement.

CHAPTER 2   LETTERS OF CREDIT: THE LIFELINE OF GLOBAL TRADE

Balancing Risk and Security: How Documentary Credits Facilitate Safe and Structured International Transactions

The buyer has a guarantee of shipment, as payment is contingent on the seller providing confirmation of shipment. Document Compliance for Customs ensures that all necessary documentation is provided for customs clearance. Finally, bank scrutiny adds an extra degree of protection as the issuing bank verifies that the documents are compliant before releasing funds.

Conversely, the Seller takes advantage of the shift in payment risk, wherein the Buyer's duty to pay is transferred to a bank that is deemed more creditworthy. Therefore, remember that documentary credits offer payment security and are irreversible without the seller's approval. The designated bank, the issuing bank, or both will make payment if the seller presents the necessary documentation. Sellers may turn to a confirming bank if they are worried about the political or economic stability of the buyer's nation.

In order to balance the interests of buyers and sellers and reduce the risks associated with international commerce, documentary credits offer an organized, controlled framework. Documentary credits make foreign transactions easier and safer by guaranteeing that payments are issued only when the requirements of the contract are met. This promotes the expansion of international trade.

The Spectrum of Documentary Credits: Types and Uses

The range of documentary credits is broad, as there are many different types of documentary credits, and each offers distinctive characteristics. When sight credits are used, the nominated bank, the confirming bank, or the issuing bank pays as soon as the documents are shown (also called "at sight"), as long as they meet the requirements of the documentary credit.

Sometimes it happens that the issuing bank agrees to honor a complying presentation at a later time, referred to as the "**maturity date**," under **usance credits**. These types of credits come in two varieties: "**acceptance credits**," which require the provision of a bill of exchange, or "drafts," which the bank will accept and pay to the beneficiary upon maturity.

Similar to acceptance credits, "**deferred payment credit**" does not call for the submission of a draft. When a portion of the amount is payable at sight and the balance is payable at a future date (or dates) in accordance with the documentary credit conditions, practitioners utilize mixed payment credits. These credits are commonly referred to as **mixed payment credits** since they combine **sight** and **usance** credits.

Based on the reimbursement modalities, we can further distinguish among credits. A negotiation credit is when the nominated bank buys drafts drawn on banks other than the nominated bank and/or documents that comply with a presentation by the nominated bank. The nominated bank then advances or agrees to advance funds to the beneficiary on or before the banking day on which the nominated bank is due for reimbursement. Credits that include both the issuing bank's and the confirming bank's irrevocable pledge to honor or negotiate, without recourse, documents that comply with the terms and conditions of the credit are referred to as **confirmed credits**.

If the beneficiary (i.e., the "first beneficiary") of a documentary credit is an intermediary trader.

If a buyer procures goods from another source, they may request the buyer to provide a transferable credit. The first beneficiary can then transfer this credit to its supplier, also known as the "second beneficiary." A **transferable documentary credit** must expressly state that it is transferable and provide the name of the nominated bank or the bank authorized to transfer.

To transfer the credit, the first beneficiary will request that the nominated or authorized bank transfer the documentary credit, either in full or in part, to the second beneficiary.

Whenever the documentary credit allows partial shipments, the first beneficiary may request a transfer to several second beneficiaries. The second beneficiary, however, cannot transfer the documentary credit to a subsequent beneficiary.

With the exception of the amount, the unit price, wherever applicable, the expiration date, and the latest date of shipping or period for presentation, which can all be reduced, UCP 600 requires the transfer to be effected under the terms and conditions in force. Additionally, you may use the applicant's name instead of the first beneficiary's.

When the documentary credit requires the presentation of an insurance document, it may adjust the amount or percentage of insurance to provide coverage as initially required. One beneficiary can submit its own invoice and claim payment for any value difference instead of the second. Nevertheless, the transferring bank may send documents collected from the second beneficiary to the issuing bank even though it doesn't submit his invoice.

There are cases where documentary credits serve the same purpose as transferable credits. Sometimes the beneficiary requires his bank to issue a new documentary credit in favor of his supplier rather than transferring the existing one to its supplier. Because banks issue these credits on the backs of original ones, practitioners usually refer to them as **back-to-back credits**.

The original documentary credit and a back-to-back credit are distinct and independent from one another. The beneficiary of the original documentary credit must be able to provide proof that meets the terms and conditions of the loan. However, the issuing bank of the back-to-back documentary credit must accept a presentation that meets those conditions under its own documentary credit. When a credit specifies a shipment schedule with specific quantities, amounts, and/or deadlines for when the products shall be shipped, it is referred to as an **installment credit**. This type of credit has a special feature in that, in case one installment is not dispatched within the time frame specified, the credit in its entirety is no longer available for any following installments, not just that one.

Rather than granting a new credit every time they place an order for the same items at the same price and terms and conditions, buyers may negotiate with vendors to issue **revolving credits**.

The terms and conditions of the current drawing "revolve" these credits, either automatically or in response to a reinstatement notification from the issuing bank.

The parties can mutually agree on the maximum amount, the number of times, or the latest date that a revolving credit will automatically reinstate.

Usually, the beneficiary submits documents that meet the requirements and conditions; documentary credits typically reimburse the beneficiary at the post-shipment stage. However, the beneficiary may receive an advance payment during the pre-shipment stage, even before they produce documentation after the items' shipment. By providing a receipt, the credit beneficiary can withdraw up to a predetermined amount. Upon delivery of the products, you must deduct the advance payment amount from the invoice amount.

Pre-shipment Financing: Understanding Red and Green Clause Documentary Credits

Pre-shipment financing can be obtained from financiers using one of two types of advance payment credits. **Red clause documentary credits**, called as such because they were once issued in letter form, banks used to type this phrase in red ink feature a clause allowing the designated bank to provide the beneficiary with an advance payment. In order to assist the beneficiary with obtaining raw materials, processing, manufacturing, packing, and exporting the goods, the bank may release a certain amount during the pre-shipment phase. The beneficiary must then submit credit-compliant documentation for the relevant shipment of goods in order to satisfy the advance payment.

Documentary credits with a **green clause** are comparable to those with a red clause. However, **green clause documentary credits** also cover pre-shipment warehousing and insurance costs in addition to providing the beneficiary with advance payment at the pre-shipment stage.

Beyond Traditional Trade: The World of Restricted and Structured Letters of Credit

International trade employs a specific type of documentary credit known as a restricted letter of credit (LC) to add an extra layer of oversight to the transaction process. If a bank agrees to the terms and circumstances set forth by the issuing bank, the beneficiary in a normal letter of credit can provide the necessary documentation to any bank that is prepared to negotiate the LC. A restricted letter of credit, on the other hand, limits this process by saying that the LC can only be redeemed at a certain bank, which is usually written in the LC itself. This limitation has a number of benefits and effects for all parties involved.

The issuing bank may exercise more control over the deal by limiting the negotiation to that particular bank. This can be particularly significant if the transaction involves high-value items, occurs in a high-risk market, or if the issuing bank and the designated bank have a relationship. The agreement makes sure that a bank that the issuer trusts is in charge of document management and LC terms execution.

Since everyone is aware of precisely which bank will handle all of the paperwork and payments, transactions can be completed with greater efficiency. This predictability might minimize delays resulting from the beneficiary locating a bank ready to discuss the LC or from different banks reading the conditions of the LC in different ways.

In an effort to more effectively manage expenditures, the applicant (often the buyer) and the issuing bank might opt for a restricted LC. By limiting the LC to a single bank, the parties may be able to bargain for more favorable conditions or leverage the advantages of preexisting banking relationships. Negotiation and handling fees can differ between banks.

A restricted letter of credit's primary drawback is the beneficiary's limited flexibility. In situations where the beneficiary has a stronger relationship with another bank or the designated bank is located in an unsuitable location, this restriction may lead to logistical issues, potentially delaying the transaction.

There may be cases where the designated bank has no headquarters in the beneficiary's country or lacks global reach. This circumstance might make the redemption process more difficult and necessitate additional arrangements, which could lead to delays and increased costs. The beneficiary must adhere to the designated bank's procedures and costs for document handling and negotiation, giving the bank significant control and potentially leading to terms that are less favorable for the beneficiary.

Notwithstanding these limitations, restricted letters of credit may represent an invaluable tool for conducting cross-border business dealings, in particular when reliability, control, and predictability are critical. When dealing with fresh partners, in high-risk markets, or when the transaction contains sensitive or highly valued items, companies have the option to apply for a restricted LC.

Ultimately, the decision to take advantage of a restricted letter of credit should stem from an in-depth assessment of the conditions of the transaction, the relationship between the parties, and the qualifications and reach of the designated bank. It's a calculated move that might enhance the efficiency and security of international trade finance, but it calls for thorough preparation and open communication between all stakeholders.

The beneficiary's bank, when it differs from the designated negotiating bank, serves as a key intermediary in the process when handling a restricted letter of credit (LC), in which the issuing bank designates a specific negotiating bank for the transaction. The beneficiary's bank advises the beneficiary to deliver the required documents directly to the designated negotiating bank in accordance with the LC terms. This includes providing instructions to the beneficiary on how to request acceptance or payment from the negotiating bank.

Pre-Forwarding Document Check: Prior to sending the documents to the negotiating bank, the beneficiary's bank may offer a document examination service. While not mandatory, this service helps ensure that the documents comply with the terms of the LC, potentially reducing the risk of discrepancies that could lead to delays or refusal of payment. However, this service is subject to fees. The beneficiary's bank follows the LC's instructions and requirements, transmitting the paperwork to the negotiating bank via banking channels after performing a preliminary check, if applicable.

With the support of the intermediary bank, the beneficiary can save a lot of time and cash by presenting the required documents directly to the negotiating bank. Reducing the number of banks involved in the document examination and transfer process may minimize associated fees and decrease the transaction timeline. This efficiency results from the established relationship and mutual understanding between the negotiating bank and the beneficiary's bank, which streamlines the document handling process.

The beneficiary's bank does not receive any extra security or protection under the Uniform Customs and Practice for Documentary Credits (UCP) as long as it does not function as the nominated bank. This implies that if the beneficiary's bank provides a document examination service without being the designated bank, it does not function with the usual protections provided to negotiating banks under the UCP. The beneficiary may have little recourse against the beneficiary's bank if the negotiating bank dishonored the documents or lost them in transit, particularly if the bank's only action was to transfer the documents without conducting a formal examination.

Submitting documents at a bank can have benefits for know your customer (KYC) and anti-money laundering (AML) compliance since banks have facilities with procedures for handling these statutory requirements. In addition to contributing strategic support, beneficiaries handling a restricted LC might save both time and money by having their bank help with the presentation of documentation to the designated negotiating bank. Beneficiaries must be aware of their bank's obligations and restrictions during this procedure, especially regarding UCP transaction security and protection.

International trade transactions might encounter particular challenges and complexities due to the use of these instruments. Even though their purpose is to give the parties more protection and control, they can cause problems at times, especially because they confine the LC to a single bank.

Dependency on SWIFT: Potential Issues to Beneficiaries

We are aware that the SWIFT network is a major source of secure, standardized communications for the global banking industry, including the transfer of LCs. If the beneficiary's bank does not have SWIFT authentication arrangements with the originating bank, direct LC transmission becomes complicated. In order to lessen this, the issuing bank may designate that bank as the restricted negotiating bank and transfer the LC through their correspondent bank in the beneficiary's nation. This reliance on correspondent banking relationships may cause the transaction to be more complex and cause delays.

Limiting the LC to a single bank significantly reduces the beneficiary's options, potentially causing inconvenience and inefficiencies, particularly if the chosen bank is not their preferred choice for managing trade transactions or if they have a stronger relationship with another. In addition to this, the beneficiary must agree to these terms if the designated bank charges greater costs or offers less advantageous terms for managing LCs.

Issues may also arise if the authorized bank's branch network does not sufficiently cover the beneficiary's business region, or if the bank lacks the necessary knowledge or resources to effectively manage specific types of LC transactions. This may cause delays in completing the LC and the underlying trade transaction, as well as logistical difficulties and higher expenses.

Nowadays, a sophisticated body of regulations, such as know your customer (KYC) and anti-money laundering (AML) procedures, apply to cross-border transactions. The verification and acceptance process for the LC may be complicated and may result in delays or extra scrutiny if the beneficiary's bank and the designated bank have differing standards or practices for compliance.

The efficient implementation of a restricted LC transaction depends on the beneficiary, his bank, the issuing bank, and the designated bank having effective communication and coordination. There could be disagreements, issues with acceptance, or non-payment if the LC conditions are not understood or communicated clearly if the paperwork is not consistent or if information is sent slowly.

The beneficiary can experience greater challenges resolving issues if the designated bank declines to abide by the LC because it fails to adhere to the letter. As the LC is limited, there are no other negotiation options, which may limit the beneficiary's options and complicate the settlement process. Special LCs, while offering security and control advantages, also pose unique challenges and intricacies that require proper handling. To keep problems to a minimum and make sure the transaction goes smoothly, both the person issuing the money and the person receiving it must be aware of these possible problems and work closely with their banks to make sure there is clear communication, good coordination, and following all rules and regulations.

When trying to address specific issues, operational preferences, or risk mitigation techniques in international trade transactions, restricted L/Cs are available in a variety of forms. By only allowing one bank or branch to present and negotiate the L/C, the parties are trying to lower their risks, take advantage of good financial conditions, or build on trusting banking relationships. In this scenario, the beneficiary's bank, which also holds the authority to verify the letter of credit, issues the letter of credit on the condition that presentation and negotiation take place through them. When the beneficiary wishes to combine their banking transactions for convenience and more favorable conditions, or when they have confidence in their bank's capacity to handle the L/C procedure successfully, this arrangement may prove advantageous. There may have been a number of reasons for the explicit exclusion of some banks from handling the L/C, such as poor terms offered by the excluded institutions, increased costs, or prior negative experiences.

An L/C may stipulate that the drawee, financier, and issuing bank can only operate from the same branch of a bank, for instance, the London office. This usually happens when the beneficiary has a preferred branch because it has better financing rates, a better location, or more experience with handling foreign transactions than the beneficiary's bank. This limitation ensures the recipient can still benefit from interacting with the selected branch despite the fact they don't have an account there, which could help them get the best terms on their trade finance.

When issuing a letter of credit (LC) from a developing nation, the inherent risks associated with the transaction, the issuing bank, and the nation's financial system may necessitate the use of a limited LC. The restriction aims to mitigate risks by mandating a bank with a more stable and reliable banking infrastructure—typically in a developed nation—to advise and negotiate the LC.

Associating the LC with a bank that has a more comprehensive risk management system and a stronger global footprint will help safeguard the beneficiary's interests. Sometimes restricted LCs put the beneficiary in a difficult situation, especially if they have no control over the particular bank's or branch's decision.

Risk management, strategic goals, or partnerships with other banks could all impact the issuing bank's choice of correspondent bank. The issuer may have a good reason for only letting one bank handle the L/C, but the beneficiary may have operational, financial, or logistical problems if the chosen bank is not their first choice or if it offers worse terms. They are used to help clients manage the intricacies of international trade finance by offering solutions that are customized to each trading party's unique requirements, risks, and preferences. Although they provide advantages for strategic financial planning and risk management, they also need to be carefully considered in light of the possible difficulties and limitations they may place on the beneficiary. To manage international trade transactions efficiently and maximize the advantages of trade financing arrangements, one must comprehend the dynamics and ramifications of restricted L/Cs.

CHAPTER 2   LETTERS OF CREDIT: THE LIFELINE OF GLOBAL TRADE

Streamlining Trade Transactions: UCP 600 and the Flexibility of Direct Document Submission

The Uniform Customs and Practice for Documentary Credits (UCP 600) regulates the use of letters of credit (LCs) in international trade. Provisions within its framework allow for flexible handling and presentation of documents during transactions. It is true that, under some circumstances, the beneficiary may communicate directly with the issuing bank rather than through designated, advising, or confirming banks, as stated in sub-articles 6a and 6d(ii) of UCP 600.

Sub-Article 6a outlines the tasks and obligations of banks participating in the LC process. It makes it clear that the main purpose of the nominated, advising, and confirming banks' engagement is to facilitate the transaction on the beneficiary's behalf.

Sub-Article 6d(ii) grants the beneficiary the ability to submit documents to the issuing bank directly, avoiding the nominated bank and any other banks acting as intermediaries. This can happen when the beneficiary and the issuing bank have the main contractual relationship, implying that other banks' participation is optional and meant to help the beneficiary. He may choose to deal directly with the issuing bank for the presentation of documentation rather than using the services of designated, advising, or confirming banks. Efficiency, financial factors, or the relationship with the issuing bank may all have played a role in this calculated decision.

Communicating directly with the issuing bank can expedite the entire process as well as save costs and presentation time for the document. By eliminating unnecessary processing and communication layers, the procedure becomes more efficient. So, while bringing paperwork directly to the issuing bank may have some benefits, it also means that the beneficiary is responsible for making sure that all of the paperwork meets the requirements of the LC.

Because there isn't a bank acting as a middleman to check or validate the paperwork before it gets to the issuing bank, the recipient needs to prepare their documentation carefully to make sure there are no errors that could result in rejection. Collecting documents directly from the beneficiary may additionally assist the issuing bank in operating more efficiently, as it may speed up the document's scrutiny processes and minimize the bank's need to communicate with other banks. The UCP 600 allows direct communication between the beneficiary and the issuing bank. However, this doesn't happen very often and depends a lot on the agreements and arrangements between the parties. It will depend on a number of factors, including transaction complexity, trust, and past connections, to determine whether direct document presentation is practical and beneficial.

Under an LC, the UCP 600 sets up a framework that gives the person receiving the documents a lot of freedom, including the choice to give the documents directly to the bank that issued the LC. This adaptability helps meet the different wants and needs of traders, but it needs careful thought about the effects, risks, and duties that come with not using middle-man banks. Nevertheless, the specific details and agreements of the LC will dictate the best course of action for all parties involved.

Structured Letters of Credit: Redefining Liquidity and Flexibility in International Trade Finance

Throughout our discussion, we have repeatedly emphasized the widespread recognition of letters of credit (LCs) as crucial instruments that secure cross-border payments in international commodities trade. However, structured letters of credit have shown that LCs can serve more than just traditional purposes. Beneficiaries can now utilize LCs as flexible financing choices rather than only as payment facilitators, thanks to these cutting-edge financial instruments. The conversion of LCs into structured formats represents a significant shift in how the global trade finance ecosystem perceives and makes use of them.

Structured letters of credit, unlike their conventional counterparts, primarily serve as financing tools instead of directly resolving trade disputes. An easy way to explain it is that a structured LC uses the deferred payment feature to give the beneficiary access to funds before the actual payment due date for the swap. This approach meets the recipients' immediate financial needs without waiting for the transaction's completion, providing them with increased liquidity and financial flexibility.

The innovative use of structured LCs calls into question their acceptability and legality, especially because of the absence of a genuine underlying trade transaction. The New York County Supreme Court's ruling in the case of Fortis Bank (Nederland) N.V. v. Abu Dhabi Islamic Bank from August 2010 serves as an important point of reference. The court's decision made it clear that the LC is still a stand-alone payment obligation, even though there isn't a real economic transaction going on. This decision highlights the artificial nature of structured long-term contracts, confirming their legality and enforceability as financial instruments.

The acceptance of this instrument as a valid financial one widens the range of options available for trade finance. For businesses in need of quick cash flow, structured LCs provide an innovative alternative by decoupling the payment mechanism from the actual trading of commodities. This flexibility is especially helpful in situations where there may be less or no access to traditional financial sources. The case also establishes a precedent for the wider acceptance and use of novel financial instruments in international finance by demonstrating how flexible the legal system can be. The trade finance industry has flourished due to the use of structured letters of credit for purposes beyond trade finance. The trade finance industry has grown by using structured letters of credit for purposes beyond trade finance. The financial markets will likely require further use and improvement as they continue to grow.

Sight LCs Streamlining Payments and the Dynamics of Deferred Payment Undertakings

In the complex world of global commerce, processing payments promptly and safely can often feel like navigating a dangerous maze. Allow us an opportunity to introduce you to the world of letters of credit (LCs), and particularly sight letters of credit (Sight LCs), which function as reliable and legitimate indicators for trade parties. Since these financial instruments only pay out when specific conditions are met, they are essential for facilitating worldwide trade. The UCP 600's uniform regulations are in place to govern them.

Securing Global Trade: The Evolving Role of Letters of Credit and Deferred Payment Agreements in Trade Finance

A Sight LC is a promise from a bank that, provided all conditions are fulfilled, money will be paid to the seller (beneficiary) right away upon presentation of the necessary paperwork. Because it offers an instant guarantee of payment, this kind of LC is the one that sellers look for in their foreign transactions. Because the Sight LC acts as an intermediary guarantee, it reduces the danger of non-payment, making it an invaluable instrument, particularly when working with unfamiliar or unidentified parties.

Its working mechanics are simple but effective. The issuing bank agrees to pay the recipient the agreed-upon amount once it receives documentation proving the shipment of goods or completion of services. This configuration ensures prompt payment to the seller upon product shipment and documentation, thereby reducing time and frustration. Before releasing the funds, the bank in turn demands a reasonable amount of time to check the paperwork, usually up to five business days. By making sure that everyone abides by the terms of the agreement, this verification procedure protects the integrity of the transaction.

Both time letters of credit (Time LCs) and sight letters of credit (Sight LCs) ensure payments, thereby fostering trade; the primary difference lies in the timing of payments. With no grace period, a Sight LC requires payment immediately following document presentation and authentication. On the other hand, a Time LC establishes a deferred payment system, allowing a predetermined period to elapse after the submission of paperwork before the payment becomes due. This essential distinction meets the different objectives of trading parties by providing sellers with more instantaneous financial liquidity through Sight LCs.

Sight LCs help both buyers and sellers by verifying the shipment of goods and protecting merchants by guaranteeing timely payment. Mutual protection cultivates trust, which facilitates more seamless and effective international trade operations. Furthermore, Sight LCs' flexibility and security enable companies to grow internationally with assurance since they reduce the risks involved with doing business globally.

Sight Letters of Credit are essential components of the framework of international trade finance, offering a safe and effective way for buyers and sellers to interact. Through the guarantee of timely payments following the completion of contractual duties, Sight LCs uphold the foundation of confidence that underpins international trade. Sight LCs will continue to be an essential tool for securing profitable and mutually beneficial trading partnerships as companies negotiate the challenges of global trade.

Documentary letters of credit (LCs) and deferred payment agreements (DPAs) are crucial because they provide buyers and sellers with protection and flexibility by guaranteeing payment only once specific conditions are satisfied. These financial instruments, which are vital to trade finance, reduce risk and increase trading partners' mutual confidence, which facilitates cross-border transactions.

We have clarified that a documentary letter of credit (LC) is essentially an irreversible promise from the importer's bank to pay the exporter a specific amount of money, subject to the exporter presenting specific documentation, typically confirming the shipment of products. We guarantee that the importer will not receive payment until they present proof of shipment, and the exporter will receive payment once they fulfill their part of the trade agreement. The Uniform Customs and Practice for Documentary Credits (UCP 600), which offers a uniform set of generally accepted guidelines, regulates LCs, a fundamental aspect of modern commercial finance.

The issuing and execution of Letters of Credit, which were previously paper-based, have progressively shifted to digital platforms like SWIFT in line with the digital revolution of the banking and finance industry. This change makes international trade more accessible and secure by streamlining procedures, increasing efficiency, and lowering the risk of fraud.

The direct right to payment that an LC confers on its recipient allows the exporter to better manage its cash flow by introducing an element of transferability. If the seller has acceptance credits or deferred payment LCs with payment scheduled for a later date, they may choose to transfer the right to payment to a financier in order to accelerate cash inflow.

In the case of Deferred Payment LCs, the seller can unlock the value of the receivable prior to its maturity by assigning the right to receive future payments, which serves as a crucial financing mechanism. As for the Acceptance Credits, receivables are transferred more easily under this arrangement. The beneficiary can change the bank's payment obligation into a negotiable instrument by delivering a draft along with the necessary paperwork. The beneficiary can easily sell this draft once the issuing bank accepts it, providing instant liquidity.

More than just financial tools, documentary LCs and deferred payment agreements are essential components that promote flexibility and confidence in global trade. They mitigate the risks associated with cross-border business by guaranteeing payment based on verifiable activities. This makes the global business environment more stable and active.

The clever use of deferred payment agreements and documented letters of credit highlights the advanced trade finance options that are currently accessible to global traders. These tools will be crucial in bridging the trust-risk divide as the digital transformation of trade progresses, guaranteeing the stability and expansion of international trade.

Deferred payment agreements and documentary letters of credit (LCs) are essential tools for guaranteeing cross-border trade and transaction security. These tools offer a structured method for controlling payment risks in addition to fostering confidence between business partners. Let's look into these crucial financial tools' mechanics in greater depth so as to acquire an improved comprehension of their workings along with their practical applications in trade finance.

CHAPTER 2   LETTERS OF CREDIT: THE LIFELINE OF GLOBAL TRADE

A documentary letter of credit is an exporter's promise to a bank that they will pay a certain amount as long as the exporter shows proof that the goods are being sent in line with the terms of the LC. Because it helps importers and exporters lower the risks associated with payment and goods delivery, respectively, this system is critical to international trade.

We will soon explore the UCP 600 and their role in global trade. This set of rules regulates the use of LCs. They provide a consistent legal framework that governs LC transactions around the world, making sure that documentary credits are consistent and reliable. Technology is advancing to the point where electronic letters of credit (eLCs) are gradually replacing or supplementing traditional paper-based LCs. Platforms like SWIFT have streamlined procedures and reduced the expenses and time required to produce traditional paper documents, enabling the digital issue and presentation of LCs.

Letters of credit with deferred payments allow the importer (or buyer) to postpone payment until a predetermined future date, adding a temporal component to the LC system. The importer may benefit most from this agreement since it gives them more time to sell the imported items before making the payment, which helps with cash flow management.

The right to payment under a deferred payment Exporters seeking instant financing can sell or assign LC to a financier. The exporter is able to obtain funds prior to the deferred payment. This sale or assignment determines the maturity date of the LC, effectively transferring the right to future payment.

Acceptance credits are a type of deferred payment letter of credit in which the recipient provides a draft and the necessary shipping documentation. Once the issuing bank accepts the draft, the bank's obligation under the LC turns into a negotiable instrument. The beneficiary can sell the instrument before the deadline to get money.

Through the strategic use of documented letters of credit and deferred payment undertakings, importers and exporters can manage and finance international trade transactions effectively. Exporters can secure rapid cash and payment assurances through the sale of payment rights, while importers can use these instruments to ensure the shipment of products prior to final payment.

Deferred payment agreements and documentary letters of credit are essential because they provide trading partners with security, adaptability, and liquidity. Participants in international trade can confidently negotiate the difficulties of cross-border transactions by comprehending and utilizing these tools, ensuring that payments and commodities move freely and securely around the world.

CHAPTER 2 LETTERS OF CREDIT: THE LIFELINE OF GLOBAL TRADE

Decoding the Global Language of Documentary Credits

The standardized Customs & Practice for Documentary Credits (UCP 600), an essential pillar of international trade, provides a set of standardized guidelines for the issuance and administration of letters of credit (LCs). The International Chamber of Commerce (ICC) developed and distributed these laws, which offer consistent legal and procedural guidelines that financial institutions, dealers, and merchants globally can utilize to foster international trade. Let's examine the main points and implications of UCP 600 in more detail. Standardizing documentary credit rules and practices around the world will make international trade easier and more predictable for everyone, and it will also get rid of any confusion or oddities in the Letters of Credit UCP 600 process.

UCP 600: The Global Standard Ensuring Security and Efficiency in International Trade Transactions

Banks and other financial institutions in 175 countries accept and use UCP 600, which covers a large portion of international trade. It is a universal language for LC transactions because of its extensive use. The 39 easily readable clauses of the regulations cover every facet of documentary credit operations, from issuance to settlement. This transparency reduces the likelihood of misunderstandings and conflicts. While providing a comprehensive framework, UCP 600 also allows for application flexibility, enabling parties to adapt it to specific contractual obligations and local laws as needed. By standardizing processes, UCP 600 plays a vital role in lowering the risks connected to international trade, such as credit risk, legal risk, and nonpayment risk.

UCP 600 emphasizes that papers, not products, services, or performances, are the medium of exchange for banks. This approach bases the decision to honor or negotiate a credit on the supplied documents' compliance with the LC's conditions, irrespective of any concerns about the underlying goods or services. The rules stipulate that no sales or other commitments can serve as the foundation for the LC. Therefore, banks focus solely on ensuring that the documents meet the requirements of the LC, avoiding any issues that may arise from the sale contract.

According to UCP 600, which specifies the exact criteria for evaluating papers, banks have up to five banking days to determine whether the documents they are submitting comply with the letter of credit's requirements. The adoption of UCP 600 offers a dependable and effective method for protecting payments and promoting the seamless completion of transactions, which has important ramifications for international trade. If those standards are met, buyers will be paid, and sellers will be paid if they meet recorded requirements. This mutual confidence is vital for the growth and dynamism of international commerce. UCP 600 embodies the cumulative knowledge of the international banking and trading community, providing a uniform yet adaptable framework to facilitate and protect international trade activities. It is a vital component of the architecture of international trade because of its broad acceptance and application, which support the efficiency and confidence that are essential to the functioning of the international LC system.

The Core Pillars of UCP 600 Simplified

The enforcement of the Uniform Customs & Practice for Documentary Credits (UCP 600) on July 1, 2007, marked significant advancements in trade finance. This set of established norms, which replaced the UCP 500, assures all parties participating in trade finance transactions that the procedures relevant to letters of credit (LCs) meet their demands. We thoughtfully designed these regulations to accommodate and adjust to the evolving dynamics of international trade. Let's look at the goals of UCP 600 and how they affect the trade finance landscape. The primary objective of UCP 600 is to standardize and regulate regulations pertaining to international trade financing. Parties in other countries frequently followed their own national laws or customs prior to the UCP.

The enforcement of the Uniform Customs & Practice for Documentary Credits (UCP 600) on July 1, 2007, marked significant advancements in trade finance. This set of established norms, which replaced the UCP 500, may persuade all parties engaged in trade finance transactions nowadays that the procedures relevant to letters of credit (LCs) match their demands. The designers thoughtfully designed these regulations to accommodate and adjust to the evolving dynamics of international trade. Let's look at the goals of UCP 600 and how they affect the trade finance landscape. The primary objective of UCP 600 is to regulate and standardize rules pertaining to financing for global trade. Previously, parties in foreign countries typically followed their own national laws or customs.

International trade requires a stable and consistent framework for Letters of Credit transactions, which UCP 600 offers. Due to the set of internationally recognized laws, businesses can trade more safely on the global market knowing that their LC-related transactions are subject to a uniform set of rules. Among the many important tasks that

CHAPTER 2   LETTERS OF CREDIT: THE LIFELINE OF GLOBAL TRADE

UCP 600 accomplishes in connection with international trade are decreased credit, operational, and legal risks. UCP 600 reduces the possibility of disagreements and the related expenses of settlement by making sure that all parties are aware of their rights and responsibilities under a letter of credit.

Under the direction of the ICC Banking Commission, industry professionals created UCP 600, which shows a thorough and practical grasp of the requirements and difficulties of contemporary trade financing. Using a bottom-up strategy guarantees that the laws are practical, current, and flexible enough to consider the intricacies of modern international trade as well as technological and communication breakthroughs. The necessity to address new concerns in the trade finance industry and to further improve and clarify the legislation in order to better serve the stakeholders drove the switch from UCP 500 to UCP 600. This action shows that, despite changes in international trade, the ICC is committed to maintaining the norms that regulate Letters of Credit. Their goal is to build a solid and dependable framework that will enable international trade to thrive, not only to offer a list of requirements for letters of credit. UCP 600 standardizes, streamlines, and lowers risk to enable seamless execution of international trade financing transactions. It represents the body of knowledge that the community has in that area and serves as a roadmap for effectiveness, safety, and equity in the area of international trade finance. Although the UCP 600 is a cornerstone in the field of international trade finance, it operates within a unique legal framework.

The UCP 600 regulations don't have legal standing, unlike laws that governments pass and uphold. Instead, the binding authority of trade finance transactions comes from the voluntary incorporation of participants into contracts. Let's examine the legal framework, application, and relationship of UCP 600 with ISBP (International Standard Banking Practice). The trade finance contract must expressly include UCP 600 for every letter of credit (LC) transaction to be applicable. All parties to the contract—the buyer, seller, and issuing bank—have committed to follow the UCP 600 rules by including them in their terms. Once added, the UCP 600 rules become a legally binding part of the contract. They control the 39 articles that make up the rules for issuing, managing, and settling LCs. One of the key benefits of UCP 600 is its versatility, which enables adaptations to satisfy the particular needs of international trade parties. In the fast-paced world of international trade, where actors from many legal systems and jurisdictions attempt to establish common ground, this flexibility is crucial.

A helpful addition to UCP 600 is ICC Publication 745, which is the International Standard Banking Practice for the Examination of Documents under Documentary Credits (ISBP). It tells you in detail how to check if a document meets the requirements of LC. Once added, the UCP 600 rules become a legally binding part of the contract. They control the 39 articles that make up the rules for issuing, managing, and settling LCs. The entire set of articles in UCP 600 govern the interpretation of credits at the time of issuance. However, the regulations allow for exceptions by specifically changing or removing the LC's provisions. This implies that although UCP 600 offers a comprehensive framework, parties have the ability to modify specific clauses for their benefit.

The UCP 600 norms will legally bind the parties who want to use them in their LC transactions, even though they are not formal statutes. The UCP 600 norms will legally bind the parties who want to use them in their LC transactions, even though they are not formal statutes. This contract integration and the fact that UCP 600 is used and adopted all over the world highlight how important it is for standardizing and making it easier to finance international trade.

At events like the ICC UK Winter Trade Finance Conference, the ICC's ongoing efforts to review, discuss, and amend UCP 600 provide more proof of its critical role in revolutionizing trade practices and rules. UCP 600 has legal force since parties to trade financing agreements accept it, even though it is not a legally binding document in and of itself. Because UCP 600 combines consistency, flexibility, and optional adoption, it is an essential tool for promoting international trade. It offers a trustworthy set of principles covering a wide range of business practices and legal systems. The entire body of laws known as UCP 600 governs the issuance and application of letters of credit (LCs), which are crucial instruments for advancing global trade. The International Chamber of Commerce (ICC) developed these standards with the goal of standardizing practices globally, promoting transparency, and reducing the risks associated with conducting business.

The Key Elements of UCP

If an LC simply states that it is subject to these rules in its language, UCP 600 is applicable. The purpose of UCP 600 is to serve as an optional addition to trade finance agreements, providing a generally recognized benchmark for documentary credits.

The regulations start with clear definitions and meanings of terms used in LC transactions in order to avoid misconceptions. This creates a common language for beneficiaries, issuers, and banks.

UCP 600 outlines the obligations and liabilities of various parties, including the beneficiary, the issuing bank, and any confirming institutions. It describes how banks should handle documentary credits and gives them flexibility when it comes to managing documents. The element of UCP 600 is the requirement for documented compliance.

Payments under an LC are subject to the fulfillment of certain requirements. The rules provide a baseline for how quickly institutions must examine documents. Banks have five banking days to determine if the provided documents satisfy the LC requirements. UCP 600 mandates the sending of a notice of denial, detailing any irregularities found in the filed papers, if they fail to comply. Since it allows for the waiving or correction of inconsistencies, this procedure is crucial for transparency.

UCP 600's independence principle states that the LC is independent of the sale and any other contracts it may contain. Banks deal with paperwork, not the goods, services, or performances they are associated with. UCP 600 outlines the responsibilities and procedures for requesting compensation from the issuing bank.

The rules clarify the transferability of an LC, enabling the original beneficiary to transfer the credit to one or more subsequent beneficiaries. This makes trading more complicated. UCP 600 covers adding confirmation to an LC.

By providing its own guarantee to maintain or negotiate an LC, a confirming bank provides the beneficiary with even more comfort. While providing a solid base, UCP 600 also allows for customization. With mutual consent, the parties may modify or remove any restriction as long as the modifications are explicit in the credit documentation. While not explicitly mentioned in UCP 600, the ISBP is a helpful addendum that provides guidance on applying UCP 600, especially with regard to document inspection.

Sixteen articles form the foundation of the UCP 600, providing a uniform framework for conducting documented credit transactions in international trade. To enable seamless and effective trade operations, it is imperative that all parties involved in such transactions comprehend these regulations. Most LC transactions around the world are supported by UCP 600, which is a complete, flexible, and fair framework that draws on the knowledge of the international trade finance community as a whole. Its extensive adoption and application have produced definite, dependable criteria for the use of documentary credits, which have greatly aided in the uniformity and efficiency of global trade.

The international Uniform Customs and Practice (UCP 600) regulations underwent a major change when transitioning from UCP 500 to UCP 600. In order to address new concerns and reflect changes in international trade practices, UCP 600 included new terminology and concepts. This included terms such as data matching, electronic papers, and updated commercial procedures. Also the language of the current regulations was changed for relevance and clarity. UCP 600 altered the rules' structure to improve readability and usage.

The purpose of this rearrangement was to simplify the document and increase user accessibility, especially by combining relevant provisions and getting rid of unnecessary ones. They made both significant and decorative adjustments. Modifications to the basic rules and procedures for documentary credits, like making it clearer what each party's roles and responsibilities are, were seen as big steps forward. On the other hand, additional opinions aim to enhance the rules' readability and presentation without changing their intended purpose.

However, they introduced further ambiguity: improving clarity and removing ambiguity in the regulations controlling documentary credits was one of the main goals of updating UCP 500 into UCP 600. Overall, by rewording, rearranging, and adding new vocabulary, UCP 600 was able to achieve more clarity. However, despite these efforts, the complexity of international commercial transactions and evolving patterns eventually led to new uncertainties in certain areas, requiring further interpretation and assistance. We changed seven important articles from UCP 500 to UCP 600, addressing various documentary credit-related issues like document review, bank responsibilities, handling contradictory documentation, and issuing credit amendments. The primary goal of these modifications was to keep the core values of the UCP while updating and modernizing the regulations to reflect current trading practices.

Taking into account changes in trade practices, new technologies, and the need for trade transactions to be more efficient and clear, the switch from UCP 500 to UCP 600 was a major turning point in the history of international trade finance rules. As a "testament" to the persistent efforts to harmonize and streamline international trade financing, UCP 600 stands. A comprehensive and inclusive process led to its creation, representing a robust global agreement among trade finance specialists. However, discussions about its revision, or lack thereof, highlight the challenges and complexities involved in modernizing such a widely used framework. Here is a clarification based on the points mentioned: The 14-year transition from UCP 500 to UCP 600 underscores the need for a meticulous and all-encompassing approach in updating these regulations.

This discrepancy demonstrates the effort to ensure that any modifications are both necessary and align with the overall consensus within the international trade community. The establishment of a consultative group of 41 individuals from 26 nations, convened on more than 15 occasions, underscores the cooperative and global aspect of the UCP's advancement. This diversity guarantees that the regulations take into account a broad spectrum of legal frameworks and business practices.

The examination of more than 5000 comments prior to the unanimous acceptance of UCP 600 in October 2006 demonstrates the extensive consultation process that ensured the recommendations are strong, thorough, and widely accepted. Many of the challenges inherent in trade finance are successfully addressed by UCP 600, as evidenced by the treaty's effectiveness and the comparatively low number of conflicts. This widespread contentment with the law is noteworthy. When disagreements do occur, they frequently center on linguistic ambiguities that were challenging to settle even during the writing process.

The topic of updating UCP 600 raises a number of issues, including the time and expense required to complete the task, the difficulty in finding specialists with the depth of experience needed to write modifications, and the regulatory ambiguity that currently exists in international markets. The landscape of international sanctions and the regulatory environment poses significant challenges for any potential revision of UCP 600.

Changes in these areas can directly impact the applicability and effectiveness of trade finance rules. The International Standard Banking Practice (ISBP) and other parts of opinions released by the ICC Banking Commission are crucial in clearing up things that aren't clear under UCP 600. This is because the rules themselves may leave room for interpretation. The fact that the system must accommodate more than 150 trade countries with varying legal and commercial contexts supports the idea that there will always be compromises in creating standards of this kind.

This fact emphasizes how the structure established by UCP 600 and its supplemental documents must be flexible and adaptable. While the international trade finance industry widely acknowledges the benefits of UCP 600, discussions over its revision reveal a deeper understanding of the challenges involved in revising such a significant treaty. Because it's hard to come up with ideas, agree on them, and make changes to regulations, as well as the fact that trade is global, any changes that are coming will need a lot of thought and cooperation from everyone.

As things are right now, UCP 600 continues to be a vital pillar of international trade, and its interpretations and clarifications are always changing to keep up with market demands. The international trade finance community is highly interested in the potential revisions to the UCP 600. The International Chamber of Commerce (ICC) created the UCP 600, which is essential to the issuing and functioning of Letters of Credit—documents that are necessary to enable international trade. We must consider numerous criteria to determine the likelihood of a revision. In 2007, the UCP 600 replaced the UCP 500.

Given the approximately 14-year interval between the prior iterations, it suggests that discussions about changes may be imminent. However, the thoroughness and overall satisfaction with UCP 600 could potentially prolong this period. Comments pointing to serious operational difficulties or emerging market conditions that the current regulations don't fully address are likely to prompt revisions to UCP 600. The ICC closely monitors this input through its various channels, including conferences and consultations. Updates to the UCP may be necessary due to the rapidly changing global trade scene, which is characterized by swift technical breakthroughs and shifting market dynamics. The digitization of trade papers, blockchain technology, and other fintech advancements may lead to the idea of adding new clauses or explanations.

Changes in the trade agreements and sanctions landscape could have an effect on how effective the UCP 600 framework is now. The ICC must assess whether the regulations have undergone updates or remain inadequately responsive to these developments to ensure conformity and relevance. It is no straightforward task to revise the UCP 600.

The Emergence of eUCP

With the advent of electronic documentation, the need for a supplementary set of rules became evident. We introduced the eUCP to bridge the gap between traditional paper-based practices and the modern digital landscape. Subsequent updates have refined the initial version of eUCP.

eUCP Version 1.0

UCP 500, the then-prevailing set of rules, introduced the first version of eUCP as a supplement. This version aimed to address the handling of electronic records and provided a framework for their presentation and examination. It defined terms specific to electronic records, established standards for electronic document presentation, and clarified the responsibilities of banks in processing these documents.

eUCP Version 2.0

eUCP Version 2.0 represented a more substantial update, addressing advances in digital technology and the evolving needs of international trade with enhanced definitions:

New definitions were introduced, such as:

- electronic record
- data processing system
- presenter

We strengthened the rules around data corruption and the handling of electronic records, ensuring robust procedures for maintaining the integrity and authenticity of documents.

CHAPTER 2   LETTERS OF CREDIT: THE LIFELINE OF GLOBAL TRADE

Detailed guidelines were provided for the presentation and examination of electronic records, including the introduction of a "notice of completeness" to signal the completion of a presentation

The ICC continues to review and update eUCP to reflect technological advancements and the evolving landscape of international trade. This ongoing process ensures that the rules remain relevant and effective in promoting secure and efficient trade practices. The eUCP has significantly contributed to modernizing trade finance by integrating electronic documentation into the traditional framework of documentary credits. Its evolution reflects the ICC's commitment to adapting to technological changes and supporting the needs of the global trade community.

Introduction to eUCP 2.1

The evolution of global trade has demanded continuous adaptation to new technologies and methodologies. The ICC's Uniform Customs and Practice for Documentary Credits (UCP 600) is a well-established framework governing letters of credit. The ICC introduced the eUCP, a supplement to the UCP that addresses electronic presentations, in response to the increasing digitization of trade. The latest version, eUCP 2.1, represents a significant update aimed at enhancing clarity and efficiency in handling electronic documents within the context of international trade.

Scope and Application

The eUCP 2.1 extends the applicability of UCP 600 to electronic presentations. This supplement clarifies that if an electronic credit does not specify the version of eUCP it adheres to, it is automatically subject to the latest version. Applying the most current standards enhances legal certainty and operational efficiency.

Definitions and Terminology

The eUCP 2.1 introduces several new definitions crucial for understanding electronic records:

- **Electronic Record**: Includes any record that contains information required in the equivalent paper document.

- **Electronic Transferable Record**: Reflects an electronic record with similar functionalities to traditional negotiable instruments.

- **Data Processing System**: A system used to process electronic records, ensuring their integrity and authenticity.
- **Presenter**: The party making the electronic presentation.

These definitions align with contemporary digital practices and provide a clear framework for all parties involved.

Presentation and Examination

To ensure clarity, eUCP 2.1 has detailed the rules for the presentation of electronic records.

- **Notice of Completeness**: Acts as a notification that the electronic presentation is complete, triggering the period for examination.
- **Examination of Records**: Banks are required to examine electronic records with the same rigor as paper documents, ensuring they meet the terms of the credit.

Data Integrity and Security

Recognizing the challenges posed by digital formats, eUCP 2.1 addresses data integrity and security.

- **Data Corruption**: Specifies the procedures for handling corrupted electronic records, ensuring that the issuing or confirming bank can access and verify the documents.
- **Liability**: Clarifies the responsibilities of banks concerning their data processing systems, emphasizing the need for robust security measures.

Force Majeure

A new article on force majeure addresses circumstances beyond control that may impact the processing of electronic records. This provision provides flexibility and protection for parties in the event of unforeseen disruptions.

eUCP 2.1 represents a significant step forward in the digitization of trade finance. By providing a clear and robust framework for electronic presentations, it facilitates smoother transactions and enhances the overall efficiency of international trade. As the global trade environment continues to evolve, the principles and guidelines set forth in eUCP 2.1 will play a crucial role in shaping the future of trade finance.

ISBP 821 or the Art of Document Examination

The International Standard Banking Practice for the Examination of Documents under Documentary Credits (ISBP 821) is an important guide that goes along with the Uniform Customs and Practice for Documentary Credits (UCP 600), which are the basic rules for letters of credit (LCs) used in international trade.

Although ISBP 821 doesn't modify UCP 600, it serves as a clarifying tool by offering particular details on how documentary credit professionals really implement UCP 600's regulations. Ensuring uniformity and lowering the percentage of document rejections owing to inconsistencies are its main goals. Let's examine the main features and advantages of ISBP 821.

The Crucial Step: Examination

Preliminary considerations in ISBP 821 establish the framework for the subsequent thorough examination guidelines. These factors highlight how crucial it is for practitioners of documentary credit to become knowledgeable about the subtleties of document inspection in order to guarantee adherence to the requirements of documentary credits. Broad guidelines apply to all documents displayed with documentary credits. This section emphasizes the significance of following the terms and conditions mentioned in the credit as well as the requirement that all documentation be detail-consistent with one another.

ISBP 821 provides comprehensive details on various types of documents frequently required for documentary credits. This includes, but isn't limited to, rules for reviewing drafts figuring out when to make payments under timely LCs; detailed information on how business invoices are looked at, including information that must match the LC; and other papers that are sent in.

If document checkers use ISBP 821 as an intelligent checklist, which explains how to follow the rules in UCP 600, they can make sure that LC requirements are met. With the aid of this exact guidance, beneficiaries can create their paperwork in accordance with international standards, greatly lowering the possibility of discrepancies that result in bank rejection of their documentation.

Also, ISBP 821's detailed explanations are very helpful for understanding how standard procedures for document evaluation work, which helps everyone involved in documentary credits. This information is crucial for creating documents that adhere to the stringent requirements of foreign trade financing. This will make transactions go more smoothly and reduce the chance of costly delays and disagreements. ISBP 821 has become an important companion to the UCP 600 because it makes sure that papers with documentary credits are compliant and standardized according to international best practices. By making it clearer how UCP 600 regulations should be applied, ISBP 821 is a key part of reducing differences, increasing efficiency, and creating a safer and more stable environment for international trade financing.

Mastering Strict Compliance for Documentary Credits

The smooth operation of transactions in the field of international trade is largely dependent upon the careful preparation and presentation of trade documents under documentary credits (DCs). These documents serve as the foundation of international trade, ensuring that purchasers receive their goods and sellers receive compensation. These documents represent a modern evolution of long-standing trading customs. The International Standard Banking Practice for the Examination of Documents under Documentary Credits (ISBP 821) and the Uniform Customs and Practice for Documentary Credits (UCP 600) are two important documents that help keep this system honest.

Here's a thorough examination of the essential elements involved in making sure document presentations are credit-compliant. Trade documentation has a long history, dating back to the days of clay tablets, paper, and increasingly, digital representations. These documents are more than just formalities; they are necessary for the operationalization of Documentary Credits, which makes cross-border payments and goods exchanges easier. Compliance and the effective execution of transactions depend on an understanding of the particular purpose and specifications of each document type under a DC. Global statistics show that banks reject an alarming number of documents when they present them for the first time due to discrepancies. Timing inconsistencies are a common problem, as are more complicated difficulties like contradicting information, missing endorsements, or inaccurate product descriptions. These differences may result in extra expenses, delays, or, in the worst situation, payment rejection. Document preparation under a DC requires a great deal of attention to detail. Generally speaking, beneficiaries are in charge of issuing any necessary documentation, unless the DC or the UCP 600 specify otherwise. It is important to minimize the inclusion of unnecessary information that could compromise compliance in order to prevent discrepancies. Include only the data required by the DC terms and the ICC standards.

Beneficiaries preparing documentation must have a thorough comprehension of both the ISBP 821 and the UCP 600. Specifically, ISBP 821 acts as a useful manual, outlining the inspection phase and providing information on the areas bank document examiners concentrate on. It highlights the importance of beginning document preparation early in the trading cycle and giving due consideration to the necessary documents, their issuers, content, and presentation.

The following are some useful pointers for document compliance:

- Contacting the designated bank for advice might help to ensure compliance and clarify expectations when unsure about the documentation needed.

- Collaborate with Other Parties: Providing a copy of the DC to the relevant third party (freight forwarder, carrier, or insurance company) ensures their understanding and ability to adhere to the DC's guidelines for documents not issued by the beneficiary.

- It is wise to ask the applicant to submit an amendment if any problems emerge.

- It is dangerous and best to avoid depending on verbal assurances for post-presentation modifications.

- In order to comprehend the international standards for document examination, beneficiaries should become acquainted with UCP 600 and ISBP 821.

We can create checklists for common document types and necessary data to help ensure compliance. To identify and fix any mistakes or omissions, the staff members who prepared the documents must give them a comprehensive examination before presenting them under a DC. The challenge of ensuring credit-compliant document presentations under Documentary Credits is intricate but doable; it calls for careful planning and a thorough awareness of international trade standards. By following the rules in UCP 600 and ISBP 821, asking banks for help, getting along well with third parties, and carefully reviewing papers, beneficiaries can greatly improve their chances of successful and legal document presentations. This enhances the stability and dependability of international trade finance arrangements, in addition to facilitating seamless commercial transactions.

When it comes to documentary credits, dealing with differences between documents requires a complex process that involves carefully comparing each document to the terms and conditions spelled out in it. These terms and conditions are usually set by the Uniform Customs and Practice for Documentary Credits (UCP 600), along with global standard banking practices and the fact that the documents are always the same. The integrity and trust that are necessary for conducting business internationally depend on this process.

When documents submitted under a documentary credit do not meet the conditions stated in the credit, a discrepancy occurs. Differences can range widely in type and degree, from small typos to substantial inconsistencies in shipment information or document authenticity.

Giving advice on differences in documents is a delicate and frequently disputed task.

For any document rejection, banks must give a thorough justification so that the presenting party is fully aware of the nature of the difference. Banks are required to provide precise and understandable explanations for document rejections. Generalizations like "Invoice not as per LC" are inadequate and useless. A thorough explanation allows the presenter to understand the discrepancy without consulting the documentary credit. To ensure efficient processing and issue resolution, presenting documents should be accompanied by a covering schedule that contains reference numbers, contact information, payment instructions, and other pertinent facts.

UCP 600 allows banks to assess the documents' compliance within a maximum of five banking days after the presentation. This standard intends to facilitate due diligence while expediting the inspection of documents. During the five-day period, the designated, verifying, and issuing banks take turns reviewing the documents to ensure compliance.

Banks have to make decisions on document compliance. Finding discrepancies does not always lead to rejection. Banks may choose to request waivers from the applicant or ignore small inconsistencies.

The issuing bank may contact the applicant to request a waiver of inconsistencies. This process could result in various outcomes, including the acceptance or rejection of the documents, depending on the applicant's response.

CHAPTER 2   LETTERS OF CREDIT: THE LIFELINE OF GLOBAL TRADE

Taking into account the terms of the documentary credit and potential bank errors, beneficiaries should carefully evaluate the validity of any found inconsistencies. Beneficiaries are better equipped to create papers that adhere to the necessary requirements when they are familiar with UCP 600 articles and the International Standard Banking Practice (ISBP) principles. This lowers the possibility of discrepancies. If discrepancies arise, what are the available options? First, to fix the inconsistencies, either replace or amend the papers. Second, in order to obtain permission to honor or negotiate in spite of the differences, ask the designated or confirming bank to get in touch with the originating bank. Last, send the documents to the issuing bank for settlement from the designated or confirming bank, being careful not to include any language implying that documentation collection procedures are applicable. Having precision and adherence from the start can greatly lessen the possibility of inconsistencies.

A thorough attention to detail and a comprehension of the relevant regulations and procedures are necessary for both the presentation and evaluation of papers. Through meticulous planning and effective communication, parties can more easily negotiate the difficulties of international trade, reducing conflicts, and promoting successful transactions when approaching documentary credits.

A crucial component of international trade finance is dispute resolution under documentary credits, which deals with differences that come up when reviewing papers to make sure they comply with the provisions of letters of credit (LCs). Despite everyone's best efforts to ensure compliance and clarity, disagreements still occasionally arise, usually over whether the presented documents truly meet the required standards. This article provides a thorough analysis of the procedures used to settle disputes involving documentary credits, emphasizing the function of the International Chamber of Commerce (ICC) and other dispute resolution tools. Under LCs, we carefully examine documents to ensure proper adherence to all credit terms. Usually, the parties can easily resolve differences without the need for outside arbitration or formal legal procedures. This simple method emphasizes how effective the documentary credit system is in promoting global trade.

When it comes to offering advice and settling conflicts involving international trade, the ICC is essential. Among its contributions are numerous publications on Uniform Customs and the ICC has published Practice for Documentary Credits (UCP) and other relevant subjects since 1933. In order to provide clarification on the interpretation of ICC regulations, particularly UCP 600, the ICC Banking Commission also offers formal opinions in answer to particular queries. For disputes pertaining to ICC regulations, including documentary credits, the Documentary Dispute Resolution Expertise (DOCDEX) provides a specialized alternative dispute resolution process. Introduced in 1997, DOCDEX provides a hastened expert decision-making process to help parties avoid the complications and expenses of going to court.

Even though the DOCDEX and ICC tools significantly reduce the necessity for litigation, some conflicts may still require resolution through the courts or arbitration. Typically, these situations involve deeper disputes that the ICC protocol cannot settle. However, because they can be expensive and time-consuming, going to court is not always the best way to resolve disputes.

The type of disagreement and the interests of the parties involved determine which conflict resolution technique is best. However, it is generally not advisable to proactively incorporate specific dispute resolution clauses in the documentary credit itself, as this could potentially signal anticipated issues that may not align with the specific type of disagreement that arises. Given their thorough examination and interpretation of ICC regulations, DOCDEX rulings and ICC Opinions are highly respected and frequently cited in court applications. They are not legally binding, but they are useful guidelines that arbitrators and courts regularly take into account when making decisions. Documentary credits require an organized resolution of issues, prioritizing efficiency, compliance, and clarity.

The ICC offers a wealth of information for comprehending and implementing documentary credit regulations through its extensive publications, opinions, and DOCDEX system. Even if it is always the intention to settle conflicts quickly and peacefully, the presence of these mechanisms guarantees that parties have access to professional advice and alternate dispute resolution choices, reducing the need for expensive and drawn-out court cases.

The Electronic Frontier and the Future of Trade Finance Messaging

Trade finance is moving more and more toward digitalization, particularly in relation to bank guarantees and letters of credit (LCs). This indicates a substantial change in the direction of more standardized and structured data flows. The Society for Worldwide Interbank Financial Telecommunication (SWIFT), which made this transition possible, has introduced new message types with the intention of streamlining interactions between banks and businesses.

SWIFT: The Game Changer

The goal of SWIFT's shift to structured data is to improve the efficiency and clarity of transactions involving standby letters of credit and bank guarantees. SWIFT aims to facilitate a smoother transaction process by reducing ambiguities and providing a more standardized approach for these transfers. However, this change comes with its own problems, mostly related to telling the difference between signals about dependent undertakings and demand guarantees, as well as the different message formats used for bank-to-bank and bank-to-corporate communication.

What are the primary obstacles? This disparity necessitates specific handling procedures, which may complicate workflow and increase operational costs. When bank-to-bank and bank-to-corporate communications use different formats, it can cause issues and make transactions less smooth. These problems show how important it is to let structured forms be used for dependent undertakings too, which would speed up the process for all assurances and undertakings.

The MT 760 for guarantee issue and MT 767 for guarantee amendment, which comprised a combination of predefined fields and a single, free-style narrative field, were the traditional forms used for bank guarantees transferred between banks. Although this format is flexible, it presents major challenges for automation, especially when it comes to extracting important elements like the guarantee amount or expiration date.

The SWIFT messaging standards have been in effect since November 2021. These standards will add structured fields for standbys and demand guarantees to bank-to-bank messages (MT 760 and MT 767), which will help solve these problems and make it easier to automate processes. The problem with automation will not go away because sureties, accessory guarantees, and other dependent agreements will still be sent through MT 759, which has a large narrative field, even though the structured approach is only used for some types of guarantees.

Structured formats for MT 760 and MT 767 communications are a beneficial step toward automating tasks and getting rid of confusion. Not including interdependent activities is a bad idea. For dependent tasks in MT 759, it requires parallel processing, which increases complexity and may result in expenses.

Further complicating matters is the alignment—or lack thereof—between bank-to-bank and bank-to-corporate messaging (mostly via MT 798). This is particularly true when working on dependent projects, which call for close attention to guarantee accurate and compliant communications.

The current state of affairs emphasizes the significance of taking a more comprehensive approach to structured communication formats, one that covers all kinds of commitments and assurances in order to assure efficiency and consistency everywhere. Moreover, it is imperative that banks, corporations, and software providers collaborate more broadly in order to improve these standards and tackle the real-world issues that all stakeholders in trade finance encounter. The development of SWIFT messaging types, which aim to improve structure, clarity, and efficiency, constitutes a major advancement in the digitization of trade finance. However, the problems with the current method make it clear that we need to keep talking, work together, and maybe even try to standardize more in order to fully enjoy the benefits of digital trade finance. The industry's overall goal should be to promote a trade finance ecosystem that is more streamlined, automated, and inclusive as it navigates these developments.

The evolution of trade finance for the digital era is among the biggest shifts in international trade. The UCP 600, which provides a common framework for the use of letters of credit (LCs), has long been the cornerstone of international trade. However, its primary application was in the world of paper, a limitation that became increasingly apparent as digital technologies gained traction. Recognizing the inevitable shift to a digital ecosystem, the International Chamber of Commerce (ICC) has worked hard to ensure that documentary credits remain a vital tool for mitigating trade risk in the digital age.

Electronic Transactions Powered by MLETR

The ICC established the eUCP as a complement to the UCP to explicitly address transactions involving electronic documents. The ICC recognized the digital revolution in trade finance with the release of version 1.0 in 2002. The ICC further improved these guidelines with the release of Version 1.1 in 2007 and the more extensive Version 2.0 in 2019, ensuring compliance with contemporary digital practices and UCP 600 terminology. The publication of the eUCP 2.0 marked a significant milestone.

This version featured a thorough overhaul to facilitate "e-compliance" and enable seamless integration with the evolving landscape of digital trade finance. July 2023 saw the release of Version 2.1, which was a major development. It made the eUCP compliant with the UNCITRAL Model Law on Electronic Transferable Records (MLETR) and the UK's Electronic Trade Regulation. The transition to electronic presentations is primarily being driven by automated compliance checking solutions for the documentary credit sector.

CHAPTER 2   LETTERS OF CREDIT: THE LIFELINE OF GLOBAL TRADE

Trade finance processes should become more effective, safe, and transparent as a result of the quick developments in artificial intelligence (AI), machine learning (ML), distributed ledger technology (DLT), smart contracts, the Internet of things (IoT), and optical character recognition (OCR). In order to keep the eUCP current and helpful in advancing documentary credits within this digital framework, the ICC regularly updates it in recognition of these advances.

Focusing on the electronic record presentation rather than the eUCP credit issue is a crucial component of the eUCP design. Knowing that the industry has been providing electronic documentary credits is the basis for this strategy. In the process of providing documentary credit under the eUCP, a few more factors come into play. First, in order to permit the presentation of electronic records, both the applicant and recipient must mutually agree. Crucial tasks include figuring out what kinds of papers can be provided electronically and making sure both parties have the technical capacity to manage such presentations. This conversation guarantees the delivery of electronic papers in an acceptable format and equips the nominated and issuing banks with the necessary tools for efficient processing. The eUCP is a proactive effort that bridges the gap between traditional trade finance methods and the digital future.

The International Chamber of Commerce (ICC) is promoting efficiency and security in international trade by offering a practical and legal framework for the use of electronic documents in letters of credit (LC) transactions. This ensures that documentary credits will always be relevant. The eUCP is proof of the flexibility and durability of international trade agreements in the face of swift technical advancement, particularly as our economy undergoes digital and ecological changes.

We have implemented stricter standards for electronic record authenticity and integrity to ensure the safety and dependability of online transactions. The recognition and acceptance of electronic signatures as legitimate and enforceable in documented credit transactions is subject to specific requirements and guidelines. We are implementing procedures such as arbitration and mediation to settle disagreements arising from electronic transactions.

With the eUCP regulations, the values and rules set by the old UCP regulations will be kept, but it will be easier to use electronic documents and transactions in international trade finance. In trade finance operations, eUCP helps lower risks, simplify procedures, and increase efficiency by offering precise norms and standards for electronic transactions. As digital technologies and electronic paperwork become more important in international trade, the eUCP laws are necessary for the growth and acceptance of electronic transactions in documentary credits.

eUCP provides a uniform framework for electronic trade finance transactions, which contributes to the improvement of global trade's efficacy, transparency, and dependability. Remember, the purpose of eUCP is to enhance and collaborate with the conventional UCP 600 standards.

UCP 600 establishes the general framework for documentary credits, while eUCP provides specific guidelines and standards for electronic transactions that take place within that framework. Regardless of whether the transaction involves paper-based or electronic papers, this integration ensures uniform and coherent trade finance procedures.

The publication of the eUCP regulations in Version 2.0 represents a significant step toward modernizing trade finance procedures, promoting electronic transactions, and maintaining the reliability and integrity of international trade finance. The Electronic Uniform Rules for Bank-to-Bank Reimbursements (eURC) and the Electronic Uniform Customs and Practice for Documentary Credits (eUCP), commonly referred to as the "eRules," are forming an evolutionary partnership that marks a significant milestone in the digitization of trade finance operations.

The International Chamber of Commerce created eRules with the intention of streamlining the records and transactions related to electronic trade finance in order to accelerate the digitization of trade finance activities. The ICC regularly examines and modifies the eRules to ensure their continued relevance and applicability in the rapidly changing digital environment, in an effort to demonstrate its commitment to keeping up with developments in trade finance and technology. Trade practitioners will regularly evaluate the content of the eRules, especially the eUCP.

The International Chamber of Commerce created eRules with the intention of streamlining the records and transactions related to electronic trade finance in order to accelerate the digitization of trade finance activities. They represent a forceful international reaction to the growing need for digital trade financing. In collaboration with eUCP, they provide a framework that manages electronic documents and transactions effectively. This makes trade finance operations easier, faster, and safer in a world that is becoming more digital. A lot of big changes and improvements were made to the way documents are shown electronically in trade finance transactions with eUCP Version 2.0. The goal was to reflect the ongoing efforts to bring trade finance practices into the digital age and make sure that electronic transactions are clear, consistent, and safe.

The eUCP version 2.1 upgrade brought about a number of noteworthy changes and improvements aimed at enhancing the efficiency and interoperability of electronic trade finance processes. The establishment of a new definition for "Electronic transferable record" was one notable update in eUCP version 2.1. This definition emphasizes the importance of electronic transferability in trade finance transactions, encompassing electronic records that hold information similar to traditional paper documents such as assignable insurance documents or negotiable bills of lading. Version 2.1 added an appendix that offers specific recommendations for SWIFT MT700 field requirements in the context of eUCP transactions. By streamlining the use of SWIFT messaging in electronic presentations, this feature hopes to improve trade finance communication efficiency and interoperability.

The alignment of eUCP version 2.1 with the UNCITRAL Model Law on Electronic Transferable Records (MLETR) is arguably the most notable modification. This alignment makes it easier to digitize trade documents and transactions by making sure that eUCP is consistent and works with new international standards for electronic transferable records. The international trade finance community has overwhelmingly approved and supported the alignment with MLETR. Stakeholders understand how crucial it is to synchronize eUCP with newly developing regulatory frameworks in order to advance digitization and simplify trade finance procedures internationally. The International Chamber of Commerce (ICC) has made a substantial contribution to the evolution of international trade law, according to UNCITRAL legal officer, Luca Castellani. He emphasized that the approval of eUCP version 2.1 and the ICC's support of UCP 600 are positive moves in the direction of updating trade finance procedures.

An important first step toward the digitization of trade papers and transactions is the harmonization of eUCP with MLETR. As more jurisdictions pass laws pertaining to electronic transferable records, eUCP version 2.1 will significantly aid international trade finance compliance and interoperability. In order to facilitate the digitalization of trade finance, eUCP version 2.1 includes significant changes and conforms to newly developing international standards. It's not over yet, as there is one more important element in this picture. The International Chamber of Commerce (ICC) created URC 522, also known as "Uniform Rules for Collections 522," as a set of guidelines to standardize the document collection process in cross-border trade. Banks typically handle documents against acceptance (D/A) and documents against payment (D/P) to settle international trade transactions, providing a framework for financial institutions to operate within. In a D/A transaction, the exporter, or seller, delivers the items and gives their bank the shipping paperwork and a bill of exchange, which is a formal demand for payment. The bank then forwards these documents to the importer's (buyer's) bank. Before obtaining the paperwork proving ownership of the items, the importer must accept (agree to pay) the bill of exchange. Typically, this acceptance signifies the importer's commitment to pay for the items at the specified later date on the bill of exchange. In order to ensure that both parties meet their commitments, the URC 522 specifies how banks should handle the paperwork and the acceptance, which streamlines the procedure.

The process of a D/P transaction is somewhat similar to that of a D/A transaction, with the exception that the importer must pay for the products before obtaining the ownership documents. This ensures that the exporter will receive payment according to the agreed terms or immediately upon delivery of the items. The rules for these transactions are in URC 522; it stresses that banks are responsible for making sure that the exchange of payments for documents is safe and consistent. The URC 522 is important for international trade because it makes the collection process more consistent and reduces the chance of misunderstandings and disagreements between importers, exporters, and their banks. It also guarantees a smoother transaction process by outlining precise rules for managing documents. The International Chamber of Commerce (ICC) has incorporated electronic versions of its trade regulations, such as the eUCP for electronic Documentary Credits and the upcoming eURC for Collections, in line with the worldwide trade trends towards digitalization. The goal of the eURC is to enable the management of electronic documents and transactions by modifying the conventional rules for collecting for the digital age. As eURC grows, specifics may change, but the main goal is to provide a framework that accommodates modern ways of doing business online while keeping the safety and dependability of the original URC 522 rules. URC 522 and its electronic version, eURC, are very important to international trade because they provide safe, standardized ways to collect money and manage trade documents. The advent of digital trade finance and the increasing trend toward electronic transactions have brought to light the shortcomings of conventional frameworks, such as URC 522, when it comes to effectively handling the subtleties of digital documentation and procedures. The creation and application of electronic rules, or eRules, for trade finance is the result of the International Chamber of Commerce's (ICC) recognition of the urgent need to adjust to these developments. The goal of these updates is to close the gap between traditional procedures and the digital environment. Examples of these updates are URC 522 and Uniform Customs and Practice for Documentary Credits (UCP 600).

CHAPTER 2   LETTERS OF CREDIT: THE LIFELINE OF GLOBAL TRADE

With the growing integration of digital transactions in global trade, the current frameworks need to adapt to allow electronic papers and conversations. Conventional regulations, while useful in transactions involving paper records, fall short in addressing the intricacies and security issues related to digital data. By offering precise instructions for managing electronic presentations, the eUCR seeks to make sure that the regulations are current and appropriate in the digital era. Electronic transactions greatly reduce the time and resources required to process trade paperwork. There is no longer a need for parties to courier physical documents back and forth, which saves money and delays. By standardizing the handling of electronic presentations, the eUCR promotes efficiency and lowers costs associated with trade transactions. Security and fraud prevention present particular difficulties when it comes to digital transactions. The purpose of the eUCR rules is to guarantee the validity and integrity of electronic documents. Through the establishment of guidelines for safe electronic communication and document management, the eUCR helps lower the possibility of fraud in global trade. One of the challenges in digital trade finance is making sure electronic documents are legal and adhere to international trade regulations.

The eUCR provides a framework that ensures the legal recognition of electronic presentations, assisting businesses in navigating the legal complexity of digital transactions. The eUCR encourages innovation in trade finance by facilitating digital transactions, which makes it possible to create new platforms and technology that help expedite trade finance procedures. Additionally, it promotes inclusion in the global commerce ecosystem by eliminating entrance barriers to international trade, such as the expense and complexity of managing paper paperwork, for smaller enterprises. We must adopt electronic regulations like the eUCR to maintain international commerce's security, efficiency, and legal compliance in the face of a shift to digital trade finance. Because it fixes the problems with current rules for electronic transactions, the eUCR makes the groundwork for a more flexible, open, and creative trade finance environment. This development is a reflection of the ICC's dedication to promoting trade in the digital age and making sure that trade finance regulations continue to be applicable and helpful to advances in international trade.

The quick development of digital technologies and their growing use in international trade have prompted the introduction of electronic rules, or eRules, for trade finance. The trade finance industry can gain a lot from these eRules, which are meant to simplify and expedite electronic operations. By dissecting the essential components mentioned, we may investigate the various benefits that eRules offer to global trade.

The digital trade sector is characterized by its rapid growth and the continuous emergence of new technologies. eRules ensure that trade finance practices remain relevant and applicable amid these changes, providing a flexible framework that can adapt to evolving digital technologies and trade practices. Transitioning from paper-based to electronic documentation significantly reduces the risk of loss, damage, or fraud associated with physical documents. eRules facilitate this shift by establishing standards and protocols for electronic transactions, thereby mitigating risks and enhancing the security of trade finance operations.

Compared to traditional paper records, electronic records have many benefits, such as improved accessibility, quicker processing, and less environmental impact. In order to ensure the integrity and legal validity of electronic records, eRules provide the procedural and legal framework required for their general acceptance and use in trade finance.

Because of varying national and regional laws and customs, the international aspect of trade financing frequently faces difficulties. eRules, which encourage harmonization across jurisdictions and ensure that electronic trade finance activities are consistent and effective worldwide, make international transactions simpler.

Interpretations of terminology and intentions can lead to misunderstandings and disagreements in international trade. To ensure mutual understanding and clarity among all stakeholders involved in trade finance, eRules standardize terminology and processes. eRules make trade financing easier and more secure in many places and economies by providing a consistent framework that goes beyond regional differences in economics and law. Because it makes it possible for companies of all sizes to compete on the world market, this inclusivity promotes international trade.

The adoption of eRules is probably going to encourage the creation of automated systems for compliance checking and electronic presentations. These developments represent a substantial breakthrough in trade finance since they will expedite the processing of documentary credits, lower the possibility of human error, and boost productivity.

Digital trade finance is being revolutionized by the integration of cutting-edge technologies such as AI, ML, DLT, Smart Contracts, and the IoT (Internet of things). We engineer the eRules to effectively integrate and utilize emerging technology, thereby augmenting automation, transparency, and efficiency in trade finance operations.

A critical first step toward modernizing and safeguarding cross-border trade transactions in the digital age is the implementation of eRules for trade finance. eRules not only make trade finance operations easier and safer, but they also foster innovation and expansion within the global trade ecosystem by tackling important issues and utilizing emerging technologies.

Guarding Global Trade: Tackling Financial Crime, Fraud, and Sanctions

Documentary credits are crucial instruments for enabling cross-border transactions in the complex web of international trade. However, this system is not without flaws, particularly when it comes to financial crimes like fraud and sanctions breaches. These problems have made it necessary to build strong procedures and technology for their control and prevention, since they are frequently harmful and difficult.

Financial crime is the umbrella term for a variety of illicit behaviors, such as tax evasion, money laundering, financing of terrorism, and sanctions violations. These offenses have the potential to negatively affect people, businesses, and even countries. The ICC Financial Crime Risk and Policy Group and other international organizations have created specific tools and rules to identify and stop suspicious transactions in trade finance because they understand the seriousness of these dangers.

Mitigating Fraud and Sanctions Risks: How to Ensure Integrity in International Trade

Throughout trade history, fraud has been a constant concern that has affected transactions, even though it accounts for a very small percentage of global trade volumes. A well-known English judge named Lord Diplock previously described fraud in documentary credit transactions as the issuer's knowing inclusion of major misrepresentations as false. To reduce financial losses and mitigate such risks, companies should establish strict protocols for spotting, reporting, and escalating such fraudulent activity. Strict inspections of the items' presence and quality, as well as paperwork correctness verification, are among them.

Sanctions, which impose limitations aimed at preserving or reestablishing international peace and security, are essential to international trade. These sanctions, which are under the control of a number of international organizations, including the

European Union, OFAC, and the United Nations, have a significant impact on companies that conduct international business. In addition to severe fines, non-compliance can seriously harm one's image.

A number of guidelines released by the ICC Banking Commission have clarified the use of sanctions provisions in documentary credits. First published in 2010 and revised in 2014, these recommendations emphasize the need for clear and restrictive wording of such terms to safeguard the independence of financial instruments such as bank guarantees and letters of credit.

Despite normally not advocating this, the International Chamber of Commerce (ICC) has recommended that penalty provisions should only relate to necessary legislation that applies to the bank in question. In order to protect themselves against financial crimes and sanctions concerns, banks and trading organizations need to put in place a number of practical steps. Keeping up internal compliance policies that instruct personnel on how to handle trade finance transactions correctly is part of this. Identifying transactions involving dual-use items, or those potentially used for both military and civilian purposes, is crucial.

Operations departments should be aware of the trading patterns and histories of their counterparties in order to spot any aberrations that would point to fraudulent activity or sanctions breaches, even though they are not usually responsible for looking into commercial transactions outside of their purview.

Financial crimes and the falsification of documented credits pose a serious threat to the integrity of international trade. Banks and enterprises may safeguard themselves against the potentially disastrous consequences of fraud and sanctions violations by following defined protocols and employing sophisticated risk management technologies. In addition to being necessary for legal compliance, this proactive strategy is also critical for preserving the confidence and dependability that are essential to international trade.

The "Strategic Duel" Between Bank Guarantees and Letters of Credit

Bank guarantees (BGs) and letters of credit (LCs) are two crucial financial instruments that operate as pillars for safeguarding transactions and fostering mutual confidence between parties. Both lower the chance of nonpayment, but they do so in different ways, accomplishing different objectives and having various effects over the course of the trade cycle.

As explained earlier, an LC is essentially a bank's promise to pay the seller on behalf of the customer, provided that the seller meets the conditions outlined in the LC, such as providing goods that meet predetermined standards.

- The process begins with the buyer filing an application for an LC at their bank (the issuing bank);

- After acceptance, the seller's bank, also known as the advising bank, receives the application.

- Subsequently, the seller ships the goods and provides their bank with the required documentation, which the bank then forwards to the bank that issued the payment permission.

Every kind of LC is made to satisfy certain trade specifications, with the purpose of guaranteeing on-time delivery and excellent quality of the merchandise. This validation benefits exporters, as the issuing bank verifies the buyer's creditworthiness prior to issuing the LC.

Being more comprehensive, BGs offer a bank financial assurance in the event that one party violates the terms of the contract. The buyer or seller can offer these guarantees in various forms such as performance, advance payment, and shipment guarantees. Each has a specific purpose in a transaction. They demonstrate their capacity to fulfill contractual obligations and serve as a safeguard for the affected party in the event of a breach. When presenting bids for business contracts, they provide an assurance that, in the event of a breach, the injured party can collect the agreed payment from the bank.

Timing and payment assurance are key differences between LCs and BGs, as LCs provide a precise payment date upon meeting specified requirements, typically leading to on-time payments. On the other hand, because the bank steps in only in response to a breach of contract, BGs are more suited for scenarios in which performance assurance is critical and may lead to late payments.

The Scope of Protection also differs, as BGs provide a wider range of protection than LCs, which mainly safeguard sellers by guaranteeing payment upon the presentation of appropriate documentation; they provide protection to both parties in the event that one or more contractual obligations, whether they pertain to performance, payment, or other terms, are not met.

As for cost implications, because of their greater coverage and propensity to protect higher-value transactions, BGs are typically more expensive than LCs. When choosing which instrument to use in their trade operations, parties must take this cost differential into account.

There are many different types of BGs:

- **Bid Guarantees** that assure the creditworthiness of the supplier and pay the buyer back in the event that the supplier is unable to deliver,

- **Performance Guarantee** that pays back the buyer in the event that the supplier breaches the terms of the agreement,

- **Advance Payment Guarantees**, which guard the buyer's upfront payments to the supplier in the event that the supplier breaches the agreement,

- **Deferred Payments Guarantees**, which indicate payment due after a predetermined amount of time after a specific transaction occurrence.

- Finally, when there is no bill of lading, the **Shipping Guarantees** are used under an LC to expedite the release of cargo from port.

Understanding the distinctions between BGs and LCs is crucial for parties engaged in international trade. Deciding which instrument to use depends on the specific needs, risks, and dynamics of the transaction at hand. LCs offer a more direct way to get paid based on following the written terms, while BGs provide a bigger safety net in case the contract isn't followed, though they might cost more. Successful navigation of these instruments can significantly enhance transaction security and trust, paving the way for smoother international trade operations.

Standby letters of credit (SBLCs) lessen the risk of the buyer not being able to pay the seller back by acting as a guarantee of payment. SBLCs are flexible enough to support a broad range of commercial, performance, and financial guarantees. The beneficiary frequently uses an SBLC as a safety measure in an effort to reduce trade-related risks.

In its most basic form, it's a bank's promise to pay, made on the client's behalf. It also serves as a "payment of last resort" due to its use in various situations. The SBLC keeps contracts from being unfulfilled in the event that a company files for bankruptcy or is otherwise unable to pay its debts. Furthermore, the existence of an SBLC typically demonstrates the buyer's creditworthiness and ability to make payments, thereby demonstrating good faith.

We complete a brief underwriting assignment to confirm the party requesting the letter of credit has good credit before posting it. Upon completion, we forward a notification to the bank of the party, usually the seller, who initiated the letter of credit request.

Under an SBLC, the issuing bank may repay a portion of the financing to the counterparty in the event of a default. Because of this, Standby Letters of Credit are used to encourage trust in businesses. A bank will evaluate a number of factors when considering an application for a standby letter of credit, but the primary one will be the ability to repay the amount promised. In essence, it serves as an insurance policy for the business entering into the contract.

Since its insurance, collateral can be required to safeguard the bank in the event of a default; this could be money or other assets like real estate. The bank and SBLC size require collateral based on risk and business viability. The bank requests information about the business's assets and potentially the owners, in addition to the typical inquiries. The bank usually sends the business owner a letter after receiving and reviewing the papers. After the delivery of the letter, the business owner is required to pay a fee for each day the standby letter of credit is overdue. If the company fulfills its contractual commitments before the deadline, it can terminate the fee without incurring extra costs.

Standby Letter of Credit (SBLC) vs. Letter of Credit

A standby letter of credit is different from a letter of credit. When called upon when criteria are not met, an SBLC is paid. On the other hand, a letter of credit serves as a guarantee of payment, provided particular requirements are fulfilled and documentation from the selling party is obtained. Because of the nature of international transactions, distance, knowledge of the other party, and legal distinctions, letters of credit help to foster trust in transactions.

When offering products to a counterparty abroad, they can use an SBLC to ensure payment to their seller. Should the seller fail to receive payment, they will forward the SBLC to the buyer's bank for payment collection. A performance-focused SBLC guarantees the fulfillment of trade requirements such as appropriateness and product quality. Construction contracts occasionally include SBLCs since the build must adhere to several quality and timeline requirements. If the contractor fails to meet these requirements, the bank can receive payment after receiving the SBLC, eliminating the need for proof of loss or lengthy negotiations.

The Application Process

The initial step is to evaluate repayment capacity. The bank first thoroughly reviews the applicant's financial accounts, cash flows, and other relevant financial indicators. This is a crucial phase in determining the applicant's capacity and stability to repay the sum that the SBLC guarantees; we conduct a credit check to assess the applicant's creditworthiness. Clearly, a positive credit history suggests a reduced default risk, potentially influencing both the bank's decision and the SBLC's requirements.

The collateral requirements come next; banks often need these to secure SBLCs and minimize the default risk. Assets can come in a variety of forms, such as cash, real estate, or other assets that the bank approves. We carefully assess the collateralized asset to ensure its value aligns with the amount the SBLC guarantees. The bank's demand for collateral might surpass that of the SBLC, contingent on the applicant's creditworthiness and projected risk.

After completing this operation and receiving approval for the application, the bank prepares legal documentation to establish a lien against the collateral. Upon completion of this operation, the collateral becomes available. By pursuing this legal action, the bank ensures they have a claim to the collateral in the event that the SBLC becomes accessible.

The next step in the process involves completing a risk analysis and evaluating the strength of the company in question. The bank evaluates the applicant's company on the basis of its overall performance and stability, including elements like market position, industry risks, and operational strengths. A robust business model suggests a less hazardous enterprise.

The guaranteed amount is a crucial factor to take into account during the application process. Investigations into larger SBLCs should be more thorough due to the greater danger involved. Banks may require extra risk mitigation measures based on the kind of transaction, the applicant's sector, and the geopolitical risks associated with the beneficiary's location.

The applicant must submit a formal application for the SBLC, detailing the terms, amount, and purpose of the program. Reviewing and submitting the application is the fourth stage. The fourth stage involves identifying the intended recipient and the contractual obligations that the SBLC aims to protect. The bank considers the application in view of its lending guidelines and risk. Negotiating terms, prices, and collateral requirements is now necessary. If the bank is pleased with the risk assessment and collateral arrangements, the beneficiary may receive the SBLC directly from the bank or via advisory banks.

CHAPTER 2   LETTERS OF CREDIT: THE LIFELINE OF GLOBAL TRADE

The application process for a small business loan (SBL) is rigorous and requires demonstrating one's financial stability, providing sufficient collateral, and meeting the bank's risk control requirements. It's a strategic tool that guarantees finances and fosters trust in company operations. To increase their chances of receiving an SBLC, applicants should prepare for a rigorous assessment of their business acumen, financial stability, and project viability. Assuring that the collateral meets the bank's requirements and completely covers the guaranteed amount is vital to safeguarding the transaction for all parties.

As well as having collateral and being financially stable, applicants for a standby letter of credit (SBLC) must also go through a strict due diligence process where the issuing bank looks into the applicant's finances as both an individual and a business. This comprehensive study ensures that the bank is fully aware of the risk profile before deciding to issue an SBLC.

In this situation, the intention is to provide the beneficiary with a solid payment assurance, ensuring they will receive funds should the applicant default on their obligations. However, the matter of non-payment under an SBLC may arise under certain circumstances. The operating status of the issuing bank and the beneficiary's compliance with the SBLC's requirements primarily determine these circumstances. It's crucial to reiterate that an SBLC guarantees the beneficiary's reimbursement from the issuing bank, subject to the submission of the necessary evidence demonstrating the applicant's noncompliance with contractual obligations. This guarantee is based on the bank's ability to fulfill its financial obligations at the time of the demand for payment.

If the issuing bank faces insolvency or serious financial difficulties that hinder its capacity to do business, non-payment under the SBLC may happen. This unique circumstance highlights how important the position and financial health of the issuing bank are when applying for an SBLC. There may be times when operational limitations or regulatory actions that momentarily freeze the bank's assets affect its ability to make SBLC payments. The recipient must abide by the specific terms and circumstances outlined in the agreement in order to be eligible for the SBLC. This means turning in the required documents in accordance with the guidelines and before the deadline.

Non-payment may occur if the paperwork fails to correctly comply with the SBLC's requirements. If the documents do not fulfill the requirements specified in the SBLC, the issuing bank has the right to refuse payment since financial institutions deal in papers rather than the underlying goods, services, or performance. The SBLC sets a deadline for the receiver to submit the necessary documentation, and failure to meet this deadline could prevent payment.

To reduce the likelihood of non-payment due to bank insolvency or operational issues, it is crucial to issue SBLCs from reliable, trustworthy businesses with strong financial positions. Beneficiaries should read the SBLC's terms carefully and ensure that any documentation they submit for payment conforms with these standards. Working with trade finance or legal experts might make it simpler to review and complete the necessary documentation.

Regular monitoring helps keep abreast of news and financial developments on the condition of the issuing bank and the political and economic stability of the country in which it operates.

An SBLC provides a strong payment guarantee, but the issuing bank's ability to meet its commitments and the beneficiary's compliance with the SBLC's conditions still leave a slight but potential risk of nonpayment. We must carefully select the issuing bank and strictly adhere to the SBLC regulations to mitigate these risks. Standby letters of credit (SBLC) costs can vary significantly depending on several factors, including the issuing bank's rules, the applicant's creditworthiness, the SBLC amount, the transaction's risk, and the SBLC's term. You can find an extensive explanation of the SBLC fee structure below:

An SBLC typically costs 1–10% of the entire amount of the credit letter. This broad range represents the different risk profiles and distinctive situations seen in different kinds of transactions and establishments. Businesses with a stable credit history and funds typically receive waived fees due to the applicant's creditworthiness, which lowers the bank's risk. The fee percentage could change based on the SBLC's total amount. Larger amounts may provide lower percentage rates but higher absolute fees due to the larger base amount. The perceived risk of the transaction, which might include the industry, country risk, and specifics of the contract, can affect the cost (transactions with more risk often have higher prices). The cost may also change based on the length of time the SBLC is given; longer durations might cost more because the bank would be taking on more risk.

The company's existing banking relationship with the issuing bank may impact its fee negotiations; long-term bank clients with several accounts may receive preferential terms. Typically, these expenses consist of issue fees, which are one-time costs incurred at the SBLC issuing point. This usually amounts to a part of the SBLC total; for SBLCs intended to last more than a year, an annual fee may be imposed. On the first day of each SBLC year, this fee, usually a portion of the SBLC, is due. If the SBLC needs confirmation or advice from a different bank, there could be additional charges; these fees compensate the advising or confirming bank for their involvement in the process. An amendment fee may apply if the SBLC's terms require alterations after its issuance.

Occasionally, the company may be able to terminate the SBLC without incurring additional costs beyond the initial agreement, provided it fulfills its contractual obligations before the SBLC is nearing its deadline. It relieves both the applicant and the issuing bank from further obligations through this termination process.

Businesses may better plan for the expenses of obtaining an SBLC by knowing the variables that affect the fees and the structure of the fee arrangement, even if the prices for Standby Letters of Credit can vary greatly. An essential part of the application process is negotiating the conditions and costs with the issuing bank, taking into account the business's creditworthiness, the transaction's risk profile, and the SBLC's duration.

It is clear that this process involves several intricate steps meant to thoroughly evaluate the applicant's financial status and any related dangers. For both the bank and the applicant, each step—from the preliminary due diligence procedure to the paperwork review, offer letter issuing, and fee payments—is crucial. Businesses can better prepare for the requirements and expectations that come with getting an SBLC if they understand these processes. This will make financial transactions go more smoothly and give them a safety net for keeping their contractual obligations.

Both the issuing bank and the SBLC applicant must make financial arrangements and commitments to fund an SBLC. By ensuring that the bank has sufficient security to satisfy any responsibility under the SBLC, the method lowers the possibility of a payment default. Pledges of monetary collateral are the most straightforward method of funding an SBLC. The applicant, or party seeking the SBLC, must deposit a certain amount of money with the issuing bank in order for the bank to fulfill its commitment under the SBLC. By supplying the SBLC, the bank mitigates its risk through this collateral. Different amounts of collateral may be required, depending on the applicant's creditworthiness, relationship to the bank, and expected risk of the transaction. Sometimes, the bank will need collateral equal to 100% (or more) of the SBLC amount, especially if there is a substantial risk or the applicant's trustworthiness is questionable.

Apart from the prerequisites for collateral, the bank levies an additional cost for SBLC supply. The bank receives payment for this fee in exchange for assuming the risk and providing the service. We frequently compute the charge as a percentage of the SBLC value.

The precise percentage may differ significantly depending on a number of variables, including the complexity of the transaction, the length of the SBLC, the total amount involved, and the bank's evaluation of the risk. The fees for the SBLC might vary from a few percent to several percent of its annual value. While cash collateral is commonly utilized,

SBLCs can also be funded through other means, especially for well-established businesses with strong banking relationships.

In addition to cash, banks may accept marketable securities, real estate, or other tangible assets as collateral. The bank will assess these assets to determine their value and suitability as collateral. Banks may award the SBLC to businesses based on their existing credit lines. The bank's lending policies and the company's creditworthiness are the main factors influencing this arrangement.

Occasionally, a third party may provide the bank with a guarantee on behalf of the applicant. This third party must have a strong credit history and be well connected to the bank.

Before giving out SBLCs, banks carefully consider all the possible risks. This includes the risk of the transaction, the applicant's financial health, and the political and economic situation in both parties' home countries.

Additionally, to ensure adherence to know your customer (KYC) and anti-money laundering (AML) standards, applicants and banks must manage legal and regulatory procedures. As a result, careful preparation and a discussion between them are necessary before funding an SBLC. If applicants want to lower the cost of getting an SBLC, they should be ready to offer enough collateral or show that they are highly creditworthy. Last but not least, the particular arrangements for funding a small Business Loan might differ significantly depending on the rules of the bank, the kind of transaction, and the level of risk.

Balancing the Ledger: Exploration of the Pros and Cons of Documentary Credits

So far, we have seen that documentary credits are essential instruments in the financing of international trade. This settlement technique has certain disadvantages but offers substantial benefits in lowering the risks involved in the international trade of goods and services. In order to present a fair assessment, we examine all perspectives here.

CHAPTER 2   LETTERS OF CREDIT: THE LIFELINE OF GLOBAL TRADE

The mitigation of risk is one of the main benefits of employing documentary credits, particularly in international trade. When interacting with unknown people or conducting business under disparate legal systems, buyers and sellers frequently experience uncertainty. Documentary credits mitigate these risks by providing a bank's promise to pay the seller upon meeting the specified paperwork criteria.

Offering a documentary credit to customers as a payment option might help vendors appear more trustworthy to them. It provides the buyer with the assurance that a bank, which has agreed to underwrite the deal, has thoroughly investigated the seller. Credits for documentaries might provide financial flexibility. Obtaining a documentary credit enables exporters to improve their cash flow by enabling them to secure bank funding before receiving the buyer's payment. This is very helpful for handling bulk orders or lengthy production runs.

By using documentary credits, a buyer can ensure that the items they receive meet the standards before making a payment. Only once all paperwork, including insurance policies, shipping records, and inspection reports, is in order can the bank release money.

The intricacy of documentary credits is one of their main drawbacks. It may be intimidating and time-consuming for both sides to go through the procedure, which calls for strict compliance and thorough paperwork. Opening and maintaining documentary credits can also come with hefty expenses, which include bank charges, administrative expenditures, and sometimes even legal fees.

Documentary credits' stringent requirements might potentially be a disadvantage. Once granted, it can be challenging to amend a documentary credit without the consent of all parties, including the issuing bank. If modifications become necessary after the credit's grant, this rigidity could lead to delays and additional costs.

Documentary credits offer protection, but they also put the issuing bank's performance and financial health at risk. Financial difficulties or administrative setbacks may cause the bank to postpone or compromise payments.

Documentary credits demand that all submitted materials closely adhere to the credit's requirements. Malicious inconsistencies between the documentation and the credit terms may lead to nonpayment, which can have severe consequences.

However, small and medium-sized businesses (SMEs) may find the cost of obtaining documentary credits prohibitive. This financial instrument necessitates significant capital reserves or credit facilities from the importer, as banks often withhold credit amounts until transaction completion. This essentially locks up important operating money that SMEs could have otherwise used to finance ongoing operations, create new goods, or enter new markets.

Documentary loans are a major capital-intensive hurdle for SMEs, particularly those with restricted access to big credit lines. Smaller enterprises, who usually have less financial stability and fewer assets than bigger organizations, may find it more difficult to achieve these standards since banks evaluate risk and creditworthiness strictly. Small and medium-sized enterprises (SMEs) may face exclusion from international trade possibilities or be compelled to pursue less secure alternative payment methods, therefore increasing their risk exposure.

Due to its restriction on liquidity, SMEs' capacity to develop and adapt in a competitive market is not only limited, but it also puts their very survival at risk. Having money frozen can cause operational problems in a commercial setting where cash flow is crucial, impacting everything from payroll to inventory control. Small and medium-sized businesses (SMEs) may find it difficult to maintain operations without the funding required to get documentary credits, which would inhibit innovation and limit growth in the larger economy.

This makes it even more important for lawmakers and financial institutions to make it easier for small businesses to get the financial products they need to do business around the world without putting their own finances at risk.

With difficulties as well as security, documentary credits provide a well-rounded strategy for controlling payment risks in international trade. They lower the chance of nonpayment, improve the legitimacy of transactions, and make financing easier, but they also come with complexity, expense, rigidity, and a dependency on banks.

Companies wishing to finance trade should carefully consider these aspects before deciding if documentary credits are the best option. This evaluation is especially crucial for transactions where the financing implications and risk balance have a significant impact on the profitability and operational flow of the deal.

CHAPTER 2 LETTERS OF CREDIT: THE LIFELINE OF GLOBAL TRADE

Summary

The important role letters of credit (LCs) play in safeguarding commercial transactions and offering a safety net for sellers and purchasers is investigated in this chapter. It emphasizes the difficulty in juggling interests across parties and names the main players engaged—applicant, beneficiary, issuing bank, confirming bank, and advising bank—who cooperate to establish confidence.

The chapter highlights various types of LCs, such as At Sight, Usance, and Red and Green Clause LCs, and outlines the ISBP and UCP frameworks that regulate these LCs, focusing on their advantages such as payment security and simplified processes. UCP 600 talks on the development of eUCP and its effects on digital trade documents and worldwide compliance, as well as on developing concerns like SWIFT dependency.

Together with the transforming power of SWIFT, MLETR, and trade finance digitization, the value of exact document scrutiny under ISBP 821 is underlined. Emphasizing the strategic use of standby letters of credit (SBLCs) in increasing corporate trust, the chapter also looks at how LCs prevent financial crime, fraud, and penalties.

Finally, from a fair standpoint, the chapter evaluates the advantages and drawbacks of LCs while underscoring their ongoing importance in a trading environment undergoing rapid change.

CHAPTER 3

Cashing In on the Opportunity: The Dynamic World of Receivables Finance

For companies trying to maximize their working capital and cash flow, receivables financing has developed into a vibrant and essential instrument. Companies are looking more and more to this type of finance as the global economy gets more linked and fast-paced to release the value locked behind exceptional invoices. This chapter investigates the expanding relevance of receivables financing, its various forms, and its transformative effect on companies of all kinds. Understanding the methods, advantages, and drawbacks of this financing option will help businesses to properly seize a great chance to support resilience and expansion in a market always evolving.

A business may successfully utilize its receivables as collateral in order to get capital based on the funds that customers owe them through a financial arrangement known as receivables finance. This specific form of finance is essential for monitoring a business's working capital and cash flow issues. It is a system that bridges the gap between providing goods or services and receiving payment by giving the seller immediate access to funds and the buyer a postponement of the payment due date.

A receivable is an asset on the seller's balance sheet and a liability on the buyer's. Every transaction results in the creation of a new receivable, which is an essential component of trade finance.

CHAPTER 3   CASHING IN ON THE OPPORTUNITY: THE DYNAMIC WORLD OF RECEIVABLES FINANCE

For a vendor, the speed of converting receivables into cash is crucial. When days sales outstanding (DSO) are lower, the seller collects payment earlier, reducing the need for additional financial resources and enhancing their cash flow condition. In an attempt to boost both their financial stability and efficiency in operation, companies try to lower their debt service obligations (DSO).

Conversely, many buyers aim to increase their days payable outstanding (DPO), a measure of how long a business typically takes to settle its invoices. By providing the buyer with an additional opportunity to use the products or services they have acquired to generate revenue before paying the owing, a longer DPO enables the buyer to keep track of and safeguard working capital.

Receivables financing serves a buyer with the aim of reconciling the conflicting goals of buyers and sellers with regard to DSO and DPO. Sellers are able to get immediate payments based on their outstanding bills through a number of receivables finance alternatives, notably asset-based lending, factoring, and discounting of invoices, which lowers their days of service. This speedy financial injection enables companies to slash their operational costs, capitalize on expansion prospects, and concentrate less on debt.

Different methods exist for funding accounts payable.

Factoring, for instance, is when an organization provides a third party (a factor) with a discount on its bills. Following that, the factor pays the buyer right away, allowing the seller the opportunity to use funds right away.

Invoice discounting, like factoring, entails the seller maintaining control over the sales ledger, collecting funds from the buyer, and repaying the financier according to the agreed-upon terms.

Credit lines or loans secured by a variety of company assets, such as stock, machinery, and receivables, are known as asset-based lending.

Receivables finance makes it possible for businesses to improve their cash flow without having to wait for the terms of payment to expire. This helps make financial planning less unpredictable and decreases the likelihood of shortfalls in funds. It is imperative for companies to weigh the positive aspects of enhanced liquidity and working capital management against the drawbacks of these agreements, which include interest rates and service fees.

A versatile instrument that matches the operational capital and cash flow requirements of both the buyers and the sellers in trade activities is receivables financing. This supports businesses in overcoming the intricacies of trade finance by providing them immediate access to funds retained in receivables, improving their operational efficiency and affordability.

The Lifecycle of Receivables Fueling the Trade Finance Engine

Receivables, which embody the essence of trade whereby products or services are traded for payment, are a basic outcome of the business relationships that fuel the global economy. Multiple levels of interaction are often involved in the process, from raw materials to the final goods, each resulting in a distinct set of receivables.

Let's begin our exploration of the processes that lead to receivables and their crucial role in facilitating trade finance. The sale and purchase arrangements naturally link to the beginning of a receivable throughout a transaction's lifecycle. Think about a raw material producer who supplies raw materials to a manufacturer. The latter now owes the producer funds because the producer created a receivable against the company. On the producer's balance sheet, this receivable appears as an asset, which reflects an anticipated cash inflow.

A new receivable against the retailer arises when the manufacturer turns the raw material into an end product and then sells it to a different party, possibly a store. Every stage of the sales process, from the procurement of raw materials to the delivery of the final product to the customer, creates receivables.

Each supply chain activity not only generates receivables but additionally indicates a potential need for funding. In order to lower days sales outstanding (DSO), sellers may look for financing options that will allow them to quickly turn these receivables into cash. This will help them run their businesses better and keep their cash flow stable. On the other hand, buyers who want to boost their days payable outstanding (DPO) could search for financing solutions that let them extend payment without harming their financial standing or their contractual ties with suppliers.

Whenever the buyer or seller generates receivables, investors may intervene by tailoring options to meet their needs. For instance, an investor might be willing to purchase the seller's receivables at a discount, providing the seller with instant cash flow in exchange for taking on the risk and work of collecting from the buyer. Alternatively, a lender could provide the buyer with a receivables-backed line of credit, giving them more control over the payment terms.

Peer-to-peer lenders and institutional investors have also become involved as a result of the development of digital platforms and blockchain technology. The potential of trade receivables as an asset class attracts these actors to the market.

Of course, trade interactions result in the production of accounts receivable, which exist as proof of successful transactions and provide access to potential funding opportunities.

The financing of receivables is becoming more complex, involving a broader spectrum of stakeholders and innovative approaches as international trade continues to evolve. Learn more about the receivables lifecycle, from where they come from to how they are paid, to better understand trade finance and the ways it can improve liquidity and financial flexibility all along the supply chain.

The Art of Enhancing Quality for Optimal Financing

The quality of receivables has a big impact on the financing options that are available under a trading agreement. This feature takes into consideration a lot more than the face amount of the receivables; it additionally takes into consideration the purchaser's creditworthiness, the conditions of the payment obligation, and the transaction's whole risk profile.

Let's begin by exploring how improving their quality can lead to more profitable financing options. Financial institutions are constantly searching for solutions that minimize the dangers inherent in financing collections. Optimizing creditworthiness to strengthen the quality of the receivable is an ordinary approach.

This may manifest in a number of ways:

- To assure the lender of the receivable's collectability, a third party, frequently a bank or other financial institution, guarantees the buyer's payment commitment.

- Credit insurance safeguards the vendor against the likelihood that the buyer will not pay, thus providing the seller with greater tranquility of mind and improving the quality of the collectible.

- Lastly, a surety company guarantees that the seller will do what they agreed to do for the buyer through surety bonds. This gives the lender an extra layer of security when it comes to receivables.

Transforming a collectible into an irrevocable payment obligation significantly strengthens its quality. There are two main ways to make this change: directly, by using language that makes the transaction itself irreversible, and indirectly, by using

CHAPTER 3   CASHING IN ON THE OPPORTUNITY: THE DYNAMIC WORLD OF RECEIVABLES FINANCE

a document like a promissory note or an irrevocable payment undertaking (IPU) for the collectible. These binding instruments establish an unambiguous commitment to payment, improving the value of the collectible.

It's important to remember that establishing this irrevocability may require a buyer to give up some rights, such as the ability to refuse compensation for defective goods, even though they still retain the right to sue the seller for those problems.

The probability and timeline of payment have a direct effect on a receivable's valuation as well. Suppliers who need time to prepare for manufacturing and shipping might be eligible to obtain funding from lenders. The overall cost of financing will, however, be a representation of the longer time between output and settlement, which will impact the collection's short-term value.

A more valuable collectible is an invoice requiring settlement in a short period of time, like 30 days. Investors find it enticing as a result of a forthcoming payment, which decreases both the risk and the price of funding.

Enhancing receivables integrity is vital for negotiating favorable funding terms in trade agreements. By strengthening credit, introducing irreversible payment commitments, and simplifying payment timetables, suppliers are able to render their outstanding debts much more appealing to financiers. This strategic enhancement not only accelerates cash flow but also fortifies the financial backbone of global trade dynamics, enabling businesses to thrive even in the face of uncertainty.

Optimizing a company's financial resources and liquidity involves thoughtful consideration of collection funding. The next step after evaluating a receivable's integrity is to focus on financing it as profitably as possible. The question of whether the account receivable constitutes an unconditional payment obligation is going to influence the source of funding choices that are readily available.

Conditional vs. Unconditional Receivables

Let us examine the variables and approaches associated with collection financing, emphasizing the distinctions between conditional and unconditional receivables.

The image in question primarily pertains to the topic of "Conditional vs. Unconditional Receivables." Conditional liabilities are receivables that come with extra duties or conditions that the seller must meet before they become an unconditional payment obligation. This can entail performing a task, supplying more items, or hitting a set of performance goals. Conditional receivables carry a performance risk to the seller, leading to lenders being cautious of them in general.

CHAPTER 3   CASHING IN ON THE OPPORTUNITY: THE DYNAMIC WORLD OF RECEIVABLES FINANCE

Once a receivable becomes an unconditional obligation for the purchaser, it becomes more financeable. This modification occurs as a result of the receivable's substantial enhancement in quality, which minimizes the financier's exposure. At this stage, the buyer's credit risk or creditworthiness takes priority.

Options do exist for funding unconditional receivables. Selling the receivable at a discount to a third party, or factor, is known as factoring. The factoring company then assumes responsibility for the buyer's payment collection, enabling the seller to have instant liquidity.

Invoice discounting is comparable to factoring in that the seller remains in charge of managing the sales ledger and is in charge of collecting payment from the client. The financier provides a cash advance based on the invoice value, which the buyer repays once they settle.

Asset-based lending refers to using receivables as security for a loan or credit line. Usually expressed as a percentage of the value of the receivable, the financing amount provides flexibility and quick access to funds.

Several crucial factors need to be considered when financing accounts receivable. This is especially important in the case of conditional receivables, where the financier assesses the likelihood that the seller will fulfill the requirements needed for converting the receivable into an unconditional obligation to pay.

When it comes to unconditional receivables, the buyer's ability to make payments is crucial. By assessing the buyer's creditworthiness, it is simpler to determine the risk involved in financing the receivable. A number of factors, including the terms of payment, the buyer's reliability history, and its legal enforceability, influence the overall quality of a receivable. This, in turn, impacts the financing options that are available.

This requires a calculated move that involves carefully weighing the conditionality of the receivable, the risks involved, and the credit standing of the buyer. Businesses can improve their liquidity and better manage their working capital by assessing these aspects and choosing the best financing option. By grasping the intricacies of receivables financing within the trade finance context, businesses can unlock the potential of their sales, propelling them toward growth and sustainability.

The intricate operations of receivables financing significantly influence the economic viability and reliability of financing arrangements. The transformation of a conditional receivable to an unconditional one presents numerous potential performance hazards, especially for investors who must closely monitor the variables that could contribute to the transformation's success. Whenever real-world transportation occurs, the whole thing becomes significantly more complex because managing ownership documents and overseeing the delivery of the products are essential elements.

The mode of transportation directly affects the level of control a financier may exercise over the receivable. As an example, a bill of lading issued for maritime freight offers a rather simple scenario since it acts as a key to unlocking a wealth of financing options, giving the possessor authority over the cargo in addition to signifying that they are on board a vessel. When the items are loaded aboard a ship, a financier with possession of the bill of lading can utilize it to convert the issuing bank's payment obligation into an unconditional one, making the receivable financeable.

Additional issues and concerns arise when financing receivables in conjunction with other modes of transportation, such as truck, rail, or air. Similar to maritime shipping, air waybills offer a similar level of control and confidence. There are more complicated logistical issues with these modes of transportation because the rules that govern transportation and the handling of goods are spread out across many jurisdictions and transportation systems. Controlling the documentation may not be as straightforward as it is with air or sea freight, which in turn affects the items involved.

We have already seen how a letter of credit (LC) may significantly enhance the quality of the receivable in situations where the supplier poses a performance risk since it is a financial instrument that guarantees payment. The issuing bank provides payment to the beneficiary upon presentation of the required documentation, including transport documents such as the bill of lading or air waybill. This reinforces the payment obligation and enhances the likelihood of financing a receivable.

A letter of credit (LC) may significantly enhance the quality of the receivable in situations where the supplier poses a performance risk. The LC is a financial instrument that:

Payment Guarantee: The issuing bank guarantees payment to the beneficiary upon presentation of the required documentation, including transport documents such as the bill of lading or air waybill. This reinforces the payment obligation and enhances the likelihood of financing a receivable. By determining when and how the payment obligation becomes unconditional, the investor directly controls the receivable's financing potential. Managing the presentation under the LC accomplishes this.

Lastly, the investor can directly influence the financeability of the receivable by controlling the terms and circumstances under which the payment obligation becomes unconditional. Controlling the presentation of the LC achieves this.

Receivable financing can benefit from extended credit terms, particularly when structured under a letter of credit. This versatility offers a buffer that can be critical to operational liquidity and financial planning, giving the buyer additional time to effectively oversee their financial resources and payment obligations.

Receivables funding relies heavily on logistics, which entails processing and transporting items as well as managing title documents. The transformation of an account receivable from a conditional to an unconditional obligation depends on these logistical factors, which significantly impact the financer's risk assessment and the overall financeability of the receivable. So, for financiers to lower performance risks and get the most out of receivable financing, they need to understand and be able to handle the logistics of different types of transportation.

Tailoring for Buyer's Flexibility

Assisting sellers in converting receivables into instant funds for the purpose of speeding up their financial operations is a topic of significant interest in the intricate field of receivables finance. However, establishing terms that help the buyer—especially by extending their payment terms—is just as crucial an element. In addition to helping the seller achieve faster liquidity, this strategy gives the interested party additional financial breathing room.

In simple terms, collections finance enables clients by allowing the lender to determine the buyer's trustworthiness and consent to defer repayment beyond the standard term that the seller grants. In doing so, the lender offers the seller a loan on the receivables and bears the risk of both the buyer's creditworthiness and the extended duration.

A comprehensive assessment of the purchaser's financial standing provides the foundation for extending payment terms.

A solid credit record gives the lending institution trust that the purchaser is going to be ready to fulfill their payments on time, regardless of whether they come in later than expected. An effective agreement requires the buyer to explicitly acknowledge that they will be responsible for payment, even if it is late.

To be able to define the terms and circumstances of the additional repayment period, this consent is mandatory.

A number of significant variables must be considered when determining whether to extend the time frame for payment. When establishing the duration for which the buyer can reimburse the deferred amount, it is crucial to carefully consider how to reconcile the seller's demand for liquidity with the buyer's handling of funds. Then, preserving the receivable's trade debt status is of the utmost importance since it affects how rating agencies and accountants perceive the receivable.

Extended repayment intervals might make it harder to determine the difference between bank and trade debts. Understanding this distinction is essential for rating and reporting purposes, given that transforming trade debt into bank debt could impact the buyer's debt-to-equity ratio and financial statements.

Providing customers with customized receivables financing creates a mutually beneficial arrangement where buyers benefit from extended repayment terms and sellers accelerate their revenue streams. However, creating these agreements requires careful consideration, assessing factors like the buyer's credit history, the certainty of payment obligations, and the influence of extended duration on debt classification. Investors may establish strategies that strengthen the financial well-being of both sellers and buyers by carefully handling all of these variables, which will strengthen the trading ecosystem as a whole.

From Traditional Methods to Digital Horizons

Received payment financing is an important part of trade finance that has changed a lot over the years to adapt to changing business needs and new technological advances. Fundamentally, receivable finance is the practice of utilizing a company's accounts receivable, or cash owed by clients, as security for loans. With the help of this approach, businesses can free up the value enshrined in unpaid invoices, improving their liquidity and cash flow management.

Two of the main components of conventional receivables finance are **forfaiting** and **factoring**, each with subtle differences affecting the seller's recourse. Under this type of factoring, the seller typically sells a receivable without any legal recourse, thereby releasing them from liability in the event of the buyer's payment default. Before selling the receivable, the seller must guarantee that the buyer's payment obligation is unconditional. Upon the sale of the receivable, the seller releases themselves from further liability and receives a discounted payment.

Factoring presents the vendor with an advance payment at a discount, much like forfaiting. Nonetheless, the buyer may not pay the component (the finance provider) in full, and the seller may receive additional money. In contrast to forfaiting, if the customer doesn't pay the receivable, the seller might have other options.

CHAPTER 3   CASHING IN ON THE OPPORTUNITY: THE DYNAMIC WORLD OF RECEIVABLES FINANCE

The use of forfaiting and factoring has expanded beyond the sale of goods or the provision of services. For instance, forfaiting transactions now encompass payment claims from financial instruments like loan agreements or letters of credit. Receivables finance has become a more versatile tool for handling liquidity as a result of its extended reach.

Supply chain finance (SCF) is a relatively recent breakthrough in receivables financing, initially made possible via digital platforms. The primary objective of SCF programs is to maximize the amount of working capital for both sellers and buyers.

They may either be buyer-led (focusing on payables) or supplier-led (focusing on receivables). SCF can prolong payment periods for buyers while granting suppliers access to finance on more favorable terms by utilizing the buyer's credit score.

The digitization of trade finance has led to the development of creative approaches that simplify receivables financing. Unconditional payment obligations have been made possible by automated data matchmaking, even though bank payment obligations (BPOs) were not as successful as expected. Receivables are created and financed much more quickly thanks to programs like the Uniform Rules for Digital Trade Transactions (URDTT) and the use of electronic shipping documents like electronic bills of lading and credit letters.

By developing systems and techniques that allow for faster and safer transactions, the fintech industry has significantly shaped the future of receivables financing. Legal frameworks are undergoing modifications to accommodate the evolving digital trade practices. Organizations like the English Law Commission are striving to upgrade laws to keep up with technological advancements, and some jurisdictions are considering adopting the UNCITRAL Model Law of Electronic Transferable Records (MLETR).

The ever-changing nature of trade finance is apparent in the growth of receivables financing from conventional techniques to digital frontiers. As companies strive to optimize their working capital and liquidity management strategies, we expect the incorporation of technology in this field to offer increasingly inventive and adaptable financing options. This continuous change improves the general effectiveness and robustness of global commerce ecosystems, in addition to helping suppliers and buyers.

As soon as an account receivable turns into an unconditional payment obligation, funders can finance, trade, or refinance these obligations. This makes the market more liquid and gives suppliers more financial options. The structure of a receivable and the procedures in place for its exchange or liability issuance determine its transactability.

Having the ability to transform receivables into arrangements that facilitate straightforward transferability and security is vital for trading them. Converting a receivable into a negotiable document like a promissory note enhances its availability. Lenders find these tools useful as they ensure payment to the holder through delivery, endorsement, or other transfer instruments. The International Trade and Forfaiting Association (ITFA) created the Electronic Payment Undertaking (ePU).

We are anticipating legislative changes that could allow the transmission of digital promissory notes. This electronic counterpart reflects the changing nature of trade finance by making it easier to trade receivables in a digital environment.

Financial institutions often purchase assets by assignment, either directly or indirectly. This entails the seller assigning the debt to the lender and notifying the payer of the allocation. With the support of these assignments, financiers might assume the position of the seller and collect payment from the buyer.

Establishing special purchase vehicles (SPVs) with the explicit purpose of purchasing assets is an innovative approach. By issuing promises to pay, backed against the debts that they buy, these SPVs fund their acquisition. The issued instruments, often consisting of promissory notes or other comparable securities, aim to enhance the market's liquidity for receivables through free trading.

Lenders frequently use the strategy of diversifying their financing arrangements by incorporating different financial partners. This partnership may involve non-bank financial investors, which has been a growing trend in the last several years. These investors' involvement in receivables acquisitions marks a substantial change, expanding the pool of capital available for financing trade transactions.

Invoice trading is an intricate sector of finance that integrates traditional approaches with cutting-edge innovations. The financial business continues to evolve by transforming debts into marketable formats, developing mechanisms for their smooth transfer, and engaging a broader spectrum of participants. These innovations further enhance the financial environment of trade finance by providing suppliers with additional possibilities for investment and by making it easier for them to manage their working capital more effectively.

Receivables financing is a vital tool for vendors to boost their liquidity. Suppliers can infuse their company with instant liquidity by trading assets as soon as possible—sometimes even before they materialize. Because of their financial adaptability, suppliers are able to provide purchasers with advantageous loan conditions, which might give them a competitive edge, while additionally including the cost of financing in the sale price to protect profits.

CHAPTER 3   CASHING IN ON THE OPPORTUNITY: THE DYNAMIC WORLD OF RECEIVABLES FINANCE

Invoice refinancing aids buyers by potentially offering extended repayment periods. These types of agreements may assist them in governing their financial resources far more effectively, which will enable them to make investments in expansion initiatives and optimize their finances. In this scenario, the customer's involvement often entails committing to an unconditional payment commitment, helping the seller obtain financing.

Receivables funding appeals to investors, particularly banking institutions, as a means of allocating cash with the objective of maximizing revenues. They have to nevertheless meticulously handle the regulatory expenditures associated with these financings. There are plenty of chances of earning significant returns if one can effectively set up these financings while managing risk. Additionally, lenders deliver the full financing structure, which facilitates more seamless trade activities.

By providing guarantees or coverage for a fee, credit support organizations may benefit from receivables financing. In spite of lowering risk and raising the attractiveness of the assets to financiers, this support enhances trust and stability across the trade finance ecosystem.

Well-structured receivables finance programs, delivering an opportunity to invest in receivables from trade without having to shell out for the starting structuring fees, are attracting a growing number of inquiries from investors. We must meticulously design these programs to accurately reflect accounts receivable and provide investors with an actual, asset-backed investment opportunity.

There are several challenges and dangers in the area of receivables finance. The Greensill Capital case shows that there is a risk with using too big of financing structures that include future speculative receivables as commercial liabilities. Such types of operations emphasize the value of conducting comprehensive research and sticking to the initial purpose of receivables funding, meaning financing backed by supplied or forthcoming products and services.

Receivables financing provides an opportunity for increasing liquidity, extending credit, and optimizing returns under a regulated framework, making it an attractive business case for all parties involved in the trade process. Even though there are a lot of options, there is a need to follow procedures that protect the integrity of financing for trade receivables. Residual finance can remain a pillar of international trade finance strategies with proper structuring and cooperation between buyers, sellers, financiers, and credit support providers.

Navigating the Capital Adequacy Maze

The Basel regime is an important part of the rules that govern the world's banking system. Its goal is to make sure that banks have enough capital to handle the risks that come with doing business, especially those that have to do with credit risk. The Basel Agreements' development, from Basel I to Basel III, is noteworthy because it demonstrates a vigorous attempt to improve financial stability and streamline banking regulation. This shift will have an enormous effect on the way banks and other financial institutions handle financing and refinancing of outstandings, which is an essential aspect of trade finance.

First implemented in 1988, Basel I established the fundamental guidelines for capital adequacy by primarily addressing credit risk, or the possibility of suffering a loss due to a counterparty's default. Unfortunately, the **one-size-fits-all method of risk weighting** quickly proved to be too simplistic to account for the diverse default risks that different borrowers face or the evolving ways that banks manage risk.

In an effort to solve these flaws, Basel II was created in 2004. It featured a more complex framework that took into account variations in default risk and pushed banks to use more sophisticated risk management strategies. It was a major step toward a more comprehensive risk assessment strategy by emphasizing the necessity for banks to keep capital for operational and market risks in addition to credit risk.

The 2007–2008 financial crisis revealed additional flaws in the world banking system, which led to the creation of Basel III. The goal of this round of regulations was to make the banking industry stronger against economic shocks by putting in place more rules like the leverage ratio and liquidity coverage ratios, as well as stricter capital requirements and better risk coverage. We have gradually implemented Basel III and continue to coordinate the global adoption of its final features.

Due to the capital adequacy requirements under Basel III, banks are now more cautious when financing receivables, particularly in cases where the buyer or seller has assumed a significant amount of credit risk. Banks can now try to mitigate this risk by using arrangements that let them sell off their exposure to other financial institutions.

The regulatory environment impacts the way banks structure debt funding deals. Banks' required capital reserves against funded receivables may vary depending on whether they fall into the category of retail or corporate exposures, for instance. Basel III has prompted more detailed evaluations of the features of receivables and portfolio diversification.

Basel III capital requirements impact strategies including credit insurance and guarantee provisioning (e.g., aval on a bill of exchange and standby letters of credit). It changes banks' capital adequacy and leverage ratios when they treat these credit enhancements as off-balance-sheet entities with a 100% credit conversion factor (CCF).

Non-bank companies involved in supply chain and collection financing have an opportunity as a result of Basel III's higher capital requirements and regulatory burden for banking institutions. By taking advantage of regulatory arbitrage, these organizations may provide competitive financing alternatives for collections without having to adhere to the same strict capital adequacy standards as banks.

The landscape of collections finance will surely change as the financial services industry struggles to adjust to the Basel III regulatory environment and as possible future Basel standard revisions loom. Regulators, banks, and the larger financial community need to keep talking to each other in order to find a balance between protecting financial stability and creating an environment that is good for debt funding. Preserving this state of equilibrium is critical for boosting global commerce and ensuring that finance is readily accessible to companies operating in different markets.

The impact of the Basel system on the financing of receivables highlights the complex relationship between financial practices and regulatory frameworks. Credit improvements and the structure of receivables financing become more intricate as banks manage the Basel Standards' capital adequacy requirements.

Legal Nuances and Financial Implications of Payment Instruments in International Trade: The Role of Guarantees, Credit Enhancements, and Non-notified Transfers

The variety of payment methods is essential to transaction settlement since it provides different levels of security and advantages to importers (buyers) and exporters (sellers). These documents, which may be anything from straightforward invoices to intricate bills of exchange and letters of credit, not only make money transfers easier but also produce receivables. These receivables are legally binding rights to payment that the beneficiary—usually the exporter—can use to get funding. Gripping these payment mechanisms' uses and limits in trade finance requires a grasp of the legal status of these instruments and the related receivables.

CHAPTER 3   CASHING IN ON THE OPPORTUNITY: THE DYNAMIC WORLD OF RECEIVABLES FINANCE

That is, how strong a receivable is legally and how easy it is for the recipient to demand payment directly affect how much it is worth as a financial asset. Similarly, to sell or use receivables as collateral, they must be transferable or possess the legal ability to assign the right to receive payment to another party. Lastly, we refer to the ease of purchasing and selling these instruments on the financial markets as their tradability, a factor that influences their liquidity and investor appeal.

The types of receivables finance that are accessible to an exporter depend on the legal status of a particular payment instrument. For instance, the Uniform Rules for Bills of Exchange globally recognize a bill of exchange, which offers a high degree of enforceability and transferability. For exporters looking to maximize their financing strategies, it is therefore essential to comprehend the legal subtleties of payment mechanisms. With this information, they may choose the best payment options to improve their access to money and financial flexibility, which in turn helps them to participate in the global commerce ecosystem.

Because the receivables engaged in international commerce are so diverse, the legal environment around payment instruments is complex. These legal tools are essential for enabling commerce because they give sellers legally binding claims against purchasers for products or services rendered. It is vital to comprehend pivotal legal factors, such as negotiability and enforceability, in order to adeptly navigate this terrain. This review examines these elements and their impact on the various payment methods in trade finance.

The foundation of any payment instrument is its enforceability, which refers to the seller's legal power to demand payment from the buyer, who, once the obligation forms, becomes the debtor. Enforceability guarantees that a receivable, which is shown in the buyer's records as payment, is actually a legitimate financial asset for the seller. The enforceability of this depends on the seller meeting all requirements in order to establish a legally enforceable payment obligation. The strength and clarity of this legal base directly affects the seller's ability to use the receivable as security in transactions or as a means of financing.

Negotiability refers to the ease with which one party can transfer ownership of a receivable to another. This attribute has a big impact on the receivable's flexibility and liquidity. Bills of exchange and promissory notes are examples of negotiable documents that enable simple transfers, usually by delivery and endorsement, without the need for substantial transfer documentation. They are ideal for secondary market trade and receivables finance because of their simplicity of transfer. The legal notion of negotiability has its origins in conventional, paper-based trade. The emergence of digital financial solutions poses a threat to the transferability of electronic negotiable instruments, particularly in countries with evolving legal systems like the UK.

Assigning non-negotiable receivables necessitates specific transfer documents and usually entails notifying the debtor. The original agreement may have transferability restrictions, which might reduce the liquidity of the receivable. Invoices and other non-negotiable receivables are nonetheless essential to the financing of receivables, notwithstanding these restrictions. The introduction of efficient computerized platforms made possible by financial technology, particularly in payables finance programs, has streamlined the legal process of buying and selling receivables. The changing digital environment prompts legal changes to enhance the establishment and transfer of electronic negotiable instruments. By keeping the benefits of being able to negotiate in a digital setting, these changes aim to keep instruments for financing receivables useful and appealing. In addition, non-negotiable receivables are becoming easier to finance and invest in because of fintech advances that are solving certain long-standing problems with them. It is important for all parties involved in international trade to comprehend the legal differentiations among various payment instrument kinds. Receivables' enforceability and negotiability affect not just how much they are worth as financial assets but also which platforms and financing methods are used. As legislative frameworks change to allow digital transactions and fintech companies provide new methods to handle receivables, the trade finance environment is becoming more inclusive and flexible.

A legal concept known as "true sale" influences the buyer of a receivable's rights and protections, particularly in cases where the original owner is bankrupt. This concept is crucial in the financial industry. This discrepancy affects the recipient's financial plans as well, regardless of whether they plan to use the receivable as collateral for financing or to pursue an outright sale.

Let's explore these methods' subtleties and ramifications. The term "true sale" refers to the complete transfer of a receivable from the beneficiary, typically the exporter or seller, to the purchaser, typically a financier or investor. This transfer, which grants the buyer complete ownership of the receivable, safeguards it from claims made by the previous owner's assets. This safeguard is essential as it shields the buyer from the original owner's creditors and provides a level of assurance for the return of the invested money. If the original owner becomes insolvent after a genuine sale, the buyer of the receivable is shielded from the insolvency procedures and is not subject to the claim priority that usually impedes recovery efforts in such cases.

CHAPTER 3   CASHING IN ON THE OPPORTUNITY: THE DYNAMIC WORLD OF RECEIVABLES FINANCE

When the transaction fails to meet the requirements for a legitimate sale, the agreement often functions as financing, using the receivable as security. In this scenario, the financier promises the receivable to secure financing or a loan, yet the original owner retains ownership of the receivable. In the case of the original owner's insolvency, financiers have a priority claim over the collateral as secured creditors. However, creditors who must receive priority may surpass their recovery. If the financier fails to properly complete the security interest over the receivable, such as by registering with appropriate authorities like Companies House in the UK, the risk to the financier increases. The financier faces significant risks when they initially frame a deal as secured finance but ultimately intend it as a real sale. The financier may find themselves in the position of an unsecured creditor, which would severely hinder their ability to collect the cash if they fail to register properly or if the transaction does not fulfill the requirements for a real sale. Many jurisdictions have quite different legal frameworks for secured transactions and real sales. Local regulations govern the definition of a real sale, the perfecting of a security interest, and the handling of secured creditors during bankruptcy proceedings. Parties engaging in international receivables transactions must seek local legal guidance to properly manage these complications and structure their deals to achieve the intended legal and financial goals.

In trade finance, the difference between actual sales and financing using receivables as security is crucial because it affects the risk profile and chances of recovery for financial transactions using invoices. People who are giving money and people who are receiving it need to be able to understand and navigate these legal nuances in order to structure their transactions in a way that minimizes risks and maximizes protections. This is especially important for cross-border transactions where different legal systems may apply. In receivables finance, the notion of independence from underlying trade transactions is fundamental, particularly when financiers want to ensure that their payment rights are protected against disagreements resulting from the initial commercial arrangement between the seller and the buyer. This distinction informs the architecture of financing agreements, a crucial step in assessing the level of risk a financier bears.

When lenders use certain payment instruments, like bills of exchange, promissory notes, letters of credit (LCs), and independent payment undertakings (IPUs), they can keep some distance from the actual business deal. These agreements set out commitments for payments that are unaffected by disagreements between the trade parties.

93

For example, disagreements over the quality of products provided under a trade contract do not absolve parties of their responsibility to fulfill a letter of credit. These instruments are attractive for non-recourse financing arrangements due to their independence. They offer a greater assurance of repayment. Unlike the instruments indicated above, an invoice's amount inextricably links to the terms of the commercial parties' contract. Due to this connection, the contract's defenses, such as allegations of non-performance or flaws in the supplied products or services, can lead to disputes over payment. Financiers may use tactics like with-recourse financing or post-performance (i.e., after the debtor's express acceptance) of receivables purchases to reduce risk. If the seller's non-performance withholds payment, the financier can demand that the seller purchase the receivable. To mitigate the risks related to contract-based receivables, the debtor may choose to issue or obtain a separate payment obligation.

This might be in the shape of an IPU, a promissory note, or a bank-issued letter of credit agreement. By separating the financier's payment entitlement from the underlying trade disputes, these instruments facilitate enforcement and recovery more clearly. In receivables finance, the capacity of a payment obligation to exist alone from the underlying trade transaction is crucial. It determines the level of financial and legal protection that financiers have against disagreements between the original trade partners as well as the risk profile of financing agreements.

Financiers can improve the security of their trade finance assets and more effectively control their exposure by carefully choosing or arranging payment mechanisms to optimize this independence. In the context of financing receivables, credit enhancement strategies play a critical role in reducing the risks associated with debtor nonpayment. These tactics transfer the debtor's share of the inherent risk of the financing arrangement to a more creditworthy party, such as a bank or another company with an improved credit rating. Getting an independent, irreversible payment guarantee from the debtor's bank is a typical method of improving credit. This guarantee essentially replaces the debtor's credit risk with the bank's more reliable risk profile, providing a safety net that ensures the financier recovers the money in the event of the debtor's default. Securing guarantees from a different business entity in the debtor's group is another strategy.

When the debtor is a member of a larger conglomerate with firms that have stronger balance sheets or better credit ratings, this strategy is very helpful. Such an organization guarantees payment to the lender, regardless of the debtor's financial situation. These security interests, which provide a concrete recovery route in the case of failure, may consist of real estate, intellectual property, or other priceless rights. Financiers are protected against losses resulting from non-payment in cross-border transactions by ECAs through insurance or guarantees. Because of different legal systems and political unrest in the debtor's home country, transactions involving foreign trade may carry higher risks. For this reason, this kind of coverage is particularly helpful. Credit insurance shifts the risk from the banker to the insurer, protecting financiers against losses brought on by debtor insolvency or payment failure. Similar to this, surety bonds provide an extra degree of protection for the financier by having a third party, the surety, guarantee the debtor's commitments. Clearly, these strategies are vital resources for financiers involved in receivables financing, offering ways to lower credit risk exposure and guarantee payback. Through the application of these techniques, financiers may more confidently negotiate the intricacies of trade finance, resulting in more seamless transactions and more mutual trust between involved parties. The dynamic nature of international commerce underscores the criticality of efficiently mitigating credit risk through these kinds of innovations.

In the legal and financial communities, there is a heated discussion about categorizing debt as "true trade debt" vs. "bank debt" and how to handle this debt during a debtor's restructuring or insolvency. Understanding this differentiation is crucial for both lenders and corporations, particularly considering the advantages that certain loans may offer in financially troubled circumstances. Let's explore the ideas and ramifications of this discussion.

Fundamentally, "true trade debt" usually refers to debts that result directly from the selling and acquisition of products and services. The inherent connection to the buying and selling of goods sets this type of debt apart from other financial commitments a business may have. The main topic of discussion is whether trade finance debt, particularly short-term liabilities directly linked to trade activities, should take precedence in the event of a debtor's restructuring or insolvency.

Prioritizing these debts in order to facilitate the flow of products and services might help firms weather challenging times and even prevent a complete collapse. Despite the lack of a universal agreement or historical precedent mandating the prioritization of trade debts in all countries, several examples exist, including the restructurings of JSC BTA Bank and JSC Alliance Bank in Kazakhstan.

However, relying on such therapy without a clear legal basis is risky and not recommended. Recent financial struggles of Abengoa and Carillion have highlighted the blurring of the distinction between trade debt and bank debt when financing agreements change payment conditions. The issue over reclassification starts when financial institutions give loans that significantly change the terms of the debtor's payments, possibly moving trade payables into the category of bank debt. Analysts and rating agencies contend that these agreements ought to cause a reclassification of the impacted receivables on a business's balance sheet. Representing these commitments as bank debt instead of trade payables could potentially impact the company's debt profile and credit rating.

These categorization arguments must be considered by those creating financial arrangements that influence the payment or financing of receivables. A company's finances, relationships with creditors, and an insolvency plan might all be impacted by misclassification or a failure to foresee how such obligations are seen. Beyond mere semantics, the distinction between "true trade debt" and bank debt significantly influences the management of debts in restructuring or bankruptcy scenarios. Financial and legal professionals should exercise caution in this area, considering jurisdictional differences and the evolving nature of trade financing. It is becoming increasingly crucial to have a thorough grasp of these classifications as the financial industry innovates, especially in the structure of financing receivables. Because of their features as outlined in the Bills of Exchange Act of 1882, negotiable instruments—especially bills of exchange and promissory notes—are essential to the ease of trade finance.

Let's examine these tools, their transferability, legal ramifications, and related credit-building strategies. These tools are described as a written, unqualified command that requires the payee to pay a certain amount to a designated individual or bearer, either immediately upon demand or at a later time. In essence, it serves as a request for payment of the purchase price from the importer (drawee) to the exporter (drawer). It is defined as an unqualified written promise by one party to another party, or bearer, to pay a specific sum of money, either immediately or at a predetermined future date. It stands for dedication.

No matter what the terms of the underlying commercial transaction are, both instruments establish an unconditional payment obligation. Because their enforcement is largely dependent on actual physical possession, they are considered tangible assets under English law; however, this legal structure does not now apply to electronic versions.

The Act deems these instruments negotiable when they meet its requirements, thereby simplifying transferability. Transferring an instrument payable to a specific person requires an endorsement, whereas a bearer instrument transfers simply through delivery. In forfaiting transactions, these instruments are often transferred without the seller's recourse, giving the buyer immediate rights against the debtor. Forfaiting agreements, however, frequently contain provisions allowing for recourse to the seller in the event that certain instrument statements are proven to be false.

Bills of exchange and promissory notes are advantageous for secondary market trading due to their transferability, which increases the liquidity and adaptability of trade finance activities.

The International Trade and Forfaiting Association (ITFA) wants to change the rules that English law puts on electronic negotiable instruments. They think that ePUs should give the same rights as physical bills of exchange and promissory notes within the context of a contract.

Securing a bank guarantee or appending an approval to the instrument is a typical enhancement approach that increases the creditor's trust in the instrument's repayment. Although England does not legally recognize the concept of an aval, it functions similarly to a guarantee by providing the financier with an extra layer of confidence. In order to reduce risk and guarantee a better level of security in the transaction, financiers frequently condition the discounting of a bill or note on the existence of such credit improvements.

Promissory notes and bills of exchange are important tools in trade finance because they provide a formal way to establish autonomous, unconditional payment commitments. Their physical characteristics and the legal framework established by the Bills of Exchange Act of 1882 highlight their dependability and effectiveness in commercial transactions. However, the development of ePUs demonstrates the need for legislative changes in order to maintain the instruments' usefulness in modern trade finance. Furthermore, credit enhancement strategies like bank guarantees and avals reinforce the confidence of financiers, further enhancing the usefulness of these instruments in promoting international commerce.

Transactions when an exporter sells items under an export contract give rise to contract receivables, which impose payment obligations on the importer. These receivables are the sums owed to the importer, as specified in the contract or on later bills the exporter sends out for completed deliveries. Unlike negotiable instruments, the details of the underlying trade agreement and its implementation closely influence the enforceability and features of contract receivables.

Payment rights are frequently subject to the exporter's compliance with the conditions of the contract. The importer and the exporter may withhold payments until they resolve a dispute, potentially altering the amounts owed through credit notes. Contract receivables are not subject to strict form requirements under English law; instead, the fundamental principles of contract formation govern them. Because of its adaptation to contemporary trading processes, this flexibility makes it easier to employ electronic contracts and invoicing. Unlike negotiable instruments, you don't need to physically hold a contract or invoice to enforce payment. This feature greatly increases the financing options that are available for these receivables.

Under English law, the process of assignment transfers contracts receivables in a legal or equitable manner. Selecting one of these two formats impacts the rights of the assignee and the degree of defense against outside claims made against the assignor's property. A legal assignment gives the assignee the legal right to the debt and protects it from the assignor's creditors. It also lets the assignee sue the debtor on its own and requires the debtor to pay the assignee directly.

The transfer must meet a number of requirements listed in Section 136 of The Law of Property Act 1925 in order to be considered a valid assignment, including the assignment's absolute character, its written form, and the debtor's receipt of an assignment notice. There are various ways to provide notice to the debtor, ranging from general notifications covering all receivables under a contract to specific notices placed on invoices. The debtor's acknowledgment strengthens the assignee's trust, but it's not legally necessary for the assignment to be considered lawful.

Contract receivables allow for the flexible and adaptable creation and enforcement of financial obligations arising from commercial transactions. Legal assignment is the most common way to transfer these receivables. It gives financiers a solid base for working with these instruments and protects them from the assignor's unstable financial situation. However, compliance with legal requirements and the details of the underlying trade contract have a major impact on the efficacy of such transfers as well as the rights of the parties involved. It is necessary to comprehend these subtleties in order to create receivables as financial assets and to use them in financing agreements.

"Non-notified transfers of receivables" refers to a specific type of receivables financing where the debtor remains unaware of the transfer of their debt obligation to a third party. In order to protect the interests of lenders and assignees, this section looks at the features, risks, and strategic considerations of non-notified transfers, as well as ways to improve credit. Even without informing the debtor, the assignment of the receivable remains fair.

This status warns the debtor that the financier or assignee may not have legal title to the debt and that later legal assignments may override their claim. Assignors often undertake not to further transfer or deal with the debt in a way that could be detrimental to the interests of the assignee in order to reduce the risks associated with non-notification. These projects are essential to preserving the worth and integrity of the allocated receivable. When transfers occur without notice, the main danger is that later assignees who notify the debtor of the assignment will take precedence. To mitigate this risk and stop unlawful transactions with the debt, the assignor and assignee must carefully craft their contractual agreement.

It is important for assignees to thoroughly examine the provisions of the parent contract to make sure that no limitations or prohibitions exist for assignment. Breaking these conditions could render the assignment void or lead to legal action.

In order to provide the financier with extra reassurance, the debtor or connected businesses may issue guarantees or security interests as credit upgrades. These guarantees' precise clauses determine their transferability and applicability to the assignee. For the buyer or financier, the debtor's acknowledgment of assignment and commitments to pay into designated accounts may greatly improve control and security over the revenues from the sale of receivables. These agreements offer a safety net by enabling the buyer to pursue legal action against the seller in the event that the debtor defaults.

Usually predetermined, the extent of recourse (full or limited) is dependent on certain risk occurrences or conditions. Converting the debt into a more secure payment instrument, like a letter of credit or a bank-guaranteed negotiable instrument, essentially substitutes the bank's risk for the debtor's credit risk, thereby enhancing the level of security. By waiving any defenses against its payment obligation, a debtor might make the obligation unconditional and unaffected by the fulfillment of the underlying contract. This improvement significantly strengthens the financier's position.

When it comes to receivables finance, non-notified transfers necessitate careful handling of contractual, legal, and risk factors. These agreements provide advantages in terms of flexibility and operations, but they also come with special difficulties that call for the application of credit enhancement strategies. Financiers and assignees can control the risks related to unnoticed transfers and maintain the stability and dependability of their financing agreements by carefully utilizing these strategies.

The Dynamics of Transferability and Tradability

Negotiable instruments, such as bills of exchange and promissory notes, are important parts of trade finance because they make it easier for people to pay each other in a way that is organized and legally binding. These instruments, which are defined under the Bills of Exchange Act of 1882, have unique qualities that make them essential to business dealings.

CHAPTER 3   CASHING IN ON THE OPPORTUNITY: THE DYNAMIC WORLD OF RECEIVABLES FINANCE

Formally speaking, bills of exchange are written, unequivocal instructions in which one party, usually the exporter, directs another, the importer, to pay a certain amount, either immediately upon demand or at a later date. The issuer must write down this directive, address it to another party, and properly sign it. Similar to promissory notes, promissory notes differ in that the importer unconditionally promises to pay the exporter a specific amount, either on the same terms of demand or at a later date. The promises also need to be in written form, bear the maker's signature, identify the payee, and indicate that the bearer will receive money.

The unconditional payment obligation that both bills of exchange and promissory notes provide—which is unrelated to the actual commercial transaction—is an essential feature. This freedom gives both sides a level of financial security and predictability by making sure that the payment obligation stays the same no matter what disagreements or problems come up with the trade agreement itself.

The legal status of these documents is inextricably linked to their physical custody. Transferring the instrument itself allows for the transfer of ownership and the rights it grants. This aspect highlights how English law has traditionally treated negotiable instruments, which do not currently accept electronic versions because of the emphasis on physical ownership. Thus, the importance of the physical document does not change.

Bills of exchange and promissory notes serve as the cornerstones of trade finance, ensuring the fulfillment of payment obligations with a high level of dependability and legal enforceability. Even though they come from old legal theories that put a lot of weight on written documents, they are still very important to modern trade because they provide important tools for managing risk and making cross-border business transactions go smoothly. Trade will also drive the development of the structures and technologies supporting these outdated instruments, potentially paving the way for their digital counterparts in the future.

Promissory notes and bills of exchange are examples of negotiable instruments that are vital to ensuring the smooth running of business since they enable a standardized and secure way to express and transfer value. The Bills of Exchange Act 1882, an English law, grants these instruments the unique ability to transfer and trade. These important features enable their widespread use in international trade finance.

As long as it meets the Act's requirements, parties can freely exchange a negotiable instrument. The negotiability of bills of exchange and promissory notes enables their use as instruments for cross-border finance and payment.

A negotiable instrument's transferring procedure depends upon whether it is payable or not. Simple delivery may transfer ownership of instruments that are specifically payable to the bearer. The instrument's ease of transfer highlights its liquidity, making it a desirable choice for simple and rapid transactions. Transferability of instruments payable to a named party requires both delivery and the specified person's endorsement. Usually written on the document itself, this endorsement certifies that the new holder has received the rights.

The current legal system highlights the transfer of physical possession. This physical exchange of the instrument transfers ownership and, crucially, the right to demand payment. Even as the financial world becomes more digitally connected, the fact that these instruments still rely on physical paperwork highlights their conventional origins.

The transfer concept is essential in a forfaiting transaction, which is the sale of receivables or negotiable instruments without the seller having any recourse. It is typical for the parties to individually agree that specific seller representations, if proven false, can allow recourse, even though the instrument may change hands without recourse. This balance preserves the negotiable nature of the instrument while guaranteeing the buyer's safety.

The new holder obtains direct rights against the debtor upon transfer, guaranteeing that payment obligations comply with the conditions of the instrument. This direct relationship facilitates the instrument's ease of trading, making it especially desirable to forfaiters and other financial institutions operating in secondary markets. These instruments are more liquid and useful in the financial sector since they are easier to purchase and sell than other payment instruments.

These instruments play a crucial role in trade finance since they are tradable and transferable; these features guarantee that these assets can function as efficient instruments for guaranteeing payment, controlling risk, and improving liquidity throughout the world economy. The principles of negotiability are unwavering as the financial industry develops, notwithstanding the potential.

Unlocking Liquidity Through Securitization

Securitization of trade receivables is a cutting-edge financial innovation that provides companies with an advanced method of releasing cash from their accounts receivable. This process transforms the anticipated future cash flows from trade receivables into marketable securities. This gives investors access to a wide range of assets and provides the person who started the process instant cash. This becomes a critical strategy as businesses learn to handle the intricacies of international commerce and look for effective strategies to manage their working capital.

We are going to talk about the history, mechanics, and purpose of trade receivables securitization in today's financial markets so that you can fully understand how it works and what effects it has. Investable assets have emerged as a prominent means by which businesses may get money and effectively manage liquidity, especially with the securitization of trade receivables. The 1980s saw the first securitization of trade receivables, a type of cash flow asset that gained popularity approximately 30 years ago.

Businesses can get cash by selling a certain group of receivables to a special purpose entity (SPE). The SPE is legally separate from the seller and doesn't have to worry about the seller going bankrupt. The SPE subsequently returns the proceeds from the sale of the collateralized notes to the original firm in exchange for these receivables. This procedure enhances the selling company's balance sheet in addition to supplying instant liquidity. Due to the prevalence of private and customized agreements, precise information about the size of the trade receivable securitization market is difficult to come by. However, estimates place the total value of outstanding securitizations between USD 80 and USD 100 billion.

The market is a flexible instrument for managing liquidity across sectors since it spans a wide variety of industries and geographical areas. Securitization of trade transactions ranges in size from USD 50 million to over USD 1 billion, with substantial variations in size. A discernible trend toward diversifying funding sources for larger transactions has emerged since the global financial crisis of 2008, indicating a change in market dynamics and risk tolerance. Furthermore, the range of currencies and regions in which these transactions take place has expanded, covering a number of invoicing nations and currencies other than the US dollar, such as euros, sterling, and Mexican pesos. This flexibility allows for the inclusion of receivables from various jurisdictions, satisfying the requirements of both domestic and international funding.

A notable feature of trade receivables securitization is that it can include sellers or issuers who are not rated or rated below investment grade as creditors. These securitizations can obtain investment-grade ratings by carefully constructing them, which will improve the underlying assets' credit profile. The seller gains from this credit arbitrage by perhaps reducing financing costs and increasing the number of investors who are prepared to participate in the offering.

CHAPTER 3   CASHING IN ON THE OPPORTUNITY: THE DYNAMIC WORLD OF RECEIVABLES FINANCE

For businesses wishing to leverage their receivables for quick cash and better liquidity management, trade receivables securitization offers a sophisticated financial approach. The method's adaptability across numerous sectors, regions, and currencies, as well as its capacity to alter the credit quality of the involved assets, highlights its usefulness as an investable asset class. Understanding this market's characteristics, possibilities, and hazards will be essential for those looking to maximize their financial strategy as it continues to change.

The fact that issuers and sellers in the trade receivables securitization market come from a wide range of industries shows how flexible and appealing this type of financing is in any economy. Businesses can lower their overall borrowing costs by using securitization as a strategy. Securitized assets have a better credit rating than traditional debt instruments; companies may access finance on more favorable terms by transforming receivables into liquid assets. Securitization offers upfront cash flows that help businesses optimize the value of their receivables. This is especially appealing when it comes to investing in expansion prospects and managing working capital needs.

Companies can remove these assets from their balance sheets by structuring securitization as a sale of receivables, which can improve financial ratios and perhaps have positive accounting effects. Issuers can shift the credit risk attached to their receivables to investors by means of securitization. Businesses trying to control the risk concentration of their receivables portfolio can particularly benefit from this risk transfer. Companies can diversify their funding sources beyond conventional bank loans or bond issuances by utilizing the securitization market. This diversity can lessen the impact of market volatility and lessen reliance on any one source of money.

The issuer's credit quality heavily influences the securitization process. Even though the structure of securitizations attempts to separate the performance of the receivables from the seller's credit risk, the issuer's creditworthiness still partially influences the pricing and availability of funding. Considering issuers usually go on servicing the receivables after sale, there is a correlation between the performance of the securitization and the issuer's financial standing. The use of a backup servicer has grown in popularity as an instrument to mitigate servicer risk, especially in transactions involving less trustworthy lenders. If the original issuer fails to meet its debt servicing commitments, a backup servicer can take over and handle the receivables, thus protecting investor interests and the performance of the securitized assets.

For an extensive range of issuers, from publicly listed behemoths to tiny businesses, trade receivables securitization presents an enticing value proposition across several industries. By understanding and planning ahead, providers can use securitization as a useful financial tool to reduce costs, increase proceeds, lower risk, and diversify their funding sources. They must be aware of how their credit score affects the deal's terms and whether investors will buy it. Trade receivables securitization is a popular investment choice among financiers and investors because it offers tools to lower risk and the chance to make a lot of money. This has been shown to perform well in the past, especially during difficult economic cycles like the global financial crisis.

This resiliency reflects the important nature of the underlying transactions, which frequently include vital products and services. As a result, the asset class usually has low rates of loss, which appeals to investors looking for steady returns. Trade receivables securitizations are unique because their structure is flexible, which lets reserve levels be changed often based on how the portfolio is doing. This dynamic protection mechanism provides investors with a layer of assurance that has worked well in a variety of economic climates by adapting to changing economic situations. Trade receivables securitizations frequently offer better yields when compared to alternative investment options with comparable risk profiles.

Trade receivables' usually brief term, which can provide investors faster returns on investment and the freedom to reallocate money more frequently, adds to their allure. Trade receivables securitizations are a safer way for borrowers to provide loans to clients with poorer credit profiles. These products can protect you from the seller or issuer going bankrupt by separating the seller or issuer's credit risk from the securitization itself. No matter how well the seller or issuer does financially, proper structuring guarantees that financiers will be able to anticipate returning their whole investment. Investing in trade receivables securitizations can be a capital-efficient strategy for regulated financial institutions. Compared to directly making identical loans, the high implicit or explicit credit ratings of these products often result in reduced regulatory capital requirements.

Trade receivables securitizations are an increasingly appealing asset class owing to their effectiveness, which allows institutions to get the most out of their capital allocation and perhaps raise return on equity. Trade receivables securitizations are a well-rounded investment option that combines risk reduction strategies with the possibility of yielding substantial rewards. Due to their structural adaptability, historical resilience, and regulatory capital efficiencies, these instruments are a favorable choice for investors and financiers, especially those who want to diversify their portfolios or lend money to a wider range of customers without significantly increasing their risk exposure. Complex financial arrangements transform receivables into investable assets, often aiming for an investment-grade rating.

This arrangement makes it easier to appeal to and accessible to a wider range of financing sources. Often, trade receivables securitizations aim to meet specific rating agency requirements, and achieving an "A" rating is a common objective. The securities' ability to acquire such a rating reflects the reduced risk profile necessary to attract institutional investors. It also makes the securities more appealing to a larger pool of investors. The emphasis on investment-grade ratings underscores the meticulous structuring of these deals to ensure their strong alignment with regulatory requirements and investors' risk tolerances. Bank-sponsored commercial paper conduits provide funding for several of them. These channels are special purpose vehicles (SPVs) that banks have set up to issue commercial paper, which is a type of short-term debt instrument, to pay for the purchase of assets like trade receivables. By using this technique, banks may manage their risk exposure by providing finance while remaining somewhat detached from the receivables themselves.

Because of their adaptability and the comparatively inexpensive finance they provide—which is backed by the sponsoring banks' credit—commercial paper conduits are appealing. Another major source of funding for trade receivables securitizations is direct financing from bank balance sheets. Banking institutions have the option to lend money using the securitized receivables as collateral or to buy these securities outright. Banks' direct engagement reflects their desire for high-quality, short-duration assets, enabling them to deploy money and manage liquidity effectively. Bank balance sheet financing frequently has the extra advantage of preexisting ties and the possibility of more specialized lending options. Trade receivables securitizations draw a broad spectrum of traditional capital markets investors, such as fixed-income asset managers, insurance firms, and pension funds, in addition to banks. The low default rates and generally steady profits of trading receivables attract investors like these.

Because the asset class's short-term and high credit quality fit their liability-driven investment strategies and regulatory capital requirements, pension funds and insurance firms in particular favor it. The beneficial effects of trade receivables securitizations for portfolio diversification and yield improvement are well-liked by fixed-income asset managers. Trade receivables securitizations are a strong and attractive financing instrument, as evidenced by their structure for investment-grade ratings. Companies can get money from traditional capital markets investors, bank balance sheets, and bank-sponsored commercial paper conduits by using the receivables they own as leverage. This can help them better manage their capital and liquidity.

CHAPTER 3   CASHING IN ON THE OPPORTUNITY: THE DYNAMIC WORLD OF RECEIVABLES FINANCE

Putting together trade receivables into securities is an important part of the financial system as a whole because it offers investors and banks a great mix of credit quality, return potential, and variety. Asset-backed commercial paper (ABCP) conduits are a special kind of financing that lets banks fund their businesses by giving out short-term loans backed by assets like trade receivables. Let's examine the main features of ABCP conduits and how they finance securitizations of trade receivables: A vital component of ABCP conduits is the sponsoring bank's supply of credit and liquidity improvements, typically in the form of a letter of credit (LC).

These improvements are crucial as they instill greater confidence in investors about the return on their investments, particularly during challenging economic times. The Global Financial Crisis highlighted the significance of these credit safeguards, as LCs' express credit protection helped to protect ABCP investors during a period of substantial market volatility. Rating agencies are required to monitor ABCP conduits due to their rating status as entities. An ABCP conduit's asset pool must include trade receivables securitizations structured in accordance with rating agency guidelines. Although each securitization that is added to the asset pool of an ABCP conduit does not always need an explicit rating, rating agencies frequently need to reaffirm the conduit's overall rating. This procedure guarantees the conduit's continued creditworthiness to investors and the general market. Securitizations of trade receivables make up a sizable fraction of the assets financed by ABCP conduits; estimates place their percentage at over 20%. There are several reasons why ABCP conduits find trade receivables appealing.

Trade receivables generally have a brief lifespan, which fits very nicely with ABCP's short-term finance structure. As a result of this feature, ABCP conduits can efficiently manage liquidity and react to shifts in the market or in investor demand. They have performed well in recessions with low loss rates. In comparison, consumer assets underperformed significantly during the Great Recession of 2007–2009. This performance stands in contrast to theirs. Trade receivables are a preferred asset class for ABCP conduits due to their strong track record, which adds to the reliability and allure of these financing options.

Through ABCP conduits, companies can secure their receivables and get cash. These conduits are an important way to finance trade receivable securitizations. The structure of these conduits ensures a steady and reliable flow of short-term financing, with help from sponsoring institutions that improve credit and liquidity and follow rating agency rules. The intrinsic attributes of trade receivables, such as their short-term and outstanding historical performance, make them an integral part of ABCP conduits' investment strategy, further highlighting their suitability as an asset class for these conduits.

CHAPTER 3   CASHING IN ON THE OPPORTUNITY: THE DYNAMIC WORLD OF RECEIVABLES FINANCE

There have been big changes in trade receivables securitization financing. For example, some banks are no longer supporting asset-backed commercial paper (ABCP) conduits and are instead using their own balance sheets to back these deals. This change has strategically reoriented banks' handling of trade receivable financing. They can now use their own credit assessment resources while still managing the market and regulations. This is a thorough explanation of the change and its effects: Several banks have moved away from the conventional ABCP conduit strategy and toward leveraging their balance sheets to directly fund trade receivable securitizations.

This change gives banking institutions more control over risk assessment and management procedures, enabling them to manage these assets internally. Banks can apply their internal credit standards and flexibilities to securities on their balance sheets, allowing them to customize their strategy for each unique transaction. This flexibility includes the way banks manage certain securitization-related issues, including excess obligor concentration management. Balance sheet financing lets banks take on more debt than the stricter rules that might apply to ABCP conduit transactions because it lets them look at specific risks and decide if they are creditworthy. Historically, the benchmark for ABCP conduits has been commercial paper (CP) rates, while bank balance sheet facilities frequently cited LIBOR (London Interbank Offered Rate). However, the financial industry's shift from LIBOR to risk-free rates has significantly changed the benchmarking of interest rates for these financing arrangements.

Generally speaking, ABCP rates have closely correlated with LIBOR, with the exception of periods of extreme market stress like the Global Financial Crisis, when CP rates spiked. It's crucial to remember that incidents involving manipulation cast doubt on LIBOR's dependability, which led to the move toward risk-free rates that are more transparent and stable. We anticipate a close correlation between ABCP and risk-free rates, assuming no further manipulation.

The shift in trade receivables securitizations toward balance sheet financing is a reflection of banks' desire for more control over their risk and investment management procedures. With this strategy, banks have the flexibility to make careful decisions on the basis of market conditions, regulatory regulations, and their evaluation of credit risk. This change might lead to more customized financing options for the market. Furthermore, the transition from LIBOR to risk-free rates is indicative of a larger industry trend toward benchmark rates that are more trustworthy and transparent. This shift has an effect on the whole financial transaction environment, in addition to the price and structuring of trade receivables securitizations. By moving toward balance sheet financing, banks are signaling a strategic shift in how they handle trade receivables securitizations. This gives them more freedom in evaluating credit and managing risk.

The transition from risk-free rates to LIBOR, along with other changes in the financial markets, underscores the ongoing efforts to enhance the integrity and stability of financing arrangements. Capital markets are very important for developing countries because they provide liquidity and money for trade receivables securitizations when traditional banking facilities and ABCP lines aren't as common or well-established. Leveraging capital markets to finance trade receivables is becoming more and more popular as regulatory restrictions on banks increase. Let's examine the subtle differences between capital market investors and bank or ABCP conduit funding. Because bank credit programs are still in their infancy and there are no ABCP conduits, emerging nations have a greater dependence on capital markets for funding trade receivables securitization. Although issuances in developed markets are less common, they still provide a sizable chance to diversify funding sources.

The changing regulatory environment, particularly with regard to bank capital needs, is leading to a rise in capital markets issuances. It is expected that this change would infuse the industry with fresh money, relieving banks of some of their duties as the main providers of trade credit. Fixed-size issuances are a common feature of capital markets transactions; this means that the total amount of capital generated stays fixed over the securitization's revolving term. In comparison, bank and ABCP conduit facilities could provide greater flexibility in adjusting the funded amount over time in accordance with the demands of the seller or issuer. This flexibility encompasses elements that are not commonly seen in capital market placements, such as the utilization of interest margins and the elimination of fees, to accommodate fluctuations in funding needs. Another factor that sets capital market issuances apart from bank-financed facilities is the duration of funding.

Securitizations of capital markets trade receivables frequently have longer durations—up to 5 years—and provide issuers with longer stretches of predictable and stable funding. Bank facilities, on the other hand, usually require yearly renewals, which call for more frequent reevaluation and negotiation and may result in increased uncertainty and administrative burden for the seller/issuer. There are important ramifications to trade receivables securitizations' growing preference for capital markets as a funding source. Companies can diversify their funding sources beyond traditional banking lines and ABCP conduit issuers by entering the capital markets. By doing so, they may be able to get better terms and attract a larger pool of investors. Capital markets offer an essential means of obtaining liquidity for emerging economies, where bank credit options may be restricted, hence facilitating economic growth and development. The move toward capital markets can lessen the reliance on bank balance sheets for trade financing, enabling banks to more effectively allocate their capital as they confront increasing regulatory capital demands.

The changing relationships among capital markets investors, bank financing, and ABCP conduits highlight a larger trend in trade receivables securitization funding toward innovation and diversity. Particularly in areas where traditional financial sources are less readily available, capital markets position themselves to play an increasingly important role in supplying liquidity and fostering the expansion of international commerce. This is especially true as regulatory environments change and markets continue to evolve. Trade receivables securitizations involve sophisticated financial structures designed to convert receivables into investable assets. These structures commonly employ various mechanisms for risk mitigation to protect the interests of investors and financiers and enhance the creditworthiness of securitization.

The foundation of risk mitigation in trade receivable securitizations is the establishment of reserves through over-collateralization. In this process, investors safeguard themselves against credit losses and dilution risks by allocating a portion of assets or cash to cover potential losses. We use the characteristics of the receivables and past performance data to determine the reserve levels. This is a logical way to predict and reduce future risks. Securitizations utilize reserves derived from the aging history of receivables to anticipate and cover potential losses due to obligor default or delayed payment. For example, Standard & Poor's standards can establish a reserve for credit losses at twice the most recent peak moving average loss experienced. This strategy ensures the securitization's resilience to unfavorable credit events within the portfolio. Dilution describes declines in the value of accounts receivable due to circumstances other than the debtor's capacity to pay, including product flaws or business conflicts.

To protect against these losses, securitization agreements usually include dilute reserves. The size of these reserves depends on how much dilution has happened in the past. Securities need to take a different approach when accounting for the time value of money since trade receivables do not naturally yield interest. People often purchase receivables at a discount, akin to the discounted structure of a financial instrument such as a US Treasury note. This discount covers the securitization's return and fees; typically, reserves for these costs are lower, especially during low-interest rate environments. Segmentation strategies need to control concentration risks in order to maximize the advantages of obligor diversity. Each obligor's credit quality determines the limits, and higher-risk obligors have minimum reserve levels imposed. Following this procedure ensures that securitization can withstand the default of one or more creditors.

CHAPTER 3   CASHING IN ON THE OPPORTUNITY: THE DYNAMIC WORLD OF RECEIVABLES FINANCE

In securitization, trade credit insurance can mitigate certain risks, such as nationwide risks or significant concentrations of obligated parties. Depending on the transaction's goals and the parties' needs, the structure of the insurance, such as co-insurance or senior/subordinated arrangements, can enhance security and facilitate the use of IFRS derecognition for risk transfer. Despite the primary goal of securitizations being to eliminate the seller's credit liability, sellers typically face expectations to provide guarantees and assert the quality of the receivables. These guarantees safeguard against fraud, deception, and dilution hazards, with vendors expected to rectify any instances of dilution. Sustaining investor trust requires efficient management and clear reporting. The Global Financial Crisis brought to light the risks associated with opaque securitizations, which resulted in more stringent reporting regulations. As part of modern securitization, detailed and regular reports may be given on things like cash flows, new debts, eligibility, reserves, and currency risks, among other things.

Trade receivables securitizations use a variety of risk management tools, such as credit insurance, reserves, and strict reporting rules, to protect investors' interests and keep the securitization's integrity. These safeguards make sure that securitizations continue to be a desirable and feasible investment choice even in the face of the inherent risks connected to trade receivables. Securitizations of trade receivables are complex financial structures closely connected to accounting, legal, and regulatory frameworks. As such, a full grasp of their ramifications on these fronts is vital. The transfer of assets from the originator to a special purpose entity (SPE) that is located outside of bankruptcy is the cornerstone of trade receivables securitization. The acknowledgment of this transfer as a real sale is necessary to ensure the formal and irreversible conveyance of the receivables to the SPE. The "true sale" opinion of counsel confirms this separation, preventing the seller's bankruptcy estate from reclaiming the receivables. Should the seller file for bankruptcy, this legal arrangement ensures the protection of the financing source, which will only act as the recipient of the cash flows from the receivables and not as a creditor involved in the bankruptcy process.

Under US Generally Accepted Accounting Principles (GAAP), FASB Accounting Standards Codification Topic 860 largely governs trade receivables securitization. Sales of receivables to the SPE and then to the financing source must follow the change of control rules for securitization process transactions involving balance sheet transactions. Due to the implementation of ASU 2016-15, businesses had to use different structures in order to keep their original cash flow reporting categories. This made it harder to report payments that were late. In order to get GAAP sale treatment, it is common to keep the seller from having any control or major involvement in the receivables beyond servicing them. Including auditors early in the structuring process is crucial to ensure adherence to GAAP rules. For securitizations seeking off-balance sheet treatment, the International Financial Reporting Standards (IFRS) pose a more demanding obstacle.

IFRS 9 (de-recognition) and IFRS 10 (de-consolidation) lay out the rules. The main requirements are giving up control over the receivables and transferring big risks and rewards related to them. Companies have created complicated models and structures to meet these requirements, as the definition of "substantial" risk transfer remains unclear. Typically, companies use trade credit insurance or multi-tranche frameworks. As with GAAP, IFRS compliance requires close coordination with auditors at all stages of the securitization process to make sure the structure achieves the desired accounting treatment. Legal and accounting issues play a significant role in shaping and carrying out trade receivables securitizations. Accounting procedures under GAAP and IFRS impact the financial statement consequences of these transactions, while the legal side focuses on ensuring a genuine sale to protect the receivables from the seller's insolvency risks. To successfully navigate different areas, you need to carefully plan your steps, get excellent advice, and strictly follow all relevant legal and accounting rules. This shows how complex trade receivables securitization architecture is. Trade receivables securitizations are a sophisticated sector of finance that provides a flexible and reliable vehicle for investment and liquidity for businesses and investors alike. The execution, structure, and market perspective of these transactions reflect their attractiveness and usefulness in the contemporary financial environment.

Most trade receivables securitizations occur in secret, with minimal to no public disclosure, underscoring the customary and private nature of these financial arrangements. The banking industry is very important for providing liquidity because banks play a big part, either directly through balance sheet financing or indirectly through asset-backed commercial paper (ABCP) conduits sponsored by banks. Depending on the seller's credit rating, variable rate spreads for these transactions might vary significantly: investment-grade sellers will pay smaller spreads (50–100 bps), while weaker sellers will pay greater spreads (200+ bps). This tiered structure reflects the risk assessment that is part of lending activity. We levy a non-usage cost, ranging from 25 to 100 bps, on unused sections of the pledged amount to encourage effective use of the available funding. We can meet the demands of a wide range of sellers and the international nature of trading by using major currencies like USD, EUR, and GBP for funding. It is possible to achieve scalability, economy, and risk diversification in a single securitization issue by including several connected firms from different countries. These facilities usually have tenors of one to three years, but there is a noticeable tendency toward continual renewal, which frequently extends the liquidity provision to more than 10 years. Public term issuances are uncommon, although they are more frequent in emerging economies.

One country that publicly registers agreements and attracts a diverse investor base is Mexico. These offerings often have set financing levels and extended tenures (3–5 years), frequently with a soft-bullet amortization structure. We expect the trade receivables securitization industry to continue its development and expand its service to more businesses globally. Securitizations continue to be a useful tool for businesses to optimize profits, diversify funding sources, and maximize working capital; this is indicative of the transactions' strategic importance in corporate finance. Trade receivables securitizations give an appealing risk-reward profile to investors, making them a feasible choice for capital deployment in a range of economic scenarios. Trade receivable securitizations are a unique and flexible tool in corporate and investment finance that can be used to create custom solutions that meet the liquidity needs of businesses and give investors the chance to make money while minimizing risk. These transactions' dynamic character, together with the market's continuous growth and their structural adaptability, emphasizes their importance as a cornerstone of financial strategy and portfolio diversification.

Securitization in the Modern Regulatory Landscape

The aftermath of a decade characterized by broad regulatory reforms and tightened controls has drastically changed the topography of bank lending and investment strategies in the securitization of global finance. The rise of synthetic collateralized loan obligations (CLOs) as a premier instrument for risk transfer from the banking industry to the large domains of non-bank investors is one of the most notable developments of this new age.

This change is shown by the fact that "significant risk transfer" (SRT) transactions, which are also called "capital relief" deals, are becoming more and more popular and have built a strong niche in the financial markets. The challenges posed by the Capital Requirements Directive IV (CRD IV) and Basel regulations have prompted a push for synthetic securitization. This is especially true in the trade finance sector. Because of these rules, the cost of capital for trade finance has gone up a lot. This has made people in the industry question the long-held belief that trade receivables shouldn't have to meet the same strict capital requirements as higher-risk asset classes because they have a historically low-risk profile. As a result, banks are using securitization more and more as a tactical instrument to maximize capital efficiency and optimize balance sheets.

CHAPTER 3   CASHING IN ON THE OPPORTUNITY: THE DYNAMIC WORLD OF RECEIVABLES FINANCE

Investor interest in trade finance synthetic securitization has increased as a result of its appealing nature. These deals have a clear reason behind them, as at least USD 5 billion in first-loss and mezzanine paper is issued every year, which is likely based on assets worth around USD 50 billion. This pattern indicates a growing recognition of trade finance securitizations as an attractive investment option that offers a careful balance between risk and return in a securitized structure while also assisting banks in managing the complex regulatory environment.

It is now appropriate to discuss the characteristics and difficulties of a particular financial industry niche market, with an emphasis on synthetic securitization, specifically in the trade finance business. There aren't many players on the market. However, the mention of several returning issuers such as Deutsche Bank and Standard Chartered suggests some activity and interest from well-known banks.

The term "synthetic side" describes synthetic securitizations, which are financial instruments that allow investors to manage credit risk without having to liquidate the underlying assets. In addition to companies that have issued these financial instruments repeatedly, there are other entities that have issued them just once.

Usually, these corporations operate on a private, bilateral basis, arranging deals directly between two parties. We can determine that this niche market is very small due to high entry barriers when compared to the larger Significant Risk Transfer (SRT) and Collateralized Loan Obligation (CLO) markets. This comparison suggests a parallel to the loan securitization industry, which is more established and more easily accessible.

One major obstacle is the demand for strong and effective administration of the CLOs. Due to the difficulty of managing these financial systems over time. We observe that integrating departments within a company, such as the trade finance and securitization departments, can be challenging. Different terminologies, objectives, and expectations present a challenge. It is also important to note that managing the short-term nature of trade finance assets and processing a sizable amount of data, including the infrastructure for managing transaction replenishment, will require a significant technological investment.

Despite the mentioned constraints, the execution of agreements containing up to USD 3.5 billion of varied trade financing assets suggests a considerable demand for these kinds of transactions. This implies that, despite the obstacles to entry, there is a sizable interest in and room for expansion in this specialized industry. Within trade finance, there is a particular specialty market area that focuses on synthetic securities. Large transactions and robust demand demonstrate the market's potential, while also drawing attention to its particular difficulties, such as the requirement for a large investment in technology and the difficulty in promoting interdepartmental collaboration.

Therefore, for financial institutions, this particular market provides a region with both major problems and opportunities. The section addresses investor interest in synthetic securitization and sheds light on the advantages of the practice for issuers, notably in the trade finance space. Issuers can keep smaller capital reserves on their loan portfolios because of statutory capital relief. The Basel framework establishes a systematic and acknowledged method for handling capital needs, which controls the calculation of this relief. Revisions to the Basel framework that went into effect in January 2019 have impacted the efficacy of synthetic securitizations for capital relief. Nevertheless, given the ongoing high volumes of issuance in 2019, it appears that banks still view this instrument as both economically feasible and essential for maximizing their capital positions.

The hedging of credit risk offers issuers yet another important advantage. This enables banks to safeguard themselves against any default losses. Prolonged pricing lock-ins also guarantee execution certainty, which is particularly helpful when starting trade financing agreements with sell-down clauses. De-risking individual assets might require less ongoing operational effort if the required program and infrastructure are in place. This efficiency makes risk management easier, which is especially important for institutions that produce a lot of tiny assets.

The synthetic securitization method allows for scalable diversification of credit risk. Banks are able to complete transactions involving assets valued at many billions of dollars, thereby increasing their capacity for hedging and improving the way they manage risk exposure. Businesses often perceive trade finance assets as lower risk than other asset types due to their self-liquidating nature and a strong incentive to repay trade loans on time to maintain trading capabilities. Investors seeking steady profits find the products intriguing due to their lower risk profile.

Investor competitiveness may be heightened by the lack of trade finance for synthetic structured risk transfer (SRT) transactions, which might result in more advantageous pricing for issuers. Issuers profit from this scarcity value since it may reduce their cost of capital. Investors favor trade finance as an asset class due to its uncorrelated returns, which significantly contribute to diversification. These assets' uncorrelated returns can perform well even when other investments in the investor's portfolio fail. This helps to spread and lower overall risk.

It's worth highlighting the two main benefits that issuers in the trade finance industry receive from synthetic securitization:

- substantial regulatory capital relief
- effective credit risk hedging

CHAPTER 3   CASHING IN ON THE OPPORTUNITY: THE DYNAMIC WORLD OF RECEIVABLES FINANCE

Trade finance assets are appealing to investors because they have a low-risk profile, competitive prices, and the chance to diversify their portfolios through returns that are not correlated with each other. Synthetic securitizations are an attractive financial instrument in the trade finance industry because of the advantages they offer to issuers and investors, even in spite of the difficulties and expenses involved in establishing and managing the infrastructure required for these programs. The early history of synthetic securitization and its innovative transactions, especially in the wake of the 2008 credit crisis, marked a change in the way financial institutions handled risk and regulatory capital during the financial crisis. These transactions are noteworthy.

The 2008 financial crisis exposed a number of flaws in the global financial system, including risks related to credit and liquidity. As a result, regulators and financial institutions looked for methods to reduce these risks, which sparked innovation in financial tools and approaches. The structure of this deal, in which the underlying assets are sold to a special purpose vehicle (SPV), which then makes securities backed by the assets, makes it one of the earliest "true sales."

Since true-sale transactions remove assets from the bank's balance sheet, they clearly relieve statutory capital requirements. Here's another illustration of a creative framework that sprang from the crisis. Citi and Santander's partnership serves as another illustration of the management and distribution of trade finance risk through securitization. This transaction exemplifies the synthetic approach, as does Deutsche Bank's TRAFIN series (2011, 2012, and the record-sized 2015). Synthetic securitizations do not include the sale of assets in contrast to true-sale transactions. Rather, they make use of financial tools like assets.

After the crisis, there has been a definite preference for synthetic structures, despite the early instances of true-sale transactions. There are a few reasons for this desire, one of which is that synthetic securities offer a more adaptable instrument for controlling the inherent volatility of the credit markets. People prefer synthetics due to their effectiveness and simplicity. Synthetics require fewer procedures than true-sale transactions because the underlying assets remain on the bank's balance sheet. This lowers transaction costs and streamlines the procedure.

Both types of transactions offer regulatory capital relief, but synthetics have become more appealing because banks can get this relief without having to sell the assets, which speeds up the process and causes less trouble. Financial institutions are looking for solutions to manage credit risk that are less capital-intensive, more flexible, and more efficient. This has led them to turn toward synthetic securitization. True-sale securitizations were used in the early days after the crisis, but now the synthetic route is

CHAPTER 3   CASHING IN ON THE OPPORTUNITY: THE DYNAMIC WORLD OF RECEIVABLES FINANCE

preferred because it is easier to use, better at controlling volatility, and makes it easier to get regulatory capital relief. These changes demonstrate how creatively and adaptably the financial sector has been able to respond to market and regulatory demands.

Naturally, the process of creating synthetic collateralized loan obligations (CLOs) involves structural elements and concerns that underscore the variety and intricacy of methods employed in these financial instruments. The special purpose vehicle (SPV) structure entails setting up a special purpose entity (SPE) that is not subject to bankruptcy and that offers notes to investors. The revenues from these notes purchase government bonds and other low-risk acceptable collateral. Next, the SPV and the issuing bank engage in a credit enhancement transaction, frequently in the form of a credit default swap (CDS) or financial guarantee. By establishing a formal division between the assets of the bank and the investment vehicle, it reduces counterparty risks for the investors as well as the issuing bank.

The SPV's structure, which aims to shield investors from the parent firm's financial risks, will protect them in the event that the issuing bank declares bankruptcy. However, it necessitates administering and setting up the SPV, which raises the cost and complexity levels. Investors may view the utilization of their money to purchase this low-risk collateral during periods of low government bond rates as inefficient due to the poor returns.

An alternate structure that involves issuing credit linked notes (CLNs) directly from the balance sheet of the issuing bank is called a direct issuance of CLNs. This strategy offers a price advantage and is considered efficient for banks with an established CLN issuing platform, as the bank can use the revenues for its general corporate objectives.

It gives banks the ability to use the revenues directly for more varied uses, which might improve the bank's financial and operational flexibility. Furthermore, because of the simplified issuing procedure and more extensive utilization of revenues, it may provide a more appealing price. Despite this, the direct correlation between investors' profits and the solvency of the issuing bank increases their risk exposure. Although they may control this risk, investors must carefully assess the underlying creditworthiness of the assets involved to effectively mitigate potential losses. (e.g., by using the CDS market or creative)

In addition, alternative agreements like pure guarantee or real sale may be used; however, specifics regarding these are not given. Different structures have pros and cons depending on the transaction and market. When creating an artificial CLO, a number of crucial factors come into play. The structure they choose impacts both issuers' and investors' risk-return profiles. We must balance efficiency, risk reduction, and return on investment.

Market liquidity and current interest rates can impact the desirability of various structures. Compliance with regulations may affect the cost and viability of solutions. Last but not least, the operational and administrative challenges of maintaining SPVs or CLN issuance platforms may have a significant impact on a synthetic CLO's overall sustainability. It's hard to make decisions about how to design a synthetic CLO structure that meets regulatory requirements, works well, and fits the risk-return preferences of both issuers and investors. Every structure has benefits and drawbacks of its own; therefore, before moving further, all parties must carefully consider them all.

Balancing Opportunities, Risks, and Regulatory Compliance

Distribution techniques are a complex system for extending investment opportunities, controlling and spreading credit risk, and optimizing capital consumption, especially through sub-participation in the trade finance sector. An originating or financing institution can share its exposure to a specific credit risk with other investors through sub-participation, also known as distribution or syndication, without directly transferring or assigning the underlying assets. The particular preferences, objectives, and operational frameworks of the parties involved will all impact the mix of strategic benefits and possible downsides associated with this method. Sub-participation provides an avenue for originating institutions to more effectively manage and optimize their capital allocation. They can increase their ability to lend money or make other investments by disbursing some of their credit exposure.

Investors can diversify the risk in their portfolio by sub-participating in a range of trade finance activities. By spreading out credit risk throughout several markets or assets, it can lessen the impact of future defaults and create an environment that is more stable for investments. Sub-participation gives investors access to trade financing possibilities that would not otherwise be available because of regulatory restrictions, size, or complexity. Smaller investors or those wishing to have exposure to particular markets or industries may find this very interesting. Sub-participation agreement architecture can be complicated and expensive, involving legal, administrative, and due diligence fees. This intricacy calls for a high degree of skill and might be difficult for certain individuals. In a sub-participation agreement, investors usually have an indirect interest in the underlying loan or credit facility, as their risk and return are dependent on the performance of the underlying assets, but they do not have direct legal rights against the borrower.

Investing in a variety of trade finance operations allows investors to diversify the risk in their portfolio. Diversifying credit risk across multiple markets or assets can mitigate the impact of potential defaults and promote a more stable investment environment. Investors who sub-participate have access to trade financing options that they would not otherwise have due to regulatory limitations, complexity, or scale. This might be highly intriguing to smaller investors or those looking to get exposure to certain areas or sectors. The architecture of a sub-participation agreement, which includes administrative, legal, and due diligence costs, can be intricate and costly. This complexity requires a high level of talent and may be challenging for some people.

Typically, investors in a sub-participation agreement have an economic interest in the underlying transaction, but they do not have direct legal rights against the borrower. Instead, their rights are governed by the agreement with the primary lender, who remains the legal creditor and bears the obligation to pass on payments received from the borrower to the investors. A combination of risk management, financial, and market expansion factors influences this strategic decision. Institutions sometimes have set limits on the amount of risk they will accept. By sharing it with other investors, distribution enables them to better manage and mitigate credit risk and adhere to their risk tolerance. Institutions disperse transactions in response to internal goals for capital adequacy and RWAs as well as regulatory obligations.

This distribution helps make the best use of capital and makes sure that regulatory capital requirements are met without affecting the institution's ability to offer financing options. Financing institutions can leverage their capital more effectively and earn greater returns on equity by selling off portions of transactions or full facilities. This method allows for better returns without increasing the borrowing costs for customers. Sub-participation and other distribution strategies create new sources of liquidity, enabling institutions to finance more projects or larger transactions than their balance sheets would normally allow. Distribution allows organizations to provide services to a larger customer base.

When clients want a simplified administrative procedure yet want to work with many banking partners, institutions might serve as their main point of contact. This method makes it easier for the client to connect with the financial system and permits more widespread involvement by means of sub-participation mechanisms.

A key technique for handling financial assets is outright sales, which enable organizations to completely remove transactions from their balance sheets and portfolios. Effective resource reallocation, credit restriction release, and assignment, endorsement, or transfer may all make this process simpler. Despite their advantages, straightforward sales have several logistical drawbacks that may compromise their viability and efficiency.

Distribution enables the pooling of resources and risk-sharing among several investors for transactions that surpass the risk-taking capabilities of a single institution. This cooperative strategy guarantees that clients' funding needs are satisfied, even for significant transactions that would be too big for a single institution to manage on its own. In the trade finance industry, the way receivables finance transactions are spread out is an example of a strategic change that meets both customer needs for all-around financing solutions and institutional needs for managing risk and capital. By using distribution approaches, financial institutions may be able to make their operations more flexible and create a trade finance environment that is more dynamic, resilient, and focused on clients.

For an outright sale to be successful, the transactions must readily divide into parts with different quantities and maturities. It is imperative that both investors and obligors can precisely recognize their respective rights and duties. The lender of record for each divided payment obligation must be specified. This clarity is particularly crucial when the obligor fails to fulfill the obligation by the maturity date, as it prompts concerns about the equitable compensation of investors for any unfulfilled payments.

When there is no requirement for a fronting bank to serve as an agent or middleman, outright sales are most efficient. Although fronting banks can streamline processes by acting as the obligor's single point of contact, their participation in conventional trade is less widespread than in the syndicated or structured finance markets. In the event of an outright sale, the obligor must formally acknowledge each new investor as the new legitimate creditor or beneficiary of the receivables, ensuring that the investor holds direct rights against the obligor under the agreement.

The lengthy and intricate nature of this identification process may make it more difficult to quickly reallocate transactions with shorter timelines, such as 30-day receivables. Different nations' legal and regulatory systems may provide further obstacles to outright sales. Certain markets are less appealing to institutions aiming to become lenders of record because of the broad range of requirements needed to complete a sale or transfer. Although outright sales provide financial transfers with a precise and unambiguous way to remove themselves from certain transactions, increasing liquidity and capital efficiency, they are not without difficulties.

The above-mentioned logistical issues make outright sales even more difficult. These include the fact that the transaction can be split up and clear lender identification, as well as the need to avoid fronting banks and make sure that new investors are recognized as debtors, making transactions more difficult; thus, navigating these possible roadblocks effectively may need to be cautious and planned.

CHAPTER 3   CASHING IN ON THE OPPORTUNITY: THE DYNAMIC WORLD OF RECEIVABLES FINANCE

Risk participation agreements (RPAs) facilitate bank-to-bank connections with various products, increasing trade finance volumes and revenue streams for all stakeholders. Due to its larger sales and origination network, one institution usually experiences a balance shift when it acts more frequently as a seller. On the other hand, the other party—which may have a smaller geographic reach—gains access to transactions that it could not have initiated on its own. These arrangements, akin to an on-demand guarantee, enable investors to assume a contingent obligation, requiring cash only in the event of transaction default. Though rapid and adaptable, the original holder bears some risk in determining the investor's capacity to fulfill future commitments.

Funded dividends, which minimize the seller's contingent risk by requiring upfront money from the investor, are more appealing to sellers. However, investors need to feel at ease with the selling bank's potential bankruptcy risks. Legal requirements in various countries can make it hard to use RPAs and affect the enforceability and usefulness of some agreements, such as the transfer of assets or the building of trust structures. In the past, the variety of RPA forms presented considerable difficulties during negotiations, prompting calls for standardization to speed up the procedure and lower legal expenses.

Acknowledging the requirement for consistency, BAFT backed the development of standardized RPAs. The 2008 publication of the Master Participation Agreement (MPA) under English law and the 2010 release of its equivalent under New York law sought to offer a standard starting point. We discovered basic differences throughout the writing process, which led to the inclusion of optional sections to accommodate varying viewpoints. These differences highlight how difficult it is to create a document that works for everyone in the global financial system.

There is also disagreement about how to allocate fraud risk: some believe that sellers, having tighter customer relationships than buyers, should take on more risk, while others think all participants should share some risk to properly represent distribution. RPAs provide financial institutions with a strategic way to manage trade finance risks and enhance their operational capabilities, particularly through master RPAs. These agreements provide opportunities for mutually beneficial collaborations and risk sharing, but they also come with challenges due to the complexity of the legal, regulatory, and negotiating frameworks.

The standardization of RPAs by BAFT and the larger financial community is a sign of the industry's dedication to improving consistency and efficiency in the trade finance sector. However, ongoing discussions and jurisdictional differences highlight the importance of continuous dialogue and updates to these instruments to ensure they meet the needs of all global financial players. Financial institutions engaging in global trade financing must carefully examine whether to structure risk participation agreements under English or New York law, particularly when it comes to funded and unfunded payouts. Each legal system offers unique interpretations and repercussions for the parties engaged in these transactions.

When it comes to unfunded participation, where the investor pledges to finance solely in response to a claim, the guiding principles of both English and New York law largely align. Rather than the basic framework of unfunded participation, the primary distinctions between the agreements lie in other areas. Under UK law, a financed sub-participation typically establishes a debtor–creditor relationship between the investor and the seller, without granting the investor any beneficial interest in the underlying transaction. This link can make it difficult for the seller to satisfy the de-recognition requirements needed to remove the asset from their balance sheet, especially in light of some internal and local accounting rules. Investors' money may mix with the seller's possessions, complicating recovery if the seller becomes insolvent.

In contrast, the Master Participation Agreement (MPA) under New York law presents the idea of a "true sale," acknowledging the investor's direct share of the risks and profits of the underlying transaction. This legal interpretation gives investors a firmer foundation for their participation in the deal and makes it easier to de-recognize the asset from the seller's balance sheet. Investors find some peace of mind knowing that their money is less likely to be entangled in the seller's estate in the event of insolvency. Additionally, New York law, which acknowledges their involvement, may permit investors to obtain funds directly from the obligor upon maturity. Although the "true sale" theory of the New York statute MPA provides distinct benefits in financed participation, its use is primarily limited to the Americas. Even if English law has limits on financed distributions, financial institutions outside this region may be more familiar with it and have greater access to English-speaking legal advice. This familiarity might influence their choice of English law.

Deciding whether to use English or New York law in risk participation agreements depends on the unique demands and hazards both the selling and investing parties must manage, as well as the kind of participation (funded vs. unfunded). In financed participations, the debtor-creditor framework of English law may pose challenges for the de-recognition of assets and the recovery of investors in insolvency cases. In contrast, New York law's "true sale" concept provides clearer pathways for balance sheet management and investor protection but faces limited adoption outside the Americas. Institutions must weigh these factors carefully, considering both legal and operational perspectives, to choose the most suitable jurisdiction for their risk participation agreements.

CHAPTER 3   CASHING IN ON THE OPPORTUNITY: THE DYNAMIC WORLD OF RECEIVABLES FINANCE

The trade finance secondary market has experienced significant developments and shifts in demand since the original release of the Bankers Association for Finance and Trade (BAFT) Master Participation Agreement (MPA) forms. As things changed, like the move toward funded distributions and the addition of open account solutions, the MPAs had to be updated to meet new needs and make the agreements better by using what had been learned. The revised MPAs include references to payables finance and receivables finance structures, recognizing the trend toward open account trade finance. This reflects the market's shift toward more flexible and diversified trade financing choices.

The change to transfer a beneficial ownership interest in the financed distributions is a big improvement to English law. It brings it more in line with the "true sale" idea that is common in New York law. This modification increases the MPA's legal strength and market utility by making a clearer financial and legal link to the underlying transactions. The English and New York law versions no longer include the specific fraud element. The justification for this is that the MPA sufficiently addresses the dangers and ramifications of fraud. This modification simplifies the agreements by eliminating unnecessary parts while acknowledging the difficulties in attributing fraud.

Working together, BAFT and IIFM introduced Sharia-compliant MPA forms in response to the unique requirements of Islamic Trade Finance. This extension guarantees the inclusion of Islamic financial institutions in the secondary market while acknowledging the worldwide variety of trade finance practices. Sub-participations add further levels of complexity to trade finance transactions, which at times reflect and intensify the field's intrinsic complexity. While they may be flexible and aid in international trade, they are not always the ideal option in every situation. In some cases, alternatives like outright sales or bundling trade assets for institutional investors may be more suitable.

The trade finance industry is undergoing a transformation due to the emergence of funds, fintechs, and other non-conventional participants, which might lead to more modifications in distribution strategies. The presence of these organizations requires continuous modifications to the MPAs and distribution procedures to account for their differing expectations and operating models. The changes made to the BAFT MPAs under both English and New York law show how trade finance distribution methods have changed over time to adapt to changing market needs and government concerns. While the original MPAs were being changed, the new ones made the secondary market more open, flexible, and welcoming by allowing Islamic finance and more closely following the idea of a "true sale." The MPAs will likely undergo more adjustments as the trade finance environment changes with the arrival of new market players. This will ensure they remain relevant and useful instruments for promoting international trade financing.

Strategic Importance and Future of Credit Enhancement in Trade Finance

Credit enhancement strategies are mathematical financial approaches employed to raise the reliability of financial instruments like promissory notes and bills of exchange. These strategies enhance the trust of financiers, investors, and other transaction stakeholders by providing additional assurances of the instrument's completion. Let's examine the details of these strategies and their importance in the context of negotiable instruments.

In trade finance, one of the most common ways to improve credit is for the debtor's bank to provide a transferable, irreversible bank guarantee for the amount mentioned in the promissory note or bill of exchange. In the event that the debtor defaults, the bank will satisfy the payment obligation, providing the holder of the instrument with a safety net. By obtaining a bank guarantee, the instrument becomes far less risky financially, increasing its appeal to lenders and customers.

While the purposes of a bank guarantee and an "aval" are similar, the implementation of an "aval" differs. A third party, typically a bank or financial institution, guarantees the payment obligation of an aval appended to a bill or note. It's important to note that English law does not specifically recognize the concept of an aval, despite its widespread acceptance and use in many nations. However, the practical impact of an aval in international trade is comparable to that of a guarantee, offering the holder of the instrument an additional layer of security.

Before discounting a bill of exchange or promissory note, financiers frequently require the availability of an aval or bank guarantee. Discounting is the process of buying the instrument from the holder before it matures at a price lower than its nominal value, giving the holder access to instant liquidity. The need for credit enhancement strategies like avales or guarantees indicates bankers' aversion to risk, which they use to mitigate.

Trade agreements give rise to contract receivables when an exporter sells goods to an importer, creating a financial claim against the latter. This claim may appear explicitly in the contract or indirectly through later delivery bills. Unlike negotiable instruments, contract receivables have some conditionality attached to them because the right to payment may depend on the completion of the underlying transaction. English law provides a broad foundation for electronic interactions by not imposing any particular formality on contracts or invoices beyond the general criteria for contract formation.

CHAPTER 3   CASHING IN ON THE OPPORTUNITY: THE DYNAMIC WORLD OF RECEIVABLES FINANCE

The idea of assignment is central to the transfer of contract receivables under English law. Differentiating between equitable and legal transfers, these transfers have subtleties that impact the rights granted to the recipient. When someone legally assigns a debt, the person who is assigning gives up all control of the debt to the person who is receiving it. This lets the assignee collect the debt on its own and protects it from claims by third parties about the assignor's assets. A written notification to the debtor is one of the elements outlined in Section 136 of The Law of Property Act 1925 that must be followed for a legal assignment to be deemed effective.

By enhancing its security and appeal, credit enhancement strategies help contract receivables become more attractive to lenders. These can include the debtor offering security or assurances regarding the payment obligation or converting the debt into a stronger payment instrument, such as a letter of credit. An agreement that provides recourse for the seller in the event of debtor default adds another layer of protection for the buyer of the receivable. These improvements successfully raise the receivable's credit quality, reducing risks for both buyers and lenders.

Credit enhancement techniques are essential to the efficient operation of trade financing. By enhancing the perceived risk profile of bills of exchange and promissory notes, these strategies promote greater involvement from financiers and investors. Consequently, businesses can more easily use their receivables to meet short-term financial demands, improving liquidity and operational flexibility.

Supply chain finance has enabled the use of creative receivables management strategies, often utilizing electronic platforms that speed up the assignment notification process. However, in cross-jurisdictional situations, complexities arise, necessitating the validation of electronic notices. Silent (non-notified) financing agreements pose a unique challenge, as improper notification to the debtor could compromise the financier's rights, underscoring the significance of contract clauses that forbid further assignment.

Contract receivables are essential components of the trade finance architecture as they represent the financial commitments that drive international trade. Stakeholders in the trade ecosystem can handle the intricacies of international transactions with more confidence and security if they have a thorough understanding of their features, transfer methods, and possibilities for credit enhancement. As the trade finance industry evolves, the strategic management of contract receivables will continue to be essential in unlocking liquidity and fostering strong business relationships.

Sailing the Legal Seas of Payment Instruments

The legality of payment instruments has a direct impact on the range of financing options available to exporters. Receivables function as a legal and financial asset; therefore, the suitability of various financing options depends on your capacity to trade, transfer, and enforce these claims. Whether through factoring, forfaiting, or using receivables as collateral for loans, the legal treatment of payment instruments shapes trade finance.

Exporters must comprehend the legal ramifications of various payment options to protect their interests and maximize financial strategies. The ability to successfully navigate the complexity of the global marketplace will depend on one's knowledge of the legal ramifications of different payment methods as international trade continues to expand.

A crucial component of the architecture of trade finance is enforceability, which ensures that transactions take place and are legal in a way that ensures security for all parties. For sellers engaged in the complex web of international commerce, establishing an enforceable payment obligation against the buyer is an essential first step toward safeguarding their financial interests. This enforceability, which specifies the exact authority to demand payment, transforms a business agreement into a legally enforceable commitment. This is essentially dependent on the seller fulfilling their end of the trade agreement and taking all the necessary actions to establish a legally enforceable claim for payment against the buyer. By transforming the trade agreement into a legally enforceable contract, the seller ensures payment choices beyond the buyer's goodwill.

As soon as the buyer establishes an enforceable payment obligation, they become the debtor. This status serves as more than just a classification; it signifies a formal recognition of a debt between the buyer and vendor, essentially a receivable that appears as payable in the client's financial records. This modification puts the transaction in a framework that permits legal action and emphasizes the financial and legal ramifications of enforceability.

It's crucial to keep in mind that obligations that the seller has already created by fulfilling their portion of the agreement are the main topic of discussion when it comes to enforceability. Unfulfilled actions or conditions render future payment obligations currently unenforceable. This distinction draws attention to the point at which a payment obligation becomes a concrete, enforceable right rather than a claim that may arise in the future.

CHAPTER 3   CASHING IN ON THE OPPORTUNITY: THE DYNAMIC WORLD OF RECEIVABLES FINANCE

This provides sellers with a means of security and redress and forms the basis for trade financing transactions. Understanding the nuances of enforceability preserves the integrity of the global trading system overall and aids sellers in negotiating international trade more skillfully.

A key idea in trade finance is negotiability, which helps to distinguish between assets that move through the financial system with ease and those that require more skill. This distinction mostly relates to documents that are negotiable, such as bills of exchange and promissory notes, and those that are not, notably invoices. Mastering the nuances of negotiability is crucial for businesses involved in trade finance, especially when it comes to secondary market trading and financing receivables.

Negotiable instruments facilitate the transfer of financial claims efficiently. The advantage of these instruments lies in their ease of transfer, typically requiring only a simple delivery and, if required, an endorsement. Because they transfer easily and don't require complex documentation, negotiable instruments are a beneficial option for financing receivables and other trade activities, giving businesses more liquidity and financial flexibility.

The capacity to exchange documents physically emphasized the legal process in a society where paper documents predominated. This is where the concept of the negotiability of instruments finds its roots. However, as the financial sector evolves with fintech advances, the legal framework governing the production and transfer of electronic negotiable instruments is facing challenges and modifications to adapt to the digital era. A key factor in increasing the effectiveness and accessibility of negotiable instruments in contemporary finance is the shift from paper to digital.

Conversely, non-negotiable receivables need a more structured method of transfer, usually in the form of assignment. This procedure calls for accurate documentation and frequently calls for informing the debtor. Various complexities can arise from non-negotiable receivable transfers, such as agreements that limit or require the debtor's approval before the receivable's sale. Even with these problems, non-negotiable receivables are still an important part of receivables financing. And financial innovators are working on ways to make legal requirements easier, especially with the help of electronic platforms and payables financing schemes.

In trade finance, the idea of negotiability includes the practical and legal differences between different types of receivables and whether they are suitable for trading and financing. A major advancement in supporting electronic negotiability is the development of legal frameworks, which comes as the financial industry continues to embrace digital solutions. This change opens up a whole new era in the ease of access and flexibility of trade finance instruments. It makes financial transactions run more smoothly and gives businesses more financing options.

Securing Financial Stability: The Crucial Role of Credit Insurance in Receivables Financing

Whenever financial transactions are based on the promise of future payments, credit insurance is necessary. In its simplest form, a receivable is an entitlement or right that one party must receive payment from another at a later date. Businesses extensively utilize this finance instrument to ensure seamless operations and extended loan periods between enterprises. However, the interim period between the issuance of the receivable and the creditor's payment is fraught with uncertainty and risk.

The main risk associated with financing receivables is the likelihood that the debtor won't be able or willing to fulfill the mutually agreed payment by the due date, known as credit risk, or the buyer's default risk. Financial instability, insolvency, or other financial troubles experienced by the buyer may give rise to this risk. Fluctuations in exchange rates may have a major impact on the receivable's worth in cross-border transactions, leading to losses for the seller or financier if the currency value declines. Political developments affecting global trade, such as import-export limitations, government involvement, or instability, may halt payments, rendering receivables worthless. In regions where politics are unstable, this threat is more obvious.

Credit insurance plays a crucial role in reducing these risks and offering comfort to both receivables owners and lenders. In this scenario, credit insurance protects the policyholder against damages brought on by a debtor's default. Subject to the terms and conditions of the policy, the insurance company compensates the policyholder with the covered amount if the debtor defaults for an extended period or becomes insolvent.

Businesses may utilize insured assets as a way to secure bank and financial institution funding. Receivables become a more enticing collateral option thanks to credit insurance, often resulting in stronger loan conditions and increased cash flow for the company. Credit insurance affords companies the trust they need to explore and grow into new, potentially unpredictable areas by decreasing political and currency risks, which may be very helpful for companies trying to expand internationally in terms of clientele.

CHAPTER 3   CASHING IN ON THE OPPORTUNITY: THE DYNAMIC WORLD OF RECEIVABLES FINANCE

Despite minimizing exposure, credit insurance companies often provide useful data on potential clients' financial standing. Providing more information can strengthen credit management decisions and strategies, thereby further reducing the chance of default. This becomes a vital risk management approach in the context of financing receivables, allowing organizations greater safety while expanding their operations both locally and globally and safeguarding against any financial losses.

An experienced insurance broker plays a crucial role in this complex environment where lenders attempt to mitigate the risks involved in funding receivables. Brokers provide expertise and guidance through the intricacies of insurance products, acting as an essential bridge between investors and the insurance market. A number of essential duties and obligations revolve around ensuring the financer receives the best coverage possible.

Acting as a counselor to the insured party—in this case, the financiers—is the main responsibility of a broker. They understand the subtleties associated with various types of insurance and have a thorough knowledge of the credit insurance sector. Because of their expertise, they can advise on the most suitable insurance options based on the particular needs of the financier. Brokers ensure financiers have access to reasonable and suitable coverage alternatives by comparing pricing bids from several insurers and utilizing their extensive industry expertise. Creditors may find it challenging to understand the complicated terminology and phrasing used in credit insurance plans. Brokers help ensure that the coverage is in line with the financer's risk management plan by facilitating the understanding and negotiation of these policy conditions.

The broker's responsibility doesn't end with the first purchase of the insurance policy. The broker ensures that the insurance solution aligns with the financer's evolving risk management requirements by providing continuous support throughout the insurance period, answering any questions the financer may have, and assisting with any necessary coverage modifications. The broker becomes the financer's most valuable ally in the case of a claim, streamlining the claims procedure by handling correspondence between the insured and the insurers. His participation is essential in claim settlement negotiations, as they use their knowledge and connections in the market to support the financier. Such an individual is essential since they not only provide access to insurance products but also provide assistance, negotiation, and consulting services. His knowledge and participation guarantee that financiers can confidently traverse the complicated world of credit insurance and obtain coverage that satisfies their unique risk management goals.

Financial institutions can also obtain their own credit insurance policies for the receivables they fund as a backup strategy. Although this entails accepting liability for insurance requirements and premium payments, this approach assures that the financier is the insured party and offers direct control over the claims procedure. Suppliers and financiers must carefully address the legal and operational difficulties to share the benefits of credit insurance. Every methodology possesses a unique combination of benefits and drawbacks, and the choice of one mostly relies on the specific circumstances and degree of risk tolerance of the investor. The ultimate goal is to find a balance between minimizing the risks and dependencies that come with getting credit insurance and making the most of its safety benefits.

For both financiers and insurance consumers, it is increasingly critical to comprehend the legal nuances of insurance plans. These policies are subject to a particular set of regulations under insurance law in addition to normal contract law. This dual legal framework makes it necessary to understand insurance contracts in greater detail and highlights the value of seeking expert legal counsel when navigating the responsibilities and possible consequences of contract violations. The cornerstone of insurance contracts is the concept of *uberrima fides*, or the highest best faith, which calls for openness and truthfulness from all parties. According to this notion, neither side can mislead the other or conceal crucial information from them. This concept is important because it regulates how judges read insurance contracts, determining the parties' responsibilities and the legality of their activities under the policy.

In the context of receivables financing, credit insurance, in particular, requires a grasp of the indemnity concept. The concept argues that the purpose of insurance is to prevent the insured from making more money than they have lost by paying for actual losses sustained as a result of an insured occurrence. This becomes even more crucial given the relationship between insurers and bankers, which transfers the risk and ownership of receivables. If a financier acquires receivables on a non-recourse basis and a debtor fails, the insurer may not consider the original owner (the insured party) to have suffered a loss, potentially complicating insurance claims. In order to protect their interests, financiers could have to seek separate insurance policies or become co-assurers.

The need for the insured to have an "insurable interest" in the insurance's subject matter is another essential idea. This implies that in the scenario where the covered event takes place, the insured must be subject to a financial loss or responsibility. The insurance contract is void if there isn't an insurable interest. Credit insurance users face challenges as the application of this approach to indemnity insurance plans, apart from marine insurance, remains unclear. The Insurance Act 2015, a historic overhaul of insurance law, further regulates non-consumer insurance policies under UK law. This law has significantly improved several key areas. The Act imposes a duty of fair presentation on the insured person, requiring them to disclose all relevant facts they know or should know or provide sufficient information to prompt further research.

As long as the breach is fixed before the loss, the new law changes the old one about warranties so that coverage is dropped instead of being suspended. In the event of false claims, the Act gives insurers options, including the ability to end the agreement and reject any and all claims filed under it. It is important that financiers and other stakeholders involved in the credit insurance industry recognize these legal principles and specific rules outlined in the Insurance Act 2015. It ensures that they can efficiently handle the complexity of insurance contracts, uphold their commitments, and maximize the insurance coverage's protective advantages.

Financiers, notably those involved in receivables finance, must navigate the complexities of insurance coverage. Understanding important terminology and its meanings can significantly impact the usefulness and reliability of credit insurance as a risk management tool. Exclusions identify circumstances in which an insurer is unlikely to compensate for losses, allowing a clear definition of the bounds of coverage. Typical restrictions might include wider market exclusions, like losses from radioactive pollution or nonpayments resulting from legitimate commercial disagreements. Financiers must carefully review these exclusions to make sure they match the perceived breadth of coverage and the risks they are trying to reduce.

As stipulated by the Insurance Act of 2015, covered parties must accurately communicate the risk to insurers. This entails revealing all relevant circumstances that are known or should be known, or at the very least, supplying enough details to elicit more questions from insurers. This presentation needs to be factually correct, concise, and presented with excellent intentions when it comes to expectations or beliefs. The Act establishes the definition of "material" information and emphasizes the insured party's responsibility to actively investigate the risk, rather than ignoring such issues.

It is essential to carefully review the coverage scope, including claim triggers and policy restrictions. Coverage typically encompasses a dynamic pool of receivables; therefore, to qualify for benefits, collections must meet specific eligibility criteria, such as being due from a debtor under approval or originating from a jurisdiction under approval. Financiers must perform due diligence to ensure they understand and adhere to the policy's requirements.

CHAPTER 3   CASHING IN ON THE OPPORTUNITY: THE DYNAMIC WORLD OF RECEIVABLES FINANCE

Due diligence is a crucial procedure that entails painstaking assessment and confirmation to guarantee that the insurance policy fulfills its intended role as a risk reduction instrument. When insurers rely on their clients' insurance policies to improve the credit quality of funded receivables, this procedure becomes even more crucial. Companies use credit insurance to protect themselves from the risk of their clients defaulting on their bills. Insurance companies generally perform risk assessments of potential consumers before underwriting a credit insurance policy. This review looks at several aspects, such as the company's financial standing, its payment history, and the state of the economy as a whole.

To ensure that credit insurance fulfills its intended function in the context of receivables finance, it is necessary to resolve specific problems and issues. To determine how the insurance plan will respond to defaulting receivables, thorough knowledge of the coverage's terms and conditions is necessary. For coverage to activate, the policy may have unique exclusions, prerequisites, and requirements. We must carefully review these specifics to ensure that receivables fall within the scope of covered risks. We must also carefully examine the creditworthiness of the receivables to fund. To make sure that the receivables fulfill the insurer's risk requirements, the lender or investor must evaluate the financial standing and credit history of the accounts payable clients.

Due diligence also includes a rigorous investigation of the insurance company's reputation and dependability. The investor has to make sure that the insurance company is financially solid and has a history of paying out claims in a timely and fair manner. This evaluation can involve looking at the insurance company's financial standing, credit rating, and claims history. Since insurers often apply strict and sophisticated standards to assess the risk profile of the insured party, it is essential to comprehend the risk assessment process utilized by the insurance company. This entails examining the underwriting procedures of the insurer, which may include evaluations of the policyholder's risk management techniques, the quality of the receivables, and the general financial stability of the insured party.

A crucial component of risk management is communication with the insurance provider. The insured must make sure that the insurer receives timely and correct information about the status and creditworthiness of the receivables. This may require frequent sharing of data on customer payments, financial accounts, and any significant changes that could affect the credit risk of the receivables. An investor must carefully consider these factors when funding receivables backed by the supplier's insurance policy to manage risks and optimize the benefits of credit insurance.

CHAPTER 3   CASHING IN ON THE OPPORTUNITY: THE DYNAMIC WORLD OF RECEIVABLES FINANCE

True Sale vs. Secured Financing

When trade finance deals with the transfer of receivables, there is an important decision to be made about the nature of the deal: whether to go for a direct transfer of ownership, or "true sale," or whether to use the receivable as collateral for a loan. This disparity has important ramifications for the parties' rights and safeguards, particularly in light of the original owner's bankruptcy. Let's analyze these two strategies to comprehend the intricacies of law and finance, as well as how they affect the people concerned.

The full transfer of ownership from the beneficiary to the purchaser occurs upon a real sale of receivables. In the event that the original owner becomes insolvent, this transaction essentially shields the buyer against claims made against the latter's assets. This protection is what makes a real sale so appealing; it gives the buyer actual ownership of the receivable and provides them the freedom to act without regard to the original owner's financial situation. In receivables financing, the idea of a real sale is fundamental since it provides a clear separation from the original owner's balance sheet and any potential complications with bankruptcy procedures.

On the other hand, borrowing against receivables does not involve a transfer of ownership. Instead, the original owner, also known as the beneficiary, uses the receivable to secure a loan. Because of the security interest given to the financier, the receivable is nevertheless listed as an asset on the beneficiary's balance sheet under this arrangement. Compared to absolute ownership, the financier's recovery prospects are less advantageous in the case of the beneficiary's insolvency. As a secured creditor, the financier's claim often falls below the mandated preferred creditors in bankruptcy proceedings.

One of the major dangers involved with structured finance transactions is the potential misclassification of a transaction as a secured loan when it was really meant to be a true sale. This recharacterization can put a financier in a challenging situation, particularly if they haven't fully finalized the security interest through registration or other necessary procedures. In nations like the UK, failure to register a security interest within the allotted time frame renders it unenforceable against insolvency practitioners, severely hindering the recovery of a financier.

The legal landscape surrounding the transfer of receivables, true sales, and secured financing varies significantly across jurisdictions. Parties engaging in international trade and finance must seek local legal advice to navigate these complexities effectively. To structure transactions that are in line with the parties' goals and offer the right level of protection, it is important to know the local laws about transferring receivables, perfecting security interests, and being bankrupt.

It is important to carefully consider the financial and legal ramifications of each option before deciding whether to pursue a real sale of receivables or use secured financing against them. This choice affects the financier's risk exposure and long-term recovery chances, in addition to the beneficiary's immediate cash and financial freedom. It is nevertheless critical for all parties involved to comprehend and navigate the subtleties of these transactions as the global trade finance ecosystem develops.

The Principle of Independence: How to Ensure Payment Amidst Disputes

In receivables finance, the idea of being separate from the underlying trade transaction is a key factor that has a big impact on how safe and appealing the financing arrangement is. This concept ensures payment to all parties involved, irrespective of the type of business relationship. It does this by protecting the lender or buyer of the receivable from possible disputes between the original trading parties.

The idea behind receivables financing comes from the financier's need for certainty, or the promise of payment even if there are disagreements or problems with the trade transaction itself. Financiers prefer a financing agreement that gives them no recourse against the sale and allows payment without any performance or other seller requirements. This degree of independence increases the investment's security, which makes some payment instrument types especially alluring.

The level of autonomy differs among various payment methods. Promissory notes, letters of credit, bills of exchange, and independent payment undertakings (IPUs) are notable examples of instruments that establish independent payment obligations. By shielding these commitments from disagreements within the underlying transaction, these without-recourse financing structures give financiers more peace of mind.

On the other hand, the underlying contract closely links amounts owed under invoices, subjecting payment to any legal defenses the debtor may have. Due to this dependence, the debtor can dispute or delay payment until they meet contractual obligations or settle disputes. This exposes financiers to risk.

In order to reduce the risks involved with financing-dependent payment mechanisms, financiers have devised various solutions. One strategy involves purchasing receivables only after ensuring the debtor has acknowledged the fulfillment of the contract. An additional tactic involves using "with recourse" financing, which gives the financier the right to demand the seller repurchase the receivable if the debtor defaults due to the seller's non-performance.

The debtor can either accept that they have to pay no matter what, or they can help make an independent payment instrument, like an IPU, promissory note, or bank-issued LC so that they can get out from under the obligation. These tools successfully separate the execution of the underlying transaction from the payment obligation, offering a strong foundation for financiers to rely on.

The principle of independence from the underlying trade transaction is a cornerstone of secure and effective receivables financing. Finance professionals can more easily handle the complicated world of trade finance if they know the differences between independent and dependent payment instruments and use risk reduction strategies. As the landscape of international trade continues to evolve, the pursuit of independence remains a key strategy for ensuring the reliability and stability of financing arrangements.

Understanding Trade Debt: Implications for Insolvency and Restructuring

The distinction between "true trade debt" and bank debt carries significant implications, especially in the context of a debtor's insolvency or restructuring. At the heart of this discourse lies the foundational understanding of "true trade debt" as obligations arising directly from the sale and purchase of goods. This debate underscores the complex interplay between trade finance and insolvency proceedings, as well as the broader financial strategies employed by companies to manage their liabilities.

There is no established precedent for the controversial notion that trade-financed debt should receive special consideration in bankruptcy or reorganization procedures. Certain cases, meanwhile, like the 2009 restructurings of Kazakhstan's JSC Alliance Bank and JSC BTA Bank, demonstrate situations in which trade-related short-term loans took precedence. The above examples show that sometimes people do recognize the important role that trade debt plays in a business's operations and the bigger picture of making sure suppliers can pay their bills.

Debates about how to classify debts resulting from financing agreements that change a debtor's obligations in other ways, such as by extending payment terms, are ongoing. Financial analysts and rating agencies have been debating how best to classify debts in financial crises as a result of high-profile examples like Abengoa and Carillion. Do we now more appropriately categorize these debts, which once resembled trade payables but underwent modifications due to financing agreements, as bank debt?

This is not just an intellectual subject; it has important ramifications for the management and perception of a company's liabilities, particularly when it comes to financial reporting and bankruptcy risk assessment. Reclassifying trade payables as bank debt may change a company's perceived creditworthiness, which may impact its future financing prospects and ability to handle financial difficulties.

These discussions highlight how crucial it is for experts involved in trade finance arrangement structuring to give serious thought to the financial and legal implications of their choices. Given the possibility of reclassifying trade debt as bank debt, a comprehensive understanding of the deliberate and inadvertent outcomes of financial innovations aimed at managing liquidity and extending payment terms is crucial. More than just a semantic argument, the difference between "true trade debt" and bank debt is important for businesses, financiers, and attorneys negotiating the complex world of trade finance, insolvency, and restructuring. It is crucial to comprehend and appropriately categorize trade-related responsibilities because the financial landscape is constantly changing, and businesses are using more complex financing arrangements to handle their commitments. For all parties involved, striking a balance between the requirements of financial stability and transparency and the necessity of flexibility in trade finance will continue to be a major problem.

From Tradition to Digital Innovation: The Role of Negotiable Instruments

Negotiable instruments have long been the cornerstones of safe and dependable transactions in the field of international trade finance. These documents, which are unrelated to the underlying economic transaction and have their roots in centuries of legal tradition, provide a simplified means of guaranteeing payment.

According to the Bills of Exchange Act of 1882, both promissory notes and bills of exchange create an independent, unconditional payment obligation from the debtor to the beneficiary. This independence is crucial as it ensures that the debtor will not withhold payment until they resolve any issues arising from the trade transaction. These instruments are essential tools in trade finance because their physical presence, combined with the required endorsements, makes them easier to transfer and enforce.

However, the development of these tools' legal structure in a world where paper was king presents challenges in a rapidly digitizing economy. Legal restrictions have slowed the transition to electronic negotiable instruments, especially in countries like England where actual possession is required for enforceability. Legal changes are being considered to close this gap. One idea for updating current laws for the digital age is to make sure that electronic versions of promissory notes and bills of trade have the same legal standing as their paper counterparts.

It is important to note that negotiable instruments are very valuable in the secondary market and for financing receivables because they are easy to trade and transfer. The ease with which these instruments can circulate is demonstrated by forfaiting transactions, in which instruments are sold without recourse.

To address the difficulties brought about by the shift to digital, creative solutions such as the electronic payment undertaking (ePU) have surfaced. The International Trade and Forfaiting Association (ITFA) has proposed ePUs, which are digital-age contractual instruments that aim to replicate the rights associated with traditional negotiable instruments. This innovation holds the potential to open up new avenues for trade finance by facilitating the simple exchange and transfer of receivables on an online platform.

Negotiable instruments, from their traditional origins to their digital application, embody the evolution of trade finance. With enhanced accessibility, efficiency, and security, the future of trade finance looks promising as legal reforms strive to bridge the divide between tradition and innovation. The introduction of ePUs represents a significant turning point in this process: the shift to digital negotiable instruments. This shift has the potential to completely change how trade finance functions in the global economy.

Strengthening Trade Finance: Techniques for Credit Enhancement

Ensuring payment and safeguarding transactions are critical for financiers and participants in the complex world of trade finance. In this procedure, credit enhancement strategies are essential, particularly when working with bills of exchange and promissory notes. By strengthening financial instruments' creditworthiness, these strategies make them more appealing to lenders and investors.

Providing a bank guarantee that is simultaneously transferable and irrevocable is one of the oldest and most commonly employed techniques for enhancing creditworthiness. In the event that the debtor defaults on the bill of exchange or promissory note, the debtor's bank will, in effect, guarantee the reimbursement of the stipulated amount. The transferable nature of the guarantee makes sure the new holder is able to make use of the financial instrument in the event that ownership changes.

Adding an aval is another way to improve credit, and it's especially important for promissory notes and bills of exchange. An aval is an endorsement that represents a third party's promise to pay the instrument, typically a bank. Many countries recognize the Aval, despite its lack of specific recognition. The appraisal provides an extra assurance of payment that fortifies the instrument's credit quality, much like a bank guarantee.

It is frequently a requirement for financiers thinking about discounting bills or notes to get an aval or bank guarantee. By lowering the perceived risk of the financial instrument, these credit enhancement strategies increase its acceptability for trading or discounting. These strategies facilitate smoother transactions and increase involvement in trade financing operations by providing financiers with assurances regarding the security, guarantees, and availability of the instrument.

Avalization and bank guarantees are two essential instruments in the trade finance toolbox for credit improvement. They mitigate risk by providing a strong assurance of payment to support promissory notes and bills of trade, going above and beyond the debtor's commitment. These strategies' significance in building confidence and enabling cross-border trade transactions doesn't wane even as the global trade finance scene changes. Participants in the trade finance ecosystem can negotiate the challenges of global trade with more assurance and confidence by strategically applying credit enhancement.

Decoding Contract Receivables

Contract receivables are essential to the intricate web of trade finance because they allow importers and exporters to deal securely and smoothly. These receivables, originating from export agreements and invoice deliveries, serve as a crucial payment entitlement, essential for maintaining the liquidity and stability of trading entities. Contract receivables arise when an exporter sells goods under an export contract, requiring the importer to pay the exporter. The contract may specifically state these receivables, or delivery invoices may illustrate them. Unlike negotiable instruments, the enforceability of contract receivables strongly links to the underlying commercial transaction. This suggests that contractual duties could condition payment, and disagreements could lead to payment withholding or adjustments through credit notes.

CHAPTER 3   CASHING IN ON THE OPPORTUNITY: THE DYNAMIC WORLD OF RECEIVABLES FINANCE

Contract receivables are special in that they can take on any shape. For instance, English law does not outline specific requirements for the invoice or contract, beyond the basic principles of contract formation. Electronic contracts and invoicing, now widely used in international trade, demonstrate this adaptability by streamlining procedures and boosting productivity.

Under English law, the process of assignment transfers contract receivables in a legal or equitable manner. By giving the assignee full legal rights to the debt, a formal assignment removes the obligation from the assignor's control and shields it from claims made by third parties against the assignor. This stops the debtor from using any set-off rights against the assignor and gives the assignee the authority to sue the debtor directly for payment.

A number of prerequisites must be satisfied for an assignment to be considered lawful, including the assignment's absolute nature, its need to be in writing and signed by the assignor, and the debtor's receipt of a notice of assignment. This notification may take different forms. Despite the debtor's acknowledgment of enhancing the assignee's security, the legal validity of the assignment does not strictly require it, as long as the debtor has received proper notification.

Trade finance relies heavily on contract receivables, which represent the rights and responsibilities that underpin global trade. Their ability to be assigned allows for the management of financial risk and liquidity, and their features strike a balance between the need for strict legality and adaptability. All parties involved in international trade will need to comprehend the nuances of contract receivables as trade finance continues to change, particularly with the growing usage of electronic papers.

Strategizing Security: Managing Risks in Receivables Financing

In the complex world of trade finance, managing the risks associated with receivables financing requires a strategic combination of legal and financial knowledge. These abilities are crucial in the implementation of credit improvement strategies and the execution of non-notified transfers. Non-notified transfers involve the transfer of debt to a third party without the debtor's awareness. This is a covert yet intricate aspect of receivables finance. This "silent" strategy offers advantages, chief among them being the maintenance of the debtor-seller business relationship. However, the assignee, a financier or other entity buying the debt, assumes an additional layer of risk by maintaining an equitable assignment until the debtor receives formal notification.

The primary worry is that another party, who notifies the debtor after receiving the same obligation, might gain priority. Assignors usually guarantee the assignee that they won't deal with the transferred debt in the future in order to reduce this risk. However, being vigilant is crucial since the assignee still needs to protect their legal and financial rights, even if the debtor is unaware of them.

In order to increase receivables' trustworthiness and give financiers more security, credit enhancement strategies are essential instruments in the trade finance toolbox. These strategies, which can include everything from contractual obligations to bank guarantees, are essential to raising the allure and security of funding agreements.

Guarantees from banks and corporations: An irreversible bank guarantee is a strong way to improve credit since it provides the financier with an extra degree of protection by guaranteeing payment even in the event of a debtor's default. Corporate guarantees can achieve similar goals, but the creditworthiness of the corporate guarantor determines the quality of the guarantee. In order to improve the financier's capacity to directly manage the proceeds of receivables, debtors may consent to direct payments into specific accounts under its control.

These offer an extra layer of protection by enabling the buyer of the receivable to pursue legal action against the seller in the event that the debtor defaults. Certain terms may apply, such as limited recourse contingent on predetermined risk occurrences or full recourse. The financier gains additional security when they replace the original loan with a more secure payment instrument, like a bank-guaranteed negotiable instrument or a letter of credit, as this transfers the risk from the corporate debtor to the bank. Persuading a debtor to forego any defenses against their payment obligation or setting up an independent payment obligation makes a receivable more secure and financeable.

In receivables finance, navigating non-notified transactions and using credit enhancement measures effectively are critical strategies. They necessitate striking a careful balance between protecting privacy and guaranteeing the safety of financial transactions. Financiers and merchants can safeguard their interests, reduce risks, and enable more seamless and secure trade finance operations by comprehending and putting these techniques into practice.

CHAPTER 3   CASHING IN ON THE OPPORTUNITY: THE DYNAMIC WORLD OF RECEIVABLES FINANCE

Strengthening Global Linkages Through Cross-Border Payables Finance

Trade finance professionals worldwide are drawn to the innovative and highly effective concept of cross-border supply chain financing (SCF) in modern commerce. Despite the increasing popularity of the term "supply chain finance," it often serves as a broad umbrella term, encompassing a diverse array of financial products, structures, and solutions. To negotiate the complexity of SCF, one must have a solid understanding due to its multitude of meanings and uses. So, it's important to start this investigation with a clear definition that sets the stage for a deeper look at the role, how it works, and many other aspects of supply chain finance within the context of global trade finance.

The best way to conceptualize supply chain finance is as an umbrella term for a variety of financial instruments, frameworks, or systems designed to assist buyers and sellers in profiting from the capital involved in each of the numerous steps of the actual supply chain on a transactional basis. The Global Supply Chain Finance Forum (GSCFF) says that supply chain finance is the use of financing and risk reduction strategies and tactics to make the most of the working capital and cash flow that is available for supply chain operations. Certain events in the supply chain initiate the use of SCF in open account trading. As a result, finance providers must be able to see the underlying trade flows, which is a process that technological platforms frequently make simpler. Supply chain finance is a broad term for a lot of different products and services. For example, receivables finance and inventory finance are both types of payables finance. However, the degree of complexity that the intertwining of payables and receivables across the supply chain introduces may even confuse experienced practitioners. Because one party's payment is another's receivable, there might be uncertainty over the best methods for monetizing the supply chain as a result of this convolution.

Leading industry groups like the ICC, BAFT, FCI, ITFA, and the European Banking Association have joined forces under the GSCFF to create a uniform vocabulary of words, definitions, and best practices, acknowledging the need for clarity and consistency in this area. The 2016 release of the Standard Definitions for Techniques of Supply Chain Finance marked the pinnacle of this coordinated effort. The project seeks to promote standardization so that capital markets, regulatory bodies, and institutional investors that are interested in trade and supply chain financing have a common understanding.

CHAPTER 3   CASHING IN ON THE OPPORTUNITY: THE DYNAMIC WORLD OF RECEIVABLES FINANCE

Payables finance, especially its buyer-centric version in the receivables finance suite, is one of the many products in the SCF portfolio that has attracted the attention of investors, regulators, and practitioners. This summary of cross-border supply chain finance not only shows how important it is to have a common framework for understanding, but it also sets the stage for a more in-depth look at the main players, how they work, and the important part that SCF plays in making international trade finance more effective and liquid. As we continue reading this chapter, we will learn more about the complexities of SCF mechanisms, their advantages for the global trade ecosystem, and the difficulties they seek to resolve in a business environment that is changing quickly.

Let's start with payables financing, a buyer-centric approach to supply chain financing, also known as authorized payables or reverse factoring. In order to validate the buyer's responsibility to pay for provided products or services, this model prioritizes the buyer's participation in validating seller invoices. This part explores the complexities of payables finance, its structural framework, methods for managing working capital, and its wider effects on supply chain security.

Payables financing is a type of finance where a financial institution, sometimes known as a financier, buys a proven receivable from a seller at a reduced rate. The financier's choice to discount is contingent upon the buyer validating the invoice. This confirmation transfers credit risk from the seller to the buyer (now the obligor) by showing that the buyer has accepted the obligation. With the help of this method, buyers may efficiently allocate their credit capacity to strategic sellers in need of funding, which maximizes resource allocation across the supply chain.

For both buyers and sellers, controlling and optimizing working capital is greatly aided by payables finance. To improve their working capital management and financial condition, the first group aims to extend their days payable outstanding (DPO) in order to hold cash for a longer period of time. Increasingly, financially sound businesses looking to improve their working capital and cash flow ratios are using this strategy. On the other hand, the latter want to reduce their days sales outstanding (DSO) in order to accelerate cash inflow, which is essential for preserving liquidity. Extended payment terms can cause sellers a great deal of stress, especially in situations when liquidity is expensive or scarce, especially for smaller or highly leveraged sellers.

Payables financing appears as a way to reconcile these conflicting demands by using the buyer's creditworthiness to provide important suppliers with liquidity at a competitive price. This helps customers achieve their DPO goals without negatively impacting the financial stability of their suppliers. By using payables finance, sellers can reduce their debt and improve their working capital position without taking on additional debt or lowering their leverage ratios. Sellers achieve this by discounting their receivables shortly after the buyer approves the invoice. Typically, the process involves electronically transmitting the authorized invoice data to the finance provider, following which the seller receives notification about the potential discount. More sophisticated systems may enable automated discounting of each accepted invoice, significantly simplifying the procedure and giving sellers instant financial relief.

Within the supply chain, payables finance is a buyer-centric, strategic strategy that is advantageous to both buyers and sellers. It provides purchasers with an effective means of controlling cash flow and maximizing working capital while maintaining the financial health of their suppliers. Through the quicker monetization of receivables, it gives sellers a crucial lifeline that allows them to increase liquidity and working capital efficiency. Payables finance is therefore a crucial part of contemporary supply chain finance, providing a fair and advantageous response to the problems that come with safeguarding international supply networks and managing working cash.

In order to optimize working capital for both buyers and sellers, payables finance integrates two unique connections that exist inside the supply chain: that of the buyer and the service provider, as well as that of the seller (supplier) and the service provider. The foundation of this approach is the buyer's approval of invoices, which makes it essentially buyer-centric.

The procedure starts with a contract between the buyer and the service provider, which is usually a bank or other financial organization, in which the buyer agrees to electronically transmit payment instructions for certain bills. These instructions usually include important information such as the seller's name, account details, payment amount, currency, due date, and invoice reference number. Interestingly, this agreement does not specifically mention funding or credit provision. The commitment of the buyer that the underlying business activities are lawful and that the stipulated monies are rightfully owed to the seller is the main emphasis of this agreement. In the event that the service provider is a bank, the agreement can also permit the bank to transfer the money to the seller and debit the buyer's account immediately on the due date. The service provider contacts the seller to acquire the verified receivable at a discount and without recourse after receiving the buyer's payment confirmation. This means that the service provider, not the seller, is taking on the buyer's credit risk. Both parties outline their obligations, rights, and duties in a separate receivables purchase agreement, which also specifies the terms under which the seller agrees to sell and the service provider agrees to purchase the receivable.

CHAPTER 3   CASHING IN ON THE OPPORTUNITY: THE DYNAMIC WORLD OF RECEIVABLES FINANCE

The seller usually enters into the transaction on a non-recourse basis, which means that in the event that the buyer defaults, the service provider will not be able to pursue payment from the seller. Under the terms of this agreement, the service provider purchases the particular receivable or pool of receivables that the buyer has verified. Upon selling the receivable at a reduced rate, the service provider immediately pays the seller, basing this payment on the net present value of the future payment the buyer anticipates making. This transaction is similar to a forfaiting transaction, except that payables financing usually uses account receivables instead of negotiable instruments and involves the sale of a future claim for its discounted present value. By keeping liquidity for extended periods of time, this arrangement enables purchasers to prolong their payment terms without negatively impacting their suppliers, maximizing their own working capital. By lowering their days sales outstanding (DSO) without taking on more debt or changing their leverage ratios, sellers get instant cash flow, enhancing their liquidity and working capital management. By purchasing the receivables without recourse, service providers reap the benefits of the discount on future payments. The buyer's creditworthiness and the clear confirmation of the bills reduce their risk.

With the help of a third-party service provider, payables finance cleverly unites the financial interests of buyers and sellers along the supply chain. In addition to ensuring that sellers get necessary money more quickly, this triangulated connection enables buyers to manage their cash flow more effectively while the service provider controls credit risk and smoothly completes the financial transaction.

To fully grasp how payables finance works from a money point of view, you need to know a lot about math, especially when it comes to finding the net present value (NPV) of discounted receivables. A few essential elements are involved in this computation: the length, the discount rate, the cost of funds, and the margin.

First and foremost is the margin, which represents the service provider's profit or premium for the transaction and covers opportunity costs, risks, and other costs. It's crucial to remember that the seller, not the buyer, pays this margin when monetizing the receivable. In order to retain program profitability and recruit sellers, the service provider must carefully manage this margin.

The cost of funds enters the scene as the starting point for obtaining money or capital. Despite the gradual replacement of Interbank Offered Rates (IBOR) by risk-free rates, their historical use persists. One of the most important components that make up the overall discount rate applied to the receivable, together with the margin, is the cost of funds. The discount rate combines the cost of funds and the margin.

For example, the total discount rate would be 150 bps if the cost of funds is 50 bps and the margin is 100 bps. We use this rate to compute the NPV of the receivable and determine the amount the seller will receive upfront. Duration refers to the remaining time between the service provider's acquisition of the receivable and its maturity, or the day the buyer is required to make payment.

The length plays a crucial role in NPV calculation since it influences the discount rate's application over time. The service provider applies the discount rate to the face value of the receivable over the designated period in order to get the net present value (NPV) of the receivable. The net present value calculation (NPV) represents the amount the seller will receive upfront for the receivable from the service provider.

The discount amount is the difference between the face value and net present value of the receivable. Assume we have a $100,000 face value receivable that is due in 90 days. If the discount rate, which we determine by adding the cost of funds and margin, is 150 bps per year, we can compute the NPV and the discount amount as follows. Note that we'll assume a linear application of the discount rate for the full ninety-day period in order to keep things simple. To determine the NPV, we must first modify the yearly discount rate to the specified length (in this example, 90 days) and then apply it to the face value.

The difference between the face value and the NPV is therefore the discount amount. This simplified example shows the basic ideas behind the discounting process in payables finance. In real life, calculations can be more complicated and use different rates, interpolation methods, and calculation approaches. To prevent any shocks, it is imperative that merchants comprehend and reach a consensus on the discounting mechanism with the service provider.

By enabling purchasers to extend credit terms without negatively affecting their supplier's financial health, payables financing provides an effective solution for sellers to increase their liquidity by receiving immediate payment for receivables. One of the most important steps in ensuring that sellers in the program participate successfully is the onboarding process in payables finance. A thorough procedure combining technical expertise, sales prowess, and painstaking due diligence is necessary to properly recruit vendors into the program. The first step is to explain to prospective seller participants the advantages of the payables financing program. The service provider should highlight the value proposition of the program and explain how participation might improve the seller's liquidity and working capital management. Getting into a contract with sellers requires a rigorous due diligence procedure. This involves confirming the authenticity of the signatures and ensuring compliance with all legal and regulatory requirements. The procedure is essential for reducing financial and reputational risks, particularly in cross-border transactions where legislation may differ greatly.

The onboarding staff has to have a special blend of technical knowledge of payables finance and sales savvy. How well they interact with the targeted merchants and solve their problems has a direct impact on program adoption. Programs that include cross-border transactions must choose a service provider with a broad worldwide reach and familiarity with local legislation. This guarantees that the software complies with various regulatory frameworks and facilitates simple seller-buyer interaction in various legal contexts. An effective onboarding campaign depends on the buyer and service provider having a solid working relationship.

To ensure that the program is in line with the buyer's working capital objectives, both sides must collaborate closely to build a strategic approach to seller engagement and selection. Crucial procedures include selecting the appropriate sellers to participate in the program and carrying out a well-planned pre-positioning strategy. In order to speed up the adoption process, this entails giving targeted sellers thorough information and messaging about the program, its workings, and its advantages. It is essential that the buyer actively promotes the payables finance program.

If the buyer supports the proposal, sellers are more likely to accept it than if a service provider approaches them directly and asks them to participate, even if they may not already be acquainted. In payable finance, successful seller onboarding is a complex process that needs meticulous preparation, thorough due diligence, and tactical cooperation between the service provider and the buyer. Programs can get greater rates of seller acceptance by focusing on these elements, which will help buyers and sellers alike accomplish their objectives related to working capital efficiency. Effective onboarding sets the stage for a long-lasting and mutually beneficial financial ecosystem and makes it easier for sellers to join the payables finance program without any problems.

Payables finance has grown significantly in recent years, demonstrating its effectiveness as a trade finance solution that benefits buyers, sellers, and service providers equally. This increase is a sign of the significant value that payables financing provides to all parties concerned. Through payables finance solutions, big corporate purchasers may prolong payment periods and maximize their working capital without negatively impacting their suppliers. Buyers benefit from improved working capital efficiency and cash flow management as a result of this optimization.

CHAPTER 3   CASHING IN ON THE OPPORTUNITY: THE DYNAMIC WORLD OF RECEIVABLES FINANCE

By paying their receivables early, sellers can reduce their days sales outstanding (DSO), enhance their working capital position, and enjoy increased liquidity. Because these programs provide high-value services to important clients and provide attractive returns with relatively minimal risk, they are profitable for service providers, primarily banks. These long-term initiatives also cultivate stronger customer relationships, paving the way for the cross-selling of additional financial services. Service providers and their clients frequently decide to continue their cooperation after implementing a payables financing program. This link includes more than just financing for payables. It also includes cash management, foreign exchange management, and liquidity management, all of which are important parts of a working capital management plan. Well-executed payables financing programs can also grant access to program sellers.

These sellers may become purchasers in their own right since they frequently have demands for working capital. They may want to set up payable finance programs for their suppliers to increase the number of customers the service provider serves. It is essential to select a service provider with a solid reputation as well as the required abilities and resources. In addition to ensuring the payables finance program runs smoothly, a fantastic service provider reduces the financial and reputational risks related to the program's documentation, process flows, and structure.

To guarantee compliance and reduce risk exposure, purchasers must extensively research possible service providers, sometimes with the assistance of tax and legal consultants. A key element in the success of these initiatives is the service provider's proficiency in payables finance. Improved working capital management for both buyers and sellers, appealing financial returns, and the possibility of strengthening and growing customer relationships through other financial services are just a few advantages that a well-selected supplier may give.

The long-term impacts of these programs on important financial metrics like DSO and DPO show how important it is to pick a service provider that can help clients reach their overall working capital goals by understanding the bigger picture of finance as well as the specifics of payables finance.

In recent years, the Global Supply Chain Finance Forum (GSCFF) has played a major role in the development and standardization of the payables finance environment, which is an essential part of supply chain finance (SCF). Let's examine the major breakthroughs and contributions that have influenced the sector: Establishing itself in 2014, the GSCFF seeks to promote supply chain finance methods in the marketplace. Its development was a determined attempt to give the many SCF practices coherence and a common meaning. The important 2016 book Standard Definitions for SCF Approaches gives clear, general explanations of several SCF approaches, such as payables finance. It has played a crucial role in bringing understanding and application of SCF across various markets and legal systems into harmony.

The Crucial Step: KYC

The know your customer (KYC) processes are one area where the ICC, BAFT, and Wolfsberg Trade Finance Principles are particularly relevant. These principles serve as a shared reference for industrial practices. The Open Account Appendix clarifies the treatment of customers and counterparties during the onboarding process from a KYC perspective, addressing the differences between the two parties in payables finance.

As for industry guidelines and updates, the Receivables Discounting Approach (2019) instruction went into great detail about receivables discounting and how to use it in the best way for this SCF approach. To make corporate accounting practices for payables finance clearer, the Payables Finance Paper (2020) talked about a subject that was becoming more important to everyone and stressed how important it is for financial reporting to be consistent and clear.

The GSCFF added three additional methods to the Standard Definitions (2021) update under the heading of "Advanced Payable": corporate payment undertaking (CPU), bank payment undertaking (BPU), and dynamic discounting (DD). This update takes into account how SCF is changing and how industrial dynamics require ongoing adaptation. With the backing of influential groups like the ICC, BAFT, FCI, ITFA, and EBA, the GSCFF has made a name for itself as the primary resource for supply chain finance-related enterprises.

Its all-encompassing strategy for lobbying, education, and standardization has greatly aided in the development and expansion of SCF practices. The forum is still essential in spreading the word about SCF's advantages, pushing for the industry to embrace its standards, and making sure the sector is flexible and adaptable to new advancements. The GSCFF has made fundamental contributions to the advancement of more comprehensive SCF methodologies as well as a uniform approach to payables finance. The forum has improved supply chain finance's overall growth, operational efficiency, and transparency by addressing new trends like dynamic discounting, defining essential concepts, and providing clarification on best practices. As the area grows, the GSCFF's ongoing work will be necessary to navigate the complicated world of international supply chains and financial transactions. This will make sure that everyone can benefit from well-planned SCF initiatives.

CHAPTER 3   CASHING IN ON THE OPPORTUNITY: THE DYNAMIC WORLD OF RECEIVABLES FINANCE

Deep Dive into a Powerful Risk Mitigation Tool

Forfaiting, a fundamental component of trade finance, has recently undergone a "back to the future" kind of rebirth. The digital revolution of the trade finance industry has been the main driver of the considerable changes in the forfaiting environment since the release of this book's second edition in August 2019.

This development emphasizes the ongoing search for the ideal digital trade responsibility, a quest in which legislative frameworks have had to keep up with the quick advancement of technical solutions. Thankfully, this disconnect between technology and legislation has not impeded development but rather shown that the technological answers required for successful forfaiting are already in place.

The fact that faith is still relevant in the current digital era shows how flexible and timeless it is. Real and projected legal changes have reevaluated the functions of digital platforms and their potential to enhance trade finance operations. This chapter will examine these changes, emphasizing how forfaiting is changing due to digitalization and how this makes it an even more alluring option for the modern, digitalized economy. As we examine the fundamentals of forfaiting, it becomes evident why this approach is so well-liked for reducing the risks connected to global commerce. In order to fully understand forfaiting in the context of trade finance, this chapter will analyze its development, the effects of digitalization, and the possibilities presented by contemporary technology.

According to the "Standard Definitions for Techniques of Supply Chain Finance," which major financial organizations like ITFA, ICC, BAFT, FCI, and EBA have published, forfaiting offers a sophisticated and organized approach to trade finance. We present the following definitions and explanations based on the provided content: One particular type of receivables purchase is forfaiting. It is the acquisition of future payment obligations, usually represented by financial instruments or payment commitments, without recourse.

These are often obtained at face value or a discount in return for a financing charge, and they are typically in the form of negotiable or transferable agreements. This definition emphasizes how faith helps sellers reduce their credit risk and maintain liquidity.

The regulation of forfaiting under international norms, namely the Uniform Norms for Forfaiting (URF800), emphasizes the practice's distinctiveness within the trade finance industry. The URF800, released by the International Chamber of Commerce in collaboration with ITFA, creates universal international guidelines for forfaiting that are similar to those for documentary credits, improving consistency and predictability.

CHAPTER 3   CASHING IN ON THE OPPORTUNITY: THE DYNAMIC WORLD OF RECEIVABLES FINANCE

The text provides a detailed list of benefits for exporters using forfaiting, including but not limited to risk mitigation. Forfaiting eliminates dangers like credit risk, exchange rate volatility, and rising interest rates. Forfaiting eliminates the need to cover 100% of the contract value, thereby increasing the seller's cash flow and liquidity.

- Competitive Edge: Gives customers the option to prolong loan terms, increasing the allure and competitiveness of items on the international market.

- Balance Sheet Management: Assists in clearing out bank loans, contingent liabilities, and accounts receivable from the balance sheet.

- Operational Efficiency: Offers quick and customized financing options while relieving the seller of the paperwork and complexity of collection.

This method becomes essential to trade finance and provides exporters with several advantages by making financing more accessible, increasing liquidity, and delivering strong risk reduction tools.

The URF800's standardization and the many benefits it offers highlight the crucial role that forfaiting plays in facilitating international commerce, making it an invaluable resource for financial professionals as well as importers and exporters.

Payment instruments or claims are crucial to forfaiting, a financing strategy that involves the acquisition of receivables without recourse. These instruments are essential to the forfaiting transactions since they form the foundation for these financial agreements. These payment instruments' qualities and nature are key factors in deciding whether or not they are appropriate for forfaiting.

Payment instruments ought to be separate entities from the transactions they support. If the forfaiter's claim against the debtor is "autonomous and abstract," it will be clear-cut and less contested, as it does not directly relate to the provision or quality of goods and services. In order to lower the legal risk associated with the forfaiting transaction, instruments must have legal certainty, which entails being acknowledged by the law as legitimate obligations to pay.

The perfect payment instrument minimizes complexity and dispute risk by being legally simple, but it also allows for some flexibility to handle certain forfaiting agreement details. A payment instrument has to be marketable in order to be forfeitable. This enhances the instrument's liquidity by ensuring its easy sale or transfer on the financial market.

CHAPTER 3 CASHING IN ON THE OPPORTUNITY: THE DYNAMIC WORLD OF RECEIVABLES FINANCE

By making the best use and allocation of capital, instruments should get the best capital treatment possible under regulatory frameworks. This will make them more appealing to financial institutions. In an ideal world, sovereign and private debt restructurings would give preferential treatment to these instruments, ensuring the preservation of their value and priority position even in challenging financial circumstances. Although promissory notes and bills of trade have historically been linked to forfaiting, their features cannot perfectly fit the stated ideal standards. Although features like the capacity to expedite payments could call for further agreements, negotiability, and legal certainty are frequently present.

Furthermore, carefully drafting the contract to increase legal clarity and reduce risk can render invoices or book receivables forfeitable, even if they are contingent on the underlying transaction. Many of the desired attributes for forfaiting include the ability to eliminate credit risk, improve cash flow, enhance liquidity, and provide non-recourse financing by selling trade receivables at a discount to a forfaiter who assumes the credit and political risk associated with the underlying transaction. More modern financial instruments, such as irrevocable payment undertakings (IPUs) and bank payment obligations (BPOs), also incorporate many of the desired attributes for forfaiting. Their inclusion underscores the versatility of forfaiting and its adaptability to a diverse array of financial instruments, underscoring the technique's flexibility. A payment instrument's appropriateness for forfaiting depends on a number of operational, financial, and legal factors.

The fact that forfaiting has expanded to encompass instruments other than the classic ones is indicative of the technique's adaptability to the evolving trade finance environment. Because of its flexibility, forfaiting continues to be a crucial instrument for controlling risk, supplying liquidity, and funding international commerce, highlighting its wide range of applications and significance in the contemporary financial industry. Two important financial services used in trade finance for the financing and management of receivables are factoring and forfaiting.

Although similar, there are some key differences that may influence which to use in certain situations. The vendor has no, or very little, recourse when using this method. In other words, the forfaiter assumes the credit risk relating to the receivables. The seller is not required to reimburse the forfaiter in the event that the debtor defaults. Generally, factoring agreements provide the seller with complete recourse. The seller is required to repurchase the unpaid receivables from the factor if the debtor fails to make payments on the account. In most cases, forfaiters finance the whole receivable's face value, giving sellers the most liquidity possible against their transactions.

CHAPTER 3   CASHING IN ON THE OPPORTUNITY: THE DYNAMIC WORLD OF RECEIVABLES FINANCE

Factors frequently subtract a reserve from the receivables' nominal value, which they do not finance. This reserve acts as a safety net in case there are disagreements or payment shortages. Forfaiting is suitable for long-term supplier credits, as it can provide access for extended periods. This competence is especially important when big projects or capital items are involved. Factoring typically prefers shorter tenors. Factoring still mostly serves short-term receivables, despite market convergence toward forfaiting's preference for shorter periods.

Mostly used for cross-border transactions, this technique aids in promoting international trade by reducing the risks associated with exporting goods to foreign countries. Factoring is mostly a domestic company. Although cross-border factoring is available, it is less flexible than forfaiting when it comes to international transactions since it needs to be adhered to on certain platforms and laws. It handles a wide range of payment instruments, such as promissory notes, bills of exchange, and bank payment obligations, in addition to invoices. This variety makes it possible for increased transaction structure flexibility. This variety primarily concentrates on book debts or invoices. Factoring is quite beneficial for companies that use a short-term credit sales strategy because of this emphasis.

Receivables finance includes both factoring and forfaiting, each of which has unique benefits suited to various requirements. Factoring offers immediate liquidity and ease of transaction, making it especially advantageous for enterprises seeking finance and administration of their domestic receivables. However, forfaiting excels in the context of global commerce, giving exporters a means of obtaining longer-term finance without having to assume credit risk. The decision between factoring and forfaiting ultimately comes down to the particular requirements of the transaction, such as the type of receivables, the trade's geographic reach, the preferred tone, and the recourse structure.

Global forfaiting transactions, as a receivables financing and risk mitigation tool, have become more standardized with the introduction of the Uniform Rules for Forfaiting (URF 800). The International Chamber of Commerce (ICC) and the International Trade and Forfaiting Association (ITFA) released this set of guidelines, which is based on the expertise of seasoned professionals from the documentary credit, forfaiting, and broader trade finance industries.

Experts in forfaiting, trade finance attorneys, and documentary credit specialists collaborated for four years to finally create URF800. The regulations are thorough and represent the demands of the sector thanks to the wide range of input received. On January 1, 2013, the URF800 formally entered into force, and for its application in a specific transaction, the relevant contracts must explicitly incorporate it. The adoption procedure for other sets of standardized trade finance regulations is comparable to this. The Forfaiting Sector intends to replace the Uniform Customs and Practice for Documentary Credits (UCP), which operates in the documentary credit business, with the URF.

This entails giving practitioners a standard structure and vocabulary to enable more seamless transactions. The fourteen clauses or articles that make up the URF800 each deal with a distinct facet of Forfaiting transactions. These include outlining the responsibilities and rights of each party engaged as well as identifying important phrases and concepts. The URF's examination of what constitutes acceptable paperwork for forfaiting transactions is one of its key topics. This contains specifications for the kind and caliber of paperwork needed to guarantee a deal's seamless completion. The document also covers the extent of sellers' remedies, another significant topic.

The URF offers security and predictability for both sellers and forfaiters by making clear the circumstances in which sellers may be held accountable for debtors' inability to fulfill their payment commitments. The URF800 improves forfaiting's dependability, efficiency, and transparency as a financing alternative by instituting standard procedures. This is especially beneficial in a market that encompasses several legal systems and jurisdictions. The "eURF," a revised version of the URF that takes into account the continuous digital transition in trade finance, is now being considered. This change tries to make sure that the URF stays useful and appropriate in a digital world that changes quickly by taking into account the new opportunities and issues that come with digitization.

Global forfaiting processes have become more formalized and standardized, thanks in large part to the URF800. It supports the expansion and development of the forfaiting market by giving participants in international trade finance a dependable framework and a set of unambiguous, globally accepted norms. The industry is always changing, especially with the introduction of digital technology. To keep the URF relevant and effective in facilitating safe and effective forfaiting transactions, upgrades like the eURF are essential. The notion of "without recourse" is a crucial component of forfaiting agreements, denoting the inability of the buyer (the forfaiter) to pursue payment from the seller in the event that the debtor defaults.

The forfaiting procedure, which provides sellers with a certain level of protection and assurance by shifting the credit risk associated with the receivables, is based on this idea. The idea that a seller in a forfaiting transaction has no redress, however, is complex and deserves further investigation. The word "forfaiting" originates from the phrase "à forfait," which denotes a transaction without recourse. Practically, endorsements of negotiable documents characterized by "without recourse" or "sans recourse" strengthen this idea by shifting the risk of debtor non-payment from the seller to the facilitator. There are several exceptions to the Forfaiting Principle, such as in situations involving fraud, even if in most cases the seller has little remedy. Furthermore, it implicitly expects the main forfaiters—those who initiated the transaction—to ensure the legitimacy, enforceability, and legality of the receivables under their care.

The Uniform Rules for Forfaiting (URF800) set up a methodical way to figure out who to go to for help by outlining in Article 13 the exact situations in which each party should be contacted. In a forfaiting transaction, this "liability cascade" makes clear the obligations and possible liabilities of each party. Article 13 outlines several grounds for recourse against the first seller, typically the one closest to the obligee.

These reasons include fraud in the underlying transaction, failure to disclose material facts, and lack of sole legal possession of the claim. In accordance with market norms, primary forfaiters are responsible for guaranteeing transaction authenticity, and subsequent sellers are required to communicate information that is currently accessible. The recourse mechanism significantly impacts obtaining a "true sale" status under the relevant accounting rules. The legal transfer of the receivable and the distribution of risks and rewards determine this status, which in turn shapes the representation of the transaction in financial statements. International Financial Reporting Standards (IFRS 9) place more emphasis on the transfer of risks and benefits than does the US accounting standard (FAS 125), which stresses the need for legal transfer.

Article 13 of the URF restricts recourse to issues that are under the seller's control in order to comply with these criteria. A contract between the forfaiter and seller, the supply and review of pertinent documentation, the computation of the purchase price, and the collection of the debt from the debtor "without recourse" to the seller are all part of the main market forfaiting procedure.

To address the issues that arise from agreement to the collection, forfaiting is complicated and drawn out. Forfaiting is characterized by the "without recourse" concept, which protects sellers from credit risk. However, this principle is subject to restrictions and exceptions, particularly in cases of fraud or failure to meet specified duties. URF800's responsibility cascade offers a thorough framework for comprehending and handling these exceptions, ensuring honesty and integrity in the finance sector.

This methodical approach guarantees that forfaiting continues to be a dependable and efficient means of funding global commerce, as does compliance with pertinent legal and accounting norms. The basis of the forfaiting is the commercial agreement between the primary forfaiter, a financier specializing in forfaiting transactions, and the initial seller of the claim, usually an exporter. Several formats for this agreement have different details and requirements.

Let's dissect the essential components and factors in these kinds of agreements, taking into account suggested procedures such as those included in the Uniform Rules for Forfaiting (URF). A master agreement, which is frequently uncommitted, establishes the broad conditions that apply to future deals. A master agreement's specific transactions need an addendum or supplement that contains the specifics of each sale.

Single transaction agreements are a unique type of agreement, specifically designed to outline the terms of a single sale of receivables. In the past, these types of payments were customary to confirm the seller's financial capability. But when the market changed, these techniques became less common. Financiers are less willing to commit resources to unknown uses, and exporters now frequently offer deals for sale later in the process. The emphasis now is on making a profit, mostly from the discount that was given when the receivable was purchased.

Forfaiting agreements, whether or not they are subject to the URF, often cover a number of important topics. This calls for a precise understanding of the commitment to purchase and sell the receivables. An uncommitted master agreement outlines the terms and conditions for offering and approving suggested transactions. The agreement outlines the process of passing the payment claim from the seller to the forfaiter, including endorsement, assignment, and other methods, to ensure a smooth and lawful transfer of ownership. The agreement plays a crucial role in the transaction by outlining the documentation required from the seller for the underlying trade and the acceptable "availability date" for their supply. Specific pricing parameters, such as the discount percentage and any other costs, define each party's obligations and liabilities in the agreement, along with the circumstances under which claims may be brought, especially in extreme cases like fraud. It clarifies legal remedies and dispute resolution by establishing the legal framework and the jurisdiction that will apply to the agreement.

This list is not all-inclusive, but it does emphasize the essential elements that Forfaiting Agreements must cover in order to guarantee the transaction's clarity, fairness, and legality. The simplicity of these agreements and the URF's cooperation in providing templates and guidelines make forfaiting a desirable financing alternative for international commerce. Through these structured agreements, exporters and forfaiters can make the best use of their working capital and handle the risks that come with collecting money from overseas customers. Clear and quick transactions accomplish this.

One of the most important steps in the forfaiting process is looking over the documentation pertaining to the payment claim and the underlying transaction. This examination guarantees the transaction's validity, enforceability, and completeness. It is the responsibility of the buyer (Primary Forfaiter) to ascertain which paperwork is required to certify the payment claim and any credit support (such as guarantees and avals). This entails determining any supporting documentation—such as side letters or assignments—that is required in order to transfer the claim or enforce it. The transaction requires proof to validate the signatories' legitimacy.

Forfaiting transactions require a more comprehensive review, in contrast to letters of credit (LoCs), where papers must merely conform "on their face" with the credit standards. We must examine documents more closely, considering them as investments, to ensure their effectiveness and the forfaiters' ability to collect repayment from the debtor.

The main market evaluation is quite thorough and goes beyond the surface level to evaluate the legitimacy, enforceability, transferability, and legality of papers. Part of the reason for this thorough analysis is the requirement to adhere to anti-terrorist funding, anti-money laundering, and know your customer (KYC) rules. Although the need for such thorough inspection may not be as strong in the secondary market, where deals between financiers take place, comparable requirements of inspection are nonetheless in place to guarantee the integrity of the exchanged instruments.

The Uniform Rules for Forfaiting (URF), which aim to achieve equilibrium, grant broad discretion to the primary forfaiter in the primary market. It places emphasis on important forfaiting (URFng transferability, the need to pay without set-off, and the validity and enforceability of papers). If forfaiters have reason to doubt a document's authenticity or legality, the URF says they can reject it even without proof. This is in line with how markets normally work. The URF stipulates that forfaiters must provide paperwork in a suitable format by a designated "availability date," which could be considered instantly available, meaning within ten business days of signing the purchase agreement.

Forfaiting transactions include a complex and crucial document evaluation procedure that requires a delicate balancing act between meticulous scrutiny and operational efficiency. While retaining discretion and flexibility, forfaiters can perform due diligence by following the guidelines established by the URF. This thorough approach to documentation supports the integrity and efficient operation of international trade finance by guaranteeing that forfaiting continues to be a dependable and safe financing technique.

CHAPTER 3 CASHING IN ON THE OPPORTUNITY: THE DYNAMIC WORLD OF RECEIVABLES FINANCE

A crucial stage in a forfaiting transaction is calculating the purchase price, which establishes the instant cash value that the seller gets in exchange for the forfaiter's payment claims. This section delves into the process of determining this price, focusing specifically on the concept of discounting, which remains the primary method for forfaiters to profit from these transactions. We will also discuss the unique situations where the seller receives payment "without recourse" and the nuances of making payments "under reserve." This approach discounts the nominal value of the payment claim using a basic, non-compounding procedure. It gives the seller's net value (NV) in an easy-to-understand formula that takes into account the nominal value (N), the discount rate (R), and the number of days (D) before maturity. A $1,000,000 payment claim, for instance, with an 850-day maturity and a 10% straight discount, would have a $763,888.89 net value. This approach, in contrast to simple discounting, takes the discount rate into account over the whole duration without compounding. The computation modifies the claim's nominal value by a factor that takes into account the discount rate that is applied during the period until maturity.

Due to the varied handling of the discount rate, the claim's net value under the identical conditions would be $808,988.76, which is a larger net value than under simple discounting. It takes the discount rate into account over the whole duration without compounding. The computation modifies the claim's nominal value by factoring in the applied discount rate until maturity. Due to the varied handling of the discount rate, the claim's net value under the identical conditions would be $808,988.76, which is a larger net value than under simple discounting. Compounding the discount rate yearly provides a more sophisticated method for longer tenures. Using the compounded rate, this technique divides the time into complete years and a final partial year. The compounded method reflects the impact of compounding on the discount calculation, yielding a net value of $797,770.88 for the $1,000,000 claim that expires in 850 days at a 10% annual discount rate.

Payments made in forfaiting transactions are paid "without recourse" to the seller, which means that in the event of a debtor failing, the forfaiter takes on the credit risk and is unable to pursue recovery from the seller. This agreement, which gives sellers a risk-free way to settle their receivables, is essential to forfaiting. Payments may occasionally be paid "under reserve," especially if some components of the transaction—typically the documentation—are not entirely satisfactory. Under this agreement, the seller agrees to make amends on any deficiencies, and the forfaiter can move forward with payment on that understanding by a given date. If the problems remain unresolved, the seller may be required to repay the forfaiter. Although less popular because of the difficulties involved—such as the requirement that the forfaiter give the seller access to a credit line—it provides a way to move forward with transactions that may otherwise be postponed. In order to demand payment from the obligor, forfaiters must make sure they have the required documents from the vendor. This encompasses not only the financial instruments but also any additional documents required by regional laws, such as proof of paid stamp taxes or local government registration.

The methods used to determine the purchase price in forfaiting transactions strike a compromise between giving the seller fair value and making sure the forfaiter is profitable. Selecting between compounded discounting, simple discount to yield, and straight discount allows for flexibility in connecting the transaction structure with the anticipated results for both parties. The clauses that let money be paid "without recourse" and, less often, "under reserve" show how complicated the duties and risks are that come with forfaiting deals. In the trade finance sector, the secondary market for forfaiting is essential for supplying flexibility and liquidity.

Institutions can more effectively manage their risk and capital by selling forfaiting transactions initiated by primary forfaiters. The following provides a thorough explanation of the traits, paperwork, liabilities, and more elements associated with the forfaiting secondary market: The secondary market, primarily an interbank marketplace, creates long chains of transactions through the sale and potential resale of transactions initiated by primary forfaiters. Some organizations work in one primary market, while others cover both. This diversity enhances the market's depth and liquidity. In many nations, the secondary market typically summarizes verbal agreements with a written confirmation, making the paperwork far less complicated than in the primary market. Many jurisdictions typically initiate negotiations over the phone and then confirm the terms in writing, ensuring they accurately reflect the economic parameters discussed verbally. But in other nations, like Germany, commercial agreements must be in writing. The URF supports both written and verbal transaction agreements, provides confirmation forms, and specifies the procedures and due dates for confirmation agreements. In the secondary market, this uniform method contributes to efficiency and clarity. Apart from fraud, the extent of each seller's obligation or recourse to their buyer in the secondary market has historically been a little hazy.

Generally, buyers should exercise caution, except in specific situations outlined by the URF. The URF says that sellers on the secondary market are mainly responsible if they don't transfer a claim with full and clear title or if they don't tell relevant facts that change the existence of the payment claim. The URF aims to increase uniformity and clarity in the secondary market's expectations of liability.

By the time a transaction enters the secondary market, its paperwork is typically complete and unchangeable. A primary financier, with insight into the requirements of the secondary market, can greatly influence the ease of selling a transaction later. According to the URF, the only grounds for rejecting a document are those related to authenticity, enforceability, legal validity, transferability, duty to pay without set-off, and certain restrictions specified in the confirmation.

This approach aims to strike a compromise between market discipline and wide discretion when rejecting materials. We also cover the procedure that sellers may use to transfer any rights of recourse against previous sellers, which can simplify claims and reduce the risk and complexity of "chain of mirror" disputes. These transfers can have a big impact on the dynamics of recourse and require the approval of all parties. With the help of the URF's defined procedures and streamlined paperwork, the secondary market for forfaiting offers crucial prospects for risk management and liquidity. It is imperative for players to comprehend the intricacies of responsibility, paperwork requirements, and the possibility of recourse rights transfer in order to operate efficiently in this market. The rules set forth by the URF are essential to preserving justice and order and guaranteeing the seamless and effective operation of the secondary market.

Fueling Commerce with the Power of Bank Loans

Bank loans make up a sizable portion of lending portfolios for banks, especially those intended to support trade activities (trade loans) and those made possible by the SWIFT system (SWIFT loans). These loans create receivables in which banks function as creditors and borrowers as debtors. Comprehending the structure and transferability of these loans is crucial for understanding their role in trade finance and the broader financial system. To enhance our comprehension of their dynamics.

Usually, banks offer these short-term loans to promote foreign trade. Among other purposes, they can finance the acquisition of commodities before their resale, provide liquidity for manufacturing procedures, or bridge payment gaps in export transactions. The SWIFT (Society for Worldwide Interbank Financial Telecommunication) system organizes and distributes these loans over an international network, ensuring swift and secure bank-to-bank communication. The use of SWIFT enables effective international loan and repayment procedures. Loan agreements contain the terms, conditions, and payback commitments for these loans. These crucial documents lay out the terms of the loan, the lender-borrower relationship, the financial commitments, interest rates, repayment plans, and any covenants or limitations that apply.

Similar to other non-negotiable receivables, parties may assign the rights to payments under bank loans. Through this technique, the original lender (also known as the assignor) can transfer the debt obligation and the right to repayment from the borrower to a different organization (also known as the assignee). Sub-participation is an alternate way to transfer the economic interest in a loan without officially changing the lender on file. These agreements allow for the sharing or transfer of loan risk—including the funding obligation—to other banks or financial institutions. Even though they don't deal directly with the borrower, these participants implicitly participate in the loan's risk and return profile by agreement with the original lender. Sub-participation may be funded, in which case the participant gives money to the original lender, or unfunded, in which case the participant promises to pay a portion of the losses in the event that the borrower defaults without contributing money up front.

Before transferring loans, whether by assignment or sub-participation, it is important to carefully think about the laws that govern them. This includes any restrictions on transfers that come from the original loan agreement or local laws. Additionally, operational factors are crucial, particularly when multiple institutions participate in or transfer loans. These factors include managing borrower relationships and overseeing loan repayments. Bank and SWIFT loans play a crucial role in facilitating international trade by providing borrowers with the necessary funding. Banks can better manage risk and liquidity by being able to transfer these loans through assignment or sub-participation agreements. This lets them support international trade while keeping their lending portfolios diverse and simple to manage. To guarantee successful implementation, however, one must have a comprehensive awareness of legal, regulatory, and operational considerations due to the complexity of loan transfer methods.

Loan agreements carefully record the terms and circumstances of these loans. These crucial documents lay forth the terms of the loan arrangement between the lender and the borrower. They provide information on the loan's financial responsibilities, interest rates, repayment plans, and any relevant covenants or stipulations.

Other parties may receive the rights to payments under bank loans, as is the case with all non-negotiable receivables. The original lender (assignor) can transfer the debt obligation and right to repayment from the borrower to the assignee using this method.

CHAPTER 3   CASHING IN ON THE OPPORTUNITY: THE DYNAMIC WORLD OF RECEIVABLES FINANCE

Sub-participation, which can take two forms, is an alternate way to transfer the economic interest in a loan without legally altering the lender on file. In Funded Sub-Participation, the participant provides funds to the initial lender; in Unfunded Sub-Participation, the participant agrees to cover a portion of the borrower's default losses without providing any initial funds; and in Sub-Participation, participants establish a contract with the original lender, avoiding direct interaction with the borrower, thereby indirectly contributing to the loan's risk and return profile.

The legal structure regulating debt transfers, whether by assignment or subparticipation, must be carefully considered. This covers any transferability limitations imposed by the original loan contract or by applicable local laws. Additionally, operational factors are crucial. This is especially true when multiple institutions participate in or transfer loans. These factors include managing borrower relationships and administering loan repayments.

Banks typically extend trade loans, which are short-term loans that support international trade. They are designed to meet various needs, such as financing the purchase of goods before resale. These loans assist companies in purchasing goods intended for sale in diverse markets.

Ensuring liquidity for production processes is crucial because trade finance instruments provide the capital needed to keep production lines running. They are particularly beneficial for manufacturers engaged in export, effectively bridging payment gaps in export transactions by covering the financial gap between shipping goods and receiving payment.

The SWIFT system, or the Society for Worldwide Interbank Financial Telecommunication, plays a key role here because it facilitates structured and disbursed loans through a global network, ensuring rapid and secure communication between banks. This global networking is critical for efficient international lending and repayment processes and plays a vital role in facilitating trade by providing necessary financing to borrowers engaged in international commerce. The ability to transfer these loans through assignment or sub-participation agreements enhances liquidity and risk management options for banks. This allows them to maintain a diversified and manageable lending portfolio while supporting global trade activities. However, the complexities of these loan transfer mechanisms necessitate a thorough understanding of legal, regulatory, and operational factors to ensure successful execution. These strategies not only support individual banking operations but also contribute to the stability and fluidity of global trade finance.

CHAPTER 3   CASHING IN ON THE OPPORTUNITY: THE DYNAMIC WORLD OF RECEIVABLES FINANCE

Bridging the Gap Between Insurance Companies and Financial Guarantees

In the complex world of global trade finance, insurance plays a crucial role by enabling businesses to manage risks and ensure smooth transactions. To fund trade, issue guarantees, credit letters, and forfait receivables, banks depend on a range of insurance products. The collaboration between banks and insurers is not without difficulties, though. Problems including information gaps, administrative roadblocks, and internal obstacles frequently impede these exchanges, reducing the effectiveness of the collaboration.

The insurance industry is one noteworthy sector where potential and reliability coexist. With surety, insurance providers ensure businesses that they will fulfill their contractual obligations to third parties. This is important because a surety bond may protect the project beneficiaries' financial interests in industries like construction. While surety bonds have long been a mainstay of the insurance industry, bank-led financial products and services have only recently started to use them in a significant way since the early 2000s.

At first, insurance firms operated only in conventional markets and industries. However, when banks began to cover certain markets by themselves, things started to change. This gave insurance firms an opportunity to break into a significant market that was previously dominated by banks and diversify their offerings beyond standard credit or political risk insurance. It's a big step forward for trade finance that these two financial institutions have formed a strong partnership. Together, they could offer more advanced and all-encompassing solutions that meet both assurance and banking needs.

According to the International Credit Insurance & Surety Association (ICISA), a surety bond is a contract that an insurance company makes to guarantee financial repayment in the event that the principal, such as a contractor, defaults on their obligations. The two main categories of surety bonds are contract surety bonds, typically used in the construction industry as proof of a contractor's adherence to the terms of a construction contract, and commercial surety bonds, which cover obligations related to non-construction-related agreements, such as compliance with state laws and regulations.

Suretyship has changed a lot over the years. It used to be simple promises from one person to another, but now there are more complicated agreements with three parties: the obligee (or beneficiary) who wants the guarantee, the principal who needs the bond, and the surety who gives it. This framework is especially crucial for situations demanding a high degree of certainty and compliance, such as public building projects.

The following might serve as an illustration of how a standard surety bond would operate in real life: A government organization, i.e., the beneficiary, grants a construction business, i.e., the principal, a contract to build a roadway; an insurance firm, i.e., the surety, provides a surety bond to the construction company; this bond ensures that the building business will carry out its obligations under the contract; and finally, the insurance company reimburses the government agency for any monetary losses in the event that the construction business is unable to finish the project on schedule. It is straightforward to see that surety bonds are an add-on to the main obligation, which is often a contract, guaranteeing the principal's performance under predetermined circumstances. Typically, the bond's whole amount serves as the underlying obligation; crucially, the bond remains unrevocable as long as the underlying commitments remain unfulfilled, ensuring continued performance and compliance.

In addition to fulfilling their contractual obligations, they must pay the bond price, defend the surety against any claims, and supply all required documentation. The beneficiary must adhere to the contract's terms, inform the surety of any significant changes or issues, and transfer the instrument to the surety upon completion of the contract. The surety is also required to handle claims professionally and not pay the principal if they have a favorable defense.

This essential tool for contemporary business offers a safety net that makes compliance and trust easier in major initiatives. Through comprehension of the roles and responsibilities delineated in surety contracts, corporations may enhance their risk management capabilities and perform their contractual duties with assurance, and at the same time, provide strong assistance in intricate, high-value transactions across sectors as they develop further.

Surety bonds are essential for improving the dependability and effectiveness of project executions and contractual obligations in a variety of industries. They benefit project owners, contractors, and other relevant stakeholders greatly by reducing performance risks and pre-qualifying contractors. By guaranteeing that the surety business will take over and expedite project completion in the event of a contractor's default, they primarily assist the project owner by lowering the level of uncertainty surrounding project completion. This assurance ensures strict adherence to the project timeframe and protects the project owner from financial damages.

CHAPTER 3   CASHING IN ON THE OPPORTUNITY: THE DYNAMIC WORLD OF RECEIVABLES FINANCE

The selection of contractors is subject to an extra level of scrutiny when a surety business is involved. Surety providers thoroughly evaluate the contractor's capacity to effectively execute the project in terms of both financial stability and technical proficiency. Then, pre-qualification removes unqualified competitors and improves the caliber of bids received by providing the project owner with reassurance that the chosen contractor is fully capable of meeting the contractual responsibilities. Surety bonds are similar to a credit line for contractors in that they give businesses the opportunity to compete on and win contracts that they may not otherwise be able to without a surety bond, especially those related to public projects. Construction firms can boost their portfolio and credibility with this skill, which can help them grow and survive.

They take on a variety of forms based on specific circumstances and requirements. If a contractor secures the contract, bid bonds ensure their ability to fulfill their obligations and secure performance bonds, which guarantee the project's completion in compliance with the contract's conditions. Payment bonds ensure the payment of suppliers and subcontractors, thereby preserving the integrity of the supply chain. Supply bonds and warranty bonds, respectively, meet specific supply chain and post-completion warranty requirements. There are more types of commercial surety bonds than just fiduciary and judicial bonds. These include permit and license bonds, which are necessary for businesses to run legally, as well as fiduciary and judicial bonds that protect the rights and obligations in those areas. Last but not least, tax bonds and customs ensure that businesses engaged in international commerce comply with tax laws and regulations.

Bank credit analysis and surety bond underwriting are comparable procedures. The process involves a comprehensive evaluation of the project's viability, the financial stability of the contractor, and the availability of collateral. Conducting a thorough investigation mitigates the risks associated with the contractor's potential default. Surety insurance providers must adhere to a strict regulatory framework that is defined by the European Union's Solvency II standards and a number of national laws that apply these requirements in certain localities. This regulatory framework permits certain national-level flexibility while guaranteeing that insurance firms function under a uniform set of regulations.

Insurance firms need to apply for a license in order to sell certain insurance products under Solvency II, the EU's core regulatory framework for the insurance sector. Solvency II increases the amount of capital that EU insurance companies must retain to lower their risk of insolvency. This framework permits an insurer to provide certain categories of insurance products, including surety bonds. The Directive 2009/138/EC from the European Parliament and the Council, dated November 25, 2009, makes it clear which non-life insurance class groups are used for Article 159. For surety bonds, "Class 14: Credit Insurance and Class 15: Suretyship" are relevant. These classifications specify the kinds of risk coverages that insurance providers may offer, encompassing suretyship as well as other credit-related insurance products.

Nations translate EU laws into national legislation differently, allowing for varying applicability and interpretations based on local legal and commercial frameworks. The Financial Services and Markets Act 2000 (Regulated Activities) Order 2001 stipulates that suretyship encompasses fidelity bonds, performance bonds, administration bonds, bail bonds, and other comparable contracts of guarantee, provided they impact non-banking organizations. The Luxembourg statute of December 7, 2015, which deals with the insurance industry, also provides guidelines for the regulation of suretyship within its jurisdiction.

It's important to realize that even though insurance rules govern suretyship, suretyship contracts are not the same as insurance contracts; they are instead referred to as "insurance activities." This distinction holds significance as it influences the capital requirements for surety bonds, the claims-handling process, and the underwriting of these bonds. Unlike typical insurance, surety bonds guarantee the execution of a contract or duty from one party to another, and correct assessment eliminates any risk of loss.

When underwriting surety, insurance firms have to carefully traverse these regulatory seas. They must manage their portfolios in a way that complies with legal requirements, maintain compliance with both European and national rules, and comprehend the particular insurance classes that apply to their surety products. Effective compliance not only mitigates the risk of fines from the authorities but also positions these businesses as reliable issuers of surety bonds, thereby fostering confidence in markets that mandate surety bonds.

The regulatory framework governing insurance firms' surety underwriting creates a controlled and safe environment that limits how these businesses may function and provide surety bonds in various countries. Insurance firms must comprehend and abide by these rules in order to operate profitably in the surety market.

The regulatory framework that followed the 2008 financial crisis dramatically altered the banking industry's operating environment, especially with regard to capital use and risk management. Banks have had to reconsider their approaches to capital allocation and risk reduction since Basel III/CRD IV introduced stricter capital requirements. In this regard, surety bonds have become an indispensable instrument for banks, serving as a means of capital relief as well as strategic company development and risk mitigation.

Surety bonds, particularly those falling under the contract and commercial surety classes, have become essential to banks' operations because they enable them to cover a wide variety of obligations, from performance guarantees to standby letters of credit. These tools play a crucial role in ensuring that parties fulfill their obligations, thereby reducing the financial risk associated with defaults.

Capital relief is one of the main benefits of surety bonds for banks. The majority of bank surety covers are CRR compliant, which can result in considerable capital utilization reductions of up to 80%. This compliance is important because it complies with regulatory requirements to uphold specific liquidity and capital ratios, allowing banks to use their capital more wisely and take on more lending and investing operations without unnecessarily raising their risk exposure.

Working together, banks and insurance companies in the surety space not only help banks manage risk but also provide them with strategic advantages such as **increased credit capacity**, as financial institutions are better equipped to service valuable customers as they can take on bigger projects and transactions without using up all of their capital. As a result of having access to surety products, banks may be able to improve their competitive position by serving new customer segments and breaking into new markets. They may also be able to keep customers longer and make them happier by improving their connections with customers through better client needs management. Finally, using insurance as a risk transfer tool may help them manage their portfolios and maximize their risk-weighted assets.

In order to guarantee mutual understanding and clarity between banks and insurers, operationalizing assurance in banking requires thorough and organized paperwork. This comprises the **master risk participation agreement (MRPA),** which serves as the framework agreement that establishes the terms and circumstances for the issuance of guarantees and the filing of claims, and the **transaction-specific agreements**, i.e., records that include the particulars of a single transaction, such as the terms, payments, and circumstances.

The International Trade and Forfaiting Association (ITFA) further standardized these procedures with the creation of the ITFA Surety MRPA, specifically designed for insurance firms to participate in unfunded risk. This standardized agreement speeds up negotiations and ensures compliance with regulatory requirements, which facilitates effective collaboration between banks and insurers. The incorporation of such a tool into banking operations offers a comprehensive solution to the issues caused by modern financial rules and market needs. Banks can use surety bonds to grow into new markets, strengthen their operational skills, and boost risk management procedures, in addition to guaranteeing compliance with strict capital requirements. Thus, this mutually beneficial partnership between banks and insurance providers is evidence of how the financial services industry is changing and how strategic innovation and teamwork promote efficiency and expansion.

Balance the Books: Weighing the Pros and Cons of Accounts Receivable Financing

Businesses may manage their cash flow and obtain finance rapidly through accounts receivable financing, also known as factoring, by selling their past-due bills to a third party at a discounted rate. To help you better grasp this funding strategy's ramifications and applicability for firms, we've broken it down into its advantages and disadvantages below.

The primary advantage of AR financing is the rapid rise in cash flow.

Companies may get cash fast—often in a matter of days—which is essential for paying for urgent requirements like payroll, inventory, and other running expenses without having to wait for clients to settle their bills.

In contrast to conventional loans, which usually demand collateral, AR financing employs the actual outstanding invoices as security. For tiny enterprises that do not have many valuable assets to pledge as security, this is very advantageous.

Small businesses with poor credit scores or no credit history may qualify for AR funding even though they might not be eligible for standard bank loans. Factors often give greater weight to the invoice holders' creditworthiness and less weight to the company selling the invoices.

Companies provide the factoring business with the task of selling the invoices to recover debts. You might be able to save time and money on late payments by taking this action.

Factoring agreements provide organizations with flexibility through their customizable form. Businesses can better manage money by selling invoices when and how.

However, the expense of AR financing is one of its main disadvantages. Fees charged by factors can differ greatly, usually based on the credit risk attached to the receivable. In the long term, this choice will cost more because of these costs, which might be significant when compared to alternative financing options.

CHAPTER 3   CASHING IN ON THE OPPORTUNITY: THE DYNAMIC WORLD OF RECEIVABLES FINANCE

It's possible for certain companies to rely too much on factoring to handle their cash flow, which can result in a loop where they sell their receivables and never quite make up lost revenue. This may hinder long-term financial planning and growth.

In the event that the factoring agreement is set up as "recourse factoring," the company that sells the invoices can still be liable if the client doesn't pay. This increases the risk since the company may have to pay back the factor for the overdue invoice.

A company's connection with its clients may suffer if it uses a third party to collect debts. The reputation of the company may suffer if the factoring company uses forceful collection tactics.Long-term contract obligations and possible hidden costs are requirements of some factoring providers, which can make a company's financial management more difficult. Businesses should carefully review and comprehend all conditions before signing a factoring agreement.

Even though immediate liquidity and streamlined credit procedures are two major advantages of accounts receivable financing, there are expenses and risks associated with it that may not make it appropriate for every type of organization. Businesses that are thinking about this kind of funding should carefully evaluate their cash flow requirements, their clients' creditworthiness, and the conditions that factoring companies provide. To choose the best course of action for managing their finances, firms should ideally weigh the advantages and disadvantages of factoring in alternative financing choices.

Summary

The important function of Receivables Finance in world business and financial stability is investigated in this chapter. Beginning "The Lifecycle of Receivables," it emphasizes the significance of accounts receivable in trade finance. "Enhanced Quality for Optimal Financing" addresses the demand of dependable receivables for bettering financial results. "Conditional vs. Unconditional Receivables" answers the dangers and flexibility of receivables agreements.

The chapter then looks at the change from conventional approaches to digital solutions in "From Traditional Methods to Digital Horizons" and emphasizes how receivables may be customized to fit buyer desire in "Tailoring for Buyer's Flexibility." Examined with an eye on liquidity generation via securitization in "The Dynamics of Transferability and Tradability" are the complexity of "Capital Adequacy" and "Legal Nuances of Payment Instruments in International Trade."

CHAPTER 3   CASHING IN ON THE OPPORTUNITY: THE DYNAMIC WORLD OF RECEIVABLES FINANCE

Furthermore discussed are their functions in reducing buyer failure risks and guaranteeing independence in payment guarantees: "Strategic Importance of Credit Enhancement" and "Credit Insurance." "True Sale vs. Secured Financing explores these differences." While "From Tradition to Digital Innovation" emphasizes the part negotiable instruments play in the digital era, "Understanding Trade Debt" discusses bankruptcy and restructuring ramifications. In "Balance the Books," the chapter ends with a discussion on controlling risks and safeguarding receivables, thereby enhancing worldwide trade, and balancing the benefits and drawbacks of accounts receivable finance.

CHAPTER 4

The Interplay Between Banks and Stakeholders in Trade Finance

Trade finance serves as the backbone of global commerce, enabling businesses to navigate the complexities of cross-border transactions. Banks and various stakeholders collaborate within this ecosystem to facilitate seamless trade, manage risks, and unlock economic opportunities. This chapter explores the pivotal roles banks and stakeholders play in trade finance, the evolution of their contributions, the impact of digital transformation, and the challenges and opportunities this landscape presents.

Understanding Trade Finance and Its Ecosystem

Trade finance encompasses a variety of financial instruments and services designed to bridge the trust gap between importers and exporters. Its significance lies in providing liquidity, risk mitigation, and operational support to businesses engaged in global trade. Diverse participants, each fulfilling a specialized function, compose this ecosystem to ensure the smooth operation of international commerce.

Banks remain central to this ecosystem, providing essential services such as letters of credit, guarantees, and trade loans. However, they are not the only actors. Other stakeholders include trade finance companies that offer tailored financial solutions, insurers and export credit agencies that manage risks, and technology providers that enable efficient processes through digital platforms.

CHAPTER 4   THE INTERPLAY BETWEEN BANKS AND STAKEHOLDERS IN TRADE FINANCE

The Role of Banks in Trade Finance

Banks are the cornerstone of trade finance, acting as intermediaries, risk mitigators, and providers of essential financial products. Their role extends beyond financing to fostering trust and stability in the global trade network.

- Bank Intermediation in Trade Transactions

    Banks facilitate trade by offering instruments such as letters of credit (L/Cs), trade loans, and performance guarantees. These tools reduce payment risks and provide the necessary working capital to exporters and importers. For instance, letters of credit guarantee payment upon meeting specific shipment conditions, fostering confidence among trading partners.

- Risk Mitigation and Trust Building

    One of the critical challenges in trade is reconciling the opposing interests of exporters and importers. Exporters desire immediate payment, whereas importers aim to postpone payment until the delivery of goods. Banks bridge this divide through mechanisms like letters of credit, which assure exporters of payment and importers of timely receipt of goods. This function not only minimizes risk but also facilitates trade in high-risk regions or industries.

- Supporting Emerging Markets

    Global banks play a crucial role in bridging the access to trade finance gap in regions like Asia and Africa. Initiatives such as the Asian Development Bank's Trade Finance Program highlight the importance of collaboration between international banks and local financial institutions to stimulate trade and economic growth.

Stakeholders in Trade Finance

The trade finance ecosystem involves a complex network of participants, each contributing unique expertise and resources. Their collaboration is integral to ensuring that global trade flows smoothly and securely.

- Importers and Exporters: At the core of the trade finance ecosystem are the businesses engaged in cross-border transactions. These entities rely on financial and risk management solutions to execute trade efficiently and cost-effectively.

- Trade Finance Companies: Trade finance companies complement traditional banking by offering specialized services, such as invoice discounting, factoring, and supply chain finance. These entities often step in where banks are unable or unwilling to provide services, addressing gaps in the market.

- Insurers and Export Credit Agencies: Insurers and export credit agencies (ECAs) add an essential layer of security to trade finance by covering risks such as non-payment, political instability, or currency fluctuations. This risk coverage is particularly valuable for businesses operating in volatile markets.

- Technology Providers: With trade finance becoming increasingly digitalized, technology providers are transforming the landscape. Platforms leveraging blockchain, artificial intelligence, and machine learning enhance efficiency, transparency, and risk management, reshaping traditional processes.

The Evolution of Banks in Trade Finance

The role of banks in trade finance has evolved significantly over time, shaped by changes in global trade patterns, technological advancements, and regulatory frameworks.

In the medieval period, European merchants faced significant challenges in conducting international trade due to risks like piracy, political instability, and the lack of standardized financial instruments. To mitigate these risks, early forms of trade finance emerged, such as bills of exchange and letters of credit, which allowed merchants to conduct transactions without the immediate exchange of cash. These instruments were crucial in facilitating trade across different regions and currencies.

By the 16th century, merchant banks began to dominate trade finance. Institutions like the Medici Bank in Italy provided services that included financing trade ventures, currency exchange, and the issuance of letters of credit. These banks played a central role in the expansion of international trade by offering financial products that reduced the risks associated with long-distance commerce.

The Industrial Revolution in the 18th and 19th centuries led to a significant increase in international trade. Banks expanded their services to include trade finance products such as documentary collections and trade loans. The establishment of global financial centers, notably London, facilitated the standardization of trade finance practices and the development of international banking networks.

The 20th century brought about significant changes in trade finance due to geopolitical events and technological advancements. The two World Wars and the Great Depression disrupted international trade, leading to the establishment of institutions like the International Monetary Fund (IMF) and the World Bank to stabilize the global economy. Post-World War II, the Bretton Woods system established fixed exchange rates, which facilitated international trade and finance.

The late 20th and early 21st centuries have seen rapid digitalization in trade finance. Technologies such as electronic data interchange (EDI), blockchain, and artificial intelligence have transformed traditional banking practices. Banks now offer digital platforms for trade finance, enabling real-time tracking of transactions, reducing paperwork, and enhancing security. These advancements have made trade finance more accessible to small and medium-sized enterprises (SMEs) and have facilitated the growth of global supply chains.

Modern Transformations

In the past, banks primarily facilitated trade through traditional instruments like letters of credit and documentary collections. These paper-based processes, while effective, were cumbersome and time-intensive. The establishment of global systems like SWIFT in the 1970s modernized communication between banks, paving the way for faster, more secure transactions.

Today, banks offer a broader range of services, including supply chain finance and factoring, which address the cash flow challenges faced by businesses. Additionally, technological integration has revolutionized trade finance. Blockchain enables real-time information sharing, reducing delays and errors, while AI automates tasks like credit scoring and risk assessment.

Impact of Digitalization on Trade Finance

Digitalization has brought about a paradigm shift in trade finance, enhancing efficiency, reducing costs, and expanding access to underserved markets.

- Streamlined Operations: The adoption of digital platforms has replaced traditional paper-based systems with streamlined processes. Tools like electronic bills of lading (eBL) and automated document management systems expedite transactions, reduce errors, and enhance overall efficiency.

- Enhanced Risk Management: Real-time access to data enables banks to monitor supply chain risks and evaluate creditworthiness more effectively. Advanced analytics and AI-powered systems detect fraud and ensure compliance with regulatory standards, reducing operational risks.

- Bridging the Trade Finance Gap: One of the most significant impacts of digitalization is its potential to address the trade finance gap, estimated at $1.7 trillion globally. Digital tools enable banks to assess the creditworthiness of small and medium-sized enterprises (SMEs) more accurately, allowing these businesses to access financing that was previously out of reach.

- Challenges in Digital Transformation: While digitalization offers numerous benefits, it also presents challenges. High implementation costs, cybersecurity risks, and a lack of standardization across platforms are significant barriers. Additionally, integrating new technologies with legacy systems requires substantial investment and expertise.

Preparing Employees for Digital Trade Finance

The successful adoption of digital trade finance solutions depends on a skilled workforce. Training programs must address the technological and operational changes brought about by digitization.

Digital Learning Platforms

Banks can use digital learning platforms to deliver flexible, on-demand training. Scenario-based modules simulate real-world trade finance scenarios, enabling employees to apply their knowledge effectively.

Continuous Upskilling

Regular updates to training programs ensure that employees stay abreast of the latest technological advancements and industry best practices. Collaborative learning environments foster knowledge sharing across departments.

Change Management

Implementing digital solutions requires a cultural shift. Clear communication of the benefits of digital tools and targeted training sessions on emerging technologies can help employees adapt to new workflows.

Several prominent banking associations play a crucial role in the trade finance sector, providing advocacy, setting industry standards, and offering educational resources. Key organizations include:

- **The Bankers Association for Finance and Trade (BAFT):** It is a prominent global financial services association that focuses on international transaction banking. It offers advocacy, thought leadership, education, and a global forum for professionals in trade finance, payments, and compliance. BAFT focuses on areas such as trade finance, payments, and compliance, providing resources like standardized legal documentation and policy updates.

- **International Chamber of Commerce (ICC):** The ICC's Banking Commission is a vital component of the trade finance landscape. It develops universally accepted rules and guidelines, such as the Uniform Customs and Practice for Documentary Credits (UCP 600), which standardize international trade practices. The ICC also offers dispute resolution services and provides training to enhance the skills of trade finance professionals.

- **International Trade and Forfaiting Association (ITFA):** ITFA is a global trade association for companies, financial institutions, and intermediaries engaged in trade and forfaiting. It promotes best practices, provides networking opportunities, and offers education on trade finance products and techniques. ITFA also engages with regulatory bodies to advocate for favorable trade finance policies.

- **Euro Banking Association (EBA):** The EBA is an industry forum for the European payments industry, focusing on the development of pan-European payment infrastructures and practices. While its primary focus is on payments, the EBA also addresses trade finance topics, particularly in relation to digitalization and regulatory developments

- **UK Finance:** UK Finance is a trade association representing the banking and financial services sector in the UK. It provides insights into international trade, offering guidance on trade finance, international payments, and foreign exchange services. UK Finance also engages with policymakers to advocate for a favorable business environment for trade finance.

- **Indian Banks' Association (IBA):** The IBA represents the banking industry in India, including public sector banks, private sector banks, and foreign banks operating in India. It addresses various aspects of banking, including trade finance, by providing a platform for discussions, policy advocacy, and the development of best practices within the Indian banking sector.

Established in 1991, the European Bank for Reconstruction and Development (EBRD) is an international financial institution that supports the transition of former Eastern Bloc countries toward market-oriented economies. Over time, the EBRD has expanded its operations to more than 30 countries across Central Europe, Central Asia, the Middle East, and North Africa.

Popular Publications by Key Trade Finance Organizations

Trade finance organizations such as BAFT, ICC, EBA, and EBRD regularly publish influential reports, guidelines, and thought leadership papers. These publications shape industry practices, promote standardization, and address emerging challenges in trade finance.

Bankers Association for Finance and Trade (BAFT)

BAFT is known for its global advocacy in transaction banking and trade finance. Its publications focus on industry standards, innovation, and compliance.

- BAFT Master Participation Agreement (MPA): A standardized framework for trade finance transactions. It helps banks and non-bank financial institutions collaborate efficiently on risk sharing in trade finance. Globally, people have widely adopted the MPA to streamline processes.

- Trade Finance Principles: Developed jointly with the International Chamber of Commerce (ICC), these principles set out best practices for managing trade finance transactions, including guarantees, documentary credits, and supply chain finance.

- Annual Global Trade Industry Report: This report provides insights into trade finance trends, the impact of technology, regulatory updates, and evolving customer needs.

International Chamber of Commerce (ICC)

The ICC's Banking Commission is one of the most influential bodies in trade finance. It has set global standards for trade and banking operations for over a century.

- Uniform Customs and Practice for Documentary Credits (UCP 600):

    A globally accepted rulebook for documentary credit transactions, used by banks and corporations worldwide to ensure consistency and reliability in letters of credit.

- ICC Trade Register Report: An annual publication offering data-driven insights into the risks and performance of trade finance instruments. It is an essential resource for banks to evaluate trade finance portfolios.

- Incoterms® Rules: These internationally recognized terms define the responsibilities of buyers and sellers in the delivery of goods. The latest version, Incoterms® 2020, reflects updates relevant to global trade practices.

- Guide to Digital Trade: A forward-looking publication that addresses digitalization challenges in trade finance and provides practical guidance on implementing digital trade solutions.

Euro Banking Association (EBA)

The EBA specializes in advancing pan-European banking infrastructure, with publications that emphasize innovation in payments and trade finance.

- EBAday Reports: Published annually, these reports provide insights from the EBAday conferences, focusing on the future of payments, trade finance innovation, and regulatory developments.

- Digital Trade Finance Ecosystem Report: This publication outlines how technology, including blockchain and artificial intelligence, is transforming trade finance processes within Europe and beyond.

- Thought Leadership Papers on Open Banking: These papers examine the implications of open banking for trade finance, focusing on opportunities for collaboration, security, and compliance.

European Bank for Reconstruction and Development (EBRD)

The EBRD focuses on fostering trade and investment in developing economies. Its publications highlight sustainable trade, emerging market trends, and green finance.

- Annual Transition Report: This flagship publication analyzes economic transitions in EBRD-supported regions, highlighting trade finance's role in facilitating growth and market stability.

- Green Trade Facilitation Programme (Green TFP) Report: Focused on sustainable trade, this report showcases EBRD's efforts to promote green technologies and materials through trade finance.

- EBRD Trade Exchange Newsletter: A quarterly publication providing updates on EBRD's Trade Facilitation Programme, including success stories, challenges, and developments in supported markets.

- The EBRD Guide to Sustainable Financing: This guide offers practical advice for banks and corporates on integrating sustainability goals into trade finance operations.

Asian Development Bank

In May 2024, the synergy between BAFT and the Asian Development Bank (ADB) led to the publishing of a paper explaining how "deep-tier supply chain finance (DTSCF)" can unlock financing for small and medium-sized enterprises, improve financial stability, and ensure complex supply chains become more transparent and resilient.

- Overview of Deep-Tier Supply Chain Finance (DTSCF): The report likely explores the potential of deep-tier SCF, which extends financing to suppliers further down the supply chain, particularly smaller or less-visible suppliers who may face greater challenges in accessing traditional financing.

- Unlocking Capital for Small Suppliers: Deep-tier SCF helps unlock capital by using the creditworthiness of larger companies to facilitate financing for smaller suppliers, ensuring their participation in the supply chain.

- Technology's Role: The report probably highlights the importance of digital platforms, blockchain, and data analytics in streamlining deep-tier SCF and providing transparency, improving access to financial products for smaller suppliers.

- Benefits for Supply Chains: By enabling smaller suppliers to access liquidity, deep-tier SCF strengthens the entire supply chain, improves the resilience of businesses, and can lead to better sustainability practices.

- Barriers and Challenges: Some barriers include the complexity of setting up deep-tier finance systems, lack of awareness among smaller suppliers, and the need for standardization in documentation and processes.

Why These Publications Matter

The collective impact of these publications lies in their ability to:

- Set Global Standards: Documents like UCP 600 and Incoterms® establish consistent practices across jurisdictions.

- Promote Innovation: Reports on digital trade finance ecosystems and green financing encourage the adoption of new technologies and sustainable practices.

- Support Policymaking: Data-driven publications, such as the ICC Trade Register Report, influence regulatory decisions and industry advocacy.

Including a section on these publications enhances the chapter by showcasing the knowledge resources that underpin trade finance's evolving landscape. This not only informs readers but also positions the organizations as central to the ongoing modernization of the sector.

The interplay between banks and stakeholders in trade finance is a dynamic and evolving relationship, influenced by technological advancements, regulatory pressures, and global economic trends. While challenges such as regulatory compliance, cybersecurity risks, and the trade finance gap persist, the opportunities offered by digitalization and innovation are immense. By investing in technology, fostering collaboration, and upskilling their workforce, banks and stakeholders can build a resilient and inclusive trade finance ecosystem that meets the demands of modern commerce.

CHAPTER 4   THE INTERPLAY BETWEEN BANKS AND STAKEHOLDERS IN TRADE FINANCE

Summary

This chapter investigates the important role banks play as middlemen and risk-reducing agents in world trade financing. It describes the trade finance ecosystem, stressing how banks help developing markets by lending and liquidity, therefore enabling transactions and trust building. The chapter tracks the evolution of trade financing from traditional intermediaries to tech-driven solutions, focusing on how digitization has enhanced transparency and efficiency. To negotiate digital trade finance, it also underlines the requirement of worker training via digital platforms and upskill initiatives. The chapter also covers the role that institutions like BAFT, ICC, EVA, EBRD, and ADB play in facilitating information exchange and promoting innovation. At last, the chapter emphasizes the need for cooperation between banks and stakeholders to solve problems, grab possibilities, and propel sustainable growth in the fast-changing trade finance sector.

CHAPTER 5

Empowering SMEs in Trade and Supply Chain Finance

Designed to maximize the movement of money throughout supply networks, supply chain finance (SCF) is a collection of technologically driven business and financial tools. This optimization lowers finance expenses and improves general company effectiveness. Fundamentally, SCF develops a financial ecosystem that links buyers, sellers, and financial institutions—that is, all the players engaged in a transaction—thereby enabling more efficient monetary transactions. The integration of technology and finance plays a critical role in ensuring that every player in the supply chain can maintain good cash flows and financial stability.

The running of SCF is mostly about meeting the financial demands of suppliers and buyers alike. In conventional transactions, depending on the conditions of the agreement, a buyer receives products or services from a provider and frequently has a 30- to 90-day or more wait in payback. This delay might affect suppliers' cash flow because they must pay for payroll, manufacturing, and other ongoing expenses before receiving payment from the buyer. By giving suppliers the choice to get early payment for their invoices at a discount, SCF solutions close this gap and guarantee they have the required working capital to run their operations without any problems.

SCF's mechanics consists of a sequence of coordinated activities enabled by technological platforms and financial institutions. A provider first presents an invoice to the buyer upon delivering goods or services. The buyer then accepts the invoice, therefore verifying that the transaction terms have been satisfied. Following approval, the supplier may opt to use a SCF program for early payment of the invoice. A financial institution advances the supplier the invoice amount, which a little finance fee helps facilitate. The buyer closes the transaction cycle by paying the entire invoice amount to the financial institution on the original due date.

For suppliers as well as purchasers, this layout has major advantages. SCF programs allow customers to prolong payment periods without compromising the supplier's cash flow. This expansion lets consumers better control their working capital, therefore releasing funds for other uses such as operational needs or other investments. Early payment at a fair price greatly lessens the financial burden on suppliers. This quick access to money guarantees that suppliers may pay their short-term debts, make investments in their companies, and keep seamless operations free from the disturbance that protracted payment cycles might bring about.

One cannot emphasize how transformingly important technology is to SCF. Using technologies such as cloud computing, blockchain, and artificial intelligence, advanced SCF systems simplify procedures, improve openness, and guarantee transaction security. These systems let buyers, suppliers, and financial institutions share real-time data and integrate themselves, therefore streamlining the SCF process and increasing its dependability. Scalable and easily available systems made possible by cloud computing can manage an enormous volume of transactions with outstanding dependability. Blockchain technology presents an unchangeable ledger that improves transaction security and openness, therefore lowering the fraud risk. Artificial intelligence (AI) and machine learning techniques in Supply Chain Finance (SCF) can examine transaction data to optimize financing terms and identify potential risks, thereby enhancing the efficiency of working capital management, credit assessment, and risk mitigation throughout the supply chain. Furthermore, the integration of these technologies into SCF systems leads to a seamless and transparent procedure. While buyers and financial institutions can monitor compliance and more effectively control risks, suppliers can track the state of their invoices and payments in real-time. This openness helps everyone engaged to develop trust, therefore promoting a more effective and cooperative supply chain.

All things considered, supply chain finance is an essential financial tool for improving the efficacy and efficiency of worldwide supply networks. Through technology-based solutions, SCF maximizes cash flow, lowers financing costs, and promotes the financial stability of all the players engaged by connecting customers, suppliers, and financial institutions. This not only boosts company efficiency in an increasingly interconnected world, but also enhances the resilience and sustainability of supply chains. With the help of cutting-edge technology, SCF is a proof that financial innovation can lead to significant changes in global trade, thereby promoting economic growth and stability.

CHAPTER 5   EMPOWERING SMES IN TRADE AND SUPPLY CHAIN FINANCE

The Growing Importance of Sustainable Supply Chain Finance

Today's corporate environment has made sustainability a top concern for businesses all over. Integration of sustainable practices into every facet of corporate operations has never been more important as global supply chains become more complicated and linked. Sustainable supply chain finance (from now on tagged as SSCF) emerges as a powerful tool to promote sustainability across supply networks in response to this need.

SSCF is a spectrum of financial strategies meant to support trade activities in ways that reduce negative effects and generate favorable social, environmental, and financial results for all participants. SSCF guarantees that sustainability performance becomes a basic factor of financial decision-making by including environmental, social, and governance (ESG) issues into conventional supply chain finance (SCF) procedures.

Fundamentally, SSCF seeks to inspire and honor environmentally friendly actions among vendors and consumers. SSCF generates incentives for businesses to adopt more sustainable practices by including ESG criteria into financial transactions, therefore addressing labor conditions, carbon emissions reduction, and ethical governance assurance. This linkage of financial incentives with environmental objectives promotes favorable change all along the supply chain.

One main way SSCF meets its goals is by giving vendors with excellent ESG performance better payment conditions. Suppliers satisfying particular sustainability standards might get early payments at reduced discount rates, trade loan access with reasonable conditions, or other financial incentives. These incentives help suppliers not only keep their financial situation better but also inspire them to keep improving their environmental standards.

Using SSCF calls for a group effort among several stakeholders—buyers, suppliers, financial institutions, and technology companies. Every one of these entities is very important for the effective inclusion of sustainability into supply chain financing.

By establishing ESG performance criteria for their suppliers, buyers—especially big global companies—can use their purchasing power to advance sustainability. By including these criteria in their SCF initiatives, consumers encourage vendors to follow sustainable practices, therefore enhancing the general viability of their supply chains. This top-down strategy ensures that sustainability is a top priority and enforced throughout the supply chain, thereby aligning with the purchasers' larger corporate responsibility goals.

SSCF will help suppliers, most notably those in underdeveloped nations or sectors with limited resources. Early payments and favorable financing conditions help reduce the financial load so that suppliers may devote more money to environmentally friendly technology and practices. These expenditures over time can result in better operational efficiency and competitiveness, therefore benefiting suppliers as well as buyers.

By creating and providing financial products integrating ESG standards, financial institutions—including banks and other financial service providers—play a vital role in SSCF. Using their knowledge of financial structuring and risk management, these companies may produce creative ideas supporting sustainable supply chains. Financial institutions satisfy the rising need for ethical investment and help push the larger agenda of sustainable economic growth by matching their products with environmental aims.

Effective application of SSCF also depends on the technology suppliers. Modern technology systems offer the required instruments for monitoring and confirming ESG performance. Blockchain, artificial intelligence, and big data analytics, among other technologies, improve openness, simplify procedures, and guarantee the integrity of sustainability statistics. Real-time monitoring and reporting made possible by these technologies lets stakeholders follow development toward sustainability objectives and make wise decisions grounded in the correct facts.

SSCF offers advantages beyond quick cash gains for customers and suppliers. SSCF helps more general society goals like environmental conservation, social fairness, and economic growth by encouraging a culture of sustainability inside supply chains. Giving suppliers that follow sustainable practices first priority, for instance, helps businesses lower their carbon footprint and lessen the effects of climate change. In the same vein, helping companies that follow fair labor policies advances social justice and enhances working conditions worldwide.

Furthermore, SSCF conforms to the rising expectations of customers, investors, and authorities of companies running ethically and sustainably. Businesses that proactively use SSCF techniques may improve their standing, attract environmentally conscious customers, and open themselves to new markets and investment prospects. In addition to promoting long-term corporate success, this proactive strategy helps to make global supply networks generally more resilient and sustainable.

Ultimately, the increasing relevance of SSCF points to a more general movement toward including sustainability at the heart of corporate activity. Through matching financial incentives with ESG performance, SSCF offers a strong means of promoting environmental change across supply chains. SSCF will become even more important in advancing a more sustainable and fair global economy as businesses, financial institutions, and technology providers keep working together and innovating. This integration is not just a means of reaching worldwide sustainability targets but also a road toward a future in which economic success and sustainability are mutually reinforcing. It is not only a commercial approach.

Integrating Sustainability into Supply Chain Finance

Supply Chain Finance (SCF) is now a necessary tool for enabling commerce and ensuring seamless operations across global supply chains. Fundamentally, SCF encompasses a spectrum of financial strategies and solutions designed to optimize cash flow for both suppliers and buyers, thereby enhancing the resilience and efficiency of supply chains. Sustainable Supply Chain Finance (SSCF) further extends these strategies to promote environmental, social, and governance (ESG) considerations, fostering more resilient and responsible supply chain practices. In the complicated and linked global trade world of today, where timely cash movement may dramatically affect a company's capacity to satisfy market needs and continue operations, this financial flexibility is especially important.

Including ESG (environmental, social, and governance) factors into SCF procedures has great potential for companies dedicated to sustainable values. This integration not only matches the increasing worldwide focus on corporate responsibility but also provides clear advantages to all parties involved. Embedding sustainability into the basic financial transactions that support a company's supply chains can help to create a more responsible supply chain that actively lowers environmental footprints, enhances social circumstances, and follows strong governance criteria.

Investigating the junction of SCF and sustainability helps one see how including ESG factors may improve supply chain finance. Through this integration, companies can reap numerous benefits. One of these benefits is better risk management, since making sure that suppliers meet certain sustainability standards usually leads to better operational procedures and a lower chance of interruptions. Embedding ESG into SCF may also improve brand perception, as stakeholders want businesses to show a real dedication to environmental policies more and more. Attracting environmentally conscious customers and investors who prioritize sustainability will help this integration promote innovation and establish new markets.

Understanding how companies may efficiently include ESG in their supply chains depends on knowing the pragmatic side of using sustainable SCF solutions. Businesses can get their suppliers to adopt and stick to higher ESG standards by creating programs that give them financial rewards for doing the right thing, like better payment terms or lower financing costs. Through a positive feedback loop, these incentives can cause a chain reaction of sustainable actions all along the supply chain. This makes everyone more responsible.

Financial institutions have had a significant influence on this paradigm shift. Essential enablers are banks and other financial service companies that deliver the required financial goods and services in accordance with ESG standards. These companies not only help their customers' sustainability objectives but also promote the more general mission of sustainable economic development by creating and advertising sustainable SCF solutions. Financial institutions can offer the knowledge and tools required to create and carry out economically feasible SCF initiatives consistent with ESG values.

Including ESG factors in SCF is a road toward promoting worldwide sustainable development, not just a corporate plan. Companies and financial institutions may cooperatively help to create a more sustainable future by encouraging a more open, accountable, and efficient supply chain. This integration helps the environment, society, and businesses all around to create a whole approach to sustainability that transcends simple compliance to become a fundamental part of company identity and strategy.

The path to sustainable SCF consists of several important phases. First, businesses must carefully evaluate their current supply chain policies to identify potential areas for incorporating sustainability. This evaluation needs to take governance criteria, social responsibility, and environmental effects into account. Businesses must then set unambiguous ESG targets that complement their general environmental objectives. These goals should be explicit, quantifiable, realistic, pertinent, and time-bound, therefore offering a road map for reaching sustainable results.

Companies may create SCF initiatives after setting objectives to motivate suppliers to achieve these levels. For suppliers who show excellent ESG performance, this might entail providing early payment reductions, reduced interest rates, or other financial advantages. Ensuring that suppliers understand the benefits of joining the program and meet the necessary criteria requires effective communication and their active participation.

Important elements of sustainable SCF also include monitoring and making decisions. Companies have to set strong procedures for monitoring development toward ESG objectives, compiling supplier data, and publishing results. This openness not only enables companies to better control their supply chains but also fosters confidence among stakeholders, who are growingly demanding responsibility and openness in company operations.

Financial institutions may help this process by offering the tools and systems required to include ESG in SCF. This includes creating financial products that support sustainability, providing consulting services to let companies create successful SCF initiatives, and using technology to increase supply chain transaction openness and efficiency.

Including ESG factors in SCF is a great way for companies trying to satisfy legal needs, improve sustainability, and attain long-term profitability. Businesses may build stronger and more ethical supply chains by using SCF's finance systems to reward environmentally friendly actions. Apart from helping particular businesses, this integration guarantees that sustainability and economic success are mutually reinforcing goals, therefore supporting the more general goal of sustainable development. Companies and financial institutions can make a big difference for the better by working together, being creative, and sticking to ESG values. This will help make the global trade ecosystem more fair and long-lasting.

The Imperative for SSCF Now

Adoption of SSCF has become more important than ever because of the confluence of numerous important events. These elements together form an atmosphere fit for implementing sustainable practices into supply chain finance, so SSCF not only makes sense but is also rather helpful for companies, financial institutions, and more generally, society.

First, the market for supply chain finance (SCF) is expanding quickly—at an amazing yearly pace of almost 20%. This steady increase in demand for SCF solutions indicates a rich platform for implementing sustainable practices. There is a great chance to include environmental, social, and governance (ESG) issues into these generally accepted financial systems as more businesses acknowledge the operational efficiency and financial advantages given by SCF. Using the growing SCF market to encourage sustainable practices throughout supply chains can generate environmental as well as financial gains. Businesses may use the growing acceptance of SCF to include sustainability in their activities, therefore guaranteeing that developments in sustainability match changes in financial systems.

Furthermore, the digitization of SCF operations is transforming supply chains and offers hitherto unheard-of chances for creativity. Perfect integration of ESG data into SCF solutions made possible by modern technology platforms improves accuracy, openness, and efficiency. Blockchain, AI, and big data analytics are some of the digital tools that make it possible to track and verify sustainability performance in real time. This facilitates companies in monitoring and managing ESG data more effectively. Complex SSCF systems that can adapt to the changing needs of global supply chains can now be created thanks to this new technology. This gives companies that put sustainability first a competitive edge. Using digital technology not only makes things easier but also makes sure that sustainability measures are tracked and reported correctly, which supports the legitimacy of SSCF projects.

Furthermore, in the present state of the economy, suppliers as well as customers depend most on working capital. SCF solutions allow buyers to stretch payment periods and provide much-needed liquidity to suppliers, hence optimizing cash flow. Managing supply chain interruptions and uncertainty call for especially this financial flexibility. Building on this advantage, SSCF links financial incentives to environmentally friendly behavior. Businesses can ensure that their working capital supports socially and ecologically friendly suppliers by incorporating sustainability criteria into SCF initiatives, thereby aligning financial success with sustainability objectives. All stakeholders benefit from this integration, which ensures the financial stability of supply chains and promotes sustainability.

Data collection and processing advances make it progressively possible to measure and confirm supplier sustainability performance. More solid and dependable ESG data results from the explosion of sustainability standards, certifications, and reporting systems. From social compliance audits to environmental impact studies, technological developments allow more exact and thorough data collection. Businesses use this enhanced data availability to make informed decisions about their supply chain partners, directing financial resources to suppliers who demonstrate outstanding sustainability performance. Since choices in SSCF projects are based on verifiable and clear evidence, this data-driven approach improves their credibility and efficacy.

Additionally, banks and other financial institutions are playing a significant role in facilitating the shift toward sustainable supply chains. Given the increasing importance of ESG elements, these companies are increasingly offering financial products and services that incorporate sustainability data. Financial institutions may attract clients and socially concerned investors by matching their products with more general ESG commitments, therefore improving their market position. Banks may also reduce credit and reputation risks connected to financing environmentally and socially conscious companies by including ESG factors into their risk assessment and lending policies. Financial service providers actively contribute to the wider adoption of SSCF, thereby promoting a more sustainable financial environment. The active participation of financial institutions guarantees that SSCF is not only a theoretical idea but also a useful and doable plan.

Ultimately, the junction of these important elements renders the demand for SSCF urgent and necessary. Together with digital transformation, the fast expansion of the SCF market, the urgent need for working capital, better data availability, and the active involvement of financial service providers offer an excellent setting for including sustainability into supply chain financing. Adopting SSCF techniques helps companies not only improve their financial performance but also support worldwide sustainability objectives by strengthening the supply chain ecosystem and thus promoting a more resilient and responsible one. This integration is not only a strategic benefit but also a required development in making sure supply chains are strong, sustainable, and in line with more general objectives of social responsibility and environmental preservation. The time to act is now, and the benefits of doing so are vast and diverse.

Leveraging SSCF for a Resilient and Responsible Global Trade

The need to implement SSCF has never been more urgent in the modern corporate scene. For companies, financial institutions, and more generally, society, several convergent elements form an atmosphere that makes incorporating sustainable practices into supply chain financing both practical and rather beneficial. This chapter investigates why now is the pivotal point for SSCF and the several advantages it presents to financial service providers, suppliers, and worldwide consumers.

CHAPTER 5   EMPOWERING SMES IN TRADE AND SUPPLY CHAIN FINANCE

At about 20%, the market for supply chain finance (SCF) is fast increasing. This strong increase indicates a growing need for supply chain finance (SCF) solutions, which provide a rich environment for incorporating environmental principles. Businesses are becoming more aware of the financial and operational benefits of SCF, so there is a good chance that environmental, social, and governance (ESG) issues will be included in these commonly used financial systems. Using the growing SCF market to push for environmentally friendly practices all along supply chains will help make sure that progress in financial systems matches progress in sustainability, which is good for both the economy and the environment.

SCF process digitalization is transforming supply chain operations and creating hitherto unheard-of innovation potential. Perfect integration of ESG data into SCF solutions made possible by modern technology platforms improves accuracy, openness, and efficiency. Blockchain, AI, and big data analytics are some of the digital tools that make it possible to track and verify sustainability performance in real time. This facilitates companies in monitoring and managing ESG data more effectively. This technical development makes it possible to develop complex SSCF systems that can fit the changing requirements of worldwide supply chains, therefore giving companies that give sustainability first priority a competitive edge.

For suppliers as well as customers in the current economic environment, working capital is very vital. SCF solutions allow buyers to stretch payment periods and provide much-needed liquidity to suppliers, hence optimizing cash flow. Managing supply chain interruptions and uncertainty particularly requires this financial flexibility. Building on this advantage, SSCF links financial incentives to environmentally friendly behavior. By incorporating sustainability criteria into SCF projects, businesses can ensure that the given working capital supports socially and ecologically friendly suppliers, thereby aligning financial success with sustainability objectives.

Data collection and processing advances make it progressively possible to measure and confirm supplier sustainability performance. More solid and dependable ESG data results from the explosion of sustainability standards, certifications, and reporting systems. From social compliance audits to environmental impact studies, technological developments allow more exact and thorough data collection. Businesses use this enhanced data availability to make informed decisions about their supply chain partners, directing financial resources to suppliers who demonstrate outstanding sustainability performance. Since choices in SSCF projects are based on verifiable and clear evidence, this data-driven approach improves their credibility and efficacy.

The change toward sustainable supply chains depends heavily on banks and other financial institutions. Given the increasing importance of ESG criteria, these companies are increasingly offering financial products and services, which include the integration of sustainability data. Financial institutions may attract clients and socially concerned investors by matching their products with more general ESG commitments, therefore improving their market position. Banks may also reduce credit and reputation risks connected to financing environmentally and socially conscious companies by including ESG factors into their risk assessment and lending policies. By means of their proactive approach, financial service providers help to promote the wider acceptance of SSCF, therefore fostering a more sustainable financial environment.

SSCF initiatives are quite helpful for worldwide consumers in fulfilling their sustainability obligations. Through including ESG criteria in financial transactions, these initiatives encourage suppliers to embrace and uphold high sustainability standards. Buyers may offer improved financing terms, such as early payments or lower interest rates, as a reward for strong ESG performance by suppliers. This not only motivates vendors to improve their environmental policies but also helps to match the supply chain with the whole corporate sustainability plan of the client. As a result, purchasers may more successfully meet their sustainable sourcing targets, therefore guaranteeing responsible production of the goods they acquire.

Additionally, crucial for improving supplier relationships and guaranteeing a consistent supply of sustainably produced commodities are SSCF initiatives. Buyers may build loyalty and commitment among their supply chain partners by giving suppliers financial incentives depending on their sustainability performance. Since suppliers are more inclined to give buyers who support their sustainability initiatives first priority, this cooperative approach reduces the hazards connected with supply chain interruptions. Investing in the financial situation of their suppliers helps buyers to guarantee that these partners stay viable and able to satisfy their needs, therefore strengthening the whole resilience of the supply chain.

Using SSCF initiatives to promote sustainability greatly improves a buyer's company's reputation. Consumers, investors, and other stakeholders in the modern market especially support businesses that show a real dedication to sustainability. Including ESG issues in their supply chain finance policies helps buyers highlight their commitment to ethical business conduct. This not only enhances a brand's image but also draws investors and ecologically and socially concerned consumers. Strong sustainability certifications help businesses comply with legal obligations and reduce any reputational concerns related to unethical supply chain operations.

For suppliers, SSCF offers much-needed access to working cash, which is vital for preserving seamless operations and supporting environmentally friendly projects. SSCF helps suppliers close the gap between product delivery and payment by offering early payment choices and suitable financing terms. This financial help helps suppliers meet running expenses, make investments in sustainable technology, and use methods to improve their ESG performance. Suppliers may therefore increase their operational efficiency and financial stability, thereby guaranteeing that they satisfy the sustainability criteria anticipated by their customers.

Programs run by SSCF give vendors that enhance sustainability real cash incentives. These initiatives inspire suppliers to use more sustainable practices and constantly enhance their environmental and social impact by tying financial incentives to ESG performance. For instance, if suppliers reach certain sustainability goals—such as lowering carbon emissions or enhancing labor conditions—they can get faster payment terms or lower financing expenses. This makes sustainability investments a strong commercial case, as suppliers directly benefit financially from their attempts to run more ethically.

Businesses that shine in sustainability can greatly improve their market position. Showing excellent ESG performance distinguishes suppliers from their competitors in a competitive market and increases their appeal to ethical consumers. Suppliers with strong environmental credentials are more likely to get contracts and long-term alliances as more businesses give sustainability top priority when choosing suppliers. This improves their standing as leaders in environmentally friendly practices in addition to their commercial prospects. This better market position can, over time, result in more client loyalty, more sales, and a more robust competitive edge.

Offering SSCF solutions helps financial service companies stand out in a very competitive industry. Banks offering SSCF solutions can draw and keep customers dedicated to ESG values as companies search for financial partners that support their sustainability objectives more and more. This market difference not only improves the bank's brand but also helps it establish leadership in sustainable financing. Developing creative SSCF products can help banks satisfy the changing expectations of their customers and profit from the increasing market for environmentally friendly financial solutions.

SSCF solutions let banks and other financial institutions meet their green financing commitments and sustainability goals. Banks may help to further the more general objectives of sustainable development and responsible investing by including ESG criteria in their lending packages. This congruence with global sustainability goals guarantees that financial institutions stay compliant and competitive by helping them satisfy investor expectations and legal criteria. Presenting SSCF goods shows the bank's dedication to having a positive social and environmental effect, thereby strengthening its corporate responsibility initiatives and improving its standing among its stakeholders.

Including ESG issues in SCF helps financial firms reduce credit and reputation concerns. By supporting ecologically and socially conscious companies, banks can reduce the possibility of being associated with unethical or negative behaviors. By means of this proactive risk management strategy, banks guarantee that they assist businesses with excellent sustainability practices—typically more stable and less prone to legal or regulatory problems. Studies show that companies with high ESG performance usually show superior financial performance and reduced default rates, therefore giving banks a more safe and solid portfolio of customers.

Ultimately, the junction of these important elements renders the demand for SSCF urgent and necessary. Together with digital transformation, the fast expansion of the SCF market, the urgent need for working capital, better data availability, and the active involvement of financial service providers offer an excellent setting for including sustainability into supply chain financing. Adopting SSCF techniques helps companies not only improve their financial performance but also support worldwide sustainability objectives by strengthening the supply chain ecosystem and thus promoting a more resilient and responsible one. This integration is not only a strategic benefit but also a required development in making sure supply chains are strong, sustainable, and in line with more general objectives of social responsibility and environmental preservation. The time to act is now, and the benefits of doing so are vast and diverse.

The Role of SSCF Models in Promoting ESG Performance

Environmental, social, and governance (ESG) principles are some of the strategies that are used in financial operations when sustainability is part of the supply chain. These systems give suppliers real incentives to improve their sustainability performance. Therefore, these systems strengthen the supply chain and increase its resilience. This chapter explores three fundamental models of SSCF.

CHAPTER 5   EMPOWERING SMES IN TRADE AND SUPPLY CHAIN FINANCE

Among the most powerful tools available in SSCF is sustainable payables finance. Fundamentally, it's about including ESG criteria into payables finance systems, which let suppliers get early payment for their bills. Payables finance initiatives historically concentrate just on increasing operational efficiency and cash flow. However, the inclusion of ESG standards transforms these initiatives into powerful tools for promoting sustainability. Strong sustainability performance—such as lowering carbon emissions, enhancing labor conditions, or following ethical governance standards—by suppliers earns favorable financing terms. These terms could include reduced discount rates for early payment or longer payment terms, therefore directly motivating suppliers to keep and improve their ESG policies. This strategy guarantees that sustainability becomes a major factor in financial transactions, therefore matching the whole supply chain with the sustainability objectives of the customer and improving the financial situation of suppliers.

Another really vital tool inside SSCF is sustainable trade loans. These loans cater to the working capital needs of vendors engaged in sustainable practices. Sustainable trade loans include ESG elements in the financing process, unlike traditional trade loans, which concentrate mostly on creditworthiness and payback capacity. Trade loans with more favorable conditions are available to suppliers that can show a dedication to sustainability—by certifications, verified ESG reports, or recorded sustainable activities.

Lower interest rates, longer loan terms, or more money for environmental projects might all fit here. Sustainable trade loans help suppliers that invest in sustainable technology and practices by tying the availability and cost of finance to ESG performance. This ensures the allocation of financial resources to companies that positively influence environmental and social outcomes, while also assisting suppliers in enhancing their sustainability credentials. This technique encourages a culture of sustainability across the supply chain over time, therefore promoting group advancement toward world sustainability targets.

A fresh technique to include sustainability in supply chain financing is smart contracts. Using blockchain technology, smart contracts enforce agreements depending on preset ESG criteria and automate tasks. These digital contracts ensure transparent tracking and confirmation of sustainability performance throughout the transaction process. For instance, you can set a smart contract to only pay a supplier once it verifies the achievement of specific sustainability targets, like reducing waste to a specific level or sourcing materials from certified sustainable sources. This level of automation and transparency ensures the consistent application of sustainability principles, thereby reducing the administrative burden associated with ESG compliance. Smart contracts, by providing a tamper-proof record of sustainability performance, also foster confidence among supply chain partners, thereby reducing the risk of greenwashing and ensuring the appreciation of genuine sustainability initiatives. Furthermore, improving the security and integrity of financial transactions via blockchain technology helps boost the dependability and resilience of the supply chain.

Including these SSCF systems in supply chain activities calls for cooperation among several stakeholders—buyers, suppliers, financial institutions, and technology companies. Setting explicit sustainability criteria and including them in their financial agreements with suppliers help buyers have a major influence. This will help them encourage the acceptance of sustainable practices all around their suppliers. Conversely, suppliers have to be ready to make investments in sustainability and keep raising their ESG performance if they are to be eligible for the financial gains SSCF systems provide. Using their knowledge of risk management and financial structure to provide creative ideas, financial institutions are essential in producing and providing SSCF products that fit with sustainability targets. By creating sophisticated platforms that provide real-time monitoring, data integration, and ESG compliance automation, technology vendors help implement SSCF systems.

Using SSCF systems has advantages beyond just quick cash gains. These systems help to achieve more general goals, including environmental preservation, social fairness, and economic development, by incorporating sustainability into financial procedures. For instance, customers may lower their total carbon footprint and help to slow down climate change by giving suppliers that follow environmentally friendly policies top priority. In the same vein, businesses may advance social justice and enhance working conditions worldwide by helping suppliers that follow fair labor standards. Furthermore, SSCF systems fit the rising expectations of customers, investors, and authorities about companies running sustainably and ethically. Businesses that aggressively embrace SSCF techniques may improve their standing, attract investors and consumers who share their values, and open themselves to new markets and investment prospects. In addition to promoting long-term corporate success, this proactive strategy helps to make global supply networks generally more resilient and sustainable.

In the end, smart contract solutions, sustainable payables financing, and sustainable trade loans are all good ways to make supply chain finance more environmentally friendly. These systems encourage a culture of sustainability and resilience throughout supply chains by giving suppliers real financial incentives to improve their ESG performance. SSCF will become more and more important in helping to create a more fair and sustainable global economy as businesses, financial institutions, and technology companies keep working and innovating together. Incorporating sustainability into financial operations is not only a strategic advantage, but also a necessary step toward maintaining robust, sustainable supply chains that align with broader environmental stewardship and social responsibility goals.

Unpacking Sustainable Payables Finance

When it comes to payables in particular, sustainable payables finance is a creative way to add ESG performance criteria to supply chain finance projects. Under this strategy, buyers can negotiate with financial institutions to provide suppliers the choice to get early payment for their bills at preferred discount rates, subject to achieving specific sustainability criteria. Examining its process, advantages for buyers, and benefits for suppliers, this chapter explores the nuances of sustainable payables finance.

Fundamental in nature, sustainable payables finance is the process by which financial institutions and purchasers cooperate to include sustainability into financial transactions. Once a customer authorizes an invoice from a supplier, the supplier has the choice to get an early payment from a financial institution discounted. However, we do not set that discount rate. Rather, it depends on the ESG performance of the supplier—as judged by the customer or a third-party rating system. Higher sustainability-rated suppliers have better financing arrangements, like speedier payment processing, lower discount rates, or both combined. This system directly finances suppliers to keep high ESG criteria in line with their sustainability performance, therefore matching their financial incentives with their performance.

Sustainable payables finance is a strong tool for consumers looking to reach their sustainable sourcing targets. Directly tying financial incentives to suppliers' ESG performance helps buyers motivate their whole supply chain to adopt and improve sustainable practices. This integration guarantees that sustainability becomes a basic feature of the supply chain and does not merely promote more acceptance of responsible actions. Buyers may use this technique to show stakeholders their dedication to sustainability, therefore strengthening their company brand. Showing a dedication to ESG values will help a company's brand image and market placement greatly in the current market when consumers, investors, and authorities give sustainability top priority.

CHAPTER 5   EMPOWERING SMES IN TRADE AND SUPPLY CHAIN FINANCE

Supporting a supply chain that meets high standards for sustainability can also lower the risks of unethical behavior, damage to the environment, and poor working conditions. This proactive supply chain management guarantees that consumers not only follow legal guidelines but also complement more general business social responsibility aims. Beyond only quick cash gains, sustainable payables finance offers purchasers long-term strategic advantages like better supplier relationships, better risk management, and more stakeholder confidence.

Sustainable payables finance gives suppliers vital financial support and instantaneous access to working cash. Early payment choices help suppliers to meet running expenses and invest in sustainable practices, therefore lessening their financial burden. Implementing new technology, enhancing labor conditions, or using environmentally friendly methods might all depend critically on financial backing. This access to liquidity could significantly impact many suppliers, especially those in cash-strapped sectors or emerging areas, enabling a transition to more sustainable corporate structures.

Sustainable payables finance's preferential rates are a real incentive for suppliers' environmental initiatives. This method makes a strong economic case for ongoing ESG improvements because suppliers directly benefit financially from their commitment to sustainable practices. Better financial conditions depending on ESG performance not only improve suppliers' operational effectiveness but also help boost their market competitiveness. Those that shine in sustainability are more likely to attract ethical consumers and earn long-term contracts, therefore supporting stability and corporate development.

Moreover, suppliers can establish a strong sustainability record through sustainable payables funding initiatives, enabling them to access various forms of sustainable funding and investment. This increasing focus on sustainable performance creates fresh chances for suppliers to increase their overall corporate resilience, draw investment, and widen their market share.

Sustainable payables finance marks a major development in including sustainability into supply chain finance. Linking financial incentives to ESG performance helps to build a more sustainable and robust supply chain, therefore benefiting suppliers as well as customers. While suppliers have instant access to working cash, financial awards for sustainability initiatives, and enhanced market positioning, buyers may fulfill their sustainable sourcing goals, boost their corporate reputation, and reduce risk. Adoption of mechanisms like sustainable payables finance will be crucial in pushing worldwide sustainability objectives and creating a more fair and sustainable economic environment as companies give sustainability top priority.

CHAPTER 5   EMPOWERING SMES IN TRADE AND SUPPLY CHAIN FINANCE

Unpacking Sustainable Trade Loans

Short-term financing solutions meant to help suppliers in the manufacturing or procurement of products and services fulfilling particular sustainability requirements are sustainable trade loans. Suppliers can access these loans at favorable rates, designed to finance initiatives with clear social or environmental benefits. Examining the nuances of sustainable trade loans and their advantages for suppliers as well as consumers, this chapter clarifies their methodology.

Financial institutions essentially base sustainable trade loans on a process where they assess the sustainability qualities of the products or services they are seeking. The process starts with suppliers seeing projects or ideas fit for stated sustainability standards. Projects eligible under this category might be those involving fair trade items, energy efficiency, renewable energy, or commodities having approved environmental advantages. After that, financial institutions assess these initiatives to find how closely they fit with sustainability objectives. Once a project qualifies, suppliers get the loan on other advantageous terms or at a cheaper interest rate, including extended payback times or fewer collateral requirements. This framework guarantees that financial support goes toward projects really benefiting the environment or society.

Sustainable trade loans provide purchasers with indirect yet major benefits. Buyers may strengthen their supply chains by making sure their suppliers are financially able to keep or enhance their sustainability practices. This helps raise the availability of sustainable goods and services inside purchasers' supply chains by matching their sustainable buying policies. When suppliers have the financial support to invest in sustainable initiatives, buyers can rely on a consistent supply of ecologically and socially conscious products, thereby enhancing the overall sustainability of their procurement procedures. Because companies can show a supply chain that actively supports more general environmental and social aims, this technique also helps purchasers fulfill their corporate sustainability pledges.

For vendors, sustainable trade loans have direct, transforming power. Access to reasonably priced funding, especially designed to help environmental projects, speeds up their capacity to use sustainable technology and practices. Improving operational performance and strengthening competitive advantage might depend heavily on this financial help. Many suppliers, particularly those in industries where sustainability projects could be too expensive or dangerous without financial help, find these loans to provide the required resources to carry out activities that are otherwise out of reach.

The preferred rates and advantageous terms make it financially feasible for suppliers to invest in renewable energy, increase energy efficiency, or create fair trade products, thereby improving their sustainability performance.

The possibility of getting sustainable trade loans encourages supplier creativity as well. These loans inspire suppliers to investigate new technologies and methods that can propel even more environmental and social advantages by lowering the financial obstacles to sustainability initiatives. This creativity helps not just the suppliers but also advances sustainable growth generally in the sector. Suppliers who embrace and improve sustainable practices create new standards for sustainability, therefore guiding others in the supply chain to match.

Furthermore, the application of sustainable trade loans advances more general objectives of sustainable economic growth. Through directing financial resources toward initiatives with obvious social or environmental advantages, these loans help to meet world sustainability goals. Leveraging their knowledge of risk assessment and financial structure, financial institutions are crucial in this process of producing loan products that fit with sustainability goals. Their involvement ensures the inclusion of sustainability in financial decision-making, thereby promoting ethical investing and the adoption of sustainable practices across various sectors.

Ultimately, a key tool in the integration of sustainability into supply chain financing is sustainable trade loans. These loans generate major social and environmental advantages by giving suppliers access to cash at favorable rates for projects satisfying particular sustainability requirements. While suppliers get direct financial help to use and grow sustainable practices, buyers indirectly benefit from improved supply chain sustainability. The stronger and more sustainable supply chain ecosystem that financial institutions, suppliers, and consumers collaborate to create supports more global goals of sustainable development. Mechanisms like sustainable trade loans will become ever more important in advancing a more sustainable and fair global economy as companies and financial institutions keep giving sustainability top priority.

The Power of Smart Contract Solutions

Smart contracts use blockchain technology to make transactions safe and automated. They also make it possible to track goods and see information about sustainability, which is a big step forward in supply chain financing. Operating on distributed blockchain networks, these contracts are self-executing agreements with straightforward written terms.

CHAPTER 5   EMPOWERING SMES IN TRADE AND SUPPLY CHAIN FINANCE

Examining their procedures, advantages for buyers and suppliers, and joint influence on the supply chain ecosystem, this chapter explores the nuances of smart contract solutions.

Smart contracts are fundamentally based on a system that immediately writes the agreement between buyer and provider straight onto the blockchain. This digital contract, powered by Supply Chain Finance (SCF) and smart contract technology, encompasses all transaction information, including product specifications, delivery schedules, and ESG performance criteria, ensuring transparency, accountability, and efficiency throughout the supply chain. The contract automatically executes and sets off payment or other predetermined actions whenever the terms specified there are satisfied.

Blockchain technology guarantees that every element of the smart contract is visible, unchangeable, and verified. This immutability guarantees that the contract conditions, once noted, remain unchangeable, providing a secure and dependable foundation for trade.

Smart contracts give consumers unmatched traceability and openness about the environmental qualities of their products. This degree of visibility helps consumers guarantee adherence to their ESG standards, therefore supporting their sustainability commitment.

Blockchain technology's open and thorough character enables consumers to follow products' route and source, confirming that they satisfy certain sustainability criteria. With customers, investors, and other stakeholders who expect responsibility in business operations, this guarantee helps to build confidence. Smart contracts' intrinsic automation also greatly lowers administrative expenses, therefore removing the need for human processing and hastening transaction completion.

Smart contracts help suppliers comply with ESG criteria by automating verification procedures and thereby lowering the manual reporting load. Blockchain's openness and security help suppliers establish credibility by means of customers who can clearly view and confirm their compliance with sustainability requirements. Furthermore, smart contract automatic execution guarantees timely payments, therefore enhancing supplier cash flow and financial predictability. This dependability lets suppliers better plan and handle their money, therefore creating a steady operating climate fit for long-term sustainable investments.

Smart contracts enable several players in a supply chain to cooperate more efficiently, thereby transcending the influence of one transaction. Smart contracts enable group action toward sustainability goals by offering a clear and safe forum for data exchange and proof of sustainability assertions. The blockchain allows everyone involved in the supply chain, from raw material suppliers to end users, to access and trust the information. This shared openness promotes responsibility and collaboration, therefore motivating group efforts to meet goals related to social, environmental, and governmental spheres.

They also aid in the integration of other SSCF systems, such as sustainable trade loans and sustainable payables finance. Smart contracts simplify the application of sustainability requirements by guaranteeing automatic verification and enforcement of them. For instance, in a sustainable payables finance agreement, we can configure a smart contract to initiate early payment reductions upon the achievement of specific ESG performance targets. Likewise, the conditions of a sustainable trade loan might be automatically changed depending on real-time blockchain validation of sustainable activities. This perfect integration makes SSCF mechanisms work better and more efficiently, which strengthens their effect on sustainability.

Smart contracts have advantages for financial institutions in addition to their inherent benefits; they also help to innovate. Blockchain technology will help banks and other financial service providers improve the security and openness of their financial goods by including them in their activities. Greater confidence and trust among customers and investors resulting from this development will help to establish financial institutions as leaders in sustainable development. Moreover, the automatic nature of smart contracts lowers the possibility of human error and fraud, thereby strengthening risk control and compliance procedures.

In the field of SSCF, smart contract solutions are quite useful instruments. Smart contracts provide a clear and reliable structure for checking and enforcing integrity objectives by using blockchain technology to automate and secure transactions. From more transparency and efficiency to better financial predictability and cooperation, the advantages for customers, suppliers, and financial institutions are really significant. Adoption of smart contract solutions will become more and more important as companies keep giving sustainability top priority in order to drive world sustainability targets and create a more fair and sustainable economic environment. Combining smart contracts with other SSCF systems enhances their impact and creates a cohesive and robust supply chain ecosystem that aligns with social, environmental, and governance objectives.

CHAPTER 5   EMPOWERING SMES IN TRADE AND SUPPLY CHAIN FINANCE

The Role of Banks and International Institutions in Advancing ESG Integration

Banks and international institutions are becoming major forces in the adoption and use of SSCF as the financial industry progressively welcomes sustainability. There are a lot of important issues that these institutions need to deal with if they want to get the most out of SSCF and make sure that their efforts are successful and also help reach larger sustainability goals.

Integration of ESG criteria into their financial goods and services is one of the main issues banks and international organizations give top importance to. This entails creating and marketing goods specifically using social, environmental, and governance guidelines. Financial institutions may guarantee that sustainability is a basic part of their business operations by including these requirements at the center of their offerings. This integration calls for a complete knowledge of ESG elements and how they affect financial risk and return. Research and development investments by institutions help to provide creative financial solutions that satisfy the changing demands of their clientele and support sustainability.

Establishing strong systems for evaluating and tracking ESG performance is also quite important. Banks and international organizations must create thorough systems for assessing the environmental credentials of their suppliers and customers. This entails applying strict evaluation procedures and defining exact criteria and standards for ESG performance. These models should be open and consistent so that benchmarking across many sectors and areas may be based on trustworthy comparisons. Institutions also have to make investments in sophisticated data collection and analysis systems to track ESG performance in real-time, thereby enabling quick responses to any problems or prospects that develop.

One cannot stress the role technology plays in enabling SSCF. Financial institutions must utilize modern technologies like blockchain, artificial intelligence, and big data analytics to enhance the security, efficiency, and transparency of their SSCF products. For instance, blockchain technology may offer a tamper-proof record of transactions and sustainability data, therefore guaranteeing that all sides have access to correct and verifiable information. Big data analytics and artificial intelligence can help examine enormous volumes of data, spotting trends and patterns that would guide risk management and decision-making. Including these technologies in their SSCF systems will enable financial firms to provide their customers with more advanced and efficient solutions.

Another important factor weighing on banks and international organizations is cooperation. These institutions have to collaborate closely with a variety of stakeholders, including governments, regulatory authorities, non-governmental organizations, and industry groups, if we are to advance the broad acceptance of SSCF. Through this cooperation, SSCF can foster the development of regulations, norms, and incentives that promote sustainable finance. Financial institutions may also learn a tremendous deal about the possibilities and difficulties related to SSCF by interacting with stakeholders all along the supply chain, therefore helping them to more precisely customize their goods and services.

Important elements of SSCF also include capacity building and education. In order to improve the knowledge and skills of their employees and clients, banks and international organizations must fund training and education initiatives. This entails offering thorough instruction on ESG standards, sustainability assessment techniques, and sophisticated technology use in SSCF. To further awareness of the advantages and relevance of SSCF among their partners and customers, institutions could also provide seminars, workshops, and other instructional activities. Financial institutions may encourage a sustainable culture that penetrates the whole supply chain by increasing the capabilities of all the players.

Another vital issue banks and international organizations should give top attention to is risk management. Including ESG criteria in financial products helps to reduce operational, regulatory, and reputational risks, as well as other risks. SSCF does, however, also have certain inherent hazards, like the possibility for greenwashing or the difficulties proving ESG performance. Institutions have to put strong risk management systems with extensive due diligence procedures, continuous monitoring, and frequent audits into action if they are to handle these hazards. Financial institutions may guarantee the integrity and efficacy of their SSCF solutions by taking a proactive attitude toward risk management.

At last, SSCF's success depends critically on openness and responsibility. Banks and multilateral organizations pledging open reporting and disclosure policies will provide clear and accurate information on their SSCF operations to stakeholders. Along with the results and effects of their SSCF projects, this involves routinely reporting on the ESG performance of their financial products. Institutions may show their clients and stakeholders their dedication to sustainability and strengthen their leadership in sustainable finance by being open and responsible, therefore fostering confidence.

Banks and international organizations are absolutely essential in promoting the acceptance of SSCF. If these institutions want to get the most out of SSCF, they need to include ESG criteria in their products and services, set up strong evaluation systems, use cutting-edge technologies, encourage cooperation, fund education and capacity building, keep risks under control, and promise to be open and responsible. Through addressing these important factors, financial institutions may significantly help to promote sustainability throughout worldwide supply chains, therefore supporting a more sustainable and strong global economy.

Revolutionizing KYC: The Integration of ESG Criteria for Risk Management and Sustainable Finance

Fundamentally employed by financial organizations to verify the identity and authenticity of the companies they support, Know Your Customer (KYC) checks are essential compliance measures aimed at preventing money laundering, fraud, and other illicit activities, while ensuring adherence to regulatory requirements. Usually, these examinations have concentrated on verifying legal conformity and evaluating financial soundness. As KYC processes start to include environmental, social, and governance (ESG) elements, the financial scene is changing significantly. This integration is crucial due to its significant impact on how financial institutions manage risk, promote sustainability, utilize cutting-edge technologies, and cultivate trust and transparency.

One of the main reasons banks are including ESG criteria in KYC processes is to improve risk management. Including ESG evaluations helps banks more effectively spot and reduce credit and reputation problems. Poor ESG companies are more likely to run into operational interruptions, legal problems, and regulatory fines—all of which can compromise their financial stability. For example, a corporation that ignores environmental rules can incur penalties or suffer closures, therefore compromising its capacity to pay back debt. By assessing ESG performance during KYC, banks may be able to identify these risks early and take steps to mitigate them, such as limiting loan terms or not lending to high-risk companies.

Furthermore, including ESG elements in KYC procedures advances environmentally friendly practices in several sectors. Financial availability that depends on meeting specific ESG criteria motivates companies to enhance their environmental and social performance. This change starts a chain reaction that promotes a more general acceptance of sustainable methods. To qualify for a loan, a manufacturing business looking for money may, for instance, use better labor standards or cleaner production techniques. Apart from improving operational efficiency and reputation, this helps the business in terms of more general social and environmental objectives. Therefore, financial institutions play a significant role in promoting sustainability, as they base their KYC procedures on ESG standards.

Modern tools improve the efficiency of KYC systems with ESG integration even further. Technologies like the Global Map of Environmental and Social Risks in Agro-Commodity Production by the IFC offer insightful analysis of sectors with significant risk. These instruments help banks do comprehensive ESG analyses, identifying areas or businesses that could create major social or environmental hazards. For a bank deciding on a loan to an agricultural company, for example, these instruments can help assess the possible social consequences and environmental effects of the project. Using these cutting-edge techniques would enable financial institutions to make better financing decisions, therefore supporting initiatives promoting sustainable development while avoiding those potentially detrimental to the environment or society.

Another important result of including ESG in KYC procedures is developing openness and trust. Showing a dedication to sustainability by means of thorough KYC checks helps a bank build credibility in a time when consumers and investors demand responsibility and ethical behavior from financial institutions. Banks may reassure stakeholders that their financing activities match ethical and sustainable values by carefully reviewing the ESG performance of their customers. This dedication to openness helps to build long-term partnerships with investors and customers that give ethical finance first priority, therefore improving the institution's market position and brand loyalty.

Moreover, KYC procedures linked to ESG fit the rising regulatory demands for financial firms to control and reveal their environmental effects. Globally, regulatory authorities are progressively requiring that banks include ESG considerations in their risk management systems. Banks not only meet legal criteria but also establish themselves as leaders in sustainable finance by aggressively including these elements in KYC procedures. By keeping ahead of regulatory trends and adjusting to changing compliance environments, this proactive approach helps financial institutions stay ahead of the risk of future regulatory breaches and related fines.

The shift to ESG-integrated KYC procedures also requires a culture change within financial institutions. Equipping staff members with the information and abilities required for thorough ESG evaluations depends on staff training and capacity development. Financial institutions have to make investments in teaching their staff about the value of ESG elements, evaluation tools, and approaches for including these elements in KYC procedures. Banks can guarantee that ESG factors permeate every facet of their activities—from customer onboarding to continuous risk management—by encouraging a culture of sustainability.

Ultimately, the inclusion of ESG criteria in know your customer (KYC) procedures is undergoing a radical change in the banking industry. Improving risk management, encouraging sustainable behaviors, using modern evaluation methods, and building trust and openness are some of the main benefits that show why this integration is important. Adopting ESG-integrated KYC procedures helps financial companies not only better control risks but also promote social and environmental change, thereby matching their activities with the ideas of sustainable finance. As the financial world changes, it will become even more important for banks and multilateral institutions that want to lead ethical and responsible finance to make sure that ESG factors are part of the know your customer (KYC) process.

Multilateral Financial Institutions: Driving SSCF and Empowering SMEs in Developing Countries

Multilateral financial institutions (MFIs), such as the European Bank for Reconstruction and Development (EBRD) and the International Financial Corporation (IFC), play a crucial role in bridging the trade financing gap, particularly for small and medium-sized businesses (SMEs) in developing countries. Their many contributions to SSCF include technical support, making it easier to get money, backing sustainable projects, building people's skills, and pushing for better laws and rules.

Getting trade credit presents major difficulties for SMEs in developing nations. These difficulties result from perceived greater risks and little collateral, which makes conventional lenders reluctant to supply the required money. By providing guarantees and preferred conditions for sustainable projects, MFIs help to close this gap and enable these businesses to more easily get the required finance. SMEs cannot engage in worldwide supply networks or help to sustain development without this backing. By providing financial support and reducing perceived risks, MFIs facilitate the inclusion of SMEs in the global market, thereby fostering economic development in developing regions.

Another important area that MFIs significantly influence is supporting sustainable initiatives. Funding for programs with obvious social and environmental advantages—such as fair trade policies, energy efficiency enhancements, and renewable energy projects—should come first. MFIs encourage companies to engage in projects that significantly enhance environmental empowerment by offering reasonable funding arrangements for these sustainable initiatives. This not only advances sustainability but also shows other financial institutions how financially feasible and powerful sustainable investments may be.

MFIs are more than just financiers; they also help companies in developing countries with technical support and capacity building. This support includes assistance in developing robust ESG plans, guidance on meeting international requirements, and training on sustainable best practices. MFIs increase the whole influence of SSCF by arming companies with the information and abilities required to raise their sustainability performance. This all-encompassing strategy guarantees not only financial support but also the empowerment of companies to properly use sustainable practices.

Another essential role of MFIs is the encouragement of legislative and legal systems that assist sustainable financing. They collaborate closely with governments and regulatory agencies to create an environment that is conducive to sustainable finance. This entails pushing openness, supporting laws and rules that include ESG issues in financial systems, and fostering responsibility. Good policy designs guarantee that financial practices include environmental factors, thereby promoting the systematic transformation of markets. MFIs contribute to creating a more suitable environment for sustainable investments and practices by affecting high-level policy.

SSCF presents a significant opportunity to align financial practices with sustainability objectives. Including ESG factors in SCF systems can help companies achieve better supply chain resilience, greater risk management, and favorable social and environmental results. To fully realize SSCF, though, cooperation among all stakeholders—including buyers, suppliers, financial institutions, and international organizations—is essential. This cooperative approach ensures that sustainability permeates every stage of the supply chain, from procurement to financing and beyond.

SSCF provides a means for global consumers to fulfill sustainable sourcing targets, improve supplier relationships, and boost business reputation through enhanced transparency, reliable ESG reporting, incentivized financing options, and promoting responsible practices across the supply chain. Buyers may establish confidence with customers and investors by making sure their supplier chains follow high sustainability criteria, therefore proving a dedication to ethical corporate behavior. Access to operating cash, financial incentives for sustainable development, and a better market posture help suppliers. By means of market distinctiveness, fulfillment of ESG obligations, and improved risk mitigation, financial institutions establish themselves as leaders in sustainable finance and benefit from it.

By allowing SMEs in developing nations access to capital, sponsoring sustainable initiatives, offering technical support, and advocating appropriate policy frameworks, multilateral financial institutions significantly help to foster sustainable development. Their involvement makes sure that sustainability is supported at all levels of the financial system and that the benefits of SSCF are generally easy to get to.

SSCF is a really effective instrument for promoting environmental growth. Including ESG issues in supply chain financing will help stakeholders build a more resilient, sustainable future for world commerce. Realizing this potential depends on the cooperative efforts of customers, suppliers, financial institutions, and international organizations; so, sustainability is not only a side effect but a fundamental element of worldwide supply chains. MFIs will become more and more crucial as the financial sector develops to support SCF, therefore guiding a future in which sustainability and economic success coexist.

Summary

The important role sustainable supply chain finance (SSCF) plays in enabling small and medium-sized companies (SMEs) in a fast-changing worldwide market is underlined in this chapter. It starts by stressing the need to include sustainability into financial systems supporting trade and supply chains, as well as the increasing relevance of SSCF. This chapter stresses the need to include social, environmental, and governance (ESG) elements into financial solutions for companies to flourish.

Discussed as means to give SMEs access to funding while matching sustainability goals are key instruments, including sustainable payables finance and trade loans. The chapter also looks at how clever contract ideas could lower risk and improve openness.

Covering the function of banks and international institutions, the emphasis is on how financial institutions may include ESG issues into their Know Your Customer (KYC) procedures, thereby guaranteeing compliance and support of ethical behavior. At last, the chapter looks at how multilateral financial institutions support the development of sustainable financial markets and their part in thus advancing a more equitable global economy.

CHAPTER 6

Unlocking Value: The Potential of Deep-Tier Supply Chain Finance (DTSCF)

Deep-tier supply chain finance, from now on referred to as DTSCF, is a significant evolution in the landscape of supply chain finance, which builds upon the foundation of traditional supply chain finance (SCF) solutions. As businesses increasingly prioritize sustainability, DTSCF emerges as a powerful tool to address the financing needs of suppliers further down the supply chain—often in the "deep-tier" segments that have historically lacked access to working capital. This new way of financing doesn't just focus on improving cash flow; it also adds sustainability to the financial ecosystem. This makes it possible for everyone in the supply chain, even smaller and more remote suppliers, to benefit from sustainable finance solutions. As SCF solutions become more environmentally friendly, it helps this change happen by giving these underserved suppliers the cash they need and building stronger, more accountable, and clearer supply chains.

DTSCF is a deliberate strategy. It is a big change in trade finance because it brings financial benefits to the lower levels of a supply chain. Unlike conventional financial instruments, DTSCF seeks to release cash at more advantageous rates for suppliers located farther down the chain who might have restricted access to credit and additional financing expenses. By reducing hazards and supporting sustainability, this strategy not only improves the financial situation of these vendors but also helps to stabilize the whole supply chain.

CHAPTER 6   UNLOCKING VALUE: THE POTENTIAL OF DEEP-TIER SUPPLY CHAIN FINANCE (DTSCF)

DTSCF has wider consequences than only those related to business activities. It guarantees that all players in the supply chain are better suited to manage economic swings by fostering an environment marked by more financial stability and better risk management. DTSCF helps to build stronger and more open supply chains by including environmental, social, and governance (ESG) ideas in trade ties. Since companies prioritize sustainable practices, aligning with ESG criteria is crucial. DTSCF is therefore a key instrument in changing conventional supply chain dynamics.

Working together, the Asian Development Bank (ADB) and the Bankers Association for Finance and Trade (BAFT) have developed the subtleties of DTSCF, stressing its creative function in funding supply chains and trade. Their guide brief explains the legal grounds needed for the DTSCF to be widely accepted and gives a detailed account of it, stating its limits and what it covers. This note's focus on DTSCF's ability to close the trade financing gap—a major obstacle still standing for many companies, especially smaller suppliers—is very vital.

Driving liquidity to the most underprivileged parts of the trade market helps DTSCF improve the openness and visibility of world supply networks. This is especially crucial in a worldwide economy because interruptions in supply chains could have far-reaching effects. The advice paper stresses how important it is for businesses to work together and for there to be strong laws and rules in place to make sure that DTSCF is used effectively on a large scale.

The ADB's release of a brief on DTSCF at the Global Trade Review (GTR) Asia in 2022 marked a significant milestone in understanding the value of this financial innovation. This initial swift action laid the groundwork for subsequent initiatives, such as the establishment of specialized working groups by ADB and BAFT. These organizations have been very helpful in investigating and suggesting approaches to expand DTSCF, therefore ensuring that the recommendations and insights are based on pragmatic, real-world use.

Deeper into the complexity of DTSCF, the guiding note offers insightful analysis of the concepts and legal frameworks required for success. It underlines the need for cooperation among several parties, including buyers, sellers, financial institutions, fintech businesses, regulatory agencies, and specialists from the accounting and legal spheres. The report also discusses how other forms of deep-tier finance, like those that use digital assets produced by financial institutions, may complement DTSCF.

The main goal of the guideline note is to make several financial instruments accessible to those engaged in worldwide supply chains. The note tries to get people to agree with this new way of doing things by giving them a lot of information about DTSCF and what it means. This will help make global trade environments more stable, long-lasting, and financially accessible for everyone.

Strengthening Global Supply Chains: The Role of Innovative Financial Solutions in Empowering Deeper-Tier Suppliers

The COVID-19 epidemic sharply exposed the flimsiness and ineffectiveness of world supply systems. In addition to recent changes in the economy and worries about geopolitics, the epidemic has made these weaknesses even worse and made world trading systems even more complicated and unstable. Also, serious issues like damage to the environment, unequal distribution of economic benefits, trafficking and exploitation of people, and the existence of slavery and child labor in supply chains have grown and need to be dealt with right away.

Innovative financial solutions targeting the often overlooked and disadvantaged segments of society have become crucial in this rapidly evolving landscape, bolstering supply chain resilience. Above all, one must be able to react successfully to unanticipated events and emergencies. Beyond direct suppliers, supply chains include deeper-tier vendors essential for the manufacturing and delivery of final products. These deeper-tier suppliers, however, usually get the least financial help and hardly gain from conventional supply chain financing (SCF).

The epidemic underscored the interdependence of global supply chains and underscored the necessity of providing financial support to all levels, particularly the lower ones, to ensure operational stability. COVID-19's disturbance exposed how brittle and linked these supply networks are, so it became clear that any weakness in one layer might have domino repercussions all over the network. Particularly for small and medium-sized businesses (SMEs), which represent the backbone of most economies, this insight has motivated a fresh focus on financial innovation to solve the ongoing funding shortages. Rising from $1.7 trillion in 2020 to a startling $2.5 trillion in 2022, the Asian Development Bank's 2023 Trade Finance Gaps, Growth, and Jobs Survey shows how dramatically trade finance is lacking worldwide.

Although SMEs play a vital role, they have considerable difficulty finding the required capital to sustain their operations and expansion, thereby losing opportunities in foreign markets.

CHAPTER 6   UNLOCKING VALUE: THE POTENTIAL OF DEEP-TIER SUPPLY CHAIN FINANCE (DTSCF)

One exciting new financial idea in SCF is the category of receivable purchase, which has gotten a lot of attention as a way to help more people, including small businesses, get cheaper loans. This technique improves cash flow management, reduces financial risk, and gives suppliers more reasonably priced financing choices by moving credit risk from the supplier to the anchor customer. This strategy guarantees that deeper-tier suppliers have the financial means they need to keep and grow their businesses, therefore strengthening the supply chain ecosystem.

Receivable buying provides advantages beyond only financial ones. This system lowers the danger of interruptions and fosters stability, therefore strengthening the whole supply chain. Usually found in smaller marketplaces or emerging areas, deeper-tier vendors are more sensitive to market swings and economic changes. By means of reasonable financing provided by receivable buy, these suppliers may guarantee timely delivery of products and services, invest in their operations, and increase efficiency. This thereby improves the dependability of the whole supply chain.

Furthermore, attending to the financial requirements of deeper-tier vendors fits more general objectives of sustainability and economic inclusiveness. Businesses may contribute to closing the economic gap and guarantee a more fair sharing of economic gains by supporting these suppliers financially. Dealing with the problems of human trafficking, exploitation, and the existence of human slavery and child labor inside supply chains depends especially on this. Deeper-tier suppliers' financial stability can enable them to improve labor conditions, follow ethical guidelines, and promote more responsible and sustainable corporate operations.

Supply chain finance clearly depends on creative financial solutions. The epidemic and later economic upheavals have underlined the necessity of a more sustainable, inclusive, and resilient strategy for world commerce. Although they help to some degree, traditional SCF systems may fall short in reaching the deeper levels of supply chains where there is the greatest need for support. Financial innovations like receivable purchases play a critical role in bridging these gaps and ensuring financial empowerment for every player in the supply chain.

Finally, the changing terrain of global commerce calls for a review of supply chain financing. Together with continuous socioeconomic and geopolitical issues, the vulnerabilities revealed by the COVID-19 epidemic highlight the need to help deeper-tier vendors. Adopting financial innovations that offer reasonably priced financing choices and reduce risks can help companies build a more sustainable and strong supply chain. This strategy not only improves operational stability but also supports ethical corporate practices and economic inclusiveness, therefore helping to create a more fair and sustainable world.

DTSCF: Expanding the Reach of SCF to Strengthen Global Networks

DTSCF is a complex method of post-shipment financing that spreads the advantages of conventional supply chain finance to every level of the supply chain. Unlike traditional approaches, which mostly concentrate on direct or tier-1 suppliers, DTSCF covers the whole supply network, therefore touching even the most deeply ingrained suppliers.

Usually a big, financially strong corporation starts financing plans for its tier-1 suppliers; DTSCF starts with the anchor customer. These agreements then flow down the supply chain, allowing every supplier to provide comparable terms of financing to their own downstream counterparts. A tier-1 supplier getting funding from the anchor customer, for instance, can then fund a tier-2 supplier, therefore extending the terms to a tier-3 provider. This generates a chain of finance closely related to the supply chain and the related products and services supplied by the anchor buyer.

Using payables finance products will help DTSCF maximize the working capital of the anchor buyer. This strategy lets purchasers present finance choices to tier-1 suppliers as well as to those outside of the immediate tier. Therefore, anchor purchasers can ensure the stability of their entire supply chain, reducing the risk of disruptions at any stage due to financial constraints.

For vendors, DTSCF offers a vital financial lifeline. Before their due dates, suppliers of goods to the customer can access the discounted value of their receivables. This preemptive access to money, usually more advantageous than what the suppliers might find on their own, comes at a financing cost commensurate with the credit risk of the anchor customer. Two benefits come from this alignment: it guarantees that finance costs stay constant and predictable across the supply chain and gives suppliers more reasonably priced choices.

DTSCF significantly affects suppliers' cash flow. Early payments to suppliers help them increase their liquidity, therefore facilitating better management of their operations. Their due dates are then easier for them to handle. Investing in new initiatives, increasing production capacity, or just daily operations stabilization may all benefit from this enhanced cash flow. DTSCF also helps to level the playing field for smaller suppliers that would otherwise find it difficult to get reasonably priced financing by matching financing costs with the credit risk of the anchor customer.

DTSCF also increases openness and efficiency. The finance plans, closely linked to the actual movement of products and services across the supply chain, ensure accurate recording and traceability of every transaction. Since every stakeholder has a clear awareness of the operational and financial processes under influence, this degree of openness helps to develop confidence among all the engaged parties.

Moreover, DTSCF can lower administrative overheads and increase general supply chain efficiency by simplifying the financing process and depending less on established financial institutions. Using DTSCF requires proper cooperation and preparation. To define the terms and conditions for the finance agreements, anchor purchasers have to collaborate closely with their suppliers. We must also consider legal and regulatory issues to ensure that the finance systems adhere to both local and international norms. Technology plays a significant role in enabling DTSCF; digital platforms provide the necessary infrastructure for transaction management, payment monitoring, and record-keeping.

DTSCF then offers a revolutionary method of supply chain management. DTSCF helps to maximize working capital, boost cash flow, improve transparency, and raise efficiency by spreading financing benefits to all levels of the supply chain. SCF provides a route to more financial stability and operational resilience for both anchor purchasers and suppliers, therefore guaranteeing that supply chains stay strong and are able to resist economic changes. In the linked worldwide economy of today, sustainable and inclusive development depends on this all-encompassing approach to supply chain financing.

Leveraging Post-Shipment Financing to Strengthen Supply Chain Resilience and Trust

DTSCF differs from other forms of trade financing mostly in that it is based on the ideas of post-shipment finance, a crucial factor. Grasping the special advantages and processes of DTSCF depends on an awareness of this focus.

Post-shipment financing, which focuses the credit risk on the anchor buyer, forms the foundation of DTSCF. Usually having superior credit than its suppliers, the anchor customer in a supply chain offers a strong basis for extending advantageous financing terms down the chain. This is much different from pre-shipment financing, which evaluates supplier performance and then affects credit availability and price depending on risk profile.

CHAPTER 6 UNLOCKING VALUE: THE POTENTIAL OF DEEP-TIER SUPPLY CHAIN FINANCE (DTSCF)

Post-shipment financing provides funding after product delivery, thereby highlighting the creditworthiness of the anchor buyer. This strategy ensures a significantly reduced risk associated with financing, as the anchor customer's ability to meet payment obligations is typically more reliable and consistent than that of the suppliers. This helps to simplify the risk evaluation and improve the appeal of the financing conditions for suppliers, therefore clarifying the financing process.

Examining the subtleties of DTSCF, the working group underlined the need to keep a clear difference between pre-shipment and post-shipment money. This separation is crucial to avoid confusing DTSCF with other types of trade financing that have distinct risk profiles and operational concerns. For example, pre-shipment funding calls for a careful assessment of the supplier's capacity to satisfy an order, therefore adding a layer of performance risk that can complicate the financing process. DTSCF makes the financial arrangements easier by focusing only on post-shipment finance. This makes the financing structure simpler and more closely matches the credit risk of the anchor buyer.

Focusing on post-shipment funding as a basic criterion of DTSCF is also very helpful in terms of cost and accessibility. Unlike conventional financing choices that could be accessible to them independently, the financing is based on the credit risk of the anchor customer, so suppliers can get money at a cheaper cost. Small and medium-sized businesses (SMEs) at the deeper levels of the supply chain especially benefit from this cost-effectiveness, as their lower credit scores usually result in higher financing expenses. DTSCF makes reasonably accessible finance more available to these important but sometimes underprivileged sections of the supply chain by using the higher credit profile of the anchor buyer.

Furthermore, a post-shipment finance emphasis helps to improve supply chain openness. The anchor buyer clearly bears the credit risk, allowing all participants to better understand the financial dynamics at play. More cooperative and strong supply chains result from this openness, building confidence among suppliers and consumers. Suppliers who are sure they can get finance depending on the creditworthiness of the anchor buyer may better schedule their activities and make investments in expansion prospects.

In the framework of DTSCF, operational efficiency is still another major benefit of post-shipment financing. DTSCF streamlines financing by doing away with the requirement to evaluate and control performance risk at every supply chain level. This efficiency not only lowers administrative overheads but also accelerates the movement of money across the supply chain, thereby guaranteeing that suppliers get payments fast and can maintain seamless operations. The streamlined post-shipment finance makes it possible for faster cash deployment, which is crucial for maintaining supply chain liquidity and operational continuity.

Ultimately, a defining feature of DTSCF is its emphasis on post-shipment finance. DTSCF offers a more easily available, reasonably priced, and effective financing solution for suppliers by focusing the credit risk on the anchor customer and using their better credit situation. More robust and cooperative relationships follow from this clarity and simplicity, improving transparency and building trust inside the supply chain. So, for DTSCF to work and be able to grow, people need to understand and stick to the difference between pre-shipment and post-shipment financing. This will make sure that it keeps its promise to help supply chains around the world stay financially stable and healthy.

Unlocking Key Advantages for Stakeholders and Strengthening Global Supply Chains

For many different supply chain participants—including anchor customers, suppliers, and financiers—deep-tier supply chain financing provides a range of major advantages. Appreciating DTSCF's transforming power requires knowledge of these advantages.

DTSCF changes how anchor purchasers see their connections with suppliers, therefore presenting them as preferred buyers. The improved financial assistance and advantageous conditions that anchor purchasers may provide through DTSCF help to explain this change in appeal to suppliers looking for consistency and predictability in their payment flows. Leveraging their better credit profiles, anchor purchasers may offer financing choices that enhance the financial situation of their suppliers, therefore cultivating loyalty and improving the whole supply chain.

For anchor customers, the improvement of supply chain robustness and openness is one of the main advantages. Anchor purchasers have improved access to their suppliers' financial situation and operating capacity because of DTSCF. This increased openness helps to see any hazards and take early action to remedy them, therefore lowering the possibility of disturbances. DTSCF also wants to make sure that all levels of the supply chain follow ESG standards. This will help the anchor customer meet their environmental, social, and governance (ESG) reporting and goals. Consistency with ESG goals not only enhances the buyer's reputation but also ensures adherence to regulatory compliance and market expectations.

CHAPTER 6   UNLOCKING VALUE: THE POTENTIAL OF DEEP-TIER SUPPLY CHAIN FINANCE (DTSCF)

From a business standpoint, DTSCF lets anchor purchasers maximize their working capital by hammering out advantageous financing terms with their suppliers. This optimization boosts cash flow, thereby reducing the need for anchor purchasers to secure capital in goods and receivables. Competitive financing rates obtained through DTSCF can also help reduce the cost of items supplied, therefore increasing profit margins. Another important benefit is the decrease in fraud and nonperformance risk, as DTSCF's strong financial integration and openness help to identify and stop dishonest behavior more easily.

Usually more advantageous than what suppliers could get on their own, DTSCF gives access to finance at costs matching the credit risk of the anchor customer. For suppliers—especially small and medium-sized businesses (SMEs) at the lower levels of the supply chain—this access to reasonably priced finance is very vital as it increases their liquidity and helps them to invest in their operations. The lower running expenses associated with independently obtaining funds significantly improve the financial stability of the suppliers.

For suppliers engaged in DTSCF, another major advantage is following ESG targets. Suppliers can raise their own ESG performance by matching the ESG criteria of the anchor buyer, therefore creating new market prospects and strengthening their brand. In the corporate context of today, this compliance also guarantees that suppliers participate in a sustainable and responsible supply chain, which is ever more vital.

By broadening their client base to include suppliers at several levels of the supply chain, DTSCF opens fresh business prospects for financiers. Because it lets financiers diversify their portfolio and access a larger market, this growth is very appealing. One obvious advantage of SMEs' credit risk mitigating strategy is that the payment commitment goes to the anchor buyer, whose credit risk is usually less. Lenders find it more reasonable to provide loans to SMEs due to this risk shift, as they would otherwise perceive them as overly hazardous.

DTSCF also produces useful information for the management of ESG risk and financial analysis. The comprehensive data on transactions, supplier performance, and ESG standard compliance helps financiers better control risks. This data-driven strategy improves the accuracy and efficiency of risk-reducing measures and financial decision-making processes.

DTSCF also gives lenders a deeper understanding of the supply chain needs of their clients. This knowledge enables financiers to more precisely customize their goods and services, therefore satisfying the particular demands of suppliers and their consumers. Improved knowledge of supply chain dynamics helps to build closer bonds between bankers and their clients, fostering more cooperative and mutually productive alliances.

To sum up, for stakeholders, deep-tier supply chain financing offers several different and notable advantages. Anchor purchasers get greater ESG compliance, strengthened financial performance, and more supply chain resilience. Improved ESG alignment, lower running costs, and access to reasonably priced credit help suppliers. Financiers reduce credit risk, open new corporate prospects, and learn a tremendous deal about supply chain dynamics. Understanding and using these advantages will help stakeholders build more sustainable, transparent, and resilient supply chains, thereby promoting the stability and development of the world economy.

Key Principles and Effective Implementation for Strengthening Global Supply Chains

Effective use of DTSCF depends on a comprehensive knowledge of its mechanics and unique qualities. Unlike other forms of supply chain financing that may involve loans to multiple supplier tiers, DTSCF is fundamentally associated with an irreversible payment obligation from the anchor customer. This dedication, the cornerstone of DTSCF, ensures that the credit risk originates from the most reliable supply chain organization.

The category of supply chain finance receivable acquisition directly influences how DTSCF functions as a financing tool. It uses the better credit standing of the anchor buyer to provide financing choices split and distributed to lower levels of the supplier chain. This strategy guarantees that the creditworthiness of the anchor customer will help even the smallest vendors, therefore preserving a constant credit risk profile all across the supply chain.

DTSCF's capacity to lock in the credit risk of the anchor buyer across the supply chain is among its most important features. As credit risk passes from one tier to the next and each layer adds new risk variables, traditional financing techniques can see credit risk worsen. On the other hand, DTSCF preserves the credit risk at the level of the anchor buyer, therefore offering financiers a consistent and predictable risk environment. Financial institutions especially find considerable attraction in this consistency, as it lowers the total risk involved in funding several layers of suppliers.

Starting with the creation of an irreversible payment obligation from the anchor buyer, implementing DTSCF effectively calls for various phases. This payment obligation guarantees that, independent of any supply chain difficulties, the anchor buyer will meet its payment obligations. The premise for providing finance to the tier-1 supplier—who may then provide comparable conditions to their downstream partners—is this

CHAPTER 6   UNLOCKING VALUE: THE POTENTIAL OF DEEP-TIER SUPPLY CHAIN FINANCE (DTSCF)

irreversible promise. Every supplier in the chain may get money at more reasonable rates by tying the financing to the credit risk of the anchor buyer, therefore enabling each other.

The procedure starts when the anchor buyer and tier-1 supplier are discussing the parameters of the receivable purchase agreement. After setting these conditions, the tier-1 supplier can offer financing options to its tier-2 suppliers, and so on. The strong credit profile of the anchor buyer guarantees that financing expenses stay reasonable and constant across the supply chain, therefore benefiting each level. From the largest buyer down to the smallest supplier, this cascade impact of financing arrangements produces a logical and effective financial ecology.

Strong technological systems are absolutely necessary to guarantee the flawless use of DTSCF. These systems help businesses monitor compliance with the agreed agreements, handle receivables, and track purchases. Maintaining openness and efficiency depends mostly on digital solutions, which also enable everyone to have real-time access to the money movements inside the supply chain. This openness not only helps the participants develop trust but also improves their capacity for proactive risk management.

Effective DTSCF implementation also depends on legal frameworks and regulatory compliance. Maintaining the integrity and legality of the transactions depends mostly on the financial arrangements following local and international rules. Standardized and clear legal documentation reduces conflicts and misunderstandings, therefore strengthening the basis for financial implementation. Collaborating with legal professionals and authorities facilitates the negotiation of cross-border transaction complexity, ensuring the safety of all participants and the robustness of financial systems.

Moreover, the success of DTSCF depends critically on effective communication and education among all the stakeholders. Suppliers, anchors, and financiers must fully grasp the advantages and DTSCF processes. By means of training courses and educational seminars, one may help to match the expectations and knowledge of every participant, thus guaranteeing that everyone agrees on the procedures and advantages of DTSCF.

For DTSCF to work, it needs to use the anchor buyer's credit risk, make payment obligations clear, and keep things open and legal by having strong technical and regulatory frameworks. Following these values will enable DTSCF to offer a consistent, reliable, and effective financing solution benefiting all levels of the supply chain, therefore promoting financial inclusion and stability in the worldwide market.

CHAPTER 6   UNLOCKING VALUE: THE POTENTIAL OF DEEP-TIER SUPPLY CHAIN FINANCE (DTSCF)

Key Principles of DTSCF: A Strategic Approach to Strengthening Global Supply Chains

Understanding the basic ideas guiding DTSCF can help one to appreciate its essence and efficient execution. These ideas guarantee that DTSCF stays in line with its fundamental goals, therefore offering a reliable and effective funding source for all levels of the supply chain.

DTSCF is fundamentally based on the salient features of trade finance. This suggests that supply chain sales and purchases of products and services must have a close connection with finance. DTSCF is naturally short-term and self-liquidating, unlike long-term financing choices. The focus on short-term financing ensures that the provided funds align precisely with specific trade transactions, expected to conclude in a relatively brief period. This short-term nature works with the business cycles of companies in the supply chain, making sure that the financing needs are met without putting too much stress on the long-term finances.

DTSCF also depends critically on the presence of an irrevocable payment commitment from the anchor buyer. This framework is the most important part of the financing plan for the tier-1 supplier because it makes sure that the anchor customer will pay in full and can't back out. Crucially, this framework allows for the splitting and transfer of the irrevocable payment obligation to lower levels of the supply chain. This transferability guarantees that the product credit risk profile of the anchor customer will flow down the supply chain, therefore giving all the engaged suppliers financial stability and predictability. The promise of an unbreakable payment obligation lowers the risk for lenders, which makes it easier for suppliers to get loans on many levels.

Another fundamental DTSCF idea is emphasizing just post-shipment financing. This suggests that DTSCF restricts financing to past-due transactions, particularly those that occur after product delivery. DTSCF firmly focuses the credit risk on the anchor customer's ability to make payments rather than on the performance risk of suppliers by emphasizing post-shipment finance. This difference is essential as it reduces the risk assessment process for financiers by removing doubts about the capacity of the suppliers to meet orders. DTSCF guarantees that the financing stays closely tied to the payment risk of the anchor buyer, which is usually more predictable and consistent by removing performance risk.

Finally, the anchor customer's supply chain must precisely connect to DTSCF finance. This direct link guarantees that the trade finance risk profile stays constant and that the funding helps meet the operational and financial requirements of the supply chain as planned. Keeping a direct link to the anchor buyer's supply chain helps DTSCF make financial transactions more transparent and simple to track. This makes it easier to manage the supply chain's finances. This relationship also guarantees that every level of the supply chain receives a fair distribution of the advantages of DTSCF, including better cash flow and lower financing costs.

The effective running and execution of DTSCF depend on these general principles. Following these values guarantees that DTSCF remains a strong and efficient financial tool able to solve the particular difficulties supply chains have. If DTSCF focuses on trade finance, uses irreversible payment commitments, limits post-shipment finance, and stays connected to the anchor buyer's supply chain, it may be able to provide a reliable, consistent, and effective way to get money. This improves the financial stability of the supply chain as well as builds more trust and cooperation among all the players, therefore supporting a more inclusive and sustainable worldwide commerce environment.

Building a Strong Legal Framework for DTSCF: Key Elements of Clarity, Protection, and Efficiency

Any outstanding financial innovation starts with the strength and clarity of its legal framework. A strong legal framework is not only helpful but also necessary for deep-tier supply chain financing (DTSCF) to realize its full possibilities. Clear, reproducible legal agreements that offer clarity, legal protection, risk management, operational efficiency, and stakeholder confidence must all fit within this framework.

In DTSCF, a strong legal framework mostly serves to offer clarity. Clear legal agreements are very vital given the complicated structure of supply chains, whereby several levels of suppliers engage with the anchor customer and lenders. These agreements define the duties, obligations, and expectations of every participant engaged. This helps them to avoid uncertainty that can cause conflicts or misinterpretations. In DTSCF, where financial transactions and commitments must be open and explicitly specified to retain confidence and efficiency, this clarity is especially crucial.

Another significant benefit of a solid legal system is legal protection. Within the framework of DTSCF, legal agreements protect all the engaged parties. These agreements guarantee the legally binding and enforceable rights and responsibilities of the anchor buyer, suppliers, and financiers. Maintaining the confidence of stakeholders depends on such protection, as it ensures that the legislation protects their interests. For example, the legally obligatory and well-specified irreversible payment commitments of the anchor customer must provide lower-tier suppliers and financiers with trust.

Good risk control also naturally relates to a disciplined legal framework. Managing credit risk is very critical in DTSCF, as the financing depends mostly on the creditworthiness of the anchor buyer. Therefore, it is crucial to include comprehensive clauses in legal agreements that outline the evaluation, distribution, and control of credit risk throughout the supply chain. This covers systems for managing various contingencies, disagreements, and defaults. DTSCF can maintain financial stability and reduce the effects of unanticipated difficulties by tackling these possible hazards within the legal system.

Another major advantage of a strong legal system is operational efficiency. Standardized legal agreements help to simplify the DTSCF implementation procedures. Knowing the established legal ground truth reduces the administrative load. Faster transaction times, reduced running costs, and better movement of money across the supply chain follow from this efficiency. Legal document standardization also helps to promote scalability and more general acceptance by facilitating simpler replication of DTSCF models throughout several supply chains and geographic areas.

DTSCF's success ultimately depends on the faith of its stakeholders. A well-defined legal framework instills trust in all participants—anchor purchasers, suppliers, and financiers—by ensuring the precise safeguarding of their positions and interests and the open and fair rules controlling their interactions. The foundation of developing solid, cooperative relationships inside the supply chain is this confidence. Stakeholders are more likely to engage actively and make long-term investments in the DTSCF model when they believe the legal framework will protect their rights and duties.

Basically, the effective use of deep-tier supply chain financing depends on the building of a strong legal framework. Underlying the whole DTSCF structure, this kind of framework offers the required clarity, legal protection, risk management, operational efficiency, and stakeholder confidence. Ensuring the clarity, enforceability, and repeatability of all legal agreements enhances the legal system and facilitates the growth of DTSCF. This supports a stronger, more open, and more efficient global supply chain network. Along with supporting the financial situation of the supplier chain, this basis advances inclusive and sustainable development in the larger economic scene.

Unlocking Financial Support for SMEs: How DTSCF Enhances Inclusivity and Overcomes Barriers in Supply Chain Finance

Though the supply chain finance (SCF) receivable buy category has high potential, especially in relation to payables finance, the system has not quite lived up to the high expectations set for it. Usually including fewer small and medium-sized businesses (SMEs) at the first tier, global supply chains reflect the tendency of big customers to interact with more established and sizable suppliers. Tier-1 suppliers—which could have first been SMEs—have grown their activities over time, therefore reducing the representation of SMEs among direct suppliers to major worldwide consumers. SMEs frequently find themselves at lower levels of supply chains due to their smaller scale and specialized activities, and conventional SCF systems occasionally disregard them as a result. This control has resulted in the category of receivable purchases failing to sufficiently reach and assist these important SMEs.

Many factors help to explain SCF's limitations in this sense. The main problem is the emphasis on either tier-1 or direct suppliers. Often quite large companies with strong financial records and more money access than SMEs, these suppliers are Given the prevalence of SMEs at lower supply chain levels, prioritizing larger, first-tier suppliers naturally limits the benefits of SCF. The result is a financial scene in which the most susceptible and usually most important supply chain linkages go underutilized.

Furthermore, especially for seller- or supplier-led products like factoring, the SCF onboarding procedures can be labor-intensive and rather costly. Effective scaling of such solutions is challenging given the time and expenses involved in onboarding these vendors. For SMEs, this is a major obstacle, as they usually lack the means to negotiate challenging onboarding processes and cannot pay the related expenses. The outcome is a system that, although nominally inclusive, is mainly unreachable to the smaller actors most in need of it.

Legal documentation's intricacy adds even another layer of difficulty. SCF entails several players working across several countries, each with its own relevant rules. This variety complicates the task of optimizing the receivable assignment. The legal complexities involved in coordinating several rules and guaranteeing compliance greatly hinder the effective use of SCF solutions. For SMEs, this complexity discourages them, as they usually lack the legal knowledge and tools to handle these obligations.

CHAPTER 6 UNLOCKING VALUE: THE POTENTIAL OF DEEP-TIER SUPPLY CHAIN FINANCE (DTSCF)

Unlocking financial assistance for deeper tiers of suppliers remains a difficult task, even if SCF has evolved throughout the years. Although they help to some degree, the current systems do not sufficiently meet the requirements of SMEs at these lower levels. Here, DTSCF shows itself as a possible way to close the gap and enable financial support for SMEs inside supply chains.

By providing financial support beyond the direct suppliers to the deeper tiers, where SMEs are more prevalent, DTSCF offers a more inclusive strategy. This strategy acknowledges the important role SMEs play in the general resilience of supply networks and the general state of health. By concentrating on the lower tiers, DTSCF hopes to guarantee a more fair distribution of financial gains among all levels of the supply chain.

Effective implementation of DTSCF depends on simplifying onboarding procedures and lowering related expenses. Streamlining processes and increasing accessibility to SMEs can greatly improve the scalability of DTSCF solutions. Furthermore, the creation of uniform legal systems applicable to several countries can lessen the complexity of legal documents. Such systems would give SMEs a more consistent foundation for the assignment of receivables, therefore facilitating their involvement in DTSCF projects.

Moreover, using technology could be rather important in conquering these obstacles. Digital platforms may help to save expenses, enable more effective onboarding procedures, and offer better legal compliance and openness. DTSCF can become a more practical and successful means of helping SMEs in supply chains by using technology's potential.

Even if SCF has certain difficulties, they are not insurmountable. The launch of DTSCF marks a hopeful path toward resolving these problems and giving SMEs in lower levels of supply chains much-needed financial aid. DTSCF has the ability to change supply chain finance and build a more robust and fair global trade environment by concentrating on inclusion, streamlining procedures, and harnessing technology. Supply chain finance's future is in its capacity to change and grow to satisfy the demands of every stakeholder, therefore enabling even the most modest and vulnerable suppliers to flourish.

CHAPTER 6   UNLOCKING VALUE: THE POTENTIAL OF DEEP-TIER SUPPLY CHAIN FINANCE (DTSCF)

Navigating Legal Challenges in DTSCF: Ensuring Clarity, Enforcement, and Global Collaboration for Effective Supply Chain Financing

DTSCF has created tremendous buzz and a rush to provide novel ideas, much as with every major invention. Although this excitement is motivating, it has also resulted in a profusion of DTSCF-labeled items with varying risk profiles. Examining these products closely demonstrates that they do not follow the fundamental ideas of DTSCF as stated in official advice. As one explores the supply chain, this departure from basic standards might lead to worsening credit risk.

One major issue is the way the market misclassifies some financial instruments as DTSCF. Many of these products are just conventional trade financing solutions used at several points of the supply chain. Such systems progressively increase credit risk at each deeper level, therefore compromising the stability and efficiency of the supply chain financing system. Some solutions also adhere to traditional purchase order finance models, portraying a top-tier customer's purchase order as a low-risk payment tool throughout the supply chain. Although these techniques look novel, they sometimes deviate from the basic ideas of DTSCF, which causes more uncertainty and risk.

DTSCF's effective application depends on rigorous adherence to the basic definitions and features described in thorough guide notes. Anchor buyers must keep their credit risk profile across several tiers intact. Not only can misclassifying several financing products with varying risk profiles cause uncertainty but could also raise default rates. Clearly defining, comprehending, and presenting the differences between DTSCF and other deep-tier financing products is therefore absolutely essential. Avoiding reputation risks that can hinder DTSCF solution scaling depends on this clarity.

The framework provided by authorized organizations for DTSCF is essential for the market to come up with effective solutions, especially for cross-border transactions that haven't been used a lot yet. Standardized definitions and principles guarantee shared knowledge among all the players, including companies, financial institutions, and authorities. For many different reasons, this shared knowledge is vital.

First of all, it offers a strong basis for legislators and authorities to develop sensible rules. These rules ensure the transparent and legally sound implementation of DTSCF. Such regulatory systems help reduce risks and safeguard all users, therefore supporting the stability and integrity of financial markets.

CHAPTER 6   UNLOCKING VALUE: THE POTENTIAL OF DEEP-TIER SUPPLY CHAIN FINANCE (DTSCF)

Second, by stimulating liquidity in underprivileged market sectors, a clear framework helps close the trade financing gap. Usually found in the lower levels of supply chains, SMEs stand to gain greatly from DTSCF. It may improve visibility and stability across worldwide supply chains by making sure these smaller suppliers have the financial means they require. Managing risks and making sure supply networks withstand interruptions depend on this higher visibility.

Thirdly, well-defined and consistent definitions help to create creative DTSCF solutions catered to the requirements of several stakeholders. Knowing the financial instruments at their disposal helps companies, for example, better plan and control their supply chain operations. Authorities can ensure that products meet strict legal and risk management criteria, while financial institutions can design goods that better align with consumer demands.

It is impossible to overestimate the need to follow the basic DTSCF concepts and ideas. A dedication to preserving the integrity and stability of the supply chain financing system must moderate the desire to launch fresh items. Ensuring that these creative ideas meet their promise to benefit SMEs, close the trade finance gap, and improve the resilience and openness of worldwide supply chains depends on clear, consistent definitions and a strong knowledge of DTSCF. The DTSCF approach creates the foundation for a more stable, inclusive, and effective worldwide trade ecosystem by encouraging shared knowledge among all stakeholders.

Implementing deep-tier supply chain financing (DTSCF) successfully requires complete knowledge and navigation of a complex array of regulatory frameworks across several countries. These legal issues, ranging from payment responsibilities to mandatory legal requirements, hold significant importance as they impact various aspects of DTSCF.

The structure of payment responsibilities is one of the main legal issues in using DTSCF. Under DTSCF, the financing arrangement depends on the anchor buyer's irrevocable payment commitment. All relevant countries must legally enforce and precisely define this responsibility. The difficulty, then, is the variation in legal systems' acceptance and execution of such responsibilities. Honoring and enforcing these payment obligations across borders is crucial for maintaining the integrity and dependability of the financial system.

The distribution of funding down the supply chain is also very important. DTSCF depends on its capacity to smoothly assign the payment responsibility of the anchor customer to lower-tier suppliers. Legal recognition of this transferability will help to guarantee that the better credit risk of the anchor buyer will benefit every level of suppliers. Different legal standards on the transfer of payment duties can create major obstacles for jurisdictions, so it is imperative to build agreements in line with the legal needs of every engaged area.

Another important factor is dispute-resolving systems. Many supply chains are globally based; hence, conflicts are prone to develop in cross-border transactions. Selecting a law and dispute resolution mechanism with global influence is crucial for minimizing legal uncertainty and enhancing the scalability of DTSCF. Most of the time, the United Nations Commission on International Trade Law (UNCITRAL) Convention on the Recognition and Enforcement of Foreign Arbitral Awards (New York Convention) makes arbitration a valid and useful option. This agreement ensures the acceptance and enforcement of arbitral rulings in over 160 countries, thereby offering a reliable solution for resolving issues arising from DTSCF transactions.

DTSCF implementations are absolutely dependent on know-your-customer (KYC) processes and anti-money laundering (AML) standards. These laws aim to prevent financial crimes and ensure the integrity of financial transactions. Different countries have different KYC and AML rules, which adds even another level of complication. Involved in DTSCF, financial institutions have to carefully negotiate these rules to guarantee compliance and enable seamless financial operations across several borders.

One of the main obstacles DTSCF has right now is the absence of a consistent legal system or framework both inside different countries and across borders. This fragmentation might put a cap on the efficiency and scalability of DTSCF systems. Contracts without sufficient addressing of enforceability concerns might become major obstacles, therefore hindering the general acceptance and duplication of DTSCF models. Consequently, it is important to draft flexible and adaptive legal agreements fit for different legal surroundings.

Legal issues also arise from the acceptance and usage of electronic negotiable instruments, including bills of exchange or promissory notes. Countries without official recognition of these instruments limit the use of DTSCF structures. Nonetheless, UNCITRAL's adoption of the Model Law on Electronic Transferable Records (MLETR) is intensifying efforts to harmonize legal frameworks. Adoption of these standards by nations such as Germany, Singapore, the UK, and the United States helps to legalize electronic records and hence lower uncertainty in cross-jurisdictional transactions.

Dealing with conflicts of laws and lowering legal ambiguity in international transactions depend on the harmonic coordination of legal systems. Legal standards alignment helps nations provide a more consistent and predictable environment for DTSCF, therefore promoting more general acceptance and application. Along with implementing MLETR and other model laws, this harmonization process promotes international collaboration and communication to guarantee that legislative changes complement one another and are consistent.

Basically, working out the legal issues in DTSCF is a tough but necessary task to make sure that this creative financial solution can be used well and be expanded. By determining payment responsibility, ensuring law enforcement, selecting effective dispute resolution methods, and adhering to KYC and AML rules, concerned parties can establish a robust legal foundation for DTSCF. This will help to harmonize different legal frameworks. Fostering confidence, lowering risk, and allowing the effective movement of money across worldwide supply chains depend on this basis. Maintaining and improving the advantages of DTSCF will depend mostly on constant adaptation and cooperation among stakeholders as legal circumstances change.

Overcoming Currency and Regulatory Challenges: Strategies for Global Supply Chain Resilience

The cross-border nature of global supply chains poses significant challenges, particularly due to the variety of currencies and the varying regulatory restrictions across different countries. These currency issues are essential for the proper use of DTSCF because they affect how complicated and possible it is for financial transactions to happen within supply chains.

Tier-1 suppliers in various foreign supply chains frequently conduct transactions in major international currencies like the US Dollar (USD), Euro (EUR), British Pound (GBP), Japanese Yen (JPY), Chinese Renminbi (RMB), and Indian Rupee (INR). Widely used and traded, these currencies provide some degree of consistency and predictability for worldwide trade. But the situation gets more complicated as we move downstream to tier-2 vendors and beyond. Often operating in local marketplaces and using distinct local currencies for their operations, downstream suppliers experience currency mismatches, which complicate the financial arrangements within DTSCF.

DTSCF systems' inherent mismatches of currencies might present a number of difficulties. First, changes in the value of foreign currencies can bring volatility and uncertainty into supplier financial operations. A tier-2 supplier paying in local currency, for example, might be seriously financially liable should the value of the local currency fall negatively relative to the anchor buyer's currency. Cash flows, company margins, and general financial stability can all change with this volatility.

CHAPTER 6   UNLOCKING VALUE: THE POTENTIAL OF DEEP-TIER SUPPLY CHAIN FINANCE (DTSCF)

Second, the necessity of converting currencies at several phases of the supply chain might cause more expenses and delays. Every currency translation entails transaction costs and processing time, which can undermine DTSCF's financial advantages and hinder the seamless flow of payments across the supply chain. Smaller suppliers, who operate with narrower margins and limited financial flexibility, may find these expenses and delays particularly burdensome.

Moreover, developing nations can impose strict foreign exchange restrictions and government regulations, closely monitoring import payments through central banks and export results. These measures aim to regulate foreign exchange, stabilize local currencies, and maintain economic equilibrium through their movement. For DTSCF, they can, however, provide major difficulties, particularly when using outside vendors. Commonly in DTSCF, tokenization or partial assignment of receivables may conflict with these regulatory systems, thereby complicating compliance and potentially disrupting the payment flow.

If we are to properly use DTSCF in such surroundings, we must engage authorities in creating strong frameworks that can fit the changing dynamics of international commerce. Regulators should be aware of the special qualities of DTSCF and how it interacts with current monetary policy and foreign currency restrictions. Legal and regulatory frameworks that make it simple for DTSCF to fit into global supply chains could be made if financial institutions, anchor customers, suppliers, and regulators are encouraged to work together.

Hedging techniques are one possible way to reduce regulatory difficulties and currency concerns. By locking in favorable exchange rates or offering defense against negative currency moves, financial instruments such as forward contracts, options, and swaps can help suppliers control exchange rate risks. Although helpful, these instruments may not be available to all providers, especially smaller ones, and call for a comprehensive awareness of financial markets.

Adoption of blockchain technology and digital currencies also provides interesting ways to solve regulatory issues and mismatches in currencies. Particularly those issued by central banks (currencies, digital currencies, or CBDCs), digital currencies can offer a stable and generally acknowledged alternative that streamlines international trade. Through real-time transaction monitoring and regulatory compliance automation, blockchain technology may improve openness, security, and efficiency in DTSCF.

Applying DTSCF depends critically on negotiating financial issues. The cross-border nature of supply chains introduces complexity due to multiple currencies and regulatory restrictions, which requires proper control to ensure the performance of

DTSCF. Stakeholders may solve these problems and fully realize DTSCF by involving authorities, using hedging techniques, and using digital technology. This all-encompassing strategy guarantees DTSCF's ability to offer comprehensive, steady, and effective financing options, supporting the resilience and expansion of world supply chains.

Overcoming Challenges: How to Ensure Sustainability and Efficiency

If the program is to be effective and sustainable, deep-tier supply chain financing (DTSCF) must properly address several operational and technological difficulties. These difficulties include restricted access to technology among SMEs, the requirement of joint ownership, the importance of distributing benefits down the chain, overcoming information barriers, and maintaining strong supply chains.

For SMEs, particularly those located in remote areas and developing countries, experience poses a significant operational challenge.

These businesses, vital components of the worldwide supply chain, often operate with limited resources and face a daily struggle for survival, which typically precedes technological investments, making it challenging for them to adapt to the complexity of modern supply networks. Apart from their limited involvement in DTSCF, this technical difference affects their general competitiveness and efficiency. Dealing with this problem calls for focused programs to provide SMEs with the required technology tools and training so they may fit very well into sophisticated supply chain finance systems.

DTSCF's success depends much on cooperative efforts among all the stakeholders; hence, collective ownership of the project is very necessary. Long-tail supply chains, like those in the automotive sector, where choosing and onboarding important suppliers calls for a coordinated effort, depend especially on this cooperation. Working together with a high degree of dedication, anchor purchasers, banks, and suppliers—especially tier-1 and tier-2 suppliers—must guarantee the seamless deployment of DTSCF. This joint ownership guarantees that all members are completely involved in the process and in line with their goals, therefore promoting shared accountability.

The willingness of vendors at every level to forward the payment advantages down the chain is another important consideration. DTSCF's success depends on this cooperation, as any resistance to benefit distribution compromises program goals. A supplier might decide to keep the money, which would disrupt the anticipated cash flow and defeat the advantages of DTSCF. Including incentives inside the scheme might help suppliers pass on advantages, therefore counteracting this. Anchor purchasers and funders have to carefully evaluate and arrange these incentives to make sure they efficiently encourage the anticipated behavior without generating unexpected results.

Informational barriers make it difficult to implement the DTSCF. Key suppliers, particularly those at tier-1, might be reluctant to provide the anchor buyer with comprehensive supply chain data due to concerns about potential omission or loss of negotiation power. Effective DTSCF implementation relies on visibility, and this opposition could potentially hinder it, as transparency is crucial for monitoring and controlling financial activities across the supply chain. By guaranteeing data integrity and offering selective visibility, advanced technology solutions can significantly help overcome these obstacles. Such solutions can protect private data and provide the required openness for DTSCF to operate as it should.

Ensuring that the finance given through DTSCF is directly tied to commodities or services unique to one anchor buyer depends on maintaining strong supply chains. This concentration prevents credit leakage, which could otherwise leverage a strong buyer's creditworthiness to fund another buyer's supply chain, thereby diminishing the effectiveness of DTSCF. Technology may help track products to make sure their source and intended usage line up with the financing arrangements. Maintaining the integrity of the financial system and preventing credit abuse depend on this traceability.

Reducing risks inside the DTSCF structure also depends on closely observing the creditworthiness of anchor purchasers. Underlying the whole system is the financial health of anchor purchasers, since their credit profile dictates the terms and conditions of financing spread along the supply chain. Any loss of the credit of the anchor customer might have a domino effect, therefore influencing the supplier ecosystem generally and especially SMEs. The supply chain financing network needs to be regularly checked, and the credit situations of anchor buyers need to be closely watched in order to keep it stable and avoid any risks.

Handling the technical and operational issues in DTSCF implementation calls for a multimodal strategy. By facilitating technology access for small businesses, encouraging stakeholder ownership, ensuring benefits flow down the supply chain, eliminating information barriers with modern technology, and maintaining strong supply chain links, DTSCF can fully realize its potential. By means of a strong, open, and transparent financial environment, these initiatives will assist in the expansion and sustainability of worldwide supply chains, therefore benefiting all those engaged.

CHAPTER 6   UNLOCKING VALUE: THE POTENTIAL OF DEEP-TIER SUPPLY CHAIN FINANCE (DTSCF)

Leveraging Technology for Scalable DTSCF: The Role of Fintech and Collaboration with Financial Institutions

Adoption of modern technology is therefore crucial for the effective deployment and scalability of DTSCF. Continuous experimental activities and pilot projects have a significant impact on the still-developing discipline of DTSCF. The platform-based strategy, a common thread across these projects, is essential for managing the complexity of DTSCF, particularly in accessing deeper levels of suppliers across multiple countries.

Among various important tasks in DTSCF, technology is the backbone for supply chain links' identification, tracking, and monitoring. Modern supply chains' complexities require advanced technology solutions to guarantee compliance, openness, and efficiency at several levels. Fintech businesses are crucial in tackling these issues, as they provide creative ideas that can simplify DTSCF procedures.

Finding pertinent ecosystem players is one of the main uses of technology in DTSCF. Modern data analytics and machine learning techniques can help identify important supply chain partners and vendors. For anchor purchasers and financiers, these tools offer insightful analysis of enormous volumes of data to find trends, relationships, and possible hazards. Understanding the structure and dynamics of the supply chain helps stakeholders make better decisions and apply more successful DTSCF initiatives.

Another vital ability that technology enables is tracking and monitoring supply chain links. For example, blockchain technology provides a transparent and safe means of documenting and verifying purchases all across the supply chain. Blockchain ensures the traceability of goods and money flows by building an unchangeable record of transactions, therefore strengthening the confidence and dependability of DTSCF systems. Maintaining the integrity of the financing process depends especially on this traceability, as it guarantees proper use of the money and helps avoid fraud.

Fintech solutions greatly assist in managing the regulated release of sensitive data across the supply chain. Any financial transaction raises significant privacy and data security issues; DTSCF is no exception. Modern encryption and data security systems help to secure private data so that only authorized users may access certain records. This deliberate information sharing improves openness and safeguards supplier and other stakeholder confidence.

CHAPTER 6 UNLOCKING VALUE: THE POTENTIAL OF DEEP-TIER SUPPLY CHAIN FINANCE (DTSCF)

Although fintech companies have made significant progress in creating technological solutions for DTSCF, the lack of a consistent framework often makes scaling difficult. Many times, lacking the required balance sheets to function as lenders or without the reach to interact with all supply chain players, fintech firms This restriction can make DTSCF solutions less often used overall. However, the financial sector remains committed to exploring DTSCF solutions, typically with the guidance and collaboration of respected financial institutions.

Overcoming these obstacles depends on fintech firms working with established banking institutions. Established financial institutions provide outstanding resources, knowledge, and reach that would complement the creative capacity of fintech companies. Working together, these organizations may create and apply scalable DTSCF solutions utilizing the respective capabilities of each other. While fintech companies may provide modern technologies and rapid development methods, financial institutions can supply the required cash and regulatory compliance.

Furthermore, one cannot understate the importance of exploratory initiatives and trial projects. Through real-world testing and refining of DTSCF solutions, these projects enable stakeholders to find any problems and make required changes before more general application. Pilot projects also offer insightful information and comments, therefore strengthening the foundation for DTSCF and enabling better dependability and efficiency. These initiatives help DTSCF's general awareness and comprehension grow as they go, therefore enabling greater general acceptance.

Fintech companies have greatly advanced recently in creating technology solutions to support DTSCF. These developments include systems within a single ecosystem that encompass a variety of financial services, from invoice finance to payment processing. These systems can automate compliance tests, streamline supplier onboarding, and offer real-time supply chain financial health analysis. These skills are crucial in managing the complexity of DTSCF and ensuring that every participant can benefit from the financing plans.

The effective implementation and scalability of deep-tier supply chain financing naturally correlate with the acceptance of sophisticated technology. Using innovative fintech solutions can help stakeholders solve the complexity of contemporary supply chains, improve openness and efficiency, and guarantee financial transaction integrity. Overcoming the obstacles and releasing DTSCF's full potential will depend on cooperation between fintech startups and traditional financial institutions, along with continuous pilot projects. As these initiatives develop, they will help to create a more robust, inclusive, and effective worldwide supply chain ecosystem.

CHAPTER 6   UNLOCKING VALUE: THE POTENTIAL OF DEEP-TIER SUPPLY CHAIN FINANCE (DTSCF)

The Platform-Based Strategy: Enhancing Real-Time Monitoring, Compliance, and Scalability

DTSCF has a complex character that calls for a strong and sophisticated technological basis. When you want to connect many suppliers, each with their own set of laws and rules, you need a system that works well with all of these different parts. This demand has led to the platform-based strategy, which is essential for DTSCF's flawless execution and scalability.

The capacity to simplify the identification of supply chain players is the core of the platform-based strategy. Modern supply chains are large, linked systems, including many companies from many countries. Finding all the pertinent player systems—he anchors the customer down to the most distant supplier—is difficult. Advanced data analytics and machine learning techniques on a strong technical foundation help to sort through vast amounts of data and precisely map the whole supply chain. This thorough identification procedure is crucial for understanding the flow of products and services and ensuring proper connectivity among all participants within the DTSCF structure.

Another crucial ability of the platform-based approach is real-time monitoring. Real-time monitoring of events and transactions is crucial in the constantly evolving landscape of global trade. Real-time access to the state of commodities, financial transactions, and contractual conditions compliance offers via a sophisticated platform to stakeholders. This level of transparency enables proactive risk management by promptly identifying and resolving any issues before they escalate. Real-time monitoring improves decision-making for financiers and anchor purchasers by giving current knowledge on the operational state and financial situation of suppliers.

Maintaining the integrity of the DTSCF process depends mostly on accurate tracking of products and financial activities. Every transaction is guaranteed to be openly and immutably recorded by a technology platform fitted with blockchain or another distributed ledger system. This feature not only stops fraud but also offers a clear audit trail on which stakeholders could depend. Along with the matching financial flows, tracking the movement of items from one level of the supply chain to the next ensures that the funding given through DTSCF is applied as planned. Cross-border transactions in particular depend on this traceability, as different laws and standards might impede compliance and execution.

CHAPTER 6   UNLOCKING VALUE: THE POTENTIAL OF DEEP-TIER SUPPLY CHAIN FINANCE (DTSCF)

Additionally, addressing the regulatory difficulties related to DTSCF requires a platform-based approach. Legal rules vary across different countries; hence, it is challenging to guarantee consistent compliance throughout the supply chain. Standardizing procedures and paperwork made possible by a single technology platform guarantees that every transaction follows pertinent legal and regulatory guidelines. For suppliers, who may otherwise find it difficult to negotiate the convoluted regulatory terrain on their own, this standardization streamlines compliance. Also, the system can do many compliance-related tasks automatically, such as KYC (know your customer) checks and AML (anti-money laundering) processes. This makes things easier for both the supplier and the banker in terms of administration.

The cooperative character of DTSCF depends on the integration possibilities of a strong platform. Effective DTSCF depends on the smooth interaction of several players, including suppliers, anchor purchasers, financiers, and legislators. A well-designed platform offers a common area where all users may coordinate their activities, share information, and communicate. This cooperative environment promotes trust and openness by enabling every member to understand how their job fits into the larger supply chain and financial ecology. Anchor purchasers, for example, may better appreciate the difficulties their suppliers have, while financiers can learn about the operational reality of the supply chain, thereby guiding wiser and more encouraging finance decisions.

Furthermore, the platform-based approach considerably improves the scalability of DTSCF. The technology platform ought to be able to scale with the development of supply chains. The scalability and adaptability provided by cloud-based solutions allow one to meet growing transaction volumes and growing supplier networks. Because these platforms are simple to update and add to, they will continue to be able to meet the needs of a growing DTSCF system without any major problems.

Finally, the effective implementation and scalability of deep-tier supply chain financing depend on the platform-based strategy, which is very important. By facilitating real-time monitoring and precise tracking of product and money movements, a robust technical platform safeguards the integrity and effectiveness of the DTSCF process. This strategy not only solves the inherent complexity of worldwide supply chains but also improves scalability, compliance, and cooperation, therefore opening the path for a stronger and more effective financial environment. The platform-based strategy will stay at the forefront of supply chain financing advances as technology develops, therefore promoting stability in world commerce and sustainable development.

Strategic Alliances Between Fintech and Traditional Banks: A Path to Scaling DTSCF

In DTSCF, fintech firms have positioned themselves at the forefront of innovation. Still, they have significant obstacles that hinder the scalability and general acceptance of their solutions. Among the most important obstacles are the financial and network restrictions present in many fintech companies, as well as the absence of a thorough and uniform framework.

For fintechs, the lack of a consistent framework is the main challenge. The use of DTSCF solutions becomes scattered and erratic without well-defined, generally agreed-upon rules and standards. This lack of cohesiveness makes it challenging for fintech firms to properly expand their solutions throughout several regions and countries. Every new deployment calls for adaptation to fit local rules, therefore generating inefficiencies and extra expenses. The outcome is a fragmented strategy that hinders the wider acceptance of DTSCF and stifles the possible advantages it might provide to worldwide supply networks.

Another major obstacle for fintech startups is financial capability. Unlike established financial institutions, fintech companies can lack the significant balance sheets required to directly credit suppliers. The efficient use of DTSCF depends on their limited capacity to offer complete financial services. The foundation of DTSCF is its capacity to provide finance across several layers of the supply chain, therefore assuring that even the smallest vendors have access to the required capital. Fintechs, running on little money, find it difficult to meet this need on their own.

Furthermore, fintech startups usually lack the large networks needed to involve all supply chain players. Long-standing partnerships between traditional banks and a broad spectrum of companies across several sectors and geographical areas abound. Reaching the many players in a supply chain—from big anchor customers to tiny, distant suppliers—these networks are absolutely vital. Though technologically advanced, fintech companies can lack the reach and impact needed to properly interact with all pertinent parties.

Fintech firms are joining with established financial institutions more and more to tackle these obstacles. The partnerships bring together the large amounts of money and power that traditional banks have with the new technologies and flexibility of fintechs. This is an example of a strategic marriage of capabilities. The development and use of scalable DTSCF solutions depend on such collaborations.

CHAPTER 6 UNLOCKING VALUE: THE POTENTIAL OF DEEP-TIER SUPPLY CHAIN FINANCE (DTSCF)

When fintechs and conventional banks collaborate, they can create a more robust and efficient DTSCF structure. Modern technology features brought by fintech organizations include digital platforms for smooth integration of supply chain players, machine learning for risk assessment, and blockchain for transaction traceability. These technologies may greatly improve the dependability, openness, and efficiency of DTSCF. Traditional banks, meanwhile, provide their wide networks of clients and partners, regulatory knowledge, and outstanding financial acumen. This mix, with the necessary financial support and regulatory compliance, ensures the large-scale implementation of the innovative ideas generated by fintechs.

Financial capacity is another problem that fintechs and banks can solve by working together. Working together, fintech companies may use the significant balance sheets of established banks to supply the necessary funding. This structure lets fintechs concentrate on creating and improving their technology solutions while depending on banks to handle DTSCF's financial needs. The outcome is a more complete and all-encompassing service that is able to serve the whole supply chain.

These alliances also help fintechs access the large networks of conventional banks. The existing ties of banks to companies in various fields can facilitate the onboarding of a wide range of supply chain players. This extensive reach ensures the widespread and successful use of DTSCF solutions, thereby assisting suppliers across all stages of the supply chain. Using these networks helps fintechs overcome their constraints in reach and connectivity, therefore improving the scalability and influence of their products.

Additionally, the cooperative efforts between fintech businesses and conventional financial institutions are opening the path for the evolution of a consistent framework for DTSCF. By means of cooperative projects and pilot programs, these alliances might help create internationally accepted best practices and norms. Standardizing will help to minimize costs, simplify the use of DTSCF solutions throughout several markets, and lessen the necessity of customizing. This harmonic approach is crucial for realizing the full potential of DTSCF and ensuring its widespread acceptance.

Strong alliances with established financial institutions provide a beneficial road forward, even if fintech firms struggle greatly to expand their DTSCF products. Combining the financial resources and networks of banks with the technological innovation of fintechs will help to overcome the constraints limiting the expansion of DTSCF. The development of scalable, efficient, and uniform DTSCF systems capable of revolutionizing worldwide supply chains depends on such cooperative efforts. Deep-tier supply chain financing will be adopted and successfully Strategic partnerships combined with advanced technological solutions will enable the identification, tracking, and monitoring of supply chain connections. This will ultimately make DTSCF initiatives more scalable and effective. These partnerships will drive these initiatives as they develop, thereby benefiting all players in the supply chain ecosystem.

Leveraging Technology for Scalable and Efficient DTSCF: The Role of Innovation and Strategic Partnerships

DTSCF has a future closely connected with the development and integration of technology. Tech will help this subject evolve and be a key tool. We should continuously explore and implement pilot projects, as they provide insightful information that enhances the technical bases necessary for successful DTSCF.

A platform-based strategy is absolutely necessary in the changing terrain of DTSCF. This method uses cutting-edge digital tools to handle the complexity of combining several layers of suppliers in several legal and regulatory environments. These systems make it possible to identify, monitor, and keep track of supply chain links in real time, which is important for keeping DTSCF operations honest and efficient. These systems can precisely map supply chains utilizing advanced algorithms and data analytics, therefore giving stakeholders a clear and all-encompassing perspective of the whole supply chain.

Fintech companies and well-established financial institutions will work together to largely address the challenges of scaling DTSCF. Fintech companies provide creative technology ideas that can improve supply chain finance's efficiency by means of simplification. Their limited financial capability and reach, however, can restrict their power to apply these ideas more broadly. Conversely, conventional financial institutions have the means and large networks needed to enable substantial use. Combining these skills will help fintechs and financial companies produce strong and scalable DTSCF solutions.

One of the exciting developments for DTSCF going forward is blockchain technology integration. Blockchain provides an unchangeable database that guarantees the traceability of commodities and money movements all along the supply chain, therefore offering a safe and open means of recording and verifying transactions. The prevention of fraud and guarantee of regulatory standard compliance depend on this traceability. Blockchain technology increases openness and confidence among supply chain players by allowing real-time transaction tracking, hence improving DTSCF dependability and efficiency.

CHAPTER 6   UNLOCKING VALUE: THE POTENTIAL OF DEEP-TIER SUPPLY CHAIN FINANCE (DTSCF)

Artificial intelligence (AI) and machine learning (ML) also stand to greatly influence future DTSCF. By using large volumes of data analysis, these technologies can spot trends, project hazards, and maximize financial judgments. By offering insights into supplier operating state and financial situation, artificial intelligence and machine learning techniques assist anchor buyers and financiers in making wise decisions. These systems may also automatically handle mundane chores such as risk assessments and compliance checks, therefore lightening administrative responsibilities and improving operational effectiveness.

Smart contracts will also eventually find prominence in DTSCF technology. Because the terms of the agreement between the buyer and seller are written into these self-executing contracts, they may be able to automatically carry out the terms of the contract without the need for a third party. Smart contracts improve financial transaction speed and dependability, lower transaction costs, and simplify procedures. By ensuring the automatic performance of contract provisions when established criteria are satisfied, smart contracts enhance the effectiveness of DTSCF, thereby reducing conflicts and delays.

Furthermore, the use of Internet of things (IoT) technologies can revolutionize the monitoring and management of supply chains. As products pass through the supply chain, IoT devices may offer real-time data on their location, condition, and status. By means of this real-time visibility, stakeholders may see any problems before they become more serious, therefore guaranteeing the seamless flow of products and financial activities. IoT integration with DTSCF systems helps supply chains become more flexible and resistant to disturbances.

Technology is not just a tool but also a pillar of DTSCF. Overcoming the difficulties with growing DTSCF depends on the constant development and application of sophisticated technical solutions. The sector may fully use DTSCF by adopting a platform-based strategy and supporting strategic alliances between fintechs and established financial institutions. Together with blockchain, artificial intelligence, machine learning, smart contracts, and IoT, these partnerships will help to identify, track, and monitor supply chain relationships with hitherto unheard-of accuracy and efficiency. DTSCF projects will therefore become more scalable and efficient, thereby promoting increased resilience, openness, and sustainability in world supply chains. The future of DTSCF technology promises a more interconnected, efficient, and secure supply chain finance ecosystem, which will benefit all stakeholders and foster equitable economic growth.

CHAPTER 6   UNLOCKING VALUE: THE POTENTIAL OF DEEP-TIER SUPPLY CHAIN FINANCE (DTSCF)

Leveraging DTSCF for ESG Compliance and Enhancement

In recent years, there has been a clear shift toward a more responsible and ecologically, socially, and governance-oriented global commerce ecosystem. Different ESG-related legislative projects and rules that have developed all throughout the world are driving this shift. Company supply chains must be researched to ensure that their operations and suppliers follow strict human rights, labor, and environmental standards. Governments and regulatory bodies agree that this is of utmost importance.

A historic piece of legislation mandating businesses to disclose the dangers of modern slavery in their operations and supply networks, Australia's Modern Slavery Act of 2018 By requiring companies to act proactively to stop forced labor, human trafficking, and other kinds of modern slavery, this legislation guarantees more responsibility and openness throughout their supply chains.

The Duty of Vigilance Act (Loi de Vigilance) mandates in France that big businesses create and follow sensible vigilance strategies. These strategies aim to identify risks and prevent significant violations of human rights, fundamental freedoms, and environmental harm resulting from their operations, as well as those of their suppliers, subsidiaries, and subcontractors.

The Supply Chain Act of Germany (Lieferkettengesetz) is yet another important step toward guaranteeing corporate accountability. This law requires businesses to find and reduce environmental hazards and human rights issues in their supply chains, therefore spreading their responsibility from their local operations to cover their whole network.

The Environment Protection Act of 1986 in India emphasizes the need for environmental preservation by mandating businesses to follow strict environmental criteria and to carry out actions meant to stop and lessen pollution. Likewise, Indonesia's Law No. 32 of 2009 on Environmental Protection and Management stresses sustainable development and the preservation of the environment, mandating companies to follow environmental rules and to guarantee sustainable practices inside their operations and supply chains.

The Environmental Quality Act of 1974 from Malaysia offers a structure for environmental protection and control of industrial contamination. This law requires businesses doing business in Malaysia to follow environmental criteria and carry out policies meant to reduce their effects.

Another important advancement in the realm of ESG control comes from Norway's Transparency Act. This legislation mandates businesses to be transparent in their operations and supply chains and reveal information on how they control the possibility of human rights abuses. This helps companies become more responsible and sustainable, as well as foster more corporate accountability.

Articles 964j et seq. of the Swiss Code of Obligations and the Due Diligence and Transparency Ordinance, which are part of Switzerland's legal system, require businesses to do their research on their supply chains. These laws stress the importance of protecting human rights and the environment. This kind of regulation stresses the need for openness and responsibility in business processes.

The Framework Act on Sustainable Development of the Republic of Korea emphasizes its dedication to corporate responsibility and sustainable development. This law helps businesses incorporate sustainable practices into their operations and supply chains, therefore balancing environmental preservation with social development and economic success.

California's Transparency in Supply Chains Act mandates that major stores and manufacturers in the United States reveal their initiatives to abolish forced labor and human trafficking from their suppliers. By revealing the actions businesses are taking to solve these important problems, this legislation seeks to educate customers and encourage corporate responsibility.

A major step toward consistent worldwide sustainability reporting standards is the recent founding of the International Sustainability Standards Board, a climate component of the International Financial Reporting Standard. This evolution is likely to inspire businesses to match with uniform ESG reporting systems and boost supply chain monitoring. The International Sustainability Standards Board seeks to empower stakeholders to make informed decisions based on similar sustainability data by means of a shared set of norms, therefore promoting better openness and accountability in worldwide supply chains.

These legal changes across several countries show how increasingly important ESG issues are to supply chain management and corporate governance. These rules make sure that companies actively manage ESG risks and opportunities in their supply chains by doing what they need to do to protect human rights, stop child labor, and protect the environment.

Beyond mere compliance, these rules inspire businesses to embrace more ethical and environmentally friendly business models. Companies that match these values help to create a more sustainable global economy, therefore advancing social fairness, environmental protection, and economic resilience.

Furthermore, a crucial first step toward more openness and comparability in ESG performance is the shift toward uniform worldwide sustainability reporting systems. Following these models helps businesses give stakeholders consistent and accurate information on their environmental policies, thereby supporting investors, customers, and authorities to make wise decisions.

The development of ESG-related rules and policies all throughout the world marks a radical change toward a more ethical and sustainable worldwide commerce ecology. These rules not only force businesses to follow due diligence on their supply chains but also promote the acceptance of best practices in human rights, labor standards, and environmental protection. Businesses have to be alert and aggressive in their approach to ESG compliance as the regulatory environment changes so that they help to create a more fair and sustainable planet. Integration of new technologies and adherence to strong ESG criteria would help DTSCF and global supply chains be more transparent, responsible, and sustainable worldwide.

Enhancing ESG Visibility and Compliance Through DTSCF

DTSCF has tremendous promise as a tool to improve visibility for reporting reasons, guarantee regulatory compliance, and encourage the accomplishment of environmental, social, and governance (ESG) standards. By using DTSCF in their business, anchor buyers can make changes in all three ESG pillars, creating a supply chain that is more open, responsible, and long-lasting.

Within the context of environmental sustainability, DTSCF provides anchor purchasers with a strong tool to encourage their vendors to reach ESG standards. Anchor purchasers can inspire suppliers to embrace more sustainable practices by connecting finance rates to The company implements ESG-aligned key performance indicators (KPIs). For instance, we could offer better financing conditions to suppliers who demonstrate significant reductions in their carbon footprint or obtain specific environmental certifications. This strategy not only drives suppliers to raise their environmental performance but also helps to match financial incentives with more general sustainability objectives.

Better visibility through DTSCF may significantly improve environmental reporting. Anchor customers can gather and examine real-time, accurate data on supplier environmental practices to gain a comprehensive understanding of the entire environmental impact of their supply chain. The better optimization of logistics made possible by this insight helps to minimize lead times and thus the carbon footprint related to inventory control and transportation. Simplifying these procedures helps businesses save waste, lower energy use, and create a more sustainable supply chain.

Anchor purchasers can use DTSCF to promote improved labor standards in their suppliers from a social perspective. Anchor purchasers may utilize DTSCF to propel positive social change based on KPIs such as fair compensation and safe working conditions. Following these KPIs can help suppliers get better financing terms, therefore motivating them to raise labor standards. This strategy guarantees employees receive fair treatment and operate in secure surroundings.

DTSCF's additional openness helps anchor purchasers to more precisely check labor rules' compliance. By using real-time data on salaries, working hours, and safety events, one may gather and examine such information to enable quick identification and correction of any problems. Proactive surveillance ensures the safety of every worker in the supply chain and aids in preventing labor violations. Moreover, by encouraging fair labor standards, anchor purchasers may improve their brand and develop closer ties with investors and customers that share social concerns.

From a governance standpoint, DTSCF improves the visibility of suppliers' compliance with operational, ethical, and regulatory norms and practices. DTSCF systems gather comprehensive information that provides anchor customers with a comprehensive understanding of their suppliers' adherence to ethical standards and legal obligations. Maintaining high standards of government all throughout the supply chain depends on this openness.

By making sure that suppliers follow operational, ethical, and legal rules, DTSCF helps lower the risks that come with not following the rules, such as legal penalties, damage to the company's reputation, and financial losses. Using robust monitoring and reporting systems, anchor buyers can monitor suppliers' adherence to governance KPIs such as anti-corruption policies, data security requirements, and ethical sourcing guidelines. Regular meetings of these KPIs will reward suppliers with improved financing conditions, therefore motivating them to maintain high levels of governance.

Using DTSCF for governance also encourages more responsibility throughout the supply chain. We expect suppliers to meet high standards, promptly identifying and correcting any deviations. This responsibility guarantees that every link in the supply chain runs with integrity. This responsibility ensures transparency and integrity, thereby fostering confidence among stakeholders and enhancing the overall resilience and sustainability of the chain.

Considering all factors, DTSCF serves as an excellent tool for enhancing reporting visibility, ensuring regulatory compliance, and promoting adherence to ESG standards. Anchor purchasers using DTSCF may significantly increase environmental sustainability, social responsibility, and governance requirements inside their supplier chains. While financial incentives matched with ESG KPIs inspire suppliers to use more sustainable and ethical practices, improved visibility and transparency make monitoring and reporting more effective. DTSCF therefore helps to build a more open, responsible, and sustainable global trade ecosystem, thereby benefiting all the parties involved.

Integrating DTSCF into ESG Strategies

DTSCF is becoming important given the growing market and legislative needs for thorough ESG reporting. DTSCF becomes increasingly important for tracking and encouraging ESG-aligned behavior as businesses try to satisfy these needs. Including DTSCF in an ESG plan calls for a complete approach and strong cooperation among all pertinent parties.

Anchor consumers first have to be proactive in including DTSCF into their ESG plans. Working closely with suppliers helps one establish reasonable ESG objectives. Among these goals should be strong government policies, social responsibility, and environmental sustainability. Through a cooperative definition of these goals, suppliers and anchor customers may make sure their ESG aims are reasonable and complement the more general supply chain goals.

Important parts of this integration process include regular monitoring and reporting. Anchor customers must set up systems to monitor advancement toward ESG objectives so that suppliers are fulfilling their obligations. Digital channels that offer real-time data on several ESG criteria—such as carbon emissions, labor conditions, and governance compliance—can help to enable this. By compiling and evaluating information from all over the supply chain, these systems provide a thorough understanding of general ESG performance.

CHAPTER 6 UNLOCKING VALUE: THE POTENTIAL OF DEEP-TIER SUPPLY CHAIN FINANCE (DTSCF)

Improving the efficacy of DTSCF inside ESG initiatives depends mostly on cooperation with financiers. For suppliers that either achieve or surpass ESG objectives, financial institutions can provide incentives, including varying financing rates. These incentives ensure the incorporation of ESG issues into the financial aspects of the supply chain while also motivating suppliers to adopt sustainable practices. Anchor purchasers and financiers may help to significantly increase sustainability throughout the supply chain by matching financial rewards with ESG performance.

Including DTSCF in ESG plans calls for even more openness and responsibility. Companies ought to be open about their ESG objectives and their development toward reaching them. Among stakeholders—including investors, consumers, and government agencies—this openness fosters confidence. Supported by data acquired via DTSCF systems, regular and thorough ESG reports help to show a company's dedication to sustainability and its effects on the supply chain.

The possibility of improving ESG reporting is one of the main benefits of including DTSCF in ESG policies. The complete and more accurate picture of a company's ESG performance that the thorough data gathered by DTSCF offers Companies can use this information to produce comprehensive reports that meet the expectations of investors and other stakeholders, as well as meet the requirements of regulatory bodies. Companies may improve the legitimacy and dependability of their ESG reporting by using the openness and traceability DTSCF provides.

Moreover, effective control of DTSCF can greatly help meet environmental targets. DTSCF encourages suppliers to adhere to policies that reduce their environmental impact, improve labor conditions, and elevate governance standards by aligning financial incentives with ESG performance. This alignment guarantees that supply chain activities center on sustainability rather than being a secondary issue.

Including DTSCF in ESG plans also helps to create an always-improving culture. Suppliers continuously enhance their methods to meet ESG criteria and secure better financing arrangements. Stronger governance structures, less environmental impact, and improved social results are just a few of the long-term gains possible from this continuous improvement cycle.

Including DTSCF in an ESG plan for a firm is a fantastic way to improve sustainability, satisfy legal criteria, and reach long-term commercial objectives. Anchor customers, suppliers, and financiers must all work holistically and cooperatively toward this integration. Companies can use DTSin to make big changes in their supply chains by setting clear ESG goals, keeping regular track of progress, and linking financial rewards to sustainability success. DTSCF therefore not only promotes improved ESG reporting and compliance but also helps to make global supply networks more generally resilient and sustainable.

Coordinating Stakeholder Efforts for Scaling DTSCF: A Call to Action for Collaborative Innovation and Harmonized Legal Frameworks

While we have laid the fundamental foundations of DTSCF, the actual development and scaling of DTSCF require coordinated work from all involved parties. This all-encompassing call to action details the required actions to fully utilize DTSCF, therefore promoting an ecology of cooperation, creativity, and shared dedication.

Establishing a committed forum that gathers all pertinent players comes first and is absolutely vital. This forum will provide a place for coordination whereby participants may exchange ideas, go over difficulties, and plan on appropriately scaling DTSCF. By bringing together anchor purchasers, vendors, financiers, attorneys, and regulatory authorities, the forum will facilitate a comprehensive approach to DTSCF, ensuring the inclusion of all perspectives in the development process. Building trust and creating a cooperative atmosphere depend on honest communication inside this forum.

In addition to the forum, the establishment of specialized working groups will prove beneficial in addressing specific issues that are crucial for the success of DTSCF. These working groups should mostly concentrate on promoting the harmonization of home law with international best practices. This entails pushing nations to match their legal systems to criteria like the Model Law on Electronic Transferable Records (MLETR), therefore enabling the usage of electronic records in global trade. Harmonized legal systems will lower legal ambiguity and complexity, facilitating the implementation of DTSCF solutions throughout several countries.

One other important chore for these working groups is providing legal analysis. Knowledge of efficient legal structures and DTSCF regulations would help stakeholders better grasp the legal scene and guarantee compliance. This common knowledge will enable the building of strong legal systems that enable flawless DTSCF transaction execution. Furthermore, unambiguous rules for anti-money laundering (AML) processes and know-your-customer (KYC) policies should be established. These rules will standardize KYC and AML, ensuring all DTSCF participants adhere to the necessary regulatory criteria, thereby enhancing system security and confidence.

CHAPTER 6   UNLOCKING VALUE: THE POTENTIAL OF DEEP-TIER SUPPLY CHAIN FINANCE (DTSCF)

Improving knowledge of DTSCF's potential depends critically on educational resources and tools. Creating instructional materials explaining the advantages, processes, and implementation techniques for DTSCF should be the main priorities of working groups. Working groups may share these materials across various fields to enhance awareness and fortify the capabilities of all participants. Further supporting these educational initiatives are partnerships with academic institutions, trade groups, and training companies so that information is generally available and accessible.

Another main goal is motivating cooperation between fintech startups and established financial institutions. Traditional banks provide financial resources and large networks; fintech companies contribute technical innovation and agility. Effective development and implementation of creative DTSCF solutions depend on cooperation between several organizations. These partnerships will combine the capabilities of both sides to produce a more scalable and unified DTSCF ecosystem.

Simplifying DTSCF operations also depends on standardizing documentation. Standardizing legal papers will help to streamline transactions, lower administrative costs, and guarantee consistency throughout several DTSCF implementations. Standardizing will facilitate smoother talks and faster transaction execution, thereby enhancing the accessibility and effectiveness of DTSCF for all parties.

Realizing DTSCF's full potential requires operational, technological, and legal issues to be addressed by open communication, team efforts, and information sharing. Stakeholders may coordinate their activities, exchange ideas, and create strategies that handle the complexity of DTSCF by means of a specialized forum and specific working groups. Important first steps toward the effective growth of DTSCF will be harmonizing legislative frameworks, creating explicit KYC and AML rules, supporting fintech alliances, and standardizing documentation.

Everyone involved in DTSCF must cooperate if we are to realize its full potential. The sector may overcome obstacles and release the transforming power of DTSCF by setting a specific forum, forming specialized working groups, and encouraging cooperation and information exchange. In addition to enhancing the transparency and efficiency of supply chains, this integrated strategy will contribute to the advancement of general sustainability and ethical corporate practices. The moment to act is now; DTSCF can transform world trade finance by working together, building a more strong and inclusive financial environment for future generations.

CHAPTER 6   UNLOCKING VALUE: THE POTENTIAL OF DEEP-TIER SUPPLY CHAIN FINANCE (DTSCF)

Revolutionizing Supply Chain Financing: How Blockchain and Invoice Tokenization Empower Deep-Tier Suppliers and Strengthen Global Trade

Maintaining effective financial operations is critical for the survival and expansion of companies at every level in the complicated and linked global supply chains of today. Smaller suppliers, particularly those situated further upstream in the supply chain, commonly referred to as deep-tier suppliers, often face significant challenges in securing reasonably priced funding sources. Usually several stages distant from the ultimate anchor buyer, these suppliers are essential for the seamless flow of products and services as they often provide specialized components or materials necessary for the end result. Deep-tier suppliers, for all their significance, can have liquidity problems. This results from a lack of exposure, poorer credit profiles, and restricted direct financial interactions with big, creditworthy buyers—many different factors.

Usually functioning with limited working capital, deep-tier suppliers are responsible for covering running expenses, such as personnel, supplies, and manufacturing costs, before they receive payment for their products or services. Normal payment cycles in many sectors often result in delays of 60–90 days or more, thereby exacerbating liquidity issues. Deep-tier suppliers typically face exclusion due to their opaque position in the supply chain, which limits their eligibility for reasonably priced financing. This exclusion increases their sensitivity to financial stress, which also increases their susceptibility to disturbances that could affect the entire supply chain.

Recognizing these challenges, recent advancements in financial technology (FinTech) have revolutionized the market by offering deep-tier suppliers new avenues to secure affordable capital. One such advance is the application of blockchain technology—more especially, the tokenizing of invoices. This technology transforms bills into digital assets on a transparent, secure ledger, enabling monitoring and movement. Deep-tier suppliers may now acquire finance at more reasonable conditions by using the better creditworthiness of anchor purchasers. Under this approach, the risk moves from the smaller suppliers and spreads throughout the supply chain, therefore reducing financing expenses and increasing capital availability.

A paradigm change in supply chain finance, invoice tokenization helps deep-tier suppliers more readily and inexpensively access working cash. Even the smallest businesses will be able to thrive in an environment that has historically favored larger, more well-known organizations thanks to this invention's ability to democratize funding across the entire supply chain. Blockchain-enabled solutions thus not only solve the liquidity problems experienced by deep-tier suppliers but also improve the general resilience and efficiency of world supply chains. Adoption of such FinTech technologies will be vital in preserving operational continuity and promoting inclusive development for all supply chain players as supply networks keep becoming more complicated.

The use of invoice tokenizing, particularly for smaller, deep-tier suppliers, is radically changing supply chain financing. Under conventional supply chain finance, only direct suppliers—usually higher tier-1 suppliers—can readily get reasonably priced financing depending on the creditworthiness of significant purchasers. Deep-tier suppliers—those deeper along the supply chain—often go unseen to financial institutions, therefore restricting their capacity to get capital. Together with worse credit profiles, this lack of visibility drives these suppliers to either operate with little working capital or seek expensive loans to meet manufacturing expenses while they wait for payment from downstream consumers.

Supply chain finance dynamics are changing with invoice tokenization. By transforming invoices into digital assets stored on a blockchain, even the tiniest suppliers at the top levels of the supply chain can access funding by leveraging the credit strength of major, reputable purchasers. Deep-tier suppliers may now obtain early payments or transfer responsibilities thanks to the democratization of financing, therefore lessening their reliance on conventional, expensive credit lines and helping them to have better cash flow. In this sense, invoice tokenization builds a more inclusive financial system inside the supply chain whereby every provider, irrespective of size or position, may access reasonably cheap financing.

Furthermore, improving supply chain resilience is invoice tokenizing. Providing suppliers at all levels with access to reasonably priced finance helps to reduce the possibility of business interruptions and liquidity shortages. Without waiting for long payment cycles, suppliers can keep running without problems, therefore reducing the risk of manufacturing slowdowns that may otherwise affect the whole supply chain. This increase in liquidity finally helps to guarantee the general financial stability of the supply chain so that all players may fulfill their responsibilities even in uncertain economic times or disturbances.

Blockchain technology also provides traceability and openness that help to ease supply chain finance process friction. Knowing real-time credit-backed invoices and payment commitments of trustworthy anchor purchasers helps financial institutions to provide beneficial conditions. This lower credit risk motivates more banks and other financial institutions to participate, as they can now confidently provide finance to further levels of suppliers. By guaranteeing more seamless movement of cash across all levels, this increased availability of finance not only helps suppliers but also improves the general efficiency of world supply chains.

Unlocking Resilience: The Transformative Power of Blockchain-Enabled DTSCF

Supply chains, which have several levels depending on one another to guarantee the seamless delivery of products and services, are rather complicated in the linked global economy of today. Among these levels, deep-tier suppliers—often small and medium-sized businesses (SMEs)—are very vital in maintaining the supply chain. Still, these SMEs are particularly sensitive to disturbances. Deep-tier suppliers deal with issues that can compromise the stability of the whole supply chain without direct access to capital markets and low financial resilience. Usually emphasizing tier-1 suppliers with which manufacturers have direct ties, traditional supply chain financing (SCF) approaches can fail to assist these important companies. This restricted visibility and access to funding causes supply chain bottlenecks that could grow during times of operational or financial instability.

Blockchain technology, however, presents a fresh paradigm for SCF as it provides unheard-of transparency and direct financing methods free from conventional constraints. Particularly for deep-tier banking, blockchain's capacity to track, validate, and safely distribute transaction data transforms it. Blockchain allows manufacturers and financiers to provide financial support straight to deep-tier suppliers, therefore assuring that these important but vulnerable businesses have the tools they need to weather interruptions. This article investigates how blockchain may transform SCF, stressing its efficiency in deep-tier finance and looking at blockchain-enabled financing plans that might reduce risks and increase resilience across multi-layer supply chains.

The Challenges Facing Deep-Tier Suppliers in Global Supply Chains

Deep-tier vendors can find it difficult to get the capital required for consistent operations, investment in expansion, and handling unforeseen difficulties. Three main factors make one vulnerable: Limited Access to Capital Because they do not have direct access to capital markets, SMEs find it challenging to get funding from institutional investors or conventional banks. They sometimes pay more for borrowing or are totally denied access to funding because of inadequate credit records or lack of collateral. This restricted access makes it more difficult for them to maintain cash flow, especially in industries that are prone to volatility or crises.

Lack of Visibility in Traditional SCF Models: Conventional SCF mostly addresses the interactions between tier-1 suppliers and manufacturers. Manufacturers have little to no awareness of the operations, financial situation, or hazards tier-2 and tier-3 suppliers experience. Manufacturers cannot proactively handle problems impacting deep-tier suppliers due to a lack of understanding, which results in frequently too-late reactionary responses that cause interruptions.

Reluctance to Share Sensitive Data: Fearing competitive disadvantages or privacy violations, deep-tier suppliers might be reluctant to provide financial or operational data to their customers or financial institutions. This resistance reduces the availability of financial support even further since manufacturers and banks lack the information required to evaluate risk and distribute resources properly.

The outcome is a financial disparity that limits proactive risk reduction. When deep-tier suppliers experience financial uncertainty, the knock-on consequences might cause supply interruptions, manufacturing slowdowns, and quality problems, thereby affecting downstream consumers and suppliers.

Blockchain Technology: A Transformative Solution for Supply Chain Finance

Blockchain brings numerous technologies that solve problems for deep-tier suppliers, thereby increasing SCF's inclusiveness, openness, and efficiency.

1. **Enhanced Visibility and Data Transparency**: The distributed ledger technology of blockchain lets one see real-time across several supply chain levels. Blockchain lets manufacturers track the financial performance and health of deep-tier suppliers without depending on direct ties with middlemen by recording transactions and financial data on an unchangeable ledger. This openness guarantees that producers may see hazards early on and act proactively to help weaker suppliers.

2. **Privacy-Preserving Verification Mechanisms**: Through cryptographic techniques like zero-knowledge proofs (ZKPs), blockchain enables deep-tier suppliers to verify their financial stability without revealing sensitive data. A supplier could show, for instance, that it has enough working capital to meet an order without revealing its whole financial portfolio. This privacy-preserving strategy fosters confidence and motivates vendors to join financing programs while safeguarding their competitive posture.

3. **Direct Financing Models**: Blockchain helps manufacturers avoid middlemen and provide loans or financial assistance straight to deep-tier suppliers, therefore facilitating direct financing models. This strategy guarantees that money finds the appropriate beneficiaries and lessens reliance on tier-1 suppliers. Direct finance may be customized to meet certain operational requirements for investing in risk reduction or manufacturing growth, thereby improving supply chain resilience.

Blockchain-Enabled Financing Schemes for Deep-Tier Suppliers

Two main finance approaches made possible by blockchain allow deep-tier suppliers' demands to be met: delegate financing and cross-tier direct funding.

- **Delegate Financing**: Under this approach, manufacturers shift money to tier-1 vendors in hopes of supporting their own suppliers downstream. Blockchain gives manufacturers visibility into money flow, therefore enabling them to confirm that finance reaches deep-tier suppliers as intended. While this technique depends on the cooperation of tier-1 suppliers and may be less efficient if they decide to keep cash, it is effective when deep-tier suppliers suffer significant financial restrictions.

- **Cross-Tier Direct Financing**: Blockchain helps companies in cross-tier finance to avoid tier-1 middlemen by allowing them to fund tier-2 and tier-3 suppliers straightforwardly. Manufacturers may track the financial situation of deep-tier suppliers and provide help according to confirmed requirements by using blockchain real-time data. Particularly fit for complicated, multi-tier supply chains, this approach provides better risk mitigation as manufacturers may motivate risk-reducing investments and react dynamically to financial demands. mitigation

Strategic Implications for Managing Blockchain-Enabled SCF

Blockchain use in SCF improves operational efficiency and robustness, therefore benefiting supply chains strategically.

- **Strengthened Supply Chain Reliability**: By facilitating direct finance, blockchain enables producers to ensure constant financial flow throughout the supply chain, reducing reliance on middlemen. At all levels, this system helps suppliers to endure financial shocks, keep manufacturing plans, and react adaptably to disturbances.

- **Improved Supplier Relationships**: The openness of blockchain helps to build closer, trust-based interactions between deep-tier suppliers and manufacturers. Reducing information asymmetry and allowing safe data exchange would help manufacturers and suppliers to participate in more cooperative, aligned partnerships that improve general supply chain integrity.

- **Cost-Efficiency**: Blockchain lowers the need for emergency sourcing and so minimizes operational disruptions, thereby generating long-term financial benefits even if it involves early setup expenses. Blockchain reduces numerous administrative chores with automated systems and smart contracts, therefore cutting operating costs and opening finance for even the tiniest suppliers.

Future Outlook: Expanding Blockchain's Role in Deep-Tier Financing

Advances like zero-knowledge proofs and distributed finance (DeFi) systems will boost direct funding methods as blockchain develops:

- **Zero-Knowledge Proof Cryptography**: By allowing suppliers to check financial circumstances without disclosing private information, ZKPs help to ensure that even the tiniest of suppliers may obtain finance without compromising confidentiality. Large-scale adoption depends on this capacity, as it fosters confidence throughout several supplier chains and helps the flow of money to people most in need.

- **Decentralized Finance (DeFi) Mechanisms**: Tokenized assets and peer-to-peer loan pools are two new financing tools DeFi presents that provide SMEs with more adaptable and easily available choices. By using blockchain's distributed architecture, these developments let suppliers get money, therefore facilitating quick access to capital—especially in crisis-torn times.

By tackling the problems experienced by deep-tier suppliers, blockchain technology might transform supply chain financing. Blockchain helps manufacturers assist their suppliers in ways that conventional SCF models cannot by offering openness, privacy-preserving verification, and direct funding choices. Adoption of blockchain in SCF would not only increase stability and resilience in worldwide supply chains but also help to promote more fair, inclusive access to finance. Blockchain promises to be a pillar of a more flexible and robust supply chain ecosystem as it develops, therefore enabling manufacturers and suppliers both to flourish among complexity and unpredictability.

Understanding the Challenges in DTSCF

Extending the problems experienced by deep-tier suppliers in worldwide supply chains clarifies the complicated financial environment these small and medium-sized businesses (SMEs) negotiate and the possibilities of blockchain to change this terrain.

Unique Obstacles DTSCF

1. Limited Capital Access

Particularly for those at the lowest levels of supply chains, SMEs generally run under major financial restrictions. Unlike bigger businesses, they usually have no established credit history and must meet strict lending criteria that make it difficult to get conventional bank loans. Their low financial means also limit their abilities to participate in large-scale, capital-intensive projects or to make investments in risk-reducing strategies, including sourcing backup suppliers or raising manufacturing capacity.

SMEs' lack of capital reduces their resilience in settings where financial shocks—such as natural catastrophes, material shortages, or quality control problems—can sweep across the whole supply chain. One disturbance at the deep-tier level may cause delays, result in costly emergency sourcing, and generate manufacturing bottlenecks affecting all the stakeholders. Under these circumstances, traditional avenues of financing become both necessary and elusive for these suppliers, leading to a situation whereby their supply chain partners are financially fragile and, thus, so are they.

2. Visibility Barriers

Manufacturers mostly engage with their immediate tier-1 suppliers, so the conventional supply chain architecture results in a "visibility barrier." This barrier makes it challenging for the manufacturer to evaluate and control the risks connected with deep-tier suppliers, as it restricts their knowledge of their operations and financial situation. For instance, the manufacturer might not know about the financial difficulty or operational troubles a tier-2 or tier-3 supplier is experiencing until they cause production to be disrupted.

Lack of visibility further muddies financial decisions. Manufacturers may find it difficult to offer focused financial help without understanding the requirements and circumstances of deep-tier suppliers. This "blind spot" in the supply chain results in inefficiencies as downstream finance programs meant to boost resilience might not be able to adequately trickle down, leaving deep-tier suppliers without the resources they need to lower risks.

3. Reluctance to Share Sensitive Data

Another challenge occurs in the few circumstances which manufacturers or finance organizations might interact personally with deep-tier suppliers: data privacy. Many times, suppliers are reluctant to provide financial information or other sensitive data that can expose their company policies, expenses, or weaknesses. A tier-2 supplier could, for instance, worry that disclosing its financial information to a tier-1 supplier or the end manufacturer will compromise its negotiating leverage or result in more demand or pressure to lower costs.

This resistance to data sharing causes a basic finance issue, as it makes it impossible for outside parties to evaluate the creditworthiness of these suppliers without correct financial data, therefore impeding their capacity to get money. Furthermore, the lack of financial transparency can cause supply chain expectations to be mismatched and impede group efforts toward risk reduction and resilience-building.

Consequences of the Finance Gap

These difficulties provide a finance gap that penetrates the supply chain, therefore affecting limited cash flows, delayed payments, and higher risk exposure for deep-tier suppliers. This disparity is particularly important in times of economic uncertainty or when erratic occurrences like world pandemics cause supply networks to be disrupted. These suppliers struggle to satisfy production needs or recover from disruptions without enough access to capital and visibility, which can lead to delays, higher costs, and lost income for downstream purchasers.

In the end, this financial disparity reduces proactive risk avoidance. While big businesses may have the capacity to withstand shocks and adapt, SMEs at lower levels often face a choice: continue operating with limited resources or cease operations entirely.

Blockchain As a Solution for Privacy-Preserving Transparency

With a privacy-preserving transparency paradigm that balances visibility and data privacy, blockchain technology offers a strong answer to these problems, allowing supply chain participants to:

- **Achieve Real-Time Visibility**: Without direct access to private financial data, blockchain's distributed ledger lets manufacturers have real-time awareness of the financial situation of deep-tier vendors. By securely recording each financial transaction, capital level, and material movement in a tamper-proof way, blockchain technology helps businesses monitor supply chain health without invading supplier privacy.

- **Implement Privacy Measures Through Cryptographic Techniques**: Zero-knowledge proofs (ZKPs) and other privacy-preserving techniques let blockchain users check the truth of financial claims, like that an account balance is enough, without seeing the sensitive data underneath. In this sense, without revealing the specific information of its accounts, a tier-2 supplier might show a manufacturer or financing institution its solvency or financial health state.

- **Direct Cross-Tier Financing Opportunities**: Blockchain creates cross-tier finance by providing verifiable but confidential information on the financial situation of deep-tier suppliers. Based on blockchain-verified data, a manufacturer may, for example, straight-finance a tier-2 or tier-3 supplier. By tier-1 suppliers, this strategy might eliminate the need for financial intermediation and guarantee that money gets to those most in need, therefore strengthening the whole supply chain.

- **Reduced Operational Costs and Faster Transactions**: Because blockchain is transparent and distributed, dependence on middlemen, such as banks or credit agencies, which often raise financing costs and slow down transaction speeds, is also decreased. Blockchain smart contracts may automatically enforce the conditions of finance agreements, thus guaranteeing that payments and transactions happen quickly and effectively, helping SMEs with limited resources.

Blockchain technology essentially offers the means for a balanced approach to visibility and privacy, allowing manufacturers to obtain the financial insights required for strong supply chain management while maintaining supplier data. Blockchain might strengthen the financial situation of deep-tier suppliers and improve the robustness of whole supply chains by bridging the finance gap, therefore enabling a more fair and stable global supply network.

Blockchain-Enabled Supply Chain Finance Models

Blockchain enables two primary deep-tier financing models: delegate financing and cross-tier direct financing.

1. Delegate Financing

With tier-1 suppliers functioning as middlemen, delegate finance uses blockchain to essentially route financial support from manufacturers to deep-tier suppliers. By use of a blockchain-enabled supply chain finance (SCF) platform, this arrangement improves transparency and control over cash flows in ways that conventional systems cannot match, therefore benefiting the manufacturer as well as lower-tier suppliers.

Key Advantages of Blockchain-Enabled Delegate Financing

Blockchain has three major benefits in delegated finance that increase the efficiency of financial support:

- **Real-Time Monitoring of Capital Flow**: From tier-1 to tier-2 suppliers, the SCF platform gives the manufacturer a safe, real-time picture of financial activities so it may monitor money as they travel. This visibility guarantees that money set for production investment or risk reduction gets to its intended use without needless delay or diversion.

- **Enhanced Verification and Security Through Privacy-Preserving Mechanisms**: Blockchain lets firms check important data about tier-2 suppliers, such as their solvency or working capital position, without revealing private financial information entirely. Blockchain allows the manufacturer to verify that tier-2 suppliers satisfy financial criteria without directly accessing private information by use of cryptographic methods like zero-knowledge proofs. Since manufacturers may evaluate risk and modify financial support based on confirmed needs, this system guarantees data privacy and helps to develop confidence in the funding process.

- **Strengthened Confidence in Funding Effectiveness**: Blockchain-enabled delegate finance helps to allay worries about fund abuse or ineffective allocation by offering information on capital availability and usage. In supply chains where manufacturers can be reluctant to provide financial help because of doubts regarding money use at the deep-tier level, this improved confidence is very vital.

Challenges and Limitations of Delegate Financing

Although delegate financing provides certain benefits, its scalability and dependability are limited, particularly in situations when the tier-2 supplier's financial restrictions are less severe.

Dependency on Tier-1 Supplier's Intermediary Role: The manufacturer uses the tier-1 supplier in delegate finance to allocate money to tier-2. Tier-1 suppliers may not completely send down the money as planned, though, if they have their own financial strains or try to keep control over cash. Delays, fewer financial rewards for tier-2 suppliers, and finance chain inefficiencies can all result from this intermediate reliance.

Limitations in Moderately Constrained Capital Scenarios: When tier-2 suppliers are significantly capital-constrained, delegated funding is most successful. In these situations, finance is obviously needed, and persuading tier-1 suppliers to provide money right away to guarantee tier-2 vendors keep production. However, in scenarios where the tier-2 supplier's capital constraints are moderate, the tier-1 supplier might retain more control over financial decisions, potentially prioritizing its own cash flow needs over downstream support. This can lead to a bottleneck, therefore compromising the robustness of the supply chain and delaying or lowering the efficacy of the funding.

Risk of Overreliance on Intermediary Control: Any disturbance or inefficiency at this level might have a domino effect, as delegate financing relies on the function of an intermediary between tier-1 suppliers. Should tier-1 suppliers fail to efficiently allocate money or have operational difficulties, the flow of funding to tier-2 and deeper providers may be compromised, therefore compromising risk and causing disturbance of production.

Optimizing Delegate Financing with Blockchain

Blockchain-enabled SCF systems can include certain tactics to leverage the advantages of delegate financing and minimize its restrictions:

Incentivizing Tier-1 Compliance: By tier-1 vendors, smart contracts might be utilized to ensure compliance by means of automated rewards or penalties depending on financing agreement adherence. Smart contracts might, for example, automatically release money to tier-2 suppliers under pre-defined circumstances, such as the receipt of products or timely delivery, therefore lessening the capacity of tier-1 suppliers to hold control unduly.

Customization of Financial Terms Based on Tier-2 Needs: Blockchain's openness allows manufacturers to customize financial support based on the particular requirements of tier-2 suppliers, such as changing advance payment terms or providing interest-free financing depending on confirmed capital limitations. This would guarantee that financial help is focused on ways that directly solve the capital constraints of deep-tier suppliers without too much intermediate reliance.

Regular Reporting and Accountability Mechanisms: By offering continuous data on the state of financial flows and performance, blockchain-enabled SCF systems may encourage responsibility all across the supply chain. Early identification of any possible interruptions or inefficiencies made possible by these reports enables the manufacturer to intervene or change financing arrangements as needed.

When Delegate Financing Is Most Effective

Delegate funding well in very limited situations when the capital demands of tier-2 suppliers are major and urgent, therefore compelling tier-1 suppliers to comply and guarantee funds reach lower tiers. Blockchain-enabled delegate finance improves supply chain visibility by balancing openness and privacy, therefore arming the manufacturer with means to track and validate financial transfers without violating supplier privacy. In situations where tier-2 suppliers have mild restrictions, this strategy might need further tools like smart contracts or direct incentives to guarantee money is efficiently directed downstream.

Blockchain helps firms provide financial support throughout supply chains indirectly by means of delegated finance. By means of blockchain visibility and privacy-preserving characteristics, one may follow, validate, and safeguard money transfers, thereby strengthening supply chain resilience. However, as with any model, its success depends on the particular financial limits of tier-2 suppliers and the cooperation of tier-1 suppliers, thereby stressing the need for properly created finance structures that fit the reality of supply chain dynamics.

Cross-Tier Direct Financing

By allowing manufacturers to avoid conventional middleman roles and directly fund deep-tier suppliers, Direct Financing Through Blockchain is a very successful approach that changes supply chain financing. Blockchain This method decreases reliance on tier-1 suppliers and minimizes the delays and expenses sometimes linked with intermediary-based models by employing blockchain, therefore generating a transparent, open finance channel.

Advantages of Blockchain-Enabled Direct Financing

Blockchain direct finance presents unique advantages that make it an intriguing substitute for more conventional financing sources:

- **Direct Incentives for Risk Mitigation**: Manufacturers might encourage particular risk-mitigating investments catered to the requirements of tier-2 suppliers by funding them straightforwardly. Manufacturers may, for example, provide financing conditions linked to better quality control or increased production dependability, therefore directly addressing supply chain weaknesses. This direct relationship between operational investment and finance helps tier-2 suppliers to increase their capacity, therefore enhancing the resilience and stability of the supply chain.

- **Elimination of Intermediary Costs and Delays**: Funds in conventional supply chain financing usually go through tier-1 suppliers, who could cause extra expenses or delays before forwarding cash to tier-2 suppliers. Eliminating this middle layer from blockchain-enabled direct finance speeds capital distribution and reduces financing transaction fees. Cash-strapped tier-2 vendors that need quick financial help to fulfill manufacturing needs or minimize interruptions would especially benefit from this simplified strategy.

- **Enhanced Transparency and Trust**: The open, unchangeable ledger of blockchain offers all users a trustworthy single source of truth. This openness helps manufacturers track tier-2 suppliers' financial and operational performance in real time, hence reducing information asymmetry between them and deep-tier suppliers. Furthermore, blockchain's privacy-preserving features help providers distribute pertinent financial data without disclosing private information, therefore fostering confidence at several levels and maintaining anonymity.

- **Reduction of Dependency on Tier-1 Suppliers**: Usually depending mostly on tier-1 suppliers to act as middlemen delivering payments to lower tiers, conventional finance methods But if tier-1 vendors opt to withhold money to preserve their cash flow or have financial restrictions, this reliance might turn problematic. By enabling manufacturers to send cash straight to tier-2 suppliers, blockchain-enabled direct finance lessens this dependency and guarantees that money reaches those most in need free from reallocation or hindrance.

- **Direct Incentives for Risk Mitigation**: Manufacturers might encourage particular risk-mitigating investments catered to the requirements of tier-2 suppliers by funding them straight-forwardly. Manufacturers may, for example, provide financing conditions linked to better quality control or increased production dependability, therefore directly addressing supply chains weaknesses. This direct relationship between operational investment and finance helps tier-2 suppliers to increase their capacity, therefore enhancing the resilience and stability of the supply chain.

- **Elimination of Intermediary Costs and Delays**: Funds in conventional supply chain financing usually go through tier-1 suppliers, who could cause extra expenses or delays before forwarding cash to tier-2 suppliers. Eliminating this middle layer from blockchain-enabled direct finance speeds capital distribution and reduces financing transaction fees. Cash-strapped tier-2 vendors that need quick financial help to fulfill manufacturing needs or minimize interruptions would especially benefit from this simplified strategy.

- **Enhanced Transparency and Trust**: The open, unchangeable ledger of blockchain offers all users a trustworthy single source of truth. This openness helps manufacturers track tier-2 suppliers' financial and operational performance in real time, hence reducing information asymmetry between them and deep-tier suppliers. Furthermore, blockchain's privacy-preserving features help providers to distribute pertinent financial data without disclosing private information, therefore fostering confidence at several levels and maintaining anonymity.

- **Reduction of Dependency on Tier-1 Suppliers**: Usually depending mostly on tier-1 suppliers to act as middlemen delivering payments to lower tiers, conventional finance methods But if tier-1 vendors opt to withhold money to preserve their cash flow or have financial restrictions, this reliance might turn problematic. By enabling manufacturers to send cash straight to tier-2 suppliers, blockchain-enabled direct finance lessens this dependency and guarantees that money reaches those most in need free from reallocation or hindrance.

Key Features of Blockchain-Enabled Direct Financing

- Automated Payment Mechanisms Through Smart Contracts: By use of smart contracts on the blockchain, manufacturers may automatically pay tier-2 suppliers according to preset criteria, like effective product delivery or quality requirements. This automation guarantees that money is issued right upon fulfillment of requirements, lowers administrative effort, and speeds payment delays. Manufacturers may guarantee that deep-tier suppliers remain financially supported and operationally driven by including terms that favor timely delivery and dependability.

- Real-Time Financial Insights: The transparency of blockchain gives manufacturers real-time access to tier-2 supplier financial situations, thereby allowing them to evaluate and modify financial support as required. Through more focused, responsive assistance from suppliers, manufacturers' continuous monitoring helps them to proactively handle possible interruptions. Real-time data may also highlight patterns in supplier performance, therefore guiding producers in strategic decisions and pointing up areas of additional risk reduction potential.

- Reduced credit risk and improved financing access for SMEs: Deep-tier vendors historically have trouble getting loans because of high interest rates and a lack of credit background. By using verified data on the blockchain as a replacement creditworthiness assessment tool, direct funding made possible by blockchain technology addresses these issues. Manufacturers may issue credit straight based on transaction history, performance measures, and verifiable financial data using blockchain, enabling SMEs to get finance free from significant collateral restrictions.

Potential Challenges of Direct Financing Through Blockchain

Although direct finance made possible by blockchain technology has many benefits, several issues have to be resolved to guarantee its efficiency:

- **Initial Setup and Integration Costs**: Direct finance systems based on blockchain technology call for large technological, integration, and personnel training investments. Establishing a completely working blockchain network for supply chain financing might prove difficult for smaller producers or those with limited means.

- **Data Accuracy and Reliability**: Effective operation of blockchain depends on correct data inputs. Mistakes or false reporting at the point of data entry could compromise blockchain records' veracity, therefore influencing funding decisions. Dependent data inputs call for strong verification systems, including outside audits or interaction with dependable data sources.

- **Regulatory Compliance and Legal Considerations**: Complicating legal and regulatory issues for cross-border supply chains are differing standards for data protection, financial transactions, and contractual duties. Particularly with financial data and cross-border payments, blockchain-based finance systems must guarantee adherence to local laws.

By letting manufacturers directly fund deep-tier suppliers, blockchain-enabled direct financing offers a potent answer to conventional supply chain finance constraints. Offering a more effective and strong substitute for conventional finance methods, this strategy simplifies money flows, improves openness, and reduces reliance on tier-1 suppliers. Direct finance via blockchain may be crucial in stabilizing supply chains, assisting SMEs, and reducing disruptions by providing focused, real-time financial support, as Foxconn's platform exemplifies.

Blockchain's capacity to create open, safe, and direct financing channels transforms supply chain finance by matching financial incentives, lowering intermediary reliance, and building resilient, flexible supply chains more suited to negotiate the complicated global markets of today.

Delegate Finance vs. Direct Finance: A Comparative Analysis

The decision between direct and delegated financing models depends on specific requirements, such as the capital profile of suppliers and the risk of disruption, in a supply chain that uses a blockchain. These models' further comparison study across important criteria follows here:

1. Visibility Impact

Both delegate and direct finance models depend on blockchain-enabled visibility, but it is more important in direct financing since:

- Delegate Financing: Under this paradigm, blockchain mostly gives visibility to track capital transfers between tier-2 suppliers, thereby making sure money gets to the proper receivers. But tier-1 suppliers function as middlemen, so the manufacturer's knowledge of tier-2's precise financial situation is fairly limited, usually confined to aggregate data or monthly reports rather than real-time updates. While visibility here facilitates tracking of money disbursement, it depends on tier-1 supplier compliance and collaboration.

- Direct Financing: Direct financing maximizes blockchain visibility as manufacturers get real-time, detailed information on tier-2 supplier operating demands and financial situations. This approach lets the manufacturer flexibly change financing levels depending on real-time data and react instantly to changes in performance criteria or capital demand. Maintaining a proactive approach to risk management depends on this visibility, which also provides customized financial assistance able to instantly handle certain risks, such as production delays or cash shortages.

While visibility enhances delegate financing, it plays a crucial role in direct financing. Real-time data enables a focused and flexible financing approach, making it the preferred option for high-risk, complex supply chains that require close control and intervention.

2. Risk Mitigation

Blockchain improves the risk-mitigating capacity of both approaches, while direct funding provides more exact and efficient risk-reducing power.

- **Delegate Financing**: The firm uses tier-1 suppliers to control risk at the tier-2 level by means of funding delegation. This strategy helps tier-2's risk management operations indirectly, as tier-1 suppliers are supposed to distribute money correctly to guarantee that tier-2 suppliers may keep production uninterrupted without disturbance. Nevertheless, tier-1 suppliers have some degree of control over capital allocation, so the manufacturer's impact on risk reduction at the deep-tier level might be restricted, especially if the tier-1 supplier has different goals or has its own limitations.

- **Direct Financing**: Direct finance lets the producer directly encourage tier-2 suppliers to participate in risk-reducing initiatives such as supply chain optimization or increased manufacturing dependability. Manufacturers may guarantee the dependability of the supply chain by funding, especially for proactive risk-reducing activities, therefore making tier-2 suppliers financially ready to manage interruptions. Since manufacturers may define precise criteria linked to risk reduction, this direct linkage helps to enable better coordination in risk management across tiers. This makes the concept especially appropriate for high-risk situations, including sensitive deep-tier suppliers.

Direct financing lets manufacturers directly incentivize and support deep-tier suppliers, ensuring that risk-mitigating actions are sufficiently funded and carried out without intermediary delays or resource diversions. This helps to manage risk at all supply chain levels.

3. Scalability

Another important consideration when evaluating delegate vs. direct funding strategies is scalability; direct financing offers more general applicability.

- **Delegate Financing**: Delegate finance well in supply chains when severe capital restrictions hinder the financial independence of tier-2 suppliers, as this technique may help cascade money from the top down when tier-1 suppliers collaborate efficiently. However, dependence on tier-1 suppliers to function as middlemen limits the scalability of this arrangement. Delegate finance may become less effective or require expensive changes to accommodate different supplier profiles if the capital restrictions or operational complexity vary greatly between levels.

- **Direct Financing**: Because it avoids tier-1 middlemen and creates direct financial ties between manufacturers and deep-tier suppliers, direct financing is intrinsically more scalable. Regardless of the particular capital profile or financial situation of each supplier, this direct relationship lets manufacturers provide customized support to any level as needed. Direct finance may be used flexibly across a range of supplier profiles and conditions, thus flexible to both high and low capital limitations, thanks to blockchain giving real-time insights and privacy-preserving validation. This approach also enables growth into bigger and more varied supply chains, where direct ties with deep-tier vendors may be preserved free from middleman coordination.

Direct finance offers a flexible approach that caters to various supplier profiles and risk tolerances. While efficient under extreme restrictions, delegated finance is constrained by its reliance on tier-1 suppliers and less sensible in complicated supply chains with varying financial demands across tiers.

The particular demands and structure of the supply chain will determine whether delegate or direct finance methods are a better fit for you:

- For supply chains with a cooperative tier-1 intermediary and significant capital restrictions at the deep-tier level, delegate finance is appropriate. When intermediary coordination can consistently flow money downstream and real-time modifications are not absolutely necessary, it offers value.

- For complicated and high-risk supply chains, however, direct financing is a more reliable, scalable, and efficient solution as it gives direct access to real-time financial data and allows customized, proactive risk reduction. This approach fits supply chains where rapid financial response and little reliance on middlemen are critical and accommodate a wide spectrum of supplier characteristics.

Although both models gain from blockchain's security and openness, direct funding shines in visibility, risk reduction, and scalability; therefore, it is the recommended solution for improving supply chain resilience and efficiency in many different contexts.

Key Managerial Implications

Particularly in terms of dependability, supplier relationships, and cost-efficiency, blockchain has transformed strategic relevance for handling supply chain financing. These advantages are set out in more detail here:

1. Enhanced Supply Chain Reliability

By giving manufacturers direct access to deep-tier suppliers, therefore avoiding middlemen, blockchain-enabled direct finance increases supply chain resiliency. This direct contact makes real-time, open financing possible, ensuring that suppliers have access to money exactly when and where they need it.

- **Minimizing Dependency on Intermediaries**: Traditional finance sometimes results in cash not reaching the intended recipients, delays, and creates bottlenecks as funds travel via intermediary tiers—like tier-1 suppliers. By means of blockchain, manufacturers may directly fund lower-tier suppliers, guaranteeing timely support and reducing financial constraints-related disturbance. Particularly in industries with intricate, multi-tier supply chains subject to manufacturing slowdowns or unplanned interruptions, this dependability is very vital.

- **Proactive Risk Management**: The transparency of blockchain lets manufacturers track their deep-tier suppliers' financial situation and performance right now. Using this information, companies may proactively handle possible hazards, modify funding, or step in before little problems become major disruptions. If a tier-2 supplier is running low on working capital, for instance, the manufacturer may swiftly provide extra money to keep manufacturing schedules and reduce the possibility of cascading delays all along the supply chain.

- **Implication**: Blockchain supports constant and strong operations even under uncertain situations by allowing flexible, direct funding that removes reliance on intermediate levels and therefore improves supply chain dependability.

2. Improved Supplier Relationships

Blockchain helps manufacturers and their deep-tier suppliers build closer, trust-based partnerships. Its open, distributed character encourages mutual confidence and transparency, which facilitates successful supplier and manufacturer collaboration.

- **Building Trust and Reducing Information Asymmetry**: The distributed ledger of blockchain gives all players in the supply chain access to one, confirmed source of truth. This openness helps to lower information asymmetry, as suppliers may be more sure they will get timely financial support without having to provide all private information. Manufacturers may similarly rely on money reaching the designated suppliers and being used for specified uses, including output growth or risk-mitigating action.

- **Greater Collaboration and Alignment**: Blockchain direct finance helps to match financial incentives and goals all across the supply chain. Manufacturers can promote certain activities or investments—such as quality control, sustainability standards, or process optimization—that fit larger supply chain goals by interacting directly with deep-tier suppliers. By means of this cooperation, a more coherent supply chain network is created whereby all players pursue common goals, thereby benefiting the whole supply chain.

- **Reducing Capital Bottlenecks**: Delays at the tier-1 level in conventional finance can lead to bottlenecks starving tier-2 suppliers of necessary funds. By allowing instantaneous cash allocation to the relevant tier, blockchain's direct finance method helps eliminate these delays and improves supplier relationships and operational flow across the supply chain.

- **Implication**: Blockchain creates trust and lowers bottlenecks by improving openness and direct cooperation, strengthening supplier connections at all levels and improving the cooperative and aligned supply chain.

3. Cost-Efficiency

Although using blockchain calls for an initial infrastructure expenditure, long-term cost benefits, and operational improvements usually exceed these setup expenses. By means of simplified procedures and less dependency on emergency responses, blockchain aids in the push of cost-efficiency.

- **Reduced Need for Emergency Sourcing**: Blockchain reduces the possibility of manufacturing delays and emergency sourcing by making sure money reaches suppliers consistently and fast. Usually more costly, emergency sourcing calls for quick manufacturing or other providers. Blockchain-enabled finance allows suppliers to keep more seamless operations and lower risks without turning to expensive last-minute actions.

- **Streamlined Financial Transactions**: By means of smart contracts, blockchain automates and simplifies financial transactions, hence lowering the administrative load of hand payments and verifications.

When pre-defined criteria are satisfied—like the successful delivery of goods—these smart contracts run payments automatically. By increasing liquidity and financial efficiency, this automation lowers labor costs, removes human mistakes, and speeds up the cash flow cycle, thereby helping manufacturers and suppliers.

- **Long-Term Operational Cost Savings**: Although blockchain systems' initial setup calls for integration and training charges, their long-term advantages usually consist of reduced running costs. Companies should see cheaper credit risk assessment costs, less payment term conflict, and lower interest rates for short-term funding as blockchain-based supply chain finance spreads. Improved supply chain dependability also implies less disturbance, fewer inventory-keeping expenses, and a more consistent manufacturing schedule.

- **Implication**: Blockchain's direct funding approach and automation help to streamline financial procedures and lessen dependency on expensive emergency solutions, therefore cutting running costs and improving supply chain profitability.

Blockchain's strategic ramifications for supply chain finance are significant; it provides means to increase dependability, strengthen supplier relationships, and lower cost efficiency. Manufacturers may build more robust, cooperative, and reasonably priced supply chains better suited to managing current complexity and disruptions by using blockchain transparency and distributed structure. Blockchain's application in supply chain finance marks a major change toward proactive risk management, effective capital allocation, and trust-driven relationships—which, taken together, increase the integrity and stability of world supply networks.

Future of Blockchain-Enabled Deep-Tier Financing

Driven by technology developments like zero-knowledge proof (ZKP) cryptography and decentralized finance (DeFi) systems, the spread of deep-tier financing applications is anticipated to quicken as blockchain adoption in supply chain finance (SCF) continues to increase across sectors. These new instruments will probably help manufacturers more by opening direct finance channels that boost the support of smaller suppliers even in uncertain times.

- **Zero-Knowledge Proof Cryptography**: Ensuring privacy and trust in deep-tier financing zero-knowledge proofs (ZKPs) are cryptographic methods wherein one party may confirm the validity of particular data without disclosing any underlying information. By allowing the following, ZKPs help to establish confidence between manufacturers and deep-tier suppliers inside SCF:

- **Privacy-Preserving Financial Verification**: By use of ZKPs, suppliers may confirm their financial situation to manufacturers without disclosing confidential information. Smaller suppliers that might be unwilling to provide manufacturers comprehensive financial data because of privacy or competitive concerns will find this capacity very helpful. By proving that they satisfy creditworthiness or liquidity criteria using ZKPs, these vendors may show that they do not compromise confidentiality and therefore enable more focused, risk-adjusted funding.

- **Enhanced Risk Assessment**: By real-time financial stability assessment of deep-tier suppliers using ZKP-enabled systems, manufacturers may spot any early warning indicators of possible disturbance. A tier-2 supplier may utilize a ZKP, for instance, to show it has enough working capital to satisfy future production needs. This verification process ensures that financing is allocated to suppliers who need it most, helping to prevent potential production bottlenecks and strengthening supply chain resilience.

- **Reduced Compliance Costs and Data Sensitivity Concerns**: ZKPs offer verifiable evidence without data exposure, therefore reducing the need for costly compliance controls and broad data sharing. By allowing manufacturers to check financial circumstances via a privacy-preserving route, this function lowers regulatory and data sensitivity concerns connected with direct data processing, therefore saving compliance expenses.

- **Implications**: As ZKP cryptography develops, it will boost confidence and openness in SCF, thereby motivating more firms to use direct financing methods based on blockchain technologies. This privacy-preserving solution is likely to be crucial in allowing firms to access smaller suppliers while protecting private data and thus expanding finance farther into their supply chains.

- **Decentralized Finance (DeFi) Mechanisms**: Expanding Access to Capital and Enabling Fluid Financing Structures. Decentralized finance (DeFi) is changing access to money and giving suppliers in the SCF ecosystem creative, flexible financing choices. DeFi systems bring fresh approaches to help deep-tier vendors via improved access to decentralized financing solutions, smart contract-based agreements, reduced transaction costs, enhanced transparency, and frictionless cross-border payments, thereby enabling more efficient and inclusive financial support throughout the supply chain.

- **Tokenized Assets and Collateralization**: Tokenization in DeFi lets real-world items such as contracts, invoices, and goods be turned into digital tokens fit for collateral for funding. Deep-tier providers might leverage these tokenized assets via DeFi platforms to get financing from a larger pool of lenders—including those outside of conventional financial institutions—by means of Small suppliers that might find it difficult to satisfy conventional banking needs would find enormous value in this access to distributed finance as it provides flexible and easily available cash.

- **Automated Smart Contracts for Real-Time Payments**: Smart contracts used by DeFi provide automatic, conditional payments, therefore enabling flawless money movement across supply chain levels. These agreements eliminate delays and lower payment conflicts by immediately completing transactions upon satisfying pre-defined criteria—e.g., confirmed delivery of goods—so removing By offering instantaneous liquidity and improving their capacity to react to changing market needs or crises without waiting for long payment cycles, this automation can help smaller suppliers.

- **Decentralized Liquidity Pools and P2P Financing**: By use of distributed liquidity pools, DeFi enables suppliers to access peer-to-peer (P2P) finance, therefore directly linking them with an international investor network. Decentralized platforms allow smaller suppliers—especially those in areas with few traditional banking choices—to obtain funding without regard to credit history or large collateral. Manufacturers and suppliers may rely on a distributed finance source through these pools, which offers quick access to capital—particularly important during supply chain interruptions.

- **Implication**: Particularly for deep-tier vendors with few conventional financing choices, DeFi systems provide unmatched adaptability and accessibility. DeFi develops a fluid finance ecosystem that lowers entrance barriers by letting these suppliers use tokenized assets, access distributed liquidity pools, and profit from automated smart contracts, thereby enabling manufacturers to more successfully support their suppliers.

Future Outlook: A Resilient and Adaptive SCF Ecosystem

Blockchain-based SCF is poised to become a highly robust, flexible ecosystem supporting providers at all levels as ZKP cryptography and DeFi systems keep improving. As these technologies proliferate, here's what we should anticipate:

- **Expanded Reach of Direct Financing in Complex Supply Chains**: Manufacturers will be more suited to engage deep-tier suppliers previously unreachable owing to privacy or regulatory concerns as ZKPs and DeFi continue to evolve and expand finance across very complicated, worldwide supply chains. Manufacturers will start to trust in helping these vendors without compromising their own control over capital flow or privacy.

- **Increased Supply Chain Agility During Crises**: Deep-tier suppliers—whether they be environmental, geopolitical, or financial—often have significant liquidity problems during times of crisis. By combining DeFi for flexible financing with ZKPs for safe verification, manufacturers will be able to react fast to these changes and provide targeted financial help to impacted suppliers to keep operational continuity and reduce rippling effects across the supply chain.

- **Strengthened Resilience Through Decentralized**: As more companies use DeFi and ZKP-enabled SCF models, we could expect a more distributed, cooperative attitude to financing. This approach creates a finance ecosystem whereby manufacturers, suppliers, and investors cooperate to guarantee stability and resilience, therefore lessening reliance on conventional banks and middlemen. By means of distributed platforms, suppliers may immediately access the required capital in this environment, therefore fostering self-sustaining, strong supply chains.

For deep-tier funding, the combination of zero-knowledge proofs and distributed financial systems into blockchain-enabled SCF is a significant breakthrough. Manufacturers will be more able to assist smaller suppliers as these technologies develop, even in crisis, therefore guaranteeing continual, adaptable financial assistance that increases the resilience of the whole supply chain. Blockchain-driven SCF is expected to become a necessary tool for managing complicated, multi-tier networks in the next few years, thus orienting manufacturers and suppliers both to negotiate obstacles with stability and trust.

Inclusive Financing for Deep-Tier Suppliers: How Invoice Tokenization Is Unlocking Access to Affordable Capital

Smaller suppliers—especially those positioned many steps away from the anchor buyer—often find considerable difficulty obtaining reasonably priced financing in the conventional terrain of supply chain finance. This is mostly because of less visibility and lower credit histories than bigger, downstream purchasers. Because their creditworthiness is either unclear or seen to be excessively dangerous, financial institutions are reluctant to provide credit to these deep-tier suppliers. Therefore, these vendors sometimes have to rely on costly short-term loans or endure long payment cycles, which can tax their operating capital and hinder their expansion.

Invoice tokenizing is rewriting this story. Smaller suppliers can receive funding based on the financial health of their downstream partners instead of their own credit ratings by tokenizing invoices and integrating the creditworthiness of anchor customers inside these tokens. This change lets deep-tier vendors get better financing rates

CHAPTER 6   UNLOCKING VALUE: THE POTENTIAL OF DEEP-TIER SUPPLY CHAIN FINANCE (DTSCF)

that match the reduced risk profile of the bigger, more credible anchor purchasers. Basically, invoice tokenization acts as a link between smaller suppliers and the financial advantages of their downstream partners' excellent credit ratings.

A basic problem for deep-tier providers is their obscurity in the supply chain. While deep-tier suppliers—such as tier-2 or tier-3 suppliers—are further distant from these buyers and therefore sometimes operate in the shadow of the supply chain, tier-1 vendors usually have direct interactions with anchor buyers. When banks look at the risk of lending money, they usually only look at the interactions between tier-1 suppliers and anchor buyers. This means that deep-tier suppliers can't get credit lines that aren't too high.

The fact that deep-tier suppliers are usually small or medium-sized businesses (SMEs) with less proven credit histories aggravates this restricted exposure. These vendors are doing well technically, but their absence of a strong credit profile will make it difficult for them to obtain favorable financing possibilities. Because of their smaller size and less transparent financials, which increase the perceived risk of default, banks and other financial institutions are often unwilling to provide reasonably priced loans to these providers.

Unlocking Affordable Capital for Smaller Suppliers: The Role of Invoice Tokenization in Redefining Trade Finance

Driven by blockchain technology, invoice tokenizing solves these problems by turning bills generated by anchor purchasers into digital tokens. Stashed on an open, unchangeable blockchain, these tokens reflect the payment responsibilities of the anchor buyer. This openness lets financial institutions see the creditworthiness of the anchor buyer buried in the token, therefore lowering the seeming risk of financing to smaller suppliers farther up the supply chain.

When a tier-1 supplier gets a tokenized invoice from an anchor customer, for instance, they could either keep the token until payment is due or forward it to a tier-2 provider. Based on the creditworthiness of the anchor customer, the tier-2 supplier may then sell this token to a factoring company or financial institution to guarantee early payment at a reasonable interest rate. This approach lets deep-tier vendors get access to financing that mirrors the strength of the credit rating of the anchor buyer, therefore bypassing the conventional obstacles of their own financial situation.

One of the best things about invoice tokenization is that it lets smaller suppliers get loans at rates that were previously only available to bigger, more well-known competitors. Due to the tokenized invoice's backing by a creditworthy anchor buyer's payment obligation and consequent reduction in default risk, financial institutions are more willing to offer competitive rates. Smaller suppliers, who frequently have interest rates much higher because of the risks often connected with their smaller size and poorer credit profiles, can benefit much from this access to less expensive funding.

For instance, a tier-2 supplier may receive high interest rate financing in a conventional supply chain finance model due to their weak credit history or lack of direct contact with financial institutions. With invoice tokenization, however, the same supplier might get financing at a reduced rate as the credit risk now rests on the good financial profile of the anchor customer. This enables the tier-2 supplier to get the operating cash required to keep operations running free from the high expenses usually connected with trade credit or short-term loans.

Revolutionizing Supply Chain Financing: How Invoice Tokenization Empowers Deep-Tier Suppliers and Strengthens Global Resilience

More than merely offering favorable rates, invoice tokenization actively closes the financing gap for deep-tier suppliers. Many of these vendors work in sectors where extended payment cycles are typical and have to properly cover their running expenditures well before their clients pay them. There aren't many credit options that aren't too expensive, which makes this problem worse because suppliers have to deal with limited liquidity, which often causes cash flow problems that make it harder for them to meet demand.

Blockchain-based solutions assist in solving cash flow problems by allowing deep-tier suppliers to get early payments via the sale of tokenized invoices. By tokenizing invoices and securing early funding, suppliers may keep better cash flow, lessen their dependency on costly loans, and lower the financial stress resulting from longer payment cycles. This thus allows companies to keep a consistent flow of goods and services to their consumers and increases their resilience to supply chain interruptions.

Additionally affecting financial inclusion throughout supply networks is invoice tokenization. This invention guarantees that smaller suppliers—who are vitally important in the manufacturing of goods and services—are no longer marginalized in favor of bigger, more visible businesses by democratizing access to reasonably priced loans. Deep-tier suppliers, previously limited to tier-1 suppliers, now have the ability to participate in supply chain financing initiatives, enabling them to expand and make more informed investments in their companies.

Consequently, invoice tokenization improves the general resilience and efficiency of worldwide supply chains as well as the financial stability of particular providers. Blockchain-enabled invoice tokenization makes sure that liquidity flows naturally across all levels of the supply chain, from the smallest tier-2 or tier-3 suppliers to the biggest anchor buyers. This creates a more fair and inclusive financial environment. This approach benefits all parties involved by reducing the likelihood of supply chain disruptions caused by liquidity issues and ensuring the seamless flow of products and services from suppliers to consumers.

Especially for deep-tier suppliers, invoice tokenization marks a revolutionary change in supply chain financing. Using the credit power of anchor purchasers, these vendors may now get reasonably priced financing that would not be possible otherwise. This better access to financing not only helps smaller suppliers have excellent cash flows but also supports the general stability and resilience of supply chains, therefore enabling even the tiniest firms to flourish in the global economy of today.

Sourcing Strategy and Supply Chain Configuration

Buyers and suppliers have different configurations in supply chains that maximize efficiency, lower risk, and lower costs. The Y-shaped and V-shaped supply[1] chains are two often used arrangements by companies to control their procurement plans. These setups specify how tier-1 and tier-2 vendors interact with the anchor buyer and affect the flow of products and services across the supply chain.

For these various supply chains, invoice tokenization—an original method leveraging blockchain technology to generate digital tokens for invoices—offers special advantages. Tokenizing invoices makes both Y-shaped and V-shaped setups more efficient and reliable by making everything more clear, lowering risk, and increasing liquidity across all supply chains. Nevertheless, the unique structure of every configuration means that the benefits of tokenization vary depending on the supply chain architecture.

---

[1] This definition has been given by the following study: "Invoice Tokenization for Deep-Tier Payables Finance": https://papers.ssrn.com/sol3/papers.cfm?abstract_id=4362566

CHAPTER 6 UNLOCKING VALUE: THE POTENTIAL OF DEEP-TIER SUPPLY CHAIN FINANCE (DTSCF)

A single tier-1 provider in a Y-shaped supply chain is in charge of acquiring components or materials from several tier-2 suppliers, thereby meeting the needs of the anchor buyer. Although their dependability, pricing, and capacity may vary, the tier-1 provider has the authority to distribute orders across various tier-2 suppliers. One tier-2 supplier may be cheaper but less reliable, while another may be more likely to cause problems. The tier-1 supplier has to manage its own profitability and risk exposure while balancing these elements to satisfy the demands of the anchor buyer.

Maximizing this balance depends much on invoice tokenizing. Invoice tokenization offers real-time transparency and new financial possibilities for all those engaged by turning invoices into digital tokens that can be readily exchanged and monitored on a blockchain. The tier-1 supplier in a Y-shaped arrangement can transfer tokenized invoices to the tier-2 suppliers, therefore enhancing the liquidity of these providers and providing more control in working capital management.

This has a significant impact on the source approach. By removing some of the financial constraints that might otherwise push tier-1 suppliers toward cheaper but riskier options, invoice tokenization helps them find tier-2 suppliers they can trust more.

If the tier-1 supplier can use tokenized invoices to guarantee early payments or offer better terms to tier-2 suppliers, it is more likely to put dependability over cost. This is because the whole supply chain's finances will be better off if it is easier to get cheap credit. Since suppliers are more suited to satisfy production and delivery schedules, this lowers the general risk of supply chain interruptions.

However, under certain circumstances, the implementation of invoice tokenization in a Y-shaped supply chain could lead to a shift in the sourcing policy, which could be detrimental to some players. If the market potential is high, for instance, the tier-1 provider may totally turn toward the more dependable (and more costly) tier-2 source, therefore depriving the less trustworthy supplier of orders. The openness and liquidity provided by invoice tokenizing simplify the process of switching between suppliers, potentially straining the long-standing relationships between tier-1 and tier-2 providers. Since their involvement in the supply chain reduces, this sourcing approach might result in negative earnings for the less trustworthy supplier.

Conversely, a V-shaped supply chain comprises the anchor buyer directly controlling relationships with two or more tier-1 suppliers, each of which sources from their respective tier-2 suppliers. In the V-shaped model, the anchor buyer has more control over sourcing decisions and order splitting than in the Y-shaped model, where the tier-1 supplier acts as a go-between for the anchor buyer and the tier-2 suppliers. This arrangement is often utilized when the anchor buyer seeks greater flexibility in its sourcing strategy or seeks to diversify its supply base to mitigate risk.

By pushing dual sourcing, invoice tokenization offers an even greater benefit in a V-shaped supply chain. Dual sourcing involves distributing orders across multiple vendors to ensure supply continuity, lower prices, and reduce risk, thereby avoiding reliance on a single provider. Invoice tokenization helps dual sourcing by making it easier for the anchor buyer to manage many supplier agreements at the same time. It does this by increasing liquidity and financial flexibility for everyone in the supply chain.

An anchor buyer may, for instance, source from two tier-1 suppliers: one working with a dependable but costly tier-2 provider and another working with a less trustworthy but more reasonably priced tier-2 supplier. By giving tier-1 suppliers liquidity, invoice tokenizing enables the anchor buyer to keep this dual-sourcing approach. The digital tokens generated from the invoices of the anchor buyer let every tier-1 supplier pay their own tier-2 suppliers more quickly, therefore lessening the financial burden resulting from longer payment cycles.

This guarantees that dependable as well as less dependable suppliers remain viable, therefore enabling the anchor buyer to more successfully manage risk and cost.

Furthermore, by lowering financial risks and offering greater liquidity, invoice tokenization helps the anchor buyer to react more dynamically to the current state of affairs. Tokenization lowers the requirement for costly short-term loans or trade credit, so the buyer may boost orders from the more trustworthy provider without raising expenses when the market potential is large. On the other hand, in times of reduced market demand, the buyer can keep its relationship with the less dependable but less expensive supplier, knowing that invoice tokenization will guarantee timely payments all along the supply chain.

The more adaptability, efficiency, and robustness, invoice tokenization provides benefits to both Y-shaped and V-shaped supply chains. In a Y-shaped arrangement, tier-1 suppliers have more control over their sourcing practices when they use tokenized invoices to help their tier-2 suppliers get more cash and feel less financial pressure. This results in more trustworthy sourcing choices, which help to balance the supply chain and lower the risk of disturbance. But when tier-1 suppliers give more dependable partners top priority over less trustworthy ones, this extra control can also cause changes in supplier relationships.

Invoice tokenization substantially helps the anchor buyer to maintain several supplier connections in a V-shaped setup. Using a dual-sourcing approach helps the buyer to guarantee that, even with market instability, its supply chain is flexible and strong. Blockchain technology's transparency and liquidity help all players in the supply chain to obtain reasonably priced finance and guarantee the timely processing of payments, therefore improving the general condition of the supply chain.

Invoice tokenizing changes Y-shaped and V-shaped supply chains by increasing financial flexibility, lowering risk, and boosting liquidity across all levels. While the specific benefits of tokenization vary depending on the supply chain configuration, they consistently offer increased efficiency, reduced disruption risk, and improved access to affordable financing for all supply chain participants. The adoption of invoice tokenization will be crucial in determining the direction of sourcing strategies and supply chain management as worldwide supply networks keep changing and become more complicated.

Reducing Financial Risk and Improving Liquidity in Supply Chains

Maintaining operational stability and efficiency in supply networks depends on proper control of risk. The possibility of cash shortages—which may cause operational interruptions or even bankruptcy—is one of the most important obstacles suppliers, particularly smaller and deep-tier providers, must confront. Delayed payments, protracted credit cycles, and restricted access to reasonably priced finance can all cause liquidity problems. Since tier-1 suppliers pay their own upstream suppliers while awaiting payment from the anchor buyer, they have historically carried much of the financial load in these supply chains. But invoice tokenization, a blockchain-based innovation, takes most of this financial burden and risk off of tier-1 suppliers and puts it more fairly on other buyers in the supply chain, especially the anchor buyer.

Invoice tokenization lessens financial burden, enhances liquidity, and decreases financing costs for all those engaged by assigning payment responsibilities to the more creditworthy anchor buyer. This not only lowers the possibility of supplier insolvency but also strengthens the whole supply chain's resiliency. This section will look at how invoice tokenization lowers supply chain expenses and financial risk.

Invoice tokenization fundamentally reduces risk by transferring financial responsibilities from tier-1 suppliers to the anchor buyer, typically the most financially stable and creditworthy company in the supply chain. Tier-1 suppliers in conventional supply chain finance frequently have to wait for long stretches—sometimes up to 90

CHAPTER 6   UNLOCKING VALUE: THE POTENTIAL OF DEEP-TIER SUPPLY CHAIN FINANCE (DTSCF)

days or more—for the anchor customer to pay for products and services supplied. Tier-1 suppliers have to figure out how to pay personnel, buy supplies, and cover overhead costs among other running expenditures during this period. The situation deteriorates when a tier-1 supplier relies on smaller, deep-tier vendors, who also require prompt payment to continue operations.

Invoice tokenization solves this problem by transforming invoices into digital tokens that parties on a blockchain can pass. Should an anchor customer send a tokenized invoice to a tier-1 supplier, the tier-1 supplier can pay off its own obligations with upstream vendors using that token. Usually more creditworthy and less likely to default on payment commitments, this approach moves the financial risk on the anchor buyer. Deep-tier suppliers can boldly take the token as payment or sell it to a financial institution for early financing as the credit rating of the anchor customer supports the invoice.

The general stability of the supply chain depends much on this change in financial risk. Previously burdened with timing the gap between paying their own suppliers and getting payments from the anchor customer, tier-1 vendors are now mostly free from much of this risk. They are therefore less prone to run over liquidity problems that can cause financial crises or bankruptcy. Industries with small or medium-sized tier-1 suppliers generally operate with low margins and limited access to reasonably priced finance; hence, this risk mitigation is especially crucial.

Apart from moving financial risk to anchor purchasers, invoice tokenization offers tier-1 providers a defense against payment default. Traditionally, if an anchor customer defaults on its payment commitments, the tier-1 supplier remains vulnerable, retaining liability for paying its upstream suppliers but receiving no payment for the products or services it provides. This could be particularly disastrous for smaller tier-1 suppliers who lack the financial reserves to handle such a shock.

By separating tier-1 suppliers from payment responsibility should an anchor buyer default, invoice tokenizing helps to reduce this risk. The tier-1 supplier can pay some or all of the tokenized invoice that the anchor buyer generates to its own suppliers. This transfer essentially places the payment responsibility on the anchor buyer, therefore absorbing the financial loss at the top of the supply chain rather than allowing it to flow down to smaller suppliers should the anchor buyer default. By separating themselves from payment responsibility, tier-1 suppliers lower their financial risk and free themselves to concentrate on their primary business without worrying about possible defaults farther downstream.

CHAPTER 6   UNLOCKING VALUE: THE POTENTIAL OF DEEP-TIER SUPPLY CHAIN FINANCE (DTSCF)

When markets are unstable because of macroeconomic events like sudden changes in demand, changes in the value of the dollar, or events in geopolitics, this risk isolation is especially helpful because payment defaults may happen. By making tier-1 suppliers less financially vulnerable to risks like defaults, invoice tokenization makes the supply chain more resilient and lowers the chance of cascading failures.

The cost of financing for every player in the supply chain is one of the most obvious advantages of invoice tokenizing. Particularly for smaller suppliers with worse credit scores, traditional finance sources, including factoring or short-term loans, can be costly. Usually reflecting the perceived risk of lending to these providers, financial institutions demand higher interest rates, therefore further stranding their already limited profits.

By allowing suppliers to access finance depending on the creditworthiness of the anchor customer rather than their own, invoice tokenization alters this relationship. Financial institutions are more ready to provide favorable financing conditions to suppliers holding tokenized invoices supported by the anchor buyer, as the buyer is usually a sizable, financially solid corporation with a strong credit rating. This leads to lower interest rates and improved financing options for tier-1 and deep-tier suppliers.

For instance, a tier-2 or tier-3 supplier who receives a tokenized invoice from a tier-1 supplier might sell that token to a financial institution at a lower discount rate, knowing that the anchors' creditworthiness will ultimately guarantee the payment. This access to reasonably priced finance lets suppliers have excellent cash flows, therefore lessening the demand for costly short-term loans or high-interest debt. Following this procedure, suppliers can reinvest the cost savings back into their operations, thereby strengthening their positions within the supply chain.

Enhancing Liquidity, Resilience, and Efficiency Across Supply Chains

Invoice tokenization improves the whole supply chain in numerous important ways by reducing financial risk and financing costs.

Enhanced Liquidity: Improved access to reasonably priced finance allows suppliers at all levels of the supply chain to preserve better liquidity. This guarantees that, without depending on costly or difficult-to-get credit, companies can pay their staff, cover their running expenses, and buy required raw materials. As a result, the likelihood of supply chain disruptions due to financial shortages is significantly reduced.

Improved Supplier Resilience: Smaller suppliers—especially those further upstream in the supply chain—are sometimes more sensitive to financial strain. Invoice tokenization helps these suppliers be more robust to outside shocks by shielding them from the financial risks related to late payments or customer defaults. This higher resilience helps the whole supply chain by lowering the possibility of interruptions brought on by financial difficulty or supplier bankruptcy.

Greater Supply Chain Efficiency: Access to reasonably priced funding helps suppliers run more effectively. Suppliers are able to meet demand more promptly and consistently, as opposed to delaying production due to resource constraints or cash flow issues. Reduced lead times, enhanced inventory control, and eventually cheaper costs for the whole supply chain follow from this increased efficiency.

Tokenizing invoices reduces the risk of cascading failures by safeguarding tier-1 suppliers from non-payment and transferring the financial risk to the anchor customer. A default by a major customer can affect the whole supply chain in conventional systems and lead to smaller supplier failure. Tokenization of invoices breaks this line of risk, thereby containing financial losses and preventing their spread to other areas of the supply chain.

Modern supply chains may greatly lower risk and cut expenses by using invoice tokenization. Invoice tokenization improves the financial stability of the whole supply chain by spreading financial responsibilities to the more creditworthy anchor customer, separating suppliers from payment problems, and reducing the cost of financing. Innovations like invoice tokenization will be especially important as worldwide supply networks change and confront growing complexity and volatility to help companies run effectively and resiliently even in the face of financial upheavals.

Though it is especially helpful for dependable tier-2 suppliers, invoice tokenization is a significant financial breakthrough with major advantages for all levels of the supply chain. Maintaining the seamless running of supply chains depends much on these vendors, who are consistent in providing premium goods or services on time. Despite their reliability, these vendors may face financial constraints such as limited liquidity and increased borrowing costs, primarily due to their unclear interactions with anchor purchasers. Invoice tokenization solves these problems by improving the quality of receivables and making it easier to get cheap loans based on the strong creditworthiness of anchor customers.

Reliable suppliers become more flexible in handling their finances and better positioned to keep fulfilling their responsibilities within the supply chain by means of invoice tokenization, therefore guaranteeing a steady and effective flow of products and services. This part talks about how invoice tokenization improves early payment security, financial health, and connections with tier-1 suppliers and anchor buyers, which in turn helps trustworthy tier-2 suppliers.

For tier-2 suppliers—regardless of their dependability—one of the main obstacles has always been the low quality of their receivables. Tier-2 vendors in many supply chains do not personally know the anchor buyer. Most of the time, they work with tier-1 vendors instead. Because the transaction is indirect and the supplier has a lower credit rating, financial institutions see their receivables as more risky. This view of risk results in higher financing costs when tier-2 suppliers attempt to factor their receivables or secure loans to meet their working capital needs.

By including the creditworthiness of the anchor buyer in the invoice token, invoice tokenization dramatically raises the quality of these receivables. A tier-1 supplier can forward part or all of a tokenized invoice from an anchor customer to a tier-2 provider for use as payment for products or services. Since the anchor buyer's credit rating supports the token, the receivable now reflects the anchor buyer's higher creditworthiness rather than the financial profile of tier-1 or tier-2 suppliers.

Reliable tier-2 suppliers view their receivables as low-risk, which helps them to obtain more advantageous financing arrangements. Knowing that a credible, sizable anchor buyer guarantees the payment, financial institutions are more willing to provide reduced interest rates or costs when factoring these receivables. This improvement in receivable quality not only decreases the cost of financing but also facilitates the availability of credit for dependable suppliers, therefore lowering their reliance on expensive short-term loans or high-interest lines of credit.

Empowering Reliable Suppliers: The Impact of Invoice Tokenization on Liquidity, Collaboration, and Growth in Supply Chains

Early payments secured through factoring at a reduced cost are one of the most direct advantages of better receivable quality. Suppliers can sell their accounts receivable to a financial institution for an instant cash advance, less a modest discount, through a financial technique known as factoring. Maintaining satisfactory cash flows and making sure they can meet running expenses without waiting for the long payment cycles that are typical in many businesses depends on early payment of dependable tier-2 suppliers.

CHAPTER 6   UNLOCKING VALUE: THE POTENTIAL OF DEEP-TIER SUPPLY CHAIN FINANCE (DTSCF)

For consistent suppliers, invoice tokenization makes factoring more accessible and reasonably priced. Under a conventional factoring contract, the cost of factoring mostly relies on the creditworthiness of the supplier; so, tier-2 suppliers with fewer credit profiles usually pay more discount rates. Tokenized invoices, however, embed the anchor buyer's credibility into the invoice, thereby shifting the risk assessment from the tier-2 provider to the anchor buyer. Financial institutions are more inclined to provide factoring services at reduced rates as the anchor buyer is usually a bigger, more financially solid company.

For instance, a dependable tier-2 supplier who has supplied goods to a tier-1 provider may receive half of the tokenized invoice from an anchor customer. The tier-2 provider can factor this tokenized invoice and receive payment immediately, unlike the tier-1 supplier, who pays the invoice after 60 or 90 days. Early payment access guarantees that trustworthy suppliers may keep liquidity, invest in their operations, and satisfy their own payment commitments to their suppliers, staff, and other stakeholders.

Not only does invoice tokenization improve the financial situation of dependable tier-2 suppliers, but it also strengthens ties between tier-1 suppliers, anchor purchasers, and each other. In conventional supply chains, delayed payments can strain the financial link between tier-1 and tier-2 suppliers, potentially leading to conflict and a decrease in confidence. Despite not receiving regular payments, reliable suppliers may experience financial pressure to meet output targets, which could compromise their ability to continue providing premium goods or services.

Improving liquidity and payment speed helps invoice tokenization enhance ties between tier-1 and tier-2 suppliers. By allowing tier-1 suppliers to transfer tokenized invoices to dependable tier-2 suppliers, tier-1 suppliers are essentially guaranteeing timely payment of these vendors. This fosters confidence and helps tier-2 suppliers to keep providing the premium goods and services that anchor consumers' needs, therefore guaranteeing the seamless running of the whole supply chain. Moreover, trustworthy suppliers are more likely to give top priority to connections with tier-1 suppliers that can provide quick payment via invoice tokenization, hence establishing a more stable and cooperative supply chain.

Even if they do not personally connect, the usage of invoice tokenizing can let dependable tier-2 suppliers create closer ties with anchor purchasers. Anchor purchasers have more awareness of the financial situation and dependability of tier-2 suppliers since invoice tokenization offers better openness in the payment process. This visibility may encourage anchor customers to maintain or even strengthen their relationships with tier-2 suppliers who consistently meet quality standards and deliver

CHAPTER 6   UNLOCKING VALUE: THE POTENTIAL OF DEEP-TIER SUPPLY CHAIN FINANCE (DTSCF)

on time. Over time, this can create more chances for trustworthy vendors to engage in bigger orders or longer-term contracts, therefore improving their position in the supply chain.

Invoice tokenization helps the supply chain to be more generally stable and flourish by helping dependable suppliers with speedier payments and improved access to reasonably priced finance. Reliable suppliers, often the backbone of the supply chain, ensure timely delivery of items and smooth manufacturing operations. Financial constraints on these suppliers might affect the whole supply chain, therefore causing delays, shortages, or quality problems. On the other hand, the whole supply chain gains from more stability and efficiency when dependable sources have access to the tools they need to run effectively.

Ensuring dependable suppliers is financially stable even in the face of obstacles like lengthy payment cycles or market changes depends critically on invoice tokenization. Invoice tokenizing helps dependable suppliers to invest in their operations, increase their capacity, and keep satisfying consumer needs by offering liquidity and lower financing costs. This improves the resilience of the whole supply chain and strengthens particular providers, therefore lowering the chance of interruptions that can affect downstream consumers.

Furthermore, a better financial situation for trustworthy suppliers creates chances for development. Reliable suppliers may invest in new equipment, increase manufacturing, or enter new markets with access to reasonably priced working cash via invoice tokenization. As it guarantees that the supply chain can satisfy rising demand and boost capacity, this development potential helps suppliers personally as well as the complete supply chain.

Reliable tier-2 suppliers benefit greatly from invoice tokenization as it enhances the quality of their receivables, enables early payment through factoring, and fosters closer collaboration within the supply chain. Tokenized invoices help to integrate the creditworthiness of the anchor buyer into tokenized invoices, lowering financing costs and increasing liquidity for dependable suppliers, enabling them to run more effectively and preserve their financial situation. This helps the supply chain to be generally stable and growable, therefore making sure that dependable suppliers may keep providing goods and services even in the face of financial difficulties. Reliable suppliers will progressively gain from this creative financial instrument as more companies use invoice tokenization, therefore improving their standing within the worldwide supply chain ecosystem.

CHAPTER 6   UNLOCKING VALUE: THE POTENTIAL OF DEEP-TIER SUPPLY CHAIN FINANCE (DTSCF)

Balancing Risk, Rewards, and Relationships in the Supply Chain

Adoption of invoice tokenizing presents difficulties even if its many advantages are clear-cut Although the system surely increases supply chain transparency, decreases financing costs, and boosts liquidity, there are certain unanticipated effects that could occur, particularly for some supply chain actors. Usually providing major benefits, invoice tokenization gives access to more reasonably priced finance and improved supply chain stability for dependable tier-2 suppliers and anchor consumers. For some players, like tier-1 suppliers and unreliable vendors, the effect may be less advantageous nevertheless.

The possible detrimental effect on unreliable suppliers—especially in Y-shaped supply chains—is one of the most important difficulties presented by invoice tokenization. A single tier-1 provider in a Y-shaped supply chain distributes orders across several tier-2 suppliers, each of whom can differ in terms of dependability, cost, and performance. Usually, the tier-1 provider has to strike a balance between sourcing from a less dependable source, who could provide less expensive items but with more risk of interruptions, and a more dependable supplier, generally with a higher cost.

Tokenizing invoices usually helps the balance to move toward more trustworthy suppliers. By adding the creditworthiness of the anchor customer to the token, invoice tokenization lowers the financial risks that come with higher-tier suppliers. This makes tier-1 providers more likely to choose reliable suppliers. Reliable suppliers can keep sending goods and services to tier-1 suppliers by taking advantage of the financial benefits of invoice tokenization, such as easier access to financing and more cash on hand. This makes them more sustainable.

This change, meantime, may marginalize less trustworthy vendors. The financial savings generated by invoice tokenization might encourage tier-1 suppliers to give more dependable providers first priority over less expensive but risky options. Unreliable suppliers might find themselves losing business because tier-1 vendors value the consistency that dependable partners offer. Previously, they could get orders based on their reduced prices. This could lead to a gradual decline in orders for unreliable suppliers, thereby depriving them of earnings or potentially removing them entirely from the supply chain.

CHAPTER 6 UNLOCKING VALUE: THE POTENTIAL OF DEEP-TIER SUPPLY CHAIN FINANCE (DTSCF)

Invoice tokenization can help to drastically change long-standing supplier relationships for these erratic vendors. Should their primary competitive advantage—lower prices—become less important given the better financing terms for dependable suppliers, they might find it difficult to stay viable in a market that prioritizes dependability over cost control more and more.

Another major obstacle to adoption is the potential for invoice tokenization to weaken the negotiating power of tier-1 suppliers. Although invoice tokenization increases liquidity, tier-1 suppliers might be under increased pressure that would affect their profitability, especially in big market environments. The rising competitive pricing pressure resulting from the transparency and efficiency offered by invoice tokenization is one main problem.

Because they act as middlemen between the buyer and the network of tier-2 and tier-3 suppliers, tier-1 suppliers in a conventional supply chain can have power over anchor buyers. They control the flow of products and services, therefore absorbing the risks and complexity involved in arranging payments and delivery. Since tier-1 suppliers carry much of the financial risk and control important parts of the supply chain, this function affords them some negotiation strength.

With invoice tokenizing, the anchor buyer bears much of the financial risk. Some tier-1 suppliers lose some control over payment flows and financial ties because invoice tokenization makes it easier for deep-tier suppliers to get affordable financing based on the buyer's creditworthiness. This makes control harder for tier-1 suppliers. With this change in risk and responsibility, tier-1 suppliers may find themselves in a worse position when bargaining with anchor customers, who now have more direct control over payments and a better view of the supply chain.

Also, in big markets with lots of competition, the fact that invoice tokenization makes it possible for deep-tier providers to have better finances might make tier-1 suppliers feel more price pressure. Tier-1 suppliers could be under pressure to pass these cost savings forward to anchor purchasers in the form of reduced prices as the cost of borrowing lowers for dependable tier-2 suppliers. Due to the efficiency that invoice tokenization produces, anchor buyers might look for tier-1 suppliers with more competitive pricing, which would reduce their profitability and squeeze their margins.

For tier-1 suppliers, the loss of negotiating leverage can have major effects on their profitability. Tier-1 suppliers can find it challenging to keep the same profit margins they had as competitive pricing pressure rises. In sectors where margins are already low, this pressure might drive tier-1 suppliers to cut their pricing to stay competitive, therefore compromising earnings.

Furthermore, since invoice tokenization improves the financial situation of deep-tier providers, tier-1 suppliers might not be able to rely on the financial leverage they previously used. Historically, tier-1 vendors may have utilized their position as the main point of contact with anchor customers to negotiate better terms or guarantee appropriate payments. Tier-1 suppliers may lose this leverage and find themselves in a less favorable position when bargaining with both buyers and upstream suppliers, as deep-tier suppliers, now able to get finance more readily via invoice tokenization, lose influence.

In some cases, invoice tokenization can even lead to disintermediation. In this case, anchor buyers make direct financial connections with deep-tier suppliers instead of avoiding tier-1 providers altogether. Although this might not be possible in every sector, the more transparent and efficient blockchain technology is, the more likely it is that buyers—especially if they can get better terms or pricing—will be able to deal straight with suppliers, lowering down the supply chain. In some markets, this might further diminish tier-1 providers' relevance and profitability.

A thorough analysis of the distribution of advantages along the supply chain is necessary for the adoption of invoice tokenization. It's clear that the change in financial dynamics will make things more efficient and cheaper for reliable suppliers and anchor buyers. However, it could disproportionately harm less reliable suppliers and tier-1 buyers. Tier-1 suppliers may exclude particularly unreliable providers in favor of dependable partners who can fully benefit from tokenization. As anchor purchasers take more control over financing arrangements and payment systems, tier-1 suppliers might also be under increasing pressure to slash prices and accept smaller margins.

To mitigate these obstacles, companies using invoice tokenization should consider measures to ensure a more equitable distribution of benefits across the supply chain. By effectively balancing cost, risk, and dependability, companies can encourage tier-1 suppliers to maintain partnerships with both reliable and less reliable providers. Anchor purchasers should regularly monitor their tier-1 suppliers to ensure that pricing pressures do not unnecessarily reduce their profitability. Offering volume-based discounts or other incentives could achieve this and maintain strong supplier relationships.

Although invoice tokenization has several advantages—improving liquidity, lowering financing costs, and increasing transparency—the adoption of it might also present problems for some supply chain players. While tier-1 suppliers may have less negotiating strength and more pricing pressure from anchor purchasers, unreliable suppliers may find themselves losing business as the efficiency of tokenization favors more dependable partners. Businesses have to carefully control these dynamics and aim to produce a better, more equal distribution of value across the whole supply chain if they are to fully enjoy the advantages of invoice tokenization.

The Transformational Potential of Invoice Tokenization: Balancing Efficiency, Risk, and Equity

The possibilities of invoice tokenization go well beyond the direct advantages of risk reduction and cost control. As companies increasingly rely on blockchain-based solutions to fortify their operational networks and enhance liquidity management, tokenization holds the potential to transform the organization and operation of supply chains in the long run. Businesses like Standard Chartered and innovative platforms like Singapore's BANCO demonstrate the use of blockchain technology in supply chain finance. This shows that more and more people are interested in tokenization as a practical way to improve financial efficiency and transparency in supply chains.

Blockchain-based invoice tokenization provides a fresh degree of financial democratization, enabling even tiny and deep-tier suppliers—who have always had trouble finding reasonably priced financing—to gain from the creditworthiness of bigger consumers. Invoice tokenization gives small suppliers the chance to acquire working capital at less cost by lessening the reliance on a supplier's own credit rating and moving risk to more creditworthy companies, like anchor buyers. For suppliers in underdeveloped areas or sectors where financial access has traditionally been restricted, this may especially be transforming.

Blockchain technology's influence in changing supply chain financing will get increasingly more evident as it develops. The world's supply chain might be better connected, more open, and more cost-effective if invoice tokenization is easily added to the larger supply chain finance ecosystem. These developments enable small and deep-tier suppliers to participate more actively in finance agreements, which were previously exclusive to larger, more established companies. Blockchain technologies allow these suppliers to tokenize invoices and get early payment, therefore strengthening their financial situation, lowering cash flow restrictions, and reinvesting in their operations.

But as invoice tokenizing becomes more popular, companies have to give much thought to the wider ramifications of these developments. Although the technology could help to build stronger supply chains, the change in financial dynamics could also bring fresh difficulties. Businesses will have to control the balance of power in the supply chain, for instance, thereby guaranteeing fair distribution of advantages like better liquidity and finance availability among several levels of suppliers. Ignoring this might have unanticipated effects such as marginalizing some providers or more competitive pressure on middlemen like tier-1 suppliers.

Ultimately, invoice tokenization offers a significant development in supply chain finance as it might improve operational efficiency, lower financial risk, and democratize access to working money. Deeper integration between financial and supply chain operations as more companies use this technology will probably result in the building of more robust, open, and sustainable worldwide supply networks. Invoice tokenization has the ability to produce long-term value for companies of all kinds throughout the supply chain with cautious deployment and an eye toward fair rewards.

Summary

The transforming possibilities of deep-tier supply chain financial (DTSCF) in filling up financial gaps and enhancing supply chain resilience are investigated in this chapter. It underlines the need for clear definitions, basic understanding, and a robust regulatory framework for efficient execution, as well as DTSCF's crucial role in helping lower-tier suppliers, particularly via post-shipment financing.

While addressing the operational and technological difficulties involved, the chapter emphasizes various advantages of DTSCF, including greater access to capital, fewer risks, and enhanced supply chain efficiency. It addresses the part technology, platform-based solutions, and fintech solutions' challenges play as well as potential technical advancements that can increase DTSCF acceptance.

Additionally covered is DTSCF's integration with environmental, social, and governance (ESG) initiatives, thus improving ESG visibility and compliance and so supporting sustainability throughout supply chains. Introduced as a creative approach to close financial gaps, lower risk, and enhance general supply chain operations is invoice tokenizing. Emphasizing DTSCF's ability to transform world supply chains by improving risk management, enabling financial access, and promoting sustainable practices close the chapter.

CHAPTER 7

Merging the Seas: The Imperative of Digital Transformation and Legal and Regulatory Reform

Digital technology is increasingly playing a significant role in modern society, transforming various sectors, including the commercial sector. Historically relying on conventional paper-based methods, this industry finds itself at a critical juncture. These paper-based systems have been the cornerstone of world trade for many years as they enable transactions and guarantee seamless flow of products across boundaries. However, as technology advances, people increasingly perceive these methods as outdated and inefficient.

The inefficiencies in paper-based systems have important consequences. First, these inefficiencies can lead to significant financial losses. Often lengthy manual procedures are involved, which causes delays, upsetting supply networks, and raising expenses. Furthermore, these methods are vulnerable to fraud due to the ease of changing or falsifying paper, thereby jeopardizing the integrity of trade transactions.

Apart from security and finances, environmental factors must be considered. By means of deforestation and the carbon footprint connected with paper manufacture and transportation, excessive usage of paper adds to environmental damage. This environmental effect is becoming more difficult to overlook in a time when sustainability is becoming more and more vital.

Furthermore, a major problem with conventional systems is how they affect small and medium-sized businesses (SMEs). The complexity and expenses connected with paper-based procedures can disadvantage these companies in the worldwide market. Small businesses may find compliance and documentation burdensome, thereby limiting their ability to compete on an equal footing with larger companies.

The digital transformation of trade operations offers the solution to these difficulties. This shift can modernize the trade industry, addressing the inefficiencies, vulnerabilities, and environmental issues associated with conventional approaches. Digital trading systems may drastically save the time and resources needed for paperwork, speed transactions, and lower the risk of fraud by itself. Moreover, they remove obstacles to access and let SMEs engage more completely in the worldwide market, therefore creating fresh prospects for them.

This digital change offers truly significant advantages. Economically, it promises to lower expenses and improve the effectiveness of world commerce. Regarding security, digital platforms may provide more traceability and openness, therefore lowering the danger of fraud and guaranteeing more ethical behavior in all kinds of transactions. Environmentally, the move away from paper-based operations fits with world sustainability objectives, therefore helping to lower the carbon footprint of trade activity.

The commerce sector has a wonderful chance to welcome the changes brought about by ongoing development in digital technology. Moving away from antiquated paper-based processes and implementing digital solutions will help the industry to achieve notable economic, security, and environmental improvements, therefore enabling a more efficient, safe, and sustainable future in world commerce.

Overcoming Legal Barriers

Thanks in enormous part to amazing developments in digital technology, the case for adopting digital trade has acquired tremendous momentum recently. These developments show the enormous possibilities digital trade and trade finance present for enhancing security and efficiency in world business. Digital procedures provide, as companies and governments both understand, a degree of speed, security, and environmental sustainability that conventional paper-based solutions just cannot match.

CHAPTER 7 MERGING THE SEAS: THE IMPERATIVE OF DIGITAL TRANSFORMATION AND LEGAL AND REGULATORY REFORM

Digital commerce offers several benefits. Digital systems streamline tasks and expedite transactions compared to the laborious processing of paper documentation. This acceleration in speed leads to a faster flow of products, faster payments, and ultimately a more dynamic global commerce environment. Besides, the security advantages are really significant. More commonly in paper-based systems, digital systems can include encryption, authentication, and traceability mechanisms that greatly lower the risks of fraud and mistakes.

Furthermore, in a society struggling with resource preservation and climate change, the environmental advantages of digital trading become ever more significant. Reducing the dependence on paper helps digital commerce operations preserve forests, decrease carbon emissions linked with paper manufacture and transportation, and save waste, thereby complementing worldwide efforts toward sustainability.

Though there are obviously significant advantages, the shift to digital trading presents certain difficulties. One of the most significant challenges is the existence of antiquated legal systems in many nations. These legal systems have not been revised to match the reality of the digital age, as paper was the sole medium used for official documentation throughout their establishment. Consequently, these systems can fail to acknowledge or meet the particular needs of electronic documents, particularly those that are absolutely vital for international trade.

Promissory notes and bills of lading, which require transferability and security, are particularly challenging due to this legal mismatch. These papers are essential for trade finance as they are the main tools for international credit and product transfers. Legal systems all throughout the world find them easily comprehended and generally approved in their conventional paper form. However, the digitalization of these records places them in a legal limbo. Many of the current regulations ignore the electronic versions of these papers, which leaves confusion and prevents the general acceptance of digital trade.

Thus, even if the rationale for digital trade is strong, it is obvious that reaching this shift would call for more than simply technological creativity. Furthermore, it will need major changes to legal systems to guarantee they fit the requirements of a digital economy. The full possibilities of digital trade will remain untapped without these legislative reforms, and the worldwide trade community will continue to suffer needless obstacles in its attempts to modernize and maximize international business.

CHAPTER 7   MERGING THE SEAS: THE IMPERATIVE OF DIGITAL TRANSFORMATION AND LEGAL AND REGULATORY REFORM

Breaking Legal Barriers, Paving the Way for Digital Trade with MLETR

The UNCITRAL created the Model Law on Electronic Transferable Records (MLETR) to resolve the legal issues preventing digital trade. This has led to change. This project directly responds to the necessity for a legal framework that fits the reality of contemporary digital trading systems.

The primary goal of the MLETR is to eliminate the existing legal barriers that would hinder the use of electronic transferable records with the same legal validity as their paper counterparts. Many countries' laws don't fully recognize or encourage the use of electronic records. International trade places significant importance on the transfer and validity of documents such as bills of lading and promissory notes across borders. By providing a legal foundation that ensures the same validity and enforceability of these electronic records as traditional paper documentation, the MLETR bridges this gap.

The MLETR is based on fundamental ideas that provide it flexibility and forward-looking capability. One of these values is the principle of not discriminating against electronic communications. This suggests that the digital nature of electronic records does not warrant their discounting or differential treatment. This idea is absolutely essential for creating a legal environment free from antiquated legal prejudices, therefore allowing digital trade to grow unhindered.

Technical neutrality is still another fundamental idea guiding the MLETR. This idea ensures the law's flexibility to accommodate various digital models, systems, and advancements, as it remains independent of any particular technology or platform. This adaptability is especially crucial in a fast-changing digital environment, as new technologies always surface and challenge established procedures. The MLETR permits the inclusion of several digital platforms, such as distributed ledger technology (DLT), which supports numerous blockchain-based applications, without favoring any specific technology. This flexibility is crucial to ensure the legislation remains relevant and efficient in facilitating digital trade, both today and in the future.

The MLETR marks major progress in the legal framework required to enable the global trade digital transition. Through the recognition and validation of electronic transferable records, UNCITRAL is opening the path for more inclusive, safe, and efficient international trade. The MLETR incorporates the principles of non-discrimination against electronic communications and technical neutrality, making it adaptable to various technological advancements and ensuring its continued relevance across various digital platforms and systems. A vital first step toward standardizing the legal regulation of digital commerce, this model law will help governments and companies to completely welcome the advantages of a digitized global economy.

Foundations of Trust: Core Concepts in the MLETR for Digital Trade

In the area of international trade, the Model Law on Electronic Transferable Records (MLETR) lays out a lot of basic ideas that are needed to understand how electronic records could be used as valid and reliable alternatives to paper documents.

Electronic transferable records are among the basic concepts of the MLETR. These are characterized as electronic records, including bills of lading or promissory notes, that capture the same data as in paper-based transferable papers or instruments. For legal acceptance, these electronic documents must meet specific requirements that ensure they possess the same legal standing and utility as their paper counterparts. This equivalency is crucial to ensure that companies and legal systems may go from paper to digital without sacrificing any of the fundamental qualities that define these documents as dependable and enforceable.

The MLETR also introduces the somewhat crucial idea "control." Control functions in the digital environment as the practical counterpart of physical world possession. This idea is important as, unlike hardcopy records, electronic ones lack a physical form that one may hold or save. Control, then, guarantees that there is only one trustworthy and authoritative form of the electronic record in use at any one point. The document's integrity is preserved throughout its lifetime, preventing duplication, just like a physical document limited to one place.

Additionally highly valued by the MLETR is the integrity of electronic records. For these records to be legally legitimate and trustworthy, they must remain whole and unchanged from the moment of production until they are no longer required. Changes in the usual flow of transmission, storage, and display—which are required for the pragmatic use of digital documents—are the sole deviations from this rule. It is crucial to uphold the integrity of digital records to ensure their trustworthiness, akin to that of paper records, without any corruption or manipulation.

At last, the MLETR's architecture revolves mostly around the idea of dependability. Reliable means that the methods used to create, maintain, and store electronic documents must regularly make sure that these files are just as trustworthy as their paper counterparts. Companies and legal systems find hope in using electronic records because they can withstand scrutiny and provide the same level of assurance as traditional documents.

In the realm of commerce, the MLETR essentially aims to ensure that electronic records can serve as actual functional counterparts of paper-based documents. The MLETR supports the digital revolution of trade while keeping the trust and safety needed for global trade. It achieves this by emphasizing fundamental concepts such as the ability to send and receive electronic records, control, honesty, and dependability.

Global Momentum: The Worldwide Adoption of MLETR

Reflecting its significance in the modernization of trade laws, the Model Law on Electronic Transferable Records (MLETR) has attracted widespread acceptance and support on the worldwide scene. The G7 countries, with some of the world's largest economies, are prominent MLETR supporters. This support from the G7 emphasizes the understanding of the MLETR's ability to adapt digital procedures, enabling more seamless, safe international trade.

Apart from the G7, several worldwide agencies have also backed the MLETR. Especially the European Bank for Reconstruction and Development (EBRD) has been instrumental in encouraging the acceptance of this model law. This is especially true in developing countries, where the switch to digital commerce could have a big effect on their growth and ability to join the global economy. The EBRD's involvement highlights the importance of the MLETR in boosting economic growth and trade efficiency.

Adoption of the MLETR is not only a theoretical activity, but it is also in progress in various countries worldwide. These nations understand they have to change their legal systems to fit the MLETR's values and clauses. Legal reform plays a crucial role in enabling these governments to establish conditions that allow the use of electronic transferable records with the same legal authority and confidence as traditional paper documents. In order to fully realize the advantages of digital trade and reduce the obstacles that have traditionally hindered the acceptance of digital processes in global trade, this reform is especially crucial.

We have created a legal reform matrix to assist countries with this challenging task of legal change. This matrix provides a complete tool for nations to assess their current legal systems and pinpoint required adjustments to match the MLETR. It offers a clear road map for carrying out the required legal and regulatory reforms, therefore providing a disciplined method of legal reform. Following this matrix helps countries to methodically close the holes and inconsistencies in their present legislation, therefore guaranteeing a seamless transition to a legal framework totally supporting digital trade.

The MLETR's worldwide backing and continuous use show a major change toward using digital solutions in global trade. More governments are implementing legislative reforms to fit this model legislation, establishing the basis for a more effective, safe, and internationally linked trading system. The G7, international agencies like the EBRD, and individual nations working together show a common will to modernize trade regulations in a way that satisfies digital age needs.

Legal Reforms As the Catalyst for Digital Trade Success

Looking ahead, effective digital transformation of world commerce depends on the execution of thorough legislative changes. Many nations firmly base their present legal systems on ideas designed for a society that relies on paper-based records, making these changes crucial. Digital trade must grow from nations changing their laws to allow the use of digital transferable records. To create a more secure and efficient commerce environment, we must eliminate the legal barriers resulting from the outdated requirement for physical documents.

Nations should evaluate these necessary adjustments by looking to countries that have made major moves in this direction. Leaders in implementing rules allowing the use of electronic records in commerce are nations like Singapore and Bahrain. Their efforts demonstrate the effective implementation of legislative changes to create an environment conducive to digital trade. Other nations can learn a tremendous deal about the possibilities and difficulties related to such changes by looking at the strategies used by these early adopters.

As benchmarks, the experiences of these countries provide useful insights that could direct other countries on their own road toward legal modernization. These nations have demonstrated that it is feasible to design a legislative framework supporting the use of electronic records that also improves the general trade accessibility, security, and efficiency. Their success stories highlight the need for a forward-looking law reform strategy that welcomes the technological developments altering the scene of world commerce.

CHAPTER 7   MERGING THE SEAS: THE IMPERATIVE OF DIGITAL TRANSFORMATION AND LEGAL AND REGULATORY REFORM

The path forward for digital trade is essentially clear: significant legislative changes must lead the way. Laws that help to use digitally transferable records will help nations remove the legal roadblocks that now hinder advancement. By leveraging these experiences, other nations can formulate their own legislative reform strategies, ensuring they can fully capitalize on the benefits of digital commerce. A completely computerized global trading system calls for careful planning, cooperation, and a dedication to changing the legal underpinnings upon which commerce is based.

The Legal Revolution for a Sustainable Future

Trade's digitization has evolved from being only a choice to a vital need for contemporary governments. The linked, fast-paced world of today increasingly perceives the conventional paper-based mechanisms that have long sustained international commerce as ineffective and outdated. The shift to digital processes promises to release a broad range of advantages necessary for the ongoing expansion and sustainability of world trade.

Among the most important benefits of digitalizing commerce are the quite remarkable gains in efficiency that are possible. Digital systems simplify operations, therefore lowering the time required to conduct transactions and transport products across borders. Eliminating the need for paper documentation and the manual processing required helps companies save time and resources, therefore directly translating into lower costs. Furthermore, the faster speed and accuracy of digital transactions aid in reducing mistakes, reducing expenses, and raising general output.

Another very vital advantage of digital trading is security. Adoption of digital signatures and electronic records helps to greatly lower the possibility of fraud and document manipulation. Digital systems can incorporate modern encryption and authentication techniques to enhance the speed and security of trade transactions compared to previous years. In a time when governments and companies are both more worried about cyberattacks, this increased security is especially crucial.

Apart from security and efficiency, digitization of commerce has significant environmental advantages. Digital trading systems help to conserve natural resources and lower carbon emissions linked with paper manufacture and transportation by lessening the need for paper. This change fits the worldwide drive for increased environmental sustainability; hence, digital trade becomes essential for a more sustainable future.

However, if we are to fully enjoy these advantages, legal systems must change to facilitate the shift from paper to digital. Many nations' present legal systems still reflect their construction around the usage of physical documents, therefore impeding the general acceptance of electronic records. To overcome these challenges, we must modify laws to recognize and facilitate the use of digital documents in commerce.

The United Nations Commission on International Trade Law (UNCITRAL) has set a clear path forward with its Model Law on Electronic Transferable Records (MLETR). This model law provides a strong basis for legal reform and guides nations in the process of changing their legislation to fit the usage of electronic records. The MLETR aims to ensure that electronic records carry the same legal weight as their paper counterparts, thereby facilitating their full substitution in commercial transactions.

Adopting the MLETR's suggested adjustments will help nations all around to open the path for a more sustainable, safe, and effective global trading system. Digitizing commerce involves a significant shift in trade practices to meet the demands of modern society, rather than merely introducing new technology. Proper legislative changes can unlock the full potential of digital trade, thereby benefiting companies, economies, and the environment.

Navigating the Convergence: The Future of Digital Trade and Sustainability Reporting Entwined

The potential convergence of electronic commerce regulations and sustainability reporting systems has revolutionized power in a society increasingly becoming digital and interconnected. Key steps toward improving digital trade are the Model Law on Electronic Transferable Records (MLETR) and the Electronic Transferable Documents Act (ETRDA). By streamlining the usage of electronic data and papers, these developments improve security and efficiency in worldwide trade. The Corporate Sustainability Reporting Directive (CSRD) and the International Financial Reporting Standards (IFRs) S1 and S2 are the newest sustainability reporting systems. They are changing the way companies are responsible and making sure that environmental, social, and governance (ESG) reporting is open and consistent. This paper investigates how the combination of these legal and regulatory developments may propel companies all around a more sustainable, safe, and smooth future.

CHAPTER 7 MERGING THE SEAS: THE IMPERATIVE OF DIGITAL TRANSFORMATION AND LEGAL AND REGULATORY REFORM

Model Law on Electronic Transferable Records is MLETR for short. UNCITRAL, the United Nations Commission on International Trade Law, adopted MLETR on July 13, 2017.

International organizations like the United Nations Commission on International Trade Law (UNCITRAL), the International Institute for the Unification of Private Law (UNIDROIT), and numerous regional bodies regularly develop model laws. Among the several legal fields they cover are business law, family law, criminal law, and environmental law.

How can we give an exhaustive definition of Model Law? It is a set of legal standards, principles, or regulations formulated by a recognized legal body or authority. These laws serve as a prototype or guideline that countries or jurisdictions can adopt, adapt, or use as a reference to develop or reform their own legislation. Model laws do not have legal force unless a jurisdiction enacts them into law, unlike binding international treaties or agreements.

Model laws offer a multitude of primary applications and significant benefits. Harmonizing laws guarantees cross-border uniformity; hence, one of the main goals is their harmonizing. Model laws enable international trade, investment, and collaboration by helping legal systems align across different countries. One outstanding illustration of this is the UNCITRAL Model Law on International Commercial Arbitration, which aims to homogenize arbitration rules all around. This standardization makes international arbitration processes more stable and predictable, which makes it easier for people from many countries to take part in confident arbitration.

Model laws are also another important goal driving legal reform. By providing a modern framework, including worldwide best practices and standards, they significantly help to modernize legal systems. Countries trying to modernize their legal systems to satisfy current global criteria depend on this modernization. Moreover, model laws help legislative procedures be efficient by offering thorough drafts that lawmakers may customize to fit local situations. This ready-made feature of model laws saves money and time, therefore allowing faster and more successful legislative changes.

One more important advantage of model legislation is capacity building. Particularly in nations with less established legal systems, they provide a well-researched and extensively screened template that is a priceless instructional tool for legislators and attorneys. These model laws provide direction, thereby improving the knowledge and skills of people engaged in the legislative process and thus strengthening the legal system generally.

One more significant benefit of model legislation is their adaptability. Jurisdictions can change these rules to fit their own legal traditions, cultural setting, and necessity. This flexibility ensures the customization of implementation to suit local conditions, thereby enhancing the relevance and efficacy of the legislation in various contexts, while maintaining the fundamental ideas and advantages of the model law.

Finally, model legislation greatly helps to provide legal clarity. Particularly helpful for companies and foreign investors, governments may improve the predictability of their legal systems by using these uniform models. This consistency provides a clear and consistent legal foundation for addressing problems, therefore helping to lower legal disputes and misunderstandings. Standardized model laws provide fewer possibilities for interpretation differences, therefore ensuring a more consistent and trustworthy legal environment.

The main goals and advantages of model laws are thus harmony of laws, legal reform, capacity building, flexibility, and legal certainty. These features, taken together, help to produce a more predictable, effective, modern legal environment that supports global cooperation and progress.

Particularly suited for nations undergoing legal reforms—especially emerging or transitional economies seeking to revamp antiquated legal systems—model laws are standardized legal frameworks designed to provide guidance and structure for developing cohesive, modern legal systems that align with international best practices and promote economic growth, legal certainty, and investor confidence. Modernizing their legal systems to fit current criteria and practices is a difficulty for many of these countries; model laws provide a thorough and well-researched basis to direct this process. These uniform laws help nations effectively modernize their legal systems, therefore guaranteeing that they conform to international standards and enable better integration into the world economy.

Model Laws as Key Tools for Legal Harmonization

Model laws are quite important in areas attempting legal harmonization to establish a more unified legal framework. Groups of nations or areas striving for economic integration and cooperation find model laws to be quite helpful in standardizing their legal systems. Trade, investment, and international mobility all depend on this harmonization, as it lowers legal disparities and advances a smooth legal scene. By adopting model laws, these places can set up a consistent set of laws that encourages economic growth and teamwork, which keeps them from fighting.

CHAPTER 7   MERGING THE SEAS: THE IMPERATIVE OF DIGITAL TRANSFORMATION AND LEGAL AND
            REGULATORY REFORM

In the field of international commerce and investment as well, model laws are absolutely necessary. For cross-border transactions and investments, they enable a predictable and stable legal environment—qualities essential for companies with worldwide operations. Model laws' predictability helps to lower legal uncertainty and conflict, therefore promoting a more suitable environment for global corporate operations. When investors and businesses can rely on a uniform legal framework guaranteeing justice and consistency, they are more likely to participate in cross-border enterprises.

Model laws provide significant advantages in newly developing legal fields such as digital trade, cyber law, and environmental rules. These disciplines are changing quickly; hence, worldwide agreement and standardization are really necessary. Model laws ensure a universally applicable strategy, thereby ensuring the logical and successful handling of emerging legal challenges. Model laws help people around the world work together and understand each other by giving developing countries a consistent set of laws. This helps countries deal with the complicated legal problems of today.

Model laws abound; one example is the UNCITRAL Model Law on International Commercial Arbitration, first enacted in 1985 and revised in 2006. Governments use this model legislation to modernize and modify their laws on arbitral processes, ensuring equity and efficiency in international arbitration. This model legislation is a pillar of international conflict resolution as it offers a consistent method that improves the dependability and predictability of arbitration processes.

Introduced in 1997, another important example is the UNCITRAL Model Law on Cross-Border Insolvency. This model law offers a complete framework for handling cross-border bankruptcy situations, therefore encouraging legal certainty for companies and creditors as well as collaboration between governments. This model law guarantees a more orderly resolution of financial difficulty across borders and helps safeguard the interests of all those engaged by enabling a coordinated response to bankruptcy problems.

Adopted in 2008, the UNIDROIT Model Law on Leasing seeks to boost the leasing sector by providing a consistent legal framework for nations to fit their own legal traditions and economic requirements. By offering a uniform set of rules and supporting investment and economic development in nations that accept this model law, it helps the leasing industry to flourish.

Model laws are essentially appropriate for nations undergoing legal reforms, sectors seeking legal harmonization, international commerce and investment, and developing legal areas overall.

Model laws make a significant contribution to the harmonization, modernization, and capacity building of legislation, which explains their exceptional suitability for various applications. Essential instruments for legal growth and change, they provide flexible yet strong frameworks that may be customized to match various legal and cultural settings. One well-known instance of such model legislation is the Model Legislation on Electronic Transferable Records (MLETR).

Approved on July 13, 2017, by the United Nations Commission on International Commerce Law (UNCITRAL), the MLETR seeks to enable the acceptance and usage of electronic transferable records in global commerce. This statute shows UNCITRAL's will to modernize and harmonize trade rules in order to match the fast-changing digital scene. Adoption of the MLETR represents a major turning point in resolving the difficulties resulting from the shift from paper-based to electronic records.

Comprising 19 pieces, the MLETR covers several facets of electronic transferable records—including their development, application, and legal recognition. Together, these papers establish a comprehensive legal framework that grants the same legal impact to electronic versions of paper-based transferable documents and instruments like bills of lading, promissory notes, and warehouse receipts. Through this, the MLETR improves the security and dependability of electronic transactions, lowers costs, and increases efficiency. Since this change fits the modern demands of international trade, it is essential for enabling more effective worldwide trade.

Enhancing Global Trade

Complementing MLETR's articles is an explanation comment that is quite important. This note offers thorough background material to help states interpret and implement the MLETR's requirements. It also provides direction to other text users, therefore guaranteeing consistent and efficient application of the rules and ideals. The explanatory note makes the legislative goal clear and gives useful analysis of the MLETR's implementation and operation, making it an essential tool for lawmakers, lawyers, and people involved in international trade.

Using the MLETR, UNCITRAL has greatly helped to enable more seamless and effective digital era global trade. This model legislation emphasizes the need for international collaboration and standardization in trade law as it helps the shift from paper-based to electronic records. Apart from modernizing trade practices, the MLETR's framework improves legal clarity and predictability, which are crucial for creating an environment fit for international commerce.

CHAPTER 7   MERGING THE SEAS: THE IMPERATIVE OF DIGITAL TRANSFORMATION AND LEGAL AND REGULATORY REFORM

Basically, meeting the changing demands of contemporary legal systems depends mostly on model legislation such as the MLETR. Promoting international harmony and collaboration, they provide a disciplined yet flexible method of law change. Model laws help to simplify legislative procedures and promote the creation of more efficient and effective legal frameworks by providing ready-made, complete drafts that can be customized to local settings. This flexibility guarantees that model laws stay applicable and helpful in many countries, hence supporting world legal growth and stability.

A law that stands out is the Model Law on Electronic Transferable Records (MLETR). Its main parts make electronic records much more flexible, easier to use, and applicable all over the world. Its technological-neutral attitude is among its best qualities. We built the MLETR without favoring any one technology, enabling the use of electronic transferable records across a wide range of technical systems. Because it is neutral, the MLETR can work with and support any system that uses a distributed ledger technology like blockchain, a token-based system, or a regular registry. This inclusive strategy guarantees that, independent of technological development, the MLETR stays pertinent and flexible. It enables companies to accept new ideas or use already-existing systems without having significant technological infrastructure changes—a flexibility often needed in the ever-changing field of international trade.

Another fundamental aspect of the MLETR is the concept of "functional equivalent." This idea proves that digitally transferable records have the same legal validity and use as conventional paper-based documentation. Should the law mandate the ownership of a transferable document, having an electronic transferable record equally meets this need. This equivalency ensures that electronic records have the same validity and effect as their paper counterparts. It makes the smooth transfer from paper-based to electronic systems easier, therefore improving efficiency, lowering costs, and encouraging more trade and business using digital solutions.

Furthermore, the MLETR is strong and able to include a broad spectrum of data and follow different industry requirements. Article 6 allows for the inclusion of additional information in electronic transferable records, which may not be present in traditional paper documents. This could incorporate digital signatures, timestamps, and metadata, thereby improving the utility, security, and accessibility of electronic documents. Article 12 guarantees that the MLETR is flexible across several industries since it can coincide with any relevant industry standard. This resilience guarantees that the MLETR stays a forward-looking and strong piece of law, therefore supporting the dynamic character of world trade and industry.

CHAPTER 7   MERGING THE SEAS: THE IMPERATIVE OF DIGITAL TRANSFORMATION AND LEGAL AND REGULATORY REFORM

As the MLETR's clauses in articles 17 and 18 show, practicality is another asset. The legislation lets an electronic transferable record replace a conventional paper-based document or instrument, and vice versa. This bidirectional flexibility guarantees that companies and people are not trapped in one format over another, therefore offering the choice to move between electronic and paper data as needed. This practical approach respects current ways of doing things while also moving them into the modern era. This leads to more acceptance and smoother transfers between different systems for keeping records.

The MLETR depends critically on cross-border recognition to be globally applicable and accepted. Article 19 asserts that merely issuing or using an electronic transferable record overseas does not negate its legal effect, validity, or enforceability. This idea solves the difficulties resulting from different legal systems throughout countries. The MLETR ensures legal clarity and consistency in cross-border transactions by ensuring universal recognition of electronic records. This clause plays a crucial role in fostering trust and collaboration among global trade partners, providing companies with the assurance that their electronic records will receive the same respect and enforceability as domestic ones.

Its technological neutrality, functional equivalence principle, robustness, practicality, and cross-border recognition are some of the most important things that make the MLETR more useful and flexible. These characteristics empower the MLETR to function as a versatile and progressive piece of legislation, capable of adapting to the evolving demands of modern international trade and commerce. The MLETR promotes efficiency, lowers costs, and builds international cooperation and confidence by enabling the use of electronic transferable records, thereby modernizing and harmonizing trade processes worldwide.

Article 19 of the Model Law on Electronic Transferable Records (MLETR) talks about cross-border recognition. This part of the law shows a strong desire to make the world a better place to do business where everyone feels welcome. This paragraph guarantees, independent of their foreign source, that digitally transferable records will have the same legal standing and validity as conventional paper-based documentation. This helps to solve a basic problem in international trade: the diverse legal systems and rules that might hinder the acceptance and use of electronic records throughout several countries.

The cross-border recognition clause largely supports the free flow of goods and services across borders. When one nation utilizes or enforces electronic transferable records, such as electronic bills of lading, promissory notes, or warehouse receipts, it eliminates any potential legal obstacles. By guaranteeing that these records, issued or used elsewhere, will not lose their legal effect, validity, or enforceability, the MLETR enhances the predictability and stability of global commerce transactions.

This clause significantly improves the effectiveness and resilience of global trade. By lowering the possibility of legal conflicts and inconsistencies resulting from different national laws, it helps to enable more consistent and dependable international trade. Cross-border recognition guarantees that, free from legal barriers, electronic records can flow across borders as easily as products and services can. Timeliness and efficient implementation of international trade agreements and contracts depend on this smooth transition.

Furthermore, the cross-border recognition clause fosters a more inclusive global trading environment by ensuring equal opportunities for nations with varying degrees of technological progress and legal development. It lets countries, at varying phases of implementing electronic records, engage in equal-footing international trade. Integration of developing economies into the global commercial system depends on this inclusiveness, which promotes economic progress all around.

Article 19 of the MLETR, through its cross-border recognition provision, essentially ensures that the source of digitally transferable records does not pose a barrier. Essential for a harmonic and inclusive international commerce environment, it supports the ideas of legal equivalency and global collaboration. This clause improves the efficiency, predictability, and resilience of international trade by helping the fluid flow of goods and services across borders, hence strengthening the linked and rich global economy.

Corporate Sustainability Reporting Directive (CSRD): Enhancing Transparency and Accountability in EU Business Practices

The Corporate Sustainability Reporting Directive (CSRD), a proposed European Union law, aims to enhance and standardize sustainability reporting among businesses. The EU's larger goal includes this regulation, among others, meant to support corporate responsibility and sustainable development. The CSRD aims to provide more openness and comparability in corporate sustainability practices by requiring that big businesses and listed small and medium-sized enterprises (SMEs) supply thorough information on sustainability issues.

The CSRD is significant because it may change the terrain of corporate reporting. Financial indicators have long dominated company disclosures, sometimes leaving environmental, social, and governance (ESG) aspects understated or inconsistently reported.

Requiring thorough reporting on a variety of sustainability problems, including climate change, social consequences, and governance policies, the CSRD closes this disparity. This change not only extends the area of corporate responsibility but also fits with expanding worldwide knowledge of the vital relevance of sustainability in company operations.

For businesses, the CSRD marks a dramatic change in legal obligations. It drives them to document their sustainability performance using more exacting, uniform methods. This covers not just their environmental impact but also reveals their policies and practices concerning corporate governance and social responsibility. The focus on thorough and open reporting in the regulation forces businesses to make investments in strong data collection and reporting systems in order to satisfy these new criteria.

The CSRD has ramifications beyond only regulatory compliance. The directive offers investors, consumers, and other stakeholders a useful tool for making better decisions. Since investors especially want to include ESG elements in their investment plans, improved comparability and openness help them. The comprehensive sustainability reports mandated by the CSRD provide a closer understanding of a company's long-term survival and risk management, therefore impacting investment choices.

Customers stand to benefit as well from the CSRD's application. Consumers are looking more and more for information on the sustainability policies of the firms they support as public knowledge of environmental and social concerns rises. The CSRD guarantees that this material is easily available so that customers may choose in line with their beliefs. Encouragement of more openness helps the directive build trust and responsibility among businesses and their employees.

Shaping a Sustainable Economy by Expanding Scope and Accountability

The CSRD also affects market dynamics and business conduct more generally. High requirements for sustainability reporting help businesses embrace more sustainable practices and incorporate issues into their main operations. As businesses look for fresh approaches to lower their environmental footprint and improve their social responsibilities, this may spur creativity. As companies that give sustainability top priority are better suited to negotiate social and environmental difficulties, over time the direction can help to create a more resilient and sustainable economy.

CHAPTER 7 MERGING THE SEAS: THE IMPERATIVE OF DIGITAL TRANSFORMATION AND LEGAL AND REGULATORY REFORM

The Corporate Sustainability Reporting Directive, a historic piece of EU law, aims to standardize and enhance corporate sustainability reporting. Its importance stems from the improved openness and comparability it offers for business sustainability policies, therefore helping investors, customers, and other stakeholders. The CSRD supports informed decision-making and encourages businesses to adopt more sustainable practices by mandating thorough disclosures on sustainability issues, therefore helping to create a more resilient economy.

The main differences between the Non-Financial Reporting Directive (NFRD) and the Corporate Sustainability Reporting Directive (CSRD) are their scope, reporting guidelines, and assurance. These changes show how the European Union's goals and rules are changing. They aim to fix the problems with the NFRD and better meet the needs of stakeholders for openness and responsibility in businesses' sustainability efforts.

First of all, the CSRD spends far more ground than the NFRD. The CSRD covers a far greater number of enterprises than the NFRD, which mostly applied to big public-interest institutions with over 500 workers, including listed corporations, banks, and insurance companies. This covers every big business as well as every listed small and medium-sized company (SME). By expanding the scope, the CSRD aims to give a fuller picture of corporate sustainability in the EU. This will make sure that a wider range of companies are responsible for their environmental, social, and governance (ESG) impacts. This development demonstrates the growing awareness among smaller companies, which collectively have a significant impact on the environment and economy, as well as larger companies, about pertinent sustainability issues.

Regarding reporting needs, the CSRD presents more exact and consistent guidelines than the NFRD. Often producing different and inconsistent disclosures among businesses, the NFRD provided a broad framework for reporting on non-financial information. On the other hand, the CSRD lays out more exact criteria that demand businesses disclose a wider range of sustainability indicators with greater accuracy. This includes full disclosures on environmental factors such as greenhouse gas emissions, water use, and effects on biodiversity, as well as social and governance factors such as labor practices, human rights, and anti-corruption policies. Improving the quality and comparability of sustainability data can help increase its value for stakeholders, including investors, customers, and legislators.

The CSRD's implementation of required third-party validation for reported data is among its most important advances. The lack of independent validation of sustainability reports under the NFRD begged questions regarding the integrity and dependability of the revealed data. The CSRD tackles this by mandating businesses get assurance from a recognized outside entity. This required third-party certification aims to make sustainability reports more reliable and trustworthy by ensuring that the information is correct, reliable, and in line with the reporting criteria that are shown in the reports. The intention behind this shift toward increased responsibility is to foster trust among stakeholders and facilitate the making of more informed decisions.

The CSRD also makes sure that its reporting rules are in line with the European Green Deal and the EU Taxonomy Regulation. This way, they work together to support the EU's overall goal of being more environmentally friendly. This guarantees that corporate sustainability reporting is not only thorough but closely connected with the main policy objectives for sustainability and climate action in the EU. The CSRD becomes even more important and influential because of this convergence. It becomes one of the main tools the EU uses to support corporate responsibility and sustainable development.

CSRD vs. NFRD

The CSRD and the NFRD differ primarily in that they cover a larger number of businesses, have stricter and more uniform reporting requirements, and require a third party to vouch for the business. These developments seek to solve the shortcomings of the NFRD, raise the caliber and dependability of sustainability data, and assist the EU's more general environmental goals. This will help the CSRD significantly promote corporate transparency and responsibility for sustainability issues.

Companies must evaluate their sustainability reporting policies holistically and improve them if they are ready for the Corporate Sustainability Reporting Directive (CSRD). Evaluating their present sustainability reporting systems and spotting any shortcomings come first in this approach. This requires a thorough look into the current ways of collecting data, the amount and quality of the data that has been recorded, and how well these methods match up with the upcoming CSRD criteria. Knowing where their present methods fall short helps businesses create a clear road map for development.

Maintaining the CSRD criteria depends on strong data collection and reporting system investment. Businesses must make sure their technical setup can record, analyze, and provide exact and comprehensive sustainability data. Under the CSRD, this might entail updating current systems or using new software solutions able to manage the higher complexity and data volume needed. Producing high-quality sustainability reports that satisfy regulatory criteria and give stakeholders insightful analysis depends on effective data management, which also forms the foundation of this.

Another crucial component of being ready for the CSRD is interacting with stakeholders. To better grasp their expectations and worries about sustainable practices and reporting, companies should aggressively ask investors, consumers, staff members, and other pertinent stakeholders. This conversation promotes more openness and trust by helping businesses match their environmental plans with stakeholder interests. Knowing the viewpoints of stakeholders also help one identify possible areas of concentration and development, therefore guaranteeing the relevance and impactfulness of environmental projects.

Preparing for the CSRD and the EU Taxonomy

Overseeing sustainability reporting depends on ensuring the required governance systems are in place. From the board level down to operational teams, this entails defining precisely the roles and duties for sustainability governance inside the company. Businesses should designate committed sustainability executives or committees charged with supervising the advancement, execution, and tracking of environmental projects as well as reporting. Robust governance systems provide the necessary control and accountability to ensure the integration of environmental practices into the entire business operation and strategy.

Companies should also get acquainted with the particular criteria and regulations the CSRD outlines. This encompasses understanding the necessary detailed reporting obligations, the types of sustainability metrics to disclose, and the mandatory third-party assurance protocols. Maintaining compliance and reaching high levels of sustainability reporting depend on being current with industry best practices and regulatory developments.

Furthermore, absolutely essential are organizational capacity building and training. Businesses should provide staff members with training so they possess the required knowledge and abilities to gather, evaluate, and fairly present sustainability data. By means of internal capacity, one may foster a sustainable culture inside the company whereby staff members at all levels recognize the need for sustainability practices and their part in supporting such initiatives.

Businesses must assess their current sustainability reporting policies, invest in dependable data collection and reporting technologies, engage with stakeholders, and establish robust governance frameworks to prepare for the CSRD. These actions will help businesses guarantee they are in a position to satisfy the CSRD criteria, improve their sustainability performance, and win confidence among their employees.

The EU Taxonomy is a comprehensive categorization system that aims to define and standardize what constitutes sustainable economic activity within the European Union. The EU's more general plan to meet its environmental and sustainability goals depends on this framework. Establishing explicit sustainability criteria helps the EU Taxonomy direct and support projects that really complement environmental objectives.

The EU Taxonomy addresses the interests of investors, businesses, and legislators, therefore serving a multifarious goal. For investors, it offers a clear, scientifically based structure that enables them to choose ecologically beneficial projects and economic operations. In a financial context where greenwashing—false assertions about the environmental advantages of investments—can be a major problem, this clarification is very vital. Investors may make better judgments by depending on the EU Taxonomy, therefore guaranteeing that their money is focused on activities that actually and favorably affect the environment.

The EU Taxonomy helps businesses match their activities with environmental sustainability criteria. It outlines specific criteria that various types of economic activities must meet to qualify as sustainable. This covers thorough technical screening standards for evaluating the environmental performance of operations in many spheres. Following these guidelines helps businesses improve their sustainability credentials, attract green investment, and support the more general environmental sustainability goal. The taxonomy motivates companies to be creative and follow policies that lower their environmental impact, therefore supporting a more sustainable economy.

The EU Taxonomy also greatly helps policymakers, as it offers a consistent framework to guide the creation and execution of policies meant to support sustainability. Standardizing a categorization system helps legislators more precisely create laws, incentives, and programs supporting sustained economic growth. This consistency guarantees that regulations complement best practices and scientific data, hence improving their efficiency in reaching environmental objectives.

One of the main goals of the EU Taxonomy is to support the EU's commitment to climate change mitigation and adaptation. The system classifies activities that support these objectives, such as sustainable land use practices, energy efficiency enhancement,

CHAPTER 7 MERGING THE SEAS: THE IMPERATIVE OF DIGITAL TRANSFORMATION AND LEGAL AND REGULATORY REFORM

and the generation of renewable energy. Through encouraging investments in these sectors, the EU Taxonomy seeks to hasten the change toward a low-carbon, resilient economy. Given the EU's Green Deal, which sets high goals for lowering greenhouse gas emissions and boosting sustainability, this is especially crucial.

The EU Taxonomy aims to evolve over time, incorporating new scientific findings and technological advancements. This dynamic feature guarantees that the categorization system stays current and efficient in handling newly arising environmental problems. The taxonomy may incorporate new sustainable technologies and methods, thereby continuously improving the framework.

Fundamentally, the EU Taxonomy is an essential instrument for promoting sustainable investment and financing. By providing a precise, scientifically based categorization of sustainable economic activity, it ensures the focus of financial resources on initiatives that truly contribute to environmental sustainability. Along with helping to address environmental problems, including climate change, this supports long-term financial stability and resilience. The EU Taxonomy is very important in promoting a sustainable future for Europe and beyond by means of its thorough and changing framework.

The EU Taxonomy offers a clear, scientifically based set of criteria that investors may use to find and assess sustainable assets, therefore greatly impacting investment decisions. This structure serves as a thorough manual, enabling investors to choose between really sustainable projects and those that fail to meet strict environmental criteria.

The main way the EU taxonomy affects investment decisions is by directing money toward clearly beneficial environmental activities. Defining what qualifies as sustainable economic activity helps the taxonomy guarantee that funding goes toward initiatives and sectors that support environmental goals like climate change mitigation, adaptation, and other sustainability targets. For instance, the Taxonomy urges investments in sustainable agriculture methods, energy-efficient technology, and renewable energy projects. Achieving long-term environmental targets and supporting the shift to a more sustainable economy depend on this deliberate distribution of money.

Moreover, the EU Taxonomy encourages responsibility and openness inside financial markets. The taxonomy provides a consistent categorization system that enhances the transparency of financial goods by identifying which investments are considered ecologically sustainable. Developing confidence between investors and the companies they fund depends on this openness. Knowing that their investments match scientifically supported environmental standards helps investors make more wise judgments.

CHAPTER 7 MERGING THE SEAS: THE IMPERATIVE OF DIGITAL TRANSFORMATION AND LEGAL AND REGULATORY REFORM

The impact of the EU Taxonomy extends to the labeling and sale of financial products. The taxonomy allows fund managers and financial organizations to create and market green financial solutions satisfying sustainability standards. This helps consumers choose goods that fit their tastes and environmental objectives. For instance, a green bond fund following EU Taxonomy requirements gives investors hope that their money supports initiatives with real environmental advantages. Consequently, the Taxonomy not only directs financial actions but also influences the evolution of financial goods available on the market.

Furthermore, the EU Taxonomy fosters a competitive environment that motivates businesses to enhance their sustainability performance. Companies looking for finance are urged to match their operations with the criteria of the Taxonomy in order to draw in investors with a concentration on sustainability. Oftentimes, this alignment entails changing environmental performance, implementing more sustainable practices, and improving reporting openness. As a result, the Taxonomy encourages businesses to innovate and raise their sustainability credentials, therefore fostering more general good environmental effects across sectors.

Additionally, crucial in determining investment decisions is the regulatory influence of the EU Taxonomy. The Taxonomy is a baseline for defining rules and norms on sustainable Regulatory agencies and policymakers also play a crucial role. This regulatory fit guarantees that investment methods complement the more general environmental policies and goals of the EU. Further underscoring the impact of the Taxonomy on investment decisions, rules requiring adherence to Taxonomy criteria force investors and businesses to match their activities to comply with these criteria.

The EU Taxonomy helps investors by offering a clear, scientifically based structure for spotting environmentally friendly assets. It directs money toward projects that improve the surroundings, assist in the shift to a sustainable economy, and increase financial market openness and responsibility. The Taxonomy is very important in guiding the change toward a better and more sustainable global economy by influencing investing habits and supporting sustainable financial solutions.

Starting with the difficulty of comprehending and interpreting the requirements established by the EU Taxonomy, companies encounter several obstacles in following the taxonomy. The EU Taxonomy is based on thorough technical screening criteria used to define a sustainable activity. These criteria, which often require a thorough understanding of environmental science, regulatory standards, and sector-specific benchmarks, can be quite detailed and complex.

CHAPTER 7   MERGING THE SEAS: THE IMPERATIVE OF DIGITAL TRANSFORMATION AND LEGAL AND REGULATORY REFORM

Navigating the Challenges of EU Taxonomy Compliance

Deciphering these criteria can be difficult for many firms, especially those without committed sustainability teams. Making sure their activities fit these standards might call for some serious learning and adaptability.

Gathering and checking the necessary information present yet another difficult task. The EU Taxonomy calls for exact and thorough information on many facets of a company's activities, including waste management techniques, energy use, and greenhouse gas emissions. Accurate data gathering requires both strong systems and procedures. Many businesses might not yet have the infrastructure in place to gather all the required data; hence, developing these skills can be resource-intensive. Furthermore, we must confirm the gathered data to ensure its dependability and correctness. This sometimes entails outside audits and third-party guarantees, which further complicate and increase the expense of compliance.

Another major challenge is incorporating the new EU Taxonomy criteria into current reporting systems. Companies that already use different sets of rules and guidelines for reporting, such as the Global Reporting Initiative (GRI) or the Task Force on Climate-related Financial Disclosures (TCFD), need to figure out how to include the EU Taxonomy's criteria without having to do extra work or make things less consistent. This integration requires rigorous planning and cooperation between several departments within the organization, including operations, sustainability, and finance, to ensure the gathering and coherent presentation of all pertinent information.

Compliance with the EU Taxonomy Standards could also call for major adjustments in company practices. Businesses may have to change their procedures, implement fresh technology, or modify their company plans to fit environmental needs. To satisfy environmental standards, for instance, a manufacturing business would have to make investments in more sustainable raw materials or cleaner technology. These operational modifications may be time-consuming and expensive, therefore affecting short-term profitability. Moreover, switching to more sustainable methods sometimes calls for a culture change inside the company, therefore encouraging a mindset that gives long-term environmental goals top priority above short-term financial success.

Apart from internal difficulties, businesses might also be under external pressure and doubt. Regulatory rules are evolving, so businesses have to always be informed about new developments inside the EU Taxonomy structure. Staff members must always invest in training and development if they are to remain current with the most recent needs and best practices. Companies also have to negotiate diverse demands and expectations from investors, authorities, and other stakeholders, each of whom can see appropriate compliance with the Taxonomy differently.

For businesses, following the EU Taxonomy essentially offers a complex task. They have to negotiate the complexity of technological criteria, create strong data collection and verification methods, include new reporting criteria in current systems, and maybe completely restructure their operations to complement sustainability objectives. Notwithstanding these obstacles, the EU Taxonomy also provides businesses with a means to improve their sustainability credentials and support a more ecologically friendly world. Through proactive handling of these issues, businesses may not only reach compliance but also establish themselves as pioneers in environmentally friendly business methods.

A key idea in sustainability reporting is that double materiality extends the range of information businesses have to provide on their activities and effects. It asks businesses to take two important factors into account: financial materiality and environmental and social materiality, therefore transcending conventional financial reporting. This double viewpoint guarantees that sustainability reporting offers a more complete and fair picture of the performance and influence of a business.

Revolutionizing Sustainability: EU's New Ecodesign Rules Set to Transform Consumer Products

Approval of a major overhaul of the ecodesign framework by the European Parliament marks a historic first toward environmental sustainability. This change represents a significant shift in the perception, use, and eventual disposal of goods within the European Union, not merely a minor alteration. With an enormous majority of 455 votes in support, this law shows a strong will to lessen the environmental effect of consumer products all throughout Europe.

This law's main goal is to greatly reduce the environmental impact of many different kinds of products. It achieves this by mandating the creation of products that are more easily recyclable, durable, and repairable. This implies that, as was often the case in past rules, the emphasis now is not just on energy economy. Rather, the new guidelines take a more all-encompassing approach, covering a whole product life. This method aims to ensure the manufacturing of objects, from daily consumer products to industrial commodities like steel, textiles, furniture, and even chemicals, with sustainability in mind from the outset.

CHAPTER 7   MERGING THE SEAS: THE IMPERATIVE OF DIGITAL TRANSFORMATION AND LEGAL AND
            REGULATORY REFORM

The extent of this law, which goes well beyond energy-related issues to embrace a wide range of product life cycle enhancements, is among its most arresting features. This law aims to change the market dynamics by motivating producers to prioritize sustainability in all aspects of manufacturing. For example, the law lays the foundation for outlawing the wastefulness of destroying unsold clothes and shoes, a habit long under criticism. This action is likely to question current production methods and force businesses to rethink how they handle unsold inventory as well as investigate more sustainable solutions for handling extra goods.

This innovative law essentially aims to change consumer behavior by promoting a culture of sustainability, which goes beyond simply creating goods that are more ecologically friendly. The European Parliament is opening the path for a consumption pattern less wasteful and more ecologically responsible by standardizing durable, repairable, and recyclable items. This idea has consequences that go well beyond Europe, as it might establish a global standard for environmentally friendly consumption. Globally, the policy may guide the design, manufacturing, and disposal of goods in other areas.

The updated ecodesign framework represents a significant shift in EU environmental policy. It signifies a clear turn toward a more sustainable future for the world economy as well as for Europe. The law questions current production standards and encourages a change to more environmentally friendly ways of consuming by setting new standards for how long products should last, how easily they should be fixed, and how easily they should be recycled. As these developments take root, they may inspire such projects abroad, therefore enabling a larger worldwide endeavor to lower the environmental effect of consumer products.

Greening the Market: How the EU's New Ecodesign Directive Targets Key Industries for Environmental Sustainability

A historic step toward sustainable consumerism, the European Union's updated ecodesign framework introduces strict environmental sustainability criteria for many different items marketed inside the EU. Under this rule, the European Commission bears a significant obligation to give particular product groupings top priority in its first working plan. The European Commission's deliberate strategy, which emphasizes specific products such as iron, steel, aluminum, textiles, furniture, tires, detergents, paints, lubricants, and chemicals, aims to address some of the most pressing environmental issues associated with modern industry.

Iron, steel, and aluminum lead this effort due to their widespread use in various sectors such as construction, automotive, packaging, and electronics. Making these metals has a significant environmental impact, mostly due to the huge carbon emissions and energy consumption involved. The EU wants to not only cut the resources used but also improve the recyclability of these metals by integrating ecodesign ideas into their manufacture and application. This might open the path for creative ideas like more effective recycling procedures and low-carbon manufacturing technologies, which would greatly lessen the environmental impact of these sectors.

Textiles—especially clothing and shoes—showcase the EU's will to address the environmental issues the fashion business presents. Renowned for its significant environmental impact, which spans chemical pollution and water consumption to trash creation, the fashion business is a prominent player in worldwide environmental damage. The EU wants more sustainable fashion by including textiles under the ecodesign framework. This could lead to the creation of more durable clothes and shoes, simplifying recycling methods, and potentially prohibiting certain harmful manufacturing techniques. Focusing on textiles also contributes to the broader adoption of a circular economy model, which prioritizes long-term use, repair, and reuse of goods, thereby reducing waste and environmental impacts.

Another important topic of attention is furniture manufacture, as the use of different materials and techniques, like deforestation and the application of dangerous chemicals, has major environmental consequences. The updated ecodesign rules aim to inspire designs that facilitate repair and disassembly for recycling, enhance manufacturing energy efficiency, and encourage the use of more sustainable materials in furniture manufacture. This all-encompassing strategy not only solves the environmental effects related to furniture manufacture but also advances sustainability all through its lifetime.

Given the difficulties with their disposal and the microplastics they create, tires have been a major concern. Tyres' ecodesign plans probably consist of steps meant to increase their lifespan, improve their fuel economy to lower vehicle emissions, and increase their recyclability. Since tires are a primary source of pollution, these developments could significantly reduce their environmental impact, particularly when it comes to the microplastics that harm ecosystems.

The order also goes after chemical products like paints, lubricants, detergents, and other compounds. It does this because these substances can harm the environment by polluting water and making hazardous waste. Ecodesign methods in this area might provide formulations free from some dangerous ingredients, more biodegradable, and less detrimental to the environment. These developments would not only help to lower the environmental hazards connected to the use and disposal of these goods but also encourage the development of better and more sustainable substitutes.

These ecodesign ideas applied among many key product groupings should result in notable environmental advantages. Focusing on lowering dangerous compounds, increasing energy and resource efficiency, and promoting recyclability at the end of the product's life, the European Commission will most likely set certain criteria for every category. This holistic approach reduces these goods' environmental impact during use and their lifetime.

Targeting these important sectors, the EU is acting strategically to help reduce some of the most major causes of environmental damage. Along with encouraging a change in consumer behavior and industry practices inside Europe, this project aims to establish a worldwide benchmark for environmental sustainability. These new rules might operate as a model for other areas when they become operative, therefore inspiring a greater global push toward more environmentally friendly industry and consumer behavior.

Empowering Consumers: The Role of Digital Product Passports in Sustainable Purchasing

The launch of digital product passports signals a significant change in enabling more informed and responsible buying decisions in a time when sustainability and openness are growingly essential to customers. Under the direction of the European Commission, this project fits into a larger plan meant to raise consumer awareness and support a market environment giving sustainability first priority.

Digital Product Passports are essentially comprehensive digital records containing detailed information about a product's entire lifecycle, including its origin, manufacturing process, composition, sustainability credentials, maintenance requirements, and end-of-life disposal or recycling options, aimed at enhancing transparency, traceability, and sustainability within supply chains. This covers information about its source, makeup, best uses, and policies for final disposal. Ensuring that this material is accurate and current will help customers to have a clear picture of the goods they are thinking about purchase. Digital product passports play a crucial role in enhancing market transparency by providing easily accessible information.

The advent of digital product passports solves a major issue for consumers: the sometimes limited and inaccurate information accessible about the goods they buy. Many times, customers remain ignorant about the environmental effects and sustainability credentials of the products they purchase. By offering a consistent and unambiguous collection of data for every product, digital product passports seek to address this gap and let customers choose more closely in line with their beliefs. This might significantly affect buying patterns by guiding buyers toward goods with less environmental effect, higher durability, or simpler repairability.

Furthermore, the availability of comprehensive product information lets customers participate in more educated comparison shopping. Consumers could be more likely to pick ecologically friendly solutions as they get more conscious of the sustainability credentials of many items. This may then stimulate market competitiveness, motivating businesses to enhance their operations to either keep or grow their consumer base. As businesses strive to meet the increasing demand for environmentally friendly products, digital product passports could potentially become a powerful tool in shifting market dynamics toward sustainability.

The European Commission wants to create a publicly available web portal to help access digital product passports. Customers will be able to quickly get information about the goods they are considering and compare many products depending on several sustainability criteria through this platform. The success of this portal will mostly rely on its design, which has to be simple and user-friendly to guarantee it is accessible to all users, even those who may not be especially tech-savvy.

Digital product passports will only be effective, though, depending on a number of important criteria. Accuracy and integrity of the given data come first. Should the data on the passports be erroneous or out-of-date, customer mistrust and resistance to system use might result. Therefore, the success of the project depends critically on the diligent maintenance and constant updating of the data. Furthermore, very vital is industry compliance. Digital product passports cannot be really successful unless all key sectors actively contribute, not just in creating these passports but also in ensuring that the information is current and complete.

Notwithstanding these difficulties, digital product passports show major progress in consumer rights and environmental campaigning. Through providing a clear window into the lifetime and sustainability of items, they enable customers to make decisions that could result in a more worldwide sustainable consumption pattern. This project has outstanding potential to spur a change toward a more open, informed, and sustainable market. However, achieving this potential will require careful implementation and robust system management to ensure it delivers on its promise of fostering a market environment that values sustainability.

Toward a Zero-Waste Future: EU Bans on the Destruction of Unsold Consumer Products

By enacting rules prohibiting the disposal of unsold consumer goods, the European Union has decisively moved toward cutting waste and promoting sustainability. Originally focusing on the garment, clothing accessories, and footwear industries, this project is a vital component of a larger legislative effort meant to reduce waste all along the supply chain and support a more circular economy.

The prohibition of burning unsold products marks a basic change in the way companies have to handle their inventory. Companies now need to reassess their inventory and manufacturing strategies to avoid accumulating excess inventory that could potentially fuel wasteful activities. This change calls on companies to use more precise demand forecasting techniques, simplify their manufacturing processes, and investigate more adaptable supply chains able to fit evolving market conditions. Overproduction to satisfy uncertain demand is giving way to a more deliberate and exact style of manufacturing that aims to balance supply with real customer demand.

For companies, this prohibition indicates a need to investigate other ways to handle unsold inventory, not only for simple compliance. We encourage businesses to consider donating unsold items to charitable organizations, repurposing resources for future use, or modifying products to attract new customers. This change is likely to inspire innovation in sectors since companies look for original solutions to manage extra inventory in line with environmental objectives. Over time, especially in the recycling and secondary markets, these methods might result in cost savings and provide new business prospects.

While firms may incur initial costs when transitioning to these new methods, especially if they need to modify their operations to align with the new regulations, the long-term benefits could be substantial. Reducing waste and finding sustainable applications for unsold goods can potentially enhance businesses' corporate responsibility profiles and reduce their environmental impact. Furthermore, adopting a circular economy model, which involves the production, consumption, and disposal of goods in waste-reducing ways, could potentially create new revenue streams and bolster a company's ability to adapt and endure.

The law also opens the path for future development by letting the European Commission classify other kinds of unsold goods under the ban. This prospect indicates a complete strategy for waste reduction, as the EU aims to address waste in several consumer groups. The possibility for more general implementation of the ban emphasizes even more the EU's dedication to its environmental goals and its vision of a more sustainable future.

Still, the execution of this restriction presents difficulties. Ensuring compliance and implementing these rules throughout the varied EU market terrain will be challenging and resource-intensive activity. Particularly considering their financial and logistical restrictions, smaller businesses may find enormous challenges in rebuilding their supply networks to follow the new requirements. Furthermore, concerns arise about the global competitiveness of European companies, given the uncertain acceptance of these criteria in other regions. If EU businesses are required to meet stricter environmental standards than their global competitors, this could potentially disadvantage them.

The EU's approach to creating a sustainable, circular economy depends much on its restriction on the disposal of unsold consumer goods. By mandating a review of the manufacturing, sale, and disposal processes, the EU is setting a precedent that could ultimately influence global consumer goods sector practices. This legislation addresses not only current environmental issues but also changes economic operations into more sustainable practices that would help the earth and next generations.

The EU's audacious posture reflects the opinion that it is time to abandon the "take, make, dispose" paradigm that has long dominated industrial output and consumer behavior. According to the new legislative framework, we should build products with sustainability at their core, ensuring that they benefit all stakeholders, respect the environment, and contribute to a better earth. This law lays the groundwork for a more responsible and sustainable attitude to consumption by making sustainable items the standard, thereby empowering customers to make wiser environmental choices, conserve energy, and embrace repairable and durable goods.

The Road Ahead for EU Ecodesign: Implementing Transformative Sustainability Standards

The European Union is poised to make sustainable products a standard among its members. One of the main components of the EU's ambitious circular economy package, the updated ecodesign guidelines are about to have a major breakthrough. The only remaining obstacle to the full application of these laws is the Council's formal ratification, a necessary procedural step that signals a shared consensus among EU member states. This approval sets the way for the law to formally come into effect and is not only a formality; it is a collaborative commitment to furthering sustainability throughout the area.

Designed to provide a strong foundation for developing sustainability criteria applicable to almost all items sold within the EU internal market, the updated ecodesign standards, proposed by the European Commission in March 2022, A few notable exceptions from these rules include food, animal feed, medical items, and living things. Aiming to encompass as many items as feasible under its sustainability umbrella, the wide breadth of the laws highlights the EU's outstanding dedication to complete environmental action.

These guidelines are a direct reaction to the growing demand from EU people for more sustainable consumption and production patterns, not only regulatory ones. The results of the Conference on the Future of Europe, where participants voiced a strong want for the EU to encourage sustainable and resilient growth, definitely mirrored this public attitude. The European Parliament is showing that it is sensitive to the issues of its people and ready to act forcefully to solve them by implementing these updated ecodesign regulations, thereby meeting their expectations.

Once the Council approves, the emphasis will move to the vital phase of execution. At this stage, the ecodesign framework's general ideas transform into specific actions and rules that directly impact product design, manufacturing, and release. The framework will guide the creation of comprehensive sustainability standards for various product categories, ensuring the creation of recyclable, repairable, and long-lasting items. The strategy aims to reduce waste and extend the lifespan of products, thereby enhancing the broader goals of the circular economy.

Crucially important elements of the implementation process will also include monitoring and enforcement. We must develop effective systems to ensure that the new guidelines not only comply but also serve their intended purposes. With an eye toward uniformity and rigor in the execution of the laws, this will call for cooperation among all EU members.

Moreover, a continuous assessment will be conducted to evaluate the new ecodesign guidelines as they begin to exert their influence. This ongoing assessment is essential as it enables changes and improvements to the regulations, therefore guaranteeing their continued relevance and effectiveness as the state of the market and technology develop. This might cause the regulations to change over time to incorporate new product categories, tougher sustainability criteria, or both.

CHAPTER 7   MERGING THE SEAS: THE IMPERATIVE OF DIGITAL TRANSFORMATION AND LEGAL AND REGULATORY REFORM

The updated ecodesign guidelines represent a significant step toward a circular economy within the EU, offering the potential to significantly reduce waste and promote sustainable development. Setting thorough sustainability criteria helps the EU not only project leadership in environmental care but also create a global baseline for product sustainability. When the Council officially accepts it, it will be the start of a new era in consumer behavior and product design—one that puts longevity, repairability, and low environmental impact above the usual linear model of production and consumption. This change may change markets, affect world standards, and help to create a more sustainable future for everybody.

EFRAG's Implementation Guidance for European Sustainability Reporting Standards (ESRS): Navigating the Future of Corporate Sustainability Reporting

Businesses all throughout Europe are expected to show more openness and responsibility in their environmental, social, and governance (ESG) policies as the value of sustainability in corporate leadership keeps rising. Produced by the European Financial Reporting Advisory Group (EFRAG), which also developed the European Sustainability Reporting Standards (ESRS), central to this change is the establishment of a comprehensive and consistent reporting framework aimed at enhancing corporate transparency, accountability, and comparability in sustainability reporting across the European Union. These criteria mark a major advance in guaranteeing that businesses offer consistent, open, comparable sustainability information. EFRAG's most recent implementation advice, especially the detailed list of ESR datapoints, is very important for businesses to meet their new reporting obligations, especially under the Corporate Sustainability Reporting Directive (CSRD).

The aim of EFRAG is to improve European public interest financial and environmental reporting. A major component of this goal is the evolution of ESRS, which offers businesses a strong structure to help them share their sustainability performance. Through encouraging openness, EFRAG's project builds confidence among many different stakeholders—including investors, authorities, and the general public. EFRAG's implementation guidelines aim to assist businesses in aligning their reporting methods with the ESRs, ensuring their sustainability disclosures align with regulatory standards, accuracy, and consistency.

CHAPTER 7 MERGING THE SEAS: THE IMPERATIVE OF DIGITAL TRANSFORMATION AND LEGAL AND REGULATORY REFORM

Published in May 2024, the comprehensive collection of ESR datapoints is one of the main components of the implementation guide. Except for ESRs 1, which emphasize broad concepts rather than particular disclosures, this Excel-style list covers all disclosure obligations across sector-agnostic criteria. Particularly for businesses getting ready to report under the CSRD beginning in January 2024, the list is a vital instrument. It provides a useful tool for planning and compiling sustainability reports, therefore enabling businesses to guarantee that their disclosures are thorough and consistent with the ESRS structure.

The direction underscores EFRAG's ongoing efforts to develop a digital ESRs XBRL taxonomy, which aims to facilitate machine-readable sustainability reporting. Though it offers a method for structuring human-readable reports, the present datapoint list is not quite translatable to this digital taxonomy. We aim to simplify further initiatives in digital tagging with this methodical approach, paving the way for more accurate and efficient digital sustainability reporting.

The direction fundamentally relies on the categorization of the datapoints into numerical, narrative, and semi-narrative elements. Every datapoint relates to a particular ESR framework disclosure need or application need. Companies use this classification since it helps them to precisely find and document the required data. Understanding the kind and nature of every datapoint helps businesses to better arrange their data collection and reporting systems, therefore guaranteeing that their sustainability statements are accurate and comply with ESRS criteria.

For businesses starting their first ESRs' sustainability reporting, the dataset is a priceless tool. It guarantees that all necessary disclosure criteria are satisfied, aids in reporting process organization, and allows data gap studies. Moreover, the guidelines separate required, conditional, and voluntary datapoints to clarify what information is required. For businesses negotiating the complexity of sustainability reporting, this separation helps them to focus on the most important elements of their disclosures.

Particularly for businesses with less than 750 employees, the implementation guidelines also provide phase-in rules. By easing their transition, these clauses aim to assist smaller businesses in gradually adhering to the full range of reporting obligations. This staggered approach offers a more doable road toward complete compliance and acknowledges the difficulties smaller businesses might have adjusting to the new criteria.

The implementation guidelines of EFRAG for ESRs mark a major development in the field of sustainability reporting throughout Europe. EFRAG gives businesses the tools they need to satisfy changing needs of stakeholders for more openness and responsibility in sustainability issues by offering a clear, comprehensive set of datapoints and outlining their application. The tools and advice EFRAG offers will be crucial for companies negotiating this new terrain in reaching compliance and proving a real dedication to sustainable business practices. Clearly, sustainability is becoming more important in corporate reporting in Europe; EFRAG's efforts in creating and enabling the use of ESRs lead the front stage in this change.

The Double Materiality Approach

Financial materiality is the impact of environmental concerns on the financial performance of a business. This component of twofold materiality centers on the opportunities and hazards that environmental, social, and governmental (ESG) elements offer to the corporate bottom line. For a company's operations, supply chains, and market demand, for example, climate change can present major hazards. Changes in regulations concerning environmental criteria could affect compliance criteria and expenses. On the other hand, businesses that follow sustainable practices can benefit from improved brand recognition, cost savings, and creativity, which can help increase financial performance. Companies give investors and stakeholders vital knowledge on how sustainability concerns could affect their financial situation and long-term viability by means of financial materiality reporting.

Conversely, environmental and social materiality studies the wider effects of a company's activity on its surroundings and society. This aspect of twofold materiality acknowledges businesses' obligations outside of their financial success. It looks at how the activities, goods, and services of a corporation influence its surroundings—that is, through waste creation, resource depletion, and greenhouse gas emissions. It also takes into account social effects like human rights, community involvement, and work methods. Reporting on environmental and social materiality forces businesses to show how their operations either contribute to or lessen more general social and environmental problems. This openness lets communities, workers, and consumers, among other stakeholders, know and assess the company's responsibility in advancing sustainability.

Reaching a more complete approach to sustainability reporting depends on the idea of twofold materiality. It guarantees that businesses take ethical and social obligations into account in addition to the financial consequences of sustainability problems. This strategy fits the increasing need of stakeholders for more openness and responsibility in business conduct. Businesses that adopt double materiality demonstrate to their stakeholders their genuine commitment to sustainability, thereby cultivating trust.

CHAPTER 7   MERGING THE SEAS: THE IMPERATIVE OF DIGITAL TRANSFORMATION AND LEGAL AND REGULATORY REFORM

When businesses use twofold materiality, they need to have good ways to find, measure, and record effects that aren't related to money. This usually entails doing extensive impact studies, interacting with a variety of stakeholders to learn their issues and expectations, and including sustainability issues in strategic decision-making procedures. It also necessitates a shift in corporate culture, transforming sustainability from a separate or auxiliary issue to a necessary component of corporate strategy.

Double materiality is a notion that forces businesses to document how their operations influence society and the environment, as well as how sustainability concerns affect their financial performance. This dual viewpoint guarantees that sustainability reporting captures the ethical as well as the financial aspects of business performance. Adopting double materiality helps businesses present a more whole and open picture of their environmental policies, therefore improving their responsibility and encouraging more involvement by stakeholders.

Empowering Stakeholders with Comprehensive Insights

For stakeholders, double materiality is essential, as it provides comprehensive and sophisticated knowledge of the environmental effects of a business and related hazards. This dual view enhances the knowledge accessible to many stakeholder groups, therefore facilitating better informed and fair decision-making.

Double materiality is especially helpful for investors as it emphasizes possible financial hazards and possibilities connected to sustainability. By concentrating on financial materiality, investors may evaluate how environmental, social, and governance (ESG) elements might affect a company's profitability and long-term survival. For example, knowing the financial effects of climate change on business operations or the possible expenses related to legislative changes in environmental legislation helps investors evaluate the risk profile of the organization. Also, looking for chances to grow the market, lower costs, or come up with new ideas through sustainable practices can help you make investment decisions that will bring you long-term value. Investors that are progressively including ESG factors into their investment plans depend on this data to reduce risks and take advantage of chances for sustainable development.

Double materiality offers information on how a business is either aggravating or reducing environmental and social concerns to other stakeholders, including consumers, staff members, and legislators. Consumers gain from knowing how a company's operations line up with their beliefs as they become more aware of the social and environmental effects of their purchase decisions. Openness in environmental policies enables consumers to choose companies that uphold moral and ethical standards. Conversely, workers are looking for businesses that show a greater dedication to sustainability and social responsibility. Understanding how a firm affects the environment and society helps staff members to be more involved and motivated, as well as to take pride in their employment.

Double materiality reporting also helps regulators and legislators as it offers a better view of a company's socially motivated and environmental regulatory compliance. More efficient regulation of standards and monitoring of them depend on this openness. By stressing areas where businesses are either leading or trailing in sustainability initiatives, it also helps to shape regulations supporting sustainable business practices. This regulatory viewpoint guarantees companies accountability for their wider effects on the environment and society.

Double materiality also promotes better responsibility and openness inside businesses themselves. It motivates companies to take a comprehensive approach to sustainability, including non-financial factors into their strategic planning and reporting procedures. A comprehensive strategy for financial accountability not only raises the legitimacy of sustainability reporting but also encourages ethical behavior and responsibility inside businesses. Businesses that adopt double materiality are better suited to establish confidence and improve their connections with every kind of stakeholder.

Double materiality is essentially crucial for stakeholders because it provides a better and more holistic view of the effects on the sustainability of a firm. While it provides consumers, staff, and authorities with insights on the company's contributions to environmental and social concerns, it also equips investors with essential knowledge on financial risks and possibilities linked to ESG elements. This dual viewpoint encourages wise decision-making, improves responsibility and openness, and finally motivates more environmentally friendly corporate operations.

Implementing Double Materiality

By following a methodical process starting with thorough materiality evaluations, companies may successfully apply double materiality in their reporting. From the financial as well as the environmental and social angles, these tests are absolutely essential in pointing out the most important sustainability concerns. Companies must carefully examine their operations, value chains, and external surroundings in order to identify which sustainability elements most apply to and influence them.

This procedure is naturally about interacting with a wide spectrum of stakeholders. Investors, consumers, staff members, vendors, local residents, and authorities comprise the stakeholders. Companies might have a full awareness of the many expectations and goals connected to sustainability by actively searching for their ideas and worries. This participation guarantees that the discovered material problems represent not only the internal opinions of the business but also the exterior perspectives and needs of people who either directly or indirectly influence the activities of the organization.

Once companies identify the material concerns, they should incorporate these revelations into their sustainability reporting systems. This entails matching their methods of reporting with accepted best standards and legal mandates. Companies should follow well-known reporting guidelines like those from the Task Force on Climate-related Financial Disclosures (TCFD), the Sustainability Accounting Standards Board (SASB), and the Global Reporting Initiative (GRI) to make sure that their reports are consistent, clear, and easy to compare. These models give thorough instructions on how to present different sustainability measures, therefore enabling businesses to properly explain their performance.

Key ideas in double-materiality reporting are openness and balance. Businesses must disclose their financial performance and the pros and cons of their initiatives for society and the environment. This all-around strategy helps the report to be more credible and builds confidence among the interested parties. Contextual information, such as the causes of certain effects and the steps taken to solve them, enhances the report's transparency and value.

Companies have to additionally make investments in strong data collection and management systems if they are to apply double materiality. Reliable and accurate data is the basis of respectable sustainability reporting. Businesses should improve or create their data collection systems to get pertinent data in all spheres of their activities. This might demand implementing new technology, enhancing data governance policies, and guaranteeing regular, methodical data collection.

Furthermore, businesses should set up solid governance systems to supervise the use of double materiality. To promote sustainability awareness at various levels within the company, it is necessary to assign specific roles and responsibilities. Senior leadership members should actively engage in setting the strategic direction for sustainability and ensuring its inclusion in the general business plan. Tasked with daily monitoring and reporting of sustainability concerns, dedicated sustainability teams or committees help to ensure the organization stays on target to satisfy its sustainability objectives.

Frequent observation of the reporting process and assessment of it are crucial. Businesses should always review the results of their materiality studies and reporting systems and make the required changes as fresh data and stakeholder comments become accessible. This iterative method keeps businesses sensitive to shifting environmental conditions and stakeholder expectations.

Businesses can effectively use double materiality in their reporting by conducting thorough materiality assessments, consulting with a wide range of stakeholders, and ensuring clear, fair reporting practices that are in line with legal requirements and best practices. Strong governance structures and reliable data collection methods help businesses present a complete and credible picture of their sustainability performance, therefore fostering responsibility and trust among their employees.

Emerging Trends in Sustainable Finance

Today's scene in sustainable finance is made up of many changing trends that show a growing desire to include environmental, social, and governance (ESG) factors in financial decisions. The rapid spread of green and sustainable bonds is one of the main trends. These financial tools specifically aim to bolster programs such as affordable housing, sustainable agriculture, clean water projects, and renewable energy initiatives that offer social or environmental benefits. As issuers and investors understand the double benefit of producing financial returns while supporting a positive society and environmental outcomes, the market for green and sustainable bonds has experienced explosive expansion.

Another obvious trend changing the financial industry is the growing curiosity in ESG investment. Beyond conventional financial criteria, investors are gradually including ESG elements into their investment plans to assess the long-term sustainability and ethical effect of their choices. Growing knowledge that ESG elements may greatly affect a company's risk profile and financial success is driving this change. Companies with excellent environmental standards, for example, could be more suited to negotiate legislative changes and resource constraints; those with strong governance systems are probably going to show more ethical behavior and responsibility. ESG investing is therefore becoming mainstream as more institutional investors and asset managers include these criteria in their portfolios to match their beliefs and satisfy changing customer expectations.

Integrating sustainability criteria into mainstream financial decision-making procedures is another important development in sustainable finance. Banks, insurance firms, asset managers, and other financial organizations are realizing more and more that sustainability is not a side issue but rather a basic component of risk management and financial analysis. This integration includes ESG factors into portfolio management plans, investment studies, and credit evaluations. This helps financial institutions evaluate the long-term sustainability and resilience of their lending policies and investments. As this trend grows, new financial products and services are appearing, such as green loans, sustainability-linked loans, and ESG-focused investment funds. These products and services must meet sustainability standards.

Transparency and responsibility are also becoming more and more important in sustainability financing. Demand for more ESG performance and impact disclosure among stakeholders—investors, legislators, and consumers—is driving change. Businesses and sectors are adopting standardized reporting systems and criteria to assess sustainability performance in a more uniform and comparable manner. Improved openness enables stakeholders to make better-informed decisions depending on accurate and verifiable data, therefore fostering trust and credibility in the market.

Technological Innovations Driving the Future of Sustainable Finance

Technological advancements have also had a significant impact on sustainability finance trends. Blockchain, artificial intelligence, and data analytics innovations are allowing more complex tracking of ESG indicators. These technologies enable investors and financial institutions to better grasp and control possibilities and sustainability hazards. Advanced data analytics, for instance, can offer a more thorough understanding of climate hazards; blockchain technology can improve the traceability and responsibility of green bonds and other sustainable financial products.

The developments in sustainable finance nowadays show a more extensive and deeper integration of ESG issues within the financial industry. The fast growth of green and sustainable bonds, the rising popularity of ESG investments, and the inclusion of sustainability factors in mainstream financial decision-making are all signs of a fundamental shift toward more responsible and sustainable financial practices. Rising awareness of the link between financial success and sustainability, technological innovation, and more openness help to promote these developments. Collectively, they show a transforming drive toward a more sustainable and strong worldwide financial system.

Technology is increasingly playing a crucial role in enhancing sustainability finance due to its improvements in openness, efficiency, and effect measurement. Technology developments are changing how businesses, investors, and financial institutions approach and include sustainability in their decision-making processes.

Blockchain technology, for instance, may greatly increase green investment traceability and responsibility. Blockchain guarantees high accuracy and openness by allowing a distributed and unchangeable record, therefore tracking the money movement. Investors, particularly in the case of green bonds and other sustainable finance tools, rely heavily on this capacity to ensure the planned use of their funds for environmental or social initiatives. From issue to final fund deployment, blockchain can record every stage of the investment process, therefore strengthening confidence and credibility in the sustainable finance sector.

Artificial intelligence (AI) and data analytics are transforming ESG risk and opportunity assessment. By allowing the processing and analysis of enormous volumes of data from many sources, these technologies give a closer understanding of a company's environmental, social, and governance policies. By spotting trends and patterns that might not be clear from conventional research, advanced data analytics helps investors and financial institutions more fully grasp the possible risks and rewards connected with ESG elements. AI systems may, for example, use satellite images to evaluate rates of deforestation or water consumption in agricultural activities, therefore offering real-time data that can guide investment decisions.

Technology also improves compliance and sustainability reporting's efficiency. Automated reporting tools and platforms help to simplify the gathering, validation, and distribution of ESG data, therefore lessening the administrative load on businesses and guaranteeing accurate and timely reports. By allowing businesses to match their reporting with different worldwide standards and frameworks, these instruments can also help improve the consistency and comparability of sustainability disclosures.

Apart from enhancing the effectiveness of reporting, technology is absolutely vital for impact evaluation. By tracking and assessing the real results of sustainable investments, sophisticated instruments give concrete proof of their social and environmental advantages. IoT sensors, for instance, may track real-time energy use and emissions reductions, therefore providing specific information on the success of environmental initiatives. This feature lets investors evaluate the actual value of their money and make better decisions regarding their next investments.

Moreover, technology encourages broader participation in sustainable financing by means of stakeholders. Between businesses and their stakeholders—including investors, consumers, and regulators—digital channels can help to enable more open and participatory communication. These sites can provide up-to-date information on environmental projects, solicit feedback, and assist groups in achieving sustainability goals. This enhanced stakeholder involvement fosters a more inclusive approach to sustainability and fosters trust.

Technology also helps in the creation of creative financial goods and services, including sustainability criteria integration. For instance, developers are developing fintech solutions that offer personalized investment options based on specific ESG preferences, allowing retail investors to align their portfolios with their values. In the same way, technology-enabled crowdsourcing sites may make it easier for more people to find sustainable investment opportunities. This means that more investors can join and support green projects.

Technology is a major facilitator driving forward sustainability finance. Technological advancements ensure the inclusion of sustainability factors in financial decision-making processes by enhancing transparency, efficiency, and impact. Blockchain enhances traceability, data analytics and artificial intelligence offer a more thorough understanding of ESG risks and possibilities, and automated reporting systems simplify compliance. These technologies used together are enabling a more responsible, effective, and powerful approach to sustainability finance, therefore building more trust and involvement among stakeholders and helping to assist the shift to a more sustainable world economy.

Embracing Circularity with ISO 59020: A Pathway to Sustainable Finance

Adoption of circular economy concepts is becoming increasingly important for companies dedicated to environmental preservation in the fast-changing terrain of sustainability. Offering a complete set of principles to enable companies to adopt circularity, the ISO 59000 series marks a major breakthrough in this change. Among these, ISO 59020 is one of the most important instruments for evaluating circularity performance—a necessary phase on the path toward sustainable finance.

CHAPTER 7   MERGING THE SEAS: THE IMPERATIVE OF DIGITAL TRANSFORMATION AND LEGAL AND REGULATORY REFORM

Fundamentally, the circular economy aims to maximize resources by means of minimum waste generation. Emphasizing reuse, recycling, and regeneration, the circular economy differs from the conventional linear economy, which uses a "take, make, dispose" approach. But changing to such a system calls for a methodical approach to measurement and financial backing, not only intention. Here, the intersection of ISO 59020 and the concept of circularity create a powerful synergy that propels the circular economy forward.

The ISO 59020 standardizes the techniques for evaluating circularity performance in many different sectors. It specifies exact computing techniques, includes both required and optional circularity indicators, and offers comprehensive data collection instructions. This degree of consistency is absolutely essential, as it guarantees that every company, regardless of size or industry, may regularly and honestly assess its circularity initiatives. ISO 59020 improves the responsibility of sustainability activities by defining defined system limits and a strong reporting mechanism, therefore facilitating companies' capacity to show their circularity commitment.

Still, quantifying circularity is simply one factor under consideration. Organizations also require the financial tools to apply sustainable practices if they are to completely embrace the circular economy. Here is where circularity financing finds use. Circuity finance is the range of financial tools and approaches meant especially to facilitate the shift to a circular economy. These include loans, green bonds, and impact investing—all meant to support initiatives improving resource economy, waste reduction, and innovation enhancement. Utilizing circularity financing gives businesses the money they need to take real steps toward sustainability, which supports economic growth and protects the environment at the same time.

The connection of ISO 59020 with circularity financing offers a whole framework for the development of the circular economy. Although ISO 59020 provides the instruments for evaluating and quantifying circularity, circularity finance provides the means to realize these evaluations. This mix guarantees that companies not only monitor their development but also have the financial means to carry out required improvements. Taken together, they provide a disciplined road map for reaching environmental targets, especially those in line with the Sustainable Development Goals (SDGs) of the United Nations.

Digital finance solutions help to further accentuate the synergy between ISO 59020 and circularity finance. One innovative way to digitize alternative finance inside the blockchain space is the circuity finance ecosystem. This ecosystem fundamentally relies on the CIFI token, a digital asset that serves both governance and settlement functions.

This digital approach to circularity financing makes sure that all financial transactions are open and efficient. This adds a new dimension to sustainability and gives circular economy projects creative ways to get money.

Companies may rapidly move to a circular economy by adopting ISO 59020 and using circularity finance's financial tools. This combined methodology ensures an accurate assessment of circularity and provides the necessary financial support to implement sustainable measures. Using these technologies is not only beneficial but also necessary for companies dedicated to environmental protection and sustainable development. The road to a sustainable future is defined by structured rules and strong financial systems, and ISO 59020, in conjunction with circularity finance, offers a clear and achievable approach to achieving it. As a whole, the ISO 59020 circularity standard is like a new common language, uniting organizations in measuring and optimizing resource use. It empowers rethinking of business models, supply chains, and product lifecycles—unlocking a world of possibilities for innovation, cost savings, competitive edge, and sustainability wins.

Strategies for Attracting Sustainable Investment

Businesses seeking sustainable investment should give top priority to creating a thorough sustainability plan that fits very well with their main corporate objectives. This approach should clearly state how the organization plans to handle social, environmental, and governance (ESG) concerns while concurrently promoting company profitability and expansion. Incorporating sustainability into their main business processes can help businesses show investors that their dedication to sustainability is sincere and strategically beneficial. This alignment emphasizes not only the company's long-term adaptability but also its proactive strategy to reduce risks related to ESG elements.

Companies trying to attract sustainable investors must clearly convey the value of their sustainability programs. This entails not just delineating environmental objectives but also offering concrete proof of development and results. Businesses should use several avenues of communication to distribute performance data, case studies, and success stories highlighting the practical influence of their environmental initiatives. Openness in communication shows investors that the business is not just establishing high goals but also reaching quantifiable achievements, therefore fostering confidence.

CHAPTER 7 MERGING THE SEAS: THE IMPERATIVE OF DIGITAL TRANSFORMATION AND LEGAL AND REGULATORY REFORM

Showcasing a company's sustainable credentials, robust data collection, and reporting techniques are fundamental. Making wise judgments depends mostly on accurate, reliable, and verified data for investors. Investing in modern data management systems would help businesses guarantee they can gather thorough ESG data in all spheres of responsibility. Publications should analyze and present this information in accordance with accepted sustainability frameworks and standards, such as the Task Force on Climate-related Financial Disclosures (TCFD) or the Global Reporting Initiative (GRI). Excellent reporting not only satisfies legal criteria but also gives investors the specific information they need to evaluate the sustainability and performance of the business.

Drawing in sustainable investment also depends critically on involving stakeholders. Businesses should aggressively solicit comments and suggestions from a wide spectrum of stakeholders, including investors, consumers, staff, vendors, and members of communities. Knowing stakeholder expectations and issues helps businesses customize their environmental plans to properly serve their interests. This involvement also demonstrates to investors the business's commitment to fostering positive relationships, its social impact, and its appreciation of stakeholder perspectives.

Companies trying to attract sustainable investment must keep updated on changing rules and market trends. The regulatory landscape for sustainability and ESG reporting is constantly changing due to the constant addition of new criteria and rules. Businesses should pay great attention to these changes and modify their operations to guarantee compliance and keep ahead of consumer expectations. Furthermore, knowing more general market trends—such as the expanding need for green technology or changes in consumer tastes toward sustainable products—helps businesses spot fresh prospects and modify their plans to grab sustainable investment.

Companies that want to attract sustainable investment have to show a sincere and purposeful dedication to sustainability. Developing a clear, coordinated sustainability plan, properly explaining its impact, maintaining strong data collection and reporting procedures, actively interacting with stakeholders, and keeping current with market and legislative developments are all part of this. By shining in these areas, firms may establish a strong image as ethical, forward-looking organizations that appeal to investors who are progressively giving sustainability top priority in their investment choices.

In the fast-changing environment of today, resilience in a company and success depend more on sustainability. Businesses that aggressively embrace sustainability reporting and integrate sustainable practices into their operations are setting themselves up to not just survive but also flourish going forward. This proactive strategy involves understanding and resolving the environmental, social, and governance (ESG) elements of their company, increasingly recognized as vital components of long-term value creation.

Including sustainability in corporate plans helps businesses better forecast and control hazards. Major obstacles influencing company operations and profitability are climate change, resource constraints, and social inequity. Businesses that recognize these hazards and seek to minimize them through sustainable practices are better able to negotiate uncertainty and constraints. Companies may save running costs and decrease the risks connected with legislative changes and resource price volatility by, for instance, lowering their carbon footprint and applying energy-efficient technologies.

Moreover, improving responsibility and openness depends heavily on sustainability reporting. Investors, clients, and other stakeholders are increasingly demanding a deeper understanding of how businesses are managing their environmental, social, and governance (ESG) impacts. Businesses that offer thorough and accurate sustainability reports show their dedication to ethical business conduct, therefore fostering confidence and trustworthiness among their customers. Being open about sustainability initiatives and having a clear plan for handling ESG risks and opportunities can help organizations attract investment as well.

Using sustainable techniques may also inspire creativity and provide new business prospects. Companies that innovate to satisfy changing customer tastes toward more sustainable goods and services may seize new markets and strengthen their competitive edge. For example, creating environmentally friendly items or implementing circular economy ideas would set a business apart from its rivals and attract a rising base of consumers that share environmental concerns.

Including sustainability in business culture also helps to improve staff retention and involvement. Worker demand is rising for environmentally and socially responsible employers who share their values. Businesses that promote sustainability may attract and keep top talent, therefore increasing motivation, production, and loyalty.

For companies as well as people, being current and involved in the changing terrain of sustainability is vital. The constantly changing regulatory landscape is incorporating new rules and criteria to address global sustainability issues. Maintaining current with these changes guarantees businesses' compliance and helps them foresee future changes in regulations. Furthermore, keeping knowledge about new trends and best practices in sustainability helps businesses maintain their leadership in sustainability and always enhance their policies.

CHAPTER 7 MERGING THE SEAS: THE IMPERATIVE OF DIGITAL TRANSFORMATION AND LEGAL AND REGULATORY REFORM

Ultimately, resilience in business and success depend on sustainability; it is not only a slogan. Businesses that adopt sustainability reporting and procedures are better suited to control risks, seize fresh prospects, and establish close bonds with their employees. Companies may guarantee their long-term viability and help the environment and society by pledging to use sustainable business practices and keeping educated about the changing sustainability scene. At last, this proactive approach will result in a more sustainable and rich future for everybody.

Green for Growth: Harnessing Nature-Based Solutions for a Thriving Nature-Positive Economy

Nature-based solutions (NBS) are becoming increasingly important in addressing growing environmental issues and facilitating the transition to a nature-positive economy. These solutions, which use ecosystems and natural processes to handle different environmental problems, are becoming more and more known for their ability to stop climate change, stop the loss of biodiversity, and improve social justice by means of their use. Adoption and integration of NBS offer a promising path toward sustainable development at a pivotal juncture in global environmental policy and practice.

Recognizing the ecological advantages of NBS is only one aspect of the change to a nature-positive economy; another is their economic potential and market dynamics. This dual awareness is crucial for mainstreaming NBS into broader economic systems and ensuring their viability and scalability. Understanding and using the economic worth of ecosystems and the services they offer can help us to promote investments in natural capital and generate new markets and economic possibilities fit for sustainable practices.

This chapter investigates the many functions of NBS in the changing economic environment. It explores the ecological benefits of these answers, stressing how they help to reduce climatic effects, protect biodiversity, and advance societal welfare. It also looks at how the financial system and market work to affect the acceptance of NBS. This includes creative ways to pay for them, legal incentives, and the worth of ecosystem services.

Understanding the market dynamics related to NBS is crucial for its successful use.

Examining present market patterns, spotting possible adoption obstacles, and investigating chances to include NBS into current economic systems are part of this. This will help us create plans that not only strengthen the resilience of natural ecosystems but also assist fair social development and sustainable economic growth.

CHAPTER 7   MERGING THE SEAS: THE IMPERATIVE OF DIGITAL TRANSFORMATION AND LEGAL AND REGULATORY REFORM

Finally, the shift to a nature-positive economy depends critically on nature-based solutions. Understanding their ecological and financial worth will help us to open fresh opportunities for sustainable development and promote a harmonic coexistence between human activities and the surroundings. This chapter seeks to give a thorough picture of NBS together with ideas on their advantages, economic possibilities, and the dynamics of the market that would define their future.

Market Trends and Dynamics in Nature-Based Solutions

Rising demand, rising investment, and changing public and private sector responsibilities define the worldwide scene for nature-based solutions (NBS) while it is experiencing a transforming change. This chapter explores the complex market trends and forces influencing the future of NBS, therefore highlighting their potential to propel a nature-positive economy.

Driven by its incorporation into international policy frameworks and increasing awareness among a wide range of stakeholders, NBS is in demand globally. Particularly in urban planning, public health, and social well-being, policymakers, businesses, and individuals are realizing the many advantages NBS provides. This broad-based awareness is generating a strong and growing market for producers of NBS, as they view these solutions as essential to solving urgent environmental problems and improving the quality of life in communities worldwide.

With around $133 billion invested in NBS worldwide, this shows a strong determination to find these answers. However, this level of investment falls far short of the ambitious targets set for preventing land degradation, protecting biodiversity, and mitigating climate change. Our NBS investments must double by 2050 and increase by 2030 to meet these goals. Emphasizing the financial possibilities of this shift, the World Economic Forum projects that by 2030, a nature-positive economy might provide up to 395 million jobs. With yearly expenditures of almost $2.7 trillion, this shift emphasizes the extent of financial dedication required to completely achieve the potential of NBS.

At 86% of all investments, the public sector now mostly funds NBS. This significant participation highlights the need for government assistance and policy programs to promote the acceptance of NBS. However, to meet the increasing investment objectives, we must further enhance the private sector's involvement. To guarantee the scalability and sustainability of NBS projects, private sector investment from 14% in 2021 to 40% by

CHAPTER 7   MERGING THE SEAS: THE IMPERATIVE OF DIGITAL TRANSFORMATION AND LEGAL AND REGULATORY REFORM

2030 has to rise. This change calls for calculated strategies that can draw private capital: building appealing investment environments, providing incentives, and highlighting effective NBS initiatives with real returns on investment.

Even if NBS clearly has advantages and demand is rising, various obstacles prevent the full-scale application and investment in these solutions. The difficulty of appreciating environmental services and the social advantages given by NBS is among the main ones. Unlike conventional infrastructure projects, NBS's long-term, sometimes diffuse, non-easily measurable effects hinder its pricing and investor attractiveness. Furthermore, the expertise and statistics on the most efficient ways to carry out NBS are lacking, which would discourage legislators and investors from funding these projects.

One more major obstacle is public financing competition. Given many conflicting demands, getting enough money for NBS might prove difficult. Overcoming these obstacles calls for strong legislative support emphasizing NBS and including it in more general environmental and financial plans. Additionally, crucial in mobilizing the required resources are creative financing structures such as green bonds, blended finance, and pay-for-performance programs. Good stakeholder involvement is equally crucial to ensure the implementation of NBS initiatives across all relevant entities, such as governments, companies, and communities.

Finally, although complicated, the dynamics and developments in the industry around nature-based solutions show great promise. Growing demand from various purchasers, notable investment increases, and changing responsibilities of the public and private sectors are shaping a new age for NBS. Realizing the full potential of NBS will depend critically on removing obstacles to investment and using chances for creative funding and stakeholder involvement. It is abundantly evident as we negotiate this change that NBS will be very essential in building a resilient, sustainable, and nature-positive economy.

GRI 101: Biodiversity 2024—A Comprehensive Guide for Sustainable Reporting

As we enter a period of more environmental consciousness, the need for biodiversity and its protection has grown ever more critical. Maintaining environmental balance and resilience depends much on biodiversity, the range of life on Earth in all its forms and interactions. Maintaining the natural systems humans and innumerable other species rely on depends on their conservation.

CHAPTER 7   MERGING THE SEAS: THE IMPERATIVE OF DIGITAL TRANSFORMATION AND LEGAL AND REGULATORY REFORM

The Global Reporting Initiative (GRI) developed a new benchmark, GRI 101: Biodiversity 2024, in response to companies' pressing need to address their environmental impacts. This standard seeks to provide companies with a complete toolkit to document their management plans and effects on biodiversity. It underlines the need for openness and responsibility in business operations with reference to biodiversity.

Overview and Importance of GRI 101: Biodiversity 2024

The Global Sustainability Standards Board (GSSB) has built a larger framework that incorporates GRI 101: Biodiversity 2024, effective from January 1, 2026. The goal of this method is to empower companies to articulate their environmental responsibilities in a clear and comprehensive manner. Clear policies and measurements help companies to evaluate, control, and document how they affect biodiversity more precisely.

The development of this standard reflects the increasing awareness of the fact that companies are rather important for the preservation of natural resources. Companies that follow GRI 101: Biodiversity 2024 will be more suited to carry out plans that help to offset their detrimental effects on biodiversity, support sustainable practices, and assist in conservation initiatives. This then helps international initiatives to preserve and rebuild ecosystems, therefore guaranteeing a better earth for next generations.

GRI 101: Biodiversity 2024 is essentially a necessary tool for companies trying to match the worldwide drive toward sustainability. It underscores the close relationship between environmental health and economic activities, advocating for a harmonious coexistence between human growth and the natural environment. Adoption of such criteria is essential for promoting a culture of environmental responsibility and preservation of the enormous biodiversity of the earth as we progress into this era of more environmentally conscious business.

In terrestrial, marine, and aquatic habitats, biodiversity is the broad spectrum of living forms that coexist. This diversity covers not only the enormous variety of species living in these habitats but also the genetic variances among individual species. Moreover, biodiversity also describes the unique qualities and traits of many ecosystems, from temperate forests and wetlands to tropical rainforests and coral reefs.

Maintaining the equilibrium and usefulness of ecosystems depends on the abundance of biodiversity. Every species, no matter how little or seems unimportant, has a special function in its environment. While many insects, birds, and animals help to poll, seed distribute, and control pest numbers, plants and trees absorb carbon dioxide and generate oxygen. Fish and coral, among other marine life, sustain intricate food webs and help to maintain ocean habitats.

Human survival depends on healthy, balanced ecosystems, as they offer several necessary functions that keep human life possible. Among the most basic offerings are meal delivery. Diverse ecosystems sustain fisheries and agriculture, providing a wide variety of crops and seafood that constitute the foundation of human meals all throughout the world. Ecosystems also control and clean the water we use. Other natural environments like wetlands and forests help to filter toxins and guarantee the supply of pure water.

Managing Biodiversity Impacts and the Role of GRI 101

Furthermore, the preservation of the quality of the air we breathe depends much on biodiversity. Through their ability to collect carbon dioxide and release oxygen, plants and trees play a crucial role in photosynthesis. This normal mechanism sustains the atmospheric conditions required for life and helps to slow down global warming. Furthermore, by stabilizing soils and controlling water cycles, different ecosystems also provide defense against natural calamities such as floods and storms.

The diversity of living forms in our world's ecosystems essentially forms the basis for human existence and well-being. The complex interactions among species, genetic variety, and environmental characteristics guarantee that ecosystems stay strong and are able to adapt to shocks and changes. Therefore, maintaining the necessary services that humans depend on for their existence and quality of life depends critically on protecting and conserving biodiversity, not merely on environmental stewardship.

Companies can significantly affect biodiversity through their various operations and the behavior of their commercial partners. Various manifestations of these effects are possible. Direct effects, for example, affect land use by means of urban development or deforestation, therefore upsetting natural ecosystems and displacing species. The use of natural resources—such as mining, fishing, or logging—which could reduce species populations and disturb ecosystem services also directly affects ecosystems. Whether it's chemicals, trash, or emissions, pollution compromises air, water, and soil, therefore influencing the health of plant life as well as animals. Organizations can also unwittingly bring invading species into new habitats, which can outcompete native species and upset nearby ecosystems.

Apart from these direct consequences, companies can indirectly influence biodiversity. Though not instantly apparent, these effects can be as important. For instance, the activities of a company might cause changes in the ecosystem services—that is, the advantages people get from the surroundings. Should these services deteriorate, human societies depending on them for food, clean water, and other needs may suffer. As communities try to adjust to the loss of these essential resources, this deterioration can also have social and economic effects.

The Global Reporting Initiative (GRI) developed the GRI 101 standard to handle these several effects on biodiversity. This criteria is meant to let companies methodically find, control, and document their effects on biodiversity. Following this criteria helps companies to better know how their operations impact the surroundings. The GRI 101 criteria offer a thorough framework that motivates companies to take into account both direct and indirect effects of their activities on biodiversity. It helps them to create plans to minimize negative effects and maximize beneficial contributions.

Integrating Digital and Sustainability Frameworks: Enhancing Efficiency and Accountability in Global Trade

Sustainability laws like the Corporate Sustainability Reporting Directive (CSRD), the European Sustainability Reporting Standards (ESRs), and the International Financial Reporting Standards (IFRS) S1 and S2 have merged with the Model Law on Electronic Transferable Records (MLETR) and the Electronic Transactions Documents Act (ETDA). This is a big step toward creating a framework that works for both technological progress and environmental protection.

The United Nations Commission on International Trade Law (UNCITRAL) designed the Model Law on Electronic Transferable Records (MLETR) as an international legal framework to facilitate the use and legal recognition of electronic transferable records. The aim of this law is to ensure that electronic records, such as warehouse receipts, promissory notes, and electronic bills of lading, possess the same legal standing as their paper-based counterparts. Technology-neutral, or MLETR, technology allows it to support distributed ledger technologies like blockchain, token-based systems, and conventional registries, among other technical platforms. The MLETR seeks to improve efficiency, lower transaction costs, and increase the dependability and security of electronic transactions by offering a uniform method to digitize transferable records.

CHAPTER 7 MERGING THE SEAS: THE IMPERATIVE OF DIGITAL TRANSFORMATION AND LEGAL AND REGULATORY REFORM

The Electronic Transactions Documents Act (ETDA) improves the MLETR by setting up legal systems for electronic transactions and documents in some places. This legislation supports digital commerce, helps to enable the shift from paper-based to electronic systems, and improves the general effectiveness of corporate operations by thus promoting digital commerce.

Putting these technological systems together with rules about sustainability, like the Corporate Sustainability Reporting Directive (CSRD), the European Sustainability Reporting Standards (ESRs), and the International Financial Reporting Standards (IFRs) S1 and S2, makes for a complete and effective way for companies to do business today. The CSRD requires businesses to submit comprehensive data on their environmental policies, therefore guaranteeing more openness and comparability. It requires big businesses and listed SMEs to reveal their social and environmental consequences, therefore complementing the more general EU sustainability objectives. Through certain criteria and standards for sustainability reporting, the ESRS guarantees uniform, comparable, and dependable disclosures.

Establishing worldwide norms for sustainability reporting helps the IFRS S1 and S2 standards improve this structure even more. While IFRS S2 especially targets climate-related disclosures, IFR S1 concentrates on generally sustainable-related financial disclosures. These criteria aim to provide investors and other interested parties with relevant and comparable insights into the climate-related risks and opportunities, as well as the sustainability performance of a firm.

Combining MLETR and ETDA with these sustainability rules ensures the natural inclusion of electronic records and transactions in reporting systems. This synergy helps businesses apply cutting-edge technology solutions to simplify reporting systems, raise data accuracy, and increase openness. With MLETR's help, blockchain technology can offer permanent records of data related to sustainability, which ensures the accuracy and integrity of the data that is recorded. Electronic signatures and documents verified under ETDA will help to effectively submit and verify sustainability reports, therefore lowering administrative costs and improving compliance.

Furthermore, this combined strategy helps to further the more general goal of building a strong and sustainable digital economy. Companies may maximize their sustainability efforts by matching technological developments with sustainability reporting criteria. This linkage encourages businesses to adopt innovative technology that supports both their environmental goals and their own. It also improves the capacity of stakeholders to evaluate the environmental performance of several businesses, thereby encouraging responsibility and wise decision-making.

CHAPTER 7   MERGING THE SEAS: THE IMPERATIVE OF DIGITAL TRANSFORMATION AND LEGAL AND REGULATORY REFORM

The combination of the Electronic Transactions Documents Act (ETDA), the Model Law on Electronic Transferable Records (MLETR), and sustainability laws such as the Corporate Sustainability Reporting Directive (CSRD), the European Sustainability Reporting Standards (ESRs), and the International Financial Reporting Standards (IFRs) S1 and S2 creates a comprehensive framework that fosters technological innovation and sustainability. By improving the efficiency, openness, and responsibility of corporate operations, this combined strategy helps to propel development toward a more sustainable and strong worldwide economy.

The Role of MLETR and ETDA in Advancing Digital Trade Documentation

Two key frameworks driving the digital revolution of trade paperwork are the Electronic Transactions Documents Act (ETDA) and the Model Law on Electronic Transferable Records (MLETR). Designed to enable the use of electronic transferable records instead of traditional paper-based ones, the Model Law on Electronic Transferable Records (MLETR)—developed by the United Nations Commission on International Trade Law (UNCITRAL)—is a legal framework that provides clear guidelines for the legal recognition, creation, and transfer of electronic transferable records, promoting efficiency, security, and legal certainty in digital trade transactions. This progress is crucial for the digitization of trade papers like bills of lading and promissory notes. These are crucial instruments in trade finance, demonstrating ownership, identifying claims, and defining responsibilities in business transactions. The MLETR enhances the efficiency, safety, and speed of trade procedures by enabling the legal use of electronic copies of these documents. This makes international trade easier by streamlining and making it easier for people to access.

Conversely, the Electronic Transactions Documents Act (ETDA) is rather important in encouraging and helping the evolution and use of electronic transactions in several spheres.

By pushing the acceptance of digital technology, the ETDA hopes to produce a more simplified, efficient, and safe environment for trading and commerce. This legislation ensures the legal validity of electronic documents and signatures, thereby ensuring the acceptance and legal enforcement of electronic transactions. The ETDA assists companies in moving from paper-based to electronic documentation by encouraging a supportive legal environment, therefore lowering the expenses and dangers involved in managing, storing, and distributing actual papers.

CHAPTER 7   MERGING THE SEAS: THE IMPERATIVE OF DIGITAL TRANSFORMATION AND LEGAL AND REGULATORY REFORM

The MLETR and ETDA taken together are quite helpful for the continuous initiatives to digital trade documentation systems. The change from conventional paper-based paperwork to electronic forms depends on their contributions, which not only improves operational efficiency but also lowers costs and improves trade finance security. Electronic documentation enables the management of trade records with enhanced dependability and security, thereby mitigating the risks of document loss, fraud, and forgery. Therefore, MLETR and ETDA play crucial roles in promoting the use of electronic records and transforming and improving the trade financing landscape.

Harmonizing Global Sustainability Reporting

A European Union legislation, the Corporate Sustainability Reporting legislation (CSRD), requires big businesses to provide thorough data on their social and environmental effects. The EU's larger plan to improve corporate responsibility and openness in sustainability depends critically on this direction. By requiring detailed reporting on a number of sustainability issues, investors, customers, and lawmakers will always have access to accurate information about how businesses are meeting their social and environmental obligations. Making wise judgments and building confidence in business operations depend on this openness.

Developed to help businesses follow the CSRD are the European Sustainability Reporting Standards (ESRs). These guidelines offer businesses a disciplined framework directing them on the particular content and style of their sustainability reports. The purpose of ESRs is to empower businesses to accurately and truthfully showcase their social and environmental performance, ensuring that the disclosed information is pertinent and beneficial for various stakeholders to inform their decisions. Following these guidelines helps businesses improve the comparability and clarity of their environmental reports, therefore facilitating stakeholder evaluation of their performance.

Introduced by the International Financial Reporting Standards Foundation, the IFRS S1 and S2 standards offer a worldwide benchmark for financial disclosures connected to sustainability. While IFRs S2 concentrate especially on climate-related disclosures, IFRs S1 contain generally relevant information on general sustainability. These criteria aim to ensure the consistency, comparability, and dependability of sustainability data across multiple countries. Businesses that use these criteria will be able to give stakeholders a clear and complete picture of their sustainability-related risks and opportunities. This will help them make better decisions and standardize sustainability reporting worldwide.

CHAPTER 7 MERGING THE SEAS: THE IMPERATIVE OF DIGITAL TRANSFORMATION AND LEGAL AND REGULATORY REFORM

When you put MLETR and ETDA together with rules for sustainability like CSRD, ESRs, and IFRS S1 and S2, you get a framework that helps with both technical progress and environmental goals. By improving the efficiency, openness, and responsibility of corporate operations, this combined strategy helps to propel development toward a more sustainable and resilient world economy. These models help businesses to make sure their trade and environmental policies complement best practices and legal obligations, therefore placing themselves for long-term success in a fast-changing corporate environment.

Along with these efforts in the EU, the International Financial Reporting Standards (IFRS) Foundation has released the IFRS S1 and S2 standards to set a standard for sustainability-related financial information around the world. The IFRS S1 standard addresses general sustainability-related information, providing businesses with a comprehensive framework for reporting on various sustainability concerns. This covers elements like governance methods, social effects, emissions, and resource utilization. On the other hand, the IFRS S2 standard specifically targets disclosures related to climate change. It describes the criteria for businesses to disclose their greenhouse gas emissions, climate-related hazards and opportunities, and policies for controlling and lessening their effects.

Businesses across many countries hope to guarantee consistency, comparability, and dependability of sustainability information through IFRS S1 and S2. Setting a global standard for these IFRS rules helps to make sustainability reporting more comparable and open. This lets investors and other stakeholders make better decisions based on consistent, high-quality sustainability data.

Significant developments in the field of sustainability reporting come from the CSRD and ESRs in the EU as well as from the IFRS S1 and S2 standards internationally. These projects aim to enhance the consistency and quality of sustainability data, thereby reinforcing institutional responsibility and facilitating the transition toward more environmentally friendly corporate operations.

Along with these efforts in the EU, the International Financial Reporting Standards (IFRS) Foundation has released the IFRS S1 and S2 standards to set a standard for sustainability-related financial information around the world. The IFRS S1 standard addresses general sustainability-related information, providing businesses with a comprehensive framework for reporting on various sustainability concerns. This covers elements like governance methods, social effects, emissions, and resource utilization. On the other hand, the IFRS S2 standard specifically targets disclosures related to

CHAPTER 7   MERGING THE SEAS: THE IMPERATIVE OF DIGITAL TRANSFORMATION AND LEGAL AND REGULATORY REFORM

climate change. It describes the criteria for businesses to disclose their greenhouse gas emissions, climate-related hazards and opportunities, and policies for controlling and lessening their effects.

By means of IFRS S1 and S2, it is hoped to guarantee consistency, comparability, and dependability of sustainability information presented by businesses across many countries.

Significant developments in the field of sustainability reporting come from the CSRD and ESRs in the EU as well as from the IFRS S1 and S2 standards internationally. These projects aim to enhance the consistency and quality of sustainability data, thereby reinforcing institutional responsibility and facilitating the transition toward more environmentally conscious company operations.

The International Financial Reporting Standards (IFRs) Foundation has put out the IFRS S1 and S2 standards. Their work around the world is similar to what the EU is doing with the Corporate Sustainability Reporting Directive (CSRD) and the European Sustainability Reporting Standards (ESRs). These criteria seek to provide a worldwide benchmark for sustainability-related financial disclosures, therefore guaranteeing consistency, comparability, and dependability of information supplied by businesses across many countries.

The IFRS S1 standard provides a complete framework for businesses to present on a wide range of sustainability concerns, therefore addressing general information on connected topics. This covers elements like government policies, societal effects, emissions, and resource utilization. Covering these several categories enables IFRS S1 to guarantee that businesses present a whole picture of their sustainability performance, which is essential for stakeholders trying to know the whole influence of a company's activities on society and the environment.

Conversely, the IFRS S2 criteria concentrate especially on disclosures connected to climate change. It describes the criteria for businesses to disclose their greenhouse gas emissions, climate-related risks and opportunities, and plans of action for controlling and lessening their effects. Given the pressing worldwide need to solve climate change and the related hazards, this focused attention on climate problems is especially crucial. IFRS S2 enables businesses to more successfully convey their climate strategies and performance to stakeholders by offering clear rules for reporting linked to climate change.

We hope to ensure that businesses provide comprehensive and standardized sustainability information through IFRS S1 and S2 standards, which will enhance comparison and transparency. Investors and other stakeholders that depend on reliable, high-quality sustainability data to make wise decisions especially benefit from this. IFRS S1 and S2 let stakeholders compare the sustainability performance of different companies and countries. This creates a better and more efficient market by using a global standard.

Significant developments in the field of sustainability reporting come from the CSRD and ESRs in the EU as well as from the IFRS S1 and S2 standards internationally. These projects aim to enhance the quality and uniformity of sustainability data, thereby fortifying institutional accountability. These rules and frameworks for reporting help businesses in their attempts to include sustainability into their operations and open their performance honestly by offering clear directions and structures. Building confidence with stakeholders and pushing the change toward more sustainable corporate practices depend on this higher responsibility and openness.

Integrating MLETR and ETDA with Sustainability Frameworks

The Model Law on Electronic Transferable Records (MLETR) and the Electronic Transactions Documents Act (ETDA), along with sustainability laws like the CSRD, ESRs, and IFRS S1 and S2 standards, create a framework that supports both technological progress and long-term sustainability goals. By improving the efficiency, openness, and responsibility of corporate activities, this combined strategy helps to propel development toward a more resilient and sustainable world. These models help businesses to make sure their trade and environmental policies complement best practices and legal obligations, therefore placing themselves for long-term success in a fast-changing corporate environment.

A calculated step toward digital and sustainable trading practices is the combination of the Model Law on Electronic Transferable Records (MLETR) and the Electronic Transactions Documents Act (ETDA) with sustainability legislation. This integration shows a thorough strategy to modernize corporate processes using technology to reach environmental sustainability objectives.

Using MLETR's electronic transferable records will help companies greatly cut their dependence on paper-based systems. This change toward digital recording makes a significant contribution to environmental sustainability in addition to being a question of operational efficiency. Reducing the use of paper directly leads to a decrease in deforestation and energy consumption associated with the production, transportation, and disposal of paper documents.

CHAPTER 7   MERGING THE SEAS: THE IMPERATIVE OF DIGITAL TRANSFORMATION AND LEGAL AND REGULATORY REFORM

For trade transactions, for example, using electronic records may greatly reduce the carbon footprint. Conventional paper-based transactions emit greenhouse gases by using a lot of physical resources and logistics. Companies may reduce these emissions by using electronic records, therefore matching their activities with worldwide initiatives against climate change. A company can meticulously record and present this reduction in carbon emissions as part of its sustainability performance. By means of thorough sustainability reporting, businesses may show their dedication to environmental protection, therefore strengthening their profile among those who give sustainability first priority.

The ETDA plays a significant role in this integration by encouraging and supporting the growth and use of electronic transactions. It offers the required infrastructure and legal framework to help the seamless shift to digital documents. Businesses depend on this help since it guarantees not only effective but also legal compliance during the change. While supporting sustainability goals, the ETDA's methodology helps companies implement digital solutions that simplify their processes, lower costs, and improve data security.

This integration fits perfectly the criteria for sustainability reporting imposed by the CSRD, ESRs, and IFRS S1 and S2 standards. These criteria demand businesses present thorough and accurate data on their environmental effects and sustainable policies. Using electronic records and transactions will help businesses increase the accuracy and openness of their sustainability information. One may measure and quantify the lower carbon footprint and improved resource efficiency brought about by digital documentation, therefore highlighting actual advancements in environmental initiatives.

Furthermore, using MLETR's electronic records helps to increase sustainability reporting's openness and responsibility. More exact tracking and transaction auditing made possible by electronic documentation helps businesses to properly estimate and explain their environmental effects. This openness is important for building trust with stakeholders like investors, consumers, and regulatory authorities, who are expecting more and more accurate and checked sustainability information.

By combining MLETR and ETDA with sustainability rules, we offer a complete strategy for reaching digital and environmentally friendly trade policies. Adopting electronic transferable records would help companies improve operational efficiency, match strict sustainability reporting criteria, and lessen their environmental effect. ETDA's help guarantees that this change is compliant with legal criteria and seamless. These projects taken together provide a more transparent, sustainable trading ecosystem that advantages the environment as well as companies.

As an example, let us take a big global manufacturing company under consideration. Using the Model Law on Electronic Transferable Records (MLETR), this company switched from paper-based bills of lading to electronic ones. By lowering the demand for paper, this change not only simplified their supply chain operations but also greatly reduced their environmental effect, therefore saving time and money related to processing actual documentation. For effective supply chain management, faster transactions, improved security, and real-time updates—all of which this digital transition enabled—are vital.

Under the Corporate Sustainability Reporting Directive (CSRD), the corporation was able to formally document these developments, therefore proving its dedication to sustainability. They recorded the environmental advantages—lower resource usage and less carbon emissions—that came from cutting paper use. This action demonstrated their will to lower their carbon footprint and their proactive approach toward more environmentally friendly corporate operations. Aligning their digital transformation with the CSRD would enable the company to openly present their environmental initiatives to stakeholders, thereby building confidence and support from investors, consumers, and authorities.

Integrating ETDA and MLETR with Global Reporting Standards in Financial Institutions

Another relevant example is a financial institution facilitating electronic trade finance transactions by means of the Electronic Transactions Development Agency (ETDA). Using electronic approaches significantly improved the institution's operational effectiveness. Using digital documentation lessened the institution's total environmental impact by reducing reliance on paper. The IFRS S2 guidelines, which focus on climate-related disclosures, recorded this change, making it highly significant.

In this case, the financial institution achieved significant progress in sustainability in addition to increasing operational efficiency by cutting processing times and simplifying document handling. Moving to electronic trade finance lessened the carbon footprint from shipping paper documents and the physical storage requirements. By pointing out these changes using IFRS S2 guidelines, the institution was able to show that it was in line with global sustainability goals. This improved its reputation with clients and investors who care about the environment. This case shows how digitization may support sustainability goals and increase operational effectiveness, therefore benefiting the company in whole.

These case studies demonstrate the practical integration of MLETR and ETDA with sustainability rules, resulting in significant operational and environmental benefits. Using electronic transferable records and electronic transactions would help companies and financial institutions reach better efficiency, lower environmental impact, and improve compliance with sustainability reporting criteria. By combining new technologies with environmental goals to create a stronger and more stable future, these examples show how digital transformation can bring about big positive changes in the business world.

There are clear benefits to combining laws on sustainability with frameworks like the Electronic Transactions Documents Act (ETDA) and the Model Law on Electronic Transferable Records (MLETR). Businesses using these systems usually find more efficiency as electronic records simplify procedures, lower manual handling, and speed transactions. Less need for physical storage, printing, and paper document transit results from this digital change, which also lowers running expenses. Another major benefit is improved security, as, with sophisticated encryption and security systems, electronic records provide stronger defense against fraud, loss, and illegal access. Particularly noteworthy are environmental advantages, as, in line with more general sustainability objectives, cutting paper use reduces a company's carbon footprint and resource consumption.

Businesses can also meet legal requirements by using these systems, like those in the Corporate Sustainability Reporting Directive (CSRD), the European Sustainability Reporting Standards (ESRs), and the International Financial Reporting Standards (IFRs) S1 and S2 criteria. Following these rules guarantees legal compliance and helps businesses to be leaders in sustainability and corporate responsibility. As stakeholders increasingly value environmental stewardship and transparency, this compliance could significantly boost a company's reputation. Improved reputation therefore may help a business be more competitive in the market and draw clients, investors, and partners that give sustainable practices first priority.

The Transition to Electronic Records in Sustainable Business Practices

However, the transition to electronic records is not without its challenges. Effective implementation and maintenance of electronic systems depend on major technological and training investments. Companies must set aside funds for the purchase of fresh technology, software, and staff continuous education to guarantee seamless integration into digital operations. Those used to conventional paper-based methods may also object to change; thus, attempts to control change and highlight the advantages of the new systems become more important. Ensuring the compatibility of several systems adds even another level of complication. Businesses have to negotiate the integration of several technologies and platforms so that they enable electronic records and transactions to flow naturally. Following several rules across many countries might complicate this process even further and call for careful coordination and strategic preparation.

Notwithstanding these difficulties, it is a worthy effort, as the long-term advantages of combining MLETR and ETDA with sustainability regulations outweigh them. Returns on investment from the gains in security, environmental impact, cost savings, and efficiency are very high. Companies that effectively navigate change position themselves for ongoing development and leadership in the evolving landscape of digital and sustainable business practices.

The move to electronic records made possible by MLETR and backed by ETDA marks a basic change toward more safe and effective trade methods. Faster transaction speeds, fewer operating overheads, and improved data security help companies. Reduced processing times, less expense connected with physical document maintenance, and less danger of document-related fraud or loss are just a few of the obvious commercial benefits these savings translate into. The environmental effect is similarly significant, as less waste and reduced carbon emissions resulting from less paper consumption help to promote world sustainability targets.

Combining these systems with sustainability rules such as IFRS, CSRD, and ESRs helps businesses to fully monitor and document their environmental effects. This openness not only satisfies legal requirements but also improves the company's reputation among those who give sustainability first priority. Clear, precise, verifiable sustainability data helps to build investor trust and can draw a larger base of ecologically minded partners and consumers.

The path to digital integration is difficult, though, and calls for large upfront costs. Businesses have to make investments in new technology, guarantee strong data security policies, and equip staff members to fit new systems. Particularly for companies firmly rooted in conventional methods, this change phase can be difficult. The common obstacle to change is resistance to it, which requires strong leadership and open communication to show the long-term advantages of digital transformation.

CHAPTER 7   MERGING THE SEAS: THE IMPERATIVE OF DIGITAL TRANSFORMATION AND LEGAL AND REGULATORY REFORM

Moreover, attaining perfect interoperability between several systems is both important and difficult. Businesses have to make sure their digital solutions follow different regional rules and fit several platforms. Usually including cooperation with technology suppliers and regulatory specialists, this calls for a systematic approach to system integration and compliance management.

Even if combining MLETR and ETDA with environmental regulations offers major difficulties, the advantages must exceed the initial obstacles. Using electronic records results in increased productivity, cost savings, better security, and especially positive environmental effects. Businesses may improve their market competitiveness and reputation by matching sustainability reporting criteria. In a world going more and more digital and sustainable, the long-term benefits of digital transformation place companies for leadership and expansion.

Integrating MLETR and ETDA with Sustainability Initiatives for a More Efficient and Sustainable Global Trade Ecosystem

Future integration of transactions based on the Model Law on Electronic Transferable Records (MLETR) and the Electronic Transactions Development Agency (ETDA) with sustainability efforts looks rather bright. Businesses should increasingly utilize the MLETR and ETDA frameworks as they recognize the numerous benefits associated with digitalization and sustainable practices. The growing understanding of how these frameworks support environmental sustainability, save costs, simplify operations, and enhance security is driving this movement.

The changing requirements of the corporate environment are projected to keep driving change in regulatory frameworks. Future rules are likely to offer stronger support and clearer instructions to facilitate the transition to sustainable practices and electronic records. This development will enable companies to more successfully negotiate compliance, therefore ensuring that they satisfy legal obligations as well as stakeholder expectations.

Technological developments will largely influence this change. Blockchain technology and other innovations seem to improve the security and efficiency of electronic records even further. Blockchain is the perfect answer for guaranteeing the validity and integrity of electronic documents because of its distributed character and capacity to offer unchangeable records. Using such technology helps companies to increase the general dependability of their digital data, lower the danger of fraud, and promote openness.

The combination of MLETR and ETDA frameworks will shape a more sustainable and effective worldwide trade ecosystem. The total consequence of more businesses using these models will be a notable decrease in paper use, less carbon emissions, and better operational efficiencies in many different areas. In addition to benefiting individual companies, this collective shift toward digital and sustainable practices will also contribute to the broader goal of environmental sustainability.

Moreover, companies will find it more and more possible to embrace and incorporate these frameworks as technical breakthroughs and regulatory authorities keep developing. The combination of digitalization and sustainability will lead to a positive feedback loop where more sustainable behaviors are encouraged by higher efficiency and lower costs.

In essence, the future combination of MLETR and ETDA with sustainability projects is ready to transform world commerce. Changing rules, new technologies, and increasing understanding of the advantages of digitalization taken together will create a more sustainable, safe, and efficient trade environment. This change will be crucial in building a strong, forward-looking global economy equipped to solve problems of the 21st century.

Businesses have a strategic opportunity, not just a legal necessity, to integrate digital and sustainable practices. Adopting MLETR and ETDA will stimulate sustainability, efficiency, and creativity, therefore fostering a more robust and responsible worldwide trading environment.

Integration of digital and sustainable practices offers strategic chances for companies to develop and flourish—far more than only a legal need. Companies may unleash major benefits going beyond simple compliance by adopting frameworks like the Electronic Trade Documents Act (ETDA) and the Model Law on Electronic Transferable Records (MLETR).

One of the main advantages of combining these techniques is the quest for more effectiveness. By cutting the time and resources required to handle paper-based paperwork, digital records simplify company processes. Real-time data access and automated systems help to increase productivity and enable faster decision-making, therefore boosting the general running effectiveness of the company. Companies may reduce costs linked to printing, storage, and document transit, therefore translating this efficiency into savings.

Apart from improvement in efficiency, using MLETR and ETDA models stimulates creativity.

Advancing Global Trade Through Technological Innovation and Environmental Responsibility

The shift to digital records promotes the application of cutting-edge technologies such as artificial intelligence, machine learning, and blockchain, among others. These technologies may improve data security, streamline supply chains, and provide fresh ideas. Blockchain, for instance, may provide unchangeable records guaranteeing document validity and integrity, while artificial intelligence can provide trend forecasting and predictive analysis. This technological development not only enhances present procedures but also creates new models and economic prospects.

Another absolutely vital component of combining these digital systems is sustainability. Using less paper greatly reduces a company's environmental impact, therefore supporting more general sustainability objectives. This modification fits world initiatives toward environmental preservation and the worldwide battle of climate change. Businesses that give sustainability first priority will be better suited to satisfy the rising demands of customers, investors, and authorities who are more and more environmental impact-oriented. Showing a dedication to sustainable practices would help a business to establish better rapport with its stakeholders and strengthen its reputation.

Improved efficiency, creativity, and sustainability taken together help to build a more strong worldwide commerce environment. Companies that follow digital and sustainable policies are better suited to manage interruptions and adjust to changing market conditions. In a global economy beset with ongoing problems from economic swings, geopolitical concerns, and environmental disasters, this resilience is very vital.

Furthermore, including these strategies emphasizes a company's obligation toward moral and environmentally friendly corporate behavior. It shows a proactive attitude to solve environmental and social problems, which could inspire more loyalty from partners and consumers. Leading companies in this integration provide a precedent for industry norms, therefore promoting more general transformation in many other areas.

In the end, using digital and environmentally friendly methods through models like MLETR and ETDA goes beyond just following the law. This presents a strategic opportunity that offers significant benefits such as enhanced sustainability, technological innovation, and heightened efficiency. These benefits help to create a more strong, responsible, and competitive global trade climate that positions companies for long-term profitability and good influence. Once again, thanks. And we appreciate our listeners coming today. With any luck, this conversation was stimulating and instructive. Stay environmental and keep inventing till next time.

Summary

The junction of digital revolution and legislative changes promoting worldwide business and environmental projects is investigated in this chapter. It starts with tackling the legal obstacles to digital trade and emphasizes, as a main facilitator, the Model Law on Electronic Transferable Records (MLETR). The chapter explores MLETR's worldwide acceptance and its function in encouraging trust and helping legal harmonization inside the digital ecosystem.

The Corporate Sustainability Reporting Directive (CSRD) and its possibility to increase openness and responsibility in corporate sustainability reporting are also covered in the chapter. It notes the EU's dedication to increase sustainability reporting by contrasting the CSRD with the Non-Financial Reporting Directive (NFRD). Examined as measures toward a zero-waste future are also the difficulties and solutions pertaining to the EU Taxonomy and new ecodesign rules, including the Digital Product Passport and prohibitions on unsold items.

The chapter emphasizes for stakeholders the significance of EFRAG's implementation rules for the European Sustainability Reporting Standards (ESRs) and the dual materiality approach. It also looks at technical developments, sustainable financial trends, and how ISO 59020 could help to support green investments and sustainability.

At last, the chapter looks at how MLETR and the Electronic Transactions Development Act (ETDA) complement sustainability frameworks, therefore enabling the shift to electronic records and in line with worldwide reporting criteria. It ends by arguing for the integration of circular economies and nature-based solutions as well as the harmonization of worldwide sustainability reporting to redefine corporate sustainability and world commerce.

CHAPTER 8

Bits, Bytes, and Legal Bites: Navigating the Digital Frontier of Trade Law and Practice

Digital trade law, rules, and practices are the collective terms for the legal frameworks, regulations, and operational standards that govern commercial activities conducted via digital platforms and networks. In today's interconnected world, when digital technology and the Internet are critical to global commerce, firms, governments, and consumers must comprehend and navigate the complexity of digital trade law. A collection of regulations known as the Multilateral Electronic Transactions Act (MLETR) aims to promote harmonization and ease cross-border electronic transactions. The norms governing the recognition and enforceability of electronic contracts, signatures, and records guarantee the lawfulness and enforceability of digital transactions in certain jurisdictions. MLETR promotes the development of uniform standards for the formation and execution of electronic contracts. The laws known as the Electronic Transactions and Digital Agreements (ETDA) regulate the creation, execution, and enforcement of digital agreements and transactions. Digital contracts, electronic payments, electronic signatures, e-commerce, and other online commercial operations are all included in these contracts. For those engaged in digital trade, the ETDA provides legal certainty and protection by defining the rights, obligations, and liabilities related to electronic transactions.

The Uniform Rules for Digital Trade Operations (URDTT) are standardized protocols and principles designed to streamline and accelerate digital trade operations. The URDTT, which promotes interoperability and efficiency by unifying norms and practices across multiple legal systems and countries, covers a number of topics related to digital trade, including data protection, payment processing, dispute resolution, contract creation, and other areas. This makes cross-border business transactions easier and more confident for businesses.

While digital commerce rules, regulations, and practices offer numerous benefits, it is important to consider the associated disadvantages and concerns. The absence of unified international standards and legislation governing digital commerce can lead to legal ambiguities and national fragmentation, complicating cross-border transactions and raising compliance costs for businesses.

Concerns over data security and privacy are intensifying as digital transactions become more widespread, necessitating the adoption of stringent security measures to protect personal information and lower cybersecurity risks. It can be hard to figure out which laws and jurisdictions would apply to settle disputes that come up from digital trade transactions when there are multiple parties and issues that span borders. In order to protect customers' rights and interests during online transactions, digital trade must have procedures in place to handle problems like fraud, misrepresentation, and non-delivery of goods or services. Laws, regulations, and practices related to digital trade facilitate and regulate the conduct of commercial operations in the digital economy. These legal tools, which define precise legal frameworks, promote interoperability, and address emerging issues, aid in the growth and development of digital trade, fostering confidence, trust, and innovation in the global marketplace. Digital commerce stakeholders need to work together and adapt as the industry grows to ensure that legal frameworks stay up to date with technological advancements and facilitate seamless cross-border digital transactions.

Transitioning from Physical to Digital

The digitalization of commerce and trade finance is transforming the legal and regulatory environment, necessitating a reevaluation of existing frameworks to facilitate the convergence of digital technology and traditional financial processes. There are several obstacles to overcome in this transformation, particularly in terms of guaranteeing adherence to financial regulations, data protection legislation, and international trade laws. Let's examine the main ideas and changes in this changing legal landscape. Historically, the legal recognition of the possession and transfer of paper led to the reliance of trade instruments like documentary credits on physical paper exchanges.

CHAPTER 8   BITS, BYTES, AND LEGAL BITES: NAVIGATING THE DIGITAL FRONTIER OF TRADE LAW AND PRACTICE

The shift toward electronic issuance and exchange of documents necessitates a legal framework that acknowledges the validity and enforceability of digital documents and electronic signatures. Legal systems have begun to recognize the possibility of possessing electronic documents. The Electronic Trade Documents Act (ETDA) in the UK, following recommendations by the UK Law Commission, marks a significant step by putting digital trade documents on the same legal footing as their paper counterparts. This recognition allows for the legal treatment of intangible digital instruments similar to that of paper documents. This makes it easier to own and transfer them in business transactions. The MLETR represents a pivotal international initiative, providing a legal framework for the dematerialization of transferable documents and instruments. The Model Law establishes functional equivalence rules, enabling the legal recognition of transferable electronic records. This brings the idea of "possession" into the digital world.

This framework supports the seamless integration of digital documents into global trade practices. The commitment of G7 digital and technology ministers and the G20's endorsement of High-Level Principles for the Digitalisation of Trade Documents underscore the international community's resolve to harmonize legal frameworks and promote the adoption of electronic transferable records. These declarations and principles aim to foster a globally compatible legal environment that supports the digitalization of trade. Unlocking the promise of digital technology in international trade requires the legal recognition of digital trade papers and the effort for international harmonization of legal frameworks. These advancements promise to increase trade processes' efficiency, security, and accessibility by facilitating the use of electronic transferable records. This will decrease transaction times and costs while enhancing transparency. We are taking proactive steps to facilitate the digital transition, as evidenced by the ICC Digital Standards Initiative (DSI) tracker and ongoing global efforts to implement MLETR and similar frameworks.

These initiatives serve as guides for countries and trade participants, encouraging the adoption of compatible legal frameworks that support digital trade. The legal framework around the digitalization of international trade and trade finance is changing dramatically. Legal and regulatory frameworks need to adapt to accommodate digital papers and electronic signatures in the future of trade. Data privacy, interoperability, and compliance are issues that the commerce sector may solve through international cooperation and the creation of standardized legal standards. These initiatives, by fully utilizing digital technology, pave the way for a trading ecosystem that is more effective, safe, and internationally integrated.

CHAPTER 8   BITS, BYTES, AND LEGAL BITES: NAVIGATING THE DIGITAL FRONTIER OF TRADE LAW AND PRACTICE

Empowering Global Trade Through Digitalization

To help with the digitalization of commercial paperwork, the United Nations Commission on International Commercial Law (UNCITRAL) developed the UNCITRAL Model Law on Electronic Transferable Records (MLETR). Its main goal is to create a solid legal framework that is in line with national laws and current conventions on documents and instruments that can be transferred, but is not dependent on technology. This will make it easier to use electronic records both within and across borders. Below is a comprehensive summary of its key attributes:

The United Nations Commission on International Trade Law (UNCITRAL) created the UNCITRAL Model Law on Electronic Transferable Records (MLETR) to aid in the digitization of trade paperwork. The primary objective of the UNCITRAL Model Law on Electronic Transferable Records (MLETR) is to establish a technology-independent legal framework that aligns with national laws and existing conventions on transferable documents and instruments. This will streamline the use of electronic records, facilitating their transfer across borders and within countries. Here is a thorough rundown of its salient characteristics:

With MLETR, you can now replace promissory notes, bills of lading, and other paper-based documents with electronic records as long as they adhere to strict reliability, integrity, and identification standards. Since it does not mandate any specific technology, the law aims to be technologically neutral, allowing for future technological improvements and flexibility. It aims to offer a uniform legal framework, reduce obstacles to global trade, and increase the efficiency of electronic business.

It outlines the criteria for deeming electronic transferable records to be functionally equal to conventional paper documents and explains what exactly qualifies as such.

Instead of using the term "possession" to refer to the physical ownership of a document, the concept of "control" describes how control can be proven to grant holders rights or interests.

The model law clarifies the potential outcomes of digitally signing and sending records. The model law ensures that the procedures are identical to those for paper documents, but tailored for digital environments. The model law also defines criteria for the upkeep and protection of electronic transferable records, along with standards to ensure their dependability and integrity. In order to facilitate cross-border transactions, MLETR urges nations to recognize electronic transferable records created under international laws that are essentially identical.

By providing a uniform legal framework, MLETR helps to reduce legal uncertainty and diversity in nations' legislation dealing with electronic records.

Using electronic transferable documents can significantly improve trade transaction efficiency while lowering costs, boosting security, and promoting openness. The technologically neutral stance encourages the use of cutting-edge technologies in trade finance, such as blockchain and distributed ledger technology (DLT).

For the model law to be effective, each state must adopt it into its own national laws. This could mean adopting something straight away or changing it to comply with current laws. Successful implementation requires the participation of all stakeholders, including governments, legal and commercial parties, and technology vendors, to ensure that the law meets the practical needs of commerce and finance.

The UNCITRAL Model Law on Electronic Transferable Records is a significant step toward the modernization of trade finance and the broader application of digital trade practices. Its goal is to increase trust in electronic transactions and make the move to digital commerce easier by making sure that records that can be sent digitally are just as reliable and safe as records that are kept on paper.

The Imperative of Digital Transformation in the Legal Sector

Digital transformation is no longer a choice in the quickly changing world of today, especially in the legal industry. The desire to remain competitive, raise efficiency, and provide better customer service is what motivates this need. The integration of digital technology into all aspects of operations characterizes the legal sector's revolution, radically altering the production of value and provision of services.

The legal industry is undergoing a multifaceted digital change. Automation of regular chores is one important component. Machine learning and artificial intelligence (AI), for example, may greatly expedite data analysis and document review procedures. AI may help legal practitioners organize and analyze documents more quickly, which will boost output and lower human error.

Blockchain technology deployment also provides unmatched legal transaction security and transparency. Blockchain can offer a transaction recorder that is impenetrable, which is very helpful for contract administration and legal document validation. This technology not only ensures that all parties involved have access to the same, unaltered documents, but also improves sensitive information security.

Digitalization also demands that law companies evolve culturally. Using digital tools and platforms calls for a flexible and always-learning attitude. To fully enjoy the advantages of the digital revolution, legal practitioners need to be prepared to adjust to new technology and approaches. This cultural change is crucial for the development of an environment where digital technologies can successfully integrate into daily activities.

Selecting between developing bespoke internal solutions and using outside platforms is one of the biggest obstacles on this digital path. Building bespoke solutions provides flexibility and control, enabling businesses to customize features to their particular requirements, as the trade finance industry has shown. This strategy, however, requires a significant investment of money and knowledge, which not many companies can afford. Purchasing current platforms, however, can speed up the use of digital technologies and give access to certain skills and information. Combining parts of both tactics, this hybrid strategy may frequently offer the best of both worlds, allowing businesses to personalize their solutions while taking advantage of the scale and experience of outside platforms.

For instance, the utilization of platforms like RIVO by Surecomp, which connects with current internal systems, shows how businesses may improve their digital capabilities without making a large initial outlay for new technology. By allowing businesses to progressively increase their online presence and adjust to changing market demands, such platforms reduce the risks involved with making significant upfront expenditures in untested technology.

The digital revolution has brought about amazing gains in productivity and service delivery in the public sector. For example, the Internal Revenue Service (IRS) of the United States used artificial intelligence (AI) and process automation to solve the problems caused by outdated technology and a scarcity of employees. The IRS greatly shortened processing times and enhanced customer service by transferring typical notices online and automating the paper return scanning process. This shift highlights the ability of digital technology to improve service delivery efficacy and efficiency, even in customarily bureaucratic and slow-moving settings.

Keeping competitiveness in a fast-changing environment, expanding client services, and increasing operational efficiency all depend on the legal industry going digital. Legal companies may negotiate the challenges of digital transformation and reap significant rewards by adopting a strategic strategy that strikes a balance between internal development and the acquisition of outside platforms. The experiences of other industries—for example, public administration and trade finance—offer insightful information about the prospects and problems that lay ahead. Accepting digital change will be essential to sustaining success and providing customers with better value as the legal sector develops further.

Overcoming Paper Paradigms

In the past, people used physical (paper) forms to show their rights to deliver goods or pay large amounts of money. The UNCITRAL Model Law on Electronic Transferable Records (MLETR) changes that. It solves a major problem that the modern banking and trade sectors are facing. In the modern digital age, this dependence creates a number of difficulties and inefficiencies.

Bills of lading, bills of exchange, promissory notes, warehouse receipts, checks, insurance policies, and certificates are all types of commercial documents and instruments that operate under the principle that you need a physical (usually paper) document to demand the delivery of goods or payment of money. These documents serve multiple purposes by proving the entitlement to goods or funds. Many of these contracts are negotiable, allowing other parties to acquire the rights they contain by endorsing or receiving the document itself. By having physical authority over the document, they offer security to the parties involved in a transaction.

However, in the context of international trade and banking, this reliance on paper has serious drawbacks. It takes money and time to physically transport paper documents across the globe. Physical documents are susceptible to fraud, loss, and damage. Paper documents can be difficult to track down and authenticate, which makes transactions less transparent. The paper-based method is less flexible when it comes to emerging technology that could simplify

By enabling the electronic depiction of these rights and obligations, the trend toward digitization provides a solution to these issues. But moving from a paper-based system to a digital one presents additional difficulties. Many legal systems base their foundation on the notion that these rights are associated with tangible records. Therefore, we need to legally recognize electronic documents to fulfill the same purpose. The transfer and recognition of control over an electronic record must be secure, just like the actual ownership of paper documents. To do this, mechanisms need to be in place. In order to avoid unwanted changes and verify the identity of holders, digital systems must guarantee the validity and integrity of electronic records.

By offering a legislative framework that permits the use of electronically transferable records, MLETR addresses these issues. This Model Law introduces the concept of functional equivalency, stating that electronic records can perform all the operations of their paper counterparts if they meet specific dependability and control requirements. By defining what it means to be in control of an electronic transferable record, similar to being in possession of a paper document, it ensures the safe transfer and acknowledgement of rights. The model law's technology-neutral structure lets different technologies be used while still meeting the legal requirements for authenticity, integrity, and control. MLETR helps to enable the digital transformation of trade and finance by addressing fundamental challenges such as legal recognition, interoperability, and security of electronic transferable records, aiming to boost productivity, lower risks, and enhance transparency and efficiency in global trade transactions.

Harmonizing Global Trade

The United Nations Commission on International Trade Law (UNCITRAL) developed the Model Law on Electronic Transferable Records (MLETR) in response to the rapidly evolving global trade and finance environment, exemplified by the growing need for trade document digitization, particularly electronic bills of lading (e-B/Ls). This change is a result of an effort to resolve enduring problems and inefficiencies related to conventional, paper-based methods.

For many years, e-bills of lading have been a complicated problem, illustrating the difficulties of switching from paper-based to digital systems in a world where trade habits have ingrained paper-based systems thoroughly. When people tried to digitize things in the past, they often ended up with technology-specific systems or laws that focused on a certain type of document or created a new category of electronic transferable records (ETRs). Although these methods produced temporary fixes, they also caused data silos and incompatible IT systems to proliferate, impeding efficiency and integration. Prior to MLETR, contracts, rather than the conventional law of bills of lading, frequently controlled e-B/Ls. This necessitated the development of specific contractual frameworks with limited applicability and no enforcement against third parties.

We introduce MLETR, a technology-neutral framework that supports a variety of systems like blockchain, distributed ledger technology (DLT), and registry-based systems. This strategy encourages smooth data transfers across many systems and interoperability. The foundation of the law is the idea of functional equivalency, which guarantees that electronic records receive the same treatment as their paper equivalents. This is essential for communicating with outside parties and using papers as security. MLETR supports contemporary digital features such as smart contracts, metadata, and

Oracle data. It also facilitates a change of medium, which addresses the usual issue with paper documents—maintaining document uniqueness to prevent repeated claims for the same performance. Through the integration of the principles of singularity and control, MLETR seeks to ensure the legal validity and reliability of electronic transferable records by establishing clear criteria for their creation, transfer, and management, thereby promoting trust and legal certainty in digital trade.

The adoption of MLETR enables the reengineering of business processes to put the transaction in front of the document itself. This makes it possible to combine all pertinent regulatory and commercial (transport and finance) papers into a single electronic record. A single electronic record that is authentic, full, accurate, and up-to-date guarantees data quality. This lowers the cost of compliance, improves credit availability, and allows for improved supply chain and trade finance oversight. MLETR further protects against fraud by lowering the possibility of errors and inconsistencies through the reduction of manual inputs.

MLETR is especially helpful for cross-border activities since it can greatly lower trade barriers by harmonizing legal procedures. The establishment of MLETR represents a significant step in digitizing trade paperwork to meet the needs of contemporary commerce and finance. MLETR provides a flexible, safe, and inclusive legal framework for emerging technologies, paving the way for a more cohesive, effective, and robust international trade system.

Digital Transformation Addressing Disruptions and Shaping the Future Commerce

You can digitize bills of lading, promissory notes, and other transferable records using the UNCITRAL Model Law on Electronic Transferable Records (MLETR), which serves as a framework for legalization. Trade disruptions caused by the COVID-19 pandemic have brought attention to the usefulness of MLETR and emphasized the importance of the law in the context of contemporary international trade.

MLETR promotes paperless trade by enabling the legal recognition of electronic transferable records. As a result, there is less need for direct contact and physical handling, which lowers the possibility of viral transmission among traders. MLETR's technology-neutral approach enables the implementation of blockchain technology, enhancing the traceability of an item's origins. This is especially important when it comes to guaranteeing the safety and authenticity of medical supplies and vaccinations, as provenance is crucial.

CHAPTER 8   BITS, BYTES, AND LEGAL BITES: NAVIGATING THE DIGITAL FRONTIER OF
             TRADE LAW AND PRACTICE

MLETR's digitization facilitation enables real-time tracking of supply chains for customs and logistics. This feature makes it possible to prioritize delivery of vital goods, like supply of vital medical equipment in the event of a pandemic, and to closely monitor them, allowing for a quicker reaction to urgent demands. By lowering compliance costs, MLETR adoption enhances trade financing governance. Consequently, this makes financing availability simpler, quicker, and more reasonably priced. The most vulnerable to economic downturns are small and medium-sized enterprises (SMEs), which would greatly benefit from easier access to trade finance.

MLETR offers various implementation options, allowing for its addition to existing laws or its passage as a stand-alone law. Adaptability has made it easier for different jurisdictions to adopt and consider.

A number of governments have passed UNCITRAL e-commerce texts to date, demonstrating the widespread agreement that legal structures are necessary to facilitate digital trade. Examples of specific acceptance are the Abu Dhabi Global Market, Singapore, and Bahrain. Moreover, countries like Paraguay and Kiribati have proposed legislation implementing MLETR. The ministerial declaration on April 28, 2021, demonstrates the G7+'s support for MLETR and its mention in Digital Economy Agreements.

Its actual use, particularly in response to the COVID-19 epidemic, demonstrates MLETR's crucial role in enhancing the robustness, effectiveness, and security of international trade. MLETR tackles current issues while also promoting a stronger economic recovery and a sustainable future for global trade by enabling paperless trade, enabling real-time tracking, and enhancing access to trade finance.

The UK's 2023 Leap into Paperless Trade

One of the most significant steps toward fully digital trade business activities is the UK's Electronic Trade Documents Act 2023 (ETDA). The UK enacted the ETDA in July 2023, and it came into effect on September 20 of the same year. The adoption of the ETDA represents a significant milestone in the ongoing debate about the need to modernize and streamline global trade. The ETDA legally recognizes electronic trade documents, such as bills of lading or bills of exchange, paving the way for more cost-effective, environmentally sustainable, and productive trade operations.

The UK Law Commission suggested a draft bill for the ETDA in March 2022. It fixed the problems with how UK law limited the use of electronic trade papers. Digital trade documents enjoy the same legal status, consequences, and capabilities as their paper counterparts. Given this significant modification, electronic papers are finally able to be used as legally enforceable contracts in commercial transactions

The ETDA seeks to significantly reduce costs associated with paper-based records, including printing, storage, and courier services, by encouraging the use of electronic records. We anticipate that the digitization of trade documentation will expedite transaction times, thereby enhancing the efficiency of trade.

The ETDA has substantial and wide-ranging implications for global trade. The Act establishes a standard for other countries to follow and positions the UK as a leader in innovative digital trade. We anticipate its implementation to bring about a number of notable changes to the global trade landscape.

We expect British companies to adopt digital trade practices to enhance their global competitiveness. Increasing the speed and security of transactions may also bring in additional foreign partners and provide new opportunities.

The transition to paperless trade fosters initiatives aimed at enhancing environmental sustainability. Eliminating the use of paper documents is consistent with more general efforts aimed at lowering waste and greenhouse gas emissions. The ETDA might serve as a catalyst for international initiatives to encourage more effective standardization and interoperability in digital commerce processes. Global standards are going to become increasingly important as nations come to recognize the benefits of digital trade documents as a way to ensure smooth cross-border transactions.

Despite the ETDA's significant advancement, successful implementation requires overcoming a few obstacles. These include concerns about cybersecurity, technical adaptation, and harmonizing international law. For businesses and legal professionals to effectively manage the changing world of digital trade, they will need to remain informed and flexible. The UK Electronic Trade Documents Act 2023 offers a roadmap for the future of global trade and is a significant step toward paperless trade. Long after the UK leaves, its influence on lowering transaction costs, enhancing productivity, and promoting sustainable trading practices is likely to shape international trade standards and practices for many years to come.

The UK's Electronic Trade Documents Act 2023 (ETDA) introduces a significant change in the legal environment by embracing the digitalization of trade documents without restricting them to a strict, comprehensive list. This strategic approach, which aims to adapt the dynamic nature of trade practices and the changing needs of business, demonstrates the Act's flexibility and foresight. The ETDA, by not adhering to a single list, ensures its applicability to a diverse array of trade-related documents that are legally or commercially necessary for duty performance.

These documents serve to illustrate the ETDA's scope; they list a number of significant instruments as examples of electronic trade papers, though this is by no means an exhaustive list. Among them are

- **Bills of Lading:** provide the holder with the right to claim the cargo and are necessary for the transportation of commodities.

- **Bills of exchange:** and promissory notes are financial instruments that guarantee payment of a predetermined amount to the holder or another authorized entity.

- **Policies for marine insurance:** agreements for coverage of cargo and vessels in the sea.

- **Warehouse receipts:** verifications of products kept in storage that grant the bearer permission to take out the stored goods.

- **Mates' Receipts:** these are initial cargo receipts that are subsequently traded in for a bill of lading.

- **Certificates of cargo insurance:** proof of coverage for products being transported.

- **Ship's delivery orders:** permits for the discharge and transportation of cargo by sea.

The shared characteristic allows the bearer to assert delivery of goods or payment, underscoring the significance of possession in the trade context. The ETDA's focus on these instruments shows that it wants to include documents that are essential to making trade possible and carried out. This solution aims to address the issue of electronic documents not being physically present in traditional legal systems.

The ETDA redefines what it means to "possess" an electronic document, which is a conceptual leap. English law has always only acknowledged material possessions, which has posed a major obstacle to the digitization of trade records. In order to address this, the ETDA creates a legal framework that recognizes the ownership of electronic documents that are intangible and converts them into assets with the same legal standing as their physical equivalents.

This evolution is essential for the digital age because it shows how legal systems must change to meet the reality of contemporary business. The ETDA enhances international trade efficiency and accessibility by enabling faster, smoother, and more affordable transactions through the "possession" of electronic trade documents.

This novel and inclusive method of addressing trade documentation guarantees that the Act will be applicable and flexible enough to accommodate new advancements in commerce and technology in the future. The ETDA represents a major advancement in the legal recognition of electronic documents by emphasizing the role and importance of possession in trade transactions. This lays a strong foundation for the global digitization of trade activities.

The groundbreaking redefining of "electronic trade documents" brought about by the Electronic Trade Documents Act (ETDA) has established a new standard for digital commerce. The documents must be put into a system that meets basic standards for authenticity, integrity, and functionality before they can be put into this new category. The ETDA pioneers a legal framework for the digital age by creating this new category, which aligns the legal status of electronic trade papers with that of their old paper equivalents.

This conversion essentially closes the gap between digital documentation and physical assets by enabling legitimate owners of electronic trade documents to assume constructive possession of the products listed in these documents. Furthermore, it empowers them to confidently demand the fulfillment of the duties associated with these items, thereby simplifying and enhancing the productivity of trade transactions. By acknowledging the critical role that digital technology plays in contemporary commerce and establishing a precedent for legal systems across the globe, the ETDA's creative approach to digital documents marks a significant advancement in the evolution of trade.

Digital Trust Unlocked

The UK's Electronic Trade Documents Act (ETDA) has established a crucial framework for the identification and management of electronic trade papers in the rapidly evolving field of digital commerce. The idea of "minimum system standards," which is a set of requirements that systems must fulfill in order to be considered dependable for the generation, storage, and transfer of electronic trade documents, is fundamental to this framework. These requirements are necessary to make sure that electronic trade documents are valid, unique, and honest, just like their paper counterparts are trusted to be.

The basis of the digital commerce environment is a "reliable system," according to the ETDA. It guarantees parties the security and legitimacy of their transactions, in addition to facilitating the legitimate development and sharing of electronic trade papers. The ETDA accepts a system as reliable only if it meets a number of essential requirements:

- **Equivalency with papers:** To preserve the legal and functional integrity of electronic trade papers, the system must guarantee that they contain all the information found in their paper counterparts.

- **Distinguishability and uniqueness:** To prevent fraud and duplication, the system must be able to tell original documents apart from duplicates.

- **Protection against unauthorized alteration:** The system must secure documents from any unauthorized changes, preserving the document's authenticity and the transaction's integrity.

- **Exclusive control:** To simulate the physical possession of a paper document, the system must restrict access in such a way that only one person can exercise control over the document at any time.

- **Accessibility and control:** The document must be accessible and straightforward for the party in charge to demonstrate control.

- **Total divestment upon transfer:** The system must make sure that, upon transferring a document, the transferee is granted complete control, totally relieving the transferor of any control over the document.

The ETDA purposely chose not to prescribe any particular methods or technology in order to future-proof the law. It makes sure it will still be useful in a world where digital technologies are growing quickly by focusing on the functional needs of systems rather than specific technological solutions. This strategy promotes creativity and adaptability, enabling the adoption of cutting-edge technology that can either meet or exceed the established criteria.

Its open-minded view on technology makes the creation and implementation of industry-accepted standards crucial. These standards will aid in the widespread use of electronic trade documents by providing platform providers and players with a crucial level of market certainty. Trade associations are expected to play a crucial role in steering these efforts and ensuring that the standards remain innovative, secure, and embody the best practices for digital trade documentation.

The minimal system standards set forth by the ETDA are a major advancement in the digital trade documentation process. It not only expedites and secures digital trade transactions but also lays the groundwork for a future where the requirement for physical documents will no longer constrain digital trade. We achieve this by establishing a robust foundation for the reliability of systems managing electronic trade documents. This chapter seeks to provide a guide for navigating the ETDA-shaped digital trade landscape by demystifying the guiding ideas behind these standards.

Digital Vaults Unsealed

Digital trade has advanced significantly with the passage of the Electronic Trade Documents Act (ETDA), particularly in terms of funding and security. By enabling the electronic custody and transfer of trade papers through a "reliable" mechanism, the ETDA ushers in a new era where electronic trade documents can successfully serve as security in financial transactions. This development is crucial because it expands the ways in which firms can use digital documents to get trade finance while also improving their acceptability and functionality.

Pledges and liens, two common possessory security mechanisms, have always been essentially dependent on the physical handling and transfer of documents. The ETDA's recognition of electronic documents as claimable instruments fundamentally transforms the existing framework. This digital twist enables the use of these documents within the existing security frameworks for trade and commodity financing. The shift to digital papers has expanded financing options due to their unparalleled speed and efficiency in managing and exchanging security.

The transition to digital possessory security arrangements calls for a major modification of market activities. Due diligence procedures will need to be expanded to include more information about how the "reliable" systems that handle these electronic documents work and how they use technology. Traditionally, due diligence procedures have concentrated on physical papers and the companies managing them. This entails being aware of the operational guidelines, system rules, and how to handle any potential technical issues. Moreover, it becomes crucial to take into account the system providers' own financial stability and insolvency concerns.

Businesses and financiers must take into account a number of intricate factors when integrating electronic trade papers into security and financing frameworks. Careful navigation is necessary due to the complexity of digital transfers, the legal frameworks controlling digital holdings, and the existence of security interests. The law must accept electronic trade documents as legitimate security instruments, and adapt financing procedures and security interest completion procedures to these digital dimensions.

CHAPTER 8   BITS, BYTES, AND LEGAL BITES: NAVIGATING THE DIGITAL FRONTIER OF
            TRADE LAW AND PRACTICE

The ETDA's rules pertaining to electronic trade papers signify a revolutionary change in the perspective on trade security and financing. By allowing these documents to serve as effective security, the ETDA paves the way for more easily accessible, effective, and secure trade financing options. But these advantages also bring with them the difficulties of adjusting to a digital trading environment, necessitating a deep comprehension of the new digital dynamics at work from all market players. The procedures pertaining to digital possession security will surely become essential components of contemporary trade finance as the business develops, changing the environment in ways that we are now learning about.

From Parchment to Pixels: The Art of Digital Possession and Transformation

Without providing a clear definition of possession, the Electronic Trade Documents Act (ETDA) provides a complex approach to the subject, basing its ideas on common law. This decision is meant to keep the current legal frameworks working well by making sure that possession is still based on actual control and the intention to possess. This strategy preserves the applicability of prior case law while giving judges the latitude to handle the nuances of digital ownership on a case-by-case basis.

The ETDA wisely chooses inclusion and flexibility in an era of rapid technological advancement. It does not make the current methods of using electronic documents in business operations obsolete. It instead recognizes the wide range of practices that exist in the business world and lets people keep using electronic documents in ways that are in line with their common goals or established norms, even if these methods don't strictly adhere to the ETDA's newly defined "electronic trade document" standards.

The ETDA's ability to facilitate smooth trade document migrations between digital and paper formats is one of its most notable features. This adaptability is a crucial feature that aims to mitigate potential risks associated with solely relying on digital or physical media, rather than merely catering to practicality. The ETDA enforces strict rules on the conversion process to ensure the accuracy and tracking of trade documents across all media. For instance, the converted documents must explicitly declare their original format and adhere to any applicable legal or contractual requirements.

By addressing real-world issues with single points of failure in digital systems and supply chains, such a clause improves resilience. Additionally, it greatly enhances cross-border interoperability by recognizing the various levels of preparedness and legal frameworks for digital documentation around the globe. The ETDA guarantees that merchants can easily traverse international waterways and exercise their rights in jurisdictions that are less accustomed to or accepting of digital trade documents by allowing documents to revert to paper form.

This careful consideration of the differences between digital and paper trade documents shows a desire to support a smooth transition to digital trade practices while respecting the variety and history of current systems. The ETDA preserves flexibility while promoting innovation by fusing the old and the new, allowing trade to go freely through both traditional and digital channels. With its skillful balance of respecting tradition and looking to the future, this legislation navigates the intricacies of possession and conversion, marking a significant step forward in the digital transformation of trade.

Digital Diplomacy and the Legal Ledger

Within a larger, ongoing effort to harmonize and update the legal frameworks facilitating international trade, the Electronic Trade Documents Act (ETDA) represents a significant step forward. Building on the goals of the 2008 Rotterdam Rules to standardize international liability standards for the maritime transport of goods, this initiative is in line with the 2017 United Nations Commission on International Trade Law (UNCITRAL) Model Law on Electronic Transferable Records (MLETR). Despite being unique to English law, the ETDA represents a significant step toward the progressive globalization of the law, establishing a standard that extends beyond the borders of the 54 Commonwealth countries and any contract subject to English law. English law documents facilitate a significant amount of international trade, which in turn significantly impacts the ETDA on a global scale.

Different countries have responded to electronic trade documentation with varying expectations. Some have fully embraced the MLETR, like Singapore's Electronic Transactions (Amendment) Act 2021, which established the idea of control as a digital equivalent of physical possession, while others have taken a more cautious approach. It's noteworthy to note that China, South Korea, and Japan have not ratified the MLETR; instead, they have adopted unique legislative provisions that outline the requirements for document possession and the processes for rights or entitlement transfers.

The formulation of the ETDA aims to accommodate unique characteristics of English law while complementing the MLETR. As more countries look into fully or partially incorporating the MLETR, there may be more differences between the model law and national laws like the ETDA. This situation emphasizes the need for more legal harmonization, which is an objective that the Digital Economy Agreements (DEAs) are actively pursuing. These agreements create the foundation for a single, worldwide digital trade ecosystem by offering a framework for bilateral and mutual recognition between countries like Singapore and the UK. The creation of such an ecosystem holds the potential to simplify operations for logistics companies, platforms, financiers, insurers, and other key players in global trade.

The push for a more digitally seamless and networked global commercial environment emphasizes how important it is that legal frameworks keep up with technology development. This development promotes a more unified environment for global trade while also making transactions easier.

Sailing Uncharted Waters

One of the most important pieces of legislation supporting the better integration and adoption of digital platforms in the trade finance industry is the Electronic Trade Documents Act (ETDA). It has given blockchain research for trade finance fresh life by acknowledging distributed ledger technology (DLT) and blockchain-based systems as potentially "reliable" technologies under its framework. This excitement makes sense given that trade finance, which relies on quick and secure transactions, closely matches the requirements of blockchain's core features—immutability, security, and transparency.

Trade finance might undergo a transformation thanks to blockchain technology, which could provide faster and safer handles than current ones. Blockchain's immutability, which renders transactions unalterable once stored, significantly reduces fraud. Furthermore, the decentralized nature of blockchain technology allows all parties involved in a transaction to access the same information in real time, thereby enhancing efficiency and transparency.

However, a range of obstacles hinder the widespread adoption of blockchain-based trade finance solutions. A key obstacle is getting enough industry support; Maersk and IBM's TradeLens platform serves as an example. The cancellation of TradeLens, which aimed to digitize the entire global supply chain, occurred due to the lack of "full global industry collaboration." This draws attention to a key obstacle facing blockchain projects in trade finance: gaining enough support and involvement from the sector as a whole to ensure the platform's viability and efficacy on a worldwide basis.

CHAPTER 8 BITS, BYTES, AND LEGAL BITES: NAVIGATING THE DIGITAL FRONTIER OF TRADE LAW AND PRACTICE

The legal recognition by the ETDA of blockchain-based systems as dependable trade document platforms may act as a spur to address these issues. The ETDA may promote DLT's usage in trade finance by offering a framework for law that recognizes the legitimacy and enforceability of blockchain transactions. This legal support is an important first step in gaining the trust of companies, authorities, and financial institutions in blockchain-based solutions, which could result in more industry cooperation and adoption.

With the ETDA's backing, the future of blockchain in trade finance appears promising, contingent on the ability of DLT projects to foster widespread industry collaboration and backing. The ETDA's framework could speed up the use of blockchain platforms, but only if these platforms keep improving and show how useful they are for making trade finance transactions safer, more efficient, and more open. The industry's collective willingness to accept these creative solutions and collaborate toward a digitalized, interconnected global trade ecosystem is the key to realizing blockchain's full potential in trade finance.

A major step forward in the digital revolution of trade finance is the ETDA's support of blockchain as a dependable system for electronic trade documentation. While the sector struggles with adoption and cooperation, the ETDA provides a legislative framework that could pave the way for a new era of blockchain-enabled trade financing. To fully achieve the immense promise of blockchain in changing trade finance, the road ahead will require both technological innovation and the promotion of international industrial collaboration.

The need to bring electronic commerce operations into compliance with legal norms, previously limited to paper documents, led to this shift. The Electronic Trade Papers Act (ETDA) and related legislative initiatives around the world mark a major advancement in the legal acknowledgement and parity of electronic and paper-based trade papers.

Before laws like the ETDA were made official, platforms like Bolero and essDocs (now ICE Digital Trade) were some of the first to use platform-specific contract frameworks. The creation of these frameworks addressed the lack of a legal foundation for electronic trade documents. Even if there weren't any laws that allowed it, parties could still trade electronically as long as they agreed that ownership and transfer of electronic documents had the same legal weight as paper documents.

We anticipate that electronic trade platforms will update their terms and conditions to incorporate the new legal realities introduced by the ETDA and related legislation. Numerous platforms have demonstrated their commitment to operational and legal efficiency in electronic trade by taking the lead in campaigning for legal reform. This shift is not without difficulties, though.

CHAPTER 8 BITS, BYTES, AND LEGAL BITES: NAVIGATING THE DIGITAL FRONTIER OF
            TRADE LAW AND PRACTICE

Legal and compliance teams are having a hard time at the start because platform-specific contracts and new laws like the ETDA are trying to work together. Due to this dual framework, it's critical to ensure that electronic commerce operations follow the law and make operational sense by having a solid understanding of both contractual obligations and legislative requirements.

We anticipate that additional countries will adopt the Model Law on Electronic Transferable Records (MLETR), which will facilitate a more broad transition from contractual to statutory frameworks. This change will improve the operational dependability and legal stability of electronic trade documents. However, this shift also requires significant changes in industry standards, particularly in the legal documentation of electronic trading instruments. For instance, we must customize electronic bills of lading to comply with national legal frameworks like the ETDA, necessitating separate jurisdiction and governing law terms from associated agreements such as charter party contracts.

It is expected that more nations will adopt the Model Law on Electronic Transferable Records (MLETR), which will enable a more widespread shift from contractual to statutory frameworks. This change will improve the operational dependability and legal stability of electronic trade documents. However, this shift also requires significant changes in industry standards, particularly in the legal documentation of electronic trading instruments. For instance, we must customize electronic bills of lading to comply with national legal frameworks like the ETDA, necessitating separate jurisdiction and governing law terms from associated agreements such as charter party contracts.

The URDTT Playbook Unlocking Digital Frontiers

With the Fourth International Chamber of Commerce Congress in 1927, more than a century ago, there is a rich historical background to the quest for unified regulations governing trade transactions. This congress initially explored the concept of standardizing export commercial credits, indicating a growing understanding of the necessity of uniform international trade practices. Wilbert Ward's comments at the time laid the groundwork for future improvements in international trade regulations, emphasizing the useful service the ICC might serve to international trade through such standardization initiatives.

In the contemporary era, the International Chamber of Commerce (ICC) persists in its objective of formulating and disseminating worldwide trade regulations that benefit the global trading community. But things have changed drastically, especially when it comes to digitalization. A reassessment of conventional paper-based procedures has become necessary due to the growing issues presented by the digitalization of trade finance.

The COVID-19 epidemic, which emphasizes how urgent it is to adopt digital solutions in trade transactions, has prompted this reevaluation. With the globe still adjusting to the pandemic's aftermath, digital technology has become an indispensable instrument for improving things and revolutionizing the economy. The G7 meeting in 2021 emphasized how crucial digital technology is to promoting economic recovery and enhancing online security.

The G7 recognized increased use of electronic transferable records in commercial transactions, including bills of lading, as one of the major interventions. Bills of lading are currently only partially electronic, which is a major missed opportunity to streamline trade procedures. The use of electronic transferable records could facilitate quicker, less expensive, and easier trade operations.

In response to these potential and challenges, the ICC UK established the Centre for Digital Trade and Innovation (C4DTI). The goal of this global initiative is to accelerate the digitization of commerce and establish transparent systems based on internationally accepted norms. C4DTI seeks to bring global trade law into the 21st century by promoting cooperation and innovation in order to develop a paperless, sustainable, and secure digital trade system.

The process of establishing a single set of regulations for commercial transactions is evidence of the continuous change in the nature of international trade. We have the chance to improve trade practices and ensure a more effective, sustainable, and equitable global trading system for future generations as we embrace innovation and digitalization.

A Shift Toward Digital and Inclusive Practices

The Uniform Rules for Digital Commerce Activities (URDTT), a noteworthy development in the area of international commerce, point to a shift in the direction of standardizing and digitizing trade operations. The URDTT is still in its infancy, having only taken effect on October 1, 2021, but it has the power to drastically alter international trading practices.

The Drafting Group specifically tasked itself with creating a high-level framework that outlined duties, regulations, and standards for the digitization of trade transactions, leading to a meticulous drafting process for the URDTT. This framework offers the foundation for maintaining consistency and clarity in digital commerce procedures.

CHAPTER 8   BITS, BYTES, AND LEGAL BITES: NAVIGATING THE DIGITAL FRONTIER OF
            TRADE LAW AND PRACTICE

In addition to the original drafting, we have developed a commercialization sub-stream to further investigate the URDTT and the ICC eRules (eUCP/eURC). The goal of this sub-stream is to evaluate the potential and challenges associated with commercializing and implementing these regulations, with plans to publish a detailed plan and suggestions in 2022.

Users can now implement the URDTT with the help of an implementation guide that offers helpful insights into several facets of digital trade transactions. This guide covers important topics such as the buyer–seller contract, legal issues, technology needs, and the use and review of electronic data. To further optimize the advantages of the URDTT, a special section on operational issues emphasizes the significance of comprehending and resolving real-world obstacles.

It's important to remember that the URDTT fully follows UNCITRAL Model Laws, especially the Model Law on Electronic Transferable Records (MLETR). This connection highlights the URDTT's worldwide relevance and application, particularly in light of initiatives like the G7's emphasis on trade digitization.

The URDTT places a strong emphasis on digital transactions exclusively, highlighting the shift away from paper-based procedures. This digital-centric approach reflects the modernization of trade procedures and the growing reliance on digital technologies in international trade.

It is important to note that the URDTT is based on a buyer–seller agreement rather than being exclusively bank-centric, acknowledging the changing financial services provider market that extends beyond traditional banks. This inclusiveness is a reflection of a progressive mindset that recognizes the wide range of stakeholders engaged in trade deals.

The debut of the URDTT marks a significant milestone in the evolution of global trade, providing opportunities for enhanced effectiveness, transparency, and security in digital trade transactions. Organizations and governments have the chance to spur innovation and open up new avenues for commerce when they adopt these regulations.

Decoding the Secrets of Digital Trade Transactions

A digital trade transaction (DTT) serves as a digital representation of the underlying business contract between the supplier and the buyer, encapsulating the method of recording and advancing transaction terms. It's crucial to remember that a DTT serves as a digital record of the terms and developments of the transaction and is separate from the actual commercial contract.

CHAPTER 8   BITS, BYTES, AND LEGAL BITES: NAVIGATING THE DIGITAL FRONTIER OF TRADE LAW AND PRACTICE

For a transaction to fall under its protection, it must explicitly state that it complies with the Uniform Rules for Digital Trade Transactions (URDTT) and accurately reflects the terms laid out in the business contract. To make the examination process easier, the DTT also has to outline the standards for evaluating compliance with electronic records.

The URDTT's emphasis on digital environments is essential since it makes it possible for participants to easily submit and exchange information online. The regulations improve efficiency for all parties involved by streamlining transaction processes and only functioning inside a digital framework.

Similar to all other International Chamber of Commerce (ICC) regulations, the URDTT upholds impartiality and independence while offering a uniform lexicon. This standardized method makes it easier to use electronic records and reduces duplication across several rulebooks.

Moreover, URDTT's association with the 'Framework for G7 Partnership on Electronic Transferable Records' highlights its dedication to advocating for legislative frameworks that are in harmony with the UNCITRAL Model Law on Electronic Transferable Records (MLETR). This alignment promotes the adoption of digital techniques in trade transactions as well as international collaboration.

One significant development made possible by the URDTT is the possibility of possessing digital Negotiable instruments, which eliminates earlier possession-related obstacles. The Unified Retail Distribution Technology (URDTT) has the potential to transform trade interactions in the digital era by adopting digitalization and complying with new legal frameworks.

The Uniform Rules for Digital Trade Transactions, or URDTT, are a significant advancement. With the adoption of these regulations, the International Chamber of Commerce takes a bold step forward in creating detailed standards for fully digital commerce transactions enabled by Internet protocols. This part takes you on an exploration of the URDTT's nuances, breaking down and evaluating its articles to find the tenets, procedures, and guidelines that support digital trade in the globally interconnected world of today.

In an era where digitization has swept through numerous industries, URDTT design adapts to the evolving nature of solely online trade transactions. By embracing the digital world, these regulations provide access to more simplified, effective, and efficient procedures for all parties involved in international trade. Given the variety of technologies and messaging standards that are prevalent in today's digital world, the URDTT maintains its neutrality. Due to their neutrality, the rules ensure adaptability and compatibility with a variety of messaging protocols and technological platforms.

CHAPTER 8   BITS, BYTES, AND LEGAL BITES: NAVIGATING THE DIGITAL FRONTIER OF TRADE LAW AND PRACTICE

The Uniform Rules for Digital Commerce Activities (URDTT), a noteworthy development in the area of international commerce, point to a shift in the direction of standardizing and digitizing trade operations. The URDTT is still in its infancy, having only taken effect on October 1, 2021, but it has the power to drastically alter international trading practices.

The Drafting Group specifically tasked itself with creating a high-level framework that outlined duties, regulations, and standards for the digitization of trade transactions, leading to a meticulous drafting process for the URDTT. This framework offers the foundation for maintaining consistency and clarity in digital commerce procedures.

In addition to the original drafting, we have developed the IA Commercialization sub-stream to further investigate the URDTT and the ICC eRules (eUCP/eURC). The goal of this sub-stream is to evaluate the potential and challenges associated with commercializing and implementing these regulations, with plans to publish a detailed plan and suggestions in 2022.

Users can now implement the URDTT with the help of an implementation guide that offers helpful insights into several facets of digital trade transactions. This guide covers important topics such as the buyer–seller contract, legal issues, technology needs, and the use and review of electronic data. To further optimize the advantages of the URDTT, a special section on operational issues emphasizes the significance of comprehending and resolving real-world obstacles.

It's important to remember that the URDTT fully follows UNCITRAL Model Laws, especially the Model Law on Electronic Transferable Records (MLETR). This connection highlights the URDTT's worldwide relevance and application, particularly in light of initiatives like the G7's emphasis on trade digitization.

The URDTT places a strong emphasis on digital transactions exclusively, highlighting the shift away from paper-based procedures. This digital-centric approach reflects the modernization of trade procedures and the growing reliance on digital technologies in international trade.

It is important to note that the URDTT is based on the buyer/seller agreement rather than being exclusively bank-centric, acknowledging the changing financial services provider market that extends beyond traditional banks. This inclusiveness is a reflection of a progressive mindset that recognizes the wide range of stakeholders engaged in trade deals.

The debut of the URDTT marks a significant milestone in the evolution of global trade, providing opportunities for enhanced effectiveness, transparency, and security in digital trade transactions. Organizations and governments that adopt these regulations stand to gain fresh insights and spur innovation in the field of international trade.

CHAPTER 8 BITS, BYTES, AND LEGAL BITES: NAVIGATING THE DIGITAL FRONTIER OF TRADE LAW AND PRACTICE

The digital trade transaction (DTT) represents the underlying commercial contract between the seller and the buyer digitally, encapsulating the process of documenting and progressing transaction terms. It's important to note that a DTT is distinct from the commercial contract itself, functioning as a digital record of the transaction's terms and progress.

For a transaction to fall under the purview of the Uniform Rules for Digital Trade Transactions (URDTT), it must explicitly state its adherence to these rules and accurately reflect the terms outlined in the commercial contract. Additionally, the DTT must specify the criteria for assessing compliance with electronic records, facilitating the examination process.

Central to the URDTT is its focus on digital environments, enabling participants to seamlessly submit and exchange information digitally. By operating solely within a digital framework, the rules streamline transaction processes and enhance efficiency for all involved parties.

As with all International Chamber of Commerce (ICC) rules, the URDTT maintains independence and neutrality, providing a standardized understanding of terms and definitions. This standardized approach minimizes redundancy across different rulebooks while facilitating the utilization of electronic records.

The fact that URDTT is in line with the "Framework for G7 Collaboration on Electronic Transferable Records" also shows that it is dedicated to promoting legal frameworks that are compatible with the UNCITRAL Model Law on Electronic Transferable Records (MLETR). This alignment not only facilitates international collaboration but also fosters the adoption of digital practices in trade transactions.

A key advancement facilitated by the URDTT is the potential for possession of Digital Negotiable Instruments, overcoming previous challenges associated with possession. By embracing digitalization and aligning with emerging legal frameworks, the URDTT stands poised to revolutionize trade transactions in the digital age.

Exploring the Articles of URDTT for Seamless Digital Trade

Uniform Rules for Digital Trade Transactions (URDTT) represent a monumental leap forward. These rules mark the International Chamber of Commerce's inaugural foray into establishing comprehensive guidelines for entirely digital trade transactions facilitated through Internet protocols. In this section, you embark on a journey to

CHAPTER 8 BITS, BYTES, AND LEGAL BITES: NAVIGATING THE DIGITAL FRONTIER OF TRADE LAW AND PRACTICE

delve into the intricacies of the URDTT, dissecting and analyzing its articles to uncover the principles, mechanisms, and standards that underpin digital trade in today's interconnected world.

The URDTT is made to meet the changing needs of trade transactions that are carried out totally online at a time when digitalization has permeated all industries. By embracing the digital world, these regulations provide more accessible, efficient, and streamlined procedures for all parties involved in international trade. They uphold neutrality in recognition of the wide range of technologies and messaging standards that are common in today's digital environment. The regulations guarantee flexibility and compatibility with a variety of message protocols and technology platforms due to their neutrality. The URDTT promotes inclusion and interoperability by rejecting bias toward particular technologies, creating an atmosphere that is favorable for seamless digital

Traditionally, trade transactions have been associated with financial organizations and banks. However, the breadth of trade transactions has grown beyond conventional bounds with the rise of non-bank suppliers of financial services and the growing digitization of company operations. By expanding into the corporate sphere, covering business transactions, and accounting for the diverse ecosystem of financial service providers, the framework aims to enhance transparency, efficiency, and accessibility across the entire financial landscape. This all-inclusive strategy is a reflection of the ICC's dedication to promoting innovation and easing trade between various entities and sectors.

The URDTT presents a progressive strategy that aims to leverage digitization's potential to revolutionize trade interactions. We will learn about the concepts and methods underlying these revolutionary norms as we go deeper into the URDTT articles, providing insight into their implications for the future of international trade.

Let's now set out to explore the nuances of the URDTT, breaking down and examining its articles to discover the tenets, workings, and norms that support digital trade in the globalized world of today.

The scope of Version 1.0 of the Uniform Rules for Digital Trade Transactions (URDTT)

Article 1 lays out the parameters for these regulations' application and scope, laying the groundwork for their use in digital trade transactions (DTTs).

The URDTT establishes a comprehensive framework that is applicable to all parties or individuals participating in a DTT. Because of their inclusivity, the rules apply to all parties involved in digital trade transactions, regardless of their specific roles or positions

CHAPTER 8   BITS, BYTES, AND LEGAL BITES: NAVIGATING THE DIGITAL FRONTIER OF TRADE LAW AND PRACTICE

within the transaction process. The URDTT aims to promote consistency and coherence in DTTs by standardizing methods and procedures throughout the digital commerce landscape by offering a uniform framework.

The URDTT establishes a comprehensive framework that is applicable to all parties or individuals participating in a DTT. This definition emphasizes the significance of electronic records in enabling and recording economic transactions in the digital sphere. It applies to all parties involved in digital trade transactions, regardless of their specific roles or positions within the transaction process.

The URDTT outlines the circumstances in which these regulations apply to DTTs. Specifically, for these regulations to apply, a DTT's terms and conditions must explicitly indicate that the URDTT governs it. This clause guarantees the parties' autonomy in deciding whether the URDTT applies to them in accordance with their choices and contractual agreements. Article 1, which highlights the need for clear agreement, encourages openness and precision in the URDTT's application to DTTs.

Article 1 emphasizes how the terms of the URDTT are binding on each party or participant in a DTT. This legally binding character highlights the rules' enforceability and each party's need to abide by the established terms. The URDTT creates a legally binding framework that promotes confidence and trust in digital trade transactions and creates an atmosphere that is favorable for their smooth execution and dispute resolution.

Lastly, it sets the basic principles of being inclusive, being clear, and being enforceable for how these rules will be put into place and enforced in digital trade activities. We shall learn more specifics and nuanced aspects of the URDTT as we read through the upcoming articles, clarifying their influence on the development of digital trade.

The Uniform Rules for Digital Trade Transactions (URDTT) Version 1.0's **Article 2** offers a thorough list of definitions that are necessary to comprehend the terms and ideas utilized inside the rules' framework. The addressee is the party or person to whom the submitter sends or authorizes access to an electronic record. This definition makes it clear who receives electronic records in digital commerce transactions and outlines their function in information sharing and communication.

The beneficiary is the seller or any other person or entity that has, in whole or in part, received the rights and advantages of a payment obligation as a transferee. This concept emphasizes the transferability of payment responsibilities in digital transactions and clarifies who is eligible to receive payments. A business day is any day that an organization or person is consistently in operation. In the context of digital trade, this concept specifies the typical time limit for carrying out commercial operations and processing transactions.

In a transaction, the buyer acts as the **buyer** of products or services. In digital trade transactions, this concept designates the party who is in charge of making purchases of products or services and fulfilling payment obligations. Data corruption refers to any loss or alteration of data. This concept emphasizes the significance of protecting digital information in commercial operations while also acknowledging the possible hazards related to data integrity.

An electronic record includes all data created, generated, sent, communicated, received, or saved via electronic means. This broad definition highlights the electronic character of trade interactions by encompassing a variety of digital information exchange formats. An electronic signature designates a data procedure that identifies a party or person. This definition acknowledges the significance of electronic signatures in the procedures of authentication and verification in digital trade transactions.

We refer to a financial institution or any other entity involved in trade transactions, other than the major party, as a financial services provider. This concept includes organizations that support financial services and transactions in the context of digital trade. A payment obligation is an unchangeable commitment by the buyer to pay the beneficiary as soon as possible after receipt or at a later time. This definition highlights the fundamental financial duty that underpins digital commerce transactions and highlights how binding it is.

In trade transactions, the **principal party** is either the buyer or the seller. This term identifies the principal parties involved in business transactions within the context of digital trade. In a transaction, the **seller** stands in for the person in charge of selling products or services. This definition makes clear the seller's responsibilities when it comes to accepting payments and providing goods or services in digital trade transactions.

We refer to the party or individual transmitting or providing an electronic record to an addressee as the submitter. The party that initiates the transfer of electronic records in digital trade transactions is defined by this term. A **transfer** is the whole or partial transfer of the beneficiary's rights and benefits under a payment obligation to one or more transferees. This term highlights the negotiable character of payment obligations in digital transactions and clarifies the method of transferring them. UTC, or Universal Time Coordinated, serves as the common time reference in digital commerce transactions. In the context of digital trade, this term creates a uniform time standard for coordinating actions and timestamps.

CHAPTER 8   BITS, BYTES, AND LEGAL BITES: NAVIGATING THE DIGITAL FRONTIER OF TRADE LAW AND PRACTICE

This article provides an extensive vocabulary of terms necessary to comprehend the regulations and guidelines guiding digital commerce transactions. These standards establish a common vocabulary and framework for conducting commercial transactions in the digital age, promoting transparency, uniformity, and interoperability among various parties and transactions.

Article 3 offers clarification on the meaning of terms and expressions used inside the rules' framework. The article establishes an interpretation principle that applies terms used in the single form to the plural form and vice versa. This implies that, within the framework of the rules, singular terms include their plural equivalents, and plural terms include their singular variants. An example of this would be a rule that defines "party" to include both "single entity" and "plural entity" contexts. If it refers to "transactions," it includes both single and multiple transactions.

This principle of interpretation ensures a flexible and inclusive application of the rules. It also makes it easier for everyone to understand their rights and responsibilities when they engage in virtual commerce. This interpretation approach is how the URDTT wants its rules to be carried out consistently and consistently across a wide range of transaction scenarios. This principle offers precise and uniform standards for interpretation, which promotes clear and consistent communication, lessens ambiguity, and increases the efficiency of digital commerce operations.

The article defines a fundamental concept to ensure consistent and inclusive interpretation of terms and expressions used within the regulations. This method of interpreting the rules promotes uniformity, consistency, and clarity in their application, which helps to facilitate the successful execution of digital trade operations.

The roles and responsibilities of the Seller as a **Principal Party** within the rules are outlined in **Article 4**. The contractual obligation pertaining to the delivery of products or the provision of services, as stipulated in the terms and conditions of the digital trade transaction, is the Seller's responsibility as a Principal Party. This involves ensuring that the buyer receives the products or receives the services in accordance with the specified conditions. In a digital trade transaction involving the sale of electronic devices, the Seller is accountable for timely delivery of the devices to the Buyer's designated location.

The seller shall supply any additional data or electronic documents needed to finalize the transaction. This could include documents pertaining to insurance, certifications from inspections, and any other documentation pertaining to the goods or services being traded. For instance, the vendor must provide Electronic Records of Inspection certificates to verify the products' compliance and quality, should the electronic equipment require certification or meet industry criteria.

CHAPTER 8   BITS, BYTES, AND LEGAL BITES: NAVIGATING THE DIGITAL FRONTIER OF
             TRADE LAW AND PRACTICE

In order to encourage accountability and openness in digital commerce transactions, Article 4 describes the responsibilities of the Seller as a Principal Party. It outlines specific obligations on the part of the Seller, including supplying necessary data, turning in necessary paperwork, and delivering goods or services on schedule. This increases transparency, simplifies transaction processes, and fosters confidence among parties engaged in digital trade.

Article 5 Financing or Risk Reduction outlines a financial services provider's responsibilities and obligations with regard to digital trade transactions. In order to provide financial support or risk mitigation services to the Buyer, the Beneficiary, or any other financial services providers participating in the transaction, a financial services provider is required.

Paying the Beneficiary in line with the conditions of the transaction is the financial services provider's responsibility. If a Principal Party or any other Beneficiary asks, the financial services provider can turn its FSP payment undertaking into a payment obligation. This means that the financial services provider is now responsible for making the payment on the due dates.

With regard to any electronic record related to the transaction, a financial services provider disclaims all liability and obligation regarding its form, adequacy, and accuracy. In the event that a financial services provider, who was originally the Electronic Record's Addressee, later takes on the role of Submitter, it bears all duty and responsibility for that particular electronic record.

When a financial services provider adds its FSP payment undertaking to a payment obligation, it is bound by the same version of the URDTT applicable to the Principal Parties involved in the transaction. By defining the role of a financial services provider and outlining its obligations and limitations within the URDTT framework, Article 5 ensures clarity, transparency, and accountability in digital trade transactions involving financial services. It delineates the specific responsibilities of financial services providers while also emphasizing their adherence to the established rules and standards governing digital trade.

The obligations of the Addressee and the Submitter in the context of digital trade transactions are outlined in **Article 6** of the URDTT. Authenticity, accuracy, and completeness: It is the Submitter's duty to make sure that an electronic record is accurate, complete, and authentic when initiating or sending one. This involves confirming, prior to submission, the accuracy and consistency of the data included in the electronic record.

In contrast to the Submitter, the Addressee, who obtains or is authorized access to an electronic record, bears no responsibility for ensuring the accuracy and completeness of the electronic record unless explicitly required by applicable laws or agreements. The electronic record was transmitted by the Submitter. Based on the Submitter's assertion, the Addressee believes the electronic record to be correct.

Except for the system they are directly in charge of, the Submitter and the Addressee are released from all obligation and responsibility for any effects resulting from the absence of a data processing system. This clause recognizes that the Submitter and the Addressee may not have any control over interruptions or malfunctions in external data processing systems, and they shall not be held liable for such events.

In digital commercial transactions, Article 6 guarantees clarity on the responsibilities and roles of both the Addressee and the Submitter. The significance of the authenticity, correctness, and completeness of electronic records is emphasized, and acceptable restrictions of liability in the event that the system is unavailable are established. Article 6 reduces potential risks and uncertainties related to data integrity and system reliability while outlining these duties and facilitating the seamless and dependable operation of digital trade operations.

The rules pertaining to electronic records in the context of digital trade transactions are described in **Article 7**. The assessment of compliance with an electronic record in a digital trade transaction necessitates a clear definition of its terms and conditions. This includes the specification of compliance terms. This ensures transparency and accountability in the transactional framework's evaluation of the veracity and accuracy of electronic records.

The Submitter shall send electronic records, or any relevant data, to the Addressee in connection with a digital trade transaction. This underscores the digital nature of the transactional process and underscores the significance of electronically submitting and transmitting pertinent data. The submission of a single electronic record satisfies the requirement for the submission of originals or copies of an electronic record. By recognizing that electronic records are equivalent to traditional paper-based documents, this rule streamlines the documentation process.

The terms and conditions of a digital trade transaction may ignore electronic records that are not required. This gives the parties to the transaction the freedom to exclude any paperwork that is superfluous or unrelated to the transactional process. Information that is part of an electronically accessible record that the addressee can access is considered to be in writing, unless the applicable law specifies otherwise. This acknowledges that electronic documentation satisfies traditional writing criteria and is legitimate legally.

Relevant law considers the placement of an electronic record under the addressee's sole control to satisfy delivery, transfer, or possession requirements. This clause facilitates the easy transfer and custody of electronic records while guaranteeing compliance with the legal frameworks governing electronic transactions. Information that is part of an electronically accessible record that the addressee can access is considered to be in writing, unless the applicable law specifies otherwise and handling of electronic records.

Article 8 of the URDTT discusses the protocols and ramifications of failing to comply with an electronic record. The Addressee should notify the Submitter in the event that an electronic record does not comply with the terms and conditions specified in the digital trade transaction or sub-article 7(b). Every explanation for the electronic record's non-compliance should be included in the notification.

After receiving notification of non-compliance, take the following actions. The non-compliant electronic record is swapped out with a compliant one by the Submitter. The terms and conditions of the digital trade transaction are updated by the Principal Parties. The non-compliant electronic record is acknowledged and accepted by the Principal Parties and any additional Obligor or Beneficiary. As soon as one of these events occurs, the resolution ensures the prompt correction of non-compliant electronic records and the continuation of the transactional process. If the Addressee fails to notify the Submitter of non-compliance by 23:59:59 UTC on the second business day after receipt, the Addressee deems the electronic record accepted. This clause establishes a timeframe for Addressees to quickly notify one another of non-compliance issues.

So as to preserve the integrity and effectiveness of the transactional process, Article 8 provides a structured method for handling non-compliance with electronic records in digital trade transactions. It places a strong emphasis on the necessity of prompt reporting, resolution, and acceptance.

Article 9 covers the management of electronic records that appear to have suffered from data corruption. The Addressee may choose to inform the Submitter of a problem if an electronic record appears to be affected by Data Corruption. In addition, the Addressee may ask the Submitter to submit the electronic record again, ideally in a format that prevents corruption of data.

A procedure for handling situations in which Data Corruption may have resulted in the compromising of electronic records is delineated in **Article 9**. Transparency and dependability in digital commerce transactions are encouraged by this provision, which permits the Addressee to notify the Submitter and seek a resubmission. This provision aids parties in promptly addressing potential issues with data integrity, safeguarding the accuracy and correctness of electronic records exchanged throughout the transaction process.

Article 10 deals with digital commercial transactions and the use of electronic signatures. The item highlights that in the event that a Party or Person uses an Electronic Signature in a digital trade transaction, it must comply with any particular terms or specifications specified in the digital trade transaction itself. This clause emphasizes how crucial it is to make sure Electronic Signatures adhere to the requirements outlined in the digital trade transaction. The article's goal is to preserve the authenticity and integrity of electronic signatures inside the transaction by stressing adherence to certain requirements.

This article lays forth rules for using electronic signatures appropriately, stressing the need to follow any requirements or restrictions specified in the digital trade transaction. By maintaining the legitimacy and dependability of electronic signatures, this strategy contributes to the growth of confidence in digital commerce transactions.

The function of data processing systems in online trade transactions is covered in **Article 11** The article states that a data processing system's simple acknowledgement of receiving an electronic record does not automatically lead to an Addressee's inspection, examination, or determination of its compliance. This clause makes it clear that a data processing system's simple acknowledgement of receiving an electronic record does not imply any kind of verification or evaluation of the electronic record's content. Rather, it functions as an affirmation of the electronic record's reception by the system.

The contrast between acknowledging receipt and actually examining or determining conformity with the terms and conditions of the digital trade transaction is emphasized in Article 11. The purpose of this essay is to dispel any misunderstanding about the importance of acknowledgment of receipt in the context of digital trade transactions.

Article 12 of the URDTT contains the provisions relating to **payment obligations** in digital trade transactions. It stipulates that the Buyer is liable to a payment obligation upon the Seller's compliance with the terms and conditions of the digital trade transaction.

If there is a condition attached to a payment requirement, it means that the Buyer's payment duty only applies if the Seller complies with the terms and conditions of the digital trade transaction. At that point, the payment obligation immediately changes from being dependent and conditional to being independent and unconditional.

A payment obligation needs to have certain data components, such as a distinct reference that connects it to the Digital Trade Agreement. The names and addresses of all other beneficiaries and the principal parties must also be included. Ensure to include both the total sum and the currency information about your interest, if any. Please provide the date of occurrence. It specifies the deadline for submitting electronic records. The terms of payment, whether they are to be paid in cash or at a later time, should also be specified. The payment obligation should be described as either unconditional or conditional relevant legislation.

Payment obligations may provide the transfer of rights and benefits to third parties if stated as transferable in their terms and conditions. Only with the consent of all pertinent parties—principal parties, financial services providers, and Beneficiaries—may payment obligations be changed or canceled. Comprehensive instructions for the creation, terms, and administration of payment obligations in digital trade transactions are outlined in Article 12. These measures aim to ensure the legal legitimacy, clarity, and transparency of the payment process, thereby fostering trust and efficiency in digital trade.

Article 13 fully describes the rules pertaining to the FSP (financial services provider) payment undertaking. This article states that a financial services provider may, at any time, choose to include their FSP payment undertaking in a payment obligation.

A financial services provider agrees to pay the payment obligation's Beneficiary when they include their FSP payment undertaking with it.

A financial services provider is required to notify the requesting Principal Party of its decision if it decides not to include its FSP payment undertaking in a payment obligation. Unconditional FSP payment undertakings function apart from and independently of digital trade transactions. A single payment obligation may have the FSP payment undertakings of many financial services providers added to it.

The financial services provider shall notify the other Principal Party and any other Beneficiary involved in the request made by a Principal Party or any other Beneficiary to add an FSP payment undertaking to a payment obligation. The submission of any electronic records must be properly validated and authenticated. Unnecessary or redundant records can be disregarded and discarded, thereby enhancing efficiency and promoting transparency in the management of digital trade operations.

Financial services providers' obligations with relation to adding FSP payment undertakings to payment obligations are outlined in Article 13. The purpose of these clauses is to encourage safe and easy online transactions by guaranteeing that the payment process is open, reliable, and follows all the rules.

The guidelines and processes for amending digital trade transactions are described in **Article 14**; per this article, every Principal Party and every financial services provider connected to the transaction must consent to any changes made to the terms and conditions of a digital trade transaction. Modifications to the terms and conditions of an FSP (financial services provider) payment undertaking, a payment obligation, or a digital trade transaction are carried out by submitting a new electronic record that includes the updated requirements. This guarantees that the amended terms are accessible to and binding on all parties. An electronic record cannot be changed or removed once it has been submitted in connection with a digital trade transaction, a payment obligation, or an FSP payment undertaking. This clause emphasizes the crucial importance of correctness and integrity in digital trade transactions, as any provided records are considered definitive and unchangeable.

The objective of **Article 14** is to create a strong and transparent framework for handling modifications to digital trade transactions. This article provides accountability, openness, and dependability during the process of changing transaction terms and conditions by requiring unanimous agreement among relevant parties and requiring the filing of new electronic records. Furthermore, the inability to change or remove electronically provided records emphasizes how careful and precise digital trade documentation management must be.

Regarding the transferability of payment obligations and FSP (financial services provider) payment undertakings within digital trade transactions, see Article 15. This provision stipulates that the Seller or any other Beneficiary acting as the transferor may carry out a transfer in line with the conditions specified in the payment obligation if a payment obligation and, if applicable, an FSP payment undertaking are designated as transferable.

The transferor shall notify the Buyer or the financial services provider of the transfer of the rights and benefits of a payment obligation and, if applicable, an FSP payment undertaking. This announcement ensures transparency and informs all relevant parties about the transfer of obligations. If an FSP payment undertaking with transferability conditions has been added to a payment obligation, it must state whether any transfers need the financial services provider's prior consent. This clause makes sure that the conditions pertaining to the transfer of FSP payment undertakings are understood and followed.

The rights and advantages of any related FSP payment undertaking shall be transferred along with a payment obligation. No transfer of the payment obligation may take place if a financial services provider has prohibited the transfer of an FSP payment undertaking unless the FSP payment undertaking has been duly modified or canceled. This guarantees the consistency and alignment of the transfer of FSP payment undertakings and payment obligations with the conditions set by all parties concerned.

CHAPTER 8   BITS, BYTES, AND LEGAL BITES: NAVIGATING THE DIGITAL FRONTIER OF TRADE LAW AND PRACTICE

A thorough structure for the transfer of FSP payment undertakings and payment obligations in digital commerce transactions is established in Article 15. This article encourages openness, effectiveness, and adherence to contractual duties throughout the transfer process by detailing the protocols, notification requirements, and conditions related to transfers.

Article 16 covers the concept of force majeure and its impact on digital trade transactions. This provision provides that neither the Seller nor any other Beneficiary shall be responsible or liable for any interference with a Beneficiary's business operations. Numerous unanticipated occurrences, including cyberattacks, terrorism, riots, civil unrest, insurrections, conflicts, and natural disasters like hurricanes, floods, and earthquakes, could cause these disruptions.

Force majeure events have the potential to significantly hinder business operations, leading to delays or the inability to fulfill contractual obligations. By including "force majeure" clauses, the URDTT recognizes the need to make it easier for parties to keep their digital business promises when unexpected and out of their control events happen.

This clause seeks to shield the Beneficiary or Seller from responsibility for events outside of their control. By explicitly stating that they are not responsible for the effects of business interruptions caused by events of force majeure, parties can reduce the likelihood of disputes arising from non-performance due to external causes.

Article 16 of the URDTT talks about how events outside of the parties' control affect their contractual duties. This gives people who are trading digitally legal protection and clarity. It's less likely that parties will fight over non-performance due to outside factors if they make it clear that they are not responsible for the effects of business interruptions caused by events of force majeure. By managing instances of force majeure, this clause promotes equity and clarity in contractual agreements.

Finding the appropriate law that regulates digital trade transactions is covered in **Article 17**. According to it, the terms and conditions of the actual transaction will determine the applicable legislation that will apply to the digital commerce transaction. This implies that the parties to the transaction are free to choose the legal jurisdiction that will apply to their contractual arrangement.

Article 17 helps make the legal framework for the transaction clear, predictable, and certain by letting the parties find the relevant law in the agreement's terms and conditions. It makes it possible for the parties to select the legal system that best suits their needs or preferences, which makes dispute resolution procedures easier to handle when problems arise. The clause embodies the idea of party autonomy, which gives the parties the opportunity to bargain over and decide on the specifics of their agreement, including which law will apply. Because of this flexibility, they are able to customize the transaction to meet their own requirements and preferences while accounting for elements like the regulatory environment, legal precedents, and jurisdictional knowledge.

Specifying the appropriate law up front avoids confusion and predictability about the legal framework guiding the transaction. It offers a precise point of reference for interpreting contractual rights and obligations and settling conflicts. By making the process of applying pertinent legal concepts more efficient, it also enhances the efficiency of legal procedures.

Article 17 emphasizes the importance of selecting the appropriate law for digital commerce transactions. The above provision gives parties the freedom to choose the law that applies to their situation, which makes the law clearer, promotes party autonomy, and speeds up the transactional process.

The ICC Uniform Rules for Digital Trade Transactions are important because they make it easier for trade transactions around the world to switch from paper to digital records. They significantly influence global trade practices. Here's how to expand on this concept: By offering thorough regulations and procedures for carrying out trade transactions utilizing digital documents, the URDTT encourages digital change in international trade. It facilitates the process of moving from traditional paper-based documentation to digital formats by providing a standardized structure.

The URDTT has a significant impact worldwide, providing consistent standards that apply in a variety of governments and areas, with enterprises operating in over 200 nations. This universal application promotes efficiency and lowers obstacles to cross-border trade by ensuring uniformity and coherence in trade processes. Although conventional banks have traditionally been essential to trade finance and documentation, the URDTT broadens its purview to include a wider range of players. This comprises businesses involved in global commerce as well as a developing network of non-bank service providers providing specific services linked to trade.

The URDTT promotes innovation and collaboration within the trade ecosystem by acknowledging the participation of non-bank service providers. It facilitates collaborations among established financial institutions, businesses, fintech startups, and other service providers by encouraging the adoption of new technology and digital solutions. The URDTT shows a move toward upgrading trade practices to meet current business needs in the digital age, when speed, efficiency, and transparency are critical. It recognizes the increasing inclination toward digital procedures and emphasizes how crucial it is to keep up with technological developments in trade documentation and financing.

CHAPTER 8 BITS, BYTES, AND LEGAL BITES: NAVIGATING THE DIGITAL FRONTIER OF TRADE LAW AND PRACTICE

The inclusion of the URDTT in platform rulebooks and the intention of technological service providers to cooperate with these regulations have marked important turning points in the development of digital trade transactions. The next stage is to seamlessly integrate with digital trading platforms and systems after technology service providers include the URDTT in their platform rulebooks. Businesses will be able to take advantage of the advantages of digitalization and uniform norms by simply adopting and implementing the URDTT standards in their current trade processes, thanks to this integration.

With the URDTT as a foundation, technology service providers are well positioned to offer cutting-edge trade products and solutions tailored to the needs of businesses engaged in digital trade transactions. These goods might include, among other things, blockchain-based trade platforms, electronic document management systems, and digital trade finance solutions. The URDTT ecosystem's adoption and growth will be largely dependent on the cooperation of multiple stakeholders, including corporations, banks, fintech companies, and regulatory agencies. Partnerships and industry consortia can support knowledge exchange, interoperability, and the creation of best practices for putting URDTT standards into effect.

State authorities and international entities' regulatory approval and adoption of the URDTT will significantly enhance its credibility and acceptance within the global trade community. Initiatives to align them with current industry norms and regulatory frameworks will promote the widespread adoption and compliance of URDTT standards. There will be an increasing demand for capacity building and training programs as enterprises move to digital trade processes controlled by the URDTT. Stakeholders can better comprehend the nuances of digital trade transactions and successfully integrate URDTT standards into their operations with the use of training programs, workshops, and educational materials.

To address new issues, technological developments, and changing business practices, the URDTT is anticipated to go through regular reviews and upgrades. We will update the regulations based on ongoing input from users and stakeholders, ensuring their applicability and efficacy in the dynamic world of digital trade. For the URDTT to have a bright future, it needs to be widely used, new products to be made based on innovation, the ecosystem to grow together, rules to be followed, people to be able to do more, and the system to keep getting better to meet the needs of people who trade digitally. The URDTT has the potential to significantly influence how international trade develops in the digital era by utilizing the combined knowledge and efforts of stakeholders.

CHAPTER 8   BITS, BYTES, AND LEGAL BITES: NAVIGATING THE DIGITAL FRONTIER OF TRADE LAW AND PRACTICE

Blockchain Unchained: Policy Considerations for a Decentralized Future

The adoption of blockchain technology in commerce and other areas presents unique concerns and obstacles, particularly in relation to blockchain interoperability and data protection. These issues influence the use, scaling, and rule compliance of blockchain technology. They are also crucial for its further integration into business and financial systems. Let's delve deeper into these factors and the emerging solutions to better understand them.

Trade requires a meticulous equilibrium between confidentiality and openness. For the supply chain to function efficiently, we can widely communicate some facts, such as the origin of the items or projected arrival times, but we must carefully protect other details, especially those crucial to business interests.

Protocols like Hyperledger and Corda have developed in response to these privacy issues. They provide tools that let you have fine-grained control over which data is visible on the blockchain. Blockchain's transparency and security characteristics allow originators to control who may access what data, protecting sensitive information from prying eyes. Although the blockchain industry is convergent around specific actors and standards, the networks themselves are frequently incompatible. Organizations find it difficult to switch infrastructures after they have selected a technological stack, which makes interoperability crucial for scalability, competitive variety, and operational efficiency.

Stable protocols like Cosmos, which facilitate communication between public blockchains, and industry-specific solutions such as DLPC CorDapp for trade instruments and Skuchain's Popskip protocol for traceability have contributed to interoperability efforts. These developments make it possible for companies operating on separate blockchains that are part of the same trading ecosystem to exchange data and trade with ease.

Data formats and papers will probably become more standardized as commerce moves toward digitizing its records. Businesses, however, are becoming less and less prepared to postpone their blockchain projects in order to reach a consensus on standards. This urgency has prompted central and commercial banks to launch stablecoins and to build new blockchain assets and standards, such as the Distributed Ledger Payment Commitment (DLPC) of the Bankers Association for Finance and Trade.

CHAPTER 8   BITS, BYTES, AND LEGAL BITES: NAVIGATING THE DIGITAL FRONTIER OF TRADE LAW AND PRACTICE

Promoting legal and legislative frameworks is crucial for the widespread acceptance and integration of blockchain technology into the existing banking and commerce systems. One fundamental step in verifying blockchain transactions and contracts in a legal setting is the recognition of electronic signatures. Making laws that protect the unique features of blockchain technology while also ensuring data security, privacy, and interoperability is key to making an environment that encourages its growth and integration into everyday business practices. The potential for blockchain technology to revolutionize commerce is enormous, providing previously unheard-of levels of efficiency, security, and openness. To truly realize this promise, though, resolving the intricate issues of interoperability and data protection is necessary. By improving blockchain protocols, making interoperability standards, and setting up legal and legislative frameworks that work together, blockchain can find the right balance between being able to grow, following the rules, and being open and private. Technology and its applications will progress in tandem with the solutions to these problems, paving the way for a global trading environment that is more integrated, effective, and secure.

Legal Frameworks for Digital Assets and Electronic Trade Documents

The digital revolution has brought not only fresh kinds of assets but also revolutionary approaches to transaction processing in the fast-changing terrain of business and finance. The requirement of clear, current legal frameworks has never been more urgent as companies and legal systems all around struggle with the more digital nature of trade. The Law Commission for England and Wales's most recent projects, which have made major efforts toward updating legal systems to fit the expanding universe of digital assets and electronic trade documents (ETDs), clearly show this urgency.

The proposed Property (Digital Assets, etc.) Bill and the most recent "Call for Evidence" from the Law Commission are absolutely essential in laying the groundwork for strong legal rules able to keep pace with technical developments. These papers bring to light an important fact: when digital transactions go beyond traditional borders of geography and jurisdiction, the clarity and adaptability of legal systems become essential for making international trade run smoothly and efficiently.

The digital transition presents significant problems for private international law because of cutting-edge technologies like the Internet, blockchain, and distributed ledger technology. Legal doctrines have long been strongly associated with physical

CHAPTER 8 BITS, BYTES, AND LEGAL BITES: NAVIGATING THE DIGITAL FRONTIER OF TRADE LAW AND PRACTICE

sites—that is, the law controlling the place of a contract made or of a piece of property. But the nature of digital assets and ETDs—including electronic bills of lading, cryptocurrency, and other trade finance documentation—fundamentally throws off traditional conventions. Usually, on a worldwide scene, these computerized instruments lack any physical link to a particular place.

Particularly in many commercial contracts without clear guiding law provisions, this dissociation from the actual locale raises major legal questions. UK courts are grappling with complex jurisdictional issues, primarily relying on established concepts of private international law to determine jurisdiction and the relevant legislation. This scenario emphasizes the urgent necessity of a legal framework able to handle the complexity of digital transactions beyond national boundaries, therefore highlighting a major void in the present system that has to be filled in order to keep up with technological development.

Dealing with the legal complexity of digital assets and ETDs calls for creative ideas able to fit the global character of the digital economy. The Law Commission is actively investigating numerous possible solutions to reduce the uncertainty digital transactions bring to private international law. One major suggestion is to tie digital assets to a physical location, such as the base of a cloud data provider or the site of a "reliable system" operator, as stated in the Electronic Trade Documents Act 2023. Still, this method has several difficulties. The flexibility and global reach of cloud providers, which occasionally operate in multiple countries or may move sites, complicate the viability of consistently designating a physical locus.

One international model the Commission is considering as it looks for a more solid structure is the Cape Town Convention on Mobile Assets. For physical items like airplanes and mining tools that often cross national boundaries, this agreement offers a disciplined legal framework. They propose the creation of an equivalent international convention for digital assets and ETDs using the Law Commission's model. Such a treaty aims to streamline the acceptance and implementation of decisions across international borders. This would make the law more stable and safe for transactions involving digital assets. This approach may provide much-needed legal stability and protection for users of the growing digital economy by bringing international law into line with the reality of the digital era.

The UK is proactively addressing the expanding digital landscape by proposing a draft bill that aims to elucidate property rights within the digital realm. This draft bill suggests a novel idea: creating a new classification of property that acknowledges digital or electronic things as personal property. This is a major change as it involves assets in action—that is, neither conventional rights nor physical objects. This new category is very broad and includes many digital things, such as blockchain systems and non-fungible tokens (NFTs). This is because property changes quickly in the digital age.

The draft bill, however, purposefully leaves out a mention of which digital assets fit under this new property category. Rather, it lets common law define this field by means of court rulings when conflicts develop. This calculated decision gives the legislation some adaptability and lets it change with time as digital technologies and their applications develop. This does, however, also bring some ambiguity, as the legal environment will need time to create clear precedents that can guide users, developers, and attorneys in knowing what qualifies as digital personal property. This time of adaptation is essential for creating an atmosphere where legal safeguards and creativity can coexist and grow.

Professionals in the trade and trade finance sectors have both possibilities and difficulties, given the rapid development of digital assets and electronic trade records. The current legal systems' existing uncertainties are not only theoretical worries; they also affect real-world problems, including higher running expenses and delays. These mostly result from the difficulties of doing due diligence and settling conflicts under dubious legal circumstances. This scenario underscores the crucial need for industrial players to actively participate in shaping the legal framework that governs their operations.

In this sense, engagement goes beyond mere passive obedience. It entails attending conferences and supporting the creation of legal systems that fairly depict the reality of contemporary corporate operations. The clarity and strength of legal systems become increasingly important as digital platforms and assets become more crucial to world trade. Working collaboratively with lawmakers, stakeholders should make sure laws not only catch up with technological developments but also improve their possibilities. We need active participation to establish a legal environment that facilitates safe, efficient, and dynamic market operations. This makes it possible for trade to take advantage of the numerous opportunities that come with new technology.

The proactive efforts of the Law Commission to demystify the legal status of digital assets and electronic trade documents (ETDs) are a noteworthy step toward simplifying the complexity of our more digitized and scattered financial scene. This forward-looking strategy sets the scene for the next wave of innovation in global business, rather than only helping one to react to change. Through active participation in this legal debate, business leaders have a special chance to shape laws protecting their interests and creating conditions fit for innovation and stable markets.

Cooperation between industry players and regulatory authorities is very vital at this turning point. It guarantees that the generated frameworks are not only thorough and forward-looking but also useful in actual situations. Such alliances can help to create legal routes that support the dynamic character of digital transactions, thereby improving confidence and enabling more seamless transitions into new forms of operation. Through coordinated efforts and ongoing communication, business leaders may help open the path for legal reforms that preserve the integrity of the market and advance sustainable development in the digital age.

The UK's Legislative Approach to Digital Assets and Property Rights

Particularly in terms of our conception, management, and protection of property, the rapid digital revolution of world economies has presented hitherto unheard-of prospects. Digital assets—including cryptocurrencies, tokenized real-world assets, and non-fungible tokens (NFTs)—have added new angles to property rights. The UK's Property and Digital Assets Bill in September 2024 is a reaction to these possibilities and problems. The purpose of this legislation is to reconsider property laws, especially in light of the expanding digital landscape.

This chapter investigates the legal changes related to digital assets in the UK, their reasons, and their worldwide consequences, while also providing a legislative background. It will examine how the government's latest legislative comment fits more general patterns in property law and digital asset management.

The fast-expanding digital asset ecosystem of the UK reflects worldwide patterns whereby digital assets increasingly account for a major share of economic value. But current rules controlling property rights have found it difficult to match this change. The complicated nature of digital ownership, problems about custodianship, and legal recognition of intangible assets call for more from traditional property law systems.

Formally introducing the Property and Digital Assets Bill into Parliament on September 11, 2024, the UK government used a legislative written statement. This law seeks to update the legal structure to handle digital property-related conflicts and ownership problems. Complementing the Law Commission's suggestions, the measure is a result of a more comprehensive endeavor to guarantee the UK stays a leader in the digital economy while safeguarding people's rights in fast-alternative surroundings.

CHAPTER 8   BITS, BYTES, AND LEGAL BITES: NAVIGATING THE DIGITAL FRONTIER OF TRADE LAW AND PRACTICE

The Property and Digital Assets Bill tackles numerous fundamental topics of interest regarding the legal position of digital assets. The following sections describe the primary clauses of the measure:

Legal recognition of digital assets as a separate category of property is one of the historic aspects of this law. Legal systems have often struggled to fit digital assets into conventional categories of "chattels" or "real property." The measure recognizes the unique character of digital assets and creates a new legal category for them, therefore offering safeguards equivalent to those of physical objects. This action helps courts and market players to be clear, therefore facilitating better settlement of ownership conflicts and application of property rights.

The measure also lays rules around digital asset custody and control. Within the framework of cryptocurrencies and distributed finance (DeFi), custodial issues have grown ever more important. Private keys enable many digital assets to be accessed, therefore enabling persons or organizations possessing these keys to essentially control the asset. Particularly in situations when digital assets are lost, stolen, or challenged, the measure seeks to resolve legal uncertainties around custody.

Apart from cryptocurrencies and NFTs, the law offers a legal framework for tokenized real-world assets. Tokenizing actual assets, like real estate or art, enables the digital display of partial ownership or more efficient trading systems on a blockchain. The legislation guarantees that these tokenized versions get the same legal treatment as their physical equivalents, therefore providing strong defense for anyone engaged in these online markets.

The recognition of digital assets as property raises concerns about how they should be managed in the event of bankruptcy or insolvency. The law provides particular standards for managing digital assets in such circumstances, therefore guaranteeing that creditors and stakeholders have clear policies for claiming or contesting digital assets during liquidation procedures.

With this measure, the UK leads the world in attempts to reform property laws and control digital assets. Though their methods vary in breadth and focus, other countries, such as the European Union (via MiCA—Markets in Crypto-Assets regulation) and the United States, are also investigating complete regulatory frameworks for digital assets. States,

The UK creates a legal framework fit for innovation by recognizing digital assets as a separate class of property, therefore providing robust consumer and investor safeguards. Promoting the UK as a worldwide hub for fintech and digital economies, this promotes the UK as an appealing destination for digital asset firms, DeFi platforms, and blockchain inventors.

The bill's introduction also emphasizes the UK's goal in establishing worldwide norms for the handling of digital property. Other countries wishing to create or change their own laws on digital assets might find influence from the legal framework. Given the global character of digital assets, future international collaboration and alignment will be absolutely vital.

Although the measure marks significant progress, various issues still exist that will call for continuous adaptation and improvement.

The digital terrain changes quickly, and it is uncertain if the present laws will stay flexible enough to support next developments like quantum computing or new blockchain technology.

Finding a balance between consumer protection and innovation promotion is a challenging task for regulation. While too little might cause systematic hazards or exploitation, too much control could inhibit creativity.

Given the transnational character of digital assets, the UK will need to engage with international authorities to make sure its legal structure conforms with worldwide norms.

Since digital assets can span several countries, implementing laws and settling cross-border conflicts might become somewhat difficult. The measure offers a basis; yet, its implementation will depend on international collaboration.

The UK's Property and Digital Assets Bill marks a significant milestone in adapting the legal system to the digital economy. The bill closes important loopholes in current property law by laying a legal basis for digital assets, therefore ensuring the UK stays competitive and forward-looking in the world digital scene. But as the digital economy develops, so too must the rules controlling it; the bill is probably the first step in a continuous legislative process of adaptation.

This move emphasizes the need for upgrading property law to represent the reality of a digital economy. The legal recognition of digital assets not only provides vital safeguards to consumers, companies, and investors, but also paves the way for more transparent, safe, and creative digital marketplaces in the future. The legislative framework of the UK will be crucial in determining the direction of property rights in the digital era as the global economy moves progressively toward digital transactions.

CHAPTER 8   BITS, BYTES, AND LEGAL BITES: NAVIGATING THE DIGITAL FRONTIER OF TRADE LAW AND PRACTICE

Summary

This chapter examines the shift from traditional paper-based trade systems to fully digitalized trading environments, focusing on its impact on international commerce and law. It starts by going over the possibilities and difficulties of digital transformation in business, stressing the importance of shifting from paper-based paradigms toward digital processes. Emphasizing the part digitalization plays in harmonizing world commerce and managing disruptions, the chapter examines the UK's legislative drive for paperless trade in 2023, therefore providing a template for other nations.

Key ideas such as digital trust and digital vaults—which illustrate how these technologies may safeguard transactions and inspire confidence in digital commerce—are covered in this chapter. It investigates the change from conventional trade tools to digital innovations, therefore rethinking ideas of possession and legal frameworks in the digital era. Important forces promoting worldwide legal harmony include digital diplomacy and the building of legal ledgers.

Beginning with the Uniform Rules for Digital Trade Transactions (URDTT), a basic rule for allowing digital commerce, the chapter describes the instruments required for flawless digital trade operations. It ends by looking at blockchain's transforming power, tackling policy issues for distributed systems, and building the basis for a strong digital future in trade law. This analysis of digital commerce enables readers to negotiate the legal and operational obstacles of a fast-changing global trade environment.

CHAPTER 9

Blockchain Breakthrough: Rewiring Trade Finance for the Digital Age

Presented as fundamental instruments for a new era of digitalized commerce, this chapter investigates the transforming power of blockchain technology and distributed ledger technology (DLT) on trade finance.

Starting with a primer on blockchain and DLT, the chapter discusses their underlying mechanics, stressing their capacity to simplify processes, improve openness, and remove inefficiencies in conventional trade finance systems. Emphasized as game-changers in automating trust and guaranteeing regulatory compliance are key advances made possible by blockchain: smart contracts and real-time data integration.

The chapter also explores how blockchain and artificial intelligence (AI) are redefining innovation in trade finance by means of their symbiotic interaction. Generative artificial intelligence and real-time analytics are among AI-powered solutions demonstrated to improve risk assessment, automate difficult tasks, and influence decisions. Smart contracts—self-executing agreements that cut reliance on middlemen—take up a large share of the conversation. Smart contracts help to create automated contracts by using real-time data and artificial intelligence, therefore guaranteeing accuracy and efficiency in trade transactions.

Examining the wider effects of blockchain and artificial intelligence for global markets, the chapter also rewrites the outsourcing scene and transforms services with more automation and openness. It provides insights on the policies needed to negotiate this fast-changing digital frontier, therefore addressing the growing ethical and regulatory issues.

CHAPTER 9   BLOCKCHAIN BREAKTHROUGH: REWIRING TRADE FINANCE FOR THE DIGITAL AGE

The chapter ends with a forward-looking view of a completely digital trade finance ecosystem in which blockchain and artificial intelligence cooperate to unlock hitherto unheard-of degrees of efficiency, trust, and invention. Promising to reshape world commerce and finance for the digital era, this change is not only technological but also institutional.

The Digital Frontier

The adoption of digital technology for documentary credits is a noteworthy development in the field of international trade finance, providing unique advantages with respect to efficacy, safety, and transparency. This trip is not without difficulties, though. Gaining a comprehensive comprehension of these obstacles is crucial to efficiently using technological breakthroughs.

As an example, the digitization of documentary credits necessitates collaboration from a broad range of parties, including banks, importers, exporters, transportation companies, and technology suppliers. Every player frequently uses multiple digital platforms, different systems, and different standards when operating.

It is imperative that these different systems become interoperable. The commerce ecosystem runs the danger of fragmenting in the absence of defined protocols, which would impede the smooth interchange of information. To get around this problem, we need to make and use universal digital standards that encourage interoperability and make sure that data flows safely and effectively throughout the world's commerce environment.

Documentary credit digitalization exposes sensitive transaction data to possible cyber risks. Ransomware, hacking, and data breach vulnerabilities may jeopardize the security and integrity of digital transactions.

Securing digital documentary credits requires implementing strict cybersecurity measures, such as the use of cutting-edge encryption technology. Frequent security practice upgrades, ongoing monitoring, and adherence to cybersecurity best practices can reduce these risks and maintain the reliability of digital transactions.

Documentary credits must traverse complicated regulatory landscapes on the digital front. Ensuring compliance with local legal requirements, data protection legislation, and international commerce restrictions is crucial.

Working with regulatory agencies to create online understandable legal frameworks may make compliance easier. Bringing digital trade finance practices into compliance with regulatory standards would also need a strong emphasis on accountability and transparency in digital transactions.

The main reasons people don't want to switch to digital documentary credits are old systems, traditions, and different levels of digital literacy among stakeholders. This opposition may actually slow down the adoption of digital technology.

Comprehensive education and training programs that highlight the concrete advantages of digitalization are necessary to address people's resistance to the digital transition. Providing strategic planning and assistance can also accelerate the adoption of digital practices.

A strategy approach that tackles acceptance, security, interoperability, legal, and regulatory issues head-on is necessary for the successful integration of digital technologies into documentary credits. It is essential that stakeholders work together to create standardized digital practices and regulations.

The trade finance sector may fully utilize digital documentary credits by addressing these issues. The objective is to establish an international commerce environment that is more open, safe, and effective for the benefit of all parties involved.

Even though digitizing documentary credits is a difficult process, the benefits might outweigh the difficulties. To usher in a new era of digital trade finance, overcoming these obstacles will require a coordinated effort from all stakeholders, leveraging cooperation, creativity, and strategic foresight.

Distributed ledger technology, often known as blockchain technology, is leading the charge to transform trade by improving efficiency, security, and transparency in all facets of business. The potential of blockchain technology is being investigated and used more often in business operations, ranging from trade finance to logistics. Let's look at some prominent platforms and initiatives and dive into the specific areas of commerce where blockchain is having a big influence.

Blockchain technology offers a decentralized framework for the secure transfer and storage of data; this is especially useful in business transactions involving numerous stakeholders from various nations. Recall that the immutable ledger of blockchain ensures transparency, traceability, and accuracy of records, which is particularly valuable in cross-border trade, supply chain finance, and regulatory compliance, where verifying and auditing transactions are essential. Since the system's immutable ledger cannot be altered, it ensures that data remains transparent and secure for all users. Researchers are increasingly exploring ways to streamline trade finance processes. Blockchain technology has the potential to significantly reduce costs, shorten transaction times, and minimize the reliance on intermediaries. This is particularly helpful in cutting down on the paperwork and complexity that are often involved with trade finance.

CHAPTER 9   BLOCKCHAIN BREAKTHROUGH: REWIRING TRADE FINANCE FOR THE DIGITAL AGE

Blockchain technology has the potential to streamline customs operations by giving authorities quick and secure access to verified transaction data. This can lower the risk of fraud, expedite the clearance of products through customs considerably, and improve the efficiency of cross-border trade.

The insurance industry is using blockchain-based technologies, such as Insurwave, to keep its data safe and look into how it can be integrated into trade single windows. These windows let everyone submit their regulatory paperwork through a single site, showing that blockchain technology has the potential to make international trade processes much easier. These windows facilitate trade by enabling parties to submit regulatory paperwork through a single site.

Lastly, blockchain may potentially protect intellectual property rights by providing a clear and open record of ownership and licensing agreements. It can increase transparency and reduce corruption in government procurement by securely keeping contracts and bids.

The Blockchain (R)evolution

Trade finance, which has always relied on paper-based processes, is about to undergo a significant shift. The digitization of documentary trade finance has faced significant challenges for a long time, with several attempts only managing to digitize a small percentage of the entire process. This chapter examines how end-to-end digital processes that are fast, affordable, and efficient might revolutionize trade finance through the use of blockchain-powered platforms. Blockchain technology, also known as distributed ledger technology, offers a potent cure for the current trade finance system's inefficiencies. Unlike past digitization initiatives that were dispersed and had a limited reach, blockchain systems are made to integrate the whole commercial process. This comprehensive approach may reduce costs, streamline operations, and enhance security and transparency. In May 2018, HSBC and ING carried out the first economically feasible blockchain-based trade finance transaction. This transaction, which involved shipping soybeans from Argentina to Malaysia for Cargill, took less than 24 hours to complete on a single shared platform, in contrast to the typical 5 to 10 days. This was a significant milestone that demonstrated the potential for blockchain to transform trade financing.

Prior initiatives to digitize documentary trade finance, including Swift's MT 798 messaging service and the Bank Payment Obligation (BPO), have not always been successful. These technologies did digitalize some aspects of the trading process, but they did not offer an all-encompassing platform that could scale effectively. Consequently, there hasn't been much adoption, and a lot of transactions still happen on paper. The main problem has been that these solutions were disjointed, resulting in digital islands as opposed to a cohesive, networked system. For a meaningful digital transformation, we must digitalize and integrate the entire trade lifecycle, involving shippers, customs officers, and port authorities.

In order to fully utilize blockchain technology in trade finance, industry players need to come to an agreement on uniform guidelines and commercial practices.

This specification will guarantee interoperability, which will also encourage wider implementation. Furthermore, some organizations must function as superconductors, including big banks, governmental bodies, and other reliable establishments. By bridging disparate networks, these superconnectors will guarantee the smooth exchange of data and preserve the integrity of the trade finance ecosystem.

Blockchain and DLT: A Primer

Trade finance is the backbone of international commerce, ensuring the smooth flow of goods, services, and payments across borders. Inefficiencies, reliance on paper-based processes, and a lack of transparency have long hampered the sector, despite its critical role. However, the advent of **Blockchain** and **Distributed Ledger Technology (DLT)** has initiated a revolution, promising to transform trade and trade finance into a streamlined, efficient, and transparent ecosystem. This chapter explores how blockchain and DLT are revolutionizing the industry, examines their key applications, and provides a foundational understanding of how these technologies work.

What Is Blockchain?

At its core, blockchain is a decentralized digital ledger that records transactions across multiple nodes in a network. Blockchain groups each transaction into a block, secures it cryptographically, and links it to the previous block to form a "chain" of records. This structure ensures:

- **Immutability:** Once a transaction is recorded, it cannot be altered or deleted.

- **Transparency:** All participants in the network have access to the same data in real time.

- **Security:** Transactions are verified through consensus mechanisms, preventing fraud and unauthorized modifications.

What Is a DLT?

DLT, or Distributed Ledger Technology, is a broader term encompassing blockchain and other decentralized systems. DLT, in contrast to traditional centralized databases, enables simultaneous data storage and updates across multiple locations. While blockchain is a type of DLT, other forms (e.g., directed acyclic graphs) offer variations tailored to specific use cases.

How Do They Work?

1. **Decentralization:**
    - In a blockchain, no single entity controls the data. Instead, all participants (nodes) maintain and validate the ledger collectively.

2. **Consensus Mechanisms:**
    - Consensus protocols like Proof of Work (PoW), Proof of Stake (PoS), or Byzantine Fault Tolerance (BFT) verify transactions.

3. **Smart Contracts:**
    - Self-executing programs stored on the blockchain automate processes based on predefined conditions.

4. **Encryption and Security:**
    - Cryptographic techniques secure data, ensuring privacy and protection against tampering.

The Transformation of Trade Finance with Blockchain and DLT

Key Innovations

1. **Digitization of Trade Documents:**

    - Traditional trade relies on physical documents like bills of lading, letters of credit, and invoices. Blockchain digitizes these instruments, ensuring they are immutable and instantly accessible to all parties.

    Example: An electronic bill of lading (e-B/L) on a blockchain eliminates courier delays and reduces the risk of forgery.

2. **Supply Chain Transparency:**

    - Blockchain enables real-time tracking of goods, ensuring provenance and authenticity. This is particularly valuable in sectors like agriculture, pharmaceuticals, and luxury goods.

    Example: A coffee exporter can use blockchain to verify the journey of their beans from farm to cup, proving ethical sourcing.

3. **Smart Contracts in Trade Finance:**

    - Smart contracts automate complex trade finance workflows, such as releasing payments upon delivery confirmation or compliance with contractual terms.

    Example: A smart contract linked to a blockchain-powered letter of credit releases funds automatically when shipping conditions are met.

4. **Improved Risk Mitigation:**

    - Immutable records reduce fraud risks, while blockchain-enabled platforms facilitate real-time KYC/AML checks, ensuring regulatory compliance.

The Future of Blockchain in Trade Finance

The blockchain revolution has demonstrated its immense potential to transform trade finance.

Key future trends include:

1. **Standardization:**
   - Industry-wide standards for blockchain implementation will enhance interoperability.

2. **Integration with Emerging Technologies:**
   - Combining blockchain with IoT (Internet of things) and AI (artificial intelligence) will further optimize trade operations.

3. **Sustainable Trade:**
   - Blockchain's ability to track carbon footprints and ethical sourcing aligns with global sustainability goals.

4. **Global Adoption:**
   - As legal frameworks evolve, more businesses and governments will integrate blockchain into their trade finance ecosystems.

The advancement of blockchain, or DLT, in trade finance is more than a technological advancement—it is a fundamental reimagining of how global trade operates. By eliminating inefficiencies, enhancing trust, and enabling new business models, blockchain and DLT are empowering businesses to thrive in an increasingly interconnected world. While challenges remain, the path forward is clear: blockchain and DLT will be at the heart of the future of trade finance.

Unlocking the Future: How Blockchain and AI Are Redefining Innovation Together

The fusion of blockchain technology and artificial intelligence (AI) has the potential to significantly alter the landscape of digital innovation. Advances in machine learning and deep learning, showing promise in various fields, are responsible for the rapid advancement of artificial intelligence. Artificial intelligence is coming into our daily lives in more and more ways, from allowing driverless automobiles to improving the capabilities of smart assistants. However, the real frontier of technological advancement lies in the integration of blockchain technology with artificial intelligence.

Blockchain provides a strong foundation for the enormous volumes of data required for AI's analytical capabilities because of its decentralized ledger. This synergy guarantees a more equal distribution of technological advantages by democratizing data access and enhancing AI's capabilities. Coinmarketcap wrote a long article about this coming together, which talks about many different blockchain-based AI projects, ranging from generative NFTs (i.e., non-fungible tokens) to health and wellness applications. This article shows how huge the blockchain potential is for this collaboration.

Like a blade in a knife sharpener, AI lives on data; the more data accessible, the sharper and more precise the results. Blockchain technology enhances this idea by generating a vast and easily accessible data pool through smart contracts and on-chain apps. This improves the accuracy of AI analytics while also adding a previously unheard-of level of depth and blocking the understanding of behavioral patterns.

The nature of the examined data, which is comparable to the public market data used for financial market transparency, lessens the risks to privacy. This ensures that the deep insights gained do not compromise personal privacy. In real life, AI and blockchain could change regulatory frameworks by allowing real-time audits, the discovery of fraud, and a better understanding of how people behave and how economies work. Beyond the advantages for regulation, this potent combination promises to open up new ways to track economic growth, identify irregularities, and support real-time policy formation. Blockchain networks empower their vast, decentralized data repositories to significantly improve economic models, prevent illnesses, and forecast market movements.

More than 100 projects that are either developing or using this combination demonstrate the endless possibilities for what blockchain and AI can do together. This alliance marks a change toward more inventive, open, and fair digital ecosystems rather than merely advancing technology.

As we teeter on the verge of this fascinating frontier, the opportunities appear almost endless. The potential for open-source innovation to drive both technologies to new heights and the richness of intelligence that blockchain + AI may provide are the two main promises of this combination. This strong connection has a bright future ahead of it. It's an exciting voyage into the unknown, and I, for one, can't wait to see where it leads.

CHAPTER 9 BLOCKCHAIN BREAKTHROUGH: REWIRING TRADE FINANCE FOR THE DIGITAL AGE

Global Trade Reimagined: The Digital Transformation Landscape

The current digital revolution in commerce has significantly changed the manner of conducting international business transactions, particularly with regard to documentary credits. Digital technology, which has the potential to fundamentally alter current practices while also enhancing efficiency, security, and transparency, is what is causing this shift. Digital technology automation streamlines crucial procedures in documentary credits from the beginning to the end. By speeding up a transaction's whole lifespan, this automation lowers the time and effort needed for manual interventions. Automated techniques are crucial in guaranteeing the adherence to the terms and conditions of documentary credits.

They can help parties communicate in real time and spot irregularities, resulting in a more streamlined and effective procedure. Digital platforms provide continuous transaction monitoring, thereby enabling prompt discovery and notification of anomalies or unforeseen occurrences. By guaranteeing that parties may promptly resolve problems, this feature improves the general dependability and security of commerce transactions.

Effective implementation of digital platforms facilitates easier communication among stakeholders in documentary credit transactions. Online portals and messaging services make secure and quick data transmission possible, which improves decision-making and encourages cooperative trading environments.

One of the main components of this digital revolution is the switch to digital documents. Digital signatures and other digital authentication methods, when combined with digital copies of crucial trade papers, guarantee the legitimacy and integrity of the documents.

Technological advancements have led to the development of sophisticated data analytics tools that businesses may use to get valuable insights on transaction patterns and industry trends. By assisting businesses in identifying opportunities and efficiently assessing risks, this data-driven approach improves decision-making for enterprises.

In August 2023, SWIFT released the industry guidelines for standby letters of credit and bank guarantees, marking the first step towards the necessary standardization and real-time visibility. APIs facilitate the addition of banking features to a wider range of systems, thereby simplifying the management of guarantees and standby letters of credit. This also makes operations run more smoothly.

Even before remote work became commonplace, the COVID-19 epidemic had already had a significant impact by hastening the deployment of digital techniques to facilitate documentary credit transactions. There are creative ways to maintain business continuity, such as accepting document presentations via email, as long as they come with better risk management and due diligence. Beyond documentary credits, digital transformation improves visibility throughout the whole supply chain. Real-time tracking of items made possible by technologies like blockchain and the Internet of things (IoT) reduces the risks associated with shipment inconsistencies.

We will have the chance to learn more about how generative AI and smart cogeneration are going to further transform the documentary credit industry. Emerging technologies have the ability to automate and improve trade finance procedures, from compliance checks to contract execution. This will create a more secure, streamlined, and interconnected global trade ecosystem. International trade is becoming more efficient, safe, and transparent, thanks to the digital revolution in global business.

Unleashing Creativity: The Dawn of Generative AI

The discussion of artificial intelligence (AI) in relation to technology has progressed from theoretical ideas to real-world uses in a wide range of sectors since the 1950s. As we explore the effects of generative artificial intelligence (GenAI) on international trade and trade finance, it is essential to comprehend the fundamental purpose of artificial intelligence (AI), according to Encyclopaedia Britannica. AI is the ability of digital computers or computer-controlled robots to perform tasks typically associated with intelligent beings. This description lays the groundwork for examining how AI, and more specifically GenAI, is changing the trade industry—particularly in the area of documentary credits. Letters of credit and other documentary credits are essential for safe payment in international trade.

Traditionally, manual examination of these documents takes time and is prone to human error. With the introduction of automation and digitalization in this field, GenAI makes it possible to process documents more quickly and accurately. Without requiring a lot of human involvement, GenAI may use machine learning algorithms to analyze the specifics of invoices, shipping papers, and other pertinent documentation to make sure they adhere to the terms and conditions of the credit.

The use of searchable digital formats and electronic images represents a significant advancement in document management. GenAI is capable of converting paper documents into digital formats, facilitating their storage, retrieval, and analysis. This digital revolution streamlines the procedures for trade finance operations by enabling faster searches and access.

CHAPTER 9   BLOCKCHAIN BREAKTHROUGH: REWIRING TRADE FINANCE FOR THE DIGITAL AGE

The trade finance sector has long placed a high value on printed paperwork, which includes bills of lading, credit letters, invoices, and other necessary documents for international trade. A single transaction may include a large amount of paperwork, making managing these papers inefficient, time-consuming, and prone to human error. The shift from paper to digital documents represents a paradigm shift in the operation of trade finance. Digital records offer remote accessibility, reduce the risk of loss or damage, and simplify handling. This shift involves adopting a new ecosystem that improves efficiency and security in trade finance as well as turning paper documents into digital ones.

In this shift, GenAI technologies are essential. They can use additional AI-driven tools and advanced optical character recognition (OCR) technology to scan and transform paper documents into electronic formats. These technologies are capable of scanning and digitizing complex documents, including those with unique formats or handwriting, enabling editing and searching. Following the digitization of documents, GenAI undergoes further processing to provide searchable data. This involves using natural language processing (NLP) to evaluate and classify the information found in texts by indexing their content. This allows us to retrieve specific information from a vast digital collection using a simple search query, just like we do for information on the Internet.

The digitalization of papers and subsequent simple retrieval have greatly streamlined the processes in trade finance. For example, it is virtually immediate to confirm that a transaction is in conformity with the associated letter of credit rather than having to go through paperwork by hand. GenAI lessens the possibility of human error by automating the review and management of documents. This includes data misinterpretation, missing important information, etc. Digital papers enhance transparency among transaction participants through secure exchange, tracking, and auditing.

Decision-making becomes more expedient and well informed with faster access to pertinent papers and data. By comparing papers, analyzing historical data, and ensuring compliance more effectively, stakeholders may improve risk management and strategic planning.

Trade finance is undergoing a radical change as a result of GenAI, moving away from the traditional paper-based documentation method and toward a digital-first approach. Along with the promise of improved operational accuracy and efficiency, this shift also makes way for cutting-edge approaches to international commerce, such as automated contract creation, real-time compliance checks, and risk management with predictive analytics. GenAI has enabled the adoption of digital papers, marking a significant milestone in the development of trade finance. This has increased trade finance's adaptability, security, and efficiency in the face of global difficulties.

CHAPTER 9   BLOCKCHAIN BREAKTHROUGH: REWIRING TRADE FINANCE FOR THE DIGITAL AGE

Trade finance is undergoing a radical change as a result of GenAI, moving away from the traditional paper-based documentation method and toward a digital-first approach. Along with the promise of improved operational accuracy and efficiency, this shift also makes way for cutting-edge approaches to international commerce, such as automated contract creation, real-time compliance checks, and risk management with predictive analytics. GenAI has enabled the adoption of digital papers, marking a significant milestone in the development of trade finance. This has increased trade finance's adaptability, security, and efficiency in the face of global difficulties.

Fundamentally, GenAI is skilled at sifting through enormous volumes of data to find patterns, trends, and anomalies. We use sophisticated algorithms to sort through intricate datasets far more rapidly and precisely than human analysts.

In the sector of trade finance, documents and transactions come together to produce massive databases containing extensive information. Through training, GenAI algorithms identify the common patterns in these papers, such as regular payee names, transaction amounts, typical shipping routes, etc. GenAI algorithms report any deviation from these norms. This ability is crucial for identifying document processing problems or strange patterns that can point to a problem, such as incorrectly labeled goods or incompletely completed invoices.

GenAI's pattern recognition capabilities go beyond identifying discrepancies to include identifying possible fraudulent activity. Trade finance fraud might involve falsified paperwork, duplicate invoices, or misrepresented items. It can also be sophisticated and difficult to identify. GenAI systems look at both past and present transactions to find signs of fraud, like shipping documents that don't match up, strange payment requests, or differences in how the items are described compared to past transactions. Its early identification of these signs prevents financial loss and legal problems. Businesses may act fast with proactive fraud detection, investigating the issue further, or halting transactions before losses occur.

Many international restrictions, such as anti-money laundering (AML) statutes, sanctions lists, and nation-specific trade regulations, apply to trade finance activities. Due to their intricacy and regular revisions, manually adhering to these standards is a difficult undertaking. GenAI automates the procedure for comparing transactions to these rules. Through constant learning and updating of its regulatory environment knowledge, GenAI is able to evaluate documents and transactions for compliance in real time. This includes checking participants in a transaction against sanction lists, confirming the legitimacy of items transferred, and making sure trade documentation follows global guidelines.

The automation of compliance checks allows for the completion of the procedure in real time or nearly real time. In trade finance, delays can result in expenses or lost business prospects; a quick response is essential. GenAI also lowers the chance of mistakes being made by humans during compliance checks, making these important checks more accurate and reliable. With its sophisticated abilities in pattern recognition, fraud detection, and automated compliance checks, GenAI is having a revolutionary effect on the trade finance sector. Businesses may use GenAI to not only improve operational efficiency and lower mistake rates but also strengthen fraud prevention measures and guarantee compliance with intricate global legislation. This is a big step toward improving the efficiency, security, and compliance of trade finance operations.

Understanding the Fundamentals of Artificial Intelligence

It's important to distinguish between narrow, or specialized, artificial intelligence (AI) and broad AI when talking about AI. This difference sets the stage for the bigger existential debates about AI's future growth. It also aids in comprehending the current applications of the technology and its potential impact on business.

Systems that lack the more general cognitive capacities of human intelligence, such as chatbot-based customer support, language translation, or autonomous vehicle operation, are known as narrow artificial intelligence (AI). It operates within a specific range or domain, excelling in specific tasks but lacking the comprehensive awareness of humans.

General AI, on the other hand, talks about made-up AI systems that are like human brains in that they can learn, understand, and use their intelligence in different ways. The systems might be able to outperform humans in almost any cognitive activity by self-learning and adjusting their knowledge. Even though general artificial intelligence (AI) sparks a lot of philosophical and ethical discussion, especially when it comes to how AI objectives connect with human values, it is still a futuristic concept rather than a reality today.

An examination of AI's core technologies is necessary to understand its implications for trade. The foundation of limited artificial intelligence is machine learning, which uses large datasets and sophisticated algorithms to generate predictions or choices without explicitly programming for a job.

ML falls into two categories: supervised learning, which trains the model on a labeled dataset to understand the relationship between input variables and the target variable, and unsupervised learning, which works with raw, unlabeled data. Without instructions, the model discovers patterns and relationships within the data set. Reinforcement learning is a dynamic method where algorithms learn to make specific choices by constantly interacting with their surroundings, getting feedback, and changing their actions to get better results.

Artificial intelligence (AI) systems can analyze and comprehend complex data types, such as words, sounds, and images, thanks to deep neural networks (DNNs), which are sophisticated structures that imitate the neural networks of the human brain. Deep neural networks (DNNs) comprise several layers that employ nonlinear functions to modify the input data, with each layer's output serving as the input for the subsequent layer. This framework enables the integration and processing of various data types, enhancing AI's ability to understand and interact with the environment in a manner more akin to human behavior.

General Purpose Machine Learning (GPML) or **GPML** is the use of machine learning tasks inside DNNs to build adaptable models that can work with different kinds of data. This adaptability is essential for AI's use in a variety of fields, including trading.

GPUs, stochastic gradient descent, and out-of-sample validation are some of the tools and methods that make narrow AI work better. These help validate models and train models more effectively. Specifically, GPUs play a key role in executing the massively parallel calculations needed to train intricate DNNs.

Artificial Intelligence (AI) is revolutionizing various industries by providing powerful tools for data analysis, prediction, and automation. For efficient use in trading or any other sector, AI requires access to large datasets. AI systems may learn from a wide range of potential scenarios, including uncommon or rare examples (sometimes known as "the tails of data"), thanks to the breadth and depth of this data. The more complete the dataset, the more precisely AI can forecast results and adjust to novel circumstances, thereby enhancing decision-making, optimizing processes, and minimizing risks.

With its wide range of uses and dependence on deep learning and machine learning technologies, narrow AI is already having a big influence on a lot of industries, including trade. Large-scale, diverse datasets are necessary for its development and implementation, as is the ongoing progress of the underlying technology. While data privacy, interoperability, and ethical usage remain important concerns, limited artificial intelligence (AI) has encouraging prospects for improving productivity, creativity, and decision-making in a variety of industries as it develops.

CHAPTER 9   BLOCKCHAIN BREAKTHROUGH: REWIRING TRADE FINANCE FOR THE DIGITAL AGE

Transforming Services and Shaping Global Markets

Artificial intelligence (AI) in trade represents a paradigm shift—a new age when automation, efficiency, and innovation become the main pillars of international trade. AI has the ability to drastically alter commerce, especially in the service industry. It will impact all facets of the economy, from high-value strategic operations to standard back-office activities. Let's examine in more detail the complex effects of AI on commerce and how they may affect global value chains in the future.

Artificial intelligence (AI) transforms industries by its exceptional ability to automate complex processes, thereby enhancing production and stimulating the development of innovative goods and services. Artificial intelligence (AI) streamlines processes to save time and money on labor-intensive jobs that were previously labor-intensive, increasing productivity and quality. Many different fields use automation, including chatbots for customer support, predictive maintenance in manufacturing, and tailored suggestions in retail. Because of its information-intensive nature, the service industry stands to greatly benefit from the incorporation of AI. AI-driven transformation is a perfect fit for services like business process outsourcing (BPO) and information technology outsourcing, which encompass a variety of back-office tasks, including account administration, medical test analysis, and loan processing. These jobs, which are frequently repetitive and standardized, are ideal for automation, which would increase productivity and free up human resources for more difficult and imaginative work. Artificial intelligence has the potential to change the conventional competitive advantages that low-cost nations hold in the service offshore market, which is one of the most significant economic ramifications of AI in trade.

Countries with lower labor costs have historically drawn outsourcing operations, leveraging their manpower to complete repetitive, low-value service jobs at reasonable prices. But as AI technologies advance and proliferate, the paradigm in service production changes from labor intensity to AI intensity. This shift implies that low-cost countries' previously experienced competitive advantage would wane as AI can accomplish the same activities faster and without the geographic constraints associated with offshore. As a result, companies can reevaluate where to locate their service activities and instead choose AI solutions that are more efficient and affordable, wherever they are.

The development of AI-powered services will significantly impact the configuration of global value chains, especially concerning service jobs. Value chain dynamics are likely to shift toward more AI-intensive activities, as AI technology may automate ordinary service functions. This shift impacts not only labor markets, economic growth plans, and international trade patterns, but also the location and mode of service delivery. Investing in AI infrastructure and capabilities can provide nations and companies with a competitive edge and increase their ability to draw in a larger portion of the world's service activity. In the meantime, in order to stay competitive, countries that depend on cheap labor for their value in the global market may need to reevaluate their economic strategy and put more of an emphasis on upskilling their workforce and encouraging innovation.

AI's role in commerce, particularly in the service industry, will significantly alter the generation, provision, and consumption of services worldwide. AI-powered automation and innovation challenge established competitive advantages and necessitate a reevaluation of global value chain structures. AI's influence on commerce will probably increase as it develops and permeates more economic sectors, bringing in a new era of productivity, creativity, and international economic dynamics.

Redefining the Global Offshoring Landscape

Global commerce is undergoing a revolution thanks to artificial intelligence (AI), which is also improving trade facilitation and marketing. AI is especially influencing the traditionally appealing offshore destinations for services. Artificial intelligence (AI) is having a significant impact on how businesses, particularly micro, small, and medium-sized companies (MSMEs), conduct international commerce. This is because AI is making the process of discovering and using export prospects less complicated. Now let's see how AI is transforming this field. The entire difference in trade costs is mostly attributable to inefficiencies in customs processes. Artificial intelligence (AI) utilizes contemporary communications technology to expedite international trade by means of digital trade facilitation. Countries can use artificial intelligence (AI) to improve tariff and duty collection and effectively detect non-compliant or illicit items by shifting from paper-based to electronic data and documentation. AI is particularly adept at sifting through massive amounts of data to find patterns and anomalies, which is essential for risk-based targeting in trading. This feature enhances overall security and compliance by enabling customs officials to concentrate their inspection resources on the products, people, and businesses that pose the biggest danger. Predictive AI may also improve risk management and readiness, especially when it comes to cargo inspection using sophisticated X-ray scanners for containers, which can make the procedure less invasive and more efficient.

AI-based services play a key role in bridging the knowledge gap and introducing businesses to profitable export markets. AI can give businesses, particularly MSMEs, customized market recommendations by processing and analyzing large global market datasets. These suggestions take into account a variety of criteria, including laws, tariffs, customs taxes, non-tariff measures, and rules of origin.

The conventional dynamics of service outsourcing are changing dramatically as AI develops. The efficacy and scalability of AI-based services are threatening the competitive advantage that low-cost nations previously had, which was primarily based on labor-intensive services. The shift in service production towards AI intensity may lessen the appeal of conventional offshore sites, which would force a reassessment of global value chains and service delivery models.

With its cutting-edge approaches to the enduring problems of trade facilitation and promotion, artificial intelligence (AI) is leading a paradigm revolution in international commerce. Artificial intelligence (AI) is increasing the ability of businesses of all kinds to engage more actively in the global economy by lowering expenses, improving productivity, and offering useful insights. A new age in international trade is being heralded by the trend towards digitization, driven by AI, which is not only changing the way trade is done but also rearranging the competitive environment. As these technologies develop further, their incorporation into trade procedures should further democratize access to international markets, promoting an environment for trade that is more dynamic and inclusive.

The Policy Frontier: Shaping the New Landscape of Regulation and Ethics

In order to balance innovation, ethics, and economic progress, the area of artificial intelligence (AI) and policy considerations—especially with regard to international trade—is rapidly developing. Early international attempts to regulate AI are indicative of a growing understanding that a united strategy is required to meet the difficulties of AI while maximizing its promise. Let's examine the essential components of trade-related AI governance and the effects of regulatory frameworks.

These guidelines represent an important first step toward reaching a broad agreement on AI governance among the main economies. They set the standard for international AI policy by emphasizing creative, human rights-abiding, diverse, and economically stimulating AI development and use. The G20's acceptance of the OECD

AI Principles and the G7's establishment of the Global Partnership on AI are examples of the global community's commitment to human-centered AI principles. These programs seek to direct ethical AI research that respects human rights and encourages diversity and inclusiveness. According to agreements like the Chile–New Zealand–Singapore DEPA and the Australia–Singapore Digital Economy Agreement, AI is a topic of discussion in contemporary trade negotiations.

These accords center on exchanging ethical AI best practices, opening up access to AI technology, encouraging business and research collaboration, and establishing a framework for trade-related AI regulation. These nations hope to avoid trade obstacles emerging from AI rules by fostering early collaboration and compatibility in these areas. This strategy emphasizes how crucial it is to unify AI governance in order to promote global commerce in AI-based products and services. The European Commission's proposal for an ex ante conformity assessment mechanism emphasizes the challenges of harmonizing international AI standards. Implementing EU-specific regulations requiring AI products to comply with EU standards and undergo testing within the EU may create trade barriers for digital products and services based on artificial intelligence.

The rule that local AI systems must retrain using EU-approved data makes regulations even more complicated and could stop AI advances from freely moving across national borders. Creating legal frameworks that encourage innovation and guarantee the moral and responsible application of AI is a difficult task. An innovation-friendly strategy highlights the necessity of early and continuous international collaboration while acknowledging the interconnectedness of AI technologies. Data must freely flow across national boundaries to advance and effectively use AI. This is because varied and sizable datasets help minimize biases and improve the performance of AI systems.

To fully utilize AI in commerce, international collaboration on data governance and trust procedures is essential. It is a difficult but necessary task to control artificial intelligence in the framework of global commerce, and it calls for a sophisticated grasp of the relevant technological, moral, and financial issues. Maintaining consistency and openness to new ideas in regulations is crucial as AI continues to transform international trade. This will help AI grow without compromising morals or economic productivity. Navigating the future of AI in commerce will require cooperation among international parties, adherence to common rules, and a commitment to transparent and reliable data flows.

CHAPTER 9   BLOCKCHAIN BREAKTHROUGH: REWIRING TRADE FINANCE FOR THE DIGITAL AGE

Automating Trust in Trade Finance

The use of smart contracts in global trade automation heralds a radical change away from antiquated, paper-based procedures and toward a more efficient, digital-first strategy. This change is essential to comprehending how technological innovations are influencing international commercial transactions, particularly when it comes to documentary credits and their digital equivalents. Let's take a closer look at this subject, focusing on the importance of automation, clarity, and artificial intelligence in influencing the direction of trade finance. Documentary credits, traditionally based on paper, are a mainstay of international trade finance, providing a safe way to make payments within the system. As a result, it becomes difficult to ensure that everyone understands the documentary credits completely.

They must be precise in their phrasing and straightforward in order to prevent misunderstandings. This need for clarity highlights how challenging it will be to ensure everyone understands these materials. Documentary credits, serving as a trust-building link between frequently geographically and legally separated parties, are essential to the financing of international trade. As long as a set of mutually agreed-upon paperwork meets a number of requirements, they promise to pay the seller. This system provides a safe way to perform transactions, which supports seamless operations. As a result, it becomes difficult to ensure that everyone understands the documentary credits completely.

These financial instruments have traditionally been paper-based, a practice with roots in trading networks that date back hundreds of years. The use of physical documents creates logistical issues, including the requirement for safe transit, the possibility of damage or loss, and the inevitable delays involved in shipping paper products over international borders. Many facets of trade finance have remained firmly rooted in this paper-based heritage. As a result, it becomes difficult to ensure that everyone understands the documentary credits completely. Even with the emergence of digital technology, this problem persists. This is partly due to the respect for past norms and the slow pace at which certain jurisdictions are adopting new regulations.

Selecting precise and understandable language for a documentary credit is crucial. This accuracy is required, not just preferred. These agreements specify the criteria for the issuance of money. Included are the types of documents (invoices, bills of lading, and inspection certificates), the dates they must be presented, and guidelines for sending items. In international trade, there is very little margin for error and significant stakes. Words that are unclear or ambiguous can cause arguments, hold-ups, and financial losses. This necessitates that all parties can easily understand the wording in documentary credits, thereby preventing a variety of interpretations that could complicate the completion of a transaction.

Due to their global scope, these transactions are more challenging. The legal systems, native languages, and cultural conceptions of business practices of the parties involved may differ. This makes it challenging to ensure that all parties fully understand the documentary credits. In addition to language and cultural obstacles, one must take legal and regulatory frameworks into account. We must design documentary credits that take into account the various legal frameworks in each country, while maintaining their primary function of enabling safe and transparent transactions. Documentary credits must be precise and unambiguous, which emphasizes the value of training and experience in international trade finance.

Experts who prepare and evaluate these contracts need to be well-versed in the language and legal complexities, as well as the operational elements of international trade, shipping, and insurance. Documentary credits, the foundation of global trade, provide a safe environment for cross-border transactions. The transition from their traditional paper-based format to digital alternatives is gradually addressing some of the logistical issues, but the fundamental need for accuracy and clarity in phrasing is still there. This need underscores the difficult task of navigating the intricate interplay of languages, legal frameworks, and trade practices that define our global economy, while ensuring that all parties involved comprehend and implement these crucial agreements.

Transitioning to a Fully Digital Environment

The idea of a "smart contract" in the digital sphere becomes challenging as it is difficult to guarantee that everyone fully comprehends the documentary credits. Smart contracts are self-executing contracts with the provisions of the agreement incorporated directly into code, in contrast to their paper-based counterparts. This change brings to light a very important difference: smart contracts automate these steps and write down the agreement's terms in a way that makes compliance automatic, while documentary credits need to be carefully worded to be clear and avoid problems. Smart contracts have significantly evolved the way we carry out contracts in the digital era. Blockchain systems embed smart contracts, unlike conventional contracts recorded on paper.

CHAPTER 9   BLOCKCHAIN BREAKTHROUGH: REWIRING TRADE FINANCE FOR THE DIGITAL AGE

This digital format allows the program to encode the agreement's conditions in computer code, making them visible, impenetrable, and immediately executable. One significant development in trade finance is the transition from paper-based documentary credits to smart contracts. For a long time, documentary credits have been an essential instrument in global commerce, providing a safe way to ensure payment after meeting certain requirements. In order to ensure compliance and resolve disputes, this procedure has traditionally relied heavily on manual monitoring and paper documentation, a process that can be laborious and prone to human error. Smart contracts automate the execution of agreements. The contract does not require human intervention to carry out the agreed-upon acts once the requirements encoded in it are satisfied. This can apply to money transfers, document releases, and any other digitally controlled operations. The logic of a smart contract encodes the conditions of the agreement, not just expressing them in words. This code automatically enforces adherence to the agreement's terms by preventing the execution of its outlined actions until all requirements are satisfied.

Traditional documentary credits require careful drafting to ensure every term is clear and unambiguous, aiming to prevent misunderstandings and disputes between parties. This process demands a high level of expertise and attention to detail. In contrast, smart contracts shift this meticulous drafting into the realm of code, where the precision of the programming language leaves little room for ambiguity. In conventional trade financing, document credit disputes can get complicated and take a long time. Financial or legal middlemen often provide assistance. Because smart contracts are self-executing, they reduce the likelihood of disagreements by guaranteeing that all parties understand the rules, which the technology automatically enforces. This lessens the need for third parties to settle disputes and expedites the transaction process. Smart contracts provide a more effective and secure means of conducting transactions by automating the execution of agreements and integrating compliance into the contract's code. This efficiency is especially important for international trade, as transaction speed and dependability have a big impact on profitability. The use of smart contracts heralds a more general movement in trade finance toward digitization.

This initiative has the potential to significantly transform international trade by simplifying procedures, reducing costs, and enhancing transparency. The digital innovation of smart contracts, which represents a paradigm shift, is replacing the previous paper-based documentary credit system. This change showcases the technological advancements in trade finance and how digitalization can surmount the limitations of traditional methods to establish a more efficient, transparent, and secure framework for conducting cross-border trade transactions.

Automation and Efficiency: The Role of AI in Smart Contracts

AI technologies automate contracts, eliminating the need for middlemen by carrying out predetermined activities when specific criteria are satisfied. This process also automates the registration, validation, verification, and ownership transfer of a wide range of documents that are crucial to global commerce, such as business and shipping documents, insurance papers, and more. Developments in AI technology have a significant impact on the efficacy and development of smart contracts. Artificial intelligence (AI) offers the processing capacity and advanced algorithms required to develop smart contracts that are able to autonomously comprehend, carry out, and uphold a contract's conditions. The management and fulfillment of contractual duties will advance thanks to the synergy between AI and smart contracts. AI technologies give smart contracts the autonomy to execute predetermined actions when certain conditions are satisfied. This capacity transforms the traditional execution of contracts, substituting manual supervision and intervention with a more efficient automated approach.

The use of AI-powered smart contracts has several benefits, one of which is the decrease—or often the complete elimination—of the need for middlemen like banks, brokers, and attorneys. These middlemen are necessary in conventional commercial transactions to confirm, authenticate, and uphold the conditions of contracts. However, smart contracts have the ability to handle these duties automatically, which might streamline the procedure and perhaps cut down on the expenses and waiting times related to using a third party. The use of AI-powered smart contracts for automation is especially advantageous when it comes to global trade. It covers a wide range of essential commercial transaction documentation, such as **shipping documents**.

Smart contracts have the ability to automatically validate the legitimacy of shipping papers, identify the dispatch of products, and even start payments as soon as it is determined that the goods have been transported or received; **commercial documents** (they may ensure that all transactions follow the conditions agreed upon by automating the issue and verification of purchase orders, commercial invoices, and other relevant documents); **insurance documents** (when it comes to transportation insurance, smart contracts can speed up the processing of claims based on predetermined criteria, such as loss or damage, which can be digitally validated); and lastly, **transfer of ownership** (they can automate the transfer of ownership of products, which is perhaps one of the most important parts of international trade).

These agreements ensure the transfer of ownership only after satisfying all requirements, including payment, delivery, and regulatory compliance. Artificial intelligence (AI) advancements are propelling the emergence of smart contracts, revolutionizing the execution of contracts in international trade. Smart contracts are a better, safer, and more cost-effective alternative to traditional methods because they automate important steps like registering, confirming, and transferring ownership of goods. This technological advancement increases the dependability and speed of trade transactions while also opening up new possibilities for innovation and optimization within the global trade ecosystem.

Real-time Data and Automated Contract Formation

When it comes to drafting contracts for international trade, having access to real-time data is revolutionary. Once we validate the required requirements, the applicable technology automatically generates contracts and papers. The underlying technology in this process evaluates the compliance of established requirements, resulting in faster and more accurate contract generation. Access to real-time data is essential in today's commercial environment. It offers current information that has a big impact on risk assessment, contract negotiations, and decision-making. All stakeholders engaged in international trade may makeinformed and timely decisions based on accurate, up-todate information. This enhances the efficiency of contract drafting, improves compliance monitoring, and reduces the risk of errors or disputes. By integrating AI and real-time data into the contract creation process, stakeholders involved in international trade can achieve greater transparency, consistency, and reliability in their transactions, ultimately fostering smoother cross-border trade operations.

We make well-informed decisions using real-time data, taking into account market pricing, currency exchange rates, and the condition of items in transit. Real-time data access transforms the process of drafting and agreeing upon contracts in this setting. The dynamic and accurate nature of contracts based on real-time data is unmatched by traditional approaches, which may rely on antiquated or static information. This adjustment lowers the possibility of disagreements over terms that may have changed in the meantime by ensuring that contracts accurately represent the most recent and pertinent circumstances.

The declaration clearly states that once the relevant technology confirms the necessary standards, it is possible to generate documents and contracts automatically.

CHAPTER 9   BLOCKCHAIN BREAKTHROUGH: REWIRING TRADE FINANCE FOR THE DIGITAL AGE

This suggests a system in which algorithms or AI-powered procedures are crucial to determining if a set of predetermined requirements has been satisfied. For instance, we can program a smart contract to initiate immediate payment once it verifies the transportation and receipt of the products based on real-time tracking data.

The declaration clearly states that once the relevant technology confirms the necessary standards, it is possible to generate documents and contracts automatically. This suggests a system in which algorithms or AI-powered procedures are crucial to determining if a set of predetermined requirements has been satisfied. For instance, we can program a smart contract to initiate payment immediately upon confirmation of product transportation and receipt based on real-time tracking data. Automating processes significantly reduces the time required to develop, evaluate, and finalize contracts. The capacity to swiftly create and carry out contracts might give an advantage in international trade when speed can be critical and prevent expensive delays. Technology that verifies the fulfillment of certain requirements greatly increases the accuracy of contracts and documentation. This could encompass tasks such as adhering to delivery schedules, confirming product specifications, and fulfilling legal obligations.

The approach ensures objective satisfaction of all requirements before contract signing, thereby reducing the risk of subjective interpretation and human error. The integration of real-time data and automated verifications generates contracts more rapidly and with greater accuracy. The technology's capacity to collect and analyze enormous volumes of data, spot pertinent trends or disparities, and apply the most recent knowledge to the contract formulation process is what gives rise to this precision. Their contract formulation incorporates real-time data and technology, which is a huge improvement in international trade. This method improves accuracy and dependability while speeding up the contracting process by automating the development and verification of agreements based on the most recent data. We anticipate that technology-driven contract formulation will transform international trade operations, reduce risks, and foster a more dynamic and responsive trading environment.

The Mechanism of Smart Contracts

The idea behind smart contracts is straightforward yet effective: "If this happens, then do that." This programmable logic makes transactions safe and easy, cutting out the need for middlemen. It accomplishes this by automatically executing a contract's terms when specific conditions are satisfied. This "digital handshake" ensures transparency and trust by compelling both parties to fulfill their commitments. "If This Happens, Then Do That!". A conditional logic framework underpins every smart contract, offering a straightforward yet sophisticated use.

This reasoning is similar to the if-then statements used often in computer programming, which only carry out operations when specific criteria are satisfied. In the context of smart contracts, the confirmation of satisfied programmed requirements triggers the automatic completion of contractual obligations, including payments and ownership transfers. Distributed ledger technologies, like blockchains, embed programmable logic at the foundation of smart contracts. These conditions will carry out the contract's provisions, and the programming outlines what will happen when those requirements are satisfied. Once implemented, the logic is translatable, requiring the agreement of all parties involved for any changes.

One of the main advantages of smart contracts is the automation of contract execution. The technology itself contains and executes the conditions of the agreement, eliminating the need for human involvement. This streamlines procedures in financial transactions, legal agreements, and other contractual arrangements by drastically lowering the time and chance of error involved in contract execution. Conventional contracts frequently call for middlemen to confirm and uphold the terms of the agreement, such as banks, attorneys, or other third parties. Smart contracts offer a safe, automated method for contract execution, which largely eliminates this necessity. This can cut expenses, speed up transactions, and lessen the chance of fraud or disputes.

Smart contracts comprise a "digital handshake," offering a secure and verifiable method for parties to agree and transact. This metaphor highlights the power of the agreement and the mutual acknowledgment between the parties, reinforced by the transparency of the contract and the unchangeable record of transactions on the blockchain. Automated smart contracts carry out agreed-upon activities immediately, if criteria are satisfied, without requiring additional permission. This obliges all parties to fulfill their obligations since the contract will execute its provisions as soon as the specified circumstances are met. This technique fosters confidence between the parties, as the contract's code guarantees the fulfillment of commitments. Smart contracts provide a secure, transparent, and efficient method for automating contractual obligations, significantly enhancing the execution of agreements and transactions. By using conditional logic, smart contracts make transactions possible without the problems and wait times that come with using traditional middlemen. This technical advancement is a potent instrument in the digital era since it not only simplifies procedures but also upholds transparency and confidence between parties.

CHAPTER 9 BLOCKCHAIN BREAKTHROUGH: REWIRING TRADE FINANCE FOR THE DIGITAL AGE

The capacity of smart contracts to function without the involvement of conventional middlemen, like banks or attorneys, is among its most revolutionary features. Smart contracts do away with the need for middlemen by depending on safe mathematical code rather than faith in an outside entity. Not only does this change make transactions easier, but it also greatly reduces the chance of disagreements, since the contract will only be carried out if certain requirements are met. Conventional transactions frequently require the use of intermediaries like banks, attorneys, or notaries to authenticate, facilitate, or enforce the transaction, particularly when it comes to legal or financial problems. Smart contracts offer a paradigm change by automating these procedures, eliminating the need for these middlemen. The blockchain executes and stores the contract, enabling automation. A smart contract's primary component is its dependence on unchangeable, secure mathematical code. This code specifies the terms of the contract and the conditions under which it will operate.

Unlike traditional contracts that depend on a third party to ensure each party meets their obligations, smart contracts trust the code itself. This code is transparent, unchangeable, and run by the decentralized network, guaranteeing that it performs flawlessly and without prejudice. A smart contract's code contains the requirements for its execution, making objective verification possible. Upon meeting the predetermined conditions, the contract automatically executes the agreed-upon activities, such as transferring money or titles. This means that there is no room for manipulation or subjective interpretation. This impartiality is important to lower the chance of disagreements because the network, not a person or institution that might be biased, is in charge of carrying out the plan, and all participants know what's going on.

Smart contracts greatly streamline transactions by eliminating the need for middlemen. The participation of several third parties enables the completion of processes that previously took days or weeks almost instantly. This efficiency is especially useful in industries where speed may lower costs and increase competitiveness, such as international commerce, banking, and real estate. Disputes are less likely since smart contracts are transparent and automatically executed. All parties have an unambiguous and shared knowledge of the parameters of the agreement since they are encoded into the contract and cannot be changed once it is implemented.

Furthermore, there is less opportunity for argument on whether the requirements have been satisfied because the execution is automated and predicated on factors that can be objectively verified. The revolutionary feature of smart contracts is their ability to do transactions using safe mathematical code rather than customary middlemen. This change not only enhances transaction efficiency and speed but also significantly reduces the likelihood of conflicts by automating contract execution and basing it on objectively verifiable conditions.

This invention has the potential to fundamentally transform the establishment of agreements across various industries, enhancing transaction security, transparency, and efficiency. The integration of smart contracts into global trade automation has significantly advanced international trade transactions. Smart contracts provide a more transparent, effective, and safe way to carry out commercial agreements by utilizing the accuracy of artificial intelligence and the effectiveness of real-time data processing. Future developments could further streamline intricate trade finance procedures, reduce the need for paper-based documentation, and pave the way for an automated and more networked global trade ecosystem.

Improving Regulatory Compliance

In international trade, regulatory compliance is crucial, as rules and regulations are always changing. In order to preserve compliance, GenAI can monitor these changes in real-time and update the systems appropriately. This flexibility guarantees seamless trade operations and lowers the possibility of non-compliance fines.

Numerous laws, rules, and regulations that differ depending on the nation and the kind of commodities or services being exchanged regulate international trade. Tariffs, trade sanctions, environmental requirements, and anti-money laundering (AML) guidelines are a few examples of these policies. The fact that these rules are dynamic and alter in reaction to shifts in global affairs, economic strategies, environmental concerns, and other variables makes compliance much more difficult.

Following these rules is a must. Serious consequences, including fines, prohibitions, and harm to a company's reputation, may arise from non-compliance. To guarantee that their transactions are compliant, companies involved in international commerce must continuously monitor and adjust to legislative changes.

Real-time monitoring and analysis of regulatory updates across jurisdictions is possible with the help of GenAI technology. This capacity is essential considering how quickly trade regulations may change. Businesses find it challenging to remain up-to-date with traditional compliance monitoring systems since they are sluggish and prone to human error, typically involving manual research and updates. GenAI is capable of incorporating this data into an organization's operational systems in addition to monitoring regulatory developments. For instance, it has the ability to automatically update transaction screening procedures, risk assessment methods, and compliance checklists. By ensuring that each transaction meets the latest regulatory criteria, this eliminates the need for manual intervention.

GenAI ensures that compliance checks are constantly based on the most recent rules, greatly reducing the risk of unintentional non-compliance. This is essential to prevent fines and legal problems that may result from breaking international trade regulations. Problems with compliance may result in delays, transaction blocks, or even the seizure of products. GenAI assists in ensuring that trade operations run smoothly and are free from the disruptions that might result from non-compliance with regulations by automating compliance checks and updates. Maintaining a competitive edge in the quick-paced world of global trade depends on this efficiency.

Businesses may operate with more agility because of GenAI systems' capacity to react to changes in regulations. With the confidence that their compliance systems will adapt to the changing regulatory environment on their own, they may join new markets and adapt to new trade agreements faster. Businesses can reduce risks, stay out of trouble, and make sure their trading activities are safe and legal by using GenAI for real-time tracking and regulatory change adaptation. This flexibility is a significant advantage in the ever-changing and intricate world of international trade laws.

The groundbreaking integration of GenAI into documentary credits automates and improves procedures previously hindered by inefficient manual labor. GenAI can automate the production and processing of financial documents by creating new content from preexisting data. This lowers the amount of time needed for decision-making and increases the accuracy and consistency of business judgments. GenAI's ability to eliminate human errors could potentially achieve previously unattainable levels of uniformity and transparency. It's important to provide a degree of security and confidence for foreign transactions in addition to expediting the process. With its continuous development, GenAI may find use in trade finance not just for documentary credits but also for risk assessment, contract creation, and even trend prediction.

A pillar of global trade, documentary credits—such as letters of credit—provide a guarantee of payment according to certain terms. However, the customary handling of these devices involves manual, paper-based procedures that are labor-intensive, prone to mistakes, and frequently opaque.

Process Automation and Improvement Using GenAI

The incorporation of GenAI into this domain streamlines the process of creating, reviewing, and handling financial papers associated with documentary credits. GenAI systems can do these jobs at a previously unheard-of level of speed and efficiency by evaluating and producing content from already-existing data. The automation that GenAI offers greatly shortens the time it takes to handle documentary credits. All parties gain from this acceleration as it speeds up the process of making business choices and completing transactions. The intelligence that GenAI brings to the system goes beyond process acceleration to enable more precise and well-informed business choices. It can analyze large amounts of data to reveal insights that manual examination might not reveal.

The capacity of GenAI to decrease human mistakes is one of its biggest benefits. GenAI guarantees greater accuracy and consistency in transactions by automating the creation and processing of papers. In trade finance, where mistakes might result in disagreements, hold-ups, or financial loss, dependability is essential. By utilizing GenAI in documentary credits, international transactions become more secure and transparent. Knowing that impartial AI algorithms generated, examined, and processed the documents in accordance with agreed-upon terms may boost parties' confidence in the process.

The use of GenAI goes well beyond documentary credits. Companies can do things like risk assessment with AI and predictive analysis for market trends. Companies leverage historical data and evolving market conditions to automatically assess transaction risks, generate contracts, and ensure legal compliance by minimizing negotiation times and creating tailored contracts for each transaction. By analyzing data from international trade to identify patterns, companies can anticipate market shifts and adjust their strategies accordingly.

Trade finance uses GenAI, particularly for managing documentary credits. This represents a significant advancement from manual processes, which are time-consuming and prone to errors, to automated, reliable, and effective ones. This shift creates new opportunities for using AI in risk management, contract formulation, and market analysis, in addition to streamlining the processing of documentary credits. The potential of GenAI technology to improve trade finance's security, accuracy, and transparency will probably grow as it develops, providing promising opportunities for the future of international trade operations. GenAI plays a revolutionary role in global commerce and trade finance, providing benefits related to efficiency, accuracy, and compliance that meet the needs of the digital era. This technology will probably become common across the trade finance industry as it develops, ushering in a new era in the management of international commerce.

Digitalizing documentary credits is a big step forward in the trade finance industry because it means switching from old, paper-based processes to a digital one. This has many benefits, both in the short and long term. This digital transition incorporates smart contracts and generative artificial intelligence (GenAI) to enhance security, boost efficiency, and reduce errors. Natural language processing and machine translation models, for example, are examples of GenAI models that enable smooth communication between speakers of various languages. This is especially important for international trade, as parties with different language origins frequently engage in transactions. Despite recent automation improvements, the issuing and revision of documentary credits often require significant manual involvement. AI-driven smart contracts can automate these procedures, reducing the risk of human error and enhancing efficiency by adhering to pre-established rules and templates.

Anti-money laundering (AML) rules, sanctions screening, and compliance with international trade norms are still primarily manual processes that carry a high degree of risk and complexity. By directly integrating regulatory requirements into their logic, smart contracts may automate compliance checks and drastically lower the risk of non-compliance. AI may also evaluate legal and regulatory materials to ensure adherence to international trade laws. Technologies such as optical character recognition (OCR) and natural language processing (NLP) can automate trade document analysis. This streamlines the process by cutting down on the time, expense, and mistakes that come with manual inspections. Resolving conflicts frequently requires a lot of effort and conversation. Smart contracts have the potential to accelerate the settlement process by automatically identifying and resolving minor issues that don't actually constitute differences based on pre-established criteria.

Smart contracts enable automatic payments, releasing money only upon the satisfaction of certain criteria, such as the receipt of legal paperwork. This guarantees accurate and rapid payouts. To evaluate the risk involved in business transactions, artificial intelligence (AI) algorithms may examine enormous volumes of unstructured data from trade contracts, market reports, and legal agreements. This facilitates decision-making by offering insights obtained from thorough data analysis.

Depending on predetermined events or triggers, using smart contracts to send tracers and alerts can ensure that all participants in a transaction receive pertinent and timely information. Because of the unchangeable and open audit trail that smart contracts offer, it is easier to follow transaction histories and modifications, which increases party confidence.

Artificial intelligence (AI) algorithms that can evaluate news stories, market reports, and other information sources can provide insightful analysis of economic indicators and global market trends. Businesses need this information in order to plan ahead and identify any changes that may impact their documentary credit transactions. The digitization of documentary credits, supported by the use of smart contracts and artificial intelligence (AI), is undergoing a revolutionary change in trade finance. This change creates new opportunities for efficiency, compliance, and worldwide connection, in addition to streamlining and securing transactions. The trade finance ecosystem will become more robust and dynamic as a result of the industry's increased ability to make better decisions, lower operational costs, and improve accuracy through the automation of complex and traditionally manual procedures.

Summary

This chapter investigates how blockchain and distributed ledger technologies (DLT) are transforming trade finance by improving efficiency, openness, and security. It explains how blockchain and DLT enable safe, distributed data sharing, therefore covering their principles. Important developments include digital trade records, quicker transactions, and smart contracts that instantly automate compliance and payments as well as other tasks.

The chapter also emphasizes how artificial intelligence is merging with blockchain to inspire more creative data processing and contract building. Looking ahead, blockchain's future in worldwide commerce promises to remodel sectors, encourage new cooperation models, and change regulatory frameworks, thereby producing a completely digital trade environment.

CHAPTER 10

Rising Titans, Falling Empires: The Epic Saga of Trade Finance Consortia in the Digital Age

In an era of lightning-fast technological progress, the field of trade finance is at a turning point, facing the huge task of adopting blockchain. A lot of new projects are trying to update old ways of financing trade because of this revolutionary technology that promises to make things more open, efficient, and safe. But the road to digitalization is not easy. People in business have to deal with legal hurdles, problems with interoperability, and systems that are stuck in their ways. This chapter goes into more detail about these significant problems, providing you with a comprehensive view of the progress.

The story then goes on to look more closely at some specific blockchain projects that have sprung up in the trade finance industry. Some of these projects have failed because they were too bold, but others have been strong and are still progressing in changing the way the industry works. Each project tells a different story of hope, creativity, and the challenging facts of combining different technologies. In this chapter, the reasons for the mistakes and the factors that led to the wins are broken down. This gives a full picture of the fast-paced and sometimes rough journey of blockchain consortiums in trade finance.

CHAPTER 10   RISING TITANS, FALLING EMPIRES: THE EPIC SAGA OF TRADE FINANCE CONSORTIA IN THE DIGITAL AGE

When you think about what has happened in this industry so far, it's helpful to think about what you can learn from these ventures. This chapter tries to gather key ideas that are necessary for the successful digitization of trade finance. These lessons show how important it is to work together, make sure that rules are followed, use methods that can be scaled up or down, and work with other systems. As the trade finance industry changes, these groundbreaking projects will provide useful lessons that will show the way to a future that is more efficient and digitally enabled.

A Blockchain Dream Deferred

It is crucial to prioritize the main projects in the trade finance industry that are based on blockchain technology, which includes examining both successful efforts and those that faced major problems resulting in their failure, with the objective of offering a comprehensive examination of the key participants, focusing specifically on those who encountered insurmountable challenges.

The Marco Polo Network, established in 2017, has become a prominent platform in the trade finance industry by utilizing blockchain technology to simplify and safeguard international trade transactions. The intricacy and ineffectiveness of traditional approaches necessitated the development of a more transparent and efficient trade finance system, which served as the main impetus for its establishment. The network rapidly gained popularity, forming partnerships with prominent financial institutions and organizations and demonstrating its ability to offer immediate visibility, minimize fraud, and enhance liquidity for firms.

Nevertheless, despite its inventive methodology and initial triumph, Marco Polo Network encountered obstacles, such as governmental impediments and commercial rivalry. The combination of these problems, together with the wider effects on the economy and changing technology environment, resulted in a decrease in its acceptance and financial sustainability. In early 2024, following thorough strategic assessments, the choice was made to terminate operations, signifying the conclusion of a noteworthy phase in the development of trade finance technology. The demise of Marco Polo Network exemplified the greater obstacles encountered by blockchain-based solutions in attaining extensive and enduring industrial transformation.

Marco Polo Network was not the only participant in the blockchain trade finance industry; it encountered substantial rivalry from several other networks and platforms. The competitive environment included both direct competitors and other prominent

CHAPTER 10 RISING TITANS, FALLING EMPIRES: THE EPIC SAGA OF TRADE FINANCE CONSORTIA IN THE DIGITAL AGE

blockchain platforms that sought to change trade finance. Although blockchain technology holds enormous potential for innovation, other platforms have faced similar obstacles, suggesting that there are underlying flaws inside the business. **we.trade** was another prominent platform in the field of trade financing whose main objective was to streamline trade processes for small and medium-sized firms (SMEs). Despite having early support from well-known European banks, it eventually had trouble growing and gaining widespread acceptance, as well as difficulties enrolling customers, integrating with established financial systems, and demonstrating consistent value to a wide range of participants. These problems emphasized the obstacles to attaining a significant number of users and maintaining the positive impact of network effects.

With the aim of digitalizing the global supply chain, IBM created **TradeLens**, a blockchain platform that shares some similarities with we.trade and Maersk. TradeLens sought to improve openness, efficiency, and security in logistics and trade documentation procedures; however, it was not just focused on trade finance. Despite establishing substantial industry relationships and conducting pilot projects, it faced harsh opposition from stakeholders who were cautious about sharing data and working together on a unified platform. These difficulties highlighted more extensive concerns about industry confidence, data confidentiality, and the intricacy of incorporating blockchain technology into current procedures.

Contour quickly established itself as a formidable contender in this industry, initially focusing on the digitization of letters of credit with the goal of making this conventional trade finance tool more efficient and straightforward. The consortium achieved faster progress than Marco Polo Network by directing its attention toward a certain target sector. Its evident value proposition, together with its triumphant pilot projects and collaborations with prominent institutions, enabled the company to establish a strong user base and showcase significant advantages from the beginning.

DLTLegers is a blockchain consortium based in Singapore, founded with the vision of harnessing distributed ledger technology to revolutionize various industries. A group of forward-thinking businesspeople and technologists founded it with the goal of building a collaborative ecosystem where companies can use blockchain for increased efficiency, security, and transparency. The consortium focuses on developing innovative solutions for sectors such as finance, supply chain, and healthcare, fostering an environment of trust and collaboration among its members. Through strategic partnerships and a commitment to cutting-edge research, **DLTLegers** has become a beacon of blockchain innovation in the Asia-Pacific region, driving the adoption of this transformative technology across the globe.

CHAPTER 10   RISING TITANS, FALLING EMPIRES: THE EPIC SAGA OF TRADE FINANCE CONSORTIA IN THE DIGITAL AGE

Finally, **Komgo** has established a specialized position in the trade finance industry, with a particular focus on the commodities trading market. The emphasis on this particular aspect enabled them to effectively tackle the distinct requirements of commodity traders, encompassing concerns pertaining to openness, security, and efficacy in trade finance procedures. Its expertise allowed it to customize its solutions more efficiently, enabling faster acceptance and incorporation into established commodities trading methods. Besides this, by adopting a strategic focus, the consortium was able to rapidly build momentum and firmly establish itself in its intended market.

A Cautionary Tale in Blockchain Finance

In 2017, a pioneering enterprise formed in the realm of finance, known as we.trade, was established with the lofty objective of transforming trade finance. This consortium rapidly gathered momentum with the backing of prominent institutions such as Deutsche Bank, HSBC, Santander, Societe Generale, and UBS, which all stand as prominent financial institutions, saw the potential of blockchain technology to optimize and safeguard trade transactions, and we.trade emerged as a pioneering force in this field. In a few years, we.trade had significantly broadened its network and enhanced its capabilities, to the point that, in 2020, IBM acquired a 7% investment in the company, strengthening its technological foundation (as a whole, the shareholders comprised a heterogeneous array of renowned financial organizations, including CaixaBank, Deutsche Bank, Erste Group, HSBC, KBC, Nordea, Rabobank, Santander, Société Générale, UBS, and UniCredit). The objective of the platform was to offer a reliable, clear, and effective method for firms to participate in international trade by utilizing blockchain, with the goal of eliminating fraudulent activities and enhancing the speed of transactions.

The technology monitored the complete supply chain process, facilitating automated payments upon delivery and verification of items. This automation is a substantial advantage for small and medium-sized enterprises (SMEs), which frequently experience the negative impact of late payments. Currently, automated payments account for 55% of all transactions conducted by we.trade, a feature that provides benefits to suppliers by guaranteeing prompt payments and also incentivizes banks to provide a wider range of financing options.

Notably, the **European Late Payment Directive** was designed to tackle the issue of delayed payments, although its effectiveness has been restricted; we.trade mitigates this issue by providing automated settlement, therefore altering suppliers' cash flow management and lowering their dependence on delayed payments as a financing option for buyers, which made the platform potentially appealing to firms seeking to enhance their liquidity and operational efficiency.

Strategic alliances and a growing presence in various regions support the we.trade business model. The platform's automated settlement feature was highly regarded, prompting the consortium to consider offering it for free for domestic payments in the Czech Republic. The strategic decision on how to charge customers for this service will be left to the banks, in line with the freemium model that is widely used in the IT industry. Its goal is to encourage wider adoption.

The platform's member banks, such as Société Générale and KBC, hold substantial market shares in different areas, being conscious of the fact that a wide network is vital for ensuring the scalability and broad reach of we.trade (for instance, in the Czech Republic, three member banks jointly represent 80% of the market). In such a picture, we.trade served a wide range of industries, particularly the industrial/manufacturing and clothing/apparel sectors, although it did not determine a distinct target consumer niche due to the many characteristics of its members. In order to tackle this issue, they instead intended to implement more functionalities and broaden its capacities, such as an improved Trader Directory and interface with ERP systems.

This crucial component was meant to incorporate negotiating and agreement conditions, creating a consolidated archive for transaction-related correspondence. In addition, we.trade had the objective of broadening its collaborations in Asia and enhancing its ERP connection to facilitate the uploading of invoices and boost customer satisfaction, and its strategy entailed substantial technological enhancements, including the migration to a more up-to-date iteration of Hyperledger Fabric. In we.trade's intentions, this update would enable on-premises hosting, provide the flexibility of numerous cloud solutions, as well as decrease the expenses associated with hosting, which now represent the platform's most significant direct cost and provide banks with more alternatives for deploying the system.

In order to increase acceptance and improve the level of protection, we.trade actively collaborated with the compliance divisions of its member institutions. The platform's governance, legal, and compliance structure, referred to as the "Rulebook," was essential for its operations, especially when it came to expanding into new countries.

Although we.trade had substantial support and employed a creative strategy, it encountered notable obstacles and at last faced challenges in attaining financial viability, continually incurring expenses without obtaining the required additional financing. As the costs increased, the initial hope started to diminish: the consortium faced a challenging financial situation as it struggled to align its lofty operational objectives with the practicalities of market acceptance and income creation.

In December 2020, the firm had a substantial deficit of €8 million compared to a revenue of €4 million, partially caused by the occurrence of the COVID-19 pandemic, which exacerbated the problem by delaying the intended financing cycle in the middle of 2020. As a result of this financial burden, the company had to lay off employees and increasingly depend on shareholder finance to survive. The slow adoption among its shareholder institutions limited their potential. Only CaixaBank and Nordea have completely implemented the solution as of mid-2020; banks that are not shareholders, despite being licensed to offer trade financing, did not make a significant contribution to the broad acceptance of this service. The final blow for the company came when they experienced a lack of leadership after General Manager Ciaran McGowan left in early 2021, which further disrupted its strategic path.

In June 2022, the unavoidable event took place, and news started to emerge that we.trade were commencing insolvency procedures. The Irish Independent disclosed that the company's banking shareholders had decided to withdraw their financial backing since they were unable to justify providing any further funds. After that, they suggested making PwC the liquidator, which would be the end of a brave but ultimately unsuccessful plan. Filing for bankruptcy was a stark reminder of how challenging it can be to integrate new technology into complex financial systems.

This narrative serves as evidence for both the possibilities and challenges of utilizing blockchain technology in the financial sector. Although the consortium could not attain sustained success, their endeavor yielded vital insights on the amalgamation of blockchain technology with conventional financial processes. Their ascent and decline underscore the significance of both technological innovation and strong financial preparation and market preparedness.

This demise provides valuable insights and contemplation for blockchain businesses operating in the fields of digital commerce and trade finance. Financial viability is paramount for the long-term success and sustainability of any organization. It involves ensuring a consistent and reliable flow of financial resources to support ongoing operations, strategic initiatives, and growth plans. Sustained funding is absolutely vital during unanticipated worldwide catastrophes, like the COVID-19 pandemic, which can interrupt regular corporate operations and impose substantial financial pressure.

CHAPTER 10 RISING TITANS, FALLING EMPIRES: THE EPIC SAGA OF TRADE FINANCE CONSORTIA IN THE DIGITAL AGE

The Emergence of Marco Polo Network

Blockchain technology in trade finance aims to transform transaction processes by improving transparency, minimizing fraud, and optimizing operations. One of the prominent participants was Marco Polo Network, formerly known as TradeIX, a trade financing network based on blockchain technology that showed significant promise but ultimately encountered insolvency. Commerzbank, BNY Mellon, and SMBC, who are prominent banks, provided assistance for this blockchain trade finance network that was originally created. By utilizing the potential of blockchain technology, the network sought to revolutionize trade finance with the support of notable investors like ING Ventures and BNP Paribas. During its prime, Marco Polo Network had more than 30 bank members, demonstrating substantial interest and support from the sector.

The consortium was created with the purpose of resolving significant inefficiencies in trade finance through the establishment of a decentralized and transparent platform for executing and monitoring transactions. Since blockchain technology has the potential to save paperwork, accelerate operations, and strengthen security, therefore reducing the risks linked to trade financing, Marco Polo Network sought to easily interface with the internal systems of banks, providing a single solution that had the potential to fundamentally transform the sector. Despite the early excitement, this project had several obstacles that impeded its advancement:

After the introduction, it took almost 6 months for the initial banks to begin operating. The prolonged schedule emphasized the intricacies associated with incorporating novel financial technology into established banking institutions. Financial organizations frequently operate within strict regulatory frameworks and hold outdated technologies that might be challenging to update. The lengthy process of bringing new users on board highlighted the challenges in matching Marco Polo's solutions with the operational and compliance requirements of potential customers. Attaining market fit entails ensuring that a product satisfies the requirements and inclinations of its intended consumer base. Marco Polo had to convince banks and financial institutions about the platform's value proposition. Sluggish adoption rate indicates that the network may not have effectively met the immediate demands of the market or that there were perceived dangers and uncertainties in using the new technology. To acquire customer confidence and commitment, it was crucial to address these issues and provide concrete, measurable advantages.

The success of Marco Polo relied on network effects, whereby the platform's value grows as more individuals join and actively engage with it. The initial sluggish acceptance sparked inquiries over the network's capacity to achieve a significant number of users. In order to fully appreciate the benefits of the network, such as increased efficiency, decreased costs, and better transparency, it is necessary to have an adequate number of active members. The challenge of attracting a sufficient number of users to establish a self-sufficient and beneficial network posed a significant obstacle. The trade finance industry is characterized by intense competition, as a multitude of well-established companies developing fintech solutions compete for a larger portion of the market. Because of this, Marco Polo had to distinguish itself not just by its technology but also by showcasing higher value in comparison to current options; the presence of rivals with established histories or perceived lower implementation risks may have contributed to the early progress's delay. It was crucial for the network to construct a persuasive argument highlighting Marco Polo's distinctive benefits in order to overcome the intense competition. Establishing confidence with stakeholders, such as banks, regulators, and corporate clients, was of utmost importance.

The slow rate of implementation suggested possible apprehensions over the dependability, safety, and adherence to the platform's regulations. Marco Polo required extensive involvement with stakeholders to tackle these issues, offer guarantees, and demonstrate successful instances of use. It became clear that building trustworthiness and showcasing tangible achievements were crucial elements in attaining wider approval. The next stage in scaling a complicated trade finance network involved implementing a strong infrastructure and support systems. The modest early uptake may be indicative of difficulties in expanding the system to handle a substantial volume of users and transactions, and it exposed the fact that it was essential for long-term success to ensure that the platform could manage rising demand without compromising performance or security. Investments in infrastructure, customer service, and scalability were essential to enabling wider acceptance. Implementing a novel technology typically requires thorough instruction and training for users, and the complexity of understanding and using the platform may have led to the delayed progress of Marco Polo.

By offering comprehensive onboarding, training programs, and continuous support, users may have a deep understanding of the platform's functionalities and effectively utilize them, resulting in a faster adoption rate. This complexity of understanding and efficiently utilizing the platform may have played a role in the delayed progress of the consortium, causing a delayed early traction that nevertheless might be attributed to several factors, including the complexity of implementation, challenges in creating network effects, competition, concerns with stakeholder trust, limitations in scalability, and the necessity for user education. In hindsight, it was vital to tackle these problems in order for the network to fully realize its potential and successfully achieve its goals of revolutionizing global trade finance.

A Case Study in Blockchain Trade Finance Challenges

Marco Polo's financial condition progressively worsened, resulting in increasing difficulties that posed a threat to company survival because of several crucial issues, such as the accumulation of debts, unsuccessful investment ventures, and the difficulty of attracting new investors. Gradually, Marco Polo's financial condition deteriorated due to the company's substantial indebtedness; its liabilities surpassed the assets by €2.5 million ($2.6 million), suggesting a concerning disparity on the balance sheet. The discrepancy indicated that the consortium was facing difficulties in fulfilling its financial responsibilities, resulting in mounting pressure from creditors and heightened financial instability. The escalating debt obligation hindered the company's ability to allocate resources toward essential operations, innovation, and expansion endeavors.

Operational and strategic issues made the financial downturn worse. The challenges encompassed issues related to platform scalability, sluggish user acceptance, and the intricacies of incorporating novel technology into conventional banking infrastructures. The company's resources were stressed, and income creation was constrained due to operational challenges. Additionally, because the anticipated sources of income did not materialize as quickly as expected, strategy errors or delays in obtaining market suitability and increasing the number of users made the financial burden worse. Marco Polo's financial stability suffered a major setback when a prospective $12 million transaction with Bank of America fell through. This agreement was largely anticipated to deliver essential funds to sustain operations, improve the platform, and stimulate expansion. Its collapse not only resulted in Marco Polo losing a significant amount of money but also had a negative impact on investor trust and belief in the deal's success. Possible factors contributing to the collapse of the agreement may have included issues over due diligence, misalignments in strategy, or external economic variables. However, the failure of the deal undoubtedly exacerbated the financial crisis. After the unsuccessful agreement with Bank of America, Marco Polo faced difficulties in finding alternative investors. Securing new investors was imperative for the firm to stabilize its financial situation and guarantee ongoing operations.

Nevertheless, the declining financial condition and lost chances probably alerted potential investors. The company's viability, market position, and capacity to fulfill its commitments posed difficulties in attracting fresh money. The company's failure to get further capital worsened its financial troubles and restricted its capacity to execute recovery initiatives. The financial difficulties encountered by Marco Polo had a consequential impact on the level of trust and assurance held by stakeholders; the company's deteriorating financial condition had a significant effect on important stakeholders, such as workers, clients, partners, and creditors. The company's future ambiguity may have resulted in personnel attrition, decreased consumer involvement, and strained partner alliances. As financial uncertainty continued, it became increasingly challenging to maintain the faith and confidence of stakeholders. Marco Polo may have had to execute cost reductions and strategy adjustments in reaction to the financial crisis, from downsizing the workforce, limiting the scope of development initiatives, to pursuing strategic alliances to distribute expenses and mitigate risks. Although essential for staying afloat, these reductions frequently have a negative effect on employee morale, creativity, and the company's competitive edge in the market.

The persistent financial difficulties sparked significant apprehension over the long-term sustainability of Marco Polo, as the company's future prospects were becoming increasingly dubious due to its obligations surpassing its assets and its inability to obtain additional capital. The circumstances necessitated immediate and calculated actions to stabilize the financial situation, regain the trust of stakeholders, and reposition the organization toward sustainable development goals. Marco Polo's financial condition declined gradually as a result of accumulated debts, operational difficulties, and strategic losses. The failure to find replacement investors following the collapse of a potential $12 million deal with Bank of America made the financial crisis worse, an event that raised serious concerns about the company's ability to survive, requiring immediate and strategic actions to stabilize and recover.

The rise and fall of Marco Polo offer several important lessons for future blockchain initiatives in trade finance. The causes of failure cannot be solely attributed to financial factors but rather may extend to encompass wider industrial difficulties. Adoption and integration are the initial items on this list. It has been observed that blockchain trade finance platforms have had difficulties becoming widely accepted and integrated within the sector. The incompatibility of legacy systems and established processes in financial institutions and trading partners hindered the adoption of new blockchain technologies. The extensive customization, training, and compliance with regulatory standards required further complicated the widespread adoption of these technologies.

CHAPTER 10 RISING TITANS, FALLING EMPIRES: THE EPIC SAGA OF TRADE FINANCE CONSORTIA IN THE DIGITAL AGE

The regulatory framework governing blockchain technology in trade finance remained ambiguous and disjointed, which caused platforms to face difficulties in ensuring compliance across borders because of the diverse needs of different countries. Then, the lack of clear regulations and the slower pace at which regulations are being adjusted have impeded the potential of blockchain platforms to expand and achieve widespread adoption.

Trust and collaboration were also another issue since building them among participants was a critical challenge, particularly in trade finance, since it involves multiple stakeholders, including banks, exporters, importers, and insurers; convincing them to collaborate on a single platform and share sensitive data required overcoming significant trust barriers proved to be challenging because of their concerns about data security, confidentiality, and competitive advantage, which made it difficult to achieve the level of collaboration necessary for blockchain platforms to succeed. It was crucial, although sometimes difficult, to consistently showcase evident benefits to all participants. Because these solutions are so complicated and new, it was hard for some blockchain trade finance systems to show clear benefits that justified switching from traditional methods. This was because they needed a strong value proposition to be widely accepted, which was not always given or achieved.

In order for a blockchain project to be successful, it is essential to attain robust market fit and scalability. These two factors are crucial for guaranteeing that the technology can not only attract and keep customers but also expand and adjust to meet growing demand and changing industry requirements. This said, in order to achieve market fit, it is essential to have a thorough awareness of the unique requirements, challenges, and preferences of the target industry. Blockchain initiatives must ascertain the specific issues they aim to address and demonstrate how their solutions offer concrete advantages compared to current methodologies; then, to successfully solve real-world difficulties, it is vital to do thorough market research, analyze competitors, and obtain direct input from potential customers in order to customize the technology accordingly.

Various sectors possess distinct needs and regulatory frameworks; adapting blockchain solutions to suit these particular circumstances is crucial for achieving market suitability. For instance, a blockchain network tailored for supply chain management will include distinct features and regulatory requirements in contrast to one specifically created for financial services. Aligning the technology with industry standards and procedures makes it more useful and appealing to potential customers. Keep in mind that scalability means that a blockchain system can handle more transactions and users without affecting its performance, security, or dependability. This requires building a strong and flexible technical framework that can support growth.

CHAPTER 10 RISING TITANS, FALLING EMPIRES: THE EPIC SAGA OF TRADE FINANCE CONSORTIA IN THE DIGITAL AGE

There are important factors to consider, such as the capacity of the network to handle data, the rate at which transactions can be processed, the amount of data that can be stored, and the ability of the system to operate together with other systems, as well as others that are essential in order to incorporate scalability into plans from the beginning in order to prevent bottlenecks and inefficiencies as usage increases.

Long-term success hinges on the capacity to change and adapt to shifting needs to accommodate emerging use cases, which requires blockchain projects to possess the flexibility to assimilate new functionalities, seamlessly interact with other systems, and effectively expand their operations. Consistent innovation and incremental development are crucial in order to maintain the technology's relevance and value for consumers.

It is crucial to involve stakeholders at an early stage in the development process in order to collect valuable ideas and input that will influence the final product, since they do encompass prospective users, professionals in the field, governing authorities, and collaborators in the technology sector. Their contribution aids in verifying assumptions, identifying crucial attributes, and ensuring that the blockchain project effectively satisfies tangible requirements. Initiating involvement at an early stage establishes a basis of confidence and cooperation, hence increasing the level of commitment from stakeholders toward achieving the project's objectives. Continuous communication with relevant parties throughout the duration of the project guarantees that the solution remains in line with the requirements of the industry and can adjust to any modifications. Likewise, regular feedback loops, pilot projects, and collaborative workshops are utilized to enhance the technology, optimize the user experience, and tackle any emergent difficulties; maintaining ongoing involvement promotes a feeling of collaboration and collective responsibility, which is essential for maintaining support and progress.

In order to get a solid market fit and the capacity to grow, blockchain projects need to clearly express their value proposition, which entails showcasing how the technology addresses certain issues, promotes productivity, minimizes expenses, or fortifies security. Case studies, proof-of-concept experiments, and measurable outcomes serve to exemplify the advantages and instill assurance among prospective users.

A project that is deemed reliable is more likely to get extensive acceptance and backing; to do this, trust is an essential element of engaging with stakeholders and achieving market suitability. According to experts, blockchain projects need to build trust by keeping their promises, making sure data is correct, being open, and using trust-building strategies like third-party audits, following rules, and giving a clear explanation of the pros and cons.

Ultimately, a combination of financial challenges, limited market penetration, and severe competition caused the network to go insolvent in Ireland

CHAPTER 10   RISING TITANS, FALLING EMPIRES: THE EPIC SAGA OF TRADE FINANCE CONSORTIA IN THE DIGITAL AGE

By early 2023, both **Marco Polo** and **Symbiont**, a fintech company specializing in blockchain technology and recognized for its partnership with Vanguard, filed for Chapter 11 bankruptcy in the United States, and their predicaments garnered considerable attention from prospective buyers. Despite being supported by significant banks like Commerzbank and financial backers like ING, BNP Paribas, and SMBC, Marco Polo ran into problems after Bank of America withdrew a sizeable $12 million investment. Notwithstanding this obstacle, other entities have expressed interest in procuring its assets, under the supervision of liquidators Ken Fennell and Andrew O'Leary. Symbiont, despite its innovative approach to using blockchain technology for institutional finance, faced severe financial difficulties that led to its bankruptcy filing. Its downfall was attributed to a combination of high operational costs, a challenging fundraising environment, and increased competition within the blockchain technology space. The company's assets have attracted interest from various firms seeking to leverage its proprietary technology and intellectual property to enhance their own blockchain-based solutions.

Despite an initial rescue effort, including $6 million in temporary finance, it eventually proved unsuccessful, and the company accrued a debt of $2.3 million to its secured creditor, LM Funding, which initially was contemplating a transition from restructuring to liquidation. Nevertheless, an agreement was made to designate a Chief Restructuring Officer with the objective of overseeing Symbiont's assets and daily activities, suggesting a possible way ahead despite past financial difficulties. This event marked the second notable collapse of a blockchain trade financing network, following we.trade's insolvency in mid-2022.

A Tale of Resilience: The Rise and Fall of Contour

Contour, first introduced as Voltron, emerged as a potential solution in the field of blockchain trade finance. With the support of a group of nine illustrious banks, including HSBC, ING, and Standard Chartered, Contour sought to use blockchain technology to convert letters of credit and other trade finance procedures into digital formats. The platform offered more transparency, less paperwork, and accelerated transaction times, which were very appealing advantages in the conventionally paper-intensive trade finance sector.

Contour implemented blockchain technology with the aim of establishing a trade financing system that is both more streamlined and highly secure. Contour aimed to diminish fraudulent activities, decrease expenses, and accelerate trade operations

CHAPTER 10   RISING TITANS, FALLING EMPIRES: THE EPIC SAGA OF TRADE FINANCE CONSORTIA IN THE DIGITAL AGE

by converting letters of credit into digital format and facilitating instant updates. The network garnered substantial attention and active involvement from prominent financial institutions, underscoring the industry's acknowledgement of blockchain's capacity to revolutionize trade finance.

Contour made a notable acquisition of crucial assets from the financially unstable we.trade in the blockchain trade finance industry. This acquisition includes we.trade's rule book and associated legal paperwork, which are essential elements for open account trade financing. It is worth noting that we.trade's primary concentration lies in this area, which sets it apart from Contour, which traditionally places more emphasis on letters of credit.

Contour, with the backing of esteemed organizations such as HSBC and Société Générale, principally enables trade finance by utilizing letters of credit. This method, which involves a significant amount of effort, guarantees payment security when items are shipped. By acquiring we.trade's assets, Contour is able to broaden its reach into open account trade finance, a kind of financing that is based on invoice transactions. Contour's strategic development is in line with its long-term objective to broaden its trade financing solutions.

The rule book obtained from we.trade adheres to the International Chamber of Commerce's (ICC) Uniform Rules for Digital Trade Transactions (URDTT), a novel standard designed to simplify digital trade procedures. The establishment of a legal framework by we.trade greatly reduces the obstacles for Contour to include this new product, hence expediting its introduction into the open account trade financing market.

The purchase of Contour is more than just a transfer of assets; it is a consolidation that signifies the start of a wider industry trend. By integrating we.trade's technology and regulatory frameworks, Contour will increase its capabilities, providing a more extensive range of trade financing options. This strategic decision establishes Contour as a frontrunner in the blockchain trade finance industry, poised to take advantage of the increasing need for streamlined and protected trade finance solutions.

In addition, the participation of Contour's Head of Product, Josh Kroeker, who has previous experience with we.trade, enables a more seamless transfer and integration process. By strategically aligning, Contour can successfully utilize the acquired assets, reducing interruptions and maximizing the value gained from the purchase.

This acquisition marked a pivotal moment in the blockchain trade finance industry. It highlights the potential for consolidation if larger or more dominant networks acquire smaller or financially challenged firms. Contour's proactive acquisition of we.trade's assets highlights the significance of agility and strategic forethought in effectively managing the challenges of blockchain finance. Furthermore, the purchase may incite other participants in the industry to reassess their strategy and pursue comparable consolidation opportunities in order to augment their competitive advantage. By combining complementary technology and regulatory frameworks, innovation and operational efficiency may be enhanced, resulting in overall benefits for the wider trade finance ecosystem.

The purchase of we.trade's assets by Contour signifies a significant advancement in the blockchain trade finance sector. By incorporating we.trade's rule book and legal paperwork, Contour is positioned to broaden its range of services, delivering a complete and resilient trade financing solution. This strategic decision not only enhances Contour's market position but also paves the way for more consolidation and innovation in the field. Strategic acquisitions will play a critical role in molding the future of blockchain-enabled trade finance as the sector continues to develop.

Contour's journey began with substantial backing from major banks, including BNP Paribas, HSBC, ING, and Standard Chartered. Despite its initial success, the platform struggled with market adoption and funding, leading to its planned shutdown. However, in a significant move, Xalts acquired Contour in early 2024 for an undisclosed amount, reportedly in the high single millions, composed of cash and stock.

Xalts, initially focused on digital assets, has pivoted toward providing blockchain and tokenization solutions. The acquisition of Contour aligns with this strategy, aiming to enhance global trade finance infrastructure. According to Everett Leonidas, Director at Citi Ventures, the merger of these two companies is expected to accelerate innovation in trade finance by combining their technological capabilities and market reach.

Ashutosh Goel, CEO of Xalts, envisions creating a "Plaid for Trade," expanding Contour's network to become a digital rail, enabling businesses to access various trade and supply chain finance solutions offered by banks, fintechs, and technology partners. This vision entails leveraging Contour's existing integrations and partnerships with major corporations like Tata, Rio Tinto, and SAIC.

One of the immediate challenges for Xalts is retaining Contour's core staff and clients. With the transition period already extending beyond three months, continuity and expertise are critical for seamless integration and ongoing operations. Despite these challenges, the acquisition presents a significant opportunity for Xalts to gain credibility and market position by inheriting Contour's mature platform and its established relationships with major financial institutions.

Xalts plans to build on Contour's foundation, aiming to enhance and expand the network's capabilities. By focusing on infrastructure and providing comprehensive blockchain solutions, Xalts seeks to foster a more efficient, secure, and transparent trade finance ecosystem. This strategic acquisition underscores the enduring potential of blockchain technology in transforming trade finance, despite the hurdles encountered by pioneering platforms.

The acquisition of Contour by Xalts marks a new chapter in the journey of blockchain trade finance networks. It highlights the resilience and adaptability required to navigate the complex landscape of digital innovation in trade finance. As Xalts integrates and expands Contour's capabilities, it aims to set new benchmarks for efficiency and innovation, reinforcing the transformative potential of blockchain technology in global trade finance.

Some Digital Roadblocks to Overcome

Although Contour had a bright beginning, it faced several challenges that impeded its growth. Adopting the digitalization that Contour, a blockchain-based trade finance network, provided, ran into significant obstacles. Although digital transformation has the potential to provide several advantages, the preparedness and adoption rates of the ecosystem, particularly in relation to electronic bills of lading (eBLs), which are essential for implementing digital letters of credit, have remained low. The sluggish acceptance of Contour hindered its capacity to attain the magnitude required for enduring viability. Below is an in-depth analysis of these difficulties: The trade finance ecosystem has been predominantly characterized by traditional, paper-based operations for a considerable period of time. For many years, many stakeholders, such as shipping firms, banks, and logistics providers, have heavily relied on these well-established procedures. Adopting digital solutions necessitates a substantial change in mentality and habits, which may encounter opposition. Stakeholders may exhibit hesitancy in relinquishing known procedures in favor of novel, unverified technology.

Deploying digital solutions such as Contour's platform required a strong and reliable technological infrastructure. Numerous participants in the trade finance ecosystem, particularly smaller enterprises and those in developing areas, may not possess the requisite infrastructure to facilitate the process of digitalization. This encompasses dependable Internet access, safe data storage, and the technological proficiency to oversee digital systems. The variation in technical preparedness within the ecosystem is a substantial obstacle to achieving general acceptance.

CHAPTER 10 RISING TITANS, FALLING EMPIRES: THE EPIC SAGA OF TRADE FINANCE CONSORTIA IN THE DIGITAL AGE

Electronic bills of lading are an essential element of digital letters of credit. They function as the digital counterpart to conventional paper bills of lading, serving as evidence of transportation and enabling the transfer of ownership of commodities. The limited acceptance rates of electronic bill of ladings (eBLs) emphasize the wider difficulties in converting commercial papers into digital formats. In 2021, the proportion of electronic bills of lading was a mere 1.2%, and this percentage slightly increased to 2.1% in 2022. These statistics suggest a gradual and careful attitude toward embracing digital documents.

The lack of compatibility and standards is hindering the acceptance of electronic bills of lading (eBLs). Various participants within the trade finance ecosystem may utilize different systems and formats for digital documents, resulting in compatibility issues. Ensuring the uniformity of electronic bill of lading (eBL) formats throughout the industry is essential for smooth integration and widespread adoption. Nevertheless, the process of reaching agreement on standards can be intricate and time-consuming, which in turn hampers the pace of adoption.

The Contour platform was reliant on network effects, whereby the value of the network increases as more users engage with it. Contour faces difficulties in achieving the necessary level of widespread acceptance for electronic bills of lading (eBLs) and other digital trade papers, which hinders the establishment of network effects. In the absence of adequate involvement from essential stakeholders, the platform is unable to provide its whole value offer, hence posing challenges in attracting and retaining users.

In order for Contour to achieve sustainability and financial viability, it is imperative that it attains a level of operation where its services are extensively utilized and provide a steady stream of income. The limited acceptance rates of digital solutions in the trade finance ecosystem impede this objective. A limited size implies a reduced number of transactions and less income, which creates financial strain on the platform and raises worries about its long-term viability.

To enhance the adoption of digital trade finance solutions, it is necessary to educate stakeholders on the advantages and functionalities of these technologies. Platforms like Contour should allocate resources toward awareness marketing, training programs, and industry events to effectively showcase the benefits of digitalization. Emphasizing accomplished case studies and pilot projects can bolster assurance and motivate additional parties to shift toward digital solutions.

Establishing strategic alliances with prominent stakeholders in the industry helps expedite the process of adopting new practices or technologies. Establishing partnerships with prominent financial institutions, shipping corporations, and regulatory authorities helps foster a conducive atmosphere for the implementation of digitalization. These collaborations can assist in establishing uniform procedures, creating compatible systems, and promoting regulatory modifications that make it easier to utilize digital records.

Offering rewards to those who embrace new technologies or ideas at an early stage might encourage curiosity and active involvement. Contour has the potential to provide stakeholders with cash incentives, reduced fees, or exclusive access to premium services as a reward for their commitment to utilizing the platform. Moreover, showing the financial benefits, operational improvements, and mitigation of potential hazards linked to digital trade finance might effectively convince additional businesses to adopt this approach.

It is crucial to interact with authorities in order to establish favorable frameworks for digital trade finance. Well-defined norms and guidelines can offer assurance and mitigate the perceived hazards linked to digital technologies. Collaborating with regulatory authorities to tackle compliance concerns and verify the legal validity of digital documents would foster confidence and promote wider acceptance.

To put it simply, the wider trade finance sector was not well equipped for the digitalization that Contour provided. The sluggish implementation of electronic bills of lading, which are crucial for digital letters of credit, emphasized the difficulties in shifting from conventional methods to digital alternatives. The sluggish acceptance of Contour's product hindered its capacity to reach the required level of growth for long-term viability. To tackle these obstacles, a comprehensive strategy is needed that encompasses education, strategic collaborations, incentives, and regulatory backing. This will promote the use of digital trade finance solutions and enable them to reach their maximum effectiveness.

Contour had substantial financial difficulties that finally resulted in its decision to halt operations. Despite the initial capital injections and a persuasive value proposition, the company faced difficulties in obtaining further financial support from its investors, resulting in financial instability. The points offer a comprehensive analysis of the specific financial challenges faced by Contour and their wider consequences. Contour garnered substantial attention and early funding from several supporters, including prominent financial institutions and key players in the sector, when it was first established. The potential for blockchain technology to transform trade finance through increased transparency, effectiveness, and security was what drove the initial investments. The first financing facilitated Contour in the development of its platform, the execution of test projects, and showcasing its capabilities.

Optimism and significant success were hallmarks of Contour's initial phase. The platform's development entailed cooperation with several industry stakeholders; additionally, strategic alliances were established to encourage the acceptance and utilization of the platform throughout its introduction. Key areas of focus include infrastructure, cybersecurity protocols, regulatory adherence, marketing strategies, and customer support services. The necessity of ongoing investment to maintain growth and foster innovation became evident.

Financial Struggles and Investor Reluctance

Despite the early excitement, Contour faced escalating challenges in obtaining new cash from its supporters. The slow adoption of digital trade financing solutions, skepticism regarding the return on investment, and the current state of the market were a few factors that contributed to investor reluctance. Investors may have been hesitant to invest more money without concrete proof of rapid and stable development.

Wider commercial and economic factors also impacted Contour's financial issues. Contour had challenges in securing the required financial backing because of economic downturns and changes in investor opinion and increased competition for investment in the fintech industry. Moreover, the collective success of blockchain projects and fintech businesses could have impacted investor confidence and their readiness to offer further financing.

Contour faced cash flow challenges due to its inability to get consistent financial backing. The lack of finances to meet operational expenditures, personnel salaries, and technology upkeep has caused substantial financial hardship. The firm faced a significant hurdle in managing its cash flow, which had a direct impact on its capacity to maintain operations and make essential investments for development.

Financial uncertainty hindered Contour's attempts to grow its platform and attract a sizable number of users. Scaling necessitates a significant allocation of resources toward marketing, user acquisition, and customer service in order to promote widespread acceptance. Due to insufficient finance, Contour faced difficulties in expanding its user base and persuading other industry participants to join the network, so restricting its potential for expansion.

In order to deal with the uncertainty in their finances, Contour probably had to adopt measures to reduce its operational expenses. These options might involve downsizing the workforce, lowering the scope of development initiatives, and

CHAPTER 10 RISING TITANS, FALLING EMPIRES: THE EPIC SAGA OF TRADE FINANCE CONSORTIA IN THE DIGITAL AGE

constraining marketing efforts. Although essential for immediate survival, these steps had a detrimental effect on the company's capacity to develop, attract new consumers, and sustain a competitive advantage.

Contour's financial condition became unsustainable due to a combination of sluggish adoption rates, investor reluctance, and financial instability. Despite diligent attempts to control expenditures and acquire supplementary capital, the firm was unable to generate adequate income or attract fresh investment to sustain its activities.

The choice to close down operations has substantial consequences for Contour's stakeholders, including staff, partners, investors, and consumers. Workers experienced layoffs, business partners had to adapt their approaches, investors suffered monetary losses, and customers were deprived of the platform's services. The shutdown emphasized the dangers and difficulties that come with being the first to develop new technology and business strategies.

Contour's experience highlights numerous crucial insights for finance businesses and blockchain projects. Ensuring consistent financial support is essential for maintaining growth and fostering innovation. Developing a persuasive value proposition that encourages quick acceptance is crucial for obtaining continuous investment. In addition, cultivating robust relationships with investors and stakeholders may assist in navigating financial difficulties and constructing resilience.

Contour faced difficulties in obtaining more money from its supporters, which resulted in financial instability and finally led to its decision to cease operations. Despite the initial capital injections and early positive outlook, the network failed to garner adequate and consistent financial backing to maintain its expansion and accomplish its strategic objectives. The difficulties encountered by Contour emphasize the significance of ongoing financial commitment, robust investor connections, and the necessity of a persuasive value proposition to stimulate acceptance and ensure long-term viability.

Operational Hurdles in Digitizing Trade Finance and Blockchain Integration Challenges

In addition to the aforementioned factors, the network had many operational difficulties: The process of converting complicated trade finance procedures into digital format poses considerable difficulties. Integrating blockchain technology with current systems and procedures is a challenging task, despite its many advantages, like enhanced transparency, security, and efficiency. In order to achieve success, this transition necessitates a significant level of industry collaboration and standardization. Trade finance comprises intricate transactions involving several stakeholders, such as exporters, importers, banks, insurers, and logistical providers. Every transaction necessitates the management of many papers, including letters of credit, bills of lading, and invoices. Digitizing these procedures involves converting complex workflows, which have historically relied on paper, into digital formats while ensuring that all stakeholders can access and utilize the information efficiently.

Trade finance is subject to extensive regulation, which includes strict compliance obligations aimed at preventing fraudulent activities, money laundering, and other illicit financial activities. The legislation differs among various nations and areas, which increases the complexity of the digitalization process. Ensuring that digital trade finance solutions adhere to all regulatory standards and maintain compliance across international boundaries is a substantial problem. A significant number of trade finance businesses utilize outdated IT systems that lack compatibility with emerging technologies such as blockchain. Incorporating blockchain technologies into these existing systems necessitates significant technical proficiency and resources. The integration must be smooth and uninterrupted to prevent any delays in operations and to guarantee that the new digital processes can coexist with existing workflows.

Another significant obstacle is the assurance of data compatibility among diverse systems. Blockchain platforms must provide efficient communication channels with diverse databases, ERP systems, and other IT infrastructure utilized by trade finance players. Standardizing data formats and communication protocols is crucial for enabling seamless data sharing and interoperability. Effective digitalization of trade finance operations necessitates cooperation among many parties, such as financial institutions, maritime firms, regulatory bodies, and technology vendors. These stakeholders must collaborate to synchronize their interests, exchange knowledge, and create cohesive solutions that yield advantages for the whole sector. Establishing a collaborative ecosystem is crucial for tackling the intricacies of digitalization and ensuring that all stakeholders are fully committed to the process of transformation.

Standardization is essential for the extensive use of digital trade finance systems. Industry standards guarantee that all parties utilize comparable technology and strictly follow the same procedures, facilitating the integration of systems and the sharing of data. The development of these standards necessitates the collaboration of industry organizations, regulatory agencies, and technology vendors in order to establish generally recognized principles and frameworks.

Blockchain technology offers significant advantages in terms of increased transparency and traceability. Transactions recorded on a blockchain are unchangeable and can be readily examined, minimizing the possibility of deceit and mistakes. The level of transparency provided is especially advantageous in the field of trade finance, as it ensures the origin and legitimacy of both papers and items are of utmost importance.

Blockchain technology provides strong security features, such as cryptographic encryption and decentralized consensus procedures. These characteristics bolster the security of trade finance transactions by safeguarding sensitive information from cyber threats and unlawful entry. The reliability of blockchain technology also fosters trust among parties, promoting seamless and dependable trading procedures.

Pathways to Efficiency and Adoption

Implementing blockchain technology to digitize trade finance procedures may greatly enhance efficiency and save expenses. Automated intelligent agreements have the capacity to optimize operations, eradicate manual processing, and expedite transaction durations. By decreasing the dependence on physical documents and reducing administrative expenses, financial savings may be achieved for all parties involved. Implementing blockchain technologies in trade finance should be undertaken in a systematic and gradual manner. Commencing with pilot projects and smaller-scale deployments enables firms to evaluate the technology, recognize obstacles, and enhance procedures prior to expanding. Implementing in phases also aids in risk management and instills trust among stakeholders.

Embracing novel technology necessitates allocating resources for the purpose of providing training and instruction to all individuals involved. Organizations must ensure that their staff has a comprehensive understanding of how to proficiently utilize blockchain technologies and is knowledgeable about the advantages and difficulties associated with them. Training programs, workshops, and ongoing learning opportunities are crucial for developing the requisite skills and knowledge.

It is crucial to initiate communication with regulatory bodies from the beginning in order to ensure that blockchain solutions adhere to compliance regulations. Engaging in cooperative endeavors with regulators can assist in shaping regulatory structures that facilitate digital transformation while also mitigating hazards. Engaging in discussions with regulators also helps in the creation of optimal methods and guidelines that are in accordance with legal and regulatory requirements.

CHAPTER 10   RISING TITANS, FALLING EMPIRES: THE EPIC SAGA OF TRADE FINANCE CONSORTIA IN THE DIGITAL AGE

If you look more closely, you can see that a more complete environment that is ready for digital change is needed for blockchain technology to work in trade finance and other areas. To get the most out of blockchain technology's benefits, like better security, speed, and openness, it's important for the whole environment to be widely adopted. This includes technologies that work with blockchain, like electronic bills of lading (eBLs). Blockchain networks will have a challenging time reaching the size and effect they need if they aren't widely used. Electronic bills of lading, or eBLs, are crucial to digital trade banking. They are like paper bills of lading, but they are digital instead of paper. They show that things were transported and who owns them. It is important for electronic bills of lading (eBLs) to be widely used so that trade finance systems that use blockchain technology can work well. Electronic bills of lading (eBLs) make it safe, easy, and clear to send trade papers, which is one of the most important benefits of blockchain technology in trade finance.

To fully digitize trade finance activities, we need to use more digital tools and technologies than just electronic bills of lading (eBLs). These include digital IDs, automated compliance systems, and electronic billing. To provide a unified and effective answer, blockchain networks must easily connect with different technologies. These extra technologies might not be included in blockchain apps, which could make them less useful overall. Resistance to change is a big problem that makes it challenging to get everyone to use supporting technology. Several important players in the trade finance environment have been using old-fashioned paper-based methods for a long time and may be hesitant to switch to digital options. It is important to show the clear benefits of digitization, give enough training, and deal with security and stability problems if you want to get past this resistance.

Making sure that different systems and platforms work together and are consistent is important for digital trade finance technologies to become widely used. It's challenging to make sure that electronic bills of lading (eBLs) and other digital papers can be sent easily between businesses and systems that don't have set procedures. Everybody in the business needs to work together to set up and follow standard formats and processes. It is important to make it simple for different systems to work together and encourage widespread acceptance. Digital tools for trade finance may not be used as much as they could be because of rules and laws. When it comes to trade paperwork, data privacy, and digital deals, different countries and regions have different rules. It is challenging to get electronic bills of lading (eBLs) and other digital papers to abide by the law and follow the rules; this requires collaborating with the appropriate officials and passing laws to support them. All the people and organizations in the trade finance value chain must work together to build a complete framework for using blockchain technology. This includes banks, shipping companies, transportation providers, insurance, government agencies, and technology vendors. In this case, working together might help people with similar interests match their efforts, share their best ideas, and come up with complete answers that meet everyone's needs.

Putting money into the digital infrastructure that is needed to make blockchain and related technologies easier to use is very important. This refers to the process of making IT systems better, strengthening defenses against cyberattacks, and making sure that everyone has a stable, nonstop Internet link. If putting money into infrastructure makes sure that everyone can use and benefit from digital trade finance solutions, then educating and training everyone involved is necessary to create a digitally equipped environment. Awareness campaigns, training programs, and workshops may help stakeholders understand the benefits of digitization, get better at using new technology, and get over any resistance to change. Participants in continuing education classes stay up to date on the newest ideas and best ways to do things. Besides this, giving rewards to early adopters is another effective way to get people to use and accept digital trade finance solutions.

Some incentives that might make stakeholders more likely to switch to digital solutions are cash prizes, lower transaction fees, and access to more features. Recognizing and rewarding people who support and accept new technologies and ideas when they are still in their early stages may set a positive example that will encourage others to do the same. Additionally, getting people to accept new technologies requires clearly showing the real benefits of digitization. There is proof that using digital trade finance systems can improve efficiency, cut costs, and lower risk through case studies, test projects, and real-world deployments.

Giving real proof of positive results boosts trust and faith in the technology. It is well known that the trade finance environment is always changing to meet new needs and take on new challenges. To keep up with these changes and make sure that digital trade finance solutions stay useful and important, they need to keep getting better. For changes and new ideas to keep coming up, it's important to keep in touch with stakeholders to get their comments and learn about new needs. We can make the benefits and advantages of blockchain even better by exploring and expanding the ways it can be used and the technologies that go with it. Blockchain technology can be used for more than just trade finance. It can be used for supply chain management, customs clearance, and trade compliance, among other things. Adding more types of applications encourages more people to use them and helps build a bigger digital environment.

CHAPTER 10   RISING TITANS, FALLING EMPIRES: THE EPIC SAGA OF TRADE FINANCE CONSORTIA IN THE DIGITAL AGE

Strategies to Secure Sustained Financial Support for a Blockchain Project's for Long-Term Success

The potential longevity and success of blockchain projects hinge significantly on securing sustained financial support. This financial support must go beyond attracting initial investment to encompass ensuring ongoing funding for continuous development, operations, and scaling. Here is an in-depth exploration of why sustained financial support is crucial and how it can be effectively secured: At the inception of a blockchain project, attracting initial investment is crucial.

This requires a compelling value proposition that clearly articulates the problem being solved, the innovative nature of the solution, and the potential market opportunity. Investors need to understand the unique benefits of the blockchain project, including how it enhances transparency, security, efficiency, or reduces costs in the target industry. A well-structured business plan is essential for attracting initial investment. This plan should outline the project's vision, mission, and strategic goals, as well as a clear roadmap for development and deployment. It should include detailed financial projections, market analysis, and risk assessments. Providing a realistic and achievable plan builds investor confidence in the project's viability and potential for success.

Investors often look at the strength and expertise of the project team. Assembling a team with a diverse set of skills, including blockchain technology, industry knowledge, business development, and marketing, is crucial. A strong team with a proven track record can instill confidence in investors, showcasing the project's capability to execute its plans effectively. Securing ongoing funding requires demonstrating consistent progress and achieving key milestones. Regularly updating investors on the development status, pilot implementations, user adoption rates, and other significant achievements help to build trust and maintain their interest. Meeting or exceeding milestones shows that the project is on track and effectively utilizing initial funds. Transparency in financial management is vital for securing sustained funding. Providing regular financial reports, budget updates, and detailed explanations of how funds are being used assures investors that their money is being managed responsibly. Transparency also helps to address any concerns or questions from investors, reinforcing their confidence in the project.

Continuous engagement with investors is key to securing ongoing support. This involves regular communication through meetings, updates, and reports. Building strong relationships with investors, understanding their expectations, and keeping them informed about the project's progress and challenges can lead to a more supportive and collaborative funding environment.

CHAPTER 10   RISING TITANS, FALLING EMPIRES: THE EPIC SAGA OF TRADE FINANCE CONSORTIA IN THE DIGITAL AGE

Relying on a single source of funding can be risky. Diversifying funding sources helps to spread risk and ensures a more stable financial foundation. Potential funding sources include venture capital, private equity, strategic partnerships, government grants, crowdfunding, and revenue from initial coin offerings (ICOs) or security token offerings (STOs). Each funding source has its own advantages and challenges, and a diversified approach can provide greater financial security. Forming strategic partnerships with established companies, industry leaders, and other blockchain projects can provide additional funding and resources. These partnerships can also offer technical support, market access, and credibility. Collaborating with partners who share a vested interest in the success of the blockchain project can lead to mutual benefits and long-term financial support. Developing and implementing sustainable revenue generation models is critical for long-term financial stability.

Blockchain projects can explore various monetization strategies, such as transaction fees, subscription services, licensing, and offering premium features. Building a steady revenue stream reduces dependency on external funding and enhances financial independence. Public funding and grants from government agencies, industry bodies, and non-profit organizations can provide vital support, especially in the early stages of a project. Compared to private investments, these funds often impose fewer restrictions. Compared to private investment, these funds often have less restrictions and can play a crucial role in financing research, development, and pilot projects. Financial planning involves forecasting, budgeting, and managing resources efficiently. This includes preparing for potential financial challenges and developing contingency plans. A robust financial plan ensures that the project can sustain operations even in the face of unexpected expenses or economic downturns. Maintaining cost control and operational efficiency is essential for maximizing the value of available funds. Regularly reviewing expenses, optimizing resource allocation, and implementing cost-saving measures help to ensure that funds are used effectively. Efficient financial management can extend the project's runway and increase the likelihood of securing additional funding.

Financial resilience involves creating buffers, such as reserve funds or emergency capital, to manage financial shocks. Building financial resilience ensures that the project can navigate periods of uncertainty or financial difficulty without compromising its core operations or strategic goals. The blockchain and fintech industries are dynamic and constantly evolving. Staying adaptable and responsive to market changes is crucial for securing ongoing funding. This includes keeping abreast of new funding opportunities, regulatory changes, and emerging trends that could impact the project's financial strategy. Investors are more likely to support projects that have a clear vision for scalability and long-term growth. Articulating a vision that extends beyond the initial implementation and includes plans for expansion, innovation, and market leadership can attract sustained investment. Demonstrating how the project will scale and evolve over time reassures investors of its long-term potential.

Securing sustained financial support is crucial for the longevity of blockchain projects. This involves not only attracting initial investment but also ensuring ongoing funding to support development, operations, and scaling. Achieving this requires demonstrating progress, maintaining financial transparency, engaging with investors, diversifying funding sources, building strategic partnerships, implementing sustainable revenue models, managing financial risks, and adapting to market changes. By taking a strategic and proactive approach to financial management, blockchain projects can build a stable foundation for long-term success.

Collaboration and Standardization as Key to Successful Blockchain Integration in Trade Finance

Integrating blockchain technology into existing trade finance processes requires more than just technological advancements; it necessitates effective collaboration and the establishment of industry standards. These elements are crucial for creating a seamless, efficient, and widely accepted digital trade finance ecosystem. Coordinated efforts from multiple stakeholders across the industry are essential to achieving this goal. Here is a detailed exploration of why collaboration and standardization are vital and how they can be effectively implemented. Trade finance involves a complex ecosystem of diverse participants, including exporters, importers, banks, insurers, shipping companies, and regulatory authorities. Each participant plays a critical role in the process, and their systems and practices must be aligned for blockchain integration to be successful. Effective collaboration guarantees that all parties are in agreement, striving toward shared objectives and utilizing their distinct strengths and viewpoints.

Collaboration helps to build trust and consensus among stakeholders. Introducing a disruptive technology like blockchain can create uncertainty and resistance. Through collaborative efforts, stakeholders can discuss concerns, share insights, and develop mutually beneficial solutions. Building trust is crucial for fostering a willingness to adopt new technologies and processes.

CHAPTER 10   RISING TITANS, FALLING EMPIRES: THE EPIC SAGA OF TRADE FINANCE CONSORTIA IN THE
              DIGITAL AGE

Collaborative efforts facilitate resource sharing and joint innovation. By pooling resources, expertise, and knowledge, stakeholders can accelerate the development and implementation of blockchain solutions. Collaboration encourages innovation by bringing together different perspectives and ideas, leading to more robust and creative solutions that address the unique challenges of trade finance. Standardization is essential for ensuring compatibility, interoperability, and efficiency in the use of blockchain technology across the trade finance ecosystem. Industry standards define common protocols, data formats, and best practices that all participants can follow. This uniformity simplifies integration, reduces complexity, and enhances the overall effectiveness of digital trade finance solutions.

Common protocols are necessary for enabling seamless communication and data exchange between different systems and platforms. These protocols guarantee that all participants comprehend and process digital documents, transactions, and data consistently. Developing and adopting common protocols requires industry-wide collaboration and agreement on technical specifications and requirements.

Standardization also helps ensure regulatory compliance across different jurisdictions. Trade finance is subject to various regulatory frameworks, including anti-money laundering (AML), know your customer (KYC), and data privacy regulations. Industry standards can provide guidelines for meeting these regulatory requirements, making it easier for stakeholders to comply and reducing the risk of legal issues. Industry associations and consortia play a crucial role in coordinating efforts among stakeholders. Organizations such as the International Chamber of Commerce (ICC), the Blockchain in Transport Alliance (BiTA), and the Global Trade Finance Consortium bring together diverse participants to develop standards, share best practices, and promote the adoption of blockchain technology. These groups provide a platform for collaboration, discussion, and decision making.

Engaging regulatory bodies is essential for ensuring that blockchain solutions meet legal and compliance requirements. Regulatory authorities can provide guidance on the necessary standards and frameworks for digital trade finance. Collaboration with regulators helps to address compliance concerns, streamline approval processes, and create a supportive regulatory environment for blockchain adoption.

Technology providers, including blockchain developers and IT infrastructure companies, are key stakeholders in the integration process. Their expertise in designing and implementing blockchain solutions is critical for developing effective and scalable systems. Collaboration with technology providers ensures that the solutions are technically sound, secure, and capable of meeting the needs of the trade finance ecosystem.

Establishing formal collaborative frameworks, such as working groups, task forces, and consortiums, provides structured environments for stakeholders to work together. These frameworks facilitate regular communication, joint problem-solving, and coordinated action. They also help to ensure that all voices are heard and that decisions are made collectively.

Pilot projects are valuable for testing and refining blockchain solutions in real-world scenarios. Collaboration pilot projects involve multiple stakeholders working together to implement and evaluate the technology. These projects provide insights into practical challenges, user experiences, and the effectiveness of the solutions. Successful pilots can serve as proof-of-concept, building confidence and encouraging wider adoption.

Developing comprehensive industry standards involves defining technical specifications, data formats, security protocols, and compliance guidelines. This process requires input from all relevant stakeholders to ensure that the standards address the diverse needs of the ecosystem. Once developed, these standards should be widely disseminated, adopted, and regularly updated to reflect evolving requirements and advancements.

Education and training programs are essential for equipping stakeholders with the knowledge and skills needed to implement and use blockchain technology effectively. These programs should cover technical aspects, regulatory requirements, and best practices. Continuous learning opportunities help stakeholders stay updated with the latest developments and standards, ensuring ongoing compliance and effectiveness.

Contour's journey highlights both the potential and the challenges of using blockchain in trade finance. While the technology offers significant benefits, its successful implementation depends on market readiness, financial viability, and extensive collaboration. As the industry continues to evolve, these lessons will be crucial for future initiatives aiming to harness blockchain's transformative power. The story of Contour serves as a reminder of the complexities involved in innovating within established industries and the importance of timing, funding, and cooperation in achieving lasting change.

CHAPTER 10   RISING TITANS, FALLING EMPIRES: THE EPIC SAGA OF TRADE FINANCE CONSORTIA IN THE DIGITAL AGE

From Boom to Bust: Lessons from Contour's Journey

When Contour was created, the goal was to change trade finance through digital innovation. Banks and businesses could use the platform to instantly issue, handle, and receive letters of credit (LCs). At its peak, Contour had a network of 21 banks and many partners in many different areas. For example, Finastra, CargoX, Bolero, and Surecomp were interface and paperwork partners.

In April 2018, global banks tested this new technology for trade finance on R3's Corda platform. This was the start of its trip. By February 2019, a global test looked into how business distributed ledger technology (DLT) could help with trade-in documents. Contour's Beta network went live for live recording in October of that same year, after going live for business in January. Big companies like Tata Power, IBM TradeLens, and the Shenzhen FinTech Institute of the People's Bank of China worked with the platform.

Even though Contour tried something new, it had trouble getting enough people to use its platform, which made it harder for it to make enough money to cover its costs. The low number of people using electronic bills of lading, which was important for the platform's growth, was still a big problem. Only 1.2% of bills of lading were electronic in 2021. That number went up to 2.1% in 2022. This slow uptake made it harder for Contour to reach the scale it needed to be sustainable.

Interoperability in the trade finance environment was one of Contour's main goals. The tool was meant to connect different groups, such as banks, businesses, and digital document partners. Making a single system that met the different wants of everyone, however, turned out to be a huge challenge. Even though Contour tried, it found that compatibility could not fix the industry's deep-seated problems on its own.

The closing of Contour is adverse news for the digital trade finance business, but it also teaches us something that we can use in future projects. Contour's problems show how important it is to be ready for the market, have effective financial management, and come up with a business plan that can work. Also, the industry needs to work on getting more people to use new technologies, making digital trade finance more open to everyone, and making it easier for systems to talk to each other.

The closing of Contour shows how hard and complicated it is to digitize trade finance. Even though new technologies have a lot of potential, they can't be used for a long time without handling basic problems like being ready for the market, making sure the business can stay in business, and working together as a whole. As the field of digital trade finance continues to change, Contour's experience will be very helpful in planning future projects and making sure that digital trade solutions are put in place successfully.

TradeLens or Centralization vs. Decentralization

In December 2022, A.P. Moller-Maersk and IBM ended their joint blockchain project known as the TradeLens initiative. This initiative has a substantial impact on the enterprise distributed ledger technology (DLT) domain, with the objective of improving the efficacy and collaboration of the global shipping sector. Despite successfully managing over 36 million electronic document exchanges, TradeLens encountered difficulties in promoting cooperation among competitors and protecting sensitive information.

TradeLens demonstrated the inconsistency between centralized and decentralized methodologies in distributed ledger technology (DLT). The platform's centralized structure, which was overseen by Maersk, was designed to facilitate rapid expansion; however, it also exacerbated trust issues among competitors. The concentration made it difficult for businesses to share commercially sensitive information.

Decentralization, which is defined by the dispersion of governance and data management among participants, offers the potential benefits of trust and security. Iov42 is of the opinion that distributed ledger technologies (DLTs) should decentralize trust in data rather than the data itself, thereby resolving privacy-related issues. It is imperative to implement this approach in order to achieve the Sustainable Development Goals (SDGs), as it facilitates transparent and inclusive collaboration across supply chains.

As the TradeLens collapse demonstrated, businesses must modify their governance structures and operations to incorporate decentralization. Successful decentralization necessitates both substantial organizational adjustments and technological innovation. Global businesses are increasingly acknowledging the benefits of decentralized systems in terms of increasing corporate productivity and promoting sustainability.

The TradeLens narrative underscores the precarious equilibrium between centralization and decentralization in blockchain projects. Although centralized methods may initially offer advantages in terms of scalability, decentralized alternatives have the potential to cultivate trust and collaboration in the long term. The success of distributed dedger technology (DLT) in corporate applications is contingent upon the establishment of a balance and the subsequent modification of business procedures.

CHAPTER 10   RISING TITANS, FALLING EMPIRES: THE EPIC SAGA OF TRADE FINANCE CONSORTIA IN THE
              DIGITAL AGE

TradeLens failed to get enough market traction and scalability, even though it was supposed to change the transportation business by making it more open and efficient. This part talks about what blockchain technology means for the transportation business as a whole, the problems it faced, and TradeLens's rise and fall.

TradeLens was founded in 2018 with the big goal of digitizing the whole global supply chain. TradeLens wanted to use blockchain technology to create a safe and open tool for tracking goods; cutting-edge technology was also instrumental in advancing industry-wide norms and system interoperability on paperwork and making it easier for everyone involved to work together. The tool was created to make things more clear and effective, which will cut down on costs and wait times in the delivery process.

Because IBM and Maersk worked together on the project, it got a lot of respect and resources. Thanks to IBM's knowledge of technology and Maersk's many years of experience in shipping, TradeLens quickly got the attention and support of major shipping lines, ports, and customs officials.

During its time in business, TradeLens reached a number of important milestones. It managed to get more than 150 people to join, including well-known shipping lines like MSC and CMA CGM. By handling millions of transportation events and transactions, the platform showed how blockchain technology could be used to make complicated supply chain processes easier.

TradeLens also played a big role in advancing industry-wide norms and the ability for systems to work together. By working together with many different groups, the platform aimed to create a stronger and more efficient global shipping environment.

Even though TradeLens had some early wins, it had to close because of a lot of problems. One of the main problems was how hard it was to get a lot of people to accept it. Some shipping companies and other interested parties were hesitant to fully commit to the platform. This was partly because they were worried about data protection, competition, and the difficulties of adding new technology to systems that were already in place.

Another problem was that TradeLens was run for business, which caused problems. In contrast to non-profit groups like the Global Shipping Business Network (GSBN), TradeLens had to make money, which led to competitive strife and people not wanting to join. The COVID-19 outbreak also caused problems that were not expected, such as more competition from new digital solutions and problems with trade around the world.

CHAPTER 10   RISING TITANS, FALLING EMPIRES: THE EPIC SAGA OF TRADE FINANCE CONSORTIA IN THE DIGITAL AGE

It was reported in November 2022 that IBM and Maersk were ending TradeLens. It was planned that the website would stop working in the first quarter of 2023, giving users time to find other options. The choice was made because the platform failed to gain the business viability and market uptake it needed to keep running.

The closing of TradeLens shows that there are many important lessons to be learned about using blockchain technology in the marine industry. At first, it stresses how important it is to reach critical mass and gain market approval. Blockchain solutions must have a lot of backing from people in business in order to work. This means that worries about data protection, connectivity, and competition need to be put to rest.

Another thing that TradeLens's experience shows is how challenging it can be to balance innovation with making money. Even though blockchain technology could be very helpful, it is essential to create a long-lasting business plan that works for a lot of different groups.

Finally, the fact that TradeLens is no longer running does not mean that blockchain technology will no longer be used in the shipping business. GSBN and other groups are still looking into how blockchain could be used to improve supply chain processes. The lessons we learned from TradeLens can help us make future efforts to make solutions that are more open, collaborative, and flexible.

This story about TradeLens shows both the possibilities and the problems that come with using blockchain technology in the shipping industry. Even though the platform ran into problems that could not be solved, its efforts to digitize and organize global supply lines have made it easier for new ideas to come up. The information gathered from TradeLens will be very helpful in creating the next generation of digital shipping options as the business world changes.

Navigating the Blockchain Waters in Shipping: The "Curious Case" of TradeLens and GSBN

Things that use blockchain to make processes more open, efficient, and safe have worked really well in the shipping business. Two well-known organizations in this field are TradeLens, which Maersk and IBM jointly founded, and the Global Shipping Business Network (GSBN), which is supported by several significant shipping lines. As well as TradeLens's rise and problems, this part also talks about its end and GSBN's plan and power.

CHAPTER 10   RISING TITANS, FALLING EMPIRES: THE EPIC SAGA OF TRADE FINANCE CONSORTIA IN THE DIGITAL AGE

A lot of people were excited when TradeLens came out because it was supposed to change the shipping business by using blockchain technology to organize and speed up the shipping process. The company was able to make a strong network and meet important people. TradeLens had a lot of potential and new technologies, but it had a lot of problems that led to its closure in late 2022.

TradeLens went out of business because of a lot of things. The idea was good in theory, but it was challenging to come up with a business plan and get people to buy into it. TradeLens was a business that wanted to make money, so they wanted to sell data. This made the business world less trustworthy and less competitive. People also thought it was cool to work with Maersk, even though it had already signed up a lot of other shipping lines. A lot of people found it challenging to join. At first, it looked like the COVID-19 outbreak would be beneficial for digital tools. There was a lot of new money put into transportation technology, though, which made the battle tougher. It was easier for these new businesses to move quickly and change their minds than for TradeLens, since they didn't have to deal with old ways of doing things and industry groups.

On the other hand, the non-profit group GSBN did things in a different way. BIG shipping lines like COSCO Shipping Lines and Hapag Lloyd back it. Their plan wasn't so much to make money off of data as it was to make a system that would let everyone work together. GSBN became a neutral player in the shipping environment by focusing on building the foundation (like an operating system) instead of specific apps. This made it simple for different players to work together and talk to each other.

CEO of GSBN Bertrand Chen said that their method was to use technology to solve real business problems instead of just using it for the sake of using it. In order to improve their services, GSBN also looked into technologies like private computers that were connected. GSBN was able to meet the goals of the business without being tied to a single tool because of this way of doing things.

Shipping companies and blockchain platforms still want to digitize a lot of shipping papers, especially bills of lading. But it has been slow to catch on. It is thought that only 1.5%–2% of bills of lading were digital. Banks, shipping lines, and companies must work together for wide use. This digital stuff is beneficial for businesses because it helps them save time and money. What about banks? They want to wait and see before deciding on a single answer because there aren't any clear market winners yet.

The Digital Container Shipping Association's (DCSA) efforts have made it simple to connect and use various electronic bill of lading (eBL) systems. It's essential that this work is done so that digital trade is easier for everyone to use and more open.

CHAPTER 10 RISING TITANS, FALLING EMPIRES: THE EPIC SAGA OF TRADE FINANCE CONSORTIA IN THE DIGITAL AGE

Things that went wrong with TradeLens and GSBN teach us a lot about how difficult it is to use blockchain in the shipping business. There aren't many products that make money and get a lot of people to use them. TradeLens failed to do both. On the other hand, GSBN's focus on teamwork and infrastructure shows how to keep new ideas coming up. A lot of work still needs to be done to fully digitize shipping, but groups like GSBN and DCSA are making progress. The work they've done shows that they want to improve the shipping business by making it safer, more open, and more efficient.

We need to learn from these early tries because they will impact how blockchain and digital trade solutions are used in the future all over the world. The story of TradeLens and GSBN shows how important it is to be adaptable, work together, and focus on making technology better rather than just making things better in the real world.

The Genesis and Evolution of the Global Shipping Business Network (GSBN)

The Global Shipping Business Network (GSBN) was established to address the pressing need for digital transformation in the maritime industry. Traditional paper-based processes became increasingly unworkable as global trade volumes increased because of their inefficiencies, delays, and fraud vulnerabilities. Recognizing these challenges, a consortium of leading shipping lines and terminal operators came together to form GSBN, aiming to leverage cutting-edge technology to revolutionize the sector.

A group of powerful companies from the industry, including COSCO Shipping, Orient Overseas Container Line (OOCL), Hapag-Lloyd, and Hutchison Ports, founded GSBN. These founding members envisioned a blockchain-powered platform that would enhance transparency, security, and efficiency across the supply chain. The network aimed to provide a trusted digital infrastructure that would facilitate seamless data exchange among all stakeholders, from shippers and consignees to port operators and customs authorities.

The journey to operationalize GSBN was not without challenges. The initial phases involved extensive collaboration to standardize processes and ensure interoperability among diverse systems. However, these efforts soon bore fruit as GSBN launched its first major initiative: a paperless cargo release system. This innovation drastically reduced the time required for cargo release from several days to mere hours, showcasing the transformative potential of blockchain technology.

CHAPTER 10   RISING TITANS, FALLING EMPIRES: THE EPIC SAGA OF TRADE FINANCE CONSORTIA IN THE DIGITAL AGE

Building on its early success, GSBN expanded its membership and scope of services. New members, such as Ocean Network Express (ONE), joined the consortium, further strengthening its global reach. GSBN also integrated advanced technologies like the Internet of things (IoT) to provide real-time traceability of shipments. These enhancements enabled the network to offer comprehensive solutions that improved visibility and control over the entire shipping process.

Strategic partnerships with various industry stakeholders, such as customs authorities and financial institutions, were a defining feature of GSBN's growth. These partnerships were crucial in driving the adoption of electronic bills of lading (eBL) and other digital documentation solutions. As the industry moves toward full digitization, GSBN remains at the forefront, committed to fostering innovation and ensuring the safe, efficient movement of goods across the globe.

The future of GSBN looks promising, with plans to further integrate artificial intelligence and big data analytics to enhance decision-making and predictive capabilities. As global trade continues to evolve, GSBN's role in shaping the digital landscape of the maritime industry will be pivotal, driving progress and setting new standards for efficiency and transparency.

From its inception to its current status as a leader in digital transformation, the Global Shipping Business Network has exemplified the power of collaboration and innovation. By harnessing blockchain technology and fostering trusted partnerships, GSBN has set a new benchmark for the shipping industry, paving the way for a more connected and efficient global supply chain.

The Blockchain Revolution in Shipping: Ensuring Safe Chemical Cargo

In the ever-evolving world of global shipping, a groundbreaking initiative is underway to enhance safety and efficiency in the transportation of hazardous materials. COSCO Shipping and Orient Overseas Container Line (OOCL), in collaboration with the Global Shipping Business Network (GSBN), have embarked on a pioneering project to integrate blockchain technology for the secure verification of chemical cargo.

The need for stringent safety measures when shipping hazardous materials has never been more critical. A stark reminder came last year when a vessel carrying 4,000

CHAPTER 10 RISING TITANS, FALLING EMPIRES: THE EPIC SAGA OF TRADE FINANCE CONSORTIA IN THE DIGITAL AGE

Porsches and Volkswagens from Germany to the United States caught fire and sank. Suspected to be caused by lithium batteries in electric vehicles, the incident highlighted the risks associated with inadequate safety verification processes.

Traditionally, safety certifications for cargo, such as those provided by the Shanghai Research Institute of Chemical Industry Testing (SICIT), are issued on paper and handed to the sender. As these documents pass through various logistics and shipping companies, there's a significant risk of alteration, potentially leading to catastrophic consequences.

Blockchain technology offers a robust solution to these challenges. By making safety certificate data immutable and easily verifiable, blockchain ensures that all parties involved in the shipping process can trust the information they receive. GSBN's proof-of-concept leverages this technology to create a digital trail that enhances transparency and security.

Gaojun Wang, IT Director at SICIT, emphasized the importance of this innovation, stating "Redefining the Safe Transportation certification process by harnessing GSBN's blockchain infrastructure is a significant breakthrough in verification. Aside from enhancing transportation safety, the streamlined digital process also increases overall efficiency and minimizes human error."

The integration of blockchain in shipping is part of a broader digital transformation sweeping through the industry. Bertrand Chen, CEO of GSBN, highlighted the industry's commitment to making bills of lading electronic, with a target of full digitization within 10 years. This move is set to unlock further opportunities for digitizing all shipping documents, revolutionizing the way cargo is managed globally.

Additionally, the project plans to incorporate Internet of Things (IoT) technology for real-time traceability, linking safety certificates to specific cargo. This development promises to provide unparalleled visibility and control over the transportation of hazardous materials, ensuring they reach their destinations safely.

While the potential benefits are immense, the transition to blockchain-based systems is not without challenges. The recent shutdown of TradeLens, another blockchain network for cargo shipping, due to significant losses and strategic missteps, serves as a cautionary tale. GSBN's success hinges on its ability to navigate these challenges, focusing on scalability, user adoption, and continuous innovation.

The collaboration between COSCO, OOCL, GSBN, and SICIT marks a significant milestone in the quest for safer and more efficient shipping. By leveraging blockchain technology, this initiative not only addresses the critical issue of safety in transporting hazardous materials but also paves the way for a more transparent and efficient global

CHAPTER 10   RISING TITANS, FALLING EMPIRES: THE EPIC SAGA OF TRADE FINANCE CONSORTIA IN THE
           DIGITAL AGE

supply chain. As the shipping industry continues to embrace digital transformation, the integration of blockchain stands as a testament to the power of innovation in driving progress and safeguarding the future.

A New Era for Shipping: ONE's Integration into the GSBN Blockchain

Ocean Network Express (ONE) has joined the Global Shipping Business Network (GSBN), a blockchain group meant to improve digitalization in logistics. This is a big deal for the shipping business around the world. In the marine sector, this merging is a key step toward streamlining processes and making them more efficient.

ONE, the sixth-largest container carrier in the world, tried GSBN's paperless cargo release system and then bought it. The traditional way to release goods at ports is through a lot of paperwork that involves many people, such as shipping lines, consignees, brokers, and terminal owners. The typical method for doing this involves hand labor over a few days, which adds time and waste.

GSBN's answer can cut this time down to just a few hours by switching to a paperless method. This will greatly improve the speed and efficiency of cargo handling. Bertrand Chen, CEO of GSBN, talked about how digitalization could change everything. He said, "The shipping industry is at a turning point where digitalization has the potential to enable a quantum leap." Collaboration based on trust is what's needed to make this work.

It's especially intriguing that ONE chose to join GSBN now that IBM and Maersk have ended their TradeLens project, which had problems despite a lot of money being spent on it. The fact that ONE has joined GSBN shows that people in the shipping business are once again hopeful about blockchain technology as a way to update shipping systems.

The fact that major container companies have all agreed to use electronic bills of lading (eBL) strengthens this confidence. The broad use of eBL is expected to further simplify paperwork processes, lower the risk of fraud, and make global trade run more smoothly overall.

When ONE joins the GSBN network, it not only makes the group stronger but also sets an example for other companies to follow. Businesses in the shipping business can make their processes more open, safe, and efficient by using blockchain technology. Working together, GSBN and its members are making a concerted effort to use the power of digitization. This will make future global trade more connected and efficient.

CHAPTER 10   RISING TITANS, FALLING EMPIRES: THE EPIC SAGA OF TRADE FINANCE CONSORTIA IN THE DIGITAL AGE

As the logistics industry changes, GSBN's blockchain solutions will be crucial for solving the problems that come up in modern logistics and making sure that things can be moved safely and quickly around the world.

Revolutionizing Global Trade Through Digital Innovation

TradeTrust is leading a significant transformation in the complex realm of international trade, where expediency and efficiency are crucial. This innovative structure is changing the way trade deals are made and fixing problems that have been around for a long time with paper-based methods. By easily checking that documents are real and come from the right place and allowing Electronic Transferable Records (ETRs), TradeTrust makes sure that digital documents are legally equivalent to paper documents.

Imagine an environment for trade where deals are not only faster but also clearer and safer. TradeTrust makes this possible by automating trade processes, which saves a lot of money, makes them more efficient, and makes them more clear. Its effect on international trade, especially in places like Singapore, shows how important it is for digital progress and economic growth.

Singapore has become a hub for digital innovation, and TradeTrust is at the front of this digital revolution. Collaboration, pilot projects, and additions to international standards were all parts of the framework's journey. This shows the power of innovation in motion. TradeTrust was one of the first companies to do business online, showing how powerful digital solutions can be in changing the way things are done now.

A big part of TradeTrust's strength is that it can adapt to how the blockchain world is changing quickly. TradeTrust supports systems like Ethereum, Polygon, and XDC, and it focuses on cooperation to make sure that different blockchain technologies work together without any problems. Because it can do so many things, TradeTrust is a system that can adapt to the constantly changing digital world.

TradeTrust is more than just a technical service; its global reach and joint efforts show that it is also a public good for companies all over the world. TradeTrust improves the speed and safety of global trade by encouraging partnerships between governments (G2G) and businesses (B2B). A paperless, efficient, and safe foreign trade system is now a tangible reality. TradeTrust is showing the way to make it a reality.

CHAPTER 10   RISING TITANS, FALLING EMPIRES: THE EPIC SAGA OF TRADE FINANCE CONSORTIA IN THE
             DIGITAL AGE

Thanks to new ideas and working together, TradeTrust has made it possible for a huge change in global trade. Businesses are moving more and more into the digital world, and TradeTrust is helping them get there. In the future, businesses will be more efficient, open, and cooperative. When trade processes are digitalized, a new era begins where speed, security, and simple merging change the way global trade is done.

In such a world, where time is valuable, speed is what people want most in foreign trade. The XDC Trade Network is dedicated to making that happen. This new system wants to change the way digital trade deals work by using a cutting-edge platform. This will change how we make, carry out, and pay for trade agreements. When the XDC Trade Network connects to TradeTrust, it makes things easier, speeds things up, cuts down on mistakes, and maintains the highest security standards. The rules of world trade have changed in a big way.

Straight-through processing (STP) is at the heart of the XDC Trade Network. It simplifies the whole trade process to make deals go more smoothly, faster, and more reliably. The goal is to create an environment where trade can happen naturally, with little to no human involvement and high accuracy. This method greatly simplifies the difficulties usually connected with trade finance, making the process faster and less likely to make mistakes.

With its unique API connection, the XDC Trade Network gives customers more freedom than any other network. Users can change their experience to fit their needs and work flows, whether they are making bills of lading (BLs) directly on the platform or importing data from other systems. Users can choose the best way to complete their trade deals because the platform is flexible. This makes the whole process more efficient and satisfying.

Security is essential to the XDC Trade Network, and they have strict measures in place to protect data and give people trust. Full security procedures make sure that all data sent is protected, can't be changed, and is completely safe. Building digital trust is important for global trade to work, and the XDC Trade Network puts this at the top of its list of priorities to make dealing safe.

The XDC Trade Network does more than just process and verify documents. It also makes it simple for exporters to get money by sending BLs and bills. This easy-to-use process links users with liquidity providers, which makes it easier for money to move around. By connecting borrowers with various liquidity sources through the platform, better rates and terms are made available to users in a competitive market.

CHAPTER 10   RISING TITANS, FALLING EMPIRES: THE EPIC SAGA OF TRADE FINANCE CONSORTIA IN THE DIGITAL AGE

In the future, the XDC Trade Network wants to use asset tokenization to adapt to changes in the market and give users more options. Environmental, social, and governance (ESG) standards are accounted for during the financial process. This shows that the platform is committed to sustainability and fair trade. The goal is clear: the XDC Trade Network is about to change the rules of world trade and trade between countries.

A new age starts as the XDC Trade Network changes the way trade banking is usually done. This platform is going to change the way people deal around the world with its focus on straight-through processing, adaptable API connections, strong security measures, and forward-thinking plans. The XDC Trade Network is leading the way toward a future of faster, safer, and more efficient global trade deals.

The XDC Trade Network is a complete answer for improving trade finance. It does this by focusing on speed, accuracy, and safety. This part has talked about the platform's most important features and where it might be going in the future, showing how it has the potential to change the industry. The XDC Trade Network is at the forefront of global trade transformation, spearheading innovative ideas and establishing new benchmarks for reliability and efficiency.

Spurring the Digital Revolution in Trade Finance

Trade finance entered a new era on a typically hot day in Singapore. Declaring the successful completion of a preshipment finance transaction, XDC Trade Network revealed an unusual use of an electronic promissory note (ePN). This amazing success was evidence of the possibilities of digital change in world trade, not only a technical one.

Using the Credore platform, the transaction was painstakingly created and included the TradeTrust utility to satisfy strict Model Law on Electronic Transferable Records (MLETR) criteria. Supported by the Bankers Association for Finance and Trade (BAFT), the ePN's issuing followed globally accepted data standards specified by the International Chamber of Commerce (ICC) and the Digital Standards Initiative (DSI). These criteria guaranteed the dependability and strength of the transaction system in addition to compliance.

Two main players—Conqoreeon Exim Private Limited, the drawer, and TradeFinex, the drawee—were important in this innovative transaction. The advanced infrastructure of the XDC Network provided the blockchain foundation for the transaction, setting the stage for this digital interaction. Carefully managed on the Credore platform, the paperwork highlights the flawless convergence of digital and legal systems.

CHAPTER 10   RISING TITANS, FALLING EMPIRES: THE EPIC SAGA OF TRADE FINANCE CONSORTIA IN THE
            DIGITAL AGE

Legal entity identifiers (LEIs) gave a layer of legitimacy and validation, therefore verifying that Conqoreeon Exim Private Limited and TradeFinex were validated entities. The jurisdiction of the Singapore courts, which only had authority over conflicts arising from the promissory note, further increased this openness and confidence.

This deal has more importance than only its immediate financial consequences. It marks a change toward more quick, safe, and effective trade finance systems. Managing a tangible paper-based promissory note historically required a labor-intensive and time-consuming process that often took several days to finish. On the other hand, the creation and transmission of the digital promissory note only took a few minutes, demonstrating the significant time savings provided by digital records.

This digital revolution offers many benefits. Apart from shortening settlement times, the accelerated method improves transaction security and openness. For shippers, this means a major drop in financing expenses and quick access to safe trade credit. Preshipment finance, which is recognized for its rigorous know your customer (KYC) requirements and intricate execution structures, benefited especially from the speed and efficiency of this digital solution.

By means of this innovative transaction, XDC Trade Network highlighted the possibilities of its whole set of distributed apps (dApps) on the XDC Network. By giving trade documents given in digital form liquidity, the platform seeks to transform the worldwide trade finance sector. The XDC Trade Network makes sure that digital trade papers are sent and approved correctly by acting as a market and making it simple for borrowers and liquidity providers to talk to each other.

This digital ecosystem depends heavily on Credore, the platform in charge of producing the electronic promissory note. Operating several locations and registered in India, Credore provides a paperless IT solution complying with MLETR, therefore improving the legal admissibility and efficiency of cross-border trade documentation. Credore guarantees the legitimacy and dependability of electronic trade documentation by using the TradeTrust tool on the XDC Network.

This deal represents a significant milestone in the digital transformation of trade finance. It emphasizes the possibility for lowered expenses, more security, and improved trade transaction efficiency. The successes of XDC Trade Network and Credore established a standard for the future of digital commerce as the global trade finance scene changes, therefore opening the path for a more linked and effective world economy.

The path XDC Trade Network follows is evidence of the force of creativity and the unrelenting search for greatness. Their innovative efforts promise to transform the sector as they keep breaking new ground in the field of digital trade finance, therefore providing new possibilities and chances for companies all across the world. Though many more milestones remain to come, this chapter in their narrative marks only the beginning.

Embracing Failure and Collaboration in the Trade Finance and Supply Chain Industries

So far, we've seen how blockchain technology has made big steps forward in digital trade finance over the past few years. There are many success stories that show how blockchain can speed up processes, make them more open, and cut costs. Along with these success stories, there have also been times when blockchain efforts in digital trade finance have not lived up to expectations, meeting a number of problems and failures. Different results like these bring up important questions about what makes blockchain projects in this field succeed or fail.

This part will go into these problems in more detail and look at the reasons why some blockchain projects in digital trade finance have failed. We will find the main problems and issues that have stopped some projects from succeeding by looking at specific case studies and getting advice from experts in the field. To fully understand why these mistakes happened, things like technical limits, regulatory issues, and how difficult it is to connect blockchain to other systems will be looked at.

The chapter will also give strategy suggestions for how to deal with these problems and be successful in digital trade finance using blockchain. It will talk about the best ways to use blockchain tools in this field, as well as new ideas, creative solutions, and ways of working together. Stakeholders can better manage the changing world of digital trade finance and use the full potential of blockchain technology by learning from past mistakes and taking advantage of new opportunities.

The field of supply chain management is changing quickly as new technologies change the way things have always been done. Businesses must be willing to fail, work together, and focus on the tasks at hand in order to survive in this constantly shifting environment. This part is very helpful because it gives you expert advice on how to do well in the supply chain business.

CHAPTER 10   RISING TITANS, FALLING EMPIRES: THE EPIC SAGA OF TRADE FINANCE CONSORTIA IN THE DIGITAL AGE

Failures are beneficial ways to learn and get better. Businesses can improve their strategies, methods, and tools by learning from mistakes they've made in the past. Companies can get better and be more successful if they see losses as a chance to do better. Figuring out the "jobs to be done" is crucial in the supply chain business. Focusing on the end goal of meeting customer wants can help businesses make sure their processes and new ideas are in line with these goals.

In the supply chain environment, working together is a key part of being successful. Businesses need to break down tough issues and work together to come up with new ways to fix them. Organizations can find chances and solve problems more efficiently when they use the knowledge and opinions of many partners. People who work together should also be willing to try new things and learn from their mistakes. It is important to use a "test and learn" method, where the goal is to quickly iterate and get better by trying new things all the time.

In today's fast-paced business world, companies need to be able to change with the times and keep up with new technologies and market trends. Being open to new ideas and innovations means keeping up with new technologies, looking into how they might be used, and proactively incorporating them into supply chain processes. Businesses can get ahead of the competition and set the standard by encouraging a mindset of constant learning and new ideas.

Collaboration is a key factor that changes things in the supply chain business. Businesses are urged to break down standard walls and form relationships that are beneficial for both sides. Organizations can deal with problems more effectively, boost productivity, and create value for everyone by working together, sharing knowledge, and pooling resources. It is essential for people in the supply chain network to trust each other and work together.

In today's fast-paced business world, it's important to accept failures, stay flexible, and encourage teamwork. A planned method can lead to long-term success. In the supply chain industry, which is always changing, expert opinions show the way to success. By being open to failure, learning from mistakes, focusing on the tasks at hand, collaborating closely with partners, and remaining flexible during changes, companies can skillfully overcome challenges and achieve their full potential. Leaders of the supply chain in the future are being told to take the initiative to succeed during this time of change.

CHAPTER 10 RISING TITANS, FALLING EMPIRES: THE EPIC SAGA OF TRADE FINANCE CONSORTIA IN THE DIGITAL AGE

Lessons Learned the Hard Way: How to Successfully Revolutionize Trade Finance with Blockchain

Have you ever had to deal with the hassle of paper-based and manual trade finance processes? The delays and flaws that plague the business are frustrating to everyone in it. We are now going to talk about how blockchain could change trade finance by sharing some shocking facts and lessons learned about this game-changing technology.

Blockchain has the ability to change many fields, and trade finance is no different. But it's important to know that trust, not speed, is what blockchains are really all about. The technology faces the "trilemma" problem, which means it needs to find a balance between security, growth, and independence. Blockchains might not be as quick as standard systems, but they are excellent at building trust and making sure that data can't be changed.

There are some important things to remember. It is essential to know what the unique problems are in the trade finance business. Blockchain can improve trust and openness, which is what should be emphasized. Blockchain can significantly reduce the waste and scam risks that are present in conventional processes.

The trade finance industry should adopt blockchain in a way that fits its unique needs. This method can help build trust, cut down on scams, and make audits easier. Each group should look at the problems it faces and plan how it will use blockchain to solve those problems.

There are different ways that blockchain can be used, depending on what problems need to be solved. For maximum value, strategic deployment is a must, especially in areas like cross-border deals and supply chain banking. By focusing on specific uses, businesses can use blockchain in the places where it will have the most effect.

Understanding the distinction between private-permissioned and public-permissionless blockchains is crucial for the success of trade finance projects. Picking the right type is important for getting the results you want because each has its own pros and cons.

It is important to think about legal rules and sustainability laws in order to improve transparency and encourage sustainable business practices. Blockchain can provide the openness needed to follow these rules, making the trade finance setting more responsible and long-lasting.

For blockchain projects to be successful, they need to be able to grow and work with other systems. Making sure that blockchain solutions work well with current systems and can handle a lot of transactions are two crucial things that determine how well they work in trade finance.

481

For digital change to go smoothly, it's important to encourage new ideas and work together with tech experts. Using new tools and encouraging a mindset of always getting better can make trade finance systems much more open and effective.

To fully use blockchain's ability to change trade finance, it's important to understand the problems that the industry is facing, see the benefits of blockchain, and use customized methods. A successful blockchain plan must take into account legal frameworks, deal with problems related to scalability, and encourage new ideas. By focusing on these areas, businesses can unlock the changing power of blockchain, get rid of waste, and create a trade finance system that is more open, reliable, and effective.

Unleashing the Potential of Decentralized Technology Amidst Regulatory and Interoperability Challenges

By design, blockchain offers a decentralized, open, and unhackable ledger system, which makes it particularly appropriate for the trade finance sector, an "industry" that has always relied on a complex web of documentation, authentication, and trust procedures. The benefits it offers include inherent security and transparency, as well as its ability to authenticate transactions without relying on a central authority. Several of these systems have progressed beyond the proof-of-concept phase and are presently at different degrees of commercial deployment. The purpose of these platforms is to streamline safe and transparent communication among all participants in the trade finance process by offering a consolidated digital setting.

Despite the evident advantages, the integration of blockchain technology in trade finance faces several challenges because of its potential to completely transform several industries, including supply chains, healthcare, and banking. Nevertheless, the current legal and regulatory frameworks do not completely support transactions that rely on it; companies and individuals that want to adopt blockchain technology face significant challenges and uncertainty due to this lack of alignment.

An essential obstacle is the absence of precise definitions and legal acknowledgment of digital assets and transactions based on blockchain technology. A significant number of nations lack explicit rules pertaining to cryptocurrencies, tokens, and other forms of digital assets. The absence of clear information results in ambiguity regarding their legal standing, ownership entitlements, and the appropriate legal treatment they should get. Smart contracts are an essential element of this technology since they can execute themselves, with the conditions of the contract put directly into code. Nevertheless, there are substantial legal uncertainties regarding their capacity to be enforced. Conventional legal systems may not acknowledge smart contracts as legally enforceable agreements, resulting in difficulties regarding the settlement of disputes and the implementation of principles of contract law.

The unalterable and transparent nature of blockchain presents challenges in complying with data privacy and security standards as legislation, such as the General Data Protection Regulation (GDPR) in the European Union, mandates that individuals possess the entitlement to access, rectify, and erase their personal data. As a result, enforcing these rights on an unchangeable blockchain might pose challenges, giving rise to questions over adherence to data protection regulations. Legal and regulatory frameworks are mostly limited to national or regional levels, but blockchain works on a global scale. This creates jurisdictional problems because many countries may have laws that are at odds with each other. It can be challenging to figure out which law applies to a blockchain transaction, especially when it involves transactions that happen in multiple countries. Transactions conducted on a blockchain, particularly those involving cryptocurrencies, have the potential to be utilized for illegal purposes such as money laundering and funding terrorist operations.

Regulators express apprehension about the level of anonymity and pseudonymity that blockchain facilitates; thus, complying with AML and KYC rules is difficult since it involves the task of identifying and validating the identities of individuals involved in blockchain transactions. Regulators frequently struggle to keep pace with the rapid rate of innovation, and the lack of clear legal norms for blockchain initiatives might impede innovation by creating regulatory ambiguity, which may discourage firms from investing in such projects. Policymakers often face a huge problem in striking a balance between the necessity of regulation to safeguard consumers and prohibit unlawful actions and the imperative to promote innovation. It is essential for governments and regulatory bodies to provide clear definitions and groups for digital assets and transactions based on blockchain technology. This includes putting different types of digital assets, like cryptocurrencies, utility tokens, and security tokens, into groups and recognizing them legally within those groups. They must also give clear definitions, which are important for figuring out how digital assets should be handled legally under current laws.

To recognize and enforce smart contracts, legal systems need to change. This means that contract law rules need to be changed to fit the unique features of smart contracts, like automation and self-execution. Regulators also need to make it clear that smart contracts can be enforced and address issues like dispute resolution and jurisdiction.

Regulators must seek methods to reconcile the transparency of blockchain technology with the need for data privacy. One possible task is to create innovative methods for handling data on blockchain, such as using privacy-enhancing techniques like zero-knowledge proofs and storing sensitive information off-chain. It is crucial to have explicit instructions on how to adhere to data protection regulations while utilizing blockchain technology.

In order to tackle the difficulties arising from diverse legal jurisdictions, it is necessary to make concerted efforts to standardize blockchain rules across various jurisdictions. Enhancing international collaboration and coordination among regulatory authorities can foster a regulatory environment that is characterized by more consistency and predictability, and global conferences, treaties, and agreements can do the rest by facilitating the establishment of universal standards for blockchain technology. Regulatory authorities should collaborate with the blockchain sector to provide efficient anti-money laundering (AML) and know your customer (KYC) solutions that make use of the distinct features of blockchain technology. A potential use is the utilization of blockchain technology to ensure safe and verified digital IDs and to monitor transactions, since compliance necessitates the presence of explicit instructions on how to execute anti-money laundering (AML) and know your customer (KYC) protocols in transactions based on blockchain.

Regulatory sandboxes offer a supervised setting for testing blockchain initiatives, ensuring compliance with regulations, as well as facilitating experimentation and innovation while guaranteeing adherence to regulatory mandates. This way, regulators can utilize the knowledge acquired from sandbox initiatives to shape the creation of suitable legislation. Improved legal and regulatory frameworks offer enhanced legal assurance for firms and users involved in these transactions since well-defined laws decrease the likelihood of legal conflicts and bolster trust in the utilization of blockchain technology. Laws that concentrate on the particular risks that come with blockchain, like fraud and unauthorized access to data, protect consumers. Legal frameworks may also set standards for openness, security, and accountability in blockchain transactions, which would boost trust and encourage widespread use. While governments may promote innovation and expansion in the blockchain industry by establishing a well-defined regulatory framework, entrepreneurs and corporations are more inclined to allocate resources to blockchain initiatives when they are presented with a stable and encouraging legal structure, thus resulting in a boost in economic activity, the generation of employment opportunities, and the progress of technology.

The current legal and regulatory frameworks are still being completely adjusted to handle transactions that are based on blockchain technology; to bridge this gap, it is necessary to establish precise definitions and classifications, enforce smart contracts, address issues over data privacy, align international legislation, improve compliance with anti-money laundering (AML) and know your customer (KYC) requirements, and encourage the establishment of regulatory sandboxes. It becomes clear that implementing these principles would provide legal clarity, safeguard consumers, and promote innovation and expansion in the blockchain industry. Despite its growing popularity in the banking sector, blockchain still suffers from a notable lack of awareness and comprehension, especially among individuals outside the financial field. The lack of information in this area presents a significant obstacle to the general acceptance and successful application of blockchain technology in many industries. Because blockchain is intrinsically sophisticated, encompassing difficult ideas such as distributed ledgers, cryptographic hashing, consensus procedures, and smart contracts, for individuals and organizations lacking technical expertise, comprehending its concepts can be challenging, as can the use of technical terminology. Lastly, its intricate nature provides a hindrance to comprehension, hence making it difficult for non-banking industries to grasp the potential uses and advantages of blockchain.

So far, blockchain has had a minimal presence beyond the financial industry. Educational institutions, professional training programs, and industry conferences, just to name a few, often prioritize conventional technology and business methodologies, which, as a result, causes those working in sectors like healthcare, supply chain, manufacturing, and government to lack adequate chances to acquire knowledge about blockchain and its potential uses.

Navigating the Complexities: Ensuring Regulatory Compliance and Financial Stability for Blockchain Projects

A big problem for blockchain projects is that they have to figure out how to work with the complicated rules that guide different businesses. Working with regulatory bodies from the start and on a regular basis helps make sure that the technology follows all the laws and rules that apply. Dealing with regulatory concerns ahead of time and showing a dedication to compliance can make adoption go more smoothly and lower legal risks.

CHAPTER 10   RISING TITANS, FALLING EMPIRES: THE EPIC SAGA OF TRADE FINANCE CONSORTIA IN THE DIGITAL AGE

The rules and regulations around us are always changing. As rules change, blockchain projects need to keep up with them and be ready to make changes to their solutions. Staying involved with governmental bodies and industry groups helps to spot and adapt to changes in regulations, ensuring ongoing compliance and market survival.

Getting more partners, users, and tools that work well together is often needed to make a blockchain project successful. Ecosystem growth encourages people to work together, come up with new ideas, and experience network effects, which make the platform more valuable as more people use it and add to it. Getting involved with a lot of different groups of people helps to create a strong and long-lasting environment that supports growth and expansion.

To get people to accept the ecosystem, you need to use smart marketing, teach users, and offer help. To get people to use blockchain, projects must clearly explain what they can do for them, offer training and tools, and provide customer help. Pilot programs, agreements, and user incentives are some of the other ways that incentives can help the ecosystem grow and involve more people.

For any blockchain project to be successful, it needs to have a favorable market fit and be able to grow. It is important to involve stakeholders early on and keep doing so to make sure the solution meets the goals of the business, follows the rules, and builds trust. Blockchain projects can deal with problems and achieve long-term growth and success by focusing on knowing what the market wants, making sure the technology is strong, showing value, and encouraging teamwork.

To be successful in the tough and quickly changing worlds of business and technology, you need to get enough support and manage your money well. With these financial plans, a business can keep running, encourage new ideas, and reach its long-term goals. Companies should also make backup plans and get money from a variety of sources in order to lower their financial risks and make their finances more stable. Here is a more in-depth look at these cash musts.

Getting the initial money you need to start and grow any business or project is important. This money can come from a number of places, such as personal funds, grants, startup capital, or angel investors. A company needs enough starting funds to be able to develop its goods or services, hire staff, spend money on marketing, and cover its operational costs in the early stages, which are very important.

In addition to the initial funds, businesses often need ongoing investments to support growth, reach new markets, and come up with new ideas. This could mean getting more than one round of funding, with each round's goal being to reach a certain

CHAPTER 10 RISING TITANS, FALLING EMPIRES: THE EPIC SAGA OF TRADE FINANCE CONSORTIA IN THE DIGITAL AGE

milestone or grow operations. Investing regularly helps keep things moving forward and gives you the tools you need to advantage of new chances and stay competitive.

Careful planning and projections are the first steps to successful financial management. Businesses need to make thorough budgets that include all of their planned costs, income, and investments. Accurate forecasting helps predict how a business will do financially in the future, which assists with making decisions and planning strategies. The company stays on track to meet its financial goals by going over and making changes to its budgets on a regular basis.

Keeping track of cash flow is important for keeping operations stable and flexible. Businesses must ensure they have sufficient cash reserves to pay their employees, meet daily expenses, and address other pressing needs. By closely monitoring cash flow and implementing measures to enhance it, such as timely invoices, effective credit control, and vigilant inventory management, businesses can prevent cash shortages and financial issues.

Controlling prices and making operations more efficient are also important parts of effective financial management. Companies should look at their costs on a daily basis and find places where they can be cut without affecting quality or performance. Taking steps to cut costs, like getting better terms with sellers, streamlining the supply chain, and using cutting-edge technologies, can help a business stay profitable and in excellent financial health.

A careful risk assessment is the first step in making backup plans. Companies need to think about the possible financial risks that come with things like market downturns, economic recessions, changes in regulations, or sudden problems like natural disasters or pandemics. Companies can plan for different events and come up with ways to lessen their effects when they understand these risks.

Setting up disaster funds or savings is an important part of planning for the unexpected. These funds give you a safety net that you can use to pay for unexpected costs or keep the business going during tough times. Having emergency funds on hand helps the business deal with short-term problems without having to take drastic steps like laying off workers or cutting back on services that customers need.

Crisis management plans are an important part of excellent backup plans. In case of a financial problem, these plans spell out what needs to be done, such as getting more money, cutting back on unnecessary costs, or moving resources around. Companies can deal with financial problems quickly and effectively when they have a clear plan that they can follow. This keeps these problems from affecting business and long-term goals too much.

Companies can take on a lot of financial risk when they depend on a single source of funding. Diversifying your investment sources makes you less reliant on a single client or source of funding. This makes your finances more stable and gives you more options. A diversified funding portfolio might include a mix of loan financing, strategic relationships, government funds, and money made from running the business.

Getting more partners is another part of diversifying your financial sources. Institutional investors, private equity companies, crowdfunding sites, and individual angel investors are all examples of this type of investor. Not only does working with a broad group of partners bring more money to the table, but they also bring new ideas, skills, and networks that can help the business.

Strategic relationships with other businesses, trade groups, or government agencies can help you get more money and resources. Partners often get something beneficial out of these relationships, like access to new markets or technology or the chance to work together on projects. By using strategic partnerships, a business can get money from more than one source and improve its place in its industry.

When financial processes are open and clear, investors, stakeholders, and workers are more likely to trust them. Companies should provide regular financial reports, communicate with partners about significant financial actions, and maintain open lines of communication. Everyone involved in the business has a clear picture of its financial health and can make smart choices, thanks to transparency.

For financial management to work well, strong financial control practices must be put in place. Setting clear rules and guidelines for financial activities, keeping accurate records, and doing frequent audits are all parts of this. Strong governance practices make sure that people are held accountable, stop theft, and improve the general honesty of financial operations.

Navigating Uncertainty: Building Financial Resilience and Leveraging Network Effects

During a crisis, businesses may have to deal with unexpected costs, less money coming in, and changes in the market. To give you an example, the pandemic caused deep economic downturns that hurt businesses in many fields. Many businesses experienced a sudden drop in demand, problems with their supply chains, and higher costs related to health and safety regulations. This showed how important it is to have a strong financial plan that includes a variety of funding sources, emergency funds, and flexible budgeting.

CHAPTER 10   RISING TITANS, FALLING EMPIRES: THE EPIC SAGA OF TRADE FINANCE CONSORTIA IN THE
            DIGITAL AGE

Furthermore, ongoing financial help ensures that groups can successfully adapt and change their strategies in response to changing circumstances.

This could mean buying new technology to help people work from home, making improvements to digital infrastructure so that clients can be reached online, or moving staff to areas where demand is higher. Firms can get through times of uncertainty without giving up on their basic operations or long-term goals if they are financially resilient. Making sure groups can stay in business by providing ongoing support isn't just about getting through tough times; it also lets them take advantage of the opportunities that arise from them. Companies with strong finances can put their money into new ideas, buy out competitors who are having trouble, or enter new markets, giving them a clear edge over their competitors. Getting ongoing funding is important for keeping an organization's finances stable and flexible. It protects against unexpected global events, keeps operations running smoothly, and lets businesses take advantage of new opportunities in a world that is changing quickly. In order to be successful, platforms that rely on network effects must have widespread acceptance by significant groups.

This is because the usefulness or appeal of a product or service increases with the number of people who use it. This trend is especially important when it comes to digital platforms, social networks, markets, and other tools that help people connect with each other in different platforms that rely on network effects have a lot of reasons why key players must accept them. The general worth of a platform goes up as more people use it and interact with it. Similarly, a social media network becomes more appealing to users as more people interact with their friends and connections on it. Also, as more sellers offer their goods, the marketplace becomes more valuable to buyers.

On the other hand, the fact that these platforms are connected creates a synergistic effect, where each new user increases the value for existing users, creating a cycle that encourages more adoption. By getting enough users, the platform can solidify its place as the market leader. Being the clear leader often leads to increased brand recognition, loyal customers, and competitive advantages that make it difficult for new competitors to catch up. Platforms that successfully cross this important level could become the best choice for customers, making it very hard for new players to get into the market. The network is stronger and better able to handle problems when it has more users. Adding more players can make the site more resistant to changes in how users use it and to shocks from outside sources. For example, if some people stop using the network or leave, it doesn't affect the whole thing as much because there are still a lot of active users. This gives users more confidence and encourages them to keep using it.

CHAPTER 10   RISING TITANS, FALLING EMPIRES: THE EPIC SAGA OF TRADE FINANCE CONSORTIA IN THE DIGITAL AGE

Large amounts of data are collected when the platform is used a lot. This data can be used to make the platform better. Platform owners can make features better, improve the user experience, and add new services that meet users' needs by looking at how they use the platform, what they like, and how they connect with it. In the same way, using a data-driven approach helps keep current users and bring in new ones, which makes network effects stronger. When a platform is popular and growing, it tries to bring in other businesses and services that work well with it. This makes the system living and connected. For example, a popular app shop encourages makers to make and offer a wide range of programs, which increases the platform's usefulness and attracts more users. More people working together in this environment can lead to more creativity, more ways to make money, and more value for everyone.

As more people use the platform, the market starts to trust and believe in it. It becomes famous and gets support from its peers, which is likely to bring in even more potential users and encourage them to get involved. Utilizing social proof can successfully lower the costs of gaining new users and speed up the growth rate. It is crucial for systems that depend on network impacts that a lot of important players agree with them. It makes the platform more appealing to users, builds a strong place in the market, guarantees the network's strength and dependability, provides useful data analysis, encourages the ecosystem's growth, and builds trust and trustworthiness. Its owners may be able to achieve long-term growth and success by putting an emphasis on steps that make it easier for many people to use. Adaptability and flexibility are important for organizations to stay competitive and do well because they need to be able to respond to changing market conditions and new technologies in order to keep growing and be successful in the long run.

Seamless Integration and Continuous Innovation

If blockchain solutions want to be widely used and successful, they need to work well with other systems and processes. To make these solutions more valuable, they also need to work together with other companies in the same field and keep coming up with new ideas. Making sure that blockchain solutions work with current systems and processes is one of the hardest things to do. Most businesses use a well-established IT framework, which includes outdated systems that might not naturally integrate with blockchain technology. For integration to work, blockchain solutions must be created that can work with these current systems without any problems. Usually, this means making APIs, middleware, and connections that let the blockchain platform and standard systems share data and work together on processes.

Integration should cause as little trouble as possible for present processes. Businesses often don't want to use new technologies if they mean a lot of downtime or need to make big changes to how they do things. Blockchain solutions need to be made so that they can work with current systems without having to completely change how things are done. Making merging paths clear and offering help can make the change easier and boost adoption.

Each company has its own set of operating needs and ways of doing things. To meet these goals, blockchain systems must be able to be changed and customized. This means letting companies change the blockchain program to fit their needs, so the technology helps their operations instead of getting in the way. Blockchain solutions can be made more flexible by adding things like smart contracts that can be changed, user interfaces that can be changed, and settings that can be changed. For blockchain solutions to have a strong community, they need to work together with other companies in the same field.

Partners, sellers, users, governing bodies, and tech companies are all part of this ecosystem. These groups can make the blockchain network stronger and more useful if they work together. For example, in supply chain management, working together with logistics providers, makers, and sellers can make it easier to track and check goods, which makes things more clear and efficient. Industry norms and interoperability models are often made when people work together. These guidelines make sure that different blockchain solutions can work with each other. This makes it easier for more people to use and integrate blockchain. A lot of work goes into making these standards, and industry alliances and working groups are crucial to making sure that blockchain technologies work with all sorts of systems and use cases.

By teaming up with big names in business, blockchain projects can use outside knowledge and resources. Partners in the same industry can help you learn more about specific problems, rules, and best practices. Working with well-known groups also gives blockchain projects more authority, which helps build trust and attract more users. For blockchain solutions to stay relevant and competitive, they need to keep getting better. Technology is always changing, with new tools, methods, and trends coming out all the time. Blockchain projects need to keep up with these changes and add them to their solutions. This could mean adding new security methods, making the system more scalable, or using new ways to reach an agreement.

CHAPTER 10   RISING TITANS, FALLING EMPIRES: THE EPIC SAGA OF TRADE FINANCE CONSORTIA IN THE DIGITAL AGE

What users want and what they say should be the driving forces behind innovation. Getting to know people and learning about their problems, needs, and experiences can help make blockchain solutions better. The technology keeps up with its users' changing needs by getting regular changes, having features improved, and adding new features based on what users say. As part of continuous growth, blockchain technology is also being looked at for new uses and purposes. Initial uses may focus on certain areas, like banking or supply chain management, but there are a lot of other ways it could be used. Blockchain projects can find new chances and increase their value by coming up with new ideas and trying out different use cases. For blockchain systems to get and keep people, they need to show clear and real benefits. Some of these perks are higher speed, lower costs, better security, and more openness. Case studies, pilot projects, and real-world applications can help build a strong value proposition by showing how blockchain can help different businesses.

Blockchain options that work well solve specific problems in a business. Blockchain projects can set themselves apart from others by focusing on fixing real problems and offering useful answers. This could mean easing complicated processes, cutting down on scams, making it easier to track things, or making compliance easier.

Trust is an important part of what makes blockchain systems valuable. Making sure that data is correct, safe, and open builds trust among users and partners. To build trust and get more people to use blockchain, projects should focus on strong security measures, open operations, and stable performance.

Bridging the Blockchain Knowledge Gap: Unlocking Potential Across Industries Through Education and Collaboration

Being often misunderstood and met with mistrust, mostly because of its connection with cryptocurrencies such as Bitcoin, blockchain is often associated only with cryptocurrencies, which feature an unpredictable nature and several regulatory obstacles. As a result, some individuals may view it as a dangerous or speculative technology, giving rise to a pessimism that might discourage firms from investigating blockchain possibilities in their particular sectors. Insufficient knowledge and comprehension of blockchain technology result in several sectors failing to seize innovative potential, losing focus on its notable advantages, which include heightened transparency, greater security, improved efficiency, and cost reduction. Organizations that fail to comprehend these advantages may persist in using older and less effective procedures, forfeiting the opportunity to exploit blockchain technology for a competitive edge.

The lack of understanding hinders the speed at which blockchain technology is adopted and integrated into non-banking businesses because decision-makers without awareness of blockchain's potential are unlikely to allocate resources toward its deployment. Similarly, the sluggish rate at which blockchain technology is being adopted is impeding the progress of industry-specific blockchain applications and causing a delay in fully realizing the technology's maximum capabilities.

Industries that do not use blockchain are likely to face the possibility of lagging behind their more inventive competitors: while some firms embrace this technology and enjoy its advantages, others that are oblivious or hesitant may have challenges keeping pace with improvements in efficiency, security, and customer satisfaction, which is clearly a serious competitive disadvantage that might result in enduring adverse effects on growth and market position. In order to address the lack of information, which represents a huge gap, it is indeed necessary to implement extensive educational efforts and training programs that specifically target blockchain technology. Universities, technical institutions, and professional training organizations ought to include blockchain courses and programs in their curricula, which should encompass essential principles, possible uses, and real-life examples in several sectors, and provide certification programs that can also enable professionals to get prestigious certifications in blockchain technology.

Besides this, conducting workshops and seminars tailored to certain industries can effectively enhance awareness and comprehension of blockchain technology; these events may be customized to suit the distinct requirements and difficulties of many industries. Showcasing how technology can effectively resolve specific issues would indeed facilitate knowledge exchange and cooperation by bringing together industry experts, blockchain developers, and potential users.

Collaborating with industry organizations can enhance endeavors to teach and enlighten their members about technology and related implications because these groups have the ability to arrange seminars, webinars, and publications that specifically concentrate on the possible uses of blockchain within their respective industries. By partnering with reputable industries, organizations may enhance the legitimacy of educational initiatives, therefore motivating a greater number of individuals to

CHAPTER 10 RISING TITANS, FALLING EMPIRES: THE EPIC SAGA OF TRADE FINANCE CONSORTIA IN THE DIGITAL AGE

participate. Public awareness campaigns can serve to elucidate blockchain technology and rectify prevalent misunderstandings since they can utilize diverse media platforms, such as social media, blogs, podcasts, and conventional media, to effectively reach a wide-ranging audience, providing them with clear and concise explanations, instances of achievements, and practical illustrations, potentially enhancing the accessibility and relevance of blockchain technology for the general public and corporate executives.

Showing how blockchain is used effectively in different areas can help show its real benefits and encourage widespread adoption. Case studies that go into detail about how companies have improved security, efficiency, and transparency by using blockchain technology can be very convincing proof of its worth. Sharing these success stories through industry magazines, conferences, and online platforms could encourage others to look into blockchain solutions.

Promoting the involvement of companies in pilot projects and proof-of-concept initiatives may provide them with hands-on experience with blockchain, facilitating businesses in conducting limited-scale experimentation using blockchain applications, evaluating their impact, and enhancing their internal expertise, because successful pilot programs can serve as a foundation for larger-scale implementations and serve as helpful examples for others in the same industry.

By participating in blockchain forums and networks, firms can stay updated on the latest advancements and optimal methods. Additionally, attending meetings and collaborating with blockchain firms and developers can provide valuable insights and learning opportunities. Lastly, establishing contacts within the blockchain ecosystem can facilitate collaborations and provide access to specialized knowledge. There is a notable deficiency in the level of knowledge and comprehension of blockchain, especially in areas beyond the financial industry, arising from the intricate nature of blockchain principles, limited opportunities for exposure and instruction, and misunderstandings and doubts. To fill this void, it is necessary to implement extensive training programs, conduct seminars tailored to specific industries, collaborate with industry groups, launch public awareness campaigns, present practical examples of blockchain applications, promote pilot projects, and actively involve blockchain communities. Sectors outside of finance may subsequently gain a deeper comprehension of and use the potential of blockchain technology, therefore stimulating innovation and gaining a competitive edge.

CHAPTER 10 RISING TITANS, FALLING EMPIRES: THE EPIC SAGA OF TRADE FINANCE CONSORTIA IN THE DIGITAL AGE

Establishing Interoperability Standards: The Key to Blockchain's Future Efficiency and Innovation

Because this industry is always getting better and more people are using it, there are now many platforms, and they all work with different protocols, consensus mechanisms, and data structures, causing fragmentation and the creation of separate systems. In order to fully harness the capabilities of blockchain, it is imperative to establish interoperability standards that guarantee smooth integration and functioning across diverse systems. Interoperability is therefore essential since it allows different networks to communicate with and interact with each other, enhancing collaboration and enabling data and asset exchange across platforms, fostering a more connected and efficient ecosystem. For instance, in supply chain management, interoperability can enable seamless tracking of goods as they move through various stages, even if different stakeholders use different blockchain systems.

The efficient integration of several systems eliminates unnecessary duplication and inefficiency because achieving interoperability among blockchains expedites the processing of transactions involving several platforms while minimizing the need for manual interventions. The enhanced efficiency can result in reduced costs, accelerated processing times, and enhanced overall performance. Then a seamless integration with well-established systems and other platforms holds the potential to significantly increase the widespread acceptance and utilization of blockchain technology, which results in businesses being more inclined to invest in similar solutions if they are certain that such systems can integrate smoothly with their existing infrastructure and other platforms, reducing the hurdles to acceptance as well as enabling a more seamless shift to blockchain-driven procedures. Interoperability promotes innovation by enabling developers to utilize the advantages of many platforms, allowing for the development of hybrid solutions that integrate the most advantageous characteristics of different blockchains, and finally promoting the exploration and creation of novel applications, thereby propelling the progress of the technology.

Many blockchain systems often utilize distinct protocols, consensus mechanisms, and data structures that provide significant technological challenges in attaining interoperability. In order to achieve effective communication across various systems, it is essential to overcome the inherent differences by creating a common language or protocol. It is also vital to ensure that interoperability solutions do not undermine the security and privacy of blockchain networks, since this should be carefully planned to ensure the data's integrity and confidentiality during its transfer across different systems, with the help of strong encryption, safe protocols for transferring data, and systems to authenticate and validate transactions. Data sharing, privacy, and financial transactions are subject to different restrictions depending on the country. Interoperability solutions need to navigate through different regulatory environments and guarantee adherence to all applicable regulations.

This intricacy introduces an extra level of difficulty to the process of creating standards that can be universally embraced, as collaboration among many industry players, such as blockchain developers, enterprises, regulatory agencies, and standards groups, is necessary for the development of interoperability standards. Such endeavors are vital in guaranteeing that the standards adequately meet the requirements and apprehensions of all parties concerned. Industry consortia and working groups provide a forum for stakeholders to collaborate, exchange knowledge, and reach agreement on interoperability solutions.

Developing standardized protocols and application programming interfaces (APIs) is an essential step in achieving interoperability, providing the guidelines and procedures for exchanging data and processing transactions on various blockchain systems (namely, standard protocols promote compatibility and provide smooth integration across diverse systems). Creating cross-chain solutions, such as bridges and interoperability layers, can enable seamless communication across diverse blockchain networks.

These solutions, known as bridges, facilitate the movement of assets and data between different blockchains, while interoperability layers establish a structured system for communication and integration, ensuring real interoperability. A winning factor is also represented by the adoption of open standards, which guarantee that interoperability protocols are clear, easily available, and not restricted by proprietary limitations. Open-source development can speed up the acceptance of interoperability solutions because such initiatives facilitate developer collaboration, contribution, and innovation in creating interoperability solutions, resulting in stronger and more universally embraced standards. Implementing pilot projects and conducting proof-of-concept activities can demonstrate the practicality and benefits of interoperability standards. They facilitate stakeholders in assessing interoperability solutions in real-life scenarios, identifying barriers, and enhancing the standards; pilot efforts that are effective have the power to establish confidence and encourage broader acceptance of interoperability standards.

Talking to regulatory agencies is important to make sure that interoperability standards follow the law and regulations. This is because these groups can give advice on things like data privacy, security, and following the rules, which can affect the creation of standards that meet legal requirements. Working together with them could also speed up the process of creating regulatory frameworks that encourage interoperability. Disseminating knowledge and instruction on interoperability standards is essential for achieving widespread acceptance since stakeholders must have a comprehensive understanding of the efficient implementation and utilization of interoperability solutions. To achieve this, training programs, workshops, and documentation are effective in developing the requisite skills and knowledge, guaranteeing the accurate and efficient implementation of interoperability standards. It is important to regularly evaluate and update these standards in order to keep up with technological breakthroughs, novel use cases, and changing regulatory environments. Governance structures with oversight make sure that standards stay useful and relevant. Regular reviews, stakeholder feedback, and small improvements all support this. All of these are necessary to make sure that interoperability standards last and are up-to-date.

In order to ensure smooth integration and operation across many systems, it is necessary to establish interoperability standards due to the existence of several blockchain platforms. Interoperability improves cooperation, enhances effectiveness, promotes wider acceptance, and stimulates creativity. To develop these standards, it is necessary to address technological, security, and legal obstacles by fostering collaboration within the industry, implementing common protocols, utilizing cross-chain technology, adopting open standards, and engaging with regulatory authorities. The process of implementing and adopting interoperability standards requires the execution of pilot projects, as well as the provision of education, training, and ongoing monitoring and evolution. To unlock the full potential of blockchain technology, the blockchain industry must tackle these problems and take aggressive measures to establish practical interoperability.

As such, the future potential of blockchain in trade finance is attributed to the continuous digital transformation initiatives and the increasing desire for more efficient, transparent, and secure trade procedures. To overcome existing challenges and facilitate broad acceptance, industry associations such as BAFT must spearhead innovation and cooperation, and clearly, the utilization of blockchain technology has the capacity to fundamentally transform trade finance by enhancing its efficiency, transparency, and security. Although there has been notable progress, the future development and wider acceptance of this revolutionary technology will rely on resolving regulatory obstacles, improving interoperability, and fostering more industry-wide comprehension and confidence.

CHAPTER 10　RISING TITANS, FALLING EMPIRES: THE EPIC SAGA OF TRADE FINANCE CONSORTIA IN THE DIGITAL AGE

Summary

This chapter documents the explosive emergence and collapse of blockchain-based trade finance consortia, therefore providing insightful analysis of the prospects and difficulties the sector has in trying to achieve digital transformation. It starts by looking at blockchain's delayed promise in trade finance and offering sobering stories of ambitious initiatives failing to live up to expectations. Examined is the rise of consortia like the Marco Polo Network and Contour, stressing their creative contributions to blockchain trade finance as well as their operational challenges. By means of thorough case studies, the chapter exposes financial difficulties, investor resistance, and the complexity of digitizing trade finance transactions, including integration issues and the requirement of standardizing. Lessons from well-known mistakes like TradeLens's limited success and Contour's fallthrough highlight the need for striking a balance between decentralization and pragmatic adoption techniques. The story explores the development of the Global Shipping Business Network (GSBN) and its attempts to transform shipping via blockchain, therefore illuminating successful integrations and important advances, including ONE's use of GSBN technology and the safe transportation of chemical cargo. Emphasizing as pillars of blockchain's future in trade finance cooperation, interoperability, and standardizing, the chapter stresses at techniques to be efficient, plans for getting long-term funding, and the need of ongoing innovation to maintain blockchain projects. The need of financial stability and regulatory compliance in negotiating the uncertainty of blockchain acceptance is a recurrent topic. Closing from a forward-looking standpoint, the chapter argues for cross-industry cooperation and education to close the knowledge gap about the blockchain. Establishing interoperability criteria and supporting a culture of resilience and creativity will help the trade finance and shipping sectors release the transforming power of blockchain technology, hence opening the path for a more transparent, linked global trade ecosystem.

CHAPTER 11

Shaping Tomorrow's Markets: The Future of Trade Finance Through Innovations

This chapter explores the revolutionary ideas shaping the direction of trade finance, focusing on Regulation Technology (RegTech), hedging instruments, and derivatives. It starts with looking at how these technologies are closing the trade finance gap, correcting information asymmetries, and changing the investing environment. The function of regulation in trade finance is outlined, therefore setting the scene for the development of RegTech from its early days (RegTech 1.0) to the intelligence-driven solutions of today (RegTech 4.0 and beyond). Detailed integration of RegTech into trade finance shows how well it can simplify regulatory compliance using main technologies such as blockchain, artificial intelligence, and workflow automation.

These instruments are improving liquidity through tokenized assets, helping trade finance to develop into tradable securities, and thus increasing investability while simultaneously lowering costs and complexity. The chapter next turns to hedging instruments and derivatives—such as container goods derivatives—which are very essential for negotiating trade finance volatility. Emphasizing their part in controlling risk and stabilizing world trade operations, the advantages and drawbacks of these instruments are investigated. Examining logistics innovation deeply reveals how improved information exchange, artificial intelligence, and interoperability standards are changing the sector.

Presenting as fundamental paths for modernizing trade finance are foundational ideas for future logistics platforms, the vision of a "physical Internet," and the cooperative creation of worldwide digital infrastructure. The last part looks at the junction of digital resources and environmental data, therefore offering a revolutionary picture of trade finance. Financial institutions may rethink approaches for inclusivity, sustainability, and economic impact by using these tools. Advocating for cooperative investment, legislative backing, and the creation of interoperable standards to build an inventive, inclusive, and resilient trade finance ecosystem for the future.

Bridging the Multi-Trillion Gap: Unlocking Trade Financing for Emerging Nations

Particularly impacting emerging nations, the discrepancy between the demand for trade financing and the approved values is a serious concern in the world economy. Estimated at a startling $2.5 trillion in 2022, this disparity highlights a major shortage that greatly affects current merchants as well as new ones in various areas. Resolving this gap is crucial for promoting economic development, as access to finance is often a major obstacle to entry and growth in the global economy.

The causes of this credit gap are many and represent a complicated interaction of elements preventing the flow of trade financing. One of the main causes is the risk aversion of creditors, which geopolitics has aggravated. These conflicts create an unstable atmosphere in which financial institutions are more wary of lending credit, particularly in areas perceived as high risk. This conservative stance reduces the availability of trade credit, therefore restricting the possibility for expansion and development in emerging countries.

Widening the trade financing gap also results from the major influence of regulatory obstacles. Financial firms must pay more for compliance and deal with more complexity as legislative criteria get stricter. These rules can provide challenges for banks and other lenders, even if they are essential for maintaining financial stability and stopping illegal activity. Compliance's weight can deter institutions from participating in trade financing, especially in areas where the regulatory climate is seen to be difficult.

Changing compliance regulations aggravates the problem even further. Global financial norms are dynamic, so institutions have to always change to fit fresh rules and standards. This ongoing adaptation calls for large resources and can cause trade

CHAPTER 11 SHAPING TOMORROW'S MARKETS: THE FUTURE OF TRADE FINANCE THROUGH INNOVATIONS

financing availability to vary. These developments can provide significant challenges for poorer nations, whose financial infrastructure and regulatory systems can already be inadequate, therefore restricting access to the required funding.

This trade financing disparity has broad effects. Lack of easily available finance limits the capacity of current traders in emerging nations to increase activities, penetrate new markets, and compete internationally. Because companies cannot fully utilize trade possibilities, this restriction stunts innovation and economic development. The obstacle to entrance grows insurmountable for future immigrants, therefore impeding their ability to engage in world commerce and gain from economic integration.

Promoting inclusive economic growth and development depends on closing this gap. Potential answers come from creative financial technologies, including risk distribution systems and securitization of trade finance assets. These technologies help close the gap by spreading risks across a larger pool of investors and increasing trade financing availability. Policymakers, financial institutions, and international organizations must thus cooperate closely to establish an environment that facilitates the flow of trade financing to underdeveloped countries.

Improving trade financing availability in these areas would help to boost global trading system inclusiveness, assist employment creation, and encourage economic development. It may provide companies with the tools they need to grow, be creative, and engage in worldwide competitiveness. It might also enable emerging nations to enter the world market, therefore promoting economic stability and growth.

Finally, a major problem requiring immediate action is the discrepancy between the demand for trade financing and the approved values. The startling $2.5 trillion deficit in 2022 highlights the major obstacles emerging nations must overcome to get credit. Dealing with this disparity calls for a multifarious strategy combining the use of creative financial technology, regulatory procedure simplification, and the reduction of geopolitical concerns. By closing this divide, we can unleash the potential of emerging nations, advance world economic development, and create a more inclusive and fair worldwide trading system.

CHAPTER 11 SHAPING TOMORROW'S MARKETS: THE FUTURE OF TRADE FINANCE THROUGH INNOVATIONS

Harnessing Data Analytics to Bridge the Trade Financing Gap: A Path to Inclusive Economic Growth

The ongoing trade financing deficit, a major obstacle to global economic development, necessitates innovative solutions. Particularly in data analytics, technology presents a bright future path to solve problems and level the playing field for companies all around. Crucially, in reducing the trade financing gap, lenders can better grasp a borrower's creditworthiness by using data analytics, therefore enabling a more nuanced and effective knowledge of this.

Often based mostly on past financial data, traditional credit assessments could not fairly represent a borrower's present financial situation or prospects. In poor countries, where financial histories are either lacking or nonexistent, this dependency can be very constrictive. By examining enormous volumes of data—including non-traditional data points—and offering a more complete and current view of credit risk, advanced analytics and sophisticated algorithms can transform this process. This innovative method contributes to increasing the availability of trade credit by helping lenders find potential customers who would have otherwise gone unnoticed.

These systems can find trends and insights by aggregating several data sources, hence strengthening lenders' confidence in borrower dependability. In developing countries, where conventional credit records are less prevalent and alternative data sources can offer vital insights on a borrower's financial behavior and prospects, this capacity is especially helpful. Credit evaluations might include, for example, information from utility payments, mobile payments, and even social media activities, therefore providing a more complete picture of creditworthiness.

Access to data determines how successful these technical fixes are. Many underdeveloped countries have inadequate data availability, which makes using sophisticated credit evaluation instruments extremely difficult. This restriction emphasizes how important strong data infrastructure and laws supporting data sharing and openness are. Not only would better data accessibility increase the efficacy of these technologies, but it would also help to promote more financial inclusion and economic growth.

Notwithstanding these difficulties, there are rather significant advantages to including sophisticated analytics in trade finance. These technologies can help close the trade finance gap by offering a more precise and all-encompassing evaluation of credit

CHAPTER 11   SHAPING TOMORROW'S MARKETS: THE FUTURE OF TRADE FINANCE THROUGH INNOVATIONS

risk, therefore enabling lenders to provide credit to underprivileged companies. More inclusive global trade systems, job creation, and economic development stimulation— all of which depend on this improved access to finance—all depend on this.

Moreover, technology-driven credit assessments might help reduce the inherent risks in trade financing and inspire additional lenders to enter this important industry. These technologies can help create a more steady and predictable lending environment by lowering uncertainty and raising credit assessment accuracy. In developing countries, where access to consistent financing may be transforming for companies wishing to grow and compete internationally, this consistency is especially crucial.

To sum up, technology—especially data analytics—helps to close the trade finance gap very significantly. Especially in emerging countries, these technologies might increase access to funding for underprivileged companies by offering more complex and effective knowledge of credit risk. Realizing the full possibilities of these developments, though, calls for better data availability and a friendly legislative framework. These technology solutions have the potential to revolutionize trade finance, boost economic development, and create a more inclusive global trading system as they keep developing and getting acceptance.

Bridging Gaps: Addressing Information Asymmetries Through Collaboration

Although the trade finance industry offers a lot of room for expansion, it also emphasizes how urgently regulatory and logistical information exchange must be innovated upon. The lack of cooperation among financial service providers, logistical businesses, and regulators— which might allow for fraud—is one of the main difficulties financial institutions confront. Although financial organizations may grant credit based on invoices for commodities, they find it challenging to confirm the validity of these records. This problem emphasizes how urgently strategic alliances should solve information asymmetries.

Working with logistics firms provides a beneficial way to solve the information asymmetry problem. Banks may verify the legitimacy and condition of items in transit by using real-time tracking data and cutting-edge technology-verified techniques. Verifying transactions and improving trade finance process security and openness depend heavily on this kind of cooperation. By tracking the flow and condition of products, financial institutions can make sure the invoices they support are supported by real, physical assets.

Working together, banks and logistics companies accomplish more than merely confirm trade document legitimacy. It also offers vital visibility into the flow of products, enabling banks to combine trade finance with compliance with environmental rules and safety. More ethical and sustainable trading methods can result from this combination. Banks may inspire companies to follow policies that give safety and environmental stewardship first priority by tying funding to compliance with these criteria.

Moreover, the greater openness this cooperation brings about can greatly lower the trade finance fraud risk. Reliable, real-time data on the products banks are funding helps them identify and stop dishonest behavior. Greater confidence among financial institutions brought about by this enhanced security motivates them to provide more credit to companies, especially in emerging nations where trade financing is absolutely vital for expansion.

Apart from lowering fraud, the better information exchange between financial institutions and logistics corporations helps to simplify the trade financing procedure. Accurate and timely data helps banks speed trade financing application examination and approval. This effectiveness helps companies by giving them faster access to the required money to participate in global commerce, therefore helping their efforts for development and expansion.

Moreover, cooperation with logistics companies can improve the general resilience of the trade financing system. The system gets stronger and more flexible to fit changing circumstances by including real-time data and sophisticated verification tools. This flexibility is crucial in a world of global trade with shifting regulatory requirements and dynamic market conditions.

In trade finance, overcoming information asymmetries via cooperation is not only beneficial but also very necessary. Financial institutions may solve the difficulties of confirming the validity of trade papers and improve openness, security, and efficiency by collaborating with logistics firms. Particularly in underdeveloped countries, this cooperation helps companies flourish, lowers the danger of fraud, and encourages more sustainable trade policies. Encouragement of such alliances will be vital as the trade finance industry develops to create a more inclusive and strong worldwide trade system.

CHAPTER 11   SHAPING TOMORROW'S MARKETS: THE FUTURE OF TRADE FINANCE THROUGH INNOVATIONS

RegTech Revolution: Transforming Compliance in Trade Finance

Trade finance, the backbone of international trade, operates in a complex environment of global regulations. These rules are designed to foster transparency, mitigate risks, and ensure compliance with laws across jurisdictions. However, the sheer volume and complexity of trade finance transactions, combined with the rapidly evolving regulatory landscape, have created significant challenges for financial institutions, corporations, and intermediaries.

Enter **RegTech**—an intersection of regulatory compliance and advanced technology. Regulation Technology, or RegTech, leverages innovative solutions such as automation, data analytics, blockchain, and artificial intelligence (AI) to simplify and enhance compliance processes. This chapter delves into the importance of RegTech in trade finance, the fundamental aspects of trade finance regulations, and the technologies driving this transformation.

The Evolution of RegTech in Trade Finance: A Historical Journey

In the bustling financial centers of the 1960s, trade finance compliance was a world of paper, ink, and meticulous human scrutiny. Picture vast rooms filled with compliance officers, their desks stacked high with documents, each piece of paper representing a crucial link in the global trade chain. This was the dawn of our journey—a journey that would transform from this paper-laden landscape into today's world of algorithmic precision and digital innovation.

From Paper to Pixels: The Early Days (RegTech 1.0)

The story begins in the manual era, where trade finance compliance was an art practiced by experienced bankers who relied on their instincts and expertise. Compliance officers would spend hours scrutinizing handwritten documents, comparing signatures, and manually cross-referencing countless lists of sanctioned entities. A single trade finance transaction could take weeks to process, as documents physically traveled across continents for verification and approval.

CHAPTER 11   SHAPING TOMORROW'S MARKETS: THE FUTURE OF TRADE FINANCE THROUGH INNOVATIONS

Trade finance teams functioned like well-tuned machinery, yet they were still human entities. Every morning, new stacks of letters of credit would arrive, each requiring careful examination. Relationship managers knew their clients personally, often through years of face-to-face meetings. While this personal touch provided certain advantages, it also meant that compliance processes were inconsistent and heavily reliant on individual judgment.

The Digital Dawn: First Steps into Technology (RegTech 2.0)

The 1990s brought the first whispers of a technological revolution to trade finance compliance. The introduction of basic computer systems marked a pivotal moment—suddenly, banks could store client information digitally, and the first primitive screening tools emerged. However, these early systems were essentially digital filing cabinets, mimicking paper processes rather than reinventing them.

SWIFT's growing network began standardizing international financial communications, creating the first universal language for trade finance compliance. Banks invested in massive mainframe computers, and the sight of compliance officers typing information into green-screen terminals became commonplace. Yet, despite these advances, the process remained largely manual, with technology serving as a support tool rather than a driving force.

The Watershed Moment: 2008 and Beyond (RegTech 3.0)

The 2008 financial crisis shook the financial world, radically changing the compliance landscape. Regulators, determined to prevent future crises, introduced waves of new requirements. Banks were overburdened with compliance obligations, and their traditional methods of managing them were unable to keep up with the volume and complexity of the new regulations. Banks were overwhelmed by the volume and complexity of new regulations, and their traditional methods of managing them were unable to keep up. This crisis became the catalyst for true RegTech innovation. Banks, faced with mounting compliance costs and regulatory pressure, began investing heavily in technology solutions. The first real-time monitoring systems emerged, capable of screening transactions against sanctions lists as they occurred. Cloud computing made its debut in trade finance, offering scalability and flexibility previously unimaginable.

CHAPTER 11   SHAPING TOMORROW'S MARKETS: THE FUTURE OF TRADE FINANCE THROUGH INNOVATIONS

The Technology Revolution Takes Hold (RegTech 4.0 and Beyond)

As we moved into the 2015s, artificial intelligence and machine learning began transforming compliance from a reactive to a proactive function. These technologies could analyze vast amounts of data, identifying patterns and potential risks that human observers might miss. Natural language processing allowed systems to understand and analyze complex trade documents automatically, while blockchain technology promised to revolutionize transaction tracking and verification.

Consider the transformation in suspicious activity monitoring: Where once a compliance officer might spend days reviewing transaction patterns, AI systems now analyze millions of data points in seconds, flagging potential issues with unprecedented accuracy. Machine learning algorithms continuously improve their accuracy, learning from each transaction they process.

Today's Landscape: The Integration of Intelligence

Modern RegTech in trade finance bears little resemblance to its paper-based ancestors. Today's compliance systems are sophisticated ecosystems that combine multiple technologies to create seamless, intelligent compliance processes. Artificial intelligence does not just flag suspicious activities; it predicts them before they occur. Blockchain networks provide immutable audit trails, while APIs enable different systems to communicate seamlessly. The modern compliance officer's workspace has transformed from a paper-laden desk to a digital command center. Multiple screens display real-time transaction monitoring, risk assessments, and regulatory updates. Automated systems handle routine checks, allowing compliance professionals to focus on complex cases requiring human judgment.

This historical journey teaches us valuable lessons about the nature of innovation in financial compliance. The evolution was not just about technology; it was about changing mindsets, adapting to new risks, and finding better ways to ensure safe and efficient trade finance operations. Just as importantly, this history shows us that successful innovation requires balance. While technology has dramatically improved efficiency and accuracy, the human element remains crucial. The best compliance systems combine technological capability with human insight, creating a hybrid approach that leverages the strengths of both. As we look forward, the pace of innovation shows no signs of slowing.

CHAPTER 11   SHAPING TOMORROW'S MARKETS: THE FUTURE OF TRADE FINANCE THROUGH INNOVATIONS

Emerging technologies like quantum computing and advanced AI promise to further revolutionize trade finance compliance. The future might bring us predictive compliance systems that can anticipate regulatory changes or autonomous systems that can adapt to new requirements in real time. Yet, as we embrace these innovations, we must remember the lessons of our journey. Each technological advance must serve the fundamental goals of trade finance compliance: ensuring security, maintaining integrity, and facilitating legitimate global trade. The story of RegTech in trade finance is far from over. Each new chapter brings fresh challenges and opportunities as we continue to push the boundaries of what is possible in financial compliance.

Streamlining Regulatory Compliance Through Regulation Technology: Collaboration and Innovation in Trade Finance for a More Inclusive Global Economy

Emphasizing the vital need for technical innovation and cooperation among all players in the trade ecosystem, the trade finance scene offers both significant problems and plenty of opportunity. Particularly in poor countries, bridging the $2.5 trillion trade finance gap calls for coordinated measures to improve data availability, increase analytics usage, and fund digital infrastructure and capacity creation. Encouragement of tighter cooperation among financial institutions, logistical companies, and regulatory authorities is essential to tackling these difficulties.

A more transparent and efficient trade finance environment can be created by these participants through better information sharing. Through process simplification and trade finance transaction speed and cost reduction, this cooperation helps companies of all kinds find trade more easily. Through pushing the acceptance of new technologies that simplify compliance procedures, regulators are absolutely vital in this ecosystem. They also have to guarantee strong systems are in place to guard against fraud and preserve trade finance system integrity at the same time. Global norms for data exchange and analytics must be developed if we are to guarantee that, regardless of size or geography, technology developments help all players.

CHAPTER 11 SHAPING TOMORROW'S MARKETS: THE FUTURE OF TRADE FINANCE THROUGH INNOVATIONS

Key Aspects of Regulations in Trade Finance

1. **Know Your Customer (KYC):**

   - KYC requires financial institutions to verify the identity of their clients to assess potential risks.

   - This involves collecting and analyzing customer data, such as business structure, ownership, and transactional behavior.

2. **Anti-money Laundering (AML) and Counter-Terrorist Financing (CTF):**

   - Institutions must monitor transactions to detect suspicious activity and report it to regulators.

   - AML compliance ensures that trade finance is not used to launder money or finance terrorism.

3. **Sanctions Screening:**

   - Transactions must comply with international sanctions imposed by bodies like the United Nations, the US Office of Foreign Assets Control (OFAC), or the European Union.

   - Screening tools are used to ensure parties in trade are not on sanctioned lists.

4. **Documentary Compliance:**

   - Regulatory bodies mandate the accuracy of trade documents such as invoices, bills of lading, and certificates of origin.

   - Misrepresentation or inaccuracies in these documents can lead to fines or the invalidation of trade deals

5. **Sustainability Regulations:**

   - Increasingly, trade finance is subject to environmental, social, and governance (ESG) standards.

   - Compliance involves adhering to regulations like the EU Taxonomy or guidelines from the Task Force on Climate-related Financial Disclosures (TCFD).

6. **Data Protection and Privacy:**
   - Trade transactions often involve sensitive data, necessitating compliance with regulations like GDPR and other data protection laws.

Bridging Compliance Complexity with Innovation: The Role of RegTech in Trade Finance

RegTech acts as a bridge between complex regulatory requirements and the entities that must comply with them. It introduces innovative solutions to address the inefficiencies and costs of manual compliance processes.

Key Technologies Driving RegTech in Trade Finance

1. **Artificial Intelligence (AI) and Machine Learning:**
   - AI-powered tools analyze vast amounts of data to detect patterns and anomalies, enabling faster and more accurate risk assessments.
   - Machine learning models adapt over time, improving their ability to identify fraud or suspicious activities.

2. **Blockchain and Distributed Ledger Technology (DLT):**
   - Blockchain ensures transparency and immutability of trade transactions.
   - It simplifies regulatory reporting by providing a single source of truth for all parties.

3. **Smart Contracts:**
   - Self-executing agreements automate compliance checks and reporting based on predefined rules.
   - For example, payments in a trade transaction may be triggered only when all compliance conditions are met.

4. **Data Analytics and Big Data:**

    - RegTech leverages data analytics to consolidate and interpret transactional data.

    - Predictive analytics can assess compliance risks and recommend preventive measures.

5. **Application Programming Interfaces (APIs):**

    - APIs enable seamless integration of RegTech solutions with trade finance platforms, automating tasks such as KYC checks and sanctions screening.

6. **Cloud Computing:**

    - Cloud-based solutions provide scalable platforms for compliance, reducing the need for extensive in-house infrastructure.

    - These platforms facilitate real-time collaboration between regulators and financial institutions.

RegTech's automated solutions can very quickly manage document integrity checks and transaction verification. Designed to scan, analyze, and validate enormous volumes of data in real time, these systems guarantee that all compliance criteria are satisfied without the need for repeated hand checks. By greatly lowering the time and expenses needed for compliance, this automation frees trading partners to concentrate more on their main operations. RegTech solutions have one of their main advantages in their capacity to simplify the paperwork process. These solutions guarantee that the required data is accessible and available all through the trade cycle by letting trading partners upload papers just once.

This flawless data integration not only facilitates the flow of money and products across borders but also reduces the friction sometimes accompanying cross-border transactions. Less paperwork and manual processing allow transactions to be finished faster and with fewer mistakes, therefore improving the general trade finance process's efficiency. RegTech products also improve compliance check accuracy and dependability. These technologies can find abnormalities and possible hazards that human reviewers might ignore by using sophisticated algorithms and machine learning. This increased degree of inspection guarantees that every transaction follows the necessary legal criteria, therefore lowering the possibility of non-compliance and the related fines. Using RegTech also helps trade financing be more transparent and secure. Because automated compliance solutions produce a thorough digital record of every transaction, audit and review processes become simpler.

This openness not only fosters confidence among trade partners but also gives authorities the instruments they need to properly monitor and enforce compliance. By means of improved security measures included in RegTech solutions, fraud and other illegal actions are prevented, therefore preserving the integrity of the trade finance system. By simplifying regulatory compliance procedures, RegTech's developments are transforming the trade finance industry at last. Automated solutions speed up the trading process, lessen the need for manual inspections, and lower the danger of mistakes and non-compliance. RegTech solutions improve trade finance security, accuracy, and efficiency by letting trading partners upload papers just once and guarantee flawless data integration. As these technologies develop, they should make global trade more safe, transparent, and accessible, therefore benefiting companies and economies all around.

Unlocking Trade Finance: How Risk Distribution Technologies Are Redefining Investment Landscapes

Long seen as a difficult and dangerous investment space, trade finance is changing significantly with the help of risk distribution tools. These financial technologies are meant to divide trade finance-related risks among a larger pool of players. This helps them to radically change the investing scene by making trade financing more appealing and easily available to a greater spectrum of investors. Traditionally, trade finance consists of several tools like invoices and letters of credit, which support worldwide commerce by giving companies the required money and assurances. Yet for a small portion of the financial world, the inherent dangers and complexity of these products have frequently restricted their attraction. Here is where risk distribution technologies are useful, as they not only help to reduce these hazards but also expand the investment base.

Securitization is the fundamental process through which these technologies function. This method pools many trade finance instruments and turns them into marketable securities, such as bonds or notes. This helps to disperse the risks and

CHAPTER 11   SHAPING TOMORROW'S MARKETS: THE FUTURE OF TRADE FINANCE THROUGH INNOVATIONS

benefits connected with these assets among a larger number of participants. By pooling and then selling trade finance assets as securities, investors have a chance to engage in trade finance without personally running into its complexity and hazards. The securitization of trade finance assets significantly alters investment dynamics. These securities are now available for purchase by investors, who will get returns contingent on the underlying trade finance asset performance.

This structure improves liquidity, allowing investors to purchase and sell these securities on the capital markets, thus increasing the attractiveness of the investment by providing a more predictable and consistent return profile. Given that it gives investors the freedom to more dynamically manage their portfolios, this greater liquidity is absolutely vital.

The securitization of trade finance assets significantly alters the investment dynamics of any individual. These solutions reduce the effect of any defaults or market swings by distributing the risk, therefore improving the general stability of the investment. Institutional investors, who are always looking for strategies to diversify their portfolios and reduce risk, find this risk-reducing action especially tempting. These developments have consequences beyond just for investors. Reducing finance costs and increasing cash availability are major advantages for companies engaged in foreign commerce. More investors ready to engage in trade financing allow companies to more quickly acquire the money they need, therefore boosting their efforts at expansion.

This then drives world commerce, therefore supporting development and economic progress. Moreover, one cannot stress the openness and efficiency these technologies bring about. Automated technologies that support the securitization process guarantee that every transaction is precisely tracked and documented, therefore producing an unambiguous audit trail. From companies and investors to authorities, this openness strengthens confidence among all the participants, thereby building a more strong and dependable trade financing system.

Risk distribution technologies are revolutionizing the trade finance industry in major measure. Encouragement of the transformation of trade finance assets into marketable securities helps to share risks across a larger pool of investors, hence increasing the appeal of trade finance. By giving companies simpler access to finance, this not only improves liquidity and stability in the investment environment but also helps global trade flourish. These technologies will progressively reinvent the trade finance and investment environments as they develop, opening fresh prospects and promoting economic growth through their evolution.

CHAPTER 11 SHAPING TOMORROW'S MARKETS: THE FUTURE OF TRADE FINANCE THROUGH INNOVATIONS

Transforming Trade Finance: Unlocking Liquidity and Growth Through Tradable Securities

A major breakthrough in the financial markets, turning trade financing into tradable securities, improves the attractiveness and accessibility of these assets. For institutional investors, this conversion is essential as it provides new opportunities to engage in trade financing with more liquidity and a larger range of exit choices. These products provide a degree of flexibility and dynamism not before possible by converting trade finance into securities sold in the capital markets. Trade finance is the variety of financial tools organizations utilize to enable global trade and commerce. These instruments comprise trade credit insurance, export credit, and letters of credit. Their illiquid character has, however, historically reduced their appeal to a wider range of investors.

Through tradeable securities, this paradigm is altered and vital, and these instruments may be purchased and sold on the open market. Since there are no long-term obligations involved, this liquidity is absolutely essential because it enables investors to sell their holdings more easily. The liquidity and exit choices included in tradeable securities appeal more to institutional investors than trade finance.

By including this new kind of investment in a diverse portfolio, investors may more properly control their risk. Trading these assets on the capital markets enables investors to react to market conditions in real time, therefore modifying their holdings to maximize profits or reduce losses. One major benefit of this dynamic administration of investment portfolios is the degree of control and responsiveness needed in the fast-paced financial climate of today. Moreover, the transformation of trade financing into tradable securities fits very nicely with the rising need for alternate investment prospects. Constantly looking for fresh approaches to improve their portfolios, institutional investors find a special mix of stability and growth potential in tradable securities created from trade finance.

These securities provide the liquidity and flexibility that investors need in addition to exposing the worldwide trade market—a basic component of the global economy. This invention has effects beyond those of the investors. Making trade financing more appealing and easily available helps boost capital flow into the world trade system. This higher investment will help international trade flourish by giving companies the required capital to develop their activities and access new markets. Therefore, turning trade money into tradable securities not only helps investors but also advances general economic growth.

CHAPTER 11   SHAPING TOMORROW'S MARKETS: THE FUTURE OF TRADE FINANCE THROUGH INNOVATIONS

The financial markets have made major progress when trade money is turned into tradable securities. It gives institutional investors more freedom and dynamic management skills, therefore improving the liquidity and appeal of trade financing. In the realm of finance, this invention is essential, as it not only provides a fresh investment path but also might help global trade flourish.

Enhancing Trade Finance: The Impact of End-to-End Workflow Automation

The inclusion of end-to-end workflow automation technologies in the trade finance industry marks a radical change in the management of these financial operations. From the origination to the distribution of trade finance securities, these sophisticated instruments automate every stage of the process, therefore offering a range of advantages like lower transaction costs and less operating risk. Adopting automation can help the trade finance sector greatly improve its speed, transparency, and efficiency, therefore enabling more scalable and easily available operations for a wider spectrum of players. Many human chores and documentation are needed in the conventional trade financing process, which frequently results in delays, mistakes, and more expenses.

End-to-end automation technologies simplify the whole process, therefore addressing these issues. Automated systems are able to easily control every step of the creation of trade finance instruments up until their final distribution as securities. This guarantees a better degree of precision and consistency, in addition to accelerating the procedure. The significant savings in transaction expenses are one of the main benefits of these automation instruments. Manual processing calls for a lot of time and effort, which drives up costs. By lowering the requirement for human involvement, automation helps to speed up processing times and cut labor costs. This effectiveness results in cost reductions that companies and investors may share, which increases the appeal and competitiveness of trade financing.

Automation also greatly lessens operational risks like data input mistakes, compliance problems, and delays. Automated systems are made to follow set guidelines and procedures, therefore guaranteeing that every transaction complies with corporate regulations and legal requirements. This increases the general process's dependability and lowers the possibility of human error. Reducing these hazards helps companies run with more confidence and security, as they know that their transactions are handled correctly and effectively.

Additionally, the increased transparency provided by automation instruments plays a crucial role in fostering confidence and trust among stakeholders. The automated systems' real-time tracking and reporting features enable all involved parties to monitor the progress of transactions at every stage. This visibility guarantees that any problems may be quickly found and resolved, thereby preserving the integrity of the system. Transparency also helps with improved decision making as it gives stakeholders access to correct, current data. Another significant advantage of end-to-end workflow automation is the speed at which transactions are handled. Automated technologies can handle a large number of transactions at once, greatly reducing processing times. In the hectic world of trade finance, where delays can have major financial consequences, this quick turnaround is very vital.

Accelerating the processing speed helps companies react faster to market possibilities and needs, therefore improving their competitiveness and future expansion. One of the main benefits of automated systems is scalability, which lets companies grow their operations free from a related rise in complexity or expenses. Automated systems can readily adjust to manage the rising workload as transaction volume rises, therefore guaranteeing constant performance and efficiency. Automation is the perfect answer for companies trying to increase their trade finance operations, as its scalability supports their development and expansion initiatives.

Finally, a major advancement with several advantages in trade finance is the adoption of end-to-end process automation systems. These instruments lower transaction costs, limit operational risk, and improve efficiency, openness, and speed by automating the whole process from origination to delivery. This change makes the trade finance process more scalable and easily available, therefore encouraging industrial development and innovation. Adoption of automation technologies will be crucial in determining the direction of trade finance as companies and investors keep looking for methods to enhance their operations.

Innovative Risk Management: Complementing Traditional Risk-Sharing Practices in Traditional Trade Finance Solutions

The arrival of creative financial technologies, particularly in risk management and distribution, has fundamentally changed the landscape of trade financing. These developments improve the current systems and increase the pool of accessible capital,

CHAPTER 11 SHAPING TOMORROW'S MARKETS: THE FUTURE OF TRADE FINANCE THROUGH INNOVATIONS

therefore complementing rather than substituting conventional risk-sharing methods between banks and credit insurers. These innovative technologies let banks and credit insurers finance a higher volume of trade operations, lower their exposure, and disperse risk more broadly by smoothly interacting with existing systems.

Historically, banks and credit insurers have been significant in reducing trade finance-related risks. Through guarantees and insurance against certain hazards, including nonpayment and political instability, they enable international trade by ensuring the security and dependability of transactions. These methods have been the pillar of trade financing, as they provide companies with the trust required to participate in cross-border commerce. A major progress is made when creative technology is included in age-old customs. These technologies improve banks' and credit insurers' capacity to control and disperse risks without compromising the current systems. They give greater possibilities for risk-sharing by increasing the pool of accessible money, therefore helping financial institutions reach more companies with their services. In the framework of world commerce, where the need for trade finance solutions is always rising, this is especially crucial.

The more effective risk distribution is one of the main advantages of combining these technologies with conventional risk-sharing mechanisms. Advanced techniques allow banks and credit insurers to better evaluate and distribute risks, therefore guaranteeing a more balanced and varied risk portfolio. This not only lessens the exposure of particular institutions but also improves the general stability of the trade finance system. Financial institutions may reduce the effect of possible losses by distributing risks across a larger base, therefore strengthening and resiliently supporting trade financing. Moreover, the combination of these technologies makes trade finance activities more scalable. Increased risk management skills enable banks and credit insurers to handle more transactions, therefore enabling the expansion of world commerce.

Meeting the growing demand for trade financing solutions—especially from small and medium-sized businesses (SMEs) aiming to grow their worldwide operations—dependent on this scalability is very vital. Giving these companies access to additional finance and improved risk management allows them to integrate creative technology, therefore promoting economic development and growth. The complementarity of these developments also guarantees that current procedures are not disturbed. While gaining from the improved capabilities offered by new technology, banks and credit insurers can keep running under their current structures. While adding changes that increase efficiency and effectiveness, this method preserves the stability and dependability of conventional risk-sharing policies. It is a harmonic strategy that embraces the possibilities of the future while respecting the tested strategies of the past. To sum up, the trade finance industry has made major progress in adding creative technology to conventional risk-sharing strategies.

These technologies improve risk distribution capacities and widen the pool of accessible capital by complementing, rather than substituting, existing institutions. These developments help to enable a higher volume of commerce by allowing banks and credit insurers to better control risks and thus promote the stability of world trade. The harmonic combination of conventional procedures and new technology will be crucial in determining the direction of the sector as the need for trade financing keeps growing.

Channeling Incremental Liquidity: The Role of Risk Distribution Technologies in Driving Inclusive Global Growth

Risk distribution systems have transformed power in trade finance as they allow significant incremental liquidity from capital market investors to be directed to underprivileged companies. For lenders and companies, especially small and medium-sized firms (SMEs) that often struggle greatly to find trade finance, this flood of cash is extremely vital. These technologies can provide much-needed liquidity into the system by making trade financing more available to institutional investors, therefore promoting economic development and a more inclusive worldwide trading climate.

Traditionally involving sophisticated and dangerous financial instruments, trade financing has limited availability for a wider spectrum of investors. By allowing trade finance assets to be securitized, risk distribution technologies are altering this terrain. Different trade finance tools are aggregated and turned into marketable securities—which are subsequently sold to investors—by securitization. By providing a consistent and steady return profile, this technique not only reduces the underlying risks but also appeals more to institutional investors who trade financial assets.

Lenders as well as companies depend on fresh cash injected via these technologies. The more liquidity there is for lenders, the more likely they are to finance more trade operations. SMEs especially benefit from this, as their low credit histories and perceived greater risks make it difficult for them to get finance. The increased liquidity brought about by institutional investors aids in bridging this funding gap, allowing SMEs to trade internationally more profitably.

CHAPTER 11   SHAPING TOMORROW'S MARKETS: THE FUTURE OF TRADE FINANCE THROUGH INNOVATIONS

The availability of additional liquidity means the required money for underprivileged companies to increase their operations and engage in worldwide commerce. Encouragement of economic development depends on the availability of funding, as it helps companies invest in new prospects, boost manufacturing, and enter new markets. This higher trade activity can have ripple effects, supporting job creation, stimulating innovation, and helping the economy to grow generally.

By allowing a larger pool of investors to access trade financing, risk distribution technologies are transforming trade finance. Further improving the efficiency and appeal of these expenditures are the automation of processes and the complementing of conventional risk-sharing systems. These solutions save transaction costs, lower operational risk, and improve openness by automating trade finance-related activities. This automation guarantees the correct and timely processing of transactions, therefore offering the degree of dependability and efficiency required in the fast-paced global trading environment.

Furthermore, affecting world commerce is one of the more general consequences of the enhanced liquidity resulting from these technologies. These developments can help level the playing field by giving companies simpler access to funding, therefore enabling more companies to engage in worldwide commerce. Promoting world economic development and guaranteeing a more fair distribution of the advantages of trade depend on this inclusiveness. The general amount of commerce is probably going to rise as more companies acquire the capacity to compete globally, therefore promoting economic growth.

Risk distribution technologies are empowered to direct small amounts of liquidity into the trade finance industry. These technologies can provide fresh liquidity into the system by allowing institutional investors to access trade financing, therefore helping lenders and underprivileged companies both. Supporting inclusive global commerce, job creation, and economic development all depends on this higher liquidity. As these technologies develop and become more accepted, they might become more important in increasing world commerce and promoting economic growth. These developments are redefining trade finance and offering a more dynamic, inclusive, and strong worldwide trading environment.

CHAPTER 11 SHAPING TOMORROW'S MARKETS: THE FUTURE OF TRADE FINANCE THROUGH INNOVATIONS

The Digital Frontier of Tokenized Assets

Particularly in the trade finance area, tokenized digital assets mark a major change in the financial sector. Tokenization turns conventional trade finance assets—such as letters of credit—into digital forms that could be more readily transferred and controlled by using blockchain and distributed ledger technologies (DLT). This technical development increases the investability of trade financing, therefore attracting a larger spectrum of investors and making it more easily available.

Fundamentally, tokenization is turning rights into an asset into a digital token kept on a blockchain. For trade finance, this procedure offers several transformative advantages. It improved liquidity first. Letters of credit and invoices are among the conventional trade financing tools that are sometimes illiquid and difficult to transfer. Tokenization lets these assets be exchanged quickly and effortlessly on digital platforms, just as stocks and bonds are traded.

This increased liquidity draws a wider range of investors, including individuals who would have considered trade financing either too complicated or absent. Furthermore, using blockchain and DLT offers unmatched security and openness. Every tokenized asset is kept on a distributed ledger, therefore guaranteeing that every transaction is unchangeable and open to all those engaged. Common issues with conventional trade finance systems, such as fraud and mistakes, are less likely with this openness. More confidence in the integrity and authenticity of the assets with which they are dealing helps investors create a more safe investing environment.

By removing entrance requirements, tokenizing also democratizes access to trade finance. Large financial organizations equipped to manage its complexity have typically dominated traditional trade financing. Smaller investors and institutions will find these products more easily available by turning trade finance assets into digital tokens. Small and medium-sized businesses (SMEs) have new chances to engage in trade financing thanks to this democratization, thereby promoting more inclusiveness and economic development.

Tokenizing also yields really significant efficiency improvements. Trade finance systems' automation and digitalization help to lower processing times and costs, streamline operations, and therefore lessen the need for middlemen. By automatically enforcing trade finance agreement norms and conditions, smart contracts—self-executing contracts with provisions explicitly put into code—increase efficiency even further. Along with accelerating transactions, this automation reduces the possibility of mistakes and delays.

Tokenization's capacity to provide improved risk management is still another main benefit. Blockchain lets all transactions and asset movements be tracked in real time, therefore enabling investors to pay closer attention to their assets and react quickly to any developing hazards. Trade finance is a more appealing investment choice as this real-time insight improves the capacity to control and reduce hazards.

Furthermore, encouraging innovation and the creation of fresh financial solutions requires the inclusion of tokenized assets in the trade finance ecosystem. Working together, financial institutions and technology companies may provide creative ideas that meet changing market demands. Tokenized trade finance assets, for example, might be combined into diverse investment products to provide investors with fresh approaches to exposure to the trade finance market while distributing their risk.

The introduction of tokenized digital assets opens up new possibilities for the trade finance industry. Tokenizing conventional trade finance tools into more liquid, transparent, and accessible digital assets by using blockchain and distributed ledger technologies enables improved efficiency, enhanced security, reduced transaction costs, and broader accessibility for small and medium-sized enterprises (SMEs) and underserved markets. This development increases the investability of trade finance, draws a larger spectrum of investors, and promotes more inclusiveness and efficiency, by means of which trade finance might evolve. Tokenized assets are likely to be crucial in determining the direction of trade finance, fostering innovation, and supporting economic development as the financial industry keeps adopting digital transformation.

Broadening Trade Finance Investability Through Tokenization: The Impact of Tokenized Digital Assets on Liquidity, Inclusivity, and Innovation

By reducing entrance obstacles for investors and democratizing access to this usually complicated industry, tokenization is transforming trade finance. These assets become more split by turning trade finance assets into digital tokens, which lets investors engage with less cash needed. This change offers trade finance to a wider investor base, including ordinary investors and smaller institutions hitherto unable to find this market accessible.

CHAPTER 11   SHAPING TOMORROW'S MARKETS: THE FUTURE OF TRADE FINANCE THROUGH INNOVATIONS

On secondary markets, traditional trade finance instruments are challenging to trade as they usually include long transfer processes and heavy documentation. Tokenization improves the liquidity of these assets, therefore addressing these problems. Improved liquidity increases the appeal of investments as it allows one to more quickly enter and exit positions. By appealing to a larger spectrum of investors looking for flexibility, this simplicity of trading lowers the long-term commitment generally needed in trade financing. Making sure transactions involving tokenized assets are transparent and unchangeable depends mostly on blockchain technology. Every transaction is noted on a distributed ledger, offering a clear, unchangeable record of ownership and transaction history. This function greatly lowers the possibility of fraud and mistakes, so trade financing products provide better security and dependability for traders. The improved security and openness inspire more investor trust, therefore promoting more trade finance market involvement.

Tokenization also simplifies trade and trade finance asset management generally. Settlement automation and fewer intermediary requirements help greatly cut transaction costs. Blockchain technology's transaction processing efficiency can help shorten settlement times from days to just a few minutes or seconds. Since it better fits the fast-paced character of contemporary financial markets, this quick processing capacity improves the appeal of trade finance investments.

Tokenization is enabling new finance models like fractional ownership, and peer-to-peer trade adds another important benefit. Owning associated fractions of a trade finance asset allows investors more freedom and chances for diversification. By distributing their money over several assets, this fractional ownership approach helps investors lower risk and improve possible returns. Platforms can also help direct trade between individuals, hence lessening reliance on conventional financial middlemen and therefore expenses.

Tokenized assets' digital character makes them readily traded internationally, drawing foreign investors and giving trade finance assets exposure to a larger pool of liquidity and investment prospects. Apart from improving the marketability of these assets, this worldwide reach diversifies the investor base, therefore lowering the concentration risk usually associated with local or regional markets. As capital moves more equally across several markets, including foreign investors, this can result in more stable and robust financial ecosystems.

Tokenization also helps in the creation of creative financial products and services meant to meet changing investor demands. Digital platforms, for instance, can provide real-time statistics and market trend data, thereby guiding investors toward wise

CHAPTER 11   SHAPING TOMORROW'S MARKETS: THE FUTURE OF TRADE FINANCE THROUGH INNOVATIONS

judgments. Further increasing the attraction of tokenized trade finance assets are these platforms, which may offer customized investment strategies depending on individual risk choices and financial goals.

Ultimately, by increasing accessibility, liquidity, and security, tokenization is expanding trade finance investability. Tokenization democratizes access to trade finance by reducing entrance barriers and allowing fractional ownership, therefore drawing a larger and more varied investor base. Blockchain technology guarantees security and openness; meanwhile, simplified procedures and fresh financial sources help to save expenses and provide more flexibility. Tokenized trade finance assets are likely to be crucial in the future of world finance as they provide more chances for development and investment worldwide.

Tokenizing presents problems that should be carefully considered, even if it has many advantages. A main focus is regulatory compliance, as the environment of regulations for tokenized assets is still developing. Institutions have to negotiate this complexity if they are to fully use tokenization's advantages. Essential is making sure tokenized assets follow know-your-customer (KYC), anti-money laundering (AML), and current financial rules. This requires a sharp awareness of both local and international regulatory systems, which differ greatly and evolve quickly.

Another major difficulty is the requirement of standardization between platforms. Tokenization cannot be successful unless these digital assets are produced, maintained, and traded with consistency. Tokenized assets become challenging, if not impossible, without consistent protocols and data formats. Lack of standardization might result in fragmented markets whereby several platforms operate in isolation, therefore lowering the general efficiency and liquidity that tokenizing seeks to attain. Overcoming this obstacle and guaranteeing that every participant may gain from the efficiency of a single system depend on the industry-wide standards developing and adoption.

In the field of tokenized assets, strong cybersecurity policies also have first importance. These assets' digital character renders them vulnerable to data breaches, fraud, and hacking, among other cyberattacks. Institutions have to make investments in cutting-edge security technology and processes if they are to safeguard their digital assets and related data. Strong encryption techniques, frequent security audits, and thorough incident response strategies are among the essential ones to apply. Strong cybersecurity not only safeguards the assets but also fosters confidence among investors, which is essential for the general acceptance of tokenized trade finance assets.

CHAPTER 11   SHAPING TOMORROW'S MARKETS: THE FUTURE OF TRADE FINANCE THROUGH INNOVATIONS

The tokenization of trade finance assets offers a transformative possibility to increase trade finance sector investability. Tokenizing increases accessibility so that a more varied spectrum of investors may join in, hence removing obstacles that have hitherto limited access to big financial institutions. Another main benefit is improved liquidity, as tokenized assets may be exchanged faster and more freely than conventional trade finance tools. This liquidity gives investors the freedom to enter and leave positions more easily, therefore enhancing the appeal of assets.

Tokenization offers a transparent, unchangeable record of all transactions, therefore improving transparency and security through the use of blockchain technology. This openness lowers fraud and mistake risk, therefore strengthening the dependability of the trade finance system. Another major advantage is fewer expenses, as tokenization automates payments and lessens the need for middlemen. Faster processing times and reduced transaction fees—benefits for all those engaged—result from this efficiency.

Tokenizing new finance models like fractional ownership and peer-to-peer trading adds more freedom and chances for diversification. Investors can own smaller portions of trade finance assets, spreading their risk over a larger portfolio. By democratizing investing, this fractional ownership approach lets smaller investors take advantage of once-unreachable possibilities. Tokenized assets' worldwide appeal further extends the advantages of tokenizing beyond local markets. Easy cross-border trade of digital tokens draws foreign investors and raises market liquidity generally. As capital moves more freely and effectively between many areas, this global connectedness can result in stronger and more durable trade finance ecosystems.

Tokenized digital assets are destined to become a major player in the global trade finance ecosystem as technology develops and rules change. The continuous development of these resources will probably lead to other inventions, therefore improving their attractiveness and usefulness. Organizations that move with the times and handle the related issues will be positioned to take advantage of the transforming power of tokenization, therefore promoting trade finance sector efficiency and growth for years to come.

CHAPTER 11 SHAPING TOMORROW'S MARKETS: THE FUTURE OF TRADE FINANCE THROUGH INNOVATIONS

Smoothing the Seas of Commerce: Hedging Tools and Derivatives in Navigating Trade Finance Volatility

Derivatives, among other hedging instruments, are significant in controlling financial risk as they offer means to protect against future price swings over several marketplaces. These tools help companies lock in rates or prices now for purchases scheduled for the future, therefore reducing the chance of negative price changes. In sectors with substantial volatility where unanticipated price changes can greatly affect profitability and financial stability, this capacity is particularly crucial.

Regarding world commerce and logistics, the idea of a market for container goods derivatives is very important. Fuel prices, geopolitics, supply chain interruptions, and seasonal demand fluctuations all affect the famously erratic speeds of container shipping. For financial institutions, logistics companies, and shippers depending on consistent transportation prices to control their budgets and pricing policies, this unpredictability can create significant hazards.

Establishing a market for derivatives of container goods seeks to provide fresh means for these participants to mitigate the inherent volatility in container shipping pricing. Using derivatives such as futures, options, and swaps helps companies guarantee stable prices for future transportation needs, therefore shielding themselves from unanticipated price swings or declines. For planning and budgeting, especially, this capacity to hedge offers a layer of financial certainty that is quite significant.

Container goods derivatives give financial institutions a chance to increase their array of hedging tools. By offering these futures, banks and other financial companies may give their customers customized solutions to control shipping cost volatility. This not only improves the value offered by these financial institutions but also assists in widening the market for goods and derivatives, thereby increasing their liquidity and strength.

Conversely, logistically speaking, container goods derivatives help suppliers control their running expenses. These suppliers frequently run on small margins; hence, their financial performance can be greatly improved by hedging against shipping rate volatility. Through derivatives, logistics firms may lock in prices and provide their customers with more consistent pricing, therefore strengthening their business ties and obtaining a competitive edge in the market.

Container goods derivatives give shippers—especially those engaged in worldwide trade—a way to guard their supply chain expenses. To guarantee that their goods stay competitively priced in foreign markets, manufacturers and exporters, for example,

CHAPTER 11 SHAPING TOMORROW'S MARKETS: THE FUTURE OF TRADE FINANCE THROUGH INNOVATIONS

can offset potential rises in transportation costs. Even in erratic market situations, this capacity to control cost risks helps companies maintain their profitability and competitiveness.

Moreover, the emergence of a container goods derivatives market can help the shipping sector to be generally transparent and efficient. The market provides comprehensive analysis of future shipping rates and useful pricing signals as more players participate in hedging operations. From creating long-term contracts to streamlining supply chain operations, this openness may let all parties make more wise judgments.

Various issues have to be resolved if one is to completely enjoy the advantages of container goods derivatives. Building a viable and dependable derivatives market mostly depends on standardizing contracts, guaranteeing regulatory compliance, and encouraging market liquidity. Overcoming these obstacles and creating a strong market for container goods derivatives would depend critically on cooperation among industry actors, financial institutions, and regulatory authorities.

Finally, by guaranteeing against future price swings, hedging instruments—especially derivatives—are absolutely essential for controlling financial risk. Particularly relevant in global commerce and logistics, the idea of a market for container goods derivatives gives creative means for financial institutions, logistics companies, and shippers to mitigate the volatility in container shipping prices. These derivatives can help companies stabilize their finances, improve competitiveness, and support a more transparent and efficient shipping sector by means of procedures to lock in future shipping prices. This market has the ability to change how transportation costs are handled as it grows, therefore helping all players in the worldwide trading system.

Mastering Hedging: The Role of Derivatives in Risk Management

A basic risk-reducing tactic used to offset possible losses in one position by occupying another position in a similar asset is hedging. Hedging's main objective is to stop losses from unanticipated market swings rather than necessarily create profit. This strategy lets companies and investors guard against negative pricing swings that can compromise their financial situation.

One must first grasp the ideas of derivatives if one is to grasp hedging. Derived from the performance of an underlying asset, index, or rate, derivatives are financial contracts. Both hedging and speculative usage of these products are possible. Among common

CHAPTER 11   SHAPING TOMORROW'S MARKETS: THE FUTURE OF TRADE FINANCE THROUGH INNOVATIONS

derivatives are futures, options, forwards, and swaps. Every one of these tools offers unique methods and advantages for controlling risk.

Futures contracts are agreements to acquire or sell an item at a certain future date and price. They are liquid and easily available as they are standardized and sold on exchanges. Companies use futures contracts to hedge against price volatility in commodities like metals, grains, or oil. An airline, for instance, might use futures to lock in fuel prices, ensuring that its expenses remain constant despite changes in the market.

Options give the right—not the obligation—to purchase or sell an asset at a designated price over a designated term. Because of this adaptability, options have become a flexible instrument for hedging. A farmer may buy a put option on grain, for instance, therefore entitizing them to sell at a certain price. Should the market price go below this level, the farmer can exercise their option and sell at the higher, set price, therefore safeguarding their income.

Though they are not traded on markets or standardized, forwards are like futures. These specially tailored agreements are set straight between two people, giving more freedom in terms and circumstances. Foreign exchange markets make frequent use of forwards, which lock in exchange rates for future transactions, thereby hedging against currency risk. This enables global companies to steady their financial performance in the face of rising exchange rates.

Swaps are two-party exchanges of cash flows or other financial instruments. Typically used to manage currency exposure or interest rate risk, one side of an interest rate swap can exchange a variable interest rate payment for a fixed rate payment, thereby controlling their borrowing costs. Similarly, a currency swap allows businesses to exchange cash flows between multiple currencies, effectively hedging against exchange rate fluctuations.

Using derivatives for hedging has as its main goal producing a balance whereby the gains in one position counterbalance the losses in another. This is especially important in industries where price fluctuations can have a significant impact on profitability. For instance, a firm dependent on raw materials can lock in pricing using derivatives, therefore safeguarding its profit margins from erosion by cost hikes. This helps them to concentrate on their main company operations without concern for negative changes in the market.

Hedging can help lower risk, but it does not totally eradicate it. Entering into derivative contracts comes with expenses; the success of a hedge relies on the correctness of the underlying assumptions and the fit of the approach. Furthermore,

CHAPTER 11   SHAPING TOMORROW'S MARKETS: THE FUTURE OF TRADE FINANCE THROUGH INNOVATIONS

market circumstances might vary suddenly, and even well-crafted hedging techniques could not work as planned.

Furthermore, derivatives may be complicated tools that require a thorough awareness of risk management techniques and financial markets. Companies and investors have to give their hedging plans extensive thought and make sure they complement their financial objectives and total risk tolerance. Furthermore, keeping current with laws and market changes that can compromise derivative contract fulfillment is crucial.

Without hedging and derivatives, contemporary risk management strategies cannot function effectively. Using these instruments allows companies and investors to stabilize their financial performance and guard against negative market swings. Effective application of hedging techniques depends on an awareness of the subtleties of futures, options, forwards, and swaps. Though it does not completely remove risk, it is a useful way to control uncertainty and improve financial resiliency. Hedging and derivatives will always be essential as markets change, as they provide fresh chances and difficulties for those who try to negotiate the complexity of the financial terrain.

Navigating Volatility: The Rise and Potential of Container Goods Derivatives in Global Trade

Early in the 2010s, the idea of selling futures contracts linked to container transportation prices surfaced. These agreements were meant to let participants lock in revenues or shipping expenses at a future date, therefore controlling the risk related to rate changes. The idea was straightforward but revolutionary: shippers, carriers, container goods derivatives, and financial institutions could hedge against the natural volatility of transportation prices, therefore guaranteeing more consistent financial results.

Though promising, at first the market for such derivatives did not get general acceptance. Many elements helped to explain this. The environment of the market at the time could not have been fit for the acceptance of such creative financial tools. Traditionally minded, the maritime sector could have lacked the knowledge or confidence required to welcome these new instruments. Furthermore, inadequate infrastructure to facilitate trading operations might have made it challenging for these contracts to acquire momentum.

CHAPTER 11 SHAPING TOMORROW'S MARKETS: THE FUTURE OF TRADE FINANCE THROUGH INNOVATIONS

Looking forward to recent years, there is growing interest in building a strong market for derivatives of container goods. This comeback occurs during a period of major global supply chain stress. These financial instruments have found a rich basis in the complexity of modern trade as well as growing container transit volumes. Driven by events including geopolitics, natural catastrophes, pandemics, and supply chain interruptions, they have underlined even more the requirement of efficient risk management strategies.

For every participant in the logistics and shipping sectors, increased volatility in shipping prices has grown to be a major concern. Shippers deal with erratic cost structures that could erode business margins and complicate budgeting procedures. Conversely, carriers find it difficult to budget for long-term investments and operating expenses as they suffer from revenue volatility. Variations in rates expose financial institutions funding trade and transportation activities to hazards that can affect their loan portfolios and investment returns.

In this regard, container goods derivatives provide a viable answer. These instruments provide a means to control financial risks and stabilize cash flows by letting parties hedge against future rate fluctuations. A shipper may, for instance, participate in a futures contract to guarantee a shipping rate for a designated term, therefore shielding their cost structure from any unanticipated rate hike. In the same vein, carriers may utilize these agreements to ensure a minimum degree of income, therefore shielding themselves from market downturns.

Container goods derivatives' growth and application depend on supporting infrastructure and a substantial degree of market openness. Standardized contracts must be created to guarantee consistency and dependability; exchanges that help to trade these contracts have to be established. Furthermore, easily available must be thorough data on shipping rates and market trends to support correct pricing and risk analysis.

Adoption of container goods derivatives also depends on awareness and education. Industry players have to know how these tools operate and how they may be included in their plans for risk management. Training courses, seminars, and workshops may be quite helpful in demystifying these financial instruments and inspiring confidence among possible users.

Furthermore, rules have to change to enable the trading of derivatives on container goods. To guarantee the integrity of the market, regulatory agencies must create well-defined policies and monitoring systems. This covers defining criteria for openness and reporting as well as putting policies in place to deter market manipulation and guarantee fair trade practices.

CHAPTER 11   SHAPING TOMORROW'S MARKETS: THE FUTURE OF TRADE FINANCE THROUGH INNOVATIONS

A well-functioning market for container goods derivatives has very significant possible advantages. These instruments can improve the stability and predictability of cash flows for every member by offering a way to counter rate volatility. More informed decision-making, improved financial planning, and more investment in the shipping and logistics industries can follow from this as well.

Moreover, the evolution of a strong market for derivatives of container goods might have more general financial consequences. These devices can help enable more seamless and effective world trade by lowering the risks associated with changes in transportation rates. Particularly in areas mostly dependent on marine trade, this can support stability and economic development.

Finally, since their introduction in the early 2010s, the idea of container goods derivatives has changed dramatically. The growing demand for efficient risk management solutions in the turbulent maritime environment of today is reflected in the fresh interest in these instruments. The possible advantages are convincing even if obstacles still exist in terms of infrastructure development, commercial acceptance, and regulatory backing. Container goods derivatives are ready to be crucial in stabilizing and improving the efficiency of global commerce as the supply chain is in constant flux.

Securing Global Trade: The Strategic Role of Container Goods Derivatives

For those engaged in worldwide commerce, container goods futures provide a significant benefit as they let participants hedge against future changes in shipping prices, therefore mitigating their impact. This ability to control risk offers a level of financial stability and predictability that is highly desirable in a volatile market. The erratic nature of shipping costs can seriously affect the financial viability of businesses depending on marine transportation. Businesses can protect themselves from unexpected and negative rate swings by locking in pricing through derivatives, therefore guaranteeing more consistent financial results.

Better price discovery follows from trading container goods derivatives as well. This approach clarifies for all players in the market future expectations on transportation expenses. Active trading of derivatives results in the collective understanding and expectations of all players reflecting in the market pricing.

CHAPTER 11   SHAPING TOMORROW'S MARKETS: THE FUTURE OF TRADE FINANCE THROUGH INNOVATIONS

This openness lets businesses change their plans depending on accurate forecasts of consumer trends. Businesses trying to negotiate the complexity of worldwide commerce would find immense value in such foresight, as it lowers uncertainty and promotes more strategic decision making.

Companies can better manage their operations if they can hedge against potential price fluctuations. Maximizing budgets, resource allocation, and long-term investments depends on this capacity for planning. A company may better organize its resources and find possible areas for cost cuts when it can more precisely forecast its transportation expenses. Based on consistent transportation prices, a company could change inventory levels and production schedules, therefore lowering storage costs and minimizing overproduction.

Moreover, the stability that container goods derivatives offer helps businesses confidently sign longer-term contracts. Since both sides can rely on consistent expenses, this long-term view helps to build better bonds with suppliers and consumers. Small and medium-sized businesses (SMEs), who frequently run with smaller margins and less financial flexibility than bigger companies, especially benefit from such stability. Reducing the risk of changing shipping prices helps SMEs compete more successfully on the international scene.

Broadly speaking, by reducing one of the main risk elements of the supply chain, container goods derivatives help to provide general security for it. Global logistics is much more concerned about the fluctuation of shipping prices, as it causes interruptions and inefficiencies most of the time. Using derivatives to control expenses helps businesses guarantee better and more consistent supply chain operations. This stability helps to maintain continuous commerce, as companies are less likely to suffer financial shocks that can affect their distribution systems and logistics.

The advantages of container goods derivatives reach the whole worldwide commerce ecosystem rather than only individual businesses. More resilient and strong supply chains result from companies that better control their transportation expenses. Global issues, including political unrest, economic downturns, and natural calamities, call for this resilience. Container goods derivatives enable larger-scale economic stability and growth by providing a tool to reduce financial risk and preserve the continuity of trade.

Moreover, the use of derivatives promotes competition and creativity in the transportation sector. Companies that use these financial products stimulate demand for more complex risk management tools and services. This need motivates technological companies and financial organizations to create new platforms and products, thereby improving the accessibility and efficiency of the derivatives market. Lower transaction costs, better market liquidity, and more engagement from many stakeholders can all follow from the subsequent advances.

Adoption of container goods derivatives also advances transportation sector openness and responsibility. More companies participate in hedging operations; hence, the data produced from these transactions offers insightful analysis of market dynamics. Regulators, analysts, and business executives may all monitor trends, evaluate risks, and create well-informed policies using this information. By creating a fair and competitive environment, more openness helps all market players.

Several advantages provided by container goods derivatives improve the general security, operational effectiveness, and financial stability of world commerce. These products are a vital tool for controlling risk in a turbulent market by letting companies hedge against future price changes. Supply chain resilience, strategic planning tools, and better price discovery brought about by the use of derivatives support improved trade flows and economic growth. The evolution of the market for container goods will probably affect the worldwide shipping sector even more as it promotes innovation and a more consistent and predictable trading environment.

Navigating Challenges and Unlocking Potential: The Future of Container Derivatives

Although container goods derivatives provide major advantages, certain issues have to be resolved if the industry is to flourish. Maintaining enough market liquidity presents one of the main difficulties. A derivatives market must have enough participants to allow traders simple access and exit if it is to be efficient. Lack of enough liquidity could make it difficult for market players to locate counterparties for their transactions, therefore increasing transaction costs and lowering efficiency. Fostering a liquid and active market depends on drawing a wide spectrum of participants—shippers, carriers, financial institutions, and speculators.

Contractual standardization is still another important obstacle. Standardizing the contracts will help to capture the subtleties of shipping rate volatility while reflecting the shared needs of market players. Standardized contracts lessen the complexity involved in writing customized agreements for every transaction and make trading easier. Still, striking the proper equilibrium in standardizing is really vital. The contracts have to be adaptable enough to include fluctuations in cargo kinds, shipping routes, and

CHAPTER 11   SHAPING TOMORROW'S MARKETS: THE FUTURE OF TRADE FINANCE THROUGH INNOVATIONS

other elements affecting freight pricing. The adoption of standardized contracts by the majority of market participants will necessitate careful consideration and collaboration among industry players.

The success of container goods depends partly on developing trust and understanding among possible market players. The advantages and strategies of employing derivatives for hedging might not be known to many of the stakeholders. Essential is teaching interested parties how these financial products could control risk and offer financial stability. Explaining the pragmatic features of trading derivatives, the possible dangers involved, and the security measures in place to guard participants is part of this instructional program. Transparency, open communication, and proving the real advantages of employing derivatives in control of shipping rate volatility help to build trust.

Establishing a strong legislative framework is still another important factor. While maintaining market integrity and safeguarding players from systematic risks, the regulatory framework has to enable the trading of container goods derivatives. This entails defining precise policies for risk management criteria, reporting requirements, and trading behavior. Regulators have to balance keeping a stable and safe market environment with encouraging invention. Building confidence among players and drawing more general acceptance depend on the market running fairly and openly.

One intriguing way to improve risk control in the worldwide commerce and logistics scene is the creation of a market for container goods derivatives. The timing appears ready for financial institutions, logistics companies, and shippers to adopt new hedging methods as the globe turns more and more toward supply chain security and efficiency. Realizing the possibilities of these creative financial products will depend on overcoming obstacles of market acceptance, liquidity, and standardization. Success in this initiative will depend on all the parties involved—industry players, authorities, and financial institutions—coordinating their efforts.

Overcoming these obstacles offers really significant advantages. A functioning market for derivatives on container goods can provide much-needed stability in a sector that is characterized by volatility. These futures allow companies to hedge against changes in shipping rates, helping to stabilize expenses and income and enabling better financial planning and investment decisions. This stability helps boost trust in world commerce, therefore motivating companies to grow their activities and enter new markets.

Furthermore, a strong market for derivatives of container goods can inspire creativity and efficiency within the transportation sector. More people involved in derivatives trading allow the market to produce insightful analyses of freight rate patterns and dynamics. This data can enable market players to maximize their supply chains, make more wise judgments, and raise general operational effectiveness.

Even if container goods derivatives have enormous potential, obtaining these advantages calls for addressing numerous important issues. Important actions in this process are guaranteeing enough market liquidity, creating standardized contracts, fostering trust and understanding among parties, and strengthening a strong legislative framework. Overcoming these obstacles will help the market for container goods derivatives to become a potent instrument for controlling risk and improving the security and efficiency of worldwide commerce and logistics. Offering the possibility for more stability, creativity, and expansion, the emergence of this market marks a forward-looking method of negotiating the complexity of the current transportation sector.

Logistics Reimagined: Navigating the Future of Information Sharing and Technological Integration

The future of logistics information will change the global supply chain, resulting in a more technologically advanced, effective, and interoperable environment than ever before. This trend depends on the growth and general acceptance of sophisticated trade-data systems meant to enable smooth data flow and cooperation across several logistics and supply chain players.

The idea of interoperability drives its development from its core. Interoperability in logistics is the capacity of several systems, companies, and nations to cooperate successfully. Standardizing data formats and communication technologies will help to achieve this so that information may flow naturally between borders and between several organizations. By lowering friction in trade processes, this standardization helps to greatly increase efficiency. Faster and more dependable supply chains depend on customs processes, for instance, which may be simplified; shipment monitoring can be improved; inventory management can be maximized.

One main driver of this new logistics scene is the incorporation of modern technology. Crucially helping are artificial intelligence (AI), blockchain, the Internet of things (IoT), and big data analytics. AI can, for example, examine enormous volumes of data to forecast demand, streamline paths, and spot any problems before they start. By using a transparent and safe method of transaction recording, blockchain technology guarantees that all participants have access to the same information, thereby lowering the fraud risk. While big data analytics can provide insights that enable businesses to make better decisions, and IoT devices can offer a real-time view into the location and state of commodities.

Trade-data systems that reflect ideas of neutrality, transparency, and control constitute the core of this approach. These platforms are meant to be impartial; hence, they are not under the control of any one entity, which helps users develop confidence by means of this neutrality. Transparency guarantees that the platforms are reachable to all pertinent stakeholders, therefore encouraging diversity and teamwork. Maintaining data integrity and security depends on oversight systems, which also guarantee that the exchanged data is correct and trustworthy.

Such systems allow different data sources to be stitched together. They can show the whole supply chain by combining and standardizing data from several platforms. From manufacturers and suppliers to logistics providers and stores, this all-encompassing viewpoint helps all parties coordinate and cooperate more effectively. Companies can therefore react faster to changes in demand, disturbances, and other difficulties.

Often referred to as standard bottlenecks, one of the long-standing problems in global trade and logistics is the absence of consistent data forms and procedures. As several systems and companies struggle to interact properly, these bottlenecks produce inefficiencies and delays.

Trade-data platforms, driven by artificial intelligence and other cutting-edge technologies, provide a shared framework for data interchange that can assist in addressing these issues. These platforms can remove many of the obstacles now impeding international trade by guaranteeing that all participants have access to consistent, reliable knowledge.

Enough data access is absolutely necessary for this vision to come to pass. Companies, governments, and other stakeholders have to be ready to freely and securely provide their data. Essential policies and rules will be those that support data sharing while safeguarding intellectual property rights and privacy. Furthermore, investments in digital infrastructure and talent development will be required to guarantee that everyone can engage in and gain from the new logistics scene.

Logistically, the future seems to be one of increasingly linked, effective, and technologically sophisticated global supply chains. Using interoperable systems, cutting-edge technology, and cooperative trade-data platforms helps the logistics sector overcome long-standing obstacles and release fresh degrees of efficiency and effectiveness. Along with improving the global flow of products and services, this change will stimulate innovation and economic development in the next few years.

CHAPTER 11   SHAPING TOMORROW'S MARKETS: THE FUTURE OF TRADE FINANCE THROUGH INNOVATIONS

Building the Future of Logistics: Neutrality, Openness, and Control in Trade-Data Platforms

The future of fast-changing global logistics depends on the creation of sophisticated systems meant to enable seamless trade-data interchange. Designed as the backbone of the contemporary supply chain, these platforms have to reflect important characteristics supporting neutrality, transparency, and control. These ideas are not just technological requirements but also fundamental ideas that guarantee these platforms can efficiently meet the many and dynamic needs of the worldwide logistics community.

The idea of neutrality is at the core of the next generation of logistics systems. This idea is essential to guaranteeing that no one entity—business, government, or organization—may have too much power over the platform. Fostering trust among users depends on neutrality, as it assures that the platform runs free from prejudice, therefore creating a fair playing field for all users.

Acting as a fair middleman, a neutral platform allows data to be shared without favoring any one side. In a global setting where logistics entails a multitude of parties with different interests and competing dynamics, impartiality is very vital. Maintaining neutrality helps the platform guarantee that every user, from different backgrounds or market influences, has equal access to its features. Small and medium-sized businesses (SMEs), who often find it difficult to compete with bigger competitors owing to resource limits, especially depend on this inclusiveness. By democratizing access to vital data and technologies, a neutral logistics platform helps SMEs engage more fully in world trade.

The technical foundation supporting a neutral platform has to be built to stop any organization from controlling or dictating the system. To monitor and enforce neutrality, this entails putting strong governance systems and openness rules into use. Furthermore, the financial and operational strategies of the platform should be set in such a way as to prevent conflicts of interest and thus guarantee that its major loyalty stays with its varied user base rather than any one stakeholder group.

Another pillar of future logistics systems is openness. From global companies to SMEs, from logistics suppliers to regulatory authorities, an open platform is meant to be reachable by a broad spectrum of entities. This inclusiveness promotes a rich ecology of players, hence improving the platform's value and efficiency.

An open platform guarantees fair and simple access to its data and services, therefore fostering greater involvement. This accessibility is crucial in a global logistics context where data exchange and cooperation are required to optimize supply chain

CHAPTER 11 SHAPING TOMORROW'S MARKETS: THE FUTURE OF TRADE FINANCE THROUGH INNOVATIONS

operations. An open platform may compile a great deal of data by letting different entities access and participate, therefore offering a whole picture of the supply chain. This all-encompassing perspective makes it possible for better coordination, more informed decision making, and increased efficiency throughout the logistics network.

The platform has to embrace open standards and protocols that enable compatibility with different systems and technology if it is to reach actual transparency. This guarantees that data may be fluidly shared among several platforms and stakeholders, therefore eradicating silos and advancing cooperation. Open standards also help to avoid vendor lock-in, thereby allowing consumers the freedom to pick the best solutions for their requirements free from limitations imposed by owned technology.

Furthermore, the platform's development and creative process are open. Through encouraging openness and teamwork, the platform may exploit the combined knowledge of its user base to propel ongoing development and innovation. Open-source projects, community-driven development, and cooperative innovation projects can all help to ensure that the platform stays sensitive to the evolving demands of the logistics sector.

Third important for future logistics systems is efficient control, which guarantees data sharing integrity, security, and dependability. Maintaining the credibility and integrity of the platform depends heavily on governance structures, which also help to solve issues with data privacy, security, and correctness.

Strong data use monitoring and management systems on a well-run platform guarantee adherence to pertinent laws and standards. This involves developing explicit rules and processes for data access, sharing, and storage, as well as putting in place cutting-edge security measures to guard against cyberattacks and illegal access.

Regular audits and evaluations to confirm the platform's performance and adherence to governance values are part of oversight as well. Committees or independent monitoring agencies might be set up to offer impartial assessments and suggestions, therefore guaranteeing that the platform runs accountably and fairly. These committees also help to resolve conflicts and handle grievances, therefore giving consumers a means to express worries and get answers.

Moreover, positive government calls for the active involvement of every participant. Through the use of inclusive decision-making procedures, whereby users have a say in determining the direction and policies of the platform, this is accomplished. The platform can create a strong and reliable ecosystem that supports its long-term viability and success by encouraging responsibility and ownership among users.

The ideas of impartiality, transparency, and control will characterize logistics platforms going forward. These characteristics are not just technical ones but also necessary ones that guarantee the platforms can efficiently meet the many requirements of the worldwide logistics community. Platforms that embrace neutrality may provide a fair playing field for every user, therefore promoting trust and inclusiveness. Openness increases general involvement and teamwork, therefore improving the usefulness of the platform. Good control guarantees the data exchange's integrity and security, thereby preserving the credibility and dependability of the platform.

These ideas will direct the creation of cutting-edge platforms that revolutionize trade-data sharing and use as the logistics sector changes. Future logistics platforms will open new degrees of efficiency, transparency, and creativity by using modern technology and creating a cooperative ecosystem, thereby guiding the global supply chain into a new era of connection and resilience.

Transforming Data Integration and Supply Chain Efficiency: The Role of Artificial Intelligence from a Regulatory Standpoint

A flawless movement of products and information throughout the world in the current logistics scene depends on the integration of innovative technology. Among these technologies, artificial intelligence (AI) is clearly a major player in changing data integration, analysis, and use inside logistics platforms. Effective and efficient information sharing depends critically on AI's capacity to manage enormous volumes of data from many sources and its ability to address compatibility problems across many data standards.

Through advanced tools for data integration, artificial intelligence will be at the center of future logistics platforms. Data is created in the logistics ecosystem from a variety of sources, including shipment manifests, customs declarations, tracking systems, and IoT devices. Every one of these sources follows distinct criteria and styles, resulting in a complicated network of knowledge that has to be harmonized for best usage. Artificial intelligence excels in this environment by utilizing sophisticated algorithms that can process, evaluate, and standardize data from various sources. This feature guarantees that data formats compatible between several systems and stakeholders may flow naturally, therefore minimizing delays and mistakes resulting from incompatible formats.

CHAPTER 11   SHAPING TOMORROW'S MARKETS: THE FUTURE OF TRADE FINANCE THROUGH INNOVATIONS

The capacity of artificial intelligence to execute sophisticated data analysis emphasizes even more its transforming power in logistics. The sheer volume and complexity of the data involved in global logistics call for more than traditional data processing techniques can manage. Artificial intelligence can sort through enormous amounts of data to find trends, patterns, and insights humans would find impossible. Maximizing supply chain operations depends on this analytical ability, as it helps businesses forecast demand, streamline paths, and spot any interruptions before they start. Using AI-driven insights helps logistics companies make better decisions, thereby improving the dependability and efficiency of their offerings.

The difficulty of matching several data standards is among the most important obstacles in logistics. The worldwide character of the supply chain implies that different areas and companies might apply different data exchange techniques and formats depending on them. As systems fight to properly interact with one another, this lack of standardization can lead to bottlenecks and inefficiencies. Acting as a middleman able to translate and harmonize data from several standards, artificial intelligence solves this challenge. By using machine learning and natural language processing, artificial intelligence can identify and adapt to different data formats, therefore guaranteeing that knowledge may be freely distributed along the whole supply chain.

Furthermore, the role artificial intelligence plays in upcoming logistics systems is improving data integrity and security. Protection of private data is critical at a time when cyberattacks are a continual worry. By seeing irregularities and possible breaches in real time, artificial intelligence (AI) may support security protocols by allowing quick reactions to reduce hazards. By always observing and verifying the data shared on the platform, artificial intelligence algorithms may also guarantee data integrity. Maintaining the correctness and dependability of the data depends on this ongoing control, which is crucial for developing confidence among all the logistics processes participants depend on.

Including artificial intelligence in logistics systems also helps to improve visibility and openness. Real-time tracking and processing features of artificial intelligence let stakeholders see the whole supply chain. This openness not only guarantees regulatory compliance but also helps to find opportunities for development and inefficiency. Moreover, artificial intelligence-powered systems may provide predictive analytics based on past data, therefore allowing proactive planning and decision-making.

The developments in artificial intelligence are absolutely entwined with the direction of logistics. The uses of artificial intelligence technology in the logistics industry will grow as it develops, therefore fostering more innovations and efficiency. The ability of AI to overcome compatibility issues, combine and analyze enormous volumes of data, and enhance security and openness demonstrates its significant influence on the development of logistics platforms in the future.

Artificial intelligence is a basic component in the development of logistics systems rather than only a technological improvement. Its capacity to easily combine and evaluate several data sets, address compatibility issues, and offer strong security measures places artificial intelligence as a main driver of efficiency and creativity in the logistics sector. Realizing the full potential of future logistics platforms will depend on the integration of artificial intelligence, enabling a more linked, efficient, and robust worldwide supply chain.

Phased Growth: Building Next-Generation Logistics Platforms with Trust and Innovation

The success and development of next-generation logistics platforms depend on a calculated, staged installation and expansion strategy. This approach starts with first focusing on certain issue areas or use cases of most relevance for target users. First, tackling these important problems would help platforms progressively establish confidence among members, inspire them to provide more data over time, and open the path for more general uses.

Usually starting with a specific pain point that has significant logistical consequences for its customers, the first step in creating a logistics platform focuses on addressing that issue. With this targeted approach, the platform can quickly demonstrate its value by resolving urgent problems and delivering tangible benefits. For example, a platform may begin by addressing challenges related to environmental data sharing.

Environmental issues are becoming more and more important in the logistics sector because of legal requirements and the need for sustainable practices. The platform may help businesses track and lower their carbon footprints, follow environmental laws, and improve their sustainability initiatives by enabling the flawless flow of environmental data.

Focusing on a particular use case, including environmental data exchange, helps the platform gain market traction. Users' trust in the system increases as they enjoy better environmental performance and simplified data flow. The encouragement of more general engagement and more thorough data sharing depends on this confidence. Participants start to view the platform as a dependable and useful tool, which encourages a readiness to interact more fully with its features.

The platform may progressively widen its reach to encompass more kinds of data and uses as trust and involvement grow. For instance, the platform may expand its capabilities to include compliance data after effective handling of environmental data sharing. For logistics firms, following several rules is a major issue, as it entails following several criteria and requirements across several countries and jurisdictions. Integration of compliance data into the platform helps customers simplify their regulatory procedures, lower their administrative load, and guarantee more effective adherence to legal requirements.

Expanding on the success of environmental and compliance data exchange, the platform may also include financial data. Important parts of the logistics sector, financial transactions, and reporting include intricate interactions among several parties. The platform may improve general financial management, lower the risk of mistakes and fraud, and facilitate the safe and open flow of financial data, thereby enhancing financial reporting. This stepwise strategy lets the platform grow progressively while naturally reacting to the most pressing demands of its customers.

Phased installation and growth address not only several kinds of data but also change the infrastructure and technology of the platform. The platform could first employ current technologies and systems to handle the particular use case under hand. The platform can include additional cutting-edge technology as it grows, like artificial intelligence, blockchain, and big data analytics. These technologies can improve the capacity of the platform to manage more data, offer deeper insights, guarantee better security and openness, and thus handle higher amounts of data.

Furthermore, the phased strategy lets one always learn and grow. Every stage of execution offers insightful comments and analysis that could guide further projects. Closely observing the performance and user experiences of the platform helps developers to see areas for improvement, handle any issues that occur, and polish the features and capabilities of the platform. This continuous method guarantees that the platform is flexible enough to meet the demands of its customers as well as those of the larger logistics sector.

CHAPTER 11   SHAPING TOMORROW'S MARKETS: THE FUTURE OF TRADE FINANCE THROUGH INNOVATIONS

The incremental implementation and expansion plan revolves mostly around the slow development of confidence. In the logistics ecosystem, effective data exchange and cooperation depend mostly on trust. Starting with a targeted strategy and proving evident benefits will help the platform build the confidence of its users, therefore motivating them to provide more data and interact more closely with its capabilities. Establishing a dynamic platform capable of supporting a wide spectrum of applications and promoting more industry-wide cooperation depends on this process of generating confidence.

The strategic strategy of staggered installation and extension of future logistics platforms helps to permit slow progress. Platforms that first concentrate on certain issue areas or use cases may rapidly show their worth, inspire more general involvement, and help users develop confidence. This confidence lays the groundwork for broadening the platform to accommodate other kinds of data and applications, thereby producing a complete and flexible tool for the logistics sector. Through ongoing education and iterative enhancements, the platform may change to satisfy the demands of its users, fostering innovation and efficiency in the worldwide supply chain.

Revolutionizing Logistics: Transforming Operations, Fostering Innovation, and Unlocking Global Economic Value

The introduction of sophisticated logistics platforms intended to enable effective data sharing is about to transform the logistics industry. These platforms will significantly alter the way operators interact with consumers, partners, and transportation hubs, thereby bringing in an era of simplified operations, redesigned industry principles, and increased economic value.

The change starts with the streamlining of present procedures, therefore enabling efficient operations. Data silos and scattered systems often lead to inefficiencies and duplicates in the conventional logistics scene. By allowing smooth data transmission, the new systems break apart these silos and combine several procedures. Real-time data sharing among shippers, carriers, and consumers, for instance, lets tracking and forecasting be more precise, thereby lowering delays and enhancing cooperation. Reducing pointless steps—such as several data entries or handwritten documentation—helps to improve operational effectiveness even further. Simplifying complicated logistics networks helps businesses save time and resources, therefore accelerating logistics operations and lowering expenses.

CHAPTER 11   SHAPING TOMORROW'S MARKETS: THE FUTURE OF TRADE FINANCE THROUGH INNOVATIONS

These platforms also inspire new business models and a reassessment of industry values, therefore fostering innovation. The logistics industry has chances for creative supply chain management as it adopts the features of contemporary technology. Sequential handoffs define traditional linear supply chains; increasingly dynamic and linked networks replace them. Businesses can use more adaptable and responsive methods, such as collaborative logistics networks or just-in-time inventory control, whereby several stakeholders instantly exchange resources and data. This modification not only increases resilience but also efficiency, as logistics systems can react quickly to demand fluctuations or disturbances.

Advanced technologies such as artificial intelligence, machine learning, and blockchain inclusion in these systems speed innovation even further. Analyzing enormous volumes of data, artificial intelligence such as machine learning algorithms can improve routing, forecast maintenance needs, and find any disruptions before they start. Blockchain technology guarantees transaction security and openness, therefore building confidence among all the engaged parties. Using this technology helps logistics companies create more proactive and intelligent plans, therefore improving their competitive advantage in a sector that is fast-changing.

Beyond specific businesses, these revolutionary developments release enormous economic value for the world economy overall. Since efficient logistical operations are crucial to global trade, these platforms' increased capacity could spur significant economic development. Companies may cut their expenses and forward savings to consumers by, for example, cutting shipment times and enhancing dependability. Faster and more consistent logistics can help companies reach consumers in new areas and distribute products more rapidly, therefore extending their markets.

Moreover, more sustainable economic development results from more efficient logistical operations, lowering environmental effects. Companies may cut their gasoline usage and greenhouse gas emissions by streamlining paths and cutting duplicity. This not only fits with world sustainability targets but also lowers running expenses, therefore benefiting the environment as well as the economy.

Additionally, effective data exchange serves as a driving force for greater cooperation across the logistics ecosystem. By working closely together and sharing common knowledge, operators, consumers, and partners can enhance coordination and improve decision-making. By removing conventional divisions and silos, this cooperative method produces a more unified and coherent logistics network. The improved visibility and openness the platforms offer help stakeholders develop trust, which motivates them to exchange more data and cooperate more successfully.

In the end, modern logistics systems' effective data exchange is going to fundamentally alter the transportation sector. These platforms will transform how logistics managers interact with consumers, partners, and transit hubs by simplifying processes, supporting innovation, and releasing economic value. Not only will the ensuing efficiency and innovations help individual businesses, but they will also propel major advantages for the world economy overall. Adoption of these platforms will be essential in determining a more sustainable, robust, and efficient future for worldwide supply chains as the logistics industry keeps changing.

Beyond Traditional 3PL Services: Transforming Global Logistics with 5PL and 6PL Solutions

Driven by the integration of new technologies that change the terrain outside the known boundaries of 3PL services, the logistics sector is about to undergo a significant metamorphosis. Fifth-party (5PL) and sixth-party (6PL) logistics services—which mark fresh levels of coordination and technical sophistication—are emerging, thanks to this growth. These sophisticated layers help logistics companies deliver a whole range of supply chain solutions that are especially suited for the needs of the digital era.

Concerning 3PL services, the conventional paradigm emphasizes supply chain operations and outsourcing of logistics. By handling several facets of logistics, including distribution, shipping, and warehouse, 3PL providers let businesses focus on their main skills. Reducing expenses and increasing efficiency have been greatly aided by this paradigm. But the restrictions of 3PL solutions become clear when supply networks get more complicated and linked. Addressing this complexity and satisfying the changing requirements of the worldwide market depend on the integration of modern technology.

In the logistics sector, the arrival of 5PL services represents a major breakthrough. Beyond only overseeing physical logistics operations, 5PL suppliers cover the whole supply chain, including strategic planning and optimization. Using technologies including artificial intelligence, big data analytics, and the Internet of things (IoT), 5PL providers provide a complete supply chain management solution. They improve supply chain visibility, control inventory levels, and predict demand by means of sophisticated data analytics. 5PL companies may provide more exact and agile logistics solutions by combining various technologies, therefore ensuring that supply chains are not only effective but also rather sensitive to changes in the market.

Furthermore, underlined by 5PL services are connectivity and cooperation. From suppliers and manufacturers to stores and final consumers, they enable flawless communication and coordination across all the supply chain participants. Modern digital platforms that allow real-time data exchange and teamwork help to reach this degree of integration. 5PL suppliers may therefore create intricate logistical networks with unmatched efficiency, thereby lowering lead times and minimizing disturbance.

With the arrival of 6PL services—the height of logistics innovation—the transformation is still in progress. Using the most sophisticated technology, 6PL suppliers provide completely autonomous and automated logistics solutions. At this level, blockchain, robots, and artificial intelligence assume a central role. Decision-making processes powered by artificial intelligence optimize every aspect of the supply chain, from purchasing to last-mile delivery. In warehouses and distribution hubs, robotics automate physical operations, hence improving speed and accuracy. Blockchain technology guarantees the openness and security of transactions, therefore fostering confidence among all the players in the supply chain.

The capacity of 6PL solutions to offer end-to-end visibility and control defines them. 6PL suppliers use IoT sensors and devices to track the location and condition of products instantly. Providers are able to anticipate and address issues before they worsen through proactive supply chain management. Moreover, 6PL systems use machine learning and predictive analytics to project future developments and modify supply chain plans. This forward-looking strategy guarantees that, in the face of evolving market conditions, logistics operations will stay flexible and strong.

The change from 3PL to 5PL and 6PL services marks a basic change in how logistics companies run, rather than only a technical improvement. It calls for a dedication to ongoing innovation and a review of conventional corporate practices. Logistics companies have to make investments in the growth of digital skills and create a culture that welcomes technology transformation. This change also requires a significant emphasis on customer centricity, as the ultimate objective is to provide clients with exceptional value by addressing their particular requirements and issues.

Moving beyond conventional 3PL solutions offers several advantages. Businesses that embrace 5PL and 6PL solutions will be able to improve supply chain resilience, operational efficiency, and cost control. Their quick response to consumer needs and changes in the market helps them gain a competitive edge in a world that is becoming more and more dynamic. Furthermore, the incorporation of cutting-edge technology helps sustainability through the best use of resources and waste minimization.

CHAPTER 11   SHAPING TOMORROW'S MARKETS: THE FUTURE OF TRADE FINANCE THROUGH INNOVATIONS

The logistics industry is finally undergoing significant change, thanks to the integration of cutting-edge technology that has allowed the growth of 3PL, 5PL, and 6PL services. These new layers of logistics services let suppliers deliver complete and very responsive supply chain solutions by representing advanced degrees of coordination and technology adaptation. Accepting these technologies would help logistics companies satisfy the needs of the digital era, therefore giving their customers more value and supporting the resilience of the world economy.

The Vision of a Physical Internet: Revolutionizing Global Logistics for a Connected and Sustainable Future

Thanks to technological developments, the idea of a physical internet is fast changing from a visionary ideal into a real-world possibility. This creative model sees logistics services radically changing the worldwide supply chain by becoming as easily available and linked as internet knowledge. Effective direct shipment, automatic replenishment, artificial intelligence-driven demand forecasting, and tech-enabled commerce will define logistics operations in this future state, thereby improving the efficiency and efficacy of world trade.

The principle of effective direct shipment drives the physical internet from its foundation. Load and route optimization for direct delivery can help logistics companies greatly reduce delays and expenses. Considering elements including traffic conditions, weather, and inventory levels, this optimization depends on real-time data and sophisticated algorithms to identify the most effective pathways for shipments. A simplified transportation procedure resulting from this shortens travel times, decreases fuel consumption, and increases overall dependability by reducing reliance on complex logistics networks and inefficient processes. Direct shipment guarantees that items get at their destinations faster and more effectively by removing needless pauses and transfers.

Automatic replenishment is yet another vital component of the physical internet. Using real-time data, logistics systems can automatically forecast and meet inventory demands, therefore preserving ideal stock levels and eliminating overstocking or shortages. Sophisticated sensors and IoT devices tracking inventories in real-time and sending data to centralized systems for analysis and demand forecasting help to allow this capacity. The system may automatically set orders to restitute supplies when inventory levels drop below a specified level, therefore guaranteeing that supply chains stay continuous and sensitive to market needs. Automatic replenishment not only improves productivity but also lessens the administrative load of the company, freeing them to concentrate on strategic operations.

AI scenario planning and demand forecasting highlight yet another transforming power of the physical internet. Artificial intelligence enables logistics companies to predict market needs with unprecedented precision, thereby guiding their planning and operation modifications. By analyzing past performance, market trends, and outside variables, artificial intelligence algorithms help businesses forecast future demand, therefore enabling active supply chain management. This foresight guarantees that logistics operations are strong and adaptable, able to minimize the risk of disturbance, and change with demand. By allowing logistics companies to replicate several scenarios and create backup plans, artificial intelligence scenario planning also helps them to maintain continuity and react to unanticipated occurrences.

Another important feature of the physical internet is tech-enabled trade, which improves the general efficiency and efficacy of world trade. From suppliers and manufacturers to retailers and consumers, advanced technologies help all supply chain participants—from seamless communication and coordination to interoperable trade-data systems that let information be securely and transparently exchanged—to accomplish this interconnection. Integrating these systems with artificial intelligence and other digital technologies would help logistics companies have better awareness and control over their operations, therefore guaranteeing that items flow naturally across borders and through several phases of the supply chain. Because logistics providers can rapidly change their operations depending on real-time data and insights, tech-enabled commerce also enables more exact and fast matching of consumer requirements.

AI in the logistics industry has enormous transforming power, along with interoperable trade-data systems. These technologies can drastically change the scene of world logistics by tackling particular pain areas, fostering confidence among stakeholders, and progressively extending the extent of change. Along with operational advantages, the move toward a more connected, technologically driven environment promises a rethink of the fundamental ideas of business. The sector may reach hitherto unheard-of degrees of agility, sustainability, and customer happiness as logistics operations become more linked and data driven.

Under this new paradigm, the physical internet supports a more strong and dynamic worldwide economy. Improved efficiency and responsiveness of logistics operations contribute to boosting global commerce and economic development by enhancing supply chain reliability, reducing costs, and ensuring faster delivery times. Businesses may reach new customers and provide goods faster and more consistently, therefore operating more competitively. Because items are delivered more quickly and precisely, consumers gain from additional options and convenience. Moreover, the physical internet supports sustainability via best utilization of resources and lessening of the environmental effect of logistical activities.

When compared to the physical internet, the logistics sector has undergone significant transformation. By means of effective direct shipment, automated replenishment, demand forecasting powered by artificial intelligence, and tech-enabled commerce, this creative paradigm transforms the opportunities for worldwide supply chains. The physical internet will eventually become a natural component of the logistics landscape as technology develops, promoting operational efficiency, innovation, and a more connected and resilient global economy by driving seamless data exchange, optimized resource utilization, and enhanced collaboration across supply chains. The future of logistics is about building a seamless, intelligent, and sustainable network supporting the changing requirements of modern society, not only about shipping things from one location to another.

Logistics Unleashed: How Enhanced Information Sharing Is Transforming Trade

The commerce and logistics sectors are at a pivotal juncture, offering significant opportunities for technological transformation to streamline processes and enhance information exchange. The current situation of products imported internationally demonstrates the complexity and inefficiency that technology seeks to solve. Shipping a single container from one nation to another, for example, is more than just a question of transportation; it entails a complex network of players, documentation, and procedures that, taken together, provide significant difficulties.

Think about the path goods travel from Kenya to the Netherlands. At least 15 distinct people can be involved in this process: exporters, importers, customs officers, shipping firms, and several regulatory authorities. Every one of these involved parties needs certain documentation and compliance checks, which results in an amazing pile of records. Usually requiring 36 papers, each of which needs several copies for several parties, the procedure runs around 240 copies overall. The heaps of papers, occasionally spanning 25 cm in thickness, clearly show the physical weight of this bureaucratic load.

CHAPTER 11   SHAPING TOMORROW'S MARKETS: THE FUTURE OF TRADE FINANCE THROUGH INNOVATIONS

This bureaucratic tsunami does more than just slow down the shipping process. With document processing alone covering up to one-fifth of total shipping costs, it greatly increases charges. Every stage of this intricate chain calls for careful processing of papers, including bills of lading, certificates of origin, business invoices, and customs declarations. Manual processing of these records takes time and is prone to mistakes, which can cause more delays and expenses.

These inefficiencies have far-reaching consequences. For companies, especially in sectors where prompt delivery is absolutely vital, the delayed and expensive shipping procedures could lower their competitiveness. These inefficiencies can translate for customers into more expensive items and longer wait times. Moreover, it is impossible to ignore the environmental effects of a lot of documentation and the related administrative tasks, as they support waste and carbon emissions.

By automating and digitizing procedures, the technological revolution in the commerce and logistics sectors promises to solve these issues. Advanced digital solutions may improve the efficiency of stakeholder contacts, lower the dependence on physical documents, and simplify the information flow. Blockchain technology, for example, provides a means to generate tamper-proof, safe digital documents that are instantly available to all pertinent parties. This will reduce the need for several copies of papers and lower the possibility of fraud and mistakes.

Including Internet of things (IoT) devices in logistics processes may also offer real-time tracking and monitoring of products, thereby enhancing coordination and openness among the several stakeholders. By handling document verification and compliance checks as well, automated solutions help to lower administrative load and speed processing times.

The possible advantages are substantial when the commerce and logistics sectors adopt these technical developments. Faster shipment times, major cost savings, and improved documentation and compliance accuracy resulting from streamlined procedures can all be achieved. This may thus increase company competitiveness, raise consumer happiness, and lower the environmental impact of shipping operations.

Ultimately, the commerce and logistics sectors find themselves at the forefront of a technology revolution meant to change global product movement. Technology might build a more sustainable, affordable, and efficient worldwide commerce system by tackling the present inefficiencies and complexity.

CHAPTER 11   SHAPING TOMORROW'S MARKETS: THE FUTURE OF TRADE FINANCE THROUGH INNOVATIONS

Overcoming Barriers to Trade Digitization: Balancing Tradition, Innovation, and Collaboration

The more conservative players in the ecosystem typically help to slow down the explosive speed of trade innovation and digitalization. The significant difficulties legacy networks and systems present—which are vital for interactions between many nations and logistical actors—drive this caution. For new competitors trying to bring technical breakthroughs, these ingrained processes impose significant hurdles. Large operators that oversee several systems and deal with the high expenses of engaging with competing platforms further complicate and raise the cost for traders trying to reach worldwide marketplaces.

The difficulty of these interactions arises from the necessity to combine several systems and guarantee flawless communication among several parties. Often out-of-date and scattered, the current infrastructure does not readily support new technology. The major expenditures needed to replace or revamp outdated systems, which big operators would be reluctant to do given the related risks and expenses, aggravate this aversion to change. As a result, the inertia of current networks greatly hinders the digital transformation of commerce.

Furthermore, certain middlemen, including freight forwarders, might find the inefficiencies in the present system advantageous. These middlemen gain from the complexity and delays that call for their services; therefore, they may be reluctant to embrace fresh, maybe revolutionary ideas that may simplify procedures and minimize their influence. This aversion to change among intermediaries inhibits the general advancement of digitization within the commerce ecosystem.

Notwithstanding these obstacles, many companies are realizing that careful data sharing may improve their competitiveness and create new prospects. Easy and safe data sharing across platforms may boost decision-making procedures, save costs, and promote efficiency. Worries about data abuse, lost intellectual property, and damaged competitive advantages can eclipse this potential. Businesses fear that divulging private data might put them in danger of intellectual property theft or unfair competition tactics.

These issues have validity. In a world going more and more digital, data security and integrity take front stage. Data sharing's advantages must be weighed against the necessity of safeguarding private data in organizations. To reduce the dangers connected with digitalization, this careful balance calls for strong data governance systems and the application of safeguarding security tools.

Moreover, the acceptance of new technology and digital approaches calls for a cultural change inside companies. Management has to create a climate that promotes innovation and ongoing development; employees have to be taught to welcome fresh tools and procedures. Particularly in sectors that have long depended on conventional approaches, this cultural change is sometimes delayed and greeted with opposition.

The difficulties of trade innovation and digitization are complex, combining cultural, financial, and technological obstacles. The sluggish rate of digital transformation is a result of ingrained legacy systems, certain intermediaries' resistance to welcome change, and worries over data security and competitive advantage. Nonetheless, the possible advantages of digitization are really great, as they provide better efficiency, lower prices, and more competitiveness. All the players in the trade ecosystem must work together to overcome these obstacles in order to support innovation, invest in new technologies, and build cooperation.

Bridging the Gaps: The Role of Interoperable Standards and Technological Solutions

In the logistics industry, the lack of compatible standards or alternative compatibility strategies prolongs fragmentation, complexity, and expensive expenses. Essential for world commerce and economic stability, this sector sometimes gets caught in a web of incompatible systems and different protocols. Although the use of new technology seeks to simplify procedures and improve efficiency, it can sometimes unintentionally raise running costs. Even the most technologically advanced companies might become overwhelmed by the need to oversee several data protocols, formats, and standards.

Globally, the logistics sector has many players, including shippers, carriers, goods forwarders, customs officers, and legal authorities. Every one of these participants usually uses different systems and data structures catered to their particular requirements and legal surroundings. Data must be translated, re-entered, and checked several times across the supply chain; a lack of uniformity results in major inefficiencies. The outcome is a fragmented industry in which flawless information flow is more of an exception than the norm.

Although their entrance into this ecosystem is meant to solve these inefficiencies, new technologies might aggravate the issue. Every technology development might have unique data protocols and needs, which adds to the already challenging terrain. After

CHAPTER 11 SHAPING TOMORROW'S MARKETS: THE FUTURE OF TRADE FINANCE THROUGH INNOVATIONS

then, companies have to commit significant funds to match these new systems with their current setup, which usually leads to more complexity and running expenses. Early promises of improved efficiency and simplified processes can quickly transform into a maze of compatibility issues and integration challenges.

Interoperable standards provide a way out of this mess. Establishing shared data formats and communication protocols helps these standards let several systems coexist together. Adoption of such criteria would help to greatly lower the requirement for data translation and re-entry, therefore enabling a more effective and simplified information flow. Realizing the full possibilities of technical developments in the logistics business depends on this interoperability.

This shift can be facilitated by technological solutions that give interoperability top priority. Blockchain-based solutions, for example, can offer a consolidated ledger wherein any participant may enter and access data in a consistent manner. This not only improves openness and confidence but also lessens the necessity of several data entry and reconciliations. Likewise, assuming the data produced by these sensors follows common standards, the Internet of things (IoT) can enable real-time tracking and monitoring of products across the supply chain.

The advantages of interoperable standards go beyond just operational effectiveness. They can also improve the sector's adaptability and fortitude. In a world where supply chain interruptions are very frequent, it is imperative to be able to quickly and effortlessly include new systems and technology. Interoperable standards guarantee that companies may embrace creative ideas free from constraints related to compatibility, therefore enabling more flexible and responsive operations.

Moreover, regulatory authorities could be crucial in encouraging the use of interoperable standards. Common data formats and communication protocols mandated by authorities help to encourage industry-wide standardization and interoperability. Knowing that interoperable technologies would be compatible with industry-wide practices and norms, this regulatory backing can provide businesses with the required drive to invest in them.

Considering all factors, the logistics industry will greatly benefit from the adoption of interoperable standards and compatible technology solutions. Although modern technologies promise simplified processes and improved efficiency, their actual value only becomes apparent via interoperability. The sector may overcome present fragmentation and complexity by giving the development and acceptance of common standards first priority, thereby creating a more robust, cost-effective logistics environment. The road toward a more connected and effective worldwide supply chain becomes clearer as stakeholders all around realize and welcome this necessity for interoperability.

CHAPTER 11   SHAPING TOMORROW'S MARKETS: THE FUTURE OF TRADE FINANCE THROUGH INNOVATIONS

Mixed-Success Initiatives and the Path Forward in the Logistics Industry: Overcoming Barriers to Digital Transformation

The logistics sector has long struggled to increase information flow and efficiency. Digitalizing bills of lading is one of the projects that clearly shows enormous promise for major savings and the opening of more world commerce prospects. These initiatives have, however, frequently had mixed results and struggled to be adopted generally across the sector. The cautious approach many logistics companies adopt toward technology investments—with just a tiny proportion of their income being committed to research and technology development—is a main cause of this resistance.

The commerce and logistics sectors must act in many key areas if they are to overcome these challenges and completely maximize the advantages of technology. Global data exchange and communication standards development and adoption help to minimize costs, ease complexity, and promote interoperability. Ensuring that several systems can interact effortlessly depends on this standardization. Furthermore, it also helps to simplify processes and improve productivity.

Furthermore, essential is cooperation among the many logistical stakeholders. To promote the acceptance of technology solutions, shipping firms, goods forwarders, authorities, and technology suppliers must coordinate more closely. Such group projects can serve to match interests, distribute best practices, and produce a more coherent approach to innovation. Working together, stakeholders may tackle shared problems and create solutions beneficial for the whole sector.

Establishing rewards for the acceptance of innovative technology might also inspire more companies to make creative investments. Companies might find it more financially appealing to adopt new technology depending on tax advantages, subsidies, or preferential treatment in regulatory compliance. These incentives enable companies to go forward and implement creative ideas by helping to cover the first expenses connected with technological investments.

Another vital action is making investments in training and education for business leaders. Companies may help overcome opposition to change by offering thorough training on the advantages and application of new technology. Teaching staff members and stakeholders how technology could streamline their operations and results will help to create a more innovative mentality.

Increasing faith in digital solutions also depends on addressing issues of data security and private information. Strong cybersecurity policies and well-defined data governance rules help safeguard private data and guarantee responsible handling of it. Businesses that show a dedication to data security help reduce worries and foster confidence in new technology.

Emphasizing effective pilot initiatives and distributing success stories may be quite motivating for more general acceptance. Real-world case studies of how technical innovation has produced observable advantages might motivate other companies to do likewise. From cost reductions to better efficiency and openness, these success tales may show the useful benefits of new technology.

Promising to make worldwide commerce more efficient, transparent, and accessible, the logistics and trade finance sectors are about to undergo a technology revolution. Stakeholders may release the enormous potential of technology to simplify the complex operations of commerce and shipping by tackling the difficulties of interoperability, investment in innovation, data security, and a cooperative ecosystem. Though the benefits are well worth the effort, embracing these changes calls for a coordinated effort from all those engaged. By means of cooperation, standardization, and a readiness to innovate, the logistics sector may advance toward a more linked and effective future.

Fostering Trade Technology Innovation: Role of Legal Frameworks and Public–Private Partnerships

Establishing a consistent and predictable legal framework is essential if investors are to boldly invest in testing and growing technologies inside the trading industry. The foundation required to build investor trust is a legislative framework including well-defined rules on digital trade practices, intellectual property rights, and data security. Investors are more ready to devote the required funds to creative trading technologies when they can predict how their investments will be managed and safeguarded.

Establishing thorough rules that handle the particular features of digital trading is essential in building such an ecosystem. These rules should precisely state the expectations and obligations of all the engaged parties, therefore guaranteeing a transparent and safe way of doing digital transactions. Likewise vital are well-defined rules on intellectual property rights. Investors want guarantees that their private data and technical advances will be kept under control against illegal access and usage.

CHAPTER 11   SHAPING TOMORROW'S MARKETS: THE FUTURE OF TRADE FINANCE THROUGH INNOVATIONS

Strong intellectual property rights enable creators to profit from their works, therefore stimulating investment in new technology. Another crucial issue needing strong laws is data protection. In a time when data is a valuable tool, security of it becomes first priority.

Strong data security policies serve to generate confidence among investors, who must know that private information will be treated carefully and maintained safe from cyber dangers. De-risking investments in the trade technology industry depends critically on public–private collaborations. These alliances might offer the first assurances or money required to inspire private sector development. Public sector cooperation with private investors might provide financial incentives meant to reduce the risks connected to creating and growing breakthrough technologies. Governments can, for instance, provide businesses engaged in trade technology with subsidies or tax advantages. They can also offer loan guarantees or generate venture capital, especially meant to support trade-related innovation.

Such public–private projects show a strong will to progress trade technologies, which draws additional private money. They also foster a cooperative atmosphere whereby the resources and regulatory knowledge of the public sector enhance the inventiveness and agility of the private sector. Developing and using innovative technology capable of transforming trade procedures depends on this synergy. Moreover, these alliances can enable the exchange of information and best practices, accelerating the adoption of fresh technology. Working collaboratively, the public and private sectors may spot and solve possible operational and regulatory obstacles early in the process, therefore guaranteeing a better route to market for creative trade ideas. A strong support network for startups and small enterprises is another major advantage of a consistent legislative environment and public–private collaborations.

Because of their low resources and increased perceived risks, these organizations can find more difficulty attracting investments. Public–private partnerships and well-defined rules help them, however, to more readily draw the money required to develop and deploy their innovations. Promoting a varied and vibrant ecosystem of trade technology innovation depends on this inclusiveness. Essentially, building circumstances for trade technology investment calls for a consistent and predictable legislative framework as well as encouragement of public–private cooperation. Investor trust depends on well-defined policies on digital trade practices, intellectual property rights, and data security. Public–private partnerships help to de-risk investments by means of required financial incentives and assistance, thereby promoting the growth and expansion of creative trade innovations. By focusing on these important areas, we can build a vibrant climate that draws investment and propels trade sector technology innovation.

CHAPTER 11   SHAPING TOMORROW'S MARKETS: THE FUTURE OF TRADE FINANCE THROUGH INNOVATIONS

Bridging Innovation: Fostering Collaboration Between Businesses and Entrepreneurs in the Trade Sector

The cooperation between businesses and entrepreneurs has become crucial in the fast-changing trade industry for promoting innovation and handling difficult problems. Platforms that encourage open innovation play a significant role in the formation of strong partnerships. Among the main tools bringing together the agility and inventiveness of entrepreneurs with the resources and market reach of established companies are incubators, accelerators, and collaborative development projects. Accelerators and incubators create a supportive atmosphere where business owners may hone their ideas, get mentoring, and find capital. These forums provide a link between companies looking for creative answers to urgent challenges. Participating in incubators and accelerators allows companies to access a fresh ideas and technology pipeline.

This symbiotic interaction speeds the creation of fresh ideas and their eventual inclusion into the larger trading ecology. Programs for joint development provide still another path for cooperation. These initiatives let businesses and entrepreneurs collaborate on particular projects, leveraging their unique capabilities to address common problems. By means of these programs, businesses profit from the creative ideas and flexible techniques that startups bring to offer while entrepreneurs acquire access to useful resources and knowledge. Usually, this kind of teamwork produces scalable and more efficient solutions than any partner could find on its own. Improving cooperation between companies and entrepreneurs depends heavily on intellectual property (IP) frameworks. These systems must combine safeguarding unique ideas with encouraging their shared use. Entrepreneurs who know their intellectual property will be protected are more likely to work together and share their ideas.

Companies have to be certain at the same time that they can use these developments without violating intellectual property rights. Maintaining long-term alliances and creating an atmosphere of open innovation depend on strong IP systems that support trust and mutual gain. Another important element enabling cooperation is interoperability. Standardizing data formats and application programming interfaces (APIs) will greatly simplify integration between many systems and platforms. Standardized APIs offer flawless data interchange and communication, thereby enabling more effective cooperation across several technologies. By lowering the technological obstacles often impeding cooperation, this standardization helps entrepreneurs to combine their ideas with the current corporate infrastructure. Consistent, generally agreed data formats improve this interoperability even further. Standardized data formats help to ease information exchange and analysis when all participants utilize them. This consistency guarantees that data may be easily combined and used amongst several systems, therefore promoting a more cooperative and effective trading industry. Furthermore, encouraging honest innovation inside companies is really essential. Companies have to be ready to welcome outside ideas and technology as they realize that teamwork may produce major competitive benefits.

Encouragement of employees to interact with outside innovators, participate in group initiatives, and keep open to fresh ideas constitutes this cultural change. On the participator side, entrepreneurs have to be ready to match their ideas with the operational reality and strategic objectives of their business associates. Knowing the particular requirements and difficulties of businesses helps entrepreneurs to more precisely customize their solutions, therefore improving the possibility of productive teamwork. Ultimately, creating platforms that support open innovation, efficient intellectual property systems, and consistent APIs and data formats will help to enable cooperation between trade sector companies and entrepreneurs. These components provide a setting in which both sides may flourish by using their own strengths to inspire creativity and address common problems. The trade industry may hasten its change by adopting these cooperative strategies, therefore improving sustainability, efficiency, and competitiveness.

Shaping Trade Technology: The Regulator's Role in Balancing Innovation, Fairness, and Consumer Protection

Regulators, who also guarantee inclusive and competitive outcomes, play a significant role in shaping the landscape of trade technology. Flexible regulatory frameworks must be created when trade technology platforms change. These models have to be flexible enough for new technologies to let the market welcome newcomers and protect consumer interests.

As they create these flexible rules, authorities must consider the quick speed at which technology is developing. This entails not only knowing present technology but also being ready for future developments that can disrupt the trade industry. Establishing rules that are wide enough to cover unanticipated changes would help authorities provide a solid yet adaptable basis for technological advancement.

CHAPTER 11   SHAPING TOMORROW'S MARKETS: THE FUTURE OF TRADE FINANCE THROUGH INNOVATIONS

Such forethought guarantees that rules can support a broad spectrum of technical advancements and prevent their rapid obsolescence. Another important duty of authorities is to guarantee equitable market access for new competitors. This entails tearing down obstacles that can impede small and medium-sized businesses (SMEs) from facing more established, bigger companies in competition.

Regulators have to design a situation whereby monopolistic behaviors or too-heavy regulations do not discourage creativity. Encouragement of competition helps authorities foster a more vibrant and varied trade technology environment, therefore benefiting consumers and the economy overall. Maintaining consumer interests comes second. Regulators have to make sure that when new trade technologies develop, they do not jeopardize consumer rights or safety. This includes defining criteria for data security and privacy, guaranteeing transaction openness, and offering customers who run into issues redress tools. Giving consumer safety first priority will help authorities establish confidence in new technology, therefore promoting more use and involvement. One calculated way to strike a balance between innovation and control is by pushing the use of regulatory sandboxes. Under the control of authorities, regulatory sandboxes allow for real-world testing of creative ideas. Without the whole weight of regulatory compliance, this controlled environment offers developers a secure place to explore and hone their solutions.

Regulators can then see these developments in use, learning a tremendous deal about their possible hazards and ramifications. Regulatory sandboxes' built-in feedback loop helps authorities as well as developers. Guidance on how to match their ideas with regulatory requirements helps developers simplify the road to market readiness. Conversely, regulators may utilize the knowledge acquired from sandbox testing to improve and modify rules, therefore guaranteeing their relevance and effectiveness. This iterative approach promotes a cooperative interaction between authorities and inventors, thereby advancing in a way that is both safe and favorable for development. Apart from regulatory sandboxes, constant communication among authorities, business players, and consumer organizations is crucial.

Such communication guarantees that consumer concerns, technical capacity, and industrial demands all shape the rules. Frequent discussions and feedback sessions enable authorities to remain current with industry changes and new issues, therefore enabling their proactive response. In regulatory support's ultimate objective is to establish a balanced ecosystem whereby consumers are safeguarded, innovation is encouraged, and competitiveness is fair. Regulators can accomplish these goals by means of flexible regulatory frameworks, guaranteed equitable market access, consumer protection as a top priority, and the use of regulatory sandboxes. This strategy guarantees that the advantages of technological developments are generally shared, as well as creating a competitive and inclusive trade technology environment.

The direction of trade technology platforms toward competitive and inclusive results depends critically on the action of regulators. By means of adaptive control, fair market access, consumer protection, and creative instruments like regulatory sandboxes, authorities may help to foster the expansion of a dynamic and fair trade technology industry. This all-encompassing strategy will help the sector fully use technological innovation, therefore promoting economic development and serving society at large.

Collaborative Digital Infrastructure: Building a Unified Ecosystem for Global Trade

In terms of world trade, a flawless and effective ecosystem depends mostly on the evolution of digital infrastructure. Building this infrastructure together will help to solve shared problems significantly more successfully than scattered initiatives of separate companies. Sharing the expenses of creation and maintenance helps to greatly lower the financial load on individual participants, therefore enabling the viability and sustainability of large-scale initiatives.

When several stakeholders collaborate to build and preserve world digital infrastructure, they provide different points of view and experience. This common knowledge guarantees that the infrastructure satisfies the many demands of the worldwide commerce community. Built on the achievements of several industries and areas, a single vision produces a more inclusive and functioning digital framework.

This kind of strategy encourages fairness and accessibility as the infrastructure is built considering the requirements of every participant, including multinational companies and small firms in underdeveloped nations. In this sense, cooperation also helps to open the path for the development of worldwide interoperability and data security norms. The flawless flow of information across several systems and platforms depends on interoperability. Without clear standards, conflicting systems cause inefficiencies and rising prices, hence fragmenting the global commerce ecology. Working collaboratively, stakeholders may create and implement these criteria so that every participant may interact effectively and without disturbance. Another vital issue that gains from teamwork is data security. Protection of private information is absolutely critical in a linked world. Through the pooling of resources and knowledge made possible by cooperative development, strong security mechanisms safeguarding data integrity and privacy are created.

This group effort can result in thorough security systems that are more resistant to cyberattacks, thereby offering peace of mind to every player in the worldwide trading environment. A team approach has advantages beyond only financial and technical ones. It encourages among stakeholders a culture of collaboration and trust. Working together toward a shared objective, entities create partnerships based on mutual respect and common interests. The long-term survival of the worldwide digital infrastructure depends on this confidence, as it motivates ongoing innovation and cooperation. Moreover, cooperative development can hasten the rate of invention. Stakeholders may test new technologies and techniques by combining resources and knowledge, thereby reducing the time it takes to bring ideas to market. This shared innovation helps the global commerce ecosystem to adapt to shifting needs and problems more quickly, hence accelerating its general progress.

The success of this kind of cooperative project depends on excellent coordination and governance. Clearly defined duties and responsibilities, together with open decision-making procedures, will help to guarantee that every interested party has a voice. Regular communication and feedback systems should quickly address any issues, maintaining alignment with the stated objective. Finally, the cooperative construction of worldwide digital infrastructure offers a convincing answer to the problems experienced by the commercial community internationally. Stakeholders may build a more inclusive, safe, and effective digital framework by distributing expenses, knowledge, and tools. This strategy not only solves financial and technical difficulties but also promotes creativity and trust in a culture. The cooperative development of digital infrastructure will be vital in guaranteeing a flawless and robust ecosystem that benefits all users as global trade keeps changing.

Unlocking Value Through Data Collaboration: Transforming Global Trade with Commercial Data Markets

For every player in the worldwide commerce ecosystem, data collaboration has the power to release immense value. Creation and success of projects like commercial data markets become possible by building strong frameworks ensuring data ownership

CHAPTER 11   SHAPING TOMORROW'S MARKETS: THE FUTURE OF TRADE FINANCE THROUGH INNOVATIONS

and rewarding contributors. Designed to enable the effective flow of vital trade data, these markets can influence more informed decision making and improve operational efficiency all throughout the industry. The commerce ecosystem is sometimes impeded in the present scene by scattered and siloed data. This fragmentation not only reduces visibility and transparency but also prevents stakeholders' capacity to act quickly and with knowledge. One transformative answer to this problem is data cooperation.

Participants may see the whole supply chain—from manufacture to delivery—by aggregating data from several sources. This all-encompassing viewpoint is quite helpful for spotting inefficiencies, trend foretelling, and quick reactions to disturbances. Concerns about data ownership and the equitable distribution of wealth from shared data have been among the main obstacles to efficient data cooperation. Overcoming these obstacles depends on well-defined systems safeguarding data ownership and honoring contributions. Stakeholders are more likely to participate in data cooperation projects if they are confident that their data will be secure and that they will receive fair compensation for sharing it. A healthy data-sharing ecosystem starts with this confidence.

Commercial data markets have demonstrated the enormous potential of data cooperation. These systems serve as middlemen for effective commerce data sharing, including shipping details. Commercial data markets help to flow information across several players, including manufacturers, logistics providers, and retailers, by offering a disciplined setting for data exchange. Several clear advantages can follow from this simplified data interchange. First of all, effective forecasting and inventory control made possible by thorough shipping data enable real-time data that allows companies to change their inventory levels and manufacturing plans, therefore lowering their risk of overproduction or stockouts. Improved customer satisfaction and cost savings follow from this resource efficiency. Moreover, data sharing improves operational effectiveness by means of improved supply chain partner coordination. Real-time data exchanged by all stakeholders helps them to more precisely coordinate their actions, thereby lowering delays and congestion.

Based on revised shipping data, for instance, logistics companies may maximize their routes and timetables, delivering faster and more dependable goods. Data cooperation has advantages outside of only operational enhancement. By providing a rich dataset for the creation of sophisticated analytical tools and technologies, it also stimulates creativity. For example, machine learning techniques may be taught on shared data to find trends and more precisely forecast future directions. These realizations can guide strategic decisions, including product development or market growth, therefore giving companies a competitive edge.

Data cooperation also helps improve responsibility and openness in the commerce system. By means of a verified record of transactions and activities, shared data helps lower fraud risk and facilitate more efficient legislative compliance. This openness enhances the integrity of the whole supply chain and helps stakeholders develop confidence. Ultimately, using data collaboration in the trade ecosystem has enormous power to unlock value and propel effectiveness. Initiatives like commercial data markets can flourish if structures guarantee data ownership and compensate contributors. These markets effectively share important trade data, therefore guiding better informed decision making and improving operational effectiveness. Data cooperation helps stakeholders transform the worldwide commerce ecosystem into a more open, effective, and creative one that benefits all the parties involved.

Harnessing Digital Assets and Environmental Data for a Transformative Financial Future

As the global financial landscape evolves, two revolutionary forces are emerging to shape the future: **digital assets** and **real-world data**, particularly **environmental metrics**. These innovations are not just tools but transformative instruments capable of redefining financial systems, expanding inclusion, and fostering sustainable economic growth. By addressing long-standing challenges such as financial exclusion, inefficiencies, and environmental risks, they are driving a paradigm shift in how financial institutions operate and influence the world around them. This chapter delves into how digital assets and environmental data are converging to build a financial ecosystem that is inclusive, resilient, and aligned with sustainability goals. Together, they hold the promise of democratizing economic opportunities while fostering a balance between economic success and environmental stewardship.

Digital Assets: Bridging Gaps and Redefining Financial Inclusion

Digital assets—ranging from cryptocurrencies to tokenized goods and blockchain platforms—are transforming financial services by addressing traditional barriers to access. These assets provide new pathways for participation in economic activities, especially in underserved regions where conventional banking systems are either unavailable or insufficient.

1. **Breaking Down Barriers:**
   - Traditional financial systems often exclude remote or underdeveloped areas due to logistical and infrastructural challenges. Digital assets, operating through decentralized financial systems, overcome these hurdles by eliminating reliance on centralized institutions.
   - This shift ensures that previously excluded individuals and communities can access loans, investments, and payment systems, fostering broader participation in the global economy.

2. **Building a Distributed Financial System:**
   - Blockchain-based platforms underpin digital assets, creating systems that are independent of conventional banking networks. This independence enhances financial resilience while providing greater flexibility and accessibility.
   - Such systems enable real-time transactions, reduce costs, and offer transparency, making financial services more inclusive.

3. **A Pathway to Economic Democratization:**
   - By bypassing geographical and institutional limitations, digital assets empower a wider spectrum of individuals to engage in economic activities. This democratization of finance promotes equity, allowing more people to benefit from opportunities that were once reserved for a privileged few.

Environmental Data: Redefining Financial Strategy

As the world grapples with climate change and sustainability challenges, environmental data has emerged as a powerful resource for financial institutions. By incorporating real-world metrics—such as ecological indicators, sustainability practices, and climate risks—into decision making, banks and other financial entities can align their strategies with global sustainability objectives.

1. **A Shift in Perspective:**
    - The inclusion of environmental data represents a fundamental change in how financial risks and opportunities are assessed. This data provides deeper insights into the interplay between economic activities and environmental impacts, enabling institutions to adopt a more comprehensive approach.

2. **Enabling Responsible Decision Making:**
    - With access to environmental metrics, financial institutions can make informed decisions that balance profitability with ecological responsibility. For instance, they can better evaluate the long-term risks associated with climate change or resource depletion when structuring loans or investments.

3. **Innovative Financial Products:**
    - Environmental data facilitates the creation of products tailored to sustainability-focused clients. These include green bonds, climate-related insurance, and sustainable investment portfolios, which cater to the rising demand for environmentally friendly financial solutions.

4. **Encouraging Ethical Finance:**
    - By integrating environmental considerations into their strategies, financial institutions can promote ethical investing and sustainable business practices, fostering a culture of accountability and responsibility.

The Intersection: Digital Assets and Environmental Data

The intersection of these innovations holds their true potential. Together, digital assets and environmental data are reshaping the financial ecosystem into one that is not only inclusive but also sustainable and forward-looking.

1. **Creating a Sustainable Financial Ecosystem:**
    - Digital assets enable broader participation, while environmental data ensures that this inclusion aligns with global sustainability goals. This synergy allows financial institutions to address pressing issues such as climate change and financial exclusion simultaneously.

2. **Customized Solutions for Modern Needs:**
    - By leveraging both digital tools and real-world metrics, financial institutions can offer tailored services that reflect the environmental values and financial goals of their clients. This personalization fosters stronger relationships while meeting the growing demand for sustainable financial products.

3. **Balancing Environmental and Economic Goals:**
    - The integration of digital assets and environmental data strikes a balance between economic growth and environmental preservation. It enables institutions to innovate responsibly, ensuring that financial success does not come at the cost of ecological harm.

Redefining Finance: The Role of Digital Assets and Environmental Data in Driving Sustainability

The strategic integration of digital assets and environmental data repositions financial institutions as key players in the transition toward a more equitable and sustainable economy. Their role extends beyond traditional financial intermediation, encompassing societal and environmental stewardship.

1. **Enhanced Risk Management:**
    - Real-world data improves the accuracy of risk assessments, enabling institutions to anticipate and mitigate challenges related to both financial and environmental factors.

2. **Meeting Consumer Expectations:**
   - Clients increasingly expect financial services to reflect their values, particularly regarding sustainability. By integrating environmental metrics into their offerings, institutions can build loyalty and trust.

3. **Driving Global Change:**
   - Financial institutions are empowered to influence industries and communities through their investments and policies. By adopting digital assets and environmental data, they can promote practices that align with a more sustainable and inclusive future.

A Transformative Vision for the Future: How Digital Assets and Environmental Data Are Transforming Finance

The convergence of digital assets and environmental data marks a significant milestone in the evolution of financial services. These innovations pave the way for a financial ecosystem that is inclusive, resilient, and sustainable—one that addresses the pressing challenges of our time while preparing for the uncertainties of the future.

By embracing these developments, financial institutions can transcend traditional boundaries and lead the way toward a more equitable and environmentally conscious global economy. The result is not just a financial revolution but a societal one, where economic growth and environmental stewardship coexist, creating a brighter future for all.

Summary

Emphasizing the vital need of closing the trade finance gap and the integration of innovative technology to solve long-standing inefficiencies, the chapter explores the transforming path of trade finance. Through cooperation and strong regulatory framework utilizing information asymmetries, the chapter emphasizes how developments in regulation technology (RegTech) have progressed from simple digital solutions (RegTech 1.0) to today's intelligence-driven tools (RegTech 4.0). By means of tokenization and risk distribution technology, these developments simplify compliance, open liquidity, and

CHAPTER 11   SHAPING TOMORROW'S MARKETS: THE FUTURE OF TRADE FINANCE THROUGH INNOVATIONS

redefine trade finance as a desirable asset class. The development of digital securities and tokenized assets emphasizes even more the growing accessibility and efficiency of trade finance, therefore opening the path for more general investor involvement.

Driven by more information sharing, interoperable standards, and AI-powered solutions, the chapter also investigates the reimagining of logistics and commerce. Future logistics systems seem to be guided by the notion of a worldwide connected "Physical Internet." Presenting a transforming power, the interaction of digital assets and environmental data promotes financial inclusion and changes financial strategies for sustainability. By means of cooperative efforts, regulatory innovation, and technology integration, this chapter sees a future whereby trade finance not only promotes worldwide trade but also supports inclusiveness, efficiency, and environmental responsibility.

CHAPTER 12

Achieving Financing Resilience and Influence on Trade Finance Through DORA

Emphasizing its part in strengthening digital resilience and compliance, this chapter explores the transforming influence of the Digital Operational Resilience Act (DORA) on the banking and trade finance sectors. It starts with looking at DORA's fundamental goals, which seek to make sure financial institutions can endure, react to, and recover from a variety of operational interruptions in an ever-digitized financial environment. The chapter unpacks the essential requirements of DORA, focusing on its mandates for operational risk management, reporting standards, and incident management. The high stakes of non-compliance, including severe penalties and reputational damage, are highlighted, underscoring the need for financial institutions to adopt a proactive approach. The pivotal role of supervisory authorities in monitoring and enforcing compliance is also discussed, showcasing their efforts to uphold digital resilience across the EU. Important new perspectives on the interaction between DORA and other laws such as GDPR and the NIS2 Directive highlight the connectivity of regulatory systems in forming a strong cybersecurity environment.

Using information rights management (IRM) and following ISO 27001 requirements are two practical compliance techniques shown. The chapter also points up and fixes flaws in ISO 27001 as businesses match their operations with DORA's more exacting standards. Examined are the ramifications of DORA for Chief Information Officers (CIOs) and Chief Information Security Officers (CISOs), providing a compliance checklist and practical operational resilience navigation guidance. To satisfy DORA's needs, the chapter stresses the requirement of dynamic data management, improved cybersecurity systems, and a thorough awareness of information rights. At last, the chapter addresses how DORA compliance would affect the trade finance industry by guaranteeing continuity across digital disruptions, enhancing confidence, and so improving transparency. Financial institutions may use DORA as a driver for innovation and resilience by planning for the future, therefore altering operational procedures in a digital-first age.

Mastering DORA: Navigating the Digital Seas of Operational Resilience and Compliance

Targeting the digital operational resilience of the financial industry, the Digital Operational Resilience Act (DORA) is a significant legislative breakthrough inside the European Union. The requirement of strong security and operational resilience has grown even more important as technology keeps profoundly merging with financial services. By means of a thorough structure meant to enable financial firms to resist, react to, and recover from disruptions and dangers connected to information and communication technology (ICT), DORA meets this requirement. This control marks a major first toward protecting the financial industry against the complexity and weaknesses of the digital age.

Fundamentally, DORA aims to create a consistent set of guidelines for the EU so that all financial institutions may run without interruption even with the unavoidable digital disturbances. The law is motivated by the necessity to standardize the digital operational resilience standards for financial firms inside the EU, therefore producing a uniform strategy to control digital risks among member states. Setting these criteria helps DORA increase the capacity of financial institutions to prevent, resist, and recover from ICT-related events—important in the sector. The control also underlines the need for financial companies to be able to react fast to and recover from such disturbances, therefore reducing the possible influence on consumer protection and financial stability.

DORA's structure lists a few main standards financial institutions have to follow. Starting with the need for thorough ICT risk management, these criteria are meant to cover several aspects of digital operational resilience. Strong systems required of financial organizations should be able to identify, evaluate, and reduce risks connected to their digital activities. This is matched by the requirement to create systems for

CHAPTER 12   ACHIEVING FINANCING RESILIENCE AND INFLUENCE ON TRADE FINANCE THROUGH DORA

instantaneous incident reporting to national and European supervisory agencies. Ensuring a coordinated reaction to threats and reducing their impact depends on rapid and accurate reporting of events, so this is absolutely essential.

The need for consistent digital operational resilience testing is yet another crucial element of DORA. These tests are demanded of financial institutions to assess their resilience against ICT interruptions, including severe yet realistic scenarios. By means of this ongoing testing, institutions can find flaws in their systems and procedures, therefore enabling their adaptation and enhancement of their defenses. Moreover, DORA gives the control and oversight of outside ICT service providers top importance. Many financial institutions rely on outside vendors, especially for cloud services; hence, it is imperative that these third parties follow DORA's guidelines. This guarantees that not only the institutions themselves but also the whole digital ecosystem keep a high degree of operational resilience.

Apart from these steps, DORA encourages financial institutions to exchange data on vulnerabilities and cyberattacks. Through encouraging cooperation and communication, the control seeks to improve sector-wide resilience against the always-changing terrain of cyberattacks.

By 2025, DORA is expected to be completely implemented, providing financial institutions with a timeframe during which they have to match their activities with the terms of the rule. This interval gives organizations enough time to modify their operational systems, risk control strategies, and agreements of contract with outside service providers. The European Supervisory Authorities (ESAs), comprising the European Banking Authority (EBA), the European Insurance and Occupational Pensions Authority (EIOPA), and the European Securities and Markets Authority (ESMA), are assigned primary responsibility for monitoring DORA's execution and guaranteeing compliance. These authorities will be crucial in helping the financial industry through the change and guaranteeing that the new criteria are efficiently included in daily activities.

Furthermore, DORA enhances current laws like the General Data Protection Regulation (GDPR) by emphasizing especially the operational resilience of ICT systems while keeping rigorous data protection and privacy requirements. This alignment emphasizes the EU's whole strategy to control the digital elements of financial services, therefore guaranteeing that operational security and data integrity come first.

Financial institutions have to examine their present ICT risk management systems closely, find areas of weakness, and improve their policies as they get ready for DORA compliance. Along with this planning, resilience testing, evaluating and maybe renegotiating third-party service agreements, and active participation in information-sharing programs must be developed along with clear and effective incident reporting processes. Although the first changes to satisfy DORA's needs might provide difficulties, they also give financial institutions a chance to improve their operational resilience, reinforce their ICT systems, and get a competitive edge in the fast-changing digital terrain.

DORA will have a significant influence on the financial industry as it will set strict criteria for digital operational resilience, therefore determining the direction of financial services in the EU. Financial institutions not only guarantee their own resilience but also help to protect the general stability and security of the financial system by acting early to follow DORA. Mastery of DORA will be crucial for negotiating the challenging seas of operational resilience and compliance as the digital age unfolds, therefore benefiting the sector and its customers.

Unlocking DORA: Navigating the Digital Frontier of Financial Resilience

The European Commission's innovative legislative initiative to improve the operational resilience of the financial industry inside the European Union—the Digital Operational Resilience Act (DORA)—represents the hazards connected with IT systems and cybersecurity have grown as digital technologies are more firmly ingrained in the financial sector, therefore endangering consumer protection and financial stability. By building a thorough framework meant to strengthen the sector's capacity to tolerate, react to, and quickly recover from operational interruptions, DORA squarely confronts these difficulties.

DORA is fundamentally based on a concentration on thorough IT and cybersecurity risk management. Emphasizing the ongoing detection and evaluation of both internal and external risks that might affect their digital operations, financial institutions are now obliged to follow policies outside the conventional range of risk management. In a climate where the pace and sophistication of cyberattacks are always changing, this proactive strategy is very necessary. DORA orders the creation of strong rules and practices meant to protect data and systems against these hazards. All of this is meant to help to lessen the possible influence of cybersecurity events: encryption technology, strict access restrictions, and thorough vulnerability management techniques.

CHAPTER 12   ACHIEVING FINANCING RESILIENCE AND INFLUENCE ON TRADE FINANCE THROUGH DORA

Important elements of DORA's approach also are incident management and reporting. Financial institutions have to set systems that let them quickly identify, handle, and document small as well as significant IT and cybersecurity events. This need guarantees rapid and efficient resolution of any disturbances, therefore reducing their influence on operations and enabling early interaction with pertinent authorities. DORA wants to build a strong financial ecosystem where disturbances may be controlled without generating general instability by implementing these ideas.

DORA's foundation also rests in the focus on business continuity management. The control emphasizes the need for having adequate continuity plans to guarantee that financial services may run without interruption even during operational interruptions. Financial organizations are supposed to create thorough plans that specify how they will keep important services operational despite different kinds of disturbances. This covers the creation of disaster recovery plans routinely verified to guarantee they can quickly restore services and data after a disturbance, as well as the deployment of backup facilities guaranteeing service continuity. By concentrating on these areas, DORA hopes to build a financial industry that is not only strong enough to withstand operational shocks but also quick enough to recover, therefore shielding the larger economy from the knock-on impacts of such disturbances.

DORA's execution depends on supervising and controlling. The control provides a structured framework that empowers national and European regulatory bodies to monitor the adherence of financial institutions to its standards. These agencies have the capabilities required for on-site inspections, requests for comprehensive operational resilience practice data, and evaluation of the success of the implemented policies by institutions. Moreover, DORA gives these supervising authorities the power to enforce compliance, hence imposing penalties and remedial actions on establishments that fall short of the accepted norms. This control is essential to guarantee that financial institutions fulfill their responsibilities under DORA with extreme seriousness and that the objectives of the law are satisfied.

DORA marks a major change in how operational resilience is seen for financial institutions.

The control not only provides a standard for IT and cybersecurity policies but also incorporates these ones into the more general operational risk management systems financial institutions have to keep. These days, institutions have to do extensive risk analyses and change their structures to fit DORA criteria. This change calls for a thorough assessment and improvement of business continuity and disaster recovery

CHAPTER 12   ACHIEVING FINANCING RESILIENCE AND INFLUENCE ON TRADE FINANCE THROUGH DORA

strategies to guarantee that operations may be kept running and rapidly rebuilt should disturbances arise. Moreover, financial institutions have to get ready for more inspections and compliance checks as supervisory agencies will be scrutinizing them more.

The adoption of DORA marks a significant milestone in the EU's efforts to ensure the operational resilience of its financial sector, particularly in light of the growing digitization and cyber risks. Following the guidelines set forth in DORA will help financial institutions not only guard against possible disruptions but also assist in the financial system remaining generally stable and honest. Financial institutions have to aggressively modify their operational resilience strategies to comply with the new regulation as DORA approaches full implementation, ensuring that they are ready to meet the challenges it presents and to grab the chances it presents for improving digital operational resilience in an ever-linked world.

DORA Unleashed: Countdown to a New Era of Digital Resilience in Finance

The Digital Operational Resilience Act (DORA) is poised to fundamentally change financial institution operational systems all throughout the European Union. DORA promises to usher in a new age of digital resilience as the formal implementation date of January 17, 2025, approaches, therefore establishing a complete set of standards meant to strengthen the financial sector's capacity to resist and recover from digital disruptions and cyberattacks. This approaching shift emphasizes the need for financial institutions to grasp the consequences of DORA and start to get ready for their demanding compliance requirements.

Fundamentally, DORA aims to unite and standardize digital operational resilience strategies among a wide range of EU financial institutions—including banks, insurance companies, investment firms, and other financial services providers. Improving IT risk management, guaranteeing business continuity, and building cyber resilience are top priorities for the legislation. Setting these criteria helps DORA safeguard the financial industry from the growing risks presented by digital disturbances, therefore compromising customer confidence and financial stability.

Given the fast approaching implementation date, financial institutions have to be proactive in order to match their operations to DORA's criteria. Doing a careful gap study comes first in this procedure. This study lets institutions evaluate their present digital resilience capacity against DORA's recommended criteria. It entails a thorough evaluation of the IT infrastructure, current cybersecurity policies, incident reporting systems, and business continuity plan strength. Financial institutions can provide a clear road map for reaching compliance by pointing out areas where their present methods fall short of DORA's requirements.

Institutions will have to revamp their policies and practices holistically in line with the gap analysis. To satisfy DORA's strict criteria, this might mean changing current cybersecurity rules, improving data security practices, and formalizing incident response plans. The control requires financial institutions to include resilience into their operational processes and organizational culture, therefore transcending simple technical compliance.

Financial institutions may also have to make investments in focused personnel training and modern technological solutions if they are to satisfy these high criteria. This investment is absolutely essential for giving staff members the tools they need to properly control digital hazards and react quickly to events. To be ready for DORA's expectations, upgrading IT infrastructure, using innovative cybersecurity solutions, and offering specialist training are all very vital.

DORA presents even another difficulty as the rule emphasizes the hazards related to outside IT service providers, particularly cloud services. Financial institutions will have to interact closely with these vendors, evaluating and maybe renegotiating agreements to guarantee that their offerings completely meet DORA's criteria. This feature of the control emphasizes the link among current financial services and the need for a strong supply chain to preserve operational stability.

Regular testing and auditing of digital resilience measures will be very vital as financial institutions migrate toward the January 17, 2025, deadline. Penetration testing and scenario-based corporate continuity exercises help institutions make sure their systems can withstand any interruptions. Additionally required are ongoing audits to confirm that every facet of DORA compliance is being kept and that any found flaws are quickly fixed.

The time before DORA is adopted provides a vital window for financial institutions to not only satisfy legal criteria but also embrace a culture of ongoing development in digital operational resilience. Compliance with DORA should be considered not just as a legislative responsibility but also as a chance to strengthen defenses against digital disruptions, thereby improving the institution's competitiveness and dependability in a world going more and more technologically driven.

CHAPTER 12   ACHIEVING FINANCING RESILIENCE AND INFLUENCE ON TRADE FINANCE THROUGH DORA

The impending launch of DORA represents a significant milestone for the EU's financial sector, underscoring the importance of digital operational resilience. Financial institutions may set themselves up to negotiate this new regulatory terrain effectively by knowing DORA's needs and acting early to comply. The road toward January 17th, 2025, is about embracing the future of financial services with resilience, agility, and confidence, so guaranteeing that they are ready for the challenges and possibilities of the digital era, not only about attaining compliance.

Bracing for Impact: Who Stands in the Path of the Upcoming DORA Regulation?

The Digital Operational Resilience Act (DORA) is likely to fundamentally change the operational scene of the banking industry of the European Union. DORA provides a complete regulatory framework meant to improve the resilience of financial organizations against such obstacles as the financial sector gets more digitalized and faces increased cyber threats. Beyond conventional banking, the broad influence of the legislation is expected to affect many important participants forming the backbone of the financial market's infrastructure, therefore impacting a variety of financial organizations.

DORA's scope is astonishingly wide, touching almost every financial sector. Among those squarely in DORA's path are credit institutions like banks and lending organizations. These organizations will have to improve their digital operational resilience to make sure their IT systems can resist and bounce back from cyberattacks and other kinds of digital disturbances. The same is true of payment and electronic money institutions, which are essential for enabling electronic transactions. These organizations have to not only strengthen their cybersecurity policies but also make sure their operations can go without stop, thereby maintaining customer confidence and the integrity of financial transactions.

Under DORA also fall investment businesses and trading platforms, which are vital for the financial markets. Maintaining market stability and safeguarding investors from possible disturbances depend on these companies making sure their digital operations are robust. By including crypto-asset service providers under DORA, DORA acknowledges the increasing awareness of cryptocurrencies and associated services as fundamental elements of the financial system. These providers will be obliged to follow the same exacting criteria of operational resilience as more conventional financial institutions, therefore transforming the control of the digital financial ecosystem.

Furthermore, companies that are vital to the securities markets—such as central counterparties and central securities depositories—must make sure they have strong systems in place to stop and fix operational interruptions. Under DORA, the insurance and reinsurance markets—including middlemen—will also undergo notable changes. These organizations have to improve their digital resilience so that, in the event of digital hazards, important activities such as risk assessment, policy development, and claim processing may go on without disturbance.

Affected equally are fund managers, in charge of overseeing other investment portfolios and alternative investment funds. By guaranteeing the resilience of their digital operations, they will be safeguarding the assets under their control, therefore preserving their clients' investments and keeping continuity of service. DORA also covers trading venues, trade repositories, and data reporting service providers, among other financial market systems. These organizations are essential to guaranteeing the stability, openness, and efficiency of financial markets; so, they have to follow DORA's guidelines to preserve the general state of the financial environment.

For these organizations, DORA has significant ramifications. Financial institutions have to thoroughly examine their present cybersecurity policies to comply with the rule and make sure they match DORA's exacting criteria. This includes putting in place strong incident response systems, improving threat detection tools, and using sophisticated risk assessment techniques. Moreover, the creation and evaluation of business continuity strategies will be very vital. Financial institutions have to be ready to keep vital activities running during and following any cyberattacks or other interruptions, therefore guaranteeing little impact on their services and the wider financial system.

Another very vital component of DORA compliance is controlling outside hazards. Financial institutions have to make sure third-party service providers—like cloud computing and IT services—which they depend on more and more comply with DORA's criteria as well. This interdependence emphasizes the requirement of a consistent strategy for digital resilience throughout the whole financial industry, as weaknesses in one area of the system can have broad effects.

Beyond the technological standards, DORA also advocates a culture change inside financial organizations. The development of a corporate culture emphasizing digital resilience is absolutely essential. Along with teaching staff members cybersecurity best practices, this entails encouraging a mentality that sees resilience as an ongoing effort rather than a one-time accomplishment. Financial institutions may better equip themselves for the difficulties presented by a society going more and more digital by including resilience into the fabric of their activities.

CHAPTER 12   ACHIEVING FINANCING RESILIENCE AND INFLUENCE ON TRADE FINANCE THROUGH DORA

DORA marks a significant milestone for the financial industry in the EU, setting a new standard for digital operational resilience. The wide scope of the regulation guarantees that all important stakeholders in the financial system are kept to a high degree of resilience, therefore reflecting the linked character of contemporary finance. Financial institutions have to move early to examine their operations, find any flaws in their digital resilience plans, and apply the required actions to follow the law as the DORA implementation date draws near. In the face of changing digital dangers, this preparation is essential not only for reaching regulatory compliance but also for enhancing the general integrity and stability of the financial market infrastructure of the EU.

Decoding DORA: Unlocking the Core Objectives of the Digital Resilience Revolution

A key legislative project meant to strengthen the operational framework of the European Union's financial industry and guarantee its resilience against digital disturbances is the Digital Operational Resilience Act (DORA). DORA lists four main goals that are absolutely necessary to reach this aim, each of which is crucial in preserving the integrity and stability of the financial system of the EU.

Improving the operational resilience of the EU's financial industry comes first for DORA. The dangers connected with cyberattacks, IT breakdowns, and other operational interruptions have become much more pronounced in a time when financial services are progressively depending on digital technology. DORA helps financial institutions to manage these risks by arming them with the tools, systems, and procedures required to resist and react properly to such disruptions. DORA's emphasis is on making sure financial services can run without interruption, regardless of the cause—malicious cyber activity, natural calamities, or technical difficulties. Maintaining daily financial sector operations as well as consumer trust and safeguarding the larger financial stability of the EU depend on this focus on operational resilience.

Apart from strengthening operational resilience, DORA gives significant focus on enhancing financial sector customer data security. Protecting private consumer data is more crucial in the digital terrain of today, when cyberattacks are always present. DORA requires that financial institutions put strong cybersecurity policies meant to guard financial and personal data from leaks and illegal access into action. DORA wants to build customer confidence in the banking system by giving data security first priority. This goal strongly corresponds with the larger framework of EU data protection rules, notably the General Data Protection Regulation (GDPR), thereby supporting the EU's dedication to defend personal privacy rights in the digital age. Apart from guaranteeing the security of private data, the emphasis on customer data protection helps create a more dependable and trustworthy financial environment for customers all throughout the EU.

By enforcing uniform criteria and standards for operational resilience within the financial sector, DORA also strives to ensure equitable competition throughout the EU. DORA guarantees that financial institutions functioning in several EU members are subject to uniform rules and expectations by unifying these regulatory requirements. This homogeneity encourages consistency and fairness inside the financial system, therefore facilitating institutions' compliance with rules anywhere. Furthermore, a fair playing field guarantees that competition in the financial industry is focused on innovation and the quality of services rather than on differences in regulatory requirements, therefore facilitating regulatory control and enforcement and so lowering chances for regulatory arbitrage. A more connected and smooth financial market throughout the EU, where all companies are held to the same high standards of operational resilience, depends on this harmonizing of all the actors.

At last, DORA underlines the responsibility of regulatory bodies in managing and implementing operational resilience in the financial industry. The control increases the authority of these authorities, thereby allowing them to more successfully monitor, assess, and handle vulnerabilities and hazards inside financial institutions. This involves doing inspections, getting comprehensive data, and, where needed, applying penalties or remedial action to cover any flaws or shortcomings. DORA guarantees that financial institutions are held responsible for their compliance with regulatory criteria and are driven to take proactive steps to improve their operational resilience by improving the supervision framework. Maintaining the integrity of the financial system and making sure every institution is sufficiently ready to manage possible disruptions depend on this more thorough supervision.

These goals taken together offer a complete and forward-looking strategy for strengthening the operational resilience of the financial sector of the EU. DORA wants to protect the stability, integrity, and trustworthiness of the EU's financial system in a world going more digital and linked by giving operational resilience top priority, improving customer data protection, supporting regulatory harmonization, and strengthening supervisory oversight top importance. Working to satisfy criteria and negotiate DORA's consequences, financial institutions are not only improving their own resilience capacity but also helping the financial ecosystem of the EU to be generally strong and stable.

Decoding DORA: Unveiling the Essential Requirements for Financial Resilience

Introduced by the Digital Operational Resilience Act (DORA), the strong framework is meant to strengthen the operational resilience of financial institutions all throughout the European Union. DORA guarantees that financial institutions are ready to resist, react to, and recover from different operational interruptions by laying down a set of basic needs. Gaining the whole breadth and relevance of DORA's influence on the financial industry depends on an awareness of each of these prerequisites.

Under DORA, one of the main criteria is that financial institutions plan and test their key business services, processes, and IT systems holistically. This procedure entails a comprehensive identification and evaluation of operational hazards, therefore enabling institutions to find weaknesses and dependencies inside their operational system. Through thorough testing, organizations learn important lessons about possible flaws that will help them to apply focused mitigating techniques that increase their general resilience. Ensuring that financial institutions may remain stable and continuous even in the face of major disruptions depends on this proactive attitude toward risk management.

DORA's emphasis on the handling of outsourcing risks is yet another important feature. DORA requires the development of strong policies to properly manage these risks as financial institutions depend more and more on outside service providers for important operations. This covers developing explicit commercial agreements defining roles and expectations as well as doing extensive due diligence on outside vendors to guarantee they satisfy the needed criteria. Furthermore, crucial are efficient monitoring systems to guarantee that these outside suppliers stay compliant with legal criteria. DORA guarantees that financial institutions keep control over their operations by tackling outsourcing risks, therefore preserving the integrity and robustness of their services even in cases of depending on outside partners.

Still another pillar of DORA's regulatory system is incident reporting. Any events that seriously affect the continuity of financial institutions' operations or jeopardize the stability of the financial system have to be promptly reported by them. This need guarantees that any hazards are promptly reported to regulatory authorities, therefore enabling them to evaluate the degree of disturbance and implement suitable corrective action. Open and thorough incident reporting not only promotes responsibility inside financial institutions but also enables a coordinated reaction to operational interruptions, therefore reducing any systemic risks that can influence the whole financial market.

DORA's main concentration is cybersecurity, which reflects the growing digital age danger presented by cyberattacks. To guard their systems and data against leaks and illegal access, financial institutions must have suitable and strong cybersecurity policies. This covers putting in place cutting-edge network security, access restrictions, encryption, threat detection, and incident response sophisticated techniques for Financial organizations may greatly lower the danger of cyberattacks by strengthening their cybersecurity systems, therefore preserving private information and keeping consumer trust.

Furthermore, fundamental to DORA's standards is a thorough risk management system. Financial institutions have to include this framework into their whole corporate plan so that operational risks are found, evaluated, and controlled in all spheres of their activities. This covers handling technological, procedural, people, and outside dependent hazards. Maintaining a strong risk management system helps financial institutions to actively spot possible hazards, put effective controls in place, and reduce risks, thereby guaranteeing their operational resilience over time.

Under DORA, governance and control are just as vital. For operational resilience, financial institutions have to define clear lines of duty and accountability; the board of directors is therefore crucial in supervising these initiatives. Making sure the organization has suitable policies, governance systems, and procedures in place to properly control operational risks falls to the board. Strong government and control systems guarantee conformity to legal criteria and help to encourage openness and responsibility, therefore strengthening resilience across the company.

Still another essential element of DORA is business continuity planning. Financial institutions have to create and keep thorough strategies to guarantee the continuation of their important business operations in case of a disturbance. These strategies have to show how to find and fix disruptions, rebuild services, and interact with stakeholders. Financial institutions may reduce the effect on their clients, keep market trust, and help the financial system to be generally stable by aggressively planning for any disturbances.

DORA stresses at last the need for consistent testing and training as fundamental elements of operational resilience. Financial institutions have to keep evaluating their resilience strategies to evaluate their success and point out areas needing work. Staff members also need to be sufficiently qualified to react to operational interruptions, therefore guaranteeing that the company is ready to meet changing risks and obstacles. Training and constant testing improve the institution's agility and preparedness, thereby allowing it to maintain operational stability and react quickly to evolving conditions.

The standards proposed by DORA offer a complete and forward-looking means of improving the operational resilience of EU financial institutions. DORA seeks to increase the stability, integrity, and trustworthiness of the EU's financial system by tackling key areas like mapping and testing, outsourcing, incident reporting, cybersecurity, risk management, governance, business continuity planning, and continuous testing and training. Financial institutions must comply with these criteria if they are to negotiate the changing digital terrain, reduce operational risks, protect financial stability, and build market trust in a world that is growingly linked.

Unveiling the DORA Effect: How Financial Institutions Will Weather the Regulatory Storm

The upcoming Digital Operational Resilience Act (DORA) is poised to fundamentally change the operational scene for European Union financial institutions. This control seems to be approaching and promises to bring a tsunami of changes that will force these institutions to rethink and adjust their activities to satisfy the new needs of digital resilience.

The major effect of DORA will be the notable rise in compliance expenses right away. To fit the strict criteria of the rule, financial institutions will be obliged to extensively spend in resources, technologies, and knowledge. Existing procedures will probably be overhauled, new systems implemented, and staff members extensively trained to guarantee they are familiar with the new compliance procedures. These developments might put pressure on institutional budgets, so intelligent resource allocation is necessary to satisfy DORA's needs while still enabling effective operation.

Apart from the financial load, DORA will cause institutions to be under more regulatory control. Enhanced powers would be given to supervising authorities to thoroughly monitor and assess financial entity operational resilience. This increased monitoring implies that financial institutions may expect more regular and thorough investigations; therefore, strong reporting systems and a proactive attitude to interact with regulatory authorities become even more important. The greater monitoring will probably force institutions to be more open and careful in recording their compliance initiatives, making sure that every element of their operations satisfies DORA's criteria.

The control will also force notable changes in corporate behavior all over the banking industry. Institutions will have to review and maybe change their present operating plans to fit DORA's requirements. This might entail reviewing outsourcing agreements to make sure outside service providers satisfy necessary risk management criteria and strengthen cybersecurity systems to protect against new hazards. Moreover, improving business continuity strategies would be very essential to strengthening operational resilience against any disturbances. These developments can call for a strategic realignment whereby institutions make operational modifications in several spheres of their operations to guarantee complete DORA compliance.

One of the main features of DORA is its focus on risk control. The control emphasizes the need for building strong risk management systems that affect every facet of the running of financial institutions. This means creating strict risk assessment systems, putting proactive risk-reducing techniques into use, and building continuous monitoring systems to find and fix possible weaknesses. The increased emphasis on risk management will not only enable institutions to comply with DORA but also be rather important in strengthening their resilience to operational interruptions, thereby guaranteeing they are better ready to manage crises when they develop.

In the end, even if DORA first poses difficulties for financial firms, the control is meant to greatly increase their operational resilience. Following DORA's guidelines can help organizations to be more resistant to and able to handle a variety of operational hazards, from different kinds of disturbances to cyberattacks and IT failures. Not only does this improved resilience help to preserve the stability of the institution, but it also helps to keep and strengthen consumer confidence and trust in the broader financial system. Institutions will find themselves more suited to negotiate the complexity of the changing digital terrain as they strengthen their systems, procedures, and controls.

Although the road to DORA compliance might be difficult, the rule acts as a driver of positive change in the financial industry. Embracing DORA's mandates will help financial institutions greatly improve their operational resilience, reduce risks more successfully, and increase their capacity to protect the interests of their stakeholders in a world going more and more technologically connected and linked. Though the road toward complete DORA compliance may be difficult, the end effect offers a future in which financial institutions emerge stronger, more robust, and better suited to flourish in the face of digital threats.

Facing the Music: The High-Stakes Consequences of DORA Regulation Non-compliance

For financial institutions functioning inside the European Union, non-compliance with the Digital Operational Resilience Act (DORA) presents major hazards. Designed to improve the operational resilience of the financial industry, the legislation comes with a strict enforcement mechanism that penalizes institutions failing to satisfy its criteria heavily. Financial institutions negotiating the regulatory terrain must first understand the seriousness of these sanctions.

The enforcement of significant administrative penalties is one of the most intimidating results of non-compliance. Should a financial institution discover a major DORA breach, penalties ranging from 10 million euros or 5% of their whole yearly turnover might be imposed. This large financial penalty is a strong disincentive that emphasizes the need to give compliance first priority. Given the possible negative effects of such fines on the financial situation of an institution, it is essential for them to make investments in strong compliance programs guaranteeing adherence to DORA's recommendations.

Apart from fines, supervisory agencies have authority to mandate corrective actions on establishments failing DORA criteria. These steps are meant to correct the found shortcomings in the operational resilience structure of an organization, not only to be punishing. Remedial efforts might call for more reporting requirements, more monitoring, or mandated institution processes and system modifications. These policies aim to force institutions to quickly and successfully solve their weaknesses, thereby improving their capacity to resist future operational interruptions.

Another major result of non-DORA compliance is public concern. Supervisory authorities might decide to publicly criticize financial organizations that fall short of legislatively mandated regulatory criteria. Signing to stakeholders, customers, and the larger financial community that the institution has not reached the necessary degrees of operational resilience, these public reprimands constitute a sort of public responsibility. A public reprimand can cause serious harm to reputation, therefore influencing investor confidence and consumer trust and maybe having wider financial consequences.

For establishments that consistently ignore legal obligations, the penalties may become more severe—that is, the removal of authorization. Supervisory agencies keep the power to cancel operational licenses of financial firms that frequently disobey DORA. The institution's survival is essentially threatened by the revocation of permission, as it means that it cannot lawfully function. This ultimate penalty emphasizes the really vital need of following legal rules as well as the possibly terrible consequences of ongoing non-compliance.

Apart from the direct fines imposed by supervising authorities, financial institutions might also be accountable for reimbursing clients or third parties for losses stemming from their non-compliance with DORA. Financial losses, damage to reputation, or other negative effects on stakeholders resulting from the institution's inability to retain operational resilience might all generate this liability. The necessity of restitution emphasizes the practical consequences of regulatory violations and reminds us sharply of the requirement of keeping strong compliance systems.

Non-compliance with DORA has serious and all-encompassing sanctions, including financial consequences, regulatory actions, public criticism, and maybe authorization loss. These effects highlight the crucial need for operational resilience in the financial industry and the EU's will to preserve the integrity and stability of its financial system. The message is obvious for financial institutions: following DORA is not only advised but also absolutely necessary for maintaining their long-term survival and prosperity. Following DORA's recommendations is essential for safeguarding stakeholders, preserving market confidence, and ensuring the institution's continuous running in an increasingly digital and linked financial environment in an environment marked by increased regulatory scrutiny and responsibility.

Guardians of Compliance: The Crucial Role of Supervisory Authorities in Upholding DORA Regulation

Ensuring the effective application and execution of the Digital Operational Resilience Act (DORA) inside the European Union mostly depends on supervising bodies. Tasked with the important job of supervising compliance with DORA's strict criteria, these agencies comprise national competent entities as well as the powerful European Banking Authority (EBA). They are indispensable protectors of the stability and resilience of the financial industry, as they play a multifarious function involving anything from thorough assessments of operational resilience to penalty enforcement for non-performance.

CHAPTER 12 ACHIEVING FINANCING RESILIENCE AND INFLUENCE ON TRADE FINANCE THROUGH DORA

Under DORA, supervising authorities have a basic duty to carefully assess the operational resilience of financial institutions. Examining important business services, IT infrastructure, and the complexity of outsourcing agreements, this approach entails a thorough and meticulous study of the resilience plans of the institutions. Whether they result from cyberattacks, IT failures, or other operational issues, the goal is to make sure these organizations have strong systems in place that can resist and react properly to such disruptions. Examining these components helps regulatory authorities determine how ready financial institutions are to keep continuity in the face of unanticipated occurrences, therefore protecting the larger financial system from volatility.

Apart from these assessments, supervisory agencies also directly and practically check compliance with DORA's directives on-site. By focusing on certain areas of risk and doing thorough analyses of their whole operations, these inspections let regulators interact with financial institutions on a detailed level. By means of these practical inspections, authorities may spot compliance flaws or shortcomings, therefore offering a concrete means of guaranteeing that institutions follow the DORA-defined regulatory guidelines. The thoroughness of these inspections reduces little space for control, therefore strengthening the integrity of the regulatory system.

Another vital area where supervisory agencies have a significant impact is enforcement. Equipped with authority to levy fines, these agencies can hold financial institutions responsible for any deviation from DORA criteria. Supervisory agencies have a wide spectrum of punishments at hand, ranging from issuing significant administrative fines to carrying out corrective action meant to address flaws. Authorities can go so far as to provide public apologies in circumstances of extreme or ongoing non-compliance, which not only discourage but also let the market and stakeholders know that the institution has fallen short of regulatory standards. Under most extreme circumstances, supervisory authorities have the last power at their disposal: the cancellation of permission, therefore preventing an organization from functioning in the financial sector. This strong enforcement authority emphasizes the vital need for compliance and the dire repercussions of neglecting DORA's guidelines.

Apart from enforcement, supervisory agencies are significant in guiding financial institutions and supporting their navigation of the complexity of regulatory compliance. In fields such as risk management, cybersecurity, and business continuity planning—where the stakes are high and the regulatory criteria are exacting—this advice is especially helpful. Supervisory authorities enable financial institutions to improve their operational resilience systems and more closely match DORA's objectives by providing best practices and professional recommendations. Along with promoting compliance, this cooperative strategy helps the financial system to be generally stable and resilient.

Under DORA, another essential quality of the supervisory authorities' responsibility is coordination. The control underlines the requirement of uniform and harmonic supervisory methods throughout the EU, which can only be reached by efficient coordination and collaboration among the several supervisory authorities. Working jointly at both national and at European levels, these agencies guarantee that DORA is enforced consistently among all member states, therefore preserving the integrity of the financial ecosystem and eliminating regulatory inequalities. Promoting a fair playing field whereby every financial institution is subjected to the same high standards of operational resilience depends on this coordinated approach.

Supervisory authorities are the vanguards of compliance, directing and enforcing conformity to DORA's strict requirements in the dynamic and ever more complicated terrain of financial regulation. Their importance is in preserving the stability and resilience of the European financial industry, therefore guaranteeing that institutions are ready to meet the demands of the digital era. Their cooperation with supervising authorities becomes a pillar of obtaining and preserving compliance as financial institutions negotiate the regulatory landscape formed by DORA, therefore ensuring the future stability and trustworthiness of the financial system.

Cracking the Code: Unraveling the Interplay Between DORA and GDPR in the EU Regulatory Landscape

Reflecting the greater regulatory environment's increasing emphasis on both data privacy and operational resilience, the link between the Digital Operational Resilience Act (DORA) and the General Data Privacy Regulation (GDPR) inside the European Union is a complex and important one. Although these two rules cover separate facets of the digital environment, their interaction forms a complicated framework that financial institutions have to negotiate precisely.

DORA and GDPR both center on a common focus on personal data protection. Though mostly concerned with improving the operational resilience of financial institutions, DORA gives these organizations significant responsibility to guarantee the security, integrity, and availability of consumer data. This need directly relates to GDPR, which is essentially focused on protection of personal data in all spheres. The junction of these two rules in the field of data security emphasizes the crucial need of safeguarding personal data, especially in the financial industry, where violations could have far-reaching effects. Therefore, financial institutions have to make sure that their data handling procedures completely comply with GDPR's strict criteria, in addition to ensuring their operations are robust against interruptions.

An additional important junction between DORA and GDPR is risk assessment and management. Though from somewhat different perspectives, both rules place strict demands on financial institutions to find, evaluate, and reduce risks. DORA emphasizes operational risks and demands that institutions have policies in place to guard against events that can compromise the availability of financial services. This includes guaranteeing company continuity, controlling outside hazards, and protecting IT systems. GDPR, in the meantime, forces companies to evaluate personal data risks and use suitable technical and organizational solutions to guard them. The similarity of these two sets of criteria emphasizes the entwined character of data protection and cybersecurity. Practically, this implies that financial institutions have to have a comprehensive approach to risk management that covers both the operational risks aimed at DORA and the data protection concerns underlined by GDPR.

The substantial penalties for non-compliance with either DORA or GDPR indicate the EU's will to vigorously enforce these rules. Should financial institutions fall short of DORA's criteria, sanctions range from 5% of their whole yearly turnover to 10 million euros, whichever is more. Again assuming the highest value, GDPR levies fines of up to 20 million euros, or 4% of the whole yearly worldwide revenue. The large financial fines connected to both rules highlight the strict regulatory framework controlling operational resilience and data protection inside the EU. This convergence reminds financial institutions of the severe consequences of non-compliance and emphasizes to them the need to give DORA and GDPR top priority.

Although DORA and GDPR are separate rules covering different facets of the larger digital and regulatory scene, their interactions are both many and important. Financial institutions that fall under both must carefully negotiate the complexities of each rule to guarantee that they have strong policies in place to comply with GDPR's data protection needs as well as DORA's operational resilience demands. Not only is it required by regulations, but also strategically, effectively managing these responsibilities in concert. Institutions may better protect consumer data and preserve the integrity of their operations in an ever-more complicated and changing regulatory environment by encouraging a culture of compliance and resilience. This double emphasis on operational resilience and data security finally helps the financial industry to withstand and react to the many difficulties presented by the digital age.

Diving Deep into DORA: Essential Insights for CIOs and CISOs

The Digital Operational Resilience Act (DORA) significantly transforms how European Union financial institutions manage operational risk, particularly by addressing cyber risks and preventing data breaches. Maintaining the resilience of their companies and guaranteeing compliance depend on Chief Information Officers (CIOs) and Chief Information Security Officers (CISOs) knowing and negotiating the complexity of this law.

DORA covers all financial institutions functioning inside the EU, including banks, insurance companies, and investment businesses, therefore affecting all financial entities. The control is all-encompassing, therefore affecting no one area of the financial system. Emphasizing that every institution, regardless of size or particular purpose, must match DORA's criteria to guarantee the stability and security of the financial system, this general applicability highlights the need for operational resilience throughout the whole financial landscape.

DORA is fundamentally meant to increase financial organizations' operational resilience. The rule requires companies to be proactive in spotting and controlling operational risks—especially those connected to data breaches and cyberattacks. DORA's focus on readiness is to guarantee that institutions can not only prevent possible hazards but also fast get back from any disturbances that do arise. DORA aims to guard financial institutions from the possibly catastrophic effects of operational failures by encouraging a resilient culture, therefore guaranteeing continuity in the face of ever-complex cyber threats.

Financial institutions have to use a multifarious strategy covering several facets of operational planning and risk management in order to follow DORA. This involves routinely assessing risks to find possible weaknesses, creating strong business continuity plans that describe ways to keep operations running during interruptions, and closely testing IT systems and processes to guarantee their resilience. Furthermore, highly valued by DORA is data security, which calls on institutions to put in place strict policies in order to secure consumer information and guarantee adherence to EU-wider data protection rules. This all-encompassing approach to compliance calls on CIOs and CISOs to constantly assess and improve their operational systems so that all possible hazards are properly reduced.

National competent authorities and the European Banking Authority (EBA) oversee and enforce DORA. These regulatory authorities are assigned to guarantee that financial institutions satisfy the rigorous criteria established by DORA. They are supposed to visit sites, provide institutions with thorough direction, and penalize non-compliance. This degree of control emphasizes the gravity with which DORA is being followed, therefore indicating to financial institutions that following the rule is not optional but rather a necessary part of their operating approach.

Failing to follow DORA carries heavy fines that reflect the strict standards of the rule and the significant consequences of preserving operational resilience. Financial firms failing DORA's criteria might be fined either 5% of their whole yearly revenue or up to 10 million euros, whichever is more. These significant financial penalties are a strong motivator for organizations to give compliance first priority and make the required investments in the tools needed to satisfy DORA's expectations. Ensuring compliance for CIOs and CISOs entails not just safeguarding their companies from outside attacks but also preventing major financial consequences resulting from regulatory breaches.

In the age of DORA, CIOs and CISOs have a significant duty as they are the main protectors of the operational resilience of their companies. They have to be proactive, closely examining and improving current risk management systems, aggressively testing IT infrastructure, and always committed to data security values. CIOs and CISOs may lead their companies toward not only compliance but also more resilience in the face of an always changing regulatory environment by adopting these imperatives and staying alert to changing legislative direction. Their leadership in this field is essential to making sure financial institutions can negotiate DORA's obstacles and come out stronger, more safe, and future-ready.

DORA Compliance Compass: The Essential Checklist for Navigating Operational Resilience

Following the road to DORA compliance calls for a thorough and systematic strategy that guarantees that every element of the operational resilience of your company is in line with the strict criteria established by the law. The road starts with a strong concentration on risk management, in which case regular risk assessments become a necessary habit. These tests are used to find and reduce operational hazards that may be ingrained in the company. Creating a strong risk management system is equally important, as it needs to be strengthened with carefully established rules, practices, and controls meant especially to protect the company from the found hazards.

Still another pillar of DORA compliance is business continuity planning. Creating a dynamic business continuity strategy is crucial, as it acts as a road map for how your company will react to operational interruptions like data leaks and cyberattacks. Yet, it is not enough to just draft this strategy; it has to be constantly improved and changed to be relevant and successful against changing hazards. Here agility is essential, as it will help your company to react quickly to fresh problems as they develop.

DORA compliance also depends much on the security policies and resilience of your IT system. Your digital defenses must stay strong; hence, regular testing of IT systems and security measures is essential. This calls for following a schedule including thorough IT system audits, vulnerability assessments, and penetration testing. These methods are meant to strengthen the defenses of your company against possible cyber enemies so that any flaws are found and fixed before they may be used.

Another vital area where planning is absolutely crucial is incident management. Charting a course of action in response to operational events depends on a strong incident management plan development. Simulations will allow you to routinely practice and improve this strategy, therefore strengthening preparedness and guaranteeing that your company can handle actual disturbances. By acting quickly and forcefully during an event, one may greatly lessen its impact, therefore preserving operational continuity and stakeholder confidence.

Both DORA and more general legal systems like GDPR have as their main emphasis data protection. Not only is safeguarding consumer data a legal obligation but also a basic one. Modern technical and organizational solutions are required to guard personal information from illegal access or breaches. Frequent audits of these policies guarantee continuous compliance and give chances for essential improvement. Maintaining confidence and making sure your company stays on the correct side of the law depend on keeping data protection regulations current.

Another area in which care is needed is the management of outsourced contacts. Ensuring that these outside partners are qualified to satisfy DORA's strict compliance criteria depends on careful due diligence when screening and supervising outside service providers and suppliers. Including DORA compliance provisions in contracts makes sure these partners maintain the same operational resilience requirements as your company and helps them answerability.

Maintaining responsibility and openness inside your company depends on effective reporting systems. Establishing strong reporting systems guarantees that important operational events and hazards are maintained under the knowledge of organizational leadership and supervisory authorities. This promotes openness, in which accurate and timely information allows stakeholders to make wise judgments and take required action. Maintaining compliance calls for a careful attitude toward monitoring at last. Regular risk assessments, internal audits, and self-assessments assist in guaranteeing that your company stays in compliance with DORA's criteria. Maintaining agility and adaptability will help your company react to legislative changes and aggressively handle new hazards. Your company may boldly negotiate the complexity of DORA compliance by adopting these basic ideas, therefore strengthening its operational resilience in an always changing regulatory environment.

DORA Data Dynamics: Unveiling Key Insights and Strategies

Setting down certain criteria that highlight the value of data quality, security, and openness, the Digital Operational Resilience Act (DORA) offers a targeted and rigorous approach to data management for European Union financial institutions. Financial institutions have to use a set of strong plans that handle the several aspects of data management and protection as described by DORA in order to negotiate this challenging regulatory terrain.

Strong data management systems are very crucial to DORA's requirements. Comprehensive data governance systems compel financial firms to guarantee the correctness, completeness, and integrity of their data. This entails not only configuring systems to track and guarantee data quality but also recording data lineage—that is, the act of following data from several systems. Such systems help organizations to keep a high degree of data dependability, which is absolutely essential for regulatory compliance as well as operational efficiency.

Under DORA, data exchange systems also play a vital role, especially in terms of preserving openness and enabling regulatory organizations like the European Banking Authority (EBA) and state supervisory authorities to oversee. Financial institutions have to have efficient systems for providing pertinent data to these authorities so that the required information is easily accessible for analysis and cooperation. Fostering confidence between institutions and authorities depends on this openness, which also helps to enable a more coherent strategy to control operational resilience throughout the financial system.

Regarding outsourcing, DORA places significant weight on making sure that such agreements do not jeopardize the operational resilience of financial institutions, especially with relation to data-related operations. Institutions have to have control over their data even if some procedures are contracted out to other service providers. This implies putting in place strict control systems to control outsourcing-related risks, therefore guaranteeing constant adherence to data governance and security requirements. Financial organizations might thereby reduce any weaknesses resulting from depending on outside partners for important data activities.

Another pillar of DORA's method of data handling is cybersecurity. Financial institutions have to have strong policies in place to protect their information from online attacks. This covers creating thorough incident response plans to quickly and successfully handle possible breaches, implementing advanced access controls to limit data access to authorized persons only, and using encryption technologies to safeguard data in transit and at rest. The focus on cybersecurity reflects the growing complexity of cyber dangers and the necessity of financial institutions to keep ahead in safeguarding their data assets.

DORA also mandates financial institutions satisfy strict reporting responsibilities. Should major events affect their data or IT systems, institutions have to notify relevant authorities—including the EBA—right away. Fast intervention and resolution depend on timely reporting, thereby preserving the integrity and security of financial data. This criterion guarantees that any disturbances that can compromise the stability of the financial system are reported to regulatory authorities, therefore enabling them to act in a suitable response to reduce risks.

Following these main ideas will help financial institutions negotiate the complex data terrain described in the DORA rule. Resilience and regulatory compliance in the digital age depend critically on strong data management systems, efficient data sharing mechanisms, control over outsourcing contracts, enhancement of cybersecurity defenses, and meeting of reporting requirements. By means of these steps, institutions not only follow DORA but also improve their general operational resilience, thereby enabling them to flourish in a financial world growing in complexity and connectivity.

CHAPTER 12   ACHIEVING FINANCING RESILIENCE AND INFLUENCE ON TRADE FINANCE THROUGH DORA

Unlocking DORA Compliance: Information Rights Management (IRM)

Aiming at assuring the resilience and security of digital operations inside financial institutions, the Digital Operational Resilience Act (DORA) outlines a set of strict criteria. In this regard, Information Rights Management (IRM) systems become indispensable instruments helping companies to reach and sustain DORA compliance. IRM technologies enable organizations to negotiate the challenging terrain of operational resilience as prescribed by DORA by offering improved capabilities in data security, risk management, and regulatory reporting.

Effective management of operational risks forms the core of DORA compliance; hence, IRM tools are rather important in this regard. These instruments let companies spot and control hazards related to the management of private information. An IRM solution helps companies aggressively handle these risks by providing insight into who accesses data and how it is utilized, and where possible, vulnerabilities reside. The ability of the application to provide real-time notifications is very important, as it lets the company know right away of any illegal access attempts or other suspicious behavior, therefore enabling a quick response to stop data breaches. Apart from DORA's strict criteria, this proactive strategy of risk management improves the general security posture of the company.

Another pillar of DORA, data protection, is much reinforced by using an IRM tool. Such a tool guarantees that sensitive data is handled with respect for its degree of sensitivity by helping to classify and label it. Strict access limits help an IRM solution to guarantee that only authorized users may access important data, therefore lowering the possibility of unapproved publication. Furthermore, the tool's capacity to track data consumption in real-time helps companies to always make sure their methods of data management stay in accordance with DORA's rules. Key values guiding DORA—consciousness, integrity, and availability of information—are preserved by an all-encompassing approach to data security.

Within the field of incident management, an IRM technology is absolutely essential, as it offers real-time warnings on operational events like data breaches. These alarms help companies to rapidly and successfully handle events, therefore reducing any harm and guaranteeing that they satisfy DORA's incident reporting criteria. Maintaining the operational resilience DORA requires depends on quick reaction to threats, as it helps to limit the effects of disturbances on the operations of the company and the larger financial system.

Regarding outsourcing, DORA underlines the need for strict control to guarantee that outside service providers follow legal criteria. An IRM solution helps with this by enforcing data security policies and making sure outside partners follow company requirements. The solution lets companies keep control over their data even if it is handled by outside vendors by giving visibility into how third parties manage it. This control is essential to make sure outsourcing agreements do not jeopardize the operational resilience of the company.

Another area in which DORA reporting responsibilities provide an excellent benefit is the IRM tool application. These instruments create comprehensive data usage, access control, and general regulatory compliance detailed reports. Meeting DORA's strict reporting requirements depends on these thorough reports, which offer the evidence required to show compliance to supervising authorities. IRM technologies enable companies to avoid possible fines and keep their reputation with authorities by supporting correct and timely reporting.

Moreover, IRM technologies directly address certain DORA articles, such as Article 5 on governance and organization and Article 6 on ICT risk management systems. Regarding governance, integrated authentication, auditing capabilities, and data encryption help to guarantee data authenticity, availability, and integrity. By means of their required strategies, policies, tools, and protection of information and ICT assets, these instruments also help to build a strong ICT risk management framework. By matching with these publications, IRM solutions support companies to create a robust basis for compliance with DORA's more general regulatory framework.

An IRM tool is an essential component of a DORA-compliant organization's toolbox. It guarantees strong data security, improves risk management techniques, helps to handle incidents, supervises outsourced projects, and supports complete reporting. IRM tools offer a complete solution for negotiating the challenging regulatory terrain that DORA presents by addressing particular requirements inside DORA, such as maintaining data authenticity, availability, integrity, and confidentiality, as well as supporting the building of an ICT risk management framework. In a financial climate going more and more digital and linked, this not only helps companies fulfill their compliance requirements but also increases their general operational resilience.

Leveraging ISO 27001 for DORA Compliance

Although the road toward DORA compliance will still be difficult, for companies that are currently ISO 27001 compliant, the path is probably more reasonable. The well-established emphasis of ISO 27001 on incompliant security management offers a strong foundation upon which the more general operational resilience needs of DORA may be developed. Especially in fields where their goals cross, the alignment between these two models has major benefits. Risk management is one of the main areas in which one finds alignment. Establishing and maintaining a satisfactory risk management system is highly valued both by ISO 27001 and DORA. Many of the risk management techniques DORA requires will already be in use for companies that currently follow ISO 27001.

This implies that these companies are probably ready in terms of spotting, evaluating, and reducing information security risks, which define the main goals of both ISO 27001 and DORA. As such, rather than a total redesign, the shift to DORA's more general operational resilience architecture may be considered an extension of the current risk management procedures. ISO 27001's extensive security control set helps DORA compliance in even another area. ISO 27001 offers a broad spectrum of controls directly meeting DORA's specifications. Through a thorough mapping process, companies may find which of these controls their present ISMS already covers and which areas could need extra improvement to satisfy DORA's particular requirements. This overlap ensures that companies can utilize their existing security systems to manage the new legal requirements, thereby streamlining the compliance process. Still another major advantage of this strategy is its efficiency. Organizations may save a lot of time and money in their search for DORA compliance by extending on an existing ISMS grounded in ISO 27001.

This strategy is by nature more effective than creating a fresh compliance program from top down. The foundations set by ISO 27001—such as established policies, processes, and controls—offer a head start in addressing DORA's needs, allowing companies to concentrate on improving and expanding their current frameworks rather than building whole new ones.

Moreover, the global acceptance of ISO 27001 is a significant advantage in proving DORA compliance. Provided the ISMS is correctly implemented and maintained to include any required improvements particular to DORA, regulators and auditors are more likely to accept ISO 27001 as proof of an organization's commitment to information security and operational resilience. This awareness may greatly expedite the regulatory review process and provide companies with hope that authorities will value their current

CHAPTER 12   ACHIEVING FINANCING RESILIENCE AND INFLUENCE ON TRADE FINANCE THROUGH DORA

compliance initiatives. Though there are obviously significant synergies between ISO 27001 and DORA, it is crucial to understand that ISO 27001 by itself cannot guarantee complete DORA compliance. DORA's needs in particular go outside what ISO 27001 addresses in some particular ways. These loopholes have to be properly closed to guarantee that a company follows the new law exactly. Therefore, even though ISO 27001 offers a strong basis and a significant head start, more effort will be required to fill these gaps and completely coincide with DORA's whole operational resilience structure. Organizations have to be ready to extend their current controls, implement new standards where needed, and make sure their operational resilience plans fully incorporate all DORA criteria.

Addressing the Gaps in ISO 27001 for DORA Compliance

Organizations already in line with ISO 27001 will have a strong basis when it comes to attaining complete compliance with DORA, but they also have to identify and fix certain holes where ISO 27001 falls short. Among such fields is business continuity management. Although ISO 27001 addresses some elements of business continuity, it does not provide the all-encompassing structure DORA requests. DORA requires financial institutions to ensure seamless operations during and after disruptions, which encompasses not only contingency planning but also a robust, ongoing ability to recover and maintain crucial activities.

Organizations could have to use ISO 22301, which is especially meant to control Business Continuity Management Systems (BCMS), to close this difference. Addressing the whole range of planning, implementation, and continual improvement DORA demands, ISO 22301 offers a more thorough and ordered method to ensure business continuity. Another area where ISO 27001 falls short is security testing. Furthering the minimum vulnerability management procedures described in ISO 27001, DORA's specifications for advanced security testing—including resilience testing and penetration testing—go further.

Although DORA demands a more exact and methodical testing technique, ISO 27001 stresses the need for spotting and reducing risks. To evaluate the robustness of their ICT systems, financial organizations have to use extra testing tools such as threat-

CHAPTER 12   ACHIEVING FINANCING RESILIENCE AND INFLUENCE ON TRADE FINANCE THROUGH DORA

led penetration testing, which replicates actual attack situations. To satisfy DORA's criteria, this type of testing is more difficult and calls for more advanced preparation and sophistication.

Companies will have to make sure they have the tools, knowledge, and procedures required to carry out these tests successfully and to use the findings to increase their general operational resilience. Another important area where ISO 27001 does not completely match DORA's objectives is supply chain risk management (SCRM). Understanding the possible vulnerabilities resulting from these interactions, DORA gives controlling the risks connected with outside ICT suppliers immense importance. Although ISO 27001 covers some elements of third-party risk, it does not fully reflect the complexity and depth needed by DORA. Organizations should take into account implementing ISO 27036, which offers a more all-encompassing framework for controlling information security risks in supplier partnerships, to close this difference.

On the other hand, under the framework of operational resilience, companies might seek various specialized models meant to manage the complexity of supply chain risk management. These extra frameworks will help companies to guarantee that they are fully compliant with DORA's strict criteria and are sufficiently controlling the risks presented by their ICT providers. Another area where DORA lays more strict expectations than ISO 27001 is incident reporting. DORA mandates that financial institutions have strong systems for promptly and thoroughly reporting ICT-related events to authorities. DORA's degree of information and reporting speed need more than what ISO 27001 recommends generally. Organizations that want to follow DORA have to set explicit policies for incident reporting that include the identification of particular roles and responsibilities, the compilation of thorough incident reports, and the building of deadlines for forwarding these reports to the relevant regulatory authorities. In line with DORA's exacting criteria, this might entail improving current procedures or creating new ones to guarantee that all occurrences are recorded faithfully and quickly. In essence, enterprises must fill up these particular gaps to completely comply with DORA, even if ISO 27001 provides a satisfactory basis for information security management.

To satisfy DORA's complete needs for operational resilience, security testing, supply chain risk management, and incident reporting, this will require establishing new procedures, improving current ones, and adhering to extra standards. By following these guidelines, companies may guarantee not just DORA compliance but also improved ability to control the complicated and changing dangers they encounter in the digital terrain of today.

Understanding the NIS2 Directive and Its Implications for Cybersecurity

The NIS2 Directive signals a major change in the European Union's attitude to cybersecurity, extending the scope and strengthening the obligations for companies inside its member states. This regulation is a thorough redesign meant to standardize and raise the degree of cybersecurity throughout the EU, not only a little step ahead of its predecessor, NIS (Network and Information Systems Regulation). Examining the main changes and outcomes NIS2 brings will help us to better grasp how it aims to strengthen the digital resilience of vital infrastructure and services.

Beyond the initial purview of NIS, the NIS2 Directive covers a greater spectrum of sectors and businesses, including those judged vital and essential. NIS2 redefines these categories, eliminating the difference and instead grouping organizations according to the criticality of the services they offer, while NIS mostly concentrated on operators of essential services (OES) and digital service providers (DSP). This shift reflects a larger knowledge that cybersecurity is not just important for sectors like digital infrastructure, health, and public administration but also for traditionally acknowledged vital infrastructure such as energy and transportation.

One of the most noteworthy features of NIS2 is its focus on the harmonizing of cybersecurity policies all over the EU. With an eye toward a more homogeneous and cooperative cybersecurity environment, this directive tackles the differences in cybersecurity maturity degrees across member nations. It requires strict incident reporting rules and mandates that public and private companies improve their cybersecurity systems. Moreover, it forces national governments to create EU-wide initiatives for cooperation and vulnerability sharing, thereby promoting a more unified and responsive cybersecurity architecture throughout Europe.

More thorough clauses on incident reporting, including certain deadlines and the contents needed in reports, NIS2 also brings. Compared to the initial NIS mandate, organizations now have to disclose events within 24 hours of discovery—a major departure in the reporting timeframe. This development emphasizes the EU's will to guarantee quick reaction and minimize the effects of cyberattacks by means of coordinated actions.

Following NIS2 has major administrative and legal ramifications in addition to a technological or operational one. The regulation creates a strong foundation for administrative penalties—including fines for non-compliance. Furthermore, it directly mandates that management bodies guarantee their companies satisfy the criteria of the regulation. Ignoring this might have dire results, including penalties or perhaps managers' temporary ban from carrying out their responsibilities.

Apart from these legislative developments, NIS2 promotes more cooperation among member states and businesses in the revealing of fresh security flaws. Improving the general cybersecurity posture of the EU depends on this cooperative approach, as it enables the quick spread of important knowledge and the application of collective defense policies against new hazards.

Establishing a European network of cyber crisis liaison organizations, or EU-CyCLone, at the core of NIS2 is meant to enable quick and efficient reaction to major cyber events or emergencies, therefore enabling member governments to coordinate their activities and provide resources where most required. Rapid reaction plans help EU-Cyclone significantly improve the resilience of the EU's digital infrastructure by means of preparation and execution.

Using NIS2 also puts major pressures on companies about security risk management. The directive mandates that companies implement organizational and technological actions commensurate with their degree of risk. This covers all aspects of risk management, including asset management, risk assessment, and governance. Supported by defined roles and responsibilities across all levels, organizations must make sure they have suitable management policies and procedures in place, under the control of top-level responsibility.

NIS2's strict criteria for service protection rules and procedures mirror its emphasis on resisting cyberattacks. Strong identification and access control policies must be followed by companies to make sure only authorized individuals and devices may access important systems and data. They also have to create strong systems and networks meant to resist cyberattacks and bounce back quickly should a breach occur.

At last, the guidance underlines the need for proactive event discovery and ongoing security surveillance. Companies should constantly monitor the security situation of their systems and networks, identifying any security flaws and monitoring the effectiveness of preventive actions. They also need to be able to aggressively find security events—even ones that avoid conventional detection systems.

Ultimately, the NIS2 Directive marks a major change in the EU's cybersecurity policy as it offers a more all-encompassing, coordinated, and strict approach to protecting services and important infrastructure. Compliance with NIS2 is not just a legal need but also a key component of firms' larger cybersecurity posture for EU members.

CHAPTER 12   ACHIEVING FINANCING RESILIENCE AND INFLUENCE ON TRADE FINANCE THROUGH DORA

The directive's emphasis on harmonization, rapid reaction, and constant monitoring guarantees that Europe is better ready to meet the rising digital age dangers by setting a new benchmark for cybersecurity throughout the continent.

Preparing for the Future: Strengthening Cybersecurity, Navigating DORA Compliance Beyond ISO 27001

It is clear as DORA and other worldwide rules like NIS2 are followed that the regulatory scene is headed toward more strict cybersecurity and operational resilience criteria. This development shows a greater awareness of the necessity of more robust defenses against the rising hazards companies encounter in the modern digital world. For financial firms and ICT providers, this transformation needs a reevaluation of their present compliance measures. Using accepted criteria such as ISO 27001 provides a strong basis for addressing these new needs, as these guidelines give a disciplined way to control information security issues. The changing character of laws like DORA implies that following current guidelines might not be enough. Organizations who want to properly negotiate this legislative change have to be ready to fill up the particular gaps between ISO 27001 and DORA.

This entails not just pointing up where their present methods fall short of DORA's standards but also acting to address those gaps. Sometimes this might require implementing more criteria, including ISO 27036 for supply chain risk management or ISO 22301 for business continuity, which provides more all-encompassing coverage of the areas DORA is most demanding on. Organizations may position themselves not just for long-term resilience but also for the January 2025 enforcement date, therefore ensuring they are totally ready. Approaching these legislative reforms actively will also assist in reducing the possibility of cybersecurity events. Organizations that are totally compliant with DORA and related rules will be more suited to react as the frequency and complexity of operational risks keep rising.

Not only does this readiness help to avoid fines from regulations, but it also helps to keep the confidence of clients, partners, and stakeholders who rely more and more on strong cybersecurity practices from the companies they deal with. Even though ISO 27001 provides a solid foundation for DORA compliance, it only marks the beginning of the journey. Companies have to surpass ISO 27001's minimum to completely satisfy the breadth of DORA's criteria. This will not only bring compliance but also greatly improve their whole cybersecurity posture. This improved resilience will be crucial in maintaining the continuous success and stability of the company in an environment where operational hazards are getting more complex and ubiquitous. Those organizations that have developed their compliance programs on a strong and flexible structure will be most suited to address future problems, head-on when rules change, therefore preserving their competitive edge and protecting their operations against new dangers.

Summary

With an eye toward trade finance especially, the chapter investigates the transforming effect of the Digital Operational Resilience Act (DORA) on the banking industry. The chapter emphasizes DORA's main goals of improving digital resilience and guaranteeing compliance in a world going more and more technologically dependent. Through a breakdown of its key needs, the book highlights how financial institutions could negotiate operational stability, risk reduction, and regulatory storm-weaving. Strategic tools for reaching and preserving compliance is a key factor, including using Information Rights Management (IRM), knowing the NIS2 Directive, and using ISO 27001.

Examining the interaction between DORA and GDPR, the chapter also explores the complex possibilities and difficulties in the EU's changing legislative scene. It emphasizes the extreme penalties of non-compliance and the critical role supervisory authorities play in maintaining DORA's requirements. Along with a thorough compliance checklist to properly negotiate operational resilience, CIOs and CISOs are given practical insights. This chapter offers DORA not only as a challenge but also as a road toward sustainable innovation and resilience in trade finance as financial institutions get ready for the new regulatory age.

CHAPTER 13

Navigating the New Normal: Reinventing Trade Finance with Blockchain, AI, and IoT in a Zero-Trust Era

This chapter delves into the reinvention of trade finance, exploring the integration of blockchain, artificial intelligence (AI), and the Internet of things (IoT) within a zero-trust security framework. It begins with an overview of the dynamic trade ecosystem, emphasizing its complexity and the growing importance of data privacy, ownership, and compliance with regulations such as GDPR. The chapter investigates how blockchain security of data collection, processing, and administration is possible.

It sets apart on-chain and off-chain data access and computation as well as permissioned from permissionless blockchains. Along with ideas for enhancing data provenance, audit trails, and content validation, key blockchain solutions for user consent management, safe data sharing, and access control are examined. The transforming power of artificial intelligence is underlined, especially in improving data retention and supporting dynamic data markets. Combining blockchain with artificial intelligence shows how incentives for data exchange and safe market structures may be created, therefore promoting a more cooperative and effective trade finance environment. The conversation then shifts to zero-trust security, including its development, ideas, and importance in protecting online commerce. Introduced frameworks with relevance to network security and application in trade finance include NIST SP 800-207 and NIST SP 800-207A.

Examined as basic components for future-proofing trade finance systems are Zero Trust Architecture's (ZTA) fundamental elements—including trust algorithms and deployment methods. The chapter ends by showing in a zero-trust environment the synergy of blockchain, artificial intelligence, and IoT. It emphasizes how IoT provides a strong data stream, artificial intelligence detects anomalies and uses predictive analytics, and blockchain guarantees security and openness. These technologies taken together provide synergistic advantages shown by use cases, including predictive supply chain analytics, improved compliance, and fraud detection. Building a strong, effective, and safe trade finance ecosystem requires a radical step toward integration.

The Dynamic Realm of Trade: A Complex Ecosystem

The intricate web of trade finance presents both opportunities and challenges for businesses and financial institutions. Understanding and addressing the key areas of concern within this complex ecosystem are crucial for sustainable growth and successful transactions.

- **Regulatory Compliance**: The ever-evolving landscape of trade finance regulations demands meticulous attention. Navigating through diverse international and domestic regulatory frameworks, including anti-money laundering (AML) and know-your-customer (KYC) requirements, is paramount for seamless cross-border transactions.

- **Risk Management**: With the inherent risks associated with global trade, effective risk management becomes a linchpin. From credit and currency risks to political and legal uncertainties, businesses must employ robust strategies to safeguard their interests and ensure financial stability.

- **Documentary Accuracy**: The abundance of trade-related documents poses a challenge, emphasizing the need for accuracy and authenticity. Errors in invoices, bills of lading, or certificates of origin can lead to delays and disputes, underscoring the importance of meticulous documentation practices.

- **Technological Integration**: Embracing technology is inevitable, but its integration must be approached with caution. Balancing the benefits of blockchain, digital platforms, and automation with security concerns and interoperability challenges is a delicate task.

- **Collaboration and Communication**: The multitude of participants in trade finance, including importers, exporters, banks, insurers, and logistics providers, necessitates seamless collaboration and communication. Efficient coordination among these stakeholders is pivotal for successful transactions.

The quick development of blockchain technology and artificial intelligence (AI) has created an atmosphere rich with chances for creativity. This mix of cutting-edge technology has enormous power to revolutionize several industries, boost efficiency, and generate fresh company models. From improved data security to more quick transactions and sophisticated predictive analytics, the creative opportunities are great.

Still, this quick progress presents some difficulties. Though exciting, the combination of blockchain and artificial intelligence presents a special set of challenges that have to be properly negotiated. These difficulties result from the different qualities and natural complexity of every technology.

For example, the distributed nature of blockchain, meant to offer security and openness, usually runs counter to the centralized data processing methods typically used by artificial intelligence systems. When trying to combine the two technologies, this basic distinction might lead to conflicts.

Moreover, scalability is quite important. While blockchain networks can become slow and less efficient as they grow, artificial intelligence needs significant processing capability and large datasets to run properly. This difference might impede the smooth integration of AI algorithms into blockchain systems, therefore restricting the performance and scalability of integrated solutions.

Data privacy and security are still important obstacles. Although blockchain security is well known, maintaining the integrity and confidentiality of AI-processed data inside a blockchain system might be difficult. Given the delicate nature of the data sometimes handled by artificial intelligence systems—personal information or secret corporate data—this is especially crucial.

The integration process also depends heavily on legal and regulatory aspects. Both artificial intelligence and blockchain are still under development; hence, their junction begs fresh issues about compliance, data security, and liability. Managing this unclear regulatory environment calls for aggressive policy adherence and smart preparation.

This chapter explores several challenges in trying to combine artificial intelligence with blockchain. It looks at the technological, operational, and legal difficulties that develop and goes over possible approaches and fixes for each. Through in-depth exploration of various domains, the chapter seeks to offer a complete knowledge of how to overcome the obstacles related to merging many strong technologies.

The aim is to guarantee that the synergy between artificial intelligence and blockchain can be fully appreciated, therefore opening fresh paths for efficiency and invention. By means of cautious thought and deliberate application, it is feasible to use the advantages of both artificial intelligence and blockchain, thus producing integrated solutions with security, scalability, and the ability to propel major developments in many sectors.

Addressing AI Privacy Concerns: The Role of Blockchain in Enhancing Data Security, Privacy, Ownership, and GDPR Compliance

The reliance of artificial intelligence on large-scale datasets for both operational and training needs raises serious privacy issues. These issues mostly surface as the proper operation of artificial intelligence systems depends on access to sensitive and personal data. Data security is a top concern as the enormous amounts of involved data increase the possibility of privacy violations and illegal access.

The General Data Protection Regulation (GDPR) has created strict rules for data processing, therefore influencing the evolution and use of artificial intelligence models. Organizations under GDPR have to make sure personal data is handled legally, honestly, and for a designated use. These rules force rigorous standards on data collection, storage, and sharing, therefore motivating artificial intelligence developers to include strong privacy protections in their systems. Compliance with GDPR might present difficulties for artificial intelligence projects, as it requires careful consideration of data minimization, user permission, and the right to be forgotten.

With its special qualities, blockchain technology offers possible answers to privacy issues. The capacity of blockchain to provide data traceability is among its main characteristics. Every transaction entered into a blockchain is transparent and unchangeable, therefore offering an unambiguous data transfer and alteration audit trail. This openness, which is required by GDPR, can aid in determining the legal management of data and demonstrating compliance during audits.

Blockchains also guarantee data integrity. Blockchain's distributed nature makes once-recorded data impossible to change or tamper with. This immutability ensures that the data utilized in AI models is constant and trustworthy, therefore lowering the possibility of data corruption or manipulation.

Another major benefit of blockchain technology is secure access management. Blockchain may enforce rigorous access limits by means of cryptographic methods, therefore guaranteeing that only authorized organizations may access private information. Protecting personal data against illegal access and guaranteeing that data privacy is kept all through the data lifetime depend on this skill.

Blockchain combined with artificial intelligence allows many of the privacy issues related to massive data consumption to be addressed. While blockchain's secure access controls can guard private data from leaks, its traceability and integrity characteristics help guarantee GDPR compliance. Blockchain technology thus presents a workable road ahead for improving data privacy and security in the framework of artificial intelligence deployment and development.

Navigating GDPR Compliance in AI Model Development: A Step-by-Step Guide

Clarifying how to comply with the General Data Protection Regulation (GDPR) in the context of artificial intelligence (AI) requires a thorough awareness of the main stages involved in AI model creation and the particular GDPR obligations connected with every stage.

Data collection forms the first phase of artificial intelligence model building. To teach the artificial intelligence system, enormous volumes of data are collected at this phase from many sources. Any personal data gathered must be done so legally and honestly under GDPR. This entails getting clear permission from people whose data is being used, thereby guaranteeing that they are well informed about how their data will be used and the particular reasons for why it is being gathered. Organizations have to be explicit about the intended use of the data and restrict their data collection to what is absolutely required for the evolution of the artificial intelligence model.

Following data collection comes data processing and preparation. To respect personal privacy at this point, the data has to be anonymized or pseudonymized. GDPR stresses the need for data minimization—that is, processing just the data required for the functioning of the artificial intelligence model. Furthermore, data accuracy is maintained to guarantee the dependability and efficacy of the artificial intelligence system. Any mistakes or pointless information should be fixed right away or eliminated.

Training the artificial intelligence model is the third step. The artificial intelligence system learns from the ready-made data in this phase to spot trends and generate forecasts. GDPR calls for people's right to know how their data is being handled and the reasoning behind any automatic decision making. Building trust and guaranteeing that data subjects know how the AI system is using their information depends on this openness.

Once trained, the artificial intelligence model moves into the deployment stage—that is, it finds practical application. At this point, GDPR is still crucial as it mandates constant performance reviews of the artificial intelligence system. Companies have to routinely check and change their data security policies to handle any fresh vulnerabilities or hazards. This entails making sure the AI system generates objective results free from prejudice or discrimination, therefore safeguarding individual liberties and rights.

Retention and destruction of data mark the last step. Personal data should not be kept longer than required for the uses for which it was gathered, the GDPR says. Clear data retention rules must be followed by firms to guarantee that once data is no longer required, it is safely erased. This lessens the possibility of illegal access and maybe data leaks.

Organizations building and implementing artificial intelligence systems must first understand these phases and their accompanying GDPR needs. Following these rules helps companies guarantee that their AI projects follow GDPR, therefore safeguarding people's privacy and building confidence in artificial intelligence technology. Along with fulfilling legal requirements, this all-encompassing approach to data security advances ethical AI development and application methods.

Ethical Data Collection for AI: Ensuring GDPR Compliance Across Diverse Sources

Reflecting the many settings in which they operate and the vast amount of data they need for proper functioning, AI models generally gather data from a broad array of sources. Web scraping—the process of gathering data from websites—is one often-used technique. This data can cover a wide range of material, including text, pictures, and metadata, maybe even the private information of people who visit or appear on these sites.

For AI models, user interactions offer yet another important supply of data. This might come from customer service contacts, Internet forums, and social media sites. Every connection provides insightful analysis of user behavior, preferences, and patterns, but it also runs the danger of gathering personally identifiable information (PII) like phone numbers, email addresses, and names.

For artificial intelligence, Internet of things (IoT) devices provide a fast-expanding pool of data. From smart household appliances to wearable fitness trackers, these technologies continually gather and broadcast data about their users. Incredibly personal and specific data from IoT devices—including location information, health measurements, and usage patterns—all of which may add to the rich datasets required to train artificial intelligence models—can be extremely detailed and intimate.

A basic component of data collection for artificial intelligence is also database collection. Companies keep large databases, including transaction history, client data, and other pertinent records. Although these databases contain a lot of PII like addresses, identification numbers, and financial information, they may be quite helpful for training artificial intelligence models. In these situations, the data subject's permission must be obtained, the processing must be necessary to carry out a contract, a legal obligation must be met, vital interests must be protected, a task must be carried out in the public interest or as part of official duties, and the data controller or a third party has legitimate interests that do not harm the data subject's rights and freedoms. It is necessary to protect vital interests, do a job in the public interest or as part of official duties, and protect legitimate interests pursued by the data controller or a third party, as long as these do not harm the rights and freedoms of the data subject.

Those using artificial intelligence must understand and follow these GDPR guidelines. It guarantees the responsible and legal conduct of personal data collection, therefore safeguarding individual privacy and fostering confidence in artificial intelligence technology. Following these rules helps companies reduce risks, prevent legal consequences, and promote a more moral attitude toward artificial intelligence growth and use.

Ensuring Data Integrity: Addressing Raw Data Challenges and Achieving GDPR Compliance

Many times, raw data—the basis for AI models and different studies—comes with multiple natural problems. These problems consist of mistakes, missing values, and outliers. Technical problems, incorrect data collection techniques, or manual entry errors are just a few of the several ways that mistakes could occur. These errors can seriously affect the quality and dependability of the data, therefore producing erroneous analyses or findings.

Another often-occurring issue in raw data is missing values. They arise in an observation when a variable lacks any recorded data value. Data entry mistakes, equipment breakdowns, or participants' non-responsiveness in surveys are just a few of the several causes this can have. As they might lower the completeness of the dataset and cause bias if not correctly managed, missing values can hinder data analysis.

Data points known as outliers deviate greatly from other observations. If not addressed, they can distort the findings of a study by means of measurement mistakes or data variability. Their discovery and management are therefore very important, as outliers can affect statistical measures and provide erroneous results.

Different processing methods are used to handle these problems and prepare the data for further investigation. Imputation is a method for handling missing values. It entails substituting values depending on the information at hand—that of the mean, median, or mode of the dataset, or by more advanced techniques, including regression or machine learning models—for missing data. This guarantees the integrity of the dataset and makes a more accurate study possible.

Outlier detection is the identification and control of data points that vary noticeably from the mean of the dataset. Outlier identification techniques could call for visual inspections, statistical approaches, or machine learning algorithms. Once found, outliers can be eliminated, changed, or corrected to lessen their effect on the research.

Normalization is the process of data scale adjustment toward a given range or distribution. Especially when the variables are measured on multiple scales, this method is essential to guarantee that various factors equally participate in the study. Depending on the kind of data and the analytic needs, normalizing might call for logarithmic transformations, z-score normalizing, or min-max scaling.

Within GDPR, **Articles 5** and **32** define fundamental data processing criteria. Article 5 underlines how closely data processing has to follow integrity, accuracy, and data security standards. Data must thus be handled in a way that guarantees its security, stops illegal access, and keeps its correctness and dependability all through its lifetime. Furthermore, underlined is the idea of data protection by design and by default, which implies that from the beginning, data protection actions have to be included in the evolution and running of data processing systems.

Article 32 mostly addresses data processing security. It calls on companies to put suitable technological and organizational policies into place to provide a degree of security fit for the risk. To guard personal data against inadvertent or illegal destruction, loss, modification, or access, this covers steps like encryption, access restrictions, and frequent security audits.

One approach that may be used to guarantee GDPR compliance is pseudonymization. It entails substituting pseudonyms or false identities for identifying data inside a dataset. This lowers the possibility of spotting people in the data while nevertheless letting the dataset remain valuable for study. Pseudonymizing may be a beneficial way to comply with GDPR rules and improve data security while also helping to safeguard personal privacy.

Following GDPR guidelines and using these processing methods can help companies guarantee that their data is accurate, safe, and compatible with legal requirements. In addition to preserving data quality and dependability for analysis, this builds confidence and trust among data subjects and organizational stakeholders on data management procedures.

Privacy-Centric Feature Engineering: Aligning AI Development with GDPR Standards

Developing artificial intelligence models depends critically on feature engineering, the act of collecting or converting unprocessed data into meaningful features that could improve the performance of machine learning systems. This technique sometimes involves changing data in ways that can unintentionally reveal sensitive personal information. Combining several data sets, for example, can provide trends revealing personal behaviors, interests, or other sensitive information not clear from the unprocessed data.

Feature engineering has to be done with a great focus on privacy and data protection, considering the possibility of exposing delicate information. The General Data Protection Regulation (GDPR) offers particular instructions to guarantee that data processing operations—including feature engineering—comply with strict privacy criteria.

Data minimization—which **Article 5(1)(c)** outlines—is one of GDPR's fundamental ideas. This concept calls for appropriate, relevant, and restricted to what is required for the intended uses of the data gathered and used. This implies that in the framework of feature engineering, data scientists have to carefully evaluate which characteristics are really required for the AI model and refrain from generating or employing features that include either needless or excessive personal data.

Articles 4(5) and GDPR's 25 address essential strategies for anonymizing and pseudonymization. Anonymizing personal data means deleting or changing it so that people cannot be uniquely recognized, therefore guaranteeing total privacy. Conversely, pseudonymizing is substituting synthetic identities or pseudonyms with recognizable data. This lowers the possibility of revealing personal identities while nevertheless enabling data to be valuable for research. In the feature engineering process, both methods are necessary to uphold personal privacy and follow GDPR guidelines.

Another basic idea ingrained in GDPR—especially in **Article 25**—is privacy by design. This idea insists that, from the very start, data protection policies ought to be included in the growth and running of processing operations. From the first phases of data collection and translation to the latter stages of model deployment, privacy issues should thus be ingrained into the process of feature engineering. This strategy guarantees that privacy is not just a top priority but rather a fundamental feature of the whole process.

Furthermore, it is vital to have clear data retention procedures, as specified in GDPR **Article 5(1)(e)**. These rules state that personal data should not be kept for any longer than is necessary for the purposes for which it is used. Within the field of feature engineering, this entails setting rules for the retention times for created features and the underlying data. Data should be safely erased or anonymized once it is no longer required to stop any possible use or illegal access.

Following these GDPR guidelines helps companies guarantee that their feature engineering procedures are consistent with data security rules and efficient. This not only protects personal privacy but also instills confidence in the data management methods of the company. Appropriately carried out, these steps can help companies maximize artificial intelligence and machine learning possibilities while preserving the best standards of data security and privacy.

GDPR-Compliant Machine Learning: Balancing Privacy and Model Development

Usually, three separate sets—training, validation, and test sets—are used to create machine learning models using datasets. Every one of these sets has a special function in the process of developing the model. The model learns patterns and relationships inside the data by means of the training set, therefore guiding it. After that, the performance of the model is evaluated, and its parameters are adjusted using the validation set, therefore preventing overfitting. At last, the test set is utilized to assess the generalization and accuracy of the model on unprocessed data, guaranteeing its performance in real-world conditions.

Many machine learning techniques and architectures are evaluated throughout this phase in search of the best-performing model. Achieving the best balance between accuracy, efficiency, and robustness depends on iteratively testing and improving.

In the framework of GDPR, numerous important criteria have to be followed during the procedure. Data reduction is one basic idea that says the gathered and used data should be restricted to what is required for the planned uses. This implies that the only necessary data needed to build the model should be found in the datasets used for training, validation, and testing, therefore reducing the inclusion of pointless or too abundant personal information.

Another absolutely vital GDPR need, as stated in Article 6, is getting previous permission. Organizations have to get clear permission from people before gathering and utilizing personal data, so they are completely aware of how it will be handled. Reflecting the personal agreement to the data processing operations, this consent ought to be freely provided, precise, informed, and clear.

Sensitive data—that which relates to religion, health, or race—must be treated especially gently. GDPR's Article 9 states that this data should be ring-fenced, meaning it should only be used under particular circumstances, like with explicit permission or for essential interests, and under more stringent protective measures. This guarantees the protection of delicate information against illegal access and usage.

Under GDPR, especially as described in Article 20, ensuring methods for data transfer is also absolutely vital. Data portability lets people access and reuse their own information across many services. Within the framework of machine learning, this entails giving people simple and safe access to and transfer of their data, hence improving openness and control over their personal data.

Article 35 of the GDPR mandates that doing data protection impact assessments (DPIs) is an absolutely vital stage in the data processing process. DPIAs enable companies to spot and reduce possible privacy hazards connected to their data handling practices. DPIAs should be carried out throughout the evolution of machine learning models to evaluate how data collection, storage, and use affect individual's privacy. This evaluation guarantees that suitable security measures are in place and that GDPR criteria are followed in the data processing operations.

Organizations may guarantee that their models are both compliant with data protection rules and successful by including these GDPR criteria in the machine learning development process. This all-encompassing strategy not only safeguards people's privacy but also builds confidence in the data management methods of the company. Following these values helps companies maintain the highest standards of privacy and data protection while nevertheless using the advantages of machine learning.

Leveraging Blockchain for GDPR Compliance: Enhancing Data Security and Ownership

Blockchain technology may greatly solve issues with GDPR compliance. Its distributed character—that data is not kept on a single, centralized server but rather dispersed across several nodes in a network—is among its most intriguing aspects. Since all modifications are noted on a public ledger viewable to all participants, this decentralization improves data transaction security and openness. This openness guarantees that every data exchange is voluntary and traceable, therefore facilitating the audit and validation of GDPR compliance.

Within the framework of data privacy management in artificial intelligence systems, blockchain features have various benefits. The immutable character of a blockchain, for example, guarantees that once data is entered, it cannot be changed or erased without leaving evidence. This immutability fits very nicely with GDPR's ideas of data integrity and security, as it offers a strong means of maintaining that data stays correct and tamper-proof. Blockchain can also provide open and safe permission handling.

Recording consents on a blockchain allows companies to show GDPR compliance by building an auditable path of user rights, therefore attesting to explicit and informed authorization.

Nonetheless, different blockchain applications must be distinguished, particularly in light of their functions in data protection and ownership. Not all blockchain systems are developed equally, and their fit for GDPR compliance will differ as well. Public blockchains, for instance, those used for cryptocurrencies like Bitcoin, provide a high degree of decentralization and openness. Still, given the public view of transactions, they might not be perfect for keeping personal information. Conversely, private or permissioned blockchains give more control over who may view and change data by limiting access to approved users. Since it strikes a balance between openness and privacy, this limited access can be more suitable for handling delicate personal data.

Moreover, blockchain lets people have more control over their personal data, therefore supporting the idea of data ownership. By means of smart contracts, people may specify and enforce the rules under which personal data is exchanged and utilized. By automating data transfers depending on established criteria, these contracts guarantee that data usage conforms to individual permission and GDPR standards. This feature enables consumers to keep control of their data even as they utilize other data-driven apps and AI systems.

Even if blockchain technology presents intriguing ways to handle GDPR compliance issues, it is important to carefully evaluate the particular uses and setups of blockchain to guarantee they fit data protection and ownership criteria. Organizations may improve their data security policies and gain confidence with the people whose data they handle by using the special qualities of blockchain, like decentralization, openness, and immutability. This careful methodology guarantees the complete realization of blockchain advantages while preserving compliance with strict data security rules such as GDPR.

Permissioned vs. Permissionless Blockchains: Tailored Solutions for Different Needs

Authorized blockchains are meant to limit write access to a designated collection of entities. Thus, only authorized participants—those who have received permission—may add to or change data on the blockchain. When data quality and sensitivity are absolutely critical, this regulated environment is very helpful. Maintaining strict control

CHAPTER 13 NAVIGATING THE NEW NORMAL: REINVENTING TRADE FINANCE WITH BLOCKCHAIN, AI, AND IOT IN A ZERO-TRUST ERA

over who may access and change sensitive data—personal identity details, financial records, or health data—involved in regulatory and governmental applications, for example, is very vital. The permissioned blockchain approach guarantees that data stays safe and that any modifications can be followed back to a verified source, therefore improving responsibility and compliance with legal criteria.

Industries requiring high degrees of data protection and control may favor this kind of blockchain. Permissioned blockchains, for instance, can be used in healthcare to safely save and handle patient information, therefore guaranteeing that only authorized staff members and healthcare professionals may access and change these records. In financial services, too, by limiting access to authorized users, including banks and regulatory authorities, permissioned blockchains can enable safe transactions and preserve the integrity of financial data. This degree of control is very necessary to stop illegal changes and guarantee that the data stays dependable.

Permissionless blockchains, on the other hand, run on another idea. They encourage a high degree of decentralization and transparency by letting any participant record data on one blockchain. Public blockchains like Bitcoin and Ethereum, where anybody may join the network, process transactions, and contribute data to the blockchain without prior permission, best show this approach. Permissionless blockchains' transparency helps to create a more inclusive and democratic system in which confidence is shared among a large network of users instead of being concentrated in a small number of reliable institutions.

Trade-offs accompany the greater decentralization and openness of permissionless blockchains. They have difficulties keeping control over integrity, even if they offer more openness and resist censorship. Everyone may contribute and receive data. Hence, there is a greater chance of malevolent players trying to change or control the blockchain. Permissionless blockchains use consensus mechanisms—such as proof of work or proof of stake—to validate and guard transactions, therefore reducing this risk. Most hostile organizations find it impossible, as these systems guarantee that changing the blockchain requires either a major computing effort or a financial commitment.

Notwithstanding these protections, permissionless blockchains' natural transparency makes them less fit for uses where data sensitivity and control are paramount. For instance, although they are perfect for establishing open and distributed financial systems or digital identities, they might not be the best choice for keeping extremely sensitive personal information or proprietary corporate data, where rigorous access control and data integrity are absolutely essential.

Blockchains, both permissioned and permissionless, have different benefits and drawbacks overall. Permissioned blockchains guarantee that only authorized users may change data, therefore offering a regulated environment perfect for uses needing outstanding security and regulatory compliance. Conversely, permissionless blockchains encourage openness and decentralization, hence allowing large-scale involvement but needing strong consensus systems to preserve data integrity. Choosing the suitable blockchain model depending on the particular demands and criteria of the application depends on an awareness of these variations.

On-Chain vs. Off-Chain Data Computing: Balancing Data Integrity and Scalability

On-chain computation is the direct data processing and operation execution mechanism inside the blockchain network. This approach guarantees security and a high degree of data immutability. Since the blockchain records all transactions and calculations, they form part of an unchangeable ledger that cannot be changed or tampered with. One of the main advantages of blockchain technology is its immutability, as it offers a strong and safe means of confirming and trusting data integrity. Every network user gets access to the same data, therefore guaranteeing accuracy and openness in the captured data.

On-chain computing does, however, have several disadvantages, mostly related to its resource-intensive nature. Direct computing on the blockchain calls for both a lot of processing capability and storage capacity. This is so because every network node has to process and retain the same data, which causes redundancy and higher resource demand. This can slow down the blockchain's speed, particularly when the complexity of calculations and transaction count rise. As such, this approach might not be appropriate for uses requiring rapid processing times and high throughput.

Conversely, off-chain computing involves handling data outside of the blockchain. Under this method, rather than inside the blockchain network itself, data is processed and calculations are done on outside systems or secondary layers. Should it be so essential, the outcomes can be entered back onto the blockchain as the procedure finishes. This approach lessens the load on the blockchain network, which greatly improves scalability and speed. The blockchain is a better fit for uses needing rapid processing and high throughput, as delegating the computing chores to other systems allows it to manage a larger number of transactions more effectively.

In terms of data integrity and security, however, off-chain processing raises possible hazards. Data modification or tampering is more likely as the processing occurs outside the blockchain's safe and unchangeable surroundings. The off-chain systems have to be reliable if we are to maintain the integrity of the data during processing. Recording the results back onto the blockchain also has to be safe to guarantee that the data stays untainted and correct. Because these other systems might not follow the same strict security criteria as the blockchain itself, this dependence on them may expose weaknesses.

Different approaches and systems may be used to guarantee that off-chain processing preserves data integrity and security, therefore reducing some hazards. Before and after off-chain operations, for example, cryptographic techniques can be employed to confirm data authenticity and integrity. Zero-knowledge proofs and multi-party computing can also offer means to do safe computations without endangering data security and privacy.

By using the inherent qualities of the blockchain, on-chain computing provides, all things considered, increased data immutability and security. For high-performance applications, it may not scale well and might be resource-intensive. While improving performance and scalability, off-chain processing raises possible security and data integrity hazards. Combining these strategies calls for a thorough evaluation of the particular requirements and demands of the application, as well as strong security measures to guard data all through the processing life.

The blockchain projects of the European Union for identity management follow a design that strikes a compromise between control and openness. The characteristics of this framework are public-to-read but permission-to-write. Anyone may access or read the blockchain data in this configuration, therefore guaranteeing great public openness. Consequently, the public may access and view the data kept on the blockchain, thereby promoting transparency and trust. This openness is essential for identity management, as it lets people and companies quickly and consistently confirm credentials and identities.

Though the data is publicly visible, one is limited in writing or adding data to the blockchain. Only authorized agencies may make modifications or additions to new information. This authority to write guarantees close control and regulation of data entry and changes. Such control is essential for identity management as it guarantees that only validated and legal data is entered and helps to stop illegal modifications. This guarantees the integrity and correctness of the identification data kept on the blockchain and helps to stop dishonest behavior.

Applications requiring both broad accessibility and strict control will find this public-to-read but permission-to-write system well suitable. In the framework of identity management, for example, it enables a wide spectrum of stakeholders—including people, companies, and government agencies—to access and validate identification information without endangering the security and integrity of the data. Simultaneously, it guarantees that the identification records may be updated and managed only by trustworthy and approved institutions, including agencies or accredited companies.

This kind of strategy will help the European Union's blockchain projects offer a strong and trustworthy mechanism for identity management. The openness guarantees that anybody may easily access and verify the identification information, therefore strengthening confidence and lowering fraud risk. Maintaining the dependability of the identity management system depends on the data remaining secure, accurate, and tamper-proof, which requires controlled write access guarantees.

This balanced strategy uses blockchain technology's advantages to build a transparent, safe, and effective identity management system that satisfies the interests of many stakeholders while following legal requirements and safeguarding personal privacy.

Enhancing Consent Management for AI with Blockchain Technology

Particularly in relation to using data in artificial intelligence models, blockchain technology has the ability to greatly enhance the way user permission is acquired and handled. This development is absolutely essential to guaranteeing that the utilized data is legal and conformable to laws, including the GDPR.

The distributed nature of blockchain management of user permissions is one of its main advantages. Blockchain spreads this data throughout a network of nodes, unlike conventional centralized systems in which consent records are kept in one place. Every node retains a copy of the consent records, hence strengthening the system's resistance to manipulation. This decentralization guarantees that user permissions stay open and unrestricted, in addition to being kept safe. The blockchain logs every instance of consent given or denied, producing an unchangeable ledger accessible at any moment. Since users can be sure that their consent preferences are honored and cannot be changed without their knowledge, this openness is absolutely vital for building confidence among them.

Furthermore, blockchain traceability allows one to track and validate every operation connected to user permission. Should a user allow their data to be utilized in an artificial intelligence model, this consent is recorded on the blockchain under a timestamp and specifics of the particular rights provided. Should the user subsequently choose to revoke their permission, this action is likewise noted. This thorough documentation guarantees a clear and verifiable history of permission choices, which is necessary to show regulatory compliance.

Blockchain may also simplify the consent-getting procedure. The consent process may be automated with smart contracts—self-executing contracts with agreement conditions directly entered into code. A smart contract can automatically seek and document user permission on the blockchain when a user interacts with a service requiring their data. This automation guarantees consistent and open obtaining of consent as well as streamlines the procedure for consumers.

A clear, consistent record of user permission is especially crucial for artificial intelligence models. A basic need for developing reliable artificial intelligence systems is that the data utilized for training and operations comes from ethical and legal sources. Using blockchain will give companies more confidence that user data is managed in line with legal criteria and personal choices.

Ultimately, by using a distributed, open, and traceable system, blockchain technology improves the process of acquiring and controlling user permission. This method guarantees regulatory compliance as well as fosters trust and responsibility—qualities important for the ethical and responsible usage of data in artificial intelligence models.

Securing AI with Blockchain: Using Blockchain to Secure Data Sharing and Access Control

Maintaining strict access control and guaranteeing the safe exchange of data are two of the primary difficulties in the field of artificial intelligence (AI). This difficulty results from AI systems sometimes needing vast volumes of data from many sources to operate as they should. Especially when handling private or secret data, securely distributing this information and making sure only authorized people have access to it can be challenging.

By providing a distributed and safe stage for data transfers, blockchain technology presents a fix for these problems. Data is kept in one place or under the control of one organization in a conventional centralized system, therefore creating vulnerabilities. Should the central server be hacked, data may be accessed or altered. By using a network of nodes, the blockchain distributes the data while each node preserves a copy of the whole blockchain. There is no single point of failure in this decentralization, therefore improving security. The remainder of the network is safe even if one node is hacked, therefore guaranteeing the integrity of the data.

Furthermore, the unchangeable character of blockchain is rather important in offering a strong structure for security and data integrity. Data entered onto the blockchain cannot be changed or erased once it is there. Every block in the blockchain has a timestamp and a connection to the one before it, therefore producing a chronological and immutable transaction record. This immutability guarantees that the data stays constant and correct over time, as any effort to change the data would require changing all the following blocks in the chain, which is practically impossible due to the computing capability needed.

This immutability guarantees dependability and tamper-proof data for AI systems, hence guiding training and decision making. Knowing that it has not been changed since it was recorded, it offers a safe place where data may be transferred with assurance. Applications that depend on historical data or call for a high degree of data accuracy depend especially on this.

Moreover, the distributed nature of blockchain helps with safe access control. Smart contracts and cryptographic keys help one control access rights. While smart contracts can automatically access control policies, cryptographic keys guarantee that only authorized persons may access certain data. A smart contract may be designed, for instance, to provide access to particular data only under particular circumstances or to particular people only under certain conditions. By means of automation, human error is less likely, and control restrictions are regularly followed.

By means of a distributed and safe platform for data transactions, blockchain technology finally solves the issues of safe data sharing and access control in artificial intelligence. Its unchangeable character guarantees data integrity and security; its distributed design reduces the risk of failure, thereby improving general system security. These characteristics make blockchain a perfect fit for handling the complicated data needs of artificial intelligence systems, guaranteeing that data stays correct, safe, and only available to authorized users.

CHAPTER 13 NAVIGATING THE NEW NORMAL: REINVENTING TRADE FINANCE WITH BLOCKCHAIN, AI, AND IOT IN A ZERO-TRUST ERA

Blockchain-Driven Transparency: Enabling Secure and Trustworthy Data Sharing for Collaborative AI

Blockchain technology guarantees that all transactions are visible and verifiable, therefore enabling safe data sharing among several parties. Fundamental characteristics of blockchain include transparency and verifiability, which give various parties a dependable way to safely exchange data without involving a central authority.

Every transaction or bit of data uploaded to a blockchain network is noted on an open, unchangeable ledger. This implies that the identical information is visible to every network user, who can thus confirm its veracity. Every transaction is time-stamped and connected to the next before it produces an endless, unchangeable chain of documentation. Since the data has been recorded, it cannot be altered; hence, this openness guarantees that every party engaged may rely on it. Independent verification of transactions helps participants develop confidence as it assures them that the data has not been altered.

In cooperative artificial intelligence settings, especially, this safe data sharing capacity is quite helpful. To operate properly, AI systems may need vast and varied datasets—typically derived from many sources. Many times, in cooperative settings, several companies or entities may have to provide their data to a shared pool. Sharing private or confidential data, however, might create questions regarding data security and integrity.

Blockchain offers a safe venue for data transfers, therefore addressing certain issues. Blockchain guarantees that every contribution is clear and verifiable when data from several sources is needed. In a joint artificial intelligence effort including healthcare data, for example, hospitals, research labs, pharmaceutical firms, and other pertinent information may all provide patient data, research findings, and other pertinent information. Every company may safely exchange their data using blockchain, knowing that the contributions are noted openly and cannot be changed. This degree of security and confidence is vital to guaranteeing that private information is safeguarded and yet available for cooperative use.

Furthermore, the distributed nature of blockchain removes the necessity of central authority for data sharing management. Under conventional data-sharing systems, a central authority usually controls access and enforces policies, which could lead to single points of failure and bottlenecks. Blockchain spreads this authority throughout the whole network. Every participant helps to validate transactions, therefore strengthening security and lowering the danger of data leaks. This distributed method is very helpful in cooperative settings where several people must constantly exchange and access data.

Blockchain can also include smart contracts to automatically handle data exchange. Smart contracts are self-executing agreements with explicitly written code terms of agreement. Under what conditions, for how long, and who may access the data—among other norms and criteria for data sharing—they can automatically enforce? This automation guarantees not only security but is also efficient and consistent with specified agreements for data exchange.

All told, blockchain technology guarantees transparent and verifiable transactions, therefore enabling safe data sharing among many parties. This openness fosters confidence among users; hence, it is a perfect answer for cooperative artificial intelligence systems when data from many sources is needed. Using blockchain allows companies to safely distribute private and important data, therefore promoting innovation and cooperation while maintaining the highest standards of data integrity and security.

Blockchain for Advanced Access Control: Enhancing Data Security with Distributed Ledgers and Smart Contracts

With its distributed ledger, blockchain technology presents a strong answer for handling access control. This solution meets a vital demand in data security by guaranteeing that only authorized people may access certain data.

Because a blockchain is distributed rather than centralized by a single authority, the control and validation of data access are dispersed among a network of nodes. Every network node copies the ledger, which logs all access rights and transactions. This arrangement offers clear, tamper-proof documentation of who has access to what information. The ledger is unchangeable; hence, any effort to change access rights without appropriate permission is almost impossible. Ensuring that only those with the necessary rights may see or change data depends on this openness and security.

Apart from the dispersed ledger, blockchain uses smart contracts to improve access control. Smart contracts are self-executing agreements whereby the terms of the agreement are explicitly coded. Without human involvement, they may immediately apply access control policies. A smart contract may be set to, for instance, allow access to a piece of data only to those who satisfy specified requirements, including owning a particular cryptographic key or having past permission. By streamlining the access control procedure, this automation lowers the possibility of human error and guarantees accurate and quick issuance of permissions.

Smart contracts, combined with the distributed ledger of a blockchain, produce a strong access control mechanism. The system may automatically check the dispersed ledger to confirm authorization when someone wants data access. Should the person satisfy the prerequisites, the smart contract will provide access. This quick and flawless approach guarantees outstanding security and efficiency.

This method is especially helpful in situations where sensitive information has to be kept free from illegal access. For instance, in the healthcare sector, smart contracts may control access to patient records stored on a blockchain. Only healthcare professionals with the necessary credentials would be able to access these documents, ensuring patient privacy and data security. In commercial environments, too, secret company information may be safely exchanged among authorized staff members under smart contracts guaranteeing that only those with the necessary rights can read or alter the data.

Organizations may better manage who accesses their data by using blockchain's distributed ledger and smart contract automation features. Through automation of the access control process, this technology not only increases security but also efficiency. Appropriate for broad spectrum of uses where data security and integrity are critical, the outcome is a strong, open, and tamper-proof approach for handling data access.

Improving Data Provenance and Audit Trails: Building Trust and Reliability in AI Through Transparent Data Histories

Data provenance is the whole record of the lifetime of data, including its sources, the procedures it has gone through, and any modifications made to it over time. This idea is like a thorough history or a clear trail that records where the data originated, how it was changed, and who or what changed it. Data provenance essentially offers a complete road map that follows data from its first production to its present condition.

For several reasons, especially with regard to the legitimacy and dependability of artificial intelligence models, ensuring precise data provenance is absolutely vital. The integrity and quality of the data AI models are trained on determining much of their behavior. The predictions and results of an artificial intelligence model may be erroneous or biased if the data used to train it is corrupted, lacking, or distorted. Thus, maintaining the authenticity and quality of the data by means of a clear and accurate record of data provenance guarantees that the data is fit for use in artificial intelligence training and operations.

Monitoring the provenance of data accurately allows us to comprehend its origins and the transformations it has undergone. Validating the legitimacy of the data depends on this transparency, as it lets engineers and data scientists go back to the original data source and evaluate its reliability. For a healthcare application, for instance, ensuring that the AI model generates accurate and reliable diagnosis or treatment recommendations depends on understanding the provenance of patient data, including which medical institution it originated from and what type of processing it has experienced.

Moreover, correct data provenance supports data integrity maintenance. Maintaining a thorough record of all modifications done to the data helps one find any illegal changes or mistakes brought about during data processing. Maintaining confidence in the data depends on this capacity to audit and confirm changes. Data provenance enables a comprehensive study to identify when and by whom any differences or problems develop, therefore helping to clarify them. The reliability of the data depends on this degree of responsibility.

Furthermore, ethical issues and regulatory compliance depend heavily on data provenance. Strict rules on data processing and privacy apply to many businesses, including government, healthcare, and finance. Accurate data provenance gives a comprehensive audit record of data use and changes, therefore proving compliance with these rules. This not only helps to prevent legal consequences but also helps to maintain ethical norms around data use and privacy.

Generally, the cornerstone of the creation and implementation of artificial intelligence models is guaranteeing correct data provenance. It supports regulatory compliance, preserves data integrity, and offers openness, thereby strengthening the credibility and dependability of the models. Through careful data tracking, companies may create more reliable and efficient artificial intelligence systems anchored on high-quality, verifiable data.

CHAPTER 13 NAVIGATING THE NEW NORMAL: REINVENTING TRADE FINANCE WITH BLOCKCHAIN, AI, AND IOT IN A ZERO-TRUST ERA

Blockchain for Data Provenance: Ensuring Data Integrity, Provenance, and Trust in AI, Healthcare, and Combatting Misinformation

Because blockchain technology boasts an unchangeable ledger, once data is entered, it cannot be removed or changed. Maintaining the integrity and dependability of data depends on this quality. Blockchain can document every transaction and change made to the data by utilizing an immutable ledger, therefore producing a permanent and unchangeable record of all activities done.

This thorough and unchangeable record offers an obvious, verifiable audit trail. An audit trail is really a thorough record of who did what and when. Within the framework of a blockchain, every data interaction marks time and is connected to a particular network participant. This implies that every addition, change, or deletion of data is transparently recorded, therefore enabling the tracking back of back every step in the lifetime of the data.

Such an audit trail greatly increases the data used for training AI models. Ensuring that the data is correct, whole, and unaltered is one of the main difficulties in creating AI models. Blockchain storage of data ensures immutability, meaning that once data is recorded, it remains unaltered and tamper-proof. Maintaining the integrity and dependability of the data depends on this assurance; it removes the possibility of illegal change or corruption that would not otherwise jeopardize the performance of the AI model.

Blockchain may be used, for example, in a financial application to monitor and document all transactions and data points required to teach artificial intelligence models fraud detection. Every transaction placed on the blockchain cannot be changed; it is permanently noted. Should efforts at data manipulation be undertaken, the audit trail would clearly show this, therefore preserving the integrity of the data. This openness helps stakeholders have faith in the accuracy of the data.

Moreover, the capacity to confirm every transaction and change improves responsibility. Blockchain records are publicly available to every network user and unchangeable, so it is simple to find and confirm who modified what and when. This degree of openness guarantees that every participant answers for their behavior, therefore strengthening the validity of the data.

In regulatory contexts, this capacity is especially appreciated. Strong data management and reporting standards apply to many sectors. By offering a consistent and verifiable record of all data-related operations, blockchain's immutable ledger

CHAPTER 13 NAVIGATING THE NEW NORMAL: REINVENTING TRADE FINANCE WITH BLOCKCHAIN, AI, AND IOT IN A ZERO-TRUST ERA

can enable companies to show compliance. In addition to helping to satisfy legal requirements, this shields the company from legal and reputational hazards related to data management.

Considering all factors, the unchangeable ledger of blockchain provides a robust method for recording every transaction and update, thereby creating a clear audit trail. By guaranteeing its quality and integrity, this function builds confidence in the data used for training AI models. Blockchain technology's openness and responsibility make it the perfect answer for upholding high standards of data quality and dependability—qualities needed for the creation of reliable and efficient artificial intelligence systems.

Blockchain technology has many benefits in the healthcare industry for patient data provenance monitoring. Provenance is the whole history of data, including information on its origins, methods of processing, and any modifications it has seen. The unchangeable ledger of blockchain guarantees that every piece of patient data is precisely traced from its source to its present state by means of a thorough recording of every transaction and update.

In the hospital, medical record accuracy and integrity are absolutely vital. Sensitive and vital information, including medical histories, diagnoses, treatment plans, and prescription records, makes up patient data. Any change—accidental or deliberate—may have major effects on patient care. For example, erroneous data could cause misdiagnoses or unsuitable treatment regimens, therefore endangering patients. Blockchain's ability to provide an open, immutable record of every data entry and modification helps to prevent such issues.

Applied to patient data, blockchain guarantees that, once recorded, information cannot be changed without notice. Every update entered into a patient's record—a new diagnosis, a therapy modification, or a test result addition—is noted with a timestamp and connected to the person making the change. This produces an exhaustive and verified medical history for the patient that may be accessed at any moment. Healthcare professionals may rely on the correct, unaltered data they are utilizing for diagnosis and treatment planning that has not been changed.

AI models applied in medical diagnoses and treatment planning depend especially on this aspect of blockchain. To provide reliable predictions and recommendations, AI models in healthcare mostly depend on high-quality data. For instance, an artificial intelligence system meant to identify early illness indications from medical imaging data must be trained on precise and dependable sets. The effectiveness of artificial

CHAPTER 13 NAVIGATING THE NEW NORMAL: REINVENTING TRADE FINANCE WITH BLOCKCHAIN,
             AI, AND IOT IN A ZERO-TRUST ERA

intelligence and the confidence in its suggestions are undermined if the underlying data is changed or defective. Blockchain guarantees that the training data stays correct and undamaged, therefore improving the dependability of the artificial intelligence model.

Moreover, blockchain openness lets all players—including patients, doctors, and government agencies—check the integrity of the data. While healthcare professionals can guarantee they are basing judgments on reliable information, patients may have more faith in the security and authenticity of their medical data. The capacity to audit patient data records helps regulatory authorities guarantee compliance with healthcare rules and standards.

Blockchain technology might thus be quite useful in the healthcare sector to monitor patient data provenance. Blockchain guarantees accurate and unaffected medical data by offering a safe, unchangeable, and transparent record of all transactions and changes. AI models in medical diagnosis and treatment planning especially depend on this capacity, as the accuracy of the data directly affects the quality of therapy given to patients. By means of blockchain, the healthcare sector may attain higher degrees of data integrity, therefore enabling improved patient outcomes and more confidence in digital health solutions.

In the information age today, disinformation and fake news pose major difficulties. These events entail the intentional dissemination of misleading or inaccurate information, therefore undermining informed decision making and eroding society's confidence. Inaccurate or misleading information can skew people's impressions of reality, therefore guiding their judgments and encouraging mistrust of credible sources of knowledge, institutions, and one another.

Blockchain technology serves as a potent tool in combating false information, enabling the verification of data integrity and validity. Operating through a distributed and unchangeable ledger system, blockchain records every piece of data in an open, tamper-proof fashion. Once data is entered into the blockchain, it cannot be changed or removed without network agreement; hence, manipulation of it is rather challenging.

Blockchain tracking of information's source and history helps one validate the source and confirm the veracity of the material. News stories, pictures, or videos, for instance, may be time stamped and registered on the blockchain at their moment of production. This procedure generates a verifiable record accessible to everyone to validate the validity of the materials. Should someone disseminate misleading information, the blockchain record can highlight differences between the original and modified versions, therefore revealing the manipulation.

Fighting false news especially depends on this capacity, as it lets fact-checkers and consumers follow back to the original source of information and evaluate its reliability. Blockchain lets one separate confirmed facts from unfounded assertions by offering a clear path. Basically, it gives people a consistent means to confirm the material they come upon, thereby enabling them to make better judgments.

Moreover, blockchain can improve responsibility among distributors and content producers. Holding people and companies responsible for the data they create and distribute becomes simpler as every transaction and change is noted and connected to a particular member of the network. This openness hinders the spread of false information, as individuals accountable may be found and punished for their activities.

Apart from confirming the validity of materials, blockchain helps to protect digital identities. This is absolutely essential to stopping the establishment and dissemination of false accounts, often used to magnify misinformation. Blockchain can lessen the effect of bots and bogus profiles that help incorrect information propagate by making sure digital identity accounts are verified.

False information and fake news significantly undermine society's trust and impair informed decision making. Blockchain technology guarantees the validity and integrity of data; hence, it may be rather important in helping to solve problems. Blockchain offers a clear, tamper-proof way to check material by means of its distributed and unchangeable ledger system, therefore building confidence and empowering people to make better decisions depending on correct knowledge. Blockchain also helps to slow down the dissemination of false information by improving responsibility and safeguarding digital identities, therefore strengthening the dependability and trustworthiness of the information environment.

Blockchain-Powered Verification: Combating Misinformation and Ensuring Authenticity in Digital Content and Social Media

For confirming the validity of digital material like photographs, videos, and news items, blockchain technology presents a strong answer. It tackles the more common, rising difficulty of separating real information from false or altered stuff in the digital era.

CHAPTER 13 NAVIGATING THE NEW NORMAL: REINVENTING TRADE FINANCE WITH BLOCKCHAIN, AI, AND IOT IN A ZERO-TRUST ERA

Blockchain's immutable ledger is the main quality allowing this to be achieved. An immutable ledger is a system of distributed, permanent record-keeping. Information entered into this ledger cannot be changed or erased once it is there. This immutability guarantees that the past of each piece of material is clear and immutable, therefore offering a trustworthy means of tracking its source and confirming its legitimacy.

Whether it is a picture, video, or news piece, digital anything generated may be time stamped and logged on the blockchain right away. Important metadata like the creator's name, the date of production, and the content's source is present in this first recording. Logging this data onto the blockchain creates a verified, permanent record.

Every later transaction or change may also be noted on the blockchain when the material is circulated, altered, or shared. This produces an extensive history of the material, including every stage it has gone through from conception to the present. Anyone interested in confirming the validity of the material can access this open trail, therefore giving them the tools to see whether the material has been changed in any way or tampered with.

Readers and fact-checkers, for instance, may follow back to the initial publication should a news item be published and logged on the blockchain. They can confirm the original wording of the piece, the qualifications of the author, and any later changes. Should someone attempt to disseminate a modified version of the article, the blockchain record will show differences between the original and the changed versions, therefore highlighting the untruth.

Blockchain can similarly record the original files and any changes or alterations made to photographs and movies. Verifying visual material notably depends on this capacity, as digital alteration of photos and movies is rather common. Blockchain guarantees that what individuals see and distribute is authentic and unaffected by offering a verifiable record of the original material.

Apart from confirming content validity, blockchain improves the responsibility of content providers and distributors. Every transaction is logged and connected to a particular network participant, so one can find who produced the material and who made any later adjustments. This degree of openness inhibits the production and distribution of erroneous information as it raises the possibility of being discovered and responsible for disseminating misleading knowledge.

Blockchain technology offers a strong overall instrument for confirming the veracity of digital material. Blockchain guarantees openness and traceability by means of an immutable ledger recording the source and history of material. This helps to separate real from false information, hence building confidence in the digital materials individuals access and distribute. Blockchain helps to create a more credible and accurate information ecosystem by improving responsibility and offering a consistent way of validation.

By means of their ability to detect or eliminate misinformation, blockchain-based verification systems have the potential to greatly improve social media networks. These systems employ the special qualities of blockchain technology to guarantee that material is real and traceable, and artificial intelligence algorithms may be used to examine material for indicators of tampering.

Blockchain-based verification systems may track original content and related information on an unchangeable ledger when material is uploaded on social media. This metadata covers specifics such as the publishing time, the creator's name, and any other pertinent information. Once entered onto the blockchain, this data cannot be changed or erased, therefore guaranteeing an open and permanent record of the source of the material.

AI systems may be used to constantly check and evaluate the material uploaded on social media sites in order to fight false information. These systems are made to identify several indicators of manipulation or fabrication, including odd text patterns, pictures or videos inconsistencies, or differences between the material and established facts. AI can examine the words of a post to find automated bot-like activity or examine a picture to look for altered signals.

The blockchain-based verification system may be used to cross-reference the flagged material with the original records kept on the blockchain when the AI algorithms find stuff that seems to be modified or maybe untrue. Verifying if the material has been changed from its original form is simpler as the blockchain offers an open and unchangeable record of its background. Should the artificial intelligence find that the material deviates from the confirmed original version kept on the blockchain, it may be reported for examination or taken from the site.

This strategy offers a two-layered method of controlling misinformation. The first layer consists of the artificial intelligence systems that actively search and evaluate material for indications of manipulation. The blockchain verification mechanism, which offers a safe and dependable way to validate the validity and integrity of the material, lies second. Combining these technologies will help social media channels build a strong system to find and correct false information.

Moreover, the application of blockchain guarantees an open and responsible verification procedure. The acts conducted by the platform may be checked and examined, as all modifications and verifications are noted on the blockchain. Because users may see the platform actively ensuring the authenticity and dependability of the material being exchanged, this openness helps to develop confidence among them.

When combined with artificial intelligence algorithms, blockchain-based verification systems provide a robust solution for reducing or eliminating false content on social media platforms. While the blockchain guarantees that the content is traceable and real, the AI algorithms examine the material for indicators of tampering. This mix improves social media platforms' capacity to identify and control false material, therefore helping to create a more dependable and trustworthy online space.

Blockchain for Data Protection: How to Improve Data Retention and Deletion Policies with Transparency and Automation

Fundamental elements of data protection are data retention and deletion policies, which guarantee that companies treat personal data ethically and in line with legal criteria. These rules control the length of time data should be kept, when it should be removed, and the way these activities should be executed. Their major goal is to reduce risks related to data breaches, illegal access, and non-compliance with legal criteria, preserving people's privacy and the integrity of the data management system.

Blockchain technology may greatly improve data preservation and deletion procedures' efficiency and openness. Operating from a distributed ledger that securely and unchangeably logs all data exchanges, blockchain Once a transaction is entered on the blockchain, it cannot be changed or deleted, therefore guaranteeing a correct and permanent record.

Within the framework of data retention, blockchain can offer an unambiguous chronology of data creation, access, and modification. Every interaction with the data logs on the blockchain and time stamps provides an open and complete history. From its first acquisition until its ultimate erasure, this thorough record-keeping guarantees that companies may readily follow the lifetime of the data. Blockchain, for instance, may automatically record compliance with a rule requiring that particular personal data be kept for a designated duration by precisely timing data exchanges.

Regarding data erasure, blockchain immutability presents a special difficulty but also presents creative ideas. Although blockchain does not permit data to be destroyed in the conventional sense, it may set systems to guarantee that data is essentially rendered unavailable or outdated. Often used is the "forget" of the data using cryptographic methods. Although the encrypted data stays on the blockchain, this entails deleting the keys required to decode the data, therefore rendering it unreadable and essentially unreachable.

Moreover, blockchain could improve responsibility and openness throughout the data deletion process. Blockchain offers an auditable trail showing adherence to deletion rules by documenting the steps taken to make data unavailable.

In regulatory settings where compliance depends on demonstrating that data has been successfully destroyed or anonymized, this is very crucial. Furthermore, used to automate data retention and deletion regulations on the blockchain are smart contracts, self-executing contracts with stipulations straight inscribed into code. Programmed to enforce retention schedules and automatically initiate deletion procedures after the data retention period is out, smart contracts can A smart contract may be configured, for example, to automatically make data unavailable after a certain period, therefore guaranteeing compliance with data security rules without calling for human involvement.

Considering all factors, the open and unchangeable ledger of blockchain provides a robust foundation for managing data deletion and retention regulations. It guarantees that every action connected to data management is precisely recorded and verified, therefore improving data protection rule compliance. Organizations may gain more openness, responsibility, and efficiency in their data management methods by using blockchain technology, thus preserving individual privacy and building confidence in their data handling procedures.

Data Retention Policies: Enhancing Security and Compliance in Finance and Beyond

Blockchain technology presents a strong instrument for implementing data retention rules, which are very vital for controlling the length of data stored and guaranteeing its safe erasure upon its disposal when it is not required. These rules restrict the storage time of personal data, therefore safeguarding individuals' privacy and enabling companies to follow legal criteria.

CHAPTER 13 NAVIGATING THE NEW NORMAL: REINVENTING TRADE FINANCE WITH BLOCKCHAIN, AI, AND IOT IN A ZERO-TRUST ERA

Blockchain allows very transparent and highly accurate data preservation rules to be applied. Every data transaction in a blockchain is permanently and securely recorded on its unchangeable ledger. Consequently, once data is uploaded into the blockchain, it cannot be changed or erased, thus offering a trustworthy and tamper-proof record of the data's life. This openness guarantees that companies may monitor precisely when data was acquired, accessed, or changed, therefore facilitating the management and application of retention policies.

Blockchain may automatically record the time and date the data was uploaded into the system, for instance, should a rule mandate that some personal information be kept for five years. To follow the retention policy, the material ought to be erased or made unavailable beyond the five-year term. Blockchain offers a clear, verifiable record of when the data retention term begins and finishes, therefore helping this procedure.

Smart contracts—self-executing agreements with terms explicitly encoded into code—can improve data retention policy execution even further. Programmable to automatically carry out activities depending on preset criteria, smart contracts Within the framework of data retention, a smart contract may be configured to track blockchain data storage age. The smart contract can set off an action to safely erase or make the data unavailable after the data ends of the retention term.

Imagine, for example, a smart contract configured with a policy stating personal data should be kept for precisely 3 years. The smart contract will track the information and, upon the end of the 3-year term, will start a deletion procedure automatically. By removing the necessity for human interaction, this automation guarantees constant compliance with data preservation laws and lowers the danger of human mistake.

Furthermore, adding another degree of security are the applications of smart contracts and blockchain. By using smart contracts, automatic retention policy execution guarantees consistent management of data under the designated guidelines. Along with improving data security, this offers a clear audit trail. The blockchain records the actions performed by the smart contracts, therefore generating an open and unchangeable record of compliance actions. For internal evaluations as well as for proving regulatory compliance, this audit trail is quite helpful.

By means of a visible and unchangeable record of data transfers, blockchain may be essentially applied to enforce data preservation laws. By automating the execution of these rules, smart contracts help to guarantee that data is kept just for the required duration and thereafter safely removed. Blockchain's safe ledger and smart contract automation features together offer a strong basis for controlling data retention, improving security, and guaranteeing legal and regulatory compliance.

Blockchain technology can be utilized in the financial industry for handling transaction data to satisfy legal needs and improve data security. Large volumes of data produced by financial transactions have to be properly controlled, kept, and finally erased in line with rigorous regulatory criteria.

The unchangeable ledger of blockchain offers a safe and open approach to documenting transaction information. The specifics of a financial transaction— including the date, time, parties engaged, and transaction amount—are entered on the blockchain. Once this data is recorded, it cannot be changed or erased, therefore guaranteeing the integrity and correctness of the transaction record. Maintaining confidence and responsibility in financial transactions depends on this unchangeable character of blockchain.

In finance, regulatory criteria can call for transaction data to be kept for a designated length of time. To comply with rules and regulations such as the Sarbanes-Oxley Act or the General Data Protection Regulation (GDPR), some financial records might, for five, seven, or even 10 years, be maintained. By offering a consistent, tamper-proof record of when the transaction data was generated and how long it has been kept, blockchain can let financial institutions satisfy these needs.

The data has to be safely erased to safeguard private information and follow laws once the mandated retention time has passed. By using smart contracts, blockchain can help ease this procedure. Self-executing bits of code running on the blockchain, smart contracts may automate data retention and erasure, among other operations.

A smart contract may be designed, for example, to track the blockchain's recorded transaction data's aging. The smart contract can start a procedure to safely destroy a certain piece of data automatically when its retention term finishes. This might entail eliminating the keys required to access the encrypted data, therefore leaving it unavailable and guaranteeing it cannot be obtained or utilized. This automatic system lowers the danger of human mistake and guarantees constant compliance with data preservation rules.

Furthermore, by offering a dispersed and decentralized network, blockchain improves data security. Blockchain's distributed character implies that transaction data is copied across several nodes in the network, unlike conventional centralized systems whereby data is kept in a single location and is prone to breaches and assaults. Because they would have to take over most of the nodes to change the data, this decentralization makes it far more difficult for malevolent actors to corrupt the data.

Blockchain technology may therefore guarantee, in the banking industry, that transaction data is safely recorded, kept for the necessary duration, and thereafter suitably erased in line with legal criteria. Blockchain improves data security and enables financial firms to keep compliance with strict regulatory criteria by offering an unchangeable ledger and applying smart contracts to automate data preservation and deletion procedures. In financial systems, this safe and effective handling of transaction data builds dependability and confidence.

Empowering Data Ownership: Blockchain and AI in Transparent and Secure Data Monetization

Blockchain and artificial intelligence taken together might transform data management and monetization, hence establishing a transparent and safe data market. Under this creative approach, people may make money from their data under control over usage.

Because blockchain technology guarantees data security and openness, it offers the basis for this business. Every bit of information may be entered on a blockchain, producing an unchangeable record following its source, ownership, and movements. Consequently, once data is placed into the blockchain, it cannot be changed or erased, hence offering a consistent and verifiable record of the information. People may boldly provide their data, knowing it will be safely kept and its use will be clear-cut.

Analyzing and interpreting the data in this sector depends much on artificial intelligence. AI systems can assess the worth of the data, link data sources with possible consumers, and guarantee ethical and efficient usage of the material. For example, businesses looking for particular kinds of data for marketing or research need AI to find and buy the pertinent data from people on the market.

One of the main advantages of this integration is data monetizing possibilities for people. Companies in the present digital economy may gather and utilize data without paying the people who provide it compensation. People may directly sell their data straight to interested parties using a blockchain-based data marketplace. This gives people a fresh income source, therefore enabling them to profit personally monetarily from their data.

Besides, people still control their information under this system. Blockchain technology makes it possible for smart contracts, which are self-executing agreements with terms directly encoded into code. These smart contracts allow one to specify under what circumstances, who may access the data, and how it may be utilized. For instance, someone could consent to selling their health records to a medical research firm but stipulate that the data can only be sold for non-commercial study. The smart contract would automatically enforce these rules, therefore guaranteeing that the data be utilized just as agreed.

Furthermore, this open and safe structure helps all users of the data market to develop confidence. Knowing that the data has been faithfully entered onto the blockchain, data purchasers may confirm its provenance and legitimacy. By seeing who is using their data and for what reason, data providers help to guarantee respect for their privacy and usage conditions.

Blockchain and artificial intelligence taken together can provide a transparent and safe data marketplace where people may profit from their data while still controlling its usage. While artificial intelligence helps data suppliers be matched with consumers, blockchain guarantees the security and openness of data exchanges. This approach enables people to profit from their data and control its use, therefore empowering them and promoting a more fair and reliable digital economy.

Decentralizing Data Trade: Blockchain-Powered Marketplaces for Transparent and Fair Data Transactions

Blockchain technology might let a distributed data marketplace be created, therefore changing the way data is purchased and traded. People may sell their data straight to AI developers in this market, therefore guaranteeing fair pay for the data providers and openness in data transactions.

Large companies or middlemen often gather and control data in conventional data marketplaces, then sell it to other companies or artificial intelligence developers. This centralized approach might result in a lack of openness whereby people are ignorant of how their data is being utilized and if they are being appropriately paid. Moreover, after their data has been gathered, people usually have very little to no control over it.

Blockchain technology allows one to create a distributed data marketplace. Data in this system is dispersed among a network of nodes rather than kept in a central repository. Because there is no single point of failure in this distributed architecture, security is improved and data breaches are less likely. Every transaction involving data is noted on an unchangeable blockchain ledger, therefore offering an open and permanent record of all data transactions.

When someone chooses to sell their data, the transaction is noted on the blockchain so that any network user may view and confirm it. Because consumers may see exactly how their data is being used and by whom, this openness helps to establish confidence among them. This openness guarantees for artificial intelligence engineers that the data they are acquiring is real and unaltered.

Moreover, blockchain technology makes smart contracts—self-executing agreements with terms straight put into code—possible. Smart contracts allow one to automate and enforce data transaction rules in a distributed data marketplace. When someone agrees to sell their data, for instance, a smart contract might define the parameters under which the data could be used, the price, and any other pertinent criteria. The smart contract runs the transaction automatically if the requirements are satisfied, therefore forwarding the data to the AI developer and the money to the data source.

This mechanism guarantees equitable pay for data input. Negotiating rates directly with AI developers allows people to avoid depending on middlemen, who could keep a substantial share of the earnings. Better remuneration for data suppliers and more competitive pricing resulting from this direct transaction model can follow. People also have control over their data, as they choose when and how to sell it.

In this regard, blockchain adoption offers another degree of protection for data exchanges. All transactions are logged on an unchangeable ledger; hence, data transfers have an obvious and verifiable history. This makes it challenging for malevolent actors to access or control data undetectably.

Ultimately, blockchain can help create a distributed data market whereby anyone may sell their data straight to artificial intelligence developers. This method guarantees an open record of all exchanges and a transparent data transaction process. It also ensures that people may negotiate costs directly and have ownership of their data, therefore properly compensating them for their information. From conventional data marketplaces, this distributed and open approach marks a major change in promoting more trust, security, and justice in the data economy.

Smart Contracts and Blockchain: Transforming Incentives and Ethical Data Sharing in Healthcare and AI

Creating incentive systems for data sharing depends heavily on smart contracts, self-executing contracts with the conditions of the agreement explicitly put into code. Operating on blockchain technology, these agreements guarantee that agreement obligations are automatically enforced without middlemen.

Using smart contracts in data exchange offers one of the main benefits in terms of rewarding people for offering high-quality data. The contracts could contain certain standards for what qualifies as high-quality data, including relevance, completeness, and correctness. As people enter their information, the smart contract may evaluate if these requirements are satisfied automatically. Should the data satisfy the necessary criteria, the smart contract activates a reward system, thereby reimbursing the data source.

This incentive structure motivates people to offer the greatest available information. Training AI models depends on good-quality data, as it directly affects their dependability and performance. To identify trends and provide accurate forecasts, artificial intelligence programs depend on vast datasets. More effective performance of the models results from accurate and complete data, therefore improving the outcomes in many different applications—from predictive analytics to tailored suggestions.

A blockchain-based data marketplace can transform medical data sharing and use in the healthcare industry. Patients have important medical records, genetic information, and treatment histories, among other things. Usually retained by healthcare practitioners, this information is not readily available for study needs. By letting patients directly exchange their medical records with researchers, a blockchain-based marketplace modulates this dynamic.

Patients may be guaranteed in this market that their information will be handled safely and morally. The transparent record of all data transactions made possible by blockchain's immutable ledger guarantees patients may view exactly how their data is being utilized and by whom. By defining that the data can only be used for particular kinds of studies and under particular circumstances, smart contracts can enforce ethical use agreements. This level of control and openness fosters patients' confidence, which increases their willingness to provide their data.

Patients also get paid for providing their data. The blockchain-based solution guarantees equitable compensation for patients by automatically managing payments, therefore addressing their needs. This reimbursement not only offers a money reward but also recognizes the worth of the patients' data, therefore encouraging involvement and support of scientific advancement.

Also greatly benefited by this arrangement are researchers. The advancement of medical research and the development of novel medicines depend on access to high-quality, varied datasets. Participating in the blockchain-based marketplace allows researchers to preserve patient privacy and rights while gathering the necessary data. This kind of data acquisition is probably more thorough and accurate, thereby improving the validity and influence of the study conclusions.

Finally, smart contracts allow one to design incentive systems for data exchange, therefore ensuring that people are paid for supplying high-quality data. This method improves the accessible data for AI training, hence raising the dependability and performance of AI models. A blockchain-based data marketplace enables patients in the healthcare sector to share their medical records with researchers, and getting paid for it guarantees ethical and safe use of their information. This approach advances the discipline of medical research by encouraging openness, trust, and teamwork, therefore benefiting patients and researchers.

The Transformative Potential of AI and Blockchain Convergence: Unlocking Synergies for Ethical and Transparent Innovation

The combination of blockchain technology and artificial intelligence has amazing chances to solve many of the integration issues. Combining the benefits of both technologies allows one to solve important concerns about data privacy, security, and transparency, thereby improving the ethical and efficient use of artificial intelligence.

Transparency and strong data security are well-known benefits of blockchain technology. Driven by a distributed ledger system with unchangeable records guaranteeing data integrity, data entered onto the blockchain cannot be changed or removed; hence, it is quite safe against fraud and manipulation once it is there. Blockchain's openness also lets all users of the network see and confirm all transactions and data inputs. The development of trust among consumers and stakeholders depends on this degree of openness.

These blockchain features may be employed in the framework of artificial intelligence to guarantee accurate, safe, and reliable data used for training and decision-making. To learn and provide predictions, artificial intelligence algorithms mostly depend on enormous volumes of data. Still, the security and integrity of this data are absolutely critical. Blockchain allows companies to produce an open and verifiable record of data origin and changes. This guarantees that the data conforms with ethical norms and privacy rules, as well as improving its dependability.

In the healthcare sector, for example, AI systems may examine patient data to offer tailored treatment suggestions. Healthcare providers may guarantee that the data stays unmodified and safe by means of blockchain, therefore empowering patients with confidence in their privacy protection. Blockchain's immutable character guarantees that patient information cannot be changed, therefore providing a safe basis for applications driven by artificial intelligence.

It is imperative to aggressively solve the problems resulting from their integration as we keep investigating the synergies between artificial intelligence and blockchain. Technical complexity, regulatory compliance, and ethical questions abound among these difficulties. Technical difficulties center on making sure blockchain systems and artificial intelligence algorithms are seamlessly compatible. Blockchain's open and auditable records help to enable regulatory compliance—that is, adherence to data protection rules and regulations.

Ensuring that artificial intelligence systems are built and used in a way that honors user privacy and prevents prejudices is part of the ethical issue.

Solving these problems calls for cooperation among technologists, legislators, and interested parties. Working together helps one create frameworks and guidelines guiding the moral and efficient application of blockchain and artificial intelligence. This proactive strategy guarantees that the advantages of modern technologies may be completely utilized for the good of society.

Finally, the combination of blockchain technology with artificial intelligence has enormous power to solve some of the difficulties in their use. The ethical and efficient application of artificial intelligence may be greatly improved by using blockchain features to guarantee data privacy, security, and transparency. It is essential to solve problems early on as we investigate the interactions between these technologies so that the advantages of blockchain and artificial intelligence may be completely realized for the good of society.

Embracing Zero Trust Architecture: Redefining Cybersecurity for Modern Enterprises

Modern corporate infrastructure in the dynamically linked world of today is defined by a sophisticated mesh of internal networks, distant offices, mobile users, and cloud services. This complex configuration has greatly exceeded the capacity of conventional perimeter-based network security systems. Historically, these methods worked under the presumption that maintaining the perimeter of the network would help to sufficiently prevent attacks. This strategy has not worked, though. Once an assailant crosses this boundary, they usually find it very simple to travel laterally across the network, therefore getting access to sensitive data and systems.

CHAPTER 13 NAVIGATING THE NEW NORMAL: REINVENTING TRADE FINANCE WITH BLOCKCHAIN, AI, AND IOT IN A ZERO-TRUST ERA

Understanding these weaknesses, the Zero Trust (ZT) cybersecurity paradigm has become a strong and flexible fix that has been somewhat well-known lately. Zero Trust questions the conventional wisdom of security based on inherent trust in network settings and marks a basic change in perspective. Zero Trust works on the idea that no environment should be seen as naturally trustworthy, rather than supposing that objects inside the network may be trusted by default. To fully safeguard business resources, this paradigm requires constant risk analysis and strict access control policies.

Covering a wide range of corporate assets, the Zero Trust model extends its protective actions to devices, apps, infrastructure elements, and users. Among these users are both human and non-human entities, including automated systems and service accounts. Zero Trust guarantees that, independent of their source or the resource they aim at, every access request is painstakingly checked.

Zero Trust Architecture's (ZTA) guiding concepts center on the idea of removing implicit trust from the network and substituting explicit verification. This entails always assessing the security posture of any entity seeking access and applying adaptive policies according to the dynamic character of contemporary cyber threats. Identity verification, device security, and network segmentation—all meant to provide several levels of defense working together to protect the corporate environment—are fundamental elements of ZTA.

Adopting a Zero Trust paradigm calls for a wholehearted cybersecurity strategy. Since it helps companies spot and react to any hazards in real time, constant risk assessment is very vital. Monitoring and evaluating network traffic, user activity, and device status helps one to find abnormalities and signs of compromise. Maintaining high degrees of visibility into all network operations helps businesses rapidly spot and reduce threats before they become major security events.

Another key component of Zero Trust is strict access restrictions. Under a least privilege approach—where users and devices are given the minimal access required to operate—this entails that organizations may lower the attack surface and lessen the possibility of illegal access by restricting access depending on roles, responsibilities, and contextual elements including location and device security state.

Zero Trust also has as its fundamental principle data protection. This entails ensuring data integrity by means of encryption and other advanced security mechanisms, therefore preventing illegal access and safeguarding data both at rest and in motion. Strong incident response and recovery strategies also help companies to rapidly and successfully react to security breaches, therefore reducing the effect on operations and data integrity.

CHAPTER 13 NAVIGATING THE NEW NORMAL: REINVENTING TRADE FINANCE WITH BLOCKCHAIN, AI, AND IOT IN A ZERO-TRUST ERA

This chapter explores the ideas and elements of Zero Trust Architecture so as to give a complete knowledge of this sophisticated security paradigm. It provides a thorough manual for companies trying to strengthen their cybersecurity posture, looking at how to apply constant risk assessment, strict access control, and data and service protection across all corporate assets. By means of this research, businesses may acquire the skills and information required to successfully negotiate the complexity of contemporary cybersecurity issues.

The techniques and tools applied to safeguard the digital terrain must change along with its evolution. Adopting Zero Trust helps companies create a strong cybersecurity system able to withstand the advanced and relentless threats defining the present threat scene.

The Evolution and Impact of the Zero Trust Concept: From Early Concepts to Modern Cybersecurity Strategy

The Zero Trust idea has its roots in projects that predate the official name. Among the first initiatives in this field was the "black core" approach of the Defense Information Systems Agency (DISA). By stressing the security of individual transactions instead of depending just on perimeter defenses, this project sought to guarantee business transactions. This strategy represented a major change in cybersecurity theory by departing from the conventional focus on the outside margins of the network.

The Jericho Forum also first proposed de-perimeterization at the same time. This idea underlined the restrictions of depending on the location of the network for security. It underlined the weaknesses and inefficiencies of conventional perimeter-based security systems, therefore hastening the development toward a more all-encompassing security solution. The observations of the Jericho Forum helped to shape a fresh perspective on cybersecurity that gave data and transaction security first priority above network security.

John Kindervag of Forrester later first used the term "**Zero Trust**." This new vocabulary captured the changing perspective that no network environment should be seen as naturally reliable. Kindervag's Zero Trust approach connected with the increasing understanding that conventional security strategies were insufficient for the new dangers of the digital era. Because of its strong commitment to cybersecurity, the

CHAPTER 13 NAVIGATING THE NEW NORMAL: REINVENTING TRADE FINANCE WITH BLOCKCHAIN, AI, AND IOT IN A ZERO-TRUST ERA

Zero Trust model soon acquired popularity in many fields, including private enterprise and higher education. Its focus on confirming every transaction and access request—regardless of source—appealing to companies struggling with ever more complex cyber threats.

Recognizing the need for more advanced security measures, federal agencies have been urged to use Zero Trust ideas by means of many legislative and regulatory actions. Establishing rules for government information security initiatives, the government Information Security Modernization Act (FISMA) forms the pillar of this endeavor. FISMA's structure emphasizes the need for a thorough and methodical approach to information security, including risk management in every facet of government activities. By means of a disciplined approach for handling security and privacy concerns, the Risk Management Framework (RMF) guarantees that federal agencies may properly identify, evaluate, and reduce risks.

The Continuous Diagnostics and Mitigating (CDM) initiative aims to improve real-time identification and response capability for cybersecurity vulnerabilities, thereby arming federal agencies with the tools and procedures required to keep a dynamic security posture.

These steps taken together seek to limit data and resource access to just approved organizations. They underline the importance of federal agencies adjusting to technological developments so that more dynamic and precise access control is possible. Federal agencies may better safeguard their data and systems by adopting these ideas in a digital terrain growing in complexity and connectivity. Adopting Zero Trust ideas marks a basic change in how government agencies handle cybersecurity—from a reactive to a proactive posture.

Beyond the public sector, the Zero Trust approach shapes cybersecurity methods across several sectors. Its ideas are now indispensable for tackling the problems presented by mobile workers, cloud computing, and the explosion of Internet of Things (IoT) devices. By guaranteeing that every access request is validated, every transaction is tracked, and every possible danger is instantly reduced, Zero Trust-adopting companies may reach a better degree of security. This strategy not only improves security but also strengthens resistance against the always-changing terrain of cyber dangers.

The path from DISA's "black core" approach and the de-perimeterization idea of the Jericho Forum to the general acceptance of Zero Trust ideas shows the continuous development in cybersecurity philosophy. The Zero Trust approach offers a strong structure for safeguarding vital systems and private data as cyber dangers grow more complex and ubiquitous. Through constant access validation and transaction security top priorities, companies may confidently and resiliently negotiate the complexity of contemporary cybersecurity issues. Emphasizing zero inherent trust and strict access control, the Zero Trust paradigm reflects the direction of cybersecurity in a society going more and more digital and linked.

Zero Trust Architecture: Redefining Cybersecurity for a Dynamic and Threat-Filled Digital World

Zero Trust marks a basic change in cybersecurity, substituting a paradigm that gives user, asset, and resource safety first priority over conventional network-based protections. This fresh perspective is based on the idea that confidence should be continually checked and validated rather than ever implicitly given. Zero confidence questions the presumption of confidence that many conventional security models make—that of entities inside the network—by demanding constant inspection of every access request.

Zero Trust Architecture (ZTA) is mostly based on its all-encompassing architecture that combines several aspects of the security posture of a company. The management of identity and credentials forms the core of this structure, as it guarantees correct identification and authentication of every user and device. This approach depends critically on access management, whereby permissions are issued based on the least privilege concept. This reduces the danger of needless exposure to sensitive data and systems by way of people and devices receiving just the minimal degree of access required to execute their activities.

Zero Trust model operations are painstakingly watched over and regulated to identify and react to possible hazards right away. Before allowing access to the network, endpoints—including computers, cellphones, and other linked hardware—must be sure they satisfy security criteria. The Zero Trust concept also spans hosting settings, including on-site data centers and cloud services, including These surroundings guarantee that the infrastructure supporting the activities of the company is safe by means of protection against illegal access and weaknesses.

Designed to enable Zero Trust ideas, the network architecture itself includes security mechanisms that dynamically change to fit the ongoing evaluation of trust. From individual devices to whole hosting environments, our all-encompassing strategy guarantees that every element is under constant security inspection. Zero Trust's overall objective is to follow the least privilege concept and allow access based just on a need-to-know basis. Users and devices are thus given just the access required to do their duties, nothing more. This reduces the possible effects of a security breach, as even if an assailant gets network access, their capacity to move laterally and take advantage of resources is much limited.

Zero trust calls for a change in how security is seen and controlled. Operating on the belief that internal entities are trustworthy, traditional models can depend on a robust perimeter to keep dangers out. This presumption has proved insufficient as cyber dangers have changed and grown more complex. By contrast, Zero Trust holds that threats might originate both within and outside of the network. Thus, independent of their source, it constantly confirms the validity of access requests.

Zero Trust's key tenet is the ongoing operation monitoring. Real-time study of network traffic, user activity, and device integrity is part of this to find any abnormalities suggesting a security risk. Maintaining high degrees of visibility in all network operations helps companies rapidly spot and reduce any hazards before they become major security events. In the digital terrain of today, where risks are always changing and growing more complex, this proactive attitude to security is very vital.

Furthermore, underlined by the Zero Trust concept is the need for endpoint security. These cover all of the devices—laptops, cellphones, tablets—that link to the network. Preventing such risks from getting a foothold depends on these endpoints satisfying strict security criteria before they are allowed access to the network. This procedure guarantees the device is free from infection, has current software, and has a security posture.

Zero Trust addresses safeguarding hosting infrastructures in addition to endpoints. Whether a company employs on-site data centers, cloud services, or a combination of both, these environments have to be kept safe from illegal access and vulnerabilities. To guarantee that the hosting infrastructure is safe, this entails putting strong security mechanisms such as encryption, multi-factor authentication, and frequent security audits into use.

Zero Trust's dynamic character calls for a network architecture able to change with ongoing trust evaluation. Security policies and controls have to be therefore adaptable to changing threat environments and flexible. Organizations may guarantee that their defenses stay strong and efficient even as threats change by putting a network architecture supporting these adaptive security measures into use.

By means of this exacting and flexible security approach, companies may better safeguard their vital resources in a digital terrain growing more complicated and dangerous. The Zero Trust method improves security as well as resilience against the always-changing terrain of cyber hazards. Organizations that constantly check access and give user, asset, and resource safety first priority will be able to confidently and resiliently negotiate the complexity of current cybersecurity issues.

Core Principles of Zero Trust: A Holistic Approach to Cybersecurity in a Dynamic Digital Era

Several fundamental ideas underlie Zero Trust and guide its approach to cybersecurity. Zero Trust is mostly based on the concept that, regardless of whether the company owns them or not, all data sources and computing tools are seen as resources. This all-encompassing perspective recognizes that security has to reach every potential endpoint and covers all tools and systems both inside and outside of the corporate boundaries

Zero Trust is fundamentally based on the need that every communication—from anywhere—be protected regardless of the network location. This idea questions the conventional wisdom that says staying inside a given network boundary suggests natural trust. Rather, every access request has to satisfy strict security criteria, therefore guaranteeing that confidence is not founded on simple network layout. This strategy deals with the fact that attacks might come from anywhere—inside and outside of the network.

Under Zero Trust, individual resource access is allowed each session. Trust is therefore constantly assessed prior to every session starting to guarantee that access is restricted to the least privilege required for the current work. Zero Trust lowers the danger of exploitation should an entity's credentials be compromised by dynamically assessing trust for every session, therefore preventing ongoing access. Minimizing the possible harm from any one breach depends on this exacting access control strategy.

Zero Trust is built on dynamic policy, which bases access on several criteria like client identification, the particular application or service sought, device condition, and other pertinent considerations. These policies change in real-time to fit the present environment, therefore improving security by customizing access limits to the particular situation of every demand. They are not fixed. Dynamic policy adaptation lets one create a more flexible and responsive security posture that can handle the fluid character of contemporary cyber threats.

A similar approach depends critically on constant asset monitoring. Every asset's integrity and security posture are under continual review to guarantee that any deviations or flaws are quickly found and fixed. This constant awareness keeps a strong security environment that can react to weaknesses and new risks. Advanced analytics and threat detection technologies are used in constant monitoring to offer real-time views of network activity and asset status.

Another aspect of Zero Trust is the rigorous use of authentication and permission. This entails the dynamic and continuous reevaluation of entities requesting access, adjusting to new information, and changing conditions to guarantee that only authorized users and devices are given access. Zero Trust guarantees that security is kept even if the operating environment changes by always confirming credentials and the validity of access requests.

At Zero Trust, thorough data collection is also absolutely vital. Companies compile a lot of data about the condition of their assets and network operations to help to constantly enhance security measures. This extensive data collection promotes proactive risk management and helps to clarify the security scene. Data trend and pattern analysis helps companies to foresee possible risks and implement preventative actions to guard their assets.

Zero Trust offers a rigorous and flexible framework for safeguarding organizational resources by following these ideas, therefore assuring that security is kept in an always-changing digital world. This architecture provides strong protection against the advanced and relentless attacks defining the current scene of cybersecurity. Zero Trust will remain crucial for protecting their key assets and keeping a safe operational environment as businesses negotiate the complexity of digital transformation.

Understanding NIST SP 800-207 and SP 800-207A: Foundations and Implementation of Zero Trust Architecture

NIST SP 800-207 and NIST SP 800-207A are both significant publications from the National Institute of Standards and Technology (NIST) that focus on Zero Trust Architecture (ZTA), but they serve different purposes and provide varying levels of detail regarding implementation.

NIST SP 800-207, titled "Zero Trust Architecture," is a foundational document published by the National Institute of Standards and Technology (NIST) that outlines the principles and practices of Zero Trust Security. This framework is designed to enhance cybersecurity by shifting from traditional perimeter-based security models to a more data-centric approach, where no entity is trusted by default.

Introduction to NIST SP 800-207

1. Core Principles: The document introduces several core principles of Zero Trust Architecture, including:

2. Components of Zero Trust: NIST SP 800-207 identifies critical components of a Zero Trust Architecture, which include:

3. Implementation Guidance: The publication provides a high-level overview of how organizations can implement Zero Trust principles within their existing IT infrastructure. It emphasizes the need for continuous monitoring, data protection, and robust identity management.

4. Use Cases: NIST SP 800-207 includes various use cases that illustrate how organizations can apply Zero Trust principles across different environments, particularly in sectors such as finance, healthcare, and government.

5. Regulatory Compliance: The framework aligns with regulatory requirements and best practices, making it particularly relevant for organizations that need to comply with standards such as FISMA (Federal Information Security Management Act).

NIST SP 800-207 serves as a crucial resource for organizations looking to adopt a Zero Trust approach to cybersecurity. By providing a structured framework that emphasizes continuous verification, least privilege access, and micro-segmentation, it helps organizations enhance their security posture in an increasingly complex threat landscape.

CHAPTER 13 NAVIGATING THE NEW NORMAL: REINVENTING TRADE FINANCE WITH BLOCKCHAIN,
            AI, AND IOT IN A ZERO-TRUST ERA

This publication is foundational for understanding how to effectively implement Zero Trust principles in various operational contexts. NIST SP 800-207A provides comprehensive guidelines for implementing Zero Trust Architecture (ZTA), particularly in cloud-native applications and multi-cloud environments. The key components of NIST SP 800-207A include:

Key Components of NIST SP 800-207A

1. Policy Engine (PE): The PE is responsible for making access decisions based on a continuous evaluation of trust levels. It integrates various data sources, such as behavioral analytics and threat intelligence, to assess whether to grant, deny, or revoke access to resources.

2. Policy Administrator (PA): The PA communicates the decisions made by the PE to the Policy Enforcement Point (PEP). It plays a crucial role in managing the policies that govern access controls and ensures that these policies align with organizational requirements.

3. Policy Enforcement Point (PEP): The PEP is the gateway that enforces access control decisions made by the PE. It intercepts access requests, authenticates users, and ensures that only those who meet the defined criteria can access resources.

4. Data Sources: These include threat intelligence feeds, security incident logs, and other relevant information that assists the PE in making informed access decisions. Data sources provide context that enhances the accuracy of trust assessments.

5. Continuous Monitoring: Ongoing surveillance of user behavior and system activities is essential to detect anomalies or potential threats. This component ensures that security measures adapt dynamically based on real-time data

6. Trust Algorithm: A systematic approach to evaluating trustworthiness based on observable behaviors and attributes from users and systems. This algorithm helps refine access policies and can adjust dynamically over time.

7. Micro-Segmentation: This involves dividing the network into smaller segments to limit lateral movement within the network, thereby reducing potential attack surfaces.

8. Identity and Access Management (IAM): Strong IAM practices are critical for verifying identities through methods like multi-factor authentication (MFA) and role-based access control (RBAC).

9. Automated Response Mechanisms: Automation of threat mitigation processes helps reduce complexity and human error in responding to security incidents.

These components collectively support organizations in establishing a robust Zero Trust framework, enhancing their ability to protect resources against evolving cybersecurity threats while maintaining compliance with regulatory standards

NIST SP 800-207 and NIST SP 800-207A both focus on Zero Trust Architecture (ZTA), but they differ in scope, detail, and specific guidance. Here are the main differences between the two publications:

Key Differences Between NIST SP 800-207 and NIST SP 800-207A

Aspect	NIST SP 800-207	NIST SP 800-207A
Purpose	Introduces the concept of Zero Trust Architecture and outlines its core principles	Provides detailed guidance for implementing ZTA, particularly in cloud-native applications and multi-cloud environments
Focus	General framework for ZTA applicable across various environments	Emphasizes practical implementation strategies for ZTA in specific contexts, such as service meshes and microservices
Implementation guidance	Offers foundational concepts without extensive implementation details	Includes systematic guidelines for organizations to adopt ZTA, focusing on application-level policies and runtime requirements
Contextual considerations	Discusses the need for a shift from perimeter-based security to a data-centric approach	Addresses contemporary challenges like remote work, cloud adoption, and compliance requirements in detail

(*continued*)

Aspect	NIST SP 800-207	NIST SP 800-207A
Trust assessment	Introduces the idea of trust but does not provide extensive methodologies for assessment	Elaborates on trust assessment mechanisms, detailing how organizations can evaluate the trustworthiness of users, devices, and applications
Use cases	Lacks specific real-world use cases or scenarios	Provides practical use cases demonstrating the application of ZTA principles in various environments
Technical components	Identifies core components of ZTA but with less technical depth	Delves into specific components like policy engines, administrators, and enforcement points with a focus on their roles in a Zero Trust model

While NIST SP 800-207 lays the groundwork for understanding Zero Trust Architecture, NIST SP 800-207A builds upon this foundation by offering comprehensive guidance tailored to modern cybersecurity challenges, especially in cloud-native environments. Organizations looking to implement Zero Trust principles will find NIST SP 800-207A to be a more practical resource with actionable insights and detailed methodologies.

A Zero Trust Perspective on Network Security: Core Assumptions and Strategies in Zero Trust Implementation

Adopting particular presumptions about network connections that drastically change conventional ideas of network security is necessary in implementing Zero Trust. Eliminating implicit trust zones is one of the fundamental ideas. Under a Zero Trust paradigm, every part of the corporate network runs under the presumption that an attacker is already there. This kind of thinking guarantees that every access request is closely examined, therefore removing any idea of a safe or trustworthy zone within the network. This change of viewpoint recognizes the reality of contemporary cyberthreats, whereby breaches may and do happen, usually from within the network itself.

The Zero Trust model's other crucial presumption is that the network contains non-enterprise-owned devices. This covers tools brought in by consumers following Bring Your Own Device (BYOD) rules. These gadgets are handled with the same degree of mistrust as any outside danger, as they are not under direct corporate control. These devices must have strict security mechanisms in order to access network resources and guarantee that they do not turn into security breach channels.

Zero Trust also requires constant assessment of asset security, so none of any device is naturally trusted. Regardless of its past security level, every gadget has to be constantly watched over and evaluated to make sure it meets security criteria both before and during network contact. This method guarantees that any security posture changes in the device are quickly identified and corrected, therefore preserving a high degree of security on every endpoint.

Zero Trust also recognizes that resources could run on infrastructure held outside of enterprises. This covers outside networks, including public Wi-Fi and cloud services, which the company has little direct control over. Security systems must thus change to safeguard data and resources even in cases of access or storage on these outside systems. In a world where mobile workers and cloud computing are the standard, this adaptability is very vital.

Zero Trust holds that local network connections should always be seen as hostile for remote users. Users operating from far-off sites have to encrypt all of their communications. perceive their local network as maybe infiltrated, and use robust security policies to protect data. In the age of remote work, when workers often connect to the corporate network from different places and devices, this idea is especially crucial.

Furthermore, essential in a zero-trust architecture is keeping a consistent security policy across several network contexts. Whether assets and processes are running over the corporate network, on outside networks, or across several settings, this consistency guarantees that they follow the same strict security postures. Applying a standard security policy helps businesses reduce risks and keep strong protection all around operations. This homogeneity guarantees that the defenses of the network are strong and helps to simplify the administration of security mechanisms.

Zero Trust presents a thorough and flexible method of network security by using these presumptions and methods. Zero Trust builds a strong security posture that can resist the complexity of contemporary cyber attacks by guaranteeing that every component and connection is always validated and shielded against any hazards. Focusing on the ongoing evaluation and verification of trust rather than depending on preset safe zones, this concept marks a major divergence from conventional security methods. The Zero Trust approach to network security offers a strong and efficient structure for safeguarding important assets and preserving the integrity of operations as businesses deal with ever more complex cyber threats.

The Core Components of Zero Trust Architecture: Building a Resilient Cybersecurity Framework

Comprising numerous fundamental logical components, Zero Trust Architecture (ZTA) may be applied either as on-site solutions or cloud-based services. ZTA is fundamentally based on the **Policy Engine (PE)**, which is absolutely vital in deciding whether access should be allowed. The PE makes these judgments by assessing enterprise policies in line with several outside inputs, therefore making sure that every access request fits the security criteria of the company and contextual background.

The **Policy Administrator (PA)** comes to complement the Policy Engine. Managing the communication channels inside the network and implementing the PE's decisions falls to the PA. It serves as the middleman, making sure policies are regularly followed and that the channels of communication in the network are correctly set to follow the security guidelines established by the PE.

The **Policy Enforcement Point (PEP)** forms ZTA's third crucial element. This component is in charge of observing and regulating the real communication between resources like data or services and topics, such as users or devices. The PEP guarantees that only permitted interactions take place and that any suspicious activity is quickly addressed by enforcing the access restrictions specified by the PE and PA.

Supporting these main elements are several more data sources that offer the required background and knowledge to implement policies successfully. Real-time information on the health and security state of network assets provided by constant diagnostic tools helps These instruments track the network environment constantly, spotting abnormalities and possible hazards, thereby offering a dynamic security posture that may change to fit newly developing dangers.

Systems of industry compliance guarantee that the company follows pertinent laws and norms. Maintaining the integrity of the security system depends on these systems, which also guarantee that all procedures and policies follow legal criteria and industry best standards. Compliance systems also point up security posture flaws and suggest changes to fit changing criteria.

CHAPTER 13 NAVIGATING THE NEW NORMAL: REINVENTING TRADE FINANCE WITH BLOCKCHAIN, AI, AND IOT IN A ZERO-TRUST ERA

Up-to-date information on possible hazards from threat intelligence feeds helps the ZTA components react to new dangers. Combining these inputs allows the policy engine and policy administrator to modify their choices and enforcement policies depending on the most current danger environment. This proactive strategy guarantees that the company is ready for possible future assaults in addition to responding to hazards.

Through comprehensive auditing and analysis made possible by precise records of all interactions and access requests maintained by activity logs, security measures may be constantly refined and improved. Post-incident analysis depends on these records, which enable security personnel to know how an incident happened and what steps should be taken to stop such events going forward. Maintaining thorough activity logs helps companies guarantee responsibility and openness in their security procedures.

Zero Trust Architecture produces a strong and flexible security architecture that constantly examines and enforces access limits by integrating these elements and data sources. This dynamic method guarantees the protection of organizational assets in an always-changing environment of threats. Modern cybersecurity depends on ZTA's flexibility and thorough coverage, as it can solve the difficult problems presented by the digital world of today.

It calls for a thorough awareness of the operating requirements of the company as well as its hazards. Organizations may create a strong security posture by using the Policy Engine's capabilities as well as ongoing diagnostics, compliance systems, threat intelligence, and activity logs—along with the Policy Administrator and Policy Enforcement Point. This all-encompassing strategy not only improves security but also fosters confidence inside the company by guaranteeing that every access request is closely examined and every possible risk is reasonably reduced.

Zero Trust Architecture is a major development in cybersecurity at last. Its focus on dynamic policy execution and ongoing verification offers a strong defense against contemporary cyberattacks. Understanding and using the fundamental elements of ZTA will help companies build a safe environment, safeguarding important assets and guaranteeing operational integrity in an ever more linked and complicated digital world.

CHAPTER 13   NAVIGATING THE NEW NORMAL: REINVENTING TRADE FINANCE WITH BLOCKCHAIN, AI, AND IOT IN A ZERO-TRUST ERA

Tailored Approaches for Enhanced Cybersecurity: Deployment Models to Implement ZTA

Several deployment strategies, each catered to distinct security requirements and operational settings, might help to implement Zero Trust Architecture (ZTA). These methods guarantee constant verification and control over access to resources, therefore giving companies flexible and strong ways to improve their security posture.

One method is device agent/gateway-based deployment. Under this paradigm, gateways stand in front of resources while agents are housed on devices. Before using any device, the agents on it make sure it follows security rules. This guarantees a first line of protection, as every gadget looking for access follows the security guidelines of the company. Gateways, in the meantime, govern and monitor the flow of data between resources and devices. By checking every access demand, these gateways strengthen security by establishing a regulated and under-observation data flow channel. When direct control of equipment is practical and desired, this paradigm is very successful.

Another paradigm emphasizing resource enclaves is enclave-based deployment. These enclaves are particular portions of the network housing important resources. The concept guarantees that only authorized traffic may enter by shielding these enclaves with gateways. This method generates a safe boundary around priceless objects, therefore stopping illegal access and lowering the possibility of lateral movement by possible network intrusions. Since it separates these important regions from the larger network, enclave-based deployment is particularly helpful for protecting sensitive data and systems that demand high degrees of security.

Subject searches are handled in resource portal-based deployment via a gateway portal. Scenarios involving Bring Your Own Device (BYOD) rules and inter-organizational cooperation call especially for this concept. Users authenticate and ask for access to resources at the gateway portal. Through centralizing access requests through this portal, the company may keep strict control over who accesses what, therefore guaranteeing security even in relation to outside or unmanaged equipment. For companies that have to oversee a wide range of devices and user scenarios and offer a flexible yet safe answer, this deployment strategy is perfect.

The Device Application The sandboxing approach runs programs on the device within safe areas, or sandboxes. This approach isolates apps from the host system, thereby preventing compromises. Should an application be hacked, the sandbox keeps the assailant off the more general system or network. This strategy especially helps to guard against harmful software and guarantees that programs execute in a safe and regulated environment. Separating programs helps companies reduce the effect of any one hacked program, hence improving general system security.

These deployment methods let companies customize their security strategy to fit their particular requirements and operating environments by providing flexible and strong ways for using Zero Trust Architecture. Every model improves security by guaranteeing constant control over access to resources, therefore providing a complete Zero Trust approach. These deployment models give the tools and frameworks required to keep a strong and flexible security posture while companies negotiate the complexity of contemporary cybersecurity.

Adopting one or more of these deployment models can help companies to properly use Zero Trust ideas, therefore producing a safe environment resistant to the changing threat scene. Every model—from device agents to secure enclaves to centralized gateways to application sandboxes—offers special benefits that add to a whole security strategy. By doing this, companies can make sure they stay alert, flexible, and safe against advanced cyberattacks.

Trust Algorithms: Ensuring Dynamic and Comprehensive Access Security

Zero Trust Architecture depends much on the trust algorithm, which carefully reviews access requests to guarantee they satisfy the required security criteria. Maintaining a strong security posture, this algorithm combines several inputs to make wise judgments on giving or refusing access.

The access request itself—which specifies who or what is seeking to access a certain resource—is a fundamental input for the trust algorithm. The program examines the characteristics of the individual making the request, including their identity, position inside the company, and any pertinent credentials. This careful review guarantees that the request comes from a reputable and authorized source, therefore complementing the security procedures of the company.

Apart from determining the topic, the trust algorithm examines the condition of the asset under access. This entails verifying if the device or system making the request conforms with the security policies of the company and is not hacked. The technique offers even another level of protection against any hazards by confirming the integrity and security state of the asking device.

The trust algorithm takes into account the needs of the resource under access as well. Various tools inside a company might have different degrees of sensitivity and particular security needs. The method guarantees that these criteria fit the credentials of the subject and present current security level. Through tighter management on more sensitive resources, this customized strategy helps safeguard important assets.

Still another important feature of the trust algorithm is including real-time threat intelligence. Integration of current data on possible hazards allows the algorithm to dynamically modify its estimate. By being proactive instead of reactive, this helps to maintain a high degree of security by allowing one to react to fresh knowledge and growing hazards. Maintaining strong security in a Zero Trust architecture depends on one being able to adjust to the changing threat scene.

Using several approaches, the trust algorithm can assess access requests. One technique is a criteria-based one whereby access is provided depending on particular requirements being satisfied. This strategy guarantees that only those fulfilling the strict requirements are granted access by defining specific criteria that a demand must satisfy.

Alternatively, the trust algorithm can use a score-based method, giving every demand a risk score depending on the several inputs. This score shows the general degree of risk connected to the request, therefore guiding or rejecting access depending on the total score. The score-based approach offers a flexible and dynamic evaluation procedure by evaluating several elements in whole, therefore giving a sophisticated assessment.

Moreover, the method may assess demands in context by considering the larger surroundings and scenario in which the demand is expressed. By means of this contextual evaluation, the algorithm may consider other aspects such as the time of access, location of the request, and previous activity patterns, thus offering a complete assessment. On the other hand, the method can evaluate requests single, concentrating just on the specifics of the particular request without regard for the larger background. Both methods have advantages and can be used to produce a fair and comprehensive assessment system.

These few techniques help the trust algorithm to guarantee a strong and flexible assessment mechanism. Maintaining security in a Zero Trust architecture—where every access request is carefully verified and validated—depends on this agility. Effective Zero Trust Architecture is mostly dependent on the trust algorithm's capacity to combine several inputs, dynamically react to threats, and use different assessment techniques.

The Zero Trust Architecture relies entirely on the trust algorithm. The method carefully examines access requests using a combination of identity verification, device status checks, resource sensitivity assessments, and real-time threat information, providing a comprehensive and flexible security solution. This extensive and dynamic assessment procedure guarantees that companies can keep a high degree of security, therefore safeguarding their assets in an always shifting terrain.

Building a Resilient Network for Zero Trust Architecture: Critical Components and Capabilities of Network Infrastructure

Effective support for Zero Trust Architecture (ZTA) depends on the network infrastructure, including numerous important characteristics and capabilities. Maintaining a strong security posture and guaranteeing closely regulated, tracked, and confirmed access to corporate resources depends on these components.

First, the network must obviously distinguish between assets held by the company and those not owned by it. This difference facilitates the use of suitable security protocols tailored to the degree of ownership and control of every asset. Differentiating between these two groups helps the network guarantee that non-enterprise-owned devices do not damage its security posture. This separation is essential as it enables the application of certain security methods for devices the company directly controls against those that are external or under user control, including those imported under Bring Your Own Device (BYOD) rules.

Monitoring all network activity is crucial for a zero-trust system. Complete monitoring guarantees that every data packet and communication flow is closely examined for any security risks. Constant observation of network activity helps the system identify abnormalities and react quickly to suspicious actions, therefore improving general security.

Early identification of any breaches and the capacity to respond before any major damage results from this continuous awareness enable one to prevent any major damage.

Another absolutely vital element of the network architecture is the division of control and data planes. While the data plane manages actual data packet transportation, the control plane is in charge of network administration tasks like policy enforcement and routing. Separating these two purposes helps the network have strong security and good performance. This separation ensures that control orders and vice versa do not disrupt data transmission, enabling more secure and seamless operations. It also clearly distinguishes management operations from data flow, therefore facilitating the enforcement of security standards and efficient network traffic management.

Enterprise resources should be available just through Policy Enforcement Points (PEPs) to provide safe channels of communication. PEPs monitor and manage access requests to corporate resources, essentially serving as gatekeepers. They guarantee that all communications follow the security regulations established by the company, therefore permitting only approved and validated exchanges. Through PEPs, the network may enforce a uniform security standard and keep tight control over who may access private resources by routing all access requests. Preventing illegal access and guaranteeing that only authenticated and authorized users and devices may interact with the network's important assets depends on this technique.

By using these elements, one guarantees that the network architecture can offer a strong and safe environment, enabling zero-trust architecture. This method guarantees strictly regulated, tracked, and confirmed access to business resources, therefore drastically lowering the possibility of illegal access and possible security breaches. These components, taken together, produce a tiered and all-encompassing security plan that handles the complexity of contemporary cyberthreats.

If the network architecture can distinguish between assets belonging to the enterprise and those not, track all network traffic, separate the control and data planes, and enforce secure communication channels through PEPs, it will be better equipped to support Zero Trust ideas. Maintaining strong security and operational integrity, this all-encompassing strategy helps companies adapt to the threat scene.

Strong security is built on the essential elements of network infrastructure for a zero-trust architecture. These characteristics will help companies establish a situation whereby access to resources is regularly checked, tracked, and under control. Supporting the general goals of Zero Trust Architecture, this approach not only improves security but also guarantees that the network stays robust and efficient in the face of developing hazards.

CHAPTER 13 NAVIGATING THE NEW NORMAL: REINVENTING TRADE FINANCE WITH BLOCKCHAIN, AI, AND IOT IN A ZERO-TRUST ERA

Adopting and Implementing Zero Trust Architecture: Core Principles, Strategies, and Cultural Transformation

Effective adoption of Zero Trust Architecture (ZTA) depends on a strong knowledge of its fundamental ideas and basic components. This technique marks a major change from conventional security models to one whereby confidence is never implicit and always subject to ongoing assessment. Through thorough and regular evaluation of trust levels, companies may apply strong access restrictions, limiting resource access to only approved entities.

Understanding Zero Trust's central tenet—never trust, always verify—helps one start this metamorphosis Zero Trust operates under the assumption that threats can originate from both within and outside the network, in contrast to conventional security models that often assume network entities are trustworthy by default. Every access request must thus be closely examined to guarantee that confidence is built depending on real-time evaluations instead of fixed credentials.

Businesses have to include constant monitoring and verification systems into their security architecture if they are to achieve this. This entails implementing cutting-edge tools and technology adept at real-time data analysis and threat detection. Constant evaluation of user, device, and network activity helps companies spot abnormalities and any hazards right away. Maintaining a strong security environment depends on this proactive attitude, as it enables a quick reaction to suspicious behavior before it may develop into major breaches.

Using a zero-trust architecture also depends critically on strict access restrictions. This calls for creating rules enforcing the least privilege concept, therefore giving users and devices just the minimal access required to carry out their activities. Real-time security assessments should dynamically change access privileges such that, should any possible danger be identified, permissions are either deleted or changed right away. This helps companies reduce the attack surface and control the possible harm from hacked devices or accounts.

Adopting Zero Trust also entails safeguarding every route of network communication. This involves encrypting data in transit and at rest, therefore guaranteeing that private information is safe even should hostile actors intercept it. Establishing safe channels of communication is important; policy enforcement points

(PEPs) serve as gatekeepers for tracking and regulating access demands. These PEPs guarantee that every contact follows the security regulations of the company, thereby enabling just-approved and authenticated communications.

Organizations also have to distinguish between non-enterprise-owned and enterprise-owned assets using suitable security policies depending on degrees of ownership and control. Given that personal devices often raise security concerns, this difference is especially crucial in settings where Bring Your Own Device (BYOD) rules are in effect. Companies may guarantee that non-enterprise-owned devices do not become weak points in their security posture by treating all devices with similar suspicion and submitting them to the same thorough security inspections.

Using a zero-trust architecture calls for a culture change inside the company. From senior executives to entry-level personnel, every employee—including Zero Trust's ideas—must know and welcome them. This covers continuous education and training to let everyone know about the newest security techniques and the need to follow them. Zero Trust cannot be properly implemented without a security-aware culture, as human error is still one of the most important weaknesses in any security system.

Organizations may significantly improve their cybersecurity posture by carefully and regularly evaluating trust levels, applying strict access restrictions, and encouraging a culture of security awareness. Strong access control systems and ongoing trust assessment guard important resources from a variety of developing hazards. This dynamic method guarantees constantly current, flexible security solutions that can react to new and developing hazards. Businesses may therefore protect their most significant assets, thereby guaranteeing the integrity and security of their operations in a digital terrain growing in complexity and hazards.

Key Aspects of Zero Trust Security in Trade Finance

1. Continuous Verification: In trade finance, every transaction and access request must be continuously verified. This means that even if a user or system is within the network, their actions should be authenticated based on real-time risk assessments and contextual factors such as location and device security status.

2. Micro-Segmentation: Implementing micro-segmentation allows financial institutions to divide their networks into smaller, more secure segments. This limits the ability of an attacker to move

laterally within the network after breaching one segment, thereby protecting sensitive financial data and transaction processes from unauthorized access.

3. Identity and Access Management (IAM): Strong IAM practices are critical in trade finance to ensure that only authorized personnel can access sensitive information. This includes using multi-factor authentication (MFA) and dynamic access controls that adjust based on user behavior and transaction context.

4. Data Protection: Zero Trust emphasizes protecting data at all stages of its lifecycle. In trade finance, this involves encrypting sensitive data both in transit and at rest, ensuring that even if data is intercepted, it remains secure.

5. Real-Time Monitoring and Analytics: Continuous monitoring of transactions and user activities helps detect anomalies that could indicate fraud or cyber threats. Advanced analytics can identify patterns that may suggest unauthorized access or other security issues.

6. Collaboration with Third Parties: Trade finance often involves multiple stakeholders, including banks, importers, exporters, and logistics providers. Zero Trust principles ensure that all third-party interactions are secure by requiring verification for every access request made by external partners.

7. Regulatory Compliance: Financial institutions must comply with various regulations governing data protection and privacy. A Zero Trust framework can help meet these compliance requirements by ensuring strict access controls and detailed audit trails of all transactions.

Adopting Zero Trust Security in trade finance allows organizations to enhance their cybersecurity posture significantly. By implementing continuous verification, micro-segmentation, robust IAM practices, and real-time monitoring, financial institutions can better protect against evolving cyber threats while ensuring the integrity of their trade transactions. This proactive approach not only safeguards sensitive information but also builds trust among stakeholders involved in international trade operations.

CHAPTER 13   NAVIGATING THE NEW NORMAL: REINVENTING TRADE FINANCE WITH BLOCKCHAIN, AI, AND IOT IN A ZERO-TRUST ERA

The co-existence of blockchain, artificial intelligence (AI), and the Internet of things (IoT) within a Zero Trust environment in trade finance creates a robust framework for enhancing security, efficiency, and transparency. Each technology contributes uniquely to addressing the complexities and challenges faced in the trade finance sector, particularly in combating fraud and ensuring compliance.

Co-existence of Blockchain, AI, and IoT in a Zero Trust Environment in Trade Finance

1. Zero Trust Principles

- Never Trust, Always Verify: In trade finance, every transaction and access request must be authenticated and authorized, regardless of whether it originates from within or outside the organization. This principle is critical for protecting sensitive financial data and preventing unauthorized access.

- Least Privilege Access: Access to trade finance systems is restricted to only those individuals or devices that require it for their roles, minimizing potential attack surfaces.

2. Blockchain for Security and Transparency

- Immutable Records: Blockchain provides a decentralized ledger that ensures all transactions are recorded immutably. This transparency is crucial in trade finance, where multiple parties (e.g., banks, exporters, importers) need to verify transaction authenticity without relying on a central authority.

- Smart Contracts: These self-executing contracts with the terms directly written into code can automate processes such as payment releases upon fulfillment of certain conditions. This reduces the risk of fraud and enhances trust among parties involved in trade transactions.

3. AI for Anomaly Detection and Predictive Analytics

- Fraud Detection: AI algorithms can analyze transaction patterns in real-time to identify anomalies indicative of fraudulent activities. For instance, AI can flag transactions that deviate significantly from historical patterns or expected pricing structures, which is critical in detecting trade-based financial crimes (TBFC).

- Predictive Analytics: By assessing historical data, AI can predict potential risks associated with specific transactions or trading partners, allowing financial institutions to proactively address threats before they materialize.

4. IoT As a Data Source

- Real-Time Data Collection: IoT devices can gather real-time data related to shipments, inventory levels, and environmental conditions (e.g., temperature for perishable goods). This data is essential for ensuring compliance with trade regulations and verifying that goods are as described in transactions.

- Enhanced Monitoring: IoT sensors can monitor logistics and supply chains continuously, providing insights that help organizations make informed decisions based on current conditions rather than outdated information.

5. Synergistic Benefits

- The integration of these technologies creates a synergistic effect: Blockchain enhances IoT security

6. Use Cases in Trade Finance

- Automated Compliance Checks: Using AI combined with blockchain allows for automated checks against sanctions lists and regulatory requirements based on real-time data from IoT devices.

- Supply Chain Transparency: Blockchain provides an immutable record of all transactions along the supply chain, while IoT devices track the movement and condition of goods. This transparency helps prevent fraud and ensures compliance with trade regulations.

Re-imagining trade finance innovation with the co-existence of Blockchain, AI, and IoT within a Zero Trust environment significantly enhances the security and efficiency of trade finance operations. By leveraging these technologies together, organizations can effectively combat fraud, ensure compliance with regulatory requirements, and build trust among trading partners. This integrated approach not only addresses current challenges but also positions organizations to adapt to future developments in the rapidly evolving landscape of global trade finance.

Summary

This chapter investigates how these technologies are changing trade finance within their zero-trust framework. Emphasizing the crucial relevance of data privacy, ownership, and compliance, the chapter investigates the complex ecology of global trade. From data collection to feature engineering and model training, blockchain's ability to improve data provenance, safe sharing, and access control guarantees GDPR compliance across AI model development workflows. Along with approaches for on-chain and off-chain data management to strike transparency and efficiency, permissioned and permissionless blockchains are contrasted.

The book also explores in a zero-trust setting the synergy of blockchain, artificial intelligence, and IoT. Blockchain guarantees security and openness; artificial intelligence finds anomalies and uses predictive analytics; and IoT provides a wealth of data for use. Through Zero Trust Architecture (ZTA), they provide transforming advantages like better data markets, incentive systems, and strong network security taken all together. Illustrating how their confluence may transform operational resilience, compliance, and creativity in an era defined by trust reduction and increased cybersecurity norms, the chapter offers a road map for using these technologies in trade finance.

CHAPTER 14

Credit Revolution: The Tokenization Tidal Wave in Global Trade

Few inventions in economic history have changed the face of international trade as dramatically as tokenization. As we approach a new age, the tokenization-driven "Credit Revolution" is not just a trend but a tsunami that is altering commerce and finance fundamentally across sectors and regions. This chapter delves into how digital tokens are transforming credit systems and fostering a global commerce environment that is more open, safe, and accessible.

Though not totally novel, the idea of tokenization has become much more popular recently as a result of blockchain technological breakthroughs. Trade of a vast range of assets across borders is made simple for companies and people by transforming tangible and intangible assets into digital tokens. This technical breakthrough is supposed to reduce the dangers usually connected to international commerce, simplify intricate trade procedures, and democratize access to cash. Tokenization is basically ready to break down established obstacles and promote a more inclusive world economy.

Fundamental to this change is the capacity to tokenize credit. Often enmeshed in inefficiency and bureaucracy, traditional lending systems are changing. Transparency and confidence between trade partners are increased in addition to transaction speed via tokenized credit. Decentralized ledgers and smart contracts reduce the need for middlemen, which lowers expenses and possible failure sites. Tokenized credit allows companies of all sizes to seize fresh chances and propel expansion in a worldwide industry that is getting more competitive.

The tokenization tide has many different and wide ramifications. Every level of the economy benefits from improving supply chain efficiency and giving small and medium-sized companies (SMEs) easier access to finance. The complexities of tokenized credit will be explored in this chapter, along with its revolutionary effects on international commerce, difficulties, and bright future. The convergence of the financial and digital worlds has led to the Credit Revolution, a new paradigm in international trade.

Public Blockchains and Asset Tokenization: Transforming Finance with Liquidity, Transparency, and Accessibility

Public blockchains and asset tokenization are causing a profound upheaval in the financial industry. As it promises to improve liquidity, openness, and efficiency across many industries, this revolution is changing the way assets are generated, maintained, and transferred.

Recall that public blockchains include Bitcoin and Ethereum. These decentralized networks enable direct transactions between people, therefore eliminating middlemen like banks and other financial institutions. Because the system is decentralized, users are assured autonomy, security, and transparency.

The Ethereum blockchain is one that sticks out especially. This blockchain is noteworthy for integrating smart contracts in addition to transactional features. A self-executing contract is one kind of contract in which the terms of the agreement are written down in code directly. This feature has made a large range of decentralized application (dApp) chances available, which has made Ethereum a platform that is dynamic and diversified inside the blockchain ecosystem.

The idea of tokenization is fundamentally changing the blockchain environment. In this procedure, one essential step is to convert assets into digital tokens that may be traded on a blockchain. These tokens stand for ownership of a particular asset, which may be anything from stocks to real estate to even arts and crafts. Tokenization removes these barriers, therefore democratizing access to investing options, which have hitherto been limited to wealthy people or organizations. By using tokenization, people may own portions of valuable assets, which broadens the range of investment options.

The public blockchains, like Ethereum and Bitcoin, provide the foundation of the tokenization method. By using tokenization, which leverages the security and transparency provided by blockchains, both asset ownership and transfer are ensured to be safe and verifiable. This technological advancement is changing the asset management scene by offering new avenues and methods for concurrent asset management and transfer.

Tokenization Milestone: The Transformational Power Revolutionizing Asset Management and Trade Across Industries

One important milestone has been attained in tokenization, the act of producing a distinct digital representation of an item on a blockchain. Blockchain-capable financial institutions will profit substantially from new revenue streams, better liquidity, and operational efficiency.

Transactions are accelerated and expenses are lowered via tokenization, which also makes real-time settlement possible. Moreover, because blockchain's immutable ledger guarantees correct record-keeping, it improves security and transparency. Though still in its infancy, this technology has the potential to completely transform the financial services sector by opening up new markets and democratizing investor access. Beyond banking, it has promise in industries like supply chain management, healthcare, and real estate, suggesting a day when assets are handled and sold digitally. The broad effects of tokenization will probably completely reinterpret the principles of asset management and trade as organizations use and improve blockchain technologies.

The Foundations and Advantages of Tokenization: Redefining Asset Ownership and Transactions in the Digital Era

Tokenization involves creating a distinct digital representation of an asset on a blockchain, producing tokens that represent a wide array of assets—intangible (e.g., intellectual property), financial (e.g., stocks and bonds), or tangible (e.g., commodities). This process has emerged as a modern alternative to traditional systems, offering significant advantages.

One primary benefit is greater efficiency. Traditional systems often involve lengthy processes, intermediaries, and manual reconciliation, increasing the risk of errors. Blockchain-powered tokenization eliminates intermediaries, enabling near-instant transactions with secure, transparent, and immutable recording through decentralized ledger technology.

Tokenization also enhances interoperability, as tokens interact seamlessly with other digital assets and applications in the blockchain ecosystem. This enables the creation of innovative financial solutions, such as fractional ownership and liquidity mechanisms, often utilized in decentralized finance (DeFi).

Perhaps the most groundbreaking aspect is programmability, achieved through smart contracts embedded within tokens. These self-executing contracts automate complex processes such as compliance checks, conditional ownership transfers, and automated payments, reducing fraud risks and ensuring reliable execution. Fractional ownership further democratizes investment, allowing access to high-value assets at lower entry barriers, while 24/7 trading on blockchain-based exchanges enhances liquidity and global investor participation.

Despite challenges like regulatory hurdles and technological integration, tokenization continues to gain traction, offering efficiency, trust, and transparency. Its applications span beyond financial institutions, enabling real-time data accuracy, reduced administrative work, and enhanced transaction speed.

The Path to Adoption and Overcoming Challenges to Unlock Liquidity and Innovation in the Financial Ecosystem

Tokenization's adoption is unfolding in waves, driven by factors like market inefficiencies, regulatory clarity, and technological complexity. Early adoption focuses on high-value assets like real estate, venture capital, and private equity, where tokenization promises improved liquidity, reduced costs, and greater transparency. As frameworks evolve, traditional asset classes like bonds and loans will follow, with tokenized markets expected to surpass $2 trillion in capitalization by 2030.

CHAPTER 14   CREDIT REVOLUTION: THE TOKENIZATION TIDAL WAVE IN GLOBAL TRADE

Key to this transition is collaboration and interoperability. Industry consortia and standardization efforts can help align tokenization practices, while the development of scalable, interoperable blockchain systems will foster seamless integration. Strategic pilot projects and partnerships can demonstrate the viability of tokenization, addressing concerns like the "cold start" issue, where low liquidity hampers initial adoption.

Success also depends on regulatory clarity. Governments must establish supportive frameworks that balance innovation and investor protection. Financial institutions can play a pivotal role by engaging with regulators, investing in advanced blockchain technology, and offering tokenized solutions tailored to customer needs.

Tokenization's future lies in overcoming obstacles like market liquidity, technical integration, and regulatory inconsistencies. Strategic alliances, MVVCs (Minimum Viable Value Chains), and proactive education campaigns will drive adoption, ensuring tokenization fulfills its potential to create a more inclusive, efficient, and innovative financial ecosystem.

Revolutionizing Asset Ownership, Liquidity, and Investment Accessibility: The Mechanics and Value Creation Through Tokenization

Making tangible or digital assets into blockchain-recorded tokens is known as tokenization. Because each token is a portion of the asset, trade and ownership options are increased. Through the simple transfer and trading of the assets on the blockchain, this novel method offers a degree of liquidiy that is sometimes unachievable with conventional asset formats.

By dividing an asset into smaller, easier-to-manage pieces, tokenization democratizes investor access. An investor may, for instance, acquire tokens that reflect a percentage of the property's worth rather than having to buy the whole thing. Thanks to this fractional ownership concept, more people can now invest in high-value assets that were previously out of their reach.

Tokenization also makes normally illiquid assets far more liquid. On the blockchain, assets like real estate, art, or collectibles may be swapped more easily than they usually take to sell and turn into cash. The ease with which asset owners can exchange their tokens for other assets or currencies makes the market more liquid.

CHAPTER 14   CREDIT REVOLUTION: THE TOKENIZATION TIDAL WAVE IN GLOBAL TRADE

Tokenization has several strong benefits, chief among them being greater security and transparency. Because blockchain technology uses cryptographic concepts and is decentralized, it is, by nature, secure. The blockchain, which creates an immutable ledger that anyone can view and confirm, records every transaction, including those involving tokenized assets. This openness guarantees that all participants have a precise and unambiguous record of ownership and transaction history, therefore preventing fraud.

Moreover, once records are included in the blockchain, they cannot be changed since tokenization uses blockchain technology. Since it ensures that the information captured is permanent and unchangeable, this immutability offers a better degree of security and confidence. Tokenization thereby improves asset trading efficiency and also increases security and dependability.

Tokenization transforms physical and digital assets into blockchain-based tokens, which also increase liquidity and permit fractional ownership. Through this procedure, people may more easily participate in high-value assets as access to investment possibilities is democratized. Blockchain technology also guarantees more security and openness, offering a reliable and effective platform for trade and asset management. Tokenization has several enticing benefits, especially in relation to liquidity possibilities. Suppose you could split up massive, often hard-to-sell assets into smaller, tradeable tokens. This approach dramatically simplifies for investors the process of acquiring and selling fractional ownership, which greatly boosts market liquidity. The market therefore becomes more lively and approachable, just as when a big, hard-to-sell property is divided into smaller, easier-to-transfer pieces.

The fact that blockchain technology provides both security and openness is still another important advantage. Blockchain is an immutable ledger, that is, every transaction is documented and cannot be altered after it has been recorded. This function greatly lessens the possibility of fraudulent conduct by guaranteeing that all transactions are safe and visible. Because blockchain technology is safe and transparent, it offers a trustworthy platform for investment management.

A key benefit of tokenization is its economy. Tokenization speeds up money transfers and lowers transaction costs by doing away with middlemen. Stated differently, you may see it as streamlining and cutting costs associated with a once-complex and costly process. This effectiveness not only saves money but also time, which makes dealings and investments much more efficient. Tokenization, generally speaking, is a very attractive substitute for modern investors since it increases liquidity, ensures security and transparency, and encourages economies of scale. All these elements help to change the investing climate.

Tokenization in Financial Services: A Paradigm Shift

Institutions always seek fresh and creative ways to increase productivity, save expenses, and create new revenue streams in the fast-paced financial market of today. Modern banking is dynamic; hence, solutions that can keep up with its rapid changes and growing complexity are needed. Based on blockchain technology, tokenization has the ability to completely change how assets are managed and transactions are completed. Currently offered, it is among the most technologically sophisticated alternatives.

Tokenization: The Transformative Power of Tokenization in Asset Management

Tokenization transforms tangible and financial assets—such as real estate, stocks, bonds, and art—into digital tokens on a blockchain. This process digitizes asset ownership, enabling seamless transactions across decentralized platforms. Blockchain's immutable and decentralized nature ensures secure, efficient, and transparent asset exchanges.

Tokenization simplifies complex asset management by eliminating intermediaries and automating processes with smart contracts. This reduces transaction costs and risks, streamlines operations, and provides traceability. A significant advantage is the introduction of fractional ownership, allowing investors to trade small portions of high-value assets, increasing liquidity, and democratizing access to previously exclusive markets.

The financial landscape benefits greatly from tokenization by enabling efficient, low-cost transfers, enhancing operational agility, and reducing time-consuming manual tasks. Tokenized assets can serve as collateral, improving liquidity and enabling innovative financial solutions. Smart contracts further automate compliance checks, payments, and ownership transfers, fostering a secure and reliable ecosystem.

Financial institutions adopting tokenization can access new revenue streams, streamline operations, and innovate their offerings. This paradigm shift bridges traditional and digital finance, unlocking new markets and enhancing global financial inclusion.

Overcoming Challenges to Unlock a Dynamic and Inclusive Future: Strategic Adoption and Future of Tokenization

Tokenization's integration into financial systems offers immense opportunities but requires strategic planning to address challenges such as interoperability, regulatory clarity, and stakeholder inclusion. Collaboration efforts among institutions, regulators, and digital innovators are crucial for developing robust frameworks and fostering market confidence.

The widespread adoption of tokenization depends on harmonized regulations that balance innovation and investor protection. Institutions must engage proactively with regulators to establish transparent guidelines and ensure compliance. Interoperable blockchain systems will facilitate seamless asset exchanges, fostering a connected and efficient financial ecosystem.

Tokenization enables financial institutions to create programmable money, automating complex operations and reducing manual oversight. This enhances risk management, transparency, and trust. Institutions leveraging tokenization can streamline processes, enhance liquidity, and expand their market reach while offering clients innovative financial products.

By addressing technical, cultural, and security challenges, institutions can position themselves as leaders in the evolving financial landscape. Tokenization represents a transformative force, promising increased automation, accessibility, and efficiency. Its integration into financial systems paves the way for a dynamic and inclusive financial future, revolutionizing asset management and transactions on a global scale.

The Digital Renaissance of Promissory Notes and Bills of Exchange

Blockchain technology has been essential to the noteworthy digital transformation that has been taking place in trade finance over the last several years. One of the more exciting advancements in financial technology is the tokenization of bills of exchange and promissory notes. This innovative approach, which may revolutionize trade processes, may lead to the streamlining of operations, the enhancement of security, and the opening of new opportunities for companies everywhere.

Here, tokenization is the act of converting bills of trade and promissory notes into secure digital tokens for handling and trading on a blockchain. This digital representation of conventional financial instruments makes trade transactions possible to conduct more transparently and efficiently. Benefiting from the irreversible character of blockchain technology, tokenization ensures that all transactions are precisely recorded and cannot be changed. Security improves, and the possibility of fraudulent behavior falls.

Trade finance is currently digitalized to a degree that reflects the growing trend of adopting technical advancements. Historically, inefficiencies, protracted paperwork, and the need for several middlemen have often impeded trade finance operations. Conversely, tokenization and blockchain technologies are making these processes more straightforward. Businesses are embracing digital platforms more and more because they make transactions easier and more affordable, which ultimately improves the company's operational effectiveness as a whole.

The simplicity with which tokenized bills of exchange and promissory notes may be traded on digital platforms suggests that this will boost the liquidity of any company. This increased liquidity offers the possibility of better money access and more adaptable financing options. Moreover, the transparency that blockchain technology provides might support the growth of greater confidence among trading partners. This is so because there is just one unchangeable transaction record available to all participants.

Nevertheless, before tokenization in trade finance can fully materialize, a number of challenges must be resolved. One big challenge that has to be solved is the need for regulatory frameworks that can supervise and enable the use of digital tokens in commercial transactions. To be accepted widely, it is important to comply with the current financial regulations and to adapt to the new technological specifications at the same time. Furthermore, for transactions to be carried out uninterruptedly across the several networks, there is a need for more interoperability across the different blockchain platforms.

Overcoming the internal corporate and cultural resistance to change is another challenge. Companies that have been using outdated processes for many years might be hesitant to switch to new digital ones because of the possibility of disruption. Driven uptake and usage of the technology will require addressing these concerns through education and proving the genuine advantages of tokenization.

Finally, the use of blockchain technology in trade finance is enabling more open, secure, and efficient trade processes. One very fascinating trend that offers businesses worldwide a plethora of benefits and opportunities is the tokenization of promissory notes and bills of exchange. Still, overcoming the obstacles presented by legal limitations, technological interoperability, and cultural resistance is essential to fully utilizing the promise of this innovation. Tokenization is expected to be crucial in determining how trade finance develops in the future and creating new opportunities for international commerce. This is so because trade finance is still evolving.

Tokenizing Trade Finance: Transforming Promissory Notes and Bills of Exchange in the Digital Era

Promissory notes and bills of exchange are two examples of trade finance instruments whose digitization is gaining traction and represents a dramatic change in the administration and use of these conventional tools. Numerous blockchain-based platforms and consortia created to make tokenization and smooth administration of these instruments easier are driving this change. Utilizing the built-in benefits of blockchain technology, these cutting-edge platforms improve the effectiveness, security, and openness of trade finance activities.

Leading this digital transformation are financial institutions, which comprise both banks and fintech startups. Their operating frameworks are being actively investigated and integrated with tokenized promissory notes and bills of exchange. The institutions' ability to use blockchain technology to improve trade transaction efficiency generally, streamline their processes, and reduce operating costs is clearly what drives the integration.

Traditionally seen as the guardians of trade finance, banks are realizing that tokenization has the power to completely transform their offerings. They may provide their customers faster and safer transaction choices by transforming actual promissory notes and bills of exchange into digital tokens. This improves the client experience and establishes banks as front-runners in the use of state-of-the-art financial technology.

Fintech firms, recognized for their adaptability and ingenuity, are seizing the opportunity to introduce innovative concepts in the trade finance sector. They are working on cutting-edge blockchain-based systems that make tokenized trade finance instruments easier to issue, transfer, and settle. Because of their intuitive and incredibly effective design, these platforms enable companies of all sizes to engage in international commerce more easily and confidently.

Thanks to the collaboration of fintech entrepreneurs and traditional financial institutions, trade finance is becoming more digital. Because they blend the technological expertise of fintech firms with the skills of existing banks, these alliances are essential. Working together, they are developing all-inclusive solutions that make use of blockchain technology to solve the challenges associated with trade financing.

The impetus behind this change is increasing as more financial institutions and companies accept the digitization of trade finance instruments. More than simply a technical improvement, the combination of tokenized promissory notes and bills of exchange signals a fundamental transformation in the way trade finance functions. Through improving these instruments' efficiency, security, and transparency, digitalization is creating a more dynamic and approachable global trade environment.

The work of fintech firms, financial institutions, and blockchain-based platforms is accelerating the digitization of trade finance instruments such as bills of exchange and promissory notes. This current change is expected to completely change the trade finance scene and provide previously unheard-of advantages and chances for companies all across the world. A more secure, efficient, and inclusive global trading system should develop as tokenized trade finance instruments become more widely used.

Tokenization in Trade Finance: Unlocking a New Era of Efficiency, Security, and Collaboration

Tokenization in trade finance has expanded remarkably, which can be attributed to the need to tighten security and increase efficiency in addition to modernizing and streamlining existing procedures. Trade finance is improving in flexibility, openness, and security as a consequence of a community effort to make use of digital transformation. Our joint efforts are what are propelling this advancement.

The present state of tokenization in the trade finance sector is being defined by several proof-of-concept tests and pilot programs. Many financial institutions, trade finance companies, and technological vendors are now looking at the feasibility of tokenizing trade finance products. Promissory note digitization, bills of trade digitization, and credit letter digitization are common instances of the use cases on which these initiatives usually focus. The implementation of these pilot projects might help stakeholders better grasp the practical applications of tokenization and identify potential challenges and opportunities.

An important development is the creation of several blockchain-based platforms and consortia, which has greatly aided in the tokenization of trade finance instruments. By using these platforms, tokenized assets will be created, traded, and agreements resolved utilizing standardized protocols and frameworks. By means of the creation of these standards, we hope to ensure that tokenized trade finance products are secure, easily marketable, and interoperable over a range of networks and systems.

Working together, more and more individuals are in the trade finance industry. Financial institutions, fintech companies, and trade finance organizations are collaborating more and more to create common standards and interoperability for tokenized assets. Entering into these alliances is essential to resolving some of the adoption-related problems. These partnerships pool a multitude of talents and resources to create more complete and strong solutions.

Furthermore, there is a shift in the regulatory framework around tokenized trade finance instruments. Although certain governments have already made the effort to provide legal certainty for digital assets, others are currently working on legislation that is appropriate for the circumstances. Noteworthy is the fact that the legal framework is a major factor that might support or oppose tokenization. Clear and beneficial policies can help establish trust and motivate more individuals to use this technology.

Trade finance tokenization still has a significant barrier in the form of interoperability issues. Systems may find it challenging to connect with one another smoothly if several blockchain platforms use distinct protocols. Building industry-wide standards and protocols is being done in an effort to address these interoperability issues and make transactions flow more easily across a range of computer systems.

With the trade finance business going more and more digital, security and cybersecurity issues are crucial. All participants should make it their top priority to safeguard tokenized assets and transactions from cyber threats and attacks. Robust security solutions and best practices are currently being thought about and developed in order to reduce risks and guarantee that the digital trade finance ecosystem stays reliable and safe.

Integration of recently created digital processes with existing legacy systems is an even more challenging undertaking. Both trade finance companies and conventional financial institutions often employ legacy systems. The conversion of these systems to tokenization is difficult. The time-consuming and intricate nature of this integration procedure can cause tokenization to be adopted slowly rather than immediately. Conversely, it is expected that the use of tokenized solutions will accelerate as long-standing companies keep upgrading their infrastructure.

CHAPTER 14 CREDIT REVOLUTION: THE TOKENIZATION TIDAL WAVE IN GLOBAL TRADE

The use of tokenization is growing to include a broad spectrum of trade finance applications. Among these uses are international trade, invoice factoring, trade credit insurance, and supply chain finance. Many times, the unique needs and goals of the people participating in the trading ecosystem dictate which use case is chosen. The numerous examples shown here illustrate the flexibility and potential of tokenization to manage a range of trade finance issues.

Even though the possible advantages of tokenization in trade finance are becoming more well known, many parties still need guidance and support in negotiating in this always shifting environment. Encouragement of increased usage requires educational initiatives and programs targeted at knowledge exchange. The sharing of information and understanding can help stakeholders make well-informed decisions and effectively use tokenization to enhance their trade finance activities.

Even though trade finance tokenization is still in its infancy, it has enormous potential to transform the industry. Tokenization in trade finance, then, seems rather promising. Pilot project execution, industry collaboration, and regulatory improvements are the means of preparing for broad adoption. We may expect that the tokenization of trade finance instruments will keep growing and evolving as long as security and interoperability concerns are resolved and regulatory frameworks are more detailed. It is exciting to watch as it develops and transforms conventional trade finance management strategies, ushering in a new era of opportunity, safety, and improved production.

Tokenization in Trade Finance: The Promise and the Challenges in Transforming Trade Finance

The tokenization of trade finance instruments offers a multitude of opportunities that might totally transform the sector. The higher efficiency that tokenization offers is among the most persuasive of the numerous strong benefits. Transaction settlements are greatly accelerated by tokenization, which also reduces the number of errors and generates significant cost savings. Reducing the requirement for paper-based procedures and human record-keeping helps to achieve this. The reduction of processing times is a particularly helpful advantage of digital transactions in the fast-paced world of trade finance.

An additional major benefit of blockchain technology is its improved transparency. As an unchangeable record, the blockchain ensures that all participants in a transaction have an open and transparent understanding of its past. Every transaction is documented and verifiable; hence, this level of transparency reduces the possibility of disagreements and fraudulent conduct. Because the blockchain is reliable, it fosters more confidence among trading partners, which facilitates and even increases the security of transactions.

The application of tokenization also raises the accessibility of the trade finance sector. Tokenization opens up a greater range of players to trade financial instruments by reducing the entrance barriers. This covers lesser businesses that could have been left out in the past. Increased economic activity and fresh opportunities for smaller companies to engage in global trade may result from this democratization of access.

One other benefit of tokenization is the capacity to boost liquidity and fractionalize assets. Fractional ownership of assets made possible by tokenization boosts liquidity and creates new investment possibilities. Additionally, there are fresh investment prospects generated. Investors' market engagement and flexibility can be increased by the capacity to purchase and sell smaller pieces of larger assets. A particular application for this ability may be in markets where liquidity has historically been an issue.

International commerce may also greatly benefit from the tokenization of transactions. By removing regulatory barriers and facilitating quicker and more effective cross-border transactions, tokenization may make international transaction processes easier. Because of the complexity of foreign transactions, this may be challenging work. The ease with which businesses will be able to do international business as a result will greatly boost world trade.

It is not without challenges, nevertheless, to get to broad tokenization in trade finance.

Financial product tokenization has to follow a plethora of national and international regulations, which might differ drastically from one country to another. This makes regulatory compliance quite difficult. Requiring cooperation from regulators and industry participants, achieving regulatory clarity and sustaining compliance is a challenging and ongoing process.

The problem of interoperability presents yet another major challenge. It is conceivable that many blockchain systems are incompatible with one another, which might cause issues with transaction execution and perfectly seamless communication. Despite ongoing efforts to standardize protocols and frameworks, achieving complete interoperability remains a challenge.

Safety concerns are also important. The digital aspect of tokenized assets may pose cyberattacks and threats even if blockchain technology is inherently secure. Strict security measures must be put in place to protect these assets and guarantee that honest transactions continue.

Adopting requires overcoming certain challenges. Given the major modifications required in the processes and systems now in place, convincing traditional financial institutions to adopt tokenization may prove difficult. Both resistance to change and the inertia of current habits may slow down the rate of adoption.

The best uses for the tokenization of bills of exchange and promissory notes are immediately obvious in a range of trade finance situations. Through the representation of invoices and payments as digital tokens, tokenization may improve supply chain financial efficiency. This makes the financing of the supply chain possible and more efficient. This may increase cash transaction efficiency and traceability internally within the supply chain.

Tokenization has the ability to improve insurance processes for trade credit insurance, ensuring that all stakeholders have access to accurate and current information. In that way, the possibility of disputes can be reduced, and confidence between covered parties and insurers can be raised.

By digitizing and simplifying a range of trade finance instruments, tokenization makes it possible to finish international transactions faster and more effectively. Companies that follow this stand a greater chance of conquering the difficulties associated with foreign trade and entering new markets.

The fascinating discovery of tokenizing bills of exchange and promissory notes may revolutionize the trade finance sector. Even though there has been a great deal of advancement, adoption, interoperability, and regulation remain unanswered. As trade finance digitizes more, those businesses that embrace tokenization have the chance to increase productivity, reduce risks, and establish themselves as leaders in the industry. This fast-expanding area is predicted to have a fascinating and revolutionary future with plenty of opportunities for growth and innovation.

Tokenization of Letters of Credit: A New Era in Trade Finance

Particularly with regard to the tokenization of letters of credit (LCs), blockchain technology has brought about revolutionary opportunities in the field of global trade finance. Through digitization and simplification of the traditional procedures related to LCs, this innovative method seeks to improve the effectiveness, openness, and security of international commercial transactions.

CHAPTER 14   CREDIT REVOLUTION: THE TOKENIZATION TIDAL WAVE IN GLOBAL TRADE

Tokenization is the process of employing cutting-edge technology like blockchain to transform valuable or significant objects into a digital form. Consider, for example, that you have a document proving your ownership or rights to a certain object. By tokenization, this tangible copy becomes a digital one. The value or ownership rights of the original paper are the same with this digital equivalent, called a token, but it is stored safely online. It is basically like possessing a virtual key to something priceless that is encrypted using cryptography. By this digital revolution, tokenization guarantees that ownership and transaction procedures are not only more effective but also far more safe and transparent.

Tokenization makes it possible to divide ownership into smaller, more manageable chunks, which makes it simpler to purchase, sell, and transfer assets within a blockchain network. This makes it possible to break ownership into smaller bits. By breaking an asset into fractions, tokenization makes it possible for a large number of users to hold a share of that asset. This also increases the asset's accessibility and liquidity.

The inclusion of blockchain technology is primarily responsible for ensuring the transparency and integrity of these transactions. The thorough documentation of each and every transaction by the blockchain results in a reliable and immutable ledger. The fact that this record cannot be altered means that every transaction is guaranteed to be safe and verifiable, which in turn increases the confidence of the participants.

The design of tokens also takes compatibility into consideration. Because of this, they are able to engage and share information or values across a variety of platforms with relative ease. The ability of tokens to work across several platforms makes their utility, and it also makes it feasible for them to be used in a wide variety of contexts. This interoperability, which also increases the efficiency of transactions, makes tokenized assets in the digital economy more valuable and flexible. Additionally, it makes the digital economy more efficient.

Tokenization offers several benefits, the main one being the chance to own a piece of an asset. As such, it suggests that clients are not required to buy the whole thing but rather can buy tiny amounts of it. This allows more people to invest in assets that were previously out of reach because of high prices or market restrictions. Many times, it was believed that these assets were too hazardous or non-liquidable for regular investors to handle. Tokenization divides ownership into smaller, more cheap pieces, therefore opening up access to these marketplaces to a larger number of individuals. Tokenization also offers the important advantage of enabling token trading without regard to regional limitations, wherever in the world. Its ability to conduct continuous trading across several time zones, thanks to its worldwide reach, guarantees that markets are continuously active and offers more chances for transactions. The flexibility and liquidity of the market are increased when investors from all over the world may trade at any time of day or night.

Blockchain technology uses cryptography to hide data, greatly enhancing the security of financial transactions. The possibility of fraudulent activity and illegal changes is much less because this cryptographic method guarantees that all transactions are safe and unchangeable. Once a transaction is documented on a blockchain, it cannot be altered, so participants have a lot of confidence in the data kept there.

Tokenization contributes to lowering the administrative expenses related to conventional asset transfers. The procedure of changing ownership of assets under traditional systems is drawn out and costly since it typically entails a lot of paperwork, intermediaries, and other fees. By using blockchain technology, tokenized transactions become more efficient and economical, as well as less administratively demanding. This cost savings helps investors and issuers equally, which eventually helps to create a more efficient and accessible financial environment.

Key problems with tokenization must be resolved if it is to be used widely and integrated smoothly into many different industries. One big issue is ambiguity about rules. Because tokenized asset legal and regulatory frameworks are still developing, it might be difficult to guarantee compliance and handle worries about jurisdictional difficulties. This always shifting environment may cause problems for businesses and investors trying to negotiate the rules, which can differ greatly from one jurisdiction to another and may change as authorities continue to change how they see digital assets. Everyone concerned can find things challenging as a result of these complexities.

Perception and adoption of tokenized assets provide yet another challenge. Because they may not be familiar with digital assets or have doubts about them, conventional investors and stakeholders might be reluctant to embrace these new investment options. The potential barrier of tokenization not being immediately apparent to those used to conventional investment methods can be significant. One major obstacle might be this reluctance. Significant education efforts and proof of the security, openness, and efficiency that tokenization may provide are needed to get over this resistance. The tokenization has to be demonstrated as well.

Tokenization of assets offers several possible solutions to long-standing issues with asset ownership, trade, and accessibility; nevertheless, in order to fully reap these advantages, tokenization-related challenges must be effectively managed.

Legal frameworks that are both explicit and consistent and that offer assurance and protection for all parties involved are essential to addressing the problems brought about by regulations. To properly manage security threats, especially those related to data integrity and digital fraud, strict technological solutions and the best cybersecurity practices must be put into practice.

Tokenized assets must gain widespread acceptance from investors and stakeholders in order to build trust and understanding. As part of this, the market should be informed about the advantages of tokenization and successful use cases that demonstrate how it may revolutionize asset ownership and trading. Part of the process is to inform the market about the benefits of tokenization. Tokenization has the potential to become a more well-recognized and integrated part of the financial scene once these regulatory, security, and acceptability issues are resolved. The industry worldwide, as well as investors, will have fresh chances as a result.

Deciphering the Complexities of Traditional Letters of Credit: Addressing Inefficiencies and Risks in Traditional Trade Finance

Traditional letters of credit (LCs) are usually labor-intensive manual procedures that are not only intricate but also sluggish. The high costs associated with courier services exacerbate this inefficiency. The current trading system is complex and operates via several phases; hence, it is a long and difficult process. According to data recently released by the International Chamber of Commerce (ICC), up to 27 papers may be submitted for a normal business transaction, nine of which are especially related to the ownership transfer. Any one of these transactions can cost up to $80,000, and it might take 2–3 months to complete.

Within the transactional business environment, there are about four billion documents being traded at any one time. Especially challenging is the creation of letters of credit (LCs) in the absence of prior banking relationships, which might cause more delays in the start of trading activities. Another study by the International Chamber of Commerce (ICC) revealed that processing a letter of credit might take more than 20 days.

Transparency and traceability are lacking in the processes already in use for the creation and distribution of conventional invoices. The difficulty to accurately depict the current market prices is increased by this lack of clarity, which increases the possibility of error. Document creation mistakes are quite common and might lead to further delays as well as significant conflicts. The financial difference widens even further when issuing banks, especially those that deal with small and medium-sized enterprises (SMEs), reject documents for the first time. The high first rejection rate makes this situation even worse.

Traditional LCs also significantly raise security-related concerns. A couple instances of this include the potential for document alteration and duplication. Because they lack any safe and unchangeable procedures, traditional letters of credit are more vulnerable to fraud and errors. Regular LCs lack these extra safeguards; tokenized LCs can, however, benefit from the automated compliance features provided by smart contracts.

Standard letters of credit transactions become much more complicated because of the many regulations that exist in many countries, especially when dealing with overseas transactions. Both the absence of international accords and penalties may impede the LC process. Though SWIFT standards are in place, the primarily paper-based verification process may cause delays and raise the risk of fraud. The problem becomes much more complicated with the lack of a global standard for party identification, such as the Legal Entity Identifier (LEI). In the UK, just 4% of companies were using the LEI system as of 2019. Restricted use of LEIs creates trust and security issues, which affect global accessibility and effectiveness. The lack of a worldwide identification standard complicates the already complex world of international trade and makes it more challenging to properly execute traditional letters of credit.

Revolutionizing Trade Finance with Blockchain Technology: Understanding Tokenization of Letters of Credit

Within a blockchain environment, tokenization is the process of transforming real assets or rights into digital tokens. Using this procedure on letters of credit (LCs) turns them from conventional LCs into programmable, digital tokens on a blockchain network. These digital tokens guarantee every transaction is safe and effective by encapsulating all the particular terms, circumstances, and responsibilities related to the LC. Commerce transactions are made safer and more transparent when LCs are represented digitally on a blockchain. This also streamlines the procedure to make it more flexible and adaptable to the needs of contemporary commerce.

CHAPTER 14   CREDIT REVOLUTION: THE TOKENIZATION TIDAL WAVE IN GLOBAL TRADE

The tokenization of LCs greatly reduces the manual processes and onerous paperwork that are typically associated with LCs. When using a digital method, the entire process—from issue to negotiation and settlement—moves more quickly. Important benefits from this digital revolution include speed and efficiency, which make the trading process more flexible and adaptable to market needs. Oracle notes that while a tokenized LC may be completed in a few hours, a physical transfer of a letter of credit can take up to 5–10 days from invoice production to eventually reaching the bank.

Blockchain technology greatly improves transparency and traceability. A tokenized limited liability's lifespan and every transaction are safely documented and traceable thanks to the blockchain's immutable ledger. Because everyone concerned has access to unchangeable transaction history, this safe and trustworthy record greatly minimizes inconsistencies and disagreements.

Tokenized limited companies are guaranteed a high degree of integrity and security by the cryptographic character of blockchain technology. Incorporating smart contracts also automates adherence to predefined conditions, which lowers the possibility of fraud or mistake. This automatic, safe setting promotes system dependability and confidence.

Tokenization also removes geographic barriers, enabling borderless transactions and global trade.

The global economy benefits especially from this capacity because the present system frequently lacks efficiency and accessibility. No matter where they are physically, blockchain technology allows different players in the commerce ecosystem to conduct transactions smoothly. eBills of Lading or Digital Letters of Credit will enhance working capital management, said 60% of SMEs in an ICC survey. This is important because, barring letters of credit, working capital is the most often used type of trade finance.

Trading domestically or internationally may be conducted at a far lower cost when letters of credit are issued and transferred digitally. With the use of paperless trade, SMEs and smaller companies may more successfully engage in international commerce by closing 50% of the trade financing gap. Along with cutting prices, this digital revolution improves inclusiveness and efficiency in the world trading system.

By providing safe and open dealings across borders, tokenized letters of credit (LCs) expedite international transactions and make procedures easier for buyers and sellers alike. The digitalization of LCs enables more efficient processing of international commerce by reducing the complexity and time typically associated with cross-border transactions. Tokenized LCs use blockchain technology to guarantee that each transaction is documented in an unchangeable ledger, therefore improving security and trust among all parties concerned.

CHAPTER 14 CREDIT REVOLUTION: THE TOKENIZATION TIDAL WAVE IN GLOBAL TRADE

Tokenized LCs may also be easily included in systems for supply chain financing. Through enhanced liquidity and capital management, this integration helps international trading companies better manage their financial resources and streamline their operations. Tokenized limited companies' increased liquidity facilitates faster and more effective payment of debts, which promotes more dependable and smooth trade. Tokenized LCs used on digital platforms build effective markets where buyers, sellers, and financial intermediaries may communicate more successfully. Better transactional and communication procedures made possible by these platforms improve the whole trading ecosystem. Tokenized LCs simplify and make the whole process more accessible by reducing the friction and delays that frequently arise in traditional trade finance by offering a centralized digital platform for these exchanges.

Tokenized long contracts provide a safe and standardized solution in the fields of financial consortia and commodity trading. By enhancing interoperability across sector players, this standardization facilitates more effective collaboration between several organizations. Furthermore, improving the dependability of trade financing in this industry is the security that blockchain technology offers, which guarantees that every transaction is free from fraud and mistakes.

Trade finance has a lot of potential to change if LCs are tokenized, as they will be more accessible, safe, and efficient. It will need industry cooperation, governmental support, and continuous technical improvements, though, for this shift to be implemented widely. Industry players must collaborate to develop and adopt standards that facilitate the use of tokenized LCs. Regulators must establish systems to guarantee the safe and authorized application of digital tokens in trade financing. To solve any outstanding issues and keep the systems supporting tokenized LCs improving, technological advancement is necessary. These components together can make tokenized LCs a mainstay of contemporary trade finance, promoting innovation and expansion in international trade.

There are some important drawbacks to take into account, even if using distributed ledger technology (DLT) to tokenize letters of credit has several advantages. One significant negative is the dearth of DLT systems that are now actively engaged in digitalizing the conventional banking industry. People wishing to use this technology will find it difficult to switch from using traditional ways to a digital framework because of the absence of well-established mechanisms.

Another important problem is the lack of international digital standards for trade. Interoperability and smooth communication are challenges for the systems that use DLT to tokenize letters of credit without these standards. The difficulty of various systems interacting with one another due to the absence of common protocols limits the usefulness and efficiency of the technology in promoting international trade.

Moreover, especially in these early phases of adoption, the procedure of completely onboarding all parties engaged in a trade into a digital platform is time-consuming and requires significant work. Every player in the transaction—buyers, sellers, banks, and other middlemen—must be persuaded of the advantages and given instructions on how to use the new system. Overcoming change aversion, resolving technical issues, and making sure all parties are at ease and adept with the new digital procedures are all part of an all-encompassing shift. There are still major challenges, even with the obvious benefits of tokenizing letters of credit with DLT. Considerable obstacles that must be overcome for effective deployment and broad acceptance include the absence of globally recognized digital standards, the absence of proven DLT systems, and the long time and work needed to onboard all stakeholders.

The Evolution from Traditional Letters of Credit: The E-Letters of Credit

The journey from traditional letters of credit to E-LCs represents a natural progression toward digitization. Initially, traditional LCs were entirely paper based, requiring extensive documentation, manual verification, and courier services to transmit these documents across borders. This reliance on paper often led to inefficiencies, delays, and vulnerabilities to fraud. In response to these challenges, the **E-LC** emerged, governed by digital frameworks such as the **eUCP (Uniform Customs and Practice for Documentary Credits for Electronic Presentation)**. E-LCs digitize the lifecycle of LCs, from issuance and document presentation to payment.

They reduce processing times, improve transparency, and align with modern trade's growing need for speed and compliance. Yet, even E-LCs retain certain limitations, such as reliance on centralized digital systems and susceptibility to data discrepancies across stakeholders. Blockchain technology and tokenization have further revolutionized E-LCs, addressing these residual inefficiencies and unlocking new capabilities.

CHAPTER 14   CREDIT REVOLUTION: THE TOKENIZATION TIDAL WAVE IN GLOBAL TRADE

Understanding Blockchain and Tokenization in E-LCs

- **Blockchain** is a decentralized, immutable ledger that records transactions securely and transparently. For trade finance, it offers a powerful solution to many long-standing inefficiencies. By leveraging **smart contracts**—self-executing agreements that automate terms and conditions—blockchain introduces automation and trust into the E-LC process.

- **Tokenization** is the digital representation of an asset or its associated rights on a blockchain. When applied to E-LCs, tokenization enables their transformation into digital assets, which can be traded, financed, or used as collateral. This makes tokenized E-LCs highly flexible and capable of driving liquidity in trade finance.

The Transition to Tokenized Letters of Credit: Strategies for Enhancing Digital Adoption of E-Letters of Credit

More digital acceptance of e-letters of credit (E-LCs) is the result of a number of strategic efforts tackling issues related to technology, regulation, and education. The technology infrastructure has to be improved first and foremost. E-LCs will need solid distributed ledger technology (DLT) solutions that are developed and implemented to easily interface with current financial frameworks.

This involves building aesthetically pleasing websites that make issuing, handling, and settling E-LCs easier. The reliability, security, and efficiency of these systems will encourage stakeholders to switch from conventional to digital solutions.

The next crucial stage is to create international digital trade standards. The lack of standardization hinders efficient transactions and communication while also preventing compatibility between various systems. Standardized procedures for E-LCs need cooperation from international organizations and trade associations. By enabling more seamless connections across different platforms, these standards will guarantee that all participants—regardless of their location or technology—can conduct trade without any problems. Because parties may be sure that their systems will work with those of their trading partners, standardization also fosters confidence.

Additionally essential to promoting digital adoption is regulatory backing. Governments and regulatory bodies must provide a definite and encouraging legal framework that acknowledges and controls the application of electronic limited companies. This entails giving rules to guarantee security and compliance as well as adapting current rules to suit digital transactions. Regulatory certainty will inspire businesses to use and invest in E-LCs because it will reassure them that their transactions are legal and protected.

Education and awareness are equally important drivers of technology adoption. Digital technology and its associated advantages may be foreign to many players in the trade ecosystem, particularly those in conventional industries. This information vacuum can be filled in part by holding training courses, seminars, and educational initiatives. Stakeholder acceptance of E-LCs will be increased by proving their efficacy, economy, and security. Case studies and success stories can help to highlight the real advantages even more and promote greater acceptance.

Encouraging cooperation among traders, financial institutions, and technology suppliers is essential. Collectively, these organizations can create integrated solutions that meet the unique requirements and worries of all participants in the trade. Working together, too, may stimulate creativity and provide more sophisticated and customized E-LC solutions that improve trading overall.

A multidimensional strategy including technology improvements, standardization, regulatory assistance, education, and cooperation is needed to increase the digital acceptance of e-letters of credit. Comprehensive treatment of these issues can speed up the shift to digital trade finance and result in a more secure, effective, and internationally linked trade ecosystem.

Application programming interfaces (APIs) are a tactical tool to help electronic letters of credit (E-LCs) be adopted and integrated. Platforms may more readily accept and use E-LCs since APIs can be easily integrated into both new and current systems. APIs facilitate easier and more effective access to the features needed to manage E-LCs by giving various software systems standardized means of communication. Businesses wishing to switch to digital trade finance solutions will find the entrance hurdles much reduced by this integration.

Utilizing interoperable distributed ledger technologies (DLTs) is another essential component of increasing the use of E-LCs. These technologies have to be able to move value and data between several systems rather simply. Interoperability, which ensures that various DLT systems can cooperate, enables a smooth flow of transactions and information.

One of the main problems in the modern digital environment is that insufficient interoperability frequently prevents effective communication across various platforms.

SWIFT's earlier this year proof of concept (PoC) is one noteworthy illustration of how APIs and DLTs are increasing interoperability. This project concentrated on enabling more safe and interoperable procedures between document issuers and the SWIFT network by means of a universal API contract. The proof of concept showed that E-LC transaction efficiency and security may be greatly improved with a standardized API. Different systems could now communicate more easily thanks to the API, which also reduced the danger and complexity of processing documents the old-fashioned way.

The proof of concept from SWIFT shows how universal APIs may simplify trade finance processes. Widespread use of E-LCs depends on platforms achieving higher security and interoperability by implementing such APIs. By guaranteeing that all transactions are carried out in a safe and open way, these developments not only increase the efficiency of the E-LC issuance and management process but also foster participant trust.

Finally, the use of interoperable DLTs and easily implementable APIs offers a workable solution to the challenges of implementing electronic letters of credit. Through smooth integration and communication across several systems, these technologies may greatly improve the security, accessibility, and efficiency of E-LCs, encouraging their wider adoption and application in the international trade finance ecosystem.

Pilot testing of electronic letters of credit (E-LCs) shows their practical application potential. These experiments are important because they make it possible to determine in real-world situations the advantages and disadvantages of E-LCs. Before a broad adoption, participants can get important information and make the required changes through these pilot tests.

An intriguing situation is covered in a GTR piece from a few years ago that had a multiparty pilot test. When combined with other essential trade papers in electronic format, this pilot successfully demonstrated the value of an electronic letter of credit. In just 2 hours, the test produced an electronic letter of credit. By contrast, the identical transaction carried out with conventional techniques would normally take 1–2 days. This noteworthy processing time decrease emphasizes how effective E-LCs are.

Compared to the old approach, which often permits just one payment per LC, another major benefit noted in the pilot test is the capacity to make several payments on a single electronic letter of credit. This feature, which also offers a more effective payment management procedure, may greatly increase the flexibility and efficiency of trade operations.

Pilot experiments essentially serve to demonstrate the practical benefits of E-LCs, such as time efficiency and the ability to manage multiple payments. Before the trade finance sector uses the system extensively, these tests guarantee that it is improved and optimized by offering a platform for spotting and resolving any possible problems. Pilot tests enable the switch from traditional to electronic letters of credit by demonstrating how E-LCs may be used in practical situations.

Facilitating a seamless transfer from conventional letters of credit (LCs) to their digital equivalents requires the development of an intuitive platform. How easily people can utilize and navigate the digital system will determine how successful this transformation is. It is therefore imperative to have an easily navigable platform.

The online platform has to provide simple ways to monitor and manage LCs. This comprises tools that let all participants in the transaction quickly track the LCs' progress and status. The platform may greatly lower confusion and increase efficiency by offering real-time updates and a transparent view of every stage of the process.

For example, customers ought to have quick access to details on the issue, modification, and settlement of LCs. To guarantee that all pertinent information is easily accessible at every step, the platform should also enable the smooth submission and retrieval of required papers. This makes the procedure easier and more transparent, therefore keeping everyone informed and involved.

To reduce the learning curve for new users, the platform's design should also give the user experience top priority. This entails adding tools for responsive help, clear instructions, and simple navigation. Its simplicity of use and understanding promote acceptance among stakeholders who might be used to conventional approaches.

The successful switch from conventional LCs to electronic ones is mostly dependent on the development of an intuitive digital platform. With real-time updates, simple information access, and an emphasis on user experience, such a platform ought to make managing and tracking LCs easier for all parties concerned. This method not only expedites the procedure but also encourages more trade finance sector adoption and usage of digital LCs.

Finally, bringing blockchain and tokenization into the field of letters of credit is a ground-breaking development that has the power to completely transform international trade finance. The industry should expect a significant and varied effect from this technological revolution.

We are bringing in a time where trade procedures become far more efficient, transparent, and safe by using the immutable record of blockchain in conjunction with the fractional ownership possibilities of tokenization. While lowering fraud, lowering risks, and improving the environment for all parties concerned, this integration quickens transaction speeds.

The broad use of these revolutionary technologies may completely change the basis of trade finance. This change has the potential to drive international trade into a more efficient, accessible, and inclusive period. Not only theoretical but also a realistic route to a better future for international commerce is the idea of a more accessible and effective trade financing system.

Accepting this chance for innovation is essential as we continue to negotiate in the ever-changing world of international trade. Establishing a more linked, effective, and profitable trading environment will need industry collaboration. The path toward this brand-new era of trade financing has already started. We can propel the industry to previously unheard-of levels of growth and dependability by cooperating. Accepting this shift will allow us to mold trade finance into a system that is advantageous to all parties involved and promotes world economic expansion.

Summary

By redefining asset representation, management, and transaction handling, tokenization is altering worldwide trade. This invention brings hitherto unheard-of degrees of openness, efficiency, and liquidity by turning tangible and intangible assets into digital currencies on blockchain networks. Tokenization is very effective in sectors like trade finance as it may fractionalize assets, simplify difficult procedures, and reduce risks, thereby transforming them. The financial services industry is seeing a paradigm movement toward digital-first solutions that promise to transform world trade as tokenized promissory notes, bills of exchange, and letters of credit become more common.

Adoption of tokenization, meanwhile, presents difficulties including infrastructure preparedness, legal obstacles, and stakeholder education. Still, its ability to solve long-standing trade finance inefficiencies—including the complexity of conventional letters of credit—makes a strong argument for reform. Blockchain technology and credit e-letter leveraging help companies lower costs, accelerate transactions, and build confidence across borders. Tokenization leads first in this change as trade finance approaches complete digitization, fostering innovation and preparing the ground for a more inclusive, strong global economy.

CHAPTER 15

The Nexus of Trade, Environment, and Sustainable Development

This chapter looks at the complicated relationship between trade, the environment, and long-term growth, focusing on the problems and chances at the level of global government. It looks at the bodies and processes of the World Trade Organization (WTO) and how environmental issues are becoming more and more connected with trade policies. Member-led projects are paving the way for a better future by showing how trade practices can be made more environmentally friendly.

The chapter stresses how important it is to involve many people in what is called the "green trade revolution," which supports environmental action that includes everyone and doesn't leave anyone behind. It is said that trade, the environment, and sustainable development must all work together, and global unity is emphasized as a way to close gaps like the gender gap in trade finance and make the global economy more fair and strong.

The conversation moves on to the important part that everyone plays in working together to stop climate change, taking advantage of the current energy for real changes in the way the world trades. The WTO is at a major turning point, and trade officials are being pushed to build futures that can handle climate change. People think that letting green subsidies go will be a big part of the future of climate-aligned trade, especially for emerging economies and countries that are sensitive to climate change.

CHAPTER 15   THE NEXUS OF TRADE, ENVIRONMENT, AND SUSTAINABLE DEVELOPMENT

The chapter also talks about how digital green lanes and global relationships could change the way global maritime trade is done. It looks at the role of different fuels, the strange case of LNG in efforts to cut down on carbon emissions, and the bigger effects of going digital and making shipping more efficient. The difficulties and opportunities of the future are talked about, with a focus on progressing toward a better future through new fuel technologies and rules.

Finally, the chapter stresses how important carbon trading systems, alternative marine fuels, and new developments in wind power are for the shipping industry's path to sustainability. Promoting the idea of "green shipping corridors" is seen as a big step toward getting zero pollution and a promise to lead the industry toward a greener future.

Aligning Trade and Environmental Policies: A Global Governance Challenge

Governments and stakeholders all over are paying more and more attention to the difficult task that trade, the environment, and sustainable development provide for global governance. Reflecting the growing agreement on the necessity to include sustainable development goals inside the framework of international commerce, this sophisticated interface has become a main focus for improved cooperation at the World Trade Organization (WTO). Celebrated in the Preamble of the Marrakesh Agreement, which founded the WTO, the dedication to sustainable development—including environmental protection—highlights the natural connection between trade policy and the state of our earth.

The debate on the junction of trade and environmental policies has changed over more than five decades, reflecting more general changes in world environmental consciousness and economic interests. Underlined at the Twelfth WTO Ministerial Conference (MC12) in June 2022, this continuous dispute has stayed a regular feature on the WTO agenda. Members here acknowledged the urgent worldwide environmental issues—from climate change to biodiversity loss—and the vital part the multilateral trading system plays in advancing the UN 2030 Agenda for Sustainable Development across its economic, social, and environmental spheres.

The debate had developed even more by the Thirteenth WTO Ministerial Conference (MC13) in February 2024, with the Ministerial Declaration underlining the need of combining commerce with environmental development. Together with many ministerial resolutions and announcements, the declaration underlined the efforts of the multilateral trade system toward environmental challenges, including climate change. This marked a significant milestone in acknowledging sustainable development as a primary objective that requires close integration with global trade policies.

Though it lacks a formal accord addressing environmental concerns, the WTO's legal structure lets countries apply trade-related environmental policies. Article XX of the General Agreement on Tariffs and Trade (GATT), which allows the adoption of measures required to protect human, animal, or plant life or to conserve exhaustible natural resources, is central to this framework since these measures do not lead to discriminating practices or act as disguised restrictions on international trade. This clause is absolutely essential in balancing the necessity of preserving free trade with the requirement of environmental preservation.

Building on this, additional WTO agreements, such as the Agreement on Technical Barriers to Trade (TBT), negotiate the careful balance between environmental regulations and the needs of free trade. These accords acknowledge that although environmental policies are crucial, they shouldn't be instruments for protectionism. To guarantee that environmental policies do not unduly hinder trade, they thus support openness, harmonization, and mutual respect of standards.

From their different angles, several bodies within the WTO address environmental concerns, therefore supporting the overall operations of the WTO, from trade negotiations and dispute resolution to policy dialogue and cooperation with other international agencies. Established in 1995, the Committee on Trade and Environment (CTE) provides a focused venue for exploring how trade and environmental policy interact. By means of its activities, the CTE has helped members to develop better understanding and cooperation, therefore enabling them to solve environmental issues in the framework of the multilateral trade system.

The emphasis has changed recently to center on particular programs meant to support environmental sustainability. Among these projects have been attempts to solve plastic waste, change fossil fuel subsidies, and boost trade of environmentally friendly goods and services. A coalition of like-minded WTO members who understand the need to match trade policies with the demands of the earth often leads such projects. Together, these groups create ideas, distribute best practices, and foster agreement on important concerns.

For instance, the WTO has become rather active in the effort to solve plastic pollution. Members understand that a coordinated response is needed for the worldwide plastic waste issue. By means of knowledge and best practices, members have investigated strategies to lower plastic waste through trade policy, namely by encouraging the sale of ecologically friendly substitutes and improving waste management practices. Similarly, the realization that such subsidies distort commerce and help cause environmental damage has motivated attempts to change fossil fuel subsidies. WTO members aim to promote sustainable development by advocating for the reduction or elimination of these subsidies.

Including environmental issues in trade policy presents difficulties as well. Reaching agreement on difficult problems is challenging given the variety of WTO membership—that of nations at different phases of development with diverse environmental goals. Still, the constant communication and WTO-based collaboration show a shared will to meet these difficulties. Ensuring that trade-related environmental measures are carried out in line with WTO regulations also depends critically on the dispute settlement system of the organization. By means of its decisions, the dispute settlement body has offered direction on the interpretation and application of important clauses, therefore clarifying the limits separating reasonable environmental measures from protectionist policies.

The WTO's influence in advancing sustainable development becomes more crucial as the world struggles with the problems of climate change, biodiversity loss, and other environmental concerns. The WTO can help to create a more fair and sustainable world by including environmental issues in trade rules. Reflecting in the Preamble of the Marrakesh Agreement and reinforced in later ministerial declarations, the dedication to sustainable development highlights the natural link between trade and the state of our earth.

Focusing on WTO procedures rather than particular rules or policies, this chapter has examined the several interactions at the WTO involving the trade and environmental interface. The WTO is significantly moving toward matching trade policies with the pressing needs of our planet by means of projects addressing plastic pollution, reform of fossil fuel subsidies, and encouragement of trade in environmental goods and services. The difficulty for global governance is still to make sure that trade and environmental policies complement one another, therefore supporting the more general objectives of sustainable development and the welfare of the next generations as the conversation changes.

CHAPTER 15   THE NEXUS OF TRADE, ENVIRONMENT, AND SUSTAINABLE DEVELOPMENT

Decades of Transformation in Trade and Development: Opportunities and Challenges for Developing Nations

Global commerce and development have undergone significant transformations during the past 60 years. Driven by the expansion of developing nations, the digital revolution, and growing environmental consciousness, these changes have transformed the scene of the world economy. It is evident from considering these decades of transformation that the dynamics behind world commerce have changed and provide chances as well as difficulties for the future.

Rising developing economies have been among the most important changes in world trade. Historically on the margins, these countries have become more and more important, greatly raising their portion in world trade. The quadrupling of their global trade involvement from 22% in 1964 to 44% by 2023 best illustrates this change. Key elements in this change have been tariff liberalization and integration into international value chains, which let these countries increase their competitiveness and economic development.

Not every growing country, meanwhile, has profited equally. Among the many difficulties least developed nations (LDCs) still confront are insufficient capital investment, poor infrastructure, and restricted access to technology. Notwithstanding these challenges, the general trend reveals a notable rise in income and stability among developing nations, therefore underlining their growing relevance in the framework of the world economy.

Another cornerstone of world trade has been maritime trade, which carries over 80% of all products transported. By standardizing the packing, shipping, and commodity handling, containerization transformed marine logistics. Along with lowering transportation costs, this invention greatly improved the efficiency of world commerce systems. Seaborne commerce volumes jumped from 2.6 billion tons to around 11 billion tons between 1970 and 2021, hence highlighting the vital role maritime logistics plays in enabling world economic connectivity.

For developing countries, the fast expansion of the digital economy offers a terrain full of possibilities as well as problems. Driven mostly by emerging nations, e-commerce sales jumped to $27 trillion by 2022. This digital revolution gives these nations a road to more economic involvement and creativity, hence expanding worldwide marketplaces to smaller companies and hitherto underprivileged populations.

CHAPTER 15   THE NEXUS OF TRADE, ENVIRONMENT, AND SUSTAINABLE DEVELOPMENT

In many developing countries, the digital economy also reveals major infrastructure gaps and digital literacy deficits, nevertheless. These countries run the danger of lagging behind in the digital race without strong logistical networks, enough Internet access, and sophisticated payment systems. Further challenges for smaller businesses in emerging nations come from the great concentration of market power among a small number of powerful companies.

Along with the economic growth of the past two decades, mounting environmental issues—especially the dramatic increase in world CO_2 emissions and the rising plastics trade—have accompanied it. Driving industrial expansion, transportation, and energy consumption, CO_2 emissions have quadrupled since 1960. This trend emphasizes how urgently sustainable manufacturing and consumption patterns must be adopted to reduce the environmental effects of world commerce.

Now worth $1.2 trillion, the plastics trade aggravates environmental damage more than others. Inappropriate waste management and the ubiquitous usage of plastics have resulted in extensive contamination, endangering ecosystems and human health. Dealing with these issues calls for creative ideas in biodegradable materials, recycling technology, and more environmentally friendly manufacturing methods.

Many underdeveloped countries still rely mostly on commodities; hence, they are sensitive to changes in world prices. With main commodity exports making over 60% of their export profits, 101 nations were labeled as commodity-dependent as of 2021. This reliance raises serious concerns as the stability of these countries' economies depends much on erratic world commodity markets.

The COVID-19 epidemic brought attention to the risks associated with this dependence, as interruptions in global demand and supply networks caused an extreme economic crisis in nations dependent on commodities. These countries have to pursue economic diversification, invest in value-added businesses, and create more strong economic policies if they are to lower these hazards.

Demand for vital minerals such as lithium, nickel, cobalt, and copper has surged along with the worldwide move toward renewable energy. Battery, electric car, and renewable energy infrastructure development depends on these minerals. This need offers both major economic possibilities and inherent difficulties for mineral-rich emerging nations.

To fully seize these opportunities, developing countries must invest in processing and manufacturing capacity, thereby advancing the value chain to generate not only raw materials but also completed goods. This shift calls for overcoming technological, infrastructure, and legal obstacles as well as handling the social and environmental effects of mining operations.

CHAPTER 15   THE NEXUS OF TRADE, ENVIRONMENT, AND SUSTAINABLE DEVELOPMENT

With emerging countries paying a large share of the $97 trillion global public debt projected in 2023, economic pressures—including the necessity for social welfare programs, infrastructure expansion, and crisis management—have fueled the rapid debt growth in many nations.

High debt levels limit the ability for investment in important areas and increase the cost of debt payment, therefore seriously impairing economic development. Developing countries have to implement sustainable fiscal policies, enhance income collection, and pursue international debt reduction and financial stability by means of international collaboration.

Environmental issues, changes in world economic power, and technological developments will continue to shape the patterns guiding worldwide commerce and development. As developing countries negotiate these challenges, the United Nations Conference on Trade and Development (UNCTAD) is rather helpful.

Ensuring that developing nations can adjust to shifting global dynamics and attain long-term economic success depends on UNCTAD's initiatives in capacity building, supporting sustainable practices, and encouraging equitable growth. Adopting these approaches will help developing countries improve their involvement in the international economy, lower poverty, and advance a more fair and sustainable planet.

Globally, trade and development have experienced amazing change within the previous sixty years. Rising developing economies, the digital revolution, and increased environmental consciousness have changed the scene of the world economy. The difficulty will be using these forces for inclusive and sustainable development so that every country may gain from the possibilities of the global economy. Guiding developing nations across this turbulent and unpredictable future will depend critically on UNCTAD's ongoing support.

Unlocking Europe's Global Potential: Revitalizing EU Trade Policy for Enhanced Competitiveness

The competitiveness of Europe depends on a strong and proactive trade policy in a world increasingly linked. Current data points to a concerning trend: the European Union (EU) underperforms in world commerce relative to its potential despite its economic weight. Apart from a rise in new technologies, inventions, and R&D expenditures in other areas, 85% of global growth is happening outside the EU; hence, the EU must better interact with other markets.

Two major economic problems for the EU's growing isolation from world markets are declining market access and less economic resilience. Rising obstacles to exporting their goods and services by EU companies limit their capacity to grow, specialize, and make research and development investments. Concurrently, the EU's economic stability is threatened by its dependence on a few sources of essential raw materials. The EU has to diversify its supply sources and provide unhindered access to modern goods, services, and technology if it is to counteract these problems. The EU has a key window of opportunity over the next five years to revive its foreign trade policy. This policy brief presents seven practical suggestions meant to improve economic resilience and market access.

The EU can greatly raise its global trade profile by modernizing current Free Trade Agreements (FTAs), negotiating targeted sectoral agreements, extending regulatory adequacy frameworks, joining the Comprehensive and Progressive Agreement for Trans-Pacific Partnership (CPTPP), deepening Trade and Technology Councils with important partners, strengthening neighborhood policies on raw materials, and launching a Trade Resilience Coalition. Emphasizing that open markets and improved competitiveness are absolutely necessary for Europe's economy, Europe Unlocked—a coalition of business organizations—argues for these policies. Europe runs the danger of trailing in global economic dynamism without strong effort to lower trade barriers and promote fresh international cooperation. The EU can guarantee a more bright future by adopting this strategic approach, using trade to propel resilience, innovation, and development.

Boosting EU Competitiveness: Overcoming Barriers to Global Market Integration and Economic Resilience

The EU's competitiveness and economic development depend much on international commerce. Acting as a dynamic engine, it greatly increases the gross domestic product (GDP) and promotes increased production and innovation among exporting businesses. Apart from increasing sales, engaging global markets is essential for obtaining the technological and creative inputs required for the EU to flourish in the worldwide economy.

Though foreign trade increases competitiveness, the EU is not completely grabbing onto these possibilities. Consistent with the EU's total economic size, the Extra-Regional Commerce Intensity Index—which gauges the value of its commerce with the rest of the world—showcases regularly values below one. This suggests that, with a tendency especially evident since 2016, the EU's foreign trade is underperforming in relation to its GDP. The minimal interaction of Europe with the outside world raises various issues. First, outside the EU is where most of the predicted global economic growth comes from.

CHAPTER 15   THE NEXUS OF TRADE, ENVIRONMENT, AND SUSTAINABLE DEVELOPMENT

While developing markets are predicted to attain growth rates between 3.9% and 4.8%, the International Monetary Fund (IMF) estimates that between 2024 and 2028, the GDP growth of the EU will vary between 1.4% and 1.7%.

The European Commission emphasizes the necessity of improved integration with worldwide markets as it notes that 85% of global development happens outside the EU. Moreover, the EU will rely more and more on outside-of-its-borders procurement of new commodities, services, and technology as developing nations push the technological frontier and modernize their own economies. The EU's capacity to export products and services is much influenced by market access—that is, lack of it. It speaks to the degree to which the EU may penetrate international markets under conditions of different tariffs, laws, and other challenges.

A lack of market access directly reduces the EU's competitiveness given the significance of exports as the engine of its economic development. Protectionist policies have developed throughout time and gone beyond conventional import barriers. From around 500 to over 12,000, European exporters suffered a more than 20-fold rise in non-tariff barriers (NTBs) between 2009 and 2023; this growth in the final four years is particularly noteworthy. For example, most NTBs were seen in 2023 among French and German exporters of vehicles, iron, steel, and metal-manufactured goods like tubes or wires.

Furthermore, affecting the EU's services—especially digital ones—is the emergence of NTBs. Over 100 data localization policies, including local storage needs and flow restrictions, the OECD discovered were imposed throughout 40 nations. Misled by non-OECD nations, these policies directly negatively impact EU businesses, particularly in industries such as comparative e-payments, cloud computing, and air travel. NTBs on services are crucial as they impede Europe's most promising businesses and its new sources of economic development. The comparative advantage of the EU abroad is moving toward a service-oriented economy. Especially in Europe's ICT services industry, this change is rather clear. Exports of ICT services increased at an average annual rate of 8.5% between 2010 and 2020, outpacing growth rates of EU exports in chemicals (2%), machinery (1.4%), and transportation equipment (1.4%).

Exceeding the value of pharmaceuticals (€129 billion), chemicals (€109 billion), and electrical equipment (€17 billion), the value of the EU's ICT services exports in 2020 climbed to €158 billion. Economic resilience is the capacity of an economy to retain its main operations while absorbing and recovering from shocks such as natural disasters, pandemics, or geopolitical conflicts. Twofold is the relevance of economic resilience for the competitiveness of the EU: it lessens reliance on outside nations and emphasizes the need to guarantee consistent access to a broad spectrum of imports, from raw materials to state-of-the-art technology. The capacity of the EU to lessen its over-reliance on a single source of imports determines its trade dependence. Out of 9,000 goods imported by the EU, just 282 products—2% (€58.5 billion) of EU total import values—could be considered reliant. Furthermore, not every commodity labeled as reliant is really vital for the EU economy.

The Russia-Ukraine war and China's strategic control over vital raw materials (CRMs) have highlighted weaknesses linked with economic reliance on minerals and energy. With imports from China making more than half of the EU's total imports of gallium, cobalt, magnesium, and manganese in 2022, the EU was quite dependent on China for these resources. The clean and digital technologies, military, and other vital sectors, including robotics, of the EU depend on CRMs. Economic resilience depends critically on safe, steady, flawless access to luxury products, services, and technologies. Still, the main obstacle to finding luxury goods usually comes from within nations themselves, not from their trading partners. The EU has created various trade and digital hurdles in recent years, like the Artificial Intelligence Act and the Carbon Border Adjustment Mechanism, which are probably going to increase import costs and perhaps cause a gulf between the EU and the world economy.

These trade obstacles seriously impair the EU's competitiveness. Comprising 30% of all imports, US companies were the top suppliers of ICT solutions to the EU market in 2020. Close to €47 billion in EU imports of US ICT services help to explain Europe's economic revolution, shown in the €158 billion of EU ICT goods sold globally. The EU's competitiveness in these new sources of economic development will suffer from EU policies imposing obstacles to the movement of products, services, and investment between the EU and its principal trade partners. Improving the EU's competitiveness calls for addressing problems with market access and economic resilience. The EU can build a more dynamic and resilient economy able to sustain development and innovation in an increasingly linked world by lowering trade obstacles and promoting deeper integration with worldwide markets.

EU Trade Policy: A Forward-Looking Agenda for 2025–2030

In the previous section, we established two key economic challenges where EU trade policy can play a crucial role in the next five years: boosting EU market access abroad and improving economic resilience, especially for critical technologies and materials needed for EU firms to be competitive. This chapter turns to policy approaches and

CHAPTER 15 THE NEXUS OF TRADE, ENVIRONMENT, AND SUSTAINABLE DEVELOPMENT

outlines a set of policy recommendations aimed at achieving these objectives. While global trade policy often seems fraught with challenges, constructive and forward-looking trade agreements are indeed happening.

Many countries are actively seeking deeper trade relations, leading to significant economic liberalization and improved economic security through diversified supplies of critical goods and technologies. The EU has participated in such negotiations with regions like Mercosur, New Zealand, and Australia. However, many initiatives have stalled, hindering the EU's ability to enhance both prosperity and security through trade. For the next five years, we propose seven actions in EU trade policy that are feasible and do not require a wholesale shift in the Union's current defensive attitude to trade. These measures connect with the objectives of market access and economic resilience, often benefiting both simultaneously.

The EU has a substantial body of Free Trade Agreements (FTAs) with various countries and regions worldwide, supporting millions of jobs within the EU. However, the recent slowdown in new FTAs and the reluctance of some EU member states to ratify agreements due to domestic reasons have impeded progress. The EU's self-imposed limitations on liberalizing sensitive sectors like agriculture further complicate securing new FTAs with key partners.

Modernizing current FTAs offers significant untapped potential for improving European market access and facilitating imports. Most existing agreements need updates to remain relevant due to changes in the economy and trade restrictions since their inception. For instance, newer FTAs like those with Canada and Japan cover more areas of the economy compared to older agreements. The EU has already started negotiations on modernizing FTAs with 12 countries, yielding new agreements with Chile and amendments to the Association Agreement with Moldova. Updating FTAs, especially with neighboring countries rich in minerals, is crucial. New EU policies like the Carbon Border Adjustment Mechanism impact trade in raw materials, making it essential to agree on better rules with raw-material-rich FTA partners. Additionally, modernizing agreements to cover services trade, particularly in ICT sectors, can significantly enhance the EU's competitive advantage.

Mini deals, targeted agreements to reduce or remove non-tariff barriers (NTBs), have become a practical trade policy tool. These agreements can focus on sectors where global regulatory requirements diverge, reducing unnecessary trade and administrative costs. The EU has already started deploying such agreements, like the digital partnership with Japan in 2022. Negotiating mini deals in digital services and e-commerce can significantly enhance EU market access and bolster economic resilience. For example, mutual recognition agreements (MRAs) in sectors like machinery and electrical equipment can reduce trade costs, boosting bilateral trade and reducing dependence on countries like China.

Expanding the adequacy framework, which certifies that a trading partner's regulations are equivalent to the EU's, can reduce trade costs and administrative barriers. This approach can improve market access and resilience by ensuring cross-border data portability and cooperation in regulatory models. The EU should create a predictable "docking station" for countries to align their regulations with the EU's, facilitating trade and avoiding increased regulatory restrictions that reduce commerce.

The EU should apply to join the Comprehensive and Progressive Agreement for Trans-Pacific Partnership (CPTPP). The CPTPP, originally a Pacific initiative, has evolved, with countries like the UK applying to join. Membership in the CPTPP can enhance market access, improve economic resilience, and counterbalance China's influence in global trade. Joining the CPTPP also offers the EU a unique opportunity to shape global digital trade norms and standards, enhancing trade in digital-intensive sectors and fostering commitments in emerging fields like AI and the data economy.

The EU-US Trade and Technology Council (TTC) and the newly established EU-India TTC present opportunities for deeper cooperation in trade, technology, and economic security. These councils can focus on global standards development, energy security, and access to raw materials, enhancing both market access and resilience. Enhancing the TTCs with more ambitious agendas and ensuring they complement ongoing FTA negotiations can maximize benefits for EU firms and strengthen trade relationships with these key partners.

The European Neighbourhood Policy (ENP) can play a vital role in diversifying imports of raw materials and energy. Strengthening ties with neighboring countries rich in important minerals can reduce the EU's dependence on suppliers like China. Expanding the Neighbourhood Policy to include partnerships on raw materials and linking it with initiatives like the Commission's New Growth Plan for the Western Balkans can enhance the EU's strategic interests and secure reliable supplies of critical raw materials.

The EU should spearhead the creation of a Trade Resilience Coalition to address global supply chain vulnerabilities and prepare for common responses to sudden trade stresses. Building on the Ottawa Group's collaboration during the COVID-19 pandemic, this coalition can focus on sectors of common relevance, such as critical raw materials. A Coalition for Trade Resilience in CRMs can support global mining and processing, reduce market barriers, and ensure a stable supply of CRMs necessary for the digital and energy transition. By implementing these seven actions, the EU can enhance its trade policy, improve market access, and bolster economic resilience, positioning itself for sustained competitiveness and growth in the global economy. These forward-looking strategies will help the EU navigate the complexities of international trade and secure a prosperous future.

Addressing Trade Policy Challenges to Reintegrate Europe into the Global Economy: Seven Strategic Recommendations for Market Access and Economic Resilience

Europe's detachment from the global economy is a growing concern, largely driven by lagging trade policy. Two significant economic hurdles—market access and economic resilience—have stifled the potential of trade to enhance Europe's competitiveness. This detachment negatively impacts job growth, innovation, and economic dependencies, leaving the EU vulnerable to global disruptions. Over the next five years, the European Commission must urgently steer Europe's trade policy toward greater market access and economic resilience. Failure to act will limit the EU's economic potential and leave it vulnerable to global disruptions. This chapter outlines seven realistic policy recommendations that can decisively improve market access and economic resilience for the EU economy, fostering greater competitiveness.

The EU has an extensive network of Free Trade Agreements (FTAs) that support millions of jobs. However, many of these agreements are outdated and do not reflect current economic realities. Modernizing existing FTAs and concluding new agreements with key regions such as Mercosur, Australia, and ASEAN countries (Indonesia, Thailand, and the Philippines) is crucial. Updating these agreements can enhance market access, reduce trade barriers, and provide more robust frameworks for cooperation in areas like raw materials and digital trade. Concluding and ratifying FTAs is a complex process requiring time and mutual willingness from negotiating parties. However, the potential benefits make it a necessary endeavor. Improved FTAs can cover more sectors, incorporate modern trade disciplines, and address new challenges, ensuring they remain relevant and beneficial for European businesses and consumers.

Mini deals are targeted agreements aimed at reducing or removing non-tariff barriers (NTBs) and enabling a reduction in bilateral trade costs. These deals are particularly effective in sectors where global regulatory requirements diverge and where the EU demonstrates a comparative advantage. Mini deals can significantly enhance market access by focusing on specific sectors like digital services and e-commerce. For example, the EU could negotiate mini deals to tackle obstacles impeding the free flow of data, foster mutual recognition of digital standards, and facilitate cross-border e-commerce. Such agreements can provide substantial economic benefits, boosting trade in sectors that are critical for Europe's future growth and competitiveness.

A transparent and efficient process for countries to demonstrate alignment with EU regulations can significantly reduce trade costs and administrative barriers. The EU should expand the existing adequacy framework, which currently applies to data protection, to other regulatory areas. This expansion would facilitate predictable market access for foreign businesses and mitigate unnecessary costs and delays associated with importing into the EU market. By creating a clear and predictable "docking station" for countries to align their regulations with the EU's, the EU can enhance both market access and economic resilience. This approach can help bridge regulatory differences, reduce trade friction, and support a more integrated global economy.

The Comprehensive and Progressive Agreement for Trans-Pacific Partnership (CPTPP) is a significant trade agreement that the EU should seek to join. Membership in the CPTPP would allow the EU to shape trade rules, counter Chinese influence, and expand its market access in the Asia-Pacific region. The CPTPP includes provisions that can enhance digital trade, protect intellectual property, and promote sustainable development—all areas where the EU has strong interests. Joining the CPTPP also offers a unique opportunity for the EU to participate in shaping global digital trade norms and standards, enhancing trade in digital-intensive sectors, and fostering commitments in emerging fields like artificial intelligence and the data economy.

The EU-US Trade and Technology Council (TTC) has the potential to advance trade and technology policies significantly. By broadening its scope and focusing on new trade and technology policies, the TTC can serve as a springboard for deeper transatlantic cooperation. Additionally, elevating the EU-India TTC is crucial, recognizing India's growing importance as a tech hub and talent pool. These councils can address global standards development, energy security, and access to raw materials, enhancing both market access and resilience. Strengthening these partnerships can provide robust frameworks for cooperation in critical areas and help the EU navigate complex global economic landscapes.

The European Neighbourhood Policy (ENP) can play a vital role in securing a reliable and sustainable supply of critical raw materials. By leveraging partnerships within the Eastern Partnership and the Union for the Mediterranean, the EU can diversify its sources of raw materials, reducing dependence on any single supplier.

CHAPTER 15   THE NEXUS OF TRADE, ENVIRONMENT, AND SUSTAINABLE DEVELOPMENT

Strengthening ties with neighboring countries rich in important minerals is crucial for the EU's digital and green transition. Expanding the Neighbourhood Policy to include partnerships focused on raw materials can enhance the EU's strategic interests and ensure a stable supply of essential resources.

The EU should spearhead the creation of a Trade Resilience Coalition, building on the Ottawa Group's efforts. This coalition would focus on building trust among members, agreeing on trade rules, and preparing for common responses to sudden trade stresses.

Such an initiative can address vulnerabilities exposed by recent global disruptions, like the COVID-19 pandemic and geopolitical conflicts. A Coalition for Trade Resilience, particularly in critical raw materials, can support global mining and processing, reduce market barriers, and ensure a stable supply of essential resources for the digital and energy transition. This coalition would enhance economic resilience and provide a framework for coordinated responses to global trade challenges. Addressing market access and economic resilience is crucial for reintegrating Europe into the global economy and enhancing its competitiveness.

By modernizing FTAs, negotiating mini deals, expanding regulatory frameworks, joining the CPTPP, deepening trade and technology councils, strengthening neighborhood policies, and initiating a Trade Resilience Coalition, the EU can create a more dynamic and resilient economy. These forward-looking strategies will help the EU navigate the complexities of international trade, secure a prosperous future, and maintain its position as a global economic leader.

Interweaving Environment and Trade: A Deep Dive into WTO Bodies and Processes Shaping Trade and Environmental Policies

Knowing how the World Trade Organization (WTO) treats the surroundings calls for careful analysis of the organizational structure and the particular agencies charged with environmental issues. Through their complicated yet coherent network of committees, councils, and projects, the WTO's dense web generates shapes that allow environmental debates to permeate the international trade accords and talks. This analysis exposes the several strategies the WTO uses to combine environmental issues with world economic dynamics.

CHAPTER 15   THE NEXUS OF TRADE, ENVIRONMENT, AND SUSTAINABLE DEVELOPMENT

Rising at the top of the WTO system, the Ministerial Conference meets biennially to discuss all issues pertaining to international trade agreements. Reflecting the collective will of the membership, this meeting guides and determines the priorities for the company. Between these meetings, the General Council takes over daily operations and convenes in specialized roles for trade policy assessments and dispute settlement. The core of the WTO, this council guarantees consistency and coherence in the operations of the body.

Three separate bodies under the General Council handle the basic categories of trade: goods, services, and intellectual property rights (TRIPS). Every one of these councils supervises several working groups and committees focused on certain trade issues. For example, the Council for Trade in Goods oversees several committees looking at many aspects of goods trade, including those having environmental consequences. Likewise, the Council for Trade in Services and the Council for TRIPS oversee groups handling environmental concerns relevant to their respective fields. Especially, groups like the Committee on Trade and Environment (CTE) and the Committee on Trade and Development (CTD) directly answer the General Council, indicating the important importance environmental issues have inside the WTO's structure.

The principal platform for discussion on the junction of trade and environmental policies is the Committee on Trade and Environment (CTE). Originally founded in 1995, the CTE offers a forum specifically for WTO members to explore environmental policies and their trade effects, therefore promoting mutual understanding and collaboration. Although mostly focused on development concerns, the Committee on Trade and Development (CTD) also covers environmental issues, especially those influencing emerging nations. These committees show how the WTO's institutional structure incorporates environmental issues, therefore guaranteeing that they are regularly addressed across many trade areas.

Originally founded with the Doha Round's 2001 start, the Trade Negotiations Committee (TNC) reflects the WTO's negotiating and rule-making capacity. Under the TNC, special sessions help to negotiate new rules, including those pertaining to commerce and environmental issues. For instance, the CTE in Special Session (CTE-SS) has been a key forum for discussions on creating worldwide disciplines on environmental issues, therefore highlighting the dynamic character of environmental talks inside the WTO. By means of these meetings, members establish accords reflecting the changing global priorities by balancing commerce and environmental goals.

CHAPTER 15   THE NEXUS OF TRADE, ENVIRONMENT, AND SUSTAINABLE DEVELOPMENT

The WTO's dispute settlement system provides a methodical judicial framework for settling trade conflicts, including maybe environmental concerns. This mechanism emphasizes, as stated in accords like the General Agreement on Tariffs and Trade (GATT), the balance between preserving trade agreements and allowing for environmental measures under particular conditions. Particularly, Article XX of the GATT allows the implementation of policies required to safeguard human, animal, or plant life or to conserve exhaustible natural resources, provided these policies do not result in arbitrary or unjustified discrimination or disguised limitations on international commerce. By means of its decisions, the dispute settlement body emphasizes the limits between reasonable environmental rules and protectionist actions, therefore fostering a more fair and predictable trade system.

Apart from official WTO agencies and procedures, member-led projects offer other means to solve environmental problems. Emphasizing the growing range of environmental issues in the WTO setting, recent projects center on environmental sustainability, plastic pollution, and reform of fossil fuel subsidies. These projects usually arise from groups of like-minded persons seeing the need to address certain environmental challenges. Working cooperatively, these members can forward ideas and gather momentum for more general WTO action.

Since the Doha Round, environmental concerns have been central to many discussions, with particular focus on efforts to create rules against overfishing and support sustainable fisheries practices as well as fisheries subsidies debates. Adopted at the Twelfth WTO Ministerial Conference (MC12), the historic WTO Agreement on Fisheries Subsidies reflects the WTO's dedication to solving environmental issues by means of its trade agreements. This agreement seeks to reduce negative subsidies supporting overfishing, therefore supporting the long-term viability of world fish supplies.

Several bodies housed by the WTO regularly address trade-related environmental policies. In addition to monitoring the implementation of WTO agreements, these committees provide avenues for exchanging information on environmental policies and resolving cooperative trade disputes. For instance, the Technical Barriers to Commerce (TBT) Committee examines regulations and policies that impact both environmental protection and commerce. These committees enable members to negotiate the difficult interaction between commerce and environmental policy by encouraging communication and openness.

The inclusion of environmental issues within the several bodies and procedures of the WTO shows the changing reaction of the institution to world environmental problems. By means of high-level decision-making bodies, specialist committees, and member-led projects, the WTO is building a multilateral trade system that recognizes and solves the need for environmental sustainability. Reflecting the intrinsic relationship between trade policy and the health of our planet, this all-encompassing strategy guarantees that environmental issues are knitted into the fabric of global trade debates.

The WTO's contribution to fostering sustainable development becomes more important as the world community keeps facing environmental problems. The capacity of the company to change and react to new environmental problems will be crucial in determining a sustainable future. By means of its several committees and procedures, the WTO not only promotes trade but also supports more general objectives of environmental protection and sustainable development. This thorough exploration of the WTO's structure and operations exposes dynamic and flexible institutions essential to the worldwide endeavor to reconcile environmental stewardship with economic development.

The Evolution of Due Diligence in Global Trade: From Voluntary Guidelines to Legally Enforceable Standards for Sustainability

The current emphasis on due diligence improvements in international commerce shows a major change in how sustainability concerns are being handled through global value chains (GVCs). Historically, voluntary instruments such as business codes of conduct, industry commitments, and voluntary sustainability standards (VSS) have been significant for sustainability governance in international commerce. Even voluntary actions have sometimes fallen short of bringing about the radical changes required to solve urgent world problems such as poverty, inequality, climate change, deforestation, and loss of biodiversity.

The awareness of these constraints has resulted in increasing focus on required due diligence rules meant to improve trade's sustainability control. Since the United Nations Guiding Principles on Business and Human Rights (UNGPs) were adopted in 2011, due diligence rules have evolved and expanded in the framework of business and human rights under somewhat different directions. Originally, due diligence was a non-binding idea meant to inspire businesses to freely implement policies guaranteeing respect of human rights inside their operations and value chains. As knowledge of corporate responsibility has developed, there has been a movement toward stronger, legally enforceable rules requiring companies to follow sustainable practices—especially with regard to human rights, labor rights, and environmental preservation.

CHAPTER 15 THE NEXUS OF TRADE, ENVIRONMENT, AND SUSTAINABLE DEVELOPMENT

Early due diligence rules were mostly focused on openness, meaning businesses had to reveal any possible flaws in their value chains together with the steps they were taking to fix these concerns. For example, these first initiatives were embodied by the European Union's Non-financial Reporting Directive of 2014 and the UK's Modern Slavery Act of 2015.

These rules sought to increase corporate responsibility by means of public exposure, therefore motivating companies to adopt more ethical behavior by subjecting their operations to closer inspection. Due diligence evolved, and stricter criteria started to be included in regulatory systems. This development is clear in the change from simple disclosure requirements to legislation imposing evolved responsibilities on businesses to deliberately minimize the negative effects of their activities. Reflecting a growing agreement that companies must go beyond openness and take proactive steps to prevent human rights abuses and environmental damage, the forthcoming EU Corporate Sustainability Due Diligence Directive and the Dutch Child Labour Due Diligence Law of 2019 reflect this trend. Concurrently, trade-based rules have become quite effective instruments for worldwide due diligence enforcement.

By forbidding the importation of commodities connected with severe crimes like forced labor or major environmental harm, these laws—including the US Uyghur Forced Labor Prevention Act of 2021 and the European Union's Deforestation Regulation—directly impact international trade. These rules go across borders and force businesses to make sure their whole supply chains follow ethical norms by tying due diligence to market access. The growth of due diligence rules also exposes a variety in their scope and emphasis. While some rules target particular problems, including deforestation or modern slavery, others cover general environmental, social, and governance (ESG) issues. Furthermore, the degree of applicability differs; some rules target all companies regardless of size, while others apply just to bigger companies depending on factors such as staff size or turnover. This divergence captures the complicated terrain of due diligence, where the practicalities of implementation across several corporate environments balance the need for universal standards.

From voluntary recommendations to a sophisticated network of legally enforceable rules spanning transparency, active mitigating, and trade-based enforcement, the terrain of due diligence in business and human rights has changed overall terms. This development highlights a rising awareness of the important role companies play in preserving environmental standards and human rights, therefore indicating a major change toward more responsible and sustainable worldwide corporate operations.

CHAPTER 15   THE NEXUS OF TRADE, ENVIRONMENT, AND SUSTAINABLE DEVELOPMENT

The Impact of Due Diligence Rules on Global Trade: Balancing Sustainability, Compliance, and Inclusivity in GVCs

Due diligence rules' fast spread and growing complexity have fundamentally changed world commerce and the framework of global value chains (GVCs). These rules affect international trade directly as well as indirectly as they grow more common, therefore changing the procurement, manufacturing, and distribution of products all across the globe.

The change in trade flows is among the most direct effects of due diligence rules. Trade diversion and segregation can result from trade-based policies forbading the importation of commodities failing to satisfy particular ethical or environmental criteria. Companies could so move their trading activity into less controlled markets, thereby avoiding strict rules enforced by some nations. Known as trade diversion, this phenomenon disturbs current trading patterns and may cause markets to enforce higher criteria to be excluded. Concurrent with this is trade segregation, whereby companies have distinct supply chains for compliant and non-compliant products, therefore complicating the world trade scene. Depending on their compliance level, this division might fracture world markets and provide separate outlets for various kinds of products. Due care rules also have another important effect: the phenomenon of sourcing deviation. Companies trying to follow these guidelines could change their procurement practices to go for vendors judged to be less risk-bearing.

Although this action could improve compliance and lower legal liability risk, it might also marginalize vulnerable suppliers—smallholder farmers—who would find it difficult to satisfy the strict standards set by big companies. These smaller businesses may therefore be left out of world supply chains, thereby aggravating inequality and lowering the inclusiveness of world commerce. Beyond these obvious consequences, due diligence rules also indirectly impact world commerce by requiring operational changes and raising compliance costs.

Companies, especially those linked to GVCs, might be compelled to combine their activities and choose bigger, more resource-rich players that can bear the extra compliance-related expenses. This consolidation might disadvantage smaller businesses, which would lack the financial or operational capacity to satisfy the new regulatory needs, thus changing the structure of GVCs and maybe reducing competition. These difficulties, in the meantime, are supplemented with possible advantages for world commerce brought forth by due diligence rules.

For example, these guidelines can help to improve the social and environmental features of GVCs by motivating the vertical integration of smallholders, hence generating new economic prospects. Furthermore, the drive toward compliance might inspire low-cost technology investments, therefore promoting general supply chain efficiency and innovation. The changing terrain of due diligence rules emphasizes the requirement of giving their effect on international trade considerable thought. Particularly in more wealthy countries, these regulations are becoming more and more fundamental to trade practices, so cooperation and support structures that enable underprivileged participants and developing nations to fulfill their commitments are increasingly needed.

Ensuring that due diligence initiatives support sustainable and equitable global trade practices rather than aggravating current inequities will depend critically on harmonizing rules and defining clear principles for execution. In essence, due diligence rules present chances for improving sustainability and social responsibility even while they seriously hinder global commerce and GVC systems. The secret is to strike a balance between enforcing these rules and the necessity to assist and include every participant in the world economy so that the advantages of ethical trade policies are shared generally.

Leaving No One Behind: Striking a Balance Between Sustainability and Inclusivity in Developing Countries

Due diligence rules, especially those like the European Union Deforestation Regulation (EUDR), have caused considerable worry among academics and politicians in developing nations. Though they are meant to encourage sustainability, these regulations provide a variety of obstacles for developing nations, particularly in terms of rising export prices, market access issues, and more general socioeconomic consequences for underprivileged populations, including smallholder farmers.

The financial weight due diligence rules place on suppliers in poor nations raise one of the main issues. Small-scale manufacturers and companies may find it costly to meet strict documentation and reporting criteria. Different types of evidence of compliance may be demanded by every customer, which would raise running expenses and cause delays. Many small-scale companies find these extra expenses unsustainable, which may force them completely out of export markets. The rapid schedule for applying these regulations aggravates the matter. With the EUDR, for example, the rule went into effect in June 2023, with complete implementation slated for December 2024.

CHAPTER 15   THE NEXUS OF TRADE, ENVIRONMENT, AND SUSTAINABLE DEVELOPMENT

Often lacking the money, experience, and infrastructure required to adapt in time, poor nations are left little opportunity to meet this short deadline and run a major danger of being left out of important export markets, including the European Union. Countries whose economies mostly rely on commodities like coffee, cocoa, or palm oil should especially find this alarming. Deeper socio-economic and environmental issues exist beyond the direct financial difficulties. The exclusion of small-scale farmers from official markets because of their incapacity to satisfy the high criteria established by due diligence rules might have grave consequences. In a desperate effort to survive, loss of revenue for these farmers might drive them toward unsustainable behaviors, including land degradation or illegal logging. Ironically, this result would contradict the precise sustainability objectives these laws are meant to accomplish, as it would cause more environmental damage instead of lessening it.

The apparent neglect of developing nations in the development of these rules is another important problem. Despite the great influence these laws have on the national economy, many believe their opinions were not sufficiently heard during the debates that resulted in the EUDR and like policies being developed. Furthermore, the rules sometimes contradict the developmental aspirations of these nations, which can include formalization of the informal sector and poverty reduction—objectives that do not necessarily accord with the more general sustainability goals imposed by outside policies. This gap can lead to injustice and discontent, especially in cases when local initiatives to solve environmental concerns are not given enough recognition.

For example, national policies meant to stop deforestation or enhance labor conditions might not be completely integrated or acknowledged inside the due diligence systems set by developed countries, undervaluing or ignoring the efforts of developing nations. Still, some in underdeveloped nations see the external pressure from due diligence rules as a possible spark for good despite these obstacles. The EUDR is considered in certain areas as a means to inspire local governments to handle long-neglected environmental problems.

These rules could provide better social and environmental results if combined with enough help and collaboration from industrialized countries. Striking a balance between applying due diligence and providing necessary assistance is crucial to enabling underdeveloped nations to comply with these rules. This help covers financial aid, capacity-building projects, and a longer transition time, thereby enabling these nations to progressively satisfy the new criteria without immediately being excluded from important markets. Moreover, the necessity of more cooperation and inclusion in the evolution of due diligence rules is becoming more and more acknowledged. Essential is ensuring sure the viewpoints and issues raised by underdeveloped nations are acknowledged and included in the rule-making process.

Furthermore, appreciating and including local initiatives as well as national standards in the more general regulatory systems might help close the discrepancy between the particular demands of underdeveloped nations and the worldwide sustainability objectives. Encouragement of a more cooperative approach helps one to apply due diligence rules in a way that fosters sustainable development worldwide without marginalizing fragile producers. In summary, even though due diligence rules have enormous potential to promote world sustainability, their use should be carefully managed to prevent inadvertent negative effects for underdeveloped nations. Ensuring that these rules enable sustainable development without leaving behind those most vulnerable calls for a balanced approach, including strong support, cooperation, and appreciation of local initiatives.

Navigating the Synergies and Challenges Between Voluntary Sustainability Standards and Due Diligence Rules in Global Trade

Particularly in the context of international commerce, voluntary sustainability standards (VSS) have become a more important part of worldwide sustainability policy. Due diligence rules such as the European Union Deforestation Regulation (EUDR) are becoming more and more important, and discussion on the part VSS may play in either supporting or complicating these new legal frameworks is developing. Complementing the Sustainable Development Goals (SDGs), VSS and due diligence rules have as their main objective improving the sustainability and justice of global value chains (GVCs). They act in different areas of environmental governance, though: VSS are essentially private, market-driven efforts, whereas due diligence rules are legally binding, typically government-enforced structures. VSS have been more important in fields such as agriculture and forestry since the 1990s, as they offer means to certify sustainable practices in compliance with international accords addressing problems including child labor, human rights violations, deforestation, and environmental degradation.

They provide companies a voluntary route to commit to sustainable practices, therefore acquiring access to markets needing certified sustainable products. Conversely, due diligence rules legally bind businesses to find, minimize, and document hazards connected to human rights, environmental sustainability, and other important concerns, including those of supplier chains. These regulations force companies to make sure their operations and supply chains follow set criteria, therefore rendering them answerable to the current legal systems. VSS and due diligence rules clearly have outstanding synergy potential. By offering companies already-existing structures fit for the due diligence process, VSS may help them prevent waste of time. By providing ready-made solutions organizations can include in their compliance strategies, the systems and tools VSS developed—such as traceability mechanisms, risk assessments, and corrective action plans—may augment the due diligence process.

These comprise encouraging ethical corporate practices, spotting and lessening negative effects, and guaranteeing continuous compliance by means of reporting systems. VSS may thus be quite helpful in lowering the expenses and complexity of following due diligence rules, especially for companies that currently run within VSS systems. Still, there are major difficulties matching VSS with due diligence rules, notwithstanding these possible synergies. The probable mismatch between the particular legal definitions, deadlines, and scopes of laws like the EUDR and the standards established by different VSS raises one of the main issues.

Variations in audit frequency, traceability standards, and the kinds of problems handled might make it challenging to completely include VSS into due diligence procedures. Furthermore, while some VSS are adjusting to these new rules by creating technologically driven tracking systems and improved risk assessment tools, these changes could not fully satisfy legal due diligence obligations. This calls on enterprises whose VSS they depend on to meet certain due diligence requirements to carefully assess. Furthermore, up for discussion is VSS's contribution to supporting due diligence rules. While companies and certain VSS groups support VSS incorporation within due diligence procedures, NGOs and some academics warn against this strategy.

They contend that depending just on VSS certification might weaken the responsibility due diligence rules are meant to impose. The consensus is that VSS certification should not be regarded as sufficient evidence of compliance, and therefore, no automatic 'green lane' or accelerated access should be granted based solely on VSS credentials. Due diligence rules are becoming more important, which will probably change the VSS scene in various respects.

These rules can cause the VSS industry to consolidate as more strong and accepted criteria acquire market share at the expense of less strict or smaller ones. This may lead to a "lock-in" effect wherein businesses restrict their procurement to VSS-certified vendors, therefore eliminating possibly non-certified firms. Furthermore, due diligence rules might reduce the market difference that VSS depends on—that which comes from being able to charge premium pricing for certified goods. This might therefore compromise the financial incentives that appeal to VSS, especially for small farmers in underdeveloped nations that rely on these premiums to cover the expenses of certification and compliance. Still, the knowledge and insights gained from VSS implementation provide tremendous help for the creation and execution of due diligence policies.

The auditing process is one important area where VSS has struggled consistently because of problems like conflicts of interest, inadequate openness, and shallow compliance inspections. The need to preserve the independence and quality of auditing procedures cannot be emphasized, as due diligence rules depend on audits more and more to guarantee compliance. Although many VSS grievance systems remain underdeveloped or ineffective, indicating a need for stronger systems inside due diligence frameworks, the grievance mechanisms set by VSS highlight the need for openness, accessibility, and effectiveness in handling non-compliance. In essence, even if VSS and due diligence rules have the same goals, they work in separate spheres and deal with different difficulties. Including VSS in due diligence systems calls for rigorous evaluation of the synergies and shortcomings among these instruments. Policymakers and companies have to negotiate this complexity to build inclusive and efficient environmental governance systems that make use of VSS's advantages as well as those of required due diligence rules. This will help to improve global sustainability initiatives and guarantee that all stakeholders—especially those in vulnerable positions—are assisted in the change toward more ethical and sustainable trading practices.

Crafting Inclusive and Effective Due Diligence Rules for Developing Nations: Key Lessons

Drawing on the experiences of voluntary sustainability standards (VSS) in poor nations provides insightful analysis for applying inclusive and effective due diligence rules inside international value chains (GVCs). These lessons underline the vital need for inclusion, justice, and the building of strong support structures that fit the special situation of these nations, therefore enabling more efficient and fair sustainable governance. One of the most important takeaways from the deployment of VSS in developing nations is that these standards, much like due diligence rules, are generally pushed from the top down. Originally from affluent nations, VSS are sometimes seen as outside demands adding layers of complexity and expense for manufacturers in developing nations.

These criteria might aggravate previously existing inequality by burdening producers who might already be struggling to compete in worldwide markets, therefore undermining equality and progress. Small-scale manufacturers have often found it more difficult to run due to the complicated and expensive compliance rules linked with VSS, perhaps leading them out of the market and widening socioeconomic inequalities. The VSS experience also emphasizes another important problem: the absence of diversity and representation in the governance of these norms. Studies show that just a tiny fraction of VSS models guarantee significant involvement of developing nation stakeholders. This exclusion might lead to standards that do not adequately represent local settings and difficulties, therefore lowering their relevance and acceptance among local producers. Developing nations should be more actively involved in both the standard-setting and decision-making procedures if due diligence rules help to prevent repeating these hazards.

This inclusiveness would assist in guaranteeing that the rules more practically and effectively promote sustainable development since they are better matched with the particular requirements and realities of these nations. Successful application of due diligence rules also depends on an awareness of and solution for the particular difficulties faced by underdeveloped nations. The South African wine sector serves as an example of how occasionally locally led sustainability projects may overlook or even aggravate already existing issues. While implementing sustainability sometimes becomes a standard expectation rather than a differentiating element that attracts higher pricing, it usually incurs large expenses. By enforcing similar standards across all sectors without addressing the extra expenses and challenges experienced by businesses in underdeveloped nations, due diligence rules may perhaps aggravate existing inequalities.

The VSS experience also emphasizes the need for offering significant financial support and capacity-building projects to enable manufacturers in developing nations to adhere to sustainability criteria. Many manufacturers in underdeveloped nations just do not have the large financial resources needed to implement these requirements. These manufacturers might be unable to satisfy due diligence criteria without enough help, thereby running the danger of being excluded from world markets. Particularly crucial in tackling issues with formalization and organization—common in emerging nations—building capacity helps to solve problems. For small-scale gold mining in Colombia, for example, the challenges of formalizing and organizing workers have hampered the acceptance of VSS even if the possible advantages—better pricing for certified goods—have been there.

These difficulties reflect larger problems that many underdeveloped and least developed nations experience, whereby legal and administrative obstacles as well as worker ignorance or lack of desire could hinder the effective execution of sustainability projects. Several important insights from the VSS experience could help to make due diligence rules more efficient and inclusive. First of all, broad consultation has to be established to guarantee that developing nations actively participate in the development and application of due diligence rules.

This strategy would guarantee that the rules be customized to meet the particular requirements and problems of these nations, therefore increasing their relevance and acceptability to local authorities. Second, strong support structures have to be in place to help manufacturers in developing nations using due diligence criteria. Financial help as well as focused capacity-building initiatives meant to handle the particular difficulties of every context—such as formalization and worker organization—should be part of this support. Furthermore, pre-existing issues such as inequality and infrastructural shortcomings must be addressed before enforcing more laws.

Good environmental governance has to be part of a larger development plan including regional-specific objectives so that due diligence projects support sustainable development without aggravating current inequalities. Finally, careful design of due diligence rules is necessary to prevent aggravation of inequality. This might entail implementing various strategies or giving especially sensitive areas and businesses more help so that the rules favor inclusiveness instead of exclusion. Finally, the knowledge gained from using VSS in underdeveloped nations provides vital direction for the execution of due diligence policies.

Embracing these lessons—especially the need for support systems, contextual understanding, and inclusivity—policymakers can create rules that are more effective, fair, and sustainable, significantly contributing to world development goals while ensuring that no vulnerable producer is left behind.

CHAPTER 15   THE NEXUS OF TRADE, ENVIRONMENT, AND SUSTAINABLE DEVELOPMENT

Balancing Sustainability and Inclusivity in Global Trade: The Role of Due Diligence Rules and Voluntary Sustainability Standards in Developing Nations

Particularly for poorer nations, including sustainability into global commerce offers a complicated range of possibilities and problems. Due diligence rules and voluntary sustainability standards (VSS) cross at global value chains (GVCs) to highlight the complex balance needed to support sustainability while guaranteeing that commerce stays fair and inclusive. The different aims, views, and economic realities across nations make this integration especially difficult as international trade regulations progressively include sustainability objectives. Establishing international trade policies that allow various economic realities is one of the main difficulties as well. Although everyone understands the need for sustainable trade, the strategies to reach it differ greatly and usually represent the interests of more industrialized countries. Particularly developing nations find it difficult to satisfy the strict environmental and sustainability criteria these countries have established.

Often without enough regard for their particular situation and capacity, the present method of including sustainability into trade is top-down impositions, wherein wealthier nations set the norms that poor nations must obey. This strategy might aggravate conflicts inside the World Trade Organization (WTO) and result in different applications of these guidelines, therefore compromising their efficiency. Using trade preferences to reward compliance might help to address this difficulty. Developed nations may promote more environmentally friendly behavior without imposing too harsh policies by providing better trading circumstances to developing countries that embrace and follow sustainability criteria.

This strategy can leverage VSS's expertise, which has had conflicting success in boosting sustainability. Although VSS have been crucial in areas like agriculture and forestry, their top-down character and related compliance costs have often alienated producers in developing nations, therefore stressing the necessity of a more balanced and inclusive approach to sustainability in trade. Adopting inclusive and comprehensive policies that solve the more general development issues confronting emerging nations is crucial in order to strike this equilibrium. Trade sustainability cannot be seen in a vacuum; it must be included in a more comprehensive development plan, including infrastructure building, poverty reduction, and educational enhancement. Dealing with these basic problems will help emerging nations be more suited to fulfill their environmental objectives and significantly support world sustainability projects. VSS's teachings can greatly guide the due diligence rules' application.

Particularly in sectors like agriculture and forestry, VSS have been vital in encouraging sustainability inside GVCs. Their developed techniques and experience provide insightful analysis on how due diligence rules could be created and followed successfully. VSS have also had major difficulties, especially with relation to compliance costs, producer ability in underdeveloped nations, and audit system efficacy. These challenges underscore the need for flexible governance instruments that are context-specific rather than universally applicable.

Integration of these governance instruments in a way that uses their individual strengths will help to optimize the synergies between VSS and due diligence rules while reducing trade-offs. Combining the particular environmental focus and adaptability of VSS with the more general, legally enforceable due diligence rules, for example, may assist businesses in simplifying compliance initiatives and prevent duplicity. Careful management of this integration will help to guarantee that the flexibility and distinctiveness of VSS are not lost in the process, therefore undermining their efficacy. Due diligence rules bring possibilities as well as difficulties for emerging nations. These rules present an opportunity to further the worldwide sustainability agenda, even if they might cause some extra responsibilities.

Establishing focused support structures that let emerging nations reach these new criteria will help minimize possible negative effects. Financial help, professional advice, and capacity-building initiatives catered to meet the particular difficulties producers in these areas confront should all be part of this support. Moreover, promoting broader inclusiveness in the rule-making process helps to guarantee that the many requirements and situations of underdeveloped nations are given enough attention. Looking forward, various issues become clear for the efficient inclusion of sustainability into world commerce. Ensuring that policy development is inclusive and including active participation of stakeholders in developing nations is among the most important ones. This inclusiveness will enable rules that not only fit more general development objectives but also are fair and efficient.

Furthermore, improved multilateral collaboration is required to further debates on due diligence and sustainability in global commerce. This cooperation needs to involve more openness among nations, international agencies, and professionals, as well as more country-wide cooperation. In this sense, South-South cooperation becomes especially crucial as it helps underdeveloped nations exchange information, resources, and tactics catered to their particular difficulties. Maintaining sustained efforts to build a more sustainable global trade system would need careful mixing of voluntary and mandatory policies, the building of strong compliance mechanisms, and continuous attempts to meet the various requirements and capacity of every nation engaged. Significant progress toward a more fair and sustainable global economy may be accomplished by using the best features of both VSS and due diligence rules, as well as by encouraging a more open and supportive international trade environment.

Supported by due diligence rules and VSS, the integration of sustainability into global commerce must ultimately be precisely tuned to reflect the particular circumstances of poor nations. This strategy will guarantee that initiatives for sustainability are not only successful but also equitable, therefore enabling global development objectives without marginalizing small producers or aggravating already existing inequality.

Charting a Greener Future: Member-Led Initiatives at the Nexus of Trade, Environment, and Sustainable Development

Driven by three important member-led efforts emphasizing commerce, environment, and sustainable development, trade and environmental debates at the World Trade Organization (WTO) have acquired tremendous momentum in recent years. These projects show a group effort by several WTO members to promote improved cooperation on urgent global environmental issues inside the WTO structure. Starting in December 2021, the projects on plastic pollution, environmental sustainability, and reform of fossil fuel subsidies provide a calculated means to foster cooperation and communication. They complement the continuous effort of other WTO bodies, most especially the Committee on Trade and Environment (CTE).

The ministerial declarations marked a significant milestone and garnered widespread backing from all WTO members. This broad support reflects the worldwide awareness of the pressing need for action on environmental sustainability in the commerce setting. Especially, these sponsorships cover a large share of world trade and feature least developed countries (LDCs) and emerging nations heavily represented. This inclusive character emphasizes the dedication to make sure every member, from different economic backgrounds, contributes to the dialogue. Every comment

CHAPTER 15 THE NEXUS OF TRADE, ENVIRONMENT, AND SUSTAINABLE DEVELOPMENT

highlights the vital requirement of a fair transition and the significant contributions that participants may make, therefore enabling honest and inclusive involvement from every WTO member.

Initiated by 53 WTO members, one of the major projects is the Trade and Environmental Sustainability Structured Discussions (TESSD). Seeking to explore paths forward and encourage more concentrated attention on these issues under the WTO's regular committee work, this project intends to enable information flow and conversation on the interconnections between environment and commerce. Reflecting its relevance and possible influence on both trade and environmental policy, TESSD has effectively attracted support from some of the world's top trading nations as well as a wide spectrum of other members. TessD helps members to share experiences, best practices, and creative ideas for including environmental issues into trade policy by building a disciplined forum for debates.

Led by China and Fiji, another major effort is the informal Dialogue on Plastic Pollution and Environmentally Sustainable Plastic Trade. This project seeks to investigate trade cooperation paths to assist worldwide initiatives to reduce plastic pollution and move toward a more circular and sustainable plastics economy. The conversation has presented a thorough work schedule to increase openness, track trade patterns, and advance best practices.

Emphasizing the need for collaboration that complements continuous worldwide efforts on plastic pollution, this project strives to match trade policies with the global drive toward lowering plastic waste and improving environmental sustainability.

Initiated by New Zealand and others, the third project is the Fossil Fuel Subsidy Reform (FFSR). This project supports openness, sharing of reform experiences, and conversation on how trade policies could promote efforts at fossil fuel subsidy reform by means of the WTO framework. Recognizing the particular difficulties and conditions experienced by developing nations and hence minimizing negative effects on vulnerable populations, the FFSR project aims to phase out ineffective subsidies that support wasteful spending. Through the reduction of fossil fuel subsidies, this project seeks to lower greenhouse gas emissions and encourage a shift toward greener energy sources, therefore supporting worldwide efforts to slow down climate change.

The momentum behind these member-led projects at the WTO exposes a growing agreement on the vital role trade policies play in tackling environmental problems and advancing sustainable development. These projects show important first steps in including environmental issues in the fabric of world trade regulation by creating venues for communication, openness, and cooperation. They also highlight the need for inclusivity and group action, making sure that initiatives to progress environmental sustainability complement more general objectives of fostering fair and sustainable development all around.

The projects show a systematic and all-encompassing approach to using trade to address environmental problems. They understand that tackling world environmental problems calls for a concerted effort including several points of view and agendas. Through encouraging communication and cooperation among members, these projects help to share knowledge, experience, and creative ideas, therefore strengthening the WTO's ability to effectively address environmental issues.

Moreover, the inclusive character of these projects guarantees that underdeveloped nations and LDCs are not behind. Through the active participation of these nations in the dialogues, the projects support a fair transition, taking into account the particular conditions and requirements of every member. Achieving sustainable development that benefits everyone—especially those most vulnerable to the effects of environmental degradation—dependent on this strategy is imperative.

The accomplishment of these projects also emphasizes the need for involving stakeholders. The projects promote a more all-encompassing and inclusive attitude to environmental sustainability by appreciating the significant contributions made by several stakeholders, including civil society, the business sector, and international organizations. This participation improves the efficacy of the projects in tackling environmental problems and helps to generate more general support for them.

Ultimately, the member-led projects on plastic pollution, environmental sustainability, and reform of fossil fuel subsidies show major progress in the WTO's attempts to include environmental factors into world trade governance. These projects highlight the need for group effort, diversity, and stakeholder involvement in tackling the intricate and linked problems of trade, environment, and sustainable development. The projects are guiding a greener future that fits trade policies with the pressing need to preserve our planet and advance sustainable development for all by building venues for communication, openness, and cooperation.

CHAPTER 15   THE NEXUS OF TRADE, ENVIRONMENT, AND SUSTAINABLE DEVELOPMENT

Engaging Stakeholders in the Green Trade Revolution: A Pathway to Inclusive Environmental Action

As a member-driven international organization, the World Trade Organization (WTO) usually works within a framework whereby non-state actors—such as NGOs, corporate representatives, and academics—have limited direct involvement in its deliberative procedures. Nonetheless, WTO members are realizing the important contributions these participants may make to many facets of the operations of the body. Several progressive actions taken since the WTO's founding clearly show this change toward inclusiveness in order to improve openness and enable more access to records and negotiations.

The WTO Public Forum, an annual event allowing public debate on a broad range of WTO-related concerns, is one of the main venues for stakeholder interaction. Reflecting a growing public interest in how trade policies may promote world environmental goals and fight climate change, the meeting has progressively concentrated on sustainability issues.

Emphasizing the services industry, digitalization, and inclusive trade policy, the 2023 Public Forum focused on trade's part in building a greener, more sustainable future. The debates at this forum not only highlight the several dimensions of trade and environmental problems but also show how different sectors may coordinate their activities toward shared objectives.

The WTO Environment Week, in which participants co-host events or present speakers, offers still another important chance for involvement. This participation emphasizes the need for cooperative communication in using trade to solve environmental problems. Environment Week activities usually showcase creative ways to include environmental sustainability into business operations, therefore giving stakeholders a forum to exchange knowledge and ideas. Furthermore, unofficial meetings inside WTO panels, such as the Committee on Trade and Environment (CTE), let stakeholders directly participate, therefore enabling direct trade-related contributions to renewable energy and environmental sustainability. These events guarantee that many opinions are heard and accounted for in the decision-making process, therefore bridging official discussions with the wider society.

Stakeholders also have means to interact with the larger deliberative framework of the WTO, including the opportunity of accreditation to participate in events of WTO ministerial conferences and WTO Secretariat attendance at briefings. Although the

WTO members' adoption of their views still rests at their will, public hearings in dispute settlement processes and the submission of amicus curiae briefs constitute other important avenues via which stakeholders may impact the WTO's decision-making. These systems for involving stakeholders show an increasing understanding of the need for openness and diversity in WTO operations.

Recent member-led projects on trade, the environment, and sustainable development best highlight the WTO's changing approach to involving stakeholders. These projects—which cover plastic pollution, environmental sustainability, and reform of fossil fuel subsidies—have specifically promised to include participants in their meetings and negotiations. The Trade and Environmental Sustainability Structured Discussions (TESSD), for example, feature sessions meant for interactions between WTO members and outside stakeholders, therefore illustrating a methodical strategy to include many points of view in trade and environmental decisions. By means of these exchanges, stakeholders provide insightful analysis that influences policies and projects meant to support environmentally friendly trading practices.

The increasing participation of stakeholders in the WTO signifies a significant shift in the WTO's approach to environmental issues and global trade. The WTO is enhancing its deliberative processes and strengthening its commitment to openness, inclusivity, and sustainability in worldwide trade practices by means of facilitating dialogue and cooperation across many platforms and initiatives, leveraging the expertise and insights of a wide spectrum of non-state actors. Engagement of stakeholders guarantees that the WTO's decisions are based on a broad spectrum of viewpoints and knowledge, therefore improving the quality of negotiations.

Dealing with difficult and linked issues like climate change, biodiversity loss, and sustainable development calls especially on this inclusive approach. Stakeholders offer a wealth of expertise and experience that can assist in spotting creative ideas and best practices. The WTO can better grasp the effects of trade policy on many sectors and communities by involving a wide range of participants, therefore producing more balanced and successful results.

Furthermore, involving stakeholders helps to create responsibility and ownership when non-governmental entities start to actively participate in the worldwide commerce and environmental control process. The development of the trust and collaboration required to properly handle world problems depends on this cooperative attitude. The WTO's dedication to stakeholder involvement shows an understanding that reaching sustainable development targets calls for group effort and the contributions of every industry in society.

CHAPTER 15   THE NEXUS OF TRADE, ENVIRONMENT, AND SUSTAINABLE DEVELOPMENT

The changing attitude toward stakeholder involvement inside the WTO marks major progress in the efforts of the WTO to include environmental issues in worldwide trade policy. The WTO is leveraging the combined knowledge of non-state players by building forums for communication, openness, and cooperation, thus enhancing its decision-making procedures and supporting its sustainability pledge. Plotting a greener future that fits trade policies with the pressing need to save our planet and advance sustainable development for all depends on this inclusive and participatory approach.

Integrating Trade, Environment, and Sustainable Development: A Pathway to Global Cooperation

Pressing transboundary environmental challenges, including climate change, biodiversity loss, and pollution, call for coherent, cooperative policy solutions spanning multiple countries that integrate trade, environment, and sustainable development. One important international platform where states may participate in inclusive conversations and measures tackling these linked issues is the World Trade Organization (WTO). This chapter defines the several WTO entry points and procedures relevant to trade, environmental, and sustainable development projects.

With its multifarious structure, the WTO offers vital forums for evaluating current policies, information exchange, best-practice discussion, promotion of common understanding, negotiation, problem solving, and litigation when needed. The other WTO bodies—including the Committee on Trade and Environment (CTE) and the Committee on Trade and Development (CTD)—help greatly to enable these operations. These bodies help members to consider how trade policies interact with environmental and developmental objectives, therefore making sure trade acts as a means of sustainable development.

Moreover, member-led projects emphasizing environmental sustainability, plastic pollution, and reform of fossil fuel subsidies have become a significant means of improving member communication. These projects not only spot and solve particular problems but also foster closer multilateral cooperation. The Trade and Environmental Sustainability Structured Discussions (TESSD), for example, give members a forum to exchange best practices and experiences, therefore fostering a cooperative approach to including environmental issues into trade policies.

The Informal Dialogue on Plastic Pollution and Environmentally Sustainable Plastic Trade, led by China and Fiji, explores trade opportunities to support global efforts to reduce plastic pollution and transition to a more circular economy. Supported by New

CHAPTER 15   THE NEXUS OF TRADE, ENVIRONMENT, AND SUSTAINABLE DEVELOPMENT

Zealand and other nations, the Fossil Fuel Subsidy Reform (FFSR) campaign promotes openness and communication on how trade policies may help to phase out ineffective fossil fuel subsidies, therefore supporting world attempts to lower greenhouse gas emissions.

Looking ahead, a coordinated effort will be required to use the WTO as a successful forum for increasing cooperation on the trade, environment, and sustainable development concerns facing the global economy. This involves a critical analysis of how new forms of collaboration and worldwide rules may proactively support trade and environmental initiatives. Reaching this target will call for high-level ministerial direction, improved national policy coherence, and ongoing, active involvement of stakeholders.

Setting the strategic orientation and priorities of the WTO's activities on trade and environment depends on high-level ministerial direction. Ministers can guarantee that trade policies complement world environmental goals and offer the political drive required to forward difficult discussions. Driving forward projects like the TESD and FFSR depends on this leadership to guarantee that they get the resources and attention required to meet their objectives.

Furthermore, absolutely essential is improved national policy coherence. Governments must guarantee that their policies on trade, ecology, and development are mutually reinforcing. Policymaking must be done holistically, with several ministries and agencies cooperating to produce synergies between environmental objectives and trade. Countries can help more successfully promote world sustainability by matching national policies with international obligations.

Another important component is the ongoing, active participation of stakeholders. Non-state players such as NGOs, corporate leaders, and academics enhance the WTO's deliberative processes. Stakeholders contribute insightful knowledge and viewpoints that help to spot creative ideas and excellent practices. Their involvement guarantees more openness and responsibility in the WTO's operations, therefore fostering confidence and support for trade policies advancing sustainable development.

Although everyone's awareness of the WTO's contribution to solving world environmental issues is growing, attaining its full potential calls for coordinated actions among all members and stakeholders. The WTO can contribute to building a more fair and sustainable worldwide trade system by encouraging innovation, communication, and cooperation, as well as by means of policies. This entails not just attending to current environmental problems but also setting the foundation for long-term, institutional transformation.

CHAPTER 15   THE NEXUS OF TRADE, ENVIRONMENT, AND SUSTAINABLE DEVELOPMENT

At the WTO, the integration of commerce, environment, and sustainable development shows a more general awareness of the links among these spheres. The problems of pollution, biodiversity loss, and climate change cannot be resolved by one sector; they call for a coordinated, cross-sectoral strategy. With its worldwide scope and all-encompassing structure, the WTO is well-suited to enable this integration and advance policies supporting both environmental sustainability and economic progress.

Although the WTO has made significant progress toward including environmental factors in its operations, more remains to be done. Leveraging the WTO's platforms and procedures will help to promote more collaboration and coherence between trade and environmental policy going forward. Essential elements of this initiative include high-level ministerial direction, national policy coherence, and active participation of stakeholders. Working together, WTO members and stakeholders can plot a course toward a greener, more sustainable future, ensuring that trade supports human welfare as well as the welfare of the earth.

Bridging the Gender Gap: Overcoming Barriers to Accessing Trade Finance and Promoting Inclusivity

In the field of international trade, women entrepreneurs encounter major obstacles that prevent their capacity to compete and flourish in worldwide marketplaces, so gender equality stays a distant target. Even though trade finance's short-term tenor, trackable character, and often self-liquidating character make it somewhat secure, many companies—especially those run by women entrepreneurs—find it difficult to get such funding. The strict collateral requirements placed by financial institutions are a main barrier for women-led companies trying to get trade credit.

Women disproportionately suffer in their capacity to get trade finance, as the typical scale of the companies they control often lacks the necessary resources to satisfy these needs. Given that younger and smaller companies, including those run by women, often lack a sufficient asset base to use as collateral against a loan, 90% of commercial banks in Africa cite the lack of collateral as the main reason they reject trade finance applications—a situation that is hardly surprising.

Another major difficulty is the intricacy of trade finance paperwork procedures. Sometimes one transaction calls for up to one hundred papers. For women and SMEs especially, this heavy bureaucratic load can be intimidating. One participant at the Global Trade Partners Meeting of the International Finance Corporation (IFC) underlined that the paperwork procedure by itself accounts for 50–60% of the transaction expenses. This complexity, together with high collateral requirements and a lack of financial knowledge, greatly hinders women's economic activity, restricting their capacity to grow companies, penetrate new markets, and boost their economic footprint.

Understanding these difficulties, the IFC has been closely involved in initiatives meant to empower women in business. Launched in mid-2019, the Banking on Women Global Trade Finance Program (BOW-GTFP) is a noteworthy effort aimed at giving women-owned companies engaged in international trade financial support and resources. Aiming to increase women's involvement in worldwide trade, the initiative has enabled approximately $260 million in transactions since its inception, therefore fostering gender parity and economic inclusiveness.

The creation of financial products that substitute alternative types of collateral or techniques to assess creditworthiness instead of conventional collateral marks a major breakthrough in breaking through these obstacles. Certain organizations are looking at using receivables as security, therefore enabling women who do not have other conventional assets or property to still get financing. Another exciting project is mixed financing, which blends commercial and concessional money. It addresses the capital and knowledge gaps many women have by offering financial resources as well as relevant training and mentoring. Digital platforms and big data, among other technological developments, are crucial in changing the way women access trade financing. These sites may help women-led companies be more visible and reduce documentation costs, therefore facilitating their worldwide competitiveness. Financial institutions can gain a hitherto unattainable understanding of the transaction histories and financial behavior of women entrepreneurs by using data analytics and artificial intelligence. This change toward a more inclusive financial system acknowledges and meets the demands of women entrepreneurs, therefore enabling their more effective participation in world commerce.

Notwithstanding these developments, robust networks and advocacy groups that can give women entrepreneurs vital assistance and education are needed. By collaboratively addressing shared obstacles such as access to money, legal constraints, or market entrance problems, networks help women to trade more successfully. Advocacy organizations can call attention to the particular requirements of women in commerce, fight for legislative reforms, and demand more institutional support on both local and worldwide levels. Overcoming the systematic obstacles encountered by women in commerce depends on the cooperative efforts of multilateral development banks

(MDBs), development agencies, and financial institutions worldwide. The IFC and its partners want to build a more fair and inclusive environment for women entrepreneurs in international commerce by supporting creative financial solutions, leveraging technology, and strengthening advocacy networks.

Silent No More: Uniting Trade, Climate, and Finance for Bold, Inclusive Change

We have to understand that breaking away from the inertia of the current global trading system is absolutely vital. The moment for complacency has passed quite clearly. We are at a critical juncture where we must not only desire but also absolutely require decisive action for the future of our planet and the welfare of future generations.

We know that little incremental adjustments will not be enough to fulfill the Paris Agreement's obligations. We have to start a dramatic change in all aspects of our societies and economies. This means a basic change in our manufacturing, consumption, transportation, investment, trading, and funding of climate solutions.

Above all, we have to release the chains of unsustainable methods that have long controlled our economic terrain. This requires saying goodbye to carbon-intensive goods and services, tearing down the obstacles to sustainable production and consumption, and transforming our logistics and transportation networks to give low-emission alternatives top priority. Our past's defining fossil fuel reliance needs to be replaced with a dedication to sustainable, renewable energy sources able to support our future.

Simply divorcing from the unsustainable is insufficient, though. We also have to make investments for the future we want to see. This means using commerce to advance and enable the creation of environmentally friendly goods and technologies that will become pillars of our combined climate solutions. International trade can spur innovation by means of green technology distribution and worldwide cooperation on climate-friendly projects. Trade can become a very effective weapon in the fight against climate change by establishing markets for sustainable products and rewarding ecologically beneficial behavior.

The pressing necessity to hasten the shift to sustainable energy sources drives the centrality of this effort. We must redouble our efforts to provide access to clean energy, significantly increase renewable energy capacity, and drive unprecedented achievements in energy efficiency.

CHAPTER 15   THE NEXUS OF TRADE, ENVIRONMENT, AND SUSTAINABLE DEVELOPMENT

We can only expect to minimize the most negative effects of climate change and guarantee a sustainable future for all by moving away from fossil fuels worldwide. With a major share of world greenhouse gas emissions, the energy sector is the one that can help us to lower our carbon footprint. Investing in solar, wind, and other renewable energy sources helps us to build a more sustainable and strong energy infrastructure.

The latest reaffirmation of the vital need for international cooperation at COP28 reminds us of the connectivity of our shared destiny. As we must cooperate to directly address the climate catastrophe, so too must we acknowledge the indispensable contribution trade may provide to this effort. Not only is international collaboration an ethical need but also a strategic one. There are no boundaries to the climate catastrophe; thus, our remedies have to be also global. Our trade policies have to match our climate goals so that the worldwide trading system supports rather than undermines our efforts to slow down global warming.

Trade ministers pledging to support sustainable development and climate action are ready to use their influence as a tool for good, guiding bold, inclusive action that will define the course of our planet for the next generations. This calls for a change in perspective as much as policy changes. Trade should be seen as a tool to accomplish more general social and environmental objectives rather than as a goal in and of itself. Including sustainability at the center of trade policy will help us to make sure that economic development does not compromise the environment.

All spheres of life must cooperate if we are to go toward a sustainable future. Together, governments, companies, civil society, and people will build a more fair and sustainable planet. Overcoming our obstacles and grabbing the chances that lie ahead depend on our working together. Though ambitious, the change we want is within our reach. By means of tenacity and group efforts, we can build a world in which trade and sustainability coexist, thereby guaranteeing a rich future for all.

The urgency of bold, inclusive transformation integrating trade, climate, and finance has never been clearer. The current situation is unsustainable; we have to welcome drastic change to save our earth and guarantee the welfare of next generations. We can build a worldwide trading system supporting environmental sustainability and economic development by divorcing harmful habits, funding sustainable innovations, and promoting international cooperation. At this critical juncture, our determination to take decisive action will shape the future trajectory of our planet. Let us grab this chance to propel significant transformation and create an inclusive, sustainable future for all.

CHAPTER 15   THE NEXUS OF TRADE, ENVIRONMENT, AND SUSTAINABLE DEVELOPMENT

Igniting the Flame: Sparking Collective Action on Climate Change

The Coalition of 60 forward-looking trade ministers has set an ambitious goal during the past year: to remove obstacles and create strong coalitions in the fight against climate change. With a strong emphasis on cooperation, they have rallied with ministries of climate, environment, finance, and development, creating a tapestry of relationships with stakeholders all around the world. Now, as the world convenes in Davos, the Coalition is gearing up for a historic ministerial roundtable, a pivotal moment where the interwoven strands of climate, trade, and finance intersect.

The Coalition aims to start a real firestorm of communication in the hallowed halls of Davos, igniting a first interchange of ideas that transcends conventional boundaries and finds unrealized chances for group action. Their vision goes much beyond simple conversation; they are the designers of a new era of sustainable trade, guiding a fair transition free from leaving any country behind. Leaders from many disciplines come together in Davos to represent not just a meeting of ideas but also a blending of missions and visions, as they are all committed to a sustainable future.

Their mission is clear: to advocate solutions that enable poor nations on their path toward sustainable commerce, therefore promoting synergies with climate financing that open hitherto unexplored horizons. From supporting net-zero, sustainable trade finance to increasing climate solutions via creative government procurement methods, they lead a transforming movement ready to change the financial scene worldwide. The Coalition understands that developing nations have the most to gain from a change to sustainable trade policies and frequently suffer the toughest obstacles. Their efforts thus are directed toward building inclusive and fair paths that guarantee that the advantages of sustainable commerce will find their way everywhere.

Still, their aspirations are not limited there. They are the designers of a new paradigm whereby trade serves as a catalyst for finance and investment in resilient development, adaptation, and climate change mitigating action. They want to use trade policies to drive the creation, dissemination, and accessibility of climate-friendly goods, services, and technologies, thereby hastening the change to a cleaner, more sustainable future. This vision sees trade as a potent tool for social development and environmental preservation rather than only a means of financial communication. The Coalition is dedicated to building an ecosystem where trade and climate action are mutually reinforcing, therefore advancing an agenda that gives both environmental protection and economic development first priority.

CHAPTER 15   THE NEXUS OF TRADE, ENVIRONMENT, AND SUSTAINABLE DEVELOPMENT

Still, they keep aware of the need for justice and balance even as they negotiate this unknown ground. They support carbon measurement and price systems that maximize climate benefits while reducing trade distortions, therefore ensuring that every action made is based on ideas of equity and justice. Their strategy stems from the conviction that, given the differing capacities and obligations of every country, successful climate action has to be fair and equitable. This means creating open, responsible systems equipped to produce significant climate results without aggravating current inequality.

For the Coalition, dismantling silos is more than just an idealistic objective. It is a dedication to stretching limits, building relationships, and moving deliberately and coherently toward significant influence. They serve as beacons of hope in a world grappling with the existential threat of climate change, aligning trade and finance with global agendas. The ministers know that real development calls for tearing down the divisions, separating many sectors and fields historically. They want to develop a whole strategy that tackles the several aspects of climate change by encouraging cooperation and harmony.

Together, they are not only writing history; they are creating a future in which resilience, wealth, and sustainability coexist. The Coalition's initiatives are meant to create a society in which environmental and economic goals are perceived as mutually reinforcing rather than as incompatible. Through their efforts, they hope to leave a legacy of environmentally friendly development upon which the next generations may build.

The path taken by the Coalition of 60 trade ministers toward a time when group action is the standard rather than the exception is audacious. Their efforts underline the need for international cooperation in tackling world problems and the transforming power of trade when matched with social fairness and environmental aims. They serve as a potent reminder that the fight against climate change calls not only for ambition but also for cooperation, creativity, and relentless dedication to justice as they keep stretching the bounds of what is feasible.

The Coalition's goal is evidence of the strength of group effort and the need to remove obstacles to bring about significant transformation. They are opening the path for a future whereby sustainable growth is within reach for all countries by aggregating trade and finance. Leaders from throughout the world find inspiration in their work in Davos and beyond to unite and act boldly toward a more resilient, fair, and sustainable planet. Through its endeavors, the Coalition ignites a spark of hope and action, guiding us toward a brighter and more sustainable future.

CHAPTER 15   THE NEXUS OF TRADE, ENVIRONMENT, AND SUSTAINABLE DEVELOPMENT

Seizing the Climate Zeitgeist: A Historic Moment for Action

In the global quest for climate action, the Inflation Reduction Act (IRA) represents a significant milestone—a robust declaration of intent from the world's second-largest greenhouse gas emitter. Unprecedented financial support from the US federal government into the field of clean energy and climate mitigation has spurred a new era of innovation and success by inspiring confidence. The IRA is a statement to the world that the United States is dedicated to spearheading the struggle against climate change, not only a legislative accomplishment.

Early signs are encouraging; studies show that since the measure's introduction, over 100,000 green jobs have been created, evidence of the transforming power of focused investment. "The more affordable it is to pursue innovation, the more you're spurring innovation," says former Canadian Ambassador to the WTO and Senior Associate at the Centre for Strategic and International Studies (CSIS). Indeed, the high subsidies of the IRA are expected to stimulate a rise in the adoption of clean technologies, thereby bridging the gap between current policy and the ambitious 2030 targets. The financial systems built inside the IRA are meant to reduce the expenses of innovation so enterprises and communities can afford to change toward sustainable practices.

Although domestic factors have resulted in protections for US-made goods, the world agrees the IRA is not favorable for the earth. Declaring, "Finally, the number one economic powerhouse says that decarbonizing is part of its trade agenda," Belgian Prime Minister Alexandre De Croo captured this attitude during the World Economic Forum's Annual Meeting in Davos. This comment emphasizes the importance of the United States' fresh dedication to climate action, which influences other countries to raise their own climate goals by means of ripple effects.

Leaders in Europe view the IRA not only as a policy project but also as a driver of worldwide competitiveness, so encouraging measures to simplify climate rules and hasten decarbonization. Emphasizing the significance of modifying state aid policies to promote innovation and competitiveness, Ursula von der Leyen, President of the European Commission, details the EU's proactive posture. "Easier calculations, simpler procedures, accelerated approvals," she says—a call to quick response in the face of a fast-changing climate scene. By raising a high standard for climate policy, the IRA forces other areas to review and improve their own regulatory systems, hence generating a positive feedback loop in global climate governance.

CHAPTER 15   THE NEXUS OF TRADE, ENVIRONMENT, AND SUSTAINABLE DEVELOPMENT

Although the EU has long been leading in terms of renewable energy financing and subsidies, the local production needs of the IRA differ from current European regulations. Unlike the EU's strategy, which gives early-stage technological research top priority without imposing localization restrictions, the IRA steers a different path, distinguished by a deliberate attempt to strengthen home manufacturing capacity. This deliberate difference draws attention to a larger discussion in the field of climate policy: how best to strike a balance between supporting national economic gains and global innovation ecosystems? Under the IRA, the US strategy seeks to establish a strong home market for clean technologies, therefore preserving the economic benefits of the green revolution inside her boundaries.

In this era of unprecedented climate action, the IRA offers hope as it demonstrates the transformative power of policy in shaping a more sustainable future for future generations. It represents a pivotal moment where legal, technological, and financial measures unite to address the pressing threat of climate change. The community closely monitors the United States' implementation of the IRA, drawing inspiration and insights to support their own environmental projects. This kind of leadership is not only about lowering emissions but also about establishing a standard for how effectively strong legislative tools may propel structural transformation.

The success of the IRA will be judged not only in terms of emissions reductions and employment creation but also in terms of its capacity to inspire and encourage such activities all around. The IRA presents a paradigm of how thorough, well-funded, and strategically planned policies can have a significant influence as countries struggle with the several issues of climate change. The cooperative efforts among governments, companies, and local groups following the IRA's execution will probably define the next stage of the worldwide climate movement.

Ultimately, the Inflation Reduction Act is a call to action, a blueprint for change, and a portent of a more sustainable future—more than just a policy. The IRA exemplifies the ability of legislative action to stimulate innovation, foster economic growth, and combat climate change at this pivotal juncture. Seizing the climate zeitgeist, the United States is not only fulfilling its own environmental obligations but also setting the path for a worldwide movement toward a more resilient, green planet. The knowledge gained from the implementation of the IRA will surely influence the upcoming generation of climate policy, therefore guaranteeing the ongoing momentum toward sustainability.

CHAPTER 15 THE NEXUS OF TRADE, ENVIRONMENT, AND SUSTAINABLE DEVELOPMENT

Turning Tides: The WTO at a Crossroads

The introduction of the Green Deal Investment Plan and the Inflation Reduction Act (IRA) has sparked a passionate discussion in the World Trade Organization's (WTO) hallways, highlighting the careful balance between world trade reform and domestic priorities. These ambitious subsidy programs provide a significant threat to the long-standing policies supporting the multilateral free trade system as they develop. Promoting domestic green businesses against following international trade rules clearly creates conflict, which prepares the ground for a turning point in WTO history.

Fundamentally, the issue is the basic non-discrimination principle. entrenched in WTO rules—an ethos that forbids trade policies favoring home manufacturers over their international counterparts and subsidies. The foundation of the worldwide trading system, this idea guarantees that every member nation runs on a level playing field. With the specter of green subsidies hovering large, the WTO finds itself at a crossroads and advises member nations to band together and negotiate the complex web of trade-related conflicts accompanying such projects. The difficulty is balancing the long-standing ideas of fair trade guiding world trade with the pressing demand for climate action.

From the perspective of WTO Director-General Ngozi Okonjo-Iweala, the issue is really significant: where will these subsidies go, and can we promote a group approach guaranteeing fair involvement for all? When considering the possible consequences, she underlines the requirement of a sophisticated and balanced subsidy structure that prevents tilting the scales in favor of particular actors on a worldwide scene. Seeking to arbitrate between the several interests of WTO members, Okonjo-Iweala's point of view emphasizes the complexity of the problem and supports solutions that advance both environmental sustainability and economic justice.

However, the implementation of local content controls (LCRs) by the IRA against WTO guidelines raises the possibility of a judicial challenge. The General Agreement on Tariffs and Trade (GATT) Article I binds WTO members to a dedication to promote fair and free competition, therefore casting doubt on the fit of these subsidies with current trade rules.

LCRs directly contradict the most-favored-nation (MFN) principle, which mandates WTO members extend any advantageous treatment given one nation to all members. The route to reconciliation is paved with difficulties since the WTO Appellate Body is still stalled in response to US resistance to new appointments, therefore endangering

CHAPTER 15   THE NEXUS OF TRADE, ENVIRONMENT, AND SUSTAINABLE DEVELOPMENT

the organization's capacity to arbitrate such conflicts. This immobility has left important questions unresolved and created a vacuum in the process of conflict resolution, therefore aggravating tensions.

The function of the WTO becomes the primary subject of dispute in this uncertain terrain. Although everyone agrees that the organization can help to guide the path toward a just and equitable settlement, questions remain about whether political reality will allow significant movement. The geopolitical scene is becoming more fractured as big powers sometimes give national interests first priority over international collaboration. Emily Benson, the Scholl Chair in International Business at the Center for Strategic and International Studies, correctly observes that we are at a pivotal juncture that could significantly shape the future of global trade governance. Benson's observation emphasizes the significant stakes involved since the choices taken during this period will determine the worldwide trade system for the next years.

There are undoubtedly significant stakes involved. Maintaining the relevance and efficiency of the WTO depends on its capacity to change with the dynamics of world trade and environmental policy. The company must navigate the delicate balance between upholding the principles of non-discrimination and fair competition and facilitating the necessary climate action. This balancing effort calls for creative thought, diplomatic grace, and a readiness to give concessions.

Growing conflicts and shifting paradigms, reflecting the evolving dynamics of global trade and the urgent need for cooperative, multilateral solutions, are threatening the WTO's future. Though there are many difficulties ahead, the road forward is also full of chances for change and rebirth. The company has to use the group will of its employees to create a road that meets both environmental sustainability and economic development.

This turning point calls for audacious leadership and creative thinking. It calls for the WTO to not only resolve current conflicts but also create the foundation for a more inclusive and robust worldwide trading system. Overcoming the present deadlock depends mostly on the organization's capacity to enable significant communication and promote cooperation among its several members.

The WTO finds itself at a crossroads, trying to negotiate the challenges of including green subsidies within the framework of global trade regulations. The difficulties presented by the IRA and the Green Deal Investment Plan highlight the need for a well-rounded strategy that upholds environmental sustainability while safeguarding non-discrimination and fair competition. The course of world trade governance will be much changed depending on the decisions the WTO takes as it negotiates this unknown territory. Though the road ahead is unknown, there is much chance for transforming change. The stakes could scarcely be higher; the world is observing. The WTO's capacity to meet this issue will define its legacy and help to shape world trade going forward.

Trading for Tomorrow: How Trade Ministers Forge a Climate-Resilient Future

Rising as an unparalleled threat, the climate crisis blankets towns all around with a shadow of destruction. Given that 1.6 billion people reside in climate-sensitive areas, the urgency of the situation is evident: lives, livelihoods, and entire ecosystems are at risk. And given estimates that this number would treble by 2050, the urgency of action grows even higher.

At the core of this global dilemma is a demand for quick, significant, and consistent cuts in greenhouse gas emissions—a need countries all around the COP27 climate conference in November 2022 reflect. The scope of the situation calls for a global response, and international cooperation is becoming absolutely essential for all of our efforts.

Presenting leaders from Ecuador, the European Union, Kenya, New Zealand, and more than 50 other countries, the Coalition of Trade Ministers on Climate is an alliance created in the furnace of need. Designed amid the hallowed halls of the World Economic Forum's Annual Meeting 2023 in Davos, Switzerland, this alliance symbolizes a historic moment of convergence—a promise to use trade as a tool for sustainable development and climate action—right here. The coalition's founding marks a paradigm shift since it acknowledges that to properly address the approaching threat, trade policies and climate solutions must be entwined.

Our objective is very clear: we want to encourage inclusive cooperation among trade ministers responding globally on climate change. Representing several points of view, different areas, phases of development, and trading conditions, our coalition is evidence of the strength of cooperation in the face of difficulty. Every member offers different ideas and perspectives, therefore building a rich tapestry of information and techniques ready for use to propel significant transformation.

Using trade and investment to accelerate the spread, development, and accessibility of climate-friendly technology, together we will map a course toward a future defined by resilience and sustainability. From the shift to sustainable energy to climate adaptation strategies, our combined desire is unbounded. Supported by strong trade policies that promote innovation and dissemination, the coalition's efforts aim to create an enabling environment where green innovations may blossom.

Still, our road is only starting. Convening with stakeholders from all around the world—from corporate executives to non-governmental organizations—we acknowledge the enormous work ahead. To turn our economy, businesses, and society for the better, we will need relentless dedication, creative ideas, and unflinching teamwork. Dealing with a wide range of stakeholders guarantees that our plans are inclusive and thorough, thereby attending to the requirements and issues of all spheres of life.

Though ambitious, the coalition's agenda is realistic. Our goal is to remove obstacles in the way sustainable practices are adopted, support trade policies encouraging the growth of green technologies, and provide access to climate finance. These initiatives aim not just at reducing climate effects but also at creating strong economies capable of surviving in an environment undergoing changes. Encouragement of a worldwide market for sustainable goods and services would help to both save our planet and boost the economy.

There are numerous obstacles on the path forward. Aligning the complicated global trading system with climate goals will require negotiating a wide range of political and financial issues. There are numerous challenges ahead. squarely with will and commitment. The coalition is dedicated to ongoing communication and cooperation so that our decisions are based on the most recent scientific findings and grounded in the reality of world commerce.

As a coalition bound by vision and goal, together we promise to spearhead the push for a better, more sustainable future for everybody. This is a specific promise to action rather than only a symbolic gesture. Including climate issues in trade decisions will help us to establish a virtuous cycle whereby sustainable commerce stimulates climate action and vice versa. Our success will depend on our capacity to be adaptable and flexible, quickly and foresightedly reacting to new possibilities and problems.

In the battle against climate change, the Coalition of Trade Ministers on Climate offers hope. Using trade's ability to propel climate action can help us to build a strong and sustainable future for all. Though difficult, the road forward has promise. We go forward knowing that our actions now will help to define the world of tomorrow. By means of group efforts, creative ideas, and relentless determination, we can reverse the trend on climate change and create a better future for the next generations.

CHAPTER 15   THE NEXUS OF TRADE, ENVIRONMENT, AND SUSTAINABLE DEVELOPMENT

Green Subsidies Unleashed: Fueling the Future of Climate and Trade

The United States and the European Union (EU) have moved boldly to increase private sector investment in renewable energy in front of the pressing need presented by climate change. Standing as a lighthouse of dedication, the US Inflation Reduction Act (IRA) promises an astounding $400 billion in investment and subsidies meant to lower the country's greenhouse gas emissions and drive the general acceptance of renewable technologies. Reducing consumer and corporate expenses will help the IRA greatly lower US environmental emissions and boost renewable energy investment. This enormous project is meant to change the energy scene in the United States, therefore promoting creativity and hastening the shift to a low-carbon economy.

Still, among the passion of advancement, divisive problems endure. Some IRA rules, especially those requiring local manufacturing of batteries and electric automobiles, have generated controversy and attracted attention since they seem to be trade-restrictive policies contradicting the ideas guiding the multilateral free-trade system. Aimed at supporting home industry, these clauses have caused concerns among US trading partners, who see them as protectionist policies possibly distorting world commerce. US trading partners, including the European Union and Japan, contend that the IRA's incentives—such as the $7500 tax credit for electric vehicle purchases and manufacturing subsidies for battery and wind turbine producers—confer unfair advantages upon domestic businesses, violating World Trade Organization (WTO) norms. Such policies run the danger of starting a trade war and inciting reprisals, therefore compromising the cooperative attitude required to address world climate problems.

In a pointed op-ed for the Financial Times, European Commissioner for Trade Valdis Dombrovskis, along with Vice President of the European Commission Frans Timmermans and European Commissioner for Competition Margrethe Vestager, expressed concerns over the IRA's potential to draw businesses to the United States, perhaps compromising the EU's industrial base for clean technologies. Although the IRA's goal is admirable, they contend that its execution runs the danger of producing a zero-sum game whereby the advantages for the United States come at the price of her trade partners. This attitude captures more general concerns about the possible division of world efforts to address climate change should nations give national interests first priority instead of group action.

743

CHAPTER 15 THE NEXUS OF TRADE, ENVIRONMENT, AND SUSTAINABLE DEVELOPMENT

Reacting to these difficulties, the European Union has presented its own ambitious response: the Green Deal Investment Plan—a €250 billion green subsidy package ready to introduce fresh tax breaks and relax bloc state aid rules in a try to further galvanize private sector investment in renewable energy. The EU's proposal guarantees that Europe stays competitive in the fast-changing green economy by matching the scope and ambition of the IRA. The Green Deal Investment Plan aims to boost creativity and help the expansion of clean technology businesses all throughout the continent by offering major financial incentives and regulatory freedom.

Although both subsidy programs show significant progress toward lowering greenhouse emissions and driving forward climate action, they also run the risk of aggravating trade conflicts and unintentionally marginalizing the needs of developing and rising nations. These nations can find themselves behind the United States and EU in the global green economy even if they usually lack the financial means and technological capacity to challenge one another. Thus, attaining sustainable and inclusive growth for all will need more general worldwide cooperation on both trade and climate fronts—a crucial need in guiding a route toward a more resilient and fair future.

There are substantial stakes here. The effectiveness of these green subsidies depends on their potential to promote international collaboration and avoid trade disputes, in addition to their capacity to lower emissions and inspire innovation. In order to achieve this aim, the United States and EU have to have open communication with their trading partners, trying to match their climate policies with international trade regulations and making sure their subsidy programs do not compromise the worldwide trade system. Such communication should seek to create shared norms and procedures supporting fair competition and hastening the change to a sustainable economy.

Furthermore, these debates have to emphasize the interests of growing and underdeveloped nations. Often most vulnerable to the effects of climate change, these nations stand to gain greatly from the worldwide move toward renewable energy. A really inclusive and sustainable global economy depends on their having access to the required technologies and financial means. Supporting these nations' attempts to decarbonize and create climate resilience calls on international financial institutions, development agencies, and private sector partners, among other players.

Contextually, the World Trade Organization (WTO) plays a vital role. The WTO has to negotiate the tricky junction of commerce and climate policy such that its policies support rather than impede worldwide efforts against climate change. This will call for careful balancing since the company wants to respect free trade values while yet allowing for the pressing need for environmental action. Maintaining the legitimacy and efficiency of the worldwide trading system depends on reforming WTO rules to better reflect the reality of the 21st century, where climate change is a central issue.

Ultimately, the IRA and the Green Deal Investment Plan are audacious moves toward a better future; nevertheless, their success will rely on the US and EU capacity to control related trade issues and promote world unity. Aligning their climate policies with international trade laws and supporting the efforts of developing and emerging economies will help them to guarantee that their green subsidies not only lower emissions but also create a more fair and sustainable global economy. Though the road ahead is difficult, it is feasible to reverse the tide on climate change and create a brighter future for everybody by means of will and cooperation.

Emerging Horizons: The High Stakes for Developing Economies

Against the backdrop of growing debt burdens and a widening financial imbalance, the call to alternative finance sources from emerging nations is especially strident. Barbados is leading the battle with its audacious suggestion for a comprehensive revamp of the international development finance system—the Bridgetown Initiative. This transforming project aims to provide growing nations with the tools and resources they need to negotiate the choppy seas of climate change and adaptation. With proposals including debt reduction, concessional financing, and more investment for climate resilience projects, the Bridgetown Initiative seeks to solve the systematic disparities in international finance. This audacious idea emphasizes how urgently a more fair financial system supporting sustainable growth has to be created.

Still, the shadow of growing inequality looms big against this creative and aspirational setting. Though clearly powerful in their goal, the green subsidies used by the US and the EU run the danger of widening the gulf between developed and developing nations. These subsidies unintentionally risk extending the fault lines of inequality by strengthening their own home industries and protecting their consumers from the most climate-related expenses. Mostly enjoyed by the developed world, the advantages of these subsidies could result in an unfair playing field whereby emerging nations struggle to keep up with the rapid improvements in green technology and renewable energy infrastructure.

CHAPTER 15   THE NEXUS OF TRADE, ENVIRONMENT, AND SUSTAINABLE DEVELOPMENT

"Developing economies are always going to be behind in a green energy race, and they don't have intellectual property rights to implement a lot of this," Dawar clearly notes. The result is… a widening of the North-South divide—a sobering reminder of the systematic injustices supporting the climate debate. This discrepancy in intellectual property rights implies that developing nations sometimes lack access to the newest advances in renewable energy and sustainable technologies, therefore aggravating their reliance on fossil fuels and antiquated infrastructure. As these countries try to fulfill their climate pledges, the technology gap combined with financial restrictions presents serious difficulties.

Still, among these difficulties, there is a ray of optimism. Emerging economies stand to gain from a "knowledge spillover" and higher production demand resulting from US and EU activities even if they lack the financial power to support green subsidies on a comparable scale. "They're takers of the innovations that result," Fried rightly says. Still, the medium term's possibility for dispersion of productive capacity is evidence of the durability and adaptability of developing nations against changing global dynamics. By means of the transfer of technology and knowledge from developed to developing countries, some of the gaps could be bridged, therefore enabling these countries to embrace and modify green technologies to fit their own situation.

We must carefully navigate the delicate balance between development and inequality, mindful of the potential impact our actions may have on the global landscape. The global community has to make sure that the advantages of innovation and green technologies are distributed fairly, therefore promoting an inclusive strategy of climate change action. This calls for a coordinated effort to enable financial support catered to the particular requirements of emerging nations, capacity building, and technology transfer. In this sense, cooperative platforms and alliances can be rather important since they offer the required means of information sharing and resource mobilization.

True progress cannot come about until the advantages of innovation and opportunity are fairly distributed throughout all countries, regardless of their level of development. This demands a rethink of global trade and financial systems where policy-making is based mostly on inclusiveness and sustainability. The demands of underdeveloped nations should come first in international accords and frameworks, therefore guaranteeing that they are not left behind in the worldwide shift toward a green economy. This all-encompassing approach to development acknowledges that, rather than being mutually incompatible, climate action and economic growth are, in fact, linked objectives that can propel mutual wealth.

The enormous stakes for developing nations in relation to the global green transition highlight the need for a fair and balanced strategy. Though it marks a major step toward reevaluating the international development finance system, the Bridgetown Initiative has to be accompanied by more general initiatives to address financial and technological gaps. Our combined dedication to equity and inclusiveness will define the success of our worldwide climate efforts as we negotiate this challenging terrain. Promoting a cooperative attitude and making sure no country falls behind will help us to build a strong and sustainable future for everybody. Along with audacious plans, the road toward this future calls for a shared vision of a society in which everyone's well-being, regardless of location or socioeconomic level, defines development.

Empowering the Resilient: Championing Climate Vulnerable Nations

Beyond the current state of affairs, it calls for a radical change in our attitude toward public and private investments. Specifically, because it is the lifeblood driving the shift to a low greenhouse gas (GHG) emissions future and promotes climate-resilient development, climate finance becomes a fundamental issue on the global climate agenda. The Paris Agreement emphasizes the need for matching financial flows with paths favorable for sustainable, climate-friendly development by acknowledging the central relevance of finance.

For developing countries, the complex and inextricable interaction among trade, finance, development, and sustainability calls for a whole and integrated strategy. Among these countries, those most vulnerable to climate change—small island developing states and least developed countries, among others—are facing an existential threat. Climate change intensifies the unrelenting assault of natural disasters that destroy livelihoods and important economic sectors, including agriculture and fisheries. Along with rebuilding following climatic shocks, these countries have to strengthen their resistance against the next onslaughts. They struggle with a terrible double bind, though, given low investment in their countries. This starts a circle of vulnerability whereby inadequate resources prevent the capacity to build resilience, thereby increasing vulnerability to next calamities.

Whether we focus on climate action, resilient development, or sustainable trade, finance, capacity building, and technology transfer consistently serve as essential building blocks. These essential enablers provide the necessary means, expertise, and

CHAPTER 15   THE NEXUS OF TRADE, ENVIRONMENT, AND SUSTAINABLE DEVELOPMENT

resources to bring about transformative change, thereby forming the foundation of sustainable development. Developing countries cannot hope to carry out the required actions to slow down the consequences of climate change or adjust to its unavoidable impacts without significant financial support. Likewise, programs for capacity development are crucial to providing these countries with the tools and knowledge needed to properly handle and apply financial resources.

Trade does, in fact, show to be a strong driver of resilience, adaptation, and climate change mitigation. It provides a dynamic means of encouraging investment in the manufacture and distribution of goods and services necessary for a sustainable economy and climate action. By means of trade, countries can organize the means required to address urgent socioeconomic issues, strengthen their resilience, and guarantee food security for their people. Including climate issues in trade policies can help nations encourage the worldwide market to support environmental sustainability by promoting the trade of green technologies and sustainable practices.

Trade, finance, and climate action's junction provides a rich environment for creative ideas and cooperative efforts. Nations can create a road toward a more sustainable, resilient, and fair future for all by using trade as a tool for positive transformation. This linked strategy calls for world solidarity and collaboration as well as the will of wealthier countries to assist their weaker peers. The fight against climate change is a common effort requiring shared responsibility and mutual assistance; hence, global society has to realize this.

Despite their low resources, developing countries sometimes have special expertise and practices that might be very helpful for efforts on world climate change. For example, conventional farming techniques can provide insights into sustainable farming practices that improve soil conditions and raise resilience to climatic unpredictability. Through trade, the whole society can gain from the many experiences and inventions of every country thereby enabling the flow of such knowledge.

Furthermore, crucial in bridging the financing gap are the functions of development agencies and foreign financial institutions. These organizations have to give projects improving climate resilience top priority for support of sustainable development in underdeveloped countries. This includes investments in renewable energy sources and financing for infrastructure projects designed to endure severe weather occurrences and campaigns supporting sustainable land and water management techniques.

Empowering climate-vulnerable countries calls for a multifarious strategy including strong trade policy, finance, capacity building, and technology transfer with regard to the world community can make sure these countries are not left behind in the shift to a low-carbon economy by realizing and tackling the particular difficulties these countries experience. By means of creative finance systems and worldwide cooperation, we can create a more sustainable and resilient future for all. Though the road toward this future calls for constant dedication and coordinated action, the benefits—which count in terms of lives saved, ecosystems protected, and communities strengthened—are almost unbounded. Let us keep in mind as we move forward that the combined successes of all countries cooperating for the common good define real development rather than the achievements of a few.

Paving the Way for Decarbonizing Global Marine Trade: Revolutionizing Global Maritime Trade Through Digital Green Corridors

A key tactic in the effort to decarbonize world marine trade has become green corridors. Zero-emission shipping solutions are used and tested extensively on these particular marine paths, which are a necessary first step toward building a sustainable and effective shipping environment. Green corridor development is a joint effort among several stakeholders, including governments, maritime businesses, fuel producers, and port authorities. By means of this cooperative strategy, greenhouse gas (GHG) emissions should be greatly lowered, and a model for the larger marine sector should be produced. Green corridors help to solve the difficult task of decarbonizing the maritime sector, which accounts for around 3% of world greenhouse gas emissions. By concentrating on specific paths, stakeholders may create and apply the required infrastructure and technologies more successfully. This focused approach shows the viability and advantages of zero-emission transport options, therefore offering a road map for industry-wide acceptance. The realization that piecemeal attempts to lower emissions throughout the whole maritime sector were inadequate started the development of green lanes.

Rather, focusing resources and knowledge on particular paths presented a more sensible and effective approach to reaching notable emissions reductions. This strategic emphasis guarantees that creative technologies and processes may be scaled up and used more generally across the sector by means of thorough testing and refining. A basic feature of green corridors is the application of zero-emission technologies. Along with the deployment of electric and hybrid propulsion systems, this also covers the use of alternative fuels such as hydrogen, ammonia, and biofuels. Reducing the carbon impact of shipping activities along certain chosen paths depends on these technologies. Green lanes' concentrated character makes it possible to build specialized infrastructure like charging facilities for electric boats and refueling stations for alternative fuels. Support for the general acceptance of zero-emission technology depends on this infrastructure. The creation of green corridors also depends on strong cooperation among several parties.

Providing regulatory support and incentives for the evolution and use of green technology depends mostly on governments. While fuel producers and port officials build and oversee the essential infrastructure, shipping businesses invest in the requisite vessels and technology. This cooperative project guarantees that every component of the green corridor is in line and aiming toward the shared decarbonization target. Moreover, green corridors provide a trial ground for creative ideas and legal systems. Concentrating efforts on certain paths allows stakeholders to test new operational policies and strategies under control. They can, for instance, apply strict emission reporting rules, maximize logistics to save fuel use and evaluate the efficacy of speed-lowering initiatives. These tests shed important light on the best strategies for lowering emissions and enhancing sustainability in marine trade. The success of green corridors might inspire more general marine sector transformation. These paths make a strong argument for more general acceptance, as they show the viability and advantages of zero-emission shipping options.

The knowledge gained from green corridors may be utilized on other paths, therefore progressively extending the reach of environmentally friendly methods across the world shipping system. Furthermore, the presence of green corridors helps to increase awareness and momentum for industrial decarbonization initiatives, therefore motivating additional players to join the environmental movement. The evolution of the green corridor presents several difficulties as well. Zero-emission technology research and implementation call for significant financial commitment; building supporting infrastructure is challenging and resource-intensive. Furthermore, it is challenging to reach an agreement among several players with different agendas and interests.

Still, the possible advantages of green corridors far exceed any difficulties. Green corridors may propel major advancements toward a sustainable marine sector by proving that zero-emission shipping is not only feasible but also financially profitable and ecologically beneficial. Ultimately, the idea of green corridors offers a revolutionary way to decarbonize world marine transportation. Concentrating efforts on certain paths helps stakeholders develop and apply zero-emission technology and infrastructure more successfully, thereby establishing a sustainable and efficient maritime ecosystem. Green corridors' cooperative character guarantees that every component points in the same direction—that of lowering greenhouse gas emissions. These corridors offer a road map for industry-wide adoption of sustainable practices as they grow and change, therefore enabling a more ecologically friendly future in maritime trade.

Seas of Change: Pooling and the FuelEU Regulations

Globally, the maritime sector finds itself poised for significant change. New rules are redefining our perspective on fuel usage, emissions, and sustainability as climate change imperatives sweep over the maritime sector. Among these transforming ideas is the ambitious FuelEU Maritime Regulation of the European Union, meant to drive the sector toward a zero-carbon future. The idea of pooling—a cooperative process providing a road to compliance and innovation—is fundamental in the execution of this control.

FuelEU Maritime arose as a component of the EU's all-encompassing plan to decarbonize its economy by 2050. By setting strict fuel energy content criteria, this control seeks to lower greenhouse gas emissions from maritime transportation. It marks a radical change in ship operation and calls for a move to greener fuels and cutting-edge technologies.

The main goal of the legislation is to progressively tighten over time and lower the carbon intensity of the fuel mix ships calling at EU ports use. Ships will be expected to cut their emissions by 40% by 2030; even more demanding goals are established for 2050. These targets have legal weight and are not only standards; they also affect ship operators greatly.

Pooling is the idea at the core of this regulatory terrain. Pooling in nautical terms is the group operation of a fleet of ships under several owners or operators who split running expenses and income. Pooling has long been a tactic used to improve operational effectiveness, best use available resources, and maximize earnings. Pooling gains another dimension under the FuelEU rules. It becomes a vital tactic for compliance since it allows shipping firms to balance the energy profiles of their fleets, therefore enabling them to jointly reach emissions targets. Pooling essentially lets businesses use a varied mix of vessels, each with different degrees of fuel economy and efficiency, to reach general compliance.

Imagine a group of shipping firms running vessels with varying degrees of carbon footprints and fuel economy. While some depend on older, less efficient vessels, others have modern ships running on low-emission fuels. For some operators, particularly those with fleets not yet tuned for low-carbon performance, individually reaching the FuelEU requirements could be an intimidating task.

CHAPTER 15 THE NEXUS OF TRADE, ENVIRONMENT, AND SUSTAINABLE DEVELOPMENT

Joining a pool allows these businesses to control the emissions of their fleet together. Acting as one, the pool distributes fuel allowances and emissions credits among its members. This strategy guarantees that the whole pool satisfies legal criteria by allowing less efficient vessels to gain from the extra allowances of more efficient ships.

In the framework of FuelEU rules, pooling presents numerous major benefits. It starts with flexibility. Based on their operational capacity and strategic objectives, companies might change their pool contributions. In a sector where market conditions and technical developments are always changing, this flexibility is absolutely vital.

Second, pooling lessens the compliance financial load. Especially for smaller operations, investing in new technologies and cleaner fuels can be quite costly. Companies can split the expenses of fleet upgrades and using green technologies by pooling resources.

Pooling also fosters invention and teamwork. It encourages participants to share responsibilities by means of which best practices may be exchanged and new ideas can be developed. Pooling marks a paradigm shift toward cooperation and common success in an industry sometimes defined by fierce competition.

Pooling has several difficulties, even if it has benefits. Good pooling calls for open government and cautious coordination. Participants have to set explicit guidelines for emissions accounting, income sharing, and methodologies of decision-making. Maintaining member confidence and cooperation depends critically on the pool's being fair and equitable. Pooling also calls for a strong legislative framework. Authorities have to give direction and control to make sure pools run legally and help to meet targets for the decrease of emissions. This entails defining precise standards for the construction and running of pools as well as systems of surveillance and enforcement.

It becomes a lighthouse of promise as the maritime sector negotiates the difficult waters of decarbonization. It reflects the creative energy and teamwork required to satisfy the demands of the FuelEU rules and, more generally, the worldwide sustainability drive.

Though there are challenges on the road toward a zero-carbon future, pooling presents a sensible and exciting road forward. It enables businesses to collectively embrace the transforming possibilities of greener, more efficient shipping, therefore transcending personal restrictions.

The maritime sector is evidence of the strength of cooperation against world problems in this new era. The FuelEU rules and the idea of pooling signify a significant change in how the globe tackles shipping—one that gives sustainability, cooperation, and invention first priority. Looking ahead, the road forward is quite clear. Through pooling, the marine sector may steer toward a sustainable future in which the oceans are managed with intent, accountability, and a shared commitment to a better world.

The Pioneering Effects of Green Corridors and Global Partnerships: Transforming Marine Trade with Sustainable Fuels and Digital Technology

Thanks to important projects and industry-wide dedication to sustainability, the evolution of green corridors in marine commerce has been much more advanced. The cooperation between the Port of Rotterdam and the Maritime and Port Authority of Singapore (MPA) is among the most ambitious initiatives under progress in this field. Establishing the longest green and digital corridor worldwide, this alliance seeks to enable low- and zero-carbon transport between three main centers. To test and develop the use of sustainable fuels and digital technology, the program is a historic endeavor combining a broad spectrum of business partners, including big shipping lines and fuel providers. Working together, the MPA and the Port of Rotterdam are a whole effort meant to handle several aspects of sustainability in marine trade. Focusing on both green and digital components, this project seeks to build a system that improves operating efficiency in addition to lowering emissions.

The core of this initiative is the utilization of renewable fuels, including ammonia, biofuels, and hydrogen. These fuels provide a beneficial substitute for conventional fossil fuels, therefore lowering the carbon impact of shipping activities. Further helping to lower emissions is the way digital technology allows real-time monitoring and performance improvement of vessels. Characteristically, this green corridor initiative is cooperative and involves a wide range of partners. Important players in the project are shipping firms, gasoline providers, technology providers, and government agencies. This inclusive strategy guarantees that the corridor has the required physical and legal backing to enable the shift to low- and zero-carbon shipping.

From fuel supply and cost to technology compatibility and regulatory compliance, these stakeholders working together can handle the difficult issues related to applying sustainable practices on such a large scale. Likewise, the ports of Los Angeles and Long Beach have started building a trans-Pacific green corridor in association with the MPA and under the sponsorship of the C40 Cities network. Two of the most important trading areas worldwide, Asia and North America, should have more sustainable and efficient transportation between them; hence, our project concentrates on these areas. This initiative intends to convert one of the busiest shipping routes into a model of sustainability by including cutting-edge digital technologies and pushing the acceptance of zero-emission fuels. The Trans-Pacific Green Corridor makes use of contemporary technologies to achieve environmental goals.

Advanced digital systems help to improve coordination and decision-making by allowing the flawless sharing of data between ports, shipping firms, and other stakeholders. Routes may be optimized using real-time data on vessel performance, fuel consumption, and emissions; this will help to lower waiting times at ports and increase fuel economy. Apart from improving operational effectiveness, this digital integration reduces the environmental impact of shipping operations.

Encouragement of the acceptance of zero-emission fuels is still another essential element of the trans-Pacific green corridor. The initiative encourages shipping companies to switch from conventional fossil fuels to greener substitutes by providing the necessary infrastructure and incentives. Reducing greenhouse gas emissions and lessening the environmental effects of marine trade depend on this change. Working together, the ports of Los Angeles and Long Beach, as well as their partners, show the viability and advantages of using sustainable fuels widely, therefore offering a model for other areas to follow. These major projects and cooperative efforts highlight the need for a coordinated and inclusive strategy for creating green corridors.

Combining several stakeholders helps these initiatives solve the several difficulties of decarbonizing marine trade. The success of these projects depends on the combined efforts of governments, industry partners, and technical innovators, all aiming toward a shared objective of sustainability. Finally, major developments in the creation of green corridors include the cooperation between the Maritime and Port Authority of Singapore and the Port of Rotterdam, as well as the trans-Pacific green corridor projects, which involve the ports of Los Angeles and Long Beach. These initiatives draw attention to the possibility of group actions to propel marine trade toward sustainability. These projects improve operating efficiency in addition to lowering emissions by including modern digital technology and sustainable fuels. Such important projects and partnerships will be absolutely vital in opening the path for a more sustainable and efficient future as the maritime sector develops.

CHAPTER 15   THE NEXUS OF TRADE, ENVIRONMENT, AND SUSTAINABLE DEVELOPMENT

The Role of Alternative Fuels and Green Corridors: Paving the Path to Sustainable Marine Trade

The formation and viability of green lanes in marine trade depend much on the research and application of alternative fuels. Green methanol and green ammonia, both generated from green hydrogen, have become intriguing contenders for general use as the shipping sector tries to lower its carbon impact. Offering great environmental advantages and complementing world sustainability goals, these alternative fuels differ greatly from conventional fossil fuels.

Green methanol is already straightforward to handle and economically feasible, which makes it appealing for quick use in the marine sector. Made from green hydrogen, green methanol may be generated from renewable energy sources, therefore reducing the carbon impact relative to traditional fuels. Its fit with current infrastructure and engines adds even more appeal as it facilitates a more seamless shift to environmentally friendly transport methods. Shipping companies can use green methanol without having to significantly alter their fleet, making adoption faster and more affordable.

Conversely, green ammonia has cost benefits and scalability, which makes it a reasonable long-term fix for the marine sector. Although its toxicity calls for strict safety regulations, green ammonia has quite a lot of potential. Green ammonia, a zero-carbon fuel, may be generated on a large scale from renewable energy to guarantee a continuous supply for the maritime sector. Common in international marine trade, long-haul journeys are fit for it depending on their energy density and storage capacity. The difficulty is resolving the safety issues related to its use; yet, these challenges may be solved with strict safety procedures and technical development.

One of the biggest dry-bulk trade routes in the world, the Australia-Japan iron-ore path is a perfect illustration of green corridor implementation. With strong governmental cooperation and major investments in green hydrogen generation in Australia driving its development, this path is a major possibility for the acceptance of alternative fuels. By using green ammonia on this path, emissions are expected to be much lowered, therefore highlighting the possibilities of focused initiatives to decarbonize marine trade. Setting a model for other paths to follow, the Australia-Japan corridor shows how well-coordinated efforts and investments may result in significant environmental advantages.

Nonetheless, the effective acceptance of green ammonia on the Australia-Japan path emphasizes the need for creative finance methods and legislative assistance to close the cost difference between alternative fuels and conventional fossil fuels. Green ammonia is still more expensive than alternative solutions right now, which makes general adoption difficult financially. Green bonds and subsidies are among the creative financing ideas that may be crucial in increasing the competitiveness of green businesses. Policy assistance from governments may also encourage the use of alternative fuels by means of tax cuts, subsidies, and laws fostering sustainability.

Alternative fuels provide purposes in green corridors beyond only environmental ones. Reducing reliance on fossil fuels would help the maritime sector become more resilient to geopolitical concerns that often cause supply lines to be disrupted as well as to changing fuel prices. Moreover, the shift to alternative fuels fits the more general objectives of energy security and economic stability as nations fund in renewable energy generation to boost their marine sector.

Including alternative fuels in green corridors also stimulates marine industry technical development and innovation. Working together to create and use these fuels, transportation corporations, fuel producers, and regulatory authorities advance allied industries like fuel storage, engine technology, and safety criteria. Along with improving the use of alternative fuels, this group effort helps the marine sector to be generally contemporary and efficient.

The viability of green corridors in marine trade depends critically on the discovery and application of alternative fuels. Derived from green hydrogen, green methanol, and green ammonia, they present intriguing ways to help the transportation sector have a lower carbon footprint. Through the acceptance of green ammonia, the Australia-Japan iron-ore route shows how focused efforts and significant political cooperation can change marine trade. Policy support and creative funding ideas are absolutely necessary if we are to fully realize the promise of these alternative fuels. A more sustainable and resilient future for world marine traffic depends critically on the inclusion of alternative fuels within green corridors as the sector develops.

LNG in Shipping: A Paradox of LNG in the Path to Decarbonization

With the shipping sector becoming a major actor in the changing terrain of global marine activities, the movement toward decarbonization has brought in a new era of environmental consciousness. Establishing strict rules meant to lower greenhouse gas

(GHG) emissions, the International Maritime Organization (IMO) has positioned itself in front of this change. These rules constitute the backbone of the worldwide plan to reach net-zero emissions by 2050, a target requiring a dramatic break from conventional fuels.

Reacting to these strict rules, the maritime sector has been turning to liquefied natural gas (LNG) as a transitional fuel more and more. LNG is praised for having far lower hazardous emissions than traditional petroleum-based fuels. Adopted as an "environmentally friendly" choice, it is backed by large expenditures in the required infrastructure and technology. Still, the acceptance of LNG as a means of addressing the carbon conundrum in shipping is rife with paradoxes that could compromise the same objectives it aims to reach.

LNG's capacity to lower emissions of sulfur oxides (SOx), nitrogen oxides (NOx), and particulate matter is the foundation for its use as a transitional fuel. LNG has been demonstrated, indeed, to reduce sulfur oxide emissions by over 95%, nitrogen oxides by over 90%, and particulate matter by 95% relative to heavy fuel oil. Given the part shipping plays in world air pollution, this drop in pollutants is absolutely vital. When one considers lifetime emissions, the environmental advantages of LNG become more complex.

"Well-to-Wake" (WtW) emissions—that is, lifetime emissions—cover the whole fuel-producing, transportation, and consuming process. When one considers LNG's whole lifetime, the picture is significantly less positive. Mostly composed of methane, a strong greenhouse gas with a global warming potential (GWP) much above that of carbon dioxide, LNG Though its quantity in the atmosphere is less than that of carbon dioxide, methane has a major influence on global warming and accounts for over 30% of the warming effect. The issue of "methane slip"—where unburned methane leaks during LNG manufacture, transportation, and combustion—exacerbates this problem, therefore reducing the total GHG emissions less than first thought.

Reports and studies such as those by the World Bank and the International Council on Clean Transportation (ICCT) have lately shown how limited LNG is in lowering GHG emissions. The results of the ICCT are especially concerning, as LNG-powered boats might produce lifetime GHG emissions more than those of conventional marine diesel oil. This stunning discovery calls into doubt LNG's long-term sustainability as a sustainable substitute and begs issues about its part in reaching net-zero emissions by mid-century.

Notwithstanding these issues, orders for LNG-powered boats have surged worldwide in the maritime sector. Representing a little but rising proportion of the global fleet, nearly a thousand LNG-powered ships are in use as of March 2024. The view of LNG as a practical solution in the maritime sector to satisfy legal criteria while somewhat lowering some of the most damaging pollutants fuels this expansion. However, this rapid development has certain difficulties, especially with regard to the building of the required infrastructure for LNG bunkering.

As a major participant in the global maritime sector, South Korea has matched its policies to the worldwide drive toward decarbonization. Seeing LNG technologies as a link to a more sustainable future, the government has instituted policies to help their development and implementation. This emphasis on LNG could eventually impede the shift to really carbon-free fuels. Dependency on LNG runs the danger of tying the maritime sector into a fuel that, albeit greener than past fuels, nonetheless feeds reliance on fossil fuels.

This dependence has important economic consequences as well. LNG infrastructure development and the rise of LNG-powered boats call for significant financial outlay. Nevertheless, the economic advantages of LNG are probably going to fade as world markets migrate toward tougher emissions targets. LNG's appeal may be further diminished by the IMO's forthcoming rules mandating shipping firms to consider the whole lifetime emissions of their fuels. This change in regulatory attention emphasizes the necessity of a more all-encompassing strategy for fuel transition that takes long-term environmental and financial consequences into account.

Strategic emphasis on LNG by South Korea also begs issues regarding the direction of its maritime sector in the face of world competitiveness. Rising leaders in this transitional era, nations like China, are fast extending their own LNG bunkering capability. The long-term feasibility of these projects relies on the state of world regulations and LNG's ongoing capacity as a bridging fuel. Should global standards tighten much more, the investments in LNG infrastructure might become liabilities, leading to stranded assets and financial losses.

LNG's dilemma in shipping decarbonization is that it might both be a solution and a possible obstacle to reaching net-zero emissions. LNG has dubious long-term sustainability, even if it provides instant advantages in lowering some kinds of pollutants. The industry's dedication to LNG shows a larger reluctance to completely accept the drastic reforms required to reach actual decarbonization. This uncertainty could slow down the introduction and growth of alternative fuels with really low greenhouse gas emissions.

Ultimately, the change to carbon-free shipping calls for a basic change in our approach to fuel sources and energy consumption, not only little tweaks in present methods. Although LNG offers a short fix for regulatory needs, its future in transportation is yet unknown. Beyond LNG, we must invest in the creation of fuels that can fulfill the promise of net-zero emissions if we are to really decarbonize the maritime

CHAPTER 15   THE NEXUS OF TRADE, ENVIRONMENT, AND SUSTAINABLE DEVELOPMENT

sector. The road forward has to be one of creativity and audacious action so that the shipping sector may satisfy the environmental concerns of the 21st century without sacrificing its long-term viability.

Digitalization in Green Corridors: Enhancing Efficiency and Sustainability in the Maritime Sector

A pillar of green corridors, digitalization is very vital for improving operating efficiency and lowering emissions in the marine sector. Digital solutions help to increase supply chain transparency and enable the smooth movement of commodities, therefore enhancing the environmental and financial gains resulting from them. Using cutting-edge technology can help stakeholders maximize marine activities, therefore guaranteeing that boats run more sustainably and effectively.

Digital commerce lanes help to provide one of the main means by which digitalization improves efficiency. Among the several stakeholders—including shipping firms, port authorities, and regulatory agencies—these channels help the transfer of pertinent data and electronic documents. This perfect information flow maximizes vessel arrival and departure, thereby lowering idle time at ports. For instance, port officials can better prepare for a ship's landing when its expected time of arrival is electronically transmitted in real time, therefore guaranteeing that berths and handling tools are available upon arrival. This cooperation helps to decrease the time ships spend idle in ports, therefore lowering fuel consumption and emissions.

The benefits of digitization go beyond the reduction of idle time. Improved data exchange makes logistical operations more plannable and efficiently executed. Real-time data allows shipping firms to modify paths depending on port congestion, current weather, and other factors, therefore guaranteeing the most effective way of operation for their trips. Green corridors' sustainability aims to benefit from these dynamic routing capabilities, helping to lower general fuel usage and emissions.

Digitalization also improves marine transportation's dependability and economy. Digital solutions help stakeholders more precisely find and fix inefficiencies by offering more openness and insight into the supply chain. Using blockchain technology, for example, can produce an unchangeable record of transactions and goods movements, therefore lowering the chance of fraud and mistakes. This increased openness helps stakeholders develop confidence and raises the general dependability of marine transportation.

CHAPTER 15   THE NEXUS OF TRADE, ENVIRONMENT, AND SUSTAINABLE DEVELOPMENT

Driving digitization initiatives along the value chain depends on cooperation among technology providers, shipping firms, and regulatory authorities. These alliances enable the creation and implementation of creative ideas addressing financial as well as environmental issues the marine sector faces. Technology suppliers may, for instance, provide sophisticated analytics and machine learning technologies to let shipping firms forecast and minimize any interruptions. Regulatory authorities may thus set guidelines and systems that guarantee the effective and safe flow of data, thereby promoting a more unified and cooperative marine environment.

The use of digital technology also helps the marine sector embrace sustainable practices. Digital systems, for instance, can enable real-time monitoring and reporting of pollutants, therefore arming shipping firms with the information required to follow environmental laws and norms. Through proactive efforts to lower their environmental impact, including fuel consumption optimization and the use of energy-efficient technology, this real-time monitoring capacity helps businesses.

Furthermore, digitalization can result in the creation of smart ports, where cutting-edge technology improves the sustainability and efficiency of port operations. Smart ports simplify operations, including cargo handling, storage, and transportation, using IoT devices, automated systems, and data analytics. Smart ports can greatly lower emissions and increase general supply chain efficiency by improving these activities.

Improved coordination and efficiency of marine operations clearly show the advantages of digitization in green corridors. Digital solutions help to greatly lower operating costs and emissions by allowing the smooth flow of commodities and enhancing supply chain openness. Technology businesses, shipping firms, and regulatory authorities working together guarantee that these digital breakthroughs are used and embraced throughout the marine sector.

Digitization is a basic element of green corridors that promotes marine sector operating efficiency and sustainability by means of driving changes in Digital technologies that help to improve supply chain transparency, streamline vessel operations, and lower emissions, therefore supporting more general objectives of environmental sustainability and economic viability. The more the sector develops, the more important digitization will be in green corridors, opening the path for a more sustainable future in world marine trade.

CHAPTER 15   THE NEXUS OF TRADE, ENVIRONMENT, AND SUSTAINABLE DEVELOPMENT

Green Corridors in Marine Trade: Overcoming Challenges to Achieve Sustainable and Efficient Shipping

The creation of green corridors represents major progress toward environmentally friendly marine traffic. These zero-emission fuel and cutting-edge technology-based corridors provide a revolutionary way to lower the environmental effect of world transportation. Though the development is encouraging, some difficult issues have to be resolved if we are to completely realize the possibilities of green corridors. Significant obstacles include the increased expenses connected with zero-emission fuels and technologies, the necessity of strong legislative frameworks, and the need for extensive cooperation among several players. Still, the possible advantages—lower emissions, improved trade efficiency, and leadership in green technologies—make these efforts worthwhile.

One of the toughest obstacles is the acceptance of zero-emission fuels such as green methanol and green ammonia. Although these fuels are better for the environment, for now, they cost more than conventional fossil fuels. The infrastructure needed for these alternative fuels—production, storage, and distribution—demands a significant financial commitment. Policy support and creative funding ideas are very vital if we are to close this cost difference. To make zero-emission fuels more financially feasible, governments and international organizations must grant subsidies, tax benefits, and support for research and development. Furthermore, alliances with private sector players can stimulate capital and hasten the building of the required infrastructure.

Another major difficulty is building strong legal systems. Effective operation of green corridors depends on well-defined rules controlling the use of zero-emission technology and fuels. Safety requirements, fuel quality, emissions reporting, and compliance monitoring need to all fall within these rules. Regulatory authorities have to cooperate to unify criteria across areas so that ships may run between and inside many green corridors without any problems. Preventing regulatory fragmentation—which can impede the general acceptance of sustainable practices—depends on this harmonizing.

Furthermore, it is necessary for the effective implementation of green corridors to have extensive cooperation among several different parties. Together, governments, shipping firms, fuel producers, technology providers, port authorities, and regulatory agencies must create and implement the required technologies and infrastructure. To guarantee that every component of the green corridor is integrated and operating as it should, this cooperation entails aligning goals, distributing knowledge, and organizing activities. Overcoming the difficult obstacles related to decarbonizing marine trade depends on these parties building confidence and encouraging collaboration among them.

Notwithstanding these difficulties, green lanes provide quite significant advantages. Green corridors help to support environmental sustainability and worldwide attempts to slow down climate change by greatly lowering emissions. Optimized routes, decreased idle periods, and better operational methods result in higher trade efficiency, which can help minimize costs and raise the competitiveness of marine transportation. Moreover, the leadership shown by implementing green technology will help businesses and nations leading the worldwide shift to a low-carbon economy to be at the forefront.

Green corridors also provide a road to reach the audacious target of zero emissions by 2050. Lessons acquired will be vital in steering the larger worldwide shipping sector toward a more sustainable future as pilot projects and demonstrations continue to grow in magnitude. These initiatives offer insightful analysis of the technical, financial, and legal facets of using zero-emission solutions. Examining the achievements and difficulties of early adopters helps stakeholders improve their policies and approaches to enable more general acceptance.

Even if the path to creating green corridors is not easy, the possible advantages make these initiatives valuable. Significant challenges that need to be faced include the higher prices of zero-emission fuels, the necessity of strong regulations, and the need for extensive cooperation among several parties. Still, it is impossible to overestimate the transforming power of green corridors in lowering emissions, improving trade efficiency, and guiding the worldwide shift to sustainable marine trade. The knowledge acquired as pilot projects and demonstrations scale will open the path for a more general shift toward a more sustainable future. Achieving the ambitious target of zero emissions by 2050 depends on the dedication to green corridors, which guarantees that the worldwide shipping sector helps to fight climate change by means of positive contribution.

Advancing Toward a Greener Future: The Path to Decarbonizing Global Shipping

With about 11 billion tons of commodities carried yearly, the shipping sector is a giant within the maze of global trade. This emphasizes its critical importance in the global economy since it equals roughly 1.5 tons per person globally. Because it depends on conventional fuels high in carbon and sulfur content, this critical industry also significantly contributes to environmental damage and accounts for roughly 3% of world CO2 emissions. Decarbonizing shipping is clearly both urgent and complicated, posing a difficult task requiring a multimodal strategy.

The shipping industry has a huge environmental footprint and requires a significant transformation to sustainable practices to help slow down climate change impact. Still, historical attempts to control emissions have faced major challenges mostly related to the international character of the sector. Shipping's worldwide reach complicates the attribution of emissions to any one government, thereby excluding it from important international climate accords such as the Paris Agreement. Setting country-level targets for lowering greenhouse gas emissions helps this historic agreement limit global warming to far below 2 degrees Celsius above pre-industrial levels. The special status of the maritime sector has required a particular strategy.

The 1997 Kyoto Protocol designated the United Nations International Maritime Organization (IMO) as the accountable party and admitted the need for industry-specific policies to handle shipping emissions. This awareness emphasizes how urgently the maritime sector should start using more environmentally friendly methods. Toward decarbonization, one must combine gains in vessel efficiency, operational adjustments meant to lower fuel usage, and exploration and implementation of alternative, less polluting fuels.

All the players—including shipping companies, governments, international organizations, and technology providers—have to work together to decarbonize the shipping sector. First of importance is the development and acceptance of greener fuels and energy-efficient technologies; equally important is a cooperative approach to build a legislative framework supporting and enabling these developments.

Admitting the scope of the difficulty starts the path toward a sustainable future for the maritime sector. For many years, traditional fuels have been the cornerstone of marine operations, but their environmental cost is now indisputable. A major stride forward has been made toward alternative fuels like biofuels, hydrogen, and liquefied natural gas (LNG). Although these fuels seem to lower greenhouse gas emissions, adoption of them is not without challenges. Technical difficulties using these fuels in current and new vessels, as well as significant infrastructure for manufacturing, storage, and distribution, call for much improvement.

Concurrent with these developments in vessel efficiency provides still another means of lowering emissions. Shipbuilding and design are changing as materials, propulsion systems, and hull design all help to increase fuel economy. Significant emission reductions can also result from retrofitting current ships with energy-saving technology such as air lubrication systems, wind-assist technologies, and more efficient engines. These developments, however, call for a large financial commitment and a readiness to welcome industry transformation.

Another absolutely vital element of the decarbonization plan are operational adjustments. Emphasizing slow steaming, where ships cruise at reduced speeds to cut fuel usage, optimizing shipping routes, and fleet management will help to greatly slash emissions. These developments demand a change in the operational perspective of the sector away from the conventional focus on speed and efficiency at the price of environmental effect.

The regulatory scene has to adjust to fit these operational and technical innovations. Driven toward decarbonization, the sector depends on a strong and consistent legislative framework. Since shipping is worldwide and fragmented state policies are inadequate, international collaboration is absolutely vital. In this sense, the IMO is significant since it develops and implements rules encouraging sustainable behavior and penalizing non-compliance.

Though there are many obstacles on the way to a better future for the maritime sector, there are also many chances. The shift to a low-carbon future can boost industry resilience to future environmental rules, inspire innovation, and generate new markets. < It can also help the sector's reputation be better matched with the rising worldwide dedication to sustainability.

Decarbonizing the maritime sector is, ultimately, not just a requirement for the ongoing viability of world trade but also an environmental one. The road forward calls for a complete strategy combining strong regulation, operational effectiveness, and technical innovation. Accepting these developments will help the maritime sector lower its environmental effect and keep serving the world economy in a more ecologically responsible way. Though the road toward a better future is difficult and multifarious, it is within our reach with enough will and teamwork.

Steering Toward a Greener Horizon: Regulatory Measures and the Future of Sustainable Shipping

The shipping sector faces an immediate challenge to reduce its significant carbon footprint since it is the lifeline of world trade. Understanding this need, the International Maritime Organization (IMO) has led the way in pushing for significant CO_2 emissions cuts, therefore indicating a more general industry sustainability commitment. With an

CHAPTER 15   THE NEXUS OF TRADE, ENVIRONMENT, AND SUSTAINABLE DEVELOPMENT

eye toward more environmentally friendly maritime operations and a road toward a better future, this chapter explores the regulatory policies carried out at both global and regional levels.

In 2018, the IMO unveiled a groundbreaking plan that aims to reduce greenhouse gas (GHG) emissions from shipping by half by 2025, compared to 2008 levels, with the aspirational goal of achieving carbon neutrality by the end of the century. This regulation marks a significant shift in the maritime sector's development toward more environmentally friendly policies. The IMO has developed a set of rules meant to discourage the use of conventional, high-polluting fuels, encouraging the sector to adopt greener alternatives and so easing this transition. The application of sanctions for non-compliance emphasizes the gravity with which these environmental goals are sought and the need for haste and dedication needed to reach them.

Regional governments and agencies have started carrying out their plans, usually in line with or even beyond IMO targets. These policies usually call for tighter emissions control inside particular maritime zones, incentives for the acceptance of green technologies, and large expenditures in research targeted at sustainable maritime fuel and engine technologies. For example, the European Union has been very aggressive in including maritime emissions in its more general climate policies, therefore establishing a model for regional solutions to the worldwide problems confronting the shipping sector.

These legislative changes force companies in the maritime industry to rethink their operational and logistical policies as a whole. Businesses today have to take the sustainability of their delivery techniques into account in addition to the environmental effects of their products. Green shipping methods, including using fuel-efficient technologies and investigating alternative fuels, have grown to be essential parts of corporate responsibility and regulatory compliance, as well as fundamental elements of achieving sustainability goals and reducing the environmental impact of global supply chains. The change toward sustainable methods marks a more general approach to environmental stewardship and a dedication to lowering the industry's carbon footprint than it is as a matter of following rules.

Decarbonizing the shipping sector will need cooperation among governments, regulatory authorities, and the maritime sector, among other things. The difficulties are severe and include the necessity of technological innovation, infrastructure development, and large financial commitment. Still, the advantages of a better shipping sector go much beyond simple commitments. Adopting sustainable practices presents the possibility for operational efficiencies, financial savings, and a significant worldwide battle against climate change contribution.

Globally and locally, the regulatory framework changes to reflect the dynamic character of marine sector environmental sustainability initiatives. Industry players who have to remain adaptable and forward-looking in their approach to sustainability must constantly adapt and innovate in this changing scene. Though there are many chances for those ready to welcome change and spearhead the drive toward a more sustainable future, the road toward a better horizon for the shipping sector is filled with obstacles.

Guiding toward a better future calls for a fundamental change in the way the maritime sector runs, not only with regard to legal compliance. The ambitious aspirations of the IMO and the proactive actions taken by regional authorities highlight the group effort needed to reach these objectives. The dedication to sustainability will not only help to minimize the environmental impact of the shipping sector but also guarantee its ongoing competitiveness and success in an environmentally sensitive global economy as it negotiates this complicated change. The future of sustainable shipping is within reach; with coordinated effort and cooperation, the sector may make notable progress toward a more ecologically friendly one.

The EU's Emissions Trading System: A Game Changer for Decarbonizing the Shipping Sector and Its Impact on Maritime Emissions

The European Parliament moved decisively in April 2023 to include the shipping sector in the EU Emissions Trading System (ETS), therefore improving environmental responsibility within the maritime sector. This historic ruling fits quite nicely with the EU's overall climate goal of at least a 55% reduction in greenhouse gas (GHG) emissions by 2030 vs. 1990 levels.

By including shipping—a major contributor to world CO_2 emissions—into the ETS, the EU uses the cap-and-trade idea to economically encourage notable emission reductions.

Offering economic incentives for reaching low pollution emissions, the cap-and-trade system offers a market-based method meant to regulate pollution. This means a strict limit on the overall volume of some greenhouse gases that can be emitted for the shipping industry as well as a cap that will steadily lower with time. This legislative framework is designed to gently prod the sector toward using more sustainable methods and greener substitutes.

Under the ETS, shipping companies—especially those running vessels of 5,000 gross tons and more—will either buy or get emission permits. These allowances are tradeable assets since each unit lets one ton of CO_2 or another greenhouse gas be emitted. The trade of these allowances creates a dynamic market for emissions reduction. Businesses that effectively lower their emissions have extra credits to offer to other businesses trying to keep inside their restrictions. This method not only promotes a competitive market for carbon reductions but also includes environmental costs into corporate models, therefore encouraging innovation and improving operational efficiency.

Over 3 years, the ETS for the shipping industry will be phased in, including both intra-EU travel and overseas trips to and from the bloc. Companies will first have to turn in allowances covering some of their emissions; this need will grow with time. The obligations for intra-EU emissions will be 100% by 2026, and for international emissions, they will be 50%. The structure calls for strict fines for non-compliance as well as a requirement to cover extra emissions in the next few years. This slow rollout gives the sector time to change operations, make investments in greener technologies, and fit the new regulatory standards.

Including the shipping sector in the EU ETS not only helps to reduce its environmental effect but also indicates a radical change in industrial behavior. Businesses now face two challenges: following rules and grabbing the chances given by a carbon-constrained planet.

Among the several ways the marine industry may reach compliance and help contribute to world climate goals are innovations in fuel economy, investment in alternative propulsion technology, and strategic operational changes. By including the shipping sector in its emissions trading system, the EU is proactively and forward-looking in ensuring that the sector answers for its environmental impact. By using market-based systems and financial incentives, the ETS is expected to significantly lower GHG emissions from one of the most important sectors worldwide. As this approach is implemented, it is anticipated to inspire a tsunami of innovative ideas and environmentally conscious policies throughout the marine industry, therefore supporting the EU's ambitious climate ambitions and establishing a worldwide environmental governance benchmark.

More than just regulatory compliance, charting a sustainable course for the maritime sector calls for a basic rethink of operational strategy and a dedication to long-term environmental care. Including shipping in the EU ETS is a crucial first step toward this objective since it uses economic tools to propel environmental improvement. The possible advantages of the industry negotiating this new terrain go much beyond only lower emissions. Adopting sustainability might result in operational improvements, financial savings, and a better name in a world going more environmentally sensitive.

Under the direction of creative legislative systems like the EU ETS, the shipping sector's future is set on a road toward more sustainability. This strategy seeks not only to reduce the negative effects of maritime activities but also to motivate the sector to welcome a period when environmental responsibility and economic prosperity coexist. By means of coordinated effort and cooperation, the marine industry can significantly contribute to a more sustainable and environmentally friendly future, therefore augmenting the worldwide campaign against climate change.

Reviving the Breeze: A Classic Twist on Wind Power Innovation

The search for green technology has become a priority as the maritime sector struggles with its significant environmental impact. Among the several options under investigation, wind power shows outstanding promise since it combines modern innovation with age-old methods. This strategy not only seeks to lower emissions but also restores a historical link to the nautical past, in which wind was the main engine propelling ships over the oceans.

In order to cut dependency on carbon-intensive fuels, modern shipping is turning to hybrid designs like sails, kites, and Flettner rotors more and more. These technologies mix time-tested techniques with modern innovations, therefore fusing the old with the new. For example, Mitsui OSK Lines' "Wind Hunter" project and efforts by businesses like NEOLINE are driving the creation of boats with sails and turbines. Along with using the wind to drive ships, these vessels create hydrogen fuel via electrolysis on voyages. Using natural wind power to generate a clean, sustainable energy supply while in transit marks a major step toward carbon-neutral shipping—this dual-purpose functionality.

Moreover, groups like the Sail Freight Alliance support a return to completely conventional sailing boats for freight movement. Emphasizing a dedication to lowering the environmental impact of marine activities, these projects give sustainability top priority over speed. These conventional boats show that the ideas of sustainability may be successfully included in modern business by depending just on wind power, therefore providing a zero-emission substitute for typical shipping routes.

Notwithstanding these developments, the general acceptance of wind power in shipping presents certain difficulties. Seas at Risk's observations highlight a clear but straightforward approach: a mere 10% speed reduction for ships will result in a 19% cut in carbon emissions. This strategy is becoming popular because of its cost advantages and simplicity in reducing environmental effects without calling for major technological changes. Slower speeds translate to reduced fuel consumption and emissions, therefore complementing the industry's more general objectives of sustainability.

Along with alternative fuels like LNG and hydrogen, the shift to green technologies—including wind power—has challenges. Significant challenges arise from the necessity for additional infrastructure, the cost of retrofitting current fleets, and changing legal environments. Retrofitting ships to incorporate sails, kites, or Flettner rotors can be costly and technically challenging, requiring specialist knowledge and large expenditure. Furthermore significant are the logistical difficulties of adding these technologies into current maritime operations and the building of infrastructure to enable hydrogen generation and storage.

Moreover, changing to match these technological developments are regulatory systems. Policymakers and business players have to work together to create criteria and incentives that guarantee safety and efficiency while nevertheless encouraging the acceptance of green technologies. These initiatives are absolutely essential to provide a conducive climate for investment and creativity as well as to enable a seamless shift toward more environmentally friendly maritime operations.

Notwithstanding these difficulties, the developments in alternative fuels and wind power are absolutely vital toward a maritime future that is sustainable and ecologically friendly. The sector is making significant progress toward decarbonizing one of the most important sectors by combining new uses with old technologies. Particularly, the comeback of wind power is a moving reminder of the maritime past and guides toward a better future.

The fresh emphasis on wind power by the maritime sector marks a larger trend toward using several environmentally friendly technologies. Projects like the "Wind Hunter" and NEOLINE's efforts show how much wind power may transform transportation, lower emissions, and open the path for carbon-neutral operations. These initiatives show a rising awareness of the necessity to strike a balance between environmental preservation and technical innovation so that the maritime sector may keep developing while reducing its influence on the earth.

CHAPTER 15   THE NEXUS OF TRADE, ENVIRONMENT, AND SUSTAINABLE DEVELOPMENT

The comeback of wind power in contemporary ships offers a harmonic fusion of history and creativity. The maritime sector is significantly moving toward sustainability by combining modern technologies with historical approaches. Although the road toward general acceptance of wind power and other green technologies is difficult, the possible advantages—lower running costs, fewer pollutants, and a cleaner environment—make the effort worthwhile. Lessons from the past and the promise of new technology will help the sector negotiate this change toward a more sustainable and responsible future.

Sailing into the Future: Green Shipping Corridors and the Quest for Zero Emissions

A daring and forward-looking approach to transform the environmental impact of the marine sector is green shipping lanes. Aiming toward the ultimate objective of net-zero carbon emissions, these designated paths, linking major ports, are only serviced by boats running sustainable technologies. These corridors originated with the Clydebank Declaration in 2021, a landmark event that set off twenty-one such projects by the next year alone. Among the most well-known examples are the transatlantic route linking Antwerp to Montreal and the corridor joining the ports of Los Angeles with Shanghai.

The development of green shipping corridors involves a whole strategy rather than only providing defined routes. This strategy fits very well with the ambitious targets established by the European Union for lowering greenhouse gas emissions in the marine industry and the International Marine Organization (IMO). To greatly reduce the carbon footprint of the maritime sector, these routes combine operational savings, alternative fuel use, and modern propulsion technologies. They represent a whole dedication to change maritime activities in favor of environmental sustainability.

Green shipping lanes have strategic importance beyond their direct environmental advantages. They act as live labs for testing and improving fresh ideas and technology that might finally be expanded all around the sector. For example, the Los Angeles to Shanghai corridor uses wind-assisted propulsion systems in addition to the most recent developments in alternative fuels, including hydrogen and liquefied natural gas (LNG). Together, these technologies help to significantly lower emissions and provide a window into the direction of marine transportation.

Another aspect of this project is the transatlantic corridor from Antwerp to Montreal, which shows how global cooperation may propel the acceptance of environmental technologies. Establishing these corridors helps ports and shipping firms make

CHAPTER 15 THE NEXUS OF TRADE, ENVIRONMENT, AND SUSTAINABLE DEVELOPMENT

investments in boats that satisfy the strict environmental criteria and infrastructure. This cooperative effort creates an ecosystem whereby environmentally friendly behaviors not only inspire but also become the standard.

The United Nations Conference for Trade and Development (UNCTAD) has underlined the value of these kinds of projects. They underline the need for a clear, multinational framework aimed at marine transport decarbonization. This call to action emphasizes the need for a coordinated worldwide approach addressing the two issues of environmental sustainability and regulatory stability. From legislators to business leaders, a coherent and well-coordinated approach guarantees that every participant is in line in their attempts to lower emissions and advance sustainable practices.

Green shipping corridors can open the path for notable decreases in world shipping emissions by encouraging an atmosphere whereby legislators and the maritime sector interact closely. Overcoming the logistical and technological obstacles inherent in switching to low-carbon maritime transportation depends on this cooperation. The hallways serve to change closely. supporting infrastructure and clean technology investment as well as a physical structure for realizing high environmental targets.

These passageways also show how financially feasible sustainable shipping methods are. They save money by lowering fuel use and raising operational efficiency, which could balance the initial outlay needed. Gaining the acceptance of industry players who can be reluctant to adopt new technology due to perceived financial concerns depends on this economic justification.

Beyond the marine sector, green shipping routes affect world trade and help to preserve a better earth. These corridors can greatly lower the carbon footprint of international shipping, a main contributor to world greenhouse gas emissions, as they expand more widely. Meeting world climate targets and reducing the consequences of climate change depend on this decrease.

The path taken to create green shipping lanes is evidence of the force of invention and global cooperation. These hallways are a proactive response in line with more general objectives of world sustainability. They draw attention to the marine sector's possibilities for radical transformation, therefore guiding other sectors.

Green shipping corridors represent a complete strategy meant to decarbonize the marine sector, not only means of passage across the sea. These corridors are a key first step toward sustainable world trade by including operational efficiencies, alternative fuels, and sophisticated propulsion techniques, as well as Overcoming the obstacles related to this shift depends on the cooperative efforts of industry leaders and legislators.

CHAPTER 15   THE NEXUS OF TRADE, ENVIRONMENT, AND SUSTAINABLE DEVELOPMENT

Green shipping lanes will be crucial in lowering emissions and advancing better earth as the maritime sector sails into the future. Not only is this path toward sustainability required, but it also promises a better, greener future for world marine transportation.

Charting a Greener Course: The Shipping Industry's Journey Toward Sustainability

The maritime sector, which plays a crucial role in supporting global trade, is currently facing significant environmental challenges. The need to solve environmental effects has changed the path the sector is following toward sustainability from an ethical quest into a necessary tactic for long-term survival. A confluence of innovative green technologies, strict regulatory systems, and a strong dedication from inside the industry itself drives this change.

Innovations, including green shipping routes, alternative fuels, and wind power applications, are guiding the sector toward a more environmentally friendly running model. Offering notable lower greenhouse gas emissions than conventional fossil fuels, liquified natural gas (LNG) and hydrogen stand out as potential alternative fuels. These technologies illustrate the industry's commitment to lower its carbon footprint since they are being progressively included in new ship designs and retrofitted into current vessels.

An old propulsion method, wind power, is being resurrected and creatively used in contemporary ships. To maximize wind energy, vessel designs include sails, kites, and Flettner rotors, hence lowering the need for carbon-heavy fuels. This mix of new and ancient technologies represents the industry's innovative effort to reach sustainability.

One other example of the industry's dedication to minimizing environmental effects are green shipping lanes. Only vessels running sustainable technologies service these exclusive routes, which connect Los Angeles with Shanghai and Antwerp with Montreal. Establishing these corridors gives the sector a concrete structure for reaching net-zero carbon emissions in marine transportation.

Concurrent with this are international rules and corporate sustainability targets seeking to lower the carbon footprint of marine logistics. Aiming high to reduce greenhouse gas emissions, the European Union and the International Maritime Organization (IMO) have created a legislative environment that supports the use of green technologies. These rules drive the sector to investigate and apply sustainable solutions by acting as catalysts for creativity rather than as requirements.

CHAPTER 15   THE NEXUS OF TRADE, ENVIRONMENT, AND SUSTAINABLE DEVELOPMENT

Corporate sustainability objectives support this regulatory drive even more since businesses understand the need to match their activities with world climate targets. Understanding that long-term success depends on balancing economic development with ecological care, the shipping sector is seeing sustainability as a central component of its business strategy more and more. Significant research and development expenditures in line with this change of viewpoint seek to provide more ecologically friendly and efficient marine operations.

As we approach this transformative era, it becomes clear that the pursuit of sustainability in shipping is not a straightforward path but rather a challenging journey across technological, legal, and financial challenges. Turning toward greener horizons depends critically on the industry's readiness to welcome change, support innovation, and follow changing environmental regulations. Achievements as well as difficulties define this path; every step forward advances the sector toward a sustainable future.

Though the road ahead is long, notable progress has been achieved in lowering pollutants and raising fuel economy. Fundamental components of this continuous trip are the acceptance of alternative fuels and renewable energy sources, the creation of green shipping lanes, and the respect for international rules. Still, a really sustainable shipping sector calls for constant work and cooperation among all the players.

The proactive actions and creative ideas of the marine industry clearly show its sustainable orientation. Projects like "Wind Hunter" by Mitsui OSK Lines and NEOLINE's efforts highlight how well green technologies might be included in regular operations. These initiatives not only help to lower emissions but also open the path for further developments in environmentally friendly marine technologies.

Furthermore, the industry's emphasis on sustainability transcends new technology development. It involves a more general culture change toward environmental responsibility. in which businesses give ecological factors top priority along with financial ones. Encouragement of a more sustainable and resilient maritime sector depends on this change.

Guiding the maritime sector toward a greener future calls for a coordinated effort with several facets. Green technologies, laws, and corporate dedication taken together are guiding the sector toward a more sustainable future. Although the road is difficult and demanding, the possible advantages are substantial and provide a means to balance ecological care with economic development. The industry's commitment to sustainability will be crucial in determining a cleaner and more ecologically responsible future for worldwide maritime transportation as it negotiates this transforming age. The continuous journey toward sustainability marks the start of a powerful and long-lasting dedication to protecting our world for the next generations.

The Power of Nature-Based Solutions for Sustainable Economic Growth: Strategic Directions for Economic Development

A multifarious strategic strategy is necessary to maximize the enormous possibilities of nature-based solutions (NBS) and propel sustainable economic growth. This chapter underlines the transforming power of these solutions on the environment and the economy, as well as the essential techniques required for including NBS in mainstream economic activities.

The integration of NBS into more general economic, environmental, and social policies depends much on policymakers. This integration calls for the creation of encouraging structures that encourage public and private NBS investments alike. Embedding NBS on national and international policy agendas helps governments build an atmosphere that would enable its acceptance and application. Such laws might call for tax breaks, subsidies, or legal requirements pushing companies and local governments to make NBS investments and applications possible. Furthermore, matching NBS with sustainable development objectives guarantees that innovative solutions get the required support and tools to flourish.

Driving the expansion of NBS equally depends on market development and innovation. Developing markets for NBS needs a dedication to creative product and service development. This entails designing innovative business models that match social and environmental results with financial gains. Businesses may create goods and services, for example, using NBS's advantages in green infrastructure solutions, ecosystem restoration services, and sustainable agricultural methods. These creative ideas provide social well-being as well as economic benefits and support environmental sustainability. Promoting entrepreneurship and cooperation between the public sector, business sector, academics, and civic society would help to produce creative NBS goods and services.

The effective use of NBS depends mostly on capacity building and the involvement of stakeholders. Training, education, and the creation of cooperative platforms combining investors, legislators, practitioners, and communities help to build capacity in many different fields. Training courses may provide people and companies with the tools they need to properly plan, run, and oversee NBS initiatives. Programs for education help to spread knowledge of the advantages of NBS and motivate a fresh generation of environmental stewards. Public-private partnerships and multi-stakeholder forums are two examples of cooperative platforms that help to exchange ideas, best practices, and resources, thus supporting a group effort toward nature-positive results.

The advancement of NBS also depends on investments in research and technology. Dealing with the knowledge gaps in this discipline calls for significant research expenditure to estimate NBS's financial advantages and provide scalable solutions. Studies can offer the proof required to show how well NBS delivers social, environmental, and financial gains as well as other advantages. Technological developments can improve NBS project design, execution, and monitoring, therefore increasing their efficiency and influence. Research and technology should be given top priority so that stakeholders may seize fresh chances for NBS and propel ongoing development in their application.

Driven by growing awareness of its several advantages, the market for natural-based solutions is ready for major expansion. Turning to a nature-positive economy calls for significant capital, creative market ideas, and encouraging laws. By attending to these demands, stakeholders may release NBS's outstanding capacity to support sustainable economic growth while simultaneously solving some of the most urgent worldwide issues. This deliberate strategy not only improves economic resilience but also guarantees a harmonic interaction between human activity and the natural surroundings, therefore securing a sustainable future for the next generations.

Tech-Driven Nature-Based Solutions: Transforming the Path Toward a Nature-Positive Economy

A nature-positive economy may be reached by means of a transforming combination of technology with nature-based solutions (NBS). Examining the historical background and development of technology, this chapter follows its path from a tool for exploitation to a driver of environmental sustainability and resilience.

Historically, technology has mostly been utilized to address human needs by means of control and exploitation of natural resources. The Industrial Revolution, a time of unheard-of machinery, manufacturing techniques, and industrial output, best embodied this model. Significant economic progress and expansion brought forth by the

Industrial Revolution allowed mass manufacturing and broad availability of products and services. This age also started a trend of resource-intensive extraction, sometimes ignoring environmental effects. The unrelenting quest for economic extraction resulted in massive destruction of habitat, pollution, and deforestation, therefore causing major environmental damage.

The view of technology changed as the negative effects of industrialization became more clear-cut. This transformation was sparked by the late 20th-century environmental movement, which also raised awareness of the pressing need to tackle ecological devastation and support sustainable living. As such, technology began to be considered not just as a tool for exploitation but also as a necessary instrument for reducing environmental damage and improving the resource economy. This change of viewpoint helped technology to lower pollution, save resources, and rebuild ecosystems to emerge.

In the modern setting, the implementation and scalability of nature-based solutions depend on technology, as it is clearly necessary. Natural processes are being supported and improved by developments in engineering, biotechnology, and information technology, therefore promoting ecological restoration and sustainability. For example, geographic information systems (GIS) and remote sensing allow exact monitoring and mapping of ecosystems, therefore supplying vital data for efficient management of natural resources. These technologies enable the identification of places requiring restoration or preservation, hence guiding priorities and effective resource allocation.

The advancement of NBS also depends much on biotechnology. Plant species are being made more resilient to climate change by means of genetic engineering and bioinformatics, thereby enhancing soil quality and so raising biodiversity. By means of natural methods, these biotechnological breakthroughs support soil conservation, water management, and insect control, thereby complementing NBS-aligned sustainable agriculture practices. Using biotechnology's possibilities helps one to design ecologically friendly farming systems that are not just profitable.

Furthermore, helping with the design and execution of green infrastructure solutions are engineering advancements. Natural components are being more and more included in cityscapes by engineers and urban designers to control stormwater, lower urban heat islands, and improve air quality. Examples of how engineering and nature could be combined to provide resilient urban landscapes supporting both human and ecological well-being are green roofs, permeable pavements, and urban woods. These ideas show how designed systems may cooperate with natural processes to solve environmental problems, therefore reflecting the synergy between technology and NBS.

CHAPTER 15   THE NEXUS OF TRADE, ENVIRONMENT, AND SUSTAINABLE DEVELOPMENT

Including technology with NBS is the domain of renewable energy. Reducing greenhouse gas emissions and tackling climate change depend on the evolution of sustainable energy technologies, including solar, wind, and hydropower. These technologies generate chances for the preservation of natural ecosystems in addition to sustainable energy substitutes. For instance, the installation of solar panels on degraded areas can offer a double advantage of land rehabilitation and renewable energy generation, therefore demonstrating the possibility of technology to serve NBS in several respects.

The function of technology becomes ever more important as March reaches a nature-positive economy. Maintaining the advancement of technological advancements that support and improve NBS is crucial so that these solutions may be successfully scaled and applied in many different settings. This entails supporting multidisciplinary cooperation, funding research and development, and designing regulations encouraging the merging of technology with NBS. This will help us to use technology to build a sustainable future in which environmental preservation and economic growth are mutually supportive.

The development of technology from a tool for exploitation to a driver of sustainability emphasizes its indispensable importance in the change to a nature-positive economy. Nature-based solutions' efficacy and scalability may be improved by using technical developments in information systems, biology, engineering, and renewable energy. Solving the urgent environmental problems of our day and reaching a harmonic balance between human activity and the natural surroundings depend on this integration.

Tech-Enabled Nature-Based Solutions: The Shift Toward a Nature-Positive Economy

Combining technology with nature-based solutions (NBS) represents a major change toward a nature-positive economy in the modern day. Thanks to digitization and technical advancements that provide fresh approaches for efficiently managing and conserving natural resources, this metamorphosis is marked by significant participation in environmental sustainability.

The development of digital technology has transformed our interactions with and perspectives on our surroundings. Modern instruments include remote sensing, geographic information systems (GIS), and big data analytics, which offer formerly unheard-of understanding of environmental conditions and biological processes.

These technologies offer exact resource monitoring, therefore facilitating more efficient management and conservation initiatives. For example, drone technology and satellite images allow one to detect deforestation, follow wildlife numbers, and instantly evaluate ecosystem health. Policymakers, environmentalists, and communities may use this abundance of information to make wise choices toward environmental sustainability.

Technological developments also greatly help towns and cities in their shift to environmentally friendly ways of life. Often marked by high degrees of pollution and environmental damage, urban settings provide special opportunities for incorporating NBS as well as obstacles. Urban sustainability is being improved using smart city technologies—which make use of sensors and data analytics—by means like Sensors may track air and water quality, for instance, offering real-time data that guarantees environmental criteria are followed and helps guide mitigating plans. Furthermore, GIS mapping helps pinpoint regions of cities that might profit from green infrastructure such as parks, green rooftops, and permeable pavements, thereby helping to control runoff, lower heat islands, and increase general urban resilience.

Communities are also using technological developments to embrace more environmentally friendly living. Online platforms and mobile apps help people to report environmental problems, participate in local conservation programs, and access instructional materials about sustainable living, thereby facilitating citizen involvement in environmental preservation activities. By using these digital technologies, one fosters a feeling of community and shared responsibility toward the environment, therefore promoting extensive involvement in attempts to preserve and repair natural ecosystems.

A nature-positive economy depends on NBS being integrated at many tiers of society and government. Policy-wise, governments are realizing more and more the need to include NBS in national and local planning systems. Policy simulation models and environmental impact assessment tools are among the technological instruments that help to examine the possible results of various policy decisions, guaranteeing that environmental factors are included in the decision-making process. Including NBS in policy and planning can help governments support sustainable development and increase community resilience against environmental threats.

This change also depends critically on the private sector. Companies seeing the long-term advantages of investing in natural capital are starting to include NBS in their sustainability plans. Technological developments help businesses to more precisely assess and control their environmental effects, spot areas for development, and apply NBS, improving resource economy and lowering environmental impact. Precision agricultural technology, including soil sensors and automated irrigation systems, for instance, maximizes water and nutrient utilization, thereby lowering waste and encouraging sustainable farming methods. In the same vein, sustainable supply chain management systems monitor the environmental effects of goods from manufacture to consumption, therefore preserving sustainability all along the value chain.

By creating creative financing tools that assist NBS, financial firms are also helping to drive a move toward a nature-positive economy. Initiatives in sustainable finance, impact investment, and green bonds draw money to projects with social and environmental advantages. Blockchain technology and technical developments in financial analytics improve openness and responsibility in these investments, therefore guaranteeing efficient use of resources to reach sustainability targets. These systems foster the broad acceptance of NBS by matching financial incentives with environmental results, therefore creating a supportive atmosphere.

The combination of technology with nature-based solutions is helping to enable the change toward a nature-positive economy. New approaches for managing and conserving natural resources provided by digitalization and technical breakthroughs help cities and communities to embrace sustainable living. Using these developments will help us to improve environmental sustainability at all levels of society and government, thereby promoting a harmonic coexistence between human activities and the surroundings. Dealing with the environmental issues of our day and guaranteeing a sustainable future for the next generations depend on this shift.

Technology As a Catalyst for Structural Change: Advancing Nature-Based Solutions for a Sustainable Future

Technology emerges not just as a tool for little changes but also as a strong motivator of structural change in the search for a sustainable and strong future. Emphasizing its critical importance in building platforms that improve connectivity among stakeholders and promote a more coherent approach to implementing nature-based solutions (NBS), this chapter explores how technology fundamentally redefines interactions between policy, markets, and corporate strategies toward sustainability.

CHAPTER 15   THE NEXUS OF TRADE, ENVIRONMENT, AND SUSTAINABLE DEVELOPMENT

Historically, changes in technology have been very crucial in determining social and economic environments. Their impact today goes farther and starts systematic alterations across conventional limits. The capacity of technology to change policy frameworks is among its most important effects. Governments all over are using technology tools more and more to create, carry out, and track programs aimed at environmental sustainability. Advanced data analytics and simulation models, for instance, let legislators forecast environmental results, evaluate the effects of different policy choices, and make wise judgments consistent with sustainability goals. This evidence-based approach guarantees not just efficiency but also adaptability of policy to changing environmental conditions.

Moreover, by changing market dynamics, technology stimulates structural change. Big data, digital platforms, and artificial intelligence have transformed the way markets run and opened fresh chances for environmentally friendly behavior. Online markets for carbon credits and ecosystem services, for example, are developing to help companies invest in NBS and enable the trade of environmental advantages. These systems give businesses scalability, openness, and efficiency, which will help them to adopt sustainable practices and enable customers to make environmentally friendly decisions. Technology encourages a change toward a more sustainable and resilient economy by including sustainability in the heart of market activities.

Thanks in significant part to technology, corporate strategies are also changing dramatically. Companies are seeing more and more the strategic advantage of including sustainability in their operations rather than only as a compliance need. Artificial intelligence, the Internet of things (IoT), and blockchain technologies enable businesses to monitor and control their environmental effects with unprecedented accuracy. Blockchain technology, for instance, guarantees traceability and openness in supply chains, thereby enabling companies to confirm the environmental viability of their goods and base choices on facts. IoT devices let businesses maximize efficiency and cut waste via real-time monitoring of resource utilization. Predictive insights provided by artificial intelligence let companies see environmental hazards and modify their plans. Companies may improve operational efficiency, build their brand, and stimulate long-term value development by including technology in their sustainability projects.

The capacity of technology to build platforms that improve connectivity among stakeholders is among its most transforming powers. Good NBS implementation calls for cooperation and coordination across several players—including governments, companies, non-governmental organizations, and local communities. Technological platforms create venues for communication, information sharing, and group action, therefore fostering this connectedness. Online portals and social media networks, for example, let stakeholders co-create solutions, exchange best practices, and debate difficulties. Using technology to unite different points of view, cooperative platforms like public-private partnerships and multi-stakeholder forums help to promote a whole approach to sustainability. Improving connection guarantees that stakeholders are in line with their activities, therefore optimizing the effect of NBS.

Furthermore, technology helps people and communities to actively engage in environmental projects. Online tools, mobile apps, and social media campaigns inform, inspire, and equip people toward environmental action. These tools democratize knowledge and resources, therefore empowering anyone to significantly help in sustainability initiatives. For instance, smartphone applications used in community-based monitoring projects gather information on local environmental conditions, therefore enabling locals to control their natural resources. Platforms for crowdsourcing let people donate money or volunteer for NBS initiatives, therefore encouraging shared responsibility and involvement. Technology supports a bottom-up approach to sustainability by enabling communities, therefore augmenting top-down policies and market-driven solutions.

Technology is a driver of structural transformation, altering connections between policy, markets, and business strategies toward sustainability. Its influence goes beyond just enabling little changes to propel major changes in our attitude toward environmental problems. Technology promotes a coherent and cooperative method of using nature-based solutions by building systems that improve connections among stakeholders. Harnessing the transforming potential of technology will be essential in driving systematic change and guaranteeing that our social and economic institutions are robust, inclusive, and nature-positive as we negotiate the complexity of a sustainable future.

Governance Systems and Future Directions for Technology Integration in Nature-Based Solutions: Building a Sustainable, Nature-Positive Economy

Looking ahead to a sustainable future, careful use of technology in nature-based solutions (NBS) depends on strong governance systems. These models are necessary to make sure that new technologies support long-term sustainability objectives and help to build a nature-positive economy by means of constructive contribution. This chapter stresses the need to include technology with environmental strategies to promote resilient and sustainable urban and rural ecosystems and investigates the crucial role of government in leading the deployment of technology in support of NBS.

Technology's adoption in NBS is a difficult process needing careful planning, coordination, and monitoring. Good governance systems give the required framework to control this complexity and guarantee that technical developments are used in ways that support social fairness and environmental sustainability. Clear regulations, standards, and guidelines established by governance structures direct the evolution, acceptance, and application of technology in NBS initiatives. These models are meant to handle several issues, including ethical questions, legal compliance, and fair sharing of rewards.

The congruence of technology with long-term sustainability objectives is one of the main features of governance systems. Clearly defined goals and targets for technology interventions in NBS help to guarantee that they support more general environmental, social, and financial results. Governance structures can, for instance, demand that technology solutions give community well-being, climate resilience, and preservation of biodiversity first priority. By matching technical developments with these objectives, governance systems serve to guarantee that the use of technology is deliberate and supports the general vision of a society based on nature.

Moreover, transparent and responsible application of technology depends much on governance systems. They set systems for tracking and assessing how technology interventions affect NBS, thereby guaranteeing that they provide the expected results and avoid inadvertent damage. Performance indicators, impact analyses, and feedback loops allowing for ongoing learning and development help to do this. Transparency and responsibility help to establish confidence among stakeholders, by which governance systems support more involvement and cooperation in NBS projects.

Another essential element of governance systems is the way technology interacts with environmental policies. This integration entails the creation of thorough plans, including technical solutions, for more general environmental management and conservation projects. Urban planning techniques, for example, may use smart technology to improve air and water quality, boost green infrastructure, and raise city resilience to climate change. In the same vein, rural development plans may maximize resource utilization, improve soil quality, and promote sustainable farming methods by the use of precision agricultural technology. Integration of technology with environmental policies guarantees that technical developments be used in a coordinated and whole manner, therefore optimizing their positive influence under governance systems.

Furthermore, underlined by governance systems is the need for involving stakeholders and inclusiveness in the application of technology. They support the participation of many stakeholders—including governments, companies, local communities, and civil society—in the execution of NBS projects. This participatory method guarantees that all stakeholders's demands and viewpoints are taken into account, therefore encouraging a feeling of responsibility for the accomplishment of NBS projects. Furthermore, governance structures encourage knowledge exchange and capacity building, therefore arming participants with the tools and expertise required to properly apply technology in support of NBS.

By means of smart technology deployment in NBS, urban and rural ecosystems may be transformed, therefore supporting a robust and sustainable global economy. The necessary basis for fulfilling this potential is provided by governance systems, which direct the use of technology in ways that complement sustainability objectives and advance favorable environmental results. These systems guarantee that technical developments are applied wisely to assist the change to a nature-positive economy by encouraging openness, responsibility, and inclusion.

Strong governance systems are absolutely essential for directing the application of technology in nature-based solutions. They match long-term sustainability objectives with technical innovations such that technology helps to build a nature-positive economy quite favorably. Integration of technology with environmental policies and encouragement of stakeholder involvement helps governance systems provide the environment required for the effective use of NBS. Establishing strong governance structures will be essential in using technology to produce resilient and sustainable urban and rural ecosystems as we travel toward a sustainable future.

International Perspectives on Nature-Based Solutions: Building a Nature-Positive Economy Through Collaboration and Innovation

It is clear from exploring worldwide viewpoints on nature-based solutions (NBS) that no one international opinion exists. Urban planners, community leaders, city officials, decision-makers, policymakers, landscape architects, entrepreneurs, students, academics, and more bring a diverse tapestry of interests and methods to the table.

CHAPTER 15   THE NEXUS OF TRADE, ENVIRONMENT, AND SUSTAINABLE DEVELOPMENT

Together, these many points of view support the foundation of a nature-positive economy, impacting investment policies, world trends, and the possibilities and difficulties presented.

The possibility of creating a nature-positive economy is much shaped by the interaction with the natural surroundings. Rich in biodiversity, areas like South America, the natural surroundings offer a strong basis for ecologically beneficial travel. Such travel helps efforts at nature protection and pro-biodiversity. For instance, sustainable tourism in areas of biodiversity hotspots not only protects special ecosystems but also presents major financial possibilities for nearby people. The flood of visitors wanting to see natural beauties benefits these areas as it helps to finance local businesses and conservation initiatives. This symbiotic link between tourism and preservation shows how NBS may be customized to fit local resources and strengths.

The deployment of NBS also depends much on the economic setting. Dealing with the twin challenges of biodiversity loss and climate change depends on investments in NBS, and this is increasingly understood. The flood of money into NBS initiatives must, however, negotiate the risk of "greenwashing," wherein supposedly sustainable investments are instead directed toward destructive operations. Economic systems anchored on rapid profit generation and growth dependence aggravate this difficulty by often overshadowing sustainable approaches. Projects that give short-term financial rewards, for example, might compromise long-term environmental and social advantages, therefore stressing the necessity of rigorous appraisal and responsibility in NBS expenditures.

The way NBS is integrated depends much on cultural settings. Many times, indigenous and local people have long-standing knowledge systems that naturally include sustainability ideas. Over decades, these knowledge systems—which have been honed—provide insightful analysis on how to sustain ecological balance and manage resources. Often these conventional strategies are undermined by dominating global economic systems, which result in cultural degradation and loss of biodiversity. A really sustainable strategy for NBS depends on realizing and incorporating indigenous knowledge into more general economic activities. For instance, including conventional land management techniques in contemporary conservation plans helps to respect cultural legacy and improve resilience and biodiversity.

Globally, political, social, and economic elements create possibilities as well as problems for NBS. Significant obstacles from overtourism, climate change, and environmental damage imperil the exact ecosystems NBS seeks to preserve. On the other hand, NBS provides chances for the improvement of local community well-being and ecological integrity. Restoring wetlands, for example, can help to reduce flood risks, enhance water quality, and generate leisure areas that benefit both people and the environment. Research shortages still exist, nevertheless, especially in fields such as sustainable tourist governance and the interaction between environmental pressures and solutions. Effective implementation of NBS depends on the close filling of these gaps by focused research and information exchange.

The success of NBS depends on efforts to raise awareness and develop capacity for it. Supported by the H2020 Connecting Nature project, programs like the UrbanByNature initiative underline the need for worldwide and local networks to promote awareness and use of NBS. These programs provide forums for information sharing, policy formulation, and investment toward environmentally friendly living. Such initiatives help to exchange best practices and creative ideas by linking players in many areas and sectors, therefore strengthening the collective ability to handle environmental issues.

Using NBS, the path to a nature-positive economy is not straightforward and varies significantly based on global circumstances. Natural, financial, and cultural components together offer a framework for knowledge and action. Supported by global collaboration and sustainable investment, this chapter emphasizes the need for an integrated strategy respecting and using local expertise and conditions. We can fully utilize NBS to build a strong and sustainable global economy by welcoming a variety of points of view and supporting cooperative efforts.

The road toward a nature-positive economy calls for a multifarious strategy combining technical developments, strong government structures, and a profound respect for ecological, financial, and cultural settings. Using the combined knowledge and dedication of stakeholders all around, we can create and use NBS that not only solves environmental problems but also advances social justice and economic resilience. This chapter demands ongoing efforts to increase capacity, promote cooperation, and guarantee that financial and technical investments line up with long-term sustainability objectives, thereby enabling a future in which people and the environment flourish together.

CHAPTER 15 THE NEXUS OF TRADE, ENVIRONMENT, AND SUSTAINABLE DEVELOPMENT

Shifting Paradigms: Toward a Nature-Positive Economy with Nature-Based Solutions

In this chapter, we explore the urgent problems and strategic suggestions vital for moving toward a nature-positive economy based on nature-based solutions (NBS). Inspired by open consultation answers and expert working group views, this synthesis summarizes the main issues and suggested solutions as stated in the entire report and consultation summary.

The open consultations turned up numerous important topics of concern for different stakeholder groups. One major problem is the use of NBS language and the predominance of greenwashing, which requires open and unambiguous guidelines. Strong measurements are very much needed to balance social, environmental, and financial effects and assess the advantages of NBS. Stakeholders also underlined the need for encouraging governmental policies that help NBS to be implemented and scaled back. Moreover, disparities in knowledge and capacity across the public and private sectors, financial institutions, and people highlight the need for thorough educational and training programs. Greater investment and community involvement are also recognized as results of NBS's economic promise. The way the phrase NBS and related greenwashing is used begs serious questions. This problem emphasizes the need for well-stated, open criteria that define what is an NBS and direct its use throughout several stages, from design and execution to maintenance. Notable programs like the NetworkNature project's emphasis on NBS quality standards highlight the important need for strict criteria in reducing criticism and preventing undesirable effects, including gentrification from greening schemes.

Developing international standards calls for the participation of business experts to produce a consistent set of criteria that support the several uses of NBS. This uniformity enhances community buy-in and investment confidence and guarantees little opportunity for greenwashing. Effective deployment and maintenance of independent experts relies on establishing certification systems and training courses to assess compliance with these criteria. Such actions guarantee the long-term viability and success of NBS projects as well as improve their reputation.

Among the stakeholders, opinions on NBS's economic value vary greatly. While some argue for integrated evaluations including biodiversity net gain and a mix of monetary and non-monetary valuation approaches, others stress the importance of realizing and measuring nature's inherent worth beyond economic measurements. Capturing the whole advantages of NBS—including ecological, social, and financial aspects—these integrated assessments are absolutely vital.

Establishing strong valuation models helps to employ several approaches, including qualitative and quantitative measures, thus completely capturing the several advantages of NBS. Furthermore, it is essential to run educational initiatives to raise understanding of the relevance and techniques of NBS valuation among interested parties. This improved knowledge can enable more initiatives for the preservation of biodiversity, therefore guaranteeing that the intrinsic and extrinsic values of nature are completely valued and included in policies of decision-making.

Leveraging Nature-Based Solutions for a Sustainable Future: Public Policy Aimed Toward NBS Implementation

Widespread acceptance of public policy frameworks depends on their effective incorporation of NBS into their structures. By using multi-level, cross-sectoral, inclusive approaches, developing these policies guarantees that NBS are fundamental in tackling issues of urban growth, biodiversity loss, and climate change. Including NBS in urban and regional development projects improves biodiversity and increases climate resilience, hence producing livable cities.

Further supporting NBS implementation using policy tools like public awareness campaigns, regulatory assistance, and financial incentives is their adoption and scaling encouragement. These laws not only provide NBS initiatives with the required support but also establish an atmosphere that promotes sustainability and innovation, by which they could flourish. Governments may guarantee that NBS becomes a fundamental component of sustainable development plans by matching public policies with the objectives of a nature-positive economy, therefore facilitating systemic transformation.

Their effectiveness depends critically on efforts to raise knowledge of NBS and develop capacity for it. Supported by the H2020 Connecting Nature project, initiatives like the UrbanByNature program underline the need for worldwide and local networks to promote awareness and use of NBS. These initiatives offer forums for information sharing, policy formulation, and financial support of sustainable activities. These projects improve the collective ability to solve environmental issues by means of the exchange of best practices and creative ideas facilitated by linking stakeholders throughout several areas and sectors.

Using NBS to move to a nature-positive economy calls for tackling several important problems and following strategic advice. Important first steps in this road include developing international standards, improving measurement and valuation techniques, including NBS into public policy frameworks, and encouraging capacity building and networking. By acting in this way, participants may fully use NBS and build a strong and healthy global economy that balances human activity with the environment. Supported by international collaboration and sustainability-oriented investment, this combined strategy opens the path for a time when people and the environment flourish together.

With nature-based solutions (NBS) at its foundation, the path toward a nature-positive economy calls for cooperation among all spheres of life. Emphasizing the requirement of educated public policies, strong standards, and thorough educational programs, this chapter provides closing suggestions for stakeholder involvement. These approaches are crucial for guaranteeing the efficient, fair, and sustainable application of NBS, thereby reducing environmental problems and improving economic possibilities.

The effectiveness of NBS depends critically on the involvement of stakeholders. Working together, governments, companies, non-governmental organizations, academic institutions, and local communities may provide NBS with a climate that is enabling. This process depends much on well-informed public policy. Policymakers have to create and carry out rules that help NBS be included in urban and rural development strategies. This covers encouraging sustainable land-use practices, rewarding green infrastructure initiatives, and making sure NBS are included in plans for climate resilience. Good public policies may help NBS to be adopted by building a structure that supports creativity and investment in sustainable solutions.

Another vital component in the change to a nature-positive economy is strong criteria. Clear, open criteria will help to define what an NBS is and direct its application. These criteria guarantee that initiatives produce real social and environmental advantages as well as assist against greenwashing. Developing worldwide standards that fit the many uses of NBS calls for cooperation among academics, legislators, and business leaders. Establishing accreditation systems and training courses for independent specialists helps to improve conformity with these criteria even more, therefore guaranteeing the efficient and sustainable use of NBS in various environments.

CHAPTER 15   THE NEXUS OF TRADE, ENVIRONMENT, AND SUSTAINABLE DEVELOPMENT

Fostering deeper knowledge and more acceptance of NBS depends on education and capacity building absolutely. By increasing awareness of the advantages of Nature-Based Solutions (NBS) and providing stakeholders with the information and tools needed to effectively implement these solutions, comprehensive educational programs can target a broad spectrum of audiences, from legislators and corporate executives to students and community members. These educational initiatives should aim to foster collaboration, inspire action, and promote the adoption of NBS as practical solutions for sustainability and resilience. Including NBS in courses at all educational levels and offering professional development chances will help us to produce leaders dedicated to environmental preservation and sustainable development.

Moreover, public awareness initiatives could be very important in changing society's perceptions of sustainability. These ads can motivate people and communities to embrace nature-based solutions by stressing effective NBS initiatives and their favorable effects. Information may be spread, and public participation in environmental projects is engaged by media sources, social networks, and community activities. Rising public knowledge and involvement may generate a wave of support for NBS, therefore stimulating demand for sustainable goods and practices as well as helping legislators give environmental concerns top priority.

Furthermore, necessary for the shift to a nature-positive economy is addressing NBS-related economic prospects. Understanding NBS's financial possibilities would help to draw money for projects such as ecotourism, sustainable agriculture, and green infrastructure, as well as boost employment in industries including NBS, which allows companies to improve their sustainability profiles, save running expenses, and enter fresh markets. Businesses that make investments in urban forests and green rooftops, for example, can gain from lower energy costs, better air quality, and a strengthened corporate reputation. Agroforestry proponents may similarly boost agriculture yields, diversify income sources, and help to preserve biodiversity.

Best practices and innovation development in NBS depend on cooperation and networking. Globally and locally, networks like the Urban By Nature project sponsored by the H2020 Connecting Nature project offer excellent forums for stakeholders to share information and coordinate NBS projects. By customizing successful models and technologies to fit local conditions and demands, these networks can help them to be transferred across many areas. Through these networks, participants may obtain technical help, keep updated on the most recent NBS advancements, and create alliances strengthening the impact and scalability of their initiatives.

The transition to a nature-positive economy with NBS at its core necessitates coordinated actions across various sectors. Stakeholders may guarantee the efficient, fair, and sustainable use of NBS by means of informed public policies, strong standards, and all-encompassing educational campaigns addressing the identified concerns. These initiatives will not only help to solve environmental problems but also improve economic possibilities, thereby strengthening the worldwide ecology. Cooperation, creativity, and a common will to protect our planet for future generations define the road toward a sustainable future.

Summary

Emphasizing their junction as both a challenge and a chance for global governance, this chapter explores the complex link between commerce, environmental stewardship, and sustainability. From revitalizing EU trade policy to addressing sustainability through WTO processes, the discussion underscores the need for a forward-looking, inclusive agenda that reconciles economic competitiveness with environmental resilience. The transformative role of voluntary sustainability standards (VSS) and due diligence regulations in reshaping global value chains (GVCs) and trade dynamics, particularly for developing countries, is explored as a pathway to achieving equitable growth.

A significant focus is placed on the maritime industry's decarbonization journey, emphasizing innovations like green corridors, alternative fuels, and digital efficiencies to reduce emissions. Complementing this, the chapter examines the shift toward a nature-positive economy, powered by technology and systemic governance aimed at scaling nature-based solutions. This chapter maps a route for world collaboration and collective climate resilience by combining trade policy change, environmental action, and sustainable development initiatives.

CHAPTER 16

Pioneering Greener Trade: Practices and Innovations in Sustainable Finance

This chapter explores the transformative journey toward sustainable finance in global trade, emphasizing greener trading practices, innovative technologies, and policy alignment. It dissects the critical role of international cooperation, fintech, and digital technologies in advancing sustainability while balancing economic growth and environmental stewardship. Positioned as a pillar of global economic and environmental resilience, this extensive chapter provides practical ideas for parties trying to negotiate the complexity of sustainable trade financing.

Greener Trading Practices in Trade Finance: Integrating Sustainability into Global Commerce

Greener trading practices in trade finance represent a significant shift toward integrating sustainability into financial transactions, particularly in the context of global trade. This approach focuses on minimizing environmental impact while maintaining economic growth, and it is becoming increasingly vital as businesses and governments strive to meet climate goals. Below is an introduction to the key elements of greener trading practices within trade finance.

Especially in the framework of world trade, greener trading practices in trade finance mark a major change toward including sustainability into financial operations. As companies and governments work to reach climate targets, this strategy—which emphasizes reducing environmental effects while preserving economic growth—becomes more and more important. The main components of more environmentally friendly trade finance trading methods are given below.

Greener trading methods are a spectrum of techniques and financial tools meant to support global commerce by means of sustainable development promotion. These strategies seek to match trade operations with environmental sustainability objectives, therefore tackling problems like social equality, resource depletion, and carbon emissions.

Key Aspects of Greener Trading Practices

- Environmental Financial Trading:
  - Green trading includes markets for emissions trading programs, renewable energy certificates, and carbon credits. These systems let companies exchange emissions allowances or make investments in greener technology, therefore motivating them to lower their environmental effect.

- Sustainable Trade Policies:
  - Good greening of commerce calls for strong environmental laws and policies supporting sustainable development and consumption. Governments are urged to include environmental issues into trade agreements and regulations so that trade policies help to achieve climate targets.

- International Collaboration:
  - Countries building confidence and cooperation will help to advance more ecologically sustainable trade. This means harmonizing sustainable finance mechanisms and fostering equitable collaboration among countries to enhance openness and governance in green trade initiatives.

- Philanthropic and Financial Support:
  - Combining trade policies, environment, and climate may be greatly facilitated by philanthropy. Funding small businesses and local communities' projects helps to guarantee that they gain from green trade policies.

- Sector-Specific Approaches:
  - By focusing on important industries with large emissions and trade volume, including manufacturing, energy, and agriculture, one may greatly lower carbon footprints and encourage sustainable behaviors.

Benefits of Greener Trading Practices

- **Climate Change Mitigation**: By promoting environmentally friendly products and practices, greener trading helps reduce greenhouse gas emissions and combat climate change.

- **Resource Conservation**: Encouraging efficient resource use minimizes the depletion of natural resources, contributing to environmental sustainability.

- **Economic Opportunities**: The growth of green technologies creates new markets and job opportunities, particularly in developing countries that adopt sustainable practices.

Challenges in Implementing Greener Trading Practices

- **Balancing Economic Development with Environmental Goals**: Developing nations may struggle to prioritize environmental protection over immediate economic needs.

- **Standardization Issues**: Differing environmental regulations across countries can complicate compliance and enforcement of green trade practices.

- **Risk of Greenwashing**: There is a potential for products to be misleadingly marketed as environmentally friendly without meeting actual sustainability standards.

Driving Sustainable Trade: The Role of Environmental Awareness and Policy in Shaping Global Markets

Growing awareness of environmental problems among people is driving demand for environmentally friendly products. This trend is predicted to accelerate the expansion of more environmentally friendly trade methods all around. Projects such as the EU's Carbon Border Adjustment Mechanism (CBAM) seek to impose tighter environmental norms in trade, therefore perhaps changing the dynamics of the world market toward more sustainable behaviors. Better trading methods constitute a vital change toward including environmental sustainability into global trade systems. Stakeholders may help to create a more sustainable world by encouraging cooperation, improving laws, and promoting creative ideas.

Fostering Green Trade: What Role Does International Cooperation Play in Green Trading?

Promoting greener trade policies and enabling the alignment of commerce with environmental sustainability objectives depend much on international collaboration. The following are the main features of how worldwide cooperation supports green trade:

Establishing Transparency and Trust

- **Trust Development**: Good green trading calls for nation-wide confidence. Through sustainable financing tools, which help to build mutual confidence in applying green trade policies, international collaboration promotes openness.

- **Harmonization of Standards**: Establishing internationally harmonized rules and guidelines that control green trade depends on cooperative efforts to guarantee that all participants follow identical environmental requirements.

Policy Alignment and Support

- **Shared Environmental Goals**: Cooperation helps countries to match their trade policies with world environmental goals, like those stated in international treaties like the Paris Agreement. Reducing the negative effects on the environment resulting from trade depends on this alignment.

- **Capacity Building**: Especially for poorer nations, international alliances can offer technical support and capacity-building projects. This helps these countries to use sustainable practices and participate successfully in green trade discussions.

Innovative Financial Mechanisms

- **Green Finance Initiatives**: Working together, creative funding ideas, including green bonds and transition money programs, might arise. These programs are meant to assist environmentally friendly projects and ease investments in sustainable technology.

- **Aid for Trade**: International collaboration may improve "Aid for Trade" initiatives, therefore enabling nations to acquire the required infrastructure and capacity to engage in efficient, sustainable commerce.

Sector-Specific Approaches

- **Targeting High-Impact Sectors**: Cooperation can concentrate on important industries with major emissions, notably energy and agriculture. Countries may more successfully lower their carbon footprints and encourage sustainable behaviors by using sector-specific policies.

- **Joint Research and Innovation**: Sustainable technology innovation may be sparked by cooperative research projects, therefore giving nations access to fresh ideas and techniques improving their capacity for green trade.

The advancement of greener trade practices depends critically on international collaboration. Countries may cooperate toward a sustainable global trade system that reduces climate change while advancing economic development by building confidence, matching policies, improving financial systems, and emphasizing important industries. These initiatives' success depends on fair cooperation, openness, and national shared commitments.

Fostering Green Trade: What Role Does Fintech Play in the Development of Green Finance Instruments?

By using technology to improve access, efficiency, and openness in funding ecologically friendly initiatives, fintech is transforming the creation of green finance instruments. The main ways fintech is helping green finance are:

1. Enhanced Accessibility to Capital

Fintech systems help small and medium-sized businesses (SMEs) that would find it difficult to get conventional finance access to money for green initiatives. These companies may more readily interact with investors by leveraging digital channels, therefore generating greater financial flow into environmentally friendly projects.

2. Crowdfunding and Peer-to-Peer Lending

Fintech makes it possible for people and businesses to directly invest in green initiatives by means of creative finance tools such as peer-to-peer lending and crowdsourcing. This widens the base of possible donors and democratizes investment possibilities.

3. Improved Efficiency and Cost Reduction

Many facets of financial transactions are automated by fintech solutions, therefore saving administrative expenses and time related to money security. Accelerating the use of green finance tools like green bonds and loans depends on this efficiency.

4. Data Analytics for Risk Assessment

More precisely, advanced data analytics tools enable evaluation of the viability and dangers connected with green investments. This capacity lets investors make wise selections, therefore boosting hope for funding sustainable initiatives.

5. Transparency and Accountability

Blockchain Technology: By means of unchangeable records of transactions connected to environmental initiatives, blockchain technology improves openness in green financing. This device can monitor money flow and guarantee that it is applied for its intended use, including funding projects aimed at carbon offsets or renewable energy sources.

6. Real-Time Monitoring

By use of IoT devices and big data analytics, fintech enables real-time monitoring of environmental consequences. This capacity guarantees that stakeholders may monitor development toward environmental objectives and assign responsibility for their promises.

7. Innovative Financial Instruments

Fintech has driven creativity in financial products meant for sustainability, like green bonds and sustainability-linked loans. Many times include performance-based incentives that match financial gains with environmental results; these tools help businesses reach sustainability goals by aligning them.

8. Integration with ESG Metrics

Environmental, social, and governance (ESG) measures are progressively included in fintech platforms' products so that investors may better assess project sustainability performance. This integration helps to meet the increasing need for choices for ethical investing.

9. Support for Policy Implementation

Fintech solutions can guarantee adherence to sustainability criteria and automate reporting procedures, therefore helping companies to comply with environmental rules. Aligning finance policies with world climate targets depends on this kind of support.

10. Public–Private Partnerships

Fintech offers platforms that support alliances aiming at funding green projects, promoting cooperation between public agencies and private investors. Such joint projects can result in more all-encompassing funding plans using public funds as well as private cash.

By expanding access to money, boosting efficiency, guaranteeing transparency, encouraging innovation in financial products, and therefore supporting regulatory compliance, fintech greatly accelerates the development of green finance instruments. Given the growing need for environmentally achieving world environmental goals and promoting sustainable economic development, it depends on fintech being included in green finance as investments keep increasing.

Leveraging Sustainable Finance: Key Instruments Supporting Green Trade Alignment with Environmental Goals

By means of the required financial assistance and structures to match trade practices with environmental sustainability objectives, sustainable finance instruments significantly improve green trade. These devices mostly help in the following important ways:

Mobilizing Capital for Green Initiatives

- **Investment in Sustainable Projects**: Sustainable financing sources provide funds into initiatives such as pollution control, energy efficiency, and renewable energy that benefit the environment. Businesses involved in green trade must mobilize funds if they are to use sustainable technology and practices.

- **Green Bonds and Financing Mechanisms:** Green bonds, along with other instruments, aid in financing environmental initiatives.

- These financial instruments inspire more companies to follow environmentally friendly trade policies by providing investors with a means to support sustainable projects while maybe yielding benefits.

Enhancing Transparency and Accountability

- **Standardized Reporting Frameworks**: Sustainable finance helps to create unified disclosure rules requiring businesses to document their environmental influence. This openness facilitates green commerce by helping consumers and trading partners to develop confidence.

- **Risk Management**: Sustainable finance helps control risks linked with climate change and other environmental issues by including environmental, social, and governance (ESG) elements into financial decision making. Businesses trying to continue their activities in a setting of changing climate depend on this risk management.

Supporting Policy Alignment

- **Regulatory Frameworks**: Sustainable finance helps governments design policies that support green investments by means of regulations. This entails matching governmental financial incentives with objectives of sustainable development, therefore promoting the use of greener trade methods in many different industries.

- **International Cooperation**: Collaborative frameworks among countries can enhance the effectiveness of sustainable finance instruments. By working together to establish common standards and practices, nations can facilitate smoother transitions to greener trade systems.

Capacity Building and Technical Assistance

- **Support for Developing Countries**: Technical support and capacity-building projects targeted at assisting lower-income nations acquire the skills and facilities required for participating in green trade can come from sustainable financing. Fair involvement in world markets depends on this assistance.

- **Pilot Projects and Innovation**: Pilot project funding helps companies—especially small and medium-sized firms (SMEs)—test innovative sustainable practices free from all the financial risk. Then successful projects may be expanded, hence improving green trade prospects.

Enhancing green commerce by means of capital mobilization toward environmentally friendly initiatives, encouragement of transparency and responsibility, support of policy alignment, and capacity building in underdeveloped areas depends on sustainable financing instruments. These initiatives taken together help to create a more sustainable global trade system that balances environmental protection with economic development.

Transforming Trade Finance: The Role of Green Technologies and Sustainability in Logistics

By increasing sustainability, raising efficiency, and promoting openness, greener technologies integrated into logistics are changing trade finance. Growing attention on environmental responsibility in worldwide supply networks combined with technical developments drives this change.

Key Drivers of Change

1. Decarbonization of Supply Chains

The drive for sustainable supply chains forces businesses to evaluate and lower the carbon intensity of their activities. Emissions data is being more and more included into financing models by trade finance providers, thereby enabling improved assessment of the environmental effect connected with trade operations and logistics. Tracking emissions throughout supply chains using technologies like artificial intelligence helps companies find opportunities for development and match their logistical plans with environmental objectives.

2. Digitalization of Trade Finance

Although trade finance is always paper intensive, digitization is changing this scene. Digital channels improve finance logistics operations' efficiency, simplify procedures, and cut documentation. This change speeds the acceptance of greener technology in addition to cutting expenses.

Blockchain and big data analytics provide real-time tracking of products and emissions, thereby giving stakeholders important new perspectives on the sustainability performance of their supply chains.

Sustainable Finance Instruments

1. Green Bonds and Loans

Projects that support sustainability in logistics, such as investments in electric cars or renewable energy sources for transportation, are funded by green bonds more often. These financial tools draw investors hoping to fund environmentally beneficial projects while maybe making profits.

Green loans provide businesses using sustainable practices in their logistical operations better financing terms, therefore motivating them to use greener technology.

2. Sustainability-Linked Financing

Sustainability-linked loans relate borrowing's cost to the accomplishment of particular environmental performance goals. This strategy encourages businesses to improve the sustainability of their logistics operations by providing lower credit rates for fulfilling set targets.

Enhancing Transparency and Accountability

1. Real-Time Emission Monitoring

Real-time emission dashboards let businesses continually assess their environmental effects and predict carbon costs. This capacity improves responsibility among trade finance and logistics-related parties, therefore promoting compliance with environmental criteria.

2. Integration with Regulatory Frameworks

Transparency emissions reporting in trade finance is being driven by regulatory projects as the Carbon Border Adjustment Mechanism (CBAM) of the European Union. Businesses have to modify their logistical plans to follow these rules, thereby underscoring even more the need for greener solutions.

By encouraging sustainable practices, improving efficiency, and raising transparency, the development of greener technology is drastically influencing trade finance by way of logistics. Integration of creative financial instruments will be vital in enabling this shift as businesses give decarbonization top priority and match with regulatory frameworks top importance. In the end, this change not only promotes world sustainability targets but also helps companies to be competitive in a market going more and more environmentally sensitive.

Transforming Trade Finance: The Impact of Digital Technologies on Reducing Carbon Emissions and Enhancing Efficiency

Digital technologies are playing a transformative role in enhancing the efficiency of carbon-intensive processes within trade finance. By leveraging innovative solutions, trade finance can significantly reduce CO_2 emissions while improving operational efficiency.

Here's how digital technologies contribute to this evolution:

1. Real-Time Emissions Tracking

Digital systems provide real-time monitoring of emissions connected to specific transactions and supply chains, therefore enabling automated carbon accounting. Companies like CarbonChain, for example, offer solutions that automate the carbon accounting process, therefore enabling trade finance providers to track the carbon footprint of their portfolio constantly. This capacity enables quick decision making to lower carbon intensity and helps find hotspots of emissions.

2. Predictive Analytics

By predicting emissions depending on different operating circumstances, advanced analytics helps businesses decide on logistics and sourcing with knowledge. Businesses may pick lower-carbon solutions early on by estimating possible emissions from various suppliers or transportation choices.

3. Enhanced Data Transparency and Accessibility

- **Blockchain for Traceability:** Blockchain technology offers unchangeable transaction records, hence improving trade finance's openness. This traceability guarantees that all those engaged may confirm the environmental claims of goods and their related emissions, therefore encouraging responsibility all along the supply chain.

- **Centralized Data Platforms:** Initiatives like SGTraDex streamline the exchange of commercial and sustainability-related data across supply chains. By centralizing access to green data, trade finance institutions can evaluate the environmental impact of financing decisions more effectively, reducing friction in accessing necessary information.

4. Optimization of Supply Chain Processes

- **Artificial intelligence and machine learning** help to maximize logistics operations by means of data analysis, therefore enhancing route planning and inventory control. Particularly important in sectors like commodities trade with a carbon footprint, this optimization lowers fuel usage and related emissions during transportation.

- **IoT devices, or the Internet of Things,** can track emissions and energy use in real time throughout several supply chain phases. This information lets businesses spot inefficiencies and quickly apply fixes, therefore helping to lower emissions generally.

5. Innovative Financing Solutions

Digital technologies help to apply sustainability-linked loans, which relate financing expenses to certain environmental performance criteria. These incentives help borrowers change their operations to include greener methods, hence lowering their carbon footprints.

Faster access to funding for initiatives meant to lower emissions thanks to digitizing bond issuing procedures helps green bond issuing and trading can be simplified via digital channels, therefore facilitating investor backing of sustainable projects.

6. Regulatory Compliance and Reporting

- **Digital solutions** enable businesses to follow changing legal criteria on emissions reporting and environmental standards. Automating compliance procedures helps companies guarantee they satisfy legal requirements and concentrate on lowering their environmental effect by means of legal duties.

- **Integration with carbon pricing mechanisms:** By means of reliable emissions data required for cost computation of carbon emissions, digital technology can help to assist the use of carbon pricing. In trade finance, this integration helps sustainable practices to be financially viable.

Digital technologies of trade finance will help to reduce CO_2 emissions and support the efficiency of carbon-intensive activities. These technologies enable trade finance institutions to be rather important in boosting sustainability within international supply chains by means of real-time tracking, greater transparency, supply chain optimization, innovative financing choices, and higher regulatory compliance. As the need for environmentally friendly solutions is rising, using digital technologies can allow us to achieve a low-carbon future in trade finance.

Optimizing Trade Finance: The Role of Greener Technologies in Enhancing Supply Chains and Reducing Carbon Emissions

By improving efficiency and lowering carbon emissions throughout supplier chains, greener technologies added into goods optimization much help to enhance trade finance. Trade finance institutions are leaning more and more on digital technology as the world demands sustainable practices to maximize operations of products. Regarding trade finance, greener technologies affect general goods optimization in the following sense:

1. Enhancing Supply Chain Transparency

- **Real-Time Emissions Tracking:** IoT and artificial intelligence technologies provide real-time emissions monitoring all across the supply chain. This openness enables trade finance providers to evaluate the carbon footprint of their sponsored projects, therefore enabling informed funding and investment decisions.

- **Blockchain for Traceability:** Blockchain technology improves the traceability of products together with their related emissions. For lenders wishing to promote better practices, stakeholders may confirm sustainability claims and guarantee compliance with environmental criteria by means of a safe and unchangeable record of transactions.

2. Optimizing Freight Operations

- **AI and Machine Learning:** By use of AI in logistics, route planning and cargo loading may be optimized, thereby greatly lowering fuel consumption and pollution. AI systems, for example, may examine past data to find the most effective paths of transportation, therefore reducing the carbon footprint connected with freight activities.

- **Telematics and Smart Technologies:** Using telematics technology lets businesses compile real-time information on driver behavior and vehicle performance. Directly helping to cut emissions in goods movement, this knowledge may help to increase operational efficiency, lower idle periods, and improve fuel economy.

3. Innovative Financing Solutions

- **Sustainability-Linked Loans:** Increasingly, trade financing institutions are providing sustainability-linked loans to encourage businesses to reach particular environmental performance goals. Tie loan terms to emissions reductions helps lenders inspire borrowers to use greener technology for their freight operations.

- **Green Bonds:** The issuance of green bonds specifically aimed at financing environmentally friendly projects in logistics is on the rise. These financial instruments attract investors focused on sustainability, providing companies with the capital needed to invest in cleaner technologies and practices.

4. Supporting Regulatory Compliance

- **Alignment with Environmental Regulations:** As regulatory frameworks like the European Union's Carbon Border Adjustment Mechanism (CBAM) come into effect, trade finance must adapt by integrating emissions data into its lending practices. Digital technologies facilitate compliance by automating reporting processes and ensuring adherence to sustainability standards.

- **Incentives for Low-Emission Vehicles:** Regulatory proposals that incentivize the use of low-emission vehicles are driving demand for greener technologies in freight transport. Trade finance institutions can support this transition by providing favorable financing terms for companies investing in cleaner fleets.

5. Fostering Collaboration Among Stakeholders

- **Partnerships for Sustainability:** Collaboration initiatives among supply chain partners are essential for successfully implementing green technologies in freight optimization. Trade finance institutions can play a key role by facilitating partnerships that promote knowledge sharing and resource pooling, ultimately driving collective action toward sustainability goals.

- **Data Sharing Platforms:** Digital platforms that enable data sharing among stakeholders enhance collaboration and transparency in emissions reporting. This collective approach allows companies to benchmark their performance against industry standards and identify opportunities for improvement.

Greener technology is very vital for freight optimization if we are to maximize trade financing by raising operational efficiency, guaranteeing regulatory compliance, and thus supporting sustainable practices across supply chains. Trade finance institutions have to adopt these technologies as digital advances change to help their customers reach sustainability targets while keeping competitiveness in a market going more and more environmentally concerned. Trade finance may greatly help to lower carbon emissions related to goods operations by using artificial intelligence, blockchain, telematics, and creative financing ideas.

CHAPTER 16   PIONEERING GREENER TRADE: PRACTICES AND INNOVATIONS IN SUSTAINABLE FINANCE

Enhancing Emissions Accuracy in Supply Chains: How Can AI Improve the Accuracy of Emissions Data in Supply Chains?

By means of several creative uses, artificial intelligence (AI) greatly improves the accuracy of emissions data in supply chains. AI helps to track and control more exact emissions by means of these ways:

1. Real-Time Data Analysis

- **Dynamic Monitoring:** AI systems can analyze real-time data from multiple sources, such as IoT sensors, to monitor emissions continuously throughout the supply chain. This capability allows companies to capture fluctuations in emissions due to changes in operational conditions, such as transportation routes or production processes, leading to more accurate reporting.

- **Predictive Analytics:** By employing predictive analytics, AI can forecast future emissions based on historical data and current trends. This helps organizations anticipate potential increases in emissions and implement corrective measures proactively, ensuring that data reflects actual conditions more accurately.

2. Optimizing Transportation and Logistics

- **Route Optimization:** AI algorithms can optimize delivery routes by analyzing traffic patterns, weather conditions, and vehicle types. For instance, companies like Walmart utilize AI to plan efficient delivery routes that minimize fuel consumption and emissions, leading to more accurate assessments of transportation-related emissions. This optimization reduces uncertainties in emissions calculations associated with logistics.

- **Load Management:** AI can also optimize load capacities by analyzing shipment data, ensuring that vehicles are used efficiently. This reduces the number of trips needed and lowers overall emissions per unit transported.

3. Enhanced Demand Forecasting

- **Accurate Inventory Management:** AI improves demand forecasting by analyzing historical sales data and market trends. Accurate forecasts help maintain optimal inventory levels, reducing overproduction and waste, which in turn decreases associated emissions from manufacturing and logistics operations. This accuracy contributes to a clearer understanding of overall emissions across the supply chain.

4. Advanced Machine Learning Models

- **Complex Data Analysis:** Machine learning models, such as Random Forests and Gradient Boosting Machines, analyze complex relationships within supply chain data to predict carbon emissions based on various factors like transportation methods and fuel types. These models provide detailed insights into the factors contributing to emissions, enhancing the accuracy of reported data.

- **Clustering Algorithms:** Techniques like K-means clustering can identify groups with similar emission characteristics within the supply chain. By pinpointing high-emission areas, businesses can focus their reduction efforts where they will have the most significant impact, leading to better-targeted interventions and more precise emissions reporting.

5. Comprehensive Reporting and Compliance

- **Automated ESG Reporting:** AI automates the collection and analysis of environmental, social, and governance (ESG) data across various supply chain stages. This automation ensures timely and accurate sustainability reporting, which is essential for compliance with regulatory requirements related to emissions disclosures.

- **Scope 3 Emissions Tracking:** AI tools are particularly effective in managing Scope 3 greenhouse gas emissions—those generated indirectly through supply chain activities—which are often the most challenging to quantify accurately. By integrating data from suppliers and logistics partners, AI helps companies gain a comprehensive view of their total carbon footprint.

6. Continuous Improvement Through Feedback Loops

- **Data-Driven Decision Making:** AI systems facilitate continuous learning by analyzing outcomes from previous interventions aimed at reducing emissions. This feedback loop allows organizations to refine their strategies over time based on what has been effective in lowering carbon footprints.

- **Scenario Simulation:** AI can simulate different operational scenarios to predict how changes (like adopting renewable energy sources or altering transportation modes) will impact overall emissions. This capability supports informed decision making that aligns with sustainability goals while improving accuracy in emissions forecasting.

Through real-time monitoring, predictive analytics, improved logistics, sophisticated machine learning models, automated reporting, and continuous improvement systems, artificial intelligence increases the accuracy of emissions data in supply chains. Using these features will help businesses to better grasp their carbon footprints, therefore guiding their decisions in line with sustainability goals and increasing operational efficiency. Reducing their environmental effect is becoming more and more important for companies, so reliable emissions tracking will be absolutely vital to satisfy legal criteria and reach climate targets.

CHAPTER 16 PIONEERING GREENER TRADE: PRACTICES AND INNOVATIONS IN SUSTAINABLE FINANCE

CO_2 Emission Reduction, Emission Tracking, Standards and Incentives in Carbon Labeling, and Sustainability Through Emission Tracking and Reporting

The integration of sustainability practices in trade finance is increasingly focused on reducing CO_2 emissions, enhancing emission tracking, establishing standards for carbon labeling, and promoting transparency through reporting. These elements are crucial for fostering a sustainable economy that aligns with global climate goals.

CO_2 Emission Reduction

Achieving global climate objectives and preventing climate change depend on lowering CO_2 emissions. Within the framework of trade finance, numerous approaches may be applied:

- **Sustainability-Linked Financing**: Financial institutions are developing sustainability-linked loans that incentivize borrowers to reduce their carbon footprints. For example, banks may offer lower interest rates for companies that meet specific emissions reduction targets or adopt greener technologies in their operations.

- **Investment in Low-Carbon Technologies**: Trade finance can facilitate investments in low-carbon technologies across supply chains. By providing capital for renewable energy projects or energy-efficient processes, financial institutions can help businesses transition to more sustainable practices.

- **Encouragement of Sustainable Practices**: Trade finance providers can promote sustainable sourcing and production methods by integrating environmental criteria into their lending decisions. This encourages companies to adopt practices that minimize emissions throughout their supply chains.

Emission Tracking

Effective emission tracking is vital for accurately measuring and managing carbon footprints within trade finance.

- **Real-Time Monitoring**: Utilizing IoT devices and AI analytics allows companies to monitor emissions continuously throughout the supply chain. This real-time data collection helps identify areas where emissions can be reduced and informs decision making.

- **Standardized Reporting Frameworks**: Establishing consistent methodologies for measuring emissions is crucial. Standards such as the Greenhouse Gas Protocol provide guidelines that help organizations quantify their emissions accurately, ensuring transparency and comparability across different sectors.

- **Lifecycle Assessment (LCA)**: Conducting LCAs enables organizations to evaluate the environmental impact of products from raw material extraction through production, use, and disposal. This comprehensive approach helps identify emission hotspots and prioritize reduction efforts.

Standards and Incentives in Carbon Labeling

Carbon labeling serves as a mechanism to inform consumers about the carbon footprint of products, influencing purchasing decisions and encouraging companies to adopt greener practices.

- **Standardization of Carbon Labels**: Developing standardized carbon labeling systems ensures that labels are meaningful and comparable across products. This helps consumers make informed choices while encouraging manufacturers to reduce their emissions.

- **Incentives for Compliance**: Governments can offer financial incentives for companies that achieve specific emissions reduction targets or adopt low-carbon technologies. These incentives may include tax breaks or access to low-interest loans for sustainable investments.

- **Consumer Engagement**: Educating consumers about the significance of carbon labels can drive demand for low-carbon products, creating market pressure for businesses to improve their sustainability practices.

Sustainability Through Emission Tracking and Reporting

Sustainability in business practices increasingly relies on effective emission tracking and reporting mechanisms.

- **Transparency in Reporting**: Regularly publishing emissions data fosters transparency and accountability among stakeholders. Companies that disclose their carbon footprints are often viewed more favorably by investors and consumers.

- **Integration with Business Strategy**: Organizations are integrating sustainability metrics into their overall business strategies. By aligning financial performance with environmental impact, companies can drive innovation while reducing their carbon footprints.

- **Collaboration Across Supply Chains**: Effective emission tracking often requires collaboration among supply chain partners. By sharing data on emissions reduction efforts, companies can collectively enhance their sustainability initiatives.

The interconnection between CO_2 emission reduction, emission tracking, standards and incentives in carbon labeling, and sustainability through reporting highlights the importance of a comprehensive approach to tackling climate change within trade finance. By implementing robust tracking systems, adhering to standardized reporting frameworks, and engaging consumers through transparent carbon labeling, organizations can significantly contribute to global sustainability efforts while enhancing their competitive advantage in an increasingly eco-conscious market. The role of trade finance in facilitating these initiatives is crucial, as it provides the necessary capital and support for businesses striving to meet their environmental goals.

CHAPTER 16 PIONEERING GREENER TRADE: PRACTICES AND INNOVATIONS IN SUSTAINABLE FINANCE

Challenges in Accurately Calculating Supply Chain Carbon Footprints: Key Barriers to Effective Emissions Control and Reporting

Precisely computing supply chain carbon footprints poses many major difficulties that impede beneficial emissions control and reporting. Based on the search results, these are the primary difficulties noted:

1. Complexity of Scope 3 Emissions

- **Definition and Scope:** Scope 3 emissions encompass all indirect emissions that occur in a company's value chain, including both upstream (e.g., emissions from suppliers) and downstream (e.g., emissions from product use by consumers) activities. These emissions can account for a substantial portion of a company's total carbon footprint—often up to 70% or more—making their accurate measurement critical but inherently complex.

- **Multiple Layers of Suppliers:** The complexity increases with multiple tiers of suppliers, where direct suppliers (Tier 1) may source materials from other suppliers (Tier 2, Tier 3, etc.). This multi-tier structure obscures the trail of emissions, making it challenging to track and quantify the full environmental impact across the supply chain.

2. Data Quality and Availability

- **Reliance on External Data:** Many companies depend on data from third-party suppliers or industry averages to estimate their emissions. This reliance can lead to inaccuracies due to variability in data quality, granularity, and methodology among different sources. For instance, if suppliers do not measure their own emissions accurately or refuse to share data due to confidentiality concerns, it can severely impact the accuracy of a company's overall emissions calculations.

- **Inconsistent Reporting Standards:** There is currently no standardized framework for carbon reporting across industries. The lack of uniform methodologies makes it difficult for companies to compare emissions data across different sources and sectors, leading to inconsistencies and gaps in reporting.

3. Measurement Methodologies

- **Hybrid Calculation Methods:** Companies often use a combination of spend-based and activity-based methods to calculate emissions. While spend-based methods use financial values to estimate emissions, activity-based methods rely on specific operational data (e.g., units produced). The hybrid approach can lead to discrepancies if not implemented correctly, as companies may struggle to gather sufficient activity data for accurate calculations.

- **Manual Data Collection:** Many organizations still rely on manual methods for data collection, such as spreadsheets. This practice is prone to human error and can complicate the understanding of emissions across the supply chain. The labor-intensive nature of manual entry makes it challenging to maintain accurate and up-to-date emissions data.

4. Lack of Technical Expertise

- **Skill Gaps in Carbon Management:** A notable challenge is the lack of personnel with the necessary technical expertise in carbon management within organizations. This skill gap makes it difficult for companies to measure, analyze, and report their emissions effectively. As sustainability practices become more critical, investing in training and expertise will be essential for improving accuracy in emissions calculations.

5. Resource Intensity

- **High Resource Requirements:** Accurately calculating Scope 3 emissions requires significant resources, including personnel, technology, and efficient data management processes. Many companies find it challenging to align these resources across their supply chains, especially when dealing with numerous suppliers who may have varying levels of commitment to sustainability practices.

The challenges of measuring supply chain carbon footprints highlight the complexity of reducing Scope 3 emissions. Many times, accurate emissions evaluations are limited by data quality, measuring methods, supplier engagement, technical understanding, and resource allocation. Dealing with these challenges requires businesses cooperating to fund better data collection technologies, standardize reporting systems, strengthen supplier ties, and acquire internal carbon management skills. Overcoming these obstacles helps companies greatly assist world climate objectives and boost their environmental activities.

Strategies for Tackling Scope 3 Emissions: Enhancing Accuracy in Tracking Indirect Emissions Across Supply Chains

Businesses can employ many strategies to tackle the inherent challenges in tracking these indirect emissions and hence increase the accuracy of Scope 3 emissions assessment. These are fundamental approaches based on knowledge acquired from several sources:

1. Enhancing Data Quality and Availability

- **Direct Engagement with Suppliers:** Companies should actively engage with their suppliers to obtain accurate emissions data. This includes encouraging suppliers to measure their own emissions and share this information transparently. Establishing strong relationships and communication channels can facilitate better data sharing.

- **Utilizing Primary Data**: Whenever possible, organizations should prioritize using primary data over secondary data or industry averages. For example, collecting specific emissions data from high-impact suppliers can provide a more accurate picture of Scope 3 emissions compared to relying solely on generalized estimates.

- **Standardized Reporting Formats**: Implementing standardized reporting formats across the supply chain can enhance data consistency and comparability. By aligning with frameworks like the Greenhouse Gas Protocol, companies can ensure that all partners use similar methodologies for emissions calculations, reducing discrepancies.

2. Adopting Advanced Measurement Methodologies

- **Hybrid Calculation Methods**: Companies can use a combination of spend-based and activity-based methods for calculating emissions. This hybrid approach allows for greater flexibility and accuracy, particularly when specific activity data is unavailable. For instance, using spend-based calculations for less impactful suppliers while applying direct measurements for major contributors can optimize accuracy.

- **Lifecycle Assessment (LCA)**: Conducting LCAs enables organizations to assess the full environmental impact of products throughout their entire lifecycle. This comprehensive approach helps identify emission hotspots and informs targeted reduction strategies.

3. Leveraging Technology for Data Collection and Analysis

- **Carbon Measurement Platforms**: Utilizing carbon measurement technologies and software platforms can streamline data collection processes. These platforms often provide tools for real-time monitoring, data visualization, and analytics, which help companies track emissions more accurately across their supply chains.

- **Automation of Data Collection**: Automating data collection processes reduces the risk of human error associated with manual entry methods. Implementing systems that integrate directly with suppliers' reporting tools can facilitate more accurate and timely data gathering.

4. Continuous Improvement and Iteration

- **Establishing Baselines and Targets**: Companies should start by establishing baseline emissions levels and setting realistic reduction targets. By continuously refining these baselines as more accurate data becomes available, organizations can improve their overall emissions measurement process over time.

- **Regular Audits and Updates**: Conducting regular audits of emissions data and methodologies ensures that calculations remain accurate and relevant. As business operations evolve or new suppliers are added, updating the emissions inventory is essential for maintaining accuracy.

5. Building Internal Expertise and Capacity

- **Training Personnel**: Investing in training programs for employees involved in carbon management can enhance internal capabilities in measuring and reporting Scope 3 emissions accurately. Developing expertise within the organization ensures that teams are equipped to handle complex calculations and understand best practices in carbon accounting.

- **Cross-Departmental Collaboration**: Encouraging collaboration between departments (e.g., procurement, sustainability, finance) fosters a holistic approach to emissions measurement. Sharing knowledge and resources across functions can lead to better data collection practices and more effective management strategies.

CHAPTER 16   PIONEERING GREENER TRADE: PRACTICES AND INNOVATIONS IN SUSTAINABLE FINANCE

Companies trying to reach significant carbon reduction targets must first increase the accuracy of Scope 3 emissions measurement. Organizations may greatly increase their knowledge of indirect emissions by improving data quality through supplier involvement, using sophisticated measuring techniques, utilizing technology, iterating on processes, and developing internal expertise. These activities promote not just adherence to legal standards but also more general supply chain sustainability projects.

- **Most Effective Methodologies for Calculating Scope 3 Emissions:** To effectively calculate Scope 3 emissions, companies can utilize several methodologies that vary in specificity, data requirements, and accuracy. The Greenhouse Gas (GHG) Protocol outlines four primary methods for calculating Scope 3 emissions, particularly for categories such as purchased goods and services. Here's an overview of the most effective methodologies:

1. Spend-Based Method

- **Description**: This method estimates emissions based on the financial value of purchased goods and services. It involves multiplying the amount spent on these goods by an emission factor that represents the average emissions per monetary unit for the relevant industry.

- **Advantages:**
  - **Ease of Data Collection**: This method is relatively straightforward as it relies on readily available financial data from accounting systems.
  - **Scalability**: Companies can easily apply this method across their operations to identify carbon hotspots.

- **Disadvantages:**
  - **Lower Accuracy**: The spend-based method is less specific because it assumes that all products within a category produce similar emissions, regardless of differences in manufacturing processes or materials.

2. Average Data (Physical Unit) Method

- **Description**: This method uses physical data (e.g., weight or quantity) of purchased materials combined with corresponding average emission factors for those materials. For example, if a company purchases a certain amount of aluminum, it would apply the average emissions associated with aluminum production.

- **Advantages**:
  - **Higher Accuracy than Spend Based**: By using physical units, this method allows for more accurate emissions calculations as it accounts for differences between products.
  - **Lifecycle Assessment Integration**: Emission factors can be derived from lifecycle assessments (LCAs), which provide a more comprehensive view of environmental impacts.

- **Disadvantages:**
  - **Data Accessibility**: Acquiring the necessary physical unit data may be more challenging compared to financial data.

3. Supplier-Specific Method

- **Description**: This approach collects detailed emissions data directly from suppliers, often through sustainability surveys or product-level carbon footprints. It provides a more precise estimate of emissions associated with specific products or services.

- **Advantages**:
  - **High Accuracy**: By using primary data from suppliers, this method yields the most accurate representation of Scope 3 emissions.
  - **Actionable Insights**: Companies can identify specific suppliers contributing to higher emissions and work collaboratively to reduce those impacts.

- **Disadvantages:**
  - **Data Collection Challenges**: Obtaining primary data from suppliers can be difficult due to varying levels of commitment to sustainability and transparency.

4. Hybrid Method

- **Description**: The hybrid method combines supplier-specific data with secondary data (such as industry averages) to fill gaps in information. This approach aims to balance accuracy and feasibility by using the most specific data available while supplementing it with broader estimates where necessary.

- **Advantages:**
  - **Improved Specificity**: By integrating both primary and secondary data, the hybrid method provides a more nuanced understanding of emissions across different product
  - **Flexibility**: This method can be tailored to different categories within Scope 3 based on data availability and significance.

- **Disadvantages:**
  - **Complexity in Implementation**: Managing both types of data can complicate the calculation process and require robust data management systems.

Calculating Scope 3 emissions mostly depends on elements such as data availability, required accuracy, and resource limits of the chosen approach. Although the spend-based approach provides simplicity of use, average data, supplier-specific, or hybrid approaches can yield more accurate judgments. Businesses should assess their particular situation and choose the strategy most in line with their reporting obligations and sustainability aims. Improving the accuracy of Scope 3 emissions estimations helps companies to better control their carbon footprints and significantly support worldwide climate projects.

Emissions can be categorized into various types based on their sources and impacts. The most commonly referenced classifications include **Scope 1, Scope 2, and Scope 3 emissions**, which are part of the Greenhouse Gas (GHG) Protocol framework. Here's a detailed overview of these categories:

1. Scope 1 Emissions

- **Definition**: Scope 1 emissions are direct greenhouse gas emissions that occur from sources owned or controlled by a company. This includes emissions from company facilities and vehicles.

- Examples:
  - **Mobile Combustion**: Emissions from fuel combustion in vehicles owned or controlled by the company (e.g., cars, trucks).
  - **Stationary Combustion**: Emissions from burning fossil fuels for energy in company-owned facilities (e.g., boilers, furnaces).
  - **Fugitive Emissions**: Unintentional emissions that escape from equipment (e.g., leaks from refrigeration systems).

2. Scope 2 Emissions

- **Definition**: Scope 2 emissions are indirect greenhouse gas emissions associated with the generation of purchased electricity, steam, heating, and cooling consumed by the reporting company.

- Examples:
  - **Electricity Consumption**: Emissions produced during the generation of electricity that a company purchases from an external provider.
  - **Purchased Steam/Heat**: Emissions associated with the production of steam or heat that is consumed by the company but generated elsewhere.

3. Scope 3 Emissions

- **Definition**: Scope 3 emissions are all other indirect emissions that occur in a company's value chain, both upstream and downstream, which are not included in Scope 2.

- Examples:

- Upstream Activities:
  - **Purchased Goods and Services**: Emissions from the production of goods and services purchased by the company.
  - **Transportation and Distribution**: Emissions from the transportation of products purchased by the company, including logistics.
  - **Waste Disposal**: Emissions resulting from waste generated in operations that are disposed of or treated.
  - **Employee Commuting and Business Travel**: Emissions from employees traveling to work or for business purposes.
- Downstream Activities:
  - **Product Use**: Emissions generated during the use phase of products sold by the company (e.g., energy consumption by appliances).
  - **End-of-Life Treatment**: Emissions associated with the disposal or recycling of products at the end of their lifecycle.

Companies trying to efficiently lower their carbon footprints depend on knowing these emission kinds. Every scope offers understanding of several places where emissions might be controlled:

- **Scope 1 and Scope 2 emissions** are typically easier to measure and manage since they relate directly to a company's operations and energy consumption.
- **Scope 3 emissions**, however, often represent the largest portion of a company's overall carbon footprint but are more challenging to quantify due to their indirect nature. Addressing Scope 3 emissions requires collaboration across the supply chain and engagement with suppliers and customers.

Organizations may better grasp their whole greenhouse gas effect and create focused reduction plans by classifying emissions into Scopes 1, 2, and 3. This categorization improves sustainability projects in several sectors in addition to helping with reporting guidelines compliance.

Revolutionizing Sustainable Trade: The Role of the Internet of Things (IoT) in Enhancing Green Technologies, Decision Making, and Sustainable Trade

By allowing real-time data collection, improving resource efficiency, and hence enabling improved decision making, the Internet of things (IoT) is changing the scene of greener technologies and sustainable trade. The relevance of IoT in several domains is summarized here:

1. Optimizing Resource Usage

- **Smart Grids:** IoT technology plays a crucial role in the development of smart grids, which connect various energy sources and consumption points. This connectivity allows for more efficient energy distribution, reducing waste and reliance on fossil fuels. By optimizing energy generation and consumption, smart grids promote the use of renewable energy sources, contributing to lower carbon emissions.

- **Water Management:** IoT sensors can monitor water usage in real time across distribution networks. This capability helps optimize irrigation in agriculture, reduce water waste, and improve overall water management practices. For instance, sensors can detect leaks or inefficiencies in the system, allowing for timely interventions 1.

2. Enhancing Energy Efficiency

- **Smart Buildings:** IoT devices can be integrated into buildings to monitor and manage energy consumption effectively. Smart thermostats, lighting systems, and appliances can adjust their operations based on occupancy patterns and preferences, significantly reducing energy waste. These technologies not only lower operational costs but also contribute to sustainability goals by minimizing overall energy consumption.

- **Demand Response Systems:** IoT enables demand response initiatives where energy consumption can be adjusted based on supply availability. For example, during peak demand periods, smart devices can reduce their energy usage or shift it to off-peak times, helping to balance the grid and reduce emissions associated with peak power generation.

3. Improving Waste Management

- **Smart Waste Solutions:** IoT technology enhances waste management by enabling real-time monitoring of waste levels in bins and containers. This data allows for optimized collection routes and schedules, reducing unnecessary pickups and associated emissions from waste collection vehicles. Additionally, it promotes recycling efforts by providing insights into waste composition.

4. Facilitating Sustainable Trade Practices

- **Supply Chain Transparency:** IoT devices can track products throughout the supply chain, providing valuable data on their carbon footprints at each stage of production and transportation. This transparency enables companies to make informed decisions about sourcing and logistics, ultimately leading to more sustainable practices.

- **Carbon Footprint Monitoring:** By integrating IoT with advanced analytics, businesses can monitor their carbon emissions in real time across various operations. This capability allows companies to identify high-emission areas within their supply chains and implement targeted strategies for reduction.

5. Supporting Smart Cities Initiatives

- **Urban Sustainability:** IoT is integral to creating eco-friendly smart cities where technology is used to enhance urban living while minimizing environmental impact. Applications include smart traffic management systems that reduce congestion and emissions, as well as environmental monitoring systems that track air quality and other pollutants.

- **Integration with AI:** The combination of IoT with artificial intelligence (AI) enhances the ability to analyze data from multiple sources for better resource management. AI algorithms can predict energy usage patterns or optimize waste collection schedules based on historical data, further driving efficiency in urban environments.

One significant facilitator of more environmentally friendly technologies and sustainable trading practices is the Internet of Things. IoT greatly helps to lower environmental impacts by means of better waste management, energy efficiency enhancement, resource use optimization, support of smart city projects, and so on. Businesses that keep implementing these technologies not only progress their sustainability objectives but also encourage a more responsible attitude to resource management in a society growingly linked by means of these technologies.

Enhancing Operational Efficiency and Sustainability in Measuring Carbon Emissions: The Role of IoT in Logistics, Tracking Carbon Emissions, and Unveiling Scope 3 Emission Calculations

Especially in measuring carbon emissions and revealing Scope 3 emission estimations, the Internet of things (IoT) is transformingly important in logistics. Using IoT technology helps businesses to increase operational efficiency, boost sustainability, and provide greater understanding of their environmental effects. IoT supports these sectors in the following ways:

Role of IoT in Logistics

- **Real-Time Tracking and Monitoring**
  - **Shipment Tracking**: IoT devices such as GPS sensors and RFID tags enable real-time tracking of shipments throughout the supply chain. This capability allows logistics companies to monitor the location and condition of goods, ensuring timely deliveries and reducing delays.
  - **Environmental Monitoring**: IoT sensors can monitor environmental conditions (e.g., temperature, humidity) during transportation, ensuring that products are stored and transported under optimal conditions. This is particularly important for perishable goods and sensitive equipment.
- **Enhanced Fleet Management**
  - **Vehicle Tracking**: IoT solutions provide detailed data on vehicle locations, fuel consumption, speed, and maintenance needs. This information helps logistics companies optimize routes, reduce fuel costs, and improve overall fleet performance.
  - **Predictive Maintenance**: By analyzing data from vehicles, IoT systems can predict when maintenance is needed before breakdowns occur. This proactive approach minimizes downtime and extends the lifespan of fleet assets.
- **Improved Inventory Management**
  - **Automated Inventory Tracking**: IoT technology allows for automated inventory management through smart shelves and connected sensors that track stock levels in real time. This reduces the risk of stockouts or overstocking, leading to more efficient resource utilization.
  - **Data-Driven Decision Making**: The data collected from IoT devices can be analyzed to improve forecasting and inventory planning, enabling businesses to align supply with demand more effectively.

Tracking Carbon Emissions

1. Accurate Emission Data Collection

a. **Real-Time Emission Monitoring**: IoT devices can track emissions from transportation vehicles in real time by monitoring fuel consumption and vehicle performance metrics. This data is essential for understanding the carbon footprint associated with logistics operations.

b. **Integration with Supply Chain Data**: By combining emissions data with logistics information (e.g., shipment distances, vehicle types), companies can gain a comprehensive view of their carbon emissions across the supply chain.

2. Facilitating Scope 3 Emission Calculations

a. **Upstream Emissions Tracking**: IoT can help track emissions from suppliers by collecting data on the materials used and their transportation methods. This information is critical for calculating Scope 3 emissions associated with purchased goods and services.

b. **Downstream Emissions Analysis**: For products sold by a company, IoT can monitor usage patterns and conditions that affect emissions during the product's lifecycle. This helps in accurately assessing emissions related to product use and end-of-life disposal.

Unveiling Scope 3 Emission Calculations

1. Data Integration Across the Value Chain

a. **Collaboration with Suppliers**: By utilizing IoT technologies to gather data from suppliers about their production processes and associated emissions, companies can improve the accuracy of their Scope 3 calculations. This collaboration fosters transparency and encourages suppliers to adopt more sustainable practices.

b. **Holistic View of Emissions**: Integrating data from various sources within the supply chain allows companies to create a detailed inventory of Scope 3 emissions, identifying hotspots where reductions can be made.

2. Enhanced Reporting Capabilities

   a. **Automated Reporting Tools**: IoT systems can streamline the reporting process by automatically compiling emissions data into standardized formats required for compliance with regulations or sustainability reporting frameworks. This automation reduces administrative burdens and improves accuracy.

   b. **Real-Time Insights for Decision Making**: With real-time access to emissions data, companies can make informed decisions about sourcing, logistics strategies, and product design to minimize their carbon footprints.

IoT integration into logistics greatly improves tracking of carbon emissions and precise calculation of Scope 3 emissions. IoT helps businesses to maximize their operations and lower their environmental effect by offering real-time data on fleet performance, environmental conditions, and shipping. Achieving transparency will depend on using IoT technology as companies concentrate more and more on environmental goals.

The Role of RPA in Ensuring Sustainable Trade and a Greener Emissions Reporting and Fostering Greener Trade Practices Across Supply Chains

Rising as a vital instrument in the search of sustainable commerce and a better future is robotic process automation (RPA). RPA greatly lowers environmental impact and increases operational efficiency by automating repetitive jobs and process optimization. RPA facilitates the shift toward greener corporate practices and helps to contribute to sustainability by means of:

1. Optimizing Resource Use and Reducing Waste

RPA helps organizations streamline operations by automating manual, resource-intensive processes. This optimization leads to reduced resource consumption, which is essential for promoting sustainability. For instance, RPA can automate data collection and reporting, minimizing the need for paper-based documentation and thereby reducing waste. By aligning operations with circular economy principles, RPA facilitates more efficient use of resources across the supply chain.

2. Enhancing Energy Efficiency

Energy management is a significant area where RPA can make a difference. Automated systems can perform energy audits, monitor consumption patterns, and identify inefficiencies in real time. By analyzing energy usage data, RPA can suggest adjustments to operations that optimize energy consumption, helping organizations lower their carbon footprints significantly. For example, automated systems can predict periods of high energy demand and adjust operations accordingly, further enhancing energy efficiency.

3. Automating Emission Tracking and Reporting

One of the primary challenges companies face is accurately tracking greenhouse gas emissions, particularly Scope 3 emissions from supply chains. RPA can automate the collection of emissions data from various sources, ensuring comprehensive and consistent reporting without the burden of manual data entry. This capability not only improves accuracy but also supports compliance with regulatory requirements and sustainability reporting standards. By providing real-time insights into emissions data, organizations can make informed decisions to reduce their environmental impact.

4. Supporting Sustainable Supply Chain Management

RPA enhances supply chain sustainability by automating vendor assessments based on sustainability criteria. This ensures that companies partner with suppliers who meet specific environmental standards, fostering a more sustainable supply chain ecosystem.

Additionally, RPA can optimize inventory management processes to reduce excess stock and associated waste, promoting cleaner operations that are less harmful to the environment

5. Facilitating Digital Transformation

The shift toward digital processes is crucial for achieving sustainability goals. RPA enables organizations to transition from paper-based workflows to digital solutions, reducing reliance on physical resources. This digital transformation not only supports broader sustainability objectives but also enhances operational efficiency by enabling faster and more accurate data processing. As companies embrace RPA, they build a foundation for further advancements in automation that align with environmental responsibility.

6. Contributing to Global Sustainability Goals

RPA aligns with global initiatives aimed at achieving net-zero emissions and other sustainability targets outlined in agreements like the Paris Agreement. By improving efficiencies across operations and supply chains, RPA helps businesses contribute to climate goals while simultaneously enhancing their competitiveness in an increasingly eco-conscious market.

A cleaner future and sustainable trade depends critically on robotic process automation (RPA). RPA gives companies the tools they need to run more sustainably by optimizing resource usage, improving energy efficiency, automating emission tracking, supporting sustainable supply chains, enabling digital transformation, and helping world sustainability objectives be reached. Integrating RPA into their operations will be crucial for significant advancement toward a sustainable future while preserving operational efficiency and competitiveness as companies under increasing pressure to embrace environmentally friendly practices seek substantial change.

CHAPTER 16   PIONEERING GREENER TRADE: PRACTICES AND INNOVATIONS IN SUSTAINABLE FINANCE

Leveraging Robotic Process Automation (RPA) to Enhance Efficiency and Reduce Greenhouse Gas Emissions

Robotic process automation (RPA) improves operational efficiency, resource consumption, and data management, thereby helping to lower greenhouse gas emissions. RPA helps to achieve this significant environmental aim in the following ways:

1. Streamlining Operations

RPA automates repetitive and time-consuming tasks, which reduces the need for manual intervention. This leads to:

- **Lower Energy Consumption**: By optimizing workflows and eliminating unnecessary steps, RPA can decrease the energy required to complete processes. For example, automating data entry or report generation reduces the time systems are active, thereby lowering overall energy use.

- **Reduced Operational Footprint**: With fewer manual processes, organizations can minimize their physical resource needs (e.g., paper, office supplies), contributing to waste reduction and lowering emissions associated with production and disposal.

2. Optimizing Supply Chain Management

RPA enhances supply chain efficiency by automating various processes:

- **Inventory Management**: Automating inventory tracking helps prevent overproduction and excess stock, which can lead to waste and increased emissions from storage and transportation. For instance, RPA can adjust orders based on real-time demand forecasts, reducing unnecessary shipments.

- **Route Optimization**: In logistics, RPA can analyze delivery routes and optimize them for fuel efficiency, thereby reducing the carbon footprint associated with transportation. This is crucial for minimizing emissions in sectors heavily reliant on logistics.

3. Automating Emission Tracking

RPA facilitates accurate tracking of greenhouse gas emissions.

- **Data Collection**: RPA can automate the gathering of emissions data from various sources within an organization, such as energy consumption logs and vehicle usage records. This ensures comprehensive data collection without the burden of manual entry.

- **Consistent Reporting**: By automating the calculation of emissions based on collected data, RPA helps maintain consistency and accuracy in reporting. This is essential for compliance with regulatory requirements and for organizations aiming to achieve sustainability certifications.

4. Enhancing Energy Efficiency

RPA contributes to improved energy management:

- **Automated Energy Audits**: RPA can perform regular audits of energy consumption across facilities to identify inefficiencies and suggest improvements. By analyzing usage patterns, organizations can pinpoint areas where energy consumption can be reduced.

- **Real-Time Adjustments**: Implementing RPA for real-time energy management allows companies to dynamically adjust their energy use based on current operational conditions, significantly enhancing overall energy efficiency.

5. Supporting Remote Work Initiatives

With the rise of remote work facilitated by RPA:

- **Reduced Commuting Emissions**: Automating tasks that employees typically handle on-site enables more remote operations, which cuts down on daily commutes and associated greenhouse gas emissions.

- **Lower Office Resource Use**: Fewer employees in physical offices lead to reduced energy consumption for heating, cooling, lighting, and powering office equipment.

By simplifying operations, optimizing supply chain management, automating emission tracking, improving energy efficiency, and enabling remote work programs, robotic process automation (RPA) dramatically helps to lower greenhouse gas emissions. RPA not only increases operational efficiency but also fits more general sustainability objectives by reducing manual procedures and better use of resources. Organizations will discover as they embrace RPA technology that these developments are necessary for a cleaner future while preserving competitiveness in a market sensitive to environmental issues.

Driving Sustainability and Operational Excellence by Leveraging IoT and Emission Tracking for a Low-Carbon Future

Particularly the Internet of things (IoT), the integration of greener technology has become more important in improving operational efficiency, measuring carbon emissions, and allowing correct Scope 3 emissions estimates.

We started by talking about the need for efficient emission tracking techniques and the reduction of CO_2 emissions. Those companies trying to properly control their carbon footprints must first understand the differences between Scope 1, Scope 2, and Scope 3 emissions. Achieving sustainability targets and complying with legal systems depend on accurate monitoring of these emissions.

The workshop covered many approaches for computing Scope 3 emissions: spend-based techniques, average data approaches, supplier-specific data collection, and hybrid approaches. Every technique has special benefits and drawbacks, which emphasizes the importance of businesses using a customized strategy depending on their particular situation and data availability.

We also looked at the importance of carbon labeling rules for several sectors and how they may inspire customer involvement and impact choice of purchase. Emphasized as a tool to support sustainable practices among companies was highlighted the part incentives play in motivating compliance with carbon labeling standards.

The discussion on IoT illustrated its transformative impact on logistics by enabling real-time tracking, improving fleet management, and enhancing inventory control. These capabilities not only optimize resource usage but also provide critical data for monitoring and managing carbon emissions throughout the supply chain.

The insights gathered so far underscore the critical intersection of technology, sustainability, and trade finance. By leveraging IoT and adopting robust emission tracking methodologies, companies can significantly improve their environmental performance while fostering transparency and accountability in their operations. As businesses increasingly prioritize sustainability in their strategies, these innovations will be essential for driving meaningful progress toward a low-carbon economy.

Summary

Emphasizing the need for sustainable finance instruments, digital technology, and creative policies, this chapter investigates how greener trading practices may be included in trade finance. It emphasizes the benefits of these approaches, which include improved openness, lower emissions, and capital mobilization for environmental projects. Green bonds and sustainability-linked loans are among the sustainable finance tools changing the sector by matching financial incentives with environmental objectives. Concurrent with these developments in logistics, driven by digitization and decarbonization, are supply chain activities being optimized and responsibility encouraged by real-time emission tracking.

The chapter also looks at how robotic process automation (RPA), the Internet of things (IoT), and artificial intelligence (AI) could help to improve the accuracy of emissions data and simplify more environmentally friendly trading practices. These technologies improve energy economy, enable effective carbon footprint monitoring, and help to promote regulatory framework compliance. Companies may create more sustainable supply chains by conquering obstacles, including Scope 3 emissions tracking and data quality. This mix of finance, politics, and technology opens the path for a time when trade finance not only promotes world sustainability but also propels economic development.

CHAPTER 17

Thriving Together: A Regenerative Power for Small and Mighty Businesses

This chapter explores the development of Regenerative Finance (from now onwards referred to as ReFi) as a vital reaction to urgent global problems, especially the socio-economic inequities and climate disaster. It starts by looking at ReFi's timely emergence and presents it as a required development in finance facing the complexity of economic exploitation and environmental damage. Historical climate movements provide insightful insights that could guide and improve the ideas of ReFi, thereby fostering resilience in ecosystems and communities.

It emphasizes the critical requirement of creative resource allocation and more openness as knowledge of problems of inequality and the limits of conventional economic models develops. Emphasizing the transforming potential ReFi can have on small enterprises, enabling them to flourish and thereby save the environment, a vision for sustainable prosperity is presented.

The story then shifts to highlight the importance of early adopters and a new generation of entrepreneurs in driving a ReFi revolution while highlighting the benefits and varied profiles among these inventors. Emphasizing how Web3 technologies and blockchain can provide new possibilities for regenerative practices, the chapter links Decentralized Finance (from now onwards referred to as DeFi) with sustainable finance.

The conversation also covers ReFi's obstacles and future prospects, including the need for compliance, real-world effects, and systems guaranteeing links between digital money and practical advantages. Through addressing the fundamental issues in the

CHAPTER 17   THRIVING TOGETHER: A REGENERATIVE POWER FOR SMALL AND MIGHTY BUSINESSES

ReFi scene—such as governance, market dynamics, and regulatory obstacles—the chapter creates a road map for a more inclusive and fair financial environment. In the end, "Thriving Together" makes a strong case for ReFi as a means of bringing about long-lasting transformation by stressing the entwined destinations of small enterprises, communities, and the earth on the road toward a more sustainable future.

A Path to Sustainable, Equitable, and Transparent Economic Systems: Understanding the Timely Emergence of ReFi

As our global civilization grapples with a range of environmental, social, and financial challenges, the concept of ReFi is gaining traction at a pivotal juncture in history. These intertwined problems create a complicated web of problems for which conventional economic models find difficult solutions.

Rising environmental issues like pollution, biodiversity loss, and climate change are causing general awareness of the unsustainable nature of our present strategy of resource management. These environmental catastrophes have a bearing on social issues, including poverty, inequality, and access to fundamental needs that are not unconnected to them. Economic systems that frequently favor short-term gains over long-term well-being exacerbate social problems.

Among these urgent issues, ReFi is becoming a transformative movement. Anchored on sustainability, equality, and openness, it seeks to build a financial system that supports and improves the welfare of people and the earth. This movement acknowledges the significant limits of current economic models, which usually overlook the actual expenses of environmental damage. These environmental catastrophes are bearing on social issues, including poverty, inequality, and access to essential needs that are not unconnected to them. Economic regimes that routinely prioritize short-term profits over long-term welfare aggravate these societal issues also social inequality.

Through financial practices and institutions, ReFi aims to create a system wherein social and ecological systems may be restored and rebuilt. This entails changing the way money is invested, stressing long-term value creation over transient benefits, and making sure that financial activities enhance the whole ecosystem. Transparency is a fundamental value as it guarantees responsibility and confidence, therefore guiding money flows to match fair and sustainable results.

ReFi first emerged when growing knowledge of our present situation was not sustainable. Novel ideas that can solve the fundamental problems driving our environmental and financial crises are desperately needed. ReFi provides a means toward a more resilient and fair society by infusing ideas of sustainability and equality into the financial system. shifts a paradigm change, stating the status quo and supporting a comprehensive strategy for economic growth that respects and promotes the interdependence of all living on Earth.

Confronting the Climate Crisis: Aligning Economic Growth with Environmental Sustainability

Most people agree that one of the most serious hazards to the earth and humans presently is the climate catastrophe. Rising sea levels, more frequent and severe weather events, and changing ecosystems all point to the increasingly alarming and unavoidable evidence of climate change. These developments not only immediately jeopardize environmental and human systems but also create long-term hazards to world stability and development.

These rising hazards are driving increasing awareness of the need for our economic systems to change to give environmental sustainability top priority. Conventional economic models, which sometimes give short-term benefits and unbridled expansion top priority, are not sufficient to handle the several problems presented by climate change. Novel ideas that can match economic activity with the demands of ecological health and resilience are much needed.

Here is where ReFi finds applications. It offers a revolutionary approach to finance, one that aims to match the goals of ecological restoration and conservation with financial activity. ReFi seeks to actively repair and regenerate natural systems, therefore generating a positive feedback loop supporting both ecological and financial health rather than only reducing environmental harm.

ReFi's guiding ideas are based on sustainability, as it is clear that long-term success depends on the state of the earth. ReFi aims to build a financial system that is not only lucrative but also beneficial for the environment by focusing money on projects and activities that support ecological balance, like renewable energy, sustainable agriculture, and conservation efforts.

ReFi also stresses how closely environmental and financial well-being are interwoven. It supports open, fair, and transparent financial methods meant to create long-term value instead of quick gains. ReFi provides a road toward a future whereby economic activities help to rejuvenate the ecological systems of the earth by means of a financial ecosystem supporting sustainable growth. It redefines the link between money and the environment, therefore offering an essentially convincing answer to the climate catastrophe. It questions the accepted economic model and presents a picture of a lackluster future in which conservation and ecological restoration are naturally entwined with commercial activity. Not only is this a moral requirement but also a pragmatic need for finance to be in line with environmental sustainability, therefore guaranteeing the long-term existence and development of the earth and humans.

Drawing Parallels: Learning from Historical Climate Movements to Enhance ReFi

As the ReFi movement gains momentum, it becomes increasingly important to learn from past initiatives in climate governance and conservation. These disciplines abound in knowledge and present both mistakes and accomplishments that would be quite helpful for the growing ReFi market. ReFi finds a complicated junction of technology, money, and environmental stewardship in its attempt to link financial systems with ecological sustainability.

To prevent repeating previous mistakes and to create a route that really helps people and the earth, one must first understand the historical settings that have molded past and contemporary climate movements. This chapter explores three important problems that have greatly affected environmental projects: the legacy of colonialism, the financialization of natural ecosystems, and the continuous fight to reconcile local requirements with worldwide strategy.

Many areas' social, economic, and environmental scenes have been profoundly and usually negatively changed by colonization. Colonial exploitation not only deprived nations of their natural resources but also imposed alien government structures, ignoring indigenous expertise and customs. These past injustices still influence modern environmental initiatives, as previously colonial populations typically have considerable difficulty recovering their natural legacy and maintaining it responsibly. For the ReFi movement, it's imperative to acknowledge and deal with these colonial relics.

CHAPTER 17   THRIVING TOGETHER: A REGENERATIVE POWER FOR SMALL AND MIGHTY BUSINESSES

It entails realizing past exploitation and making sure present financial policies do not support inequality. ReFi has to work to build inclusive systems that empower nearby areas and respect indigenous knowledge, promoting real sustainability and resilience.

An additional important problem influencing environmental governance is the financialization of natural ecosystems. This process gives ecological services—including biodiversity, water purification, and carbon sequestration—economic worth. This strategy poses major hazards even when it might encourage conservation by increasing the economic value of ecosystems more obviously. One main issue is that it can reduce intricate ecological systems to simple commodities, therefore compromising their inherent worth and encouraging exploitation and damage. Furthermore, the financialization of nature usually helps financial institutions and big businesses at the expense of nearby populations depending on natural ecosystems for their means of survival. ReFi depends on creating financial systems that acknowledge and protect the various values of natural environments. This entails building protections to stop exploitation and making sure that, especially in underprivileged areas, financial gains are fairly shared among all the parties.

In climate governance and conservation, juggling local demands with worldwide solutions continues to be difficult. Global projects can stress broad solutions that might not fit local settings and goals. Conflicts and opposition might result from this top-down approach, as local expertise and needs could be overlooked. Good environmental care calls for active participation of local stakeholders in decision-making procedures and a sophisticated knowledge of local settings. ReFi's distributed finance focus helps to solve this problem by encouraging more inclusive and participatory methods. ReFi can build open and responsible systems using blockchain technology and other distributed technologies that empower local communities and guarantee that their views are heard in worldwide environmental plans.

The ReFi movement will surely run against challenges similar to those of previous environmental and social justice movements as it expands. Navigating ReFi's future successfully depends on learning from past mistakes. For example, the fight for environmental justice has demonstrated how closely attaining sustainability depends on resolving social and economic disparities. ReFi has to give social justice first priority and aim for financially fair systems as well as ecologically friendly ones. This entails building inclusive venues that enable the involvement of underprivileged groups and making sure that financial resources are distributed to support social as well as environmental well-being.

The lessons learned from past initiatives in climate control and preservation underline the need to combine several points of view and knowledge sources. ReFi gains from the knowledge of indigenous people, grassroots groups, and other players who have long participated in environmental care. ReFi may provide more complete and successful answers to financial and environmental problems by encouraging cooperation and alliances between many sectors and levels.

Ultimately, the ReFi movement finds a turning point when it can use the rich knowledge of previous and contemporary climate movements to map a fair and sustainable future. ReFi may avoid repeating previous errors and build a really regenerative financial system by knowing and addressing the history of colonialism, the financialization of natural ecosystems, and the requirement of balancing local demands with global plans. This movement has to stay dedicated to learning from the past and embracing the complexity of environmental and social justice so that its creative solutions really help people and the earth.

Rising Awareness of Inequality and Exploitation: Redesigning Economic Systems for Justice, Equality, and Sustainability

The enormous social disparities, economic exploitation, and unsustainable industrial practices defining our planet have become increasingly known in recent years. This increased awareness results from seeing how often conventional economic systems—often to the negative effect of both people and the earth—priest profit before all else. This emphasis on profit maximization has led to severe inequalities, whereby a tiny proportion of the population accumulates severe riches while most of society stays underprivileged and excluded. Furthermore, this profit-driven attitude has resulted in extreme environmental damage when natural resources are used without consideration for their long-term viability.

The widespread nature of these problems emphasizes the basic shortcomings of our present economic systems. Short-term financial benefits' prioritizing sometimes ignores social and environmental consequences, hence sustaining cycles of inequity and environmental damage. This has created a pressing need for economic models that go beyond just wealth generation for a small number of people to support justice, inclusion, and social responsibility.

CHAPTER 17   THRIVING TOGETHER: A REGENERATIVE POWER FOR SMALL AND MIGHTY BUSINESSES

ReFi, or ReFi, answers these firmly ingrained issues. Emphasizing the need for justice and inclusion will help us to reinvent the ideas governing our economic systems. ReFi supports economic policies that guarantee everyone has access to resources and opportunities, therefore lowering social disparities. It also emphasizes the need for social responsibility, therefore motivating companies and financial institutions to take into account the wider effects of their activities on their surroundings and society.

ReFi wants to build a more fair and sustainable future by advocating economic models that respect people and the earth along with profit. This entails changing conventional methods of industry and finance to support long-term social well-being and ecological health. ReFi's goal is not just to lessen the negative effects of present economic systems but also to actively promote conditions whereby everyone in society may flourish and natural ecosystems may rebuild and grow.

ReFi is essentially a transformative solution for the important problems of social injustice, economic exploitation, and environmental sustainability. beneficial It questions the traditional focus on profit and suggests instead a complete approach combining social equality, environmental care, and economic success. This redesigned economic model promises a more fair and sustainable society in which financial institutions serve the greater good instead of extending damage and disparity.

Shifting from Profit Maximization to Long-Term Sustainability and Resilience: The Limits of Traditional Economic Models

Every year that goes by highlights the flaws in traditional economic systems. Often giving immediate financial advantages top priority above long-term environmental and social well-being, these conventional approaches often fail to generate the required incentives for sustainable activities. They are therefore unprepared to satisfy the sophisticated requirements of our globally linked and networked society.

The tendency of these economic systems to ignore the social and environmental costs related to economic activity is one of their main shortcomings. Usually rewarded for increasing profits, industries and companies employ unsustainable resource extraction, pollution, or labor exploitation, even if their practices entail these aspects. This profit-driven strategy results in major ecological damage and socioeconomic inequalities as the wider effects of these methods are not sufficiently considered or reduced.

Moreover, conventional economic models sometimes find it difficult to fit the fast-changing dynamics of a globalized world. Their foundations lie on out-of-date ideas that fail to adequately acknowledge the interdependence of communities, ecosystems, and the world economy. This isolation produces inadequately responsive economic policies and practices to meet global issues such as climate change, biodiversity loss, and rising inequality.

ReFi shows up as a visionary answer to these ingrained problems. It advocates the development of economic systems that actively support and incentivize sustainable and regenerative behaviors, therefore calling for a basic change in our attitude toward economic activity. ReFi sees an economic system in which efforts to restore and improve the natural environment, promote social fairness, and create resilient communities match the financial benefits.

ReFi wants to close the voids created by conventional economic models by including such systems. It suggests fresh approaches to appreciating and funding initiatives benefiting the earth and society. This covers helping companies and initiatives emphasizing circular economy ideas, sustainable agriculture, and renewable energy, where waste is reduced and resources are repurposed. ReFi further underlines the need for openness and responsibility, guiding money flows toward really sustainable and regenerative results.

ReFi's support for a paradigm shift signals a shift away from an economy that places a focus on short-term gains alone and toward one that emphasizes long-term sustainability and resilience. It questions accepted economic knowledge and works to include social and environmental factors at the center of economic decision-making. ReFi presents a convincing picture of a future in which economic activity supports the health and well-being of people and the earth, therefore filling in the major voids and restrictions of conventional economic systems.

Leveraging Technology for Efficient and Equitable Resource Allocation

Though there are plenty of resources in the world, their distribution usually falls short of what people most need. This misallocation is a major problem, mostly resulting from natural conflicts within the present financial system. These friction points show themselves as ineffective methods of resource allocation and money transfer.

Bureaucratic obstacles, antiquated infrastructure, and a lack of openness all help to slow down traditional financial systems and hence contribute to the inefficient allocation of resources.

Among the main problems are the inefficiencies of money transfer systems, especially worldwide. Moving money across borders may be sluggish, costly, and full of obstacles that hinder timely and sufficient help for underprivileged people and individuals. These delays and expenses can greatly diminish the value of financial aid and investments meant to promote growth and help lower poverty.

Furthermore, the way traditional financial institutions allocate resources sometimes favors well-known, well-connected businesses over others that might be more worthy or in greater need. This can cause resources to be concentrated in places where they are already plentiful instead of being spread to locations and people where they could have a significant impact. Lack of openness and responsibility in these procedures aggravates the situation even more, as it makes it challenging to guarantee that resources are focused on their most efficient usage.

Emphasizing distributed and effective resources, ReFi offers a transformative answer to these structural problems. It uses cutting-edge technologies such as DeFi and blockchain to simplify financial transactions and lower the friction points that conventional systems cause. ReFi seeks to remove middlemen who often slow down processes and raise expenses by distributing the financial infrastructure, therefore simplifying and cost-effectively transmitting money and resource allocation where most needed.

ReFi's emphasis on openness and responsibility also guarantees equitable and efficient resource allocation. ReFi guarantees that money and resources reach their intended users without unnecessary delay or diversion by means of transparent, distributed networks, therefore enabling real-time tracking and validation of financial transactions. This strategy not only improves effectiveness but also fosters confidence among stakeholders, as they can directly observe the results of their efforts.

ReFi uses these systems to try to correct the flaws and inequalities of the present financial system. It sees a society in which, rather than current power structures or connections, resources are distributed according to need and possible effects. ReFi presents a viable route toward a more fair and sustainable global economy by tackling the underlying causes of misallocation and using contemporary technology to enable fair and efficient resource distribution.

CHAPTER 17   THRIVING TOGETHER: A REGENERATIVE POWER FOR SMALL AND MIGHTY BUSINESSES

Harnessing Blockchain for Unprecedented Transparency and Accountability

A significant issue with existing economic frameworks is the lack of transparency, which enables unprincipled actors to profit at the expense of others and the environment. ReFi, leveraging blockchain technology, introduces a level of transparency and accountability previously unattainable in traditional financial systems. This transparency ensures that all actions and transactions are visible, traceable, and accountable, reducing opportunities for exploitation and corruption. The lack of openness of present economic systems is a major issue as it allows unscrupulous people and businesses to gain at the expense of others and their surroundings. This opacity in financial systems provides chances for exploitation, corruption, and environmental damage by allowing actions usually invisible to public attention to be carried out. Holding these unprincipled people responsible becomes difficult without transparent access to financial transactions and policies, therefore sustaining a cycle of damage and inequality.

Through blockchain technology, ReFi presents a solution for this ubiquitous problem. A distributed digital ledger, blockchain offers a degree of openness and responsibility absent from conventional financial institutions. Every transaction entered into a blockchain cannot be changed or erased; rather, it is publicly available and unchangeable, which allows one to trace back its beginnings. This guarantees that everyone can clearly and verifiably see all money activity, therefore promoting an honest and trusting culture.

Blockchain technology offers revolutionary transparency. It lets participants monitor money and resources in real time, therefore guaranteeing their intended usage. This degree of awareness discourages unethical activity as it makes it far more difficult to participate in frauds without being found. Companies cannot, for example, readily hide exploitative work conditions or ecologically damaging policies, as they will be noted and shown on the blockchain. Blockchain technology also imposes responsibility on every player involved in the financial system. Transactions may be watched by investors, authorities, and the general public, who can also hold individuals accountable for their activities. This lessens the chances for corruption and exploitation, as every activity is under public and legal control and has to resist public and legislative supervision. Blockchain transactions by nature are traceable; hence, any effort at misusing money or resources can be found and corrected quickly.

ReFi wants to create a more ethical and sustainable economic framework by fostering such high degrees of openness and responsibility. This fosters confidence and integrity inside the financial system, in addition to shielding the surroundings and sensitive populations from abuse. It motivates every actor to follow moral guidelines and helps to distribute resources more fairly. The lack of openness in current economic systems has let unprincipled people flourish at the expense of others and their surroundings. ReFi uses blockchain technology to bring unheard-of openness and responsibility by making all activities and transactions transparent, trackable, and under examination. By greatly lowering chances for exploitation and corruption, this transforming strategy opens the path for a more fair and sustainable financial system.

Redefining Wealth, Sustainability, and Social Justice in Economic Systems: A Vision for Sustainable Prosperity

Beyond only building a new financial system, ReFi encompasses a vision for a world in which wealth is shared fairly, sustainability is a fundamental concept, and economic activities favorably impact both society and the environment. This idea presents a complete framework and the required instruments to create a financial system very closely aligned with these principles.

ReFi is really about redefining the basis of finance. It aims to create a system whereby chances and riches are shared equally, therefore guaranteeing that everyone gains from economic development. With an eye toward a more inclusive and fair economic environment, this strategy solves the inherent inequalities in conventional financial systems. ReFi guarantees that economic operations are not only lucrative but also ecologically conscious by including sustainability into its basic ideas. This implies encouraging long-term ecological health, waste reduction, and methods of regeneration of natural systems.

Given the several challenges our planet is experiencing, the launch of ReFi is very important. From social inequities and economic uncertainty to climate change, these linked issues call for creative ideas not fit for established financial models. ReFi offers a financial system supporting ecological balance, social fairness, and sustainable growth, thereby reflecting a timely and required reaction to these many challenges.

ReFi offers a creative and hopeful road forward as we negotiate the urgent problems of our day. It uses contemporary technologies such as distributed finance and blockchain to build open, responsible, and quick financial systems. This technical basis guarantees that financial transactions support the greater good as well as improve their integrity. ReFi uses technology's capacity to propel positive change by matching economic operations with more general objectives of society, such as well-being and environmental stewardship.

ReFi is really about creating a future whereby economic systems coexist peacefully with the earth and its occupants, not only about financial reform. It sees a society in which social justice or environmental health does not suffer in order for economic development. Rather, it aims to establish a symbiotic link among fairness, sustainability, and wealth. ReFi presents a transforming way to create a financial system that really serves the greater good by providing a strong framework and useful instruments for reaching these objectives.

A Transformative Impact on the Financial Ecosystem for Environmental and Social Renewal

Aspiring to build a system that is sustainable and healing, ReFi marks a basic change in the financial industry. It is committed to building a financial ecosystem that actively regenerates the environment and improves society's well-being, unlike conventional economic models that can drain natural and social resources for temporary advantages.

ReFi's basic values center on the concept of not just reducing damage but also producing favorable effects. This implies creating financial policies and structures supporting environmental recovery, including sustainable agriculture, renewable energy projects, and forestry programs. ReFi seeks to simultaneously improve social circumstances by pushing economic models that provide equitable access to resources and opportunities, thus lowering inequality and supporting community development.

Growing knowledge of the restrictions and harm old, exploitative economic systems create drives this paradigm shift. Many times, these systems have put profit above social justice and environmental health, resulting in notable ecological damage and socioeconomic inequalities. ReFi, on the other hand, aims to match financial incentives to methods that support and rebuild social and ecological systems.

ReFi is getting traction as more people, companies, and governments understand the need for this change. Technological developments include blockchain and distributed finance, which offer the means to put open, effective, and responsible financial systems

CHAPTER 17   THRIVING TOGETHER: A REGENERATIVE POWER FOR SMALL AND MIGHTY BUSINESSES

into use and support the movement. These tools guarantee that investments go toward initiatives with actual regeneration potential and allow real-time tracking of money. ReFi's growing popularity suggests that it is nearing a significant milestone. The movement is likely to grow quickly as more participants adopt regenerative practices and observe the clear advantages of sustainable and restoring investments. This broad acceptance will probably inspire more creativity and teamwork, therefore magnifying the beneficial effects of ReFi on society and the surroundings.

ReFi's possible influence is significant. ReFi can help solve some of the most urgent issues of our day, like social injustice, climate change, and biodiversity loss, by changing the financial system to give regeneration first priority. It presents a bright picture of the future, whereby a more fair society and a better world result from economic activity.

Aiming to create a sustainable and restoring system, ReFi is essentially a transforming method of finance. It shifts from conventional extractive paradigms toward a financial ecosystem actively supporting environmental regeneration and social improvement. ReFi is likely to reach a vital tipping point as this paradigm change gathers momentum, therefore offering a major positive influence on our planet.

Traction and Recognition: Uniting Business Leaders, Policymakers, Scholars, and Citizens for a Sustainable Future

Respected corporate executives, legislators, scholars, and common people are among the many social sectors that the ReFi movement is drawing in. These several groups are coming together in search of new financial models that stress long-term ecological sustainability and social equality instead of short-term profitability.

Business executives are realizing more and more that the conventional emphasis on quick financial gains sometimes comes at a significant cost to the community and the environment. ReFi presents a convincing structure that not only lessens negative effects but also actively helps to restore natural and social systems as they look for methods to match their activities with more general sustainability objectives. Many forward-looking businesses are starting to give sustainability top strategic importance as they realize that long-term performance depends on the condition of the ecosystems and communities they run across.

As they consider the shortcomings of present economic systems in handling urgent global issues, policymakers are also focusing on ReFi. Concerning problems such as social inequality, economic instability, and climate change, conventional financial models have sometimes fallen short. ReFi offers a hopeful substitute that combines social and environmental goals with economic operations, therefore providing a road toward laws supporting social justice and sustainable growth.

By offering the theoretical underpinnings and research required to test and hone these new financial models, academics are helping the ReFi movement. Their research underlines the need for a complete approach to finance by showing the links among social well-being, ecological health, and economic activity. Scholars are working to build a strong ReFi framework that can be used practically by linking theory and practice.

Common people are realizing the flaws in the present financial system more and more. Demand for financial models that can produce more fair and sustainable results rises as public awareness of problems like social injustice, wealth disparity, and environmental damage increases. People are searching for ways to put their money to use by supporting companies that mirror their ideals and help the earth and society.

ReFi's increasing attractiveness is a result of people realizing the limits of the current financial system. ReFi's transforming power is becoming more appealing as more people and organizations realize that conventional approaches are insufficient for handling the intricate problems of our day. This movement is about radically redesigning and reorganizing the financial system to better serve people and the environment, not only about little changes.

The ReFi movement is essentially becoming popular throughout a wide range of societies. Seeking financial models that give long-term ecological and social goals top priority over short-term profits, business executives, legislators, scholars, and people are joined in this effort. ReFi's transforming power to build a more sustainable and fair society appeals more as knowledge of the shortcomings of the present financial system keeps growing.

Approaching the Tipping Point for a Sustainable and Equitable Financial Future

Once it hits a tipping point—a pivotal time when its acceptance and acknowledgment become widespread enough to cause a significant change in financial practices and attitudes—ReFi is ready to surge in momentum. Many important elements will be driving this tipping point and providing a rich foundation for the ReFi movement to grow.

CHAPTER 17   THRIVING TOGETHER: A REGENERATIVE POWER FOR SMALL AND MIGHTY BUSINESSES

The growing degree of environmental problems is one of the main causes of this approaching tipping point. Adoption of sustainable financial practices becomes indisputable as climate change continues to show up as increasingly regular and severe natural catastrophes, loss of biodiversity, and ecological degradation. These environmental catastrophes expose the shortcomings of conventional financial models that give quick profits top priority without thinking through long-term environmental consequences.

Consequently, there is increasing understanding that successful addressing of these urgent environmental challenges depends on a basic transformation in our attitude toward money.

In addition to environmental factors, society's expectations of more equitable economic systems also drive the drive toward ReFi. People are demanding financial models that more equitably share income and opportunity, therefore lessening the inequalities brought about by current economic policies. Economic systems should, it is becoming clear, serve all people rather than only the favored few. ReFi appeals to these needs by advocating financial systems that encourage community development, social justice, and fair access to resources, therefore stressing social equality and inclusion.

Moreover, ReFi is becoming more appealing as people grow unhappy with conventional, extractive financial arrangements. Often profiting from natural and human resources, these traditional methods are under scrutiny for their part in sustaining social injustice, economic instability, and environmental damage. The quest for alternative financial systems grows increasingly pressing as more individuals and companies realize the limits and negative effects of these extractive activities. ReFi is a realistic and appealing substitute for the status quo, as it offers a transforming vision that fits social responsibility and environmental aims for financial activity.

The convergence of five factors—increasing environmental concerns, society's expectations for equality, and discontent with conventional financial structures—determines ReFi's path to reaching its threshold. Adoption of ReFi ideas and practices is predicted to quicken when this time occurs, therefore transforming the way finance is done. This change will not only redefine financial practices but also change perceptions of money, investment, and economic development, thereby including sustainability and social equality at the center of the financial system.

Driven by growing environmental issues, societal demand for more equitable economic systems, and growing dissatisfaction with current financial models, ReFi is essentially about to become very popular. These forces are likely to propel ReFi to a critical juncture where its widespread adoption initiates a substantial transformation in the financial sector, thereby fostering a more sustainable and equitable future.

CHAPTER 17   THRIVING TOGETHER: A REGENERATIVE POWER FOR SMALL AND MIGHTY BUSINESSES

The Role of a New Generation: Achieving a Sustainable and Equitable Financial System

The values and objectives of the next generation joining the workforce will be a major determinant of the general acceptance of ReFi. Protecting the environment and helping their local communities is essential to this growing group of young professionals and future leaders. Advancement and acceptance of ReFi's ideas will depend greatly on their shared values and way of thinking.

Deeply ingrained concern for sustainability and social responsibility defines this generational change. Today's young workforce is more motivated by a desire to significantly change the world than earlier generations, who might have given financial success and conventional career pathways top priority. They are well aware of the urgent environmental problems confronting the earth, including the loss of biodiversity, pollution, and climate change. This understanding shapes their personal and professional choices by means of a dedication to sustainability.

Professionally, these young people are looking for jobs and companies that fit their ideals. They want to work for businesses that give ethical behavior, social fairness, and environmental preservation top priority. This change in tastes is forcing companies to embrace more environmentally friendly and community-oriented methods to draw in and keep top personnel. Rising to senior roles, these young professionals are likely to advocate for and use ReFi ideas inside their companies, therefore promoting a larger cultural and operational change toward ReFi.

Furthermore, this new generation is quite involved in concerns about social justice and community welfare. They understand that economic systems should be inclusive and equitable as well as lucrative. Their commitment to generating positive social effects fits with the objectives of ReFi, which aim to create a financial system supporting social fairness and environmental balance. Supporting projects that uphold these ideals will help ReFi be adopted faster in many different fields.

Young professionals are impacted outside of the business sphere on the larger economic scene. Consumers, investors, and business owners will all help to determine demand and market trends based on their choices. Their inclination for environmentally friendly goods and services would inspire companies to use ReFi techniques in order to satisfy the rising market demand. Today's young workforce is more motivated by a desire to make a significant positive impact on the world than earlier generations, who might have prioritized financial success and traditional career pathways. This shift in values toward sustainability and community-oriented behaviors greatly facilitates the acceptance and growth of Regenerative Finance (ReFi) as a transformative approach to creating a more equitable and resilient economy.

Young professionals and future leaders will be crucial in changing the financial system as they incorporate their values into their work, companies, and investments. ReFi's commitment to environmental preservation and positive contributions to society will hasten its adoption and implementation, paving the way for a more just and sustainable future.

Advantages for Early Adopters: Shaping the Future of Sustainable and Equitable Financial Systems

Early adopters of ReFi have a special benefit and possibility that distinguish them in this developing discipline. Acting as early movers, they are in a perfect position to influence the direction and growth of the ReFi system. These trailblazers may establish best practices, set standards, and impact the laws that will ultimately control this new financial paradigm.

Being among the first to use ReFi enables these early adopters to lead in determining how this system runs. They can play around with creative ideas and solutions consistent with social fairness and environmental responsibility. Their knowledge and experiences will be priceless in pointing out what works and what doesn't, therefore offering a road map for others to follow. This inventiveness not only guarantees that ReFi's fundamental features are strong and efficient but also stimulates creativity and innovation.

Apart from defining operational guidelines, early ReFi adopters had the chance to create best practices that would direct future users. Through proving effective approaches and techniques, they may build a body of knowledge available for others entering the ReFi environment. This shared learning improves the general quality of the ReFi ecosystem and speeds the adoption process.

Moreover, early adopters might change the environment of regulations around ReFi. The thoughts and comments of these pioneers will be vital in guiding policies that support and foster the expansion of ReFi as governments and regulatory agencies start to pay attention to this expanding industry. Early adopters who actively interact with legislators may fight for laws that support innovation while maintaining sustainability and equality values intact.

Early adopters are establishing the foundation for future attendees, not only for attending ReFi. Their efforts guarantee that the ReFi movement keeps expanding and changing, therefore laying a strong foundation from which others could develop. Leading this revolution not only helps them gain from early involvement's benefits but also significantly contributes to the institutional change ReFi stands for.

CHAPTER 17   THRIVING TOGETHER: A REGENERATIVE POWER FOR SMALL AND MIGHTY BUSINESSES

Early ReFi adopters overall have a special position of power and potential. First movers are crucial in determining the ReFi system's development, standards, and regulatory structures. Their creative ideas and solutions set standards and provide a framework for future generations of participants. These pioneers are essential for the effective expansion and sustainability of ReFi as they use their leadership and knowledge.

Building Resilience and Inclusivity Through Diverse Early Adopters

The resilience and potency of this new system depend on the variety of early adopters in the field of ReFi. A variety of perspectives and experiences help to create an inclusive and comprehensive financial model. This diversity guarantees that ReFi is built with a broad spectrum of demands and settings in mind, therefore strengthening its resilience and adaptability to different difficulties.

Including many voices helps solve complex global social, environmental, and economic concerns. ReFi may provide solutions responsive to local conditions and particular difficulties by combining ideas from several industries, areas, and communities. This method guarantees that ReFi can react properly to a variety of situations and challenges, as well as increasing its relevance and usefulness. The capacity of a financial system to adapt is directly related to its robustness, so variety is a major force behind this adaptation.

More than just a theoretical idea, ReFi is a useful, changing movement ready to reinvent financial ideas and behaviors. ReFi, as it gains traction thanks to a new generation of ecologically and socially conscious individuals and a variety of early adopters, has the potential to develop a financial system that balances economic success with ecological and social well-being. This alignment is absolutely vital as it marks a change from conventional financial models that sometimes give short-term gains top priority above long-term sustainability and equity.

ReFi's increasing popularity points to a larger social change. The younger generation entering the workforce is bringing about this transition because of their commitment to sustainability and social justice. Their aims and ideals align with ReFi's key ideas of transparency, justice, and rebirth. These forward-thinking executives and young people who support and apply ReFi techniques are creating the conditions for a radical change in the financial scene.

The path toward ReFi is one toward a more fair, sustainable, and regenerative future. This change departs greatly from conventional financial paradigms, which have sometimes been exploitative and extractive. ReFi presents a vision of finance instead that supports the general well-being of society, fair allocation of resources, and regeneration of natural systems. This movement promises not just to rethink financial practices but also to build a system that naturally prioritizes and fosters the connectivity of social, environmental, and economic health.

ReFi's development and efficacy depend essentially on the variety of early adopters it attracts. Their many points of view help to create a strong, inclusive, and thorough financial model. Driven by a generation dedicated to sustainability and equality, ReFi is transforming from a theoretical concept to a practical reality that helps to reinvent finance in a way that promotes a sustainable, fair, and regenerative future. This offers optimism and a clear road toward a better society, therefore marking a significant departure from conventional wisdom.

An On-Going Revolution: Charting the Transformative Journey from DeFi to Sustainable Finance

ReFi is a major step beyond DeFi, therefore changing our views and interactions with financial institutions. This reform entails using digital innovations—most notably blockchain technology—to transform conventional value exchange and financial flow systems, therefore bringing them into line with ideas of regeneration and inclusion. From DeFi to ReFi, the path reflects a development that drastically alters the financial scene. With its distributed character, the removal of middlemen, and increased accessibility and transparency, DeFi has already upended established banking systems. ReFi advances this, though, by integrating regenerative economic ideas into the center of financial interactions. Blockchain technology runs at the core of ReFi. Along with security and openness, this technology makes programmable money flows possible.

Customizing these programmable flows to promote regenerative practices—funding sustainable initiatives, encouraging circular economic models, and promoting fair income distribution—allows one to assist Blockchain's programmability feature lets one design financial instruments that naturally complement social equality and environmental sustainability. ReFi transforms conventional finance by changing the emphasis from simple profit maximization to a more all-encompassing approach that includes social and environmental effects. This novel method reorders financial systems to enable, rather than deplete, the regeneration of supporting systems. It supports funding for initiatives restoring ecosystems, advancing renewable energy sources, and creating strong local communities.

ReFi also wants to build inclusive financial systems that anybody, from all walks of life, may use. It lowers entrance restrictions by using distributed networks, therefore offering financial services to underbanked and unbanked groups. This inclusion also permeates decision-making procedures wherein stakeholders may influence the distribution of financial resources, therefore promoting a sense of community and shared accountability.

ReFi has the power to create systemic change by matching financial actions with regenerative ideas, therefore tackling some of the most urgent issues of our day, like resource depletion, inequality, and climate change. It marks a paradigm shift in the definition of value toward a model whereby the beneficial effects on people and the earth define the measurement of financial success rather than only economic gain. It represents a radical departure from DeFi, thereby altering financial systems through the application of digital technologies such as blockchain technology. Also, it reprograms conventional value exchange and money flows by inserting regenerative and inclusive ideas into the heart of financial systems, therefore supporting sustainability, equality, and systemic transformation. This development has broad consequences that may completely change our perspective on and interaction with money in relation to world problems.

The digital tools that drove the emergence of DeFi are now being reused in the field of ReFi to create advanced value exchange systems. These instruments help to incorporate social and environmental values into the core structure of financial systems, therefore transcending simple transactions. The pillar of DeFi, blockchain technology, is well known for guaranteeing decentralization, security, and openness. ReFi uses this technology to build value exchange platforms that go considerably beyond simply asset transfers. The transparent and unchangeable record of blockchain lets one design programmable financial instruments fit to support and advance regenerative activities. It may incorporate certain social and environmental requirements right into the center of financial transactions by leveraging blockchain.

Smart contracts, for example—self-executing contracts with the parameters of the agreement explicitly encoded into code—can be created to automatically award money to initiatives satisfying particular sustainability criteria or social impact goals. This automation guarantees that finance flows match more general regeneration goals without middlemen.

CHAPTER 17 THRIVING TOGETHER: A REGENERATIVE POWER FOR SMALL AND MIGHTY BUSINESSES

Embedding values into financial systems enables every transaction to be assessed not just on its economic benefits but also on its impact on social and environmental well-being. This transforming capacity makes it possible to produce financial goods and services that naturally give social fairness and environmental sustainability first priority. Investments might be focused on initiatives restoring natural ecosystems, supporting renewable energy, or improving community resilience, thereby guaranteeing that financial development does not come at the price of the earth or underprivileged populations.

Blockchain technology's distributed nature also democratizes financial service access. It promotes inclusiveness by lowering obstacles for both people and companies to engage in the financial system. In areas or populations where conventional financial institutions have historically been underserved, this is especially important. ReFi helps these groups to participate in and gain from regenerative economic activity by giving them access to finance and financial instruments. Its use of blockchain and other digital tools basically marks a dramatic change in the way value is traded and evaluated in financial institutions. It turns financial transactions from simple economic exchanges into activities with the potential for beneficial social and environmental results. This creative method opens the path for a financial system that supports and magnifies the ideas of sustainability and inclusiveness, therefore enabling a more regenerative and fair planet.

Integrating the fundamental infrastructure and guiding concepts of DeFi with the transforming ideas of regenerative economics, ReFi expands on them. This integration marks a change from the single objective of income generation toward a more complete approach stressing beneficial effects on communities and ecosystems. It essentially keeps the fundamental DeFi values—that people should have autonomous control over their money and that financial transactions should be open and freely available. DeFi's distributed character guarantees that users are not depending on established financial institutions, therefore providing more independence and empowerment.

ReFi is founded on a foundation of transparency and sovereignty. It goes beyond these basic ideas, though, to include an emphasis on producing results that go beyond just financial benefit, seeking to generate money in a way that simultaneously promotes and rejuvenates the environment and society, as the integration of regenerative economic ideas calls for such an approach. a financial system in which the performance of economic operations is judged not just by profit but also by their capacity to assist community well-being through the restoration and ability of natural ecosystems.

CHAPTER 17   THRIVING TOGETHER: A REGENERATIVE POWER FOR SMALL AND MIGHTY BUSINESSES

ReFi uses blockchain technology and the distributed architecture of DeFi to enable transactions that are not only simple and quick but also fit with regenerative objectives. This helps to provide financial goods and services that naturally promote environmentally friendly living. Investments can be focused, for instance, on initiatives to restore damaged land, lower carbon emissions, or empower nearby populations via fair resource sharing. Emphasizing positive influence also entails infusing social ideals into economic systems. This might include funding projects aiming at social justice, education, and healthcare, or strengthening the rights of underprivileged groups.

Blockchain's programmable character lets these values be recorded into financial contracts, therefore guaranteeing that the distribution of resources always promotes regenerative results. ReFi also works to make financial possibilities more inclusive, therefore democratizing them. Reducing the entrance obstacles guarantees that a wider spectrum of people and communities may use financial services. As more individuals are enabled to engage in and support regenerative economic activities, this inclusiveness promotes a feeling of shared responsibility and group progress. Combining its infrastructure and ideas with the forward-looking ideas of regenerative economics, it marks an advancement of DeFi. This mix not only keeps individual autonomy, openness, and accessibility first but also broadens the emphasis to include beneficial social and environmental effects. Thus, it redefines wealth creation by stressing the importance of financial systems supporting the health and sustainability of ecosystems and communities.

Fundamentally based on universal accessibility, ReFi systems are painstakingly crafted. Particularly in areas that have historically been underserved or totally excluded from conventional banking institutions, this quality is vital for promoting financial inclusion. ReFi's worldwide accessibility helps it to go beyond traditional obstacles that have long prevented fair financial participation. Accessibility is one of its most important features, as it allows individuals living in underprivileged places to. Many countries have traditional banking systems that are either lacking entirely or just insufficient. For people and communities, this lack of access to fundamental financial services poses major challenges that limit full involvement in economic activity. ReFi solves this by using distributed technologies—blockchain, for example—that do not depend on actual financial infrastructure. Rather, they do business on digital platforms available from anywhere with an Internet connection.

This implies that ReFi allows people to access financial services even in the most isolated or economically underprivileged areas. The system's architecture also naturally fights regional restrictions and censorship. Conventional financial systems are subject

CHAPTER 17 THRIVING TOGETHER: A REGENERATIVE POWER FOR SMALL AND MIGHTY BUSINESSES

to local rules and constraints and frequently run inside national or regional borders. These limits can restrict people from using financial services for political, social, or economic reasons. On the other hand, ReFi is built on distributed networks free from geographical boundaries or centralized authority's control. This worldwide reach guarantees that anyone may participate in financial transactions without concern for censorship or exclusion, depending on their location or political situation. Moreover, its inclusiveness goes beyond geographical reach. It also covers a wider range of financial instruments and possibilities that those without strong financial means or contacts usually cannot access. ReFi enables people to engage in hitherto out-of-each economic pursuits by democratizing access to these instruments. This covers loan availability, investment prospects, and other financial services meant to greatly raise their quality of life and financial situation. Its worldwide availability further fosters financial transaction openness and confidence.

Conventional banking systems can be opaque, with unclear user processes and costs. Such systems, on the other hand, run on blockchain technology, a clear, unchangeable ledger of all transactions. Since consumers may view and confirm every transaction for themselves, this transparency helps to establish confidence among them. Common problems in conventional financial systems, such as fraud and corruption, also become less likely thanks to it. They are ultimately meant to be universally accessible, a quality that is absolutely essential for advancing financial inclusion—especially in underprivileged or unbanked areas. ReFi removes conventional cases such as censorship and geographical constraints by using distributed technology, therefore enabling everyone, wherever they are, to engage in and profit from the financial system. Apart from democratizing financial possibilities, this worldwide accessibility fosters openness and confidence, therefore enabling a more inclusive and fair economic future.

ReFi systems are remarkably able to immediately translate desired behaviors into financial systems. This implies that certain actions and results may be ingrained in financial procedures so that transactions automatically complement more general objectives. including social welfare and environmental sustainability. A ReFi app may be designed, for instance, to automatically offset carbon emissions with every transaction or to distribute some transaction fees to community development initiatives. This degree of automation not only simplifies these procedures but also guarantees that economic operations favorably contribute to environmental and social goals.

Another outstanding benefit is the flexibility of the tools and platforms ReFi makes use of. systems that are made to be more adaptable, unlike conventional financial systems, which may be stiff and sluggish to evolve. They may be quickly adjusted to fit shifting

CHAPTER 17 THRIVING TOGETHER: A REGENERATIVE POWER FOR SMALL AND MIGHTY BUSINESSES

market conditions, include fresh scientific discoveries, or grab newly presented prospects. This adaptability guarantees that those systems stay current and efficient, therefore optimizing their beneficial influence all the time. Particularly in the framework of cross-border transactions, traditional financial systems are sometimes beset by inefficiencies and restrictions. These systems may be expensive, sluggish, and complicated, generating conflict that distorts resource flow. ReFi uses distributed technologies that cut many of these friction points to solve these problems. It makes financial services more traditional; financial systems occasionally experience inefficiencies and restrictions, particularly in the context of cross-border transactions. more effective and smooth resource transfers.

ReFi's capacity to offer smoother and more effective financial services can be transforming in underdeveloped areas, where financial inclusion presents a major obstacle. It lessens the time and expenses involved in cross-border transactions, therefore facilitating both personal and company international commerce and commercial activity. This accessibility might propel general development, empower nearby areas, and stimulate local businesses.

Moreover, it helps to incorporate desired behaviors into economic systems so that social equality or environmental health is not sacrificed in order to promote economic growth. ReFi guarantees inclusive and regenerative economic growth by including welfare goals and sustainability at the heart of financial transactions. More balanced and sustainable development results from this alignment of economic activity with more general societal and environmental goals. These systems essentially have the special power to translate desired behaviors into financial systems, thereby automating tasks such as community funding and carbon offsetting. Their versatility lets quick changes in response to changing circumstances ensure constant relevance and effect.

ReFi improves financial accessibility, notably in underdeveloped areas, by reducing inefficiencies and obstacles, especially in cross-border transactions, therefore facilitating easier resource transfers. This transforming strategy guarantees that social welfare and environmental sustainability complement economic progress, thereby promoting a more inclusive and fair world. These systems often provide much quicker and more flexible transactions than conventional finance. Improving the distribution and flow of several resources, including cash, ideas, and goods, depends much on this higher efficiency. ReFi guarantees faster and seamless movement of resources by simplifying transactions, therefore enabling more dynamic and responsive economic exchanges.

This fluidity not only speeds up operations but also enables more flexible answers to possibilities and problems. ReFi systems have one main benefit in that they can cross geographical and legal barriers. They run on distributed networks that are naturally

CHAPTER 17   THRIVING TOGETHER: A REGENERATIVE POWER FOR SMALL AND MIGHTY BUSINESSES

worldwide, unlike conventional financial systems, which are sometimes constrained by the legal systems of certain countries. ReFi systems can start with companies and organizations functioning in a variety of legal contexts. In any one country-state, this kind of organization offers a notable degree of resilience against the hazards connected with political instability or policy changes.

ReFi systems can help to lessen the effects of negative legislative changes or economic uncertainty in one nation by not being limited to one jurisdiction. This worldwide reach guarantees that, even in cases of disturbance in one specific area, the activities and transactions enabled by ReFi can go on without stop. In the linked world of today, where local policy decisions may have significant effects, this resilience is especially important. Furthermore, ReFi's capacity to function in several regulatory contexts lets it take advantage of local strengths. Businesses could, for example, benefit from advantageous laws in one nation while continuing operations in another. This versatility and general resilience improve their potential to flourish in a variety of political and financial environments.

Apart from their speed and fluidity, ReFi transactions gain from the natural security and openness given by blockchain architecture. This openness not only fosters confidence among the participants but also lowers the possibility of corruption and fraud, therefore improving the dependability and effectiveness of the use of resources. Fast transactions, worldwide access, and outstanding transparency combined make ReFi an outstanding instrument for contemporary financial management. Ultimately, ReFi systems' often quicker and more flexible transactions than conventional finance help to allocate resources—including cash, ideas, and products—more effectively and create a flow of information. They usually start with companies functioning in several regulatory contexts and are not limited to one country. This global character guarantees a strong and flexible financial ecosystem that can survive in many situations by resisting the hazards presented by policy changes or instability in any one country-state.

ReFi aims to build a genuinely regenerative financial environment, not only to offer financial services. This regenerative approach means building systems that naturally promote social development and environmental protection. It was founded on the idea that financial activities should maximize profit and benefit the environment. ReFi systems' design is deliberate in supporting environmentally friendly living. ReFi guarantees that every purchase and investment serves more general objectives of ecological health and community well-being by putting ideas of environmental stewardship and social responsibility into the heart of financial operations. This implies that ecological sustainability and financial development are not considered mutually incompatible but rather complemented in a way that enhances each other. Its focus on worldwide accessibility is absolutely vital. ReFi systems may reach people and communities all around, independent of their location or socioeconomic level, by using distributed technology.

This global connectivity removes conventional obstacles that have historically kept economically underprivileged populations out of involvement in the financial system. ReFi allows those who have been underserved by traditional banking—often owing to geographic isolation or financial clarity—access to a suite of financial services. Eliminating these obstacles has enormous ramifications for economic empowerment. ReFi lets people and communities on the margins of the global economy participate more completely in economic operations. Enhanced economic possibilities, more financial stability, and a better quality of living can follow from this. It works to create equal opportunities by providing the necessary tools and platforms to participate in financial markets, thereby promoting a more inclusive and equitable global economy, and its inclusive character also helps local businesses grow.

Economically underprivileged populations can invest in nearby enterprises, infrastructure, and social projects if they have access to finance and financial services. This local investment promotes resilience and self-sufficiency by stimulating ground-up economic development. Apart from financial advantages, such a regenerative approach encourages social welfare. ReFi systems help to enhance society generally by giving initiatives supporting social equity—such as affordable housing, education, and healthcare—first priority. This whole strategy guarantees that financial operations complement the objective of building a more fair and equitable society. ReFi is about building a naturally regenerative financial environment, not only about giving access to financial services. It has the ability to empower economically underprivileged areas and people by building systems that naturally result in beneficial environmental and social consequences, making financial systems internationally accessible, and removing conventional obstacles.

This empowerment promotes a more equitable and inclusive global economy in which economic development supports social well-being and environmental sustainability. ReFi's basic tenet is aligning sustainable aims with economic growth. ReFi guarantees that environmental and social goals coincide with financial development by automatically including beneficial measures. Promoting sustainable development depends on this alignment, as it ensures that the quest for economic expansion does not compromise the welfare of the earth or society. The automation inside ReFi systems further improves this alignment. ReFi designs a system whereby every economic activity helps to achieve sustainability goals by including social and environmental factors into the core framework of financial transactions.

Thus, activities like carbon offsetting, financing local projects, and supporting renewable energy projects are easily included in financial procedures, naturally resulting in sustainability from economic development. ReFi systems' distributed and multi-jurisdictional character adds even further to their robustness. They run on distributed platforms spanning several areas and regulatory regimes, unlike conventional financial institutions, which are sometimes exposed to geopolitical threats, policy changes, and economic instability inside specific nations. This worldwide distribution lessens their sensitivity to isolated disturbances. It guarantees that, even in certain places with unfavorable conditions, the system stays stable and effective.

ReFi may also use different regulatory environments thanks to its distributed strategy, which keeps a large operational base while using favorable conditions in several countries. This adaptability not only strengthens ReFi systems but also helps them to react quickly to changes, therefore guaranteeing ongoing alignment with sustainable goals. ReFi marks a dramatic change from DeFi. It refines its emphasis on building a regenerative, inclusive, and sustainable economic system while keeping the technology characteristics of DeFi—that of transparency, security, and user autonomy. Emphasizing the value of ecological health, social equality, and community resilience, this change in emphasis departs from the conventional profit-centric strategy.

ReFi's ability to change not only the financial industry but also more general social and environmental environments becomes ever clearer as it develops. It creates an economic climate whereby growth supports and improves the well-being of people and the earth by including sustainability at the center of financial systems. Its transforming ability places ReFi as a formidable instrument for promoting positive change in the future, in which social, environmental, and financial objectives are harmonically combined.

Web3 Revolution: Transforming the Digital Economy for Inclusivity, Sustainability, and Fair Wealth Distribution

Web3 represents a revolutionary trend in the digital sphere that transcends the traditional limits of Internet evolution. It ushers in a new era that will see significant technological and philosophical advancements driven by a dedicated global community.

CHAPTER 17   THRIVING TOGETHER: A REGENERATIVE POWER FOR SMALL AND MIGHTY BUSINESSES

Core to Web3 is a dedication to building user-centric digital environments and services that value inclusion, decentralization, and universal accessibility, thereby transcending boundaries like background, nationality, and socioeconomic level.

Decentralization and democratization are the foundations of this transforming Web3 concept. Unlike the conventional Internet, where a small number of big companies often hold all the power and authority, Web3 seeks to fairly share control among its users. Along with empowering people by providing them more control over their data and online activities, this change promotes a more inclusive and strong digital environment.

Web3's inclusiveness is very important. Web3 removes the obstacles that have historically kept many people of different socioeconomic backgrounds from completely engaging in the digital economy by building platforms that are accessible to everybody. This inclusion also applies to the design of digital environments whereby people from many backgrounds may engage, cooperate, and invent on equal footing.

Web3's transforming power depends much on its connection with the ideas of sustainability and fair economic distribution. Here is where the idea of ReFi finds application. ReFi strives to establish financial systems that are not just distributed and user-centric but also regenerative and inclusive, so it is intimately tied to the concept of Web3. ReFi wants to create financial ecosystems supporting sustainability and equitable wealth distribution by using Web3's technological innovations.

ReFi represents the belief that financial systems ought to improve the environment and society. It sees a day when, rather than draining or exploiting natural resources and social systems, economic activities will be meant to restore and support them. The synergy between Web3 and ReFi emphasizes how likely these technologies are to propel notable social and financial transformations. A new paradigm of digital finance results from combining the decentralization and inclusiveness of Web3 with ReFi's sustainability objectives. This paradigm opens the path for a more fair and sustainable future by giving human and community well-being first priority, as well as environmental health.

Web3 marks a revolution in the digital sphere marked by philosophical and technological changes motivated by a worldwide community dedicated to changing the digital terrain. Fundamentally, it is a commitment to design inclusive, distributed, and easily available digital environments. This vision fits very well with its objectives, which emphasize fair distribution of wealth and sustainability. Together, Web3 and ReFi are prepared to transform not just the digital economy but also the larger social and environmental settings, therefore fostering a future where socially beneficial and technical development coexist.

Web3: Empowering Users with Sovereignty, Decentralization, and Open-Source Innovation

Beyond just its cutting-edge technology, Web3 stands out for a set of design principles that emphasize user sovereignty, decentralization, and an open-source attitude. These ideas directly address the limitations and centralization observed in Web2, when big companies have substantial influence over user interactions and data. In Web2, the power dynamics are distorted toward a few dominant firms that control and profit from user data, usually without clear permission or fair benefit to the users themselves. Web3 is really about trying to turn this power back to consumers. It aims to build a digital world in which people own and manage their information completely. Under this new approach, distributed networks help to enable user interactions and transactions rather than centralized authority mediating or controlling them. Data ownership is therefore restored to the consumers, thereby enabling them to control the usage, sharing, and monetization of their information.

Blockchain, which distributes data over a network of nodes, thereby guaranteeing that no one party has total control, helps Web3 to achieve decentralization. Because data is freely available and verified by all network users, this design improves security, openness, and trust. Furthermore, Web3's distributed nature reduces the risk of data breaches and misuse, which are common in centralized systems.

Web3's open-source philosophy promotes invention and teamwork. Web3 promotes community-driven development by allowing the public access to fundamental technologies and platforms. This transparency guarantees that the development process is inclusive and transparent, in addition to hastening technical achievements. The developments in the Web3 ecosystem will help and benefit anybody.

Moreover, Web3 encourages user sovereignty by letting people interact peer-to-peer, free from middlemen. Transactions, communications, and other digital interactions may therefore happen straight between users, thus reducing reliance on outside platforms usually in charge of controlling and profiting from these interactions. Web3 reduces costs, improves privacy, and speeds up digital transactions by doing away with middlemen. Ultimately, a collection of design ideas that give user sovereignty, decentralization, and an open-source mindset top priority characterizes Web3. It results from the limits and centralization of Web2, in which big companies mostly control data and user interactions. Web3 aims to give consumers more control over their data and interactions so that a centralized authority does not mediate them. This change not only helps people but also creates a more safe, open, and creative digital ecology.

CHAPTER 17   THRIVING TOGETHER: A REGENERATIVE POWER FOR SMALL AND MIGHTY BUSINESSES

Blockchain Technology: The Foundation of Web3's Transparency, Security, and Automation

Fundamentally based on a distributed ledger system guaranteeing transparency, security, and immutability, blockchain technology is driving the Web3 movement. Blockchain runs on a network of distributed nodes, unlike conventional centralized databases run under one corporate management. Every node has a copy of the whole ledger, which logs all transactions in a way that anybody may confirm.

Because of its openness, blockchain technology promotes trust by ensuring that every network user can see every transaction. By letting users independently check transactions, this visibility helps to lower the possible fraud risk and improve the general confidence in the system. Furthermore, once a transaction is entered on the blockchain, it is practically impossible to change or erase. This immutability guarantees that the transaction history stays whole and tamper-proof, therefore offering an accurate and dependable record over time.

Another significant feature of blockchain security is that the distributed nature of the ledger makes it less susceptible to conventional centralized systems' single points of failure. Every transaction is cryptographically encrypted and connected to the one before it in a chain of blocks, which makes data manipulation challenging for malevolent parties. This strong security system safeguards user privacy as well as data integrity.

Smart contracts and distributed apps (dApps) created by blockchain technology are among the most transformative capabilities made possible. Operating on blockchain systems, decentralized apps may run free from central supervision. By means of this distributed system, dApps guarantee consumers dependable and continuous service via resistance to censorship and outages.

Another development enabled by blockchain is smart contracts, self-executing contracts with explicitly defined terms straight into code. These agreements eliminate middlemen by automatically running and enforcing the terms of an agreement based on predetermined criteria. By improving the efficiency of interactions and transactions inside the Web3 ecosystem, this automation lowers possible human error risk and helps to save expenses.

Blockchain technology essentially allows a fresh degree of security and automation for Web3 ecosystem transactions and interactions. It helps with the creation of smart contracts and distributed apps, which are very essential to realizing the goal of a distributed web. Blockchain technology guarantees Web3 runs on values of trust, dependability, and decentralization by offering a visible, safe, and unchangeable ledger, thereby advancing the push toward a more open and fair digital future.

Web3 and ReFi: Overcoming Challenges to Create a Fair and Sustainable Financial Future

Web3 and ReFi present significant difficulties, even if they present a transforming future vision. The technological complexity connected with these systems presents one of the difficulties. Blockchain's sophisticated character and distributed technologies' difficulty in grasping and applying the need for certain knowledge and expertise. Another obstacle is regulatory uncertainty. Regulations are typically vague or changing as these technologies grow, which leaves developers and consumers in erratic surroundings. This ambiguity might impede the broad acceptance and integration of ReFi and Web3 technologies.

Cooperative efforts are absolutely necessary to meet these difficulties. Working with regulators, technologists must create unambiguous rules that support creativity while safeguarding consumers. Ensuring that these technologies fit sustainability and equitable objectives also depends critically on environmentalists and supporters of social justice. Realizing the possible advantages for the environment and society, the worldwide community has to unite to assist and advance the acceptance of Web3 and ReFi.

Fulfilling its goals will depend on the ongoing development and integration of Web3 technologies, which will be essential looking forward. Web3 has enormous power to produce transparent, sustainable, and more fair financial systems. Its capacity to distribute power, incorporate underprivileged areas, and give wide access to financial services makes it a major actor in determining the direction of finance.

Finally, Web3 marks a trend toward a more fair and sustainable future rather than only a technical development. Web3 creates the foundation for ReFi by adopting decentralized, inclusive, and transparent ideas. This new paradigm guarantees that economic activities help the earth as well as people, therefore redefining our perspective and interaction with financial institutions. By means of constant innovation and cooperative efforts, the goal of Web3 and ReFi can come to pass, therefore providing a more fair and sustainable financial future.

CHAPTER 17   THRIVING TOGETHER: A REGENERATIVE POWER FOR SMALL AND MIGHTY BUSINESSES

From DeFi to ReFi: A Paradigm Shift

ReFi has its roots firmly in the ideas developed by DeFi. First, one must appreciate how DeFi has transformed the financial scene in order to appreciate its importance.

DeFi became a revolutionary movement that distributed power over cash, therefore changing the established financial system. This decentralization marked a fundamental change from the traditional banking and financial organizations that have always controlled management and money flow. These institutions manage access to financial services and set transaction terms, therefore serving as middlemen in conventional finance. For many people, especially those in underprivileged or economically depressed areas, this frequently means limited access and a lack of openness.

DeFi uses blockchain technology, on the other hand, to build a financial ecosystem in which a network of participants distributes control over money instead of a small number of central authorities concentrating their power. People may directly oversee their own assets without depending on banks or other financial middlemen. Smart contracts—self-executing contracts with terms of the agreement directly encoded into code—ensure that transactions are carried out openly and automatically when the required criteria are satisfied.

Because this decentralization has democratized access to financial services, anybody with an Internet connection may join the worldwide financial system. In a more transparent and open environment, people may now lend, borrow, trade, and invest. The reliance on conventional financial institutions is lessened, if not completely removed; the obstacles to entry are much diminished. A pillar of DeFi, this increased accessibility enables people to have more financial freedom and inclusiveness.

Blockchain technology's intrinsic openness also means that every transaction is noted on a public ledger. Since this public ledger is unchangeable, once a transaction is entered, it cannot be undone or changed. This openness builds system confidence as users may independently check transactions without depending on the guarantees of a central power.

DeFi's openness and accessibility have not only distributed financial services but also encouraged financial sector innovation. Often with the intention of addressing particular issues or serving historically underserved niche markets, new financial products and services are under constant development. This tsunami of invention has produced a more vibrant and responsive financial ecosystem.

ReFi expands on the strong foundation DeFi lays, adding another level of intent to these distributed networks, whereas DeFi has concentrated on decentralizing control and improving openness and accessibility. It aims to use DeFi's technological

CHAPTER 17   THRIVING TOGETHER: A REGENERATIVE POWER FOR SMALL AND MIGHTY BUSINESSES

developments and ideas to design financial systems, giving sustainability and inclusion top priority. It thus seeks to create financial systems and products that not only offer more control and transparency but also help to produce social and environmental results in addition.

DeFi's concepts have established a crucial foundation for ReFi through the decentralization of financial governance, enhancement of transparency, and facilitation of more accessible financial transactions. This democratization of money has empowered people and lowered reliance on traditional banks while also encouraging creativity. ReFi aims to further change the financial system by including sustainability and inclusion into its core, therefore generating a more complete and regenerative approach to finance based on these ideas.

From the basic ideas set out by DeFi, the development of ReFi follows naturally. It marks a radical improvement in the financial scene by combining the ideas of DeFi with the ideas of regenerative economics. Fundamentally, DeFi has transformed finance by distinctively sizing control and improving openness and access. ReFi expands on this basis, though, by adding the ideas of regenerative economics, which center on building economic systems that preserve the health of our world and its populations. This change shows a diversification of emphasis, including social and environmental aspects beyond only financial ones.

ReFi is a basic reevaluation of the part money may play in solving world problems, not only a development of DeFi. Sometimes, traditional financial systems prioritize short-term benefits and efficiency over environmental and social well-being. ReFi, on the other hand, aims to design financial systems that actively support social justice and help rebuild natural ecosystems.

ReFi stands out from the competition primarily because of its commitment to incorporating environmental sustainability into business operations. This implies creating financial systems to assist programs meant to help in the preservation of natural resources. ReFi programs could call for funding sustainable agriculture, supporting forestry initiatives, or financing renewable energy projects. It aids in environmental improvement by focusing financial resources on these regenerative projects.

Apart from environmental sustainability, ReFi gives social welfare top importance. This entails building financial institutions that guarantee equality and inclusiveness so that every member of society may benefit from economic activity. This might include sponsoring initiatives that advance social justice, giving underprivileged areas access to financial services, or funding companies that give fair labor standards first priority. Its aim is to build a more fair and equal economic system by including these social elements.

Its whole approach to finance has enormous transforming power. ReFi generates a financial system that is not only distributed and open but also sustainable and inclusive by combining the ideas of DeFi with the aims of regenerative economics. This is a major change from conventional financial systems, which sometimes run in silos and concentrate mostly on economic results without thinking through their wider consequences for society and the environment.

One defining quality of ReFi is its focus on building a system that actively promotes the well-being of its people and the state of our planet. It acknowledges that the health of the environment and society is naturally entwined with the state of the economy. Its goal is to build a stronger and more sustainable future by encouraging financial habits that encourage inclusiveness and regeneration.

The development of ReFi expands on the basis of DeFi by entwining its ideas with the theories of regenerative economics. This integration incorporates social and environmental aspects with economic processes, therefore transcending DeFi's conventional financial concentration. ReFi is a whole new and transforming approach to finance, not just about decentralization but also about building a financial system that actively supports the well-being of its people and the health of our earth.

Embracing Openness, Transparency, and Responsibility in the Path to a Sustainable Financial Future: The Reality of the ReFi Movement

Like their forerunner, DeFi, the ReFi movement is based on core ideas of openness and creativity. ReFi is really based on open access, open code, and open data. These values build a basis whereby openness and teamwork are given top priority, therefore enabling everyone to engage, help, and invent inside the ecosystem.

The ReFi movement is meant to be inclusive, as open access emphasizes that people and businesses from all backgrounds and areas may interact with and gain from its projects. A broad-based and varied community depends on this inclusiveness, which also drives invention and creativity. The movement may use a broad range of ideas and viewpoints by making sure that geographical, financial, or institutional obstacles do not limit access to ReFi tools and platforms, therefore advancing fresh solutions and uses.

Another essential component of ReFi's basis is open code. Making the fundamental ReFi project codes open to developers and innovators will enable them to freely examine, copy, and enhance current work. This openness guarantees the projects' integrity and security as well as quickens the rate of invention. More strong and effective solutions result from developers working internationally, sharing improvements, and group troubleshooting of problems. This open-source strategy democratizes the development process, therefore enabling a worldwide community to help ReFi flourish and change.

By guaranteeing that information produced inside the ReFi ecosystem is easily available to all users, open data enhances the ideas of open access and open code. Real-time tracking and transaction verification made possible by this openness help build responsibility and confidence by means of trust. The ReFi movement gives academics, legislators, and the general public free access to data so they may examine and evaluate the effectiveness and impact of measures and initiatives. This open data philosophy promotes ecosystem continual development and evidence-based decision-making.

Its transparency encourages free creativity and opens the path for a broad spectrum of uses addressing urgent worldwide problems. Tokenizing environmental assets—that is, turning real-world assets such as carbon credits, biodiversity credits, or renewable energy projects into digital tokens readily exchanged and managed on blockchain systems—is one such use for tokens. This improves the liquidity and openness of these assets, as well as funds and motivates environmental preservation projects.

Funding public goods via distributed, open systems is another exciting use. Underfunding and inefficiencies in conventional financial systems may plague public goods, including infrastructure, education, and healthcare. By using distributed money transparently, pooling resources, and guaranteeing responsibility in their use, ReFi can transform the way these vital services are financed by means of distributed platforms.

The ReFi movement's physical initiatives and strong community participation help to define its authenticity. The blockchain and Web3 areas clearly show this realism; several ReFi projects are already having an influence here. Constantly evolving and carrying out projects highlights its pragmatic advantages and real-world possibilities. The movement is strengthened even more by active engagement and community cooperation, as stakeholders together propel forward its goals and vision.

This movement is essentially driven by the ideas of openness and creativity. ReFi offers a rich ground for creativity and broad-based involvement by supporting open access code and open data. While the movement's actual accomplishments and active participation in the blockchain and Web3 communities highlight its authenticity, this openness allows for a wide range of advantageous applications and codebases, from the tokenization of environmental assets to the funding of public goods.

CHAPTER 17   THRIVING TOGETHER: A REGENERATIVE POWER FOR SMALL AND MIGHTY BUSINESSES

The defining openness of the ReFi movement gives users access to a wide range of creative financial services and improved transparency, therefore benefiting them. This transparency creates a space where people may interact and investigate different initiatives, thereby learning about their underlying technology and activities. This openness also means that users need to use caution and start a proactive approach to guarantee their security and prevent any hazards.

Using ReFi and Web3 services means that users must assume the enormous responsibility of doing thorough research before joining any project or service. This implies committing time to carefully explore and grasp the several facets of a project. One must be well familiar with the basic technologies involved in running a project. Users should explore the particular protocols and tools used, as well as blockchain technology and smart contract applications. Strong knowledge of the technological basis helps users evaluate the validity and relevance of the project, therefore guaranteeing their informed judgments.

Just as crucial is knowing the project's business plan. Users should look at the way the project creates value, where it gets money and the financial incentives for volunteers. This information offers an understanding of the sustainability and expansion possibilities of the project. Examining the business model helps consumers decide whether the aims of the project are reasonable and whether they fit their own values and financial situation.

Another important factor for users is compliance. ReFi and Web3 services' regulatory environment is still changing as different nations have different legal systems and criteria. Users must confirm if the project carries the required licenses or permissions and follows pertinent rules. By helping to ensure regulatory compliance, one may help reduce the risks related to legal penalties or operational closures, therefore adding further protection for participants.

Not less important is knowing the group driving the initiative. Users should look into the backgrounds and past performance of the developers, consultants, and other important players engaged. A team with demonstrated knowledge and experience can significantly increase the credibility and chances of success of a project. On the other hand, the lack of reliable data on the team or the presence of people with dubious backgrounds ought to cause worry and inspire more investigation.

Transparency creates chances for dishonest behavior, even while encouraging creativity and accessibility. Unethical players may take advantage of the dispersed nature of the ecosystem to produce misleading initiatives that abet naive consumers. Therefore, when evaluating new projects, it is crucial to approach them with a critical mindset and a healthy dose of skepticism. To support the validity of a project, users should look for official evidence of the idea, outside audits, and positive community comments.

Additionally, active participation in the ReFi community is quite helpful. Users may learn a lot and remain current on possible hazards and new trends by engaging in discussion forums, talking with other people, and following reliable sources of information. The community's combined expertise and experience is a useful tool for spotting worthy initiatives and dodging fraud.

Basically, even if the openness of the ReFi movement presents many chances, it also makes consumers accountable to apply prudence. Essential actions to guarantee safe involvement are doing extensive due diligence, knowing the technology and business strategy, confirming compliance status, and investigating the personnel behind a project. Following these values will help consumers negotiate the terrain more boldly and shield themselves from any risks.

Building Trust and Resilience in ReFi: The Role of Compliance, Transparency, and Community Engagement

To guarantee their operations are compliant and safe, many ReFi programs actively work with financial regulators and industry associations. Building confidence and trust inside the ReFi ecosystem depends mostly on this cooperative approach. These initiatives show a dedication to following legal and industry norms by closely engaging with regulatory authorities, therefore supporting their validity.

Financial authorities' participation usually implies that such initiatives have to satisfy defined compliance criteria and are under close examination. Know your customer (KYC), anti-money laundering (AML), and other financial rules meant to stop fraud and guarantee openness can all help here. ReFi reduces the possibility of illegal activity and provides a safer environment for consumers by following these rules.

Additionally, crucial in this cooperative endeavor are industry bodies. These companies provide recommendations that let projects run more ethically and successfully, hence setting the best standards and practices for the sector. ReFi initiatives gain from the collective knowledge and experience of the sector by following these criteria, therefore improving their operational procedures and general security.

Initiatives, financial authorities, and industry organizations working together help to build a foundation of dependability and confidence. Projects that are open about their compliance efforts and supported or acknowledged by credible regulatory and industry

CHAPTER 17   THRIVING TOGETHER: A REGENERATIVE POWER FOR SMALL AND MIGHTY BUSINESSES

bodies will inspire users to trust them more. In the fast-changing and occasionally unpredictable environment of distributed finance, where the danger of fraud and false schemes might be great, this assurance is especially crucial.

Moreover, these cooperative efforts may result in creative ideas that improve the user experience and compliance. For example, although smart contracts can automatically verify compliance checks and guarantee that transactions follow legal criteria, developments in blockchain technology can enable more effective and safe KYC procedures. These developments not only make projects more useful but also show their proactive attitude toward security and compliance maintenance.

ReFi projects' active cooperation with financial regulators and industry entities basically fulfills many functions. By guaranteeing that the projects satisfy strict regulatory criteria, it offers users an additional degree of security by lowering the risk of fraud and non-compliance and promoting an innovative environment that always enhances the safety and efficiency of this regenerative ecosystem. ReFi projects' increasing popularity and success may be mostly attributed to this cooperative approach, as it lays a strong basis of trust and dependability necessary for long-term development and stability.

Transparency of its codebases, which are often made available for public review, is a basic strength of ReFi. This transparency is absolutely essential, as it lets everyone, even regular users and developers, see the fundamental code running projects. Such initiatives show a dedication to openness and responsibility by making the code freely available, therefore fostering trust in society.

This openness goes beyond mere code availability. It covers ReFi's whole ecosystem, where blockchain activities and transactions are subject to public audit. The blockchain records every transaction, smart contract execution, and system modification on it, therefore offering an unchangeable, verifiable record of all activity. This public auditability guarantees that there are no covert manipulations or false activity by anybody with the required knowledge and interest, therefore verifying the validity and integrity of the operations.

Public scrutiny of the code and transactions greatly increases the credibility of the ReFi system. The projects users work on should not use dishonest methods or hide harmful code. In a distributed environment where conventional control systems might not be available, this is very critical. Allowing independent auditors and community members to examine the code helps to quickly find any possible flaws or unethical behavior, therefore preserving the integrity of the system.

Moreover, this degree of openness promotes better security and quality criteria. Developers are motivated to follow the best standards and create cleaner, safer code, knowing that their work will be in public view. Apart from enhancing the particular project, this peer review process helps the ReFi ecosystem to be more resilient and healthy.

The twillarency of codebases and transactions also contributes to a cooperative environment. Projects can benefit from the worldwide contribution of developers who help them grow and flourish. By pointing out flaws, suggesting fixes, and offering ideas, they may help to create a dynamic and responsive development process that gains from group wisdom and experience. More creative and strong financial solutions result from this open cooperation, as many points of view and abilities are applied to shared problems.

ReFi's codebases' openness and public auditability of their transactions are the main assets supporting the system's dependability and confidence. This transparency guarantees that users and developers may both confirm the integrity of the projects, support better security and quality standards, and foster a cooperative and creative atmosphere for both of them. These elements, taken together, help ReFi become more and more credible, as they provide a strong basis of trust and responsibility in the distributed financial scene.

Top blockchain security firms play a crucial role in maintaining the integrity and security of projects by conducting thorough technical audits, also known as code reviews. In order to find any potential flaws that malicious actors might exploit, these audits meticulously examine the project's codebase. The expertise of these security firms ensures that even the most subtle and complex issues are uncovered and addressed. This process makes the system stronger and reassures users and investors that these projects are safe.

In addition to professional audits, ReFi platforms often implement bug bounty programs as a proactive measure to fortify their security. These programs invite ethical hackers and security researchers from around the world to test the system for vulnerabilities. Participants who successfully identify and report security flaws are rewarded financially. This incentivizes a diverse group of individuals to scrutinize the system, significantly expanding the pool of experts working to ensure its security.

The combination of technical audits by top blockchain security firms and the implementation of bug bounty programs creates a multi-layered defense mechanism for new projects. Technical audits provide a structured and professional evaluation of the code, often using advanced tools and methodologies to detect weaknesses. On the other hand, bug bounty programs leverage the creativity and varied perspectives of a global community of security experts. Together, these approaches help to uncover and address vulnerabilities that might otherwise go unnoticed.

This comprehensive approach to security significantly strengthens ReFi platforms. It not only helps in identifying and fixing existing vulnerabilities but also in anticipating potential future threats. By continuously improving their security posture through these audits and programs, ReFi projects can build greater trust and credibility within the community.

Moreover, these security measures highlight the commitment of ReFi projects to transparency and user protection. By publicly disclosing their engagement with reputable security firms and the results of their bug bounty programs, ReFi projects demonstrate a proactive stance on security. Users can feel secure knowing that strict and ongoing security measures are protecting their assets and data, thanks to this openness.

Key blockchain security companies regularly conduct technical audits, and bug bounty programs actively participate in ensuring the security and robustness of projects. These measures not only identify and address vulnerabilities but also enhance the overall trust and credibility of the ReFi ecosystem, making it a safer environment for users and fostering a more resilient financial system.

The foundation of the success of this new area is the active community of consumers and developers inside it. This vibrant community is an active and involved collective that greatly helps initiatives grow and flourish, rather than being a passive gathering of individuals. Their participation is essential in seeing and fixing different problems that could develop, therefore guaranteeing the resilience and ongoing development of these programs.

ReFi users contribute a variety of viewpoints and experiences that enable developers to identify possible issues and opportunities for development that might not be immediately clear-cut. Based on users' suggestions for improvements or problems, developers respond by making the necessary updates and modifications. Requests are responded to by developers providing the required updates and modifications. The community then tests and uses these improvements, therefore generating more comments and a cycle of ongoing development. This procedure guarantees that initiatives stay pertinent and effective, as well as encouraging community involvement and ownership.

Furthermore, the community participates, not just in terms of technical support. Frequent educational events by community members serve to increase knowledge of ideas and technology, therefore promoting awareness. They plan and participate in forums, seminars, and debates to promote awareness and knowledge exchange. The expansion of the ReFi ecosystem depends on this instructional feature, as it helps to onboard developers and new users, therefore strengthening the community and improving its collective capacities.

Furthermore, protecting against such hazards requires substantial community support. Many eyes on the system allow vulnerabilities and suspicious behavior to be rapidly found and resolved. This group awareness improves projects' security and integrity, therefore preventing malicious actors' system exploitation difficulties.

The vibrant and powerful user and developer community in ReFi's industry is largely responsible for its success. Their ongoing engagement in seeing and fixing problems as well as their teamwork to enhance the system guarantees that initiatives stay strong, creative, and resilient. Apart from improving the security and functioning of ReFi projects, this community-driven strategy helps participants develop trust and belonging, therefore supporting the general sustainability and expansion of the ReFi ecosystem.

Grounding Web3 in Real-World Impact and Sustainability Through ReFi

Among the Web3 scene, ReFi stands out for precisely tying sophisticated blockchain technology with observable, real-world impact. ReFi is unique in its foundation in pragmatic applications, especially those that address sustainability and social effects, while many Web3 apps mostly concentrate on technological advances or radical deviations from existing financial systems. Its special posture enables it to not only take advantage of blockchain's innovative features but also apply these technologies to relevant problems in significant ways.

The emphasis ReFi places on producing favorable social and environmental results defines its strategy. Unlike other Web3 apps that might emphasize abstract technological advancement or the decentralization of financial systems for their own sake, its motivation is to achieve quantifiable gains in sustainability and social equality. This realistic approach guarantees that its "inventions" directly address some of the most urgent problems confronting society today, like economic inequality, resource depletion, and climate change.

The sense of community within ReFi strengthens its influence even more. A varied mix of stakeholders—including developers, environmentalists, social activists, and regular users—often helps initiatives be created and funded. This broad-based involvement creates a cooperative and inclusive atmosphere where many points of view and experiences help ideas develop. Apart from improving the relevance and quality of these initiatives, the active participation of society promotes responsibility and confidence in the ecosystem.

CHAPTER 17 THRIVING TOGETHER: A REGENERATIVE POWER FOR SMALL AND MIGHTY BUSINESSES

ReFi's potential to become the first main real-life use case of Web3 technology is one of the most important features, among which it offers a convincing illustration of the useful uses of distributed technology by showing how blockchain may be utilized to produce actual outcomes. Enterprises emphasizing tokenizing environmental assets, including carbon credits, or developing distributed finance systems for public goods and social enterprises clearly show this real-life influence. These uses highlight how ReFi may both offer financial value and efficiency and propel positive change.

ReFi's emphasis on quantifiable results and open procedures highlights its practical approach. Whether in terms of less carbon emissions, more financing for social programs, or more economic prospects for underprivileged areas, projects inside this domain are meant to provide obvious, verifiable advantages. Blockchain technology's intrinsic openness guarantees that these results can be confirmed and accepted, therefore strengthening the validity and influence of ReFi programs.

Considering all factors, ReFi sets itself apart in the Web3 landscape by adeptly integrating contemporary blockchain technologies with practical applications motivated by sustainability and social impact. Rooted in pragmatic solutions and community engagement, its pragmatic approach positions itself as a pioneering agent in proving the clear advantages of Web3 technology. This alignment with real-world concerns and its potential for significant influence highlight its position as a lighthouse in the evolving landscape of distributed finance.

Real-World Connection and Utility: Pragmatism and Adaptability in Leveraging Blockchain for Real-World Sustainability and Social Impact

Deeply entwined with people's lives and real-world assets, including carbon credits, ReFi is therefore quite relevant and powerful. This strong relationship emphasizes blockchain technology's practical value and its ability to propel major and favorable transformations.

ReFi shows how blockchain may be used to solve practical problems by connecting financial systems with physical assets like carbon credits. Crucially important weapons in the battle against climate change are carbon credits, which lower greenhouse gas emissions. By means of ReFi, these credits may be tokenized and sold on blockchain

CHAPTER 17   THRIVING TOGETHER: A REGENERATIVE POWER FOR SMALL AND MIGHTY BUSINESSES

systems, therefore facilitating a more open and quick procedure. This not only facilitates the tracking and lowering of carbon emissions but also encourages environmentally friendly behavior among companies and people.

Blockchain technology's inclusion in asset management guarantees transparent, unchangeable, and safe transactions. Every carbon credit token is sourced and can be tracked on the blockchain over its whole lifetime. Participants' trust is developed by this openness, as it allows them to confirm that the credits they are trading are real and that their actions really support environmental sustainability.

ReFi's influence also goes beyond advantages for the surroundings. It gives people and communities new economic possibilities by enabling the trade of actual assets on distributed systems, therefore empowering them. Small companies and neighborhood initiatives using sustainable practices, for example, may now reach worldwide markets and draw financing using tokenized assets. More people may participate in sustainable projects thanks to this democratization of financing, thereby creating a more inclusive and fair economic scene.

Its practical uses also show how blockchain technology may cut inefficiencies and expedite procedures. With many middlemen and complicated documentation, conventional approaches to managing and trading assets like carbon credits may be laborious. By automating transactions using smart contracts, therefore decreasing administrative loads and transaction costs, blockchain streamlines these procedures. This effectiveness helps the participants as well as hastens the general acceptance of sustainable living.

Its intimate proximity to people's lives and actual assets basically emphasizes the transforming power of blockchain technology. ReFi shows how distributed technology could enable significant and beneficial change by bringing pragmatic utility to sharp attention. It features the real-world advantages of blockchain by means of improved transparency, economic opportunity, or process simplification, therefore portraying it as a potent instrument for promoting sustainability and social impact.

Understanding that achieving their goals often requires making crucial compromises, the community often adopts a pragmatic and adaptable approach toward the concepts of Web3. ReFi's basic goal of planetary regeneration and societal development depends on its ability to be more accessible and flexible to meet real-world demands; hence, its practical approach helps it fulfill these goals.

Using this adaptable strategy will help the community negotiate the difficulties of combining cutting-edge technologies with useful applications. Initiatives are therefore ready to change or adapt the fundamental ideas of decentralization and transparency inherent in Web3 when it would benefit the project or improve its efficacy, even while they follow these values. This flexibility makes it simpler to apply ideas that are not only creative but also immediately beneficial for the surroundings and people.

The ReFi group clearly shows pragmatism in how they give concrete results first priority above strict ideological loyalty. For initiatives aiming at lower carbon emissions or the assistance of local communities, for instance, the emphasis is on what would best accomplish these objectives rather than rigorously adhering to theoretical models. Projects are more successful and powerful as this results-oriented attitude guarantees that efforts are based on reality and customized to solve particular difficulties.

This practical adaptability also facilitates the link between conventional systems and creative blockchain ideas. ReFi may interact with current institutions, regulatory authorities, and other stakeholders who might be reluctant about or ignorant of Web3 technology by being transparent about cooperation and compromise. This inclusive strategy facilitates better transitions and more scalability by helping initiatives be more widely accepted and integrated.

Moreover, the community's readiness to make trade-offs helps it fulfill its goal of social progress and planetary rebirth. Initiatives may generate sustainable solutions that fully address social and environmental concerns by concentrating on practical uses and effects. This entails creating finance systems that advance social fairness, biodiversity, and renewable energy initiatives. ReFi stays current and efficient in its goal as it is flexible enough to change and grow in response to fresh data and changing conditions.

Considering all factors, the community's pragmatic and adaptable approach to Web3 ideas enables it to make requests, improving its accessibility and flexibility to real-world demands. This kind of thinking helps fulfill its main goals of societal welfare and planetary regeneration by allowing the creation of creative ideas based on sensible reality. This strategy guarantees its fundamental ideals remain true while efficiently addressing social and environmental concerns.

CHAPTER 17   THRIVING TOGETHER: A REGENERATIVE POWER FOR SMALL AND MIGHTY BUSINESSES

Real-World Impact of ReFi: Transforming Carbon Markets and Agriculture with Blockchain for Sustainability and Fair Financial Access

Using tokenization of carbon credits, ReFi shows its usefulness and simplicity in the field of carbon markets. Tokenizing carbon credits simplifies the process and increases access by turning them into digital assets available on blockchain systems. By allowing project developers to sell their carbon credits straight to consumers, this digital revolution helps to eliminate middlemen and related expenses. Both sides gain financially as a result: consumers may get carbon credits at less expense, and project developers get a larger portion of the earnings. Its method also includes converting royalties into carbon tokens, therefore guaranteeing that project creators will always have financial assistance. Maintaining and growing climate-positive projects depends on developers' continuous support, which the partnerships provide. Projects aiming at lowering greenhouse gas emissions, encouraging reforestation, or supporting other environmental goals depend on this kind of financing.

The integration results in a symbiotic interaction between environmental initiatives and investors. Investors are motivated to support significant projects as the success and longevity of these initiatives immediately affect the value and return on their investments. Simultaneously, project developers gain from a consistent flow of money that helps them grow their activities and increase their environmental influence. ReFi's creative application of blockchain technology in the carbon market best illustrates its ability to propel significant transformation. It not only improves the efficiency and efficacy of carbon markets but also creates a more sustainable and fair financial environment by simplifying transactions, lowering costs, and guaranteeing continuous support for climate-positive projects. This strategy shows how it may provide real, favorable results in the battle against climate change by matching financial incentives with environmental advantages.

Projects like EthicHub provide a clear illustration of how ReFi may be used. Ethichub simplifies cross-border loans between investors and borrowers using a certain currency. For regenerative farmers, who frequently struggle greatly to obtain finance via conventional banking channels, this creative solution is very helpful. The mechanism of EthicHub helps these farmers more readily and effectively get the required money. The platform gets over many of the obstacles usually impeding cross-border lending by using blockchain technology and a separate digital currency. This simplifies and lowers the expenses often associated with international transactions by enabling a more direct and economical movement of funds from investors to farmers. EthicHub gives investors the benefit of higher interest rates than more traditional investing options. This gives investors a strong incentive to become involved, as they may support significant and worthwhile initiatives and get greater returns. The open character of the platform guarantees that investors may plainly observe the use of their money and the resulting rewards. therefore promoting responsibility and confidence. Simultaneously, EthicHub's methodology clearly rewards people and initiatives helping to address climate change.

Through funding for regenerative farmers, the site actively supports agricultural methods meant to improve the surroundings. These methods help fight climate change by means of soil regeneration, increased biodiversity, and less dependence on chemical inputs, thereby improving the ecosystem. EthicHub basically shows how ReFi may establish a mutually beneficial relationship between borrowers and investors. While investors get substantial profits and help promote environmental sustainability, farmers have simpler access to the money required to use sustainable practices. At the same time, this model demonstrates how ReFi can support and magnify climate-positive projects by matching financial incentives with ecological and social advantages, therefore highlighting its potential to cause notable positive change.

Connecting Web3 and the Real World: The Key Role of ReFi in Supporting Sustainability and Economic Inclusion

Often under less focus in conventional DeFi, ReFi is greatly bridging the gap between the creative Web3 area and actual real-world effects. It distributes financial value from the cryptocurrency domain straight into real-world economies, unlike DeFi, which mostly aims at decentralizing financial services and optimizing profits inside the digital sphere. Particularly for small-scale carbon farmers and other players involved in sustainable activities, this strategy has significant consequences.

ReFi distinguishes itself primarily in its ability to translate digital financial resources into support for concrete social and environmental projects. Small-scale carbon producers, for example, may gain from the money flows created inside the Bitcoin ecosystem. It lets these farmers access worldwide markets and get money straight through blockchain transactions by tokenizing commodities like carbon credits. This procedure gives these farmers the tools they need to maintain and grow their regenerative agriculture methods, as well as lowering the obstacles to funding they sometimes encounter.

Its ability to be included in actual economies shows how likely it is to provide a more fair and sustainable financial structure. It translates the abstract value created in the digital sphere into useful applications with quantifiable social and environmental advantages. For instance, the financial support given to carbon farmers not only enables them to carry on their vital job but also supports the more general aims of climate action. This direct infusion of money into environmentally friendly initiatives highlights its pragmatic value and part in building a more equitable economic paradigm.

Adoption and view of blockchain technology also depend much on its capacity to direct financial value created from cryptocurrencies into practical uses. It shows how effectively blockchain can be a vehicle for promoting positive change rather than only a speculative financial instrument. This useful application promotes more general adoption and involvement in many spheres of life by helping to establish confidence and trust in the technology.

Moreover, its influence goes beyond advantages for the surroundings. ReFi supports social fairness and economic inclusion by giving underprivileged groups—including small-scale farmers—financial resources. Often excluded from conventional financial institutions, these groups find fresh chances for personal development. This inclusive strategy guarantees a more equitable distribution of the advantages of blockchain technology and cryptocurrencies, therefore balancing the economic environment.

Fundamentally, ReFi is innovating a fresh approach to applying blockchain technology for practical effect. Not only does it improve the practical worth of digital financial systems, but it also supports sustainability and social well-being by bridging the gap between the Web3 area and actual results. This conversation emphasizes how it is establishing this link and underlines its ability to transform the course of finance going forward in a more inclusive and regenerative way.

The Flow of Financial Value in ReFi: Bridging the Gap Between Digital and Real-World Economies for Sustainability and Inclusion

Under ReFi systems, the flow of financial value goes beyond the digital sphere and into real-world economic operations, therefore directly affecting individuals' livelihoods and surroundings. This method is essentially different from conventional financial systems

CHAPTER 17   THRIVING TOGETHER: A REGENERATIVE POWER FOR SMALL AND MIGHTY BUSINESSES

that sometimes stay in the abstract, digital domain. Its solutions essentially close the gap between digital finance and real-world applications by allowing the smooth flow of funds from Bitcoin holdings into physical, real-world entities. Consider a small-scale carbon farmer. By means of initiatives, this farmer may directly profit from the value created inside the Bitcoin ecosystem. Tokenized carbon credits, which the farmer may sell or trade on blockchain systems, could be one way these advantages show up. These sales may then be directly put into the farmer's bank account, giving them instant cash help.

This system guarantees that the financial value produced in the digital sphere of cryptocurrencies is not isolated but rather directly reaches those involved in environmentally friendly activities. It lets the farmer access money fast and effectively without using conventional middlemen, who may slow down the process and cause extra expenses. ReFi systems therefore help farmers not only with their livelihood but also with their ecologically friendly methods.

ReFi has a major real-world impact as it renders blockchain technology useful and advantageous for regular economic operations. Farmers, who may previously have restricted access to worldwide financial markets, can now engage directly and find fresh income sources to help with their labor. This influx of money enables them to make investments in improved technology and practices that can increase their environmental impact and production even further. Moreover, these systems help to create a more fair and sustainable financial environment by including financial value in concrete economic operations.

They guarantee that those who are changing the world—small-scale carbon farmers, among other things—receive the advantages of digital banking. In ReFi's translators, power is shown by this coupling of financial incentives with environmental aims, therefore illustrating how sophisticated technology may be used for practical benefit. ReFi systems essentially help to shift financial value from the digital sphere into real-world economic activity, therefore directly influencing people and the environment. The practical and favorable uses of blockchain technology are shown by this smooth movement of cash from digital assets to physical objects like a farmer's bank account, therefore supporting their importance in building a more inclusive and sustainable financial system.

Under conventional DeFi systems, financial transactions often stay limited to the digital realm. This implies that instead of being turned into conventional fiat currencies like euros or dollars, the money in these ecosystems usually remains in digital form, like cryptocurrencies. This quality distinguishes DeFi from ReFi systems significantly. Inside the DeFi ecosystem, money moves mostly within the confines of digital assets. Although users participate in several financial activities like lending, borrowing, and trading, these operations are mostly limited to Bitcoin exchanges and platforms. The money moves around distributed apps (dApps) and digital wallets to form a self-contained financial loop that doesn't usually interact with the conventional economy. This insensitivity reduces the direct influence DeFi can have on regular financial transactions and actual economic activity. The money remains in the form of cryptocurrencies; hence, it is less likely to be utilized for daily, pragmatic costs usually requiring fiat money.

DeFi's capacity to affect local economies, challenge established banking institutions, and enable real changes in lives is thus still limited. By converting digital assets into real-world financial rewards, ReFi seeks to close this disparity. Its systems are meant to move financial value from the crypto scene straight into real-world economic operations like financing environmental projects or sustainable agriculture. This method guarantees that the financial benefits produced in the digital sphere transfer into useful, real-world effects, therefore improving the relevance and value of blockchain technology in daily life.

Such initiatives guarantee that financial gains are accessible and usable in conventional economic settings by allowing the flawless movement of cash from cryptocurrency assets to fiat currencies. Showcasing a more direct and powerful use of blockchain technology, this integration helps sustain livelihoods, promote economic inclusion, and achieve beneficial social and environmental consequences.

Mechanisms Enabling Real-World Connection: Bridging Digital and Physical Economies with Tokenization, Smart Contracts, and Banking Integration

Using tokenization, ReFi closes the distance between digital finance and actual assets. Tokenization is turning physical objects—like agricultural goods or carbon credits—into digital tokens. These tokens reflect the value of the underlying tangible assets and have actual worth rather than only abstract form. Tokenized once, these digital tokens are sold inside the Web3 ecosystem.

Blockchain technology allows assets usually connected to physical or geographical restrictions to now be globally accessible and tradeable. A farmer's food, or a carbon credit, for instance, may be turned into a digital token that anybody with Web3 platform access can subsequently purchase, sell, or trade. Along with democratizing access to these resources, this procedure improves their market reach and liquidity. Tokenizing actual assets is essential, as it creates a direct link between the digital financial realm and physical objects.

This relationship guarantees that the value produced and shared in the digital sphere is based on genuine, physical objects, therefore offering a strong basis for transactions. It also implies that investments made online can have actual, observable effects on the ground. Buying tokenized carbon credits, for example, directly supports environmental programs meant to lower emissions. ReFi establishes a smooth interface wherein digital transactions can result in real-world results by including real-world assets in the digital economy via tokenization. This not only makes blockchain technology more practically useful but also helps to match financial activity with more general objectives of sustainability and economic inclusiveness. Thus, a key technique that allows the transfer of digital financial value to real-world applications, thereby promoting a more linked and powerful economic system, is tokenization.

Smart contracts let ReFi improve financial transaction security and automation. Smart contracts are self-executing agreements with explicitly written code terms of agreement. These agreements are meant to automatically enforce the terms after specific requirements are satisfied, therefore eliminating middlemen. Within this space, smart contracts may be set to send money straight from platforms or investors to recipients—like carbon farmers. This procedure starts with the development of a smart contract outlining the circumstances under which money will be moved. A contract may provide, for instance, that a carbon farmer is paid upon proving a specific degree of carbon reduction or completion of a sustainable project. The smart contract immediately moves money from the investor's digital wallet to the recipient's account whenever these requirements are met. Automation replaces manual processing, thereby reducing the possibility of errors and delays. It guarantees the correct and quick distribution of money, thereby immediately reaching people meant to get it.

Another absolutely vital advantage of smart contracts is their security component. These contracts run on blockchain technology; hence, all transactions are logged on a distributed ledger that is open and unchangeable. This openness lets all the relevant parties monitor money flow, therefore guaranteeing that transactions are carried out as planned and lowering the possibility of mismanagement or fraud. Blockchain's unchangeable character ensures extra security and trust, as once a transaction is documented, it cannot be changed.

CHAPTER 17   THRIVING TOGETHER: A REGENERATIVE POWER FOR SMALL AND MIGHTY BUSINESSES

ReFi improves financial transaction dependability and openness in addition to streamlining by using smart contracts. This guarantees proper and efficient use of money set aside for particular uses, including helping carbon farmers. Smart contracts' security combined with automation helps systems' financial operations be more reliable and efficient, which eventually helps them to be successful and significant.

As a vital step in closing the distance between the digital cryptocurrency world and the physical, fiat money-based economy, enterprises are progressively interacting with conventional banking institutions. Particularly for people not generally engaged in the crypto area, the practical utility and accessibility of digital financial advances depend on this integration. Let us dissect this process and consider its consequences.

Initiatives often use gateways or platforms acting as middlemen to help cryptocurrencies be converted into fiat currencies (such as USD, EUR, etc.). These systems may be collaborations with established institutions, digital wallets with conversion tools, or crypto exchanges, easing the process of converting digital currencies into fiat, therefore enabling people and companies to make more use of the financial value created in the crypto realm in their regular economic operations.

To offer flawless transaction experiences, certain ventures work with already-existing banks. This can entail configuring systems for direct Bitcoin account-to-bank account transfers. Initiatives may gain credibility and legitimacy by following regulatory criteria, which helps them integrate with conventional financial institutions and therefore build user confidence; they can make consumers more familiar with traditional banking by connecting with established financial infrastructures. This broadens the user base to include companies and less tech-savvy individuals compared to typical crypto enthusiasts. This integration can also be crucial for financial inclusion, as it lets individuals in areas without access to conventional banks engage in the worldwide economy via digital means.

Digital assets must be converted into fiat money if they are to be used in the real-world economy, in which case fiat is still the main transaction medium. This lets people and companies make daily expenses, investments, or savings out of their digital income. For companies, operations like salary payments, material purchases, and other running costs depend on their capacity to translate digital assets into fiat money.

The volatility in the crypto market is well known. Encouragement of the conversion to fiat helps people and companies protect themselves against changes in the crypto market. By not having all cash locked in cryptocurrencies, integration with standard banking lets one further diversify assets and lower financial risk. ReFi initiatives combined with conventional banking systems are a major step toward increasing the accessibility and usefulness of digital finance. It converts Bitcoin profits into generally usable fiat money, therefore enabling the movement of money between the digital and physical worlds. The projects' practical value in the real-world economy improves their appeal and accessibility as well as their attractiveness, therefore strengthening the inclusive financial ecosystem.

Transforming Trade Finance for Sustainability, Inclusion, and Economic Resilience: The Emergence of ReFi

Particularly with relation to small and medium-sized businesses (SMEs), the combination of digital assets derived from the real world via ReFi concepts has enormous promise in the always-changing terrain of trade and finance. Along with modernizing trade finance, this innovative synergy closes the trade finance gap and promotes resilience and inclusion in the global economic context.

ReFi is the set of financial tools and strategies meant to promote sustainability and regeneration while simultaneously improving the environment, society, and economy. It stresses developing financial systems that benefit society, the environment, and local communities overall, unlike conventional finance, which sometimes concentrates mostly on producing income. It considers the wider consequences of financial activities on social justice, environmental health, and community resilience, thereby matching financial actions with principles that support long-term sustainability. The development of inclusive financial institutions that support community-owned enterprises, advance economic justice, strengthen regional economies, and provide financial resources to poor or disenfranchised populations is central to this idea.

ReFi supports activities that reduce negative environmental effects and, if feasible, help to restore ecosystems as it understands the interdependence between economic systems and the surroundings. It also helps microbusinesses, social entrepreneurs, and sustainable agriculture, thereby empowering communities and advancing strong, self-sustaining economies. It also questions short-term profit-maximizing tactics that may aggravate social inequity and environmental damage by emphasizing long-term, sustainable value creation that transcends simple financial benefits.

ReFi depends on cooperation among several stakeholders—including financial institutions, companies, communities, and legislators—if it is to reach its objectives. Establishing alliances lets resources and knowledge be pooled to handle difficult issues, therefore converting the financial services industry from one that creates problems to one that actively promotes positive change. Its financial operations are in line with sustainability, resilience, and regeneration, thereby honoring the reciprocal reliance of social, economic, and environmental systems.

This paradigm shift marks a basic change in the interaction of finance with society and the surroundings. For trade finance companies, combining digital assets with physical objects opens fresh prospects. Tokenizing real-world assets (RWA), like items, stocks, or industrial facilities, helps SMEs get liquidity and creates new development and expansion chances. Emphasizing long-term viability, diversity and inclusion, and the restoration of both economic and environmental value, this strategy marks a significant change in the financial scene. By supporting environmental and social initiatives in addition to trade, it seeks to change the accepted financial model.

ReFi emphasizes investments that have favorable effects on environmental, social, and governance (ESG) aspects and concentrates on incorporating sustainable practices into trade financing. Funding programs that support ethical supply chains, sustainable initiatives, and renewable energy sources go under this heading as well. The concept revolves around encouraging inclusion and elevating communities, thus providing chances for underprivileged groups to guarantee that the advantages of trade financing projects cover a wider spectrum of society and so lower inequality.

ReFi encourages investments that provide quantifiable social and environmental benefits alongside financial returns, unlike conventional trade financing, therefore attaining long-term positive consequences. This means helping projects aiming at the well-being of the next generations. It also supports the creation of creative financial mechanisms associated with the ideas of the circular economy, green bonds, and impact investment funds that promote sustainability goals.

Keystones of this strategy include responsibility for reaching sustainability goals and openness in investing methods. Companies and financial institutions have to show and evaluate the results of their investments, therefore promoting responsibility and confidence. In this regard, coordination among several stakeholders—corporations, governments, financial institutions, and NGOs—is essential to maximize the favorable effects of trade financing projects while generating significant changes.

Since it offers financial goals together with social and environmental responsibilities, it clearly marks a major development in the trade financing sector. It presents trade finance as a means of tackling important issues and thus aiding economic growth and promoting positive global developments. As this idea gains momentum, it has the potential to significantly impact the financial industry and foster a more equitable and responsible global economy. ReFi is not only a tool for reaching more general social and environmental goals but also a means of economic development, therefore redefining the financial terrain. Definitely, it can help build a strong and vibrant worldwide economy that benefits all participants by encouraging sustainable behaviors and equitable growth.

A Way Ahead for Being Inclusive: The Promise of Digital Assets to Mitigate Trade and Supply Chain Finance Inequalities

The combination of digital assets with theories of ReFi presents a fresh paradigm in trade finance, therefore greatly increasing capital availability. Beyond the simple accumulation of money, this development aims to build an inclusive financial environment that lets smaller businesses flourish and significantly influence world commerce.

Fundamentally, ReFi alters how money engages with its environment and society. It prioritizes sustainability and regeneration, focusing on benefits for the economy, society, and environment. It also stresses building financial systems that benefit the larger community, environment, and local businesses, unlike conventional finance, which frequently gives income-generating first priority. This strategy supports regional enterprises, community-owned companies, and inclusive financial institutions that advance economic justice, therefore helping underprivileged populations by means of financial resources. companies, and

Its junction with digital assets has the power to close the trade financing gap and create SMEs' chances, revolutionizing trade finance. By addressing trade finance disparities, this special synergy may guarantee equitable involvement in world trade and advance global economic growth. Using current technologies, including blockchain, digital platforms, and electronic records, several paths and techniques may be followed to promote inclusiveness in trade financing. Smaller companies that might lack the means for conventional, paper-based transactions will find these solutions to simplify processes and improve access and efficiency.

CHAPTER 17 THRIVING TOGETHER: A REGENERATIVE POWER FOR SMALL AND MIGHTY BUSINESSES

Realizing this objective depends on teaching underprivileged communities and SMEs about trade financing prospects. Developing a deeper understanding of these instruments is crucial for effectively managing risks and promoting fair competition. Moreover, it is essential to develop creative financial plans and risk-reducing initiatives catered to the particular requirements of smaller companies or areas. These techniques might call for customized financial services meant to fit various risk profiles, credit upgrades, or risk-sharing agreements.

To assist SMEs in obtaining trade credit, governments, financial institutions, and international organizations must work together. By unifying laws and documentation requirements across countries, public–private partnerships can offer guarantees or credit enhancements, hence lowering entrance barriers and streamlining trade finance systems. Policies and procedures for standardizing help to improve accessibility for all those engaged.

Just as crucial is funding technical support and capacity-building projects, which provide companies in underdeveloped countries with the tools they need to participate in worldwide commerce. Technology-based education in financial literacy, global standards adherence, and technology use will equip these companies to engage more successfully in worldwide marketplaces.

Smaller businesses can also control working capital and reduce working capital restrictions by looking at alternative financial solutions such as factoring, invoice discounting, and supply chain financing. Including social and environmental factors in trade finance systems promotes ethical and sustainable business practices, therefore drawing in investors and creating new business prospects for those following ESG policies.

Improved information availability and openness in trade finance procedures help to develop confidence among trade finance users, especially for those just starting their international trading. Promoting policies that encourage inclusive trade finance by corporate groupings, financial institutions, and government agencies can help increase the efficacy of these activities by encouraging advocacy efforts.

By using these approaches, trade finance's scope of inclusion may be expanded, therefore creating potential economic growth for every participant, regardless of their financial situation or location. Maintaining a more fair trade finance environment depends on constant innovation and adaptability to changing market dynamics, technological developments, and worldwide trade rules.

CHAPTER 17   THRIVING TOGETHER: A REGENERATIVE POWER FOR SMALL AND MIGHTY BUSINESSES

Digital assets are a major help to this change. These assets—which comprise digital currencies and other electronic resources—are becoming more and more important for their capacity to close the trade finance gap. Smaller players can participate in the trade finance sector and utilize their real assets to acquire working capital and grow their companies by allowing fractional ownership via the tokenization of actual assets.

The unique qualities of digital assets make them desirable in trade finance. Their immaterial character makes it simple to move or exchange them via electronic systems, therefore facilitating quick international transactions. Once recorded, blockchain-based digital assets are distributed and unchangeable, therefore offering a high degree of security and openness. This guarantees ownership rights' integrity and financial transaction honesty.

Digital assets tokenize once-illiquid assets, including invoices or bills of lading, therefore increasing their accessibility and liquidity. This procedure releases cash, therefore opening fresh investment opportunities to a larger spectrum of players. The underlying blockchain technology guarantees a visible and unchangeable record, therefore lowering the fraud risk and giving all those engaged real-time information access. This openness fosters greater confidence in the trade finance system.

Moreover, digital resources simplify cross-border transactions, removing geographical restrictions and promoting global trade inclusiveness. By means of less paperwork and manual procedures, their implementation in trade finance results in significant cost savings, therefore lowering administrative expenditures and removing the need for middlemen.

The growing popularity of digital assets stimulates trade finance industry innovation, which results in the development of fresh financial goods and services to meet the changing demands of companies. These assets provide adaptable, contemporary answers to long-standing trade finance problems, improving accessibility, speeding procedures, reducing risk, and thus promoting a more open and effective trading environment. Digital assets have the ability to revolutionize corporate behavior and trade transaction finance as they become more widely accepted, therefore fostering a more linked, flexible, and inclusive global trading environment.

 The combination of digital assets and ReFi theories presents a unique opportunity to revolutionize trade finance. This strategy supports economic development by means of sustainability, inclusiveness, and long-term value generation, thereby addressing important worldwide issues. As it gains momentum, this idea has the potential to significantly transform the financial landscape, thereby fostering a more equitable and responsible global economy.

CHAPTER 17   THRIVING TOGETHER: A REGENERATIVE POWER FOR SMALL AND MIGHTY BUSINESSES

Navigating the Headwinds: The Complex Challenges Facing ReFi

Pioneers and innovators in the growing field of ReFi must negotiate a terrain full of complexity and obstacles. Many difficult questions surface when they try to combine sustainable environmental practices with distributed finance. These obstacles are firmly ingrained in the socioeconomic and cultural fabric driving the movement, not only technological ones. This chapter explores the main challenges as noted by important participants, therefore clarifying both internal and external elements that can compromise the admirable goals of the project.

Regulatory ambiguity presents one of its most major obstacles. For many governments throughout the globe, the integration of blockchain technology and distributed finance into conventional financial systems still leaves a grey area. Often leading to a fragmented and inconsistent regulatory scene, governments, and regulatory organizations are still figuring out the ramifications of these technologies. Projects find a difficult environment created by this ambiguity since they have to negotiate multiple legal frameworks and compliance requirements throughout many countries. Its development and acceptance may be hampered by the absence of explicit policies and established standards since companies and investors can be unwilling to participate in marketplaces where the laws are unclear or subject to rapid changes.

Blockchain networks' technical dependability and scalability present still another important obstacle. Blockchain technology has many benefits, although it is not without restrictions. The broad acceptance of ReFi may be seriously hampered by problems including network congestion, costly transaction fees, and energy usage. Handling the rising transaction volume as the market expands depends on blockchain solutions being scalable. Blockchain networks' security is also absolutely crucial to stop fraud and hacking. Investing in strong and safe technological infrastructure is crucial since technical problems or security breaches may erode confidence in systems and compromise their legitimacy.

Two major challenges are also market adoption and stakeholder education. The ideas of distributed finance and regenerative economics may not be known to many stakeholders—including companies, investors, and the general public. Greater acceptance depends on these players learning the advantages and their mechanics.

Still, this educational initiative calls for smart communication as well as large resources. Building trust and proving the clear advantages of projects helps one to overcome doubt and opposition to change. Deeper knowledge of this "discipline" will help stakeholders to be more at ease with the creative ideas and technologies supporting the movement.

In the realm of distributed finance, liquidity issues and price volatility provide natural difficulties. Digital assets—including tokenized carbon credits—have considerable volatility depending on things like market speculation, changes in regulations, and the economic situation. Investors and companies depending on consistent asset prices for planning and budgeting may find this volatility dangerous. Furthermore, even if tokenization seeks to increase liquidity, markets might not reach enough depth and maturity to guarantee seamless trade and price stability. Stabilizing prices and improving market liquidity calls for strong risk management techniques and systems to control these hazards.

Important problems that must be addressed if systems are to be seamlessly integrated are standardizing and interoperability. The absence of shared criteria could result in market fragmentation and ineffective policies. Enabling interoperability between several blockchain systems and guaranteeing that tokenized assets may be readily traded and transferred depend on the industry-wide standards and protocols being developed and adopted. To build a coherent and integrated market, this standardizing endeavor calls for cooperation among industry players, authorities, and standard-setting organizations.

Though they remain difficult to reach, trust and openness are fundamental for success. The first priority is making sure the fundamental social and ecological credits are genuine and faithfully expressed in digital tokens. Maintaining ReFi programs' integrity depends on strong auditing and verification systems being established. Stakeholders' confidence is developed via openness in the tokenization process, including thorough disclosures on the environmental impact and credit verification. Systems can build more market confidence and involvement by upholding strong norms of integrity and openness.

Its adoption and success are much influenced by socioeconomic and cultural elements as well as by financial ones. Deeply ingrained traditional financial institutions and economic policies call for a cultural change as one moves toward it. This metamorphosis entails shifting attitudes and practices to inspire participants to give long-term social and environmental benefits top priority over transient financial gain. The inclusivity and reach of projects can also be affected by socioeconomic differences and technological access. A more fair and inclusive financial system depends on solutions being available to underprivileged populations and removing socioeconomic obstacles.

Notwithstanding these obstacles, ReFi has great potential to propel favorable socio-ecological impact. Overcoming these challenges calls for a multifarious strategy including legal clarity, technical innovation, stakeholder education, risk management, standardizing, and cultural change. To solve these issues and fully utilize them, cooperation among industry players, legislators, and the larger society is absolutely vital.

Ultimately, negotiating the obstacles confronting ReFi calls for addressing a multifarious range of difficulties across regulatory, technical, market, and sociopolitical spheres. By means of proactive removal of these challenges, stakeholders can foster a climate conducive to efforts to flourish. Though the path to a regenerative financial system is difficult, the benefits—a fair and sustainable future—are well worth the work. It shows the promise of finance to propel significant and long-lasting change in the face of global problems as it develops and matures, providing an optimistic and forceful road forward.

Establishing Standards and Safeguarding Integrity in Decentralized Climate Action

The drive toward distributed systems in the fast-changing terrain of ReFi offers both amazing possibilities and major obstacles. The pressing necessity to create strong industry standards and defensive policies against possible rogue actors drives most of these difficulties. This need results from the intrinsic character of distributed, permissionless systems that, while encouraging creativity and inclusiveness, also let abuse and manipulation get through.

One cannot stress enough the critical role standards play in ReFi, as they foster confidence and functionality in every technology environment, not just operational needs. In this new context, where the aim is to encourage climate-positive projects, the lack of consistent standards could lead to duplication of efforts—such as in the case of carbon credit reporting—and maybe compromise the main advantages of the technology. Establishing industry standards guarantees that several projects and uses not only coexist but also cooperate toward shared environmental goals. These guidelines help to ensure interoperability, therefore facilitating smooth integration and cooperation among several projects. They also give a structure for confirming the validity and efficiency of climate policies, therefore building confidence among participants and guaranteeing that initiatives really help to ensure environmental sustainability.

However, the permissionless nature of blockchain technology presents both advantages and disadvantages. It lets anyone produce and innovate without asking previous permission. therefore promoting rapid diversification and expansion of the market. This transparency speeds up invention and distributes financial tools and opportunity access.

Still, this independence also renders the system open for exploitation. For instance, initiatives such as the tokenization of seaweed as carbon credits have the potential to emerge beyond the conventional understanding of carbon markets. This emphasizes the crucial requirement of interoperability standards among several blockchain systems to avoid problems like the duplication of carbon credits, thereby guaranteeing that a credit sold on one blockchain isn't fraudulently sold on another. Establishing these criteria will call for coordinated efforts among industry leaders, technologists, and authorities to create norms that preserve the integrity of this ecosystem while maintaining its inventive potential.

Complicating the scene even more are difficulties with data coordination and openness. Blockchain's decentralizing of data presents major difficulties for scaling and controlling the enormous volumes of climate data needed for successful action. For grassroots programs, traditional infrastructure for climate data is frequently unaffordable and inaccessible.

Blockchain technology could democratize this information so that more people may access it and hence influence the outcomes. Its requirement for a re-architected, strong data infrastructure becomes clear, though, as it enters storing vast amounts of data, including soil moisture levels and rainfall records. Without this, the promise of distributed data could not be able to propel significant climate action as it deserves. A project's success depends on data integrity, accuracy, and accessibility; hence, modern data management methods and cooperation with climate scientific and technology specialists will be absolutely vital.

Another crucial chore for this group is cutting through the hoopla over blockchain and its uses in climate action. Sometimes the practical reality of using such technologies is subordinated to the thrill created by the promise of creative solutions. Not all blockchain-based initiatives significantly help to slow down global warming. For individuals in this community, it becomes imperative to evaluate and separate between what actually helps the environment and what might be only technological hope. This requires a comprehensive assessment of project concepts, focusing on tangible outcomes and quantifiable impact. This movement has two goals: it promotes innovation while upholding a strict criterion of review to stop the spread of useless or maybe dangerous initiatives. Its community can make sure its efforts are focused on significant and effective climate solutions by establishing high standards and supporting a culture of critical evaluation.

Not only a technological need but also a fundamental need that will define the integrity and efficacy of climate action projects is the development of industry standards and processes to prevent undesirable actors in this area. By means of well-defined procedures and cooperative network building across projects, ReFi can use the special advantages of blockchain technology while minimizing its natural hazards. The movement's sustainable expansion as well as its impact on world climate targets depend on this careful balance between invention and control. The development of strong governance systems and regulatory frameworks will be crucial in determining the course of this ecosystem and guaranteeing its alignment with more general environmental and social objectives as it grows.

Ultimately, although there are many difficulties on the path toward a regenerative financial system using distributed technologies, there is plenty of possibilities. Its success depends on industry standards being established, efficient data management, critical project review, and strong government. By confronting these issues head-on, the community can build a strong and reliable ecosystem that not only promises environmental regeneration but also runs sustainably inside its larger socioeconomic setting. ReFi's future relies on our collective capacity to negotiate this complexity and leverage technologically transforming potential for the benefit of all. It may propel significant advancement toward a sustainable and fair future by means of cooperation, creativity, and unwavering integrity and commitment.

Bridging Technological Gaps: Enhancing User-Friendly Interfaces

The rapid development of ReFi offers blockchain technology transforming chances for climate action. Still, the complexity of its user interfaces poses a major obstacle to its general acceptability and efficiency. The ecosystem makes clear the need for interfaces that serve not just tech-savvy people but also a larger audience, including farmers, scientists, and local communities. The success of projects depends on this inclusion since it directly affects the capacity of several players to engage properly in these creative financial systems.

Blockchain and Web3 technologies' present scene sometimes shows interfaces that demand a substantial degree of technical knowledge. Those outside the usual tech demographic, especially those engaged in environmental management and climate action who might not have the same degree of comfort with digital tools, can find this alienating. Crucially, interfaces that mirror more known systems—such as conventional Geographic Information System (GIS) software applied in environmental research and urban planning—are demanded. Professionals from conventional industries would find it simpler to grasp and apply these new technologies if they were familiar with innovative platforms, therefore facilitating their shift.

Integration of community members into the space depends critically on efficient onboarding systems. For example, the seamless integration of forest initiatives onto the NEAR platform shows how powerful well-considered user interfaces can be to enable more general adoption. When onboarding is flawless, consumers may concentrate on the advantages instead of the system's complexity since it lessens the friction related to using new technology. Moreover, teaching consumers about the advantages and workings of blockchain initiatives would help them to be much more involved. Projects can enable users to overcome the first technological obstacles by offering clear, intelligible information, therefore encouraging ownership and competence.

Even though blockchain offers unique capabilities for managing climate data and facilitating carbon credit exchanges, its complexity can have drawbacks. Still, a major obstacle is the digital divide, whereby lack of access to digital tools can prevent important populations from engaging. In areas where digital infrastructure is limited yet climate action is most desperately needed, this exclusion is especially troublesome. Furthermore, the natural complexity of blockchain can discourage non-technical users, hence supporting current disparities in information access and technology capability. Dealing with this difficulty calls for a team effort to streamline user interfaces and enable a varied audience to access them.

Projects must prioritize creating interfaces that, regardless of technical experience, are not only effective but also understandable for every user going ahead. This calls for iterative design approaches, constant user input, and a dedication to instructional outreach. By means of user needs and pain spots, one can guide the design of user-friendly input and successful interfaces. Furthermore, iterative design techniques, including user input, help to guarantee that interfaces develop to satisfy the needs of users.

Bracing the technology divide also depends on a dedication to educational outreach. Offering online resources, seminars, and training courses will enable consumers to acquire the knowledge and abilities required to traverse systems. Demystifying blockchain technology and increasing accessibility will enable more people to engage in projects, therefore empowering educational campaigns. This can therefore improve the impact and reach of projects, thereby ensuring a more fair distribution of their advantages.

Not only are simplifying interfaces and improving user education beneficial steps toward reaching the broad acceptance and effect the community envisions. ReFi's capacity to be inclusively available will determine its success. It can democratize financing for climate action by tackling the technological complexity and making blockchain technology user-friendly, thereby allowing many stakeholders to participate in and gain from this creative financial system.

The movement's capacity to involve a broad spectrum of people will determine whether or not it can propel significant climate action and advance sustainability as it expands. Unlocking this potential will mostly depend on the creation of user-friendly interfaces together with strong educational outreach. Making ReFi available to anyone will help us use blockchain technology to build a more fair and sustainable future.

Navigating Dual Worlds: Integrating Crypto and Non-Crypto Audiences in ReFi

The sector is particularly situated at the intersection of DeFi and climate governance, confronted with the challenging task of uniting two distinct communities: crypto enthusiasts and traditional climate activists. For ReFi, which seeks to use blockchain technology to affect real-world ecological improvements rather than only technological innovations, this paradox presents a special set of potential and obstacles.

It is impossible to overstate the cultural and technological gap separating these populations. On one side, heavily ingrained in the Web3 culture, crypto aficionados are familiar with ideas including the metaverse and non-fungible tokens (NFTs.). Within the crypto world, these digital developments are considered fresh and full of possibilities. Conversely, conventional climate experts like scientists and city designers sometimes see new technologies with mistrust. For many, the avant-garde character of blockchain can seem more like a diversion than a useful tool for climate action. This difference emphasizes the need for programs to concentrate on concrete, real-world value, thereby making sure that technical solutions immediately help to guarantee environmental advantages.

Crucially, we must create a varied community bridging this divide. This entails building a foundation covering people from traditional sectors of climate action as well as crypto-savvy people. New projects can use a broad spectrum of knowledge to create significant change by including professionals including climate scientists, engineers, and data analysts who might be unfamiliar with blockchain. Harmonizing these many points of view into a coherent group with a shared objective of improving climate action is a difficulty. This calls for a culture of mutual respect and education whereby many points of view are appreciated and included in the more general goal.

The integration depends much on communication and engagement techniques. Dealing with so many groups effectively calls for customized strategies. Companies sometimes interact with every target category using distinct platforms and designs. The crypto community might, for example, meet on Discord and Twitter, adopting a laid-back, jargon-heavy vocabulary that speaks to its tech-savvy members. On the other hand, contacts with traditional companies and corporate clients could happen across more official channels like LinkedIn, emphasizing analytics, updates, and professional conversation.

Writing messages that are relevant and easily available for every group helps close the technological and cultural gaps and promotes more cooperation. Furthermore, posing special difficulties is the function of anonymity and openness. Transparency becomes absolutely vital in the distributed world of blockchain, where anonymity can be the rule while handling climate governance. In the climate space, stakeholders may demand a certain degree of transparency on who is behind a project, their goals, and their approaches. Effective climate action depends critically on trust, which this openness helps create. On the other hand, the inclination for anonymity in DeFi circles can occasionally contradict these expectations; hence, a careful balance is needed to keep credibility and confidence among all user bases. Projects have to negotiate this conflict by making sure they satisfy the demands of climate governance stakeholders while still respecting the privacy and autonomy of their participants with enough openness.

Emphasizing successful case studies where blockchain technology has directly led to observable environmental results is one way to help bridge these two realms. ReFi can show conventional climate community critics the practical advantages of blockchain technology by highlighting initiatives that have efficiently applied it for climate action. By means of this evidence-based approach, misunderstandings may be dispelled and support for blockchain projects inside the environmental sector can be developed.

Furthermore, improving the legitimacy and impact of initiatives is encouraging cooperation between crypto innovators and conventional climate groups. Strong synergies can result from cooperation combining the scientific rigor of climate experts with the technical knowledge of the crypto community. These alliances can help to guarantee that blockchain solutions are built on solid environmental research and intended to efficiently solve practical problems. Working together, these many groups may use their strengths to propel significant climate action.

Future development depends on addressing these inherent difficulties of connecting two quite distinct populations. Success in this effort would not only guarantee that climate-related blockchain projects are inclusive, fair, and in line with more general objectives of global sustainability but also improve the efficacy of those activities. ReFi offers a hopeful route to handle the pressing issues of our day by combining the creative pace of cryptocurrency with the strict demands of climate action.

Ultimately, negotiating the two worlds of crypto and non-crypto viewers in the calls for a multifarious strategy that meets technological, cultural, and communication issues. ReFi can close the divide between these two groups by creating a varied community, using customized communication techniques, striking a mix between anonymity and openness, and supporting cross-sector alliances. Not only is programs' success dependent on this integration, but it also helps to further world sustainability goals. Its capacity to harmonize these several points of view will be essential as it develops in order to propel significant and inclusive climate action.

Navigating Labor Dynamics and Balancing Governance Models for Sustainable Climate Action

The labor dynamics inside the community draw attention to both the commitment and the difficulties experienced by people working at the nexus of blockchain technology and climate action. The expectations placed on employees are strong and varied, representing a special mix of enthusiasm, dedication, and complexity as they try to combine creative financial mechanisms with tangible environmental impact.

CHAPTER 17   THRIVING TOGETHER: A REGENERATIVE POWER FOR SMALL AND MIGHTY BUSINESSES

Many of the participants in the growing community are closely entwined with their jobs and sometimes handle several tasks across several projects. This situation is especially common among people who work entirely in the industry. These people show a high degree of dedication and the fluid character of work in this profession since they regularly participate in extra-voluntary roles or handle responsibilities across several projects. The variety of jobs and the necessity to balance several obligations draw attention to the dynamic and always-changing character of this environment, in which creativity and adaptation are first priorities.

Programs allow some people part-time involvement that requires juggling several jobs. People who try to fulfill the expectations of their roles while juggling other professional obligations may find beneficial stress and extended work hours resulting from this setup. The outstanding dedication needed sometimes goes beyond regular full-time hours, reflecting the enthusiasm and dedication common in society but also drawing attention to possible sustainability problems related to personal well-being and work-life balance. Sometimes the substantial degree of participation blurs the boundaries between personal and professional life, which causes burnout and tiredness among participants.

One should give considerable attention to the sustainability of such working methods. Participants worry about the long-term feasibility of committing significant hours without enough personal rejuvenation. The distributed ethos of the blockchain community, which values freedom and adaptability, stands quite different from the strong centralization of responsibility observed in many projects. Particularly if important people experience burnout or are otherwise unable to carry on their responsibilities, this centralizing might provide serious hazards. The substantial dependence on a small number of committed people makes the whole system prone to disturbances; hence, labor practices must be reviewed to guarantee long-term sustainability and resilience.

Especially in governance and project management, initiatives may show a mix of distributed goals and centralized reality despite the dispersed ideal promoted by many in the blockchain community. The conflict among these models reflects a larger industrial challenge: juggling the ideological commitment to decentralization with the need for leadership and direction. Many projects thus aim for more distributed governance structures, but the road is complicated and full of difficulties with regard to coordination, openness, and efficiency. Establishing successful distributed governance calls for thorough preparation, open communication, and strong systems for responsibility and decision-making.

One of the special features of working for ReFi is the vital need of human relationships in preserving project integrity and continuity. Though they can also cause weaknesses, the personal links between project leaders and team members typically help to sustain efforts. Should important people go or fail to perform their jobs, whole projects—and maybe more general ecosystem segments—may fall apart. This makes the continuous attempt to distribute not just a strategic objective but also an essential progression for sustainability. The long-term success of projects depends on building a strong and distributed workforce free from excessive reliance on any one person.

High participation, substantial personal effort, and the continuous difficulty of juggling creative decentralization with efficient administration and governance define the labor demands inside the community. The health and durability of the larger movement as well as the success of individual initiatives depend on these dynamics. Dealing with personnel issues will be essential to fully realize the sector and propel significant climate action as it expands and changes.

Navigating employment dynamics requires balancing centralized and distributed governance approaches, fulfilling participant's high demands, and promoting sustainable labor practices overall. Focusing on these areas will help the community build a more strong, inclusive, and efficient movement using blockchain technology's advantages to further world sustainability targets. The future depends on its capacity to change and grow such that the enthusiastic people behind this movement are enabled to carry on their important work.

Governance Challenges in the ReFi Landscape: Balancing Decentralization, Community Participation, and Effective Management

Governance is a complex responsibility, especially considering the distributed attitude of blockchain technologies against the needs for efficient community and project management. It involves running operations, and ensuring ethical alignment, openness, and participation—all of which are essential to project survival. Maintaining distributed values and attaining effective and open management simultaneously produces a complex governance scene that calls for cautious navigation.

CHAPTER 17   THRIVING TOGETHER: A REGENERATIVE POWER FOR SMALL AND MIGHTY BUSINESSES

ReFi uses a range of digital tools to oversee governance systems and community contacts. The main means of communication are well-known sites like Discord and Telegram, which help everyday operations, community debates, and decision-making procedures to be conducted. These instruments help participants to feel immediacy and involvement as well as to communicate in real time. The difficulty, then, is controlling the "digital noise" that can overwhelm participants and hence compromise the quality of involvement and decision-making. The continuous flow of data might make it challenging to give important talks top priority and guarantee that every voice is heard. In this sense, effective governance calls on striking a balance between open communication and methodical decision-making procedures that may condense insightful knowledge from the chorus of opinions.

Many projects center on developing a distributed governance architecture that stands sharply apart from conventional centralized management systems. Still, this change is difficult and full of obstacles. Usually starting with a centralized method under the direction of a small number of founders or leaders, projects progressively move toward more dispersed governance structures like decentralized autonomous organizations (DAOs). This change calls for both meticulous preparation and the implementation of mechanisms enabling increasing decentralization. While eventual decentralization empowers the community to take on governance roles, assuring its lifetime and consistency with its decentralized spirit, initial centralization gives the direction and stability needed to create the project.

Many groups use what is sometimes known as an "exit to community" or "exit to DAO." Starting with a more centralized governance structure and progressively decentralizing as the project develops and the community becomes stronger and more engaged, this approach ensures stability in the early stages while gradually transferring decision-making power to stakeholders. This phased model allows for structured growth, increased participation, and sustainable governance evolution. For instance, members of the community could get governance tokens with voting rights and project future stakes in mind. Maintaining active and significant participation depends on these incentives matching the long-term objectives of the project.

From crypto aficionados to conventional climate campaigners, bridging the divide between many community sectors offers serious governance issues. Every group approaches the project in different ways and expects different things. Corporate partners could want formal communication and thorough reports, for example; the crypto community might interact more informally on social media sites like

CHAPTER 17   THRIVING TOGETHER: A REGENERATIVE POWER FOR SMALL AND MIGHTY BUSINESSES

Twitter or Discord. Dealing with these different expectations calls for sophisticated communication techniques and sometimes different participation tactics to properly serve every audience. Customizing messages to fit the demands and preferences of many stakeholders guarantees that every group feels important and informed, therefore strengthening the unity and cooperation in society.

Governance relies critically on addressing and dispersing power inside the ecosystem. The participation of large investors, or "whales," who can affect project paths more than that of lesser players aggravates this difficulty. Projects' legitimacy and ethical position depend on power dynamics not reflecting those of conventional financial systems. Structures of governance have to be made to guarantee openness and responsibility as well as to fairly distribute authority. Mechanisms like quadratic voting, in which the voting power of individuals is diluted according to the number of tokens they possess, help reduce the impact of big stakeholders and advance more democratic decision-making procedures.

At last, the capacity to adjust and meet both internal community requirements and outside regulatory and commercial forces determines the sustainability of governance systems rather directly. Lack of transparency, centralized risk, and poor stakeholder involvement can cause governance breakdowns endangering the whole project. Long-term sustainability calls for constant observation and improvement of governance structures, community feedback inclusion, and keeping tuned to changing legal environments. Governance systems ought to be strong and adaptable, ready to change with the project and its population.

Governance is not only about administrative control but also about creating a participative, open, fair environment fit for the dispersed and regenerative attitude of society. The constant improvement of governance models will be essential in overcoming natural obstacles and guaranteeing the long-term survival and influence of projects as this sector develops. Effective governance is about striking a balance between pragmatic management demands and decentralizing principles, thereby enabling communities while maintaining project integrity and sustainability. ReFi can negotiate its governance issues and fulfill its vision of a more fair and sustainable financial environment by means of deliberate design and continuous adaptation.

CHAPTER 17   THRIVING TOGETHER: A REGENERATIVE POWER FOR SMALL AND MIGHTY BUSINESSES

Navigating Market Dynamics, Competition, and Regulatory Challenges for Sustainable Success

Significant elements influencing the course of projects are market conditions and competition. These components sometimes define not only the feasibility but also the strategic orientation of projects in the distributed Web3 environment. Achieving long-term success and effect requires knowledge of and the ability to negotiate these factors as ReFi develops.

The success and durability of projects can be directly impacted by the natural volatility of the Bitcoin markets. Usually showing erratic variations in a short period, cryptocurrency values are quite volatile. This volatility in initiatives can cause delayed token releases, therefore affecting project schedules and investor confidence. When the token value of a project falls, it can compromise the financial resources meant for development and execution, erasing the faith of possible investors and stakeholders. Some projects overcome these obstacles by using their relationship to real-world assets, such as carbon credits, therefore preserving openness and confidence in spite of market volatility. This strategy offers a barrier against the volatility usually associated with digital assets lacking physical support. Projects can present a more consistent and reliable investment offer by linking digital tokens to quantifiable and verifiable environmental effects.

The rapid growth of the market presents both possibilities and problems. On the one hand, the arrival of fresh rivals can inspire creativity and enable improvement of products. Projects aiming at raising their technology, user interfaces, and general value propositions are motivated by competition. Significant field developments resulting from this competitive pressure will eventually help the larger ecosystem. Conversely, fierce competition might force already-existing projects to keep innovating or risk obsolescence under constant pressure. Strong rivals could compromise the market share of a project or expose flaws in technology applications or user experiences. For example, a project that falls behind user expectations or technical developments may rapidly lose relevance and cause lower user involvement and investment.

A specific difficulty for public initiatives is the creation of private blockchain solutions, usually supported by established financial institutions like banks. Conventional companies cautious of the openness and decentralization of the public blockchain may find the more regulated environments these projects provide appealing. Many conventional companies look for—security, regulatory compliance, and predictability—which private blockchains may offer. The ability of private blockchains to apply strict policies and interfaces catered to conventional business could make them direct rivals to public initiatives, therefore endangering the acceptance and expansion of the latter. The appeal of private blockchains is their capacity to provide familiar operational models inside the new digital environment, which may deflect interest from public projects.

Maintaining a balance between openness and transparency while developing sufficiently to keep ahead of private rivals is one of the fundamental issues within the community. ReFi runs a genuine risk of replicating the conventional centralized systems it seeks to transform, complete with intermediaries and opaque activities that might compromise the basic ideas of decentralization and openness as it is sold. Projects aiming to uphold their values must constantly show the value of openness and decentralization as well as their effectiveness in producing social and environmental impact. This entails not only technical innovation but also strong community involvement and education, therefore guaranteeing that progress stays anchored on its guiding ideas.

Apart from fluctuations in the internal market, outside regulatory surroundings are quite important. The legal environment around blockchain technology and cryptocurrencies is still changing; hence, government measures could either provide major restrictions or help ReFi projects expand. Good rules help investors to be clear and secure, thereby motivating more involvement in projects. On the other hand, tight rules can impede the growth and acceptance of relevant technologies, therefore reducing their possible influence. Further complexity arises from the connection between new projects and legacy carbon market registries since regulatory criteria and compliance concerns apply. Initiatives should match current environmental rules; hence, it is important to advocate policies that foster innovation while also ensuring that they complement current environmental laws by means of constant communication with authorities and legislators.

Projects in this field must carefully negotiate these complex issues as competition within the industry changes and the space gets more crowded. The ongoing success and effect of projects in the larger scene of climate action and sustainable finance will depend on finding the proper mix between innovation, openness, regulatory compliance, and competitive positioning. This calls for a systematic strategy that takes into account the several requirements and expectations of stakeholders, the erratic character of digital markets, and the regulatory systems controlling both financial and environmental sectors.

Negotiating market dynamics and competitiveness in the environment calls for a sophisticated interaction of elements that shapes project operational success and strategic orientation. Projects can position themselves for long-term success by knowing these dynamics and aggressively tackling the issues they present, therefore promoting significant climate action and helping to create a more sustainable financial environment. The ability to adapt, innovate, and keep its dedication to openness and decentralization will determine its future and help to make sure it stays a potent tool for positive change in the world.

Navigating the Regulatory Terrain of ReFi: Balancing Innovation with Legal Compliance

For this new "industry," regulatory action presents one of the most important opportunities as well as a problem. This issue results not only from official agencies but also from legacy climate groups with significant impact in the field of environment. The operational and strategic frameworks of projects are shaped by their dynamic interaction with conventional regulatory bodies, therefore influencing their capacity to innovate and apply fresh ideas successfully.

The choice of the carbon offset registry Verra to forbid the tokenizing of carbon credits is one clear case of regulatory influence. Verra's position is that, particularly as retired credits should be permanently removed from circulation, not tokenized; tokenization may cause confusion in the voluntary carbon market. This choice adversely affected initiatives depending on tokenizing carbon credits, changing revenue models, and pushing projects to review their plans. Tokenizing carbon credits was considered as a means of increasing carbon market openness and accessibility, therefore facilitating simpler tracking and trading of these credits. Verra's ban brought attention to the conflict between creative blockchain ideas and the conventional systems meant to guarantee the integrity of carbon credits.

Developing confidence inside the conventional voluntary carbon market still presents a difficult task. Projects may not advance or be accepted until older authorities slowly adjust to blockchain technologies. Many conventional environmental groups and legislators are wary of implementing new technology they believe to be untested or may be detrimental to accepted wisdom. Recent events, however, point to increasing transparency among conventional authorities like Verra and Gold Standard to interact with the ecosystem. Though sluggish, this participation includes public comment times meant to help understand how to combine blockchain technologies with conventional carbon credit systems. Though much more research is needed to close the gap between old and new systems, these actions imply a readiness to investigate how blockchain can improve the efficiency and dependability of carbon markets.

Another major danger is the possibility for regulatory authorities to enforce requirements, including know your customer (KYC) checks on tokenization techniques. Such criteria could be quite different from the distributed ethos of blockchain and Web3, therefore possibly impeding innovation and acceptance in the domain. Decentralization's values of privacy, autonomy, and less reliance on middlemen help. Although meant to prevent fraud and guarantee legal compliance, KYC criteria seem to contradict these values. This regulatory conflict emphasizes the need for initiatives to negotiate a careful balance between following legal criteria and preserving the fundamental characteristics of decentralization that appeal to many participants in the blockchain ecosystem.

Additionally, crucial in determining the regulatory environment are governmental agencies. American government initiatives to grasp the interaction between blockchain technologies and climate action, for instance, show a proactive strategy to include these technologies in more general climate measures. For ReFi initiatives, such government interest can present both possibilities and difficulties. Supporting rules can, on the one hand, give clarity and inspire investment in blockchain-based climate solutions. Conversely, tight rules could restrict the extent of initiatives and force them to negotiate a convoluted web of legal limitations. The US government's involvement in blockchain technology for climate action shows a greater awareness of the possibility of digital developments to improve environmental management. Initiatives can influence policy formation and argue for frameworks that foster innovation while assuring responsibility and efficacy by means of their participation in these regulatory conversations.

Regulatory activities present chances for legitimizing and integrating projects inside existing financial and environmental systems, even while they also impose constraints and problems. Projects can become more credible and accepted among stakeholders who might otherwise be dubious of new technologies by means of regulatory interaction. They can develop trust and encourage more general acceptance by proving compliance with legal criteria and highlighting the clear advantages of their solutions. Navigating this terrain successfully calls for projects to promote strategic engagement with both governmental and conventional climate regulating authorities, as well as thorough knowledge, cooperation, and engagement in policy debates, which will help to guarantee that the community's views are reflected and help to create favorable regulatory surroundings.

CHAPTER 17   THRIVING TOGETHER: A REGENERATIVE POWER FOR SMALL AND MIGHTY BUSINESSES

The future rests much on how closely it can match, influence, and adjust to the legal systems controlling environmental and financial markets. Projects aim to innovate ethically within the global climate action framework, so building strong relationships with regulatory authorities and proving the efficacy and dependability of blockchain solutions will be absolutely vital. They can open the path for significant influence and sustainable development by aggressively interacting with authorities and helping to create supporting policies. Navigating this regulatory terrain will be a continual effort requiring vigilance, flexibility, and a dedication to the values of openness, responsibility, and innovation underpinning the movement.

Ultimately, negotiating regulatory terrain requires knowing how intricately creative blockchain ideas interact with conventional legal systems. Ventures can overcome legal obstacles and realize their full potential by developing trust, interacting with authorities, and supporting laws that foster invention while guaranteeing responsibility. Success depends on its capacity to negotiate these legal minefields and create an atmosphere where blockchain technology might flourish and support world climate ambitions.

The Looming Shadow of Climate Change: Challenges and Resilience in ReFi

For the industry, climate change poses an existential threat and a major outside obstacle to success. Participants in the movement recognize that their efforts to mitigate or adjust to climate change may face overwhelming challenges, thereby creating a sense of urgency and complexity. This insight emphasizes how urgent and complicated their task is.

Projects are especially aware of the triple threat presented by the volatility of the voluntary carbon market, economic recessions resulting in increased deforestation for subsistence, and the accelerated effects of climate change, including widespread fires and famine, in the face of this enormous challenge. These difficulties are not isolated but rather closely entwined with the environmental and economic stability of areas like Africa and Brazil, which are vital for the success of many of them. For those depending on the consistent price and trading of carbon credits, for example, the volatility of the carbon market can compromise their financial stability. In the same vein, economic crises can force communities to give immediate survival first priority above long-term environmental preservation, hence aggravating deforestation and environmental damage.

CHAPTER 17   THRIVING TOGETHER: A REGENERATIVE POWER FOR SMALL AND MIGHTY BUSINESSES

Regarding objectives in light of climate change, the focus now moves from prevention to preparation. Although it may be too late to totally "stop" climate change, participants understand that effective coordination of resources is still essential to being ready for its unavoidable effects. This entails a deliberate concentration on reducing additional harm to ecosystems and strengthening community resilience to survive and adjust to evolving climatic conditions. Projects can significantly help lessen the worst consequences of climate change and assist underprivileged groups by appreciating the reality of it and emphasizing adaptable alternatives.

Participants are hopeful about the possible influence of their activities, even if climate change presents difficult issues. They see the ability of group efforts and technical innovation to develop flexible plans to maintain ecological and human well-being. This hope stems from a will to create answers that can lessen the consequences of climate change and raise world resilience. Resiliency is in its capacity to use blockchain technology to produce scalable, open, and effective solutions for environmental action. Projects can promote more inclusiveness and involvement in climate initiatives by allowing distributed and community-driven approaches, therefore enabling local communities to take responsibility for their environmental destiny.

The reality of climate change tests the movement to act quickly and creatively. The potential to adapt and respond to these difficulties will not only prove its resilience but also its power to innovate under duress, therefore contributing significantly to world climate action initiatives. To create a strong and flexible ecosystem, this calls for a multifarious strategy including policy campaigning, community involvement, and technology developments. Initiatives can provide synergies that improve the general impact and sustainability by encouraging cooperation among many stakeholders.

The emphasis on creating climate resilience through nature-based solutions and community-driven projects is one fundamental component of this adaptation plan. Projects can help with attempts at ecosystem restoration, sustainable farming, and reforestation to increase the natural resilience of surroundings and communities. ReFi can guarantee the openness and responsibility of climate actions by combining these methods with blockchain technology, therefore offering verifiable, quantifiable impacts that establish credibility and confidence among relevant parties.

Certain initiatives also have to negotiate the complexity of the voluntary carbon market and economic forces pushing environmental damage and deforestation. ReFi can solve the underlying causes of environmental damage by designing creative financial systems that reward sustainable behaviors and offer cash substitutes for deforestation.

< This entails creating market-based solutions that match economic incentives with environmental objectives so that communities may reach economic development without endangering their natural resources.

The sector ultimately faces major difficulties in the shadow of climate change, but it also affords a chance to show resilience and creative ability. Projects can significantly contribute to worldwide climate change efforts by concentrating on adaptive techniques, harnessing technological developments, and encouraging community involvement. Resilience stems from its capacity to negotiate these obstacles and produce answers that maintain human and environmental well-being against a future of unknown climate. The movement's dedication to tackling the effects of climate change and creating a sustainable and fair future keeps its members motivated even as it develops. ReFi can meet the challenge and significantly influence the worldwide fight against climate change by means of group action and technological innovation.

Summary

This chapter looks at the emergence of ReFi as a timely reaction to the climate catastrophe and systematic inequities built into conventional economic models. The chapter investigates how previous climate movements and growing awareness of exploitation have formed ReFi's vision for sustainable prosperity, defined by openness, responsibility, and fair distribution of resources. Especially with Web3 technologies and blockchain's promise for real-world application and sustainable outcomes, ReFi's transforming impact—gaining traction and recognition—positions early adopters—diverse in demographics and industries—front and first in this financial revolution.

Examining its methods for linking digital assets to real-world effects and its part in reducing trade and supply chain finance inequality, the chapter explores the paradigm shift from DeFi to ReFi. The latter has great difficulties despite its potential in terms of standards, overcoming technology gaps, encompassing different audiences, and negotiating government complexity. ReFi provides a strong road map to counteract climate change, promote inclusion, and release the potential of digital assets to build a regenerative and fair financial environment by tackling these obstacles.

CHAPTER 18

Data-Driven Dynamics: Linking Real-World Insights to Trade Finance

This chapter investigates how real-world knowledge and technological advances are ushering in a new era of digital commerce and the transforming power of data in changing trade finance. It starts by stressing the development and spread of digital commerce and the need to include real-world data to close the gap between operational efficiency in trade finance, compliance, and independence.

Essential instruments for opening possibilities through ethical data integration are highlighted as cooperative frameworks and technology innovations like blockchain and artificial intelligence. Examining the tokenization of goods helps one to understand its mechanics, practical uses, and transforming power. Tokenizing tangible assets helps to democratize wealth creation, remove conventional obstacles, and open the path for a more equitable global commerce and investment environment. Examining the technological, operational, and legal issues related to commodity tokenization, the chapter investigates the prospects and drawbacks. Tokenized goods' flawless integration into trade finance shows how well they may improve liquidity, openness, and accessibility while negotiating challenges influencing their acceptance in practical use.

A special section on voluntary carbon markets and carbon credits shows how increasingly trade finance and sustainability connect. The chapter explores how blockchain technology is utilized to produce safe, traceable, and transferable assets, thereby unpacking the tokenization of carbon credits. Along with case studies showing its pragmatic application and potential for increasing carbon trading efficiency, the effect of tokenized carbon credits on companies, ESG policies, and worldwide markets is investigated.

CHAPTER 18   DATA-DRIVEN DYNAMICS: LINKING REAL-WORLD INSIGHTS TO TRADE FINANCE

The story ends with a look at how tokenized assets—especially carbon credits—will mix into worldwide markets. It highlights best practices for using tokenization to match ESG initiatives and stresses the legislative and policy issues vital to their acceptance. Through stressing the transforming potential of data-driven dynamics, the chapter emphasizes how real-world insights, creative technologies, and tokenization are reshaping trade finance in a sustainable, inclusive, and technologically enabled global economy.

Embracing Tomorrow: The Evolution and Expansion of Digital Trade

Welcome to a major part of our thorough investigation into the direction of digital trade. Here, we explore the transforming events changing the scene of global trade. Along with introducing you to new trends and technology, our trip through these pages will highlight the possible paths and obstacles ahead.

The world of digital trade is about to undergo a major transformation, given the speed of technical development and changing worldwide requirements. The future scenarios' presentation in this context fulfills several functions. Examining possible futures helps us better get ready for changes in regulatory settings, technical innovation, and market dynamics. These situations help companies, legislators, and interested parties create more solid plans resistant to future uncertainty. Knowing future possibilities stimulates creativity and enables organizations to more successfully adjust to approaching developments. Moreover, these situations help us spot possible hazards and possibilities, thereby guaranteeing more wise decisions.

Considered the pillar of conventional trade finance, the independence principle guarantees that financial commitments in trade financing are free from the underlying commercial transaction. In the digital sphere, this idea is changing. We could see its spread and adaptation to new digital commerce systems in the future, therefore improving security and confidence in worldwide transactions.

Widely debated nowadays, tokenization is turning rights into an asset into a digital token on a blockchain. This is going to transform promissory notes and letters of credit (LCs) among trade finance instruments. Many advantages come from tokenizing these assets; it may simplify procedures, lower documentation, enable more liquid and readily marketable securities, and speed transactions. Through this change, small and medium-sized businesses (SMEs) also have improved access to trade money.

CHAPTER 18 DATA-DRIVEN DYNAMICS: LINKING REAL-WORLD INSIGHTS TO TRADE FINANCE

Digital trade's future is closely entwined with our capacity to gather and apply actual data. By using technologies such as the Internet of things (IoT), artificial intelligence (AI), and big data analytics, real-time data integration into trading platforms may greatly improve decision-making by offering more accurate and timely information.

Leveraging Real-World Data in Trade and Trade Finance: Enhancing Efficiency, Transparency, and Compliance

The integration of real-world data with trade and trade financing systems presents a tremendous opportunity in modern global commerce. This combining of data streams has the ability to drastically change trade policies, therefore increasing efficiency and encouraging openness everywhere. Maintaining competitiveness in the global market depends mostly on the capacity to capture and use real-time data, as companies depend on it more and more to make wise judgments.

Real-world data flowing into trade activities helps companies simplify their operations, lower delays, and maximize supply chains. Accurate and current knowledge helps businesses better forecast market trends, control inventory levels, and react quickly to demand fluctuations. This improved efficiency not only lowers expenses but also speeds the whole trade cycle, from manufacture to distribution, helping all the participants.

Transparency is another major advantage resulting from the combination of trading systems with actual statistics. Greater awareness of every stage of the trade process allows stakeholders to closely check transactions to make sure all activities follow industry standards and legal criteria. This openness lowers the risk of fraud, builds confidence among business partners, and helps transactions go more smoothly.

Even with these significant advantages, one should approach the integration of real-world data carefully. Especially with regard to documentary credits, maintaining the basic values of independence and rigorous compliance is absolutely vital. These ideas guarantee that every transaction is carried out equitably and that the integrity of the trade finance system is maintained.

In this sense, independence is the objectivity of the trade finance participants toward. Avoiding conflicts of interest and ensuring the integrity of every participant by following their different duties and obligations is absolutely essential. This objectivity helps to maintain the dependability and confidence necessary for commerce internationally.

Conversely, strict compliance means following all the laws, rules, and contractual requirements. Regarding documentary credits, this implies making sure every document shown satisfies the particular terms and circumstances specified in the credit agreement. This exacting attention to detail helps to avoid conflicts and delays, therefore enabling better transactions and a stable commercial climate.

It is indeed necessary to negotiate this terrain cautiously, even though the convergence of real-world data with trade and trade finance systems has enormous potential to transform world commerce. Realizing the full advantages of this integration and preserving the integrity and dependability of international trade procedures relies on upholding the values of independence and rigorous compliance. Imagine a scenario where data from the real world seamlessly integrates with trade and finance platforms. This integration can offer unparalleled insights into supply chains, market dynamics, and risk assessments. From weather patterns impacting agricultural production to geopolitical shifts influencing market trends, real-world data enriches decision-making processes.

Balancing Compliance and Independence: Integrating Real-World Data into Trade and Trade Finance Systems

Maintaining strong regulatory framework compliance becomes critical among the integration of real-world data into trade and trade finance systems. Data utilization must be closely matched with financial compliance rules, international trade policies, and current data privacy legislation. Maintaining the integrity of the commerce system depends on data use following moral and legal standards. Following data privacy regulations guarantees that personal data of people is safeguarded, therefore stopping illegal access or usage. Following international commerce rules guarantees that all operations satisfy worldwide criteria and helps to ensure seamless transactions across borders. Meanwhile, financial compliance rules serve to prevent fraud and money laundering, therefore preserving the general security of financial systems.

Striking this equilibrium between compliance and data use calls for careful attention. Using the advantages of real-world data is absolutely vital without sacrificing moral or legal limitations. This entails building strong systems that can effectively handle and utilize data while guaranteeing that all regulatory needs are satisfied. The difficulty is using data to improve trade processes while nevertheless honoring and supporting these strict rules.

Apart from regulatory compliance, it is imperative to balance using actual data with guaranteeing abstraction and independence. Enough abstraction of the data flow should help to avoid direct entity or person identification. Maintaining privacy and secrecy on this abstraction also guarantees that sensitive or personal data is neither leaked nor used improperly. Data should be handled and used in such a way that private business information is safeguarded and people remain anonymous.

Moreover, keeping independence in data integration is essential to avoid bias or too strong an effect. This implies making sure that the integration of data does not distort judgments or generate conflicts of interest. All parties involved in trade and trade finance can trust each other because data handling independence ensures the integrity of the data used. It advances an objective and fair atmosphere in which decisions are taken according to correct and objective knowledge.

Including real-world data into trading systems has many advantages and should be done with a dedication to rigorous compliance and independence. Harmonizing data usage with regulatory systems and guaranteeing privacy, secrecy, and impartiality helps one leverage data to transform world trade practices without violating moral or legal norms.

Achieving Data Harmonization in Trade Finance: Leveraging Blockchain and Collaborative Frameworks for Secure Integration

Harmonizing trade finance with real-world data calls for outstanding cooperation across several players. The development of strong frameworks that enable data interchange while following compliance, abstraction, and independence depends on this cooperative effort. Stakeholders may design systems that efficiently incorporate real-world data into trade finance processes by combining several points of view and knowledge without sacrificing important legal and ethical norms.

In this context, stakeholders comprise trade organizations, financial institutions, regulatory authorities, and technological companies. Every one of these organizations is very important in making sure that data interoperability is attained in a way that honors compliance criteria. For instance, financial organizations have to make sure their systems, following financial rules, can safely manage private information. Regulatory authorities guarantee the required control to make sure that all activities follow legal criteria. While trade companies use these systems in pragmatic, real-world situations, technology companies offer creative ideas that enable data integration.

Blockchain and distributed ledger systems are among the creative technologies that show outstanding potential to provide safe and open data recording in trade finance. With its distributed nature, blockchain technology provides a means to permanently record transactions, therefore guaranteeing that input data cannot be changed. Since every transaction is checked by multiple parties before being noted, this immutability offers a degree of legitimacy. Because all participants have access to the same data, this verification procedure not only improves security but also promotes openness.

Blockchain and distributed ledger technology are particularly well-liked for their openness in trade finance. From the first agreement to the last settlement, these technologies let all those engaged in a transaction see every step clearly. This degree of awareness guarantees that all activities follow legal criteria and helps to prevent conflicts. Furthermore, the adoption of these technologies helps preserve data's freedom, as the distributed nature of blockchain precludes any one party from controlling the data excessively.

Furthermore, by letting data be exchanged and checked without disclosing private information about people or companies engaged in the transactions, these technologies reinforce the idea of abstraction. Abstracting data in this way allows one to maintain privacy and secrecy while also using the advantages of real-time data integration. Maintaining confidence among parties and making sure data integration improves trade finance without sacrificing ethical norms depend on this harmony.

The harmonization of trade finance with real-world data is a difficult process that requires cooperation among parties and the application of creative technology. Secure, open, and compliant data integration may be attained by building strong frameworks for data interoperability and using blockchain and distributed ledgers. This strategy guarantees that the advantages of real-world data may be completely appreciated in trade finance, thereby promoting efficiency, authenticity, and independence in international trade policies.

CHAPTER 18   DATA-DRIVEN DYNAMICS: LINKING REAL-WORLD INSIGHTS TO TRADE FINANCE

Building a Balanced Future: Integrating Real-World Data into Trade Finance with Compliance, Abstraction, and Independence

Accepting the inclusion of actual data into international commerce and finance might open hitherto unheard-of chances for development, effectiveness, and openness. By means of this junction of data and commerce, companies can transform their operations and create fresh paths for development and enhancement. Real-time data allows businesses to improve their competitiveness in the worldwide market, simplify their processes, and make more wise judgments.

Realizing these possibilities, though, calls for a rigorous strategy that gives compliance, abstraction, and independence top importance. Ensuring that all data usage fits legal and regulatory systems depends on compliance, thereby preserving the integrity of the trading system and preventing any abuses. To maintain trust and dependability in trade operations, one must thus follow data privacy laws, international trade rules, and financial compliance criteria.

Since abstraction entails data management that prohibits direct identification of people or objects, it is also equally crucial. Abstracting data helps companies safeguard confidentiality and privacy, therefore guaranteeing that private information is neither leaked nor used improperly. This cautious data processing helps businesses maximize their advantages while preserving the best standards of ethical behavior.

Another fundamental idea is independence, which guarantees that data integration does not result in too strong an impact or bias. Maintaining independence implies that judgments are grounded on accurate and objective knowledge, data is handled impartially and free of conflicts of interest, and this promotes an open and fair trade environment in which every player may rely on the integrity of the procedures engaged in.

A responsible course of action will help companies and stakeholders open the path for a day when trade finance and data integration live peacefully. By allowing more effective and open operations while maintaining the values of compliance, abstraction, and independence, this balanced approach encourages development and inclusivity in worldwide business. Consequently, a more strong and reliable global trade system results, from which the advantages of data integration are completely realized, promoting development and creativity in the worldwide market.

CHAPTER 18   DATA-DRIVEN DYNAMICS: LINKING REAL-WORLD INSIGHTS TO TRADE FINANCE

Unlocking the Vault: Revolutionizing Real-World Asset Investments Through Commodities Tokenization

Blockchain technology is opening the path for the tokenization of goods, therefore changing the financial scene. This innovative method is changing our perspective on and financial commitment to the physical objects of the actual world. Tokenizing goods marks a dramatic break from conventional investment paradigms and provides hitherto unheard-of democratization of access to assets formerly thought out of reach for the average individual. This chapter explores the radical process of commodity tokenization and its significant consequences for asset ownership and investing methods.

Fundamentally, the tokenization of goods is the generation of digital tokens that stand for ownership of tangible items such as gold, oil, or agricultural products. Safely kept and exchanged on a blockchain, a distributed digital record renowned for security and openness, these tokens blockchain technology lets real-world assets become digital tokens, therefore enabling a more liquid, quick market for commodities investments.

High obstacles to entrance, limited access, and considerable complexity have traditionally defined the conventional commodities market. Investing in commodities sometimes called for large funds, extensive knowledge, and access to specialist trading venues. Many possible investors were left excluded by this exclusivity, unable to engage in what would be a profitable market. Tokenization, on the other hand, is tearing down these restrictions so that more investors may interact in commodities markets.

The possibility of commodity tokenization to democratize asset ownership is among its most fascinating features. Tokenization, via fractional ownership, lets investors acquire tiny amounts of a product instead of having to buy the whole asset. This fractionalization allows even those with little means to now make investments in high-value assets like real estate or gold. For instance, a digital token allows an investor to acquire a portion of an ounce of gold instead of a complete ounce, therefore reducing the financial barrier to entry and creating chances for a more varied pool of investors.

Tokenizing also brings fresh degrees of liquidity to the commodities market. Conventional physical commodity investments can be difficult and illiquid; sometimes, long and complicated transactions are needed to purchase or sell. On blockchain systems, though, digital tokens may be traded instantly, offering a more flexible and dynamic market. By allowing more consistent trading activity, this enhanced liquidity not only facilitates investor entrance and exit positions but also serves to stabilize the market.

CHAPTER 18   DATA-DRIVEN DYNAMICS: LINKING REAL-WORLD INSIGHTS TO TRADE FINANCE

Blockchain technology's inherent security and openness help to increase the attraction of commodity tokenization even more. Every transaction is entered onto an unchangeable ledger so that transaction history and ownership may be quickly checked. This openness helps market players build confidence and lowers the possibility of fraud. Furthermore, the distributed character of blockchain implies that no one entity controls the ledger, therefore lowering the danger of manipulation and so strengthening the general system security.

Tokenizing is also transforming methods of investing. Using smart contracts—self-executing agreements with the terms of the agreement explicitly put into code—investors can simplify and automate many facets of the investment process. For example, token holders may get automatically disbursed dividends or rental income from tokenized assets, thereby lowering administrative costs and raising efficiency. More complicated investment strategies—such as pooling money for group investments or using automated portfolio rebalancing—may also be facilitated by smart contracts.

Beyond personal investors, the tokenization of commodities has major ramifications for institutional investors and the larger financial system. Tokenizing allows financial organizations to provide fresh goods and services, including asset-backed securities or tokenized commodities funds. This creativity can generate fresh income sources and improve the financial institutions' competitiveness in a fast-changing environment.

In the framework of commodity tokenization, regulatory issues become absolutely crucial. Regulatory systems have to change as this technology picks momentum to guarantee investor protection and encourage innovation. Policymakers and industry players have to work together to create thorough rules addressing problems including investor rights, market integrity, and anti-money laundering policies. Building trust and guaranteeing the steady expansion of the tokenized goods market depend on a well-regulated environment.

Though the road toward broad acceptance of commodity tokenization is still under development, the possible influence is quite great. Blockchain technology's development and increasing tokenization of additional assets point to a more inclusive, transparent market as it develops. Along with helping individual investors, this change will help to ensure the resilience and stability of the world financial system. The tokenizing of goods marks a paradigm change in our perspective on and investment in actual assets. Driven by blockchain technology, this innovative method is rethinking investment methods, increasing market liquidity, and democratizing access to assets.

As we enter this transformative era, it is clear that the power of digital tokens is reshaping the landscape of commodities investing. Although the road toward a completely tokenized financial environment is difficult and demanding, the possible benefits are outstanding and will create a more dynamic and easily available market for all.

Breaking Down the Barriers, Democratizing Commodities Investment: The Transformative Power of Tokenization

Investing in commodities like precious metals, oil, or rare minerals used to be quite difficult historically. Average investors found it challenging to engage in markets demanding significant funds, thorough market knowledge, and access to special financial institutions behind these obstacles. Purchasing, storing, and selling these tangible goods brought layers of complexity that further limited involvement to those with the means and knowledge to negotiate these markets. The rise of tokenization is tearing down these divisions and providing many transforming benefits.

Enhanced accessibility is one of the most important changes tokenizing brings about. Investing in commodities historically sometimes involved buying whole units of an asset. such as a barrel of oil or a full bar of gold, which would have required a significant financial outlay. Many investors found this high entrance level intolerable. Tokenizing these goods into fractional tokens lets investors own portions of an asset without having to buy it whole. This fractional ownership approach greatly reduces the entrance criteria, allowing more people to vary their investment portfolios. Smaller, more reasonably priced pieces of valuable goods allow a wider spectrum of investors to interact with markets once out of reach.

One more area where tokenization transforms the commodities market is liquidity. Conventional physical commodity investments sometimes entail time-consuming and labor-intensive transactions with notable delays in buying and selling. One important disadvantage of this lack of liquidity is limited investors' capacity to react quickly to changes in the market. Conversely, tokenized assets offer significantly more liquidity than traditional commodities markets and may be purchased and sold on digital exchanges rather reasonably easily. More dynamic investing strategies are encouraged by this simplicity of transaction, which lets investors quickly change their positions in reaction to market swings. Through increased steady trading activity, the improved liquidity also serves to stabilize the market.

CHAPTER 18 DATA-DRIVEN DYNAMICS: LINKING REAL-WORLD INSIGHTS TO TRADE FINANCE

Two main advantages of tokenization are transparency and security; they help to solve long-standing issues in the conventional commodities market. The foundation of tokenization, blockchain technology, guarantees that each transaction is noted in a tamper-proof ledger. With this unchangeable record, investments become more transparent, and investors may follow the token's past to confirm its legitimacy. Blockchain's transparency lowers fraud risk, therefore strengthening the security and confidence in the investing process. Knowing that the blockchain ledger offers a precise, unchangeable record of ownership, investors may have more faith in the validity of their assets.

Blockchain security gains go beyond only preventing fraud. Blockchain's distributed character causes no one entity to have control over the ledger, therefore lowering the danger of manipulation and raising the general system security. This distributed system guarantees that investments remain safe and secure by shielding against possible cyber dangers. Furthermore, blockchain transparency promotes confidence among market players, therefore strengthening the inclusive and fair investing environment.

Tokenizing also helps to streamline the logistical difficulties related to physical commodity investment. Conventional investments sometimes demand that investors plan for the costly and complicated transfer and storage of actual assets. Tokenized assets solve logistical issues since investors possess digital tokens reflecting their ownership, and trusted custodians safely store the physical goods. For a wider spectrum of investors, this simplicity makes commodity investments more reachable and under control.

Including tokenization into the commodities market marks a major change in our view and interaction with physical objects. Tokenization democratizes the financial environment by removing the obstacles that have previously limited access, therefore enabling more people to engage in markets once the exclusive province of rich and well-connected investors. Greater openness and diversity in the financial community resulting from this democratization help to balance and fairly distribute wealth.

Ultimately, tokenization is removing the obstacles long preventing access to commodity investments. Tokenization is changing our investment in physical assets by improving accessibility, liquidity, security, and transparency, by means of which we can access them. As this innovative strategy keeps becoming popular, it promises to produce a more inclusive, dynamic, and safe investment environment, creating new chances for investors from all backgrounds and financial situations. Blockchain technology is changing the nature of commodity investments and ushering in a new financial world period of accessibility and creativity.

Tokenizing Commodities: Revolutionizing Asset Investment through Blockchain

Tokenizing a commodity is a painstaking procedure that turns a tangible asset into a digital form fit for simple trading and management. This procedure starts with asset choosing, in which a certain item is found for tokenizing. This item can be a diamond collection, an oil barrel, or a gold bar. The first choice of the asset is significant since it forms the basis of the whole tokenizing procedure.

The selected item is verified and valued after it is decided upon. This stage comprises an extensive evaluation of the asset to ascertain its worth and a procedure of authentication to confirm its ownership. First and most importantly is making sure the asset satisfies all legal and regulatory criteria for tokenization. This includes authenticating its provenance and proving it free of any legal entanglements or conflicts. Creating digital tokens that fairly depict the value of the asset depends on a clear, transparent valuation of it, which the assessment and verification procedure provides.

Token generation comes next after verification and value. Blockchain technology is then quite relevant here. Designed utilizing particular blockchain standards, digital tokens reflecting asset shares are produced. Tokens might, for instance, follow the ERC-20 criteria on the Ethereum blockchain, which guarantees their fit with a broad spectrum of digital wallets and exchanges. These tokens are created by encoding the value and ownership information of the asset into the blockchain, therefore producing a digital representation fit for simple management and exchange.

Distribution and trading come last in the tokenizing process. Investors—who may keep the freshly produced coins in digital wallets—are given them. After that, one may easily buy and sell these tokens on digital asset markets. Blockchain technology guarantees tamper-proof ledger recording of every transaction, hence offering security and openness. All inside a safe and open digital environment, investors may readily move tokens, track their ownership, and participate in trading activities.

Tokenizing goods thereby changes the conventional investment model by increasing access, efficiency, and openness. It lowers entrance barriers, lets investors own a fraction of highly valuable assets, and increases liquidity. From asset choosing to distribution and trading, the tokenization process uses blockchain technology's ability to establish a fresh paradigm in asset investment. This invention is changing the way goods are purchased, sold, and handled, therefore generating fresh chances for investors and a more inclusive market.

Tokenizing goods affects the larger financial ecosystem, thereby influencing not only the individual investor. Around tokenized assets—like asset-backed securities and commodities funds—financial institutions can create new goods and services. In a fast-changing environment, this can generate fresh income sources and improve the financial institutions' competitiveness. Furthermore, the openness and security blockchain technology offers can help to build more confidence in the market, therefore drawing more players and strengthening the financial system.

The tokenization of goods is essentially a thorough process, starting with the meticulous selection and evaluation of an asset, then using blockchain technology to create digital tokens, and finally distributing and trading these tokens on digital markets. By using blockchain technology, this procedure democratizes access to valuable assets, improves market liquidity, and guarantees security and transparency. Tokenization is a major invention changing our investment in and management of real-world assets as the financial terrain develops. As we negotiate this fascinating border, the definition of commodities investing is changing and presents both new opportunities and problems.

The Transformative Power of Tokenization Across Industry: Real-World Applications and Impact

Tokenization has enormous potential to transform several industries by using blockchain technology, surpassing the simple investing simplification. The commodities markets clearly show one of the most quick and significant effects of tokenization. Tokenization democratizes access to high-value goods by separating them into fractional tokens, therefore enabling a larger spectrum of investors to engage. This enhanced accessibility might result in a diversification and extension of commodities markets, hence generating fresh liquidity and creative investment ideas. Previously barred because of strong entrance requirements, investors can now trade commodities, therefore creating a more dynamic and inclusive financial market.

Regarding supply networks, tokenizing goods provides major improvements in traceability and openness. Representing a fraction of a physical item, every token is entered on a blockchain and offers an unchangeable, verifiable ledger of transactions. This capability enables customers and companies to track products with unprecedented accuracy, tracing their origin, ownership, and movements. Tokenization, for instance, allows the food sector to monitor produce's path from farm to table, therefore guaranteeing authenticity and adherence to safety criteria. This openness helps consumers to develop trust, lowers fraud risk, and increases general supply chain effectiveness. By maintaining a comprehensive and responsible record of their activities, businesses may better control their stocks, maximize logistics, and react quickly to any disturbances.

The arrival of tokenization will benefit ethical and environmental investments, especially. Those who give ethical sourcing and environmental effect first priority can now select coins reflecting assets consistent with their principles. By allowing investors to support businesses and projects dedicated to sustainability and ethical behavior, this strategy encourages responsible investing. Tokens representing fair-trade goods or shares in renewable energy projects, for example, give investors an effortless approach to supporting environmentally conscious projects. This change will inspire businesses to adopt more sustainable and conscious standards by motivating more responsibility and openness in sectors usually afflicted by opaque practices.

Tokenizing has real-world uses in many other fields too. Tokenization in real estate lets fractional ownership lower the financial barrier for private investors and boost the market liquidity, thereby transforming property investments. Trading tokenized real estate on digital channels simplifies purchasing, selling, and property asset management. Along with democratizing real estate investment, this invention creates fresh paths for portfolio diversification.

Tokenization is transforming art purchase, sale, and ownership in the creative sphere. By allowing fractional ownership and making expensive art available to a larger audience, digital tokens can symbolize shares in precious pieces. By means of blockchain's immutable records, this technique can improve liquidity in the art market, generate fresh income sources, and safeguard the origin and validity of artworks.

Tokenization is causing change in the banking industry itself. Tokenizing classic financial securities like bonds and stocks can help to improve transparency, lower transaction costs, and boost liquidity. Digital exchanges allow traders of tokenized securities more freedom and access to worldwide markets. This invention lowers the need for middlemen, simplifies the investing procedure, and advances a more effective capital allocation.

Tokenization clearly shows itself in the regulatory scene as well. Governments and regulatory agencies are realizing they have to change with the times and create policies that encourage creativity while nevertheless guaranteeing investor protection and market integrity. Fostering confidence and advancing the sustainable expansion of tokenized markets depend on well-defined, thorough rules. Policymakers are closely collaborating with industry players to handle problems such as anti-money laundering policies, investor rights, and market stability, so fostering an atmosphere fit for the general acceptance of tokenization.

Tokenizing has enormous transforming power and offers advantages in many different spheres that affect different facets of the world economy. Tokenizing investments more easily, improving supply chain transparency, and encouraging responsible investing help to change the way assets are exchanged and handled. Although the path toward general acceptance of tokenization is still under development, the opportunities it reveals are really great.

Ultimately, the practical uses and effects of tokenization are broad, transforming supply chains, investment policies, and commodities markets as well as supply chains. Tokenization involves removing obstacles, improving openness, and pushing sustainability by using blockchain technology. The possibility for positive change is enormous if businesses keep embracing this innovation, therefore ushering in a new era of efficiency, inclusivity, and responsibility in the worldwide economy. Tokenization is changing the direction of asset management and investing, therefore opening the path for a more fair and sustainable financial environment.

Tokenization Trials: Navigating the Challenges and Considerations

Though exciting, the development of tokenizing goods comes with a lot of issues and questions that need to be answered if we are to fully grasp its possibilities. The road from concept to broad acceptance is paved with complexity, including legislative uncertainty, market adoption rates, and the need for a robust infrastructure to facilitate trading and custody of tokenized assets. Among the major challenges that have to be surmounted are ensuring adherence to world financial rules and fostering trust among conventional investors.

In the field of tokenization, regulatory uncertainty is maybe the most urgent problem. Blockchain and cryptocurrency regulations are still changing, and the inclusion of tokenized goods adds yet another level of complication. Different countries have different laws, and there is no one global framework to control tokenization of assets. Legal uncertainty resulting from this lack of regulatory clarity might complicate company navigation of the compliance terrain. Companies have to keep current with evolving rules and closely coordinate legal professionals to make sure their tokenizing systems follow current legislation. This can call for a lot of time and money, which complicates the acceptance of tokenized assets.

CHAPTER 18 DATA-DRIVEN DYNAMICS: LINKING REAL-WORLD INSIGHTS TO TRADE FINANCE

The regulatory scene also has to strike a mix between investor protection and creativity. Regulatory authorities are assigned to make sure tokenized assets do not turn into means of money laundering, fraud, or other illegal activity vehicles. Creating rules that safeguard investors while encouraging creativity calls for serious thought and cooperation between legislators and business leaders. A robust and reliable tokenization market depends on finding this equilibrium.

Adoption rates of markets present still another major obstacle. Although tokenizing has obvious advantages, convincing established institutions and investors to follow this fresh strategy might prove challenging. Many investors are used to conventional approaches to investing and may be cautious of digital tokens due to their connection with cryptocurrencies, which have suffered volatility and legislative scrutiny. Essential is teaching investors the benefits of tokenization—that is, more liquidity, transparency, and fractional ownership. Showcasing the feasibility of tokenized goods and providing effective case studies and use cases would also help boost confidence.

Encouragement of market adoption depends on a basic problem that has to be addressed: trust. To guarantee the security and validity of their investments, traditional investors sometimes depend on well-known companies and legal systems. One can be suspicious of blockchain technology given its somewhat young and changing character. Tokenized assets must be supported by verifiable, legally sound evidence if one is to foster confidence. Further boosting reputation is working with respectable financial institutions and getting support from regulatory authorities. Moreover, earning investor confidence depends on the strict security policies implemented to guard against cyber dangers and fraud.

Another important factor is the need for strong infrastructure to assist in trading and custody of tokenized assets. Though novel, blockchain technology depends on safe platforms and large computational capability to run efficiently. Essential elements of the required infrastructure are establishing digital exchanges able to manage the trade volume of tokenized assets, guaranteeing interoperability across several blockchain systems, and creating safe digital wallets to keep tokens. To protect transactions and assets from possible breaches, this entails large technological and cybersecurity investments.

Tokenized asset infrastructure also reaches into custody solutions. Concerning assets on behalf of investors, traditional financial markets depend on custodians to safely retain and handle them. Within the realm of tokenized goods, the responsibility of custodians has to change to fit digital assets. It is vital to create dependable custody solutions that give the same degree of security and confidence as conventional custodians. This covers regular audits to guarantee the integrity of the custodial services, strong access limits, and safe storage of private keys.

Dealing with the technological constraints of present blockchain systems is another aspect of negotiating the difficulties of tokenization. Areas needing constant research and development are scalability, transaction speed, and energy consumption. The underlying blockchain technology has to change as the acceptance of tokenized goods rises to meet growing demand sustainably and effectively.

Even if the tokenization of goods has tremendous promise, it comes with a number of difficulties that have to be gently negotiated. Important factors that call for coordinated efforts among all the stakeholders are regulatory uncertainty, market acceptance rates, and the necessity of strong infrastructure. Overcoming these obstacles mostly depends on ensuring compliance with world financial rules, fostering trust among conventional investors, and creating safe and effective technical solutions. Cooperation among legislators, business leaders, and technological experts will be vital as the sector develops to shape a future where tokenized goods can flourish, present new prospects, and change the scene of asset investment.

Tokenization of Real-World Assets: The Future of Commodity Investment

More than a passing trend, the tokenization of goods marks a fundamental change in the character of asset ownership and investing. Real-world asset tokenization is likely to become the norm as blockchain technology develops and regulatory systems get stronger. This development profoundly changes the investment environment by providing a more inclusive, open, and efficient approach to interacting with the worldwide economy.

The merger of the physical and digital spheres drives this change at its core. Tokenization builds a link, allowing investors to safely and openly own a piece of the real world. Investors can interact with commodities in a way never possible by turning physical objects into digital tokens. This technique democratizes access to valuable assets, therefore enabling a larger spectrum of players to engage in markets long the exclusive province of rich and well-connected investors. Owning fractional shares of assets like gold, oil, or real estate gives those with limited means diversified portfolio exposure to several commodities.

CHAPTER 18 DATA-DRIVEN DYNAMICS: LINKING REAL-WORLD INSIGHTS TO TRADE FINANCE

Blockchain technology develops and offers improved security and efficiency to the investing process. Every transaction involving tokenized assets logs on a tamper-proof blockchain ledger, guaranteeing openness and lower fraud risk. This unchangeable record helps investors to believe in the system's legality and the validity of their possessions. Blockchain's distributed nature also lessens reliance on middlemen, therefore simplifying transactions and cutting costs. Consequently, a more efficient market where assets may be traded fast and safely helps to create a more dynamic investing environment.

Increasing inclusiveness also defines the direction of commodity investment in the future. Tokenization helps to destroy conventional entrance obstacles, including complicated logistical plans and hefty financial needs. This inclusiveness covers institutional participants as well, going beyond personal investors. By using tokenization, financial institutions can create new goods and services, such as asset-backed securities and commodities funds, thus improving market liquidity and widening their offers. Tokenized assets being included in mainstream financial markets can stimulate innovation, increase competitiveness, and open fresh development prospects.

The direction of commodity investment is substantially shaped by regulatory systems. Governments and regulatory authorities are creating policies that strike a mix between innovation and investor protection as they get better knowledge of blockchain technology. Stable conditions for the expansion of tokenized markets are created by clear, thorough rules, therefore guaranteeing that they run with integrity and openness. Policymakers addressing issues including anti-money laundering policies, investor rights, and market stability are closely collaborating with industry stakeholders. A tokenized asset's sustainable and trustworthy ecosystem depends on this cooperative approach.

Tokenization affects more general social and economic results than just the financial markets. For sectors including agriculture, mining, and manufacturing, for instance, tokenization can increase traceability and responsibility by improving supply chain openness. By verifying the source, ownership, and movement of products, consumers and companies help to support sustainable practices and ethical procurement. This openness can propel positive change by motivating businesses to use more ecologically friendly methods of operation.

Regarding ethical and environmental investments, tokenization presents a powerful instrument for encouraging smart behavior. Tokens representing assets consistent with their principles let investors support initiatives dedicated to sustainability and ethical standards. This method not only helps businesses follow better standards of social and environmental governance but also ensures that investment strategies match personal views. Tokenization can help to create a more fair and sustainable world economy.

The tokenization of real-world assets combined with blockchain technology is changing the financial environment fundamentally. Tokenization of goods is poised to become a pillar of modern investing strategies as the technology develops and regulatory systems confirm. In line with the needs and possibilities of the digital era, this creative approach promises to generate a more accessible, diversified, and efficient market.

Ultimately, the tokenization of assets is redefining what commodities investment means going forward. This transforming process marks a basic change in our view and interaction with investments, not only a trend. Tokenization presents a safe, open, and inclusive approach to investing in the worldwide economy by linking the real and digital worlds. Adoption of tokenized assets will probably become common as blockchain technology develops and regulatory systems change, therefore ushering in a new era of investment marked by more accessibility, efficiency, and congruence with modern ideals. The road toward this future is long-lasting, and the possible advantages are enormous; they promise a more vibrant, fair, and sustainable financial environment for all.

Commodity Tokenization: Revolutionizing Investment Accessibility, Liquidity, and Security

Tokenizing commodities marks a paradigm change in how investors interact with tangible assets such as gold, oil, or agricultural products. Fundamentally, this approach is blockchain-based digital token distribution of the ownership of these physical goods. Every token represents a fractional ownership in the real item, therefore enabling investors to purchase, sell, or retain a bit of a tangible good in digital form. These markets are more open and inclusive since this invention reduces the entrance obstacles for private investors and streamlines the investment procedure in goods.

The road of commodity tokenization starts with the choice of a physical object. This might cover agricultural products as well as precious metals and energy sources. After that, the selected goods are digital and broken out into smaller, reasonable tokens. By allowing investors to own portions of costly goods without having to make a whole unit investment, this fractional ownership model democratizes access to high-value assets.

Combining these digital tokens into a blockchain comes next once the asset is fractionalized. Blockchain systems guarantee a visible, unchangeable, safe ledger of ownership. This distributed ledger logs every token, making tracking of token ownership and transactions easier. This technique generates a trustless environment for vendors and buyers whereby trust is ingrained in the technology itself instead of depending on middlemen or centralized authorities.

Like cryptocurrencies, the digital tokens denoting these goods can then be sold on specialist markets. This interaction with digital exchanges improves the liquidity of the tokenized assets, therefore enabling investors to enter or leave holdings with simplicity. The more dynamic and responsive commodities markets are made by the rising liquidity, which promotes more active trading.

The more accessibility tokenizing goods provide is one of their most important benefits. A wider spectrum of investors can engage in the commodity markets, which were historically controlled by big investors or specialized funds, by fractionalizing goods into reasonable tokens. This inclusivity creates a more varied investment scene so that those with little funds may interact with high-value assets and diversify their portfolios.

By allowing their simple trade and transfer on digital platforms, tokenization also boosts the liquidity of physical assets. More dynamic and responsive commodity markets result from this liquidity potential since investors may quickly react to changes in the market. Trading digital tokens using blockchain systems lowers the friction related to purchasing, selling, and storing actual goods, therefore optimizing the investing process.

In the framework of commodity tokenization, the security and openness offered by blockchain technology take first priority. Every transaction involving tokenized assets is noted on a distributed ledger, therefore reducing fraud risk and guaranteeing the integrity of the ownership documentation. Because investors may confidently confirm the legitimacy and provenance of their holdings, this substantial degree of openness builds trust among them. Blockchain technology's security elements guard against illegal access and manipulation, therefore preserving investors' funds.

Still another important advantage of tokenizing goods is market stability. Tokenized commodities are rooted in the real-world assets they reflect, unlike highly volatile cryptocurrency. The inherent worth of these coins is related to real supply and demand dynamics; they provide investors some consistency and predictability. For individuals looking to invest in assets with real value and less volatility, tokenized goods are appealing because of their stability.

Though commodity tokenization has many advantages, some issues must be resolved if it is to be embraced widely. As governments all around struggle with how to identify and control these digital assets, regulatory clarity is still changing. The absence of a consistent worldwide regulatory framework might result in legal ambiguities and uncertainty, therefore complicating business navigation of compliance obligations. Policymakers and business players have to work together to create rules safeguarding investors and encouraging innovation by means of policies.

The success of tokenized goods also depends on the evolution of strong and safe digital exchanges able to manage such transactions. These systems have to be able to guarantee flawless blockchain technology integration, support big trading volumes, and give investors an intuitive interface. Furthermore, the conventional markets for commodities have to welcome this change in technology and fit the new tokenized asset model.

Commodity tokenizing is choosing a tangible asset, digitizing and fractionalizing it into tokens, combining these tokens onto a blockchain, and trading them on digital markets. This creative strategy improves accessibility, streamlines the investing process, raises liquidity, and offers security and openness. To be widely adopted, though, calls for overcoming legal obstacles, building strong trading systems, and winning acceptance from established markets. Commodities tokenization has the potential to transform the investing scene, increase inclusiveness, dynamism, and alignment with digital age needs as these challenges are overcome. The redefining of commodities investment presents fresh prospects and changes the way investors interact with actual assets.

Digital Alchemy: Transforming Commodities into Tokens

With blockchain technology, the introduction of tokenized goods represents a radical turn toward democratizing access to several asset classes. Investors can own, trade, and invest in fractions of previously unattainable tangible goods by turning physical assets into digital tokens, therefore empowering themselves. This digital alchemy changes the investing scene and provides a deeper view of some of the most fascinating instances of tokenized goods transforming digital age investment.

Long valued as a secure refuge and inflation hedge, gold takes front stage in this change. Tokenizing gold lets one digitally control actual gold kept in safe vaults. This strategy not only streamlines transactions but also offers liquidity and openness, therefore enabling a larger audience to access gold investment. Investors can own fractional shares of gold and trade them readily on digital platforms and gain from the same security and stability that physical gold offers instead of worrying about the complexities of storing and safeguarding actual gold.

CHAPTER 18   DATA-DRIVEN DYNAMICS: LINKING REAL-WORLD INSIGHTS TO TRADE FINANCE

Likewise, another valuable metal—silver—gives much advantage from tokenizing. Tokens allowing fractional ownership of physical silver let investors invest in silver free from the practical difficulties of storage and shipping. This opens the silver market to more people, enabling wider participation in the investment possibilities presented by this adaptable metal. Tokenized silver lets the market open to a more varied spectrum of investors by reducing the entrance obstacles.

Particularly with regard to oil and gas reserves, the energy industry makes a sizable share of the global economy. By use of tokenization, oil and gas reserves can be digitalized, therefore enabling direct buyer participation in energy projects. This creativity creates fresh investment prospects in the sector's expansion and earnings as well as new finance sources for energy companies. Including digital tokens connected to real-world energy assets helps investors diversify their portfolios and more readily and transparently participate in the worldwide energy market.

Tokenization also reaches the agriculture industry, where tokens could stand for ownership of several crops or animals. By directly investing in the manufacturing and selling of agricultural products, this not only gives farmers and producers other funding sources but also lets investors diversify their portfolios. By means of this integration of technology into agriculture, investors and the sources of their investments become more directly connected, therefore improving transparency and sustainability in the agricultural supply chain.

Essential for modern technologies and renewable energy sources, rare earth metals provide a special investment potential. Tokenization allows individual investors to enter these specialist markets, therefore permitting fractional ownership in metals vital for making electronics, electric cars, and more. In addition to diversifying investment portfolios, this democratization of rare earth metal access helps to drive the creation of sustainable energy solutions and sophisticated technology.

By divorcing property ownership into digital tokens, real estate tokenization drastically reduces the entrance obstacles to real estate investing. In real estate portfolios, this approach enables fractional ownership, liquidity, and diversification, therefore enabling high-value property investments for a wider spectrum of investors. Without significant cash or complicated administration duties, people can now invest in parts of properties, sell these tokens on digital markets, and profit from real estate appreciation.

Tokenizing carbon credits offers a clear and effective market for trading carbon offsets in response to the pressing demand for climate action. By letting businesses and people trade carbon credits to help offset their carbon footprint, this promotes investments in sustainability projects. Tokenized carbon credits help to promote environmental projects and follow legal obligations, therefore promoting a more sustainable and responsible world economy.

Tokenization also changes the rather exclusive art and collectibles market. Fractional ownership of collectibles and artwork dissipates access to high-value assets. For artists and collectors, this not only creates fresh income sources but also offers a means of more individuals investing in and profiting from the appreciation of rare and costly objects. Owning and trading digital tokens as shares of artwork gives a market usually marked by opacity and exclusivity, liquidity, and openness.

These illustrations show the wide possibilities of tokenized goods to change the scene of investments in several fields. Tokenization presents a more inclusive, quick, and open approach to investing in the assets of the actual world by using blockchain technology. This digital revolution promises to close the distance between conventional investment channels and the future of the digital economy, therefore fostering a more dynamic and accessible market for all.

Finally, the act of turning goods into tokens is a kind of digital alchemy that may completely change investing plans. Investors can interact with the worldwide economy in hitherto unthinkable ways by separating tangible assets into digital tokens. Tokenization of goods will probably become a natural component of the investing scene as blockchain technology develops and gains adoption since it presents fresh chances for development, diversification, and financial inclusion. This creative strategy is transforming investment going forward and announcing a new era of digital asset management and ownership.

Democratizing Wealth in the Digital Age: The Power of Tokenization in the Digital Era

Tokenizing the commodities market has many different appeals and provides transforming advantages going beyond simple technological innovation. This invention is changing the environment for investors and the larger commodities market and bringing in a period of more accessibility, efficiency, and openness. One may understand its significant influence on the democratization of wealth in the digital age by looking at the convincing benefits that make tokenizing a revolutionary force.

The introduction of tokenization marks a revolution for investors, creating profitable prospects hitherto the only realm of privileged or institutional investors. Democratized access allows anybody to now own a portion of a gold mine or fund worldwide agricultural projects. Tokenizing reduces the cost barrier for admission, therefore fostering a more inclusive investing environment in which a more diverse range of investors may engage. This increased inclusivity lets those with little means interact with valuable assets, diversifying their portfolios and exposing themselves to markets once beyond reach.

Tokenization's resulting higher liquidity improves the appeal of this investment approach even more. With investments locked in for long stretches, traditional commodities markets are sometimes defined by rigidity and a glacial pace. Tokenization adds liquidity to this system so that investors may quickly purchase, sell, or exchange tokens on digital platforms at any moment—representing actual assets. Apart from more flexibility, this 24/7 market operation helps to improve pricing discovery and market efficiency. The ability to quickly enter and exit positions gives investors a more agile and responsive investment experience that fits very well with the dynamic character of contemporary financial markets.

Another major benefit of tokenization is fractional ownership, which democratizes investment by letting people own tiny portions of pricey assets. This allows an investor to diversify their portfolio without using large amounts of cash by holding some of a barrel of oil or a share of a precious metal. More customized risk management and investment strategies made possible by such granularity in investment possibilities help to satisfy different financial goals and risk tolerance. Diversity with smaller assets also reduces risk by acting as a barrier against market volatility.

Blockchain technology—which offers an unchangeable database for tracking ownership and transactions—is fundamental in tokenization. This invention tackles long-standing problems with opacity and possible fraud common in conventional markets for commodities. Every change in ownership and transaction is open, verifiable, and safe, hence building confidence among the participants. Blockchain technology's increased openness and security guarantee that every player in the market has access to correct and dependable information, therefore supporting integrity and fairness in the investing process.

Tokenization has similarly convincing effects on the commodities market. One of the main benefits is increased efficiency since tokenization simplifies several market operations, including trade finance and post-transaction settlement. Tokenization speeds transaction times and lowers operating costs by removing the need for copious documentation and manual validation. Along with reducing obstacles to market entrance, this higher efficiency makes commodities trading more appealing to a wider spectrum of investors.

Tokenizing also gives issuers fresh financing options. Accessing a worldwide pool of capital allows issuers to reach investors who were hitherto excluded because of financial or geographic restrictions. This flood of capital can greatly increase liquidity, therefore supplying the required money for commodities sector innovation and expansion. Access to many sources of finance helps propel development and expansion, thereby strengthening the more dynamic and competitive market.

Still another major benefit of tokenization is enhanced traceability. For goods, this function provides unmatched openness that lets one follow the lifetime of assets from manufacture to final sale. Tokenization guarantees that every link of the supply chain for agricultural products, minerals, and other goods is recorded and traceable. This traceability helps to confirm the ethical sourcing of goods and authenticity, thus supporting sustainability and moral behavior. Making better-informed decisions by consumers and investors helps businesses and initiatives that line with their beliefs.

The tokenization of goods marks a basic change in the investing scene and provides transforming advantages that distribute wealth in the digital era. Tokenizing gives investors democratized access, more liquidity, fractional ownership, more transparency, and more security. Regarding the commodities market, it offers better traceability, fresh financing sources, and more efficiency. It will probably become the norm as blockchain technology develops and gains adoption since it will help to close the distance between conventional investing methods and the direction of the digital economy. This invention will open the path for a new era of financial empowerment and sustainability by promising to produce a more inclusive, efficient, and transparent investing environment.

Unlocking the Future of Investment: The Seamless Journey of Commodities Tokenization

Though complicated, commodity tokenization follows a graceful and orderly procedure to turn physical objects into digital tokens that represent value and ownership. This method not only disrupts commodities' investment access but also creates fresh opportunities for using digital assets. The trip starts with valuation, where the market value of the commodity is determined based on current market conditions and relevant pricing benchmarks. This is the vital stage of valuation, in which the commodity's market value is determined. Experts examine many elements, including market trends, supply and demand dynamics, and particular commodity properties such as the grade of a metal, the quality of agricultural produce, or gemstone features. Tokenization is built on this valuation, which guarantees that the digital form of the commodity faithfully captures its actual worth.

CHAPTER 18 DATA-DRIVEN DYNAMICS: LINKING REAL-WORLD INSIGHTS TO TRADE FINANCE

The asset is actually tokenized following valuation. This entails breaking up the asset into smaller, reasonable chunks or tokens, each reflecting a fractional ownership in the good. These tokens are then generated and encrypted using blockchain technology, guaranteeing validity and security. By letting the physical commodity be owned, exchanged, and controlled digitally, this digital revolution bridges conventional commodities with the digital finance ecosystem. Token production is a painstaking procedure that guarantees every token is exactly a mirror of the value of the underlying asset.

Choosing a suitable trading platform or digital exchange comes next with the produced tokens. Tokens can be posted, bought, and traded on these platforms, which act as their market. Designed on blockchain technologies, they provide open and safe transactions. Choosing the correct platform is really vital since it will affect how quickly and safely traders of tokens may operate. The platform choice also determines the token's visibility and liquidity, impacting their market performance.

The tokens go for trade after they are posted on a selected platform. By buying tokens, investors have fractional ownership in the underlying good. Trading tokenized goods is like trading stocks or cryptocurrency; market supply and demand affect prices. Every transaction on the blockchain ledger provides a clear, unchangeable record of ownership and exchanges. Because investors may track the history of their tokens and confirm their legitimacy, this openness helps them to build confidence.

Following a trade, the buyer gains the token—and so, indirectly, the ownership share in the real asset it stands for. Blockchain technology helps to guarantee precise ownership records and security of transactions, therefore enabling this smooth settlement procedure. The instantaneous character of blockchain settlements removes the delays sometimes connected with conventional commodity trading, therefore improving the efficiency and investor friendliness of the process.

Tokenized goods have uses in finance outside of trade. Token collateral in lending, for example, gives lenders and borrowers a safe and liquid asset. By means of staking yield farming, or liquidity provision, they can also be included in distributed finance (DeFi) projects, therefore enabling token holders to earn possible rewards. These creative applications of tokenized products show the adaptability and possibilities of this technology in contemporary banking.

The subtleties of commodity tokenization expose a deliberately orchestrated dance between the real and digital spheres. This technique not only streamlines and guarantees investing in commodities but also opens the path for creative financial uses by turning physical assets into transferable digital tokens. Tokenization democratizes access to valuable assets, therefore allowing a greater spectrum of investors to engage in marketplaces once off-limits. By increasing liquidity and openness, it also improves market efficiency, facilitating investor buying, selling, and asset management.

The possibility of tokenized goods to transform the global economy becomes ever more important as the technological and legal environments change. Gradually changing to fit this new asset class, regulatory systems offer legal certainty and investor protection. Concurrent with these developments in blockchain and digital finance are increasing opportunities for tokenized assets by including them into more general financial ecosystems.

The flawless path of commodity tokenization marks a fresh phase of asset management and investment. This procedure closes the distance between conventional goods and the digital economy by using blockchain technology, providing a more inclusive, effective, and open approach to investing in actual assets. Tokenization promises to change the financial environment as it becomes more adopted, therefore generating fresh chances for wealth creation, innovation, and expansion. Investment in commodities going forward is digital; the path of tokenization is just starting.

The Trials and Triumphs of Commodities Tokenization: Challenges, Opportunities, and Future Potential

Negotiating the innovative field of commodity tokenization, participants discover themselves on the brink of a huge and mostly unexplored digital terrain. This creative mix of modern blockchain technology with established commodities markets marks a fresh period of investing prospects. Still, the road is not without difficulties and considerations; one must carefully negotiate a complicated and changing surroundings.

The scene of regulations around commodity tokenization is changing. The laws and norms controlling these new kinds of investment change as governments and financial regulatory agencies negotiate the effects of blockchain technology and digital assets. For both issuers and investors who have to keep current with evolving legal systems across several countries, this unpredictability presents a complicated navigating terrain. The absence of consistency in rules might impede international investments and need for careful compliance and legal structure approach. Before completely committing to this creative investment strategy, potential investors and issuers—who search for stability and clarity—often hesitate due to this regulatory uncertainty. Therefore, the development of coherent and comprehensive regulatory frameworks that promote innovation while guaranteeing investor protection depends on continuous communication among authorities, industry stakeholders, and legal experts.

The technological framework of commodity tokenization is its foundation; it must be strong and safe to enable the issuing, trading, and administration of digital tokens. Creating such platforms calls for a substantial degree of technological knowledge and significant financial commitment. The necessity of these platforms to be user-friendly while guaranteeing the best levels of security to guard against fraud, hacking, and other cyber dangers adds to the difficulty. The difference in the quality and security of platforms gets more evident as the market for tokenized goods expands. Due care is therefore a crucial component of platform choice for investors as well as issuers. The first priority is making sure the selected platform offers the required technological capabilities, regulatory compliance, and security measures. Moreover, constant investments in cybersecurity, system enhancements, and technical support are crucial to preserving the integrity and dependability of these systems in the face of changing hazards.

Tokenized commodities, among other emerging markets, often face initial difficulties with liquidity and price discovery. Any market's proper operation depends on liquidity—that is, the simplicity with which tokens may be purchased and sold without appreciably influencing their price. Early on in the commodities tokenization process, the market might show low trade. volumes, which would restrict liquidity. Potential investors, who could be worried about their capacity to quickly and effectively enter or leave positions, may be discouraged by this lack of liquidity. Likewise, in the absence of a critical mass of market players and open trading data, it can be difficult to build dependable pricing discovery mechanisms and channels via which the market sets the price of tokenized commodities. Overcoming these obstacles calls for strategic market growth initiatives and patience, as well as a long-term investment viewpoint. Attracting a wide spectrum of participants—including institutional investors, retail investors, and market makers—who can supply the required trading volume and market depth—building a vibrant and liquid market for tokenized commodities requires

Realizing the full potential of this creative investment model will depend first on addressing these issues as the market for tokenized goods develops. Stakeholders have to be agile in navigating the changing regulatory terrain, make investments in creating and verifying strong technological platforms, and support market conditions fit for accurate price discovery and adequate liquidity. Overcoming these challenges will depend mostly on cooperation among technology companies, authorities, and industry players. Together, these players may establish consistent procedures, distribute resources and information, and build a friendly environment for the expansion of tokenized marketplaces.

The emphasis should be on creating a robust and strong market infrastructure going ahead that can help tokenized goods grow long-term. Investing in education and awareness campaigns to let possible investors know about the advantages and drawbacks of tokenized goods, creating creative financial products and services using tokenization, and so promoting a transparent and trustworthy market culture. Stakeholders can open fresh chances for expansion, diversity, and innovation in the worldwide commodities market by confronting these issues head-on and implementing a proactive attitude toward market development.

Although the road to general acceptance of commodity tokenization is paved with difficulties, the possible benefits of converting conventional asset classes into easily available digital investments are enormous. By gently navigating these uncharted territories, stakeholders can create new opportunities for growth, diversity, and innovation in the global commodities market. Although the road may be difficult, the end point offers a more inclusive, quick, and clear investment environment that uses blockchain technology to democratize wealth and generate value for investors all around. As the world welcomes the transforming possibilities of commodity tokenization, the challenges of today will open the path for the successes of tomorrow.

Tokenization Transformed: The Dawn of a New Investment Era

The field of investing and asset management is undergoing a dramatic change with the growing area of commodity tokenization. This is not just a fleeting trend, but rather a profound shift in how we engage with tangible objects, thereby bridging the gap between the digital and physical realms. This change promises to democratize investment possibilities, simplify market operations, and bring hitherto unheard-of degrees of openness. Looking ahead, the junction of increasing technology with legislative certainty is poised to spur more adoption and generate a range of creative uses.

CHAPTER 18   DATA-DRIVEN DYNAMICS: LINKING REAL-WORLD INSIGHTS TO TRADE FINANCE

One of the most intriguing stories of commodity tokenization is how it can let a larger audience access the financial universe. Fractionalizing physical asset ownership into digital tokens reduces the entrance hurdles, often keeping common investors away. Historically, purchases of commodities like gold, oil, or real estate needed large capital, therefore restricting involvement to affluent people or institutional investors. Tokenizing lets people buy tiny parts of very valuable goods, therefore upsetting this paradigm. Along with diversifying the investor base, this democratization brings fresh cash into markets, hence encouraging development and innovation. More diversified pools of investors provide fresh ideas and cash, which drives more dynamic market conditions and increases economic involvement by means of both.

Tokenizing simplifies the transactional environment of commodity markets. Blockchain technology significantly reduces transaction times and costs by bypassing the bureaucratic processes of traditional trading and settlement procedures. Transactions in conventional marketplaces often have many middlemen, each adding layers of time, money, and complexity. By use of a single, unchangeable ledger where transactions are securely recorded, blockchain technology streamlines these procedures. Not only are investors benefited by this efficiency gain, but issuers—who can more easily access worldwide markets—also win. Reduced transaction times and costs improve liquidity and enable more nimble market reactions, therefore helping all the players in the ecosystem.

Trust among market players is much enhanced by this quality. The opacity of ownership and transaction data can cause problems, including fraud, double-spending, and market manipulation in conventional markets. Because every transaction on a blockchain is accessible and verifiable, its open ledger answers these issues. By clearly seeing the origins, ownership history, and transactional integrity of the asset, investors help to reduce the risks connected with market manipulation and fraud. This improved openness helps to build market confidence and trust, therefore motivating more strong involvement and investment.

Widespread tokenization's roadmap is closely entwined with the change in regulatory environments. While governments all around struggle with the consequences of digital assets, the next few years will probably witness harmonization of laws that stimulate invention while safeguarding investor interests. Tokenized assets operate in a disorganized regulatory environment where different governments apply diverse methods of control and supervision. This inconsistency could generate uncertainty and stop market expansion. As authorities grow more comfortable with blockchain

CHAPTER 18   DATA-DRIVEN DYNAMICS: LINKING REAL-WORLD INSIGHTS TO TRADE FINANCE

technology and its ramifications, we should anticipate more coherent and encouraging legislative settings to develop. Encouragement of a stable and flourishing ecosystem for tokenized goods depends on this regulatory maturity.

Clear, uniform rules will give the legal confidence required to draw more investors and issuers, hence promoting additional market adoption and innovation.

Tokenizing gold bars or oil barrels is only one aspect of digitization; another is rethinking asset use. Tokenization opens up a world of opportunities for creative financial applications. For example, it enables micro-investments in large infrastructure projects, allowing individuals to contribute to funding initiatives that were previously inaccessible. This democratization of investment access can revolutionize the financing of development projects and critical infrastructure, making it more inclusive and efficient. Moreover, tokenization can generate new financial instruments that provide exposure to previously non-liquid assets. For instance, tokenizing real estate properties—typically challenging to trade quickly—enables their trading on digital marketplaces, enhancing liquidity and accessibility. This shift towards more efficient, transparent, and fractionalized asset ownership has the potential to reshape traditional investment landscapes and broaden participation in wealth creation.

Furthermore, including tokenized goods into decentralized finance (DeFi) systems could transform our lending, borrowing, and yield-generating distributions. DeFi systems use smart contracts to automate and safeguard transaction-distributed systems. It will increase the value and attraction of tokenized assets as well as provide fresh approaches for investors to control risk and create profits. Tokenized assets, for example, might be loan collateral, therefore offering liquidity without having the underlying asset sold. Token holders could also engage in yield farming, staking their tokens to get interest or incentives, hence improving the value proposition of tokenized goods.

The birth of commodity tokenization marks a new investment era marked by democratized access, improved market efficiency, more transparency, and limitless invention based on changed access. Tokenization is changing our investments in and management of real assets by closing the gap between conventional assets and digital technologies. The possibility of tokenized goods to revolutionize the world economy becomes ever more important as technology develops and legislative systems change. A turning point in the development of the investment scene, the road ahead promises to open fresh chances for growth, diversification, and financial inclusion.

CHAPTER 18   DATA-DRIVEN DYNAMICS: LINKING REAL-WORLD INSIGHTS TO TRADE FINANCE

Sealing the Vault: The Transformative Journey of Asset Tokenization

Offering a link between conventional commodity investments and the efficiency and accessibility of blockchain technology, commodity tokenization is poised to revolutionize our interaction with and investment in the real world. This sector promises to make commodity investments more inclusive, liquid, and transparent as it develops, therefore profoundly changing the world economy.

Tokenization's significant influence on the investment community as well as the commodities market at large appeals to both. Tokenization is laying the groundwork for a more accessible, reliable market by connecting the agility and transparency of blockchain technology with the actual value of real-world goods. Previously excluded investors because of strong entrance restrictions can now engage in markets once restricted for institutional players or the wealthy. Along with widening the investor base, this democratization brings fresh cash into the market, therefore encouraging invention and economic progress.

Tokenization simplifies the transactional environment of commodities markets, therefore improving market efficiency. Typical features of traditional commodity trade are many middlemen, long settlement times, and expensive transaction expenses. By offering a single, unchangeable ledger where transactions are securely and publicly noted, blockchain technology cuts around this red tape. This lowers the risk of fraud or mistakes, speeds transaction times, and helps to save expenses. The capacity of issuers to easily access worldwide markets changes everything and presents fresh opportunities for capital raising and market expansion.

Tokenizing is really about the promise of increased security and openness. Blockchain technology guarantees that every transaction is entered on a transparent, unchangeable ledger, therefore offering a clear view of the provenance, ownership past, and transactional integrity of the item. This helps to foster confidence among market players by reducing the hazards connected with fraud and market manipulation. Accurate and verified information allows investors to make wise judgments that help to create a more stable and dependable market.

The path toward general acceptance of commodity tokenization is closely related to the change of legal environments. The regulatory scene is always changing while authorities all around struggle with the consequences of digital assets. Fostering a stable and growing ecosystem for tokenized goods depends on harmonizing laws to stimulate invention while safeguarding investment interests. Clear regulations will give the legal certainty required to draw more issuers and investors, hence promoting additional market adoption and innovation.

Tokenization has endless possibilities for driving creative ideas. Tokenizing goes beyond digitizing gold bars or oil barrels to allow one to rethink asset use. For big infrastructure projects, for example, it makes micro-investments possible so that people may help to fund previously unattainable undertakings. This might democratize access to investments in development projects and key infrastructure, therefore transforming the financing for large-scale projects. Tokenizing can also produce new financial instruments with exposure to hitherto illiquid assets, hence improving liquidity and accessibility.

Tokenized goods included in distributed finance (DeFi) systems could transform lending, borrowing, and yield generation. Using smart contracts to automate and safeguard transactions, DeFi platforms run free from conventional intermediaries. Including tokenized goods into these systems will increase the value and attraction of tokenized assets as well as provide fresh approaches for investors to control risk and create profits. Tokenized assets, for example, might be loan collateral, therefore offering liquidity without having the underlying asset sold. Token holders could also engage in yield farming, staking their tokens to collect interest or incentives, hence augmenting the value proposition of tokenized goods.

A more inclusive, efficient, and transparent market environment is clearly promised by commodity tokenization as we stand on the cusp of this digital revolution. From negotiating legal environments to guaranteeing technological resilience, the road ahead will surely provide difficulties. First and foremost is making sure the selected platforms provide the required technological capacity, regulatory compliance, and security features. Maintaining the integrity and dependability of these systems in the face of changing threats depends on continuous investments in cybersecurity, system enhancements, and technical support.

Our economic fabric could be profoundly changed by our shared search of this tokenized future. Stakeholders may open fresh chances for development, diversification, and financial inclusion by deftly negotiating these obstacles and welcoming blockchain technology's transforming power. As the world embraces the transforming potential of commodity tokenization, today's challenges will open the path for tomorrow's achievements.

CHAPTER 18   DATA-DRIVEN DYNAMICS: LINKING REAL-WORLD INSIGHTS TO TRADE FINANCE

The transforming trip of asset tokenization marks a major turn toward a more democratized and open worldwide economy. Tokenization is changing our investment in and management of real assets by closing the distance between conventional assets and digital technologies. The possibility of tokenized goods to revolutionize the world economy grows ever more important as technology develops and rules change. Digital will be the future of commodity investment; the path of tokenization is only starting and promises a new period of economic empowerment and invention.

Carbon Currency: Exploring the World of Carbon Credits and Voluntary Carbon Markets

In response to the escalating effects of climate change, the world is urgently seeking solutions to reduce greenhouse gas emissions. Stressing the need to limit global warming to 1.5°C above pre-industrial levels is essential to preventing the most catastrophic effects of climate change, the Intergovernmental Panel on Climate Change (IPCC) has issued severe warnings about. Reaching this ambitious target calls for a major decrease in greenhouse gas emissions, mostly resulting from burning fossil fuels for energy, deforestation, and certain industry operations.

Carbon trading, a market-based method using financial incentives to inspire companies to lower their carbon footprint, is one creative way to help lower emissions. Underlying this scheme is a special kind of money called carbon credits. Essential elements of carbon trading systems, carbon credits are concrete markers of emissions cuts. Every carbon credit marks the avoidance or removal from the atmosphere of one metric ton of carbon dioxide or similar greenhouse gases. Purchasing and selling these credits on foreign markets gives businesses financial incentives to lower their emissions.

By essentially pricing carbon emissions, the idea of carbon credits helps to turn the environmental cost of greenhouse gas emissions into a business cost. Businesses have a strong financial incentive from this pricing structure to reduce their emissions and make investments in greener, more sustainable technologies. Carbon credits directly help businesses that follow environmentally friendly policies by giving emission reductions a financial worth.

Grasping their function in carbon trading systems depends on knowing how carbon credits are produced. Many programs aiming at either lowering or eliminating greenhouse gas emissions can generate carbon credits. Among these initiatives could be those involving renewable energy sources, reforestation, energy efficiency enhancements, and more. Many times, strict verification procedures surround the development of carbon credits to guarantee that the promised emissions reductions are actual, quantifiable, and permanent.

Carbon credits help to offset difficult or impossible to completely eliminate emissions inside the carbon trading system. To offset their own emissions, businesses can buy credits, therefore balancing their carbon footprint. This system gives companies flexibility so they may keep running and expanding while nevertheless reaching their emissions goals. Furthermore, the exchange of carbon credits creates a market for emissions reductions, therefore promoting creativity and investment in green solutions in several spheres.

They have various effects on companies and the surroundings. For companies, the establishment of a carbon trading mechanism adds a fresh level of strategic planning. Businesses have to take into account their environmental effects and adherence to emissions rules in addition to their operational and financial objectives. This all-encompassing strategy can force companies toward more sustainable practices and cause notable changes in corporate behavior.

From an environmental standpoint, the broad acceptance of carbon trading and the use of carbon credits show enormous potential for significant greenhouse gas emissions to decrease. Carbon credits help everyone try to slow down climate change by motivating emissions cuts. Additionally helping the development and implementation of innovative technology that significantly reduces emissions are the financial gains connected with carbon credits.

Looking ahead, the possibilities of carbon credits and carbon trading to support worldwide initiatives against climate change remain great. The carbon market is probably going to grow as international cooperation and regulatory frameworks change, providing more chances for environmental protection and emissions lowering. Maintaining the integrity and potency of carbon trading systems will depend on the ongoing improvement of verification criteria and regulatory control.

In the fight against climate change, carbon credits serve as an effective tool as they transform emissions reductions into a traded commodity. This market-based strategy encourages companies to use greener methods as well as innovation and sustainable technology investment. Carbon credits and carbon trading will be crucial in determining a more sustainable future as the globe struggles with the pressing need of lowering greenhouse gas emissions.

CHAPTER 18   DATA-DRIVEN DYNAMICS: LINKING REAL-WORLD INSIGHTS TO TRADE FINANCE

Carbon Credits: A Vital Tool in the Global Effort to Combat Climate Change

One sort of environmental asset that shows a reduction or elimination of greenhouse gas emissions are carbon credits. They are essentially a gauge of "avoided" emissions, a means of gauging the amount of carbon dioxide or similar greenhouse gases kept from reaching the environment. Carbon credits mostly serve to motivate companies and people to participate in actions lowering their environmental effect, thereby helping to reduce greenhouse gas emissions.

Different activities that either eliminate already existing greenhouse gases from the environment or help to lower their emissions provide carbon credits. From solar power plants and wind farms to reforestation and afforestation projects absorbing carbon dioxide through photosynthesis, these projects span a broad spectrum. By proving quantifiable greenhouse gas emissions reduction, every kind of initiative helps to create carbon credits.

Each of the numerous forms of carbon credits corresponds with a different kind of emission reduction project and is under control by different criteria and rules. Projects running under the Clean Development Mechanism (CDM) of the Kyoto Protocol provide certified emission reductions (CERs). By letting developed nations engage in emission reduction programs in developing nations, this international convention seeks to lower greenhouse gas emissions. These programs obtain CERs, which developed countries can utilize to fulfill part of their Kyoto Protocol emission targets.

Created by initiatives run under the Joint Implementation (JI) framework of the Kyoto Protocol, another type of carbon credit is the emission reduction unit (ERU). ERUs, unlike CERs, are given for emission-reducing projects in developed nations pledging Kyoto Protocol emissions reductions. This system lets these nations work on projects lowering emissions inside their own borders, therefore supporting their national aims.

Apart from CERs and ERUs, projects not under Kyoto Protocol coverage provide verified emission reductions (VERs). Usually, businesses and people utilize VERs to willingly balance their own carbon emissions. Independent third-party companies confirm these credits' integrity and validity of the claimed emission cuts. For those who want to own their carbon impact outside of legal systems, VERs provide a voluntary and flexible means.

The credibility and efficacy of carbon credits depend on their measurement and validation. This procedure entails estimating the greenhouse gas emissions that a project has either lowered or eliminated and thereafter confirming these changes by unbiased audits. The type of project and the applicable rules and standards will affect the particular techniques for measurement and verification. Maintaining confidence in the carbon credit system depends on strict validation procedures that guarantee the credits reflect real and quantifiable environmental advantages.

Understanding carbon credits calls for a respect of the intricate systems supporting their origination and validation. The credibility of carbon credits depends on open, strong methods that precisely measure and confirm emission reductions. Maintaining the integrity of carbon markets and guaranteeing that they significantly support world initiatives to slow down climate change depend on this credibility.

The function of carbon credits in enabling and motivating these reductions becomes even more important as the globe struggles with the pressing need of lowering greenhouse gas emissions. Carbon credits give companies and people a financial incentive to follow eco-friendly policies, therefore transforming the emission reduction into a real financial advantage. Carbon credits promote invention and investment in sustainable technology and practices by helping a market for emission reductions.

The future of carbon credits and carbon trading as a tool for addressing climate change appears quite promising. The carbon market is probably going to grow as international cooperation and regulatory frameworks change, providing more chances for environmental protection and emissions lowering. Maintaining the integrity and efficiency of carbon trading systems depends on the development of strict verification rules and regulatory control.

Overall, carbon credits serve as a highly effective tool in encouraging the reduction of greenhouse gas emissions. They give companies and people financial incentives to embrace cleaner living by turning emissions cuts into a tradable good. Along with major environmental advantages, this market-based approach helps the more general worldwide effort to slow down climate change. The part they play in determining a more sustainable future will surely become increasingly important as we go forward.

Financial and Strategic Impacts of Carbon Credits on Businesses: Navigating the Green Transition

Both financially and in terms of their sustainability policies, carbon credits, and trade can have major effects on companies. The need to interact with carbon credits and the development of carbon trading systems produce a dynamic scene for businesses negotiating their environmental obligations.

Financially speaking, carbon trading offers companies both expenses and possibilities. Large greenhouse gas-emitting companies may find their running expenses rising since they have to buy carbon credits to offset their emissions. This need can be costly, particularly for sectors with significant carbon footprints, as they have to consider every ton of carbon dioxide produced.

Still, this method also creates possible revenue-generating opportunities. Businesses that are successful in lowering their emissions below the mandated cap will build extra credits. By selling these extra credits to other businesses that have failed to reach their reduction targets, a fresh income source is generated. This feature of carbon trading makes emissions reductions a possibly profitable activity with a clear financial incentive for companies to make investments in environmentally friendly methods.

Furthermore, the financial ramifications of carbon trading go into choices about capital investment. Attaching a price to carbon emissions naturally makes renewable energy and other low-carbon technologies more financially appealing. The cost of carbon credits can tilt the scales in favor of investments in greener, more efficient technology above conventional, fossil fuel-based substitutes. Through lower energy costs and compliance expenses, this change not only fulfills environmental sustainability aims but also advances long-term financial gains.

Furthermore, affecting corporate sustainability plans are the effects of carbon credits on companies. The need to manage carbon credit portfolios motivates businesses to include environmental factors into their main strategy and operational planning. From energy efficiency increases to the deployment of renewable energy sources and the application of more sustainable supply chain management methods, this integration usually results in the acceptance of more sustainable practices.

The ability of businesses to control carbon credits and lower emissions becomes a competitive advantage. Those who shine in these areas not only gain from the sale of extra credits but also improve their business reputation. Showing a dedication to sustainability will help to build brand loyalty, draw environmentally concerned consumers, and give a competitive edge in markets where consumer pressure for green practices is growing and regulations are supporting this.

Beyond individual businesses, the impact of carbon credits on businesses spans more general industry patterns. Industries as a whole may move toward greener methods as more companies participate in carbon trading and give emissions cuts first priority. As businesses invest in new technologies and systems to lower their carbon footprints and seize the financial possibilities afforded by carbon trading, this group action can stimulate invention.

Moreover, the environment of regulation around carbon trading can greatly affect company activities. Businesses have to keep current with changing rules and guidelines to guarantee compliance and maximize their carbon credit plans. This legislative environment promotes a proactive attitude toward sustainability since companies try to predict changes and modify their operations in line with them.

Carbon credits impact companies in various ways, including financial, strategic, and operational aspects. Carbon trading has benefits as well as expenses, which motivates businesses to balance their emissions and maximize the possible income from extra credits. The need to buy and oversee carbon credits encourages investment in greener technologies, therefore promoting a change toward more sustainable corporate operations. This method not only helps environmental objectives but also gives companies a competitive edge in a society that is more and more environmentally conscious. The global endeavor to slow down climate change depends critically on carbon credits in forming corporate plans and operations as sectors change and regulatory systems keep developing.

The Role of Carbon Credits and Trading in Shaping a Sustainable Low-Carbon Future

Carbon credits and trade have become rather effective instruments in the worldwide endeavor to lower greenhouse gas emissions in view of the growing climate problem. Pricing carbon helps them convert the environmental cost of emissions into business costs, therefore motivating them to lower their emissions and fund greener technologies. This market-based strategy not only meets the immediate demand for emissions reduction but also includes environmental responsibility into the financial structure.

Crucially in this system are carbon credits, the currency of carbon trading. Purchased, sold, and traded in carbon markets, they offer a real count of "avoided" emissions. This generates a financial incentive for reducing emissions, motivating companies to actively participate in environmentally friendly operations. The dynamic character of carbon markets lets one be flexible and creative, therefore promoting a competitive atmosphere in which businesses try to reduce their carbon footprints.

Carbon trading provides companies both a possibility and a difficulty. For high-emitting businesses, it can raise expenses, so they are driven to buy carbon credits to offset their extra emissions. This extra expense motivates businesses to seek more environmentally friendly solutions in order to lower their financial load. Conversely, businesses that can successfully lower their emissions below their allocated cap stand to make money from selling their extra credits. Businesses are much inspired to invest in greener, more efficient technologies by this possibility for income generation.

Moreover, carbon trading can stimulate competitiveness and creativity inside sectors. Reducing emissions forces businesses to investigate and use cutting-edge technology and methods that not only lower emissions but also raise general efficiency. A stronger, more resilient business sector more suited for the low-carbon future can result from this technical development. Companies that aggressively include carbon trading into their sustainability plans not only lower their carbon footprint but also position themselves well for a time when carbon emissions are probably going to be progressively limited and valuable.

Future directions for carbon credits and trading seem bright. Growing awareness of the need for market-based solutions to solve climate change drives continuous legislative and technological innovation to help expand and deepen carbon markets. The worldwide reach and influence of these markets are projected to expand as more nations and industries adopt carbon trading systems, therefore offering a strong basis for ongoing emissions reductions.

Yet, the success of carbon trading in lowering world emissions will rely on a number of important elements. The efficiency of carbon markets will be much influenced by the stringency of emission limitations. More demand for carbon credits resulting from stricter limitations increases their value and motivates more major emission reductions. The integrity of carbon credits is equally crucial since the legitimacy and openness of emission reductions guarantee that carbon trading really helps the environment. Maintaining integrity will depend on thorough validation procedures and technological developments in emissions tracking.

Moreover, the degree of success of companies will be much influenced by their readiness to participate in carbon trading. Businesses have to actively participate in carbon markets and see the long-term advantages of funding sustainable activities. Along with helping them to comply immediately with rules, this involvement helps more general climate aims and promotes group efforts toward a low-carbon future.

The possibilities of carbon credits and carbon trading to help create a sustainable, low-carbon future should not be undervalued as we negotiate these obstacles. Carbon trading presents a workable route to significant emissions cuts by matching financial incentives with environmental goals. It inspires creativity, increases clean technology investment, and advances a more environmentally friendly corporate operations method. The function of carbon credits and carbon trading will be more important in forming a resilient and sustainable global economy as the world addresses the urgent problem of climate change.

Carbon Credits in Cap-and-Trade: Driving Emission Reductions Through Market-Based Solutions

In carbon trading, a market-based strategy meant to reduce greenhouse gas emissions, carbon credits are absolutely important. The foundation of this system is "cap and trade." Under this approach, the total emissions of some greenhouse gases allowed by companies, power stations, and other installations are limited or "capmed." Over time, this cap is gradually lowered such that overall emissions match environmental targets.

Every ton of carbon dioxide a company covered by the cap-and-trade system must carry one carbon credit. Two main methods one can get these credits are either by buying them from other businesses that have lowered their emissions and so have surplus credits or by means of an allocation from the government, either free or bought via auction. Since selling extra credits helps businesses financially, this method directly motivates them to reduce their emissions.

Carbon markets enable corporate trade of these credits. These networks let businesses with extra credits sell them to others that need more credits since they have lowered their emissions more than necessary, therefore addressing their needs. This dynamic guarantees that the total cap on emissions is kept while giving businesses freedom on how they reach their cuts.

CHAPTER 18   DATA-DRIVEN DYNAMICS: LINKING REAL-WORLD INSIGHTS TO TRADE FINANCE

The cap-and-trade system lets businesses save money by selling extra credits, therefore motivating them to cut their emissions. A corporation can sell more credits and thereby create income the more emissions it can cut. Conversely, businesses that fail to sufficiently lower their emissions have to buy extra credits, which increases their running expenses. This financial drive inspires ongoing efforts in industry-wide emission reduction.

There are several ways one might trade carbon credits. Although direct sales between businesses are somewhat prevalent, credits can also be traded on carbon exchanges or through brokers. Supply and demand inside the market define the cost of carbon credits. The stringency of the emission cap, the cost of lowering emissions, and projections about future market conditions all affect this price.

Thus, a key component of the cap-and-trade system, carbon credits help to turn the environmental need of lowering greenhouse gas emissions into an economic activity. Carbon trading stimulates invention and investment in greener technology by pricing emissions. Knowing that successful emission reductions can generate financial benefits, businesses are driven to create and apply plans that minimize their carbon footprint.

Carbon credits serve purposes in carbon trading beyond simple compliance. They reflect a change in our approach to climate change by including environmental objectives into economic systems. This strategy not only helps to reach emission goals but also creates a market for environmentally friendly technologies and methods. Carbon trading encourages a proactive attitude to lower greenhouse gas emissions by matching financial incentives with environmental responsibilities.

Furthermore, the changing character of carbon markets points to the future possible influence of more impact. Demand for carbon credits is probably going to grow as national rules and international accords get stricter. As businesses want to maximize the financial gains from selling extra credits, this could lead to more cuts in emissions. Maintaining the integrity and efficiency of carbon markets depends on the ongoing development of strong regulatory systems and open trading venues.

Carbon credits are essential for the operation of carbon trading systems since they offer an economic incentive for lower emissions as well as a means of emission control. By means of the cap-and-trade concept, carbon credits transform the difficulty of greenhouse gas reduction into a controllable and financially feasible choreography. This market-based strategy not only helps to comply with environmental rules but also stimulates invention and investment in sustainable practices, therefore supporting the larger endeavor to slow down global warming. Looking ahead, carbon credits will continue to be essential for carbon trading to help to shape a more sustainable and economically strong planet.

CHAPTER 18 DATA-DRIVEN DYNAMICS: LINKING REAL-WORLD INSIGHTS TO TRADE FINANCE

Navigating the Challenges of Carbon Trading: Risks, Complexity, and Strategic Considerations for Businesses

Although carbon trading has several advantages, companies have to negotiate some possible hazards and difficulties as well. The fluctuation of carbon prices presents one major risk that can impede investment preparation. Changes in regulatory rules, market demand, and the general state of the economy all affect the price of carbon credits. This erratic nature can make it difficult for companies to precisely project expenses and benefits, therefore influencing long-term strategic decisions and financial planning.

A further difficulty arises from the intricacy of carbon markets. For companies—especially those new to carbon trading—navigating the complex web of rules, standards, and verification procedures can be intimidating. Knowing the several kinds of carbon credits, project eligibility requirements, and measuring and verifying processes calls for specific expertise and tools. This intricacy could pose a barrier to entry, especially for smaller businesses that lack the capacity to manage these regulatory criteria.

Furthermore, although carbon trading encourages emission cuts, it does not always guarantee that these cuts will be attained in the most environmentally friendly or economical way. Sometimes companies would find it more affordable to buy carbon credits than to fund their initiatives for emission reduction. While following carbon trading rules, this strategy might not necessarily coincide with more general environmental objectives. For example, a corporation can decide to purchase credits from less successful worldwide emissions-reducing projects instead of putting strong emissions-reducing policies into place inside their operations.

This relationship emphasizes a major difficulty: juggling the demand for real and efficient emission reductions with the financial incentives given by carbon trading. The general effectiveness of carbon trading in slowing down climate change may be compromised if companies give cost cuts over environmental damage top priority. Maintaining the integrity of the system depends on carbon credits reflecting actual, verifiable, and significant emissions decreases.

Moreover, the scene of regulations regarding carbon trading is always changing. Availability and cost of carbon credits might vary depending on changes in national regulations, international agreements, and market conditions. Companies have to be alert and flexible, always changing their plans to follow fresh rules and seize fresh possibilities. This necessity for continuous modification introduces yet another level of risk and complexity.

The natural uncertainty and possible difficulties related to carbon trading call for companies to use a deliberate and educated approach. Good involvement in carbon markets calls not only for a dedication to sustainability but also for a thorough awareness of environmental effects, market processes, and regulatory systems. To balance economic and environmental issues and reach their emission reduction targets, businesses must make investments in knowledge and resources to negotiate this challenging terrain.

Carbon trading is not without risks and difficulties, even if it presents an excellent possibility for lowering greenhouse gas emissions. Businesses have to take into account price volatility, market complexity, government costs, and the possibility of less-than-ideal environmental results. Dealing with these difficulties calls for a calculated and informed strategy that guarantees that carbon trading makes a significant contribution to the worldwide endeavor to slow down global warming. The objective still is to establish a sustainable and efficient method for lowering emissions and safeguarding our planet while companies and governments keep honing and improving carbon trading systems.

The Future of Carbon Credits and Trading: Key Trends and Developments in Climate Action

The need to solve climate change is more urgent, so the importance of carbon credits and trading is going to grow. Several important trends and possible developments will define the direction of these market-based systems as the terrain of climate action changes.

The important role market-based systems like carbon trading may play in tackling climate change is becoming increasingly acknowledged right now. As part of their national plans, more nations are either implementing or contemplating carbon pricing systems—including carbon trading plans. Companies as well are increasingly conscious of the financial hazards connected to climate change and the possible benefits of moving to a low-carbon economy. This change in viewpoint is helping carbon trading to be more accepted and used as a practical instrument for emissions control.

Carbon markets should expand and deepen in the foreseeable future. More nations and industries will probably be included in the framework of carbon trading systems as part of this growth, therefore extending the worldwide influence and impact of these markets. Furthermore, there is possibility for further connection between several carbon markets, which would allow international carbon credit trading. Such interdependence could improve market efficiency, therefore offering more freedom and chances for worldwide emissions reductions.

Furthermore, on the horizon are developments and ideas inside the carbon credit system. Improving the carbon credit measuring and verification procedures is one area with enormous promise. Blockchain and remote sensing, among other technological developments, could completely change the way emissions are recorded and validated. These technologies could guarantee that promised reductions are real and quantifiable, therefore boosting the legitimacy and openness of carbon credits. Maintaining confidence and efficiency in carbon markets depends on this enhancement in responsibility.

The emergence of new kinds of carbon credits that reward different kinds of climate action is also rather fascinating. Credit systems could be created, for example, to honor initiatives in carbon capture and storage or steps meant to improve climate resilience. These new kinds of credits would widen the range of carbon markets and support different creative solutions to address climate change.

Future carbon trading will be shaped in significant part by government control and international agreements. While international agreements set the aims and incentives driving carbon trading, regulatory frameworks offer the required guidelines and rules controlling carbon trading. A historic worldwide agreement on climate change, the Paris Agreement emphasizes the need for carbon pricing in reaching its objective of restricting world warming to much below 2°C. Under this accord, nations are working together to create guidelines for a new worldwide carbon market, hence potentially increasing carbon trading activity.

The larger worldwide endeavor to fight climate change will entwine carbon credits and trading into its future. Carbon markets are probably going to become a more important component of our approach to lowering greenhouse gas emissions as more nations and industries participate in carbon trading and as technological and regulatory developments improve the system's efficiency. The ongoing development of these markets calls for a balanced strategy combining creativity with strong regulation to guarantee that carbon trading efficiently helps to create a sustainable and resilient future.

Considering all factors, the future of carbon credits and carbon trading holds significant potential. Together with technological advancements and supportive laws, the expanding reach of carbon markets lays the foundation for these mechanisms to play a significant role in global climate action. Achieving significant decreases in greenhouse gas emissions and lessening of the effects of climate change will depend on the incorporation of carbon trading into national and international climate policies as we proceed. Though the road ahead will be difficult, with a combined effort, the future of carbon credits and carbon trading can greatly help to create a better earth.

Tokenizing Carbon Credits: Revolutionizing Global Markets for Environmental Sustainability

Combining environmental stewardship with the creative potential of blockchain technology, the tokenization of carbon credits marks a revolutionary advancement in the struggle against climate change. This procedure creates digital currencies on a blockchain using carbon credits—certificates denoting a particular amount of carbon dioxide or other greenhouse gases either decreased, avoided, or removed from the environment. By improving the openness, efficiency, and accessibility of carbon credit markets, this creative solution transforms the way these natural resources are traded and managed.

The path of carbon credits starts with the identification and confirmation of actions that either eliminate or lessen greenhouse gases. Among other things, these projects might be forestry campaigns, renewable energy sources, and energy efficiency enhancement efforts. Once confirmed by reputable companies, carbon credits—which show the measured environmental advantages—are granted. Traditionally, trade of these credits has been tainted by possible fraud, inefficiency, and lack of openness. Blockchain technology offers a safe, unchangeable, open ledger for tracking and storing carbon credits, therefore addressing these problems head-on.

Starting with the digitization of carbon credits, tokenization converts them into digital assets fit for simple blockchain trade. By means of fractionalization of carbon credits made possible by this digital representation, smaller, more easily accessible units can be purchased and sold by a larger spectrum of investors. Tokenization democratizes access to carbon credit markets by lowering the entrance barriers, thereby motivating more involvement from people and companies dedicated to lowering their carbon footprint.

The more openness tokenizing carbon credits gives to the market, one of their most important benefits is that every token transaction leaves an unambiguous, unchangeable track of ownership and movement on a blockchain. This openness guarantees that every player in the market may confirm the validity of the carbon credits they are trading, therefore lowering the possibility of double-counting and fraud. Blockchain records are unchangeable; hence, once a carbon credit is retired—that is, used to offset emissions—it cannot be reused, maintaining market integrity.

Tokenizing carbon credits also helps greatly with efficiency. Conventional carbon credit marketplaces sometimes call for time-consuming procedures comprising many middlemen and thorough documentation. By allowing direct peer-to-peer transactions and therefore lowering the need for middlemen and quickening transaction times, blockchain technology simplifies these procedures. This efficiency not only makes trading more practical but also lowers transaction costs, therefore enabling participants to participate in carbon-offsetting operations to be more financially viable.

The worldwide character of blockchain systems helps to improve access even more. By means of international trading, carbon credits tokenized on a blockchain help to break down geographical limitations and foster a more homogeneous and effective worldwide market. Tokens may be bought and sold around the clock, therefore enabling a more dynamic and responsive market and more liquidity worldwide. Trade of carbon credits abroad also helps to create a more homogeneous and harmonic global carbon market, which is absolutely vital for properly tackling climate change on a worldwide basis.

Another fascinating development in this area is the inclusion of tokenized carbon credits into distributed finance (DeFi) systems. DeFi systems use smart contracts to automate and safeguard transactions, therefore running without conventional middlemen. Including tokenized carbon credits into these platforms helps to establish new financial instruments and services that provide creative means for investors to earn returns while supporting environmental sustainability. Tokenized carbon credits, for example, might be collateral for loans, therefore giving investors liquidity without having the underlying commodity sold. Furthermore, encouraging the retention of carbon credits, yield farming, and staking prospects helps to support the stability and expansion of the market.

Still, there are obstacles to the way tokenized carbon credits are used widely. Tokenized carbon credits must be acknowledged and approved across several countries, depending on regulatory clarity and harmony. Working together, policymakers and regulatory authorities may create systems that foster innovation while safeguarding investor interests and guaranteeing carbon credit environmental integrity. Overcoming these legal obstacles and creating a reliable market for tokenized carbon credits will depend on public and business sector cooperation.

The success of tokenized carbon credits depends also on technological robustness. Blockchain systems have to be scalable, user-friendly, and safe if they are to enable effective management and trade of these digital assets. Protecting against any hazards and guaranteeing the dependability of the platform depends on continuous expenditures in cybersecurity, system upgrades, and technical support. Furthermore, ongoing innovation and development are needed to match the changing needs of the market and incorporate new capabilities, improving the value and utility of tokenized carbon credits.

A more transparent, efficient, and easily accessible carbon credit market is the transforming result of tokenizing carbon credits. This creative solution solves long-standing problems with conventional carbon credit markets by using blockchain technology, therefore opening the path for a more inclusive and successful worldwide effort to counteract climate change. The possibility for tokenized carbon credits to transform investment and trade practices becomes increasingly clear as the technology and legislative environment change. A major change toward a better and more sustainable future is the promise of a more democratized and transparent global economy, where environmental sustainability is effortlessly included in financial markets.

Tokenizing Carbon Credits: Revolutionizing Carbon Markets for a Sustainable Future

Tokenized carbon credits are a novel merging of modern digital technology with environmental responsibility. On a blockchain, these digital depictions of carbon credits capture the environmental advantage of lowering, avoiding, or eliminating one metric ton of carbon dioxide or its equivalent in other greenhouse gases. By converting carbon credits into digital tokens offered, acquired, and exchanged on different blockchain-based systems, this creative solution democratizes access to carbon markets and improves the efficiency and openness of these vital environmental tools.

The basic idea of carbon offsetting is central to tokenized carbon credits. Certificates known as carbon credits go to companies working to lower greenhouse gas emissions. These projects could range in nature from reforestation campaigns and energy efficiency gains to renewable energy projects, including solar or wind farms. Every carbon credit represents the avoidance, reduction, or removal of a specific quantity of CO_2 or its equivalent in other greenhouse gases from the atmosphere, verified through accredited projects. Usually marked by inefficiency, opacity, and limited access, over-the-counter markets have long been the venue for trading carbon credits.

Blockchain technology presents a transforming answer to these problems. Tokenizing carbon credits: these natural resources become digital tokens logged on a blockchain. By means of this distributed ledger technology, every token offers a visible, unchangeable record that guarantees the verifiable provenance, ownership, and transaction history of the carbon credits. One of the main problems with conventional carbon markets is the possibility of double-counting or fraud; this openness solves this one. Every tokenized carbon credit is different and cannot be replicated or distorted, therefore building more confidence among players in the market.

Tokenizing carbon credits starts with the certificates themselves being verified and issued. Accredited companies evaluate and certify the environmental advantages of different initiatives, verifying that the promised greenhouse gas reductions or removals are actual, quantifiable, and extra. Once confirmed, a blockchain system allows these carbon credits to be turned into digital currency. Each credit is digitally represented and recorded on the blockchain, where it may be traced and traded with unheard-of security and openness.

Tokenized carbon credits have several clear benefits over their conventional equivalents. First of all, by reducing the entrance obstacles, they democratize access to carbon markets.

Trading carbon credits in conventional markets sometimes calls for enormous financial resources and access to specialist platforms, therefore restricting involvement to big companies and institutional investors. Smaller entities—including people and small businesses—can engage in carbon offsetting with tokenization. Purchasing fractional shares of carbon credits allows these new players to support worldwide efforts on emissions reduction and gain from the financial possibilities the carbon markets offer.

Tokenized carbon credits also help the carbon markets be more liquid. With transactions sometimes including long talks and middlemen, traditional carbon trading may be slow and difficult. By allowing direct peer-to-peer transactions and thereby lowering transaction times and costs, blockchain technology simplifies this procedure. A more dynamic and responsive market results from the simpler purchase and sale of carbon credits made possible by this higher liquidity. Furthermore, supporting a more flexible and easily accessible market environment is the possibility to exchange tokens on digital platforms all around the clock.

CHAPTER 18   DATA-DRIVEN DYNAMICS: LINKING REAL-WORLD INSIGHTS TO TRADE FINANCE

Tokenized carbon credits' legitimacy depends critically on the security and openness blockchain technology offers. Every transaction is entered on a distributed ledger that offers a clear, unchangeable ownership and movement record. This openness guarantees correct portrayal of the environmental advantages of the carbon credits and helps to reduce fraud risk. By verifying the validity of their carbon credits, companies and investors help to boost market confidence and more strong involvement by supporting their legitimacy.

Tokenized carbon credits can also be included in distributed finance (DeFi) systems, therefore providing fresh financial innovation opportunities. DeFi systems use smart contracts to automate and safeguard transactions, therefore running without conventional middlemen. Tokenized carbon credits allow new financial instruments and services, including collateralized loans, yield farming, and stake possibilities, to be developed on these systems. By including carbon credits into the financial ecosystem, these developments not only give investors fresh approaches to create returns but also help to promote the wider acceptance of them.

Blockchain systems' worldwide character emphasizes even more the possibilities of tokenized carbon credits. Geographical and legal constraints often divide traditional carbon markets, therefore restricting cross-border trading and market integration. Blockchain technology allows flawless worldwide transactions, therefore transcending these constraints. Globally traded tokenized carbon credits help create a more homogeneous and efficient market, supporting worldwide cooperation in the battle against climate change. This worldwide reach helps projects with significant environmental effects anywhere to transfer funding to where it is most needed, therefore supporting initiatives regardless of their location.

Regulatory clarity and uniformity will be crucial to guaranteeing the general acceptance and success of tokenized carbon credits as their market develops. Working together, policymakers and regulatory authorities may create systems that foster innovation while safeguarding investor interests and guaranteeing carbon credit environmental integrity. Overcoming legal obstacles and creating a reliable market for tokenized carbon credits will depend on public and private sector cooperation.

Using blockchain technology to improve the openness, efficiency, and accessibility of carbon markets, tokenized carbon credits offer a transforming method of environmental asset management. This creative answer democratizes access to carbon offsetting, boosts market liquidity, and guarantees transaction security and integrity by turning carbon credits into digital tokens. Tokenized carbon credits clearly have the ability to transform the fight against climate change as long-evolving technology and regulatory systems develop. Promising to be more inclusive, efficient, and transparent worldwide economy, this new era of digital carbon markets will encourage more cooperation and investment in sustainable development by means of their influence.

Tokenizing Carbon Credits: Revolutionizing the Carbon Market Through Blockchain Technology

By cleverly combining blockchain technology with environmental science, the tokenization process for carbon credits turns conventional carbon credits into digital commodities readily traded and controlled. Starting with the creation and validation of carbon credits and ending in their distribution as digital tokens on blockchain systems, this process consists of numerous important stages.

The path begins with the creation of carbon credits by different operations meant to lower greenhouse gas emissions. Projects involving renewable energy sources, such as the installation of solar panels or wind turbines, reforestation initiatives involving tree planting to absorb CO_2 from the atmosphere, and energy efficiency enhancements lowering the required energy consumption for particular operations, can all be part of these activities. Each of these projects reduces, avoids, or eliminates a designated quantity of CO_2 or another greenhouse gas, which is subsequently tallied as carbon credits.

These carbon credits must be confirmed by reputable criteria like the gold standard or the verified carbon standard to guarantee they really provide environmental advantages. Certification is a thorough process whereby the environmental impact of the projects is evaluated to guarantee that the reductions are actual, quantifiable, and extra—that is, they would not have happened without the particular project. In this stage, third-party auditors are absolutely important since they independently verify the assertions made by the project developers. Maintaining the integrity and believability of the carbon credits depends on this certification and verification process.

Digitalization comes next once the carbon credits are validated and certified. During this phase, a blockchain platform turns the confirmed carbon credits into digital coins. Every token has metadata including comprehensive details on the source, certification, and carbon credit environmental impact. This metadata guarantees traceability from the source of every tokenized carbon credit, therefore fostering openness and responsibility. The digital version of the carbon credits produced by the digitizing process facilitates exchange and management of them.

Using smart contracts signifies the next crucial turn in the tokenization process. Smart contracts are self-executing agreements with directly written-in code terms of agreement. These agreements guarantee that the terms and conditions—including ownership rights and transferability—are followed without middlemen by automating the token issuing and management. Smart contracts help to improve the security and efficiency of the tokenization process, therefore lowering the danger of fraud and human mistakes.

Smart contracts help to produce digital tokens. Original holders of the carbon credits, including project developers or companies who created the credits by means of their environmental operations, can be awarded these tokens. Alternatively, the tokens can be offered to investors engaged in the tokenizing platform, who buy them to help environmental programs and maybe get a profit on their investment. The tokens can be readily accessed for trading by means of digital wallets after they are issued.

Trading and management of the tokenized carbon credits marks the last stage in the tokenizing process. By use of distributed exchanges, these digital tokens enable real-time trading of carbon credits, therefore offering a liquid market. Blockchain technology guarantees that every transaction is entered on an open, unchangeable ledger, therefore strengthening responsibility and confidence among market players. Knowing that the background and legitimacy of every token are verifiable, investors may purchase, sell, and exchange tokens with confidence. This openness promotes a more dynamic and efficient market where carbon credits may be rapidly and simply traded.

Carbon credits' tokenization has a number of major benefits. It democratizes access to carbon markets, therefore enabling a wider spectrum of investors—including people and smaller companies—to engage in carbon offsetting. More investment in environmental projects driven by this higher involvement helps to speed efforts to lower greenhouse gas emissions. Furthermore, the improved liquidity given by blockchain-based trading systems facilitates market participants' entrance and exit from positions, therefore promoting a more responsive and flexible market.

Moreover, many of the difficulties related to conventional carbon markets are addressed by the openness and security blockchain technology offers. Since every tokenized carbon credit is unique and cannot be replicated or distorted, the possibility of fraud and double-counting is much lowered. By guaranteeing that all market activities are traceable and verifiable, the clear, unchangeable record of transactions helps to foster trust among participants and hence uphold the integrity of the market.

Ultimately, the tokenizing of carbon credits offers a revolutionary way to trade and manage these important environmental resources. Using blockchain technology improves carbon market openness, efficiency, and transparency, therefore facilitating the participation of a wide spectrum of investors in the battle against climate change. A more inclusive, dynamic, and efficient worldwide endeavor to lower greenhouse gas emissions is made possible by the clear possibility for tokenized carbon credits to transform the carbon markets as the technologies and regulatory frameworks continue to change.

Transforming Carbon Markets: The Blockchain Technology Behind Carbon Credit Tokenization

Underlying the tokenization of value access, blockchain technology provides three key characteristics that improve the effect and functionality of carbon markets. A basic feature of blockchain, decentralization, runs on a distributed network that replaces central intermediaries, therefore removing their necessity. This distributed character guarantees that no entity controls the whole system and lowers the possibility of manipulation.

Blockchain improves system security and resilience against manipulation and false activity by spreading the control and validation procedures throughout a network of nodes.

Still, another essential quality of blockchain technology is transparency. Every transaction is entered into a public ledger, therefore enabling complete openness and traceability of carbon credit ownership and transfers. This openness guarantees that every transaction is traceable and publicly accessible, therefore greatly lowering the possibility of fraud and duplicate counting of carbon credits. Investors, authorities, and environmental groups, among other stakeholders, may boldly confirm the validity of every carbon credit, thereby building more market confidence.

Blockchain technology also revolves mostly around security. Its cryptographic systems provide data security and integrity, therefore stopping fraud and illegal modification of data. Every transaction generates an unchangeable chain of records by encryption and links to the one before it. Once data is entered on the blockchain, its cryptographic security guarantees that it cannot be changed or deleted without network consensus, therefore preventing false activity and guaranteeing the authenticity of carbon credits.

Smart contracts help to considerably increase efficiency. These self-executing agreements speed transactions by automating and simplifying procedures, therefore lowering administrative expenses. Without middlemen, smart contracts enforce token terms and conditions, including ownership rights and transferability, hence defining the token. By cutting the time and expenses connected with conventional carbon credit transactions, this automation helps to make the market more accessible and efficient.

Tokenized carbon credits show the transforming power of blockchain technology in improving market accessibility, transparency, and efficiency. Digitizing these environmental assets will help tokenization increase carbon market participation and enable more efficient and broad carbon offsetting projects. The ability of this technology to transform investment and trade practices globally becomes more clear as it develops and gains adoption, therefore indicating a major change toward a more democratic and open global economy.

The improved openness and traceability blockchain technology offers are among the most important advantages. Every tokenized carbon credit is noted in an unchangeable ledger with information on certification, provenance, and ownership history. This degree of openness guarantees that every transaction is traceable and publicly available, therefore lowering the possibility of carbon credit double counting and fraud. Stakeholders may boldly confirm the validity of every credit, thereby building more market confidence.

This also greatly increases liquidity and market accessibility. Illiquidity, in which purchasing and selling carbon credits can be labor-intensive and time-consuming, plagues many conventional carbon credit markets. Tokenization solves this by letting carbon credits be fractionalized into smaller pieces sold on digital platforms. This raises the liquidity of carbon credits, therefore facilitating buyer and seller entrance and exit from the market. Tokenizing carbon credits also democratizes access to them by allowing smaller investors to join the market, therefore expanding the investor base and improving market dynamics.

Further advantages of carbon credit tokenization are lower transaction costs and inefficiencies. Traditionally, the carbon credit market consists of several middlemen—brokers, registries, and auditors—who can increase transaction expenses and generate inefficiencies. Tokenizing uses smart contracts to automate and enforce transaction terms, therefore simplifying the process. These self-executing agreements greatly minimize administrative expenses and the time needed to finish transactions by doing away with middlemen. Faster and more cost-effective transactions in a more efficient market follow.

Two important issues blockchain technology addresses are ensuring authenticity and eliminating double counting. Double counting happens when more than one party claims the same carbon credit, therefore erasing the validity of carbon offsetting initiatives. The unchangeable ledger of blockchain and cryptographic security features guarantee that every tokenized carbon credit is original and cannot be replicated. This guarantees that every carbon credit is just used once and helps to avoid double counting, preserving the integrity of carbon offset claims. Blockchain's distributed character also makes it impossible for one entity to access the records, preventing fraud even further.

Tokenizing carbon credits also greatly facilitates worldwide cooperation. Often sold internationally, carbon credits include complicated legal contexts and compliance requirements. Tokenization offers a consistent digital framework that is easily flexible enough to fit various regulatory systems, therefore simplifying cross-border transactions. This increases the worldwide scalability of carbon markets and helps international cooperation on carbon offset initiatives.

Tokenizing carbon credits offers a transforming chance to improve the effectiveness and scope of carbon offset programs. Tokenization can stimulate more major participation in carbon markets by means of improved transparency, liquidity, and efficiency, as well as by guaranteeing authenticity and tokenization, therefore supporting worldwide initiatives against climate change. From negotiating legal environments to guaranteeing technological resilience, the road ahead will surely provide difficulties. Still, the group's search for this tokenized future has enormous power to fundamentally alter our economic fabric.

The blockchain technology underlying carbon credit tokenization provides important characteristics improving market accessibility, transparency, and efficiency. Tokenization can change the way carbon credits are exchanged and handled by using these characteristics, therefore improving the inclusive, efficient, and reliable nature of the market. The possibility for tokenized carbon credits to transform carbon markets and assist worldwide sustainability projects becomes ever more important as technology and regulatory systems keep changing. A major change toward a cleaner and more sustainable future is the promise of a more democratized and transparent global economy, where environmental sustainability is naturally included in financial markets.

Overcoming Challenges in Tokenizing Carbon Credits: Legal, Technological, and Market Barriers

Although tokenizing carbon credits has many advantages, it also poses significant dangers and problems that need to be properly controlled to guarantee the viability and success of this creative solution. Stakeholders that want to properly negotiate the complexity of tokenized carbon markets must first understand these obstacles.

Tokenizing carbon credits presents one of the main difficulties since negotiating the legal terrain is crucial. Various national and international rules govern carbon credit markets, and tokenization adds yet another level of complication. Avoiding legal traps requires ensuring adherence to current financial rules and environmental legislation. Tokenized carbon credits may also be difficult to adopt since companies and investors can be reluctant to participate in marketplaces where policies are not clear or changeable. Environmental and financial rules are dynamic and require constant monitoring and adaptation; thus, stakeholders must keep informed and flexible in their compliance plans.

Though they have many benefits, blockchain technology's technical features also carry serious hazards. Automated transactions under smart contracts call for careful programming to prevent mistakes that can cause operational interruptions or financial losses. The accuracy needed in coding these contracts offers limited space for mistakes; any error might have major consequences. Blockchain network security is also absolutely crucial. Blockchain systems are not immune to hacking or cyberattacks, notwithstanding their strong security measures. Maintaining belief in tokenized carbon credits depends on the technology's security and dependability. This entails always updating systems to guard against changing hazards and putting strict cybersecurity policies into effect.

Another difficulty tokenized carbon credits must negotiate is market adoption. Unfamiliarity or perceived hazards could cause traditional investors and companies to be reluctant to embrace new technologies. Gaining more general acceptance requires a higher understanding of the concrete advantages of tokenization. To show how tokenizing might improve market efficiency, openness, and accessibility, thorough education and outreach initiatives are needed. Furthermore, a continuous issue is blockchain systems' scalability. The fundamental technology has to be able to manage rising transaction volumes without sacrificing performance or security as the market for tokenized carbon credits expands. To support the growing market, continuous technological infrastructure and innovation investment is thus necessary.

Tokenization can bring volatility into the market even while improving liquidity. Tokenized carbon credits' value could vary depending on market demand, legislative changes, and more general economic circumstances. Price fluctuation might endanger companies depending on consistent carbon credit rates for planning and budgeting as well as investors. Control of this volatility calls for strong risk management techniques and systems for steady pricing. Furthermore, even if tokenization seeks to increase liquidity, markets might not reach enough depth and maturity to guarantee seamless trade and price stability. As the market grows, players in it have to be ready for the first phase of instability and adjustment.

Lack of standardization and compatibility among many tokenizing systems and blockchain networks presents still another major obstacle. Common standards help to prevent the fragmentation of the market, therefore impeding the flawless trading and tokenized carbon credit transfer. Ensuring interoperability and enabling more general market involvement depend on industry-wide standards being developed and adopted. The main goals of standardizing initiatives should be to establish consistent protocols and procedures that let several systems interact effortlessly, thereby fostering a coherent and integrated market.

Blockchain's promise of more openness does not solve a major problem with trust. Stakeholders have to believe the underlying carbon credits are legitimate and the tokenizing procedure fairly shows the claimed environmental advantages. Maintaining belief in tokenized carbon credits depends on strong verification and auditing systems being established. Third-party audits and open reporting policies should be among these systems to guarantee that every carbon credit satisfies high criteria. Developing and maintaining market confidence depends on all participants following high norms of integrity and openness. This entails, among all market players, building an ethical conduct and responsibility culture.

Successful application and broad acceptance of tokenized carbon credits depend on addressing these difficulties and reducing related risks. Stakeholders can fully realize tokenization's ability to improve the efficacy and reach of carbon offset projects by aggressively addressing legislative, technological, and market acceptance challenges. Overcoming these challenges and creating a strong and trustworthy market will depend mostly on cooperative efforts among authorities, technology suppliers, and market players.

The next section will look at case studies and actual uses of tokenized carbon credits, therefore stressing success stories and lessons learned from early adopters in this field. These case studies will explain how tokenization is actually being used and highlight

CHAPTER 18 DATA-DRIVEN DYNAMICS: LINKING REAL-WORLD INSIGHTS TO TRADE FINANCE

its ability to inspire creativity and influence in the worldwide endeavor to slow down climate change. Through analysis of these practical uses, interested parties can learn best practices and techniques for effectively deploying tokenized carbon credits.

Case Studies in Carbon Credits Tokenization: Real-World Applications and Lessons Learned

Tokenized carbon credits are becoming more and more useful in many different fields since several initiatives proved the efficiency of this creative strategy. Analyzing actual cases helps us to better appreciate the concrete advantages and possible difficulties in using tokenized carbon credits.

One such instance is Veridium's partnership with IBM. Pioneer of environmental fintech Veridium teamed with IBM to tokenize carbon credits on the Stellar blockchain. This cooperative effort seeks to streamline corporate carbon offset procedures. Veridium guarantees the traceability and openness of carbon credits by leveraging blockchain technology, therefore enabling businesses to more easily monitor their carbon footprint and balance it. IBM's participation adds more technical knowledge and credibility, enabling more market acceptability. This cooperation emphasizes the need for using seasoned technology experts to improve the dependability and scalability of tokenized solutions.

Another intriguing case study is provided by AirCarbon Exchange (ACX). To build a more liquid and open carbon market, this Singapore-based technology tokenizes carbon credits.

Using real-time pricing and enhanced market access, ACX lets companies and investors exchange tokenized carbon credits just like any other commodity. The platform's success is shown by its expanding user base and rising transaction volumes, therefore stressing the feasibility of tokenization in improving carbon market effectiveness. ACX's strategy emphasizes how easily blockchain technology might change established markets by raising liquidity and access.

Blockchain-based carbon offset market ClimateTrade lets businesses buy tokenized carbon credits straight from certified projects. ClimateTrade guarantees the veracity and traceability of every carbon credit by using blockchain technologies. Many transactions made possible by the platform have let businesses easily include carbon offsetting into their ESG plans. One particularly outstanding example of effective carbon credit tokenizing is ClimateTrade's simple interface and strong verification system. This project shows how thorough verification and user-centric design could propel market acceptance and confidence.

One striking success story comes from Microsoft's carbon offset program. The behemoth in technology has included tokenized carbon credits into its whole environmental plan. Microsoft has been able to buy and retire carbon credits more quickly by collaborating with blockchain systems. This strategy, which fits their dedication to reach net-zero emissions, has improved the openness and traceability of their carbon offset projects. Microsoft's success emphasizes the possibility for big businesses to use tokenized carbon credits in reaching their ESG targets, therefore proving that even the biggest companies can gain from the agility and openness of blockchain technology.

MCO2 tokens—certified carbon credits—have been created by the Brazilian environmental portal Moss.Earth. Moss.Earth offers a special and powerful approach for people and businesses to offset their carbon emissions by tokenizing carbon credits from Amazon rainforest preservation programs. The project has become rather popular since MCO2 tokens are traded on main bitcoin markets. This result emphasizes how appealing and scalable tokenized carbon credits are in tackling world environmental issues. The strategy of Moss.Earth shows how tokenization can promote important environmental projects and include a large audience by means of easily available digital platforms.

These case studies show the possible advantages and uses of tokenized carbon credits as well. They teach important lessons on technical resilience, market cooperation, technical compliance, and stakeholder education. Tokenized carbon credit initiatives' legality and profitability depend on their adherence to both local and global rules. Early interaction with regulatory authorities lays a strong basis for market operations and helps negotiate the convoluted legal terrain. Market acceptance depends on stakeholders being taught the advantages and mechanics of tokenized carbon credits. Transparency and open communication help to create trust and inspire involvement, hence strengthening the inclusive and dynamic market environment.

Preventing technological failures and security breaches depends on putting dependable blockchain technologies into use. Maintaining platform performance and safeguarding against developing cyber threats depends on constant technical assistance and maintenance. Market acceptance can be increased and credibility improved via market cooperation involving relationships with well-known companies and industry leaders. Cooperation guarantees their long-term viability and influence by providing the required tools and knowledge to properly expand tokenizing efforts.

Learning from these practical examples can help companies and investors better use tokenization in their ESG plans, thereby promoting more efficient and open carbon offset projects. These case studies show that reaching sustainability targets and encouraging more environmental responsibility across sectors depend critically on tokenized carbon credits.

The future possibilities of tokenized carbon credits will be discussed in the next section, together with estimates of market growth and technological developments that can improve their influence even further. Analyzing new trends and breakthroughs helps us to understand how tokenized carbon credits will develop and keep influencing worldwide attempts against climate change. The path toward a more transparent and sustainable carbon market is long-term, and the knowledge gained from these innovative initiatives will direct the next actions and motivate fresh methods of environmental care.

Unlocking the Future of Tokenized Carbon Credits: Market Growth, Technological Innovation, and Environmental Impact

Tokenized carbon credits have enormous market potential; creative technological developments and growing integration of these digital assets into world markets define their future. Tokenized carbon credits are likely to become a major player in the worldwide endeavor to slow down climate change as environmental issues keep growing and the globe strives toward more sustainable living.

In the next few years, the market for tokenized carbon credits is predicted to rise rather significantly. Rising sustainability priorities by governments, businesses, and people are driving demand for carbon credits. Driven by both governmental constraints and voluntary company pledges to carbon neutrality, industry analysts estimate that the carbon credit market might reach several billion dollars by the end of the decade. Growing awareness of the pressing need to solve climate change and the part carbon offset can play in reducing environmental effects fuels this development.

Tokenizing carbon credits improves their liquidity and accessibility, therefore drawing more investors and raising market involvement. Fractionalizing carbon credits lets smaller investments be made possible, hence democratizing access and promoting more general adoption. Tokenized carbon credit trading will become simpler and faster as additional blockchain systems and markets open up, hence accelerating market development. This more accessibility not only expands the pool of investors but also helps the flow of money into initiatives lowering greenhouse gas emissions, thus boosting worldwide sustainability projects.

Several technical developments should improve the acceptance and efficiency of tokenized carbon credits even more. More scalable and secure networks, as well as other developments in blockchain technology, will strengthen the dependability tokenization will have. Higher transaction volumes and seamless integration across several blockchain systems will be facilitated by innovations such as cross-chain interoperability and layer-2 scaling solutions. These developments will guarantee that blockchain systems may manage the increasing demand for carbon credit transactions without compromising security or performance.

Artificial intelligence (AI) and Internet of things (IoT) devices combined in monitoring and validating carbon offset projects will provide real-time data and analytics, therefore guaranteeing the correctness and integrity of tokenized carbon credits. While artificial intelligence can examine data to confirm compliance and project future performance, IoT sensors assess environmental conditions and carbon sequestration efforts. This mix of technologies will improve the dependability and openness of carbon credit markets, therefore facilitating stakeholders' trust and investment in these assets.

Advanced smart contracts will minimize transaction costs by automating complicated transactions and compliance procedures, hence lowering the demand for middlemen. These agreements can also allow dynamic pricing schemes, therefore changing the value of carbon credits depending on supply conditions and market demand. Smart contracts will simplify and reduce trading carbon credits by automating these operations, hence improving market efficiency and liquidity.

By including tokenized carbon credits into distributed finance (DeFi) systems, new financial instruments, including carbon credit-backed loans, and yield farming prospects will result. This will boost liquidity and give investors further incentives to join carbon markets. Using smart contracts to automate and safeguard transactions, DeFi platforms run free from conventional intermediaries. Tokenized carbon credits will open fresh chances for returns and risk management, so appealing to a wider spectrum of investors by including them into these platforms. They have future possibilities beyond only market expansion and technological innovation. These digital resources have the opportunity to revolutionize our approach to environmental sustainability and facilitate the meaningful action that both people and businesses can do against climate change.

Tokenization can increase involvement in carbon offset projects by offering a clear, effective, and easily available market for carbon credits, therefore supporting a more sustainable and resilient worldwide economy.

Tokenized carbon credits hold enormous promise as we head forward. Technology innovation, market expansion, and growing environmental consciousness taken together are generating a strong drive for transformation. Leveraging blockchain technology's benefits and combining it with new developments in IoT, artificial intelligence, and DeFi will help the tokenized carbon credit market to be significant in the worldwide endeavor to address climate change.

Driven by growing demand for sustainable practices and legislative pressure, the industry is projected to expand noticeably. Technological developments will improve the security, openness, and efficiency of carbon credit markets, hence increasing their appeal to a wider spectrum of investors. These digital assets will offer strong instruments for tackling climate change and advancing sustainability as they grow more linked to worldwide markets. There is much promise on the road ahead, and the effects of tokenized carbon credits on the world economy and ecology will be significant.

Shaping the Future of Tokenized Carbon Credits: The Integration of Tokenized Carbon Credits in Global Markets

Several important factors are predicted to influence the integration of tokenized carbon credits into world markets as their technology and market infrastructure keep developing. These trends will affect how companies, governments, and investors interact with carbon offset programs, therefore bringing about notable changes in environmental sustainability methods.

Rising corporate acceptance of tokenized carbon credits is one of the most important developments. Targeting more openness and responsibility, companies are under increasing pressure to improve their environmental, social, and governance (ESG) plans. Using blockchain technology can help businesses better monitor and document their carbon offset projects, therefore raising their ESG scores and drawing in investors focused on sustainability. Blockchain's transparent and unchangeable character guarantees that every carbon credit transaction is verifiable and reliable, therefore strengthening corporate reputation and investor trust. This integration lets companies show their dedication to sustainability, compliance with laws, and response to customer demand for ecologically friendly methods.

Another vital trend enabled by tokenized carbon credits is the evolution of worldwide carbon markets. These digital resources will simplify cross-border carbon trading and promote worldwide cooperation on climate projects, therefore enabling the development of more integrated and effective global carbon markets. Standardized digital frameworks will facilitate nations' ability to trade carbon credits across borders, therefore meeting their targets for emissions. Dealing with climate change depends on this worldwide integration since it guarantees the more efficient use of resources and knowledge, therefore ensuring the coordination and impactfulness of efforts at carbon reduction.

The development of dispersed carbon markets will transform tokenized carbon credit trading even more. These markets will offer easily available, open trading venues that let buyers and sellers direct exchanges. Decentralized markets will enable a wider spectrum of players to engage in carbon trading by lowering transaction costs and raising market efficiency. More companies and people will be encouraged to engage in carbon offset projects by this democratization of carbon markets, hence increasing market liquidity and promoting innovation in carbon-reducing technologies.

Successful integration of tokenized carbon credits into world markets depends on improved regulatory structures. Clearer rules and standards for these digital assets will be developed by governments and regulatory agencies, therefore offering legal clarity and encouraging market trust. Establishing strong systems that guarantee the integrity and durability of tokenized carbon credits will depend critically on cooperation between authorities and industry players. This legislative clarity will help safeguard investors, stop fraud, and guarantee that carbon credits really have positive effects on the surroundings. Regulations will have to strike a compromise between the necessity for innovation and the requirement to protect environmental integrity as they change.

As knowledge of the advantages of tokenized carbon credits increases, more general investor involvement is predicted. Attracted by the possibility of financial gains and the chance to assist sustainability projects, institutional investors, private equity companies, and individual stakeholders will progressively engage in the market. This higher involvement will stimulate creativity and liquidity, hence boosting the market for tokenized carbon credits.

New financial products and services will develop as more investors join the market, therefore offering companies and people more reasons to participate in carbon offset projects.

With huge market potential, technology developments, and growing integration into worldwide markets, tokenized carbon credits have excellent future prospects. Using these digital resources will enable stakeholders to lead more efficient and open carbon offset projects, therefore supporting worldwide efforts against climate change and in favor of sustainability. A sustainable future and full realization of the advantages of tokenized carbon credits depend on continuous cooperation, legislative clarity, and technological innovation as the market develops.

By including tokenized carbon credits in international markets, we will change our approach to environmental sustainability and open fresh chances for investment, innovation, and cooperation. We can create a more open, effective, and inclusive carbon market by using blockchain technology's capabilities and supporting a legislative environment change. This metamorphosis will be crucial in tackling the pressing issue of climate change and helping us to build a more resilient and sustainable global economy. Driving the acceptance and success of tokenized carbon credits will depend critically on the combined efforts of companies, governments, and investors as we advance, thus opening the path for a cleaner and more sustainable future.

Navigating the Regulatory and Policy Landscape: Integrating Tokenized Carbon Credits into ESG Strategies

Businesses wishing to include tokenized carbon credits into their ESG plans must negotiate the regulatory terrain. The legal framework now in place for carbon credits differs greatly among various countries. While some areas are still in their early years of building such systems, others have clearly defined rules for carbon trading and environmental markets.

Compliance depends on an awareness of these rules, which also helps to reduce legal risks.

Companies operating in countries with existing carbon markets have to follow particular guidelines and regulations controlling the creation, certification, and trading of carbon credits. Along with rules for guaranteeing the additionality and permanency of carbon offset projects, these laws sometimes call for monitoring and reporting of emissions reductions. Maintaining the authenticity and integrity of carbon credits depends on adherence to these guidelines. For instance, the European Union Emissions Trading System (EU ETS) boasts a strong regulatory structure, including strict monitoring, reporting, and verification (MRV) requirements. Companies functioning inside the EU have to make sure their carbon credits satisfy these strict criteria in order to be market players.

On the other hand, companies run uncertainty and even legal risks in areas where carbon market regulatory systems are still developing. In these situations, businesses ought to keep current with changes in legislation and be ready to modify their plans as fresh laws are adopted. Dealing with legislators and regulatory authorities will enable companies to shape the evolution of these frameworks and guarantee their conformity with industry standards and best practices. For example, companies have to negotiate a complicated terrain of different rules and norms in developing countries like Southeast Asia and Africa, where regulatory systems are still developing.

Policymakers should give many important ideas some thought in order to promote the acceptance of tokenized carbon credits. It is imperative to harmonize laws concerning blockchain technology and carbon markets. Working toward a coherent regulatory environment that promotes the global expansion of tokenized carbon credit systems, governments and regulatory organizations should establish harmonized rules. Such regulations would improve market efficiency and enable cross-border trade, thereby helping companies to effectively participate in global carbon markets.

Still, another crucial policy issue is improved openness. Establishing clear, open reporting criteria will help to guarantee the integrity of tokenized carbon credits. This covers criteria for issuers to reveal pertinent data about the tokenizing process itself and underlying carbon offsets. The development of confidence and credibility in the market depends on openness in the tokenization process. For example, mandating thorough disclosures on the environmental impact and carbon credit verification will help to prevent fraud and guarantee that the credits actually show real emissions reductions.

By offering financial support, tax incentives, or regulatory exemptions for businesses using tokenizing technology, policymakers can also encourage creativity in the carbon markets. Promoting the creation of fresh platforms and solutions meant to solve environmental problems will inspire creativity and improve the success of carbon offset programs. Giving grants or tax benefits to entrepreneurs and companies creating tokenized carbon credit systems, for instance, can inspire creativity and investment in this new area.

Another excellent way to see whether tokenized carbon credit systems are feasible in a controlled environment is by building regulatory sandboxes or pilot projects. These projects let authorities learn about the possible hazards and advantages connected to these technologies before putting more general legislative plans into effect. By offering a secure environment for creativity and experimentation, regulatory sandboxes help to spot and solve possible regulatory obstacles early on. For example, the UK Financial Conduct Authority (FCA) has effectively tested new financial technology using regulatory sandboxes, therefore offering insightful data that shapes more general legislative policies.

Given the worldwide character of carbon markets and blockchain technology, international collaboration and standardizing initiatives are absolutely vital. Common protocols, interoperable systems, and best practices for tokenized carbon credits can be established via cooperative efforts among governments, industry players, and standard-setting bodies. In tokenized carbon credit markets all around, international cooperation can help to improve market efficiency, enable cross-border transactions, and build confidence and credibility. For instance, the International Organization for Standardization (ISO) is working on creating worldwide standards for blockchain technology and carbon credits, therefore offering a shared foundation for companies and governments.

Through proactive handling of legislative and regulatory issues, stakeholders can establish an environment that makes tokenized carbon credits widely adopted possible. On a worldwide basis, this will progress ESG goals as well as environmental targets. Good control and policy support can guarantee that tokenized carbon credits be utilized to attain real emissions reductions, stimulate innovation, and advance responsibility and openness in the carbon markets. Ongoing cooperation among authorities, industry players, and legislators will be crucial to achieving the full possibilities of this creative strategy to counteract climate change and support sustainability as the market for tokenized carbon credits keeps expanding.

Implementing Tokenization for ESG Strategies: A Path to Enhanced Sustainability and Accountability

Including tokenized carbon credits into an environmental, social, and governance (ESG) plan calls for a number of important actions that can greatly improve company accountability and efforts toward sustainability. Using blockchain technology can help companies increase the impact, openness, and efficiency of their carbon offset projects, therefore enhancing their whole ESG performance.

The approach starts with a close examination of the ESG goals of the company. This entails assessing present sustainability targets pertaining to business accountability, environmental stewardship, and carbon emissions lowering. Understanding how tokenized carbon credits could support these goals will help companies match their whole ESG approach. This alignment guarantees that the integration of tokenization technology complements more general environmental projects and is deliberate. Companies must clearly see how tokenized carbon credits would enable them to reach particular goals, such as net-zero emissions or improved environmental effects.

The next stage is to inform important corporate stakeholders about the idea of tokenized carbon credits and their part in ESG projects after the ESG goals are precisely stated. Executives, board members, sustainability teams, and other decision-makers must fully grasp the advantages, drawbacks, and implementation techniques connected with tokenization technology. Workshops, seminars, and thorough lectures outlining the mechanics of blockchain, the ideas of carbon credits, and the benefits of tokenization can all be part of this educational program. Organizations can create internal support and encourage the effective acceptance of tokenized carbon credits by means of a strong awareness among stakeholders.

Including tokenized carbon credits in ESG plans depends mostly on interacting with carbon markets. Essential is building rapport with players in the carbon market, including carbon registries, verification agencies, and project developers. Knowing the criteria and processes for creating, verifying, and trading carbon credits in line with pertinent criteria—such as the gold standard or the verified carbon standard (VCS)—ensures that the carbon credits used in tokenization are credible and satisfy high environmental criteria. This involvement guarantees that companies' carbon offset projects are successful and influential, as well as helping them negotiate the complexity of the carbon markets.

Another vital phase of the implementation process is choosing a suitable tokenizing system. Companies have to investigate and assess tokenizing systems focused on carbon credit markets. Carefully thought of should be security, scalability, regulatory compliance, and user experience. The selected platform ought to satisfy the technological needs of the company and fit its risk tolerance and strategic goals. Choosing a trustworthy and strong platform helps companies guarantee that their tokenizing initiatives are sustainable and safe.

Tokenizing the carbon credits of the company comes next after a suitable platform is decided upon. This entails working with blockchain builders and carbon market analysts to translate carbon credits into digital currency. Following industry standards and best practices—including open issuing, unchangeable record-keeping, and interoperability with current carbon registries—the tokenization procedure must also follow robust and open

Tokenization of carbon credits helps to increase their authenticity and develop confidence among stakeholders. The last stage of deployment is including tokenized carbon credits into the ESG reporting system of the company. Including these digital assets in ESG reporting will let companies give stakeholders auditable, open data on environmental impact measurements, token trades, and carbon emissions cuts. This integration lets companies explain how tokenizing technology might help to improve the transparency and credibility of their ESG reports. By showing the public, authorities, and investors the company's dedication to sustainability and ethical business practices, open reporting helps to establish confidence.

Finally, using tokenization for ESG plans calls for a sequence of calculated actions that might greatly improve the sustainability initiatives of a company. Businesses can use blockchain technology to drive more efficient and open carbon offset initiatives by matching tokenized carbon credits with ESG goals, educating stakeholders, interacting with carbon markets, choosing a strong tokenizing platform, tokenizing carbon credits, and including them in ESG reporting. This all-encompassing strategy helps the company to meet sustainability targets as well as improve corporate responsibility and raises the general ESG performance. Businesses can open fresh chances for creativity, efficiency, and impact in their path toward a more sustainable future as they negotiate the complexity of including tokenized carbon credits into their plans.

Best Practices for Integrating Tokenized Carbon Credits into ESG Plans: Compliance, Collaboration, and Impact Measurement

Including tokenized carbon credits into an ESG plan means following best practices and policies meant to guarantee compliance, cooperation, and accurate impact assessment for a firm. Businesses can efficiently use tokenization to show their dedication to sustainable development goals and drive positive environmental impact by keeping strong internal controls, interacting with industry peers, and using the tools and resources at hand.

CHAPTER 18 DATA-DRIVEN DYNAMICS: LINKING REAL-WORLD INSIGHTS TO TRADE FINANCE

In the world of tokenized carbon credits, maintaining compliance is absolutely critical. Businesses must keep current with legislative changes since the environment under the control of carbon markets and blockchain technologies is always changing. To reduce legal and reputational risk, companies have to guarantee continuous adherence to pertinent laws and rules. This entails putting strong corporate controls and governance systems into use to monitor and assign responsibility for tokenization projects. Compliance checks and frequent audits help to confirm that all operations follow legal criteria and industry standards.

Businesses that keep a proactive attitude toward compliance will show their dedication to moral behavior and help to establish trust with their employees.

Another essential element of properly including tokenized carbon credits into ESG plans is working with colleagues in the sector. Working groups, industry associations, and cooperative projects aiming at promoting tokenization technology and sustainable finance might present excellent chances for information exchange and innovation when joined. Through peer-based interactions, companies can exchange best practices, lessons discovered, and creative ideas, thus advancing toward common ESG goals. Working together can also help to solve shared problems and create uniform tokenizing techniques, improving the market's general legitimacy and efficiency. Attending industry events and conferences helps to further networking and idea sharing, hence strengthening a community of practice committed to tokenizing sustainability.

To determine how well-tokenized carbon credits meet ESG targets, one must first monitor and evaluate their impact. By means of key performance indicators (KPIs), companies can track the evolution of their tokenizing efforts over time. These KPIs have to be in line with the particular ESG goals of the company and comprise environmental results, token transaction data, and carbon offset programs. Frequent monitoring and assessment helps companies to track development, pinpoint areas needing work, and make data-driven decisions to strengthen their efforts at sustainability. Showing the value of tokenized carbon credits and fostering confidence in the ESG projects of the company depends on open reporting of these indicators to stakeholders.

Businesses can use a variety of tools and resources to help with the introduction of tokenized carbon credits. Tools for blockchain development offer the required framework to create tokenized carbon credit solutions. These systems provide smart contract capability, thereby securely automating token issuing, trading, and settlement procedures. By means of these platforms, companies may guarantee the security and integrity of their digital assets and simplify their tokenizing initiatives. Dealing with

CHAPTER 18 DATA-DRIVEN DYNAMICS: LINKING REAL-WORLD INSIGHTS TO TRADE FINANCE

blockchain experts and developers will help to improve the efficacy of these solutions even more since they are customized to the particular needs and objectives of the company.

Making beneficial decisions requires access to carbon market data and analytics. Navigating the ever-changing carbon markets requires real-time market information, pricing data, and regulatory insights available from carbon market data providers and analytics systems. Maintaining knowledge of legislation changes, supply-demand dynamics, and industry trends helps companies maximize their carbon offset programs and make strategic decisions. By means of these data sources, companies can also see new prospects and hazards, enabling their strategic adaptation.

Improving openness and comparability in ESG disclosures depends on familiarizing oneself with generally accepted ESG reporting systems. Standardized reporting on ESG performance comes from frameworks such as the Global Reporting Initiative (GRI), the Task Force on Climate-related Financial Disclosures (TCFD), and the Sustainability Accounting Standards Board (SASB). Matching ESG disclosures with these models guarantees that stakeholders receive clear communication of the sustainability initiatives of the company. This linkage helps ESG reports to be more credible and enables benchmarking against peers in the sector, therefore offering insightful analysis of the development of the company toward its environmental objectives.

Businesses can successfully include tokenized carbon credits into their ESG plans by adhering to the best standards and using the resources at hand. This all-encompassing strategy not only improves the environmental impact but also strengthens the organization's standing and dedication to the objectives of sustainable development. Following these rules will be crucial for companies negotiating the complexity of tokenization to get real and long-lasting effects on their environmental initiatives.

Using tokenized carbon credits for ESG plans calls for keeping compliance, working with colleagues in the sector, and tracking impact using set KPIs. Further helping these initiatives are access to carbon market data, alignment with accepted ESG reporting systems, and blockchain development platforms. Businesses can significantly advance toward their sustainability goals and help to create a more sustainable future by using these best practices and using their resources as they are at hand. Successful integration of tokenized carbon credits into ESG initiatives offers a potent weapon for tackling climate change and encouraging environmental stewardship, hence strengthening the global economy and rendering it more robust and sustainable.

Revolutionizing ESG Strategies and Climate Action Through Blockchain: The Transformational Power of Tokenized Carbon Credits

At the junction of blockchain technology and environmental sustainability, the tokenization of carbon credits marks a revolutionary invention. This strategy presents notable gains in openness, liquidity, efficiency, and accessibility, which makes it appealing for strengthening carbon credit markets and thereby promoting ESG objectives.

Tokenization provides increased security, openness, and tradeability by turning actual assets into digital tokens on a blockchain. This translates for carbon credits into a more easily available and quick market. Digitizing carbon credits helps to simplify the complexity of conventional carbon markets, therefore facilitating corporate and investor involvement in carbon offset projects. Blockchain technology's immutable character guarantees that every transaction is securely and publicly recorded, therefore lowering the fraud risk and strengthening market participant confidence.

Tokenizing carbon credits offers many different advantages. With a clear, unchangeable record of all transactions, the procedure enhances traceability and openness. Maintaining the integrity of carbon offset projects depends on this openness guaranteeing that carbon credits are legitimate and verifiable. By letting carbon credits be sold on digital platforms, buyers and sellers may more easily enter and exit the market, hence improving liquidity and market accessibility. The efficiency of the market is further enhanced by the lower transaction costs, which also makes carbon offset programs more affordable. Tokenization also guarantees the authenticity of carbon credits by stopping double-counting and supporting safe and open verifying mechanisms.

By offering a consistent digital framework that can be readily modified to fit various regulatory regimes, this strategy also promotes worldwide cooperation on climate projects, therefore facilitating international collaboration. Notwithstanding these advantages, there are major obstacles and hazards that must be addressed if we are to completely realize the possibilities of tokenized carbon credits. A big issue is regulatory compliance since companies have to negotiate a changing terrain of financial and environmental rules.

CHAPTER 18   DATA-DRIVEN DYNAMICS: LINKING REAL-WORLD INSIGHTS TO TRADE FINANCE

Technical robustness is also essential since blockchain systems have to be scalable and safe to manage growing transaction volume. Another difficulty is market acceptance since stakeholders have to be informed about the advantages and mechanics of tokenization in order to propel more general acceptance. A stable and effective market depends on the management of price volatility and liquidity issues. Prevention of market fragmentation depends on standardizing and compatibility among several tokenizing systems. Tokenized carbon credits' authenticity and success depend critically on building trust and guaranteeing openness.

Effective initiatives including Veridium and IBM, AirCarbon Exchange, and ClimateTrade show the useful advantages and possible value of tokenized carbon credits. These case studies underline the need for technical security, market cooperation, regulatory compliance, and stakeholder education. By means of their Stellar blockchain collaboration, Veridium and IBM seek to simplify the carbon offset process for businesses, thereby improving traceability. and openness. Tokenizing carbon credits, Singapore-based AirCarbon Exchange aims to establish a more liquid and open carbon market. Using a blockchain, ClimateTrade's marketplace lets businesses buy tokenized carbon credits straight from certified projects, guaranteeing validity and traceability.

Tokenized carbon credits have the opportunity to completely change how companies and investors handle sustainability and carbon offsets. Tokenization can increase involvement in carbon markets and support more efficient environmental stewardship by offering a clear, quick, and easily available trading carbon credit platform. Including tokenized carbon credits into company ESG plans will help them to strengthen their sustainability credentials, increase openness, and draw ESG-oriented investors. Tokenized carbon credits present a new asset class for investors that fits their sustainability objectives and can yield possible financial returns. Furthermore, they can help nations and businesses to cooperate more successfully on lowering greenhouse gas emissions, therefore facilitating worldwide climate change projects. Blockchain technology's traceability and standardizing guarantees that carbon offset projects are reliable and significant, therefore supporting world decarbonizing initiatives.

Looking ahead, the tokenization of carbon credits stands out as a potentially beneficial invention that might greatly increase the reach and efficacy of carbon offset programs. Stakeholders can fully utilize tokenized carbon credits to propel significant development in the battle against climate change by overcoming obstacles and using technological developments. Accepting this creative method calls for cooperation, clear regulations, and ongoing technological and market practice improvement. With these components in place, tokenized carbon credits can be significant in reaching a sustainable and decarbonized future, therefore matching economic incentives with environmental objectives for the advantage of all.

Summary

The transforming possibilities of including actual data in the trade finance scene are investigated in this chapter. The chapter emphasizes the development of digital trade as well as the increasing need for cooperative frameworks and technical breakthroughs in linking compliance with data independence. It underlines how careful data integration guarantees openness and regulatory compliance, therefore opening fresh possibilities in global trade.

The chapter also explores the radical influence of carbon credit tokenization and commodities. Tokenizing real assets into digital tokens helps to democratize wealth creation, improve liquidity, and allow flawless commodities and carbon market investments. From the blockchain technology driving tokenization to the hazards of carbon trading, case studies and practical applications highlight the advantages and difficulties of these developments. The chapter ends with best practices and recommendations for using tokenization in ESG policies, hence establishing tokenized assets as pillars of sustainable and inclusive worldwide markets.

CHAPTER 19

Afterword: Digital Trade As an Evolved Digital Governance

Often referred to as the "dark ages" in Europe, the Middle Ages were the prosperous traders of Italian city-states such as Florence and Venice who developed creative financial instruments and systems to enable commerce both inside and outside of Europe. Among the first to create a complex system for funding and transportation of commodities were these traders. Rather than only transporting their own commodities from one city-state to another, these Italian traders invented the use of credit instruments such as promissory notes and bills of exchange, therefore facilitating commerce across vast distances. This reduced risk and created new trade prospects by letting businesses fund significant goods shipments without physically transporting gold or silver. Their inventions established the framework for what we now understand as contemporary trade finance by laying the foundation for many of the financial methods and instruments being employed in worldwide commerce today. Trade finance has changed very slowly in its basic components throughout the centuries since its beginnings. Although technology has advanced and globalization has grown, the basic mechanisms and framework of trade finance remain shockingly identical to those evolved centuries ago. If one looks with an open mind at the fundamental framework of current trade finance, it is evident that some phases of a transaction are not all that different from those utilized during the time when the rich and powerful exponents of Florentine arts and crafts dominated world commerce. For example, the foundation of modern trade finance still consists of letters of credit, bills of exchange, and guarantees—instruments honed in the busy trading centers of Italy during the Renaissance. Like they are now, these devices were utilized back then to reduce the dangers related to long-distance trading. Echoing the trust-based institutions of the past, the modern world also depends on intermediaries—banks, insurance companies, guarantors, or otherwise. Thanks to developments in logistics and communication, the main distinction now is the frequency of these exchanges. In the era of technology, the underlying complexity—the layers of documentation—as well as the manual procedures required in confirming, securing, and completing a trade finance contract might still seem rather outdated. Like the Florentines previously led in financial innovation during their time, this sluggish progression emphasizes the need for more rapid invention to keep pace with the dynamic character of global commerce today.

Navigating the Future of Trade Finance: The Urgent Shift Toward Digital Transformation

In the worldwide economy of today, even a single cargo delivery—regardless of size or importance—involves a large network of players dispersed over many nations. Modern trade has come to define this complexity; however, it brings significant problems as well as fresh chances for development and cooperation. Managing significant operational changes is very challenging, particularly in relation to deploying new technology or quickly embracing creative ideas. Getting all the stakeholders—banks, companies, logistics providers, and legislators—to line up and welcome innovative ideas is one of the most urgent issues confronting the trade finance sector.

The global supply chain is naturally fractured, and every participant usually runs with its own systems, which makes standardizing operations or integrating new technology very difficult. Moreover, the terrain gets even more complicated with the always-rising amount of laws and regulations these organizations have to follow. Constantly under pressure to simplify compliance procedures, cut processing times, and limit errors—all without increasing expenses—banks and companies are striving to adopt innovative solutions that enhance efficiency while maintaining cost-effectiveness. This changing environment is prompting conventional trade finance firms more and more to turn their attention to digital solutions. Adoption of new technologies, including blockchain, artificial intelligence, and IoT, is no longer a dream but a vital reality engulfing the financial sector.

The significant impetus behind this change is shown by the reports in 2020 of 79 national and international banks actively supporting different blockchain projects. Blockchain is not only a catchphrase in this situation. For many of the inefficiencies afflicting trade finance, it offers a real fix. Blockchain presents a more safe and effective way of doing transactions internationally by use of a distributed, unchangeable, open system. Through smart contracts, these technologies allow real-time monitoring of commodities, instantaneous document validation, and payment process automation—all of which may significantly save the time and expense related to trade finance activities. But a set of shared commercial and technological standards is absolutely necessary if digitalization is to gain general acceptance and use.

Blockchain and other digital technologies have very limited promise without consistent rules. Regardless of its size, sector, or location, these criteria are essential to guarantee seamless contact and collaboration among all the stakeholders. A coordinated strategy will provide a special synergy that not only promotes simple implementation but also global acceptance of these digital technologies throughout the whole trade finance ecosystem. No player should fall behind in this quest. Inclusivity will determine the direction of trade finance as it guarantees that every participant—from small enterprises to multinational companies—has access to and gains from the efficiency and innovations that digital solutions may offer.

This change toward a more digitized, standardized, and transparent system will help safeguard the future of world commerce, thereby opening the path for more effective, reasonably priced, and safe activities. For the trade finance sector, the digital world presents a bright future. With their increasing acceptance and practical applications, digital technologies might solve long-standing industry problems and boost international commerce to unprecedented levels. Accepting this change is not voluntary; rather, it is a required progression in a world when competitiveness depends on speed, compliance, and efficiency.

Digital Governance: A Harmonized Form of Interaction

Poor old Messer Aldobrandino Aldobrandeschi finds himself perplexed. Having spent his life navigating the world of ledgers—first the traditional ones and later highly centralized digital ones—the concept of "distributed" is a foggy notion to him. It is not surprising. The implications of digital technologies are far-reaching, and for someone used to centralized control, it can be difficult to grasp how spreading out the power and data across many nodes offers tangible benefits to all stakeholders.

CHAPTER 19   AFTERWORD: DIGITAL TRADE AS AN EVOLVED DIGITAL GOVERNANCE

Messer Aldobrandino is forced to witness the rise of blockchain-based ecosystems, struggling to comprehend the fundamental shift they represent. In today's world, digitally native ecosystems have ascended to the status of "virtual hubs," where innovation and standards are empowered to ignite a revolution in global trade. Unlike the rigid, centralized systems of the past, open-source solutions provide a neutral and agnostic foundation, creating an ideal scenario for the development of common technical, regulatory, and business practices. Their decentralized nature serves as a common ground for collaboration, allowing diverse stakeholders to align on operational practices and standards. This unique structure enables the integration of "code" with legal frameworks, thereby bridging the divide between technology and governance. As a result, these open ecosystems can redefine global trade practices, setting the stage for harmonized worldwide adoption.

The neutral nature of open-source technologies makes them a powerful enabler for this transformation, offering a platform where technical standards, business protocols, and regulatory compliance can converge seamlessly. For the first time, it becomes possible to build an environment where technology and law work together in concert to shape a more efficient and inclusive global trade system. A global approach is essential in this transformation, particularly in identifying relevant local business and technical standards led by industry innovators.

This global outlook is crucial because it enables a unique form of comparison and collaboration across markets. By setting a common path, this approach paves the way for the development of a seamless and unified trade process—from the digitization of documents to the tokenization of assets and the streamlining of cross-border clearing and settlement operations. For Messer Aldobrandino, it might seem like a strange distant reality, but for the industry, the rise of fully digital ecosystems signals an exciting new era. As the world moves toward a more digitized and decentralized future, the ability to establish global standards will determine the success of this transformation, ensuring that trade finance can meet the demands of modern commerce in a secure, efficient, and globally harmonized way. Digital technologies, particularly DLTs and blockchain, serve as the cornerstone of the (R)evolution in trade finance, a concept that Messer Aldobrandino and many others will soon comprehend and ultimately adopt.

CHAPTER 19   AFTERWORD: DIGITAL TRADE AS AN EVOLVED DIGITAL GOVERNANCE

Raising the Bar: The Next Challenge

Though it may appear utopian, even impractical, open-source technologies naturally evolve in breaking down the "silos" upon which so many technological solutions are typically based. Though intended for particular use, these silos often generate obstacles that stifle creativity, teamwork, and worldwide problem-solving. Destroying these separate buildings and creating a scene where ideas may interact, share knowledge, and create harmonic, multidisciplinary frameworks marks the next logical step in this road map. There will be many advantages when these silos fall apart. The approach will foster an environment in which several systems, industries, and solutions may interact, exchange information, and establish a shared set of standards addressing world issues.

Unlocking the full potential of digital ecosystems will depend on interoperability and cooperation, whether in banking, supply chain management, healthcare, or climate solutions. Digital Trade Finance is clearly a major facilitator of this worldwide trend in this evolutionary process. Its hybrid, interdisciplinary nature makes it particularly suitable for bridging the divide between technology, business, and government. Digital Trade Finance cannot, however, really propel this change if we continue to lock ourselves into new silos while simultaneously advocating decentralization.

Decentralization's idea is based on openness and inclusion, in which case answers are available to everyone and no one viewpoint rules. Strong relationships across many groups and sectors, open communication, and cooperation will be very vital to accomplishing this. We have to create a setting where different stakeholders—banks, companies, authorities, or technology developers—may cooperate transparently and amiably. Success depends on allowing interoperability and defining standards at both technical and corporate levels. Though only if they are used to promote integration rather than fragmentation, digital technologies have the ability to transform world industry. In the realm of "Digital Trade Finance," this entails creating solutions that can operate across borders, sectors, and platforms, thereby enabling companies and governments to participate in flawless, quick, and safe commerce. As open-source technologies develop, cooperation over rivalry and communication over division must take front stage. We can only fully realize distributed technology and propel the type of major innovation the planet so sorely needs by building a really linked ecosystem.

Digital Trade Finance's and global problem-solving's future depends on our capacity to combine many points of view, destroy silos, and create a coherent framework fit for everyone. Though it may appear utopian, even impractical, open-source technologies naturally evolve in breaking down the "silos" upon which so many technological solutions are typically based. Though intended for particular use, these silos often generate obstacles that stifle creativity, teamwork, and worldwide problem-solving. Destroying these separate buildings and creating a scene where ideas may interact, share knowledge, and create harmonic, multidisciplinary frameworks marks the next logical step in this road map. There will be many advantages when these silos fall apart.

The approach will foster an environment in which several systems, industries, and solutions may interact, exchange information, and establish a shared set of standards addressing world issues. Unlocking the full potential of digital ecosystems will depend on interoperability and cooperation, whether in banking, supply chain management, healthcare, or climate solutions. Digital Trade Finance is clearly a major facilitator of this worldwide trend in this evolutionary process. Its hybrid, interdisciplinary nature makes it particularly suitable for bridging the divide between technology, business, and government. Digital Trade Finance cannot, however, really propel this change if we continue to lock ourselves into new silos while simultaneously advocating decentralization. Decentralization's idea is based on openness and inclusion, in which case answers are available to everyone and no one viewpoint rules.

Strong relationships across many groups and sectors, open communication, and cooperation will be very vital to accomplishing this. We have to create a setting where different stakeholders—banks, companies, authorities, or technology developers—may cooperate transparently and amiably. Success depends on allowing interoperability and defining standards at both technical and corporate levels. Though only if they are used to promote integration rather than fragmentation, digital technologies have the ability to transform world industry. In the realm of digital commerce finance, this entails creating solutions that can operate across borders, sectors, and platforms, thereby enabling companies and governments to participate in flawless, quick, and safe commerce. As open-source technologies develop, cooperation over rivalry and communication over division must take front stage.

We can only fully realize distributed technology and propel the type of major innovation the planet so sorely needs by building a really linked ecosystem. Digital Trade Finance's and global problem-solving's future depends on our capacity to combine many points of view, destroy silos, and create a coherent framework fit for everyone.

CHAPTER 19   AFTERWORD: DIGITAL TRADE AS AN EVOLVED DIGITAL GOVERNANCE

An Interdisciplinary, Extended Form of Governance

Though most people agree with the idea of open source, we still have to traverse another step. This next stage will force us to focus on finding fresh chances to enable worldwide blockchain adoption. We must thus improve cooperation at several levels and concentrate on hastening the acceptance of open-source technologies by means of technical, commercial, legal, and regulatory standard development, discussion, and adoption. These criteria will redefine global norms and provide a shared regulatory framework across sectors, therefore promoting innovation and guaranteeing a harmonic universal acceptance. This is about changing the governance structures that have governed our activities over the previous two demanding years, not only about realizing the possibilities of blockchain. We are at a crossroads right now and have to ask: How may things develop? What actions have to be taken to guarantee development?

The solution is in our joint shapes of our attitudes and approaches. First, we have to reconsider our presumptions, approaches, and ideas by including ideas from several points of view and philosophical stances of life. Mindets serve as group frameworks that help to shape behavior and forward knowledge. In an open-source environment, it's imperative to let go of constrictive ideas and substitute fresh paradigms. This is where the idea of an "open source culture" becomes relevant paradigms that can only flourish under "open minds." These attitudes inspire stakeholders to see outside their own silos and foster creativity, diversity, and teamwork. In this framework, we may see the emergence of a "Consortium of Communities," driven by what can be called "Meta technologies for open mindsets." Consider it as a network of nodes, where these ones represent communities of knowledge rather than only technical points in a ledger. The real assets of this partnership are harmonized business models, shared use cases, and multidisciplinary expertise that permits flexible cooperation across industries.

This progress extends the conventional definition of a transaction. Transactions nowadays are more than simply the exchange of currency; they are "Transactions of Collaborations," in which the interaction of human beings—sharing information, ideas, and tools—creates richer, more powerful systems. Cooperation must be given top priority going ahead as a main engine. Cooperation will enable us to make use of the common knowledge about digital technology and create new communities rich in interdisciplinary knowledge, enhancing our shared perspective. "It's not just about building new systems; it's about creating the adapters to connect them." Alfonso Govela remarked. This means that the future is about how we combine several ideas to operate peacefully rather than only about standalone inventions.

CHAPTER 19 AFTERWORD: DIGITAL TRADE AS AN EVOLVED DIGITAL GOVERNANCE

Since trade is the foundation of both human interaction and the world economy, it needs to be the center of this next stage. Almost everything we do in our economic systems comes from trade; so, commerce is where blockchain democratizing power may have the largest influence. The objective is hardly less than "democratization through technology." We can utilize technology to democratize access to markets, resources, and information by removing obstacles, encouraging transparency, and allowing all players—big and small, local and worldwide—to engage on equal footing. This is the next aim, the next phase.

We can transform sectors and society itself by supporting open mindsets, cooperative efforts across groups, and acceptance of democratic technology, including blockchain. This is about rethinking our interactions, transactions, and global teamwork, not only about little steps forward. In this new paradigm, technology serves as a powerful equalizer, providing opportunities for everyone, regardless of location. With it, inclusion, creativity, and common growth characterize the future of world trade and human connection.

Bridging the Silos: A Journey Through Trade Finance from Ancient Roots to Digital Futures

Writing my book, *Quantum Leap: Innovative Strategies for Trade Finance in the 21st Century and Beyond*, I imagined it as a trip, one that starts in the far past and leads readers across a dispersed but intentional road into the most current and future-oriented incarnations of trade finance. This method reflects the interconnections in trade and the nonlinear growth of human civilization. We obtain a whole knowledge of the development of trade finance by investigating how old trade networks operated and developing that story through the growth of banks, international trade, and now digital assets.

Like technology, commerce has never been a straight path of advancement; the book's dispersed, apparently "messy" journey reflects this fact. Rather, it is a dynamic area formed by several elements, civilizations, and inventions. In the same sense, I see "breaking the silos"—moving past segmented approaches to commerce, banking, and technology. Trade finance's future resides in "bridging the silos," therefore uniting not just systems and technology but also many backgrounds, ideas, and disciplines.

CHAPTER 19 AFTERWORD: DIGITAL TRADE AS AN EVOLVED DIGITAL GOVERNANCE

From prehistoric barter networks to the complexities of blockchain and digital ecosystems, the book stresses that real development results when these traditionally separate fields interact. The concept is to create something considerably more than the sum of its parts by developing hybrid, cross-disciplinary solutions combining the technological, legal, and financial domains. A really integrated, completely digital environment for trade finance depends on cooperation across several spheres of competence.

By the conclusion of this journey, the authors aim to inspire a future in which the silos are not only broken but also connected in a way that permits more profound cooperation and innovation, thereby pushing trade finance into new frontiers.

Bibliography

Trade Finance and SCF

- *International Trade Finance From the Origins to the Present: Market Structures, Regulation, and Governance Olivier Accominotti and Stefano Ugolin:* https://eprints.lse.ac.uk/102191/1/Accominotti_history_of_international_trade_finance_accepted.pdf

- *Introduction to Letters of Credit | 2024 Guide (TFG—Trade Finance Global:* https://www.tradefinanceglobal.com/letters-of-credit/)

- *Everything You Need to Know About Letters of Credit: A Comprehensive Guide to Documentary Credits (TFG—Trade Finance Global:* https://www.tradefinanceglobal.com/letters-of-credit/baft-guide/it/)

- *BAFT and TFG Launch a Comprehensive Letter of Credit Guide:* https://www.baft.org/document/baft-and-tfg-comprehensive-letter-of-credit-guide/

- *ITFA Structured Letters of Credit Guide:* https://itfa.org/wp-content/uploads/2021/05/ITFA-Structured-Letters-of-Credit-Guide%5EJ-May-2021.pdf

- *HTC Inc. (n.d.). Digitalization of Trade Finance: Why Should It Be a Top Priority? Retrieved from* https://www.htcinc.com/resources/digitalization-of-trade-finance-why-should-it-be-a-top-priority/

- *Deutsche Bank: Guide to Receivables Finance, 3rd Edition:* https://corporates.db.com/publications/White-papers-guides/guide-to-receivables-finance-third-edition

BIBLIOGRAPHY

- *A Guide to Receivables Finance, 3rd Edition, ITFA:* https://itfa.org/wp-content/uploads/2021/10/Guide-to-Receivables-Finance-3rd-Edition_comp.pdf

- *Deutsche Bank. (2024). A Guide to Digital Trade Finance—Corporates and Institutions. Retrieved from* https://corporates.db.com/publications/White-papers-guides/a-guide-to-digital-trade-finance

- *Santander Corporate and Investment Banking. (n.d.). Digitise-to-distribute: How technology is expanding the scope of trade finance investors. Retrieved from* https://www.santandercib.com/insights/innovation/digitise-distribute-how-technology-expanding-scope-trade-finance-investors

- *Trade Finance Global. (2019). Digital Ecosystems in Trade Finance. Retrieved from* https://www.tradefinanceglobal.com/blockchain/digital-ecosystems-in-trade-finance/

- *Infosys. (n.d.). Being Resilient: Revitalize Trade Finance Digitization. Retrieved from* https://www.infosys.com/industries/financial-services/insights/documents/revitalize-trade-finance-digitization.pdf

- *Society for Worldwide Interbank Financial Telecommunication (SWIFT), History and Milestones, 2023:* https://www.swift.com/news-events/news/reflecting-year-shared-progress

- *International Finance Corporation (IFC), 2023 Trade Finance Gap Report:* https://www.ifc.org/content/dam/ifc/doc/2023/ifc-annual-report-2023-highlights-en.pdf

- *Matthew Hatton, Digital Negotiable Instruments Ideally Suited to Combating Late Payment:* https://www.tradeforprosperity.co.uk/digital-negotiable-instruments-ideally-suited-to-combating-late-payment/

- *BCG Boston Consulting Group (2019-24), Digital Ecosystems in Trade Finance: Seeing Beyond the Technology:* https://www.bcg.com/digital-ecosystems-in-trade-finance-seeing-beyond-the-technology

BIBLIOGRAPHY

- ITFA & TFG LAUNCH A NEW WHITEPAPER: "ARE WE DOING ENOUGH TO BRIDGE THE TRADE FINANCE GAP? November 2024: https://itfa.org/itfa-tfg-launch-a-new-whitepaper-are-we-doing-enough-to-bridge-the-trade-finance-gap-november-2024/

- Deep-Tier Supply Chain Finance: Unlocking the Potential (by ADB and BAFT): https://www.adb.org/publications/deep-tier-supply-chain-finance-unlocking-potential

- Electronic Trade Documents Act 2023: https://www.legislation.gov.uk/ukpga/2023/38/contents

- What Is the URDTT and Why Is It So Important?: https://www.tradefinanceglobal.com/posts/what-is-urdtt-why-is-it-so-important/

- A New Rulebook for Digital Trade, URDTT: https://www.tradefinanceglobal.com/posts/introduction-to-the-icc-uniform-rules-for-digital-trade-transactions-urdtt/

- Implementing URDTT: Uniform Rules for Digital Trade Transactions: https://www.iccitalia.org/prodotto/implementing-urdtt-uniform-rules-for-digital-trade-transactions/

- DLPC Working Group of the Innovation Council BAFT DLPC Distributed Ledger Payment Commitment Business Best Practices: https://www.tradefinanceglobal.com/wp-content/uploads/2020/06/baft-dlpc-business-bps-final.pdf

- ICC Trade Register 2024—Global Market Dynamics and Risk in Trade Finance (by ICC and BCG)

- 2024 World Investment Report Investment Facilitation and Digital Government by UNCTAD

- David Meynell, "From deficient to smart Unlocking efficiency and transitioning the documentary credit in a digital environment" (ICC UK)

- Baft & Asian Development Bank, Deep-Tier Supply Chain Finance: Unlocking the Potential, May 2024

BIBLIOGRAPHY

- David Meynell, "Amara's Law and Digital Trade Finance," ICCUK—Nov 2024

- Key Trade Documents and Data Elements Digital Standards Analysis and Recommendations (ICC DSI—ICC UK)

- ICC Trade Register 2024 Global Market Dynamics and Risk in Trade Finance

- "Digital Negotiable Instruments Ideally Suited to Combating Late Payment"—ICC UK, Apr 2024

- "Speeding Up the Adoption of Digital Trade Documents," Sunil Senapati, Chief Executive Officer, XDC Trade Network—ICC UK, Apr 2024

- Scaling the Use of Digital Identities in Trade—ICC UK

- Seizing the Moment, Unleashing the Potential of Trade Digitalisation. Improving Liquidity, Reducing Risk, Increasing Profitability (ICC UK)

- "The English Arbitration Reforms as They Apply to International Arbitration," Costas Frangeskides, Partner, Wordley Partnerships (ICC UK—Dec 2023)

Sustainability and ESG

- Green Corridors: https://globalmaritimeforum.org/green-corridors/

- World's Longest Green and Digital Corridor: https://www.maritimegateway.com/worlds-longest-green-and-digital-corridor/

- Singapore, Long Beach, Los Angeles Ports Unveil Green, Digital Shipping Corridor Partnership Strategy: https://www.maritimeinformed.com/news/singapore-long-beach-los-angeles-ports-co-1626091755-ga-co-1659532976-ga-co-1661745263-ga-co-1696599249-ga.1701951847.html

BIBLIOGRAPHY

- *Green Corridors: A Lane for Zero-Carbon Shipping:* https://www.mckinsey.com/capabilities/sustainability/our-insights/green-corridors-a-lane-for-zero-carbon-shipping

- *How Green Corridors Can Enable the Transition to Zero-Emission Shipping:* https://www.weforum.org/agenda/2022/01/green-corridors-zero-emission-shipping/

- *"Net Zero" Oil Company: Climate Action or Oxymoron? Assessing the Climate Strategy of Occidental Petroleum (Oxy), April 2024*

- *"Underfinanced. Underprepared. Inadequate Investment and Planning on Climate Adaptation Leaves World Exposed" by UNEP, 2023*

- *"Carbon Removals: How to Scale a New Gigaton Industry" by McKinsey Sustainability, Dec 2023*

- *"Environmental Rule of Law: Tracking Progress and Charting Future Directions" by UNEP, 2023*

- *"A Guide to the Next Sustainable Finance Agenda Limitations of the Current Framework and Recommendations for an Effective Transition" A Finance Watch Report, Jan 2024*

- *"Voluntary Standards and Initiatives for Carbon Management Navigating the landscape," IISD, Jan 2024*

- *Climate Finance Provided and Mobilised by Developed Countries in 2013-2021, OECD*

- *Digital Revolution in Sustainable Business Models and Finance Management, MUDPI*

- *The State of ReFi A Closer Look at Web3 Regenerative Finance, ReFi DAO Q1 2024*

- *Regenerative Finance "ReFi" Blockchain for Climate Action, Nov 2022. Authors: Sophie Hartley, Professor Ellie Rennie*

- *"The Role of Carbon Credits in Scaling Up Innovative Clean Energy Technologies How High-Quality Carbon Credits Could Accelerate the Adoption of Low-Emissions Hydrogen, Sustainable Aviation Fuels and Direct Air Capture," IEA—GenZero*

BIBLIOGRAPHY

- "The Rise of Sustainability Themed Investing and Its Impact on Promoting Sustainable Development," ESG Newsletter, Olaniwun Ajay, Apr 2024

- Adaptation & Resilience Impact: A Measurement Framework for Investors, Apr 2024

- Trade and Development Report Update, Apr 2024 by UNCTAD

- Environmental Rule of Law: Tracking Progress and Charting Future Directions by UNEP

- IETA Guidelines for High Integrity Use of Carbon Credits, VCM Guidelines, Apr 2024

- Monitoring the Transition to a Low-Carbon Economy: A Strategic Approach to Local Development (EU-LEED-OECD)

- From Disruption to Opportunity: Strategies for Rewiring Global Value Chains, WHITE PAPER, May 2024—WEF

- GRI 101: Biodiversity 2024 (GRI Standards)

- Limitations of LNG in Shipping Decarbonization—Why LNG-Powered Vessels Are Killing the Planet—SFOC Solutions for Climate

- A Compendium of Market Practices How the EU's Taxonomy and Sustainable Finance Framework Are Helping Financial and Non-financial Actors Transition to Net Zero, Jan 2024

- Accountability for Nature: January 2024 Comparison of Nature-Related Assessment and Disclosure Frameworks and Standards, WWF—UNEP, Jan 2024

- "An Open-Source Approach for Measuring Corporate Impacts on Ecosystem Services and Biodiversity," Communications Earth & Environment

- Biodiversity Credits: A Guide to Support Early Use with High Integrity WHITE PAPER DECEMBER 2023 (WEF)

- Biodiversity Finance Metrics for Impact Reporting Supplement to IFC Biodiversity Finance Reference Guide

- *Blockchain for Scaling Climate Action WHITE PAPER APRIL 2023 (WEF)*
- *Key Enablers for a Circular Economy (ICC UK)*
- *Make Climate and Environment Action Everyone's Business: A Toolkit for Delivering Sustainable Global Value Chains (ICC UK)*
- *ICC Principles for Sustainable Trade Finance, Oct 2024*
- *ICC Principles for Sustainable Trade—Wave, 3 Nov 2024*

Blockchain, IoTs, AI, and Technology

- *"Trading with Intelligence: How AI Shapes and Is Shaped by International Trade" by WTO*
- *Trade Finance Blockchains Consolidate into we.trade:* https://www.ledgerinsights.com/trade-finance-blockchain-consolidate-wetrade-batavia/
- *Trade Finance Blockchain Contour Acquires Assets from we.trade:* https://www.ledgerinsights.com/trade-finance-blockchain-contour-acquires-assets-from-we-trade/
- *Blockchain Trade Finance Consortia Face Challenges as They Go Live:* https://www.ledgerinsights.com/blockchain-trade-finance-consortia-challenges/
- *Marco Polo Lowers Barriers to Entry for Blockchain Trade Finance:* https://www.ledgerinsights.com/marco-polo-lowers-barriers-to-entry-for-blockchain-trade-finance/
- *Amazon Simulates Tokenized Seller Receivables Settled with Stablecoins:* https://www.ledgerinsights.com/amazon-simulates-tokenized-seller-receivables-settled-with-stablecoins/
- *SC Ventures-Backed SWIAT, Olea Partner for Tokenized Trade Finance:* https://www.ledgerinsights.com/sc-ventures-backed-swiat-olea-partner-for-tokenized-trade-finance/

BIBLIOGRAPHY

- *Standard Chartered: Tokenization Market to Reach $30.1 Trillion by 2034. Trade Finance Will Be Significant:* https://www.ledgerinsights.com/standard-chartered-tokenization-market-to-reach-30-1-trillion-by-2034-trade-finance-will-be-significant/
- *Tokenization Firm Xalts Acquires Contour Trade Blockchain:* https://www.ledgerinsights.com/tokenization-xalts-acquires-contour-trade-blockchain/
- *MAS, UNDP Launch Universal Trusted Credentials Initiative for MSME Financing:* https://www.ledgerinsights.com/mas-undp-universal-trusted-credentials-initiative-msme-financing/
- *Shipping Network GSBN Partners Ant's ZAN to Tokenize Bills of Lading:* https://www.ledgerinsights.com/tokenize-bills-of-lading-gsbn-ant-zan/
- *MUFG Joins Contour Blockchain Trade Finance Network:* https://www.ledgerinsights.com/mufg-contour-blockchain-trade-finance-letters-of-credit/
- *Blockchain Trade Finance Network Contour to Shutter:* https://www.ledgerinsights.com/contour-blockchain-trade-finance-network-shutter/
- *Maersk, DBS in First International Shipment Using TradeTrust Blockchain:* https://www.ledgerinsights.com/tradetrust-blockchain-maersk-dbs-shipment/
- *Bankruptcies of Blockchain Firms Marco Polo, Symbiont Attract Bidders:* https://www.ledgerinsights.com/marco-polo-symbiont-bankruptcies-enterprise-blockchain/
- *Trade Finance Blockchain Contour Acquires Assets from we.trade:* https://www.ledgerinsights.com/trade-finance-blockchain-contour-acquires-assets-from-we-trade/
- *HSBC, SocGen, IBM Backed Blockchain Company We.Trade Starts Insolvency Procedure:* https://www.ledgerinsights.com/hsbc-socgen-ibm-backed-blockchain-company-we-trade-starts-insolvency-procedure/

BIBLIOGRAPHY

- *HSBC, DBS Trial Blockchain Trade Platform GSBN for Trade Finance:* https://www.ledgerinsights.com/hsbc-dbs-trial-blockchain-trade-platform-gsbn-for-trade-finance/

- *SDX Partners with FQX for Promissory Note Trading as Digital Assets:* https://www.ledgerinsights.com/sdx-partners-with-fqx-for-promissory-note-trading-as-digital-assets/

- *HSBC, DBS, BOC Join Trade Finance Advisory Group of GSBN Blockchain Network:* https://www.ledgerinsights.com/hsbc-dbs-boc-trade-finance-advisory-group-gsbn-blockchain/

- *Limitations of LNG in Shipping Decarbonization—Why LNG-Powered Vessels Are Killing the Planet*

- *GSBN Partners with HSBC-Backed Contour for Blockchain Trade Finance:* https://www.ledgerinsights.com/gsbn-partners-with-hsbc-backed-contour-for-blockchain-trade-finance/

- *Citi, HSBC, ING Back Blockchain Trade Finance Network Contour's Series A+:* https://www.ledgerinsights.com/citi-hsbc-ing-blockchain-trade-finance-network-contour-series-a/

- *DBS Bank Goes Live on Blockchain Trade Finance Network Contour for Four Asia-Pacific Markets:* https://www.ledgerinsights.com/dbs-bank-blockchain-trade-finance-network-contour/

- *Tradelens Blockchain Competitor GSBN Signs First Deal with Bank of China HK:* https://www.ledgerinsights.com/gsbn-blockchain-deal-with-bank-of-china-hk/

- *Automated Trade Payments Prove Popular for we.trade Blockchain:* https://www.ledgerinsights.com/wetrade-blockchain-trade-finance-automated-payments/

- *Tradelens, we.trade to Integrate Anti-Fraud Trade Finance Blockchain MonetaGo:* https://www.ledgerinsights.com/tradelens-we-trade-to-integrate-anti-fraud-trade-finance-blockchain-monetago/

BIBLIOGRAPHY

- *IBM, Maersk Shutter Shipping Blockchain TradeLens:* https://www.ledgerinsights.com/tradelens-blockchain-ibm-maersk-shutters-shipping/

- *Streamlined Global Commerce: The Role of Digital Assets (CITI Treasury and Trade Solutions)*

- *Tokenization: Realizing the Vision of a Future Financial Ecosystem, Apr 2024 (Deloitte)*

- *AI for Social Good: Improving Lives and Protecting the Planet. McKinsey & Quantum Black*

- *BIS—Bank for International Settlements, Project Viridis, A Climate Risk Platform for Financial Authorities, Jun 2024*

Index

A

ABCP, *see* Asset-backed commercial paper (ABCP)
Accelerators, 556
Access control
    in AI, 621
    blockchain, 623, 624
    blockchain's secure, 607
    and data integrity, 616
    policies, 621
Accessibility, 858
ACX, *see* AirCarbon Exchange (ACX)
Adaptability, 676
ADB, *see* Asian Development Bank (ADB)
Agreement on Technical Barriers to Trade (TBT), 697
Agricultural methods, 882–883
AI, *see* Artificial intelligence (AI)
AI model development
    data accuracy, 608
    data collection, 607, 608
    deployment stage, 608
    privacy and building confidence, 608
    retention and destruction, 608
    training, 608
AirCarbon Exchange (ACX), 970
Alternative fuels, 749, 769, 772
    energy security and economic stability, 756
    green corridors, 756
    green hydrogen generation in Australia, 755
    maritime future, 769
    roles, 755, 756
AML, *see* Anti-money laundering (AML)
Anti-money laundering (AML), 14, 31, 227, 246, 417, 432, 435, 464, 509, 523, 873
Antwerp, 5, 6
APIs, *see* Application programming interfaces (APIs)
Application programming interfaces (APIs), 496, 511, 556, 557
Artificial intelligence (AI), 239, 507, 510, 804, 806, 808, 826, 835, 915, 973
    advancements, 428
    anomaly detection and predictive analytics, 665
    automation/efficiency, 427, 428
    banks/international institutions, 202
    blockchain, 405, 412–413, 620 (*see also* Blockchain)
    building trust and reliability, 624–632
    capacity, 539
    consent management, 619, 620
    conventional dynamics, 422
    creation and implementation, 625
    cutting-edge approaches, 422
    data, 538
        collection, 609, 610
        integration, 538
        privacy management, 614
        security, 606
    deep neural networks, 419

INDEX

Artificial intelligence (AI) *(cont.)*
    developments, 540, 603
    development with GDPR standards, 611–613
    digital identities, 629
    economies, 422
    framework, 640
    fraud detection, 626
    fundamentals, 418, 419
    GDPR, 606
    GenAI, 415 (*see also* Generative artificial intelligence (GenAI))
    global offshoring landscape, 421, 422
    GPML/machine learning, 419
    integration process, 606
    integrity and confidentiality, 605
    international collaboration, 423
    legitimacy and dependability, 624
    logistics, 539, 540, 547
    in medical diagnosis and treatment planning, 628
    MLETR trade finance, 58
    model development, 607, 608
    privacy concerns, 606, 607
    real-time data, 428, 429
    regulation/ethics, 422, 423
    security protocols, 539
    supervised/unsupervised learning, 419
    supply chain finance, 182
    sustainable finance, 333
    tracking of information's source, 628
    trade and supply chain finance, 16
    trade law/rules/practices, 363
    transformative potential, 640, 641
    transforming power, 603
    transforms industries, 420, 421
Asian Development Bank (ADB), 178, 210
Asset-backed commercial paper (ABCP), 106, 107, 111
Asset management, 669
Assets, 669
Asset tokenization, 668, 669, 946
Audit trails, 603, 607, 626, 627, 634, 663
Automated reporting tools, 829
Automated systems, 507, 515, 516, 830
Automated technologies, 513, 516
Automating tasks, 860
Automation, 515, 516, 856, 859, 866, 886, 887
Awareness, 838, 842, 846, 876, 912

B

BAFT, *see* Bankers Association for Finance and Trade (BAFT)
Bankers Association for Finance and Trade (BAFT), 122, 174, 176, 210
Bank guarantees (BGs)
    bank financial assurance, 66
    cost implications, 67
    different types, 67
    financial instruments, 65
    SBLCs payment, 67, 68
    standards, 66
    timing and payment assurance, 66
Banking industry, 636
Banking on Women Global Trade Finance Program (BOW-GTFP), 732
Banking systems, 855, 858, 859, 888
Bank payment obligations (BPOs), 86, 150
Banks, trade finance
    emerging markets, 170
    evolution, 171
    merchant banks, 172
    risk mitigation/trust building, 170

role of, 170
transformations, 172
Basel system, 90, 91
BCMS, *see* Business continuity management systems (BCMS)
BGs, *see* Bank guarantees (BGs)
Big data, 511
Big data analytics, 534
Bills of exchange, 674–677, 681
Bills of trade digitization, 677
Biotechnology, 776
BiTA, *see* Blockchain in Transport Alliance (BiTA)
Bitcoin, 668, 882, 884, 885, 888, 906
Blockchain, 672, 689, 801, 918, 988, 989, 994
   advantages, 617
   with AI, 418, 603 (*see also* Artificial intelligence (AI))
   application, 632
   balanced strategy, 619
   based verification, 631–634
   consent management, 603, 619, 620
   data integrity, 607
   for data protection, 632–640
   data provenance, 626–629
   in data security, 606, 607
   data transaction, 634
   ESG strategies and climate action, 983–985
   European Union's projects, 619
   framework, 626
   GDPR compliance, 606, 607, 614, 615
   guarantees, 627, 628
   in healthcare industry, 627
   immutability, 633
   immutable ledger, 630
   inherent qualities, 618
   integration process, 606
   openness and responsibility, 627
   ownership, 606, 607
   permissioned *vs.* permissionless, 615–617
   privacy, 606, 607
   quick development, 605
   readers and fact-checkers, 630
   safe ledger and smart contract, 634
   scalability, 605
   secure access management, 607
   securing AI, 620–624
   security and transparency, 664
   and smart contracts, 621, 639–641
   synergistic benefits, 665
   traceability, 620
   transformative potential, 640, 641
   unchangeable ledger, 635
Blockchain-based ecosystems, 990
Blockchain-based tokens, 672
Blockchain in Transport Alliance (BiTA), 464
Blockchain networks, 507, 893
Blockchain-powered tokenization, 670
Blockchain projects, 901
Blockchain-recorded tokens, 671
Blockchain security, 923
Blockchain technology, 510, 672, 679, 682, 686, 759, 779, 780, 855, 920, 925, 936, 944
   accountability, 846
   adaptability and flexibility, 490
   adoption and view, 883
   advantages, 458
   AI, 412, 413 (*see also* Artificial intelligence (AI))
   asset management, 879
   assets, 885

Blockchain technology (*cont.*)
   banks/international institutions, 202
   benefits, 893
   capabilities, 898
   carbon market, 881
   case studies, 900
   centralization *vs.* decentralization, 467–469
   chemical cargo, 472–474
   climate action, 896, 897, 910
   collaborations, 463–465, 473, 480, 493–496
   continuous engagement, 461
   continuous growth, 492–494
   contour, 466, 467
   contour implementation, 449–452
   conventional legal systems, 483
   cryptocurrencies, 492
   data distribution, 865
   decentralization, 482–485, 896
   deep-tier financing models, 258–275
   deep-tier suppliers, 250–256
   DeFi, 856, 868
   definition, 408, 409
   democratization, 896
   demystifying, 899
   development, 866
   digital innovation/TradeTrust, 475–477
   digital ledger, 846
   digital revolution, 478–480
   digital roadblocks, 452–455
   digital trade law/rules/practices, 397, 398
   distributed ledger technology, 376–378
   distributed nature, 857
   DLT (*see* Distributed ledger technology (DLT))
   efficiency/adoption, 458–460
   electronic bills, 453–456
   ETDA, 355
   environmental, social, and governance, 195
   features, 866
   financial operation, 249–251
   green financing, 797
   GSBN/TradeLens, 470–473
   interoperability standards, 495–497
   inventive competitors, 493
   investor reluctance, 455, 456
   investors, 461
   invoice tokenization, 276, 291
   LoCs (*see* Letters of credit (LoCs))
   legal and regulatory frameworks, 485–488
   legal environment, 907
   Marco Polo Network (*see* Marco Polo Network)
   monetization strategies, 462
   non-technical users, 898
   ONE, 474, 475
   openness and responsibility, 846, 847, 866, 868
   operational difficulties, 456–458
   permissionless, 895
   practical value, 878
   privacy-preserving transparency, 256–258
   private/public-permissionless, 481, 482
   programmability feature, 855
   programmable character, 858
   real-world advantages, 879
   ReFi, 899
   regulatory agencies, 496
   regulatory bodies, 458
   regulatory compliance, 485–488

resilience/leveraging network, 488–490
resiliency, 912
seamless integration, 490–492, 495–497
secure financial support, 461–463
significant obstacle, 457
smart contracts, 199, 886
sophisticated character and distributed technologies, 867
stakeholders, 460
standardization, 457, 463–465
standardized protocols, 496
strong security features, 458
supply chain finance, 182
supply chain management, 479, 480
sustainable finance, 333
synergistic effect, 489
traceability, 805
trade and supply chain finance, 16
trade finance, 412
trade law/rules/practices, 363
transactions, 846, 866
    records, 803
    security and openness, 543
transparency, 846
transparent and unchangeable record, 856
unique problems, 481
and Web3, 866, 867, 898
Xalts, 451
BOW-GTFP, *see* Banking on Women Global Trade Finance Program (BOW-GTFP)
BPOs, *see* Bank payment obligations (BPOs)
Bretton Woods system, 8, 9
Bring Your Own Device (BYOD) rules, 653, 656, 659, 662
Business Continuity Management Systems (BCMS), 597
Business continuity strategy, 591
Business executives, 849
Business process outsourcing (BPO), 420
Business strategies, 813

C

Cap-and-trade system, 953, 954
Capitalization, 670
Carbon Border Adjustment Mechanism (CBAM), 794, 802, 806
CarbonChain, 803
Carbon credits, 871, 878, 879, 881, 882, 884, 886, 894, 896, 906, 908, 910, 946–950
    in cap-and-trade, 953, 954
    carbon markets
        through blockchain technology, 963–965
        for sustainable future, 960–963
    global markets for environmental sustainability, 958–963
    into ESG plans, 981–984
    legal, technological and market barriers, 968–970
    trends and developments, 956–958
Carbon credits tokenization, 964
    case studies, 970–972
    integration, tokenized carbon credits, 974–976
    market growth, technological innovation and environmental impact, 972–974
    regulatory and policy landscape, 976–978

INDEX

Carbon emissions
   data collections, 828
   scope 3 emissions, 828
Carbon footprint monitoring, 825
Carbon-intensive fuels, 768
Carbon labeling, 812, 813, 834
Carbon management, 815
Carbon markets, 965–968
Carbon pricing mechanisms, 804
Carbon trading, 946, 947, 949–952, 955, 956
   plans, 956
   systems, 947
CBAM, see Carbon Border Adjustment Mechanism (CBAM)
CDM, see Clean Development Mechanism (CDM); Continuous diagnostics and mitigating (CDM)
CDS, see Credit default swap (CDS)
Centralization, 467–469
Centre for Digital Trade and Innovation (C4DTI), 379
CERs, see Certified emission reductions (CERs)
Certified emission reductions (CERs), 948
C4DTI, see Centre for Digital Trade and Innovation (C4DTI)
Chief Information Officers (CIOs), 589
Chief Information Security Officers (CISOs), 589, 590, 602
CIOs, see Chief Information Officers (CIOs)
Clean Development Mechanism (CDM), 948
Climate action, 747, 900
Climate catastrophe, 734, 839, 840, 912
Climate change
   collective action, 735, 736
   effects, 912
   natural disasters, 747
   objectives, 911
   participants, 911
   projects, 911
   reality, 911
   resilience, 911
   sector, 912
Climate crisis, 741
Climate experts, 899
ClimateTrade, 970
Climate-vulnerable countries, 748
Climate-vulnerable nations, 747–749
Climate Zeitgeist, 737, 738
Cloud computing, 511
CLNs, see Credit linked notes (CLNs)
CLOs, see Collateralized loan obligations (CLOs)
Clustering algorithms, 809
Coalition
   developing nations, 735
   ecosystem, trade and climate action, 735
   goal, 736
Coalition of Trade Ministers on Climate
   climate action, 741, 742
   climate change, 741
   greenhouse gas emissions, 741
   obstacles, 742
   sustainable development, 741
   trade and investment, 741
Code reviews, 875
Collaboration, 671, 674, 677, 679, 687, 693
Collateralized loan obligations (CLOs), 112, 113, 116
Colonization, 840
Commerce transactions, 685

Committee on Trade and
    Development (CTD), 710
Committee on Trade and
    Environment (CTE), 697, 710
Commodity, 924
Commodity tokenization,
    931–933, 937–945
Communication and engagement
    techniques, 900
Communities, 778
Community bridging, 900
Complex ecosystem
    AI privacy concerns, 606, 607
    blockchain
        consent management for AI,
            619, 620
        for GDPR compliance, 614, 615
        permissioned *vs.*
            permissionless, 615–617
    collaboration and communication, 605
    cutting-edge technology, 605
    data integrity, 610, 611
    documentary accuracy, 604
    ethical data collection for AI, 609, 610
    GDPR
        compliance in AI model
            development, 607, 608
        compliant machine learning,
            613, 614
    on-chain *vs.* off-chain data
        computing, 617–619
    privacy-centric feature
        engineering, 611–613
    regulatory compliance, 604
    risk management, 604
    technological integration, 605
Compliance, 915, 916
    regulations, 500

systems, 507
The Comprehensive and Progressive
    Agreement for Trans-Pacific
    Partnership (CPTPP), 702, 706–709
Conditional *vs.* unconditional
    receivables, 81–84
Consortium of Communities, 993
Container goods derivatives
    adoption, 529, 532
    advantages, 526, 530–532, 534
    emergence, 526
    financial institutions, 525
    financial risks/cash flows, 529
    global trade, 530–532
    growth and application, 529
    idea, 530
    legislative framework, 533
    market, 525, 526, 530, 533
    shippers, 525
    standardization, 532
    success, 533
    suppliers control, 525
Contemporary technologies, 848
Continuous diagnostics and mitigating
    (CDM), 644
Contour implementation
    blockchain technology, 449
    digital roadblocks, 452–455
    investor reluctance, 455, 456
    trade finance, 466, 467
    Xalts, 451
Contract receivables, 137, 138
Controlling misinformation, 631
Conventional authorities, 908
Conventional farming techniques, 748
Conventional investments, 923
Conventional physical commodity
    investments, 922

Conventional trade finance, 914
Cooperation, 993
Cooperative efforts, 867, 874
Corporate partners, 904
Corporate Sustainability Reporting Directive (CSRD), 301
   component, 312
   EFRAG project, 325
   environmental performance, 313
   EU Taxonomy regulations, 311, 313–316
   investors, businesses, and legislators, 313
   MLETR (*see* Model Law on Electronic Transferable Records (MLETR))
   NFRD differences, 310–312
   organizational capacity, 312
   reporting policies, 313
   sustainability issues, 311
   sustainability reporting, 309–312
   transparency/accountability, 308, 309
Counter-Terrorist Financing (CTF), 509
CPTPP, *see* The Comprehensive and Progressive Agreement for Trans-Pacific Partnership (CPTPP)
Credit default swap (CDS), 116
Credit instruments, 987
Credit letter digitization, 677
Credit linked notes (CLNs), 116
Credit Revolution, 667, 668
Cross-disciplinary solutions, 995
Crypto aficionados, 899, 904
Crypto and non-crypto viewers, 901
Crypto community, 900, 901
Cryptocurrencies, 562, 883–885, 887, 906, 932
Cryptography, 682, 683
Crypto innovators and conventional climate groups, 901
Crypto market, 887
CSRD, *see* Corporate Sustainability Reporting Directive (CSRD)
CTD, *see* Committee on Trade and Development (CTD)
CTE, *see* Committee on Trade and Environment (CTE)
Cultural and technological gap, 899
Cutting-edge technologies, 845, 865
Cybersecurity, 647, 648

D

dApp, *see* Decentralized application (dApp)
DAOs, *see* Decentralized autonomous organizations (DAOs)
Dark ages, 987
Data access, 535
Data analysis, 809
Data analytics, 502, 503, 511, 797, 801
Data breaches, 637
Data collaboration, 562
Data collection, 609, 815, 833
Data computing, 617–619
Data cooperation, 561, 562
Data deletion, 633
Data-driven decision making, 810, 827
Data exchanges, 592, 638
Data harmonization, 917, 918
Data integration, 511
Data integrity, 610, 611
   and access control, 616
   data provenance, 625
   and dependability, 626

guaranteeing, 640
and medical record accuracy, 627
and operations, 642
and quality, 627
and security, 618, 640
and validity, 629, 631
verification, 628
Data interoperability, 917, 918
Data management, 626, 627, 919
Data marketplace, 637, 638
Data minimization, 612
Data monetization, 636, 637
Data ownership, 636, 637
Data points, 610
Data portability, 614
Data preservation laws, 634
Data protection, 642
cryptographic methods, 633
data deletion, 633
data ownership, 636, 637
data retention, 632–636
decentralizing data trade, 637, 638
deletion policies, 632
distributed ledger, 632
regulatory settings, 633
smart contracts and blockchain, 639–641
Data protection impact assessments (DPIs), 614
Data provenance
blockchain, 626–629
blockchain-based verification, 631–634
clear and accurate record, 625
data integrity maintenance, 625
ethical issues and regulatory compliance, 625
history/clear trail, 624

monitoring, 625
Data retention policies
blockchain, 634
data stored and guaranteeing, 633
and deletion regulations, 633
framework, 632
smart contracts, 634, 635
Data security, 635, 636
AI, 606
with distributed ledgers and smart contracts, 623, 624
policies, 555
Data sharing
in healthcare and AI, 638–640
management, 622
secure and trustworthy, 622, 623
Data sources, 535
Data trade, 637, 638
Data transactions, 637, 638
Days payable outstanding (DPO), 78, 141
Days sales outstanding (DSO), 78, 141
DCs, *see* Documentary credits (DCs)
DCSA, *see* Digital Container Shipping Association's (DCSA)
DEAs, *see* Digital Economy Agreements (DEAs)
Decades of transformation, trade and development
developing nations
COVID-19 epidemic, 700
demand, vital minerals, 700
developing economies, 699
digital economy, 699, 700
digital revolution, 699, 701
environmental issues, 700, 701
high debt levels limit, 701
implement sustainable fiscal policies, 701

1015

INDEX

Decades of transformation, trade and development (*cont.*)
  invest, processing and manufacturing capacity, 700
  world trade, 699
  global commerce and development, 699
  LDCs, 699
  plastics trade aggravates environmental damage, 700
  underdeveloped countries, commodities, 700
Decarbonization, 764
Decarbonize global marine trade, 749–751
Decarbonizing shipping, 763
Decentralization, 467–469, 482–485, 864, 865, 867–870, 877, 902, 903, 906–908, 991, 992
Decentralized application (dApp), 668
Decentralized autonomous organizations (DAOs), 904
Decentralized finance (DeFi) systems, 271, 943, 959, 962
  blockchain technology, 856
  climate governance, 899
  concepts, 869
  distributed character, 857
  financial transactions, 884
  fundamental infrastructure and guiding concepts, 857
  local economies, 885
  money, 885
  openness and accessibility, 868
  revolutionary movement, 868
  technology characteristics, 863
  values, 857
Deep neural networks (DNNs), 419

Deep-Tier Supply Chain Finance (DTSCF), 178
  adaptive ecosystem, 274, 275
  advantages, 216–218
  anchor buyer, 276, 277
  anchor customers, 216
  balancing cost/risk/dependability, 290–292
  blockchain technology, 258–275, 291
  clarity/enforcement/collaboration, 225–228
  collaboration, 287–289
  consistent definitions, 226
  cooperative efforts, 230
  cost-efficiency, 270, 271
  cross-tier direct financing, 261
    direct finance, 264, 265
    elimination, 261
    features, 263, 264
    intermediary costs and delays, 262
    real-time access, 263
    risk-mitigation, 261, 262
    tier-1 suppliers, 262, 263
    transparency and trust, 262, 263
    unique advantages, 261
  currency/regulatory issues, 228–230
  delegate finance, 258
    benefits, 258, 259
    cryptographic methods, 258
    funding Effectiveness, 259
    intermediary control, 259
    limitations, 259
    real-time monitoring, 258
    restrictions, 260
    scalability/dependability, 259
    tier-1/2 suppliers, 260

1016

deliberate strategy, 209
direct/delegated models, 265
   risk-mitigation, 266, 267
   scalability, 267, 268
   visibility, 266, 267
dispute-resolving systems, 227
effective financial operations, 248–250
effective implementation, 218, 219
efficiency/sustainability, 230, 231
ESG integration
   legislative projects and
     rules, 240–242
   strategies, 244–246
   visibility/compliance, 242–244
finance gap, 256
financing gap, 277, 278
fintech
   conventional banks, 237
   cooperative efforts, 237
   deployment and scalability,
     232, 233
   financial capacity, 237
   implementation and
     scalability, 233
   strong alliances, 237
   traditional banks, 236–238
harmonization process, 228
hedging techniques, 229
informational barriers, 231
innovation and strategic partnerships,
   238, 239
innovative financial solutions, 211
international currencies, 228
invoice tokenization, 291, 292
legislators and authorities, 225
liquidity/resilience/efficiency, 283–285
macroeconomic events, 283
managerial implications
   advantages, 268
   intermediary tiers, 269
   proactive risk management, 269
   reliability, 268, 269
motivating cooperation, 247
operational interruptions/
   bankruptcy, 281–283
payment obligation, 218
payment responsibilities, 226, 282
platform-based strategy, 234, 235
post-shipment financing, 214–216
privacy-preserving
   transparency, 256–258
real-time monitoring, 234
smaller suppliers, 275, 276
smart contracts, 239
SMEs, 223, 224
stakeholders, 218, 247, 248
strategic approach, 220, 221
strong legal framework, 221, 222
strong legal system, 222
suppliers, 217, 269
technical and operational issues, 231
technological systems, 219
tier-1/tier-2 supplier, 219
traditional approaches, 213, 214
transformative power, 250
   capital access, 255
   DeFi, 254
   direct financing models, 252
   factors, 250, 251
   finance approaches, 252
   numerous technologies, 251, 252
   sharing sensitive data, 256
   strategic implications, 253
   visibility barriers, 255
   zero-knowledge proofs, 254
underprivileged market sectors, 226

INDEX

Deep-Tier Supply Chain
   Finance (DTSCF) (*cont.*)
  world supply systems, 211–213
  Y-shaped supply chains, 288
  Y-shaped/V-shaped supply, 278–281
  zero-knowledge proof (ZKP), 271–274
Defense Information Systems Agency
   (DISA), 643, 644
Deferred payment agreements (DPAs), 37
Demand response systems, 825
Democratization, 864, 869, 879, 935–937
Deployment models, 656, 657
Developing economies, 746
Digital alchemy, 933–935
Digital assets, 885, 887–890, 892, 894,
   912, 937
  financial future, 562
  financial inclusion, 562, 563
  financial institutions, 565, 566
  financial services, 566
  intersection, 564, 565
Digital channels, 801
Digital commerce, 759
Digital Container Shipping Association's
   (DCSA), 470
Digital content and social media, 629–632
Digital economy, 682, 699, 700
Digital Economy Agreements (DEAs), 376
Digital ecosystems, 991
Digital governance, 989, 990
Digital innovations, 855
Digitalization, 173, 759, 760
Digital material, 630
Digital noise, 904
Digital Operational Resilience Act (DORA)
   addressing ISO 27001, 597, 598
   banking and trade finance sectors, 569

banking industry, 602
CIOs and CISOs, 589, 590
compliance checklist, 590–592
core resilience objectives, 578–580
digital technologies, 572–574
EU financial institution's
   resilience, 574–576
GDPR, 587–589
high stakes, 569
impacts, 570
IRM, 594, 595
ISO 27001, 596, 597
new perspectives, 569
NIS2 Directive, 599–601
operational resilience and
   compliance, 570–572
practical compliance techniques, 569
requirements for resilience, 580–582
upcoming regulations, 576–578
Digital operational resilience testing, 571
Digital platforms, 807
Digital revolution, 686
Digital service providers (DSP), 599
Digital solutions, 554
Digital systems, 803
Digital technology, 760, 777, 802, 804–806,
   856, 989, 992
Digital tokens, 894, 920, 922, 937
Digital tools, 856, 857, 898, 904
Digital trade, 914
Digital trade finance solution, 991, 992
   change management, 174, 175
   continuous upskilling, 174
   key organizations, 174
   learning platforms, 174
   UK Finance, 175
Digital trade law/rules/practices, 359

assets/property rights, 401–403
blockchain technology, 397, 398
cryptocurrencies, 402
data security and privacy, 360
digitalization, 360, 361, 364
digital transformation, 363–365
electronic contracts, 359
electronic issuance/exchange, 361
electronic trade documents (ETDs), 398–401
platforms and networks, 359
stable protocols, 397
UNCITRAL MLETR, 362, 363
URDTT (see Uniform Rules for Digital Trade Transactions (URDTT))
Digital trade's future, 915
Digital trade transaction (DTT), 380–383
Digital trading, 554
Digital transformation, 831
   commerce sector, 294
   conventional systems, 294
   CSRD ramifications, 309–316
   digital product passports
      accuracy and integrity, 321
      comprehensive product information, 321
      consumers, 321
      inventory and manufacturing strategies, 322
      sustainable purchases, 320–322
   double materiality approach, 327, 328
      component, 327
      environmental and social materiality, 327
      holistic view, 329
      methodical process, 329–331
      regulators/legislators, 329
      reporting method, 327
      reporting process and assessment, 331
      solid governance systems, 330
      stakeholders, 328, 329
      twofold materiality, 328
   ecodesign framework, 317–320
      chemical products, 320
      components, 323
      comprehensive standards, 324
      consumption and production patterns, 324
      continuous assessment, 324
      environmental impact, 317
      environmental sustainability, 318
      furniture manufacture, 319
      innovative law, 318
      representation, 318
      sectors, 319, 320
   EFRAG project, 325–327
   EU Taxonomy, 316, 317
   GRI 101, 342–345
   legal system, 294, 295
   MLETR, 296
   nature-based solutions, 339–341
   paper-based systems, 293
   regulations/sustainability reporting systems, 301–303
   secure/efficient commerce environment, 299, 300
   significant advantages, 294
   sustainability, 300, 301, 344–358
   sustainable finance
      circuity finance ecosystem, 335
      conventional financial criteria, 331
      investment, 336–339
      ISO 59000 series, 334–336
      stakeholders, 334

INDEX

Digital transformation (*cont.*)
    technological
      advancements, 332–334
    transparency and
      responsibility, 332
    trends, 331, 332
  trade operations, 294
  unsold consumer goods, 322, 323
Digital wallets, 885–887
Digitization, 676
DISA, *see* Defense Information Systems Agency (DISA)
Distributed apps (dApps), 866, 885
Distributed concept, 989
Distributed finance (DeFi) systems, 938, 945, 962
Distributed Ledger Payment Commitment (DLPC), 397
Distributed ledgers, 640
  data security with, 623, 624
  systems, 918
Distributed ledger technologies (DLT), 296, 363, 366, 405, 510, 520, 687–691
  AI, 415–418
  bill of lading (e-B/L), 411
  centralization *vs.*
    decentralization, 467–469
  consensus protocols, 410
  decentralized systems, 410
  digital technology, 406–408
  documentary credit digitalization, 406
  documentary credits, 414, 415
  encryption and security, 410
  physical documents, 411
  regulatory compliance, 432, 433
  risk mitigation, 411
  smart contracts, 410, 411
  automation, 430–433
  digital environment, 425, 426
  digital format, 426
  digital handshake, 430
  documentary credits, 424–426
  global trade automation, 424, 425
  real-time monitoring and analysis, 432
  streamline transactions, 431
  traditional contracts, 431
  supply chain transparency, 411
  technological advancements, 414
  trade finance, 409
Distributed networks, 845, 856, 859, 860, 865, 868
Distributed technologies, 858, 860, 897
DLPC, *see* Distributed Ledger Payment Commitment (DLPC)
DLT, *see* Distributed ledger technologies (DLT)
DNNs, *see* Deep neural networks (DNNs)
Documentary credits (DCs), 19, 40, *See also* Letters of credit (LoCs); Uniform Customs and Practice (UCP 600)
  advising bank, 22
  banking institutions, 13, 14
  business transactions, 21, 22
  compliance/effective execution
    banks, 53
    beneficiaries, 52
    checklists, 52
    components, 54
    differences, 53
    DOCDEX and ICC tools, 55
    document presentations, 51
    generalizations, 53
    pointers, 52

INDEX

    presentation/evaluation, 54
    resolution technique, 55
    trade documents, 51
definition, 20
development of, 10
document types
    acceptance credits, 26
    back-to-back credits, 28
    beneficiary, 27
    installments, 28
    insurance document, 27
    negotiation credit, 27
    requirements/conditions, 26, 28
financial instruments, 13
goals/requirements, 22
history of, 10
ISBP 821, 50
issuing bank issues, 22
ledger balance
    benefits, 73
    capital-intensive, 75
    disadvantages, 74
    financial instrument, 74
    lawmakers and financial institutions, 75
    payment option, 74
    requirements, 74
    restriction, 75
    risk mitigation, 74
    security, 75
lifeblood of international commerce, 11
nominated bank, 23
payment risk/security, 26
payment terms, 13
pre-shipment financing, 28
red/green clause, 29
reimbursement claim, 23

    risk management techniques, 14
    traditional trade finance, 12
    transferring bank, 23
Documentary Dispute Resolution Expertise (DOCDEX), 55
DORA, *see* Digital Operational Resilience Act (DORA)
DORA Compliance Beyond ISO 27001, 601
DORA data dynamics, 592, 593
DORA's compliance criteria, 591
DORA's compliance monitoring authorities, 571
DORA's digital frontier
    business continuity management, 573
    disaster recovery plans, 573
    EU's efforts, operational resilience, 574
    execution, supervising and controlling, 573
    incident management and reporting, 573
    IT and cybersecurity policies, 573
    IT and cybersecurity risk management, 572
    IT systems and cybersecurity, 572
    operational resilience change, 573
    operational resilience strategies modification, 574
    supervising authorities, 573
DORA's effect
    business continuity strategies, 583
    corporate behavior changes, 583
    improved operational resilience, 583
    increased regulatory control, 582
    operational hazards handling, 583
    rising compliance expenses, 582
    risk control, 583

INDEX

DORA's requirements
    business continuity planning, 581
    consistent testing and training, 582
    cybersecurity, 581
    efficient monitoring systems, 580
    EU's financial system, 582
    governance and control, 581
    incident reporting, 580
    operational hazards identification and evaluation, 580
    outsourcing risks handling, 580
    risk management system, 581
DORA's resilience objectives
    enforcing uniform criteria and standards, 579
    enhancing customer data security, 578
    forward-looking strategy, 579
    GDPR, 579
    homogeneity, 579
    improving operational resilience, 578
    regulatory bodies responsibilities, 579
    regulatory criteria, 579
    regulatory harmonization, 579
    risk management, 578
    strong cybersecurity policies, 578
DORA's structure, 570
DORA's upcoming regulations
    business continuity strategies, 577
    controlling outside hazards, 577
    credit institutions, 576
    crypto-asset service providers, 576
    culture change, 577
    fund managers, 577
    high degree of resilience, 578
    insurance and reinsurance markets, 577
    investment businesses and trading platforms, 576
    ramifications, 577
    regulatory framework, 576
    securities markets, 577
    trading venues, 577
DPAs, *see* Deferred payment agreements (DPAs)
DPIs, *see* Data protection impact assessments (DPIs)
DPO, *see* Days payable outstanding (DPO)
DSO, *see* Days sales outstanding (DSO)
DSP, *see* Digital service providers (DSP)
DTSCF, *see* Deep-tier supply chain finance (DTSCF)
DTT, *see* Digital trade transaction (DTT)
Due diligence rules, global trade
    corporate responsibility, 713
    developing nations, VSS, 719–724
    GVCs
        compliance, 714, 715
        inclusivity, 714, 715
        sustainability, 714, 715
    importation of commodities, 713
    improve trade's sustainability control, 712
    international commerce, 712
    openness, 713
    sustainability *vs.* inclusivity, developing countries, 715–717
    UNGPs, 712, 2011
    voluntary instruments, 712
    VSS, 717–719
Dynamic monitoring, 808

E

EBA, *see* European Banking Authority (EBA)
eBLs, *see* Electronic bills of lading (eBLs)

EBRD, *see* European Bank for Reconstruction and Development (EBRD)
ECAs, *see* Export credit agencies (ECAs)
Economic crises, 910
Economic frameworks, 846, 847
Economic models, 840, 842, 843
    conventional, 837–839, 844, 848, 912
    limits, 838
Economic operations, 847
Economic regimes, 838
Economic systems, 838, 839, 843, 846, 851, 860
    conventional, 842, 844
    development, 844
    openness, 847
    paradigm shift, 848
    shortcomings, 850
    and surroundings, 888
    tendency, 843
    traditional, 843
EDI, *see* Electronic data interchange (EDI)
Efficiency, 915
EFRAG, *see* European Financial Reporting Advisory Group (EFRAG)
EIOPA, *see* European Insurance and Occupational Pensions Authority (EIOPA)
e-LCs, *see* Electronic letters of credit (e-LCs)
Electronic (eUCP)
    data integrity and security, 49
    definitions, 47
    electronic documents, 57–64
    evolution of, 48
    force majeure, 49
    MLETR (*see* Model Law on Electronic Transferable Records (MLETR))
    presentation/examination, 49
    scope/application, 48
    terminology/definitions, 48
    version 1.0/2.0, 47
Electronic bills of lading (eBLs), 366, 452–455, 459, 470, 472, 474
Electronic data interchange (EDI), 172
Electronic letters of credit (e-LCs), 39, 688–692
Electronic payment undertaking (ePU), 87, 136
Electronic promissory note (ePN), 477–479
Electronic trade documents (ETDs), 398–401
Electronic Trade Documents Act 2023 (ETDA)
    digital documentation/physical assets, 371
    digital trade law, 361
    digital trust unlocked, 371–373
    diplomacy, 375, 376
    distributed ledger technology (DLT), 376–378
    electronic trade documents, 371
    essential requirements, 371
    legal and compliance teams, 378
    legal recognition, 377
    paperless trade, 368–371
    paper trade documents, 375
    possession/transformation, 374, 375
    reliable system, 371
    shared characteristics, 370
    TradeLens platform, 376
    vaults, 373, 374
    wide-ranging implications, 369
Electronic Transactions and Digital Agreements (ETDA), 359

INDEX

Electronic Transactions Documents
    Act (ETDA)
  blockchain technology, 355
  cutting-edge technologies, 357, 358
  digital trade documentation, 346, 347
  financial institution, 352, 353
  IFRS reporting system, 345
  legal systems, 345
  sustainability efforts, 355–357
  sustainability reporting
      system, 347–350
  technological progress/long-term
      goals, 350–352
  transition/electronic records, 353–355
Electronic Transferable Documents
    Act (ETRDA), 301
Electronic transferable
    records (ETRs), 366
Electronic Uniform Rules for Bank-to-
    Bank Reimbursements (eURC), 59
Emerging economies, 746
Emission reductions, 763
Emission reduction units (ERUs), 948
Emissions trading system (ETS),
    766–768
Emission tracking techniques, 834, 835
Employees, 901
Employment dynamics, 903
Enclave-based deployment, 656
Energy management, 830
Enhanced accessibility, 922
Enterprise resources, 660
Enterprises, 878, 887
Environmental care, 841
Environmental catastrophes, 838, 851
Environmental data, 565
  financial institutions, 565, 566
  financial services, 566
  financial strategies, 563, 564
  intersection, 564, 565
Environmental governance, 841
Environmental issues, 838, 851
Environmental metrics, 562
Environmental monitoring, 827
Environmental problems, 851, 852
Environmental projects, 840
Environmental recovery, 848
Environmental regulations, 806
Environmental, social, and governance
    (ESG), 183, 187, 210, 216, 509, 797,
    799, 810, 889, 974, 979
  advantages, 195
  banks/international institutions
    elements, 203
    factor weighing, 203
    financial issues, 202
    integration, 202
    multilateral organizations, 203
    strong systems, 202
    utilize modern technologies, 202
    vital issue, 203
  CSRD system, 308
  CSRD vs. NFRD, 310–312
  deep tier suppliers, 244–246
  double materiality approach, 327, 328
  fresh technique, 194
  implementation guidance, 325
  integration, 185
  KYC process, 204–206
  legislative projects and rules, 240–242
  loans, 194
  promoting sustainability, 194
  reporting system, 301
  resilient/responsible, 190
  smart contracts, 194, 195
  stakeholders, 195

1024

strategies, 193
sustainable finance, 331, 336–339
visibility/compliance, 242–244
Environmental sustainability, 839
Environment and trade
   Council for Trade
      in Goods, 710
      in Services, 710
      TRIPS, 710
   WTO bodies
      categories of trade, 710
      CTD, 710
      CTE, 710
      environmental concerns, 711
      environmental issues, 711
      settlement system, 711
      sustainable development, 712
      TNC, 710
      trade-related environmental policies, 711
ePN, see Electronic promissory note (ePN)
ePU, see Electronic payment undertaking (ePU)
ERUs, see Emission reduction units (ERUs)
ESAs, see European Supervisory Authorities (ESAs)
ESG, see Environmental, social, and governance (ESG)
ESMA, see European Securities and Markets Authority (ESMA)
ETDs, see Electronic trade documents (ETDs)
Ethereum, 668
EthicHub, 881, 882
ETRDA, see Electronic Transferable Documents Act (ETRDA)
ETRs, see Electronic transferable records (ETRs)
ETS, see Emissions trading system (ETS)
EU competitiveness
   China's strategic control, 704
   comparative advantage, 703
   dynamic engine, 702
   economic resilience, 704
   Economic resilience, 703
   European Commission, 703
   foreign trade, 702
   international commerce, 702
   lack of market access, 703
   NTBs, 703
   Russia-Ukraine war, 704
   trade obstacles, 704
   Twofold, 703
EU-CyCLone, 600
EUDR, see European Union Deforestation Regulation (EUDR)
EU Emissions Trading System (ETS), 766–768
EU ETS, see European Union Emissions Trading System (EU ETS)
EU financial institution's resilience, DORA
   cloud services, 575
   digital operational resilience strategies, 574
   gap study, 574
   implementation date, 574
   institution's competitiveness and dependability, 575
   making investments, 575
   milestone, 576
   regular testing and auditing, 575
   revamping policies and practices, 575

European Bank for Reconstruction and Development (EBRD), 175, 177, 206–208, 298
European Banking Authority (EBA), 175, 177, 571, 585, 590
European Financial Reporting Advisory Group (EFRAG), 325–327
European Insurance and Occupational Pensions Authority (EIOPA), 571
The European Neighbourhood Policy (ENP), 706, 708
European Securities and Markets Authority (ESMA), 571
European Supervisory Authorities (ESAs), 571
European Sustainability Reporting Standards (ESRs), 325
  Electronic Transactions Documents Act (ETDA), 347
  MLETR (*see* Model Law on Electronic Transferable Records (MLETR))
European Union Deforestation Regulation (EUDR), 715–717
European Union Emissions Trading System (EU ETS), 977
EU trade policy, 701, 702
  agreements to reduce/remove NTBs, 705
  Coalition for Trade Resilience, CRMs, 706
  CPTPP, 706
  ENP, 706
  FTAs, 705
  Trade Resilience Coalition creation, 706
  TTC, 706
EU-US Trade and Technology Council (TTC), 706, 708
Export credit agencies (ECAs), 171

F

FCA, *see* Financial Conduct Authority (FCA)
Federal Information Security Management Act (FISMA), 644, 649
FFSR, *see* Fossil Fuel Subsidy Reform (FFSR)
Finance models, 524
Finance systems, 880
Financial authorities, 873
Financial Conduct Authority (FCA), 978
Financial industry, 848, 863
Financial institutions, 571, 811, 841, 869, 906
  and companies, 843, 889
  container goods derivatives, 525, 526
  conventional, 846, 857, 863, 868, 883, 887
  development, 888
  digital assets, 565, 566
  environmental data, 565, 566
  industries and communities, 566
  and logistics corporations, 504
  logistics firms, 504
  possible losses, 517
  and technology companies, 521
  traditional, 845, 894
Financial markets, 514, 515
Financial models, 850, 851
Financial organizations, 520, 531
Financial product tokenization, 680
Financial services, 858–862, 868, 872, 882, 891
Financial support, carbon farmers, 883
Financial systems, 844, 857
  advocating, 851

capacity, 854
conventional, 847, 858, 859, 861, 870, 871, 883, 893
core structure, 856
creation, 841, 847, 848, 852, 869
decentralization, 877
development, 854, 888
digital, 883
and ecological sustainability, 840
embedding values, 857
fosters confidence and integrity, 847
importance, 858
limits, 850
opacity, 846
redesigning and reorganizing, 850
ReFi, 859
regenerative, 842, 895, 897
reordering, 856
traditional, 845, 846, 860, 869
Financial technology (FinTech), 248, 501, 512, 516, 796–798
Financial transactions, 635, 845, 848, 857, 859, 860, 863, 869, 885–887
FinTech, *see* Financial technology (FinTech)
FISMA, *see* Federal Information Security Management Act (FISMA)
Forward-looking businesses, 849
Fossil Fuel Subsidy Reform (FFSR), 725, 730
Fractional ownership, 670–673, 680, 920, 922, 926, 928, 931, 934–936, 938
Fraud detection, 665
Free Trade Agreements (FTAs), 702, 705, 707, 709
FTAs, *see* Free Trade Agreements (FTAs)
FuelEU Maritime, 751

FuelEU Regulations, 751–753
Funding programs, 889

G

GATT, *see* General Agreement on Tariffs and Trade (GATT)
GDPR, *see* General Data Privacy Regulation (GDPR); General Data Protection Regulation (GDPR)
GDPR compliance
  AI development with GDPR standards, 611–613
  in AI model development, 607, 608
  blockchain, 614, 615
  data challenges and achieving, 610, 611
  data collection for AI, 609, 610
  data processing, 606
  machine learning, 613, 614
  pseudonymization, 611
GenAI, *see* Generative artificial intelligence (GenAI)
Gender gap, 731–733
General Agreement on Tariffs and Trade (GATT), 697, 711
General Data Privacy Regulation (GDPR), 587–589
General Data Protection Regulation (GDPR), 571, 579
  and Articles 4(5), 612
  Articles 5 and 32, 611
  Article 5(1)(e), 612
  Article 6, 613
  Article 9, 613
  Article 20, 614
  Article 25, 612
  Article 35, 614

INDEX

General Data Protection
      Regulation (GDPR) (*cont.*)
  framework, 613
  guidelines, 611, 612
  or Sarbanes-Oxley Act, 635
General purpose machine learning
      (GPML), 419
Generative artificial intelligence (GenAI)
  automation, 418
  decision-making process, 416
  digitalization, 416
  documentary credits, 434, 436
  documentation, 415
  fundamental tech, 415
  international restrictions, 417
  pattern recognition capabilities, 417
  process automation/
      improvement, 434–436
  smart contracts, 435
  trade finance, 416, 417, 434
Geographic Information
      System (GIS), 898
GIS, *see* Geographic Information
      System (GIS)
GIS mapping, 778
Global economy, 707, 845, 862, 890, 892
Global governance, 698
Global issues, 844
Global projects, 841
Global Reporting Initiative (GRI),
      342–345, 982
Global Shipping Business
      Network (GSBN)
  chemical cargo, 472
  Chen, Bertrand, 470
  COSCO Shipping Lines, 470
  genesis and evolution, 471, 472

  ONE's integration, 474, 475
  paperless cargo release system, 471
  strategic partnerships, 472
  TradeLens, 468–472
Global supply chain, 988
Global Supply Chain Finance
      Forum (GSCFF), 140, 146
Global Sustainability Standards
      Board (GSSB), 342
Global trade, 746
  commercial data markets, 560–562
  container goods derivatives, 530–532
  digital infrastructure, 559, 560
Global Trade Review (GTR), 210
Global trading system, 733
Global value chains (GVCs), 714, 715,
      717, 722
Good environmental
      governance, 721
Governance, 902, 903
  groups, 904
  improvement, 905
  investors, 905
  projects center, 904
  structures, 905, 993
  sustainability, 905
  systems, 781–783
Green ammonia, 755, 756, 761
Green bonds, 806
  and subsidies, 756
Green corridors, 750
  advanced digital systems, 754
  alternative fuels application, marine
      trade, 756
  Australia-Japan iron-ore path, 755
  awareness and momentum, industrial
      decarbonization initiatives, 750

INDEX

  decarbonize maritime sector, 749
  development, 749
  digitalization, 759, 760
  feature, 749
  in marine trade, 761, 762
  Maritime and Port Authority of Singapore *vs.* the Port of Rotterdam, 754
  reduce greenhouse gas emissions, 751
  renewable fuels utilization, 753
  roles, 755, 756
  stakeholders, 754
  success, 750
  sustainable marine sector, zero-emission shipping, 750
  zero-emission fuels acceptance, 754
  zero-emission technology research and implementation, 750
Green Deal Investment Plan, 744, 745
Green economy, 746
Greener future
  decarbonizing global shipping, 762–764
  member-led projects
    environmental sustainability, 724, 726
    FFSR project, 725
    global environmental issues, 724
    greener future, 726
    informal Dialogue on Plastic Pollution and Environmentally Sustainable Plastic Trade, China and Fiji, 725
    plastic pollution, 726
    reform of fossil fuel subsidies, 726
    stakeholders, 726
    TESSD, 725
Greener technology, 807

Greener trading methods, 792
Greenhouse gas (GHG) emissions, 749, 819, 958
Greenhouse Gas Protocol, 812
Green methanol, 755, 761
Green shipping corridors
  carbon footprint, international shipping, 771
  decarbonize marine sector, 771
  development, 770
  Los Angeles to Shanghai corridor, 770
  net-zero carbon emissions, 770
  transatlantic corridor, Antwerp to Montreal, 770
  UNCTAD, 771
  world shipping emissions, 771
Green shipping routes, 772
Green subsidies
  developed world, 745
  Green Deal Investment Plan, 744, 745
  growing and underdeveloped nations, 744
  international collaboration, 744
  IRA, 743, 745
  local manufacture, batteries and electric automobiles, 743
  reduce greenhouse emissions and climate action, 744
  substantial stakes, 744
  US and the EU, 745
  WTO, 744
Green technology, 768
Green trade
  accessibility to capital, 796
  crowdfunding, 796
  data analytics, 797
  efficiency and cost reduction, 796
  ESG, 797

INDEX

Green trade (*cont.*)
    financial instruments, 797
    financial mechanisms, 795
    peer-to-peer lending, 796
    policy alignment and support, 795
    policy implementation, 798
    public–private partnerships, 798
    real-time monitoring, 797
    revolution, 695
    sector-specific approaches, 795, 796
    transparency and accountability, 797
    transparency and trust, 794
Green Trade Facilitation Programme (Green TFP), 178
GRI, *see* Global Reporting Initiative (GRI)
GSBN, *see* Global Shipping Business Network (GSBN)
GSCFF, *see* Global Supply Chain Finance Forum (GSCFF)
GSSB, *see* Global Sustainability Standards Board (GSSB)
GTR, *see* Global Trade Review (GTR)
GVCs, *see* Global value chains (GVCs)

H

Harmonization, 918
Healthcare, 626–629, 640
Human civilization, 994
Hybrid calculation methods, 815

I

IAM, *see* Identity and access management (IAM)
IBA, *see* Indian Banks' Association (IBA)
ICC, *see* International Chamber of Commerce (ICC)
ICISA, *see* International Credit Insurance & Surety Association (ICISA)
ICOs, *see* Initial coin offerings (ICOs)
ICT, *see* Information and communication technology (ICT)
ICT-related events, 598
Identity and access management (IAM), 651, 663
IFC, *see* International Financial Corporation (IFC)
IFRS, *see* International Financial Reporting Standards (IFRS)
IMF, *see* International Monetary Fund (IMF)
Immutable records, 664
IMO, *see* International Maritime Organization (IMO)
Incident management plan development, 591
Independent payment undertakings (IPUs), 133, 134
Indian Banks' Association (IBA), 175
Inflation Reduction Act (IRA), 737–739, 743–745
Information and communication technology (ICT), 570
Information rights management (IRM), 594, 595, 602
Ingenuity, 676
Initial coin offerings (ICOs), 462
Innovative method, 920, 921
Innovative technology, 538, 553, 555, 566
Innovators, 893
Institutional investors, 513–515, 518, 519
Intellectual property (IP), 556, 557
Intergovernmental Panel on Climate Change (IPCC), 946
Intermediaries, 988

Internal Revenue Service (IRS), 364
International Chamber of Commerce (ICC), 14, 40, 43, 46, 54, 57–59, 61, 65, 174, 176
   contour implementation, 450
   DTT, 381–384
   URDTT digital frontiers, 378, 379
International collaboration, 792
International commerce, 680
International Credit Insurance & Surety Association (ICISA), 161
International Financial Corporation (IFC), 206, 732
International Financial Reporting Standards (IFRs), 111, 153, 301
   MLETR (*see* Model Law on Electronic Transferable Records (MLETR))
   S1/S2 standards, 347
International Maritime Organization (IMO), 757
International Monetary Fund (IMF), 172
International Organization for Standardization (ISO), 978
International Standard Banking Practice (ISBP), 25, 46, 54
   preliminary considerations, 50, 51
International trade, 731
   finance (*see* Trade and supply chain finance)
International Trade and Forfaiting Association (ITFA), 87, 97, 165, 175
Internet of things (IoT), 239, 473, 549, 609, 644, 804, 835, 915, 973
   data source, 665
   energy efficiency, 824, 825
   greener technology, 834
   logistics, 827, 835
   resource usage, 824
   smart cities, 826
   sustainable trade practices, 825
   synergistic benefits, 665
   trade and supply chain finance, 16
   waste management, 825
Interoperability, 670, 671, 675, 678, 682, 688, 690, 691
Interoperable standards, 552
Inventory management, 809, 827, 832
Investments, 857, 858
Investors, 514, 554, 881, 882, 893, 905
Invoice tokenization
   advantages, 290
   anchor purchasers, 286
   balancing cost/risk/dependability, 290–292
   blockchain, 291
   collaboration, 287–289
   deep-tier providers, 289
   dual-sourcing approach, 280
   factoring process, 285
   financial inclusion, 277, 278
   financial operations, 248–250
   financial risk/liquidity, 281
   liquidity management, 291
   liquidity/payment, 286
   liquidity/resilience/efficiency, 283–285
   long-standing relationships, 289
   negotiation, 289
   operational efficiency, 292
   reliable suppliers, 284, 287
   resilience/efficiency, 278
   smaller suppliers, 275–277
   suppliers, 286
   tier-1/2 suppliers, 280, 288, 290
   trustworthy vendors, 288
   wider ramifications, 291

Invoice tokenization (*cont.*)
    Y-shaped supply chains, 288
    Y-shaped/V-shaped supply, 278–281
IoT, *see* Internet of things (IoT)
IoT devices, 797, 804
IP, *see* Intellectual property (IP)
IPCC, *see* Intergovernmental Panel on Climate Change (IPCC)
IPUs, *see* Independent payment undertakings (IPUs); Irrevocable payment undertakings (IPUs)
IRA, *see* Inflation Reduction Act (IRA)
IRM, *see* Information rights management (IRM)
Irrevocable payment undertakings (IPUs), 81, 150
IRS, *see* Internal Revenue Service (IRS)
ISBP, *see* International Standard Banking Practice (ISBP)
ISO, *see* International Organization for Standardization (ISO)
ISO 27001 and DORA, 596, 597
ITFA, *see* International Trade and Forfaiting Association (ITFA)

J

Joint Implementation (JI), 948

K

Key performance indicators (KPIs), 242, 981
K-means clustering, 809
KPIs, *see* Key performance indicators (KPIs)
Know your customer (KYC), 14, 31, 147, 155, 227, 246, 509, 523, 873, 874, 909

banking industry, 206
digital revolution, 478
ESG criteria, 204
modern tools, 205
organizations, 204
procedures, 205
standardization, 464

L

Labor dynamics, 901
LCAs, *see* Lifecycle assessments (LCAs)
LCRs, *see* Local content controls (LCRs)
LDCs, *see* Least developed nations (LDCs)
Least developed nations (LDCs), 699
Legal entity identifiers (LEIs), 478, 685
Legal frameworks, 554, 678, 684, 690
Legal nuances/payment instruments
    actual sales/financing issues, 93
    assignor/assignee, 99
    categorization arguments, 96
    commercial transaction, 96
    debtor nonpayment, 94
    disagreements, 94
    enforceability, 91
    English law, 98
    enhancement approach, 97
    exporters, 91
    financiers, 93–95
    importer/exporter, 97
    instruments, 94, 96
    international commerce, 91
    legal and financial communities, 95
    legal assignment, 98
    negotiability, 92
    non-negotiable receivables, 92
    non-notified transfers, 98

INDEX

obligations, 97
products/services, 95
promissory notes/bills, 97
requirements, 93
secure payment instrument, 99
security/advantages, 90
transferability, 96
true sale influences, 92
true trade debt, 95
Legal systems, 591
Legal uncertainty, 927
Legislative systems, 768
LEIs, *see* Legal entity identifiers (LEIs)
Lenders, 500, 502, 503, 518, 519
Letters of credit (LoCs), 19, 681, 914
    application process
        banking relationship, 71
        bank insolvency/operational issues, 71
        collateral requirements, 69
        contractual obligations, 69
        investigations, 69
        issuing bank, 70, 72
        non-payment, 70
        regular monitoring, 71
        risk analysis/evaluation, 69
        risk process, 73
        SBLC requirements, 70
        small business loan, 70
        strong banking relationships, 73
        termination process, 72
    banks, 170
    beneficiary, 20
    BGs (*see* Bank guarantees (BGs))
    business transactions, 21, 22
    conditional *vs.* unconditional receivables, 83
    confirming bank, 24
    contour, 466
    digital tokens, 685
    documents, 19
    electronic documents, 57–64
    financial crimes, 64, 65
    fraud/sanctions risks, 64, 65
    independent commitments, 20
    instrument/agreement, 20
    ISBP 821, 50, 51
    ISBP/UCP 600, 25
    issuing bank, 24
    nomination, 24
    payment risk/security, 26
    payments/dynamics, 36
        acceptance credits, 39
        buyers/sellers, 37
        components, 37
        deferred payment, 38, 39
        documentary, 37
        issuing bank, 37
        issuing/execution, 38
        primary difference, 37
    primary risk, 25
    reimbursement claims, 24
    restriction/structured trade, 29
        advantage, 30
        beneficiary's bank, 30
        benefits, 31
        handling fees/negotiation, 29
        intermediary bank, 30
        issuing bank, 29
        negotiating bank, 30
    risk mitigation, 24, 155
    securitization process, 106
    standard transactions, 685
    standby letter of credit, 68

INDEX

Letters of credit (LoCs) (*cont.*)
   streamlining interactions, 55
   SWIFT game changer, 56–58
   SWIFT network
      beneficiary, 32
      efficient implementation, 32
      issuing bank, 34
      negotiating bank, 31
      operational preferences, 32
      redefining liquidity and flexibility, 35
      regulations, 32
      risk management system, 33
      risk mitigation techniques, 32
      strategic goals/partnerships, 33
      trade transactions, 31, 34, 35
      UCP 600, 34
   trade transaction, 23
   traditional LCs, 684, 685, 688
   transferring bank, 24
   transparency and traceability, 684
   UCP 600 (*see* Uniform Customs and Practice (UCP 600))
LIBOR, *see* London Interbank Offered Rate (LIBOR)
Lifecycle assessments (LCAs), 812, 817, 820
Liquefied natural gas (LNG) in shipping
   carbon conundrum, 757
   carbon-free shipping, 758
   economic advantages, 758
   LNG-powered boats, 757
   lower hazardous emissions, 757
   lowering GHG emissions, 757
   methane slip, 757
   reduce sulfur oxide emissions, 757
   shipping decarbonization, 758
   South Korea, 758
   strategic emphasis, South Korea, 758
   transitional fuel, 757
   WtW emissions, 757
Liquidity, 668, 670, 672, 675
Load management, 809
Local content controls (LCRs), 739
LoCs, *see* Letters of credit (LoCs)
Logistics
   accessibility, 536
   adoption, 544
   AI, 539, 540
   audits and evaluations, 537
   bottlenecks, 535
   capabilities, 541
   characteristics, 538
   and commerce, 526, 533, 534, 567
   companies, 545
   cutting-edge technology, 541
   data, 537
   data exchange, 541–544
   data silos and scattered systems, 542
   data standards, 539
   development, 540
   efficient control, 537
   environmental issues, 540
   future, 535
   global setting, 536
   global supply chain, 534
   installation and extension, 542
   interoperability, 534
   layers, 545, 546
   modern technologies, 534
   neutrality, 536
   openness, 536–538
   operations, 543
   performance and user experiences, 541

INDEX

phased installation and growth
address, 541
3PL services, 544
5PL services, 544, 545
6PL services, 545
procedures, 542
sophisticated systems, 536, 542
supply chain management, 543
sustainable economic
development, 543
technologies, 543
trade-data systems, 547
trade finance sectors, 554
use case, 541
Logistics firms, 503, 504, 525, 541
Logistics sectors, 548, 549, 551, 553
London, 3–8
London Interbank Offered Rate
(LIBOR), 107
Low-carbon economy, 835
Low-carbon technologies, 811, 812
Low-emission vehicles, 807

M

Machine learning (ML), 239, 363, 419, 510,
804, 806, 809
GDPR-compliant, 613, 614
Marco Polo Network
cautionary tale, 440–442
collaborative workshops, 448
contour, 439
crucial component, 441
DLTLegers, 439
factors, 447
financial burden, 442
financial condition, 445, 446
financial organizations, 443

history of, 438–440
institutions/trading partners, 446
investments, 444
Komgo, 440
long-term sustainability, 446
network effects, 443
obstacles, 438
operational and strategic issues, 445
payment directive, 440
platform's member banks, 441
prominent financial
institutions, 440
prominent platform, 439
regulatory frameworks, 447
slow rate implementation, 444
stakeholders, 448
strategic alliances, 441
substantial support, 441
TradeIX, 443
TradeLens, 439
transaction process, 443–445
trust and collaboration, 447
valuable insights/contemplation, 442
Marine sector, 771
Marine trade, 761, 762
Maritime sector, 752, 772
greener future, 773
LNG, 757
Market-based systems, 956
Market dynamics, 908
Market growth, 906
Master Participation Agreement
(MPA), 120–122
Master risk participation agreement
(MRPA), 165
MCO2 tokens, 971
Member-led projects, 726, 729
Methodical testing technique, 597

1035

INDEX

MFA, *see* Multi-factor authentication (MFA)
MFIs, *see* Multilateral financial institutions (MFIs)
Micro, small, and medium-sized companies (MSMEs), 421
Mindets, 993
ML, *see* Machine learning (ML)
MLETR, *see* Model Law on Electronic Transferable Records (MLETR); Model Legislation on Electronic Transferable Records (MLETR)
Model Law on Electronic Transferable Records (MLETR), 57–64, 227, 246, 359
   blockchain technology, 345
   control functions, 297
   digital platforms, 296
   digital trade, 296
      finance, 63
      sector, 63
   documents against acceptance (D/A), 60
   documents against payment (D/P), 60
   e-compliance, 57
   effective, safe, and transparent, 58
   electronic communications, 296
   electronic papers/conversations, 62
   electronic rules (eRules), 62
   electronic transferable records, 297, 298
   ETDA (*see* Electronic Transactions Documents Act (ETDA))
   eUCP design, 58
   eURC rules, 61, 62
   global commerce ecosystem, 62
   ICC eRules, 59
   interpretations, 63
   legal and regulatory reforms, 299
   modernization, 298, 299
   national and regional laws, 63
   reform/guides nations, 301
   stricter standards, 58
   sustainability reporting system, 301
   trade papers and transactions, 60
   TradeTrust, 477
   traditional paper records, 63
   transaction process, 61
   UNCITRAL, 60, 344
   URDTT (*see* Uniform Rules for Digital Commerce Activities (URDTT))
   values/rules setting/UCP, 58
   Version 2.1 (eUCP), 60
   worldwide agencies, 298
Model Legislation on Electronic Transferable Records (MLETR)
   cross-border recognition, 307, 308
   functional equivalent, 306
   global trade, 305–308
   harmonization, 303–305
   model legislation, 306
   UNIDROIT Model Law, 304
Modern banking, 673
Modern shipping, 768
Modern trade, 988
Money transfer systems, 845
Monitoring, reporting, and verification (MRV), 977
MPA, *see* Master Participation Agreement (MPA)
MRAs, *see* Mutual recognition agreements (MRAs)
MRPA, *see* Master risk participation agreement (MRPA)
MRV, *see* Monitoring, reporting, and verification (MRV)

Multi-factor authentication (MFA), 651, 663
Multilateral Electronic Transactions Act (MLETR), 359
Multilateral financial institutions (MFIs), 206–208
Mutual recognition agreements (MRAs), 706

N

Natural language processing (NLP), 416, 435
Nature-based solutions (NBS), 339–341
    advantages, 341, 787
    biotechnology, 776
    cultural settings, 784
    deployment, 784
    dynamics and developments, 341
    ecological advantages, 339
    environmental impact assessment tools, 778
    environmental issues, 339
    governance systems, 781–783
    implementation using policy tools, 787
    international perspectives, 783–785
    investments, 340
    market dynamics, 339
    market trends and forces, 340, 341
    nature-positive economy, 340, 775, 777, 778, 785–788, 790
    NetworkNature project, 786
    policy simulation models, 778
    political, social, and economic elements, 784
    public financing competition, 341
    smart technology deployment, 783
    stakeholders, 790
    sustainable economic growth advancement, 775
    advantages, 774, 775
    economic, environmental, and social policies, 774
    market development and innovation, 774
    national and international policy agendas, 774
    stakeholders, 774
    technological developments, 775
    sustainable future, public policy, 787–790
    technology, 776, 777, 782
    valuation models, 787
Nature-positive economy, 775, 781–786
    NBS, 778, 786–788
    NBS-related economic prospects, 789
    open criteria, 788
    tech-driven nature-based solutions, 775–777
    tech-enabled nature-based solutions, 777
NBS, *see* Nature-based solutions (NBS)
Network infrastructure components and capabilities, 659, 660
New technologies adoption, 988
NFTs, *see* Non-fungible tokens (NFTs)
NIS2 Directive, 599, 600
NIST SP 800-207
    automated response mechanisms, 651
    continuous monitoring, 650
    data sources, 650
    IAM, 651
    implementation guidance, 649
    micro-segmentation, 651
    vs. NIST SP 800-207A, 652, 653
    PA, 650

INDEX

NIST SP 800-207 (*cont.*)
    PE, 650
    PEP, 650
    principles, 649
    regulatory compliance, 649
    trust algorithm, 650
    use cases, 649
NIST SP 800-207A *vs.* NIST SP 800-207, 652, 653
NLP, *see* Natural language processing (NLP)
Non-DORA compliance, 584, 585
Non-Financial Reporting Directive (NFRD), *see* Corporate Sustainability Reporting Directive (CSRD)
Non-fungible tokens (NFTs), 400, 401, 899
Non-state players, 730
Non-tariff barriers (NTBs), 703, 707
NTBs, *see* Non-tariff barriers (NTBs)

O

Ocean Network Express (ONE), 474, 475
OCR, *see* Optical character recognition (OCR)
OES, *see* Operators of essential services (OES)
OFAC, *see* Office of Foreign Assets Control (OFAC)
Office of Foreign Assets Control (OFAC), 509
On-chain *vs.* off-chain data computing, 617–619
ONE, *see* Ocean Network Express (ONE)
OOCL, *see* Orient Overseas Container Line (OOCL)
Open source culture, 993

Open-source technologies, 990, 991
Operators of essential services (OES), 599
Optical character recognition (OCR), 416, 435
Orient Overseas Container Line (OOCL), 472

P, Q

PA, *see* Policy Administrator (PA)
Paper-based instrument
    Bretton Woods system, 8, 9
    evolution, 3
    negotiable bill of exchange, 9, 10
    standardization, 9
    trade finance hub/Post-World Wars
        acceptance houses, 6
        architecture and tools, 4
        banking systems, 4
        commercial rules/practices, 5
        credit/liquidity characteristics, 6
        European liquidity issues, 7
        history of, 4
        law merchant, 5
        period spanning, 6
        reconstruction, 4
        regional bankers/merchants, 3
        resources/methods, 4
        significant driver, 6
        World War I, 7
Paradigm shift, 844, 856, 889, 912
PE, *see* Policy engine (PE)
PEPs, *see* Policy enforcement points (PEPs)
Permissioned *vs.* permissionless blockchains, 615–617
Personally identifiable information (PII), 609

Physical assets, 878
Physical internet, 500, 546
    automatic replenishment, 546
    direct shipment, 546
    vs. logistics sector, 548
    paradigm, 547
    tech-enabled trade, 547
    transforming power, 547
PII, *see* Personally identifiable information (PII)
Pioneers, 853, 854, 893
Platforms, 556
Policy Administrator (PA), 650, 654
Policy enforcement points (PEPs), 650, 654, 660, 661
Policy engine (PE), 650, 654
Policymakers, 850
Pooling, 752–754
Pragmatism, 880
Precision agricultural technology, 778
Predictive analytics, 808
Pricing carbon, 951
Privacy-centric feature engineering, 611–613
Private blockchains, 907
Professional audits, 875
Professionals, 900
Profit-driven strategy, 843
Profit maximization, 842
Project developers, 881
Project management, 902, 903
Promissory notes, 675–677, 681
Public awareness, 850
Public blockchains, 668, 669
Public goods, 871, 878
Public initiatives, 906
Public–private partnerships, 555, 798, 891

R

RBAC, *see* Role-based access control (RBAC)
Real-time emission monitoring, 828
Real-time monitoring, 812
Real-world applications, 884, 886, 912
Real-world assets (RWA), 871, 878, 886, 889, 906
    investments, 920–922
    tokenization, 929–931
Real-world data, 562
    balancing compliance and independence, 916, 917
    build balanced future, 919
    efficiency, transparency and compliance, 915, 916
    with trade financing systems, 915
Real-world metrics, 563
Receivables finance
    asset-based lending, 78, 82
    aval/bank guarantee, 137
    avalization and bank guarantees, 137
    bank loans, 158–160
    Basel agreements, 89, 90
    buyers/sellers, 78
    capital adequacy, 89
    capital and cash flow issues, 77
    conditional *vs.* unconditional receivables, 81–84
    contract receivables, 137, 138
    credit conversion factor (CCF), 90
    credit enhancement strategies, 123, 124
    credit insurance, 127
        collateral option, 127
        creditors, 128
        crucial component, 131

INDEX

Receivables finance (*cont.*)
    financial institutions, 129
    financiers and insurance
        consumers, 129, 130
    fluctuations, 127
    insurable interest, 129
    rigorous investigation, 131
    risk reduction instrument, 131
  definition, 77
  distribution techniques, 117
    BAFT and IIFM, 122
    bank-to-bank connections, 120
    beneficial ownership interest, 122
    distribution, 118, 119
    diversifying credit risk, 118
    fraud risk, 120
    handling financial assets, 118
    identification process, 119
    investors, 117
    logistical issues, 119
    requirement, 120
    risk participation agreements, 121
    standardization, 120
    sub-participation, 117
    trade finance, 122
    true sale theory, 121
    unfunded participation, 121
  factoring agreements, 166, 167
  funding lifecycle, 79
  independent payment undertakings
    (IPUs), 133, 134
  insolvency/restructuring, 134, 135
  insurance companies/financial
    guarantees
    banks/insurance companies, 165
    banks/insurers, 165
    categories, 161
    collaboration, 161
    construction, 162, 163
    contractions, 163
    contractual obligations, 162
    insurance firms, 161, 163
    regulatory framework, 164
    roles/responsibilities, 162
    supply/warranty bonds, 163
    surety bonds, 165
    suretyship, 164
  intricate operations, 82
  invoice discounting, 78
  irreversible bank guarantee, 139
  irrevocable payment obligation, 80
  KYC processes, 147
  legal nuances (*see* Legal nuances/
    payment instruments)
  negotiable instruments, 126, 135, 136
  payment instruments, 125–127
  products/services, 79, 80
  quality financing, 80, 81
  risk mitigation tool
    agreement outlines, 154
    autonomous/abstract, 149
    cross-border transactions, 151
    document evaluation, 156
    elements, 154
    essential components/factors, 154
    examination guarantees, 155
    financial instruments, 150
    forfaiting transactions, 148, 151,
      152, 156, 157
    fundamental component, 148
    handling technique, 156
    key differences, 150
    KYC rules, 155
    legal transfer, 153

market discipline/wide
  discretion, 158
market evaluation, 155
methodical approach, 153
payment instruments/claims, 149
secondary market, 157
security and predictability, 152
seller's cash flow and liquidity, 149
single transaction agreements, 154
technology and legislation, 148
SCF (*see* Supply chain finance (SCF))
secured financing *vs.* true sale, 132, 133
securitization (*see* Securitization
  process)
strategizing security, 138, 139
strengthening financial instruments,
  136, 137
SWIFT system, 158
tailoring options, 84, 85
tradable and transferable, 101
traditional methods/digital horizons
  components, 85
  factoring/forfaiting, 85, 86
  funding appeals, 88
  funding process, 88
  invoice trading, 87
  SCF programs, 86
  suppliers, 87
  unconditional payment, 86
transferability, 101–103
true trade debt, 135, 136
versatile instrument, 78
ReFi, *see* Regenerative Finance (ReFi)
Regenerative Finance (ReFi), 837
  activities, 888
  adaptable strategy, 880
  aims, 838

automation, 859, 862
basic tenet, 862
basic values, 848
basis of finance, 847
benefits, 859, 860
blockchain, 878
  security, 875, 876
  technology, 846, 883, 899 (*see also*
    Blockchain technology)
capacity, 860, 861, 899
carbon markets, 881
challenges, 893–895
climate action, 911
climate community critics, 900
climate governance and conservation,
  840, 841
climate movements, 840
codebases, 875
community, 876, 877, 900
  issues, 907
  members, 898
  participants, 902
compliance, 874
concept, 838
concerning problems, 850
conventional cases, 859
conventional finance, 855, 860, 861
cooperative efforts, 874
defining quality, 870
dependability and confidence, 873
design, 861
development and efficacy, 855, 869, 870
digital assets, 890, 892
distributed/multi-jurisdictional
  character, 863
distributed technology, 879
early adopters

INDEX

Regenerative Finance (ReFi) (*cont.*)
    advantages, 853, 854
        resilience and potency, 854, 855
    ecological restoration and
        conservation, financial activity,
        839, 840
    economic models, 843, 844
    economic systems, 838, 843, 844,
        848, 851
    emphasis, 877, 878
    engagement, 877
    environmental
        damage, 911
        justice, 841
        and social justice, 841, 842
        sustainability, 869
    features, 878, 903
    financial accessibility, 860
    financial advantages, 862
    financial arrangements, 851
    financial environment, 861
    financial goals, 890
    financial methods, 840
    financial systems, 839, 841, 842, 845,
        847, 856, 864, 870
    financial tools/strategies, 888
    flow of financial value, 883–885
    global connectivity, 862
    governance issues, 905
    ideas and practices, 851
    inclusive systems, 841
    industry bodies, 873
    information, 871
    interoperability, 894
    investments, 889
    knowledge, 842
    money, 890
    movement, 871
    negative legislative/economic
        uncertainty, 861
    next generation, 852, 853
    obstacles, 895
    open access, 870
    open code, 870
    openness, 845, 871–874
    paradigm shift, 844
    people and communities, 879
    planetary regeneration/societal
        development, 879
    possibilities, 898
    programs, 873
    projects, 874, 881, 882, 895–898
    public scrutiny, 874
    real-world effects, 882, 884
    regulatory environments, 863, 872
    responsibility, 845
    security, 876
    services, 872
    significant, 849
    small-scale carbon producers, 882
    social fairness/economic
        inclusion, 883
    social welfare, 869
    societies, 850
    stakeholders, 889
    structural problems, 845
    sustainability, 839, 847
    sustainable and restoring system, 849
    systemic change, 856
    team, 872
    terrain, 909
    theoretical idea, 854
    tokenization, 885
    transactions, 858, 861, 875
    transformative movement, 838
    transformative solution, 843

translators, 884
transparency, 871, 872, 874
   and sovereignty, 857
universal accessibility, 858
users, 872, 873, 876
values, 870
Web3, 867, 878, 880
RegTech, *see* Regulation technology (RegTech)
Regular risk assessments, 592
Regulations, 867
Regulation technology (RegTech), 505, 566
   automated solutions, 511, 512
   developments, 512
   evolution, 505, 507
   products, 511
   RegTech 1.0 (paper to pixels), 505, 506
   RegTech 2.0 (digital dawn), 506
   RegTech 3.0 (watershed moment), 506
   RegTech 4.0 (revolution), 507
Regulators, 557, 558
Regulatory activities, 909
Regulatory ambiguity, 893
Regulatory compliance, 641, 649, 767, 917
Regulatory environments, 909
Regulatory frameworks, 533, 557, 559, 566
Regulatory organizations, 592
Renaissance, 987
Renewable fuels, 753
Resilient development, 747
Resilient network, 659
Responsibility and openness, 592
Risk distribution technologies, 513, 518, 519
Risk management framework (RMF), 644
Risk participation agreements (RPAs), 120

RMF, *see* Risk management framework (RMF)
Robotic process automation (RPA), 835
   automating emission tracking, 830, 833
   digital transformation, 831
   energy efficiency, 833
   global sustainability goals, 831
   optimization, 830
   remote work initiatives, 833
   reporting, 830
   streamlining operations, 832
   supply chain management, 830, 832
   sustainability objectives, 834
Role-based access control (RBAC), 651
Route optimization, 808, 832
RPAs, *see* Risk participation agreements (RPAs); Robotic process automation (RPA)
RWA, *see* Real-world assets (RWA)

S

Sanctions screening, 509
Sarbanes-Oxley Act, 635
SASB, *see* Sustainability Accounting Standards Board (SASB)
SBL, *see* Small business loan (SBL)
SBLCs, *see* Standby letters of credit (SBLCs)
Scenario simulation, 810
SCF, *see* Supply chain finance (SCF)
Scholars, 850
Scope 1 emissions, 822, 823
Scope 2 emissions, 822, 823
Scope 3 emissions
   activities, 823
   approaches, 834

INDEX

Scope 3 emissions (*cont.*)
    calculation methodologies, 816, 819
        average data method, 820
        hybrid method, 821
        spend-based method, 819
        supplier-specific method, 820, 821
    collaboration, 823
    complexity, 814
    continuous improvement, 818
    data collection and analysis, 817
    data integration, value chain, 828
    data quality and availability, 816, 817
    definition, 822
    elements, 821
    internal expertise and capacity
        collaboration, 818
        training personnel, 818
    IoT, 829
    measurement methodologies, 817
    reporting capabilities, 829
    tracking, 810
SCRM, *see* Supply chain risk
    management (SCRM)
SDGs, *see* Sustainable Development
    Goals (SDGs)
Sector-specific approaches, 793
Securing AI with blockchain
    access control, 623, 624
    characteristics, 621
    data transfers, 621
    distributed and safe platform for data
        transactions, 621
    immutability guarantees, 621
    smart contracts and cryptographic
        keys, 621
    transparency, 622, 623
    unchangeable character, 621
Securitization process, 512

ABCP conduits, 106–109
adaptability, 105
agreements, 109
amortization structure, 112
banking institutions, 107
capital markets, 108
commercial paper (CP), 105, 107
currencies, 111
cutting-edge financial innovation, 101
financiers and investors, 104
IFRS 9 (de-recognition)/IFRS 10
    (de-consolidation), 111
investment-grade sellers, 111
issuers/sellers, 103
liability, 105
LIBOR/risk-free rates, 107
liquidity, 102, 103
notable feature, 102
regulatory reforms/controls
    bank lending/investment
        strategies, 112
    benefits, 114
    capital relief deals, 112
    characteristics/difficulties, 113
    constraints, 113
    credit risk offers, 114
    financial crisis, 115
    investor competitiveness, 114
    market liquidity/current interest
        rates, 117
    problems and opportunities, 114
    pure guarantee/real sale, 116
    regulatory capital relief, 115
    SPV's structure, 116
    strong/effective administration, 113
    synthetic securitization, 114
    synthetic side, 113
    true-sale transactions, 115

risk concentration, 103
risk management tools, 110
risk mitigation, 109
risk reduction strategies, 104
segmentation strategies, 109
short-term finance, 106
significant concentrations, 110
structure of, 103
trade receivables, 104
trade transactions ranges, 102
vital products/services, 104
Security policies and resilience, 591
Security testing, 598
Security token offerings (STOs), 462
Self-executing contracts, 668, 670
Sensors, 778
Shanghai Research Institute of Chemical Industry Testing (SICIT), 473
Shared regulatory framework, 993
Shipment tracking, 827
Shipping industry, 763
Shipping process, 548, 549
Shipping sector
  decarbonization, 765
  EU ETS, 767
  future, 766
  IMO
    CO_2 emissions cuts, 764
    GHG emissions, 765
    regional governments and agencies, 765
  legislative changes force companies, 765
  regulatory framework changes, 766
Short-term financial benefits, 842
SICIT, *see* Shanghai Research Institute of Chemical Industry Testing (SICIT)

Sight LCs, *see* Sight letters of credit (Sight LCs)
Sight letters of credit (Sight LCs), 36, *see also* Letters of credit (LoCs)
Significant risk transfer (SRT), 112
Small and medium-sized businesses (SMEs), 74, 206–208, 211, 215, 217, 517, 520, 531, 536, 558, 796, 888–891, 914
  blockchain, 254
  conventional systems, 294
  deep-tier suppliers, 250–256
  DTSCF finance system, 223, 224
  DTSCF technology, 276
Small and medium-sized company (SME), 310
Small and medium-sized enterprises (SMEs), 75, 172, 173, 368
  blockchain technology, 440
  CSRD system, 308–315
Small and medium sized firms (SMEs), 439, 518, 800
Small business loan (SBL), 70
Smart buildings, 824
Smart contracts, 510, 633–635, 638, 664, 668, 670, 673, 685, 686, 689, 856, 866, 868, 874, 879, 886, 887, 921, 964
  automation/efficiency, 427, 428
  benefits, 427
  and blockchain, 639–641
  commercial documents, 427
  contract law, 483
  data security with distributed ledgers and, 623, 624
  digital environment, 425, 426
  GenAI, 435

INDEX

Smart contracts (*cont.*)
   global trade automation, 424
   insurance documents, 427
   mechanism, 429–432
   real-time data, 428, 429
   shipping documents, 427
Smart grids, 824
Smart ports, 760
Smart technology, 806
Smart waste solutions, 825
Social circumstances, 848
Social media and digital content, 629–632
Social responsibility, 852
Social sectors, 849
Society for Worldwide Interbank Financial Telecommunication (SWIFT), 55–57, 158
SPE, *see* Special purpose entity (SPE)
Special purchase vehicles (SPVs), 87
Special purpose entity (SPE), 102, 110, 116
Special purpose vehicles (SPVs), 105, 116
Spend-based method, 819
SPVs, *see* Special purpose vehicles (SPVs)
SRT, *see* Significant risk transfer (SRT); Synthetic structured risk transfer (SRT)
SSCF, *see* Sustainable supply chain finance (SSCF)
Stakeholders, 553, 554, 559, 560, 727, 730, 786, 794, 877, 889, 893, 900, 988, 991, 992
Stakeholders engagement, green trade revolution
   changing attitude, 729
   create responsibility and ownership, 728
   non-state actors, 727
   2023 Public Forum, 727

WTO, 728
   Environment Week, 727
   Public Forum, 727
Standby letters of credit (SBLCs), 67, 68, 71
STOs, *see* Security token offerings (STOs)
STP, *see* Straight-through processing (STP)
Straight-through processing (STP), 476
Supervised learning, 419
Supervising authorities, 585–587
Suppliers
   collaboration, 828
   direct engagement, 816
   multiple emissions, 814
   multiple tiers, 814
   primary data, 820
Supplier-specific method, 820
Supply chain carbon footprints
   data quality and availability, 814
   measurement methodologies, 815
   resource intensity, 816
   scope 3 emissions, 814
   technical expertise, lack of, 815
Supply chain finance (SCF), 86
   artificial intelligence, 182
   blockchain technology, 182
   buyer-centric version, 141
   buyers and sellers, 141, 142
   cloud computing, 182
   conceptualization, 140
   credit terms, 144
   cross-border finance, 140
   DTSCF (*see* Deep-Tier Supply Chain Finance (DTSCF))
   face value, 144
   financial ecosystem, 181
   GSCFF roles, 146
   industry groups, 140

key element, 146
long-term impacts, 146
net present value (NPV), 143, 144
onboarding campaign, 145
payables financing, 141, 145
payment instructions, 142
receivables finance, 124
risk-free rates, 143
service providers, 146
smart contract
    advantages, 201
    buyers and suppliers, 200
    clear and reliable structure, 201
    integration, 201
    transaction information, 200
    verification procedures, 200
SSCF (*see* Sustainable supply chain finance (SSCF))
suppliers/buyers, 181
sustainable payables finance, 196, 197
third-party service, 143
trade loans
    benefits, 198
    integration, 199
    objectives, 199
    products/services, 198
    short-term solutions, 198
    suppliers, 199
transaction, 143
Supply chain management, 543–545, 547, 830, 832
Supply chain partners, 813
Supply chain risk management (SCRM), 598
Supply chains, emissions data
    carbon footprints, 810
    comprehensive reporting and compliance, 810
    continuous improvement, 810
    demand forecasting, 809
    feedback loop, 810
    ML models, 809
    real-time data analysis, 808
    transportation and logistics, 808
Supply chain transparency, 666, 825
Sustainability, 852
Sustainability Accounting Standards Board (SASB), 982
Sustainability-linked loans, 801, 804, 806, 811, 835
Sustainable development goals (SDGs), 335, 467
Sustainable finance
    capacity building, 800
    mobilizing capital, green initiatives, 798
    policy alignment, 799
    technical assistance, 800
    transparency and accountability, 799
Sustainable future, maritime sector, 763
Sustainable shipping, future, 766
Sustainable supply chain finance (SSCF)
    advantages, 184
    businesses, 186
    data collection and processing, 188
    digitization, 188
    elements, 187
    ESG (*see* Environmental, social, and governance (ESG))
    ESG factors, 185–187
    financial decision-making, 183
    financial institutions, 189
    financial service providers, 184
    imperative, 187–189
    integration, 189

INDEX

Sustainable supply chain finance (SSCF) (*cont.*)
   MFIs, 206–208
   payment terms, 186
   resilient/responsible
      advantages, 189
      banks/financial institutions, 191
      consumers, 191
      data collection and processing, 190
      digitalization, 190
      elements, 193
      environmental/social impact, 192
      objectives, 192
      operational benefits, 190
      risk management, 193
      service companies, 192
      supplier relationships, 191
      technical development, 190
   rising expectations, 184
   stakeholders, 183
   strategies/solutions, 185
   vendors/consumers, 183
Sustainable trade, 747
SWIFT, *see* Society for Worldwide Interbank Financial Telecommunication (SWIFT)
SWIFT standards, 685
Synthetic structured risk transfer (SRT), 114

T

Task Force on Climate-related Financial Disclosures (TCFD), 982
TBFC, *see* Trade-based financial crimes (TBFC)
TCFD, *see* Task Force on Climate-related Financial Disclosures (TCFD)
Tech-driven nature-based solutions nature-positive economy, 775–777
Tech-enabled nature-based solutions nature-positive economy, 777–779
Technical audits, 875
Technical Barriers to Commerce (TBT) Committee, 711
Technological developments, 546, 778, 848
Technologies, 890
Technology as catalyst, structural change NBS, sustainable future
   advanced data analytics and simulation models, 780
   coherent and cooperative method, 781
   cooperative platforms, 781
   corporate strategies, 780
   online markets, carbon credits and ecosystem services, 780
   policy frameworks, 780
   smartphone applications, community-based monitoring projects, 781
   stakeholders, 780
   structural transformation, 781
   social and economic environments, 780
Technology-based education, 891
Technology developments, 551
Telematics technology, 806
TESSD, *see* Trade and Environmental Sustainability Structured Discussions (TESSD)

Time LCs, *see* Time letters of credit (Time LCs)
Time letters of credit (Time LCs), 37
Tipping point, 850
TNC, *see* Trade Negotiations Committee (TNC)
Token generation, 924
Tokenization, 520–522, 670–672, 689, 886, 894, 913, 914, 920, 923, 925, 926, 934, 935
    adoption, 670
    carbon credits, 881, 896
    carbon market, 908
    description, 682
    environmental assets, 871
    for ESG strategies, 978–980
    in financial services, 673
    foundations and advantages, 669, 670
    future, 671
    of LoCs (*see* Letters of credit (LoCs))
    physical objects, 885, 886
    promissory notes and bills of exchange, 675
    strategic adoption and future, 674
    transformative power, 673
Tokenization of goods, 925
Tokenization trials, 927–929
Tokenized assets, 499, 520–524, 673, 678, 683, 684
    infrastructure, 928
    perception and adoption, 683
Tokenized commodities, 940
Tokenized goods, 944
Tokenized LCs, 685–687
Tokenized transactions, 683
Trade
    adaptation, 748
    climate change mitigation, 748
    resilience, 748
    socioeconomic issues, 748
Trade and environmental policies
    climate change to biodiversity loss, 696
    global governance, 698
    governments, 696
    multilateral trade system, environmental challenges, 697
    stakeholders, 696
    WTO, 697
        agreements, 697
        legal structure, 697
        membership, 698
        plastic pollution, 697
        procedures, 698
        sustainable development, 698
Trade and Environmental Sustainability Structured Discussions (TESSD), 725, 728
Trade and supply chain finance, 1
    AI, 16
    blockchain technology, 16
    broad acceptance, 17
    conventional trade finance, 15
    digitalization, 17
    digital technologies, 15, 17
    financial institutions, 16
    global financial institutions, 14, 15
    history, 1–3
    instruments (*see* Paper-based instrument)
    IoT devices, 16
    Middle Ages, 2
    streamline processes, 16
    trading centers, 2
Trade-based financial crimes (TBFC), 665

INDEX

Trade, climate, and finance
    climate catastrophe, 734
    international trade, 733
    sustainable development, 734
    sustainable future, 734
    unsustainable methods, 733, 734
Trade-data platforms, 535
Trade-data systems, 535, 547
Trade diversion, 714
Trade, environment, and sustainable development integration
    environmental factors, WTO, 731
    global economy, 730
    high-level ministerial direction, 730
    improve national policy coherence, 730
    Informal Dialogue on Plastic Pollution and Environmentally Sustainable Plastic Trade, China and Fiji, 729
    member-led projects, 729
    transboundary environmental challenges, 729
    WTO awareness, 730, 731
    WTO bodies, 729
Trade finance, 169, 675, 891, 892, 987
    AI (*see* Artificial intelligence (AI))
    approved values, 500, 501
    automation and digitalization, 520
    availability, 501
    banks, 170, 504 (*see also* Banks, Trade finance)
        and credit insurers, 517, 518
    blockchain (*see* Blockchain)
    carbon labeling, 812, 813
    CO_2 emissions reduction, 811
    collaboration, stakeholders, 807
    complex ecosystem (*see* Complex ecosystem)
    credit evaluations, 502
    credit gap, 500
    data access, 502
    data analytics, 503
    decarbonization, 800
    derivatives, 525, 526
    digital (*see* Digital trade finance solution)
    digitalization, 173
    digital technologies, 805
    digitization, 801
    ecosystem, 169
    effects, 501
    emission tracking, 812
    end-to-end workflow automation, 515, 516
    expansion, 503
    financial data, 502
    financial institutions, 504
    financial tools, 514
    financing gap, 500
    financing solutions, 804, 806
    freight operations, 806
    global economic development, 502
    green bonds and loans, 801
    greener trading practices, 791
        awareness, 794
        benefits, 793
        challenges, 793
        key aspects, 792
    hedging
        derivatives, 526–528
        futures contracts, 527
        instruments, 525, 526
        objective, 526
        options, 527
        risk management, 528
        swaps, 527

information asymmetries, 504
information exchange, 504
institutions, 805, 807
instruments/services, 169, 522
integration, regulatory
    frameworks, 802
liquidity, 513
logistics companies, 504
lower carbon emissions, 807
modernizing, 500
organizations, 176–179
predictive analytics, 803
publications, 179
real-time emission dashboards, 802
real-time monitoring, 803
RegTech (*see* Regulation Technology
    (RegTech))
regulations, 509
regulatory compliance, 806, 807
    and reporting, 804
risk distribution
    technologies, 513, 519
    tools, 512
risk-sharing methods, 517, 518
securitization, 513
sophisticated analytics, 502
stakeholders, 170, 171
supply chain, 804, 805
sustainability, 813
sustainability-linked loans, 801
teams, 506
technology-driven credit
    assessments, 503
tokenization, 521, 522
    asset management, 522
    digital assets, 523, 524
    liquidity, 522, 523
    transactions, 524
tokenized assets, 499
tradeable securities, 514
transformation, 514
transparency and accessibility, 803
transparent and efficient, 508
trends and insights, 502
use cases, 666
ZT (*see* Zero-trust (ZT))
ZTA (*see* Zero-trust architecture (ZTA))
ZT security, 662–664
Trade finance tokenization, 678
    accessibility, 680
    bills of exchange and promissory
        notes, 681
    boost liquidity and fractionalize
        assets, 680
    efficiency, security and
        collaboration, 677–679
    industry collaboration, 679
    international commerce, 680
    interoperability, 680
    pilot project execution, 679
    regulatory improvements, 679
    safety concerns, 680
    transparency, 679
    uses, 679
Trade finance tools, 518, 524
Trade innovation and digitization, 550
    data sharing, 550
    difficulties, 551
    freight forwarders, 550
    interactions, 550
    management, 551
TradeLens, 467–473
Trade Negotiations Committee (TNC), 710
Trade sector, businesses and
    entrepreneurs, 556, 557
Trade segregation, 714

INDEX

Trade technology platforms, 559
Trade transactions, 510
TradeTrust, 475–477
Trading assets, 879
Trading methods, 794
Traditional commodity trade, 944
Traditional LCs, 684, 685, 688
Traditional lending systems, 667
Transactions, 669, 846, 993
Transactions of Collaborations, 993
The Trans-Pacific Green Corridor, 754
Transparency, 516, 535, 813, 838, 900, 915
Trust algorithms, 657–659

U

UNCITRAL Model Law, 304
UNCITRAL Model Law on Electronic
    Transferable Records (MLETR)
  digital transformation, 363–365,
    367, 368
  digitization, 362, 363
  e-commerce, 368
  harmonization, 366, 367
  physical (paper) forms, 365, 366
Uniform Customs and Practice (UCP 600),
    11, 25, 34
  ambiguity, 45
  articles, 44
  comprehensive/inclusive process, 45
  definitions/meanings, 43
  elements, 43–47
  enforcement of, 41
  eUCP (*see* Electronic (eUCP))
  events, 43
  examination, 45
  international trade finance, 44

  international trade transactions, 40, 41
  ISBP 821, 50, 51
  payments, 44
  regulations, 42
  requirements and difficulties, 42
  stable and consistent
    framework, 41
  trade agreements and sanctions, 47
  trade finance transactions, 41
Uniform Rules for Digital Commerce
    Activities
  digital trade transaction
    (DTT), 380–383
  international trading practices,
    379, 380
Uniform Rules for Digital Trade
    Operations, 359, 379, 380
Uniform Rules for Digital Trade
    Transactions (URDTT), 86
  articles, 383–396
  contour implementation, 450
  version 1.0, 384–397
Uniform Rules for Forfaiting (URF),
    154, 155
United Nations Commission on
    International Commerce Law
    (UNCITRAL), 305, 362
United Nations Commission on
    International Commercial Law
    (UNCITRAL), 362
  MLETR (*see* Model Law on Electronic
    Transferable Records (MLETR))
United Nations Commission on
    International Trade Law
    (UNCITRAL), 344
The United Nations Conference for Trade
    and Development (UNCTAD), 771

United Nations Guiding Principles on Business and Human Rights (UNGPs), 712
UrbanByNature program, 787
Urban planning techniques, 782
Urban sustainability, 778, 826
URF, *see* Uniform Rules for Forfaiting (URF)
US Generally Accepted Accounting Principles (GAAP), 110

V

VCS, *see* Verified carbon standard (VCS)
Vehicle tracking, 827
Verified carbon standard (VCS), 979
Verified emission reductions (VERs), 948
VERs, *see* Verified emission reductions (VERs)
Voluntary sustainability standards (VSS), 717–724
VSS, *see* Voluntary sustainability standards (VSS)

W

Wang, Gaojun, 473
Waste management, 825
Water management, 824
Web2, 865
Web3, 863
    aim, 865
    and blockchain, 866, 867, 898
    decentralization/democratization, 864
    design principles, 865
    digital sphere, 864
    distributed nature, 865
    ideas, 880
    inclusiveness, 864
    open-source philosophy, 865
    power distribution, 867
    and ReFi, 864, 867, 877
    regulatory environment, 872
    services, 872
    technological advances/radical deviations, 877
    transforming power, 864
    user sovereignty, 865
"Well-to-Wake" (WtW) emissions, 757
Widespread tokenization's roadmap, 942
Wind power, 772
    advantages, 770
    applications, 772
    challenges, 769
    contemporary ships, 770
    innovation, 768–770
    maritime future, 769
    maritime sector, 769
    in shipping, 769
World trade framework, 791
World Trade Organization (WTO), 695, 722
    agreements, 697
    Appellate Body, 739
    audacious leadership, 740
    awareness, 730
    commerce and climate policy, 744
    commerce, environment, and sustainable development integration, 731
    conflicts and shifting paradigms, 740
    creative thinking, 740
    environmental concerns, 697
    environmental issues, 711
    Environment Week, 727
    FFSR project, 725

INDEX

World Trade
      Organization (WTO) (*cont.*)
  function, 740
  General Council, 710
  geopolitical scene, 740
  global environmental issues, 724
  green subsidies within global trade regulations framework, 740
  legal structure, 697
  LRS, 739
  member-led projects, 725
    environment, 728
    environmental sustainability, 726
    plastic pollution, 726
    reform of fossil fuel subsidies, 726
    sustainable development, 728
    trade, 728
  Ministerial Conference, 710
  multilateral trade system, 712
  non-discrimination principle, 739
  non-state actors, 727
  non-state players, 730
  organizational structure analysis, 709
  plastic pollution, 697
  stakeholders, 727, 728
  sustainable development, 696, 698, 712
  TESSD, 725
  trade and environmental interface, 698
  trade policies, 698
  trade-related environmental measures, 698
  trade-related environmental policies, 711
  2023 Public Forum, 727
  world trade and environmental policy, 740
  world trade governance, 740
  world trade reform and domestic priorities, 739
WTO, *see* World Trade Organization (WTO)

X, Y

XDC Trade Network, 477, 478

Z

Zero-carbon future, 752
Zero-emission fuels, 754, 761, 762
Zero-emission shipping solutions, 749
Zero-emission technology, 750
Zero-knowledge proofs (ZKPs), 252, 257, 271–274
Zero-trust (ZT)
  access restrictions, 642
  CDM, 644
  central tenet—never trust, 661
  components, 649
  concept, 643–646
  corporate assets, 642
  cybersecurity, 642, 643, 645, 649
  data collection, 648
  data protection, 642
  deployment models, 657
  DISA, 643, 644
  dynamic characters, 646
  environment, 664
  FISMA, 644
  model operations, 645
  network communication, 661
  on network security, 652–654
  operation monitoring, 646
  principles, 647, 648, 650, 664

public sector, 644
RMF, 644
safeguarding hosting infrastructures, 646
security in trade finance, 662, 663
Zero-trust architecture (ZTA)
auditing and analysis, 655
concepts, 642
constant monitoring and verification systems, 661
culture change, 662
cybersecurity, 655, 662
data sources, 654
deployment models, 656, 657
elements, 642, 655
ideas and components, 661
industry compliance guarantee, 654
management of identity and credentials, 645
NIST SP 800-207 (*see* NIST SP 800-207)
NIST SP 800-207A (*see* NIST SP 800-207A)
non-enterprise-owned and enterprise-owned assets, 662
PA, 654, 655
PE, 654, 655
PEP, 654, 655
real-time security assessments, 661
resilient network, 659, 660
security policy, 653
strict access restrictions, 661
strong and flexible security, 655
trust algorithms, 657–659
up-to-date information, 655
ZKPs, *see* Zero-knowledge proofs (ZKPs)
ZT security in trade finance
collaboration with third parties, 663
continuous verification, 662
cybersecurity, 663
data protection, 663
IAM, 663
micro-segmentation, 662
real-time monitoring and analytics, 663
regulatory compliance, 663

The manufacturer's authorised representative in the EU is Springer Nature Customer Service Centre GmbH, Europaplatz 3, 69115 Heidelberg, Germany. If you have any concerns regarding our products, please contact ProductSafety@springernature.com

Printed and bound by CPI Group (UK) Ltd, Croydon, CR0 4YY

29/03/2026

02080605-0001